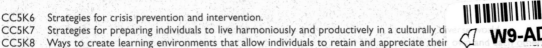
CC5K6   Strategies for crisis prevention and intervention.
CC5K7   Strategies for preparing individuals to live harmoniously and productively in a culturally di
CC5K8   Ways to create learning environments that allow individuals to retain and appreciate their own and others' respective language and cultural heritage.
CC5K9   Ways specific cultures are negatively stereotyped.
CC5K10 Strategies used by diverse populations to cope with a legacy of former and continuing racism

Skills:
CC5S1   Create a safe, equitable, positive, and supportive learning environment in which diversities are valued.
CC5S2   Identify realistic expectations for personal and social behavior in various settings.
CC5S3   Identify supports needed for integration into various program placements.
CC5S4   Design learning environments that encourage active participation in individual and group activities.
CC5S5   Modify the learning environment to manage behaviors.
CC5S6   Use performance data and information from all stakeholders to make or suggest modifications in learning environments.
CC5S7   Establish and maintain rapport with individuals with and without exceptional learning needs.
CC5S8   Teach self-advocacy.
CC5S9   Create an environment that encourages self-advocacy and increased independence.
CC5S10 Use effective and varied behavior management strategies.
CC5S11 Use the least intensive behavior management strategy consistent with the needs of the individual with exceptional learning needs.
CC5S12 Design and manage daily routines.
CC5S13 Organize, develop, and sustain learning environments that support positive intracultural and intercultural experiences.
CC5S14 Mediate controversial intercultural issues among students within the learning environment in ways that enhance any culture, group, or person.
CC5S15 Structure, direct, and support the activities of paraeducators, volunteers, and tutors.
CC5S16 Use universal precautions.

Special Education Content Standard #6: Communication

Knowledge:
CC6K1   Effects of cultural and linguistic differences on growth and development.
CC6K2   Characteristics of one's own culture and use of language and the ways in which these can differ from other cultures and uses of languages.
CC6K3   Ways of behaving and communicating among cultures that can lead to misinterpretation and misunderstanding.
CC6K4   Augmentative and assistive communication strategies.

Skills:
CC6S1   Use strategies to support and enhance communication skills of individuals with exceptional learning needs.
CC6S2   Use communication strategies and resources to facilitate understanding of subject matter for students whose primary language is not the dominant language.

Special Education Content Standard #7: Instructional Planning

Knowledge:
CC7K1   Theories and research that form the basis of curriculum development and instructional practice.
CC7K2   Scope and sequences of general and special curricula.
CC7K3   National, state or provincial, and local curricula standards.
CC7K4   Technology for planning and managing the teaching and learning environment.
CC7K5   Roles and responsibilities of the paraeducator related to instruction, intervention, and direct service.

Skills:
CC7S1   Identify and prioritize areas of the general curriculum and accommodations for individuals with exceptional learning needs.
CC7S2   Develop and implement comprehensive, longitudinal individualized programs in collaboration with team members.
CC7S3   Involve the individual and family in setting instructional goals and monitoring progress.
CC7S4   Use functional assessments to develop intervention plans.
CC7S5   Use task analysis.
CC7S6   Sequence, implement, and evaluate individualized learning objectives.
CC7S7   Integrate affective, social, and life skills with academic curricula.
CC7S8   Develop and select instructional content, resources, and strategies that respond to cultural, linguistic, and gender differences.
CC7S9   Incorporate and implement instructional and assistive technology into the educational program.
CC7S10 Prepare lesson plans.
CC7S11 Prepare and organize materials to implement daily lesson plans.
CC7S12 Use instructional time effectively.
CC7S13 Make responsive adjustments to instruction based on continual observations.
CC7S14 Prepare individuals to exhibit self-enhancing behavior in response to societal attitudes and actions.

Special Education Content Standard #8: Assessment

Knowledge:
CC8K1   Basic terminology used in assessment.
CC8K2   Legal provisions and ethical principles regarding assessment of individuals.
CC8K3   Screening, pre-referral, referral, and classification procedures.
CC8K4   Use and limitations of assessment instruments.
CC8K5   National, state or provincial, and local accommodations and modifications.

Skills:

CC8S1   Gather relevant background information.

CC8S2   Administer nonbiased formal and informal assessments.

CC8S3   Use technology to conduct assessments.

CC8S4   Develop or modify individualized assessment strategies.

CC8S5   Interpret information from formal and informal assessments.

CC8S6   Use assessment information in making eligibility, program, and placement decisions for individuals with exceptional learning needs, including those from culturally and/or linguistically diverse backgrounds.

CC8S7   Report assessment results to all stakeholders using effective communication skills.

CC8S8   Evaluate instruction and monitor progress of individuals with exceptional learning needs.

CC8S9   Create and maintain records.

Special Education Content Standard #9: Professional and Ethical Practice

Knowledge:

CC9K1   Personal cultural biases and differences that affect one's teaching.

CC9K2   Importance of the teacher serving as a model for individuals with exceptional learning needs.

CC9K3   Continuum of lifelong professional development.

CC9K4   Methods to remain current regarding research-validated practice.

Skills:

CC9S1   Practice within the CEC Code of Ethics and other standards of the profession.

CC9S2   Uphold high standards of competence and integrity and exercise sound judgment in the practice of the professional.

CC9S3   Act ethically in advocating for appropriate services.

CC9S4   Conduct professional activities in compliance with applicable laws and policies.

CC9S5   Demonstrate commitment to developing the highest education and quality-of-life potential of individuals with exceptional learning needs.

CC9S6   Demonstrate sensitivity for the culture, language, religion, gender, disability, socio-economic status, and sexual orientation of individuals.

CC9S7   Practice within one's skill limit and obtain assistance as needed.

CC9S8   Use verbal, nonverbal, and written language effectively.

CC9S9   Conduct self-evaluation of instruction.

CC9S10   Access information on exceptionalities.

CC9S11   Reflect on one's practice to improve instruction and guide professional growth.

CC9S12   Engage in professional activities that benefit individuals with exceptional learning needs, their families, and one's colleagues.

Special Education Content Standard #10: Collaboration

Knowledge:

CC10K1   Models and strategies of consultation and collaboration.

CC10K2   Roles of individuals with exceptional learning needs, families, and school and community personnel in planning of an individualized program.

CC10K3   Concerns of families of individuals with exceptional learning needs and strategies to help address these concerns.

CC10K4   Culturally responsive factors that promote effective communication and collaboration with individuals with exceptional learning needs, families, school personnel, and community members.

Skills:

CC10S1   Maintain confidential communication about individuals with exceptional learning needs.

CC10S2   Collaborate with families and others in assessment of individuals with exceptional learning needs.

CC10S3   Foster respectful and beneficial relationships between families and professionals.

CC10S4   Assist individuals with exceptional learning needs and their families in becoming active participants in the educational team.

CC10S5   Plan and conduct collaborative conferences with individuals with exceptional learning needs and their families.

CC10S6   Collaborate with school personnel and community members in integrating individuals with exceptional learning needs into various settings.

CC10S7   Use group problem-solving skills to develop, implement, and evaluate collaborative activities.

CC10S8   Model techniques and coach others in the use of instructional methods and accommodations.

CC10S9   Communicate with school personnel about the characteristics and needs of individuals with exceptional learning needs.

CC10S10 Communicate effectively with families of individuals with exceptional learning needs from diverse backgrounds.

CC10S11 Observe, evaluate, and provide feedback to paraeducators.

continues on back inside cover

SEVENTH EDITION

Exceptional Children

An Introduction to Special Education

William L. Heward

The Ohio State University

Merrill
Prentice Hall

Upper Saddle River, New Jersey
Columbus, Ohio

Library of Congress Cataloging-in-Publication Data

Heward, William L.,
 Exceptional children : an introduction to special education/William L. Heward.—7th ed.
  p. cm.
 Includes bibliographical references and index.
 ISBN 0-13-099344-1
  1. Special education—United States. 2. Exceptional children—United States. I. Title.
 LC3981 .H49 2003
 371.9'0973—dc21   2002023113

Vice President and Publisher: Jeffery W. Johnston
Editor: Allyson P. Sharp
Development Editor: Gianna Marsella/Heather Doyle Fraser
Production Editor: Mary M. Irvin
Design Coordinator: Diane C. Lorenzo
Photo Coordinator: Valerie Schultz
Text Design: Pisaza Design
Cover Design: Ali Mohrman
Cover Photo: Index Stock
Production Manager: Pamela D. Bennett
Director of Marketing: Ann Castel Davis
Marketing Manager: Krista Groshong
Marketing Coordinator: Tyra Cooper

Photo Credits: see page following the index

This book was set in Berkeley by Carlisle Communications, Ltd., and was printed and bound by R. R. Donnelley & Sons Company. The cover was printed by The Lehigh Press, Inc.

Pearson Education Ltd.
Pearson Education Australia Pty. Limited
Pearson Education Singapore Pte. Ltd.
Pearson Education North Asia Ltd.
Pearson Education Canada, Ltd.
Pearson Educación de Mexico, S.A. de C.V.
Pearson Education—Japan
Pearson Education Malaysia Pte. Ltd.
Pearson Education, *Upper Saddle River, New Jersey*

Merrill
Prentice Hall

10 9 8 7 6 5 4 3 2
ISBN 0-13-099344-1

For my parents: Helen M. and Joe W. Heward.

Mom and Dad, you are the best.

About the Author

William Lee Heward grew up in Three Oaks, Michigan, rooting for his hero Ernie Banks and the Chicago Cubs. He majored in psychology and sociology as an undergraduate at Western Michigan University, earned his doctorate in special education at the University of Massachusetts, and joined the special education faculty at The Ohio State University in 1975. In 1985, Bill received Ohio State University's highest honor for teaching excellence, the Alumni Association's Distinguished Teaching Award. He has had several opportunities to teach and lecture abroad, most recently in 1993 when he served as a Visiting Professor of Psychology at Keio University in Tokyo.

Bill's current research interests focus on "low tech" methods classroom teachers can use to increase the frequency with which each student actively responds and participates during group instruction and on methods for promoting the generalization and maintenance of newly learned skills. His research has appeared in the field's leading journals, including *Behavioral Disorders, Education and Training in Mental Retardation and Developmental Disabilities, Exceptional Children, Journal of Special Education, Learning Disabilities Research & Practice, Research in Developmental Disabilities, Teacher Education and Special Education*, and *Teaching Exceptional Children*.

Bill has coauthored four other textbooks, and he has written for the popular market. His book *Some Are Called Clowns* (Crowell, 1974) chronicled his five summers as a pitcher for the Indianapolis Clowns, the last of the barnstorming baseball teams.

Preface

Special education is an ongoing story of people. It is the story of a preschool child with multiple disabilities who benefits from early intervention services. It is the story of a child with mental retardation whose parents and teachers work together to ensure she participates in classroom and extracurricular activities with her peers. It is the story of a middle school student with learning disabilities who helps his parents and teachers plan his instructional program that builds upon his strengths and addresses his weaknesses. It is the story of the gifted and talented child who brings new insights to old problems, the high school student with cerebral palsy who is learning English as his second language, and the young woman with visual impairments who has recently moved into her own apartment and rides a city bus to work. Special education is also the story of parents and families of exceptional children and of the teachers and other professionals who work with them.

I hope you will find the seventh edition of *Exceptional Children* an informative, accessible, and interesting introduction to the ongoing story of special education, a rapidly changing field that is still in its formative years. Whether you are an undergraduate enrolled in or thinking of applying to a preservice teacher training program or a general education teacher with years of experience, I encourage you to continue your study and involvement with children and adults with special needs. For you, too, can make a worthwhile contribution to the still unfinished story of special education.

TEXT ORGANIZATION AND STRUCTURE

My goals for this book are to present an informative, readable, and responsible introduction to the professional practices, trends, and research that define the field while at the same time conveying the diversity and excitement that characterize contemporary special education. To this end, the book begins with "A Personal View of Special Education"—eight perspectives on the purpose and responsibilities of special education—followed by fifteen chapters organized into two parts.

Part 1—Foundations for Understanding Special Education—includes four chapters. Chapter 1 presents an overview of terminology, laws, policies, and practices that are consistent with the Individuals with Disabilities Education Act (IDEA) and the exceptional child's right to receive an appropriate education in the least restrictive environment. Chapter 2 examines the referral, assessment, and placement of students in special education. Chapter 3 describes how to respect, appreciate, and respond appropriately to the cultural and linguistic differences that some children with special needs bring to the classroom. Chapter 4 discusses the important role parents and families play in the decision-making process for planning the individual education needs of their children and how special educators can form effective partnerships with parents.

Part 2—Educational Needs of Exceptional Students—is organized around nine categorical chapters within a developmental lifespan perspective. Chapter 5 opens Part 2 with a look at early childhood special education and the critical role early intervention plays in nurturing the development of young children with special needs and those who are at risk for acquiring disabilities. Chapter 15 closes Part 2 with a discussion of transition from secondary school and the responsibility educators and parents share in preparing students with exceptionalities for adulthood. Chapters 6 through 14, the chapters that fall between early intervention and transition, introduce you to the definitions, prevalence, causes, historical background, assessment techniques, instructional strategies, placement alternatives, and current issues and future trends for specific categories of exceptional educational needs, including children who are gifted and talented.

 ## KEY TEXT FEATURES

 ### ESSAYS BY SPECIAL EDUCATION TEACHERS

New to this edition, each chapter opens with a first-person essay by a special education teacher. For example, you will get to know Douglas Jackson of El Paso, Texas, a special educator with 17 years experience who uses puppet plays to teach students who are deaf and hard of hearing. Diane Ellis shares some of her multifaceted responsibilities as a special educator

who selects and designs assistive technologies for students with autism and severe disabilities in Nebraska. Michelle Fundora San, just beginning her second year of teaching students with emotional and behavioral disorders at a middle school in Miami, describes her experience and perspectives as a newcomer to the profession. Jeanna Mora Dowse shares her experiences working as an itinerant teacher of Navajo children with visual impairments in Arizona. Drawn from urban, suburban, and rural school districts across the country, the 15 featured teachers share personal experiences and wisdom on topics such as "what I like best about being a special educator," "my biggest challenge," "my most significant accomplishment," and "suggestions for someone considering a career in special education." After reading each teacher's essay, you can learn more about his or her classroom and students by visiting the Teacher Feature module on the Companion Website (www.prenhall.com/heward).

 ### FOCUS QUESTIONS

Each chapter begins with five questions that provide a framework for studying the chapter and its implications. These Focus Questions serve as discussion starters for introducing, overviewing, concluding, or reviewing. Open-ended questions can be found on the Message Board on the Companion Website (www.prenhall.com/heward), which allows you to engage in interactive discussions with your classmates.

CEC PERFORMANCE-BASED STANDARDS AND PRAXIS II TESTS

Although special education teacher certification and licensure requirements vary from state to state, all special educators are expected to demonstrate a common set of competencies. The Council for Exceptional Children's (CEC) Performance-Based Standards for Beginning Special Education Teachers is a comprehensive set of knowledge and skill standards organized within 10 domain areas (e.g., Foundations, Individual Learning Differences, Instructional Strategies, Assessment). The CEC Standards were developed in collaboration with the Interstate New Teacher Assessment and Support Consortium (INTASC) and serve as the basis for curriculum content of teacher preparation programs approved by the National Council for the Accreditation of Teacher Education (NCATE). The PRAXIS II™ tests—the Subject Assessment/Specialty Area Tests of the PRAXIS Series of Professional Assessments for Beginning Teachers™—assess students' knowledge of these content standards. Many states require a passing score on one or more PRAXIS II tests for licensure or certification as a special education teacher.

Through joint agreements with CEC and the Educational Testing Service, new margin notes link critical text content to specific knowledge and skill statements from CEC's Performance-Based Standards for Beginning Teachers and to material covered on PRAXIS II™ tests for special educators. Look for margin notes such as the one shown here with CEC and PRAXIS icons throughout the text.

Criterion-referenced tests

Council for Exceptional Children Content Standards for Beginning Teachers of Students with LD: Terminology and procedures used in the assessment of individuals with LD (LD8K1) (also CC8K4). **PRAXIS** Special Education Core Principles: Content Knowledge: III. Delivery of Services to Students with Disabilities, Assessment, Use of assessment for making instructional decisions.

EFFECTIVE TEACHING STRATEGIES

Educating students with exceptional learning needs has always posed complex and difficult challenges. Yet more is expected of today's special education teachers than ever before. For example, today's special educator must ensure students' access to the general education curriculum while at the same time teach them functional skills needed for daily living and successful transition from school to life in the community and workplace. Today's special educator is expected to collaboratively plan and carry out inclusive practices with their general education colleagues while being responsive to the needs and wishes of families. Today's special educator must manage a mountain of paperwork and the challenge of preparing students for state proficiency tests from which students with disabilities have previously been exempted. The special educator must respond to all of these important and sometimes competing demands.

But what matters most in special education, the foundation without which everything would fall apart, is good instruction, day in and day out. And at the level where it matters most, special education is ultimately about the quality of instruction provided by teachers.

Reading a single textbook will not prepare you to be an effective teacher of exceptional children. Your introductory study of special education should, however, inform you about the critical elements of good instruction and provide numerous examples of their application. Each chapter includes one or more Teaching & Learning feature boxes that describe a wide range of effective teaching interventions—from classroom management and peer support strategies for inclusion to curriculum modifications and suggestions for effective error correction procedures. These boxes provide clear and practical guidelines for designing, implementing, and evaluating instruction of students with disabilities. All of the strategies described in the Teaching & Learning features are classroom-tested and supported by research documenting their effectiveness.

PROFILES OF PEOPLE/PERSPECTIVES OF ISSUES

Each chapter contains one or more Profiles & Perspectives boxes that highlight the personal struggles, triumphs, and stories of persons with disabilities or share the views of parents, special educators, and other professionals about the achievements, challenges, and future directions of special education. For example, in Chapter 2, Michael Giangreco ("Moving Toward Inclusive Education") and Douglas and Lynn Fuchs ("Inclusion versus Full Inclusion") offer different perspectives on whether or not all students with disabilities should be educated in regular classrooms.

In essays in Chapters 9 and 12 ("My Communication System" and "I Was Thinking About Black Holes"), physicist Stephen Hawking contributes his thoughts on living with a degenerative disease that causes him to continually adapt his lifestyle but does not affect his intellectual ability. In Chapter 13 ("The Autism Wars") Catherine Maurice, author of the powerful best-seller *Let Me Hear Your Voice,* describes the enormous difficulties faced by parents of children with autism in choosing scientifically tested interventions from the many myths, fads, and miracle cures that surround autism.

STUDENT SUPPLEMENTS TO SUPPORT, ENRICH, AND EXTEND THE STUDY OF EXCEPTIONAL CHILDREN

STUDENT STUDY GUIDE

The Student Study Guide provides you with a useful resource for learning about exceptional children, their families, and the field of special education. Chapter objectives, chapter overviews, chapter-at-a-glance tables, guided reviews, "What Do You Think?" activities covering current and controversial issues, and self-check quizzes allow you to review course content, apply new knowledge and skills, and prepare for tests and exams.

COMPANION WEBSITE

To see examples of the graphs and other instructional materials used by Mr. Wood and his students, go to the Teacher Feature module of the Companion Website at **www.prenhall.com/heward**

A user-friendly Companion Website (www.prenhall.com/heward), designed to complement this text, is integrated into the textbook via margin notes. Identified by the Companion Website logo, these notes direct you to online materials that will assist in reviewing chapter content, doing research online, and accessing related materials and professional resources.

Each chapter of the Companion Website contains the following features that enable students to:

- **Study for Tests**—*Essential Concepts, Chapters-at-a-Glance, Guided Reviews, Focus Questions,* and interactive true-false and essay *Chapter Quizzes* help you gauge your understanding of chapter content.
- **Learn More about Teaching Exceptional Students**—The *Teacher Feature* module provides real artifacts from inservice teachers who teach students with the disabilities covered in the text.

- **Learn More about Chapter Topics**—*Web Links* to sites covering pertinent areas of study help students access additional information on chapter topics. The *Feature Boxes* module allows students to view various resources that discuss and illustrate topics covered in the text as well.
- **Engage in Activities**—The *In-Class Activities* module offers different types of activities for each chapter, including *Group Activities* and *Response Card Activities.*
- **Work on Specialized Assignments**—The assignments module houses different types of assignments to help you through the topics studied in the text. These assignments include *Position Papers, What Do You Think?,* and *Make It, Use It* activities.
- **Communicate with Your Peers**—You can collaborate and communicate with other students enrolled in classes like yours all across the country using the *Message Board* and *Chat* features.

 DEVELOPING QUALITY IEPS: A CASE-BASED TUTORIAL CD-ROM

This free CD-ROM packaged with every copy of the text walks you through the development of Individualized Education Programs (IEPs) and familiarizes you with criteria for assessing their quality. The CD-ROM provides two interactive tutorials, six case studies with related exercises, and a variety of additional resources, including web links, journal articles, assessment and annual review evaluation forms, checklists, and tips and guidelines for developing and evaluating IEPs. Margin notes in Chapter 2 direct you to relevant information and activities on the CD-ROM.

 ADDITIONAL SUPPLEMENTS AND RESOURCES FOR THE INSTRUCTOR

 VIDEO LIBRARY

Course instructors receive a complimentary set of five compelling videos that can be used to supplement and extend information and issues introduced in the text. Two of the videos are new to this edition: *Heather's Story* chronicles the experiences of a fourth grade child with Down syndrome as she joins an inclusive classroom for the first time. *Guidelines for Making Decisions About IEP Services,* produced by the Vermont Department of Education, helps IEP team members, including families, make informed decisions about what special education and related services are necessary and appropriate for children with disabilities. The popular *A New IDEA for Special Education* highlights critical aspects of the Individuals with Disabilities Education Act (IDEA). *Together We Can!,* produced by the Juniper Gardens Children's Project in Kansas City, describes a classwide peer tutoring program in which every student in a general education classroom participates as both tutor and tutee. *LifeLink* highlights a program that provides opportunities for secondary students with disabilities to learn independent living skills and prepare for life in the adult community.

 COMPANION WEBSITE

Located at http://www.prenhall.com/heward, the user-friendly website that accompanies this text provides online resources for professors as well as students.

The passcode-protected Faculty Lounge for professors includes downloadable PowerPoint lectures; supplemental lectures corresponding to PRAXIS and CEC standards and competencies; an online version of the Instructor's Manual; suggested discussion questions, class activities, and homework assignments; answers to activities printed in the Student Study Guide; and additional resources for effective instruction. Communication tools include a faculty-only message board and chat room. The Syllabus Builder tool allows instructors to create and customize syllabi online. To obtain a passcode to enter the Faculty Lounge, contact your local Prentice Hall sales representative.

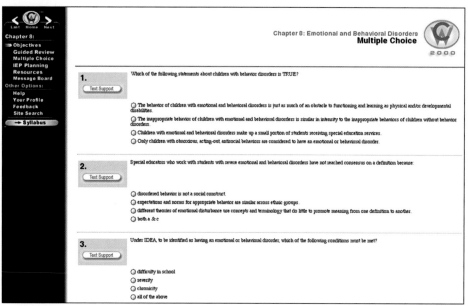

INSTRUCTOR'S MANUAL

An expanded and improved Instructor's Manual includes numerous recommendations for presenting and extending text content. The manual consists of chapter objectives and overviews of essential concepts; connections to CEC and PRAXIS standards; class discussion and essay/position paper topics; in-class activities such as cooperative group activities, SAFMEDS, response card activities, and ideas for debates; guest speakers; application exercises; and homework assignments. Additional video and Internet resources are also provided for each chapter.

OVERHEAD TRANSPARENCIES/POWERPOINT SLIDES

A package of color acetate transparencies is available for use with the text. The transparencies highlight key concepts, summarize content, and illustrate figures and charts from the text. There are also 156 transparencies available in PowerPoint format on the Companion Website (www.prenhall.com/heward).

TEST BANK

A printed test bank of more than 600 questions—all new for this edition—also accompanies the text. These objective and essay questions can be used to assess students' recognition, recall, and synthesis of factual content and conceptual issues from each chapter. The computerized version of the test bank is available in a Windows and Macintosh format, along with assessment software allowing professors to create and customize exams and track student progress.

Acknowledgments

Many people contributed ideas, insights, and suggestions that greatly enhanced the substance and quality of the seventh edition of *Exceptional Children*. As with previous editions, a highly talented team of publishing professionals at Merrill/Prentice Hall provided assistance and support throughout the planning, manuscript development, and production stages of this revision. Ann Castel Davis, who served as Acquisitions Editor for the previous three editions, is now Marketing Manager for Merrill Education. Ann was instrumental in getting the ball rolling on this edition and made significant contributions to the revision plan. Allyson Sharp was promoted to Acquisitions Editor in the early stages of the revision and has been a source of much appreciated support and enthusiasm. Developmental Editor Gianna Marsalla was a source of numerous suggestions and valued constructive criticism while I worked on the manuscript. Gianna left Merrill in the later stages of the revision process to explore other opportunities. I appreciated her thoroughness and relentless energy for the project and wish her well in her new pursuits. Heather Doyle Fraser assumed the role of Development Editor and provided able and patient assistance as the manuscript was completed.

Dawn Potter copyedited the new manuscript with the same balance of technical skill and respect for an author's writing style as she did with the previous edition. Thanks to proofreader Maggie Diehl's eegle eye, there is not a mispeled word in this hole book. The effective and meaningful portrayal of special education requires excellent photographs, and the contributions of Photo Editor Valerie Schultz are evident throughout this edition. Finally, without the many skills and hard work of Production Editor Mary Irvin, the seventh edition would never have made it to the printing press. The final appearance and accuracy of the book are the product of Mary's diligent attention to detail and ability to keep countless elements of the production process on schedule.

No one author can capture the many perspectives and areas of expertise that make up a field as diverse and dynamic as special education. Many special education teachers and researchers have contributed to the currency and quality of this text. The first-person essay by a practicing special educator that begins each chapter is a major new feature of this edition. I am grateful to the 15 special educators who graciously shared their knowledge and personal experience with prospective members of the teaching profession: Jeanna Mora Dowse (Pinon and Ganado Unified School Districts, Apache County, AZ), Diane Ellis (Bellevue Public School District, Bellevue, NE), Steven Everling (Northwest Elementary School, Largo, FL), Barbara Horvath (Monroe County Community School Corporation, Bloomington, IN), Roxanne Hudson (Kimball Wiles Elementary School, Gainesville, FL), Douglas Jackson (El Paso Regional Day School Program for the Deaf, El Paso, TX), Patricia Concepcion Lambert (Hunter College

Elementary School, New York, NY), Kimberly Lundy (Spiritridge Elementary School, Bellevue, WA), Carol Richards (Swanton Central Elementary School, Swanton, VT), Mary Kate Ryan-Griffith (Judith A. Resnik Elementary School, Gaithersburg, MD), Michelle Fundora San (Centennial Middle School, Miami, FL), Denise Smith (Miles Middle School, Tucson AZ), Ronni Hochman Spratt (Hastings Middle School, Upper Arlington, OH), Sandie Trask (Blendon Middle School, Westerville, OH), and Chuck Wood (Barth Elementary School, Romulus, MI). The individual and collective talents, wisdom, and accomplishments of these teachers provide great optimism for the future of special education.

The following scholars and teachers contributed Profiles & Perspectives or Teaching & Learning essays exclusively for this text: Sheila Alber (University of Southern Mississippi); Patty Barbetta (Florida International University); Anne Bauer (University of Cincinnati) and Mary Ulrich (Miami University), Sue Brewster and Lyn Dol (Toledo Public Schools); (Judy Carta, Juniper Gardens Children's Center); Jill Dardig, (Ohio Dominican College); Glen Dunlap, Bobbie Vaughn, and Lise Fox (University of South Florida); Gail Fitzgerald (University of Missouri) and Louis Semrau (Arkansas State University); Marsha Forest and Jack Pearpoint (Centre for Integrated Education and Community, Toronto); Douglas Fuchs and Lynn Fuchs (Vanderbilt University); Michael Giangreco (University of Vermont); Bonnie Grossen (University of Oregon); Margo Mastropieri and Tom Scruggs, (George Mason University); Catherine Maurice (author of *Let Me Hear Your Voice*); Diane Sainato (Ohio State University); Barbara Schirmer (Miami University) and Albert Ingram (Kent State University); Elaine Silliman and Jill Beasman (University of South Florida); Marti Snell (University of Virginia) and Rachel Janney (Radford University); John Umbreit (University of Arizona); and Jo Webber and Brenda Scheuermann (Southwest Texas State University).

The idea of creating margin notes to link text content to the PRAXIS tests and CEC Standards was conceived by my wife, Jill Dardig. I am grateful to Ruth Mendoza and Michelle Szpara at Educational Testing Service, and to Margie Crutchfield, director for program accreditation at the Council for Exceptional Children, for helping me turn Jill's great idea into reality.

The following professors—all of whom teach introductory special education courses at other colleges and universities—reviewed the previous edition and provided comments and suggestions that contributed to this edition: Joanne Rossi Becker, San Jose State; Jay Graening, University of Arkansas, Fayetteville; James Mason, California State University–San Bernardino; and Regina Panasuk, University of Massachusetts–Lowell; Ellen Brantlinger, Indiana University, Bloomington; Albert N. Bugaj, University of Wisconsin, Marinette; Sheila Drake, MidAmerican Nazarene University; Christine Givner, California State University, Los Angeles; Patrick Grant, Slippery Rock University; Kathleen Gruenhagen, North Georgia College and State University; Joseph E. Justen, Arkansas State University; Karen Keller, University of Missouri, St. Louis; Reid J. Linn, James Madison University; Kathryn A. Lund, Arizona State University; Sheldon Maron, Portland State University; Tes Mehring, Emporia State University; Susan J. Peters, Michigan State University; J. Lyn Rhoden, University of North Carolina, Charlotte; Phyllis Robertson, The University of Texas at Austin; Rex Shahriari, Central College; Sally M. Todd, Brigham Young University; John F. Vokurka, Western Kentucky University; Carol Moore, Troy State University at Phenix City; Gwendolyn Webb-Johnson, The University of Texas at Austin; and James Yanok, Ohio University. The perspectives, experience, and recommendations of these reviewers were instrumental in guiding the revision process.

I am indebted to Vivian Correa (University of Florida) for again co-authoring Chapter 3—Special Education in a Culturally and Linguistically Diverse Society—and to Jane Piirto (Ashland University) for co-authoring Chapter 14—Giftedness and Talent. Sheila Alber (University of Southern Mississippi) and David Bicard (Florida International University) co-authored the Student Study Guide and the Instructor's Manual. The Test Bank was prepared by Jim Persinger (Emporia State University). This group of special educators produced a very strong set of ancillary materials, and I am confident that students and instructors will appreciate and benefit from their hard work and creativity.

Finally, I will always be grateful to Mike Orlansky, a former colleague, friend, and co-author of the first four editions of *Exceptional Children*.

Most of all, I am lucky to have the unwavering support of my family—Jill, Lee, and Lynn.

Contents

Chapter 6

Mental Retardation   196

Chapter 7

Learning Disabilities   238

Chapter 8

Emotional and Behavioral Disorders 280

Chapter 9

Communication Disorders 322

Chapter 10

Hearing Loss   360

Chapter 11

Blindness and Low Vision   400

Chapter 15

Transition to Adulthood   566

Postscript

Developing Your Own Personal View of Special Education   606

Note: Every effort has been made to provide accurate and current Internet information in this book. However, the Internet and information posted on it are constantly changing, so it is inevitable that some of the Internet addresses in this textbook will change.

Special Features

✳ Teaching & Learning

Strategy	Application	Text Location

Profiles & Perspectives

Exceptional Children

Prologue

A Personal View of Special Education

My primary goal in writing this book is to describe the history, practices, advances, problems, and challenges that make up the complex and dynamic field called special education in as complete, clear, up to date, and accurate a manner as possible. This, of course, is much easier said than done: an author's personal views are surely implicit in those descriptions—between the lines, as they say. Because my personal beliefs and assumptions about special education—which are by no means unique, but neither are they held by everyone in the field—affect both the substance and the tone of the book, I believe I owe you, the reader, an explicit summary of those views.

People with disabilities have a fundamental right to live and participate in the same settings and programs—in school, at home, in the workplace, and in the community—as do people without disabilities. That is, the settings and programs in which children and adults with disabilities learn, live, work, and play should, to the greatest extent possible, be the same settings and programs in which people without disabilities participate. People with and without disabilities have a great deal to contribute to and learn from one another. We cannot do that without regular, meaningful interaction.

Individuals with disabilities have the right to as much self-determination as we can help them achieve. Special educators have no more important teaching task than that of helping children with disabilities learn how to increase their level of decision making and control over their own lives. Thus, self-determination and self-advocacy skills should be significant curriculum components for all students with disabilities.

Special education must expand and improve its efforts to serve effectively all learners with exceptional educational needs. These include the gifted and talented child, the preschooler with disabilities and the infant who is at risk for a future learning problem, the exceptional child from a different cultural or ethnic background, and the adult with disabilities. In support of this belief, this text includes a chapter on each of these critical areas of special education.

Both the meaningfulness and the effectiveness of special education are enhanced by school and family partnerships. Professionals have too long ignored the needs of parents and families of exceptional children, often treating them as patients, clients, or even adversaries instead of realizing that they are partners with the same goals. Some special educators have given the impression (and, worse, believed it to be true) that parents are there to serve professionals, when in fact the opposite is more correct. We must recognize parents as a child's first—and, in many ways, best—teachers. Learning to work effectively with parents is one of the most important skills the special educator can acquire. Thus, a chapter is devoted to the parent-professional partnership.

The efforts of special educators are most effective when they incorporate the input and services of all of the disciplines in the helping professions. It is foolish to argue over territorial rights when we can accomplish more by working together within an interdisciplinary team that includes our colleagues in psychology, medical and health services, counseling, social services, and vocational rehabilitation.

All students have the right to an effective education.   As educators, our primary responsibility is to design and implement effective instruction for academic, social, vocational, and personal skills. These skills are the same ones that influence the quality of our lives: working effectively and efficiently at our jobs, being productive members of our communities, maintaining a comfortable lifestyle in our homes, communicating with our friends and family, and using our leisure time meaningfully and enjoyably. Instruction is ultimately effective when it helps the students we serve acquire and maintain positive lifestyle changes. To put it another way, the proof of the process is in the product. Therefore, . . .

Teachers must demand effectiveness from the curriculum materials and instructional tools they use.   For many years conventional wisdom has fostered the belief that it takes unending patience to teach children with disabilities. I believe this view is a disservice to students with special needs and to the educators—both special and general education teachers—who teach them. Teachers should not wait patiently for exceptional students to learn, attributing lack of progress to some inherent attribute or faulty process within the child, such as mental retardation, learning disability, attention-deficit disorder, or emotional disturbance. Instead, the teacher should use direct and frequent measures of the student's performance as the primary guide for modifying instruction in order to improve its effectiveness. This, I believe, is the real work of the special educator. Numerous examples of instructional strategies and tactics demonstrated to be effective through classroom-based research are described and illustrated throughout the text. Although you will not know how to teach exceptional children after reading this or any other introductory text, you will gain an appreciation for the importance of explicit, systematic instruction and an understanding of the kinds of teaching skills a competent special educator must have.

Finally, the future for individuals with disabilities holds great promise.   We have only begun to discover the myriad ways in which to improve teaching, increase learning, prevent and minimize the conditions that cause disabilities, encourage acceptance, and use technology to compensate for disabilities. Although I make no specific predictions for the future, I am certain that we have not come as far as we can in learning how to help exceptional individuals build and enjoy fuller, more independent lives in the school, home, workplace, and community.

Part 1

Foundations for Understanding Special Education

Chapter 1
Defining Special Education

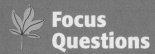

Focus Questions

- When is special education needed? How do we know?

- If categorical labels do not tell us what and how to teach, why are they used so frequently?

- Why have court cases and federal legislation been required to ensure that children with disabilities receive an appropriate education?

- How can a special educator provide all three kinds of intervention—preventive, remedial, and compensatory—on behalf of an individual child?

- What do you think are the three most important challenges facing special education today? Why? Read your answer again after finishing this book.

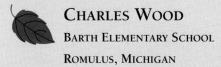

CHARLES WOOD

BARTH ELEMENTARY SCHOOL
ROMULUS, MICHIGAN

Education • Teaching Credentials • Experience
- B.S in Psychology, Western Michigan University, 1994
- M.Ed. in Special Education, The Ohio State University, 1998
- Michigan, Mentally Impaired, K–12; Ohio, Developmental Handicaps, K–12
- 4 years teaching experience

My Classroom and Students   If you walked into Barth Elementary School, you would be able to quickly find my classroom—it's usually the loudest room in the building! You might hear the boom of my students' voices as they respond aloud and in unison during a reading lesson or the roar of our cheers and applause as Chad reaches a new high score on his timed reading checkout.

I teach K–6 students with learning disabilities. This year I have 14 students, ages 5 to 12. My students spend most of the day in their general education classrooms and come to the resource room to work on reading, writing, and math for about an hour each day. I enjoy teaching in the resource room because I get to work with students at every grade level. It makes teaching more challenging and exciting.

I team-teach science lessons with a first-grade teacher twice a week. The first-grade teacher has three of my resource room students in her class, so this gives me an opportunity to work with my students in their regular classroom. During science, I use teaching strategies such as choral responding so all of the students can participate.

Most of my students need help with academic tool skills, especially reading. Here are brief descriptions of two of my students and examples of their IEP goals. Ricky is a star on his T-Ball team. Like most first graders, Ricky loves Pokémon, Dr. Seuss books, and recess. Ricky has excellent handwriting. His teacher often gives him a "check double plus" for neatness on his schoolwork. Ricky was identified as learning disabled when he was in kindergarten. He needs help with basic reading and math skills.

Annual goal 1.0.   Ricky will develop phonetic/word analysis skills.
  Instructional objective 1.1.   Ricky will recall short vowels, long vowels, and vowel combinations with 80% accuracy on curriculum-based assessments.
  Instructional objective 1.2.   Ricky will blend sounds into words with 80% accuracy on curriculum-based assessments.
Annual goal 2.0.   Ricky will develop/increase math computation skills.
  Instructional objective 2.1.   Ricky will recall single-digit addition and subtraction facts with 80% accuracy on curriculum-based assessments.
  Instructional objective 2.2.   Ricky will compute two-digit whole numbers without regrouping using the operations addition and subtraction with 80% accuracy on curriculum-based assessments.

Fourth-grader Kyle is involved in several extracurricular activities. This year he began playing the bass drum in the elementary school band. Kyle's mom, who has to endure his practice sessions at home, wishes he had chosen a quieter instrument. Kyle loves sports. He plays on a Romulus youth football team called the Flyers and is the captain of his bowling team. During his first couple of years in school, Kyle struggled mightily with everything academic. Prior to entering the third grade, he was identified as learning disabled. Kyle has made tremendous progress since he began receiving individualized instruction in the resource room.

Annual goal 1.0. Kyle will develop/increase reading comprehension skills.

Instructional objective 1.1. Kyle will recall "who, what, where" in a paragraph with 80% accuracy on informal, teacher-made assessments.

Instructional objective 1.2. Kyle will sequence sentences from a story in logical order with 80% accuracy on informal, teacher-made assessments.

Annual goal 2.0. Kyle will develop/increase spelling skills.

Instructional objective 2.1. Kyle will spell words with regular patterns with 80% accuracy on informal tests.

Instructional objective 2.2. Kyle will identify and correct spelling errors with 80% accuracy on informal tests.

Curriculum Materials and Teaching Strategies I have had great success using the Direct Instruction (DI) model and curriculum materials. This model provides carefully sequenced lessons that require active student participation. The DI reading series enables me to provide explicit phonics instruction to promote students' mastery of basic decoding skills. The series also includes daily checkouts, which test students' rate and accuracy using the stories they've read. After the timed checkouts, my students graph their daily reading progress. Each student fills in a bar graph from the reading workbook to record his or her reading rate. A goal for my sixth graders is to read more than 120 words per minute with no more than three errors. Their graph only goes up to 150 on the vertical axis. Recently, Chad and Misty have been reading at rates over 150 words per minute. They call this "bustin' through the top." Chad likes to say he's "going for 200!" The information gained from these daily assessments lets me know if my students are "getting it" and whether or not I need to review the material or try a new teaching strategy.

To see examples of the graphs and other instructional materials used by Mr. Wood and his students, go to the Teacher Feature module of the Companion Website at **www.prehall.com/heward**

Collaboration and Teaming This year I've been given the added responsibility of coordinating our school's child study team (CST). The team includes the building principal, the psychologist, the social worker, the speech and language pathologist, the learning specialist, and myself. The CST meets weekly with teachers and parents of students who are not currently receiving special education services but are having difficulty in school academically and/or socially. The team recommends strategies or services to improve students' learning, evaluates those efforts, and, when needed, refers students for a multidisciplinary evaluation to determine eligibility for special education services. Although it's a lot of work, participating on the CST gives me the opportunity to help design instructional programs that may prevent children from experiencing more significant learning achievement problems later on.

What I Like Most about Being a Special Educator When school begins in the fall, I hear some of my new students complain about how much they don't know or describe in detail everything they can't do. In the spring, it's fun to hear those same students bragging to one other about how much they know and how much they can do. "That's easy! Give me somethin' hard!" they say. I love seeing my students' confidence grow throughout the year.

Advice for Someone Considering a Career in Special Education I was fortunate to have had a wide-range of experiences with special populations before I began teaching.

During summer breaks in college, I worked as a camp counselor at a day camp for children with disabilities. During the school year, I worked as a part-time teacher's aide in a special school for students with severe disabilities and students with autism. I also got involved in a college program called Best Buddies, where I served as a mentor for a high school student with mild disabilities. Several classroom field placements and my student teaching experience allowed me to further explore the range of possible careers in special education. All those different experiences helped me know for certain that I wanted to be a special education teacher at the elementary level. Get as much experience as you can with special populations. This will help you decide if a career in special education is right for you.

The Most Difficult Thing about Being a Special Educator   It's difficult to find enough time in each school day to cover all subject areas and meet each student's unique needs. Scheduling and planning lessons with a limited amount of instructional time continues to be a challenge. However, I enjoy the challenge of finding ways to do more with my students in less time.

A Memorable Moment   Last spring the mother of one of my younger students made a chocolate cake for me. This cake was huge, about the size of a large television! The cake was made to look like an old-fashioned storybook. The words written in icing on its opened pages read, "Once there was a special little boy named Colton who had a wonderful, caring teacher named Mr. Wood." Colton's mother said she wanted to show me how much she appreciated my helping her son learn to read. It was very heartwarming. It's the little things (well, in this case, it was a huge thing!) that make teaching so great.

E ducating children with special needs or abilities is a difficult challenge. Teachers and related professionals who have accepted that challenge—special educators—work in an exciting and rapidly changing field. To begin to appreciate some of the action and excitement—as well as the persistent and emerging challenges— that characterize this important and dynamic field, it is necessary to examine some concepts and perspectives that are basic to understanding exceptional children and special education.

To better understand the topics that will be covered in this chapter, go to the Essential Concepts and Chapter-at-a-Glance modules in Chapter 1 of the Companion Website at **www.prenhall.com/heward**

WHO ARE EXCEPTIONAL CHILDREN?

All children exhibit differences from one another in terms of their physical attributes (e.g., some are shorter, some are stronger) and learning abilities (e.g., some learn quickly and are able to remember and use what they have learned in new situations; others need repeated practice and have difficulty maintaining and generalizing new knowledge and skills). The differences among most children are relatively small, enabling these children to benefit from the general education program. The physical attributes and/or learning abilities of some children, however—those called **exceptional children**—differ from the norm (either below or above) to such an extent that they require an individualized program of special education and related services to fully benefit from education. The term *exceptional children* includes children who experience difficulties in learning as well as those children whose performance is so superior that modifications in curriculum and instruction are necessary to help them fulfill their potential. Thus, *exceptional children* is an inclusive term that refers to children with learning and/or behavior problems, children with physical disabilities or sensory impairments, and children who are intellectually gifted or have a special talent. The

Definition of exceptional children

Council for Exceptional Children   Content Standards for Beginning Teachers—Common Core: Similarities and differences of individuals with and without exceptional learning needs (CC2K5).

TABLE 1.1   Definitions of impairment, disability, and handicap

Term	Definition
Impairment	Any loss or abnormality of psychological, physiological, or anatomical structure or function.
Disability	Any restriction or lack (resulting from an impairment) of ability to perform an activity in the manner or within the range considered normal for a human being.
Handicap	A disadvantage for a given individual, resulting from an impairment or a disability, that limits or prevents the fulfillment of a role that is normal (depending on age, sex, and social or cultural factors) for that individual.

Source: World Health Organization. (1993). *International classification of impairments, disabilities, and handicaps* (pp. 27–29). Geneva, Switzerland: Author.

Definition of impairment, disability, handicap, and at risk

Council for Exceptional Children Content Standards for Beginning Teachers–Common Core: Similarities and differences of individuals with and without exceptional learning needs (CC2K5).
PRAXIS Special Education Core Principles: Content Knowledge: I. Understanding Exceptionalities, Definitions of disabilities.

term *students with disabilities* is more restrictive than *exceptional children* because it does not include gifted and talented children. Definitions of several related terms will help you better understand the concept of exceptionality.

Although the terms *impairment, disability,* and *handicap* are sometimes used interchangeably, the terms are not synonymous (see Table 1.1). **Impairment** refers to the loss or reduced function of a particular body part or organ (e.g., a missing limb). A **disability** exists when an impairment limits the ability to perform certain tasks (e.g., to walk, to see, to add a row of numbers) in the same way that most persons do. A person with a disability is not *handicapped*, however, unless the disability leads to educational, personal, social, vocational, or other problems. If a child who has lost a leg, for example, can learn to use an artificial limb and thus function in and out of school without problems, she is not handicapped.

Handicap refers to a problem or disadvantage that a person with a disability or impairment encounters in interacting with the environment. A disability may pose a handicap in one environment but not in another. The child with an artificial limb may be handicapped (i.e., disadvantaged) when competing against nondisabled peers on the basketball court but may experience no handicap in the classroom. Individuals with disabilities also experience handicaps that have nothing to do with their disabilities but are the result of negative attitudes and inappropriate behavior of others who needlessly restrict their access and ability to participate fully in school, work, or community activities.

The word *handicapped* is thought to come from a game that involved the "cap in the hand," and it has the contemporary meaning of assigning extra weight (a handicap) to better performers to "level" a playing field and enhance wagering (Treanor, 1993). Unfortunately, the word conjures up the negative image of a person with disabilities begging in the street. In most instances today, the person-first descriptor *with disabilities* is preferred over the term *handicapped*.

At risk refers to children who, although not currently identified as having a disability, are considered to have a greater-than-usual chance of developing a disability. The term is often applied to infants and preschoolers who, because of conditions surrounding their births or home environments, may be expected to experience developmental problems at a later time. The term also refers to students who are experiencing learning problems in the regular classroom and are therefore at risk of school failure or of being identified for special education services.

Some exceptional children share certain physical characteristics and/or patterns of learning and behavior. These characteristics fall into the following categories of exceptionality:

- Mental retardation
- Learning disabilities

- Emotional and behavioral disorders
- Communication (speech and language) disorders
- Hearing loss
- Blindness and low vision
- Physical and health impairments
- Traumatic brain injury
- Severe and multiple disabilities
- Autism
- Giftedness and special talents

As stated earlier, all children differ from one another in individual characteristics along a continuum; exceptional children differ markedly from the norm so that an individually designed program of instruction—in other words, special education—is required if they are to benefit fully from education. It is a mistake, however, to think that there are two distinct kinds of children—those who are exceptional and those who are regular. Exceptional children are more like other children than they are different. Keep this critical point in mind as you read about the exceptional children described in this text.

HOW MANY EXCEPTIONAL CHILDREN ARE THERE?

It is impossible to state precisely the number of exceptional children for many reasons, such as (1) the different criteria used by states and local school systems to identify exceptional children, (2) the relative resources and abilities of different school systems to provide preventive services so that an at-risk student does not become a special education student, (3) the imprecise nature of assessment and the large part that subjective judgment plays in interpretation of assessment data, and (4) the fact that a child may be identified as eligible for special education at one time in his school career and not eligible (or included in a different disability category) at another time.

The most complete and accurate information on how many exceptional children live in the United States is derived from the child count data in the U.S. Department of Education's annual report to Congress on the education of the country's children with disabilities. More than 6.3 million children and youth with disabilities, ages 3 to 21, received special education services during the 2000–2001 school year (U.S. Department of Education, 2002). Table 1.2 shows the number of school-age students who received special education under each of the disability categories used by the federal government.

Let's take a quick look at some other numerical facts about special education in the United States.

- The number of children and youth who receive special education has grown every year since a national count was begun in the 1976–1977 school year.
- New early intervention programs have been major contributors to the increases since 1986. During the 2000–2001 school year, 598,922 preschoolers (ages 3 to 5) and 230,418 infants and toddlers (birth through age 2) were among those receiving special education.
- Children with disabilities in special education represent approximately 8.8% of the resident population ages 6 to 17.
- The number of children who receive special education increases from age 3 through age 9. The number served decreases gradually with each successive age year after age 9 until age 17. Thereafter, the number of students receiving special education decreases sharply.

TABLE 1.2 **Number of students ages 6–21 who received special education services under the federal government's disability categories (2000–2001 school year)**

Disability Category	Number	Percent of Total
Specific learning disabilities	2,879,445	50.0
Speech or language impairments	1,092,105	18.9
Mental retardation	611,878	10.6
Emotional disturbance	472,932	8.2
Other health impairments	291,474	5.1
Multiple disabilities	121,954	2.1
Autism	78,717	1.4
Orthopedic impairments	73,011	1.3
Hearing impairments	70,662	1.2
Developmental delay	28,683	0.5
Visual impairments	25,927	0.4
Traumatic brain injury	14,829	0.3
Deaf-blindness	1,318	<0.1
All disabilities	5,762,935	100.0

Source: From U.S. Department of Education. (2002). *Twenty-third annual report to Congress on the implementation of the Individuals with Disabilities Act* (p. AA3). Washington, DC: Author.

Relative prevalence of disabilities

PRAXIS Special Education Core Principles: Content Knowledge: I. Understanding Exceptionalities, Incidence and prevalence of various types of disabilities.

- Eighty-eight percent of all children and youth ages 6 to 21 receiving special education are reported under four disability categories: (1) learning disabilities (50%), (2) speech and language impairment (18.9%), (3) mental retardation (10.6%), and (4) emotional disturbance (8.2%).
- The percentage of students receiving special education under the learning disabilities category has grown dramatically (from 23.8% to 50%), whereas the percentage of students with mental retardation has decreased by more than half (from 24.9% to 10.6%) since the federal government began collecting and reporting child count data in 1976–1977.
- About twice as many males as females receive special education.
- The vast majority—approximately 85%—of school-age children receiving special education have mild disabilities.
- The "typical" child receiving special education in the United States is an elementary-age boy with learning disabilities who spends part of each school day in the regular classroom and part in a resource room.
- Although special education for children who are gifted and talented is not mandated by federal law as it is for children with disabilities, during the 1998–1999 school year, 43 states reported serving more than 2 million students in K–12 gifted programs (Council of State Directors of Programs for the Gifted, 2000).

WHY DO WE LABEL AND CLASSIFY EXCEPTIONAL CHILDREN?

Centuries ago, labeling and classifying people was of little importance; survival was the main concern. Those whose disabilities prevented their full participation in the activities necessary for survival were left on their own to perish or, in some instances, were even killed. In later years, derogatory labels such as "dunce," "imbecile," and "fool" were applied to people with mental retardation or behavior problems, and other demeaning words were used for persons with other disabilities or physical deformities. In each instance, however, the purpose of classification was the same: to exclude the person with disabilities from the activities, privileges, and facilities of everyday life.

Many educators believe that the labels used to identify and classify exceptional children stigmatize them and function to deny them opportunities in the mainstream (e.g., Danforth & Rhodes, 1997; Reschly, 1996; Stainback & Stainback, 1991). Others argue that a workable system of classifying exceptional children (or their exceptional learning needs) is a prerequisite to providing the special educational services those children require (e.g., Kauffman, 1999; MacMillan, Gresham, Bocian, & Lambros, 1998). Classification is a complex issue involving emotional, political, and ethical considerations in addition to scientific, fiscal, and educational interests (Luckasson & Reeve, 2001). As with most complex issues, there are valid perspectives on both sides of the labeling question. The reasons most often cited for and against the classification and labeling of exceptional children are the following:

Although children with disabilities have special instructional needs, they are, above all, children.

Possible Benefits of Labeling

- Labeling recognizes meaningful differences in learning or behavior and is a first and necessary step in responding responsibly to those differences.
- Labeling may lead to a protective response in which children are more accepting of the atypical behavior of a peer with disabilities than they would be if that same behavior were emitted by a child without disabilities. (A protective response—whether by peers, parents, or teachers—toward a child with a disability can be a disadvantage if it creates learned helplessness and diminishes the labeled child's chances to develop independence [Weisz, Bromfield, Vines, & Weiss, 1985].)
- Labeling helps professionals communicate with one another and classify and evaluate research findings.
- Funding and resources for research and other programs are often based on specific categories of exceptionality.
- Labels enable disability-specific advocacy groups (e.g., parents of children with autism) to promote specific programs and to spur legislative action.
- Labeling helps make exceptional children's special needs more visible to policymakers and the public.

Pros and cons of labeling

Council for Exceptional Children — Content Standards for Beginning Teachers–Common Core: Issues in definition and identification of individuals with exceptional earning needs (CC1K5).
PRAXIS Special Education Core Principles: Content Knowledge: I. Understanding Exceptionalities, Labeling of students, Implications of the classification process.

Possible Disadvantages of Labeling

- Because labels usually focus on disability, impairment, and performance deficits, some people may think only in terms of what the individual *cannot do* instead of what she *can or might be able to learn to do.*
- Labels may stigmatize the child and lead peers to reject or ridicule the labeled child. (Not all labels used to classify children with disabilities are considered equally negative or stigmatizing. One factor possibly contributing to the large number of children identified as learning disabled is that many professionals and parents view "learning disabilities" as a socially acceptable classification [MacMillan, Gresham, Siperstein, & Bocian, 1996].)
- Labels may negatively affect the child's self-esteem.

Effects of labels on behavior of others

 Council for Exceptional Children — Content Standards for Beginning Teachers–Common Core: Teacher attitudes and behaviors that influence behavior of individuals with exceptional learning needs (CC5K4).
PRAXIS Special Education Core Principles: Content Knowledge: I. Understanding Exceptionalities, Labeling of students, Implications of the classification process.

- Labels may cause others to hold low expectations for and to differentially treat a child on the basis of the label, which may result in a self-fulfilling prophecy. For example, in one study, student teachers gave a child labeled "autistic" more praise and rewards and less verbal correction for *incorrect* responses than they gave a child labeled "normal" (Eikeseth & Lovaas, 1992). Such differential treatment could hamper a child's acquisition of new skills and contribute to the development and maintenance of a level of performance consistent with the label's prediction.
- Labels that describe a child's performance deficit often mistakenly acquire the role of explanatory constructs (e.g., "Sherry acts that way *because* she is emotionally disturbed").
- Even though membership in a given category is based on a particular characteristic (e.g., hearing loss), there is a tendency to assume that all children in a category share other traits as well, thereby diminishing the detection and appreciation of each child's uniqueness (Gelb, 1997; Smith & Mitchell, 2001).
- Labels suggest that learning problems are primarily the result of something wrong within the child, thereby reducing the systematic examination of and accountability for instructional variables as the cause of performance deficits. This is an especially damaging outcome when the label provides educators with a built-in excuse for ineffective instruction (e.g., "Jalen hasn't learned to read because he's learning disabled").
- A disproportionate number of children from some minority and diverse cultural groups are included in special education programs and thus have been assigned disability labels.
- Special education labels have a certain permanence; once labeled, it is difficult for a child to ever again achieve the status of simply being just another kid.
- Labels may provide a basis for keeping children out of the regular classroom.
- Classifying exceptional children requires the expenditure of a great amount of money and professional and student time that might be better spent in planning and delivering instruction (Chaikind, Danielson, & Brauen, 1993).

Clearly, there are strong arguments both for and against the classification and labeling of exceptional children. On the one hand, most of the possible benefits are experienced not by individual children but by groups of children, parents, and professionals who are associated with a certain category. On the other hand, all of the potential negative aspects of labeling affect the individual child who has been labeled. Of the possible advantages of labeling listed previously, only the first two could be said to benefit an individual child directly. However, the argument that disability labels associate diagnosis with proper intervention is tenuous at best, particularly when the kinds of labels used in special education are considered. What Becker, Engelmann, and Thomas (1971) wrote three decades ago is still true today: "[The labels] rarely tell the teacher who can be taught in what way. One could put five or six labels on the same child and still not know what to teach him or how" (p. 436). (See Profiles & Perspectives, "What's in a Name? The Labels and Language of Special Education," later in this chapter.)

Although the pros and cons of using disability category labels have been widely debated for several decades, neither conceptual arguments nor research has produced a conclusive case for the total acceptance or absolute rejection of labeling practices. Most of the studies conducted to assess the effects of labeling have produced inconclusive, often contradictory, evidence and have generally been marked by methodological weakness. Let's look at how the use of categorical labels affects a child's access to special education services and the likelihood of interventions designed to prevent more serious problems as the result of disabling conditions.

 LABELING AND ELIGIBILITY FOR SPECIAL EDUCATION

On one level, the various labels given to children with special learning needs can be viewed as a means of organizing the funding and administration of special education services in the schools. Under current law, to receive special education services, a child must be identified as having a disability (i.e., labeled) and, with few exceptions, must be further classified into one of that state's categories, such as mental retardation or learning disabilities. In practice, therefore, a student becomes eligible for special education and related services because of membership in a given category. (IDEA allows children ages 3 to 9 to be identified as *developmentally delayed* and receive special education services without the use of a specific disability label.)

If losing one's label also means loss of needed services, the trade-off is not likely to be beneficial for the child. In the 1970s, for example, the definition of mental retardation was changed; and children who had previously been classified under the subcategory of "borderline mental retardation" no longer met the definition. As a result, they were no longer eligible for special education services designed for children with mental retardation. Although many of this large group of declassified youngsters receive services under other disability categories (notably learning disabilities), some do not receive needed services (MacMillan et al., 1998).

 LABELING AND PREVENTION OF MORE SERIOUS PROBLEMS

Kauffman (1999) maintains that labels are a necessary first step in serving students with important differences in behavior and learning and that our unwillingness to label children's behavior problems impedes prevention of more serious disabilities:

> Although universal interventions that apply equally to all, regardless of their behavioral characteristics or risks of developing disorders, can be implemented without labels and risk of stigma, no other interventions are possible without labels. Either all students are treated the same or some are treated differently. Any student who is treated differently is inevitably labeled. . . . We need to use the least offensive labels that clearly describe the problem, but we need not believe the fantasy that the label is the problem or that a new label will fool people for long. . . . When we are unwilling for whatever reason to say that a person has a problem, we are helpless to prevent it. . . . Labeling a problem clearly is the first step in dealing with it productively. (p. 452)

 ALTERNATIVES TO LABELING

A number of alternative approaches to classifying exceptional children that focus on educationally relevant variables have been proposed over the years (e.g., Adelman, 1996; Hardman, McDonnell, & Welch, 1997; Iscoe & Payne, 1972; Sontag, Sailor, & Smith, 1977). For example, Reynolds, Zetlin, and Heistad (1996) have proposed a system they call "20/20 analysis" as an alternative, nonlabeling approach to the traditional, categorically driven model of special education. The lowest-achieving 20% and the highest-achieving 20% of students would be identified and eligible for broad (noncategorical) approaches to improvement of learning opportunities.

> In 20/20 Analysis, we begin with measuring progress of students in important areas of learning and identifying those at the margins—those who are not learning well and those showing top rates of learning. . . . At all times the focus is on outcome variables. . . . The idea is to look to the margins in learning progress and to identify those who most urgently require adapted instruction. (Reynolds & Heistad, 1997, p. 441)

Some noted special educators have suggested that exceptional children be classified according to the curriculum and skill areas they need to learn.

> But if we shouldn't refer to these special children by using those old labels, then how should we refer to them? For openers, call them Rob, Amy, and Jose. Beyond that, refer to them on the basis of what you're trying to teach them. For example, if a teacher wants to teach Brandon to compute, read, and comprehend, he might call him a student of computation, reading, and comprehension. We do this all the time

Labeling and prevention

Council for Exceptional Children | Content Standards for Beginning Teachers—Common Core: Teacher attitudes and behaviors that influence behavior of individuals with exceptional learning needs (CC5K4).
PRAXIS Special Education Core Principles: Content Knowledge: I. Understanding Exceptionalities, Causation and prevention of disability, Implications of the classification process.

What's in a Name?
The Labels and Language of Special Education

Some years ago at the annual convention of the Council for Exceptional Children, hundreds of attendees were wearing big yellow and black buttons that proclaimed "Label jars, not children!" Wearers of the buttons were presumably making a statement about one or more of the criticisms leveled at categorizing and labeling exceptional children, such as labeling is negative because it focuses only on the child's deficits, labeling makes it more likely that others will expect poor performance or bad behavior from the child, and labels may hurt the child's self-esteem.

Labels, in and of themselves, are not the problem. The dictionary defines *label* as "a descriptive word or phrase applied to a person, group, theory, etc., as a convenient generalized classification" (Webster's New World Dictionary, 1986, p. 785). Most special educators agree that a common language for referring to children who share instructional and related service needs is necessary. The words that we use as labels, and even the order in which they are spoken or written, do, however, influence the degree to which those words effectively and appropriately communicate variables relevant to the design and delivery of educational and other human services. For example, although they may convey a general set of common educational needs, terms such as *the handicapped* or *the retarded* imply negative connotations that are unwarranted and inappropriate. Such blanket labels imply that all persons in the group being labeled are alike; individuality has been lost (Gelb, 1997). At the personal level, when we describe a child as a "physically handicapped boy," we place too much emphasis on the disability, perhaps suggesting that the deficits caused by the disability are the most important thing to know about him.

How, then, should we refer to exceptional children? At the personal level, we should follow Tom Lovitt's advice and call them by their names: Linda, Shawon, and Jackie. Referring to a child as "Molly, a fifth-grade student with learning disabilities," helps us focus on the individual child and her primary role as a student. Such a description does not ignore or gloss over Molly's learning problems but acknowledges that there are other things we should know about her.

It is important for everyone, not just special educators, to speak, write, and think about exceptional children and adults in ways that respect each person's individuality and recognize strengths and abilities instead of focusing only on disabilities. Simply changing the way we talk about an individual with a disability, however, will not make the problems posed by her disability go away. Some disabled people have begun to speak out against the efforts of those without disabilities to assuage their feelings with language that may be politically correct but that ignores the reality of a disability. Judy Heumann, former director of the U.S. Office of Special Education and Rehabilitation Services and a person who has used a wheelchair since she was 18 months old, explains her position:

As our movement has evolved, we have been plagued by people, almost always not themselves disabled, attempting to change what we call ourselves. If we are "victims" of anything, it is of such terms as *physically challenged, able-disabled, differently-abled, handi-capables,* and *people with differing abilities,* to name just a few. Nondisabled people's discomfort with reality-based terms such as *disabled* led them to these euphemisms. I believe these euphemisms have the effect of depoliticizing our own terminology and devaluing our own view of ourselves as disabled people. . . .

I have a physical disability that results in my inability to walk and perform a number of other significant tasks without the assistance of another person. This cannot be labeled away and I am not ashamed of it. I feel no need to change the word "disabled." For me, there is no stigma. I am not driven to call myself a "person with a disability." I know I am a person; I do not need to tell myself that I am. I also do not believe that being called a "person with a disability" results in my being treated any more like a human being. Maybe putting the word "disabled" first makes people stop and look at what, as a result of society's historical indifference to and/or hatred of people like me, is a critical part of my existence. . . .

Let the disabled people who are politically involved and personally affected determine our own language. . . . A suggestion to those of you who do not know what to call me: ask!

Donald Cook, an educational researcher, contributed these comments to an Internet discussion of how to speak to and about people with disabilities:

I am handicapped by post polio syndrome and must use a wheelchair and/or a walker. The other day I was referred to, for the first time, as "differently-abled." The context was benign: the speaker had noticed a beach with special wheelchairs that went across sand and into the water, and thought I would like to know about it. Still the term "differently-abled" stunned me. I asked whose feelings were being spared here, mine or hers? This question angered her—a possible sign of a question with a point. It seems clear to me that my condition is not merely different in some abstract dimension but one of a loss of function. So I prefer "handicapped" or some term which acknowledges that. (*CompuServe Education Forum,* July 11, 1994)

Bernard Rimland (1993a), director of the Autism Research Institute in San Diego and the father of a son with autism, is a severe critic of those who are trying to change the language of special education under the

Changing the label used to identify or classify Jeffrey's disability won't lessen the impact of his disability. But referring to him as "Jeffrey, a third grader," instead of "a mentally retarded boy," helps us recognize his strengths and abilities—what he can do—instead of focusing on the disability as if it were his defining characteristic.

arrogant assumption of the moral high ground . . . certain that their way is the only way. . . . They insist that words such as "autistic," "retarded," and "handicapped" not be used. They insist that the silly euphemism "challenging" be used to describe severely self-injurious or assaultive behavior. . . . It deprives the handicapped of their most valuable asset—the recognition of their disability by the rest of us. Yes, there are people on the borderline between normal and handicapped. Does that mean that no one is handicapped? Yes, there are shades of gray. Does that mean there is no black and white? Does twilight disprove the difference between day and night? (p. 1)

Michael Goldfarb, executive director of the Association for the Help of Retarded Children, offers some provocative and insightful thoughts on the language of special education:

Consider the following lists of words:

crippled
handicapped
disabled
challenged

inmate
patient
resident
client
program participant

feeble minded
retarded
person with mental retardation
person

institution
state school
developmental center

Consider the words on the top of each list, the old and unfashionable ones. The names at the bottom are new and more acceptable. Many professionals in this field have made it a matter of deep personal commitment to get you to use the most up-to-date expressions.

Every one of these changes has been presented as an essential act of consciousness raising. Every one of these changes has been proposed by numbers of enlightened, progressive, and intelligent professionals with the genuine intent of changing the image and role of disabled people in this society. Every one of these linguistic reforms has been followed several years later by newer and "better" names. Every one of these changes has failed to make the world different.

Linguistic reform without systemic change conceals unhappy truths. Social problems may be reflected in the way we speak, but they are rarely, if ever, cured by changes in language. It is certainly true that liberals feel better when they use the most acceptable phrase, but this should not obscure the fact that the oppressed continue to be oppressed under any label. (Perhaps we should not call people "the oppressed"; perhaps it would be better to call them "people with oppression.")

Our real problem in this and many other societies is that we respect only intelligence, stylish good looks, and earning potential. This society denigrates people who are not intelligent, who are deemed unattractive, or who are poor. Referring to retarded people as "people with men-

tal retardation" will not make them brighter, prettier, richer. These names leave the old prejudices intact. Society's attitudes and the values that underlie them must be changed. This will take far more than trivial linguistic changes. Can you imagine a Planning Board meeting at which a local resident says, "We don't want any retarded people living in our neighborhood! But people with mental retardation? That's different. They can move in anytime." I can't.

Changing attitudes and values is more difficult than changing language. Perhaps that is why we spend so much time changing language.

Sources: Long excerpt reprinted from Heumann, J. (1993). Building our own boats: A personal perspective on disability policy. In L. O. Gostin & H. A. Beyer (Eds.), *Implementing the Americans with Disabilities Act: Rights and responsibilities of all Americans.* Baltimore: Paul H. Brookes Publishing Co., Inc. Used by permission of the publisher and the author.
Final segment adapted from Goldfarb, M. (1990, Spring). Executive director's report. *AHRC Chronicle.* Used by permission.

with older students. Sam, who attends Juilliard, is referred to as "the trumpet student"; Jane, who attends Harvard, is called "the law student." (T. C. Lovitt, personal communication, January 14, 2002)

In a system such as this, called **curriculum-based assessment,** students would be assessed and classified relative to the degree to which they are learning specific curriculum content (Deno, 1997; Howell, 1998; Jones, 2001; Steeker & Fuchs, 2000). Educators who employ curriculum-based assessment believe that it is more important to assess (and thereby classify) students in terms of acquisition of the knowledge and skills that make up the school's curriculum than to determine the degree to which they differ from the normative score of all children in some general physical attribute or learning characteristic.

Even though curriculum-based assessment is being used more frequently, use of the traditional labels and categories of exceptional children is likely to continue. The continued development and use of educationally relevant classification systems, however, make it more likely that identification and assessment will lead to meaningful instructional programs for children, promote more educationally meaningful communication and research by professionals, and perhaps decrease some of the negative aspects of our current labeling practices.

Curriculum-based assessment

 Council for Exceptional Children Content Standards for Beginning Teachers–Common Core: Basic terminology used in assessment (CC8K1).
PRAXIS Special Education Core Principles: Content Knowledge: III. Delivery of Services to Students with disabilities, curriculum-based assessment.

WHY ARE LAWS GOVERNING THE EDUCATION OF EXCEPTIONAL CHILDREN NECESSARY?

 ### AN EXCLUSIONARY PAST

It is said that a society can be judged by the way it treats those who are different. By this criterion, our educational system has a less than distinguished history. Children who are different because of race, culture, language, gender, or exceptionality have often been denied full and fair access to educational opportunities (Banks & Banks, 2001). (Past practices were not entirely negative. Long before there was any legal requirement to do so,

Historical background

PRAXIS Special Education Core Principles: Content Knowledge: II. Legal and Societal Issues, Historical movements/trends affecting connections between special education and the larger society.

many children with special needs were educated by devoted parents and teachers [cf. Safford & Safford, 1996]).

Although exceptional children have always been with us, attention has not always been paid to their special needs. In the past, many children with disabilities were entirely excluded from any publicly supported program of education. Before the 1970s, many states had laws permitting public schools to deny enrollment to children with disabilities (Murdick, Gartin, & Crabtree, 2002). Local school officials had no legal obligation to grant students with disabilities the same educational access that nondisabled students enjoyed. One state law, for example, allowed schools to refuse to serve "children physically or mentally incapacitated for school work"; another state had a law stipulating that children with "bodily or mental conditions rendering attendance inadvisable" could be turned away. When these laws were contested, the nation's courts generally supported exclusion. In a 1919 case, for example, a 13-year-old student with physical disabilities (but normal intellectual ability) was excluded from his local school because he "produces a depressing and nauseating effect upon the teachers and school children. . . . he takes up an undue portion of the teacher's time and attention, distracts attention of other pupils, and interferes generally with the discipline and progress of the school" (Johnson, 1986, p. 2).

When local public schools began to accept a measure of responsibility for educating certain exceptional students, a philosophy of segregation prevailed—a philosophy that continued unchanged until recently. Inclusion of exceptional children into regular schools and classes is a relatively recent phenomenon. Children received labels—such as mentally retarded, crippled, or emotionally disturbed—and were confined to isolated and segregated classrooms, kept apart from the other children and teachers in the regular education program. One special education teacher describes the sense of isolation she felt and the crude facilities in which her special class operated in the 1960s:

> I accepted my first teaching position, a special education class in a basement room next door to the furnace. Of the 15 "educable mentally retarded" children assigned to work with me, most were simply nonreaders from poor families. One child had been banished to my room because she posed a behavior problem to her fourth-grade teacher.
>
> My class and I were assigned a recess spot on the opposite side of the play yard, far away from the "normal" children. I was the only teacher who did not have a lunch break. I was required to eat with my "retarded" children while other teachers were permitted to leave their students. . . . Isolated from my colleagues, I closed my door and did my thing, oblivious to the larger educational circles in which I was immersed. Although it was the basement room, with all the negative perceptions that arrangement implies, I was secure in the knowledge that despite the ignominy of it all I did good things for children who were previously unloved and untaught. (Aiello, 1976, p. 14)

Children with mild learning and behavioral problems usually remained in the regular classroom but received no special help. If they did not make satisfactory academic progress, they were termed "slow learners" or simply "failures." If their deportment in class exceeded the teacher's tolerance for misbehavior, they were labeled "disciplinary problems" and suspended from school. Children with more severe disabilities—including many with visual, hearing, and physical or health impairments—were usually placed in segregated schools or institutions or kept at home. Gifted and talented children seldom received special attention in schools. It was assumed they could make it on their own without help.

Society's response to exceptional children has come a long way. As our concepts of equality, freedom, and justice have expanded, children with disabilities and their families have moved from exclusion and isolation to inclusion and participation. Society no longer regards children with disabilities as beyond the responsibility of the local public schools. No longer may a child who is different from the norm be turned away from school because someone believes that he is unable to benefit from typical instruction. Recent legislation and court decisions confirm that all children with disabilities have the right to a *free, appropriate program of public education in the least restrictive environment.*

The provision of equitable educational opportunities to exceptional children has not come about by chance. Many laws and court cases have had important effects on public education in general and on the education of children with special needs in particular. And the process of change is never finished; legal influences on special education are not fixed or static but fluid and dynamic (Yell, 1998).

 SEPARATE IS NOT EQUAL

The recent history of special education, especially in regard to the education of children with disabilities in regular schools, is related to the civil rights movement. Special education was strongly influenced by social developments and court decisions in the 1950s and 1960s, especially the landmark case *Brown v. Board of Education of Topeka* (1954). This case challenged the practice of segregating students according to race. In its ruling in the *Brown* case, the U.S. Supreme Court declared that education must be made available to all children on equal terms:

> Today, education is perhaps the most important function of state and local governments. Compulsory school attendance laws and the great expenditure for education both demonstrate our recognition of the importance of education to our democratic society. It is required in the performance of our most basic responsibilities. . . . In these days, it is doubtful that any child may reasonably be expected to succeed in life if he is denied the opportunity of an education. (***Brown v. Board of Education,*** 1954)

The *Brown* decision began a period of intense concern and questioning among parents of children with disabilities, who asked why the same principles of equal access to education did not apply to their children. Numerous court cases were initiated in the 1960s and early 1970s by parents and other advocates dissatisfied with an educational system that denied equal access to children with disabilities. Generally, the parents based their arguments on the 14th Amendment to the Constitution, which provides that no state shall deny any person within its jurisdiction the equal protection of the law and that no state shall deprive any person of life, liberty, or property without due process of law.

PARC case and equal protection

PRAXIS Special Education Core Principles: Content Knowledge: II. Legal and Societal Issues, Federal laws and legal issues related to special education.

 EQUAL PROTECTION

In the past, children with disabilities usually received differential treatment; that is, they were excluded from certain educational programs or were given special education only in segregated settings. Basically, when the courts have been asked to rule on the practice of denial and segregation, judges have examined whether such treatment is rational and whether it is necessary (Williams, 1977). One of the most historically significant cases to examine these questions was the class-action suit *Pennsylvania Association for Retarded Children [PARC] v. Commonwealth of Pennsylvania* (1972). The association challenged a state law that denied public school education to certain children considered "unable to profit from public school attendance."

The lawyers and parents supporting PARC argued that even though the children had intellectual disabilities, it was neither rational nor necessary to assume they were ineducable and untrainable. Because the state was unable to prove that the children were, in fact, ineducable or to demonstrate a rational need for excluding them from public school programs, the court decided that the children were entitled to receive a free, public education.

In addition, the court maintained that parents had the right to be notified before any change was made in their children's educational program.

The wording of the PARC decision proved particularly important because of its influence on subsequent federal legislation. Not only did the court rule that all children with mental retardation were entitled to a free, appropriate public education, but the ruling also stipulated that placements in regular classrooms and regular public schools were preferable to segregated settings.

> It is the Commonwealth's obligation to place each mentally retarded child in a free, public program of education and training appropriate to the child's capacity. . . . placement in a regular public school class is preferable to placement in a special public school class and placement in a special public school is preferable to placement in any other type of program of education and training. (*PARC v. Commonwealth of Pennsylvania*, 1972)

In addition to the *Brown* and *PARC* cases, several other judicial decisions have had far-reaching effects on special education. The rulings of some of these cases have been incorporated into subsequent federal legislation, notably the Individuals with Disabilities Education Act.

THE INDIVIDUALS WITH DISABILITIES EDUCATION ACT

In 1975 Congress passed Public Law 94-142, a landmark piece of legislation that has changed the face of education in this country. P.L. 94-142 was originally called the Education for All Handicapped Children Act. Since it became law in 1975, Congress has reauthorized and amended P.L. 94-142 four times, most recently in 1997. The 1990 amendments renamed the law the Individuals with Disabilities Education Act—often referred to by its acronym, IDEA.

IDEA has affected every school in the country and has changed the roles of regular and special educators, school administrators, parents, and students with disabilities in the educational process. Its passage marked the culmination of the efforts of a great many educators, parents, and legislators to bring together in one comprehensive bill this country's laws regarding the education of children with disabilities. The law reflects society's concern about treating people with disabilities as full citizens with the same rights and privileges that all other citizens enjoy.

The purpose of IDEA is to

> assure that all children with disabilities have available to them . . . a free appropriate public education which emphasizes special education and related services designed to meet their unique needs, to assure that the rights of children with disabilities and their parents or guardians are protected, to assist states and localities to provide for the education of all children with disabilities, and to assess and assure the effectiveness of efforts to educate children with disabilities. (IDEA, 20 U.S.C. § 1400[c])

IDEA is directed primarily at the states, which are responsible for providing education to their citizens. The majority of the many rules and regulations defining how IDEA operates are related to six major principles that have remained unchanged since 1975 (Turnbull & Cilley, 1999; Turnbull & Turnbull, 2000):

Public Law 94–142

PRAXIS Special Education Core Principles: Content Knowledge: II. Legal and Societal Issues, Federal laws and legal issues related to special education, Public Law 94–142.

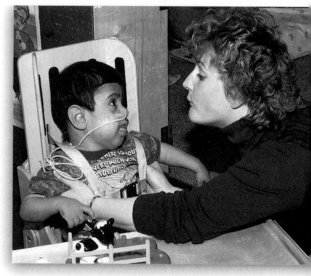

In the past, many children like Roberto were denied access to education in public schools.

 **SIX MAJOR PRINCIPLES OF IDEA**

Zero Reject   Schools must educate *all* children with disabilities. This principle applies regardless of the nature or severity of the disability; no child with disabilities may be excluded from a public education. The requirement to provide special education to all students with disabilities is absolute between the ages of 6 and 17. If a state provides educational services to children without disabilities between the ages of 3 to 5 and 18 to 21, it must also educate all children with disabilities in those age groups. Each state education agency is responsible for locating, identifying, and evaluating all children, from birth to age 21, residing in the state with disabilities or who are suspected of having disabilities. This requirement is called the *child find system*.

Nondiscriminatory Identification and Evaluation   Schools must use nonbiased, multifactored methods of evaluation to determine whether a child has a disability and, if so, whether special education is needed. Testing and evaluation procedures must not discriminate on the basis of race, culture, or native language. All tests must be administered in the child's native language, and identification and placement decisions cannot be made on the basis of a single test score. These provisions of IDEA are known as *protection in evaluation procedures*.

Free, Appropriate Public Education (FAPE)   All children with disabilities, regardless of the type or severity of their disability, shall receive a free, appropriate public education. This education must be provided at public expense—that is, without cost to the child's parents. An **individualized education program (IEP)** must be developed and implemented for each student with a disability. The IEP must be individually designed to meet the child's unique needs.

Least Restrictive Environment (LRE)   IDEA mandates that students with disabilities be educated with children without disabilities to the maximum extent appropriate and that students with disabilities be removed to separate classes or schools only when the nature or severity of their disabilities is such that they cannot receive an appropriate education in a general education classroom with supplementary aides and services. IDEA creates a presumption in favor of inclusion in the regular classroom. The law requires that a student's IEP contain a justification and explanation of the extent, if any, to which a child will not participate with nondisabled peers in the general academic curriculum, extracurricular activities, and other nonacademic activities (e.g., lunch, recess, transportation, dances). To ensure that each student with disabilities is educated in the least restrictive environment appropriate for her needs, school districts must provide a continuum of placement and service alternatives. (The LRE and the continuum of services are discussed in detail in Chapter 2.)

Due Process Safeguards   Schools must provide due process safeguards to protect the rights of children with disabilities and their parents. Parental consent must be obtained for initial and all subsequent evaluations and placement decisions regarding special education. Schools must maintain the confidentiality of all records pertaining to a child with disabilities and make those records available to the parents. When parents of a child with disabilities disagree with the results of an evaluation performed by the school, they can obtain an independent evaluation at public expense. When the school and parents disagree on the identification, evaluation, placement, or special education and related services for the child, the parents may request a due process hearing. States are also required to offer parents an opportunity to resolve the matter through mediation by a third party before holding a due process hearing. Parents have the right to attorney's fees if they prevail in due process or judicial proceedings under IDEA.

Parent and Student Participation and Shared Decision Making   Schools must collaborate with parents and students with disabilities in the design and implementation of special education services. The parents' (and, whenever appropriate, the student's) input and wishes must be considered in IEP goals and objectives, related service needs, and placement decisions.

OTHER PROVISIONS OF THE LAW

Extending Special Education Services to Infants, Toddlers, and Preschoolers   Noting that states were serving at most about 70% of preschool children with disabilities and that systematic early intervention services for infants and toddlers with disabilities from birth through age 2 were scarce or nonexistent in many states, Congress included provisions in the Education of the Handicapped Act Amendments in 1986 (P.L. 99-457) to expand services for these segments of the population. Beginning with the 1990–1991 school year, each state was required to fully serve all preschool children with disabilities ages 3 to 5—that is, with the same services and protections available to school-age children—or lose all future federal funds for preschoolers with disabilities.

P.L. 99-457 included an incentive grant program to encourage states to provide early intervention services to infants and toddlers with disabilities and their families—that is, children from birth through age 2 who need early intervention services because they are experiencing developmental delays or because they have a diagnosed physical or mental impairment likely to result in developmental delays. With the most recent reauthorization of IDEA in 1997 (P.L. 105-17), Congress reaffirmed the nation's commitment to a system of early intervention services. Rather than mandate special services for this age group, IDEA encourages each state to "develop and implement a statewide, comprehensive, coordinated, multidisciplinary, interagency program of early intervention services for infants and toddlers with disabilities and their families." The encouragement is in the form of a gradually increasing amount of federal money to be awarded to states that identify and serve all infants and toddlers with disabilities. Various education and human services agencies within each state work together to provide services such as medical and educational assessment, physical therapy, speech and language intervention, and parent counseling and training. These early intervention services are prescribed and implemented according to an **individualized family services plan (IFSP)** written by a multidisciplinary team that includes the child's parents. (IFSPs are discussed in Chapter 5.)

▲ School districts must provide related services to students with disabilities— such as transportation in specially equipped vans or buses—so they may have access to and benefit from a public education.

Related Services and Assistive Technology   Children with disabilities have sometimes been prevented from attending regular schools or benefiting from educational activities by circumstances that impede their access or participation. A child who uses a wheelchair, for example, may require a specially equipped school bus. A child with special health problems may require medication several times a day. A child with an orthopedic impairment may need physical therapy to maintain flexibility and use of her arms and legs. IDEA requires schools to provide any **related services** (e.g., special transportation, counseling, physical therapy) and **assistive technology**—devices and services such as visual aids, augmentative communication devices,

TABLE 1.3 **Types and definitions of related services that students with disabilities may need to benefit from education**

Related Service	Definition
Audiology	(1) Identifying children with hearing loss. (2) Determining the range, nature, and degree of hearing loss. (3) Providing habilitative activities, such as auditory training, speech reading, hearing evaluation, and speech conservation. (4) Creating and administering programs for prevention of hearing loss. (5) Counseling and guidance of pupils, parents, and teachers, regarding hearing loss. (6) Determining the child's need for group and individual amplification, selecting and fitting an appropriate hearing aid, and evaluating the effectiveness of amplification.
Counseling services	Services provided by qualified social workers, psychologists, guidance counselors, or other qualified personnel.
Early identification and assessment	Implementing a formal plan for identifying a disability as early as possible in a child's life.
Medical services	Services provided by a licensed physician to determine a child's medically related disability that results in the child's need for special education and related services.
Occupational therapy	(1) Improving, developing, or restoring functions impaired or lost through illness, injury, or deprivation. (2) Improving ability to perform tasks for independent functioning when functions are impaired or lost. (3) Preventing, through early intervention, initial or further impairment or loss of function.
Orientation and mobility services	Services provided to children who are blind or have visual impairments to assist them in traveling around their school or environment.
Parent counseling and training	Assisting parents in understanding the special needs of their child and providing parents with information about child development.
Physical therapy	Services provided by a qualified physical therapist.
Psychological services	(1) Administering psychological and educational tests, and other assessment procedures. (2) Interpreting assessment results. (3) Obtaining, integrating, and interpreting information about child behavior and conditions relating to learning. (4) Consulting with other staff members in planning school programs to meet the special needs of children as indicated by psychological tests, interviews, and behavioral evaluations. (5) Planning and managing a program of psychological services, including psychological counseling for children and parents.

Related services

PRAXIS Special Education Core Principles: Content Knowledge: III. Delivery of Services to Students with Disabilities, Integration of related services.

specialized equipment for computer access—that a child with disabilities may need in order to access and benefit from special education. Table 1.3 provides definitions of the types of related services included in the IDEA regulations.

Federal Funding of Special Education   Laws and regulations calling for special education would be of limited value if the schools lack the necessary financial resources. Congress backed up its mandate for free, appropriate public education by providing federal funds to help school districts meet the additional costs of educating children with disabilities. However, educating students with disabilities is very expensive. Chaikind et al. (1993) reported a per-pupil annual cost of approximately $7,800 in 1989–1990 dollars, or about 2.3 times the cost of educating

TABLE 1.3 *continued*

Related Service	Definition
Recreation	(1) Assessment of leisure function. (2) Therapeutic recreation services. (3) Recreation programs in schools and community agencies. (4) Leisure education.
Rehabilitative counseling services	Services provided by qualified personnel in individual or group sessions that focus specifically on career development, employment preparation, achieving independence, and integration in the workplace and community.
School health services	Services provided by a qualified school nurse or other qualified person.
Social work services in the schools	(1) Preparing a social or developmental history on a child with a disability. (2) Group and individual counseling with the child and family. (3) Working with those problems in a child's living situation (home, school, and community) that affect the child's adjustment in school. (4) Mobilizing school and community resources to enable the child to learn as effectively as possible.
Speech pathology	(1) Identification of children with speech or language impairments. (2) Diagnosis and appraisal. (3) Referral for medical or other professional attention. (4) Provision of speech and language services for the habilitation and prevention of communicative problems. (5) Counseling and guidance of parents, children, and teachers regarding speech and language impairments.
Transportation	(1) Travel to and from school and between schools. (2) Travel in and around school buildings. (3) Specialized equipment if required to provide special transportation for a child with a disability (e.g., special or adapted buses, lifts, and ramps).
Assistive technology devices and services	Devices and related services that increase, maintain, or improve the functional capabilities of children with disabilities.

Source: IDEA regulations, 34 C.F.R. § 300.13.

each pupil in regular education. They found that costs of special education services varied considerably by disability category, ranging from under $1,000 per student with speech and language impairments to more than $30,000 per student with deaf-blindness.

State and local educational administrators contend that federal financial assistance for the education of students with disabilities has not been sufficient and that schools are hard pressed to meet the requirements in IDEA. When Congress passed IDEA in 1975, its intent was to provide federal funds for 40% of the total costs of educating children with disabilities. However, during the 1998–1999 school year the federal government provided only 8% of the average dollar amount needed to educate a student with disabilities over and above per-pupil expenditures to provide general education services (Parrish, in press).

States cannot use federal funds to serve more than 12% of their school-age students in special education. IDEA requires that 75% of the federal funds received by the states be passed on to local school districts; 25% of the funds may be used by the state educational agency for administration, direct and supportive services for students with disabilities (e.g., support to state residential schools for students with sensory impairments), supervision, and compliance monitoring. In addition, each state is required to develop a *comprehensive system for personnel development,* including in-service training programs for regular education teachers, special education teachers, school administrators, and other support personnel.

Tuition Reimbursement   Parents and school officials sometimes disagree about whether placement in a private school is the most appropriate way to meet the needs of a student with disabilities. IDEA stipulates that, in cases in which an appropriate education cannot be provided in the public schools, children with disabilities may be placed in private school programs at no cost to their parents. This has proven to be a particularly controversial aspect of the law (Yell, 1998).

 LEGAL CHALLENGES BASED ON IDEA

Although IDEA has resulted in dramatic increases in the number of students receiving special education services and in greater recognition of the legal rights of children with disabilities and their families, it has also brought about an ever-increasing number of disputes concerning the education of students with disabilities. Thousands of due process hearings and hundreds of court cases have been brought about by parents and other advocates. Due process hearings and court cases often place parents and schools in confrontation with each other and are expensive and time-consuming (Lanigan, Audette, Dreier, & Kobersy, 2001).

It is difficult to generalize how judges and courts have resolved the various legal challenges based on IDEA. There have been many different interpretations of *free, appropriate education* and *least restrictive environment*. The law uses these terms repeatedly; but in the view of many parents, educators, judges, and attorneys, the law does not define them with sufficient clarity. Thus, the questions of what is appropriate and least restrictive for a particular child and whether a public school district should be compelled to provide a certain service must often be decided by judges and courts on consideration of the evidence presented to them. Some of the key issues ruled on by the courts are the extended school year, related services, disciplinary procedures, and the fundamental right to an education for students with the most severe disabilities. (Table 1.4 on pages 28–29 summarizes key judicial decisions that have had significant impact on special education and the lives of individuals with disabilities.)

Tables 1.4 and 1.5

PRAXIS Special Education Core Principles: Content Knowledge: II. Legal and Societal Issues, Federal laws and legal issues related to special education.

Extended School Year   Most public school programs operate for approximately 180 school days per year. Parents and educators have argued that, for some children with disabilities, particularly those with severe and multiple disabilities, a 180-day school year is not sufficient to meet their needs. In *Armstrong v. Kline* (1979), the parents of five students with severe disabilities claimed that their children tended to regress during the usual breaks in the school year and called on the schools to provide a period of instruction longer than 180 days. The court agreed and ordered the schools to extend the school year for these students. Several states and local districts now provide year-round educational programs for some students with disabilities, but there are no clear and universally accepted guidelines as to which students are entitled to free public education for a longer-than-usual school year.

Rowley and Tatro cases

PRAXIS Special Education Core Principles: Content Knowledge: II. Legal and Societal Issues, Federal laws and legal issues related to special education, Rowley re: program appropriateness, Tatro re: related services.

Related Services   The related services provision of IDEA has been highly controversial, creating much disagreement about what kinds of related services are necessary and reasonable for the schools to provide and what services should be the responsibility of the child's parents. The first case based on IDEA to reach the U.S. Supreme Court was *Board of Education of the Hendrick Hudson Central School District v. Rowley* (1982). Amy Rowley was a fourth grader who, because of her hearing loss, needed special education and related services. The school district had originally provided Amy with a hearing aid, speech therapy, a tutor, and a sign language interpreter to accompany her in the regular classroom. The school withdrew the sign language services after the interpreter reported that Amy did not make use of her services: Amy reportedly looked at the teacher to read her lips and asked the teacher to repeat instructions rather than get the information from the interpreter. Amy's parents contended that she was missing up to 50% of the ongoing instruction (her hearing loss was estimated to have left her with 50% residual hearing) and was therefore being denied an appropriate public school education. The school district's position was that Amy, with the help of the other special services she was still receiving, was passing from grade to grade without an interpreter. School personnel thought, in fact, that an interpreter might hinder Amy's interactions with her teacher and peers. It was also noted that this service would cost the school district as much as $25,000 per year. The Supreme Court ruled that Amy, who was making satisfactory progress in school without an interpreter, was receiving an adequate education and that the school district could not be compelled to hire a full-time interpreter.

The second P.L. 94-142 case to reach the Supreme Court was *Irving Independent School District v. Tatro* (1984). In this case, the Court decided that a school district was obligated to provide catheterization and other related medical services to enable a young child with physical impairments to attend school. In the 1999 *Cedar Rapids v. Garret F.* case, the Supreme Court reaffirmed and extended its ruling in the *Tatro* case. (See Chapter 12 for further discussion of the *Tatro* and *Garret* cases.)

Disciplining Students with Disabilities   Some cases have resulted from parents' protesting the suspension or expulsion of children with disabilities. The case of *Stuart v. Nappi* (1978), for example, concerned a high school student who spent much of her time wandering in the halls even though she was assigned to special classes. The school sought to have the student expelled on disciplinary grounds because her conduct was considered detrimental to order in the school. The court agreed with the student's mother that expulsion would deny the student a free, appropriate public education as called for in IDEA. In other cases, expulsion or suspension of students with disabilities has been upheld if the school could show that the grounds for expulsion did not relate to the student's disability. In 1988, however, the Supreme Court ruled in *Honig v. Doe* that a student with disabilities could not be expelled from school for disciplinary reasons, which meant that, for all practical purposes, schools could not recommend expulsion or suspend a student with disabilities for more than 10 days.

The IDEA amendments of 1997 (P.L. 105-17) contain provisions that enable school districts to discipline students with disabilities in the same manner as students without disabilities, with a few notable exceptions. If the school seeks a change of placement, suspension, or expulsion in excess of 10 days, the IEP team and other qualified personnel must review the relationship between the student's misconduct and her disability. This review is called a **manifestation determination** (Katsiyannis & Maag, 2001). If it is determined that the student's behavior is not related to the disability, the same disciplinary procedures used with other students may be imposed. However, the school must continue to provide educational services in the alternative placement.

Right to Education   The case of *Timothy W. v. Rochester School District* threatened the zero reject philosophy of IDEA. In July 1988, Judge Loughlin of the district court in New Hampshire ruled that a 13-year-old boy with severe disabilities and quadriplegia was ineligible for education services because he could not benefit from special education. The judge ruled in favor of the Rochester School Board, which claimed that IDEA was not intended to provide educational services to "*all* handicapped students." In his decision, the judge determined that the federal law was not explicit regarding a "rare child" with severe disabilities and declared that special evaluations and examinations should be used to determine "qualifications for education under PL 94-142."

In May 1989, a court of appeals overturned the lower court's decision, ruling that public schools must educate all children with disabilities regardless of how little they might benefit or the nature or severity of their disabilities. The three-judge panel concluded that "schools cannot avoid the provisions of EHA [Education of the Handicapped Amendments] by returning to the practices that were widespread prior to the Act's passage . . . unilaterally excluding certain handicapped children from a public education on the ground that they are uneducable."

Challenges to existing services and differing views on whether a particular program is appropriate or least restrictive are certain to continue. Although the courts will probably grant some requests in the future and deny others, it is now a well-established principle that

Honig case

PRAXIS Special Education Core Principles: Content Knowledge: II. Legal and Societal Issues, Federal laws and legal issues related to special education, Honig re: discipline.

Manifestation determination

Council for Exceptional Children   Content Standards for Beginning Teachers–Common Core: Laws, policies, and ethical principles regarding behavior management planning and implementation (CC1K2).

TABLE 1.4	Major court cases that have influenced special education and the lives of individuals with disabilities	
Date	**Court Case**	**Educational Implications**
1954	*Brown v. Board of Education of Topeka* (Kansas)	The case established the right of all children to an equal opportunity for an education.
1967	*Hobson v. Hansen* (Washington, DC)	The court declared the tracking system, in which children were placed into either regular or special classes according to their scores on intelligence tests, unconstitutional because it discriminated against African American and poor children.
1970	*Diana v. State Board of Education* (California)	A Spanish-speaking student in California had been placed in a special class for children with mental retardation based on the results of intelligence tests given in English. The court ruled that children cannot be placed in special education on the basis of culturally biased tests or tests given in other than the child's native language.
1972	*Mills v. Board of Education of the District of Columbia*	Seven children had been excluded from the public schools in Washington, DC, because of learning and behavior problems. The school district contended that it did not have enough money to provide special education programs for them. The court ruled that financial problems cannot be allowed to have a greater impact on children with disabilities than on students without disabilities and ordered the schools to readmit the children and serve them appropriately.
1972	*Pennsylvania Association for Retarded Citizens v. the Commonwealth of Pennsylvania*	This class-action suit established the right to free public education for all children with mental retardation.
1972	*Wyatt v. Stickney* (Alabama)	The decision declared that individuals in state institutions have the right to appropriate treatment within those institutions.
1979	*Larry P. v. Riles* (California)	The court ruled that IQ tests used to place African American children in special classes were inappropriate because they failed to recognize the children's cultural background and the learning that took place in their homes and communities. The court ordered that IQ tests could not be used as the sole basis for placing children into special classes.
1979	*Armstrong v. Kline* (Pennsylvania)	The case established the right of some children with severe disabilities to an extension of the 180-day public school year.
1982	*Board of Education of the Hendrik Hudson Central School District v. Rowley* (New York)	This was the first case based on P.L. 94–142 to reach the U.S. Supreme Court; while denying the plaintiff's specific request, the Court upheld for each child with disabilities the right to a personalized program of instruction and necessary supportive services.

TABLE 1.4 *continued*

Date	Court Case	Educational Implications
1983	*Abrahamson v. Hershman* (Massachusetts)	The court ruled that residential placement in a private school was necessary for a child with multiple disabilities who needed around-the-clock training and required the school district to pay for the private placement.
1984	*Department of Education v. Katherine D.* (Hawaii)	The court ruled that a homebound instructional program for a child with multiple health impairments did not meet the least-restrictive-environment standard and called for the child to be placed in a class with children without disabilities and provided with related medical services.
1984	*Irving Independent School District v. Tatro* (Texas)	The court ruled that catheterization was necessary for a child with physical disabilities to remain in school and that it could be performed by a nonphysician, thus obligating the school district to provide that service.
1984	*Smith v. Robinson* (Rhode Island)	The court ordered the state to pay for the placement of a child with severe disabilities in a residential program and ordered the school district to reimburse the parents' attorney fees. The U.S. Supreme Court later ruled that P.L. 94–142 did not entitle parents to recover such fees, but Congress subsequently passed an "Attorney's Fees" bill, leading to enactment of P.L. 99–372.
1985	*Cleburne v. Cleburne Living Center* (Texas)	The Supreme Court ruled unanimously that communities cannot use a discriminatory zoning ordinance to prevent establishment of group homes for persons with mental retardation.
1988	*Honig v. Doe* (California)	The court ruled that children with disabilities cannot be excluded from school for any misbehavior that is disability-related (in this case, "aggressive behavior against other students" on the part of two "emotionally handicapped" students) but that educational services could cease if the misbehavior is not related to the disability.
1989	*Timothy W. v. Rochester School District* (New Hampshire)	The U.S. Appeals Court upheld the literal interpretation that P.L. 94–142 requires that all children with disabilities be provided with a free, appropriate, public education, unconditionally and without exception. The three-judge appeals court overturned the decision of a district court judge, who had ruled that the local school district was not obligated to educate a 13-year-old boy with multiple and severe disabilities because he could not benefit from special education.
1999	*Cedar Rapids v. Garret F.*	U.S. Supreme Court rules that a local school district must pay for the one-on-one nursing care for a medically fragile student who required continuous monitoring of his ventilator and other health-maintenance routines. The case reaffirmed and extended the Court's ruling in the 1984 *Tatro* case that schools must provide any and all health services needed for students with disabilities to attend school as long as performance of those services does not require a licensed physician.

each student with disabilities is entitled to an individualized program of special instruction and related services that will enable him to benefit from an education in as integrated a setting as possible.

 RELATED LEGISLATION

Gifted and Talented Children   Although IDEA does not apply to gifted and talented children, other federal legislation has addressed the specialized needs of these students. P.L. 95-561, the Gifted and Talented Children's Education Act of 1978, provides financial incentives for state and local education agencies to develop programs for students who are gifted and talented. The law provides for the identification of gifted and talented children and includes special procedures for identifying and educating those from disadvantaged backgrounds. The law makes funding available for in-service training programs, research, and other projects aimed at meeting the needs of gifted and talented students.

In 1982 the Education Consolidation Act phased out the federal Office of Gifted and Talented and merged gifted education with 29 other programs. Federal dollars to support these 30 wide-ranging education programs (K–12) are sent to the states in the form of block grants. Each state has the responsibility to determine what portion, if any, of the block grant funds will be used to support programs and services for students who are gifted and talented.

Congress passed the Jacob K. Javits Gifted and Talented Student Education Act in 1988 as part of the Elementary and Secondary Education Bill. This moderately funded act (approximately $10 million in 1996) provides federal money for special projects, a national research center, and a position within the U.S. Department of Education with responsibility for gifted education.

Section 504 of Rehabilitation Act

PRAXIS Special Education Core Principles: Content Knowledge: II. Legal and Societal Issues, Federal laws and legal issues related to special edition, Section 504.

Section 504 of the Rehabilitation Act of 1973   Another important law that extends civil rights to people with disabilities is Section 504 of the Rehabilitation Act of 1973. This regulation states, in part, that "no otherwise qualified handicapped individual shall, solely by reason of his handicap, be excluded from the participation in, be denied the benefits of, or be subjected to discrimination in any program or activity receiving federal financial assistance." This law, worded almost identically to the Civil Rights Act of 1964 (which prohibited discrimination based on race, color, or national origin), has expanded opportunities to children and adults with disabilities in education, employment, and various other settings. It requires provision of "auxiliary aids for students with impaired sensory, manual, or speaking skills"—for example, readers for students who are blind and people to assist students with physical disabilities in moving from place to place. This requirement does not mean that schools, colleges, and employers must have all such aids available at all times; it simply means that no person with disabilities may be excluded from a program because of the lack of an appropriate aid.

Section 504 is not a federal grant program; unlike IDEA, it does not provide any federal money to assist people with disabilities. Rather, it "imposes a duty on every recipient of federal funds not to discriminate against handicapped persons" (Johnson, 1986, p. 8). "Recipient," of course, includes public school districts, virtually all of which receive federal support. Most colleges and universities have also been affected; even many students in private institutions receive federal financial aid. The Office of Civil Rights conducts periodic compliance reviews and acts on complaints when parents, disabled individuals, or others contend that a school district is violating Section 504.

Architectural accessibility for students, teachers, and others with physical and sensory impairments is an important feature of Section 504; however, the law does not call for a completely barrier-free environment. Emphasis is on accessibility to programs, not on physical modification of all existing structures. If a chemistry class is required for a premedical program of study, for example, a college might make this program accessible to a student with physical disabilities by reassigning the class to an accessible location or by providing assistance to the student in traveling to an otherwise inaccessible location. All sections of all courses need not be made accessible, but a college should not segregate students with disabilities by assigning them all to a particular section regardless of disability. Like IDEA, Section 504 calls for nondiscriminatory placement in the "most integrated setting appropriate" and has served as the basis for many court cases over alleged discrimination against individuals with disabilities, particularly in their right to employment. (Table 1.5 summarizes federal legislation regarding the education and rights of individuals with disabilities.)

The Americans with Disabilities Act requires employers to make reasonable accommodations to allow a person with disabilities to perform essential job functions.

Americans with Disabilities Act

The Americans with Disabilities Act (P.L. 101-336) was signed into law in 1990. Patterned after Section 504 of the Rehabilitation Act of 1973, the Americans with Disabilities Act (ADA) extends civil rights protection of persons with disabilities to private sector employment, all public services, public accommodation, transportation, and telecommunications. A person with a disability is defined in ADA as a person (1) with a mental or physical impairment that substantially limits her in a major life activity (e.g., walking, talking, working, self-care); (2) with a record of such an impairment (e.g., a person who no longer has heart disease but who is discriminated against because of that history); or (3) who is regarded as having such an impairment (e.g., a person with significant facial disfiguration due to a burn who is not limited in any major life activity but is discriminated against). The major provisions of ADA are as follows:

Americans and Disabilities Act

PRAXIS Special Education Core Principles: Content Knowledge: II. Legal and Societal Issues, Federal laws and legal issues related to special education, Americans with Disabilities Act (ADA).

- Employers with 15 or more employees may not refuse to hire or promote a person because of a disability if that person is qualified to perform the job. Also, the employer must make reasonable accommodations that will allow a person with a disability to perform essential functions of the job. Such modifications in job requirements or situation must be made if they will not impose undue hardship on the employer.
- All new vehicles purchased by public transit authorities must be accessible to people with disabilities. All rail stations must be made accessible, and at least one car per train in existing rail systems must be made accessible.
- It is illegal for public accommodations to exclude or refuse persons with disabilities. Public accommodations are everyday businesses and services, such as hotels, restaurants, grocery stores, and parks. All new buildings must be made accessible, and existing facilities must remove barriers if the removal can be accomplished without much difficulty or expense.
- Companies offering telephone service to the general public must offer relay services to individuals who use telecommunications devices for the deaf (e.g., text telephones) 24 hours per day, 7 days per week.

TABLE 1.5 Federal legislation concerning the education and rights of exceptional children

Date	Legislation	Educational Implications
1958	National Defense Education Act (P.L. 85–926)	Provided funds for training professionals to train teachers of children with mental retardation
1961	Special Education Act (P.L. 87–276)	Provided funds for training professionals to train teachers of deaf children
1963	Mental Retardation Facility and Community Center Construction Act (P.L. 88–164)	Extended support given in P.L. 85–926 to training teachers of children with other disabilities
1965	Elementary and Secondary Education Act (P.L. 89–10)	Provided money to states and local districts for developing programs for economically disadvantaged and disabled children
1966	Amendment to Title I of the Elementary and Secondary Education Act (P.L. 89–313)	Provided funding for state-supported programs in institutions and other settings for children with disabilities
1966	Amendments to the Elementary and Secondary Education Act (P.L. 89–750)	Created the federal Bureau of Education for the Handicapped (today's Office of Special Education)
1968	Handicapped Children's Early Assistance Act (P.L. 90–538)	Established the "first chance network" of experimental programs for preschool children with disabilities
1969	Elementary, Secondary, and Other Educational Amendments (P.L. 91–230)	Defined learning disabilities and provided funds for state-level programs for children with learning disabilities
1970	Education Amendments of 1970 (P.L. 91–230)	Mandated a study of the gifted that resulted in the *Marland Report* (1972), which many states used as a basis for building programs for gifted and talented students
1973	Section 504 of the Rehabilitation Act (P.L. 93–112)	Declared that a person cannot be excluded on the basis of disability alone from any program or activity receiving federal funds
1974	Education Amendments (P.L. 93–380)	Extended previous legislation; provided money to state and local districts for programs for gifted and talented students for the first time; protected the rights of children with disabilities and their parents in placement decisions
1975	Developmental Disabilities Assistance and Bill of Rights Act (P.L. 94–103)	Affirmed the rights of citizens with mental retardation and cited areas in which services must be provided for people with mental retardation and other developmental disabilities
1975	Education for All Handicapped Children Act (EAHCA) (P.L. 94–142)	Mandated free, appropriate public education for all children with disabilities ages 6 to 21; protected the rights of children with disabilities and their parents in educational decision making; required the development of an IEP for each child with a disability; stated that students with disabilities must receive educational services in the least restrictive environment.
1978	Gifted and Talented Children's Education Act of 1978 (P.L. 95–561)	Provided funds for in-service training programs, research, and other projects aimed at meeting the needs of gifted and talented students

TABLE 1.5 *continued*

Date	Legislation	Educational Implications
1983	Amendments to the Education of the Handicapped Act (P.L. 98–199)	Required states to collect data on the number of youth with disabilities exiting their systems and to address the needs of secondary students making the transition to adulthood; gave incentives to states to provide services to infants and preschool children with disabilities
1984	Developmental Disabilities Assistance and Bill of Rights Acts (P.L. 98–527)	Mandated the development of employment-related training activities for adults with disabilities
1986	Handicapped Children's Protection Act (P.L. 99–372)	Provided authority for the reimbursement of attorney's fees to parents who prevail in a hearing or court case to secure an appropriate education for their child
1986	Education for the Handicapped Act Amendments of 1986 (P.L. 99–457)	Required states to provide free, appropriate education to all 3- to 5-year-olds with disabilities who were eligible to apply for federal preschool funding; included incentive grants to encourage states to develop comprehensive interdisciplinary services for infants and toddlers (birth through age 2) and their families
1986	Rehabilitation Act Amendments (P.L. 99–506)	Set forth regulations for the development of supported employment programs for adults with disabilities
1988	Jacob K. Javits Gifted and Talented Students Education Act	Provided federal funds in support of research, teacher training, and program development for the education of gifted and talented students
1988	Technology-Related Assistance for Individuals with Disabilities Act of 1988 (P.L. 100–407)	Created statewide programs of technology assistance for persons of all ages with disabilities
1990	Americans with Disabilities Act (P.L. 101–336)	Provided civil rights protection against discrimination to citizens with disabilities in private sector employment; provided access to all public services, public accommodations, transportation, and telecommunications
1990	Individuals with Disabilities Education Act Amendments (IDEA) of 1990 (P.L. 101–476)	Renamed the EAHCA; added autism and traumatic brain injury as new categories of disability; required all IEPs to include a statement of needed transition services no later than age 16; expanded the definition of related services to include rehabilitation counseling and social work services
1997	Individuals with Disabilities Education Act (IDEA) of 1997 (P.L. 105–17)	Restructured IDEA and added several major provisions: increased emphasis on parent participation and shared decision making; a regular education teacher must be a member of the IEP team; students with disabilities must have access to the general education curriculum; beginning at age 14, the IEP must identify transition services related to his course of study; the IEP must address positive behavior support plans where appropriate; students with disabilities must be included in state- or district-wide testing programs; orientation and mobility services added to the list of related services; if a school seeks to discipline a student with disabilities resulting in change of placement, suspension, or expulsion for more than 10 days, a "manifestation determination" by the IEP team must find that the student's misconduct was not related to the disability

WHAT IS SPECIAL EDUCATION?

Special education can be defined from many perspectives. One may, for example, view special education as a legislatively governed enterprise. From this viewpoint, one would be concerned about issues such as due process procedures for informing parents about their right to participate in decisions about their children's education programs and the extent to which all of the school district's IEPs include each component as required by IDEA. From a purely administrative point of view, special education can be seen as the part of a school system's operation that requires certain teacher-pupil ratios in the classroom and that uses special formulas to determine levels of funding for related services personnel. And from a sociopolitical perspective, special education can be seen as an outgrowth of the civil rights movement, a demonstration of society's changing attitudes about people with disabilities in general. Each of these perspectives has some validity, and each continues to play an important role in defining what special education is and how it is practiced. None of these views, however, reveals the fundamental purpose or essence of special education as *instructionally focused intervention*.

 ### SPECIAL EDUCATION AS INTERVENTION

Special education is, first of all, purposeful intervention. Successful interventions prevent, eliminate, and/or overcome the obstacles that might keep an individual with disabilities from learning and from full and active participation in school and society. There are three basic types of intervention: preventive, remedial, and compensatory.

Preventive Intervention   Preventive intervention is designed to keep potential or minor problems from becoming a disability. Prevention can occur at three levels.

- **Primary prevention** is designed to eliminate or counteract risk factors so that a disability is never acquired; it is aimed at all relevant persons.
- **Secondary prevention** is aimed at reducing or eliminating the effects of existing risk factors; it is aimed at individuals exposed to or displaying specific risk factors.
- **Tertiary prevention** is intended to minimize the impact of a specific condition or disability; it is aimed at individuals with a disability.

Preventive efforts are most promising when they begin early—even before birth, in many cases. In later chapters, we explore some of the promising new methods for preventing and minimizing the effects of disabilities. Unfortunately, primary and secondary prevention programs have only just begun to affect the incidence and severity of disabilities in this country. And it is likely that we will be well into the 21st century before we achieve a significant reduction in the incidence of disabilities. In the meantime, we must rely on remedial and compensatory efforts to help people with disabilities achieve fuller and more independent lives.

Remedial Intervention   Remediation attempts to eliminate the effects of a disability. Remedial programs are supported largely by educational institutions and social agencies. In fact, the word *remediation* is primarily an educational term; the word *rehabilitation* is used more often by social service agencies. Both have a common purpose: to teach the person with disabilities skills for independent and successful functioning. In school, those skills may be academic (reading, writing, computing), social (getting along with others; following instructions, schedules, and other daily routines), personal (eating, dressing, using the toilet without assistance), and/or vocational (career and job skills to prepare secondary students for the world of work). The underlying assumption of remedial intervention is that a person with disabilities needs special instruction to succeed in typical settings.

Levels of preventive intervention

PRAXIS Special Education Core Principles: Content Knowledge: I. Understanding Exceptionalities, Causation and prevention of disability.

Remedial and compensatory interventions

 Content Standards for Beginning Teachers–Common Core: Models, theories, and philosophies that form the basis for special education practice (CC1K1).

Compensatory Intervention Compensatory interventions involve teaching the use of skills or devices that enable successful functioning in spite of the disability. This third type of intervention involves teaching a substitute (i.e., compensatory) skill that enables a person to perform a task in spite of the disability. For example, although remedial instruction might help a child with cerebral palsy learn to use her hands for some tasks, a headstick and a template placed over a computer keyboard may compensate for her limited fine motor control and enable her to type instead of write lessons by hand. Compensatory interventions are designed to give the person with a disability an asset that nondisabled individuals do not need—whether it be a device such as a headstick or special training such as mobility instruction for a child without vision.

SPECIAL EDUCATION AS INSTRUCTION

Ultimately, *teaching* is what special education is most about. But the same can be said of all of education. What, then, is special about special education? One way to answer that question is to examine special education in terms of the who, what, how, and where of its teaching.

Who We have already identified the most important *who* in special education: the exceptional children whose educational needs necessitate an individually planned program of instruction. Teachers, both general education classroom teachers and special educators (those who have completed specialized training programs in preparation for their work with students with special needs), provide the instruction that is the heart of each child's individualized program of education. Working with special educators and regular classroom teachers are many other professionals (e.g., school psychologists, speech-language pathologists, physical therapists, counselors) who help provide the educational and related services that exceptional children need. This interdisciplinary team of professionals, working together with parents and families, bears the primary responsibility for helping exceptional children learn despite their differences and special needs.

What Special education can sometimes be differentiated from general education by its curriculum—that is, by *what* is taught. Although every student with disabilities needs access to and support in learning as much of the general education curriculum as possible, the IEP goals and objectives for some special education students will not be found in state standards or the school district's curriculum guide. Some children with disabilities need intensive, systematic instruction to learn skills that typically developing children acquire naturally. The term *functional curriculum* is often used to describe the knowledge and skills needed by students with disabilities to achieve as much success and independence as they can in daily living, personal-social, school, community, and work settings. For example, self-help skills such as dressing, eating, and toileting are a critically important component of the school curriculum for many students with severe disabilities. Also, some children are taught certain skills to compensate for or reduce the handicapping effects of a disability. A child who is blind may be taught how to read and write in braille, whereas a sighted child does not need these skills.

How Special education can also be differentiated from general education by its use of specialized, or adapted, materials and methods. This difference is obvious when you observe

Most of all, special education is about teaching.

a special educator use sign language with students who are deaf or witness another special educator teach a child how to communicate his wishes by pointing to pictures in a special booklet he carries with him. When watching a special educator gradually and systematically withdraw verbal and physical prompts while helping a student learn to perform the steps of a task, you may find the differentiated nature of special education instruction less obvious; but it is no less specialized. It should be noted that many of the special methods for adapting curriculum and instruction developed for students with disabilities are also effective for students without disabilities.

Definitions of educational placements

PRAXIS Special Education Core Principles: Content Knowledge: III. Delivery of Services to Students with Disabilities, Placement and program issues.

Where   Special education can sometimes be identified by where it takes place. Although the majority of children with disabilities receive most of their education in regular classrooms, the others are someplace else—mostly in separate classrooms and separate residential and day schools. And many of those in regular classrooms spend a portion of each day in a resource room, where they receive individualized instruction. (Table 1.6 lists the definitions of six educational placements used by the U.S. Department of Education.) (See Teaching & Learning, "Signaling for Help," later in this chapter.)

Special educators also teach in many environments not usually thought of as "school." An early childhood special educator may spend much of his time teaching parents how to work with their infant or toddler at home. Special education teachers, particularly those who work with students with severe disabilities, are increasingly conducting *community-based instruction*, helping their students learn and practice functional daily living and job skills in the actual settings where they must be used (Owens-Johnson & Hamill, 2002).

Nearly three out of four school-age children with disabilities received at least part of their education in regular classrooms during the 1999–2000 school year (see Figure 1.1). This includes 47.3% who were served in the regular classroom and 28.3% who were served for part of each school day in a resource room, a special setting in which a special educator

TABLE 1.6   **Federal government's definitions of educational placements for students with disabilities**

Educational Setting	Definition
Regular classroom	Students receive a majority of their education program in a regular classroom and receive special education and related services outside the regular classroom for less than 21% of the school day.
Resource room	Students receive special education and related services outside the regular classroom for at least 21% but no more than 60% of the school day.
Separate classroom	Students receive special education and related services outside the regular classroom for 61% to 100% of the school day.
Separate school	Students receive special education and related services in a public or private separate day school for students with disabilities, at public expense, for more than 50% of the school day.
Residential facility	Students receive special education and related services in a public or privately operated residential facility in which children receive care or services 24 hours a day.
Homebound/hospital	Students receive special education and related services in a hospital or homebound program.

Source: Adapted from U.S. Department of Education. (2000). *Twenty-second annual report to Congress on the implementation of the Individuals with Disabilities Education Act* (p. II-14). Washington, DC: Author.

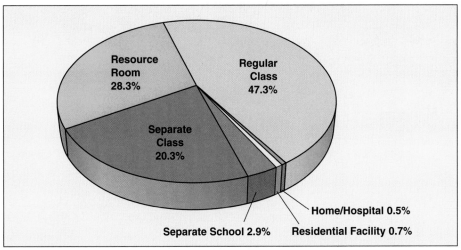

FIGURE 1.1

Percentage of all students with disabilities ages 6 through 21 served in six educational placements (1999–2000 school year)

Source: From U.S. Department of Education. (2002). *twenty-fourth annual report to Congress on the implementation of the Individuals with Disabilities Education Act* (p. AB2). Washington, DC: Author.

Notes: Separate school includes both public and private separate school facilities. Residential facility includes both public and private residential facilities

provides individualized instruction. About one-fifth of all children with disabilities are educated in separate classrooms within a regular school. About 3% of school-age students with disabilities—usually students with severe disabilities—are educated in special schools. Residential schools serve less than 1% of all children with disabilities, as do nonschool environments such as homebound or hospital programs.

The vast majority of children in the two largest groups of students with disabilities spend at least part of the school day in regular classrooms: 84% of children with learning disabilities and 94% of children with speech or language impairments (see Table 1.7). In contrast, only 43% of children with mental retardation, 35% of children with autism, 30% of children with multiple disabilities, and 25% of children with deaf-blindness were educated in regular classrooms for part of each day during the 1999–2000 school year, although these figures represent increases over those of previous years.

TABLE 1.7 **Percentage of students ages 6 through 21 served in six educational environments (1999–2000 school year)**

Disability Category	Regular Classroom	Resource Room	Separate Classroom	Separate School	Residential Facility	Homebound or Hospital
Specific learning disabilities	45.3	37.8	15.8	0.7	0.2	0.2
Speech or language impairments	87.5	6.7	5.3	0.4	0.1	0.1
Mental retardation	14.0	29.5	50.5	4.9	0.6	0.4
Emotional disturbance	25.8	23.4	32.8	13.0	3.5	1.5
Other health impairments	44.9	33.2	17.2	1.6	0.3	2.7
Multiple disabilities	11.2	18.7	43.1	21.9	2.7	2.5
Autism	20.6	14.5	49.9	13.3	1.3	0.4
Orthopedic impairments	44.4	21.9	27.7	4.1	0.3	1.6
Hearing impairments	40.3	19.3	24.5	7.1	8.6	0.2
Developmental delay	44.3	29.9	24.4	0.8	0.1	0.3
Visual impairments	49.1	19.5	17.7	6.7	7.4	0.6
Traumatic brain injury	31.0	26.6	31.6	7.2	1.3	2.3
Deaf-blindness	14.9	10.2	39.4	17.3	16.6	1.7
All disabilities	47.3	28.3	20.3	2.8	0.8	0.5

Source: From U.S. Department of Education. (2002). *Twenty-fourth annual report to Congress on the implementation of the Individuals with Disabilities Education Act* (Table AB2). Washington, DC: Author.

Signaling for Help

Resource rooms are busy places. Students come and go throughout the school day, each according to an individualized schedule. Each student who comes to the resource room does so because of a need for intensive individualized instruction. The IEP objectives for any given group of students in a resource room at any one time often cover a wide range of academic and social skills. Because of the varied skill levels and the ever-changing student groupings in the resource room, the special education teacher must often manage several types and levels of instruction at once. To accomplish this, students are often assigned individualized learning activities. Resource room teachers face a difficult challenge: the need to be in several places at once. While students work at their desks, learning centers, or computers, the teacher moves about the room, providing individual students with prompts, encouragement, praise, and corrective feedback as needed.

Students in a resource room are usually working on the skills for which they need the most help—that is, difficult material they have not yet mastered. Therefore, an effective and efficient system with which students can signal the resource room teacher for assistance is needed. Hand raising, the typical attention-getting signal in the classroom, poses several problems. It is difficult to continue to work while holding one's hand in the air, a situation that results in a great deal of down time while students wait for the teacher to get to them. In addition, if several students are waving their hands in competition for the teacher's attention, it is distracting to other students and to the teacher. If unsuccessful in getting the teacher's help, students may give up

Defining features of special education

 Council for Exceptional Children Content Standards for Beginning Teachers–Common Core: Models, theories, and philosophies that form the basis for special education practice (CC1K1).
PRAXIS Special Education Core Principles: Content Knowledge: III. Delivery of Services to Students with Disabilities, Background knowledge, Conceptual approaches.

 DEFINING FEATURES OF SPECIAL EDUCATION

What, then, is special education? At one level, special education is an important part of society's response to the needs of exceptional children and the rights of individuals with disabilities—a response brought about by parental advocacy, litigation, legislation, and, increasingly, self-advocacy by disabled persons themselves. At another level, special education is a profession with its own history, cultural practices, tools, and research base focused on the learning needs of exceptional children and adults. But at the level where exceptional children most meaningfully and frequently contact it, *special education is individually planned, specialized, intensive, goal-directed instruction.* When practiced most effectively and ethically, special education is also characterized by the use of research-based teaching methods, the application of which is guided by direct and frequent measures of student performance (Bushell & Baer, 1994; Greenwood & Maheady, 1997). Table 1.8 on page 40 shows the dimensions and defining features of special education.

 CURRENT AND FUTURE CHALLENGES

Special education has accomplished a great deal in recent years, and there is legitimate reason for those in the field to feel good about the progress. Much has been accomplished in terms of making a free, appropriate education available to many children with disabilities who were pre-

trying whenever they run into difficulty. Even worse, students who are unsuccessful in obtaining the teacher's assistance may stop discriminating their need for help and simply continue to practice errors.

Students need an effective, quiet means of signaling for help that allows them to keep working with the assurance that their teacher will recognize their need for help. In Ronni Hochman Spratt's resource room for middle school students with disabilities, each student has a small flag made of colored felt, a dowel rod, and a 1¼-inch cube of wood. (You'll read more about Ms. Spratt and her classroom in Chapter 7.) When one of Ronni's students needs assistance or wants her to check completed work, the student simply stands the flag up on his desk. While waiting for the teacher, the student can either go on to another item or work on materials in a special folder. With this simple and inexpensive system, down time is greatly reduced; and neither Ronni nor her students are distracted by hand waving or calling out. (An effective signaling device can also be made from an empty can wrapped with red and green construction paper [Kerr & Nelson, 2002]. Students turn the can on one end or the other to signal "I'm working" or "I need help.")

Ronni asked her students to write what they thought of the signal flag system after using it for about 3 months.

This is one of the best way to work in sted of raising your hand you raise your flag and keep on working but if you raise you hand you can't keep working. That is special because I get more work done. If she is working

Signal flags are a simple and effective way for students to obtain teacher assistance and feedback.

with some one els you raise it and she will get to you as fast as she can. (Brent)

The flags in Miss Hochmans room are used for assistance from the teacher. When Miss Hochman is working you rais you flag and she will help you as soon as she has time. But you keep on working, like going on to the next problem. (Pam)

viously denied access to an education. Much has been learned about how to effectively teach children with severe disabilities—children who many previously had assumed were incapable of learning. Special educators and parents are learning to work as partners on behalf of exceptional children. Technological advances have helped many students overcome physical or communication disabilities. Throughout the remaining chapters, we describe many of these advances; but it is difficult to describe the state of the art of a large and ever-changing discipline such as special education. It is even more difficult to predict what special education will look like and be able to accomplish in the future.

Although the beginnings of the field can be traced back several centuries (Safford & Safford, 1996), in many respects special education is still in its formative years. There is a great deal that must be done to make special education most useful to those who need it most. Here are four areas that many in the field consider critical.

BRIDGE THE RESEARCH-TO-PRACTICE GAP

Special education can be nothing more, or less, than the quality of instruction provided by teachers (Heward & Dardig, 2001). Contrary to the contentions of some, special education research has produced a significant and reliable knowledge base about effective teaching practices (Lovitt, 2000; Spear-Swerling & Sternberg, 2001; Vaughn, Gersten, & Chard, 2000). No knowledgeable person will argue that research has discovered every-

TABLE 1.8   Dimensions and defining features of special education instruction

Dimension	Defining Features
Individually planned	• Learning goals and objectives selected for each student based on assessment results and input from parents and student • Teaching methods and instructional materials selected and/or adapted for each student • Setting(s) where instruction will occur determined relative to opportunities for student to learn and use targeted skills
Specialized	• Sometimes involves unique or adapted teaching procedures seldom used in general education (e.g., constant time delay, token reinforcement, self-monitoring) • Incorporates a variety of instructional materials and supports—both natural and contrived—to help student acquire and use targeted learning objectives • Related services (e.g., audiology, physical therapy) provided as needed • Assistive technology (e.g., adapted cup holder, head-operated switch to select communication symbols) provided as needed
Intensive	• Instruction presented with attention to detail, precision, structure, clarity, and repeated practice • "Relentless, urgent" instruction (Zigmond & Baker, 1995) • Efforts made to provide incidental, naturalistic opportunities for student to use targeted knowledge and skills
Goal-directed	• Purposeful instruction intended to help student achieve the greatest possible personal self-sufficiency and success in present and future environments • Value/goodness of instruction determined by student's attainment of outcomes
Research-based methods	• Recognize that all teaching approaches are not equally effective • Instructional programs and teaching procedures selected on basis of research support
Guided by student performance	• Careful, ongoing monitoring of student progress • Frequent and direct measures/assessment of student learning that inform modifications in instruction

thing that is important to know about teaching exceptional students. There are many questions to be answered, the pursuit of which will no doubt lead to other questions yet to be asked.

While there is a significant gap between what is relatively well understood and what is poorly understood or not understood at all, the more distressing gap may be between what research has discovered about teaching and learning and what is practiced in many classrooms. For example, scientific research has helped us discover a great deal about areas such as how to design instruction to promote students' generalization and maintenance of what is taught, what features of early reading instruction will reduce the number of children who later develop reading problems, how to teach students the skills they need to more effectively self-determine and self-manage their lives, and what components of secondary special education programs increase students' success in making the transition from school to work. It is fundamentally and critically important for special education to bridge the research-to-practice gap regarding effective instruction (Carnine, 1997; Gersten, 2001; Vaughn, Klingner, & Hughes, 2000). Instructional practices supported by scientific research are featured in the Teaching & Learning boxes and described throughout this text.

Using research-based practices

Council for Exceptional Children Content Standards for Beginning Teachers–Common Core: Methods to remain current regarding research-validated practice (CC9K4). **PRAXIS** Special Education Core Principles: Content Knowledge: III. Delivery of Services to Students with Disabilities, Critical evaluation and use of professional literature.

INCREASE THE AVAILABILITY AND INTENSITY OF EARLY INTERVENTION AND PREVENTION PROGRAMS

It is better to intervene earlier than later. The recent growth in providing special education and family-focused services for infants, toddlers, and preschoolers who have disabilities or are at risk for developmental delay is a positive sign. Increased efforts must be made, however, to ensure that early intervention and special education preschool programs become more widely available and intensely delivered.

 ## IMPROVE STUDENTS' TRANSITION FROM SCHOOL TO ADULT LIFE

When special education is judged by its ultimate product—the youth who leave secondary school programs—it becomes clear how much further the field must progress. Too many young adults with disabilities are unsuccessful and unhappy in their postschool adjustment. Special education must improve the transition of youth with disabilities from school to life in their communities.

 ## IMPROVE THE SPECIAL EDUCATION–GENERAL EDUCATION PARTNERSHIP

In addition to the 10% to 12% of school-age children with disabilities who receive special education, another 10% to 20% of the student population experience difficulties with learning or behavior problems that interfere with their ability to succeed in school. Special and general educators must develop strategies for working together and sharing their knowledge and resources to prevent these millions of at-risk students from becoming failures of our educational system.

The ultimate effectiveness of special education must be measured by its ability to help secondary students with disabilities make a successful transition to adult life.

These four areas are by no means the only important issues facing special education today. We could easily identify numerous other challenges that many in the field would argue are equally important. For example:

- Increasing the availability and quality of special education programs for gifted and talented students
- Applying advances in assistive technology to greatly reduce or eliminate the disabling effects of physical and sensory impairments
- Combating the pervasive effects of childhood poverty on development and success in school (one in five American children under the age of 5 is living in poverty and nearly 4 in 10 African American and Hispanic children live in poverty [Fujira & Yakima, 2000])
- Developing appropriate accommodations and alternative assessments so that the participation of students with disabilities in district- and state-wide tests provides fair and valid measures of their learning
- Increasing access to technologies that can enhance the educational performance and personal independence of individuals with disabilities
- Helping students with disabilities acquire self-determination and self-advocacy skills
- Improving the quality of pre- and in-service training programs to ensure that all special educators meet professional standards (CEC, 2002)
- Providing mentoring programs for beginning special education teachers and ongoing professional support for teachers to increase the effectiveness and retention of the teaching force
- Improving the behavior and attitudes of people without disabilities toward those with disabilities

- Opening up more opportunities for individuals with disabilities to participate in the full range of residential, employment, and recreational options available to nondisabled persons

We do not know how successful special education will be in meeting these challenges. Only time will tell. And, of course, special educators do not face these challenges alone. General education; adult service agencies such as vocational rehabilitation, social work, and medicine; and society as a whole must all help find the solutions to these problems. But we do know that a large and growing group of people are working hard to respond to these challenges—people with and without disabilities, people within and outside special education. Whatever professional and personal goals you follow, I hope your introductory study of special education will encourage you to become part of that group.

For more information on defining special education, go to the Web Links module in Chapter 1 of the Companion Website at **www.prenhall.com/heward**

 SUMMARY

WHO ARE EXCEPTIONAL CHILDREN?

- Exceptional children are those whose physical attributes and/or learning abilities differ from the norm, either above or below, to such an extent that an individualized program of special education is necessary.
- *Impairment* refers to the reduced function or loss of a particular body part or organ; a disability exists when an impairment limits the ability to perform certain tasks in the same way that most persons do.
- *Handicap* refers to the problems a person with a disability encounters when interacting with the environment.
- A child who is at risk is not currently identified as having a disability but is considered to have a greater-than-usual chance of developing a disability if intervention is not provided.

HOW MANY EXCEPTIONAL CHILDREN ARE THERE?

- Children in special education represent approximately 9% of the school-age population.
- The four largest categories of children with disabilities receiving special education are learning disabilities, speech and language impairments, mental retardation, and emotional disturbance.
- The vast majority of children receiving special education have mild disabilities.
- Three out of four students with disabilities receive at least part of their education in regular classrooms.

WHY DO WE LABEL AND CLASSIFY EXCEPTIONAL CHILDREN?

- Some believe that disability labels can have negative effects on the child and on others' perceptions of her and can lead to exclusion; others believe that labeling is a necessary first step to providing needed intervention and that labels are important for comparing and communicating about research findings.
- In curriculum-based assessment, students are assessed and classified relative to the degree to which they are learning specific curriculum content.

WHY ARE LAWS GOVERNING THE EDUCATION OF EXCEPTIONAL CHILDREN NECESSARY?

- Before the 1970s, many states had laws permitting public schools to deny enrollment to children with disabilities. When local public schools began to accept a measure of responsibility for educating certain exceptional students, a philosophy of segregation prevailed.

- Special education was strongly influenced by the case of *Brown v. Board of Education* in 1954, in which the U.S. Supreme Court declared that education must be made available to all children on equal terms.
- In the class-action lawsuit *PARC* (1972), the Court ruled that all children with mental retardation were entitled to a free, appropriate public education and that placements in regular classrooms and regular public schools were preferable to segregated settings.
- All children with disabilities are now recognized to have the right to equal protection under the law, which has been interpreted to mean the right to a free public education in the least restrictive environment.
- All children with disabilities and their parents have the right to due process under the law, which includes the rights to be notified of any decision affecting the child's educational placement, to have a hearing and present a defense, to see a written decision, and to appeal any decision.
- Court decisions have also established the rights of children with disabilities to fair assessment in their native language and to education at public expense, regardless of the school district's financial constraints.

THE INDIVIDUALS WITH DISABILITIES EDUCATION ACT

- The passage of IDEA by Congress in 1975 marked the culmination of the efforts of many educators, parents, and legislators to bring together in one comprehensive bill this country's laws regarding the education of children with disabilities. The law encompasses six major principles:
  - *Zero reject.* Schools must educate all children with disabilities. This principle applies regardless of the nature or severity of the disability.
  - *Nondiscriminatory identification and evaluation.* Schools must use nonbiased, multifactored methods of evaluation to determine whether a child has a disability and, if so, whether special education is needed.
  - *Free, appropriate public education.* All children with disabilities shall receive a free, appropriate public education at public expense. An individualized education program (IEP) must be developed and implemented for each student with a disability.
  - *Least restrictive environment.* Students with disabilities must be educated with children without disabilities to the maximum extent appropriate, and they should be removed to separate classes or schools only when the nature or severity of their disabilities is such that they cannot receive an appropriate education in a general education classroom.
  - *Due process safeguards.* Schools must provide due process safeguards to protect the rights of children with disabilities and their parents.
  - *Parent and student participation and shared decision making.* Schools must collaborate with parents and with students with disabilities in the design and implementation of special education services.
- IDEA requires states to provide special education services to all preschoolers with disabilities ages 3 to 5. This law also makes federal money available to encourage states to develop early intervention programs for disabled and at-risk infants and toddlers from birth to age 2. Early intervention services must be coordinated by an individualized family services plan (IFSP).
- Court cases have challenged the way in which particular school districts implement specific provisions of IDEA. No trend has emerged, but rulings from the various cases have established the principle that each student with disabilities is entitled to a personalized program of instruction and related services that will enable him to benefit from an education in as integrated a setting as possible.
- The Gifted and Talented Children's Education Act (P.L. 95-561) provides financial incentives to states for developing programs for gifted and talented students.

- Section 504 of the Rehabilitation Act forbids discrimination in all federally funded programs, including educational and vocational programs, on the basis of disability.
- The Americans with Disabilities Act (P.L. 101-336) extends the civil rights protections for persons with disabilities to private sector employment, all public services, public accommodations, transportation, and telecommunications.

WHAT IS SPECIAL EDUCATION?

- Special education consists of purposeful intervention efforts at three levels: preventive, remedial, and compensatory.
- Special education is individually planned, specialized, intensive, goal-directed instruction. When practiced most effectively and ethically, special education uses research-based teaching methods and is guided by direct and frequent measures of student performance.

CURRENT AND FUTURE CHALLENGES

- Among the many challenges faced by special education today are the following:
  - Bridging the research-to-practice gap
  - Making early intervention programs more widely available to infants, toddlers, and preschoolers who have disabilities or are at risk for developing disabilities
  - Improving the ability of young adults with disabilities to make a successful transition from school to community life
  - Working more effectively with general education to better serve the many students who have not been identified as disabled but who are not progressing in the general education program

To check your comprehension of chapter content, go to the Guided Review and Quiz modules in Chapter 1 of the Companion Website at **www.prenhall.com/heward**

Chapter 2
Planning and Providing Special Education Services

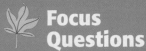

- Why must the planning and provision of special education be so carefully sequenced and evaluated?

- Why does the effectiveness of special education require collaboration and teaming?

- How should the quality of a student's individualized education program be judged?

- Is the least restrictive environment always the regular classroom? Why?

- What elements must be in place for special education to be appropriate in inclusive classrooms?

CAROL RICHARDS
SWANTON ELEMENTARY SCHOOL DISTRICT
SWANTON, VERMONT

Education • Teaching Credentials • Experience
- B.S., Special Education, Bloomsburg State University, Pennsylvania, 1975
- M.A., Special Education, Johnson State College, Vermont, 1985
- Vermont Professional Level II Certification in Special Education, K–12
- 27 years of teaching experience, 25 years as a special educator

Current Position/Duties   I team with a "house" of second- and third-grade regular education teachers. The students on my caseload this year have a wide range of mild to severe disabilities and are served under various IDEA categories such as learning disabilities, mental retardation, behavioral disorders, physical and health impairments (including ADHD), and students with multiple disabilities. I team with teachers to develop individualized goals, behavior plans, and accommodations for their students' programs. I provide direct instruction to students, design accommodations to help students be successful in the regular classroom, and help teachers plan how to incorporate students' IEP goals into regular class activities. I also coordinate and conduct comprehensive evaluations to determine special education eligibility. Other important components of my work in a typical week include data collection to measure students' progress on IEP goals, coordinating support from related services specialists, training paraeducators, and scheduling IEP team meetings.

Collaboration and Teaming   Our school uses a collaborative team model to plan and provide special education services. We set up core and extended teams around kids. A core team may be the regular classroom teacher and parents, the special educator and paraeducator, and the speech-language pathologist. The extended team might also include a physical therapist (PT), an occupational therapist (OT), a school psychologist, an administrator, the school nurse, a family worker in the home, or a consultant from the Vermont interdisciplinary team. There are so many variations in team makeup, depending on who needs to be involved in a child's program and to what degree. I interact weekly with teachers, parents, paraeducators, the school psychologist and guidance counselors, the Title I teacher, the administrators, and other special educators. Throughout the year I am involved with and receive input from physicians, parent advocates, agency workers supporting families, consultants, neuropsychologists, the school nurse, an OT, a PT, and any other people who can add to the quality of a child's program. The staff members of the Swanton schools believe it takes a community to raise a child, and our collaborative teaming helps us put our beliefs into practice.

We collaborate on everything: overall program development at the school level, IEP development, delivery of instruction, and problem solving. We delegate

and share tasks to keep programs running smoothly. The classroom teachers whom I work with are awesome; they take responsibility for their students and are savvy at knowing what they need from other team members.

IEP Goals　　All of our IEP goals are written to address Vermont state curriculum standards. We develop short-term instructional objectives using a rubric of four levels of performance: just learning, getting there, good, and great. Here are examples of IEP goals and objectives for two of our current students:

Annual goal.　　By 2/13/02, Tara will write and edit a paragraph as described at the "great" level in the rubric below.
　　State standard addressed: 1.5.　　Students draft, revise, edit, and critique written products so that final drafts are appropriate in terms of purpose, details, organization, and voice or tone.
　　Short-term objective 1. By 6/13/01, when writing about a topic, Tara will write at the "getting there" level.
　　Short-term objective 2. By 11/13/01, when writing about a topic, Tara will write at the "good" level.
　　Short-term objective 3. By 2/13/02, when writing about a topic, Tara will write at the "great" level.

Annual goal.　　By 11/10/02, Jeffrey will improve his ability to stop and think and use skills he has practiced to manage his anger and control his impulsiveness at the "great" level as described in the rubric on page 49.
　　State standard addressed: Healthy choices.　　Students make informed, healthy choices that positively affect the health, safety, and well-being of themselves and others.
　　Short-term objective 1.　　By 1/20/02, when beginning to feel stressed or angry, Jeffrey will verbalize and work through the steps in his "stop and think" plan at the "getting there" level.
　　Short-term objective 2.　　By 6/1/02, when beginning to feel stressed or angry, Jeffrey will verbalize and work through the steps in his "stop and think" plan at the "good" level.
　　Short-term objective 3.　　By 11/10/02, when beginning to feel stressed or angry, Jeffrey will verbalize and work through the steps in his "stop and think" plan at the "great" level.

Teaching Strategies　　I use the following teaching strategies frequently:

Think-alouds.　　Having students talk as they try to solve a problem or perform a task allows me to evaluate their understanding of skill sequences and where their understanding breaks down or is inconsistent. It also helps students become aware of what they

Just Learning	Getting There	Good	Great
Has great difficulty writing several complete sentences and a topic sentence	Writes a sentence to start her paragraph but has difficulty sticking to the topic and making detail sentences complete	Writes a paragraph with a topic and detail sentences but needs an adult or peer to help her identify and correct incomplete sentences	Writes a paragraph with a topic and detail sentences and checks and corrects structures when sentences are incomplete
Needs the assistance of the teacher or peer to help her form the sentences and write them so they are complete	Corrects errors mostly with teacher or peer support		Needs adult coaching to add new details but is able to put ideas into sentences within her paragraph

are thinking. The think-aloud strategy helps students be consistent from one situation to the next (generalization) in the way in which they approach a task.

Checklists and scripts.　All students in our school are encouraged to use checklists to help them get their materials ready for an activity or to guide them through revising and editing their written work. Most special education students need direct instruction and lots of modeling and practice to learn to use checklists effectively. I use the same checklists that the students do, so my modeling reinforces or teaches their use. When needed, I help develop individualized checklists for special situations, with input from the teachers. Some students do better in a step-by-step skill, such as regrouping in subtraction, with a checklist or script for each problem: e.g., "Is the bottom number bigger? If yes, then. . . ." I have created behavioral checklists to remind students to use proper body behavior to demonstrate attending. A small card on the desk or somewhere in the student's materials can have stick-figure drawings and a few key words to remind a student to keep feet on the floor and hands on his desk, face his body toward the speaker, and look at the speaker. The checklists are gradually withdrawn and replaced with self-talk in which a student begins to internally monitor his body. This strategy is paired with feedback from the teacher during and/or after the practice sessions.

In-school homework.　After I have observed a student be fairly fluent with a skill in a controlled setting, she and I will discuss a plan about where she is going to use the skill independently throughout the day. The student then reports back to me on her use of and success with the skill. This process strengthens a student's awareness of what she is thinking and reinforces her ability to recall information or apply a skill across settings and situations. This takes lots of practice, and it helps when the classroom teacher or paraeducator reminds the student or praises her for appropriately using her new knowledge or skill.

Peer tutoring.　Peer tutoring can be very effective for teaching curriculum content such as math facts, science or social studies facts, vocabulary or sight words. A peer presents five or six flashcards that include three or four known and two unknown

 To learn more about teaching strategies used by Ms. Richards, go to the Teacher Feature page on the Companion Website at **www. prenhall.com/heward**

Just Learning	Getting There	Good	Great
With his counselor in a one-on-one setting, when not angry or frustrated, verbalizes steps in the sequence that he will use to help him stop and think and control his anger and impulsiveness	With his counselor in a one-on-one setting in a situation that produces stress, identifies his escalating behavior and verbalizes steps that allow him to stop and think and keep his behavior under control In classroom situations in which the adult identifies his escalating behavior and with the adult coaching him to follow the steps of his plan, stops and thinks and keeps his behavior under control	In a real classroom situation that produces stress, identifies his escalating behavior and verbalizes steps that allow him to stop and think and keep his behavior under control, with adult reminders to use his skills	In a real classroom situation that produces stress, identifies his escalating behavior and verbalizes steps that allow him to stop and think and keep his behavior under control, without reminders and on a consistent basis In less structured settings, such as the playground and gym, in which the adult identifies his escalating behavior and with the adult coaching him to follow the steps of his plan, stops and thinks and keeps his behavior under control

items. As the unknown cards are learned, they become known cards; and older knowns are replaced with new information. Charts can be used to record results, and the cards with known information can be recirculated into the drills so the knowledge is not forgotten.

What I Like Most about Being a Special Educator   I enjoy helping students figure out how to learn. It is exciting to watch a child at the moment of understanding after lots of effort. When the student sees how a strategy works or suddenly understands a concept, it is so exciting and makes all the hard work more than worth it!

Personal Qualities Important for Special Educators   A special educator needs to be an efficient consumer of time. I often have an IEP progress report on the computer and work on it whenever a short block of time is available, even if it is only 10–15 minutes. I eat lunch with a different teacher each day so I can have regular time to address student programs. A special educator should also enjoy helping others, not only students but also teachers, paraeducators, and parents. Special educators are constantly trying to problem-solve, offer empathy, observe, and offer constructive and positive feedback. The special educator should be able to motivate students and adults and be a good facilitator.

Advice for Someone Considering a Career in Special Education   Develop a clear sense of your philosophical beliefs about education in general and how that relates to students requiring special education. Then find and work in a school system or setting that practices those beliefs.

The CD-ROM packaged with this text will walk you through the process of developing quality IEPs. It contains an overview of the IEP and the special education process, two interactive tutorials, six case studies with practice exercises, and additional resources.

To better understand the topics that will be covered in this chapter, go to the Essential Concepts and Chapter-at-a-Glance Modules in Chapter 2 of the Companion Website at **www.prenhall.com/heward**

In Chapter 1, *special education* was defined as individually planned, specialized, intensive, goal-directed instruction. But how do teachers know what kinds of modifications to curriculum and instruction an individual child needs? And toward what goals should instruction be directed? In this chapter, we examine the basic process by which special education is planned, devoting particular attention to four critical aspects of educating students with disabilities: (1) the importance of teaming and collaboration among professionals, (2) the individualized education plan (IEP), (3) the least restrictive environment (LRE), and (4) inclusion.

THE PROCESS OF SPECIAL EDUCATION

IDEA mandates a particular sequence of events that schools must follow when identifying and educating children with disabilities. Although the rules and regulations that state and local school districts must follow to implement IDEA are formal and sometimes redundant for legal purposes, the process is designed to answer a sequence of questions that makes both educational and common sense:

- Which students might need special education?
- Does this particular child have a disability that adversely affects his educational performance? In other words, is this student eligible for special education? If the answer is yes, then. . . .
- What are the specific educational needs that result from the child's disability?
- What specialized methods of instruction, accommodations, curricular modifications, related services, and/or supplementary supports are necessary to meet those needs so

the student can be involved and progress in the general curriculum and life of the school?

- Who is best suited to provide the special education and related services needed by the student?
- What placement is the least restrictive environment in which the student can be provided with an appropriate education?
- Is special education helping the student make progress? Is it working?

Figure 2.1 identifies the major steps in the sequence of planning, implementing, and evaluating special education and highlights some of the key procedures, elements, or requirements of each step. With the exception of the first step, prereferral intervention, each step in the process is required by IDEA. (Although not required to do so, some states follow a process similar to the one shown in Figure 2.1 on pages 52–53 for planning individualized education programs for gifted and talented students.)

For a review of the special education process, access the section *How are Students Identified?* in Part 1 of the CD-ROM.

 PREREFERRAL INTERVENTION

A child who may need special education usually comes to the attention of the schools because (1) a teacher or parent reports concern about differences in learning, behavior, or development or (2) the results of a screening test suggest a possible disability. (Screening tests are relatively quick, inexpensive, and easy-to-administer assessments given to large groups of children to find out who might have a disability and need further testing. For example, most schools administer vision screening tests to all elementary children.) Before referring the child for more formal testing and evaluation for special education, however, most schools initiate a process known as *prereferral intervention.*

Prereferral intervention is an informal, problem-solving process with two primary purposes: (1) to provide immediate instructional and/or behavior management assistance to the child and teacher and (2) to reduce the chances of identifying a child for special education who may not be disabled (Salvia & Ysseldyke, 2001). Many schools use *intervention assistance teams* (also called *student support teams* or *prereferral assistance teams*) to help classroom teachers devise and implement adaptations for a student who is experiencing either academic or behavioral difficulties so that she can remain in the regular classroom (Logan, Hansen, Nieminen, & Wright, 2001). Prereferral intervention has the potential to prevent or reduce the frequency of future student problems by strengthening the teacher's capacity to effectively intervene with a greater diversity of children (Fuchs, Fuchs, Bahr, Fernstrom, & Stecker, 1990).

When prereferral intervention is successful in ameliorating the problems that originally caused teachers or parents to be concerned about the child, it also prevents the costly and time-consuming process of assessment for special education eligibility. A school district may not, however, use prereferral intervention to delay formal evaluation and assessment of a student who is eligible for special education (Yell, 1998). Although they are not required by federal law, many states either require or recommend that local school districts use prereferral interventions for students suspected of having a disability.

Prereferral intervention

 Content Standards for Beginning Teachers–Common Core: Screening, pre-referral, referral, and classification procedures (CC8K3).
PRAXIS Special Education Core Principles: Content Knowledge: III. Delivery of Services to Students with Disabilities, Assessment, Pre-referral.

 EVALUATION AND IDENTIFICATION

Teachers seldom refer children for minor or frivolous learning or behavior problems. In practice, about 90% of children who are referred are formally evaluated for special education, and about 73% of those who are tested are found eligible for special education (Ysseldyke, 2001). IDEA requires that all children suspected of having a disability receive a nondiscriminatory **multifactored evaluation (MFE).** Either the school or parents can request that a child be evaluated for special education. Regardless of the source of the referral, the parents must be notified of the school's intent to test their child, and they must give their consent to the evaluation. IDEA is explicit in describing some do's and don'ts for the evaluation

Multifactored evaluation

Content Standards for Beginning Teachers–Common Core: Legal provisions and ethical principles regarding assessment of individuals (CC8K2).
PRAXIS Special Education Core Principles: Content Knowledge: III. Delivery of Services to Students with Disabilities, Assessment, Procedures for referral.

and identification of children for special education. Sometimes referred to as *protection in evaluation procedures* (Yell, 1998), the rules in IDEA for nondiscriminatory, multifactored evaluation and identification of children require the following:

- Technically sound instruments must be used to assess the student across four domains: cognitive, behavioral, physical, and developmental.
- Tests must not discriminate on the basis of race or culture.
- Tests must be provided and administered in the child's native language or other mode of communication.
- Standardized tests must have been validated for the specific purpose for which they are used.
- Standardized tests must be administered by trained and knowledgeable personnel in accordance with any instructions provided by the publisher of the tests.
- The child is assessed in all areas related to the suspected disability.
- The evaluation process must not rely on any single procedure as the sole criterion for determining whether the student has a disability, the student's program, or placement. (IDEA, Sec. 1414[b])

The multifactored evaluation is conducted by a school-based *evaluation team,* sometimes called a *child study team,* which includes the child's parents. The team examines the test results and all other relevant information to determine if the child has a disability and needs special education. An MFE must do more than just provide information on the existence of a disability for determining eligibility for special education. IDEA requires evaluation reports to also provide information about the child's educational needs and how to meet them.

 PROGRAM PLANNING

If the evaluation team determines that a child has a disability that is adversely affecting his educational performance, an individualized education program (IEP) must be planned and provided. The IEP process determines the *what* (learning goals and objectives, specialized

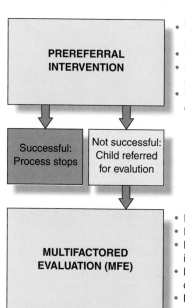

PREREFERRAL INTERVENTION	• Teacher or parent reports concern with child's learning, behavior, or development, or results of screening test indicate possible disability. • Parents are notified. • Intervention assistance team works with classroom teacher to plan and help implement modifications in curriculum and instruction in an attempt to solve the problem. • Prereferral intervention is not required by IDEA; it may not be used to delay referral and evaluation of an eligible student.

Successful: Process stops

Not successful: Child referred for evaluation

MULTIFACTORED EVALUATION (MFE)	• Parent consent for testing and evaluation must be obtained. • Evaluation must not discriminate on basis of race, culture, language, or gender. • MFE considers all areas related to the suspected disability (e.g., academic performance, general intelligence, social behavior, vision, health). • MFE uses a variety of assessment tools and strategies (e.g., formal tests, direct observations in classroom, parental input). • MFE should provide information to help determine if the child has a disability, what kinds of related services may be needed, and how the child can participate in the general education curriculum.

(continues)

FIGURE 2.1 **The basic steps in planning, providing, and evaluating special education**

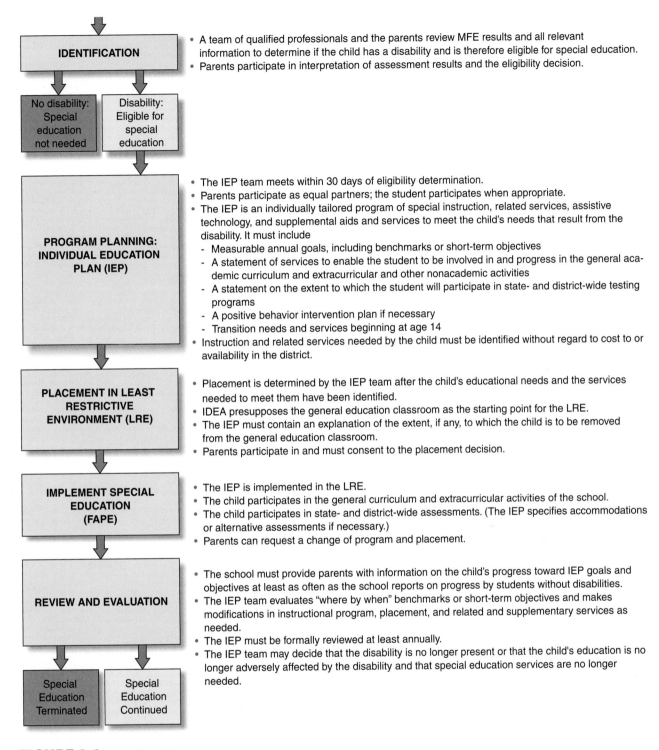

| IDENTIFICATION | • A team of qualified professionals and the parents review MFE results and all relevant information to determine if the child has a disability and is therefore eligible for special education.
• Parents participate in interpretation of assessment results and the eligibility decision. |

| No disability: Special education not needed | Disability: Eligible for special education |

PROGRAM PLANNING: INDIVIDUAL EDUCATION PLAN (IEP)

• The IEP team meets within 30 days of eligibility determination.
• Parents participate as equal partners; the student participates when appropriate.
• The IEP is an individually tailored program of special instruction, related services, assistive technology, and supplemental aids and services to meet the child's needs that result from the disability. It must include
  - Measurable annual goals, including benchmarks or short-term objectives
  - A statement of services to enable the student to be involved in and progress in the general academic curriculum and extracurricular and other nonacademic activities
  - A statement on the extent to which the student will participate in state- and district-wide testing programs
  - A positive behavior intervention plan if necessary
  - Transition needs and services beginning at age 14
• Instruction and related services needed by the child must be identified without regard to cost to or availability in the district.

PLACEMENT IN LEAST RESTRICTIVE ENVIRONMENT (LRE)

• Placement is determined by the IEP team after the child's educational needs and the services needed to meet them have been identified.
• IDEA presupposes the general education classroom as the starting point for the LRE.
• The IEP must contain an explanation of the extent, if any, to which the child is to be removed from the general education classroom.
• Parents participate in and must consent to the placement decision.

IMPLEMENT SPECIAL EDUCATION (FAPE)

• The IEP is implemented in the LRE.
• The child participates in the general curriculum and extracurricular activities of the school.
• The child participates in state- and district-wide assessments. (The IEP specifies accommodations or alternative assessments if necessary.)
• Parents can request a change of program and placement.

REVIEW AND EVALUATION

• The school must provide parents with information on the child's progress toward IEP goals and objectives at least as often as the school reports on progress by students without disabilities.
• The IEP team evaluates "where by when" benchmarks or short-term objectives and makes modifications in instructional program, placement, and related and supplementary services as needed.
• The IEP must be formally reviewed at least annually.
• The IEP team may decide that the disability is no longer present or that the child's education is no longer adversely affected by the disability and that special education services are no longer needed.

| Special Education Terminated | Special Education Continued |

FIGURE 2.1 *continued*

A PDA in Hand . . .

by Anne M. Bauer and Mary E. Ulrich

Seventh-grader Mei is sitting at her desk, working on her math practice sheet. Periodically she picks up what appears to be a large calculator to check her computation. At one point in her work, she hears a soft chirp. She picks up the instrument and reads the note that says, "11:30—medication." Mei pushes a button, gets up from her seat, and nods to her teacher as she goes to see the school nurse to get her medication.

As students enter junior high school, demands for independence and responsibility increase significantly. Though challenging for all students, these demands are exacerbated when the student has a disability. In addition, parent communication typically decreases as students grow older, although the need for family-school collaboration continues. One way to support students in their efforts toward independence and in communication with parents is through the use of *personal digital assistants* (PDAs).

Personal digital assistants, also called "palms" or "handhelds," are becoming commonplace in community and business settings but are only emerging in schools as productivity tools for teachers and students. PDAs may be affordable, motivating ways to support students in general education and in home-school communication. Not only are handheld computers commercially available and decreasing in price; parents are often already familiar with their use. Students are already comfortable with handheld technology through video games. In our work in inclusive classrooms, we have found that students quickly learn to use PDAs and develop creative applications for them.

Classroom Applications

There are many possible applications for PDAs in inclusive classrooms. These include both in-class motivational and academic supports.

- *Calculator and spell checker.* A PDA eliminates the need for the student to carry a spell checker, a dictionary, a calculator, or a plan book. One tool addresses all of these needs.

- *Self-management tool.* Students may use the easy-to-set alarms on handhelds as reminders to take medication, begin a new task, or self-check if the correct task is being completed. PDAs include "to do lists," allowing the student to record activities and assignments that must be completed by a designated time. PDAs may include long-term project planners, which may break longer assignments into manageable segments. In addition, students can track their own grades on their handhelds.

- *Instructional support.* PDAs may provide instructional supports for teachers and students. A study buddy can beam notes or assignments to a classmate with disabilities. Providing a PDA to the study partner may be a motivating way to engage natural supports for the student with disabilities. Tools that supplement instructional needs may include software programs such as measurement converters, graphing calculators, project planners, homework organizers, or drill and practice programs.

- *Word processing.* Software and keyboards allow teachers and students to use word processing programs compatible with desktop computer programs. Teachers can beam overhead transparencies or lecture notes to students, eliminating the need for an intermediary note taker. Students can synchronize the beamed notes or assignments with their home computers, printing out copies to review. Written assignments may be completed and edited using handhelds.

- *Motivational and behavior management plans.* Students may self-cue and self-record their behavioral data on the PDA. A student or teacher may enter reminders into the PDA, with alarms set throughout the day. In addition, flashcard sets, self-quizzes, and quiet problem-solving games are avail-

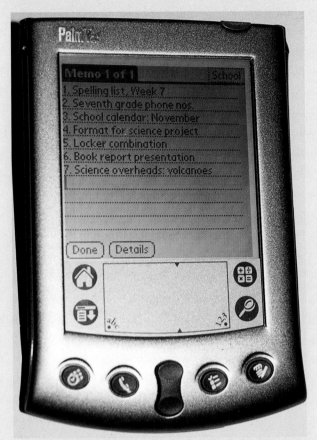

Students learn to use PDAs quickly and for a wide variety of classroom applications.

A PDA can function as a portable homework hotline for parents.

able, allowing the student to quietly busy himself or herself by reviewing or relaxing.

Home-School Communication

PDAs also have great potential for enhancing home-school communication.

- *Parent-teacher communication.*   Teachers are able to write notes to parents and other caregivers, identify school events, develop the classroom schedule or calendar, or provide the class phone list and beam the information to students. Parents then check the PDA, which is less likely than a paper note to be lost or crumpled in the bottom of a book bag.

- *Homework communication.*   Teachers and peers may enter homework and long-term assignments on their handhelds and beam them to students with disabilities for whom recording assignments is difficult. Parents could use the PDA to send messages back to the teacher regarding the amount of time the assignment took or any challenges in completing the assignment.

With new programs available as free shareware on almost a daily basis, the potential ways in which PDAs can be used to support students with disabilities seems endless.

Guidelines and Considerations

Here are several considerations for the use of PDAs in the classroom. First, inputting information may be difficult for some students. However, the PDA may be a motivating way for a peer to enter the information for a student with a disability. The teacher may also enter information on his or her PDA and beam it to students who require that level of support.

Second, handhelds are most useful if they are constantly available to the students. They do take up space, especially if the student is using a keyboard. They also don't bounce. Protective cases are essential. Passport wallets worn around the neck or a belt pack may be an option for younger children. Simply having enough room on the desk for a PDA, a keyboard, a book, paper, a pencil, and a PDA stylus may be a challenge.

Batteries pose an additional yet pesky problem. Although students can be reminded to tell a parent or teacher if the battery indicator shows that the power level is low, they may forget or try to get one more day out of the current batteries. If the batteries are dead for any period of time, all information on the PDA, outside of the basic programs, may be lost. However, many newer models automatically recharge their batteries when the instrument is placed in the synchronization stand. The need to frequently synchronize the PDA with a desktop computer may be a challenge, especially when the student's home computer is not compatible with the school computer. In our work it became apparent that we needed a way for the students to synchronize frequently at school and that keeping a supply of fresh batteries at school was helpful.

Here are some additional considerations when using PDAs to support students:

- *There are bad programs and inappropriate programs.* Care must be taken in downloading programs from the Internet. Pilot any program before using it. In addition, some programs and games have content inappropriate for school. Inappropriate or unneeded programs may use up memory the student actually needs for school supports.
- *Management.* Students quickly learn how to beam to each other, including notes and even homework. They may trade handhelds. Teachers need to pay attention to what students are actually doing with their handhelds.
- *Teachers may be less motivated than students to use handhelds.* Students usually find it fun to try new

programs; some teachers may find it a hassle. Teachers who are far less trusting of technology prefer the comfort of paper and pencil. Effective use of PDAs could easily be built into pre- and in-service teacher training programs.

However, these issues are easily managed and are minimal in comparison with the potential for PDAs in supporting students in inclusive classrooms. Given their increasing popularity and universal design, a PDA can be a status-enhancing accommodation instead of a stigma. Students are ready, able, and eager to use handheld technology.

Anne Bauer is a member of the teacher education faculty at the University of Cincinnati, where she teaches in the early childhood/early childhood special education program and conducts research related to supporting young children in general education. Her son and daughter, who both have learning disabilities, use PDAs to support their inclusion. Mary Ulrich is also the parent of a young adult with disabilities. She is a member of the special education faculty at Miami University in Oxford, Ohio, where she studies issues of inclusion.

instruction, and related services), *who* (teachers and related service providers), and *when* (frequency of specialized instruction and related services) of a child's special education program. A critically important element of special education practice—some would say the centerpiece—the IEP will be described in detail later in this chapter. (Some students' IEPs specify assistive technology as a related service to support their access to the general education curriculum. See Teaching & Learning, "A PDA in Hand. . . ," on pages 54–56 in this chapter.)

PLACEMENT

After the child's educational needs and the special education and related services necessary to meet those needs are determined, the IEP team decides on the least restrictive environment (LRE) in which an appropriate education can be provided to the child. The placement of children with disabilities is one of the most debated and often misunderstood aspects of special education and IDEA and will be discussed in depth later in this chapter and throughout the text.

"Here's another idea we could try." Intervention assistance teams plan strategies to help children with learning or behavioral problems remain in the regular classroom.

REVIEW AND EVALUATION

In addition to being specialized, intensive, and goal-directed education—when it is properly practiced—special education is also continuously evaluated education. All aspects of a child's IEP—progress on goals and short-term objectives, delivery of specialized instruction and related services, appropriateness of placement—are reviewed and open for change. The IEP must be thoroughly and formally reviewed on an annual basis. However, schools must notify parents of their child's progress in the general curriculum and toward IEP goals and objects at least as often as parents of nondisabled students receive information about their children's school performance.

No matter how appropriate the goals and benchmarks or short-term objectives on a student's IEP, the document's usefulness is limited without direct and ongoing monitoring of student progress (Fuchs & Fuchs, 1996; Ysseldyke, 2001). Unfortunately, many teachers do not collect and use student performance data to evaluate the effectiveness of their instruction. Although three-fourths of the 510 special education teachers in one survey indicated that frequently collected student performance data are "important," many indicated they most often relied on anecdotal observations and subjective measures (e.g., checklists, letter grades) for determining whether or not IEP objectives were met; and 85% said they "never" or "seldom" collected and charted student performance data to make instructional decisions (Cooke, Heward, Test, Spooner, & Courson, 1991). Giek (1992) and Farlow and Snell (1994) describe a variety of practical procedures for obtaining and using student performance data to monitor student progress toward IEP objectives.

 ## COLLABORATION AND TEAMING

Special education is a team game. The fourth-grade teacher who works with Sharelle in the regular classroom, the speech-language pathologist who meets with Sharelle's teacher each week to co-plan language activities, and the special education teacher who provides Sharelle with intensive reading instruction each day in the resource room and collaborates with her regular classroom teacher on instructional modifications for Sharelle in math and science are all members of a team that plans, delivers, and evaluates a program of special education and related services designed to meet the individual needs that arise from Sharelle's disability. Without open, honest, and frequent communication and collaboration between and among the members of Sharelle's team, the quality of her education is likely to suffer.

 ### COLLABORATION

Collaboration has become a common and necessary practice in special education (Friend, 2000; Heron & Harris, 2001; Walther-Thomas, Korinek, McLaughlin, & Williams, 2000). Teachers who work with students with disabilities and other students who are difficult to teach have discovered they are better able to diagnose and solve learning and behavior problems in the classroom when they work together (Giangreco, Cloninger, Dennis, & Edelman, 2000; Snell & Janney, 2000a, 2000b). Three ways in which team members can work collaboratively are through coordination, consultation, and teaming (Bigge, Stump, Spagna, & Silberman, 1999).

Coordination is the simplest form of collaboration, requiring only ongoing communication and cooperation to ensure that services are provided in a timely and systematic fashion. Although an important and necessary element of special education, coordination does not require service providers to share information or specifics of their efforts with one another. Fortunately for Sharelle, the three educators on her IEP team do much more than simply coordinate who is going to work with her when.

In *consultation*, team members provide information and expertise to one another. Consultation is traditionally considered unidirectional, with the expert providing assistance and advice to the novice. However, team members can, and often do, switch roles from consultant to consultee and back again. Sharelle's fourth-grade teacher, for example, receives expert advice from the speech-language pathologist on strategies for evoking extended language from Sharelle during cooperative learning groups but takes the consultant's role when explaining details of the science curriculum to Sharelle's resource room teacher.

Monitoring student progress

 Council for Exceptional Children Content Standards for Beginning Teachers—Common Core: Evaluate instruction and monitor progress of individuals with exceptional learning needs (CC8S8).
PRAXIS Special Education Core Principles: Content Knowledge: III. Delivery of Services to Students with Disabilities, Assessment, On-going program monitoring.

Types of collaboration

Council for Exceptional Children Content Standards for Beginning Teachers—Common Core: Models and strategies of consultation and collaboration. (CC10K1).
PRAXIS Special Education Core Principles: Content Knowledge: III. Delivery of Services to Students with Disabilities, Professional roles, Collaborator with other teachers.

TEAMING

Intervention assistance team, child study team, IEP team: each step of the special education process involves a group of people who must work together for the benefit of a child with special needs. For special education to be most effective, these groups must become functioning and effective teams (Clark, 2000; Thomas, Correa, & Morsink, 2001). *Teaming* is the most difficult level of collaboration to achieve; it also pays the most dividends. Teaming "bridges the two previous modes of working together and builds on their strengths while adding the component of reciprocity and sharing of information among all team members through a more equal exchange" (Bigge et al., 1999, p. 13). There are several levels or ways in which this can happen. Table 2.1 shows examples of coordination, consultation, and teaming activities by special educators.

Although there are many variations of the team approach in terms of size and structure, each member of a team generally assumes certain clearly assigned responsibilities and recognizes the importance of learning from, contributing to, and interacting with the other members of the team. Many believe that the consensus and group decisions arising from a team's involvement provide a form of insurance against erroneous or arbitrary conclusions in the complex issues that face educators of students with disabilities. In practice, three team models have emerged (McGonigel, Woodruff, & Roszmann-Millican, 1994).

Multidisciplinary Teams   *Multidisciplinary teams* are composed of professionals from different disciplines who work independently of one another. Each team member conducts assessments, plans interventions, and delivers services. Teams that operate according to a multidisciplinary structure risk the danger of not providing services that recognize the child

Teaming models

Content
Standards for
Beginning Teachers–Common
Core: Models and strategies of
consultation and collaboration.
(CC10K1).
PRAXIS Special Education
Core Principles: Content
Knowledge: III. Delivery of
Services to Students with
Disabilities, Professional roles,
Teacher as multidisciplinary
team member.

TABLE 2.1   Examples of coordination, consultation, and teaming activities in special education

Activity	Examples
Coordination	• special and general education teachers working out class schedules and support schedules for students • therapists and general and special education teachers working out schedules for therapy interventions • general and special education teachers coordinating grading procedures and policies • special education teachers working with job coaches and transition teachers to set community-based experience schedules for students
Consultation	• special education teachers assisting general education teachers • vocational education teachers working with community employers • related service personnel providing support to special education and general education teachers
Teaming	• special and general education teachers, administrators, counselors, support staff, and school psychologists working together on prereferral teams to design and implement interventions in general education classrooms • special and general education teachers co-teaching in the classroom • paraprofessionals working with general education teachers • special and general education teachers serving together on curriculum-planning teams • team of professionals working together to determine whether a child is eligible for special education services • IEP teams working together to assess the current performance of a student to determine continued eligibility for special education services

Source: Reprinted from Bigge, J. L., Stump, C. S., Spagna, M. E., & Silberman, R. K. (1999). *Curriculum, assessment, and instruction for students with disabilities* (p. 14). Belmont, CA: Wadsworth. Used by permission.

as an integrated whole; they tend to "splinter" the child into segments along disciplinary lines. (An old saying described the child with disabilities as giving "his hands to the occupational therapist, his legs to the physical therapist, and his brain to the teacher" [Williamson, 1978].) Another concern is the lack of communication among team members.

Interdisciplinary Teams   *Interdisciplinary teams* are characterized by formal channels of communication between members. Although each professional usually conducts discipline-specific assessments, the interdisciplinary team meets to share information and develop intervention plans. Each team member is generally responsible for implementing a portion of the service plan related to his discipline.

Transdisciplinary Teams   The highest level of team involvement, but also the most difficult to accomplish, is the transdisciplinary team. Members of *transdisciplinary teams* seek to provide services in a uniform and integrated fashion by conducting joint assessments, sharing information and expertise across discipline boundaries, and selecting goals and interventions that are discipline-free (Gallivan-Fenlon, 1994; Giangreco, Edelman, & Dennis, 1991). Members of transdisciplinary teams also share roles (often referred to as *role release*); in contrast, members of multidisciplinary and interdisciplinary teams generally operate in isolation and may not coordinate their services to achieve the integrated delivery of related services. Regardless of the team model, team members must learn to put aside professional rivalries and work collaboratively for the benefit of the student.

INDIVIDUALIZED EDUCATION PROGRAM

The individualized education program (IEP) is the centerpiece of the special education process. IDEA requires that an IEP be developed and implemented for every student with disabilities between the ages of 3 and 21. (*Individualized family service plans [IFSPs]* are developed for infants and toddlers [from birth until age 3] with disabilities. IFSPs are described in Chapter 5.) The law is specific about what an IEP must include and who is to take part in its formulation (U.S. Department of Education, 2000).

IEP TEAM

Each IEP must be the product of the joint efforts of the members of an *IEP team*, which must include the following members:

IEP team membership and components

PRAXIS Special Education Core Principles: Content Knowledge: II. Legal and Societal Issues, Federal laws and legal issues related to special education, Public Law 105–17 (IDEA '97).

1. The parents (or surrogate parent) of the child;
2. At least one regular education teacher of the child (if the child is, or may be, participating in the regular education environment);
3. At least one special education teacher, or if appropriate, at least one special education provider of the child;
4. A representative of the local education agency (LEA) who—
   i.   Is qualified to provide, or supervise the provision of, specially designed instruction to meet the unique needs of children with disabilities;
   ii. Is knowledgeable about the general curriculum; and
   iii. Is knowledgeable about the availability of resources of the LEA;
5. An individual who can interpret the instructional implications of evaluation results, who may be a member of the team described above;
6. At the discretion of the parent or the school, other individuals who have knowledge or special expertise regarding the child, including related service personnel as appropriate; and
7. The student, if age 14 or older, must be invited. Younger students may attend if appropriate. (34 CFR 300.344)

For additional information on the IEP team, access the section *Who Creates an IEP?* in Part I of the CD-ROM.

For strategies to encourage and facilitate the effective participation of students in their own IEPs, see Teaching & Learning, "Someone's Missing: The Student As an Overlooked Participant in the IEP Process," later in this chapter.

 IEP COMPONENTS

All IEPs must include the following seven components:

To review the necesssary parts of an IEP, access the section *What Components Make Up IEPs?* in Part I of the CD-ROM.

1. A statement of the child's present levels of educational performance, including
   i. How the child's disability affects the child's involvement and progress in the general curriculum; or
   ii. For preschool children, as appropriate, how the disability affects the child's participation in appropriate activities;
2. A statement of measurable annual goals, including benchmarks or short-term objectives, related to
   i. Meeting the child's needs that result from the child's disability to enable the child to be involved in and progress in the general curriculum; and
   ii. Meeting each of the child's other educational needs that result from the child's disability;
3. A statement of the special education and related services and supplementary aids and services to be provided to the child, or on behalf of the child, and a statement of the program modifications or support for school personnel that will be provided for the child
   i. To advance appropriately toward attaining the annual goals;
   ii. To be involved in and progress in the general curriculum and to participate in extracurricular and other nonacademic activities; and
   iii. To be educated and participate with other children with disabilities and nondisabled children in [such] activities;
4. An explanation of the extent, if any, to which the child will not participate with nondisabled children in the regular class and in the activities described in paragraph (3);
5. A statement of
   i. Any individual modifications in the administration of State or district-wide assessments of student achievement that are needed in order for the child to participate in such assessment; and
   ii. If the IEP team determines that the child will not participate in a particular State or district-wide assessment of student achievement (or part of an assessment), a statement of (A) Why that assessment is not appropriate for the child; and (B) How the child will be assessed;
6. The projected date for the beginning of the services and modifications described in paragraph (3) and the anticipated frequency, location, and duration of those services and modifications; and
7. A statement of
   i. How the child's progress toward the annual goals described in paragraph (2) will be measured; and
   ii. How the child's parents will be regularly informed (through such means as periodic report cards), at least as often as parents are informed of their nondisabled children's progress, of (A) Their child's progress toward the annual goals; and (B) The extent to which that progress is sufficient to enable the child to achieve the goals by the end of the year. (20 U.S.C., Sec. 1414[d][1][A])

IEPs for older students must also include information on how the child's transition from school to adult life will be supported:

Beginning at age 14, and updated annually, a statement of the transition service needs of the child under the applicable components of the child's IEP that focuses on the child's courses of study (such as participation in advanced placement courses or a vocational education program);

Beginning at age 16 (or younger if determined appropriate by the IEP team), statement of the needed transition services for the child, including, when appropriate, a statement of the interagency responsibilities or any needed linkages before the student leaves the school setting. (20 U.S.C., Sec. 1414[d][1][A])

IEP FUNCTIONS AND FORMATS

▲ Jeremy takes an active role on his IEP team by indicating the learning goals most important to him.

The IEP is a system for spelling out where the child is, where she should be going, how she will get there, how long it will take, and how to tell if and when she has arrived. Thus, a good IEP serves as both a road map and a guide book for meeting the challenges posed by a student's disability. The annual goals and benchmarks identify the destinations for the journey and provide signposts along the way.

The IEP provides teachers and parents with the opportunity (and, we might add, the responsibility) to first be *realistic* about the child's needs and goals and then to be *creative* about how to meet them. Being realistic does not mean taking a pessimistic or limited view of the child's capabilities or potential. It means analyzing how specially designed instruction and related services can help the student get from her present levels of performance to future goals.

The IEP is also a measure of accountability for teachers and schools. Whether a particular school or educational program is effective will be judged, to some extent, by how well it is able to help children meet the goals and objectives set forth in their IEPs. Like other professionals, teachers are being called on to demonstrate effectiveness; and the IEP provides one way for them to do so. The IEP is not a legally binding contract. A child's teacher and school cannot be prosecuted in the courts if the child does not achieve the goals set forth in the IEP. Nevertheless, the school must be able to document that a conscientious and systematic effort was made to achieve those goals (Huefner, 2000). The IEP is, however, much more than an accountability device. Its potential benefits are improved planning (including planning for the student's needs after he leaves school), consistency, regular evaluation, and clearer communication among parents, teachers, and others involved in providing services to the student (Lytle & Bordin, 2001; Menlove, Hudson, & Suter, 2001).

IEP formats vary widely across school districts, and schools may go beyond the requirements of the law and include additional information. Bateman and Linden (1998) caution against overreliance on standardized forms and computers for creating IEPs. "Forms by their very nature tend to interfere with true individualization. . . . a proper form will contain all the required elements in the simplest way possible, allowing for the most flexibility and creativity" (p. 57). Figure 2.2 shows the "non-form" for IEPs recommended by Bateman and Linden. The first page identifies the student, IEP team members, and special factors to consider as required by the 1997 IDEA amendments. The "heart of the IEP" (p. 96) begins on the second page in the form of a three-column sequence from needs and present levels of performance, to services that will be provided, to goals and objectives.

To better understand how a student's present level of performance is the foundation of the IEP, complete the *Present Level of Performance Tutorial* in Part II of the CD-ROM.

FIGURE 2.2 **Example of an IEP form**

Individualized Education Program

Student's Name _____ Date of IEP Meeting _____
Date of Birth _____ Grade _____ Primary Contact Person/Case Manager _____

Copies of this IEP will circulate among staff members who are working with this student.
Please observe the Federal and state laws that protect the student's right
to confidentiality of education records.
Do NOT share with unauthorized persons,
and do NOT include sensitive information such as disability category or IQ.

Participants		Special Factors to Consider
Signature	Position	For all students, consider: ❑ Strengths of the student ❑ Concerns of the parent(s) ❑ Need for assistive technology

Special Factors to Consider

For all students, consider:
- ❑ Strengths of the student
- ❑ Concerns of the parent(s)
- ❑ Need for assistive technology

If behavior impedes learning of the student or others, consider:
- ❑ Strategies, including positive behavioral interventions
- ❑ Supports to address behavior

If the student has limited English proficiency, consider:
- ❑ Language needs as they relate to the student's IEP

If the student is blind or visually impaired, consider:
- ❑ Instruction in the use of Braille (unless the IEP team decides instruction in Braille is inappropriate)

Consider communication needs (language & communication needs for students with hearing impairments), including:
- ❑ Opportunities for direct communication with peers and professionals in the student's language and communication mode
- ❑ Opportunities for direct instruction in the student's language and communication mode

Unique Educational Needs, Characteristics, and Present Levels of Performance (PLOPs)	Special Education, Related Services, Supplemental Aids & Services, Assistive Technology, Program Modifications, Support for Personnel	Measurable Annual Goals & Short-Term Objectives or Benchmarks • To enable the student to participate in the general curriculum • To meet other needs resulting from the disability
(include how the disability affects the student's ability to progress in the general curriculum)	*(include frequency, duration, & location)*	*(include how progress toward goals will be measured)*
	[This is the most important part of the IEP. See Figure 2.3 for sample entries.]	

Source: Reprinted from Bateman, B. D., & Linden, M. L. (1998). *Better IEPs: How to develop legally correct and educationally useful programs* (pp. 97, 98, 99). Longmont, CO: Sopris West. Used by permission.

FIGURE 2.2 *continued*

Progress Reports

The parents will receive regular reports about (the student's)
(a) progress toward achieving annual goals
(b) and the extent to which that progress is sufficient to enable achievement of goals by the end of the year
Progress reports will take the form of _____

and the parents will receive them _____ times/year (which is at least as often as parents of children who are not on IEPs receive progress reports). Reports will include **specific** information about progress on each IEP goal.

Participants With Nondisabled Students

Explanation of the extent to which (the student) will **not** participate with nondisabled children in (a) regular classes _____
_____
_____
_____

(b) special education services _____
_____
_____
_____
_____

Participation in State- and District-Wide Assessments

(The student) needs the following modifications in the administration of state- or district-wide assessments _____
_____

The IEP team has decided that (the student) will **not** participate in any state- or district-wide assessments
(a) because _____
_____

(b) (The student) will instead be assessed by _____
_____
_____

Transition Planning

(The student) has reached age 14, and (his or her):
(a) goals for life after high school include _____
_____

(b) course of study is linked to student transition goals by
_____

(The student) has reached age 16, and:
(a) the following activities are needed to promote transition to post-high school life

• Instruction _____
_____

• Related services _____
_____

• Community experiences _____
_____

• Development of employment and other adult living objectives _____
_____

• Acquisition of daily living skills and functional vocational evaluation _____
_____

(b) (The student) does not need one or more of the activities listed above because _____
_____

(The student) will reach the age of majority under state law on (date). (He or she) has received notice (at least a year in advance) of all rights under the IDEA that will transfer to (him or her) at that time.

_____
Student's Signature

The IEP form concludes with additional IDEA requirements and, for older students, transition components.

Figure 2.3 shows portions of the IEP for Curt, a ninth grader and low achiever seen by the school district as a poorly motivated student with a disciplinary problem and a bad attitude. Curt's parents see their son as a discouraged and frustrated student with learning disabilities, especially in written language.

One of the most difficult tasks for the child study team is determining how inclusive the IEP document should be. Strickland and Turnbull (1993) state that the definition of special education as "specially designed instruction" should be a key element in determining what should go into a student's IEP.

The determination of whether instruction is "specially designed" must be made by comparing the nature of the instruction for the student with a disability to instructional practices used with typical students at the same age and grade level. If the instructional adaptations that a student with a disability requires are

Role of the IEP team

Council for Exceptional Children — Content Standards for Beginning Teachers–Common Core: Develop and implement comprehensive, longitudinal individualized program in collaboration with team members (CC7S2).
PRAXIS Special Education Core Principles: Content Knowledge: III. Delivery of Services to Students with Disabilities, Background knowledge, Role of IEP team.

the roles of each team member, and procedures that will be followed. Videotaped presentations of real or staged IEP meetings can be an excellent way to prepare students for their own conference. Role playing can also help emphasize and define the responsibilities of all team members, including those of the student. Students should rehearse appropriate and expected behaviors. The following are suggested rules for student behavior during the IEP conference:

- Remain seated throughout the meeting.
- Maintain eye contact with those who are addressing you.
- Respect others as they speak by listening without interruption.
- If you don't understand, excuse yourself politely and ask the speaker to explain again.
- Wait your turn before offering your opinion and recommendations.
- When you disagree, state your case without being loud or impatient; offer your own suggestions instead.
- Respond to direct questions.

Creative intervention by teachers is sometimes necessary to convince parents of the advantages of student involvement in the IEP conference. Parents may be persuaded by talking to others who have involved their child in the IEP conference. Parents can be invited to participate in or view videotapes of classroom preconference activities. In some cases, administrators may also need to be reminded of students' right to participate and be encouraged to advocate for them in this regard.

Conference participation. Students who have been involved in other phases of the IEP process will be better prepared for the conference experience. The more active the student has been, the more likely she will be successful in the IEP meeting itself. When something should not be discussed in front of the child (e.g., controversial issues, policy decisions, disagreements), the student can enter the meeting near its conclusion to meet with team members, listen to suggested goals and objectives, and hear comments relating to her progress.

With parental cooperation, team commitment, prior preparation, and involvement in other phases of the IEP process, students can be successfully integrated as team members. The student might report her own progress, contribute to discussions, and help formulate goals and objectives at the conference. Once these are agreed on, the student should co-sign the completed IEP document, just as other team members do.

ASSESSMENT
- Determines preferences
- Self-evaluates
- Sets goals/ assists in writing objectives

IEP CONFERENCE
- Preconference preparation
- Conference participation

INSTRUCTION
- Comonitors progress
- Engages in regularly scheduled meetings
- Reassesses program
- Self-manages program/ goals

FIGURE A Student participation in the IEP process

Instruction

In co-monitoring their progress, students participate in classroom activities that remind them of the goals they have helped set. Daily, weekly, and monthly activities can be designed to include students in the ongoing collection of data, assessment of progress, and reevaluation of goals. Teachers can help students tally stickers, tokens, points, or grades they have earned. These can be recorded on a chart or other visual representation related to identified student goals. Students can select items to include in a portfolio of academic or other work products (Salend, 2001; Wesson & King, 1996). Younger students can color bar graphs or collect small items or cards to signify their progress.

Students can also co-monitor their progress in meetings with other students. These meetings should be positive, encouraging group cooperation, support, and problem-solving opportunities. Self-management, self-monitoring, and self-instruction techniques may also help students meet the goals they have helped set (Kerr & Nelson, 2002; Lovitt, 2000).

Including students in a process designed expressly for them is often overlooked, but there are numerous possibilities for student participation in the IEP process for educators who wish to implement instruction *with* students—not just *for* them.

Adapted from Peters, M. T. (1990). Someone's missing: The student as an overlooked participant in the IEP process. *Preventing School Failure,* 34(4), 32–36. © 1990. Used with permission of the Helen Dwight Reid Educational Foundation. Published by Heldref Publications, 1319 Eighteenth Street, NW, Washington, DC 20036-1802.

FIGURE 2.3 Portions of an IEP for Curt, a ninth grader with learning disabilities and a history of disciplinary problems

Unique Educational Needs, Characteristics, and Present Levels of Performance (PLOPs)	Special Education, Related Services, Supplemental Aids & Services, Assistive Technology, Program Modifications, Support for Personnel	Measurable Annual Goals & Short-Term Objectives or Benchmarks • To enable student to participate in the general curriculum • To meet other needs resulting from the disability
(include how the disability affects the student's ability to progress in the general curriculum)	*(include frequency, duration, & location)*	*(include how progress toward goals will be measured)*
Study Skills/Organizational Needs: How to read text Note taking How to study notes Memory work Be prepared for class, with materials Lengthen and improve attention span and on-task behavior Present Level: Curt currently lacks skill in all these areas.	1. Speech/lang: therapist, resource room teacher, and content area teachers will provide Curt with direct and specific teaching of study skills, i.e. Note taking from lectures; Note taking while reading text; How to study notes for a test; Memorization hints; Strategies for reading text to retain information. 2. Assign a "study buddy" for Curt in each content area class. 3. Prepare a motivation system for Curt to be prepared for class with all necessary materials. 4. Develop a motivational plan to encourage Curt to lengthen his attention span and time on task. 5. Provide aide to monitor on-task behaviors in first month or so of plan and teach Curt self-monitoring techniques. 6. Provide motivational system and self-recording form for completion of academic tasks in each class.	Goal: At the end of academic year, Curt will have better grades and, by his own report, will have learned new study skills. Obj. 1: Given a 20-30 min. lecture/oral lesson, Curt will take appropriate notes as judged by that teacher. Obj. 2: Given 10-15 pgs. of text to read, Curt will employ an appropriate strategy for retaining info.—i.e., mapping, webbing, outlining, notes, etc.—as judged by the teacher. Obj. 3: Given notes to study for a test, Curt will do so successfully as evidenced by his test score. Goal: Curt will improve his on-task behavior from 37% to 80% as measured by a qualified observer at year's end. Obj.1: By 1 month, Curt's on-task behavior will increase to 45%. Obj. 2: By 3 months, Curt's on-task behavior will increase to 60%. Obj. 3: By 6 months, Curt's on-task behavior will increase to 80% and maintain or improve until end of the year.
Academic Needs/Written Language: Curt needs strong remedial help in spelling, punctuation, capitalization, and usage. Present Level: Curt is approximately 2 grade levels behind his peers in these skills. Adaptations to Regular Program: • In all classes, Curt should sit near the front of the class. • All teachers should help Curt with study skills as trained by spelling/language specialist and resource room teacher. • Curt should be called on often to keep him involved and on task. • Teachers should monitor Curt's work closely in the beginning weeks/months of his program.	1. Provide direct instruction in written language skills (punctuation, capitalization, usage, spelling) by using a highly structured, well-sequenced program. Services provided in small group of no more than four students in the resource room, 50 minutes/day. 2. Build in continuous and cumulative review to help with short-term rote memory difficulty. 3. Develop a list of commonly used words in student writing (or use one of many published lists) for Curt's spelling program.	Goal: Within one academic year, Curt will improve his written language skills by 1.5 or 2 full grade levels. Obj. 1: Given 10 sentences of dictation at his current level of instruction, Curt will punctuate and capitalize with 90% accuracy (checked at the end of each unit taught). Obj. 2: Given 30 sentences with choices of usage, at his current instructional level, Curt will perform with 90% accuracy. Obj. 3: Given a list of 150 commonly used words in writing, Curt will spell with 90% accuracy.

Source: Reprinted from Bateman, B. D., & Linden, M. L. (1998). Better IEPs: How to develop legally correct and educationally useful programs (pp. 97, 98, 99). Longmont, CO: Sopris West. Used by permission.

FIGURE 2.4   Some do's and don'ts for IEP annual goals

Do	Don't
• Include at least one goal for every area of functioning (e.g., academic, social, vocational) adversely affected by the disability. • Ask how a potential goal will increase the student's access to and benefit from the general education curriculum and other school activities. • Ask to what extent achieving a potential goal will improve the child's present and future life. • Prioritize the goals within each area of functioning. • Make sure each goal includes objective criteria by which the student's progress can be measured (e.g., "By June, Martin will read grade-level text at 100 wpm with 5 or fewer errors"). • Write two or three measurable, short-term objectives or benchmarks that will enable families, students, and educators to monitor progress during the year and, if appropriate, revise the IEP. • Ask the parents and, when appropriate, the student if the goals and objectives "look right."	• Include goals for areas of the general education curriculum and functioning that are not adversely affected by the disability (e.g., the IEP for a student with a physical disability who has no special needs in academics does not need to address goals in math or science). • Write goals and objectives in unmeasurable terms (e.g., "Geoff will improve his math skills" or "Suzie will be successful in the regular classroom"). • Select goals from a preprinted or computerized list (though in some curriculum areas, such as math, a hierarchy of sequenced short-term objectives can be used once the goal has been determined). • Select goals based on the availability of services. • Select goals because other students in the school with the same disability have those goals on their IEPs. • Choose goals based on the present or presumed future placement of the student. IEP goals and the specially designed instruction needed to meet those goals must be determined before the IEP team discusses placement.

(1) significantly different from adaptations normally expected or made for typical students in that setting, and if (2) the adaptations are necessary to offset or reduce the adverse effect of the disability on learning and educational performance, then these adaptations should be considered "specially designed instruction" and should be included as part of the student's IEP, regardless of the instructional setting. (p. 13)

Each area of functioning that is adversely affected by the student's disability must be represented by an annual goal on the IEP. Goals are measurable statements of what the IEP team believes the student can accomplish in one year if the special services provided are effective. Figure 2.4 includes some do's and don'ts concerning IEP annual goals.

For help writing meaningful annual goals and objectives, complete the *Developing Quality IEPs* Tutorial in Part III of the CD-ROM.

PROBLEMS AND POTENTIAL SOLUTIONS

Since its inception, the IEP process has been problematic (Huefner, 2000; Yell & Drasgow, 2000). Twenty years ago, Gallagher (1984) wrote that the IEP is "probably the single most unpopular aspect of the law, not only because it requires a great deal of work, but because the essence of the plan itself seems to have been lost in the mountains of paperwork" (p. 228). Studies of actual IEPs seem to support Gallagher's contention (Smith, 1990a, 1990b; Smith & Brownell, 1995). Smith and Simpson (1989), for example, evaluated the IEPs of 214 students with behavioral disorders and found that one-third of the IEPs lacked necessary mandated components. A study that examined IEPs for high school students found that transition-related goals included vague outcomes (e.g., "will think about best place to live," "will explore jobs"), no evaluation procedures, and very few adaptations in activities or materials (Grigal, Test, Beattie, & Wood, 1997).

But properly including all of the mandated components in an IEP is no guarantee that the document will guide the student's learning and teachers' teaching in the classroom, as intended by IDEA (Drasgow, Yell, & Robinson, in press). Although most educators support the idealized concept of the IEP, inspection and evaluation of IEPs often do not reveal consistency between what is written on the document and the instruction that students experience in the classroom (Smith & Brownell, 1995). Bateman and Linden (1998) contend:

> Sadly, most IEPs are horrendously burdensome to teachers and nearly useless to parents and children. Far from being a creative, flexible, data-based, and individualized application of the best of educational interventions to a child with unique needs, the typical IEP is "empty," devoid of specific services to be provided. It says what the IEP team hopes the student will be able to accomplish, but little if anything about the special education interventions and the related services or the classroom modifications that will enable him or her to reach those goals. (p. 63)

Special and regular educators are working together to create procedures for developing IEPs that go beyond compliance with the law and actually serve as a meaningful guide for the specially designed instruction a student with disabilities needs. Several tools have been developed to assist IEP teams in the critical process of designing a truly appropriate education, including a variety of strategies for involving all IEP team members and writing good goals and objectives (Gibb & Dyches, 2000; Lignugaris/Kraft, Marchand-Martella, & Martella, 2001; Lytle & Bordin, 2001; Menlove et al., 2001; Rock, 2000; Walsh, 2001). For example, Choosing Outcomes and Accommodations for Children (COACH) is a field-tested IEP process that guides child study teams through the assessment and planning stages of IEP development in a way that results in goals and short-term objectives directly related to functional skills in integrated settings (Giangreco, Cloninger, & Iverson, 1998).

 ## LEAST RESTRICTIVE ENVIRONMENT

IDEA requires that every student with disabilities be educated in the **least restrictive environment (LRE).** Specifically, the law stipulates that

> to the maximum extent appropriate, children with disabilities, including children in public or private institutions or other care facilities, [will be] educated with children who are not disabled, and that special classes, separate schooling or other removal of children with disabilities from the regular educational environment [may occur] only when the nature or severity of the disability is such that education in regular classes with the use of supplementary aids and services cannot be achieved satisfactorily. (20 U.S.C. § 1412[a][5])

Thus, the LRE is the setting that is closest to a regular school program and also meets the child's special educational needs. Least restrictive environment is a relative concept; the

---

Additional Resources in Part IV of the CD-ROM will help you develop and implement quality IEPs that serve as a meaningful guide for teaching students with special needs.

IEP goals and objectives

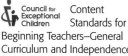 Content Standards for Beginning Teachers–Common Core: Develop and implement comprehensive, longitudinal individualized program in collaboration with team members (CC7S2).
PRAXIS Special Education Core Principles: Content Knowledge: III. Delivery of Services to Students with Disabilities, Curriculum and instruction, IEP process.

Least restrictive environment

Content Standards for Beginning Teachers–General Curriculum and Independence Curriculum Referenced Standards: Principles of normalization and concept of least restrictive environment (GC1K8) (IC1K7).
PRAXIS Special Education Core Principles: Content Knowledge: III. Delivery of Services to Students with Disabilities, Background knowledge, Least restrictive environment.

LRE for a 10-year-old student who is blind might be inappropriate for another 10-year-old with a similar visual impairment. And the LRE for both children may change over time. Since the passage of IDEA, there have been many differences of opinion over which type of setting is least restrictive and most appropriate for students with disabilities. Some educators and parents consider any decision to place a student with disabilities outside the regular classroom to be overly restrictive; most, however, recognize that full-time placement in a regular classroom is restrictive and inappropriate if the child's educational needs cannot be adequately met in that environment.

 A CONTINUUM OF SERVICES

Children with disabilities and their families need a wide range of special education and related services. Today, most schools provide a *continuum of services*—that is, a range of placement and service options to meet the individual needs of students with disabilities. The continuum can be symbolically depicted as a pyramid, with placements ranging from the regular classroom at the bottom to special schools, residential facilities, and hospital or homebound placements at the top (see Figure 2.5). The fact that the pyramid is widest at the bottom indicates that the greatest number of children with disabilities are served in regular classrooms and that the number of children who require more intensive and specialized placements gets smaller as we move up the continuum. As noted in Chapter 1, the majority of children receiving special education services have mild disabilities. As the sever-

ity of a disability increases, typically the need for more specialized services also increases, while the number of students involved decreases. However, the fact that a larger proportion of children with severe disabilities are educated in placements outside of the regular classroom does not mean that the LRE for a student with severe disabilities is necessarily a special class or separate school.

Five of the eight placement options depicted in Figure 2.5 are available in regular public school buildings. Children at the first three levels on the continuum have full-time placements in general education classrooms and receive various degrees and types of support by special teachers who consult with the children's regular teachers. In a *resource room*, a special educator provides instruction to students with disabilities for part of the school day, either individually or in small groups. Children who require full-time placement in a *separate classroom* are with other children with disabilities for most of the school day and interact with children without disabilities only at certain times, such as during lunch, recess, or perhaps art and music. Although the separate classroom provides significantly fewer opportunities for interaction with nondisabled children than the regular classroom does, it provides more integration than does placement in *special schools* or *residential facilities*, which are attended only by children with disabilities. A student in a *homebound* or *hospital* setting receives special education and related services on an individual basis and has few opportunities to interact with other students.

The least restrictive environment is a relative concept; the LRE for one child may be inappropriate for another.

Continuum of services

Council for Exceptional Children   Content Standards for Beginning Teachers–General Curriculum and Independence Curriculum Referenced Standards: Continuum of placement and services available for individuals with disabilities (GC1K5) and (IC1K4).
PRAXIS Special Education Core Principles: Content Knowledge: III. Delivery of Services to Students with Disabilities, Background knowledge, Continuum of services.

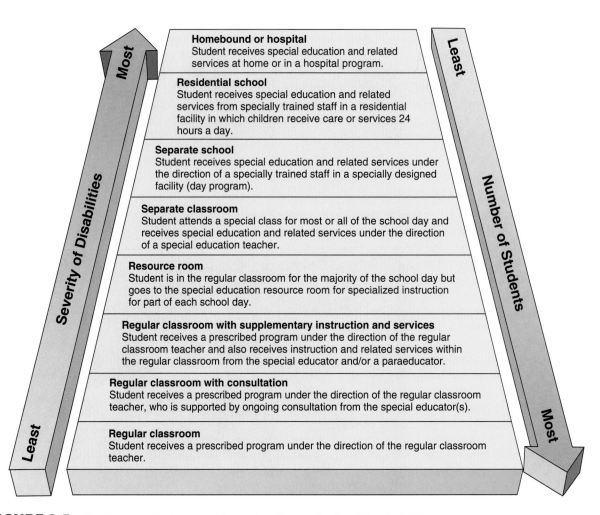

FIGURE 2.5 **Continuum of educational services for students with disabilities**

 DETERMINING THE LRE

The IEP team determines the proper placement for a child after the child's needs that result from the disability and the special education and related services necessary to meet those needs have been determined. For many years special education operated like this: (1) a student found eligible for special education was labeled with a disability category; (2) the student was placed into a program for students with that particular disability; and (3) a not-so-individualized version of the already-in-place program was written down and presented as the student's IEP, even though the program continued as usual whether or not the "new" student was in it. This is the wrong way.

The legally mandated and educationally sound process goes like this: (1) the school must determine whether the child has a disability and is therefore eligible for special education; (2) the child's needs must be determined and an IEP developed that specifies the special education and related services that will be provided to meet those needs; and (3) the child is then placed in the least restrictive environment in which an appropriate program can be provided and the child can make satisfactory educational progress.

Bateman and Linden (1998) describe the difference between the wrong way and the IDEA way:

> For many, the old way is deeply ingrained and it seems practical. . . . for example, "Joe is learning disabled, so we'll put him in the resource room for learning disabled students and then have the resource teacher write up one more copy of the ongoing program in that room and call it the IEP." Instead, one should have said, "Joe is eligible, Joe's individual needs are X, Y, Z, and can be met by services A, B, C (his IEP) which we can implement in placement P." Districts have tried to fit children into programs, . . . rather than flexibly and creatively designing new programs one child at a time. (p. 67)

The general education classroom is the starting point for the IEP team's discussion of placement. Before considering that instruction and related services will be delivered in any setting other than the regular classroom, the IEP team must discuss if the IEP goals and short-term objectives can be achieved in the regular classroom. Removal of a child with disabilities from the general education classroom should take place only when the nature and severity of the child's disabilities are such that an appropriate education in that setting cannot be achieved.

Placement of a student with disabilities should not be viewed as all or nothing at any one level on the continuum. The IEP team should consider the extent to which the student can effectively be integrated into each of three dimensions of school life: the general academic curriculum, extracurricular activities (e.g., clubs), and other school activities (e.g., recess, mealtimes). The LRE "provision allows for a 'mix and match' where total integration is appropriate under one dimension and partial integration is appropriate under another dimension" (Turnbull & Cilley, 1999, p. 41).

In addition, placement must not be regarded as permanent. The continuum concept is intended to be flexible, with students moving from one placement to another as dictated by their individual educational needs. The IEP team should periodically review the specific goals and objectives for each child—they are required to do so at least annually—and make new placement decisions if warranted (Giangreco, 2001). The child's parents must be informed whenever any change in placement is being considered so that they can either consent or object to the change and present additional information if they wish.

Because neither IDEA nor the regulations that accompany it specify exactly how a school district is to determine LRE, numerous conflicts have arisen; some have led to court cases. After reviewing the rulings of four LRE disputes that reached U.S. courts of appeals, Yell (1995) concluded that "for some students with disabilities, the appropriate and least restrictive setting will not be the regular education classroom. . . . The IEP team, as the courts have indicated, needs to employ a balancing test, weighing the desirability of integration against the obligation to furnish an appropriate education" (p. 402).

Determining LRE

Council for Exceptional Children — Content Standards for Beginning Teachers–Common Core: Issues, assurances and due process rights related to assessment, eligibility, and placement within a continuum of services (CC1K6).

PRAXIS Special Education Core Principles: Content Knowledge: III. Delivery of Services to Students with Disabilities, Background knowledge, Least restrictive environment.

INCLUSIVE EDUCATION

Although often confused, the terms *inclusion* and *least restrictive environment* are not synonymous. **Inclusion** means educating students with disabilities in regular classrooms; the LRE principle requires that students with disabilities be educated in settings as close to the regular class as possible in which an appropriate program can be provided and the child can make satisfactory educational progress. Much discussion and controversy and many misconceptions have arisen regarding the inclusion of students with disabilities in regular classrooms (Kauffman & Hallahan, 1994; Kavale & Forness, 2000; Sasso, 2001).

Many parents of children with disabilities strongly support inclusion; others have resisted it just as strongly, thinking that the regular classroom does not offer the intense, individualized education their children need. For example, a recent study of parents of children with severe disabilities found some parents in favor of and some against inclusion (Palmer, Fuller, Arora, & Nelson, 2001). Another study found that most parents of elementary students with learning disabilities who received reading instruction in resource rooms had strong positive attitudes toward the resource room program and were reluctant to have their children reintegrated into general education classes for reading instruction (Green & Shinn, 1995).

As we have seen, what the law does call for is the education of each child with disabilities in the least restrictive environment, removed no farther than necessary from the regular public school program. IDEA does not require placement of all children with disabilities in regular classes, call for children with disabilities to remain in regular classes without necessary supportive services, or suggest that general education teachers should educate students with disabilities without help from special educators and other specialists. Although not all children with disabilities attend regular classes, it is true that regular classroom teachers are expected to deal with a much wider variety of learning, behavioral, sensory, and physical differences among their students than was the case just a few years ago. Thus, provision of in-service training for general educators is an important (and sometimes overlooked) requirement of IDEA. General education teachers are understandably wary of having children with disabilities placed in their classes if little or no training or support is provided. The role of regular classroom teachers is already a demanding one; they do not want their classes to become any larger, especially if they perceive exceptional children as unmanageable. Regular classroom teachers are entitled to be involved in decisions about children who are placed in their classes and to be offered continuous consultation and other supportive services from administrators and their special education colleagues (Kennedy & Fisher, 2001; Kochar, West, & Taymans, 2000).

We know that simply placing a child with disabilities in a regular classroom does not mean that the child will learn and behave appropriately or be socially accepted by children without disabilities (Cook & Semmel, 1999; Division for Learning Disabilities, 2001; Freeman & Alkin, 2000). Nor, it should be pointed out, does placement in a special education setting guarantee that a child will receive the specialized instruction he or she needs (e.g., Moody, Vaughn, Hughes, & Fischer, 2000). It is important for special educators to teach appropriate social skills and behavior to the child with disabilities and to educate nondisabled children about their classmates. Examples of effective inclusion programs can be found at age levels ranging from preschool (Sandall, Schwartz, & Joseph, 2000) to high school (Bauer & Brown, 2001), and they include children whose disabilities range from mild (Hock, Schumaker, & Deshler, 1999) to severe (Fisher & Ryndak, 2001). Numerous strategies for successfully including students with disabilities in the general education program can be found in Beninghof (1998), Friend & Bursuck (1999), Kochar et al. (2000), Lewis and Doorlag (1999), Mastropieri & Scruggs (2000), Salend (2001), and Wood (2002). (See Teaching & Learning, "Classwide Peer Tutoring: Collaborative Learning for Students with Disabilities in Inclusive Classrooms," later in this chapter.)

Facilitating inclusion

 Content Standards for Beginning Teachers–General Curriculum and Independence Curriculum Referenced Standards: Barriers to accessibility and acceptance of individuals with disabilities (GC5K1) & (IC5K2).

PRAXIS Special Education Core Principles: Content Knowledge: III. Delivery of Services to Students with Disabilities, Background knowledge, Inclusion.

 ARGUMENTS FOR AND AGAINST FULL INCLUSION

Some special educators believe that the continuum of services should be dismantled and all students with disabilities placed in regular classrooms. For example, in a paper widely cited by advocates of full inclusion, Taylor (1988) contends that the LRE model

1. *Legitimates restrictive environments.* To conceptualize services in terms of restrictiveness is to legitimize more restrictive settings. As long as services are conceptualized in this manner, some people will end up in restrictive environments.

2. *Confuses segregation and integration with intensity of services.* As represented by the continuum, LRE equates segregation with the most intensive services and integration with the least intensive services. The principle assumes that the least restrictive, most integrated settings are incapable of providing the intensive ser-

vices needed by people with severe disabilities. However, segregation and integration on the one hand and intensity of services on the other are separate dimensions.

3. *Is based on a "readiness model."* Implicit in LRE is the assumption that people with developmental disabilities must earn the right to move to the least restrictive environment. In other words, the person must "get ready" or "be prepared" to live, work, or go to school in integrated settings.

4. *Supports the primacy of professional decision making.* LRE invariably is framed in terms of professional judgments regarding "individual needs." The phrase "least restrictive environment" is almost always qualified with words such as "appropriate," "necessary," "feasible," and "possible" (and never with "desired" or "wanted").

5. *Sanctions infringements on people's rights.* The question imposed by LRE is not whether people with disabilities should be restricted, but to what extent.

6. *Implies that people must move as they develop and change.* As LRE is commonly conceptualized, people with disabilities are expected to move toward increasingly less restrictive environments. Even if people moved smoothly through a continuum, their lives would be a series of stops between transitional placements.

7. *Directs attention to physical settings rather than to the services and supports people need.* By its name, the principle of the LRE emphasizes facilities and environments designed specifically for people with disabilities. The field has defined the mission in terms of creating "facilities," first large ones and now smaller ones, and "programs," rather than providing the services and supports to enable people with disabilities to participate in the same settings used by other people. (from pp. 45–48)

There is no clear consensus in the field about the meaning of inclusion. To some, inclusion means full-time placement of all students with disabilities into regular classrooms; to others, the term refers to any degree of integration into the mainstream. Stainback and Stainback (1996), strong advocates and leaders of the inclusion movement, define an *inclusive school* as "a place where everyone belongs, is accepted, supports, and is supported by his or her peers and other members of the school community in the course of having his or her educational needs met" (p. 3). Giangreco et al. (2000) contend that "inclusive education is in place only when all five features [shown in Figure 2.6 on page 77] occur on an ongoing, daily basis" (p. 294).

Virtually all special educators support the responsible inclusion of students with disabilities in regular classrooms and the development and evaluation of new models for working more cooperatively with general educators to serve all students (e.g., Kochar et al., 2000; Smith & Hilton, 1997; Schwartz, 2000; Vaughn, Schumm, & Brick, 1998). Descriptions of many research-backed model programs and strategies for successfully and meaningfully including students with disabilities as full members in the academic and social life of regular classrooms are provided throughout this text. (See Profiles & Perspectives, "Moving toward Inclusive Education," later in this chapter.)

Most special educators, however, are not in favor of eliminating the LRE concept and dismantling the continuum of alternative placements. The Council for Exceptional Children, the major professional organization in special education, supports inclusion as a "meaningful goal" to be pursued by schools but believes that the continuum of services and program options must be maintained and that IEP planning teams must make placement decisions based on the student's individual educational needs (see Figure 2.7 on page 77). Position statements on inclusion by the Council for Learning Disabilities, the Learning Disabilities Association of America, and The Association for Persons with Severe Handicaps (TASH) can be found in Chapters 7 and 13. The discussion of inclusion continues throughout the text. (See Profiles & Perspectives, "Inclusion versus Full Inclusion," later in this chapter.)

Shared activities with individualized outcomes and a sense of belonging and group membership for all students are two defining features of inclusive education.

Classwide Peer Tutoring: Collaborative Learning for Students with Disabilities in Inclusive Classrooms

Meaningful inclusion of students with disabilities into the academic and social life of the regular classroom presents a difficult challenge. The regular classroom teacher is not only accountable to deliver individualized instruction to these and other students whose learning is at risk but is also expected to ensure all other learners' academic success and integrate the whole class socially. In-class tutoring is one method that has been used to individualize instruction without requiring students to leave the classroom. Often untapped but always available sources of tutoring help in every classroom are the students themselves.

Although the idea of peer tutoring (same-age classmates teaching one another) is not new (Lancaster, 1806), it has become the focus of much interest and research in special education. Traditional peer tutoring involves singling out students who have not mastered a particular skill for special help from a few high-achieving students who are assigned as tutors. In contrast, *classwide peer tutoring* (CWPT) includes low achievers and students with disabilities as full participants in an ongoing, whole-class activity. In one of the videos that accompanies this text, "Together We Can: Classwide Peer Tutoring for Basic Academic Skills," you will observe students participating in a CWPT program (Greenwood, Delquadri, & Carta, 1997). Depicted in this video is a diverse group of students engaged in the learning/teaching process in which all students have the opportunity to tutor and be tutored.

Characteristics of Effective Classwide Peer Tutoring
The classwide peer tutoring system shown in the video "Together We Can" is one of several CWPT models that have been shown to reliably produce significant academic gains by students with disabilities—and their classmates without disabilities (e.g., Fuchs et al., 2001; Fulk & King, 2001; Maheady, Harper, & Mallette, 2001; Miller, Barbetta, & Heron, 1994). They all have several characteristics in common.

- *Clearly defined learning tasks/responses.* CWPT programs are based on clearly defined learning

tasks and explicitly defined peer tutoring roles and teaching responsibilities. Tutoring procedures are often scripted, and each tutor is expected to use standard procedures with little variation.
- *Individualized instruction.* In CWPT, teachers give frequent pre- and post-tests to determine learning tasks that match the current needs of each student. Additionally, because CWPT uses a one-on-one tutor/pupil ratio, each learner's performance can be observed, checked, and redirected in ways not otherwise possible in traditional teacher-led instruction.
- *High rates of active student responding (ASR).* Well-designed CWPT programs provide each student with many opportunities to respond. Depending on the learning task, students may make 100 or more responses during a 10-minute peer tutoring session. Total ASR is increased further in reciprocal CWPT programs because each student responds to the academic task in the role of tutee (initial responses to tutor's prompts, repeating missed items) and tutor (prompting responding, discriminating between correct and incorrect responses, and providing instructional feedback).
- *Immediate feedback and praise for correct responses.* Peer tutors provide feedback and praise to their tutees, and the teacher provides feedback to the tutors as a means of promoting high-quality peer teaching and learning during CWPT sessions. Formal point/reward systems are used in many CWPT programs to motivate participation and make learning fun.
- *Systematic error correction.* Tutors immediately and systematically correct mistakes by their tutees. Accurate error correction by tutors who themselves are learning the material can be achieved by using materials that show the correct response to the tutor or by a "tutor huddle" procedure described later in this box.
- *Measurement of student progress.* All research-backed CWPT programs incorporate direct and frequent mea-

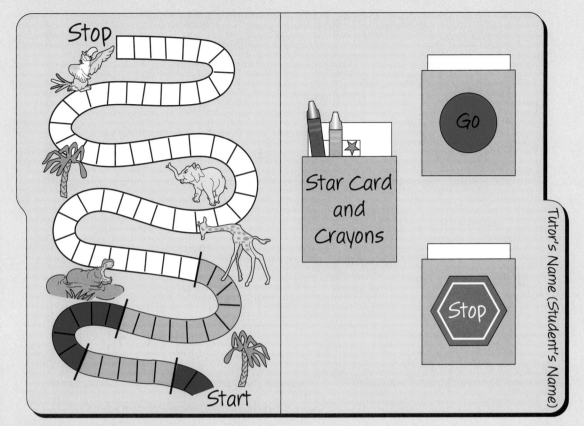

FIGURE A Peer tutoring folder.

Source: Adapted from "Total Tutoring for Special and General Educators [Instructor's Manual]" by T. E. Heron & W. L. Heward, 2000. Columbus, OH: The Ohio State University Special Education Program. Used by permission.

surement of each student's progress. These data are obtained in a variety of ways, such as daily end-of-session assessments given by tutors, regularly scheduled teacher-administered "check outs" of students' performance, and weekly pre- and post-tests. In some programs, items missed on follow-up assessments are put back into the student's folder for additional practice.

Example of a Reciprocal Classwide Peer Tutoring System

A CWPT system originally developed for teaching basic reading and math skills in the primary grades (Cooke, Heron, & Heward, 1983; Heward, Heron, & Cooke, 1982) has been replicated and extended by hundreds of classroom teachers in elementary, middle, and secondary schools across a wide range of curriculum areas such as spelling, science facts and vocabulary, algebra, geometry, reading fluency, foreign language vocabulary, and social studies (e.g., Gardner et al., 2001; Miller et al., 1994; Wright, Cavanaugh, Sainato, & Heward, 1995). Each student serves as both tutor and tutee each day. In the role of tutee, each child responds to questions posed by his or her partner (tutor) over an individualized set of unknown facts, problems, or items determined by a teacher-given pretest.

Tutoring folders. Each student in the class has a tutoring folder containing a set of 10 task cards on specific curriculum content (see Figures A and B). Each card identifies one word, problem, concept, or fact to be taught to the child's tutoring partner. The task cards are placed in a GO pocket on one side of the folder. Also in the folder is a track to record the tutee's progress, markers to use for recording, and a STOP pocket to collect learned cards.

Tutor Huddle. When the questions or answers on the task cards are not obvious to the tutors (e.g., abstract words that the tutor is also learning), the daily peer tutoring session begins with children getting their folders and participating in a 5-minute "tutor huddle" with two or three other tutors. In the huddle, the tutors take turns orally presenting the words or problems they will shortly be responsible for teaching to their partners. (Meanwhile, their partners are in other tutor huddles working on the content that they, too, will soon be teaching.) Fellow tutors confirm correct responses by saying yes and help identify words a tutor doesn't know. The teacher circulates around the room, helping tutor huddles that cannot identify or agree on a given word. Careful construction of the tutor huddles usually ensures that at least one student in each group will know or be able to recognize

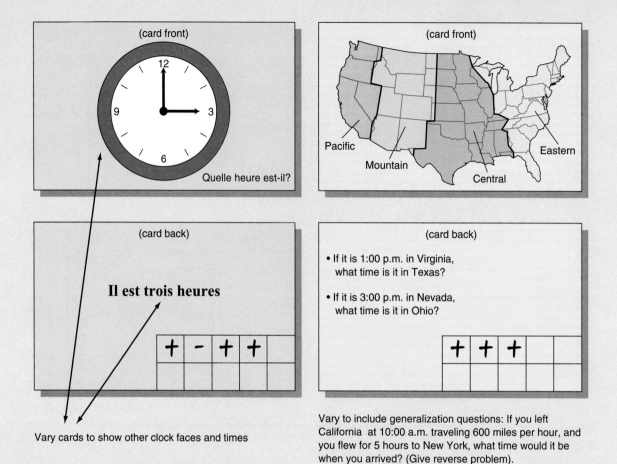

(card front)

Quelle heure est-il?

Il est trois heures

+	-	+	+		

Vary cards to show other clock faces and times

(card front)

Pacific
Mountain
Central
Eastern

(card back)

• If it is 1:00 p.m. in Virginia,
  what time is it in Texas?

• If it is 3:00 p.m. in Nevada,
  what time is it in Ohio?

+	+	+			

Vary to include generalization questions: If you left
California at 10:00 a.m. traveling 600 miles per hour, and
you flew for 5 hours to New York, what time would it be
when you arrived? (Give reverse problem).

FIGURE B   Examples of peer tutoring flashcards in different subject areas showing variations in presentation and response modes. Tutor marks plus and minus signs to record partner's performance during testing

Source: Adapted from "START tutoring: Designing, training, implementing, adapting, and evaluating tutoring programs for school and home settings" by A. D. Miller, P. M. Barbetta, & T. E. Heron, 1994. In R. Gardner III, D. M. Sainato, J. O. Cooper, T. E. Heron, W. L. Heward, J. Eshleman, & T. A. Grossi (Eds.), *Behavior analysis in education: Focus on measurably superior instruction* (pp. 274–275). Pacific Grove, CA: Brooks/Cole. Used by permission.

each task card. A tutor huddle is unnecessary for curriculum content with standard questions and answers provided on the backs of cards for the tutor to see (e.g., math facts, geometric shapes, equations).

Practice.   After the tutor huddle, partners pair up to practice their words. One child begins in the role of tutor, presenting the task cards as many times as possible during a 5-minute practice period, shuffling the set of cards after each round. Tutors are trained to praise their partners' correct responses from time to time. When a student makes an error, the tutor says, "Try again." If the student still does not respond correctly, the tutor says, for example, "This word is *tree;* say *tree.*" A timer signals the end of the first practice period, and the partners switch roles. While students are tutoring, the teacher walks around the room, prompting and rewarding good tutoring behaviors, answering questions, and generally supervising the activity.

Testing.   After the second practice period, the students reverse roles again; and the first tutor tests her partner by presenting each task card once with no prompts or cues. The teacher gives tutors about 5 minutes each to test and record their tutees' progress. Cards that a tutee reads or answers correctly are placed in one pile and missed cards in another. Roles are then switched again, and the first tutor is now tested on the words she practiced. The tutors then mark the back of each card to identify if it was "correct" or "incorrect" during the test. Each tutor records his tutee's daily progress on the chart. When a child correctly responds to a task card on the test for three consecutive sessions, that item is considered learned and is moved to the folder's STOP pocket. When all 10 cards have been learned, a new set of words is placed in the GO pocket. The session ends with tutors praising and complimenting each other for their good work.

Inclusive education is in place when each of these five features occurs on an ongoing, daily basis.

1. *Heterogeneous Grouping*   All students are educated *together* in groups where the number of those with and without disabilities approximates the *natural proportion*. The premise is that "students develop most when in the physical, social, emotional, and intellectual presence of nonhandicapped persons in reasonable approximations to the natural proportions" (Brown, Ford, Nisbet, Sweet, Donnellan, & Gruenewald, 1983, p. 17). Thus, in a class of 25 students, perhaps there is one student with significant disabilities, a couple of others with less significant disabilities, and many students without identified disabilities working at various levels.

2. *A Sense of Belonging to a Group*   All students are considered members of the class rather than visitors, guests, or outsiders. Within these groups, students who have disabilities are welcomed, as are students without disabilities.

3. *Shared Activities with Individualized Outcomes*   Students share educational experiences (e.g., lessons, labs, field studies, group learning) at the same time (Schnorr, 1990). Even though students are involved in the same activities, their learning objectives are individualized and, therefore, may be different. Students may have different objectives in the same curriculum area (e.g., language arts) during a shared activity. This is referred to as *multi-level instruction* (Campbell, Campbell, Collicott, Perner, & Stone, 1988; Collicott, 1991; Giangreco & Meyer, 1988; Giangreco & Putnam, 1991). Within a shared activity, a student also may have individualized objectives from a curriculum area (e.g., social skills) other than that on which other students are focused (e.g., science). This practice is referred to as *curriculum overlapping* (Giangreco & Meyer, 1988; Giangreco & Putnam, 1991).

4. *Use of Environments Frequented by Persons without Disabilities*   Shared educational experiences take place in environments predominantly frequented by people without disabilities (e.g., general education classrooms, community worksites).

5. *A Balanced Educational Experience*   Inclusive education seeks an individualized balance between the academic/functional and social/personal aspects of schooling (Giangreco, 1992). For example, teachers in inclusion-oriented schools would be as concerned about students' self-image and social network as they would be about developing literacy competencies or learning vocational skills.

The Council for Exceptional Children (CEC) believes all children, youth, and young adults with disabilities are entitled to a free and appropriate education and/or services that lead to an adult life characterized by satisfying relations with others, independent living, productive engagement in the community, and participation in society at large. To achieve such outcomes, there must exist for all children, youth, and young adults with disabilities a rich variety of early intervention, educational, and vocational program options and experiences. Access to these programs and experiences should be based on individual educational needs and desired outcomes. Furthermore, students and their families or guardians, as members of the planning team, may recommend the placement, curriculum option, and the exit document to be pursued.

   CEC believes that a continuum of services must be available for all children, youth, and young adults. CEC also believes that the concept of inclusion is a meaningful goal to be pursued in our schools and communities. In addition, CEC believes children, youth, and young adults with disabilities should be served whenever possible in general education classrooms in inclusive neighborhood schools and community settings. Such settings should be strengthened and supported by an infusion of specially trained personnel and other appropriate supportive practices according to the individual needs of the child.

FIGURE 2.6
Components of inclusive education

Source: Reprinted from Giangreco, M. F., Cloninger, C.J., Dennis, R.E., & Edelman, S. W. (2000). Problem-solving methods to facilitate inclusive education. In R. A. Villa & J.S. Thousand (Eds.), *Restructuring for caring and effective education: Piecing the puzzle together* (2nd ed.), (p. 294). Baltimore: Brooks. Used by permission.

Components of inclusive education

 Council for Exceptional Children   Content Standards for Beginning Teachers–Common Core: Use strategies to facilitate integration into various settings (CC4S1).
PRAXIS Special Education Core Principles: Content Knowledge: III. Delivery of Services to Students with Disabilities, Integration of related services.

FIGURE 2.7   **CEC's policy on inclusive schools**

Source: Reprinted from the supplement to *Teaching Exceptional Children, 25*(4), May 1993. Used by permission.

Moving toward Inclusive Education

by Michael F. Giangreco

In the early 1980s, when I first heard about efforts to include students with moderate and severe disabilities within general education classrooms, I must admit I was somewhat skeptical. I wondered how the educational needs of the students in my own special education class, who had labels such as autism, deaf-blindness, severe mental retardation, and multiple disabilities, could be appropriately addressed within a general education classroom. I knew it wouldn't be enough merely to have students physically present in a classroom, separated within the class, or programmatically isolated from their peers.

Over the next few years I had opportunities to help develop inclusive educational opportunities for students with disabilities by working collaboratively with other team members (e.g., parents, general educators, related services staff, paraprofessionals). Despite the initial apprehensions of some school staff, once people got to know their new student with disabilities and designed appropriately individualized curriculum and instruction, they usually felt positive about the situation. Equally as important, many teachers came to realize that the steps they had taken to ensure educational integrity and appropriate inclusion of the student with disabilities (e.g., collaborative teamwork, activity-based learning, cooperative experiences, data-based instruction, creative problem solving, peer-to-peer supports) were also applicable for meeting the widely differing educational needs of students without disability labels. Qualified general education teachers with inclusive attitudes and appropriate supports found that they could successfully teach students with disabilities, in part because the basic principles of teaching and learning are the same whether a student has a disability label or not.

In recent years the term *inclusive education* has been a source of some controversy. Sometimes people's concerns about inclusive education are based on speculation rather than actual experiences with inclusion. Other times their concerns are less about inclusion than about the process of change. Often they had been exposed to something labeled "inclusive education" when it wasn't. Some of these well-intentioned but mislabeled situations were only partial implementation efforts. Too often they were simply examples of bad educational practice. As my colleague, Michael Hock, likes to say about inclusive education, "Doing it wrong doesn't make it wrong." So when someone tells me a horror story about a student with a disability who was dumped into a classroom, or how the teacher wasn't supported, or how a student's needs weren't met, I remind them that such situations are inaccurately labeled as inclusive education.

Inclusive education means:

1. All students are welcomed in general education classes in their local schools. Therefore, the general education classroom in the school that a student would attend if he did not have a disability is the first placement consideration, given individually appropriate supports and services.

"PAROLE APPROACH" TO SCHOOL INCLUSION

Source: *"Absurdities and Realities of Special Education: The Best of Ants. . ., Flying. . ., and Logs—Full Color Edition"* by Michael F. Giangreco © 2002. Reprinted with permission. Available from Peytral Publications, Inc. 952-949-8707 www.peytral.com

2. Students are educated in classes where the number of those with and without disabilities is proportional to the local population (e.g., 10% to 12% have identified disabilities).

3. Students are educated with peers in the same age groupings available to those without disability labels.

4. Students with varying characteristics and abilities participate in shared educational experiences while pursuing individually appropriate learning outcomes with necessary supports and accommodations. In cases where students have substantially different learning outcomes, this can occur through differentiated instruction, multi-level instruction, or curriculum overlapping.

5. Shared educational experiences take place in settings predominantly frequented by people without disabilities (e.g., general education classroom, community worksites).

6. Educational experiences are designed to enhance individually determined, valued life outcomes for students and therefore seek an individualized balance between the academic/functional and social/personal aspects of schooling.

7. Inclusive education exists when each of the previously listed characteristics occurs on an ongoing daily basis.

At its core, inclusive education is a set of values, principles, and practices that seeks more effective and meaningful education for all students, regardless of whether they have exceptionality labels or not.

People occasionally ask me, "Are there any students who cannot successfully be included in general education?" If you are looking for the rare exception, it can usually be found. At the same time, it is important to acknowledge that where such exceptions exist it is usually because we, as a field, have not yet figured out how to include certain students or have chosen not to. The exclusion of many students with disabilities often has less to do with their characteristics than ours. For example, 20 years ago it was quite rare for students with Down syndrome to be educated in general education classrooms. Today in many school districts it is commonplace. The range of characteristics presented by students with Down syndrome are the same now as they were then. What has changed are our attitudes and practices. But clearly more needs to be done.

Our attention and energy may be more constructively focused on asking questions such as "How can we successfully include more students with disabilities who are still being educated in unnecessarily restrictive environments such as special education schools and classes?" We know that far too many students are unnecessarily excluded because children with similar characteristics and needs who live in one community are educated in general education classes with supports while in other communities they continue to be sent to special education classes and schools, often without any real consideration being given to general class placement. Being included should not depend on where you live, but currently it does. We need to continually remind ourselves that special education—namely, specially and individually designed instruction—is a portable service, not a place.

We have moved beyond knowing whether inclusive education is viable; it has been demonstrated to be so for an ever widening array of students in increasing numbers of schools over many years. As this change progresses, it will require a continued shift in how we think about educating diverse groups of students and how schools operate. Students' lives should be better as result of having been in school. Inclusive education provides a foundation for that to occur for students with disabilities in ways that are not possible in special education schools and classes. Ultimately, this job will be easier, approached with greater enthusiasm, and maybe even with a greater sense of urgency, when we demonstrate that we truly value people with disabilities by including them, welcoming them, and helping them learn skills and develop supports that result in meaningful outcomes in their lives.

Michael F. Giangreco is a research associate professor at the Center on Disability and Community Inclusion at the University of Vermont. His research and writing focus on the education of students with disabilities in inclusive classrooms and community settings.

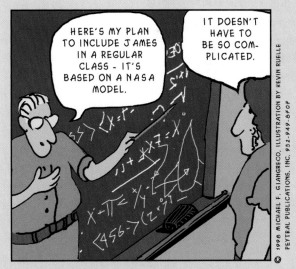

FRANK LEARNS THAT INCLUSION DOESN'T HAVE TO BE ROCKET SCIENCE.

Inclusion versus Full Inclusion

by Douglas Fuchs and Lynn S. Fuchs

WHAT IS INCLUSION?

Inclusionists believe that regular classroom teachers and special educators can help children with disabilities acquire important skills, knowledge, and behaviors that, for many, will facilitate high school (or even college) graduation and a good job. Such achievement depends on a continuum of special education placements, which includes the regular classroom.

In principle, each special education placement on the continuum offers specialized, individualized, and intensive instruction that is continuously evaluated for its effectiveness. Teachers in these special settings are instructional experts. To the fullest extent appropriate, these special educators and their students work on the general education curriculum and understand the level of academic accomplishment and social behavior necessary for success in regular classrooms.

Nevertheless, although classrooms can and should be made more flexible and responsive to a broad range of children's instructional needs, there is a limit to how much a classroom can be expected to change and how many students any teacher can responsibly teach. First, the number of children in regular classrooms is large. And second, the students in the regular classrooms are not all performing on grade level. Researchers have found few teachers who differentiate their instruction to address this broad range of academic achievement (Baker & Zigmond, 1990; Fuchs, Fuchs, & Bishop, 1992; McIntosh, Vaughn, Schumm, Haager, & Lee, 1993). Instead, many teachers present the same lesson and instructional materials to all students.

When teachers do implement research-backed instructional methods such as cooperative learning or classwide peer tutoring, their responsiveness to diversity increases as does student achievement, including the achievement of many special-needs children. Even so, some children with disabilities typically fail to respond to these best practices, suggesting that even knowledgeable and dedicated teachers cannot address the special instructional needs of all children in the regular classroom.

WHAT IS FULL INCLUSION?

Full inclusionists believe the primary job of educators is to help children with disabilities establish friendships with nondisabled persons. Moreover, educators should (1) help change stereotypic thinking about disabilities among normally developing children and (2) help children with disabilities develop social skills, which will enable them to interact more effectively within a broad network of acquaintances, co-workers, family members, and friends. Friendship making, attitude change, and social skills development can only occur, say full inclusionists, in regular classes for the simple reason that these objectives require the presence of age-appropriate, nondisabled children.

In addition, full inclusionists claim that the placement of special-needs children in regular classrooms must be full time (e.g., Lipsky & Gartner, 1991; Stainback & Stainback, 1992). First, only full-time placement confers legitimacy on special-needs children's membership and place in regular classrooms. Second, as long as special education placements exist, educators may use them as dumping grounds for the difficult-to-teach student. Full inclusionists predict that by eliminating special education placements, classroom teachers will have to transform their classes into settings responsive to all children. However, this will require fundamental changes in the roles of special and regular educators and the entire teaching and learning process. These changes include a radical constructivist vision of teaching and learning and a concomitant de-emphasis, even rejection, of standard curricula, directed instruction, and accountability standards. "From a holistic, constructivist perspective, all children simply engage in a process of learning as much as they can in a particular subject area; how much and exactly what they learn will depend upon their backgrounds, interests, and abilities" (Stainback & Stainback, 1992, p. 72).

MANY CHILDREN, MANY NEEDS

How does one explain the dramatic differences between the inclusionists and the full inclusionists? They advocate for different children with different needs. Most inclusionists speak for children with sensory impairments and high-incidence disabilities such as learning disabilities, behavior disorders, and mild mental retardation. Most full inclusionists represent children with severe disabilities. So when full inclusionists argue for regular class placements for children with disabilities, they are motivated by the concern that "their" children make friends, influence attitudes about disability, and improve social skills. If the children's learning of academic, functional, or vocational skills suffer, this is a sacrifice many full inclusionists seem willing to make. Inclusionists, by contrast, are primarily concerned that "their" children get appropriate academic instruction; if this is most likely to happen in a resource room, separate class, or even a special school, most inclusionists say, "So be it."

WHY THE FULL INCLUSION MOVEMENT WILL NOT SUCCEED

There are several reasons why the full inclusion movement will not succeed.

Uncompromising and presumptive. To ensure a place in regular classrooms for children with severe disabilities, full inclusionists have pressed for an elimination of special education placements for all children with disabilities. Their antipathy toward special education placements is based on a conviction that, as long as such programs exist, children with severe disabilities will most likely be assigned to and confined in them. They presume to speak on behalf of parents and professional advocates of deaf children, blind children, and children with learning disabilities, behavior disorders, and mild mental retardation. This puts full inclusionists in direct conflict with many in the disability community. For example, Bernard Rimland (1993b), a well-known advocate and father of a child with autism, writes: "I have no quarrel with [full] inclusionists if they are content to insist upon inclusion for their children. But when they try to force me and other unwilling parents to dance to their tune, I find it highly objectionable and quite intolerable. Parents need options" (p. 3).

Accommodating all in one place. Full inclusionists have an unquestioned belief in the capacity of regular education to accommodate all children. However, the limits of the regular classroom and the need for a variety of special education placements are recognized even in Vermont, a state with nearly double the national average of students with disabilities in regular classrooms and long known as a leader in inclusive education (Sack, 1997). Several years ago, Rutland, Vermont, school officials began The Success School, a separate program for disruptive students in grades 6 through 12. According to Rutland's director of special services, Ellie McGarry, the goal for most students is to return to the regular classroom full time. For others it is gaining the skills necessary to find a job. A handful of students, Ms. McGarry said, "wouldn't be in school at all if it weren't for [The] Success [School]" (Sack, 1997, p. 6). The district's superintendent, David Wolk, says The Success School is "a common-sense way to help the inclusion pendulum settle in the middle. It's clear this is the best environment for those children" (p. 3).

Special education accountability. We acknowledge that there are major problems with how special education is practiced in many school districts. For example, few special educators document their effectiveness in teaching students with disabilities. And separate special education placements become terminal assignments in the educational careers of too many children. There is insufficient evidence that special education teachers facilitate movement along the continuum of special education services so that children in special day schools, for example, transition into resource rooms or those in resource rooms reintegrate into regular classrooms, where eventually they may be decertified.

For too long, accountability in special education has been defined in terms of process—for example, by whether school districts can produce legally correct IEPs. Our field, however, is in the midst of redefining accountability in terms of student progress in academic, social, and school-behavior domains. Although this redefinition will be difficult to accomplish, it is an important endeavor. We are confident that time will tell that student progress requires options in instruction, curricula, materials, and placements.

―――――――――
Douglas Fuchs and Lynn Fuchs are professors of special education at Vanderbilt University. Their research interests focus on developing classroom-based techniques such as curriculum-based measurement and peer-assisted learning strategies that strengthen the academic performance and social integration of students with and without disabilities. They are the coeditors of the *Journal of Special Education.*

WHERE DOES SPECIAL EDUCATION GO FROM HERE?

The promise of a free, appropriate public education for all children with disabilities is indeed an ambitious one. The process of bringing this goal about has been described in such lofty terms as a "new Bill of Rights" and a "Magna Carta" for children with disabilities (Goodman, 1976). Weintraub and Abeson (1974) wrote nearly 30 years ago in support of IDEA: "At the minimum, it will make educational opportunities a reality for all handicapped children. At the maximum, it will make our schools healthier learning environments for all our children" (p. 529). Today, most observers acknowledge that substantial progress has been made toward fulfillment of that promise.

IDEA has had far-reaching effects. As Turnbull and Turnbull (2001) observe, the student is no longer required to meet the requirements of the school, but the school is required to fit the needs of the student. Schools today provide far more than academic instruction. In effect, they have become diversified agencies offering services such as medical support, physical therapy, vocational training, parent counseling, recreation, special transportation, and in-service education for staff members. In place of the once-prevalent practice of excluding children with disabilities, schools now seek the most appropriate ways of including them. Schools are committed to providing wide-ranging services to children from diverse backgrounds and with different learning needs.

Most citizens—both within and outside the field of education—have welcomed the inclusion and participation of children with disabilities in their schools and communities. Additionally, the greater involvement of parents and families in the educational process and the emphasis on team planning to meet individual needs throughout the life span are widely regarded as positive developments. Reports from teachers and students, as well as a growing number of research studies, indicate that many children with disabilities are being successfully educated in regular schools and that, for the most part, they are well accepted by their nondisabled schoolmates.

Despite this ample evidence of progress toward providing equal educational opportunity, it is equally true that many people—again, inside and outside the field of education—have detected significant problems in the implementation of IDEA (e.g., Finn, Rotherham, & Hokanson, 2001). Many school administrators maintain that the federal government has never granted sufficient financial resources to the states and local school districts to assist them in providing special services, which are often very costly. Special education teachers express dissatisfaction over excessive paperwork, unclear guidelines, and inappropriate grouping of students with disabilities. General education teachers contend that they receive little or no training or support when students with disabilities are placed in their classes. Some parents of children with disabilities have voiced opposition to full inclusion. Some observers find that the schedules and procedures used in some inclusion programs actually allow for relatively little integration (Sansone & Zigmond, 1986). There are many other problems, real and perceived, and no quick fix or easy solution can be offered.

Special education is at a crossroads. Once, access to educational opportunity was the primary issue for children with disabilities. Would they receive an education at all? Could they be served in their local community? Some access problems persist (e.g., particularly for children who live in poverty or in extremely isolated areas), but now the primary issue of concern is the appropriateness and effectiveness of special education.

Regardless of where services are delivered, the most crucial variable is the quality of instruction that each child receives.

For more information on special education services, go to the Web Links module in Chapter 2 of the Companion Website at **www.prenhall.com/heward**

Can we fulfill the promise of a free, appropriate public education for all students with disabilities? The answer depends in part on the ability of professionals to work together, assume new roles, communicate with each other, and involve parents, families, and individuals with disabilities themselves. But ultimately, educators must realize that the most crucial variable in the effectiveness of special education is the quality of instruction that children receive.

Special education is serious business. The learning and adjustment problems faced by students with disabilities are real, and their prevention and remediation require intensive, systematic intervention. Regardless of who does it or where it takes place, good teaching must occur. Exceptional children deserve no less.

 SUMMARY

THE PROCESS OF SPECIAL EDUCATION

- IDEA mandates a particular sequence of events that schools must follow in identifying and educating children with disabilities.
- Prereferral intervention is an informal, problem-solving process used by many schools to (1) provide immediate instructional and/or behavior management assistance to the child and teacher and (2) reduce the chances of identifying a child for special education who may not be disabled.
- All children suspected of having a disability must receive a nondiscriminatory multifactored evaluation (MFE) for determining eligibility for special education and to provide information about the child's educational needs and how to meet them.
- An individualized education program (IEP) must be planned and provided for each child with a disability that is adversely affecting her educational performance.

COLLABORATION AND TEAMING

- Coordination, consultation, and teaming are three modes of collaboration that team members can use.
- Three models for teaming are multidisciplinary, interdisciplinary, and transdisciplinary. Transdisciplinary teams conduct joint assessments, share information and expertise across discipline boundaries, and select discipline-free goals and interventions.

INDIVIDUALIZED EDUCATION PROGRAM

- An IEP planning team must include at least (1) the parents of the child; (2) one regular education teacher of the child; (3) one special education teacher; (4) a representative of the local education agency; (5) an individual who can interpret the instructional implications of evaluation results; (6) other individuals who have knowledge or special expertise regarding the child, including related service personnel as appropriate; and (7) the student, if age 14 or older, must be invited. (Younger students may attend if appropriate.)
- Although the formats vary widely from district to district, each IEP must include these seven components: (1) the child's present levels of educational performance; (2) measurable annual goals, including benchmarks or short-term objectives; (3) the special education and related services and supplementary aids and services to be provided to the child; (4) an explanation of the extent, if any, to which the child will not participate with nondisabled children in the regular class; (5) any individual modifications in the administration of state- or district-wide assessments of student achievement that are needed for the child to participate in such assessment (or alternative assessments); (6) the projected date for the beginning of the services and modifications described in number 3 and the anticipated frequency, location, and

duration of those services and modifications; and (7) how the child's progress toward the annual goals will be measured and how the child's parents will be regularly informed of their child's progress.

- Beginning when the student reaches age 14, IEPs must also include information on how the child's transition from school to adult life will be supported.
- Without direct and ongoing monitoring of student progress toward IEP goals and objectives, the document's usefulness is limited.
- The IEP is a measure of accountability for teachers and schools; however, a teacher and a school cannot be prosecuted if the child does not achieve all of the goals set forth in the IEP.

LEAST RESTRICTIVE ENVIRONMENT

- The LRE is the setting closest to the regular classroom that also meets the child's special educational needs.
- The LRE is a relative concept; the LRE for one child might be inappropriate for another.
- The continuum of services is a range of placement and service options to meet the individual needs of students with disabilities.
- The IEP team must determine the LRE after it has designed a program of special education and related services to meet the child's unique needs.

INCLUSIVE EDUCATION

- Inclusion describes the process of integrating children with disabilities into regular schools and classes.
- Studies have shown that well-planned, carefully conducted inclusion can be generally effective with students of all ages, types, and degrees of disability.
- A few special educators believe that the LRE principle should give way to full inclusion, in which all students with disabilities are placed full time in regular classrooms.
- Most special educators and professional organizations, such as CEC, support inclusion as a goal but believe that the continuum of services and program options must be maintained and that placement decisions must be based on the student's individual educational needs.

WHERE DOES SPECIAL EDUCATION GO FROM HERE?

To check your comprehension of chapter content, go to the Guided Review and Quiz Modules in Chapter 2 of the Companion Website at **www.prenhall. com/heward**

- The promise of a free, appropriate public education for all children with disabilities is an ambitious one, but substantial progress has been made toward fulfillment of that promise.
- Implementation of IDEA has brought problems of funding, inadequate teacher training, and opposition by some to the inclusion of children with disabilities into regular classes.
- Regardless of where services are delivered, the most crucial variable is the quality of instruction that each child receives.

Chapter 3
Special Education in a Culturally Diverse Society

by Vivian I. Correa and

William L. Heward

- What effects does the changing diversity in the population have on students and schools?

- Why are culturally and linguistically diverse students disproportionately represented in special education?

- How can a teacher become a culturally proficient educator?

- What assessment, curriculum, and instructional methods are effective for students with disabilities from culturally or linguistically different backgrounds?

- Does it make a difference if a child's limited English proficiency is caused by a cultural difference or by a disability?

ROXANNE HUDSON
KIMBALL WILES ELEMENTARY SCHOOL
GAINESVILLE, FLORIDA

Education • Teaching Credentials • Experience
- B.A. in Political Science, Gonzaga University, 1989
- M.Ed. in Exceptional Children, Western Washington University, 1994
- Elementary and endorsement in Exceptional Children, K–12 (Washington); Varying Exceptionalities, K–12 (Florida)
- 5 years of experience teaching elementary students with disabilities; 3 years as a teacher assistant in residential treatment center for adolescent boys

Current Teaching Position and Students   I have taught in self-contained settings of one sort or another for most of my career, mostly with primary-age students with behavioral and emotional disabilities. In rural western Washington my students were primarily Caucasian. When I moved to Florida, I began teaching at Kimball Wiles Elementary in a self-contained class for students with behavioral problems and learning disabilities. I was teaching in another monocultural class, but this time all of my students were African American. My students and I took a while to get used to each other; we both were in a bit of a culture shock and had to learn to communicate with each other. Now they had a northern teacher who "talked funny," and I had moved to a southern state with many different expectations for teachers and students.

I had many concerns about my ability to teach students from a cultural background different from mine. Growing up in the Pacific Northwest, I hadn't had much experience with African Americans and didn't know much about the cultural background of my students. I quickly realized I needed to do some investigation and learn about their lives. I went on home visits in the first month of school to meet the students' families and see their neighborhoods. I asked my African American teaching assistant about how parents and children interact and what works best with the students, and I asked the students what they found helpful in my teaching and discipline. I read about the history of the local African American community in Gainesville and watched how families interacted around me. I tried my best to learn where my students were coming from and how I might best teach them. Through this, I gained confidence and believe I teach them well.

Teaching Strategies   I use a social justice perspective in my teaching, and this permeates all of my educational choices—from the subjects I teach to how I interact with students and families. I focus on literacy because I see literacy as power in our society and want all my students to have a chance to participate as powerful agents in our culture. Real opportunities to read and write are integrated throughout the day, along with more traditional skills-based direct teaching and fluency development.

Because of my social justice perspective, I have grounded my curriculum in the students' lives and adapted it to meet their individual needs. While teaching in Washington, I noticed that my monocultural students had no understanding of people of other cultures and races and used biased epithets without really understanding what they meant or how they could hurt someone. So I decided to focus some time on learning the history of various groups in our country. Through music, art, drama, reading, and writing and by discussing the lives of African Americans, Hispanics, the Jewish community, and Asians, the students developed understanding, tolerance, and respect for others—no small feat for a group of six- to eight-year-olds with severe emotional and learning disabilities!

In Florida, the needs of my students were different. They understand the dominant culture well but need to learn about their own culture and develop pride in themselves and their heritage. I thus integrate information from African American culture and history into everything we do, from reading to science to social studies. For example, during shared and independent reading, we often enjoy books written in various dialects, books about skin color and hair texture (e.g., *All the Colors of the Earth* by Sheila Hamanka and *Happy to Be Nappy* by bell hooks), and biographies of important people of all cultures. I try to integrate information about African Americans and culture as a matter-of-fact part of the curriculum rather than as something separate and special. I have asked my African American teaching assistant to share her experiences living in the south during segregation and desegregation.

Each year, I begin with the theme of friendship and community building; and during that time, we focus on students' families and each child's unique family history. We put up a timeline, and each child interviews members of his or her family about important dates such as birthdays, ancestors' immigration to the United States, as well as languages spoken in the family and important family stories and sayings. The students then share this information, make signs to put up on the timeline, and, after studying biographies in language arts, write their own autobiographies. As we move through the year studying social studies and science, we add important discoveries and historical time periods to the timeline and compare them to important dates within the children's families. In this way, the curriculum is brought into the real lives of the students; and they can understand, for example, that their great-grandmother and Mary McLeod Bethune lived at the same time in Florida.

I also feel it is critical for my students, some of whom are going to the middle school next year, to develop more cultural capital in how to be successful in a school setting dominated by Caucasian teachers and cultural expectations. After all, every one of my students is in my class because he or she was unable to function successfully in general education classes. We discuss issues such as dialects and how everyone has a different way of talking but that we all need to write in what I call "book language." This discussion tends to take place during writing time. I encourage students to use invented spelling supported by Elkonin boxes. Because they spell what they say as I conference with them, I have an opportunity to talk about differences in how people talk and write. We find examples of book talk for what they are saying, and I tell them that everyone (including me) has to learn to write this way.

The discussion of dialects is helped by the fact I come from the north and speak very differently from them. We talk about how I use different words for the same meaning and that there are certain times when we can talk or write like we do at home and certain times when we have to be more formal. I believe it is important for the students to feel powerful and invested in how the rules are made, so we discuss why schools have rules and what things might be like without them. The students and I collaboratively come up with the class rules and the consequences for breaking them. We focus heavily on problem solving among the students and developing social skills that will help them succeed in the dominant culture while still supporting their cultural values and behaviors.

Working with Families I try to use what Beth Harry and Maya Kalyanpur call "cultural reciprocity" with the families of my students. When I first came to Florida from

To find a list of readings suggested by Ms. Hudson for increasing your understanding of other cultures, go to the Teacher Feature page on the Companion Website at **www.prenhall.com/heward**

Washington, I didn't know about my students' lives, so I went on home visits early in the school year. This way, I began to develop the partnerships with families that I consider critical to my success as a teacher. During IEP meetings, we collaborate to develop goals and objectives for the students, and I make sure to explain the reasoning behind my recommendations and explain the ramifications of each choice so the parents can make an informed decision about services and goals. We discuss their vision for the future of their child and what we need to do now to meet it.

A Meaningful Moment   I will always cherish this memory of my students taking activism to heart. We had been studying ecology and plants in science, and during story time I read them a wonderful book by Susan Jeffers called *Brother Eagle, Sister Sky,* which is a beautifully illustrated version of a letter that Chief Seattle wrote. At the end, it implores the president of the United States to take care of the land because we are all connected. The book shows the results of what will happen if we don't by including an illustration of a clearcut forest. The students and I talked about the book, and I asked them what we could do to help protect the forest. I thought they would say we should recycle our paper or use less. Instead, they decided they wanted to plant trees to help the forest and decided they would start in our schoolyard. They wrote a letter explaining the project to the principal; raised money from their families and the school staff; went on a class trip to a nursery to pick out an apple tree; and then designed invitations to their families, the principal, and the school superintendent to come to our tree-planting ceremony. I was proud and amazed by their enthusiasm and by how a simple, everyday activity like story time led them to this act. What a strong lesson in their own power to change things around them!

My Continuing Education   I am currently a doctoral student in the special education program at the University of Florida, where I am focusing on the prevention of reading disabilities and studying children from culturally and linguistically diverse families. I want to learn more about how to promote the acquisition of English literacy skills among children from different cultural backgrounds while maintaining and strengthening their first-language skills.

The United States is a society composed of people from many cultural groups, and the students in our schools reflect this great diversity. Not only have new waves of immigrants brought greater diversity to the country, but the children of these families bring a rich heritage to the classroom that can enhance the educational experience of all students. Teachers play a critical role in assuring that these students' experiences, values, and beliefs are the foundation for culturally responsive curriculum and pedagogy. If culturally diverse students are not positively oriented toward both their own and the dominant culture (Sparks, 2000), they can become marginalized, and their chances for success in school will be jeopardized.

The educational system serves many students and their families well. However, because the achievement of ethnic groups such as African Americans, Hispanics, and Native Americans is similar to white students' in the early grades but falls further behind the longer the students stay in school (Banks, 1994b), there is reason for concern about the role our educational system may be playing in limiting the achievement of students from different cultural groups. The basic problem is that good teaching, good programs, and good schools are not available to all students, especially those from diverse racial and ethnic backgrounds

To better understand the topics covered in this chapter, go to the Essential Concepts and Chapter-at-a-Glance Modules in Chapter 3 of the Companion Website at **www.prenhall.com/heward**

and who live in poverty (Hernandez, 2001; Nieto, 2000a). Minority and low-income students in urban schools are more frequently taught by teachers who are "inadequately prepared, inexperienced, and ill-qualified" (Darling-Hammond, 1995, p. 470).

The reasons for these inequities are complex. However, low student achievement, low rates of retention, and high dropout rates are not inherently a function of the family or social or ethnic background of the students. Thus, for all students to succeed in schools, significant changes in educational policies and school practices must occur. To overcome these challenges, policymakers, educators, and the public will have to recognize that *all* students are entitled to receive a rich, challenging, and thoughtful curriculum and be taught by a fully qualified and certified teacher.

Each student in this classroom benefits from the diverse cultural and ethnic perspectives, values, and problem-solving approaches they experience by working with one another.

 ## CHALLENGES FOR EDUCATION

The increasing cultural and linguistic diversity of the United States is having significant effects on schools (Gollnick & Chinn, 2002). The demographic trends in race/ethnicity, poverty, and dropout rates and the disproportionate relationship between race and disability are reasons for concern about the role of our educational system.

 ### CHANGING DEMOGRAPHICS

In 2000, the U.S. census codified the population on the basis of membership in one race or two or more races. The race categories included white; American Indian, Eskimo, or Aleut; black; Asian or Pacific Islander; and other. Additionally, the census considered race and Hispanic origin to be two separate and distinct concepts. Table 3.1 shows race and ethnic comparisons in the 1980, 1990, and 2000 censuses.

Most surprising was the growth of the Hispanic population in the United States. For the first time Hispanics have surpassed the nation's black population. Furthermore, the 2000 data reveal how multiracial and multiethnic our nation truly is. Today's educators need to recognize that multiracial/multiethnic children must be included and supported in the multicultural landscape of education (Wardle, 2000).

African Americans, Latinos, Asian Americans, and American Indians form 30% of the nation's population. About 65% of U.S. population growth in the next two decades will be "minority," particularly from Hispanic and Asian immigrants (Hodgkinson, 2000). Minority groups are expected to make up more than 40% of the population by 2020 and 50% of the population by 2040 (Gollnick & Chinn, 2002).

POVERTY

The demographic trends for poverty in the United States continue to be alarming. It is estimated that 20% of children in the United States live in poverty (Children's Defense Fund, 2000) and that culturally and linguistically diverse students are more likely to experience poverty than are white students (Alder, 2000). Nearly 4 in 10 African American and His-

TABLE 3.1 **U.S. census comparisons**

Population Group	Percent of Total		
	1980	1990	2000
Non-Hispanic white	79.8	75.6	69.1
Black	11.5	11.7	12.1
Hispanic	6.4	9.0	12.5
Asian	1.6	2.8	3.7
American Indian	0.6	0.7	0.7
Some other race	0.1	0.1	0.2
Two or more races	NA	NA	1.6

Source: Kent, M., Pollard, K., Haaga, J., & Mather, M. (2001). *First glimpse from the 2000 U.S. census.*
Available at http://www.prb.org/AmeriStatTemplate.cfm

panic children live in poverty, the majority of them in female-headed, single-parent house-holds (Dalaker & Naifeh, 1998). Fujiura and Yamaki (2000) reported that poverty and single-parent families are the two variables most highly correlated with increased risk for childhood disability. Overall, culturally and linguistically diverse students are more likely to experience challenges and barriers in school achievement, especially if those students also experience poverty (Díaz-Rico & Weed, 2002).

 ## SCHOOL DROPOUT

The statistics on school dropout rates among culturally and linguistically diverse students further illustrate the disparities in the educational system. Culturally and linguistically diverse students drop out of school at a much higher rate than white students do. In 1999, the dropout numbers were highest for the Hispanic group, with 28.6% of Hispanic youths ages 16–24 dropping out of school compared to 12.6% of blacks, 7.3% of whites, and 4.3% of Asian/Pacific Islanders (National Center for Education Statistics, 2000). American Indian/Alaska Native students were included in the general category of Asian/Pacific Islanders. Yet data reported in 1994 indicated that 25.4% of American Indian/Alaska Native students who should have graduated in 1992 dropped out of school (National Center for Education Statistics, 1994). Furthermore, African American and Latino students who do manage to graduate from high school are much less likely than whites to go to college (Education Trust, 1996). Compounding this problem is the fact that dropout rates are higher for students with disabilities (Horn & Berktold, 1999).

The distinguishing characteristics of race and ethnic background, socioeconomic status, and disability place these students in jeopardy for dropping out of school and not attaining success in postschool settings. Utley (1995) observed that some culturally and linguistically diverse students "face quadruple jeopardy due to a combination of factors, such as poverty, language, culture, and/or disabling condition and this has devastating effects on their educational opportunities and makes them vulnerable to placement in special education" (p. 303).

 ## DISPROPORTIONAL REPRESENTATION IN SPECIAL EDUCATION

Culturally and linguistically diverse students are both under- and overrepresented in special education (Artiles, Aguirre-Munoz, & Abedi, 1998; Artiles & Zamora-Durán, 1997; Baca & Cervantes, 1998; Correa, Blanes-Reyes, & Rapport, 1995; Daugherty, 2001; Ford, 1998; MacMillan & Reschly, 1998; Oswald & Coutinho, 2001; Oswald, Coutinho, Best, & Singh, 1999; Patton, 1998). The 1998–1999 school year was the first time that individual states were required to report the race and ethnicity of children served under IDEA. Those reports show some disparities with the distribution of race/ethnicity in the general student population (see Table 3.2). Black and American Indian students were overrepresented in special education programs, while Asian and white students were underrepresented. Hispanic students were generally represented among the special education population at a rate comparable to their proportion in the resident school-age population.

Although somewhat controversial, the meaning of disproportionality has been difficult to pinpoint. MacMillan and Reschly (1998) believe that all of the indices and data must be considered for an accurate representation of the enrollment patterns among culturally and linguistically diverse students, including (1) percentage of total student enrollment by group, (2) percentage of special program enrollment by group, and (3) percentage of group in the special program. Harry (1994) emphasized that the concept of disproportionality is relative rather than absolute. She believes there is great variability in over- and underrepresentation in special education among states and local school districts. She argues that there is a problem when the percentage of minority students in the special education program is larger than the percentage of that group in the general educational system. The lack of consistent criteria and the collection of disaggregated enrollment data continue to hinder the examination of this problem. Nonetheless, invalid assessments and placement of diverse students in special education is problematic because they can stigmatize students and deny them appropriate educational interventions that match their full learning capacities. Additionally, some culturally and linguistically diverse students served in special education have difficulties that were pedagogically induced and acquired their disability label because instruction was not adjusted to fit their individual needs or background.

Special educators facing these challenges seek to provide a relevant, individualized education to students with disabilities from diverse backgrounds. Our public school system is based on a philosophy of equal educational opportunity. IDEA is only one of many significant steps toward implementing equal educational opportunity. Besides prohibiting discrimination in schools because of intellectual or physical disability, court decisions and legislation have forbidden discrimination in education and employment on the basis of race, nationality, gender, or inability to speak English. Special programs now provide financial support and assistance to schools that serve refugee and migrant students and provide self-determination in education for Native Americans.

TABLE 3.2 **Percentage of students ages 6 through 21 in different race/ethnicity groups who received special education, by disability category, in the 1998-1999 school year**

Disability	American Indian	Asian/Pacific Islander	Black (non-Hispanic)	Hispanic	White (non-Hispanic)
Specific learning disabilities	1.4	1.4	18.3	15.8	63.0
Speech and language impairments	1.2	2.4	16.5	11.6	68.3
Mental retardation	1.1	1.7	34.3	8.9	54.1
Emotional disturbance	1.1	1.0	26.4	9.8	61.6
Multiple disabilities	1.4	2.3	19.3	10.9	66.1
Hearing impairments	1.4	4.6	16.8	16.3	66.0
Orthopedic impairments	.8	3.0	14.6	14.4	67.2
Other health impairments	1.0	1.3	14.1	7.8	75.8
Visual impairments	1.3	3.0	14.8	11.4	69.5
Autism	.7	4.7	20.9	9.4	64.4
Deaf-blindness	1.8	11.3	11.5	12.1	63.3
Traumatic brain injury	1.6	2.3	15.9	10.0	70.2
Developmental delay	.5	1.1	33.7	4.0	60.8
All disabilities	1.3	1.7	20.2	13.2	63.6
Resident population	1.0	3.8	14.8	14.2	66.2

Source: U.S. Department of Education. (2000). *Twenty-second annual report to Congress on the implementation of the Individuals with Disabilities Act.* Washington, DC: Author.

Despite these important efforts, equal educational opportunity for all is not yet a reality (Banks & Banks, 2001; Grossman, 1995; Nieto, 2000a). The problem of disproportionate numbers of culturally diverse students in special education is not simple, and the solutions require significant changes in schools and communities (Artiles et al., 1998; Artiles & Trent, 1994; Artiles & Zamora-Durán, 1997; Baca & Cervantes, 1998; Gollnick & Chinn, 2002; Harry, 1994; Oswald et al., 1999; Patton, 1998; Smith, 2001). However, understanding the multivariate nature of the problem is a first step in identifying effective solutions to improving educational services for all culturally and linguistically diverse students and their families.

WHY ARE THERE DISPROPORTIONATE PLACEMENTS OF CULTURALLY DIVERSE STUDENTS IN SPECIAL EDUCATION?

The fact that culturally diverse students are identified as having mental retardation, emotional disturbance, or learning disabilities is not, in itself, a problem. All students with a disability that adversely affects their educational performance should receive special education services, whatever their racial or ethnic background. The presence of large numbers of culturally diverse students, however, raises several important concerns about our education practices. Understanding the reasons for the disproportionality phenomenon in special education is not simple. Several factors must be considered, including the sociopolitical context of schools and communities in the United States (Nieto, 2000a). However, three areas that have been identified as integral to this problem include (1) incongruity in interactions between teachers and culturally diverse students and families, (2) inaccuracy of the assessment and referral process for culturally diverse students in special education, and (3) ineffective curriculum and instructional practices for culturally diverse students. Subsequent parts of this chapter addresses possible solutions to these three concerns.

INCONGRUITY BETWEEN TEACHERS AND CULTURALLY DIVERSE STUDENTS

The incongruity between teachers and diverse students has been discussed in the literature from diverse perspectives. Nieto (2000a) describes multiple theories of why children fail in school. She concludes that a combination of factors can help explain the massive failure of many students. Among those factors, Nieto includes "the school's tendency to replicate society and its inequities, cultural and language incompatibilities, the unfair and bureaucratic structures of schools, and the political relationship of particular groups to society and the schools" (p. 245).

The cultural and language incompatibility factor has gained much attention in the literature (Harry, Rueda, & Kalyanpur, 1999; Gollnick & Chinn, 2002; Grant & Gomez, 2001; Hernandez, 2001). Predominately white, middle-class educators are teaching a growing number of culturally and linguistically diverse students (Fox & Gay, 1995; Pavri, 2001). In fact, Nieto (2000a) reports that the proportion of white teachers increased from 88% in 1971 to 90.7% in 1996. The National Education Association (2001) predicts that by early in the 21st century the percentage of minority teachers will shrink to an all-time low of 5%, while 41% of American students will be minorities.

Teachers, administrators, school psychologists, and counselors generally require or expect certain behaviors of students. The danger is when those expectations are based on stereotypes, prejudices, or misunderstandings. For example, they assume that most children will learn to respond to the teacher's instructions and be positively motivated by verbal praise and attention. Children, however, are strongly influenced by their early contacts with family members, neighbors, and friends. If the expectations and values of home and school environments are vastly different, children may have serious problems. Behaviors considered

Cultural differences between teachers and students

Council for Exceptional Children Content Standards for Beginning Teachers–Common Core: Impact of the dominant culture on shaping schools and in the individuals who study and work in them (CC1K9).
PRAXIS Special Education Core Principles: Content Knowledge: III. Delivery of Services to Students with Disabilities, Professional roles, Influence of teacher attitudes, values, and behaviors.

problems by school personnel might be related to differences between the standards of behavior in the home and in the school. For example, a teacher might characterize a silent and shy child as overly withdrawn and refer him to a school counselor. In fact, however, the child may be behaving according to the standards of his home.

The idea of cultural incongruity between home and school can also be seen in instruction. The learning preferences of diverse students can influence their ability to receive and process information (Banks & Banks, 1995; Bennett, 1999; Swisher, 1992). A common mode of instruction in dominant U.S. classrooms is analytical, verbal, and competitive, whereas the learning preferences of some culturally diverse learners is more imaginative, nonverbal, and cooperative (Daniels, 2001; Harry, 1992a; Hernadez, 2001). For example, some culturally diverse students might find it difficult to recite mathematics facts in front of the whole class and compete to win on the weekly spelling bee. However, the same students might become more engaged in instruction if the math facts were embedded in an ethnic cooking activity with small groups of peers and the spelling bee were turned into a dramatic play activity in which they were asked to perform the history of their ancestors using the week's spelling words. Such conflicts can interfere with a child's learning and behavior and are thus a legitimate concern of all special educators. At the same time, teachers should be cautious of oversimplifying and stereotyping students' learning preferences solely on ethnicity or culture (Nieto, 2000a).

Without a solid understanding of how culture influences both students and school personnel, the cultural conflict between the home and school will continue to exist. School staff can better understand cultural incongruity with students and families from diverse cultures if they recognize the definition of culture, the heterogeneity within cultures, and the existence of microcultures.

Cultural differences between students

 Council for Exceptional Children Content Standards for Beginning Teachers—Common Core: Differing ways of learning of individuals with exceptional learning needs including those from culturally diverse backgrounds (CC3K5).

PRAXIS Special Education Core Principles: Content Knowledge: I. Understanding Exceptionalities, Characteristics of students with disabilities including cultural and linguistic factors.

Dimensions and effects of culture

Council for Exceptional Children Content Standards for Beginning Teachers—Common Core: Effects of cultural and linguistic difference on growth and development (CC6K1).

Definition of Culture Culture "consists of the values, traditions, social and political relationships, and world view created, shared, and transformed by a group of people bound together by a common history, geographic location, language, social class, and/or region" (Nieto, 2000a, p. 139). Because a social group adapts to and modifies the environments in which it lives, *culture* can be defined as "the way of life of a social group; the human-made environment. Although culture is often defined in a way that includes all the material and nonmaterial aspects of group life, most social scientists today emphasize the intangible, symbolic, and ideational aspect of culture. . . . Cultures are dynamic, complex, and changing" (Banks, 1994a, pp. 50–51).

A culture, then, is determined by the "world view, values, styles, and above all language" shared by members of a social group (Hilliard, 1980, p. 585). Although an outsider can learn to speak the language of another social group or use some of its tools, such accomplishments do not confer complete access to or understanding of the group's culture. While the language, artifacts, and other things associated with a particular group are sometimes presented as its culture, this view is only partly accurate.

People who share a particular culture's ideas and values usually interpret events in similar ways. Although membership in a specific cultural group does not determine behavior, members are exposed to (socialized by) the same set of expectations and consequences for acting in certain ways. As a result, certain types of behavior become more probable (Banks, 1994b). However, Nieto (2000a) warns us that culture gives us just one way in which to understand differences among students. "The assumption that culture is the primary determinant of academic achievement can be over simplistic, dangerous, and counterproductive because, while culture may influence, it does not determine who we are" (p. 141).

Gollnick and Chinn (2002) outline four basic characteristics of culture that give us a background for considering the special needs of culturally diverse students with disabilities and their families.

1. *Our cultural heritage is learned.* It is not innately based on the culture in which we are born. Vietnamese infants adopted by Italian American, Catholic, middle-

class parents will share a cultural heritage with middle-class Italian American Catholics, rather than Vietnamese in Vietnam.

2. *Culture is shared.* Shared cultural patterns and customs bind people together as an identifiable group and make it possible for them to live together and function with ease. Groups may not realize the common cultural aspects as existent in the cultural group—the way they communicate with each other and the foods they eat.

3. *Culture is an adaptation.* Cultures have developed to accommodate certain environmental conditions and available natural and technological resources. Thus, Eskimos who live with extreme cold, snow, ice, seals, and the sea have developed a culture different from the Pacific Islander. The culture of urban residents differs from rural residents, in part because of the resources available in the different settings.

4. *Culture is a dynamic system that changes continuously.* For example, the replacement of industrial workers by robots is changing the culture of many working-class communities. (pp. 7–8)

Heterogeneity within a Culture The importance of understanding and respecting inter- and intraindividual differences cannot be stressed too strongly. Ethnic groups can be extremely heterogeneous; for example, Native Americans today comprise 510 federally recognized groups and 278 reservations (including pueblos, rancherias, and communities) and speak 187 languages (Coburn et al., 1995). Although many Native Americans share a certain cultural heritage and world view, differences among the groups are very real, and group affiliations are quite important (Little Soldier, 1990). Navajo Indians, for example, are culturally diverse from Sioux Indians. Asian Americans are an extremely diversified group, coming from more than 24 countries and speaking more than 1,000 languages and dialects (Leung, 1988). There can be dramatic cultural differences among members of the black population if they identify themselves as African American, Nigerian American, or West Indian. Heterogeneity is also seen across Hispanic groups such as Mexican Americans, Central and South Americans, Puerto Ricans, and Cubans.

Microcultures The degree to which a student inherits a distinct cultural background varies immensely. Remember, a student's cultural group is just one of the social groups that influence her values and behavior. Each student is simultaneously a member of a number of *microcultures* such as race, ethnicity, social class, religion, gender, and disability. Each of these groups exerts various degrees of influence on a student's ways of interpreting and responding to the world. (See Profiles & Perspectives, "The So Called," later in this chapter.)

For example, a child in the classroom is not just Hispanic, but also female, Catholic, and from a working class family living in inner city Los Angeles. Her view of reality and her actions based on that view will differ from those of a Hispanic boy or a Hispanic girl living in Ruskin, Florida, a rural agricultural area. A teacher's failure to consider the integration of race, social class, and gender could lead at times to an oversimplified or inaccurate understanding of what occurs in schools. (Grant & Sleeter, 1989, p. 49)

This student's behavior and values are influenced not only by her membership in a specific cultural group but also by her social class, gender, and exceptionality.

The So Called

by Pazcual Villaronga

I am mixture
similar to h2O
I am american pie
the black-eyed peas
with plenty of salsa

I am the rhythm and blues
the classical lines
the pro-cu-ta-ca-ca-mambo

I am a potpourri of values and
    attitudes
the fact that men don't cry
but in reality they do
and don't die

I am a mixture
of beautiful paints
that picture
psychedelic tones
african blood
spanish blood
and Indian blood

transported
by economical
social
or political fact

from an island of joy
under a damn
cynical
implemented
ploy

to a jungle of cement
metal
and glass

to become a confused entity
a confused being
of meatloaf
and oxtails
and arroz con pollo

of Beethoven
Isaac Hayes
and eddi palmieri

to struggle with my culture
their culture
and the loss of mine

goodbye three kinds
hello christmas
and its mad capitalistic
season

the cropping of my accent
the implementation of
another language

I am Puerto Rico
the u.s. of a.
and new york

spinning
trying to lose myself
in the sun
on the penthouse
in my place
in my slums
trying to become
what will constantly be denied

I am black
white
brown
uptown
downtown
all around
the damn town

I am here
I am there
I am everywhere
spread thin
so that my existence
my consistency
my reality

can be denied
mesmerized
until I boil down to nothing
at the bottom of the pot
"El Pegao"

which they don't know is the best
part of the meal
especially because I survive
to eat it

I am the music you can't exploit
because you don't
understand
comes from our corazones
speaks of our culture
our history
our minds

in a language you find
easier to destroy
becausee yours is better

I am caught in a flight
over a sea
of controversy

I am a piece of a puzzle
that doesn't fit
here or there

because both my vehicles of expression
are dulled and
downed
by my own
and my own

I am what has always been there
only with a different name
to fit the purpose
to play the game
for someone's fame
other than mine

I am the P.R.
the rican
the spic
he new click
the so called New-Yor-Rican

Pazcual Villarongu is a bilingual teacher in
the Lola Rodriguez School in Manhattan's
District 4, in New York City's "El Barrio."

Although this chapter emphasizes issues related to culturally and linguistically diverse students from African American, Hispanic, Asian, and Native American backgrounds, it is important to define diversity in a much broader way.

> [Diversity] encompasses not only those individuals whose ethnic heritage originates in another country, but also those among us who may have special educational and other needs . . . , those who may share significantly different lifestyles (rural and urban children, children who live in extreme poverty, drug dependents), those whose identity is critically influenced by gender, and those who are significantly influenced by variations in class and religion. (Cusher, McClelland, & Safford, 1992, p. 7)

In other words, as we think about diversity, we must remember that Appalachian, gay and lesbian, homeless, or Muslim students deserve the same respect, understanding, and acceptance from educators as other diverse groups do.

 ## INACCURATE ASSESSMENT AND REFERRAL

A second major reason for the disproportionate numbers of culturally diverse students in special education is bias in assessing and referring these students. Tests are widely used in special education. However, the testing methods used to identify students for special education services are an inexact science at best and at times little more than guesswork (Correa et al., 1995; Langdon, Novak, & Quintanar, 2000; Ortiz, 1997; Utley & Obiakor, 2001). The likelihood of obtaining valid, accurate, and unbiased assessment results is lower when the student in question is from a culturally different background. Figueroa (1989) calls the current practice of psychological testing of children from culturally and linguistically diverse groups "random chaos" because it is so fraught with problems.

The biggest challenge for special educators is to try to disentangle English-language skills and/or culturally linked behaviors from academic or learning skills. Barrera (1995) notes that there are three potential sources of learning problems in children who come from culturally and linguistically diverse backgrounds: (1) unrecognized cultural/linguistic diversity, (2) deficits stemming from chronic poverty or trauma, and (3) disabilities. Inappropriate referral to special education can occur if educators and school psychologists are unable to correctly separate the presence of unrecognized diversity or deficits from disability.

> Learning problems associated with unrecognized cultural or linguistic diversity are, in contrast to those stemming from disabilities, not reflective of "within the child" conditions. These problems are, rather, social and dynamic in nature and, thus, more dependent on external contexts than on internal conditions. They demonstrate intact learning abilities within their home setting(s). Problems typically arise only when these children are placed in a different context with significantly different expectations and norms (e.g., a preschool setting). It is, thus, not their abilities, but rather the dissonance between cultural and linguistic contexts that interferes with their performance. (Barrera, 1995, p. 57)

The second source of potential learning problems is associated with learning deficits stemming from chronic poverty and trauma. Learning deficits do not result from diversity of sociocultural beliefs, values, world views, and preferences. "Rather, they result from the constraints that chronic poverty or unaddressed trauma can place on a child's access to the experiences and knowledge deemed normative for all children by the cultural group(s) with which their families affiliate" (p. 58). Barrera (1995) contends that special education services are neither appropriate nor most efficient for learning difficulties that are not the result of inherent disabilities.

> If, for example, a child has experienced trauma that remains unaddressed, simply reducing task complexity will not be a sufficient response. Or if, on the other hand, the

Cultural and linguistic differences and assessment

 Council for Exceptional Children Content Standards for Beginning Teachers–Common Core: Issues in identification of individuals with exceptional learning needs, including those from culturally and linguistically diverse backgrounds (CC1K5). **PRAXIS** Special Education Core Principles: Content Knowledge: III. Delivery of Services to students with Disabilities, Assessment, How to select and conduct nondiscriminatory and appropriate assessments.

child has intact learning abilities and an age appropriate repertoire of skills, but cannot understand the language of instruction, it is equally inappropriate and wasteful of both financial and human resources to generate a complete interdisciplinary assessment and special education program instead of simply providing needed linguistic support. It is important, therefore, to understand the specific difficulties that may stem from unrecognized diversity or deficits. Once understood, pre-referral intervention can be directed toward eliminating their impact and assessing whether any difficulties remain. It is these difficulties, that remain after diversity and deficit have been addressed, that are the appropriate target for special education. (p. 64)

The current practices of high-stakes assessments may place children with disabilities who are from diverse backgrounds at further risk for discrimination or marginalization. Thurlow and Liu (2001) found that English-language learners with disabilities essentially are not currently included in state and district assessments. Some states are using alternative assessment approaches for children with disabilities, but to date, no accommodations have been provided for English-language learners.

 INEFFECTIVE CURRICULUM AND INSTRUCTION

A third reason that disproportionate numbers of culturally diverse students are placed in special education may be because educators do not provide effective academic instruction to students from diverse backgrounds. "Traditional schools require conformity, passivity, quietness, teacher-focused activities, and individualized, competitive, non-interactive participation of students" (Shade & New, 1993, p. 318). The idea that curriculum and instructional strategies that are effective for white, middle-class students will benefit all students has dominated American education (Winzer & Mazurek, 1998). However, since the context of a culturally diverse student's life is often different from a middle-class student's, "sameness of treatment does not always equate with equality of treatment" (p. 126).

If the student's cognitive functions, learning styles, and communication modes do not conform to the traditional educational patterns, the student is likely to lag behind expected learning benchmarks. Educators who do not adapt the curriculum for the diversity in schools today will most likely perpetuate the disproportionate referral of culturally diverse students into special education. If one believes that diverse cultures foster diverse learning styles, then providing a "one size fits all" instructional approach to education will most likely create a mismatch between the learners' style and the instructional style. For example, field-independent (analytical) students learn well through books, lectures, and worksheets. Field-dependent students (often members of underrepresented groups), on the other hand, learn best in context through hands-on, authentic tasks rather than out of context (Daniels, 2001; Gollnick & Chinn, 2002). The teacher's own instructional style (especially if she comes from the dominant white, middle-class culture) may be incompatible with the natural learning styles of students from diverse cultural backgrounds. For example, some culturally diverse students may not respond well to timed tests and may fail to complete an examination within the allotted time. This does not mean that students from cultural backgrounds cannot, or should not, be taught to perform academic tasks at faster rates.

Further accentuating the problems between the traditional curriculum and culturally diverse students are the textbooks selected by teachers for instruction. Many educators do not evaluate the validity of a textbook's content even when they are highly dependent on textbooks for instruction. Curriculum materials that do not reflect the images and voices of culturally diverse students may fail to engage such students in active classroom participation. Furthermore, teaching styles that clash with the unique characteristics of culturally diverse students will most likely result in referral to special education, tracking, or discrimination and bias against students.

Culturally influenced learning styles

Council for Exceptional Children Content Standards for Beginning Teachers–Common Core: Differing ways of learning of individuals with exceptional learning needs including those from culturally diverse backgrounds (CC3K5).

PRAXIS Special Education Core Principles: Content Knowledge: III. Delivery of Services to Students with Disabilities, Professional roles. Teacher as multidisciplinary team member.

Special Education Core Principles: Content Knowledge: I. Understanding Exceptionalities, Characteristics of students with disabilities including cultural and linguistic factors.

The ultimate goal of multicultural education is to meet the individual learning needs of each student so that all students can progress to their fullest capacity. This goal has not been reached in the past, partly because educators have been unable to effectively use the cultural backgrounds of students in providing [appropriate curriculum materials] and classroom instruction. (Gollnick & Chinn, 2002, p. 350)

Understanding the complex issues related to the disproportionate numbers of culturally diverse students in special education requires that educators understand the incongruity between a teacher's interactions with students and families from diverse cultures, the assessment and referral process in special education, and ineffective instructional and discipline practices (Craig, Hall, Haggart, & Perez-Selles, 2000; Ford, 2000; Townsend, 2000). To better meet the needs of students with disabilities from culturally diverse backgrounds, educators should address three areas. First, school staff must become culturally responsive to students and families. Second, school staff must implement appropriate assessment strategies for determining the educational needs of culturally diverse students. Third, educators should implement culturally responsive practices that support a multicultural approach to curriculum and instruction.

BECOMING A CULTURALLY PROFICIENT EDUCATOR

Given the challenges that face schools today, it is critical that educators become culturally responsive or culturally proficient. "As a culturally proficient instructor, you open the minds and hearts of your learners, affirming that differences are not deficits" (Robins, Lindsey, Lindsey, & Terrell, 2002, p. 149). Culturally proficient educators deal sensitively with different learners by using a variety of skills and strategies and modifying their methodology to match changing needs. Developing cultural proficiency in our nation's teachers requires quality teacher education, ongoing professional development, and a strong commitment to equity for all learners.

Robins et al. (2002) believe that teachers vary in their ability to understand the needs of culturally and linguistically diverse learners. They conceptualize cultural proficiency on a continuum of teacher awareness and actions across six phases.

1. *Cultural destructiveness:* the elimination of another cultural group or the suppression of the cultural practices. Teachers at this phase fail to include people of color and issues of racism or oppression in their classroom curricula.
2. *Cultural incapacity:* treatment of members of nondominant groups based on stereotypes and with the belief that the dominant group is inherently superior. Teachers at this phase of the continuum hold low expectations for culturally diverse students. They might believe that it is pointless to expect higher reading levels out of a group of students who come from "the projects."
3. *Cultural blindness:* failure to see or acknowledge that differences between groups often make a difference to the groups and their members. Teachers at this phase of the continuum might say, "I really want to be fair to all my students, so I treat them all alike."
4. *Cultural precompetence:* behavior or practices that seek to acknowledge cultural differences in healthy ways but that are not quite effective. Teachers at this phase of the continuum might understand the importance of recognizing children's cultural backgrounds and establish a thematic unit on foods and costumes of Spain, China, and Scotland.
5. *Cultural competence:* effective interactions with individuals and groups of people from different ethnic and social cultures; use of the essential elements as the standards for individual behavior and organizational practice. Teachers at this phase of the continuum create a classroom environment that reflects students' diverse backgrounds by using multicultural literature and instructional materials.

Continuum of cultural proficiency

 Content Standards for Beginning Teachers–Common Core: Culturally responsive factors that promote effective communication and collaboration with individuals with exceptional learning needs, families, school personnel, and community members (CC10K4).
PRAXIS Special Education Core Principles: Content Knowledge: III. Delivery of Services to Students with Disabilities, Professional roles, Reflecting on one's own teaching.

6. *Cultural proficiency:* practices that reflect knowing how to learn and teach about different groups; having the capacity to teach and learn about differences in ways that acknowledge and honor all people and the groups they represent. Teachers at this phase of the continuum realize that some of the Haitian students in their school are struggling with English and decide to take a community leisure and recreation course on speaking Haitian Creole. They include Haitian families and community members at their weekly storytelling time (adapted from Robins et al., 2002, p. 126).

The task of becoming a culturally proficient instructor is not easy. Before teachers and other staff members can implement culturally responsive assessment, curriculum, and instructional procedures, they must develop self-awareness and an appreciation of diversity.

TEACHER AWARENESS AND DEVELOPMENT

To understand and fully appreciate the diversity that exists among the students and families that special educators serve, we must first understand and appreciate our own cultures. All cultures have built-in biases, and cultural self-awareness is the bridge to learning about other cultures. "It is not possible to be truly sensitive to someone else's culture until one is sensitive to one's own and the impact that cultural customs, values, beliefs, and behaviors have on practice" (Lynch & Hanson, 1998, p. 39). (See Profiles & Perspectives, "A Cultural Journey," later in this chapter.)

Self-awareness is the first step on the journey toward becoming a culturally proficient teacher. Educators must also become aware of their own biases and prejudices: "Teachers are human beings who bring their cultural perspective, values, hopes, and dreams to the classroom. They also bring their prejudices, stereotypes, and misconceptions to the classroom. The teacher's values and perspective mediate and interact with the teacher and influence the way that messages are communicated and perceived by their students" (Banks, 1994b, p. 159).

Fortunately, multicultural education is becoming a required component in many teacher education programs, and educators are learning how to become more accepting and supportive of cultural differences (Artiles et al., 2000; Banks & Banks, 2001; Dilworth, 1998; Dinsmore, 2000; Hernandez, 2001; Montgomery, 2001; Nieto, 2000b; Voltz, 1998). As a measure of their beliefs about culture and its importance to teaching, for example, both practicing and prospective teachers can complete an instrument such as the Multicultural Self-Report Inventory (Slade & Conoley, 1989) (see Figure 3.1). Items with a zero in the far lefthand column have no positive or negative relevance and are included to lessen the probability of giving answers just because they are socially acceptable. Items with a minus are scored negatively. The lower the score, the more accepting and supportive the person's attitude about cultural differences. A low score indicates less multicultural bias; a high score suggests greater discomfort with the concept.

Once teachers are aware of their own ethnic attitudes, behaviors, and perceptions, they can begin an action program designed to change their behavior if necessary (Banks, 1994b) and gain knowledge about other cultures. Methods for gathering information about cultures include but are not limited to reading books, searching the Internet, studying ethnograms, and interviewing cultural informants (persons from a particular culture who are familiar with families' beliefs and patterns). Teachers can increase their understanding and

▲ Having students teach one another about their ethnic, linguistic, and historical backgrounds is a good way to increase multicultural understanding and appreciation by teachers and students.

Cultural self-awareness

Council for Exceptional Children Content Standards for Beginning Teachers—Common Core: Personal cultural biases and differences that affect one's teaching (CC9K1).
PRAXIS Special Education Core Principles: Content Knowledge: III. Delivery of Services to Students with Disabilities, Professional roles, Reflecting on one's own teaching.

A Cultural Journey

Culture is not just something that someone else has. All of us have cultural, ethnic, and linguistic heritages that influence our current beliefs, values, and behaviors. To learn more about your own heritage, take this simple cultural journey.

ORIGINS

- When you think about your roots, what country(ies) other than the U.S. do you identify as a place of origin for you or your family?
- Have you ever heard any stories about how your family or your ancestors came to the U.S.? Briefly, what was the story?
- Do you or someone else prepare any foods that are traditional for your country(ies) of origin? What are they?
- Does your family continue to celebrate any celebrations, ceremonies, rituals, or holidays that reflect your country(ies) of origin? What are they? How are they celebrated?
- Do you or anyone else in your family speak a language other than English because of your origin? If so, what language?
- Can you think of one piece of advice that has been handed down through your family that reflects the values held by your ancestors in the country(ies) of origin? What is it?

BELIEFS, BIASES, AND BEHAVIORS

- Have you ever heard anyone make a negative comment about people from your country(ies) of origin?
- As you were growing up, do you remember discovering that your family did anything differently from other families because of your culture, religion, or ethnicity that seemed unusual to you?

- Have you ever been with someone in a work situation who did something because of his or her culture, religion, or ethnicity that seemed unusual to you? What was it? Why did it seem unusual?
- Have you ever felt shocked, upset, or appalled by something that you saw when you were traveling in another part of the world? If so, what was it? How did it make you feel? Pick some descriptive words to explain your feelings. How did you react? In retrospect, how do you wish you would have reacted?
- Have you ever done anything that you think was culturally inappropriate when you have been in another country or with someone from a different culture? In other words, have you ever done something that you think might have been upsetting or embarrassing to another person? What was it? What did you do to try to improve the situation?

IMAGINE

- If you could be from another culture or ethnic group, what culture would it be? Why?
- What is one value from that culture or ethnic group that attracts you to it?
- Is there anything about that culture or ethnic group that concerns or frightens you? What is it?
- Name one concrete way in which you think your life would be different if you were from that culture or ethnic group.

Source: Reprinted from Lynch, E., & Hanson, M. (1998). *Developing cross-cultural competence* (2nd ed., pp. 87–89). Baltimore: Paul H. Brookes Publishing Co., Inc. Used by permission of the publisher and the authors.

appreciation of different ethnic and cultural groups by developing the following competencies:

- Knowledge of and sensitivity toward the history and culture of student language and ethnic groups
- Ability to work with an interpreter in assessment and instruction
- Knowledge of different cultural perceptions of disabling conditions
- Knowledge of the educational implications of social class and the process of acculturation
- Knowledge of tests and techniques used for evaluative purposes
- Knowledge of general instruction methods applicable to English-language learners with disabilities
- Knowledge of both special education and bilingual education legal issues
- Knowledge of how to integrate teaching techniques from both bilingual education and special education
- Knowledge of techniques for developing materials especially for English-language learners with disabilities
- Knowledge of methods for dealing effectively with parents and families (adapted from Gallegos & McCarty, 2000)

Understanding Verbal and Nonverbal Communication Styles Another important aspect of teacher awareness and cultural competence involves understanding the patterns of verbal and nonverbal communication of ethnic groups (Gollnick & Chinn, 2002). Although some white, middle-class teachers will probably not find it feasible to adopt the nonverbal behaviors of another culture, teacher-student and teacher-parent communication may be enhanced by some knowledge of the different significance attached to touch, interpersonal distance, silence, dress, and gestures.

Understanding Multicultural Terminology In preparing to work with culturally and linguistically diverse students and their families, school personnel must also have a common understanding of correct terminology for working with a diverse population. Many terms have been applied to members of culturally diverse populations. As we have learned elsewhere in this book, it is difficult to use labels effectively. Although labels can sometimes serve a useful purpose in identifying relevant factors, they are just as likely to convey misleading or inaccurate generalizations. This unfortunate effect is especially evident in several terms that have been used to refer to children from different cultural backgrounds.

In the United States, the term *minority* essentially represents an attempt to categorize by race, not by culture (Harry, 1992a; Nieto, 2000a). Furthermore, the term implies that the racial group being referred to constitutes a recognizable minority in society. Yet in many communities and regions of the country, "minorities" constitute the predominant population. An African American child in Detroit, a Hispanic child in Miami or Los Angeles, or a Navajo child on a reservation in Arizona could be considered part of a minority only in respect to the national population, a comparison that would have little relevance to the child's immediate environment. The *majority* of students now enrolled in the 25 largest public school systems in the United States are from ethnically diverse minority groups (Zawaiza, 1995). In addition to suggesting that the population of the group is small, the term *minority group* carries some negative connotations of being less than other groups with respect to power, status, and treatment (Gollnick & Chinn, 2002).

The term *culturally diverse* is preferred when referring to children whose backgrounds are different enough to require, at times, special methods of assessment, instruction, intervention, or counseling. This term implies no judgment of a culture's value and does not equate cultural diversity with disability. Furthermore, the names used to describe ethnic groups have also changed. *Asian American* has replaced Oriental; *African American* has replaced black; *Latino* in

FIGURE 3.1 Multicultural Self-Report Inventory

MULTICULTURAL SELF-REPORT INVENTORY

SA = Strongly Agree
MA = Moderately Agree
U = Undecided
MD = Moderately Disagree
SD = Strongly Disagree

		SA	MA	U	MD	SD
	1. I am interested in exploring cultures different from my own.	1	2	3	4	5
(−)	2. I have enough experience with cultures different from my own.	1	2	3	4	5
(0)	3. I seem to like some cultures and ethnic groups better than others.	1	2	3	4	5
(−)	4. Part of the role of a good teacher is to encourage children to adopt middle class values.	1	2	3	4	5
(−)	5. I feel that cultural differences in students do not affect students' behavior in school.	1	2	3	4	5
(−)	6. As students progress through school, they should adopt the mainstream culture.	1	2	3	4	5
	7. I am comfortable around people whose cultural background is different from mine.	1	2	3	4	5
	8. I can identify attitudes of my own that are peculiar to my culture.	1	2	3	4	5
	9. I believe I can recognize attitudes or behaviors in children that are a reflection of cultural or ethnic differences.	1	2	3	4	5

Source: From "Multicultural Experiences for Special Educators" by J. C. Slade & C. W. Conoley. *Teaching Exceptional Children, 22*(1), 1989, p. 62. © 1989 by the Council for Exceptional Children. Reprinted with permission.

some parts of the country has replaced *Hispanic;* and specific tribal names, rather than *Native American,* are preferred. It is important for all educators to respect and keep up with changes that represent increasing group identity and empowerment (Lynch & Hanson, 1998).

WORKING WITH CULTURALLY AND LINGUISTICALLY DIVERSE FAMILIES

Family involvement in the educational process is important for students' success in school. The positive influence of parental involvement on children's academic achievement and school adjustment should be of great concern to school staff. A strong correlation between parental involvement in school and the at-risk child's development of self-confidence, motivation, and sense of cohesiveness is evident in the literature (Harry, Kalyanpur, & Day, 1999; Hernandez, 2001; Hidalgo, 1997; Siu, Bright, Swap, & Epstein, 1995; Valdés, 1996). Furthermore, Rumberger, Ghatak, Polous, Ritter, and Dornbush (1990) reported that families of students who did not drop out and succeeded in school participated in their children's school decisions, demonstrated motivating and nonpunitive action concerning grades, and were involved to different degrees within the school environment. (Parent involvement is examined in detail in Chapter 4.)

Involving families who come from diverse backgrounds in school activities is often challenging. The demands and challenges faced by families who are less educated, poor, or iso-

FIGURE 3.1 *(continued)*

		SA	MA	U	MD	SD
	10. I feel I can take the point of view of a child from a different culture.	1	2	3	4	5
(−)	11. It makes me uncomfortable when I hear people talking in a language that I cannot understand.	1	2	3	4	5
(−)	12. Values and attitudes learned in minority cultures keep children from making progress in school.	1	2	3	4	5
(−)	13. Only people who are part of a culture can really understand and empathize with children from that culture.	1	2	3	4	5
(−)	14. I have had few cross-cultural experiences.	1	2	3	4	5
	15. Multicultural education is an important part of a school curriculum.	1	2	3	4	5
(0)	16. I am prejudiced in favor of some ethnic or cultural group or groups.	1	2	3	4	5
(−)	17. Some ethnic groups make less desirable citizens than others.	1	2	3	4	5
	18. Some ethnic groups are more reluctant to talk about family matters than other cultural groups.	1	2	3	4	5
	19. Children from differing ethnic groups are likely to differ in their attitudes toward teacher authority.	1	2	3	4	5
(−)	20. Personally, I have never identified any prejudice in myself.	1	2	3	4	5
(−)	21. I am prejudiced *against* some ethnic or cultural groups.	1	2	3	4	5
(−)	22. In the United States, given equal intelligence and physical ability, every individual has equal access to success.	1	2	3	4	5

Working with culturally diverse families

Council for Exceptional Children

Content Standards for Beginning Teachers–Common Core: Culturally responsive factors that promote effective communication and collaboration with individuals with exceptional learning needs, families, school personnel, and community members (CC10K4).

PRAXIS Special Education Core Principles: Content Knowledge: III. Delivery of Services to Students with Disabilites, Professional roles, Directing parents and guardians to groups and resources that can address student and family concerns in a culturally responsive way.

lated from the dominant American culture may prevent them from becoming actively involved in school partnerships. The literature on culturally diverse families supports the following six notions about these families (Cartledge, Kea, & Ida, 2000; Correa & Jones, 2000; Gollnick & Chinn, 2002; Harry, 1992b; Hernandez, 2001; Kalyanpur, Harry, & Day, 1999; Lian & Fontánez, 2001; Lynch & Hanson, 1998; Park, Turnbull, & Park, 2001; Thomas, Correa, & Morsink, 2000).

1. *Many families may be English-language learners, be less well educated, have low socioeconomic status, or be undocumented immigrants.* Thus, practitioners should provide materials in both the native and English language and preferably communicate with the family directly through home visits or by telephone. Some parents are not able to read their native language and may depend on older children who are English-dominant to translate materials for them.

2. *Practitioners must understand that, although the parents may not have finished school or are unable to read, they are "life educated" and know their child better than anyone else does.* In Spanish, the term *educado* (educated) does not mean "formal schooling" but means that a child is skilled in human relations, well mannered, respectful of adults, and well behaved.

3. *If families are undocumented immigrants, they are naturally fearful of interaction with anyone representing authority.* Our role as special educators is not to engage in the activ-

ities of the Office of Immigration and Naturalization Services. Our focus is on educating children, who by law are not a suspect class (Correa, Gollery, & Fradd, 1988). Building families' trust and cooperation, even if they are undocumented immigrants, is important.

4. *Families from culturally diverse backgrounds tend to be family-oriented.* Extended family members—*compadres* or *padrinos* (godparents) in the Hispanic culture—may play important roles in child rearing and family decisions. A child's disability or even a mild language problem may be an extremely personal subject for discussion with outsiders, and solutions for problems may lie within the family structure. It is important for educators to respect this informal kinship system of support and to understand that we may represent a much more formal and impersonal support service for these families. The close, insular aspect in a family is a strength that assists the family in functioning and coping with the stresses sometimes associated with raising a child with a disability (Bailey, Skinner, Correa, Arcia, et al., 1999a; Dunst, Trivette, & Deal, 1988).

5. *It is important to know that culturally diverse families may have different experiences with and views about disability, and some may hold idiosyncratic ideologies and practices about the cause and treatment of disability.* For example, in some Hispanic cultures, parents may believe that God sent the child with disabilities to them as a gift or blessing, while others may believe the child was sent as a test or a punishment for previous sins. In recent studies on Latino families, parents acknowledged transforming their lives since the birth of their child by becoming better parents (Bailey, Skinner, Correa, Arcia, et al., 1999; Bailey, Skinner, Correa, Blanes, et al., 1999). Most families were positive in describing the child with disabilities, and very few reported the presence of the child with disabilities as a negative sign or punishment from God for sins. The role of faith in God was extremely important for families coping with the child, more so than formal religious activities such as church attendance or Bible studies (Bailey, Skinner, Correa, Blanes, et al., 1999; Skinner, Correa, Skinner, & Bailey, 2001). Interestingly, among many Native American groups, it is not considered negative or tragic to have a child born with a disability. "It is assumed the child has the prenatal choice of how he wishes to be born and, if [disabled], is so by choice" (Stewart, 1977, p. 439).

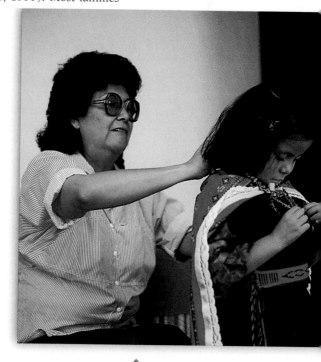

Although previous literature has reported the existence of folk beliefs and alternative treatments for disabilities in some cultural groups, more recent research finds that for Puerto Rican and Mexican families such beliefs are not prevalent (Bailey, Skinner, Correa, Blanes, et al., 1999; Skinner et al., 2001). Families did report knowing about *el mal ojo* (the evil eye) or *el susto* (a scare or fright experienced by the pregnant mother) as explanations given for disabilities but did not believe them to be true of their own children with disabilities. They reported that some family members (usually the elders) might believe that, to cure the child, the family must make *mandas* (offerings to God or a Catholic saint) or seek the help of a *curandero* (a local healer). However, almost all families interviewed used traditional western medicine to treat the child with disabilities.

▲ A culturally responsive educator strives to develop awareness of and sensitivity for the beliefs and values held by parents and family members from different cultural groups.

6. *The educational system—in particular, the special education system—may be extremely intimidating to the family.* Although this may be true for many white families as well, for the family from a non-English–language background or one that is less well educated

and poor, professionals' use of educational language and jargon, their nonverbal communication, and their possible insensitivity may be especially intimidating. Furthermore, parents with disabilities may also find themselves just as disenfranchised from their child's special education program, often not wanting to engage in any school-home interaction. Some families may even put the professional on a pedestal and, believing the professional is the expert, not question or comment on their own wishes for their child's education.

Ethnically diverse parents of children with disabilities have seldom used the modern idea of consumer involvement in service delivery (Lynch & Hanson, 1998; Thomas et al., 2000; Valdés, 1996). Parents or caregivers may not participate in a partnership with us because (for example) parent education groups do not address their needs or the ways in which we educate and propose solutions to child-rearing issues may be inappropriate or impractical for the culturally diverse family. Further, discrepancies between what teachers interpret as involvement and what parents view as involvement have been reported. In a study of transition planning beyond school, parents often reported a high level of involvement in their child's transition, while educators felt parents were not actively involved in the process (Geenen, Powers, & Lopez-Vasquez, 2001).

Antunez (2000) outlines several barriers that might exist in working with parents and families from culturally diverse backgrounds.

- *Language skills.*   Inability to understand the language of the school is a major deterrent to the parents who have not achieved full English proficiency. In these cases, interactions with the schools are difficult, and, therefore, practically nonexistent.
- *Home/school partnerships.*   In some cultures, such as many Hispanic ones, teaming with the school is not a tradition. Education has been historically perceived as the responsibility of the schools, and parent intervention is viewed as interference with what trained professionals are supposed to do.
- *Work interference.*   Work is a major reason stated by parents for noninvolvement in school activities. Conflicts between parent and school schedules may mean parents cannot attend school events, help their children with homework, or in other ways become active participants in their children's education.
- *Knowledge of the school system.*   A great number of low-income parents view schools as an incomprehensible and purposefully exclusionary system. Lack of trust is often the result of misunderstanding the perceived intentions of each party. Sending home communications in English only and scheduling meetings at times when parents cannot attend serve to reinforce parent apprehension. The lack of involvement that results from mistrust and apprehension is often misperceived by schools as a lack of concern for the children's education.
- *Self-confidence.*   Many parents of English language learner students believe that their participation does not help schools perform their jobs as educational institutions; as a result, they separate themselves from the process. Parents who feel uncomfortable in the school setting are less likely to be involved than those who have developed a sense of equal partnership are.
- *Past experiences.*   Many non-English speaking parents have had negative education experiences of their own, and these memories linger through adulthood. In some cases, these parents have fallen victim to racial and linguistic discrimination by the schools. Negative feelings toward home-school interaction are often reinforced when schools communicate with parents only to share bad news about their children. (pp. 4–5).

To overcome these barriers Christensen (1992) advised that teachers should understand a broad range of families' cultural aspects. She reported the following 12 areas that teachers thought were necessary for understanding families from culturally diverse backgrounds:

- General understanding of culture
- Child-rearing practices
- Family patterns
- Views of exceptionality
- Availability and use of community resources
- Linguistic differences
- Acknowledging own culture and biases
- Beliefs about professionals
- Nonverbal communication styles
- Views of medical practices
- Sex roles
- Religion

Additionally, Dennis and Giangreco (1996) advised that teachers should understand a broad range of families' cultural aspects. A good way to gain knowledge and understanding of family values and priorities for a child with disabilities is to conduct family interviews. Dennis and Giangreco suggest that professionals seek help from cultural interpreters before the interview and carefully ascertain the literacy and language status of family members. In conducting the interview, professionals should be prepared to adapt the time frame to meet the needs of the family and be flexible and responsive to the family's interaction style. (Specific strategies for communicating with parents and families are examined in Chapter 4.)

APPROPRIATE ASSESSMENT OF CULTURALLY DIVERSE STUDENTS

VARIED AND ALTERNATIVE METHODS OF ASSESSMENT

Alternative, nonstandardized methods of assessment seem to be more appropriate for some culturally and linguistically diverse students. Alternative assessments supplement the results of standardized testing with relevant and useful information regarding student performance that is valuable in making appropriate instructional decisions (Baca & Cervantes, 1998; Díaz-Rico & Weed, 2002; Ellwein & Graue, 2001; Fradd & McGee, 1994; Gollnick & Chinn, 2002; Gonzalez, Brusca-Vega, & Yawkey, 1997). Alternative assessment models integrate a variety of measures and data collection methods with multiple criteria, such as direct observations, portfolios, self-reports, inventories, and interviews. For example, Rueda (1997) identifies several types of portfolios that can be used as the basis for collecting and examining achievement as well as meeting the accountability demands usually achieved by more formal testing procedures (p. 13):

Alternative assessment methods

PRAXIS Special Education Core Principles: Content Knowledge: III. Delivery of Services to Students with Disabilities, Assessment, alternatives to norm-referenced testing including portfolio assessment.

1. *Student portfolios* inform the student and document self-reflection.
2. *Working portfolios* are designed for the teacher's daily use and as a primary tool for developing and modifying instruction on a short-term basis.
3. *Showcase portfolios* inform the parents and surrounding educational community.
4. *Cumulative portfolios* are designed for accountability and evaluative purposes.

Furthermore, alternative assessment allows for exploration of the numerous factors and confounding variables (e.g., environmental deprivation, poverty, health problems, language and cultural differences) that affect the performance of culturally diverse students and that could result in a misdiagnosis:

*Misinterpretation of cultural
differences*

 Content
Standards for
Beginning Teachers–Common
Core: Ways of behaving and
communicating among cultures
that can lead to misinterpreta-
tion and misunderstanding
(CC6K3).
PRAXIS Special Education
Core Principles: Content
Knowledge: I. Understanding
Exceptionalities, Characteristics
of students with disabilities
including cultural and linguistic
factors.

Nondiscriminatory assessment

 Content
Standards for
Beginning Teachers–Common
Core: Administer nonbiased
formal and informal assess-
ments (CC8S2).
PRAXIS Special Education
Core Principles: Content
Knowledge: III. Delivery of
Services to Students with
Disabilities, Assessment, How
to conduct non-discriminatory
and appropriate assessments.

Ishil-Jordan (1997) states that behavior is culture-related; and when there is "a great disparity between a cultural interpretation of a child's behavior and the school's inter- pretation of that behavior, there is also likely to be a disagreement on how that behav- ior is viewed and handled" (p. 30). Along with objective observation and recording of behavior, a child's social and cultural background should be taken into account when assessing performance. What is normal and acceptable in a child's culture may be re- garded as abnormal or unacceptable in school and may result in conflict, mislabeling, or punishment.

Gallimore, Boggs, and Jordan (1974) offer the example of several native Hawaiian chil- dren, who sought help from other children on tests and tasks and seemed to pay little at- tention to the teacher. This behavior was interpreted as cheating and inattentiveness. Closer observation of the children's home and community environments, however, revealed that the Hawaiian children were typically peer-oriented. It was normal for them to share in the responsibility of caring for each other, and they often worked cooperatively on tasks rather than following the directions of an adult. Some Asian American students internalize their reactions to environmental and intrapersonal stimuli by not expressing how they are feel- ing or demonstrating negative emotions. Educators might interpret this behavior negatively as docile and unhealthy.

Nondiscriminatory assessment requires that decisions be based on varied and accurate information. Building rapport with children before testing them; observing their behavior in school, home, and play settings; and consulting with their parents can help teachers and examiners become more aware of cultural differences and reduce the number of students inappropriately placed in special education programs. The National Research Council (2000) recommends the following for reducing bias in assessment and accommodating English-language learners in the process:

- Allowing extra time, extra breaks, or other flexibility in scheduling;
- Administering the test in small groups when applicable;
- Simplifying or translating the directions;
- Using dictionaries or glossaries;
- Reading questions aloud or allowing students to dictate answers or use a scribe;
- Assessing in students' native language or allowing students to respond in native language;
- Allowing students to choose either English or native-language versions of test ques- tions;
- Administering the test by a person familiar with test-takers' primary language and cul- ture. (pp. 25–26)

 ATTENTION TO LANGUAGE

As Brown (1982) notes, limited use of language is not synonymous with limited intellec- tual ability: "Some culturally different children are virtually silent in the testing situation, and the examiner may need to listen to the child in play with other children to hear a rep- resentative sample of the child's language" (p. 170). Standardized tests in English are not likely to give an accurate picture of a child's abilities if he comes from a non- English–speaking home. "In fact, if the student's primary language is Spanish, Navajo, or Tagalog, the only justification for testing in English is to determine the student's facility in this second language" (Lewis & Doorlag, 1999, p. 427).

IDEA specifies that assessment for the purpose of identifying and placing children with disabilities must be conducted in the child's native language. Unfortunately, when an examiner does wish to use the child's native language, few reliable tests are available in languages other than English; and translation or adaptation of tests into other lan- guages poses certain problems (Díaz-Rico & Weed, 2002; National Research Council,

2000). DeAvila (1976) points out the great variety in language within Hispanic populations and notes that when Mexican American children were given a test in Spanish that was developed with a population of Puerto Rican children, they performed even more poorly than on an admittedly unfair English test. To illustrate the confusion that may result from inappropriate translations, DeAvila observes that a Spanish-speaking child may use any one of several words to describe a kite, depending on the family's country of origin: *cometa, huila, volantin, papalote,* or *chiringa.* Thus, although translation of tests and other materials into a child's native language may be helpful in many instances, care must be taken to avoid an improper translation that may actually do a disservice to the linguistically different child.

It is not always easy to distinguish between children whose learning and communication problems result from disabilities and those who are solely in need of instruction in English. The high number of language-minority students in special education classes, however, implies a need for tests and referral procedures that will help untangle disability from cultural or linguistic factors.

Language-proficiency tests coupled with an analysis of real or authentic conversational factors provide the opportunity to assess communicative competence. Figure 3.2 provides a checklist for assessment of communicative competence skills in four areas: grammatical, sociolinguistic, discourse, and strategic.

 AVOIDING DISCRIMINATION AND BIAS

Bias and discrimination can also occur in the referral process, when children's records are reviewed and decisions are made about what types of services to provide. In the opinion of some educators, a child's race, family background, and economic circumstances—rather than actual performance and needs—unfairly influence the label she is likely to receive and the degree to which she will be removed from the regular classroom.

Ortiz and Garcia (1988) developed a prereferral process as a means of making sure that curriculum and instruction are responsive to the linguistic and cultural needs of Hispanic students who are experiencing difficulty in the regular classroom *before* they are referred for formal assessment to determine special education placement. Ortiz (1991a, 1991b, 1997) further developed and evaluated the efficacy of the model by addressing the issues of prereferral, assessment, and intervention of students from non-English–language backgrounds. The steps and features of the Assessment and Intervention Model for the Bilingual Exceptional Student (AIM for the BESt) model are listed in Figure 3.3. Although the model was presented in reference to Spanish-speaking students, it is a sound approach to improving the quality of regular education for any student who is experiencing academic difficulty. By systematically addressing the questions as illustrated in the model, both special and regular educators can work together to improve the student's performance in the dominant U.S. classroom before moving him to a more restrictive environment.

Prereferral assessment and intervention

 Content Standards for Beginning Teachers–Common Core: Screening, pre-referral, referral, and classification procedures (CC8K3).
PRAXIS Special Education Core Principles: Content Knowledge: III. Delivery of Services to Students with Disabilities, Assessment, How to conduct non-discriminatory and appropriate assessments.

 CULTURALLY RESPONSIVE CURRICULUM AND INSTRUCTION

Culturally and linguistically diverse students come to school with rich and complex cultural backgrounds that may be influenced by the family, home, and local community. Culturally responsive educators struggle with the balance between accepting and respecting the unique characteristics of students from diverse backgrounds and preparing them for postschool environments in the dominant American culture. In fact, Brower (1983) suggests that culturally and linguistically diverse students may need to be taught about expectations and values of the dominant culture so that they can become more forthright and assertive in educational and employment situations.

FIGURE 3.2 Checklist for skills that illustrate communicative competencies

Grammatical

- ☐ Uses noun/verb agreement
- ☐ Uses pronouns correctly
- ☐ Uses proper syntax
- ☐ Uses verb tenses appropriately
- ☐ Uses dialectical variations
- ☐ Uses complex sentence structure

Sociolinguistic

- ☐ Demonstrates various styles of social register in speech, for example, when interacting with peers or adults
- ☐ Uses diminutives
- ☐ Uses terms of endearment
- ☐ Uses courtesy, etiquette terms, and titles of respect
- ☐ Uses appropriate variations in intonation

Discourse

- ☐ Retells an event with attention to sequence
- ☐ Explains activity in present or near future
- ☐ Shares experiences spontaneously
- ☐ Tells stories with personal emphases
- ☐ Switches languages for elaboration
- ☐ Switches language to clarify statements
- ☐ Switches language to experiment with new language

Strategic

- ☐ Joins groups and acts as if understands activities
- ☐ Demonstrates expressive ability
- ☐ Counts on friends for help
- ☐ Switches language to resolve ambiguities
- ☐ Observes and imitates language patterns
- ☐ Asks for information
- ☐ Reads to gain information
- ☐ Uses a dictionary
- ☐ Asks for repetition
- ☐ Takes risks and guesses at language meaning
- ☐ Attempts difficult words and constructions

Source: From "From Tests to Talking in the Classroom: Assessing Communicative Competence" by G. Zamora-Durán & E. Reyes. In A. Artiles & G. Zamora-Durán (Eds.), *Reducing Disproportionate Representation of Culturally Diverse Students in Special and Gifted Education* (1997, p. 51). Reston, VA: Council for Exceptional Children. © 1997 by the Council for Exceptional Children. Reprinted with permission.

Culturally responsive instructional practices

Council for Exceptional Children

Content Standards for Beginning Teachers–Common Core: Develop and select instructional content, resources, and strategies that respond to cultural, linguistic, and gender differences (CC7S8). **PRAXIS** Special Education Core Principles: Content Knowledge: I. Understanding Exceptionalities, Characteristics of students with disabilities including cultural and linguistic factors.

A CULTURALLY RESPONSIVE PEDAGOGY

Culturally responsive instructional practices enhance students' opportunities to reach their fullest potential. The need for a culturally responsive pedagogy is even more critical when referring to culturally diverse students with disabilities (Ford, 2000; Gersten & Scott, 2000; Gollnick & Chinn, 2002). The place to begin to prepare students for the real world is the classroom. Teachers can begin to balance respect for one's culture and preparedness for postschool settings by accommodating and adapting their instructional programs and curricula and by adopting a culturally responsive pedagogy. Correa et al. (1995) describe the characteristics of a culturally responsive pedagogy:

- *Context-embedded instruction.* Context-embedded instruction facilitates the development of responsive classroom environments for all children by providing meaningful content that is culturally responsive and uses students' experiences as tools for

FIGURE 3.3 **The AIM for the BESt model for culturally diverse students**

The Assessment and Intervention Model for the Bilingual Exceptional Student (AIM for the BESt) describes a service delivery system designed to (1) improve the academic performance of limited English proficient (LEP) students in regular and special education programs, (2) reduce the inappropriate referral of LEP students to special education, and (3) ensure that assessment produces are nonbiased. AIM for the BESt consists of six major steps:

Step 1: **The regular classroom teacher uses instructional strategies known to be effective for language-minority students.**   The project staff trained general, bilingual, and special education teachers on using a reciprocal interaction approach to oral and written communication that emphasized higher-order thinking and problem solving. In particular, the teachers were introduced to the shared literature (Roser & Firth, 1983) and writing workshop approaches (Graves, 1983).

Step 2: **When a student experiences difficulty, the teacher attempts to resolve the difficulty and validates the problem.**   The project staff trained the teachers in diagnostic/prescriptive approaches that included sequencing instruction by (a) observing and analyzing student performance to design instructional programs, (b) implementing the program, (c) monitoring the progress, and (d) redesigning instruction as necessary.

Step 3: **If the problem is not resolved, the teacher requests assistance from a school-based, problem-solving team.**   The project staff, teachers, and support personnel formed cooperative teams to assist teachers with student-related problems by developing interventions and follow-up plans to resolve the difficulties.

Step 4: **If the problem is not resolved by the school-based, problem-solving team, a special education referral is initiated.**   The team's records describing the intervention plans from Step 3 accompanied the referral for special education services. The records were beneficial in assisting the referral team in designing appropriate evaluations and making recommendations.

Step 5: **Assessment personnel incorporate informal assessment procedures into the comprehensive individual assessment.**   Project staff trained personnel in using alternative assessment instruments and strategies to support standardized testing. In particular, curriculum-based assessment in both the native language and English were used with the students.

Step 6: **If the child had a disability, special educators used instructional strategies known to be effective for language-minority students.**   Special education teachers used the reciprocal interactive strategies for instruction. The holistic strategies described in Step 1 also included (a) encouraging expression of students' experiences, language background, and interests to foster success and pride and (b) peer collaboration and peer approval.

Source: Adapted from Ortiz, A. A., & Wilkinson, C. Y. (1991). *Assessment and Intervention Model for the Bilingual Exceptional Student* (AIM for the BESt). *Teacher Education and Special Education,* 14, 35–42. Used by permission.

building further knowledge (Baca & Cervantes, 1998; Bennett, 1999; Cummins, 1989; Scarcella, 1990). Delpit (1995) reported that African American teachers who successfully taught mathematics to African American students who speak a dialect confirmed that the use of cultural context and students' prior experience is essential in helping students learn. In one case, Delpit found that students connected with mathematics problems that related to a familiar locale and the amount of money needed to buy a leather jacket more than to a problem that involved unfamiliar locales and the number of milk cans needed by a farmer.

- *Content-rich curriculum.*   Researchers have shown that students who receive instruction within a content-rich curriculum develop a positive attitude about learning, a heightened self-concept, and pride in their culture (Duran, 1988; Scarcella, 1990). In addition, a content-rich curriculum should be integrated across broad fields of subject matter. For example, Gonzalez et al. (1997) describe the P.I.A.G.E.T. programs, where pre-K–12 teachers incorporate all subject matter around the thematic units of self, family, living things, and transportation. The orientation provides meaningful experiences from multiple perspectives focused on a unitary set of common learning (e.g., transportation). The classroom becomes a "mosaic of students' personalities along with their social, emotional and cultural overlays" (p. 87).

- *Equitable pedagogy.* An equitable pedagogy, which varies according to students' needs and teachers' styles, focuses on providing an appropriate educational experience for all children regardless of their disability or ethnolinguistic background. Instructional practices that facilitate and promote academic success among students within a pluralistic and democratic setting allow students to develop positive ethnic and national identifications (Villegas, 1988). In fact, Banks (1994a) advocates for a "transformative curriculum that challenges the basic assumptions and implicit values of the Eurocentric, male-dominated curriculum institutionalized in U.S. schools, colleges, and universities. It helps students to view concepts, events, and situations from diverse racial, ethnic, gender, and social-class perspectives. The transformative curriculum also helps students to construct their own interpretations of the past, present, and future" (p. 103). (See Teaching & Learning, "An Ethnic Feelings Book," later in this chapter.)

- *Interactive and experiential teaching.* Interactive and experiential teaching approaches have been reported by researchers to promote feelings of responsibility, self-pride, and belongingness in diverse learners (Obiakor, Algozzine, & Ford, 1993; Voltz & Damiano-Lantz, 1993). This hands-on approach empowers learners as they share the responsibility for the learning process while teachers provide guidance in the construction of knowledge.

- *Classroom materials and school environment.* Classroom materials and school environment should reflect students' diverse backgrounds (Freeman & Freeman, 1993). Materials selected on the basis of their content and their relevance and significance to the students' cultural and ethnic backgrounds generate a more meaningful and student-centered learning experience. (See Teaching & Learning, "Questions Teachers Should Ask about a New Culture or Ethnic Group," later in this chapter.)

Teachers are most effective when curriculum content and instructional methods are responsive to the cultural, ethnic, and linguistic diversity among their students.

BILINGUAL SPECIAL EDUCATION

It is especially challenging for students who are both linguistically different and disabled to succeed in school. Not only must they work to overcome the difficulties posed by their disability, but they also must do so in an environment in which instruction occurs in a foreign language and opportunities to use their native language are infrequent. English-language learners comprise about 7.3% of the population, and the vast majority spend most of their days in monolingual English classrooms (Nieto, 2000b).

For these children, a program of bilingual special education may be needed. Baca and Cervantes (1998) define **bilingual special education** as

the use of the home language and the home culture along with English in an individually designed program of special instruction for the student in an inclusive environment. Bilingual special education considers the child's language and culture as foundations upon which an appropriate education may be built. The primary purpose of bilingual special education is to help each individual student achieve a maximum potential for learning. (p. 21)

Some people object to bilingual special education on the basis that it is too much to ask special educators, who already face the difficult task of teaching basic skills to a child with a disability, to also teach in a second language. Baca and Cervantes (1998) reply that the opposite is true:

> The imparting of basic skills may be facilitated considerably if one understands that the child's culture and language are the foundations upon which an appropriate education may be built. . . . Building on children's existing knowledge base is fundamental to sound educational practice. In actuality, Anglo cultural skills and English are the new subject matters for the linguistically or culturally different child. (p. 21)

Most general bilingual education programs emphasize either a transitional or a maintenance approach. In a *transitional* program, the student's first language and culture are used only to the extent necessary to function in the school until English is mastered sufficiently for all instruction. Transitional programs are an assimilationist approach in which the limited English proficient (LEP) student is expected to learn to function in English as soon as possible (Gollnick & Chinn, 2002). The home language is used only to help the student make the transition to English. The native language is gradually phased out as the student learns to speak English.

The *maintenance* approach to bilingual education, however, helps the LEP student function in both the native language and English, encouraging the student to become bilingual and bicultural in the process. Cummins (1989) stresses the importance of encouraging children to develop their first language (L1) skills. He cites several studies suggesting that a major predictor of academic success for linguistically different students is the extent to which their native language and culture are incorporated into the school program. Cummins states that even where programs of bilingual education are not offered, school staff can encourage and promote children's skills and pride in their first language. Figure 3.4 lists several specific strategies through which school staff can create a climate for promoting children's use of their first language.

Although most bilingual educators support the maintenance approach to bilingual education, the majority of programs in existence are transitional (Gollnick & Chinn, 2002). In fact, all state and federal laws providing support for bilingual education favor only transitional models. However, as Baca and Cervantes (1998) point out, the laws do not prevent school districts from offering maintenance programs if their staff members desire to do so.

A *restoration* model of bilingual education seeks to restore the students' ancestral language and cultural heritage that have been lost or diminished through cultural assimilation. *Enrichment* programs of bilingual education are designed to teach a new language and cultural ways to a group of monolingual students; for example, some school districts now offer language immersion schools in which all or most instruction is provided in a second language. (Spanish and French are the most common.)

Maintenance and promotion of first language skills

Council for Exceptional Children — Content Standards for Beginning Teachers–Common Core: Ways to create learning environments that allow individual to retain and appreciate their own and each others' respective language and cultural heritage (CC5K8).

Some bilingual education programs help students function in both their native language and English, encouraging the child to become bilingual and bicultural.

Educators disagree about the most effective methods for teaching bilingual students. Former U.S. secretary of education William Bennett (1986) wrote that the choice of specific methods to teach bilingual children should be a local decision, but he argued strongly that "all American children need to learn to speak, read, and write English as soon as possible" (p. 62). Some professionals and legislators have called for the designation of English as the exclusive official language of the United States. Adopting such a

FIGURE 3.4 Strategies for encouraging children to develop proficiency in their first language (L1)

- Reflect the various cultural groups in the school district by providing signs in the main office and elsewhere that welcome people in the different languages of the community.
- Encourage students to use their L1 around the school.
- Provide opportunities for students from the same ethnic group to communicate with one another in their L1.
- Recruit people who can tutor students in their L1.
- Provide books written in the various languages in the classroom and in the school library.
- Incorporate greetings and information in the various languages in newsletters and other school communications.
- Provide bilingual and multilingual signs.
- Display pictures and objects of the various cultures in the school.
- Create study units that incorporate the students' L1.
- Encourage students to write contributions in their L1 for school newspapers and magazines.
- Provide opportunities for students to study their L1 in elective subjects and in extracurricular clubs.
- Encourage parents to help in the classroom, library, playground, and in clubs.
- Invite second-language learners to use their L1 during assemblies and other official school functions.
- Invite people from ethnic minority communities to act as resource people and to speak to students in both formal and informal settings.

Source: From New Zealand Department of Education. (1988). *New Voices: Second Language Learning and Teaching: A Handbook for Primary Teachers.*, Wellington: Author; cited in "A Theoretical Framework for Bilingual Special Education" by J. Cummins. *Exceptional Children, 56,* 1989, pp. 113–114. © 1989 by the Council for Exceptional Children. Reprinted with permission.

policy, however, would probably discourage schools from offering instruction in students' native languages.

Conversely, the English Plus group advocates for linguistic pluralism and encourages educational programs to offer opportunities to learn a second language and develop cultural sensitivity (National Council for Languages and International Studies, 1992). Banks (1994b) observes that the nation's language policies and practices are at a crossroads and exemplify the second-language ambivalence held by people in the United States.

Research in bilingual education has not provided clear guidelines for methodology. There is general agreement, however, that children acquire English most effectively through interactions with teachers, parents, and peers (Gersten & Baker, 2000). A child who engages in and talks about interesting experiences will be more likely to develop good English skills than will a child whose exposure to English is limited to classroom instruction and teacher correction of errors. Efforts should be made to give bilingual exceptional children a variety of opportunities to explore the world through language.

THINKING ABOUT YOUR OWN PRACTICE

How can educators prevent the inappropriate referral and placement of culturally diverse students in special education while providing special education to all students who need services? The answer is not simple. Daugherty (2001) outlines six promising practices to reduce disproportional representation in special education:

- *Special education reform.*   Reform efforts should encourage a greater emphasis on inclusive education, noncategorical service models, and collaborative problem-solving approaches.
- *Prereferral intervention.*   Prereferral intervention programs are effective in reducing special education referrals.
- *Training.*   Training through ongoing professional development will help make school personnel aware of their attitudes, values, and perspectives toward diversity and provide them with knowledge and skills about culturally responsive instructional strategies.
- *Recruit and retain.*   It is essential to recruit school personnel who reflect the diversity of the school environment as well as personnel who are qualified and enthusiastic about working with diverse students.
- *Family involvement.*   Parent-family input should be solicited and incorporated into all aspects of the child's school experience. Culturally responsive interactions with families is critical, and information should be provided in the families' native language.
- *Alternative assessment strategies.*   Innovative assessment approaches should be linked to prevention and intervention, not solely to eligibility for services.

Many of the promising practices begin with culturally responsive curriculum and instructional practices in the general education classroom that enable all students to achieve at their highest potential. And achievement (i.e., learning meaningful academic and social skills) should be the focus of every classroom activity. Focusing on achievement helps us recognize another fundamental form of diversity in the classroom:

> While gender, social class, race, ethnicity, and language difference increasingly characterize U.S. classrooms and influence equitable access to the benefits of educational programs, every classroom can also be characterized by students' *skill diversity*. Some children learn quickly and easily apply what they learn to new situations. Other children must be given repeated practice to master a simple task and then may have difficulty successfully completing the same task the next day. Some children are popular and have many friends. Others are ostracized because they have not learned how to be friendly. (Heward & Cavanaugh, 2001, p. 295)

For the most part, good systematic teaching is good systematic teaching. But when a student with disabilities has the additional challenge of learning in a new or different culture or language, it is even more important for her teacher to plan individualized, culturally responsive activities; convey expectations clearly; observe and record behavior precisely; and provide specific, immediate reinforcement and feedback in response to performance. In a study of effective teaching practices for English-language learners with and without disabilities, Gersten and Baker (2000) found that "effective instruction for English-language learners is more than just 'good teaching.' It is teaching that is tempered, tuned, and otherwise adjusted, to the correct 'path' at which English-language learners will best 'hear' the content (i.e., find it most meaningful)" (p. 461). This special modulation, coupled with a helpful and culturally sensitive attitude, will increase the culturally different child's motivation and achievement in school.

An Ethnic Feelings Book

by B. A. Ford and C. Jones

The self-contained classroom for students with developmental disabilities consisted of four boys and eight girls from 9 to 12 years old. All of the children were African Americans. Their teacher, Charles Jones, was concerned about his students' self-perceptions and levels of self-esteem. Their informal verbal discussions about themselves, their aspirations, and their interpersonal interactions with each other were often negative. When frustrated academically or socially, the students frequently engaged in ethnic name calling, which was often associated with skin color and their African heritage (e.g., "You're black"; "I'm not black"; "You're like those dirty Africans"; "My ancestors don't come from Africa!"). Self-deprecating statements, such as "I'm crazy," were also heard. When asked, "What do you want to do for a living when you're an adult?" the children's responses typically involved sports, working in a fast-food restaurant, and motherhood, suggesting a limited view of future possibilities. Collectively, the students did not feel good about themselves, nor did they appear comfortable with their ethnicity. Difficulty in performing academic tasks seemed to reinforce their feelings of inadequacy in general and their negative perceptions of their ethnicity in particular.

Working with Bridgie Alexis Ford, a faculty member in special education at the University of Akron, Mr. Jones developed and implemented a cultural awareness project for his students. The project was designed to help the students learn factual information about the historic experiences and contributions of African Americans. Jones and Ford believed that as a result of learning about their ancestors' experiences and examining their own feelings about those experiences, the students would develop positive feelings about their ethnic heritage.

The cultural awareness unit took 30 to 45 minutes each day for 10 weeks and revolved around the creation of an

The most effective teachers are, by definition, responsive to change (or lack of change) in an individual student's performance. Therefore, it can also be argued that the effective teacher needs as many different ways of teaching as there are students in the classroom—regardless of cultural backgrounds. This argument is basically true. But it pushes us to question how cultural and language differences affect a child's responsiveness to instruction and hence whether those effects warrant different approaches to teaching. So although the basic methods of systematic instruction remain the same, teachers who will be most effective in helping children with disabilities from culturally diverse backgrounds to achieve will be those who are sensitive to and respectful of their students' heritage and values. A teacher

ethnic feelings book. The feelings book included both factual information about African Americans and the students' interpretations of the feelings of their ancestors during various periods. The unit began with the positive aspects of African life before the slave-trade era, discussed slavery and segregation, identified actions by African Americans to create freedom and equal opportunity, and focused on the students' positive characteristics and capabilities. After covering each part of the unit, the students created another section of their feelings book. The emphasis throughout the unit was on highlighting positive aspects and contributions and dispelling negative stereotypes.

Historical information and personal accounts were presented via low-vocabulary, high-interest, well-illustrated books and filmstrips, recordings, and West African artifacts. African American leaders from the local community also visited the classroom and discussed their accomplishments and feelings with the students. These were some of the instructional activities that were part of the unit:

- *Brainstorming.* This helped the teachers acquire background information about what the students already knew about their African ancestors.
- *Adoption of a tribe.* Each student adopted one of the tribes portrayed in the books or filmstrips and prepared a report about it. The class selected one of the reports, edited it, and included it in the feelings book.
- *Discussions about negative terminology and stereotypes assigned to slaves.* Ethnic name calling was also discussed.

- *Segregation simulation.* At the beginning of one school day, half the class tied blue strings around their waists to designate themselves as segregated students (SS). Throughout the rest of that day, these students were treated in a discriminatory manner: they did not get to use recreational equipment during recess, they could not use the rest rooms at the times the non-SS students were using them, and they received no verbal attention or tangible reinforcement during normal class routines. The next day, the students switched roles so that everyone experienced the feelings of segregation.
- *Identification of positive attributes.* Positive characteristics of relatives and community leaders whom the students admired were discussed. The students submitted typed paragraphs describing their talents and interests and indicating the types of jobs they believed they could pursue.

The students exhibited a great deal of enthusiasm and cooperative behavior throughout the project. Name calling decreased; and when it did occur, the students began to reprimand one another.

Multicultural activities are often restricted to a special day or week during the school year. For students with developmental disabilities, Ford and Jones believe that an ongoing, systematic approach to cultural awareness is imperative.

Source: Adapted from Ford, B. A., & Jones, C. (1990). An ethnic feelings book: Created by students with developmental handicaps. *Teaching Exceptional Children, 22*(4), 36–39. © 1990 by the Council for Exceptional Children. Used by permission.

does not have to share his students' culture and native language to serve them effectively, but he will likely be quite ineffective in helping his students achieve in the classroom if he ignores those differences.

The teacher of culturally diverse children with disabilities should adopt a flexible teaching style, establish a positive climate for learning, and use a variety of approaches to meet individual student needs. With a caring attitude, careful assessment and observation of behavior, and the use of appropriate materials and community resources, the teacher can do a great deal to help culturally and linguistically diverse children with disabilities and their families experience success in school.

 For more information on cultural diversity in special education, go to the Web Links module in Chapter 3 of the Companion Website at **www.prenhall.com/heward**

Questions Teachers Should Ask about a New Culture or Ethnic Group

1. *What is the group's history?* While you will not become a scholar on the history of a given group, you can become well informed by reading some general books and articles. It is important to be able to recognize names, places, and events that are important to the group in question. It is also important to understand how historical events influenced the ways in which members of this group see things now.

2. *What are the important cultural values of the group?* It is critical to understand the important values of a group. Does the group value family issues over individual concerns? How do members of the group view themselves and others?

3. *Who are outstanding individuals who claim membership in this group?* There will be artists, writers, inventors, historical figures, athletes, and others who are members of the group and who have standing in the local, national, and international communities. Knowing who these people are is helpful to teachers, making it easier to understand who children are talking about and who can act as positive role models. Furthermore, teachers can help the other children in the class appreciate the leaders of different cultural communities through introducing and discussing these cultural personalities.

4. *What are the group's major religions and beliefs?* The answers provide information on values and events in children's lives and are important in explaining to other children what their classmates

are doing and how they see things.

5. *What are the current political concerns?* Knowing about these issues means knowing about what is important in the children's home community. Sometimes these concerns will affect the school directly, sometimes they will not; but in all cases, they are issues the children will hear about in the neighborhood and at home.

6. *What are the group's political, religious, and social celebration days?* These are events that are important to the community and, as such, are days children will discuss at school. Good teachers will make use of this information in understanding their students and in planning curriculum.

7. *What are the educational implications of the answers to the preceding questions?* Very often, the answers are important because they affect individual students, and because they have a bearing on the entire class. It is important to know when students will miss school for religious holidays that are not part of the Christian calendar, just as it is important to discuss the political issues facing a specific group with all the students in the class. Because everyone should have an appreciation of the issues facing students of color, integrating these issues into the curriculum is a good instructional strategy.

Source: From Grant, C., & Gomez, M. L. (2001). *Campus and classroom: Making schooling multicultural* (2nd ed.), (pp. 131–132). Upper Saddle River, NJ: Merrill/Prentice Hall. © 2001 by Merrill/Prentice Hall. Reprinted with permission.

SUMMARY

WHY ARE THERE DISPROPORTIONATE PLACEMENTS OF CULTURALLY DIVERSE STUDENTS IN SPECIAL EDUCATION?

- Although cultural diversity is a strength of our society, many students with disabilities still experience discrimination because of cultural, social class, or other differences from the majority. Educators must avoid stereotypes based on race or culture and become culturally responsive to differences in students from diverse backgrounds.
- Students who are members of culturally diverse groups are typically underrepresented in gifted programs and overrepresented in special education.
- Three factors may account for the disproportionate placement of students in special education: (1) incongruity in interactions between teachers and culturally diverse students and families, (2) inaccuracy of the assessment and referral process for culturally diverse students in special education, and (3) ineffective curriculum and instructional practices implemented for culturally diverse students.

BECOMING A CULTURALLY PROFICIENT EDUCATOR

- It is necessary for educators to become culturally self-aware before becoming responsive to students and families from diverse backgrounds.
- Teacher education programs should include curriculum and field-based experiences related to teaching culturally diverse students.
- Understanding family values and beliefs about education, disabilities, and the school involvement of culturally diverse students informs teachers about their diverse students.

APPROPRIATE ASSESSMENT OF CULTURALLY DIVERSE STUDENTS

- Assessment of students for placement in special education should be fair; referral should be based on each child's needs rather than on background.
- Language plays a major role in the assessment of a student's educational and emotional needs.

CULTURALLY RESPONSIVE CURRICULUM AND INSTRUCTION

- Multicultural approaches to curriculum include an equitable pedagogy that matches the student's learning style and the teacher's teaching styles and focuses on providing an appropriate educational experience for all children regardless of their disability or ethnolinguistic background.
- Cooperative learning can be an effective strategy for students from diverse backgrounds.
- Bilingual special education uses the child's home language (L1) and home culture along with English in an individually designed education program.
- Most bilingual special education programs take either a transitional or a maintenance approach.

THINKING ABOUT YOUR OWN PRACTICE

- Skill diversity is a fundamental form of diversity in the classroom.
- Regardless of their cultural background, all children benefit from good, systematic instruction.
- The teacher must be sensitive to the effect of cultural and language differences on a child's responsiveness to instruction.

To check your comprehension of Chapter content, go to the Guided Rrview and Quiz modules in Chapter 3 of the Companion Website at **www.prenhall. com/heward**

Chapter 4
Parents and Families

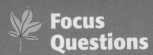

- What can a teacher learn from the parents and families of children with disabilities?

- How does a child with disabilities affect the family system and roles of parents?

- How can a teacher who is not the parent of a child with a disability communicate effectively and meaningfully with parents of exceptional children?

- How might the nature or severity of a child's disability change the objectives of family involvement?

- How much parent and family involvement is enough?

Denise Smith Stappenbeck
Miles Exploratory Learning Center
Tucson Unified School District, Tucson, Arizona

Education • Teaching Credentials • Experience
- B.A. in Deafness, American Sign Language, and the American Deaf Community, University of Rochester, 1995
- M.A. in Special Education, Deaf and Hard of Hearing, University of Arizona, 1997
- Arizona, General Education, K–8; Arizona, Hearing Handicapped, K–12; California, Communication Handicapped, K–12
- 5 years of teaching students with hearing impairments

Current Teaching Position and Students   Miles is a K–8 public school. In grades six through eight, there are approximately 90 students, 15 of whom are deaf/hard of hearing (DHH). Our DHH students are fully integrated into regular classes in what we call a co-enrollment environment. Most classes are team-taught by a special educator and a regular educator. This creates a student-teacher ratio of about 15 to 1 and enhances the curriculum for all students. All classes are multi-age (6–8); and the majority of Miles students attend our middle school for the full 3 years, which allows teachers to build strong relationships with students.

Communicating with My Students and Their Families   The cultural, linguistic, and economic backgrounds of my students vary tremendously. One lives on the Tohono O'odham reservation; another lives on a farm in Marana. Many come from Spanish-speaking families, but some are affluent Anglo-Saxon students. Although most families don't use sign language, some do to a small extent. One family does not speak any English and does not sign in Spanish. However, I am fortunate to have a few actively involved ASL-using parents. There is no single method of communication that works for all families, so we employ a variety of strategies.

In past years we used a three-way journal to facilitate communication between parents, students, and teachers. Each teacher in the middle school was assigned a group of students and parents to correspond with. Students were given time in school to write to either parents or teachers. But I had one student, Jared, who rode the bus an hour to and from school. He wrote to me in his journal regularly on those trips, not only about school and personal issues but sometimes just about "regular stuff" like the Yankees versus the Mets. To his parents he would write about his day or how he felt about a family topic. Jared was profoundly deaf, and his parents did not sign, so this communication opened up a forum for them that had not existed before.

This year, Miles has an e-mail distribution list for parents and families. In addition to the paper copy of school activities that students take home, parents

receive notices and reminders via e-mail. Our school website offers parents additional information. My students developed the website and update it regularly.

Although the website is effective for a majority of families, not every family has access to a computer. Therefore, all students have an assignment/communication book. Teachers and parents are expected to check the assignment books at least once a week, but notes can be written in at any time. In addition, we use midquarter reports, IEP updates, report cards, and phone calls to keep communication open.

To visit the website constructed and operated by Ms. Stappenbeck's students, go to the companion website and click on Teacher Feature module on the Companion Website at **www.prenhall.com/heward**

Working with Families   Over the years I have established several strong relationships with parents and families. Some I consider true friends. I met Jenny while working with her son Brian, first as a student teacher when he was a third grader and then for the last three years of middle school. She has asked me for advice and support on issues that are critical to Brian's well-being. It's crucial to establish trust and a positive rapport with parents. As an educator, you have the ability to influence the minds of those you teach; and parents need to feel secure about your values and abilities. I will go with Jenny and Brian to visit several high schools over the next few months, confident that he is prepared, proud of his accomplishments, and sad that my chapter with him is ending. But when my perspective counts for something in the eyes of a parent, that is a compliment.

On the other end of the spectrum, I have had to chase parents in parking lots and stand in front of their cars to get their attention. I have driven to houses to pick up parents and children for meetings. Working with the children of uninvolved parents can be a challenge. For example, Gwen recently came to us from another state with little to no language and a first-grade reading level. Like many other deaf students, she watches TV and movies with no sound; and guess what kind of reality she walks away with? I worked with Gwen on a family life curriculum with a focus on human sexuality. Getting her to understand that kissing does not equal pregnancy was my first success. My second success was to teach her that males and females have different anatomies. Nevertheless, I could not convince Gwen's parents that they needed to communicate with their middle school daughter about issues and relationships between boys and girls.

Parents have the power, if only more would use it! I treasure the families who can sign, who are inquisitive and participate at IEP meetings, the ones who question me and the system. The discouraging moments of my job involve trying to work with parents who would rather leave the parenting to me. I try to get them to look beyond the disability. I tell them their child can do everything except hear, and accepting who that child is will make all the difference in the world.

If I Could Change One Thing about Special Education   I honestly can't think of one thing that I would like to change about my job except to have more than 24 hours in a day. I'm still new enough at this to feel invincible. Ask me this question again in a few years, but I'm hoping my answer won't change.

A Memorable Anecdote   Andrea is a former student who is now a junior in high school. She was an eighth grader my first year at Miles; and although I was her teacher for only 1 year, we established a relationship that has developed into a lasting friendship. Andrea was one of the students I kept a three-way communication journal with that year. As the year progressed, our journaling developed into a two-way correspondence that discussed school, home, the future, fears, beliefs, literature, personal reflections, and just the whims of the week. I spent at least 1 hour every weekend just writing to her, although she must have spent countless hours during the week writing to me. By the end of the year, we had worked our way through five spiral notebooks. Over the years, Andrea and her family invited me to their house, included me in family events such as Andrea's high school performances, and were active in planning my wedding.

When Andrea was in ninth grade, she wrote a paper for an English class titled "My Hero." It was about my role in her life and the impact I have made on her. The paper is framed and hanging on the wall in my house. I look at it for support in times of success and discouragement. It is one of my most prized possessions because it encompasses everything I've strived to be as a teacher.

The family is the most powerful and pervasive influence in a young child's life. Long before a professional with the job title "teacher" arrives, parents and family members help the child learn hundreds of skills. A parent is a child's first teacher, the person who gives encouragement, prompts, praise, and feedback. With rare exceptions, no one ever knows or cares about a child as much as a parent does. Yet only recently have special educators begun to understand these fundamental truths.

For years, many educators viewed parents as either troublesome (if they asked too many questions or, worse, offered suggestions about their child's education) or uncaring (if they did not jump to attention whenever the professional determined the parent needed something—usually advice from the professional). Parents, too, have often seen professionals as adversaries. But today, parent involvement and family support are understood as essential elements of special education. Special educators have given up the old notions that parents should not be too involved in their children's educational programs or that they should not try to teach their children for fear of doing something wrong. Educators now realize that parents and families are powerful and necessary allies.

 To better understand what will be covered in this chapter, go to the Essecial Concepts and Chapter-at-a-Glance Modules in Chapter 4 of the Companion Website at **www.prenhall.com/heward**

SUPPORT FOR PARENT AND FAMILY INVOLVEMENT

A number of forces have combined to focus attention on the importance of a strong parent-teacher partnership based on mutual respect and participation. Although many factors have contributed to the increased emphasis on collaboration between parents and teachers in the education of exceptional children, three issues are clear: (1) parents want to be involved, (2) research and practice have shown that educational effectiveness is enhanced when parents and families are involved, and (3) the law requires collaboration between schools and families.

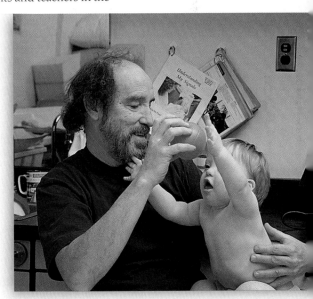

▲ A parent is a child's first teacher.

PARENTS ADVOCATE FOR CHANGE

For decades, parents of exceptional children have advocated for equal access to educational opportunities for their children, and they have done so with impressive effectiveness. As we learned in Chapters 1 and 2, parents played the primary role in bringing about litigation and legislation establishing the right to a free and appropriate public education for all children with disabilities. Not surprisingly, parents themselves have been most responsible for their greater involvement in planning and evaluating the special education services their children receive.

The first parent group organized for children with disabilities was the National Society for Crippled Children, formed in 1921. The United Cerebral Palsy Association, organized in 1948, and the National Association for Retarded Citizens (now called The Arc), organized in 1950, are two national parent organizations largely responsible for making the public aware of the special needs of children with disabilities. The Learning Disabilities Association of America (LDA), formed in 1963, also organized by and consisting mostly of parents, has been instrumental in bringing about educational reform. Parent members of The Association for Persons with Severe Handicaps (TASH), founded in 1975, have been forceful and effective advocates for family-focused educational services and the inclusion of students with severe and multiple disabilities in neighborhood schools and general education classrooms. Many parent organizations continue today to advocate for effective education, community acceptance, needed services, and rights of individuals with disabilities. For example, Mothers From Hell 2 is a national, grass-roots parent group that offers support and empowerment for families of individuals with special needs.

Families have the greatest vested interest in their children and are usually the most knowledgeable about their needs. The developers of a highly regarded program for planning and implementing inclusive educational programs for students with disabilities agree. They present four powerful arguments for viewing active family involvement as the cornerstone of relevant and longitudinal educational planning:

Family involvement as cornerstone for planning

 Council for Exceptional Children **Content Standards for Beginning Teachers–Common Core:** Family systems and the role of families in supporting development (CC2K4).

- *Families know certain aspects of their children better than anyone else does.* As educators, we must remind ourselves that we spend only about half the days of the year with our students, seeing them less than a third of each of those days. Nonschool time may provide key information that has educational implications, such as the nature of a student's interests, motivations, habits, fears, routines, pressures, needs, and health. By listening to families, educators can gain a more complete understanding of the students' lives outside school.
- *Families have the greatest vested interest in seeing their children learn.* In our professional eagerness to help children learn, we sometimes convey the message to parents that teachers care more about children than parents do. Of course, this is rarely the case.
- *The family is likely to be the only group of adults involved with a child's educational program throughout her entire school career.* Over the course of a school career, a student with special educational needs will encounter so many professionals that it will be difficult for the family to remember all of their names. Some of these professionals will work with the child for a number of years, others for a year or less. Eventually, even the most caring and competent among them will depart because they are professionals who are paid to be part of the student's life. Professionals are encouraged to build upon an ever-evolving, family-centered vision for the child rather than reinventing a student's educational program each year as team membership changes.
- *Families must live with the outcomes of decisions made by education teams all day, every day.* People rarely appreciate having someone else make decisions that will affect their lives without being included in the decision making. As professionals making decisions, we must constantly remind ourselves that these decisions are likely to affect other people besides the child and have an effect outside of school. (Giangreco, Cloninger, & Iverson, 1998, pp. 19–22)

EDUCATORS STRIVE FOR GREATER EFFECTIVENESS AND SIGNIFICANCE

To meet the special needs of children with disabilities, educators must expand the traditional role of the classroom teacher. This expanded role demands that we view teaching as more than instructing academic skills in the classroom. Today's special educator attaches high priority to designing and implementing instructional programs that enable students with disabilities to use and maintain academic, language, social, self-help, recreation, and other skills in school, at home, and in the community. As part of their home and community life, children may participate in some 150 different kinds of social and physical settings (Dunst, 2001). The large number of nonschool settings in which children live, play, and learn illustrates two important points. First, the many different settings and situations illustrate the extent of the challenge teachers face in helping children use newly learned skills throughout their daily lives. Second, the many different settings and social situations children experience in home and community provide extended opportunities for learning and practicing important skills. It is clear that to be maximally effective, teachers must look beyond the classroom for assistance and support, and parents and families are natural and necessary allies.

Extensive evidence shows that the effectiveness of educational programs for children with disabilities is increased when parents and families are actively involved (e.g., Cronin, Slade, Bechtel, & Anderson, 1992; Guralnick, 1997; Hardin & Littlejohn, 1995; Keith et al., 1998). At the very least, teachers and students benefit when parents provide information about their children's use of specific skills outside the classroom. But parents can do much more than just report on behavior change. They can provide extra skill practice and teach their children new skills in home and community. When parents are involved in identifying what skills their children need to learn (and, just as important, what they do not need to learn), the hard work expended by teachers is more likely to produce outcomes with real significance in the lives of children and their families.

 LEGISLATORS MANDATE PARENT AND FAMILY INVOLVEMENT

Parent involvement was a key element in the Education of All Handicapped Children Act (P.L. 94–142), the original federal special education law. Each reauthorization of the law has strengthened and extended parent and family participation in the education of children with disabilities (ERIC/OSEP, 2001). Congress reaffirmed and made clear its belief in the importance of parent and family involvement in the introduction to IDEA 1997: "Over 20 years of research and experience has demonstrated that the education of children with disabilities can be made more effective by . . . strengthening the role of parents and ensuring that families of such children have meaningful opportunities to participate in the education of their children at school and at home" (U.S.C. 601[c][5][B]).

Parent participation in the form of shared decision making is one of six basic rules, or principles, of IDEA that form the general framework for carrying out national policies for the education of children with disabilities. IDEA provides statutory guidelines that schools must follow with parents of children with disabilities with regard to referral, testing, placement, and program planning and evaluation. In addition, the law provides due process procedures if parents believe that their child's needs are not being met.

We have identified three factors responsible for increased parent and family involvement in the education of exceptional children: parents want it, educators know it's a good idea, and the law requires it. But the most important reasons why parents and educators should strive to develop working partnerships are the benefits to the child with disabilities:

- Increased likelihood of targeting meaningful IEP goals
- Greater consistency and support in the child's two most important environments
- Increased opportunities for learning and development
- Access to expanded resources and services

To learn how a parent-teacher partnership built upon communication and mutual respect benefited a student, his family, and his teacher, see Profiles & Perspectives, "In Support of Jay," later in this chapter.

 UNDERSTANDING FAMILIES OF CHILDREN WITH DISABILITIES

When parents and teachers work together for the mutual benefit of a child with disabilities, they make a powerful team. To work together, they must communicate with one another.

IDEA and parent participation

PRAXIS Special Education Core Principles: Content Knowledge: II. Legal and Societal Issues, The school's connections with families of students with disabilities, parent partnerships and roles.

In Support of Jay

by Ann P. Turnbull and Mary E. Morningstar

ANN'S PERSPECTIVE

Jay was in Mary's class for the last year of his high school program, and it was a very positive experience for him and our entire family. The first evening that our family met Mary, we were impressed with her energy, state-of-the-art knowledge, and obvious commitment to her students. Mary quickly earned our confidence in terms of the programming that she was doing, and we were totally together in our values for integration, productivity, and independence.

Mary organized an in-service program that allowed teachers and parents to work together and to share information about disabilities with the typical students in the school to help prepare them for positive interactions. It gave us a chance to go to classes, meet students and teachers, and feel like part of the school. Right away, Mary got Jay established as a manager of the football team, helped facilitate relationships between Jay and typical students (an opportunity he had never really had before), and helped him dress cool, walk cool, and generally fit into the school.

In terms of family contact, Mary treated us, Jay's parents and sisters, with respect and dignity. There have been times in the past when I have felt judged by teachers, and often it made me feel defensive. To the contrary, I always felt that Mary was able to see my strengths and to value how conscientiously our family was trying to support Jay.

We exchanged a notebook back and forth, and I always looked forward to reading Mary's positive messages. It was a great source of connection and camaraderie for all of us. It was as if we had a visit each day.

I also remember how wonderful it was for Mary to bring Jay and his classmates to our house a couple of days a week for their domestic training. It was a bonus for Jay to be able to learn domestic skills in his own setting, and it was certainly a bonus for our family to have assistance in housekeeping.

One of the confidences that I had throughout the entire year was that Jay was in a quality program and that Mary knew exactly what she was doing. It was an incredible relief for our family to not feel that we had to advocate during every spare minute to ensure opportunities for Jay. We knew that Mary was doing a good job, and we could relax and spend time in family recreation rather than in evening advocacy meetings. What a relief from previous years!

Effective communication is more likely when each party understands and respects the responsibilities and challenges faced by the other. For educators, an important initial step in developing a partnership with parents and families is to strive for an understanding of how a child with disabilities might influence the family system and the many interrelated roles of parenthood.

 THE IMPACT OF A CHILD WITH DISABILITIES ON THE FAMILY

The birth of a baby with disabilities or the discovery that a child has a disability is an intense and traumatic event. Consider this parent's feelings: "All I wanted was a baby and now I've got doctors' appointments, therapy appointments, surgeries, medical bills, a strained marriage, no more free time. . . . When you have a handicapped child, you don't just have to deal with the child and the fact that he's handicapped. You have to adjust to a whole new way of life. It's a double whammy" (Simon, 1987, p. 15).

MARY'S PERSPECTIVE

The most crucial part of my school program always started during that first meeting with the family. I have always preferred that my first visit take place in the family's home. This puts the family more at ease, lets me get a feel for how the family lives, and lets me meet the brothers and sisters.

As with all of my families, my first visit with Ann, Rud, Jay, Kate, and Amy included completing a parent inventory and a skill preference checklist. The inventory included such items as Jay's daily schedule. What did he do each day? What did he need help with? What was important to him and to his family? I also identified his level of performance and past experiences with certain functional activities, such as grocery shopping, domestic chores, riding a public bus, and having a job. Finally, it looked at future goals. Where did Jay want to work? Where was he going to live? Who would be his friends?

From this inventory, we moved to the preference checklist. On the basis of Jay's activities and skill levels, we figured out what Jay should spend his time learning while in school. Once all of this was done, we picked specific goals and objectives to work on for that year and plugged them into a weekly schedule. What seemed to me to be "just doing my job as a special education teacher" often had a profound effect on families. I remember Ann and Rud's being awed by this process. As parents of a young man with disabilities, they greatly valued the opportunity to work with the schools to tailor a program for their son. Their enthusiasm and excitement about Jay's program helped sustain me through some of the more trying school days.

Continued communication with the family is critical to the success of any school program. Like all of my students, Jay carried his home-school communication notebook back and forth with him each day. This was my lifeline with the family. Any issues, problems, great ideas, changes in schedule, or good things that happened were written down in that notebook. In fact, it was such an important chronicle of our school year that when Jay graduated, we fought over who would keep the notebook! Our compromise was to make a copy for me as a keepsake.

Parent-professional partnerships require give-and-take on both sides. What was most important to me in my relationship with the Turnbulls was their willingness to support me and follow through with Jay's program at home. Ann mentioned that Jay was the manager of the football team, but what she left out was that Rud and Kate enthusiastically attended just about every game, both home and away. They were there not only to cheer the Whitman Vikings but also to support Jay and, through Jay, me and my program.

Knowing that Ann and Rud were there to support my efforts was the most critical component of Jay's successful year. Their involvement provided me with the sustenance to continue my efforts and to improve my program. A school- and community-based program requires more than an 8-hour day. It touches the lives of not only the student and teacher but also the family, school friends, neighbors, employers, store workers, bus drivers, and all who come into contact with that student and family. Establishing a positive and mutually beneficial family-professional partnership requires much effort and skill, but the outcomes of such a relationship far outweigh the efforts.

Source: Adapted from "Family and Professional Interaction" by A. P. Turnbull & M. E. Morningstar, 1993. In M. E. Snell, *Instruction of students with severe disabilities* (3rd ed.), (pp. 31–32). Upper Saddle River, NJ: Merrill/Prentice Hall. Reprinted with permission.

Parental responses to disability

 Council for Exceptional Children — Content Standards for Beginning Teachers–Common Core: Concerns of families of individuals with exceptional learning needs and strategies to help address these concerns (CC10K3).

Many studies have been conducted on the emotional responses and adjustments of parents of children with disabilities (Blacher, 2001; Eden-Piercy, Blacher, & Eyman, 1986; Frey, Fewell, & Vadasy, 1989; Johnson, 1993). This research showed that most parents go through an adjustment process, trying to work through their feelings. For example, widely cited research by Blacher (1984) found three consistent stages of adjustment. First, parents experience a period of emotional crisis characterized by shock, denial, and disbelief. This initial reaction is followed by a period of alternating feelings of anger, guilt, depression, shame, lowered self-esteem, rejection of the child, and overprotectiveness. Finally, parents reach a third stage in which they accept their child. Based on their observations of 130 participants in two parent support groups over a period of several years, Anderegg, Vergason, and Smith (1992) have developed a revised model of Blacher's work they call the grief cycle, which consists of three stages: confronting, adjusting, and adapting.

Poyadue (1993) suggests a stage beyond acceptance or adapting that involves appreciation of the positive aspects of family life with a child with a disability. There is growing research evidence supporting this concept. For example, Patterson and Leonard (1994) interviewed couples whose children required intensive home care routines because of chronic and complex health care needs and found roughly equal numbers of positive and negative responses. Among the positive responses was that caregiving brought the couple closer together and created a stronger bond among family members. In another study, the majority of 1,262 parents of children with disabilities agreed with the following statements about being the parent of a child with a disability: "The presence of my child is very uplifting. Because of my child, I have many unexpected pleasures. My child is the reason I am a more responsible person" (Behr, Murphy, & Summers, 1992, p. 26). Skinner, Bailey, Correa, and Rodriguez (1998) found many of the 150 Latina mothers in their study believed that having a child with disabilities made them better mothers. And parents in several studies reported not only coping successfully with the challenges posed by a child with disabilities but said that their families experienced benefits because of the child (Bradley, Knoll, & Agosta, 1992; Meyer, 1995: Naseef, 2001; Stainton & Besser, 1998).

Educators should refrain from expecting parents of children with disabilities to exhibit any kind of typical reaction. Relying on any stages of adjustment theory as the basis for planning or delivering family services poses two potential problems. First, it is easy to assume that all parents must pass through a similar sequence of stages and that time is the most important variable in adjustment. In fact, parents react to the arrival of a child with disabilities in many ways (Lin, 2000; Turnbull & Turnbull, 2001). For some parents, years may pass, but they still are not comfortable with their child. Yet other parents, as we have just discussed, report that having a child with disabilities has strengthened their life or marriage (Scorgie & Sobsey, 2000). The sequence and time needed for adjustment are different for every parent. The one common thread is that almost all parents and families can be helped during their adjustment by sensitive and supportive friends and professionals.

A second concern is that some stages of adjustment theories have a distinct psychiatric flavor, which may lead professionals to mistakenly assume that parents must be maladjusted in some way and in need of counseling.

> It may be that many parents do respond in ways that are well described by the stage model. But it is dangerous to impose this model on all parents. Those who exhibit different response patterns might be inappropriately judged as "deviant." Parents who do not progress as rapidly through the "stages" might be considered slow to adjust. And those who exhibit emotions in a different sequence might be thought of as regressing. (Allen & Affleck, 1985, p. 201)

THE MANY ROLES OF THE EXCEPTIONAL PARENT

Parenthood is an awesome responsibility, and parenting any child requires tremendous physical and emotional energy. All parents share a great deal in common. Hart and Risley (1995), who conducted a longitudinal study of 42 families with young typically developing children, noted: "Raising children made all the families look alike. All the babies had to be fed, changed, and amused. As we went from one home to another we saw the same activities and lives centered on caregiving. . . . Most impressive of all that the parents had in common was the continual and incredible challenge a growing child presents" (pp. 53, 55).

Parents of children with disabilities, however, sometimes experience added stress caused by a child's physical, emotional, and financial demands. Educators who are not parents of a child with disabilities or chronic illness cannot know the 24-hour reality of being the parent of such a child (Patterson, Barber, & Ault, 1994). Nonetheless, they should strive to understand how a child with special needs affects (and is affected by) the family system.

In addition to providing love and affection, parents of children with disabilities must fulfill at least nine other varied and demanding roles.

Roles of exceptional parents

Council for Exceptional Children Content Standards for Beginning Teachers–Common Core: Concerns of families of individuals with exceptional learning needs and strategies to help address these concerns (CC10K3) (also CC2K4).
PRAXIS Special Education Core Principles: Content Knowledge: II. Legal and Societal Issues, The school's connections with families of students with disabilities, parent partnerships and roles.

Caregiver   Taking care of any young child is a demanding task. But the additional care-giving requirements of children with disabilities can be tremendous and cause added stress. And the level of care needed by some children with severe disabilities or chronic health conditions can be nonstop:

> Mike sleeps when he wants to, mostly during the day. He sleeps with a heart monitor on which alarms several time per night, because he stops breathing frequently. Usually I'm up by 8:00 and often cannot go to bed until 12:00 or 1:00 because of Mike's feedings, medication. It's hard to fit all of this into a day and still have time for sleep.

> Douglas's tube caught on the door handle and his trach came out. I panicked, but Douglas's father was home and he "simply" reinserted the trach and reattached the tube to the ventilator machine. Douglas meanwhile had turned gray, then blue for just a minute or less. I was crying as he began breathing again and his color came back. (Bradley et al., 1992)

Although many parents receive help from extended family members and friends in caring for a child with disabilities (Burns, 2000), the amount and level of help is often insufficient. Respite care can reduce the mental and physical stress on parents and families created by the day-to-day responsibilities of caring for a child with disabilities (see Figure 4.1).

Provider   Food, clothing, shelter, music lessons: parents pay a lot of money to raise a typically developing child from birth to adulthood. Providing for a child with disabilities, however, often means additional expenses, sometimes in the tens of thousands of dollars. For example, consider these parents of a child with physical disabilities and chronic health problems:

> We had to find another place to live with first floor bedroom, widened doorways, enlarged front porch, central air, ramp, van. House renovation: $10,000. Van: $18,500. Air: $1,450. Porch: $1,400. Ramp: $1,000. Furnishings to accommodate supplies: $800. We've got the following equipment: Suction machine, portable suction machine, generator for emergency power, hospital bed, air pressure mattress, wheelchair, room monitor, humidifier, bath chair, oxygen, air cleaner, gastronomy tube pump, breathing treatment machine. And all the following expenses have gone up: formula, diapers, appliances, utility bills, medications. (Bradley et al., 1992)

It is not just parents of children with physical disabilities or health conditions who face financial burdens. Many parents of children with learning and behavioral problems pay thousands of dollars for specific treatments, behavioral intervention programs, and in-home therapy. While some families receive federal, state, and/or private assistance for such extra expenses, most families have to pay their own way. On top of the additional expenses, families of children with disabilities often have reduced income because one parent works part time instead of full time or withdraws from the workforce altogether in order to take care of the child at home (Barnett & Boyce, 1994).

Teacher   Most children learn many skills that no one tries to teach them. Children with disabilities, however, often do not acquire new skills as naturally or independently as their typically developing peers do. In addition to learning systematic teaching techniques, some parents must learn to use and/or teach their children to use special equipment and assistive devices such as hearing aids, braces, wheelchairs, and adapted eating utensils (Parette & Brotherson, 1996).

Counselor   All parents are counselors in the sense that they deal with their children's changing emotions, feelings, and attitudes. But in addition to all of the normal joys and pains of raising a child, parents of a child with disabilities must deal with the feelings their child has as a result of his particular disability: "Will I still be deaf when I grow up?" "I'm

FIGURE 4.1   Respite care: Support for families

Parents of nondisabled children frequently hire others to care temporarily for their children. The range of day care options available to families of children with disabilities, however, is severely limited. Many parents of children with severe disabilities identify the availability of reliable, high-quality child care as their single most pressing need (Grant & McGrath, 1990; Warfield & Hauser-Cram, 1996). One study found that 56% of parents of children with disabilities reported having difficulty finding child care, compared to only 3% of parents of children without disabilities reporting the same problem (Emlen, 1998). In response to this need, many communities have developed respite care programs. **Respite care** is the short-term care of a family member with disabilities to provide relief for parents from caretaking duties.

Quality respite care can reduce the mental and physical stress on parents and families created by the day-to-day—in some cases, moment-to-moment—responsibilities of caring for a child with disabilities. Respite care has also been correlated with reduced requests for long-term residential placement of children with disabilities and improved family functioning (Neef, Parrish, Egel, & Sloan, 1986). The mother of a son born with a neurological condition that produces frequent seizures and extreme hyperactivity describes her family's experience with respite care:

> During the first four years of Ben's life, we averaged four hours of sleep a night. We were wearing ourselves out; I have no doubt we would have completely fallen apart. My husband, Roger, used his vacations for sleeping in. The respite program came along just in time for us. It was hard at first. There's an overwhelming guilt that you shouldn't leave your child. We didn't feel like anyone else could understand Ben's problems. But we had to get away. Our church gave us some money, with orders to take a vacation. It was the first time Roger and I and our 12-year-old daughter, Stacy, had really been together since Ben was born.

Another parent expressed what respite care has meant to her family:

> Our son Tom's autism has meant a lot of restrictions in our family life for the past 25 years, bringing with it many problems and much resentment. At last we have been given a no-strings-attached, low-cost way to loosen some of those restrictions. Funny thing is, our Tom is such a nice guy—it's sure good to be able to get far enough away every so often to be able to see that.

Families and their advocates can locate respite service providers in their communities by calling the National Respite Locator Service at this toll-free number, (800) 773-5433, or visiting their website, www.respitelocator.com.

Respite care

Council for Exceptional Children   Content Standards for Beginning Teachers–Common Core: Concerns of families of individuals with exceptional learning needs and strategies to help address these concerns (CC10K3).
PRAXIS Special Education Core Principles: Content Knowledge: II. Legal and Societal Issues, The school's connections with families of students with disabilities, Teacher advocacy for student and families.

not playing outside anymore; they always tease me." "Why can't I go swimming like the other kids?" Parents play an important role in how the child with disabilities comes to feel about himself. Their interactions can help develop an active, outgoing child who confidently tries new experiences or a withdrawn child with negative attitudes toward himself and others.

Behavior Support Specialist   All children act out occasionally, and all parents are challenged and frustrated from time to time by their children's noncompliance and misbehavior. But the frequency and severity of challenging behaviors exhibited by some children with disabilities can make it nearly impossible for some families to experience and enjoy normal routines of daily life (Dunlap, Robbins, & Darrow, 1994). Turnbull and Ruef (1996) interviewed 14 families with children with mental retardation who frequently exhibited problem behavior. The parents reported that their children frequently engaged in at least one of four categories of problem behavior: aggression toward others, property destruction, self-injurious behavior, or pica (eating inedible objects). The children's problem behavior fell into one of two domains, according to the behavior's impact on the child and the family: dangerous behavior (e.g., "He punches his face a lot on the jaw line—his cheek bone, his mouth, occasionally his forehead. . . . He will eventually bleed from his mouth") and difficult behavior (e.g., "When I am around him it is constant noise. He talks or squawks. By afternoon I am frazzled") (p. 283). Such behavior demands specialized and consistent treatment, and some parents of exceptional children must become skilled in behavior support techniques to achieve a semblance of normal family life (e.g., Boulware, Schwartz, & McBride, 2001; Delaney & Kaiser, 2001; Peck, Peterson, Derby, Harding, Weddle, & Barretto, in press; Vaughn, Clarke, & Dunlap, 1997). To learn how educators and one family worked together to provide positive behavioral support for a young boy with challenging behavior, see Teaching & Learning "A Parent-Professional Partnership in Positive Behavioral Support," later in this chapter.

Parent of Siblings without Disabilities   Like studies investigating parental reactions to a child with disabilities, results of research on the effects of children with disabilities on their siblings have varied. Some studies have found negative effects, such as a higher incidence of emotional or behavioral problems (Orsillo, McCaffrey, & Fisher, 1993) or lower self-esteem (McHale & Gamble, 1989) in siblings of children with disabilities. But other studies found siblings of children with disabilities had fewer behavioral problems (Carr, 1988) or were more likely to display prosocial behavior (Stoneman, Brody, Davis, & Crapps, 1989), nurturing, and affection toward their brother or sister with disabilities (Stoneman, 1998) than were siblings of children without disabilities. The positive relationships between a sibling and his or her brother or sister with disabilities often last well into adulthood (Orsmond & Seltzer, 2000).

It is clear, however, that children are deeply affected by having a brother or a sister with special needs (Caro & Derevensky, 1997; Wilson, Blacher, & Baker, 1989). Brothers and sisters of a child with disabilities often have concerns about their sibling's disability: uncertainty regarding the cause of the disability and its effect on them, uneasiness about the reactions of friends, a feeling of being left out or being required to do too much for the child with disabilities (Dyson, Edgar, & Crnic, 1989). Parents play key roles in determining the nature of the relationship between their children and the extent to which their children without disabilities develop into happy, well-adjusted adolescents and adults.

Marriage Partner   Having a child with disabilities can put stress on a marriage. Specific stressors can be as diverse as arguing over whose fault the child's disability is; disagreeing about expectations for the child's behavior; and spending so much time, money, and energy on the child with disabilities that little is left for each other (Cohen, Agosta, Cohen, & Warren, 1989). It is a mistake, however, to assume that the presence of a child with disabilities has a negative effect on marital relations. Some studies have found that a child with disabilities strengthens a marriage in part because of a couple's shared commitment to the child (Sandler & Mistretta, 1998; Scorgie & Sobsey, 2000).

Nondisabled brothers and sisters often have special needs and concerns because of their sibling's disability.

Information Specialist/Trainer for Significant Others   Grandparents, aunts and uncles, neighbors, the school bus driver: all of these people can have an important influence on a child's development. While parents of a child without disabilities can reasonably expect her to receive certain kinds of treatment from significant others, parents of children with disabilities know they cannot necessarily depend on others' appropriate actions and reactions. These

A Parent-Professional Partnership in Positive Behavioral Support

by Glen Dunlap, Bobbie J. Vaughn, and Lise Fox,
University of South Florida

Our research group at the University of South Florida has focused on children and families affected by disabilities and problem behavior. We have tried to find effective and efficient ways for resolving serious behavior problems that result in durable, meaningful changes for the child and concerned family members, friends, and professionals. Millie Bucy was a part-time member of our group. She helped families enrolled in our early intervention program understand their children's challenges and obtain needed services from schools and agencies. Millie was well suited to this role because she is the mother of a 9-year-old boy with a severe disability.

Her son Jeffrey was born with Cornelia de Lange syndrome, a condition associated with significant, chronic medical challenges and severe intellectual disabilities. Jeffrey had a history of disruptive and destructive behaviors. He did not talk; he communicated through gestures, vocalizations, and behaviors that included whining, scratching, yelling, biting, hitting, throwing, and head banging. For example, when his mother tried to move him from his favorite spot near the doors of the grocery store, he cried, screamed, and dropped to the floor. If she tried to pick him up, he scratched her face and arms and banged his head on the floor. Yet despite his challenging behaviors, he was a fun-loving child with a great smile.

Jeffrey often exhibited intense aggression and tantrums, especially in public, which increased the difficulties for Millie, her husband Bob, and Jeffrey's 11-year-old brother Chris. Scratched and bruised by Jeffrey's attacks, Millie was reluctant to let him accompany her on errands. Bob, a truck driver, was often out of town, and Millie had no reliable help with Jeffrey.

When she eventually revealed the severity of her son's behavior, we formed a support team that included Millie, ourselves, and our colleague Shelley Clarke, an experienced researcher and support provider. As a team, we agreed to pursue two goals: (1) develop and implement a plan to reduce Jeffrey's problem behaviors and help him establish more congenial patterns of public interaction and (2) document the process carefully so that our experience might benefit other families in similar circumstances. Existing research literature gives little insight into the actual experiences of families affected by a child's severe behavior problems, and little is known about the impact of behavioral support programs on families' day-to-day functioning as well as feelings, expectations, and hopes.

Our work with Millie and Jeffrey was a true partnership. Millie participated as a full member of the behavioral support and research team. Each member had different roles and expertise, but all views were respected and incorporated into decisions. Millie was involved in assessment and intervention. She made final decisions about settings and procedures, and her views and preferences were instrumental in determining specifics of the research.

To address Jeffrey's behavior, we used *positive behavioral support,* which uses findings from applied research literature (especially applied behavior analysis) to construct a comprehensive, individualized program of intervention designed to reduce (or eliminate) problem behaviors while developing alternative patterns more agreeable to the child and the people around him. Positive behavioral support is based on person-centered values. Procedures are intended

parents must try to ensure that, as much as possible, other people interact with their child in ways that support their child's dignity, acceptance, opportunities for learning, and maintenance of adaptive behaviors. One mother describes her response to anyone who stares at her son with Down syndrome: she looks the person squarely in the eye and says, "You seem interested in my son. Would you like to meet him?" (Schulz, 1985, p. 6). This usually ends the staring and often creates an opportunity to provide information or begin a friendship.

to preserve the child's dignity and promote his ability to engage with the environment while striving for outcomes that enhance his lifestyle. Positive behavioral support plans are individualized to the child and his circumstances. Specific intervention procedures are derived from a *functional assessment* process that produces an individualized understanding of the child and how his behavior relates to the environment.

For Jeffrey, functional assessment included conversations with Millie and observations in the three community settings that she identified as most problematic: a large grocery store, a fast-food restaurant, and a drive-through bank. The process involved two weeks of information gathering and team discussion. Observations confirmed that Jeffrey exhibited high rates of severe problem behaviors in the three settings. Particularly serious tantrums occurred when he was expected to go through store and restaurant doorways. The team surmised that tantrums occurred because he liked the doorways very much (especially the electronic doors), and disruptions prolonged his proximity to them. We hypothesized that his aggression and tantrums in the store, restaurant, and bank related to boredom and an absence of interesting, reinforcing things to occupy his attention.

We linked our assessment-based hypothesis statements to intervention strategies that (1) were appropriate for the designated settings and (2) Millie considered feasible to use while she was running errands. A number of components were tailored to each of the settings. The plan included techniques for increasing the positive features of Millie's interactions with Jeffrey (e.g., reducing her number of corrections) and promoting appropriate engagement with the routines. When he needed to wait (e.g., in the car at the bank, in the booth at the restaurant, in line at the grocery store), he was given toys to secure his attention and interest or a special picture book depicting favored items and activities. To encourage his participation in shopping, he had a pictorial shopping list so that he could anticipate and identify items to be placed in the grocery cart. To reduce tantrums during transitions through doorways, we provided a powerful, competing reward. Immediately before a transition, he was handed a picture of a highly desired, noisy toy that would be waiting for him in the car. This motivated him to move quickly through the doors.

Although Millie always implemented the support plan as if she were alone with Jeffrey, the support team was on site for coaching during the first few sessions in each setting.

During subsequent sessions, members were present to inconspicuously collect data but remained in the background. After an average of seven sessions per setting over a period of about 3 months, Millie was handling the community outings without any on-site assistance. Formal follow-up observations were conducted 5 to 6 months after intervention began.

Support efforts produced important outcomes for Jeffrey and his family. His severe behaviors were virtually eliminated in each targeted setting. The store took longer than the other settings, perhaps because he was learning to use the picture schedule while participating actively in shopping. Tantrums during transitions were reduced substantially. Millie's instructions and interactions with Jeffrey changed positively, with reprimands declining and activity-specific praise increasing over the course of the study. She described the changes as extremely significant and reported restored confidence in being able to manage Jeffrey's behavior, even in awkward circumstances. She felt a new sense of hope for his future as a member of her family and the community:

> I'm feeling a lot more optimistic now and I think that things are really working. I'm seeing differences every day in Jeffrey, little things that he's learning to do. This has just had a really powerful impact on him and on us too.
>
> We decided that we would stop in the grocery store on the way home. . . . it was amazing how well he did. . . . And another thing that was kind of rewarding was that people in the store recognized him and said "hi" to him. . . . I think that helps me and hopefully helps him to feel like he's a part of the community and that was one of our major goals.

We learned a great deal from Millie and Jeffrey and from our efforts to work as partners in seeking meaningful solutions to difficult problems. We gained an appreciation for the value of respectful collaboration and learned that trusting relationships with family members can yield valuable insights. We also learned more about the deep impact that severe problem behaviors can have on all aspects of a family's life. As we learn more about supporting children and their families, we must remain sensitive to the many challenges they encounter every day. That sensitivity will help us be even more effective partners in working with families to make life with their children more rewarding, productive, and satisfying.

For a more detailed account of this case, see Vaughn, Dunlap, Fox, Clarke, and Bucy (1997).

Advocate IDEA not only defines the rights of parents of children with disabilities but also requires specific efforts and responsibilities. Although some involvement in the educational process is expected and desirable for all parents, involvement is a must for parents of exceptional children. They must acquire special knowledge (e.g., different kinds of related services) and learn special skills (e.g., how to participate effectively in IFSP/IEP meetings) and be consistent and firm in presenting their wishes regarding learning goals and placement options for their

TABLE 4.1 The four life-cycle stages of a person with disabilities: Issues and strategies for family members

	LIFE-CYCLE STAGES	
	Early Childhood, ages 0–5	**Childhood, ages 6–12**
Issues for Parents	• Obtaining an accurate diagnosis • Informing siblings and relatives • Locating early intervention services • Participating in IFSP meetings • Seeking to find meaning in the exceptionality • Clarifying a personal ideology to guide decisions • Addressing issues of stigma • Identifying positive contributions of exceptionality • Setting great expectations	• Establishing routines to carry out family functions • Adjusting emotionally to educational implications • Clarifying issues of mainstreaming versus special class placement • Advocating for inclusive experiences • Participating in IEP conferences • Locating community resources • Arranging for extracurricular activities • Developing a vision for the future
Issues for Siblings	• Less parental time and energy for sibling needs • Feelings of jealousy because of less attention • Fears associated with misunderstandings about exceptionality	• Division of responsibility for any physical care needs • Oldest female sibling may be at risk • Limited family resources for recreation and leisure • Informing friends and teachers • Possible concern about younger sibling surpassing older • Issues of mainstreaming into same school • Need for basic information on exceptionality
Enhancing Successful Transitions	• Begin preparing for the separation of preschool children by periodically leaving the child with others. • Gather information and visit preschools in the community. • Encourage participation in Parent to Parent programs. (Veteran parents are matched in one-to-one relationships with parents who are just beginning the transition process.) • Familiarize parents with possible school (elementary and secondary) programs, career options, or adult programs so they have an idea of future opportunities.	• Provide parents with an overview of curricular options. • Ensure that IEP meetings provide an empowering context for family collaboration. • Encourage participation in Parent to Parent matches, workshops, or family support groups to discuss transitions with others.

Family life-cycle stages

 Council for Exceptional Children

Content Standards for Beginning Teachers–Common Core: Concerns of families of individuals with exceptional learning needs and strategies to help address these concerns (CC10K3).
PRAXIS Special Education Core Principles: Content Knowledge: I. Understanding Exceptionalities, The influence of an exceptional condition throughout an individual's life span.

child (Hanson et al., 2001). In addition, many parents of children with disabilities have concerns over and above those of most parents; they must often advocate for effective educational services and opportunities for their children in a society that devalues persons with disabilities (Kozloff & Rice, 2000; Yell & Drasgow, 2000). For example, while all parents may be concerned about having adequate community playgrounds, the parents of a child who uses a wheelchair may find themselves having to fight long and hard for an accessible playground.

CHANGING NEEDS AS CHILDREN GROW

Another way to increase our understanding of how a child with disabilities might affect his or her family and vice versa is to examine the likely impact of the child's and family's changing needs at various ages (Blacher, 2001). Table 4.1 identifies possible issues and concerns that parents and siblings face during four life-cycle stages and suggested strategies for supporting families as they transition in and out of the stages.

TABLE 4.1 *continued*

LIFE-CYCLE STAGES		
	Adolescence, ages 12–21	**Adulthood, ages 21–**
Issues for Parents	• Adjusting emotionally to possible chronicity of exceptionality • Identifying issues of emerging sexuality • Dealing with physical and emotional changes of puberty • Addressing possible peer isolation and rejection • Planning for career/vocational development • Arranging for leisure activities • Expanding child's self-determination skills • Planning for postsecondary education	• Addressing supported employment and living options • Adjusting emotionally to any adult implications of dependency • Addressing the need for socialization opportunities outside the family • Initiating career choice or vocational program • Planning for possible need for guardianship
Issues for Siblings	• Overidentification with sibling • Greater understanding of differences in people • Influence of exceptionality on career choice • Dealing with possible stigma and embarrassment • Participation in sibling training programs • Opportunity for sibling support groups	• Possible issues of responsibility for financial support • Addressing concerns regarding genetic implications • Introducing new in-laws to exceptionality • Need for information on career/living options • Clarify role of sibling advocacy • Possible issues of guardianship
Enhancing Successful Transitions	• Assist families and adolescents to identify community leisure activities. • Incorporate into the IEP skills that will be needed in future career and vocational programs. • Visit or become familiar with a variety of career and living options. • Develop a mentor relationship with an adult with a similar exceptionality and an individual who has a career that matches the student's strengths and preferences.	• Provide preferred information to families about guardianship, estate planning, wills, and trusts. • Assist family members in transferring responsibilities to the individual with an exceptionality, other family members, or service providers as appropriate. • Assist the young adult or family members with career or vocational choices. • Address the issues and responsibilities of marriage and family for the young adult.

Source: Adapted from Turnbull, A. P., & Turnbull, H. R. (1990, 1997, 2001). *Families, professionals, and exceptionality: Collaborating for empowerment* (2nd ed., pp. 134–135; 3rd ed., p. 149; 4th ed., p. 173. Upper Saddle River, NJ: Merrill/Prentice Hall. Used by permission.

 ## ESTABLISHING PARENT-TEACHER PARTNERSHIPS

Principles of effective communication

 Council for Exceptional Children — Content Standards for Beginning Teachers–Common Core: Foster respectful and beneficial relationships between families and professionals (CC10S3).
PRAXIS Special Education Core Principles: Content Knowledge: III. Delivery of Services to Students with Disabilities, Professional roles, Communicating with parents.

Effective parent-teacher partnerships are characterized by family members and professionals who are jointly pursuing shared goals in a climate of mutual respect and trust. Parents are provided with supports in the form of the knowledge and resources that empower them to participate as full partners. Regular two-way communication with parents is the key operational element of an effective parent-teacher partnership. Without open, honest communication between teacher and parent, many of the positive outcomes we have examined cannot be achieved.

 ### PRINCIPLES OF EFFECTIVE COMMUNICATION

"A good conversation is neither a fight nor a contest. Circular in form, cooperative in manner, and constructivist in intent, it is an interchange of ideas by those who see themselves not as adversaries but as human beings come together to talk and to listen and to learn from one another" (Martin, 1985, p. 10). Wilson (1995) recommends five principles for effective communication between educators and parents.

FIGURE 4.2 Active listening

The following excerpts contrast the communication styles of two early childhood teachers, a passive listener and an active listener, while discussing IEP goals with a parent.

Passive Listening

Parent: I would very much like to have my child use his communication board on a more regular basis. Currently, he becomes very frustrated because he can't tell us what he needs. [The parent frowns and looks sad.]

Passively listening teacher: All the students in my class are able to speak. We will have the speech language pathologist work with Andy so that he can speak as well. [The teacher is fiddling with papers she needs for her next parent conference.]

Parent: Perhaps you didn't read Andy's file carefully. His cerebral palsy is so involved that he isn't able to make any understandable speech sounds. We have already had him evaluated by a speech therapist, and he created the communication board for Andy so he could develop his language skills.

Passively listening teacher: [Still looking at her other papers.] We have an excellent speech language pathologist. She will have Andy talking in no time. Andy can work with her during circle time since that is oral and Andy wouldn't be able to participate.

Parent: We don't want Andy to miss out on circle time. He loves to be a part of the group. We can choose appropriate pictures to put on his communication board so he can respond with the rest of the children. He gets very frustrated when he is not allowed to be with the rest of the students.

Passively listening teacher: Oh, we don't let the children bring toys to the circle. He has to be able to speak up like everyone else. Also, I've been meaning to talk to you about his behavior. He has been refusing to cooperate with our group activities. I'd like to send him to time out when this happened.

Parent: [She gives a big sigh.] As I've said, Andy gets very frustrated when he isn't able to communicate and when he isn't a part of the group. I don't think time out would be the right answer for this problem.

Passively listening teacher: Well, if you don't allow us to control his behavior, I don't know how Andy is ever going to be able to be a part of this class. [She looks at her watch, ready to end the meeting.]

Parent-teacher communication is enhanced when teachers value what parents say and listen well.

Accept Parents' Statements   Accepting parents' statements means conveying through verbal and non-verbal means that what parents say is valued. Parents are more likely to speak freely and openly when they believe that what they say is respected. Acceptance means conveying, "I understand and appreciate your point of view." It does not mean the teacher must agree with everything that a parent says.

Listen Actively   Good listeners attend and respond to a conversation partner in a sincere and genuine manner. A good listener pays attention to the content of what is being said, noting who said it and how he said it. For example, in an IFSP/IEP conference attended by extended family members, an educator should notice if a grandparent seems to be speaking for the child's parents or if the mother and father express different opinions about an issue through tones of voice or body language. An active listener not only interprets, sorts, and analyzes what the speaker says but responds to the speaker's message with animation and interest (Howard, Williams, Port, & Lepper, 2001). Figure 4.2 illustrates the skill of active listening.

Question Effectively   To the extent possible, educators should use open-ended questions when communicating with parents, especially during conferences. For example, an open-ended question such as "What did Sharena do with her homework project last week?" is

FIGURE 4.2 *continued*

Active Listening

Actively listening teacher: We didn't address this in our last IEP meeting, but I think Cherise has matured in her language and self-help skills enough that she is ready to start toilet training. What do you think about this? [Teacher leans forward and looks parent in the eye.]

Parent: Do you really think she could learn to go by herself? If would be such a relief not to have her in diapers, now that we are expecting another child. [The parent smiles.]

Actively listening teacher: [Nods enthusiastically.] I just want to explain what this would involve and make sure we can work on this at both home and school. I'd like to check her every 15 minutes to see if there is a pattern to when she is wet and then start putting her on the potty at those most likely times each day. Can you do the same thing when she is at home with you in the afternoon and evening? [The teacher watches the parent's face and notices that her mouth falls a little.]

Parent: I don't think I could check every 15 minutes. We have the two older ones, so I'm always driving them to activities; and Cherise's therapy sessions usually run at least 45 minutes and I don't like to disturb her once she's started a session. [The parent sits back in her chair, pushing away from the table.]

Actively listening teacher: Of course, you are probably on the go so much there isn't a lot of down-time when you could stop and do this every 15 minutes. Is there any period of time, like maybe the hour just before bed that you could work on this? I find kids learn toilet-training so much faster when we work on it at school and at home. [The teacher raises her eyebrows in a hopeful gesture.]

Parent: Maybe I could ask my husband to watch Cherise when I take her older sister to her dance lessons. That way she'd be home for the two hours before bed. Would that be enough to make a difference?

Actively listening teacher: I appreciate you rearranging your hectic schedule. I think that could make a big difference, and once Cherise is out of diapers, you'll have a little more free time with the new baby.

Parent: I'm so glad you think we can do this. It would make a big difference not to have two in diapers, and Cherise will be happier if she can be like the big girls. [She hesitates.] But what if I can't carry through at home? What if she doesn't learn?

Actively listening teacher: I know it's hard to do these things at home when your hands are full. We'll keep working on it at school. Cherise might not learn right away, but I've got some ways to motivate her. You just let me know if you don't think it's going well at home and we'll go back to the drawing board.

Parent: Thank you for being so understanding. I'll give it my best shot. I'm so glad you thought to work on this. It's like you read my mind.

Source: Adapted from Howard, V. F., Williams, B. F., Port, P. D., & Lepper, C. (2001). *Very young children with special needs: A formative approach for the 21st century* (2nd ed.) (pp. 448–450). Upper Saddle River, NJ: Merrill/Prentice Hall. Used by permission.

more likely to evoke a descriptive and informative reply from parents than is the closed-ended question "Is Sharena having trouble with her homework?" which might result in a yes or no response. Questions to parents should not focus solely on problems or deficits, and teachers must respect families' desire to keep some things private and "in the family" (Turnbull & Turnbull, 2001).

Encourage It is important for parents to hear good news about their son or daughter. Describing or showing parents specific instances of their child's good behavior or improved performance encourages parental involvement. When parents need to be informed of an academic or behavioral problem, educators might use the "sandwich" technique: presenting the concern between two positive comments or examples of progress.

Stay Focused Although greetings and some small talk are desirable before getting down to business, conversations between parents and teachers should focus on the child's educational program and progress. Educators must be sensitive to cultural differences and the idiosyncratic conversational styles of individual families (Dennis & Giangreco, 1996; Wilson & Hughes, 1994). But they must also learn to distinguish when extended small talk is drifting too far from the purpose at hand so that they can refocus the conversation.

Active listening

Council for Exceptional Children Content Standards for Beginning Teachers–Common Core: Foster respectful and beneficial relationships between families and professionals (CC10S3).
PRAXIS Special Education Core Principles: Content Knowledge: III. Delivery of Services to Students with Disabilities, Professional roles, Communicating with parents.

IDENTIFYING AND BREAKING DOWN BARRIERS TO PARENT-TEACHER PARTNERSHIPS

Let's face it: parents and teachers do not always communicate effectively and cooperate with one another. They may sometimes even seem to be on opposite sides, battling over what each thinks is best for the child. The child, unfortunately, never wins that battle. She needs to have the people responsible for the two places where she spends most of her life—home and school—work together to make those environments consistent with supportive of her job of learning. Teachers should work to increase the likelihood that their interactions with parents and families are characterized by cooperation. They must be responsive to the practices and beliefs of families from diverse cultural backgrounds and identify and eliminate attitudes and behaviors that block family involvement.

Cultural Differences   Differences in the cultural and linguistic beliefs and practices of professionals and families often serve as barriers to parent involvement (Greenen, Powers, & Lopez-Vasquez, 2001; Harry, Kalyanpur, & Day, 1999). Teachers who fail to recognize and respect differences between their own cultural perspectives and the culturally based values and beliefs of families are prone to make biased and faulty judgments about parents that weaken the parent-teacher relationship. Educators can increase parent involvement by using culturally responsive and respectful strategies such as the following (Al-Hassan & Gardner, in press; Parette & Petch-Hogan, 2000):

Cultural and linguistic differences

 Council for Exceptional Children   Content Standards for Beginning Teachers–General Curriculum & Independence Curriculum Referenced Standards: Potential impact of differences in values, languages, and customs that can exist between the home and school (CC1K10) (also CC3K4, CC6K3, and CC10K4). **PRAXIS** Special Education Core Principles: Content Knowledge: III. Delivery of Services to Students with Disabilities, Professional roles, Influence of teacher attitudes, values, and behaviors.

- Have native-speaking individuals make initial contacts.
- Use trained interpreters during conferences.
- Conduct meetings in family-friendly settings.
- Identify and defer to key decision makers in the family.
- Recognize that families from diverse cultures may view time differently from the way professionals do and schedule meetings accordingly.
- Provide transportation and child care to make it easier for families to attend school-based activities.

Educators should also work toward understanding how differing values and belief systems may influence families' perspectives, wishes, and decisions. For example, a special educator who views disability as a physical phenomenon that can be measured and treated in an objective way may have difficulty developing an effective partnership with parents from a culture that views disability as a blessing or a punishment that is to be treated with spiritual perspective (Harry, Kalyanpur, & Day, 1999; Skinner et al., 1998). Understanding differences between our own perspectives and those of people from other cultures and ethnic groups requires careful examination of our own cultural background and belief system. The questions and issues posed in Profiles & Prespectives, "A Cultural Journey" (on p. 100 in Chapter 3), suggest one way to begin such a personal assessment, the initial step in working toward cultural reciprocity. (See Profiles & Perspectives, "Building Cultural Reciprocity," later in this chapter.)

Cultural reciprocity

Council for Exceptional Children   Content Standards for Beginning Teachers–General Curriculum & Independence Curriculum Referenced Standards: Culturally responsive factors that promote effective communication and collaboration with individuals with exceptional learning needs, families, school personnel, and community members (CC10K4) (also CC3K4 and CC6K3).

Professional Roadblocks to Communication   In addition to being insensitive to cultural differences, some parents and teachers make assumptions about and hold attitudes toward one another that are counterproductive. Teachers sometimes complain that parents are uninterested, uncooperative, or hostile. Parents may complain that educators are negative, unavailable, or patronizing. We should examine factors that cause friction between parents and teachers not to determine fault but to identify what we can change and improve. Professionals who recognize that some of their own behaviors may diminish the potential for productive partnerships with parents are in a better position to change their actions and obtain the benefits that such relationships can provide.

While educators cannot directly change the attitudes of parents, they can—and, as professionals, must—identify and eliminate attitudes that may serve as barriers to communication with families. Some professionals hold stereotypes and false assumptions about what parents of children with disabilities must be like and what they need (Adelman, 1994; Dyson, 1996; Voltz, 1994). These attitudes often lead to poor relationships between parents and professionals. We should not be surprised if parents feel intimidated, confused, angry, hostile—or just terminate their involvement altogether—when educators interact with them in any of the following ways:

- *Treating parents as vulnerable clients instead of equal partners.* Professionals who see parents only as helpless souls in need of assistance make a grave mistake. Teachers need parents and what they have to offer as much as parents need teachers (Sonnenschein, 1981).
- *Keeping professional distance.* Most professionals in human services develop some degree of distance to avoid getting too involved with a client—supposedly to maintain objectivity and credibility. But aloofness or coldness in the name of professionalism has hindered or terminated many parent-teacher relationships. Parents must believe that the educators working with their children really care about them (Soodak & Erwin, 2000).
- *Treating parents as if they need counseling.* Some professionals make the faulty assumption that having a child with disabilities causes a parent to need therapy or parent education. A mother of a child who attended a preschool for students with developmental delays described her frustration: "Everybody who came here was aimed at me. Everybody is telling me 'You need parent counseling.' I mean I have lived for 30 years. I never needed help and all of a sudden I need help on how to do this and help on how to do that. I feel like they are saying John is not the problem, I am the problem" (Rao, 2000, p. 481).
- *Blaming parents for their child's condition.* Some parents do feel responsible for their child's disability and, with a little encouragement from a professional, can be made to feel completely guilty. A productive parent-professional relationship focuses on collaborative problem solving, not on laying blame (Singer, Powers, & Olson, 1996).
- *Disrespecting parents as less intelligent.* Teachers sometimes give too little recognition to parents' information and suggestions. Parents are considered too biased, too involved, or too unskilled to make useful observations (Lake & Billingsley, 2000). Some professionals concede that parents have access to needed information but contend that parents are not able to, or should not, make any decisions based on what they know. "They treat me like I'm undeducated. They break down things into real small pieces and then ask me to repeat things. I have gone to nursing school. I can read. Maybe they met other people who cannot read but they can ask me 'Rose, can you read?' They treat you like you are a child" (Rao, 2000, p. 481).
- *Treating parents as adversaries.* Some teachers expect the worst whenever they interact with parents. Even when that attitude can be partially explained by previous unpleasant encounters with unreasonable parents, it often becomes a self-fulfilling prophecy and is at best a negative influence on new relationships.
- *Labeling parents.* Some educators seem eager to label parents (Sonnenschein, 1981). If parents disagree with a diagnosis or seek another opinion, they are *denying;* if parents refuse a suggested treatment, they are *resistant;* and if parents insist that something is wrong with their child despite test evidence to the contrary, they are *anxious.*

Roadblocks to communication

 Content Standards for Beginning Teachers–Common Core: Foster respectful and beneficial relationships between families and professionals (CC10S3).
PRAXIS Special Education Core Principles: Content Knowledge: III. Delivery of Services to Students with Disabilities, Professional roles, communicating with parents.

Conflict Resolution through Dialoguing Not all ineffective parent-teacher relationships are caused by professional mishandling. Some parents are genuinely difficult to work with or unreasonable. There are situations in which parents fight long and hard for services for their child. But after services are found and the child is receiving an appropriate education, the parents continue their intense advocacy until minor issues with professionals become major confrontations. One mother stated, "For years I have scrapped and fought for services. Now I come on like gangbusters over issues that are really not that important. I don't

Building Cultural Reciprocity

A service provider and a family member meet for the first time. If the parent's perspective of the world is similar to the service provider's, then a positive connection generally occurs. However, if the parent holds a belief system different from the service provider's, difficulties typically arise. According to Beth Harry, a faculty member at the University of Miami, the source of the difficulty often is a point of view that is defined and limited by cultural orientation.

According to Harry, stumbling blocks often arise when service providers and families do not recognize and accept the other's culture.

> For example, I found that individuals from Puerto Rican backgrounds tended to view disabilities as more severe conditions than do people from the mainstream United States—in fact, many of our high-incidence disabilities were not seen by them as disabilities, but simply as individual characteristics within the normal range. We observed that when parents from Puerto Rico realized their views were not valued by Anglo service providers, they stopped participating in their children's educational process.

The process of acculturation takes time, and professionals who are hoping to make a difference for children must be willing to take the initiative in building a bridge between the cultures of diverse families and the culture of schools.

To build this bridge, Harry advocates that professionals initiate a two-way process of information sharing and understanding called *cultural reciprocity*. The cultural reciprocity process is recursive, meaning that each step informs the others.

Step 1: Identify the cultural values that are embedded in your interpretation of a student's difficulties or in a recommendation for service. Ask yourself which values underlie your recommendation. Next, analyze experiences that contributed to your holding of these values. Consider the roles of nationality, culture, socioeconomic status, and professional education in shaping your values.

Step 2: Find out whether the family being served recognizes and values your assumptions and, if not, how their view differs from yours.

Step 3: Acknowledge and give explicit respect to any cultural differences identified, and fully explain the cultural basis of your assumptions.

Dialoguing to resolve conflicts

Council for Exceptional Children

Content Standards for Beginning Teachers–Common Core: Foster respectful and beneficial relationships between families and professionals (CC10S3).
PRAXIS Special Education Core Principles: Content Knowledge: III. Delivery of Services to Students with Disabilities, Professional roles, Communicating with parents.

like what has happened to me. I've ended up to be an aggressive, angry person" (Bronicki & Turnbull, 1987, p. 10).

Although some teachers voice concern that parents of children with disabilities are unrealistic and make too many demands of schools (e.g., Chesley & Calaluce, 1997), most recognize that these parents, like all parents, are simply advocating for the best possible educational services and outcomes for their children. When someone sees things differently from us and we both have vested interests in the outcome, we often resort to argument in an attempt to resolve our differences. Although a teacher may "win" an argument with parents—if one defines winning as forcing the parents to agree verbally or simply give up their perspective—arguing is rarely a useful tool in a partnership. *Dialoguing* is an approach to conflict resolution in which both parties try to see each other's point of view. Gonzalez-Mena (2002) points out differences between a dialogue and an argument.

- The object of an argument is to win; the object of a dialogue is to gather information.
- The arguer tells; the dialoguer asks.
- The arguer tries to persuade; the dialoguer seeks to learn.

Step 4: Through discussion and collaboration, determine the most effective way of adapting your professional interpretations or recommendations to the value system of this family.

Harry points out that "by developing your own cultural self-awareness, you are able to recognize the cultural underpinnings of your professional practice. This, in turn, enables you to facilitate conversations with the families. Through the process, families also acquire knowledge about the special education system, which supports them in making informed decisions about services. "With cultural reciprocity, we find not only better relationships, but more reasonable goals that are implemented."

ONE TEACHER'S PERSONAL ACCOUNT

"Before learning the reciprocity process, I was somewhat closed-minded," shares Yamile Llano, a Miami, Florida, high school teacher who is Hispanic of Cuban origin. As a graduate student in one of Professor Beth Harry's special education courses, Llano was required to participate in a number of activities with families based on Harry's cultural reciprocity research. One activity involved attending a social event with one of her students and his family. Llano selected Jack, an African American youngster, and arranged to attend church with him and his family. Following is an excerpt from Ms. Llano's journal entry:

> I was very nervous. I was on my way to a Baptist church in a predominantly black neighborhood. My stomach was in knots. . . . I am of Catholic faith and I was not sure what to expect. As I waited for the family, many people looked at me as if were lost. I really did not fit in; I stood out like a sore thumb. . .

I felt as if I were intruding. As people stared at me, I simply smiled and said, "Hello." I just wanted to disappear. When I saw Jack's family, I felt more comfortable. They welcomed me very warmly, and Jack shook my hand for the first time. It was then I felt I was in a very warm atmosphere. The church felt like one big family—very different from the church I regularly attend. At my church, when people walk in, they are very quiet and very careful not to make the slightest noise. At Jack's church, everyone was happy and no one whispered. This made me feel good. Jack's family interacted with everyone. I noticed that everyone greeted Jack—just like everyone else. No one treated him differently. Jack was accepted as he is. I tried to see if anyone treated Jack differently, but I saw no evidence of that. Instead, what I saw was a close-knit community that was accepting of Jack's disability.

Many times we make assumptions about people based on race, religion, and other factors that hinder us from mixing and mingling with other people. I thought people in the church would not be accepting of me because of my race and my religion—but I was wrong!

According to Llano, that experience taught her a lot about herself. She encourages other teachers to move outside their circles and experiences and into the lives of their students and families. "You will feel richer for the experience."

Source: Adapted from ERIC/OSEP Special Project. (2001). *Family involvement in special education.* (Research Connections in Special Education, no. 9), (pp. 4–5). Arlington, VA: ERIC Clearinghouse on Disabilities and Gifted Education.

- The arguer see two opposing views and considers hers the valid or best one; the dialoguer is willing to understand multiple viewpoints. (p. 110)

Most of us are better at arguing than we are at dialoguing. That's probably because we have had much more practice with the former. We tend to argue first and think rationally (if we do at all) later. But later might be too late if in "winning" the argument, we have damaged the parent-teacher relationship.

> So how does one switch from an argument to a dialogue in the heat of the moment? Start by noticing your body language. Sometimes you can just change your body language, and an energy switch will follow. Then it's a matter of doing one simple thing: listening to the other person. To truly listen, one must suspend judgements and focus on what's being said rather than just gathering ammunition for the next attack. Really hearing someone is extremely simple, but it's not easy. (Gonzalez-Mena, 2002, p. 111)

After adopting open body language and beginning to listen, Gonzalez-Mena (2002) recommends using the RERUN approach: reflect, explain, reason, understand, and negotiate.

- *Reflect*   Acknowledge what you perceive the other person is thinking or feeling. If you understand what the person is feeling, you might say, "I think you're looking at it this way." If you perceive the other person is very emotional, acknowledge that perception: "You sound really upset." Such responses invite the person to talk some more. People who know that their feelings and thoughts are received and accepted are more likely to listen and be open to your thoughts.
- *Explain*   Remember, we have two ears and one mouth; that's a reminder that we should listen twice as much as we talk.
- *Reason*   The explanation of your perspective should include the reason you believe or feel the way that you do.
- *Understand*   Next comes the hardest part. Tune in to both thoughts and feelings and try to understand the situation from both points of view. You don't have to say anything out loud at this point; just be sure you have clarity. You may have to talk inwardly to yourself to get it. Self-reflection is an important part of the process. When you think you understand, you're ready for the next step.
- *Negotiate*   Try brainstorming together until you can find a mutually satisfying solution. Don't give up. Refuse to taken an either-or attitude. If you don't get stuck in a dualistic frame of mind, you can probably find a third or fourth solution that is different from or combines both of your stances on the matter. Creative negotiators can open up new avenues of action that no one has ever thought of before. (adapted from Gonzalez-Mena, 2002, p. 111)

For additional suggestions on resolving conflicts and disagreements with parents, see Heron and Harris (2001), Lambie (2000), Margolis and Brannigan (1990), and Simpson (1996).

 ## METHODS OF HOME-SCHOOL COMMUNICATION

 ### PARENT-TEACHER CONFERENCES

Although parent-teacher conferences are as common to school as recess and homework, they are not always an effective vehicle for communication. Too often, parent-teacher conferences are stiff, formal affairs with anxious teachers and worried parents who wonder what bad news they will hear this time. Fortunately, parents and teachers are learning to talk with one another in more productive ways. In a face-to-face meeting, parents and teachers can exchange information and coordinate their efforts to assist the child with disabilities in school and at home. Parent-teacher conferences should not be limited to the beginning and end of the school year but scheduled regularly.

Preparing for the Conference   Preparation is the key to effective parent-teacher conferences. It entails establishing specific objectives for the conference, obtaining and reviewing a computer printout or list of the student's grades, selecting examples of the student's work and perhaps a graph or chart showing the student's cumulative progress, and preparing an agenda for the meeting (Courson & Hay, 1996; Dodd, 1996; Stephens & Wolf, 1989). Figure 4.3 shows a parent-teacher conference outline that can be used for preparing an agenda and recording notes of the meeting.

Conducting the Conference   Most parent-teacher conferences for school-age children are held in the child's classroom because (1) the teacher feels comfortable in familiar surroundings; (2) the teacher has ready access to student files and instructional materials; (3) the class-

Planning and conducting parent-teacher conferences

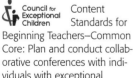

Council for Exceptional Children   Content Standards for Beginning Teachers–Common Core: Plan and conduct collaborative conferences with individuals with exceptional learning needs and their families (CC10S5).
PRAXIS Special Education Core Principles: Content Knowledge: III. Delivery of Services to Students with Disabilities, Professional roles, Communicating with parents, meeting with parents to discuss student concerns, progress, and IEPs.

FIGURE 4.3 **Outline for a parent-teacher conference**

Conference Outline

Date _____2-14-03_____   Time _____4:30 - 5:00_____

Student's Name _____Jeremy Wright_____
Parents' Name(s) _____Barbara and Tom Wright_____
Teacher's Name _____Tim G._____
Other Staff Present _____None_____

Objectives for Conference: (1) Show graph of J's reading progress, (2) find out about spelling program,

   (3) get parents' ideas: intervention for difficulties on playground/in gym, (4) share list of books for leisure reading

Student's Strengths
- good worker academically, wants to learn
- excited about progress in reading fluency

Area(s) Where Improvement Is Needed:
- continue w/spelling @ home
- arguments & fighting w/other kids

Questions to Ask Parents:
- Interactions w/friends while playing in neighborhood?
- How would they feel about f'dback from classmate re: playground/gym behavior?
- Consequences?

Parent's Responses/Comments:
- very pleased w/reading - want to build on it.
- wondering how long w/in-home spelling?
- willing to give rewards @ home: playground/gym

Examples of Student's Work/Interactions:
- graph of corrects/errors per min.: reading
- weekly pre- & post-test scores: spelling.

Current Programs and Strategies Used by Teacher:
- reading: silent read, two 1-min. time trials, self-charting comprehension practice
- spelling: practice w/tape recorder, self-checking

Suggestions for Parents:
- continue spelling games (invite friends)
- Show interest in/play fantasy games (Dung. & Dragons) w/J

Suggestions from Parents:
- Try using some high-interest spelling words (e.g., joust, castle)
- Matt & Amin could help with playground/gym program

Follow-up Activities: (Agreed to in conf)

   Parents:
- Continue to play spelling game 2 nights per week
- Take J to library for adventure books

   Teacher:
- Ask J for high-interest words & use 3-4 in his weekly list.
- Develop peer intervention strategy w/Matt, Amin & J (group contingency?)

Date to Call for Follow-up:

    Feb. 28 (Wednesday) _____   (check when called)

---

room itself serves as a reminder to the teacher of things the child has done; and (4) the classroom, with its desks, chairs, and teaching materials, reminds both teacher and parents that the purpose of the conference is their mutual concern for improving the child's education. Wherever parent conferences are held, the area should be arranged so that it is conducive to partnership interactions (Courson & Hay, 1996). Teachers should not make the mistake of hiding behind their desks, creating a barrier between themselves and the parents, or of seating parents in undersized chairs meant for students.

Stephens and Wolf (1989) suggest a 4-step sequence for parent-teacher conferences:

1. *Build rapport.* Establishing mutual trust and the belief that the teacher really cares about the student is important to a good parent-teacher conference (Perl, 1995). A minute or two should be devoted to relevant small talk. The teacher might begin with something positive about the child or family instead of a superficial statement about the weather or traffic.

2. *Obtain information.* Parents can provide teachers with important information for improving instruction. As suggested earlier, teachers should use open-ended questions that cannot be answered with a simple yes or no. For example, "Which activities in school has Felix mentioned lately?" is better than "Has Felix told you what we are doing now in school?" The first question encourages the parent to provide more information; the teacher is trying to build a conversation, not preside over a question-and-answer session. Throughout the conference, the teacher should show genuine interest in listening to parents' concerns, avoid dominating the conversation, and stay focused on the purpose of the meeting. Above all, teachers should refrain from making comments that lecture ("Do you realize. . . ."), criticize or judge ("That was a mistake. . . ."), or threaten ("Unless you take my advice. . . ."), all of which block communication (Simpson, 1996; Turnbull & Turnbull, 2001; Wilson, 1995).

3. *Provide information.* The teacher should give parents concrete information about their child in jargon-free language. The teacher should share examples of schoolwork and data on student performance—what has already been learned and what needs to be learned next. If the student has not made much progress, parents and teacher should look together for ways to improve it.

4. *Summarize and follow up.* The conference should end with a summary of what was said. The teacher should review strategies agreed on during the conference and indicate the follow-up activities that either party will do to help carry out those strategies. Some teachers record notes on a laptop computer during the conference, printing out a copy at the conclusion of the meeting so that parents will also have a record of what was said or agreed to.

By showing parents specific examples of their children's progress, teachers set the occasion for parental praise and approval of student effort.

These strategies are relevant to all types of parent-teacher meetings. However, IEP and IFSP planning and evaluation meetings, which are discussed in Chapters 2 and 5 respectively, entail additional procedural requirements. Detailed suggestions for planning and conducting parent-teacher conferences can be found in Jordan, Reyes-Blane, Peel, Peel, and Lane (1998); Kroth and Edge (1997); Simpson (1996); and Turnbull and Turnbull (2001). For some families, holding a conference in the home might be appropriate and appreciated (Edens, 1997).

WRITTEN MESSAGES

Although much can be accomplished in face-to-face meetings, they require considerable time to plan and conduct, so they cannot take place frequently. But parent-teacher conferences should not be the sole means of home-school communication. Written messages, especially when part of a systematic program of ongoing information exchange, can be an excellent way of maintaining home-school communication.

Teachers should never rely on written messages, regardless of their form, as the sole method of communicating with parents. Teachers must also be sensitive to the cultural and linguistic backgrounds and educational levels of parents (Al-Hassan & Gardner, in press). For example, Harry (1992a) reports that because one group of Hispanic parents had to spend a great deal of time translating and trying to understand a school's written messages, they viewed those messages as a nuisance that further alienated them from their children's school.

Happy Grams The easiest and quickest type of home-school written message are short notes informing parents of something positive their child has accomplished at school. Many teachers regularly send happy grams home with their students, giving parents an opportunity to praise the child at home and stay abreast of activities in the classroom. A book by Kelly (1990) includes tear-out masters of school-home notes that can be duplicated and used for a variety of communication purposes.

Two-Way, Home-School Note Systems A two-way, parent-teacher communication system can be built around a reporting form or notebook that the child carries between home and school. Teachers can develop and use a standard form or checklist, such as the one shown in Figure 4.4, to inform parents about their child's homework assignments and behavior in the classroom (Cronin et al., 1992; Olympia, Andrews, Valum, & Jensen, 1993; Sicley, 1993). Parents sign the form to indicate they have received it and can use the form themselves to provide information or request assistance from the teacher(s). To be most effective, home-school communication forms should be simple to use, with spaces for teachers and parents to circle or check responses and to write short notes to one another.

Home-school dialogue notebooks offer another form of written communication between parents and teachers. Williams and Cartledge (1997) describe a notebook system that Williams used to communicate regularly with the parents of children with emotional and behavioral disorders. The children attended an urban school, and all came from low socioeconomic backgrounds. Williams and Cartledge emphasize the importance of being organized, persistent, and flexible in expectations for parent participation. Figure 4.5 shows some sample parent-teacher notebook exchanges.

> Parent responses are needed to make the notebook system work. How did we get parents to respond regularly and meaningfully? The secret is the teacher's consistency, persistence, and caring. . . . I found that to make the system work, I had to be well organized and disciplined. I had to read 10 notebook entries every day and make my own entries. In my classroom, I placed a basket near the door. . . . As soon as the students entered the classroom, they were to put their notebook in the basket before going to breakfast. I would read the parent notes while the students were eating breakfast, and I also used lunch or periods when students attended art, music, and physical education classes as times to review parent messages. I usually wrote to the parents during the afternoon recess period.
>
> Needless to say, not all parents immediately embraced this communication system. This is where persistence became important; I refused to give up. I always tried to respond positively to every parent, and I worked to help them gradually increase their levels of participation. Some parents were comfortable with just signing their names on the notebook to let me know that they had read my message; some were comfortable writing about their child's activities during the previous night; and some would go further to share special or personal events that they felt would be of significance to their child's schooling. (Williams & Cartledge, 1997, p. 32)

Home-school written communications

Council for Exceptional Children Content Standards for Beginning Teachers—Common Core: Involve the individual and family in setting instructional goals and monitoring progress (CC7S3).
PRAXIS Special Education Core Principles: Content Knowledge: III. Delivery of Services to Students with Disabilities, Professional roles, Communicating with parents, writing reports directly to parents.

FIGURE 4.4 Home-school communication form for monitoring homework and in-school behavior

Assignment Monitoring Sheet

Name _____ Date: _____

PERIOD	ASSIGNMENT	FEEDBACK			COMMENT	SIGNATURE
1		HWC HWNC	CWC CWNC	AB UB		
2		HWC HWNC	CWC CWNC	AB UB		
3		HWC HWNC	CWC CWNC	AB UB		
4		HWC HWNC	CWC CWNC	AB UB		
5		HWC HWNC	CWC CWNC	AB UB		
6		HWC HWNC	CWC CWNC	AB UB		
7		HWC HWNC	CWC CWNC	AB UB		

KEY:
HWC = HomeWork Completed   HWNC = HomeWork Not Completed
CWC = ClassWork Completed   CWNC = ClassWork Not Completed
AB = Acceptable Behavior   UB   = Unacceptable Behavior
****

Parent Feedback/Assistance Request
Feedback or Issue of Concern:
_____
_____
_____

Action Requested: phone conference   _____
                      conference at school   _____
                      none   _____
Best day/time to contact: day: _____
                              time: _____
Parent Signature: _____ Phone: _____

Source: From "Home-School Partnerships" by M. E. Cronin, D. L. Slade, C. Bechtel, and P. Anderson, 1992, *Intervention in School and Clinic,* 27(5), 286–292. © 1992 by PRO-ED, Inc. Reprinted with permission.

FIGURE 4.5   Sample parent-teacher notebook exchanges

The teacher said:
William had a great first day at school. He did as much as he could with his hand. Please go through the papers that he brought home and explain them to him. He had a great start, and I am sure that he is just going to do fine.

Then the parent said:
William had a great evening. He was very anxious about school. His goal for this semester is to have straight *A*s. Thanks so much for being so kind with him.

The teacher said:
Mrs. R, thank you very much for attending our class feast yesterday. That was very nice of you, and I want you to know that it was greatly appreciated. I am pleased that Jason is making progress both academically and socially—which could not have happened without your support and cooperation.

Then the parent said:
Mrs. W., thank you very much for the lunch. It was very good. I am glad that Jason is making progress especially with his behavior. I hope this will continue. Jason misplaced his homework and could not find it. Would you please send another homework home today so that he will be able to get the credit?

The parent said:
I checked some of Jermain's papers. Please don't accept sloppy work. He is making some mistakes, and I think he is not paying attention to his work. He loves to come to school, and he is making some new friends. He said you have been very helpful. He had a great weekend.

Then the teacher said:
Jermain had a pleasant day at school today. He did his assignments and followed directions. I talked with him about his writing and taking time with his work. He promised to do better. Let me know when you want to come in for the conference so that I can make time to be available for you before Thursday.

The parent said:
Matt practiced his spelling words. He finally gave me his spelling book this morning. When is the science project due? Matt could not remember when. He read a cookbook for a half-hour and made out a grocery list for supper from the recipes.

Then the teacher said:
Matt's day at school was fine. He did his assignments and followed directions on the playground. The science project is due in tomorrow morning. He is concerned that he might not be able to put it together before tomorrow. I told him that he should do his best and bring whatever he has in. We will be doing our cooking on Friday, and you are welcome to attend if it is convenient for you.

Source: Reprinted from Williams, V. L., & Cartledge, G. (1997). Passing notes to parents. *Teaching Exceptional Children, 30*(1), 32. Used by permission of the Council for Exceptional Children, Reston, VA.

Home-School Contracts   A home-school contract specifies parent-delivered rewards for the child contingent on her behavior or academic performance in the classroom (Smith, 1994). For example, Kerr and Nelson (2002) describe a home-school contract developed by the teacher and parents of a child who interrupted the teacher and disrupted other students during math and social studies classes. The student received a checkmark for each class period that he participated in class discussions instead of disrupting others; when he earned 50 checkmarks, his parents agreed to buy him a gerbil. Home-school contracts use parent-controlled rewards, build in parent recognition and praise of the child's accomplishments, and involve the teacher and parents together in a positive program to support the child's learning.

Class Newsletters and Websites   Class newsletters or websites are additional methods of fostering home-school communication. Even though putting together a class newsletter or designing a website requires a lot of work, in many cases it is worth the effort. Most teachers today have access to a computer and word processing software. A one- to three-page monthly newsletter can give parents—especially those who do not attend meetings or open houses—information that is too long or detailed to give over the telephone. A newsletter is also an excellent way to recognize parents who participate in various activities. By making the newsletter or website a class project, the teacher can include student-written stories and news items and can create an enjoyable learning activity for the entire class.

 To see the website constructed and operated by Ms. Stappenbeck's students, go to the Companion Website and click on Teacher Feature page at **www.prenhall.com/heward**

Telephone Calls   Regular telephone calls can be an effective and efficient way to maintain home-school communication and parent involvement (Gartland, 1993). A brief conversation that focuses on a child's positive accomplishments lets parents and teachers share the child's success and recognize each other's contributions. Short, positive calls from the teacher also reduce parents' fear that calls from school always indicate a problem. Teachers should set aside time on a regular basis so that each child's parent receives a call at least once every two or three weeks. Teachers should ask parents what times they prefer to receive calls. Keeping a log helps to maintain the schedule and reminds teachers of any necessary follow-up.

Telephone answering machines are a convenient, low-cost technology for home-school communication. By recording daily messages on an answering machine, teachers can give parents a great deal of information for relatively little cost. Parents can call and listen at their convenience, literally 24 hours a day. Recorded telephone messages can provide schoolwide and classroom-by-classroom information, good news (e.g., citizen of the month), and suggestions for working with children at home (Heward, Heron, Gardner, & Prayzer, 1991; Minner, Beane, & Prater, 1986; Test, Cooke, Weiss, Heward, & Heron, 1986). Parent callers can also leave messages on the machine, pose a question, offer an idea or suggestion for the teacher, and so on.

Daily recorded telephone messages can increase parent-teacher communication and improve student achievement. One teacher of a primary learning disabilities class recorded brief messages on an automatic telephone answering machine. Parents could call five nights per week from 5:00 P.M. until 7:00 A.M. and hear a recorded message like this one:

> Good evening. The children worked very hard today. We are discussing transportation. They enjoyed talking about the airport and all the different kinds of airplanes. The spelling words for tomorrow are train, t-r-a-i-n; plane, p-l-a-n-e; truck, t-r-u-c-k; automobile, a-u-t-o-m-o-b-i-l-e; and ship, s-h-i-p. Thank you for calling. (Heward & Chapman, 1981, p. 13)

The number of telephone calls the teacher received from the parents of the six children in the class each week was recorded for the entire school year. The teacher received a total of only 5 calls from parents during the 32 weeks when the recorded messages were not available (0.16 calls per week) compared with 112 calls during the 6 weeks the message system was in operation (18.7 per week). During the nonmessage phases of the study, the next day's spelling list was sent home with the children each day, and parents were asked to help their children with the words. Nonetheless, scores on the daily five-word spelling tests improved for all six students only when the recorded messages were available.

Although no single method of communication will be effective or even appropriate with every parent and family, teachers can increase the number of families they reach and the frequency of communications with those families by making several methods of home-school communication available to parents. Some parents and families prefer face-to-face meetings; others appreciate receiving written messages or phone calls; still others communicate more frequently and efficiently via e-mail or fax machine. Teachers should ask parents which methods of communication they prefer. Whatever modes or forms of parent-teacher communication are used, educators should consider the suggestions in Teaching & Learning, "Guidelines for Communicating and Working with Parents," later in this chapter.

 # OTHER FORMS OF PARENT INVOLVEMENT

 ## PARENTS AS TEACHERS

Typically developing children learn many skills that children with disabilities do not learn without systematic instruction. For children with disabilities, the casual routines of everyday life at home and in the community may not provide enough practice and feedback to teach them important skills. Many parents of exceptional children have responded to this challenge by systematically teaching their children self-help and daily living skills or by providing home-based academic tutoring to supplement classroom instruction.

Parents can serve as effective teachers for their children, a conclusion supported by numerous research studies and parent involvement projects in which parents have successfully taught their children at home (e.g., Barbetta & Heron, 1991; Leach & Siddall, 1992; Thurston & Dasta, 1990). Research shows that parents can enhance the development of children with disabilities by teaching them at home (e.g., Baker, 1989; Delaney & Kaiser, 2001; Snell & Beckman-Brindley, 1984; Wedel & Fowler, 1984). And the majority of parents who participate in systematic home tutoring programs describe it as a positive experience for them and their children. A mother and father who participated in a home-tutoring program organized by their child's school wrote: "We really enjoyed teaching M. to tell time, and he enjoyed working with us. He learned so quickly and we were so happy and proud to see the progress he was making. We have two other children. Doing this program allowed us to spend time alone with M." (Donley & Williams, 1997, p. 50).

Usually, if parents wish to tutor their children at home, they can and should be helped to do so. Properly conducted, home-based parent tutoring strengthens a child's educational program and gives enjoyment to both child and parent. Guidelines for home-based parent tutoring include the following (Bowen, Olympia, & Jensen, 1996; Hudson & Miller, 1993; Lovitt, 1982):

- *Keep sessions short.* Aim for 15- to 20-minute sessions three or four days per week.
- *Make the experience positive.* Parents should praise the child's attempts.
- *Keep responses to the child consistent.* By praising the child's successful responses (materials and activities at the child's appropriate instructional level are a must) and providing a consistent, unemotional response to errors (e.g., "Let's read that word again, together"), parents can avoid the frustration and negative results that can occur when home tutoring is mishandled.
- *Use tutoring to practice and extend skills already learned in school.* For example, use spelling or vocabulary words from school as the questions or items for an adapted board game (Wesson, Wilson, & Higbee Mandelbaum, 1988).
- *Keep a record.* Parents, like classroom teachers, can never know the exact effects of their teaching unless they keep records. A daily record enables both parents and child to see gradual progress that might be missed if subjective opinion is the only basis for

Guidelines for communicating with parents

 Council for Exceptional Children Content Standards for Beginning Teachers–Common Core: Foster respectful and beneficial relationships between families and professionals (CC10S3) (also CC1K7 and CC9S7).
PRAXIS Special Education Core Principles: Content Knowledge: III. Delivery of Services to Students with Disabilities, Professional roles, Communicating with parents.

Parents as tutors

 Council for Exceptional Children Content Standards for Beginning Teachers–Common Core: Assist individuals with exceptional learning needs and their families in becoming active participants in the educational team (CC10S4) (also CC1K7).
PRAXIS Special Education Core Principles: Content Knowledge: III. Delivery of Services to Students with Disabilities, Professional roles, Communicating with parents, encouraging parent participation.

Ten Guidelines for Communicating and Working with Parents

Regardless of the mode or form of parent-teacher communication, the following suggestions are valuable guidelines for educators in their interactions with parents and families. Contrast these 10 guidelines with the professional roadblocks to communication described earlier in the chapter.

Don't assume that you know more about the child, his needs, and how those needs should be met than his parents do. If you make this assumption, you will usually be wrong and, worse, will miss opportunities to obtain and provide meaningful information.

Junk the jargon. Educators who use technical terminology will have difficulty communicating effectively with parents (or with anyone else, for that matter). Speak in clear, everyday language and avoid the alphabet soup of special education (e.g., FAPE, IFSP, MFE).

Don't let assumptions and generalizations about parents and families guide your efforts. If you are genuinely interested in what a father or mother feels or wants, ask. Do not assume a parent is in the x, y, or z stage and therefore needs a, b, or c.

Be sensitive and responsive to the cultural and linguistic backgrounds of parents and families. The information and support services desired by families from different cultural and ethnic groups vary, and majority educators must work to be sensitive to those differences (Harry, Rueda, & Kalyanpur, 1999; Lynch & Hanson, 1998).

Don't be defensive toward or intimidated by parents. Unless you are one, you cannot ever really know what being the parent of a child with disabilities is like. But as a trained teacher, you do know something about helping children with disabilities learn. That's your job; it's what you do every day with lots of children. Offer the knowledge and skills you have without apology, and welcome parents' input.

Refer families to other professionals when needed. If you are a child's teacher, you interact with parents and families in an effort to improve the child's educational program. In that role, you are not a marriage counselor or a therapist. If a parent or a family member indicates the need for non-special education services, offer to refer him to professionals and agencies qualified to provide those services.

Help parents strive for a realistic optimism. Children with disabilities and their families benefit little from professionals who are doom-and-gloom types or who minimize the significance of a disability. Help parents analyze, plan, and prepare for their child's future (Giangreco et al., 1998; Turnbull & Turnbull, 2001).

Start with something parents can be successful with. For many parents, involvement in their child's educational program is a new experience. When parents show an interest in helping their child at home, don't set them up to fail by giving them complicated materials, complex instructions, and a heavy schedule of nightly tutoring. Begin with something simple that is likely to be rewarding to the parent and the child.

Allow and respect a parent's right to say, "No." Most educators are eager to share what they know with parents and to help families plan and carry out shared teaching goals. But professionals sometimes "fail to recognize the more basic needs of families, one of which is to not need a professional support person!. . . there comes a time when parents and other members of the family wish to be left alone" (Howard et al., 2001, p. 452).

Don't be afraid to say, "I don't know." Sometimes parents will ask questions that you cannot answer or request services you cannot provide. The mark of a real professional is knowing the limits of your expertise and when you need help. It is okay to say, "I don't know." Parents will think more highly of you.

evaluation. Most children do make progress under guided instruction, and a record documents that progress, perhaps providing the parent with an opportunity to see the child in a new and positive light.

It is important for professionals to consider carefully to what extent parent tutoring is appropriate. Not all parents want to teach their children at home or have the time to learn and use the necessary teaching skills—and professionals must not interpret that situation as an indication that parents do not care enough about their children. Teachers must not assume that parents who choose not to participate in home teaching programs are disinterested in their children. Some parents may choose not to do home tutoring because they feel it may compete with other activities in the home and negatively affect their family's overall quality of life (Parette & Petch-Hogan, 2000).

Properly conducted, home-based parent tutoring sessions strengthen the child's educational program and are enjoyable for the child as well as the parent.

For specific programs and techniques teachers can use to help parents who do wish to tutor their children at home, see Bowen et al. (1996) and Miller, Barbetta, and Heron (1994). For suggestions for supporting parents who want to help their children with homework and study skills, see Jayanthi, Bursuck, Epstein, and Polloway (1997); Jensen, Sheridan, Olympia, and Andrews (1994); and Luckner (1994).

PARENT EDUCATION AND SUPPORT GROUPS

Education for parenting is not new; programs date back to the early 1800s. But as a result of greater parent involvement in the education of children with disabilities, many more programs are offered for and by parents. Parent groups can serve a variety of purposes: from one-time-only dissemination of information on a new school policy, to make-it-and-take-it workshops in which parents make instructional materials to use at home (e.g., a math facts practice game), to multiple-session programs on IEP/IFSP planning or behavior support strategies.

Parent education and parent support groups

PRAXIS Special Education Core Principles: Content Knowledge: III. Delivery of Services to Students with Disabilities, Professional roles, Communicating with parents, directing parents to parent-educators or to other groups and resources.

There is consistent agreement in the parent education literature on the importance of involving parents in planning and, whenever possible, actually conducting parent groups (Kroth & Edge, 1997; Turnbull & Turnbull, 2001). To determine what parents want from a parent program, educators should use both open and closed needs assessment procedures. An open needs assessment consists of questions like these:

The best family time for my child is when we _____.

I will never forget the time that my child and I _____.

When I take my child to the store, I am concerned that she will _____.

The hardest thing about having a special child is _____.

I wish I knew more about _____.

A closed needs assessment asks parents to choose, from a list of possibilities, topics they would like to learn more about. For example, educators can give parents a list of topics (e.g., bedtime behavior, interactions with siblings, homework, making friends, planning for the future) and ask them to check any item that is something of a problem and circle any topics that are of major concern or interest.

Bailey and Simeonsson (1988a) have developed a family needs survey consisting of 35 items organized into six categories (e.g., information, support, finances, family functioning). Because they have obtained different profiles of responses for mothers and fathers, they recommend that both mothers and fathers complete the survey. They also recommend combining open-ended questions with an overall assessment of family needs. They simply ask parents to list on a piece of paper their five greatest needs as a family. By examining the results of needs assessment questionnaires, parents and professionals together can plan parent education groups that respond to families' real needs.

The Beach Center on Families and Disability at the University of Kansas provides technical assistance for a national network of Parent to Parent support programs. Visit the Beach Center website at www.lsi.ukans.edu/beach/beachhp.htm.

 PARENT TO PARENT GROUPS

Parent to Parent programs help parents of children with special needs become reliable allies for one another (Santelli & Poyadue, 2001). Parent to Parent gives parents of children with disabilities the opportunity to receive support from a veteran parent who has experienced or still is experiencing similar circumstances and challenges. The program carefully matches trained and experienced parents in a one-to-one relationship with parents who have been newly referred to the program. "Because the two parents share so many common disability and family experiences, an immediacy of understanding is typically present in the match. This makes the informational and emotional support from the veteran parents all the more meaningful" (Santelli et al., 1997, p. 74). The first Parent to Parent program, called Pilot Parents, was formed in 1971 by the parent of a young child with Down syndrome in Omaha, Nebraska. Today, there are more than 550 active local Parent to Parent groups and 29 statewide programs.

 PARENTS AS RESEARCH PARTNERS

Researchers in special education are concerned about the social validity of their studies (Schwartz & Baer, 1991). Are they investigating socially significant variables? Are the methods used to change student performance acceptable? Did the changes observed make any real difference in the child's life? Who better than parents can identify meaningful outcomes, observe and measure performance in the home and community, and let researchers know if their ideas and findings have any real validity?

A model research-partnership program conducted at the Fred S. Keller School in New York embraces parents as full partners in conducting action research with their children. "The parents are the scientists, and they conduct empirical studies under the supervision of the schools' parent educators" (Donley & Williams, 1997, p. 46). Parents are assisted in the development of their research projects by their child's teachers, other parents, and a paid parent educator. The experience culminates with a poster session presentation at the end of the school year during which the parent-scientists display the academic, social, and affective gains achieved by their children. Donley and Williams recognize that some school programs do not have the resources to hire a parent educator. They provide several suggestions for schools with more limited resources to approximate their model.

Kay and Fitzgerald (1997) believe that collaborative action research projects foster closer bonds between teachers and parents and provide parents with the satisfaction of knowing what works with their child and why. They recommend that parents participate in action research by helping brainstorm research questions, collect performance data on their children, and share the outcomes with other parents and teachers. Kay and Fitzgerald recognize that involving parents in home-based research experiences can, at times, be overwhelming; but they view the benefits as far outweighing the disadvantages. Whether the parents participate as paid or volunteer members of a research team, they are involved in collecting performance data on their children, talking about these data on a regular basis with other parents, and displaying them in an informal and supportive environment at the end of the year (Donley & Williams, 1997).

 HOW MUCH PARENT INVOLVEMENT?

It is easy to get carried away with a good concept, especially one like parent and family involvement, which has so much promise for positive outcomes. But teachers and everyone else involved in providing special education services to children with disabilities must not take a one-sided, unidirectional view of parent involvement. Sometimes the time and energy required for parents to participate in home-based tutoring programs or parent education groups cause stress among family members or guilt if the parents cannot fulfill teachers' expectations (Callahan, Rademacher, & Hildreth, 1998; Turnbull & Turnbull, 2001). The time required to provide additional help to a child with disabilities may take too much time and attention away from other family members (Parette & Petch-Hogan, 2000).

Kroth and Edge (1997) describe the mirror model for parent involvement (see Figure 4.6), which recognizes that parents have a great deal to offer as well as a need to receive services from special educators. The model attempts to give parents an equal part in deciding what services they need and what services they might provide to professionals or other parents. The top half of the model assumes that professionals have certain information, knowledge, and skills that should be shared with parents to help them with their children. The bottom half of the model assumes that parents have information, knowledge, and skills that can help professionals be more effective in assisting children. The model assumes that not all parents need everything that professionals have to offer and that no parent should be expected to provide everything. All parents should be expected to provide and obtain information, most parents will be active participants in IEP planning, and fewer parents will participate in or contribute to workshops and extended parent education groups.

When helping families assess their strengths and needs, professionals must not overlook the importance of leisure time.

 CURRENT ISSUES AND FUTURE TRENDS

Special educators and families of children with disabilities will continue to develop more effective ways of working together. These efforts will be increasingly driven by the complimentary values of family-centered services and family empowerment. Family-centered services are predicated on the belief that the child is part of a family system and that effective change for the child (who is one part of the system) cannot be achieved without helping the entire family (the whole system) (Turnbull & Turnbull, 2001).

The rationale for family empowerment is based on the belief that families are the primary and most effective social institution, that families cannot be replaced, that parents are and should remain in charge of their families, and that the role of professionals is to help parents in their capacity as family leaders (Callister, Mitchell, & Talley, 1986). Empowerment can be viewed as a process of enabling families to take control of their lives by providing information and resources and helping families learn to use them. The specific actions and supports that result in meaningful and effective empowerment will vary across families and even change across time and instances within a specific family (Jones,

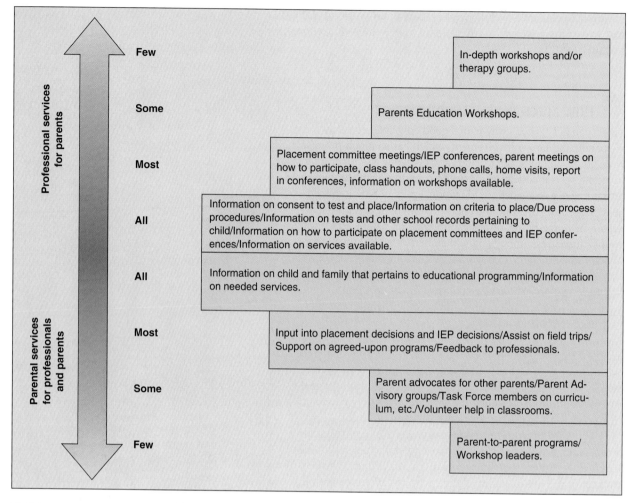

FIGURE 4.6 Mirror model for parent involvement

Source: From Kroth, R. L., & Edge, D. (1997). *Strategies for communicating with parents of exceptional children* (3rd ed.). Denver: Love. Reprinted by permission.

Mirror model for parent involvement

Council for Exceptional Children Content Standards for Beginning Teachers–Common Core: Models and strategies of consultation and collaboration (CC10K1).
PRAXIS Special Education Core Principles: Content Knowledge: III. Delivery of Services to Students with Disabilities, Professional roles, Communicating with parents, encouraging parent participation.

Garlow, Turnbull, & Barber, 1996). Dunlap and Fox (1997) define family supports as "any and all actions that serve to strengthen and sustain the family system, especially as these actions pertain to the family's assimilation and understanding of the child's disability" (p. 4).

Another emerging perspective, particularly with families involved in early intervention programs for infants and toddlers, is the movement toward a *strength-based approach* to conceptualizing and providing family supports:

A strength-based philosophy is a critical belief, an all-pervasive attitude that informs all of the professional's interactions with families. It assumes that all families have strengths they can build on and use to meet their own needs, to accomplish their own goals, and to promote the well-being of family members. The family-professional relationship starts not from an assessment of problems related to the child with a disability but from an attempt to fully understand the way in which the family successfully accomplishes its goals and manages its problems. (Powell, Batsche, Ferro, Fox, & Dunlap, 1997, p. 4)

Professionals and parents are working to develop and provide a wide range of supportive services for families of children with disabilities. Programs are being implemented to help parents plan effectively for their family's future; develop problem-solving skills; and acquire competence in financial planning, coping with stress, locating and using community services, and finding time to relax and enjoy life—to name just a few areas of emphasis.

Parents and family are the most important people in a child's life. Effective and caring teachers should be next in importance. Working together, teachers, parents, and families can and do make a difference in the lives of exceptional children.

For more information about parents and families of exceptional children, to to the Web Links module in Chapter 4 of the Companion Website at **www.prenhall.com/heward**

SUMMARY

SUPPORT FOR PARENT AND FAMILY INVOLVEMENT

- Three factors are responsible for the increased emphasis on parent and family involvement in the education of children with disabilities: parent advocacy, educators' desire to increase their effectiveness, and legislative mandates.
- A successful parent-teacher partnership provides benefits for the professional, the parents, and—most important—the child.

UNDERSTANDING PARENTS AND FAMILIES OF CHILDREN WITH DISABILITIES

- All parents and family members must adjust to the birth of a child with disabilities or the discovery that a child has a disability. This adjustment process is different for each parent, and educators should not make assumptions about an individual parent's stage of adjustment.
- Parents of children with disabilities fulfill nine roles and responsibilities: caregiver, provider, teacher, counselor, behavior support specialist, parent of siblings without disabilities, marriage partner, information specialist/trainer for significant others, and advocate for school and community services.
- A family member's disability affects parents and siblings without disabilities in different ways during the different life-cycle stages.
- Respite care—the temporary care of an individual with disabilities by nonfamily members—is a critical support for many families of children with severe disabilities.

ESTABLISHING PARENT-TEACHER PARTNERSHIPS

- Five principles for effective communication between educators and parents are accepting what is being said, listening, questioning appropriately, encouraging, and staying focused.
- Differences in the cultural and linguistic beliefs and practices of professionals and families often serve as barriers to parent involvement.
- Attitudes of and behaviors by professionals that serve as barriers to communication with parents and families include making assumptions about the services and information that parents need, treating parents as clients or adversaries instead of partners, keeping professional distance, blaming parents for their child's disability or performance, acting as if parents need counseling, disrespecting parents' suggestions, and labeling parents who don't act the way the professional believes they should.
- Dialoguing is an approach to conflict resolution in which both parties try to see each other's point of view.

METHODS OF HOME-SCHOOL COMMUNICATION

- The three most common modes of home-school communication are parent-teacher conferences, written messages, and telephone calls.

- Here are 10 guidelines for working with parents and families of children with disabilities:
  - Don't assume you know more about a child than the parents do.
  - Junk the jargon and speak in plain, everyday language.
  - Don't let assumptions or generalizations guide your efforts.
  - Be sensitive and responsive to cultural and linguistic differences.
  - Don't be defensive toward or intimidated by parents.
  - Refer families to other professionals when needed.
  - Help parents strive for realistic optimism.
  - Start with something that parents can be successful with.
  - Allow and respect parents' right to say no.
  - Don't be afraid to say, "I don't know."

OTHER TYPES OF PARENT INVOLVEMENT

- Many parents can and should learn to help teach their child with disabilities.
- Parents and professionals should work together in planning and conducting parent education groups.
- Parent to Parent groups give parents of children with disabilities support from veteran parents who are experiencing similar circumstances and challenges.
- Parents who serve as action research partners help brainstorm research questions, collect performance data on their children, and share those data with other parents and teachers.
- The mirror model of parent involvement assumes that not all parents need everything that professionals have to offer and that no parent should be expected to participate in everything.

CURRENT ISSUES AND FUTURE TRENDS

- Professionals who work with parents should value family needs and support families in maintaining control over the services and supports they receive.
- The rationale for family empowerment is based on the belief that families are the primary and most effective social institution, that families cannot be replaced, that parents are and should remain in charge of their families, and that the role of professionals is to help parents in their capacity as family leaders.
- Family-centered services are predicated on the belief that the child is part of a family system and that effective change for the child cannot be achieved without helping the entire family.
- A strength-based approach to family supports assumes that all families have strengths they can build on and use to meet their own needs, accomplish their own goals, and promote the well-being of family members.

To check your comprehension of chapter contents, go to the Guided Review and Quiz Modules in Chapter 4 of the Companion Website at **www.prenhall. com/heward**

Part 2

Educational Needs of Exceptional Students

Chapter 5
Early Childhood Special Education

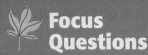

KIM LUNDY
SPIRITRIDGE ELEMENTARY SCHOOL

BELLEVUE, WASHINGTON

Education • Teaching Credentials • Experience
- B.A. with major in English and minor in Elementary Education, Whitman College, 1994
- M.Ed. in Early Childhood Special Education, University of Washington, 1996
- Early Childhood Special Education, Birth–Grade 3, and General Education Elementary, K–8 (Washington)
- 6 years of teaching preschoolers with and without disabilities

Current Teaching Position and Students   I have the greatest job! I teach two half-day sessions of integrated preschool each day. Of my 20 total preschoolers (9 in the morning and 11 in the afternoon), 15 qualify for special education services because of a developmental delay in one or more of the following areas: cognitive, adaptive (self-help), social, gross and/or fine motor, and communication. A few of my students qualify for special education services under the IDEA categories of health impairments or autism. Four of my students are nonverbal or just learning to talk, and four come from families that speak English as a second language.

Meet Some of My Students   I wish I could introduce you to all of my students, but here's a picture of four of them. Abby is a delightful 3-year-old girl who loves bubbles, the color purple, and being around her friends. She has several significant disabilities that make her nonverbal, nonmobile, and medically fragile. Abby has a really cool special chair and a prone stander, and she takes great pride in being able to activate toys that have a switch! Four-year-old Ben enjoys the sensory table and cars. He is eager to learn how to talk but gets overwhelmed by sudden noises, changes in routine, and large groups of children. Grace is a 3-year-old with a beautiful smile and a diagnosis of autism. She is mostly nonverbal and requires a high level of assistance to participate appropriately and safely in most classroom activities. Grace receives a full day of special education services from the school district: she participates in intensive one-on-one instruction in the morning and attends my integrated preschool in the afternoon. Four-year-old Sam is a typically developing child. He enjoys art, music, blocks, and the house area and is a great friend to all of the children.

There is no way I could teach all of my terrific students alone; I am fortunate to have wonderful classroom aides (three in the morning and two in the afternoon) and a team of excellent speech, physical, and occupational therapists.

IEP Goals   I teach skills that increase children's independence and give them a base for future learning. Children's learning goals include following directions; transitioning from one activity to another; playing appropriately; attending;

- Why is it so difficult to measure the impact of early intervention?

- How can we provide early intervention services for a child whose disability is not yet present?

- What do you think are the most important goals of early childhood special education?

- What are some ways in which early childhood special education differs from special education for school-age children with disabilities?

- How can a play activity or an everyday routine be turned into a specially designed learning opportunity for a preschooler with disabilities?

taking turns; communicating; participating in group activities; pre-academic skills (such as counting and identifying colors, shapes, and letters); and functional skills such as toileting, washing hands, and coat skills. Because all preschoolers need to learn these skills, they are incorporated into thoughtfully planned classroom activities. When necessary, these skills are addressed by children's IEP goals and objectives, as in the following examples.

Cognitive skills IEP goal. Abby will improve her cognitive skills so that she will be able to participate in developmentally appropriate activities.

Short-term objective 1. With adult assistance to arrange opportunities, Abby will use eye gaze to correctly identify (a) 5 pictures of familiar objects and/or people by (date); and (b) 10 pictures of familiar objects and/or people by (date) on 3 separate days, as measured by monthly classroom data collection.

Short-term objective 2. With adult assistance to arrange opportunities and assistive technology, Abby will follow adult directions to "turn it on/make it go" and "turn it off/make it stop" (a) 2 times daily by (date) and (b) 4 times daily by (date) on 3 separate occasions, as measured by monthly classroom data collection.

Adaptive skills IEP goal. Ben will improve his adaptive skills to be better able to independently care for his own needs.

Short-term objective 1. Ben will complete all steps of the handwashing process (a) 2 times daily with visual/gestural prompts as needed by (date) and (b) 2 times daily independently by (date) on 3 separate days, as measured by monthly classroom data collection.

Short-term objective 2. Ben will unfasten his coat, take his coat and backpack off, and put them in his cubby (a) 1 time daily with verbal/gestural prompts by (date) and (b) 1 time daily independently by (date) on 3 separate days, as measured by monthly classroom data collection.

I think that the present levels of performance (PLOP) section of the IEP is just as important as, if not more so than, the goals and objectives. PLOPs communicate how you think about a child. If you think about a child in terms of strengths and challenges instead of deficits and describe what she can do well, parents are much more willing to listen and work with you on identifying some objectives for areas of improvement. For example, here is the PLOP I wrote to address Abby's cognitive and adaptive skills:

Abby really enjoys preschool! One of her favorite parts of the day is circle. . . . she loves music and beams her famous smile at everyone when we start singing! She is able to direct her eye gaze to choose a picture of the song she wants to sing. She is also able to visually track objects horizontally, vertically, and in a circular motion when they are moved slowly. Abby is beginning to demonstrate discrimination of objects and colors placed in or near her hands, and has been observed pushing the correct item/color when given a direction such as, "Give me the red bird/car/person/." She is unable to independently access classroom materials and toys; hence, we've done many trials with different switch styles and positions and have found that a small switch mounted near her right fist is very successful. With this, she can activate toys and communication devices by herself. Abby's limited mobility and communication skills impair her ability to access and play in her school environment and impact her independent participation in developmentally appropriate activities. Objectives in this area should focus on building her emerging cognitive skills.

Teaching Strategies I tell anyone who asks that my classroom isn't that different from the tuition-based preschool next door. I begin with general education preschool activities and add structure and accommodations as necessary. One of the most important things I do takes place before the children even arrive. During the summer, I give a lot of thought to arranging the physical classroom environment, designing boundaries, minimizing distractions, allowing for adequate space to play, arranging the space to be accessible to all students, and making sure that all the areas and materials in my room are fun and that children and teachers will want to play.

I emphasize structure and routine. I have an overall classroom schedule and individual schedules as needed to ease transitions and teach independence. I try to make learning *meaningful* for my students: I purposefully plan opportunities for communication, I embed learning trials into naturally occurring (but thoughtfully designed) activities, and I use natural reinforcers whenever possible. And I have tons of fun with my kids! I love to play with them. In doing so, I build friendships and connections with them that make my teaching all the more effective.

How do I know that all of this stuff works? Every year, I get better at collecting data on the children's learning. The data tell me if what I am doing is working. Equally important, the data tell me when something is not working and it's time to try a different strategy.

Communicating with Parents and Families   As the older sister of a young woman with Down syndrome, I have a very personal view of the role and significance of families. You just can't take a child out of the context of his or her family. I have an open classroom policy, which means that families can come and visit any time—no advance warning needed. When writing and presenting IEPs to families who are new to special education, I write out acronyms and try to avoid using any jargon or technical terms. I send home a weekly newsletter called "The Adventures of Room 45." I do home visits and help plan birthday parties. I love to have siblings come and visit for a day. I phone and e-mail families often.

A Memorable Lesson for Me   Last year, I had a 3-year-old who missed a lot of school. When Joey did come to school, he wore dirty, stinky clothes; sometimes he came to school sick. Joey's mom *never* came to any scheduled meetings or events, even when she told me she would come. I started thinking some pretty negative things about her. One evening, I took Joey home after another student's birthday party. Since his mom hadn't attended Joey's IEP meeting, I decided to talk with her right then and there. I discovered she was a single parent who loved her two children very much and that after providing food, shelter, and child care for them, her financial and personal resources were totally exhausted. I gained a lot of respect for Joey's mom that night and lost some for myself for not discovering and understanding her situation sooner.

What I Like Most about Being a Special Educator   I believe that we can all make significant contributions to society. I count my blessings every day because I am in the position to teach children the skills they will need to do this. I spend my days with a very precious future; I embark on a different adventure every day and strive to make a difference in each adventure. Being a special education teacher is not easy. The field is full of paperwork and miles of red tape. But it's even more full of wonderful children who need your help. If you want to make a difference, want a challenge, and want to learn a lot along the way, then this is the job for you!

To see examples of activity schedules and data collection forms used by Ms. Lundy, go to the Teacher Feature page on the Companion Website at **www.prenhall.com.heward**

Most children learn a phenomenal amount from the time they are born until they enter school. They grow and develop in orderly, predictable ways, learning to move about their world, communicate, and play. As their ability to manipulate their environment increases, so does their level of independence. Normal rates and patterns of child development contrast sharply with the progress experienced by most children with disabilities. If they are to master the basic skills that most children acquire naturally, many preschoolers with disabilities need carefully planned and implemented early childhood special education services.

To better understand what will be covered in this chapter, go to the Essential Concepts and Chapter-at-a-Glance Modules in Chapter 5 of the Companion Website at **www.prenhall.com/heward**

Early childhood experts agree that the earlier intervention begins, the better. Child development expert Burton White, who has conducted years of research with typically developing infants and preschoolers at Harvard University's Preschool Project, believes that the period between 8 months and 3 years is critical to cognitive and social development: "to begin to look at a child's educational development when he is 2 years of age is already much too late" (White, 1975, p. 4). If the first years of life are the most important for children without disabilities, they are even more critical for the child with disabilities, who, with each passing month, risks falling even further behind typically developing age mates. Yet parents concerned about deficits in their child's development used to be told, "Don't worry. Wait and see. She'll probably grow out of it."

Over the past 25 years, the "extraordinary vulnerability of young children at risk for developmental problems . . . as well as those with established disabilities has been recognized" (Guralnick, 1998, p. 319). Today, early childhood special education has become one of the most prominent and growing components in education, and the creation of an effective system of early intervention services has become a national priority.

 ## THE IMPORTANCE OF EARLY INTERVENTION

 ### DEFINING EARLY INTERVENTION

In the early childhood and special education literature, the term *early intervention* sometimes refers only to services provided to infants and toddlers from birth through age 2, and *early childhood special education* refers to educational and related services provided to preschoolers who are ages 3 to 5. In this book, the two terms are used interchangeably in most instances to describe special education services provided to children from birth to age 5 and their families. **Early intervention** consists of a wide variety of educational, nutritional, child care, and family supports, all designed to reduce the effects of disabilities or prevent the occurrence of learning and developmental problems later in life for children presumed to be at risk for such problems. McConnell (1994) provides an excellent definition of early intervention:

> [The term refers to] home- and classroom-based efforts that provide (1) compensatory or preventative services for children who are assumed to be at risk for learning and behavior problems later in life, particularly during the elementary school years, and (2) remedial services for problems or deficits already encountered . . . . Simply put, early intervention must provide early identification and provision of services to reduce or eliminate the effects of disabilities or to prevent the development of other problems, so that the need for subsequent special services is reduced. (pp. 75, 78)

 ### EXAMINING THE EFFECTIVENESS OF EARLY INTERVENTION

Does early intervention work? If so, what kinds of interventions work best? Hundreds of studies have been conducted in an effort to answer these questions. We'll look at a few of those studies here. First, we'll consider two widely cited examples of what Guralnick (1997) calls first-generation research: studies that try to answer the question "Does early intervention make a difference for children and their families?" Then we'll look at three examples of second-generation research studies designed to find what factors make early intervention more or less effective for particular groups of children.

Skeels and Dye   The earliest and one of the most dramatic demonstrations of the critical importance and potential impact of early intervention was conducted by Skeels and Dye (1939). They found that intensive stimulation, one-to-one attention, and a half-morning kindergarten program with 1- to 2-year-old children who were classified as mentally re-

Skeels & Dye study and Milwaukee Project

Council for Exceptional Children   Content Standards for Beginning Teachers of Early Childhood Students: Historical and philosophical foundations of services for young children both with and without exceptional learning needs (EC1K1).

tarded resulted in IQ gains and eventual independence and success as adults when compared to similar children in the institution who received adequate medical and health services but no individual attention. Although the Skeels and Dye study can be justly criticized for its lack of tight experimental methodology, it challenged the widespread belief that intelligence was fixed and that little could be expected from intervention efforts. This study served as a catalyst for many subsequent investigations into the effects of early intervention.

The Milwaukee Project   The goal of the Milwaukee Project was to reduce the incidence of mental retardation through a program of parent education and infant stimulation for children considered to be at risk for retarded development because of their mothers' levels of intelligence (IQs below 70) and conditions of poverty (Garber & Heber, 1973; Heber & Garber, 1971; Strickland, 1971). The mothers received training in child care and were taught how to interact with and stimulate their children through play. Beginning before the age of 6 months, the children also participated in an infant stimulation program conducted by trained teachers. By the age of 3½, the experimental children tested an average of 33 IQ points higher than did a control group of children who did not participate in the program. (Play is critically important to children's learning and development. See *Teaching & Learning*, "Selecting Toys for Young Children with Disabilities," later in this chapter.)

Although the Milwaukee Project has been criticized for its research methods (e.g., Page, 1972), this study is sometimes offered as evidence that a program of maternal education and early infant stimulation can reduce the incidence of mental retardation caused by psychosocial disadvantage. (**Psychosocial disadvantage**, a combination of social and environmental deprivation early in a child's life, is generally believed to be a major cause of mild mental retardation.)

A stimulating, language-rich environment enhances the social and cognitive development of all young children.

The Abecedarian Project   The Abecedarian Project was designed as an experiment to test whether mental retardation caused by psychosocial disadvantage could be prevented by intensive, early education preschool programs (in conjunction with medical and nutritional supports) beginning shortly after birth and continuing until children enter kindergarten (Martin, Ramey, & Ramey, 1990). Children in the Abecedarian Project received early intervention that was both intensive and long: a full-day preschool program, 5 days per week, 50 weeks per year. Compared with children in a control group who received supplemental medical, nutritional, and social services but no daily early educational intervention services, children in the early intervention group made positive gains in IQ scores by age 3, were 50% less likely to fail a grade, and scored higher on IQ and reading and mathematics achievement tests at age 12.

A related finding was that children of low-IQ mothers benefited most from early intervention. For the mothers with IQs below 70 who were in the control condition, all but one of their children had IQs in the mentally retarded or borderline intelligence range at age 3. In contrast, all of the children in the early intervention group tested in the normal range of intelligence (above 85) by age 3.

This finding supports the concept of *targeted intervention*, which indicates that primary prevention of childhood disorders is more likely for certain subgroups than for others (Landesman & Ramey, 1989). Because the majority of children with mild and moderate mental retardation come from families with extremely low resources and with parents who have limited intellectual resources themselves, these families are the ones that are most in need of early intervention and are those that benefit the most in terms of outcomes valued by society. (Ramey & Ramey, 1992, p. 338)

Selecting Toys for Young Children with Disabilities

In 1916, John Dewey said, "Children learn by doing." He might just as well have said, "Children learn by playing." Play provides children with natural, repeated opportunities for critical learning. It is how they explore the world and discover their own capabilities. An infant bats a mobile with her hand, repeats the action, and begins learning about her world. As a toddler, her interactions with play materials teach her to discriminate and compare shapes and sizes and to learn concepts such as cause and effect and fast and slow (Hughes, Elicker, & Veen, 1995). A preschooler's increasingly complex play develops gross and fine motor skills, requires her to communicate and negotiate plans with others, and exposes her to pre-academic math and literacy skills (Morrison, 1999; Weber, Behl, & Summers, 1994).

If play is the work of childhood, then toys are the child's tools. Ideally, play materials, whether store-bought toys or everyday household items such as pots and pans, should provide meaningful, motivating activities that serve as a precursor to more complex learning (Brewer & Kieff, 1996; Mann, 1996; Perlmutter & Burrell, 1995). Not all toys, however, are accessible to children with disabilities.

The National Lekotek Center is a nationwide, nonprofit network of play centers, toy lending libraries, and computer loan programs dedicated to making play accessible for children with disabilities and to those living in poverty. Diana Nielander, planning and information officer at Lekotek, recommends keeping the following 10 tips in mind when selecting toys for young children with disabilities:

1. *Multisensory appeal.* Does the toy respond with lights, sounds, or movements? Are there contrasting colors? Does it have scent? Texture?
2. *Method of activation.* Will the toy provide a challenge without frustration? What force is required to activate it? What are the number and complexity of steps required?

Project CARE Project CARE compared the effectiveness of home-based early intervention in which mothers learned how to provide developmental stimulation for their infants and toddlers with center-based early intervention such as that provided in the Abecedarian Project (Wasik, Ramey, Bryant, & Sparling, 1990). Children who received the full-day, center-based preschool program five days per week, supplemented by home visits, showed gains in intellectual functioning almost identical to those found in the Abecedarian Project. A disappointment was that the intellectual functioning of children in the home-based–only treatment group did not improve. Ramey and Ramey (1992) suggest, "One plausible interpretation of these results is that the home-based treatment was not sufficiently intensive, on a day-to-day basis, to produce the same benefits that occur when a more formally organized and monitored center-based program is provided year round" (p. 339).

The Infant Health and Development Program The Infant Health and Development Program (IHDP) provided early intervention services to infants who were born prematurely and at low birth weight (less than 2,500 grams, or about 5½ pounds), two conditions that place children at risk for developmental delays (Ramey et al., 1992). This large-scale study involved nearly 1,000 children and their families in eight locations throughout the United

Play provides children with natural, repeated opportunities for critical learning.

7. *Potential for interaction.* Will the child be an active participant during use? Will the toy encourage social and language engagement with others?
8. *Safety and durability.* Are the toy and its parts sized appropriately given the child's size and strength? Can it be washed and cleaned? Is it moisture resistant?
9. *Where the toy will be used.* Will the toy be easy to store? Is there space in the home? Can the toy be used in a variety of positions (e.g., by a child lying on his side) or on a wheelchair tray?
10. *Current popularity.* Is it a toy almost any child would like? Does it tie in with popular books, TV programs, or movies?

Information on specific toys can be found in Lekotek's *Toy Guide for Differently-Abled Kids!,* a free resource published in conjunction with Toys "R" Us and endorsed by the National Parent Network on Disabilities. The catalog includes pictures and descriptions of more than 100 toys that have been tested with preschoolers with disabilities. Each toy is identified according to its likelihood of promoting growth in 10 developmental or skill areas: auditory, language, visual, tactile, gross motor, fine motor, social skills, self-esteem, creativity, and thinking.

Information about Lekotek and its services to families can be obtained at its website (http://www.lekotek.org). Lekotek also operates a toy resource helpline at (800) 366-PLAY, a toll-free service that anyone can use to talk directly to trained play experts who will recommend appropriate toys and play activities for a particular child as well as make referrals to other disability-related resources for families.

3. *Adjustability.* Does the toy have adjustable height, sound, volume, speed, or level of difficulty?
4. *Opportunities for success.* Can play be open-ended with no definite right or wrong way?
5. *Child's individual characteristics.* Does the toy provide activities that reflect both developmental and chronological ages? Does it reflect the child's interests?
6. *Self-expression.* Does the toy allow for creativity and choice making? Will it give the child experience with a variety of media?

States. Home visits were conducted from shortly after birth through age 3. Because of health problems associated with prematurity and low birth weight, the children did not begin attending the center-based early education program until 12 months of age and continued until age 3. Improvements in intellectual functioning were noted, with babies of comparatively higher birth weight showing increases similar in magnitude to those found in the Abecedarian Project and Project CARE.

The IHDP study found a positive correlation between how much children and their families participated in the early intervention and the intellectual development of the children. The percentages of children whose IQ scores fell in the mental retardation range based on tests administered at age 3 for each of the groups were 17% for the control group, 13% for those with low participation, 4% for medium participation, and less than 2% for high participation. The most active participants had an almost ninefold reduction in the incidence of mental retardation compared to the control group.

Together, these three second-generation studies provide strong evidence that children at risk for developmental delays and poor school outcomes respond favorably to systematic early intervention. They also point to two factors that appear highly related to the outcome effectiveness of early intervention: the *intensity of the intervention* and the *level of participation* by the children and their families (Ramey & Ramey, 1992).

Intensity of early intervention and level of participation

PRAXIS Special Education Core Principles: Content Knowledge: I. Understanding Exceptionalities, Causation and prevention of disability.

Summarizing the Research Base   Numerous methodological problems make it difficult to conduct early intervention research in a scientifically sound manner. Among the problems are the difficulties in selecting meaningful and reliable outcome measures; the wide disparity among children in the developmental effects of their disabilities; the tremendous variation across early intervention programs in curriculum focus, teaching strategies, duration, and intensity; and the ethical concerns of withholding early intervention from some children so that they may form a control group for comparison purposes (Bricker, 1986; Guralnick, 1998; Strain & Smith, 1986).

Despite these problems, most educators agree with Guralnick (1998), who concluded that, when taken as whole, comprehensive early intervention programs reveal a "consistent pattern of effectiveness as these programs are able to reduce the decline in intellectual development that occurs in the absence of intervention" (p. 323). Our national policymakers also believe that early intervention produces positive results for young children with disabilities, those who are at risk for developmental delays, and their families. Citing research and testimony from families, Congress identified the following outcomes for early intervention in the 1997 amendments to IDEA (P.L. 105–17, Sec. 1431):

In addition to helping young children with disabilities make developmental gains, early intervention can help prevent secondary disabilities, provide needed support for parents and families, and reduce the need for special education services when children reach school age.

a. to enhance the development of infants and toddlers with disabilities and to minimize their potential for developmental delay;

b. to reduce the educational costs to our society, including our Nation's schools, by minimizing the need for special education and related services after infants and toddlers with disabilities reach school age;

c. to minimize the likelihood of institutionalization of individuals with disabilities and maximize the potential for their independently living in society;

d. to enhance the capacity of families to meet the special education needs of their infants and toddlers with disabilities; and

e. to enhance the capacity of State and local agencies and service providers to identify, evaluate, and meet the needs of historically underrepresented populations, particularly minority, low-income, inner-city, and rural populations.

IDEA AND EARLY CHILDHOOD SPECIAL EDUCATION

When Congress passed P.L. 94–142 in 1975 (the original IDEA), it mandated a free, appropriate public education for all school-age children with disabilities ages 6 through 21. The law also required a state to provide special education services to all preschool children ages 3 to 5 with disabilities if that state already provided general public education for children in that age group. To encourage states to begin programs for preschoolers with disabilities, P.L. 94–142 included an incentive grant program that provided funds for establishing or improving preschool programs for children with disabilities.

Since 1975, Congress has enacted four bills reauthorizing and amending the original IDEA. The second of those bills, P.L. 99–457, has been called the most important legislation ever enacted for children with developmental delays (Shonkoff & Meisels, 2000). Before passage of this law, Congress estimated that states were serving at most about 70% of preschool children with disabilities, and systematic early intervention services for infants and toddlers with disabilities from birth through age 2 were scarce or nonexistent in many states. P.L. 99–457 included a mandatory preschool component for children with disabilities ages 3 to 5 and a voluntary incentive grant program for early intervention services to infants and toddlers and their families. With the passage of IDEA in 1997 (P.L. 105–17), Congress reaffirmed the nation's commitment to a system of early intervention services.

 EARLY INTERVENTION FOR INFANTS AND TODDLERS

If a state chooses to provide comprehensive early intervention services to infants and toddlers and their families, it can receive federal funds under IDEA's early intervention provisions. Currently, all states are participating; each state receives federal funds under this program based on the number of children, newborns through age 2, in the state's general population. In 2000, approximately 230,000 infants and toddlers were served nationally (U.S. Department of Education, 2002).

The law covers any child under age 3 who meets the following criteria:

a. Needs early intervention services because of developmental delays (as measured by appropriate diagnostic instruments or procedures) in one or more areas of cognitive development, physical development, social or emotional development, or adaptive development.
b. Has a diagnosed physical or medical condition that has a high probability of resulting in developmental delay.
c. Each State may also, at its discretion, serve infants and toddlers who are at risk of experiencing a substantial developmental delay if early intervention services are not provided.

Thus, states that receive IDEA funds for early intervention services must serve all infants and toddlers with developmental delays or established risk conditions. Although not required to do so, states may also use IDEA early intervention funds to serve infants and toddlers who fall under two types of *documented risk,* biological and environmental.

- *Developmental delays* are significant delays or atypical patterns of development that make children eligible for early intervention. Each state's definition of developmental delay must be broad enough to include all disability categories covered by IDEA, but children do not need to be classified or labeled according to those categories to receive early intervention services.
- *Established risk conditions* include diagnosed physical or medical conditions that almost always result in developmental delay or disability. Examples of established risk conditions are Down syndrome; fragile-X syndrome; fetal alcohol syndrome (FAS); and other conditions associated with mental retardation, brain or spinal cord damage, sensory impairments, and maternal acquired immune deficiency syndrome (AIDS). (Down syndrome, fragile-X syndrome, and FAS are discussed in Chapter 6.)
- *Biological risk conditions* include pediatric histories or current biological conditions (e.g., significantly premature birth, low birth weight) that result in a greater-than-usual probability of developmental delay or disability.
- *Environmental risk conditions* include factors such as extreme poverty, parental substance abuse, homelessness, abuse or neglect, and parental intellectual impairment, which are associated with higher-than-normal probability for developmental delay. (See Profiles & Perspectives, "Educating Young Children Prenatally Exposed to Illegal Drugs," later in this chapter.)

IDEA and early intervention

 Content Standards for Beginning Teachers of Early Childhood Students: Laws and policies that affect young children, families, and programs for young children (EC1K3). **PRAXIS** Special Education Core Principles: Content Knowledge: II. Legal and Societal Issues, Federal laws and legal issues related to special education.

Definitions of developmental delays risk conditions

 Content Standards for Beginning Teachers of Early Childhood Students: Laws and policies that affect young children, families, and programs for young children (EC1K3). **PRAXIS** Special Education Core Principles: Content Knowledge: I. Basic concepts in special education, definitions of specific categories and specific disabilities.

Educating Young Children Prenatally Exposed to Illegal Drugs

by Judith J. Carta

About 14 years ago, several of my colleagues and I became aware that children who had been identified as being prenatally exposed to drugs, especially cocaine, were entering our local preschool and child care settings. At that time, the media were publishing reports describing a new population of children like no other previously seen. These children were described as out of control with no ability to focus attention, lacking in affect, and unable to tell the difference between right and wrong. Understandably, teachers felt afraid and ill-equipped to handle such children, and potential foster and adoptive parents were hesitant to open their homes and families to them.

These fears were based on several myths and misconceptions that are conveyed in questions people most frequently asked about children prenatally exposed to drugs.

Do they all have behavior problems or learning difficulties? Children whose prenatal histories include their mothers' use of drugs represent a wide range of abilities. Some have physical and mental disabilities; others appear unaffected. Some are passive and socially withdrawn; others are aggressive. Some are unattached; others constantly seek attention and affection. No profile or set of characteristics defines this group of children. Some studies have reported that approximately 30% of these children perform lower than typically developing children. But this average figure masks the considerable variation in the way in which individual children may be affected (from a lot to not at all). It also fails to convey the many other factors in children's lives that may account for their developmental outcomes.

What accounts for the growing number of inner-city children's sudden episodes of violence, difficulties in attention, or lack of social skills, which appear more often in our classrooms? Aren't these problems caused by mothers' drug use? It is interesting that only behavior problems in inner-city schools are linked to prenatal drug use. Such a conclusion suggests that only mothers in the urban areas use drugs. In reality, the problem of illegal drug use by pregnant women is not unique to the inner city nor to any particular racial or ethnic group. No one group "owns" the problem of prenatal substance exposure. It is as likely to occur in rural areas as in urban areas or the suburbs.

IFSP

Council for Exceptional Children Content Standards for Beginning Teachers of Early Childhood Students: Laws and policies that affect young children, families, and programs for young children (EC1K3). **PRAXIS** Special Education Core Principles: Content Knowledge: III. Delivery of Services to Students with Disabilities, Curriculum and instruction, IFSP.

Individualized Family Services Plan IDEA requires that early intervention services for infants and toddlers be delivered according to an **Individualized Family Services Plan (IFSP).** The IFSP is developed by a multidisciplinary team that includes the child's parents and family and must include each of the follow eight elements:

1. a statement of the child's present levels of physical development, cognitive development, communication development, social or emotional development, or adaptive development, based on objective criteria;

2. a statement of the family's resources, priorities, and concerns relating to enhancing the development of the family's infant or toddler with a disability;

3. a statement of the major outcomes expected to be achieved for the infant or toddler and family, and the criteria, procedures, and timelines used to determine the degree to which progress toward achieving the outcomes is being made and whether modifications or revision of the outcomes or services are necessary;

Although prenatal substance exposure may be a factor in explaining the wide-ranging types of problems occurring with greater frequency in our schools, many risk factors associated with living in poverty and less-than-adequate caregiving may also be responsible (Carta et al., 2001). For example, two other factors are associated with a drug-using lifestyle in poverty: violence and drug trafficking. Violence is a fact of life in communities where trafficking occurs. A large percentage of children witness violence in neighborhoods as well as in their homes. Mothers are often victims of abuse, as are the children themselves. A growing body of research on the effects of exposure to violence or maltreatment of children points to many of the same behavioral symptoms attributed to prenatal drug exposure.

Another factor associated with behavioral and learning difficulties is the quality of caregiving that children receive in a substance-using lifestyle. Substance abusers are often inconsistent caregivers, behaving one way toward their children when they are straight, another when they are high or coming down. Attempting to get straight often requires a period of separation from children because many residential treatment centers do not allow children to reside or visit there. Drug-using parents are often socially isolated and lack a network of friends or family. They have difficulty getting the things they need for themselves and their children, such as child care, jobs, and education. The lack of support, resources, and sometimes bare necessities challenges any parent's caregiving.

These risk factors and many others can act in combination with each other as well as with prenatal exposure to drugs, producing behavior and learning problems. Such factors can threaten a child's developmental and educational outcomes and challenge teachers, caregivers, and parents, who affect a child's development and educational success.

Will children prenatally exposed to drugs require specialized interventions that have not yet been developed? Currently, no evidence suggests that these children exhibit a unique set of problems requiring a unique curriculum or set of educational or caregiving procedures. Not all children prenatally exposed to drugs have problems, and those who do, have difficulties that are also exhibited by other children. Some children who are prenatally exposed may have language or social problems; others may have cognitive, motor, or adaptive deficits. Effective interventions are available for improving skills in each of these areas. There is no evidence that these interventions are not effective for children with a history of prenatal exposure to illegal drugs as they have been for other children. We do not need a curriculum or intervention aimed at the population of children who have been drug exposed; what we do need is a set of instructional procedures to address the problem behaviors and skill deficiencies exhibited by these children. Therefore, our suggested approach to determining interventions for children who are prenatally exposed to illegal drugs is identical to the approach we use for all children:

- Identify specific behaviors that require remediation.
- Determine specific interventions that address those behaviors.
- Systematically implement those interventions.
- Monitor the effects of the interventions on the specified behaviors.

What do require special attention, however, are the risks these children face growing up in drug-using lifestyles. Until we begin to comprehensively address the risks associated with living in concentrated poverty, our efforts to provide interventions for children will have little chance of producing lasting effects.

Judith J. Carta is a Senior Scientist and Director of Early Childhood Research at the Juniper Gardens Children's Project of the University of Kansas.

4. a statement of the specific early intervention services necessary to meet the unique needs of the infant or toddler and family, including frequency, intensity, and method of delivering the services;
5. a statement of the natural environments in which early intervention services shall appropriately be provided, including a justification of the extent, if any, to which the services will not be provided in a natural environment;
6. the projected dates for initiation of services and anticipated duration of services;
7. the identification of the service coordinator from the profession most immediately relevant to the infant's or toddler's or family's needs who will be responsible for implementation of the plan and coordination with other agencies and persons; and
8. the steps to be taken to support a successful transition of the toddler with a disability to preschool or other appropriate services. (P.L. 105–17, Sec. 1436)

IFSPs differ from IEPs in several important ways (Bruder, 2000). Unlike the IEP, an IFSP does the following:

- Revolves around the family system as the constant and most important factor in the child's life
- Defines the family as being the recipient of early intervention services rather than the child alone
- Focuses on the natural environments in which the child and family live, extending the settings in which services can be provided beyond formal, contrived settings such as preschools to everyday routines in home and community
- Includes interventions and services provided by a variety of health and human service agencies in addition to education

The IFSP must be evaluated once a year and reviewed with the family at 6-month intervals. Recognizing the critical importance of time for the infant with disabilities, IDEA allows for initiation of early intervention services before the IFSP is completed if the parents give their consent. Figure 5.1 on pages 172–173 shows portions of an IFSP developed with and for the family of a 26-month-old child with disabilities.

 SPECIAL EDUCATION FOR PRESCHOOLERS

IDEA requires states to provide special education services to all children with disabilities ages 3 to 5. The regulations governing these programs are similar to those for school-age children, with the following exceptions:

- Preschool children do not have to be identified and reported under existing disability categories (e.g., mental retardation, orthopedic impairments) to receive services. This provision of IDEA also allows, but does not require, states to serve at-risk students from ages 3 through 9
- Each state, at its discretion, may also serve children (from ages 3 through 9) who are
  a. experiencing developmental delays as defined by the State and as measured by appropriate diagnostic instrument and procedures in one or more of the following areas: physical development, cognitive development, communication development, social or emotional development, or adaptive development; and
  b. who, by reason thereof, need special education and related services. (Sec. 1401)
- IEPs must include a section with suggestions and information for parents.
- Local education agencies may elect to use a variety of service delivery options (home-based, center-based, or combination programs), and the length of the school day and year may vary.
- Although preschool special education programs must be administered by the state education agency, services from other agencies may be contracted to meet the requirement of a full range of services. For example, many preschoolers with disabilities are served in community-based Head Start programs (Odom et al., 2000).

 SCREENING, IDENTIFICATION, AND ASSESSMENT

Assessment and evaluation in early childhood education is conducted for at least four different purposes, with specific evaluation tools for each purpose (Bondurant-Utz, 2002; Bricker, Pretti-Frontczak, & McComas, 1998; McLean, Bailey, & Wolery, 1996; Neisworth & Bagnato, 2000):

Screening: quick, easy-to-administer tests to identify children who may have a disability and who should receive further testing.

Diagnosis: in-depth, comprehensive assessment of all major areas of development to determine a child's eligibility for early intervention or special education services.

Program planning: curriculum-based, criterion-referenced assessments to determine a child's current skill level, identify IFSP/IEP objectives, and plan intervention activities.

Evaluation: curriculum-based, criterion-referenced measures to determine progress on IFSP/IEP objectives and evaluate the program's effectiveness.

 SCREENING TOOLS

Before young children and their families can be served, they must be identified. Some children's disabilities are so significant that no test is needed. As a general rule, the more severe a disability, the earlier it is detected. In the delivery room, medical staff can identify certain disabilities, such as microcephaly, cleft palate, and other physical conditions, as well as most instances of Down syndrome. Within the first few weeks, other physical characteristics such as paralysis, seizures, or rapidly increasing head size can signal possible disabilities. But most children who experience developmental delays are not identifiable by obvious physical characteristics or behavioral patterns, especially at very young ages. That is where screening tools come into play.

The Apgar Scale   The Apgar scale, which measures the degree of asphyxia (oxygen deprivation) an infant experiences during birth, is administered to virtually all babies born in U.S. hospitals. The test administrator—nurse, nurse anesthesiologist, or pediatrician—evaluates the newborn twice on five physiological measures: heart rate, respiratory effort, response to stimulation, muscle tone, and skin color. The child is given a score of 0, 1, or 2 on each measure according to the criteria described on the scoring form (see Figure 5.2).

The first administration of the test, which is conducted 60 seconds after birth, measures how the baby fared during the birth process. If the newborn receives a low score on the first test, the delivery room staff takes immediate resuscitation action. The scale is given again 5 minutes after birth. At that point a total score of 0 to 3 (out of a possible 10) indicates severe asphyxia, 4 to 6 moderate asphyxia, and 7 to 10 mild asphyxia. Some stress is assumed on all births, and the 5-minute score measures how successful any resuscitation efforts were. A 5-minute score of 6 or less indicates follow-up assessment to determine what is causing the problem and what interventions may be needed.

The Apgar has been shown to identify high-risk infants—those who have a greater-than-normal chance of developing later problems. Research has shown that oxygen deprivation at birth contributes to neurological impairment, and the 5-minute Apgar score correlates well with eventual neurological outcomes.

Developmental Screening Tests   A widely used screening tool for developmental delays is the Denver II (Frankenburg & Dodds, 1990). It can be used with children from 2 weeks to 6 years of age, using both testing-observation and a parent report format. The Denver II assesses 125 skills arranged in four developmental areas: gross motor, fine motor–adaptive, language, and personal-social. Each test item is represented on the scoring form by a bar showing at what ages 25%, 50%, 75%, and 90% of normally developing children can perform that skill. The child is allowed up to three trials per item. A child's performance on each item is scored as "pass" or "fail" and then interpreted as representing "advanced," "OK,"

IDEA requires states to provide special education to all children with disabilities ages 3 to 5.

Screening tests

Council for Exceptional Children   Content Standards for Beginning Teachers—Common Core: Screening, pre-referral, referral, and classification procedures (CC8K3).
PRAXIS Special Education Core Principles: Content Knowledge: III. Delivery of Services to Students with Disabilities, Use of assessment for screening.

FIGURE 5.1 Portion of an IFSP written with the family of a 26-month-old child with disabilities

INDIVIDUALIZED FAMILY SERVICE PLAN (IFSP) for Children Birth to Three Years   SANTA CLARA COUNTY

Child's name: _Cathy Rae Wright_   Birth Date: _11-15-00_ Age: _26_ months Sex: _F_

Parent(s)/Guardian(s): _Martha and Gary Wright_   Address: _1414 Coolidge Drive Cupertino_   Zip: _95014_
Home phone: _408 398-2461_ Work phone: _408 554-2490_ Primary language of the home: _English_ Other languages _____

Date of this IFSP _____ Projected periodic review _____ Projected annual review _____ Tentative IFSP exit _____
(at 6 months or before)

Service Coordinator Name	Agency	Phone	Date Appointed	Date Ended
Sandy Drohman	Regional Center	408-461-2192	12/10/01	/ /

Family's strengths and preferred resources (With the family, identify the family strengths and the resources they might find helpful in addressing family concerns and priorities.)   Mr. and Mrs. Wright are well-educated and constantly seek additional information about Cathy's condition. They are anxious to help Cathy in any way possible. Mrs. Wright's family is very supportive. They provide child care for Cathy's older brother. Because of Cathy's tendency to be medically fragile, Mr. and Mrs. Wright prefer a home based early intervention program. They appreciate receiving written materials to help them understand how to work with Cathy. Mrs. Wright wants to be home when the home visitor comes so she can learn from her.

Family's concerns and priorities   (With the family, identify major areas of concerns for the child with special needs and the family as a whole.)   Mr. and Mrs. Wright are very concerned about Cathy's delays in walking, using her fingers to pick up things, and in talking with other children. They also worry about her small size. Cathy is their second child and was born at 24 weeks gestation. Mr. and Mrs. Wright would like to have more information on the issues of prematurity and they would like to find an appropriate support group for themselves.

CHILD'S STRENGTHS AND PRESENT LEVELS OF DEVELOPMENT

With the family, identify what the child can do and what the child is learning to do. Include family and professional observations in each of the following areas:

PHYSICAL *Based on parent report and HELP Strands

Health   _Cathy is said by her parents to be healthy but is very petite. Her parents are working with a nutritionist to help Cathy gain weight._

Vision   _Cathy has had corrective surgery for strabismus._

Hearing _She has had numerous ear infections and currently has tubes in her ears._

Gross Motor (large movement)   _Cathy stands on tiptoes, runs on toes, makes sharp turns around corners when running, walks upstairs with one hand held_

Fine Motor (small movement) _Cathy grasps crayon adaptively and points with index finger; imitates horizontal strokes, builds 6 block tower, turns pages one at a time; has trouble picking up small objects._

COGNITIVE (responsiveness to environments, problem-solving) _Cathy finds hidden object; attempts and succeeds in activating mechanical toy; demonstrates use of objects appropriate for age_

COMMUNICATION (language and speech)
RECEPTIVE (understanding) _Cathy points to body parts when asked; obeys two part commands._

EXPRESSIVE (making sounds, talking) _Cathy names 8 pictures, interacts with peers using only gestures; attempts to sing songs with words_

SOCIAL/EMOTIONAL (how relates to others) _Cathy expresses affection, is beginning to obey and respect simple rules, tends to be physically aggressive_

ADAPTIVE/SELF-HELP (sleeping, eating, dressing, toileting, etc.) _Cathy can put on socks and shoes, verbalizes need to use the toilet, but is not potty trained, feeds self_

DIAGNOSIS (if known) _____

INDIVIDUALIZED FAMILY SERVICE PLAN (IFSP) for Children Birth to Three Years   SANTA CLARA COUNTY

Child's name: _____Cathy Rae Wright_____

IFSP OUTCOMES
With the family, identify the goals they would like to work on in the next six months. These should be directly related to the family's priorities and concerns as stated on page one.

OUTCOME: _Cathy will increase her attempts to vocally communicate in order to make her needs known and to positively interact with others._

Strategy or activity to achieve the outcome	Service Type (Individual = I Group = G) Location	Frequency of sessions / Length of each sesssion	Start Date	End Date (anticipated)	Responsible Agency/ Group Including payment arrangements (if any)
Strategy or activity to achieve the outcome (Who will do what and when will they do it?) AIM Infant Educator will model for Mr. and Mrs. Wright techniques to solicit Cathy's vocalization efforts. **Criteria** (How will we know if we are making progress?) Increased vocalization will be observed by parents and infant educator.	I — Home-based infant program	1 hour each week	1-23-03	11-10-03	AIM (funded by SARC) Family
Strategy or activity to achieve the outcome (Who will do what and when will they do it?) Mrs. Wright will take Cathy to play with neighborhood children and will invite children to her home. She will encourage play and vocalization. **Criteria** (How will we know if we are making progress?) Mrs. Wright will observe and note extent of interaction	G — Home and in the neighborhood	once each week for at least 30 minutes	2-1-03	ongoing	Mrs. Wright
Strategy or activity to achieve the outcome (Who will do what and when will they do it?) Cathy will be assessed by a speech pathologist by 2-15-03 and followed on an as needed basis. **Criteria** (How will we know if we are making progress?) A follow-up report will be submitted.	I — Regional Center Speech and Language Clinic	1 hour play based assessment	2-1-03	as needed	Sandy Drohman will make arrange-ments (funded by SARC)

OUTCOME: _Mr. and Mrs. Wright will join Parents Helping Parents in order to receive peer parent support and learn more about Cathy's condition._

Strategy or activity to achieve the outcome	Service Type / Location	Frequency / Length	Start Date	End Date	Responsible Agency/ Group
Strategy or activity to achieve the outcome (Who will do what and when will they do it?) Sandy Drohman will provide all referral information to Mr. and Mrs. Wright and will accompany them to their first meeting if they desire. **Criteria** (How will we know if we are making progress?) Mr. and Mrs. Wright will find satisfaction in increased support and knowledge.	G — Parents Helping Parents	(up to parent's discretion)			Sandy Drohman Mr. and Mrs. Wright Parents Helping Parents
Strategy or activity to achieve the outcome (Who will do what and when will they do it?) AIM Infant Educator will assist Mr. and Mrs. Wright in obtaining additional information about Cathy's condition. **Criteria** (How will we know if we are making progress?) Mr. and Mrs. Wright will express satisfaction over the assistance received in becoming more informed.	I — Home	ongoing	2-1-03	11-10-03	AIM Infant Educator

Source: Adapted from Cook, R. E., Tessier, A., & Klein, M. D. (2000). *Adapting early childhood curricula for children in inclusive settings* (5th ed.), (pp. 139–143). Upper Saddle River, NJ: Merrill/Prentice Hall. Used by permission.

FIGURE 5.2 The Apgar evaluation scale

			60 sec.	5 min.
Heart rate	Absent Less than 100 100 to 140	(0) (1) (2)	 1	 2
Respiratory effort	Apneic Shallow, irregular Lusty cry and breathing	(0) (1) (2)	 1	 1
Response to catheter stimulation	No response Grimace Cough or sneeze	(0) (1) (2)	 1	 2
Muscle tone	Flaccid Some flexion of extremities Flexion resisting extension	(0) (1) (2)	 1	 2
Color	Pale, blue Body pink, extremities blue Pink all over	(0) (1) (2)	 0	 1
	Total		4	8

"caution," or "delayed" performance by comparing the child's performance with those of the same age in the standardized population. The Denver II is most often administered by physicians, and the test form was designed to fit the schedule of well-baby visits recommended by the American Academy of Pediatrics.

No one observes a child more often, more closely, and with more interest than his parents. Mothers' estimates of their preschool children's levels of development often correlate highly with those that professionals produce by using standardized scales, and parental involvement in screening has been found to reduce the number of misclassifications (Henderson & Meisels, 1994). Recognizing this fact, early childhood specialists have developed a number of screening tools for use by parents. One such tool is the Ages & Stages Questionnaire (ASQ) (Bricker & Squires, 1999; see also Squires, Bricker, & Twombly, 2002). The ASQ includes 11 questionnaires to be completed by the parents when the child is 4, 6, 8, 12, 16, 18, 20, 24, 30, 36, and 48 months old. Each questionnaire consists of 30 items covering 5 areas of development: gross motor, fine motor, communication, personal-social, and adaptive. Many of the items include illustrations to help the parents evaluate their child's behavior. Figure 5.3 shows part of the 8-month questionnaire.

DIAGNOSTIC TOOLS

Developmental domains

Council for Exceptional Children — Content Standards for Beginning Teachers–Common Core: Typical and atypical growth and development (CC2K1).
PRAXIS Special Education Core Principles: Content Knowledge: I. Human development and behavior as related to students with disabilities.

When the results of a screening test raise suspicion that a disability or developmental delay may be present, the child is referred for diagnostic testing. The specific diagnostic tests to be used depend upon the suspected delay or disability (Bondurant-Utz, 2002; McLean et al., 1996). Tests that seek to determine if a child is experiencing a developmental delay usually measure performance in five major developmental areas or domains:

- *Motor development.* The ability to move one's body and manipulate objects within the environment provides a critical foundation for all types of learning. Motor development involves improvements in general strength, flexibility, endurance, and eye-hand coordination and includes gross- or large-muscle movement and mobility (such as walking, running, throwing) and small-muscle, fine-motor control (like that needed to pick up a toy, write, tie a shoe).

III. Fine Motor   *(Be sure to try each activity with your child.)*

	Yes	Sometimes	Not Yet
1. Does your baby reach for a crumb or Cheerio and touch it with her finger or hand? (If she already picks up a small object, check "yes" for this item.)	☐	☐	☐
2. Does your baby pick up a small toy , holding it in the center of her hand with her fingers around it?	☐	☐	☐
3. Does your baby *try* to pick up a crumb or Cheerio by using her thumb and all her fingers in a raking motion, even if she isn't able to pick it up? (If she already picks up a crumb or Cheerio, check "yes" for this item.)	☐	☐	☐
4. Does your baby usually pick up a small toy with only one hand?	☐	☐	☐
5. Does your baby *successfully* pick up a crumb or Cheerio by using her thumb and all her fingers in a raking motion? (If she already picks up a crumb or Cheerio, check "yes" for this item.)	☐	☐	☐
6. Does your baby pick up a small toy, with the *tips* of her thumb and fingers? You should see a space between the toy and her palm.	☐	☐	☐

FIGURE 5.3 Sample items from the 8-month Ages & Stages Questionnaire

Source: Reprinted from Bricker, D., & Squires, J. (1999). *Ages & Stages Questionnaires (ASQ):™ A parent-completed, child-monitoring system* (2nd ed.). Baltimore: Brookes. Used by permission.

- *Cognitive development.*   Children use cognitive skills when they attend to stimuli, perform preacademic skills such as sorting or counting, remember things they have done in the past, plan and make decisions about what they will do in the future, integrate newly learned information with previously learned knowledge and skills, solve problems, and generate novel ideas.
- *Communication and language development.*   Communication involves the transmission of messages such as information about needs, feelings, knowledge, desires, and

so forth. Children use communication and language skills when they receive information from others, share information with other individuals, and use language to mediate their actions and effectively control the environment. This domain encompasses all forms of communication development, including a child's ability to respond nonverbally with gestures, smiles, or actions and the acquisition of spoken language—sounds, words, phrases, sentences, and so on.

- *Social and emotional development.* Children who have developed competence in social skills share toys and take turns, cooperate with others, and resolve conflicts. Children should feel good about themselves and know how to express their emotions and feelings.
- *Adaptive development.* As young children develop self-care and adaptive skills such as dressing/undressing, eating, toileting, toothbrushing, and handwashing, their ability to function independently across multiple environments increases, which provides and enhances opportunities for additional kinds of learning.

Assessment of developmental domains

 Council for Exceptional Children Content Standards for Beginning Teachers–Common Core: Use and limitations of assessment instruments (CC8K4).
PRAXIS Special Education Core Principles: Content Knowledge: III. Delivery of Services to Students with Disabilities, Assessment, Procedures and test materials for referral.

Generally, these five areas are broken down into specific, observable tasks and sequenced developmentally—that is, in the order in which most children learn them. Sometimes each task is tied to a specific age at which a child should normally be able to perform it. This arrangement allows the examiner to note significant delays or gaps as well as other unusual patterns in a high-risk child's development. These developmental domains are not mutually exclusive. There is considerable overlap between domains as well as across skills within a specific domain. Most activities by children in everyday settings involve skills from multiple domains. For example, playing marbles typically requires a child to use skills from the motor, cognitive, communication, and social domains.

Two widely used tests for diagnosing developmental delays are the Battelle Developmental Inventory (Newborg, Stock, Wnek, Guidubaldi, & Suinicki, 1988) and the Bayley Scales of Infant Development—II (Bayley, 1993). The Battelle can be administered to children with and without disabilities from birth through age 8, and it has adapted testing procedures for use with children with different disabilities. The Bayley II evaluates development in motor, adaptive, language, and personal-social in infants from 2 to 30 months.

The Bayley Scales can be used to diagnose developmental delays in children from 2 months to 30 months.

Curriculum-based assessment in ECSE

Council for Exceptional Children Content Standards for Beginning Teachers of Early Childhood Students: Select, adapt and use specialized formal and informal assessment for infants, young children and their families (EC8S2).
PRAXIS Special Education Core Principles: Content Knowledge: III. Delivery of Services to Students with Disabilities, Assessment, Procedures and test materials for ongoing program monitoring.

PROGRAM PLANNING AND EVALUATION TOOLS

A growing number of early intervention programs are moving away from assessments based entirely on developmental milestones to curriculum-based assessment (CBA). CBA tools enable early childhood teams to (1) identify a child's current levels of functioning, (2) select IFSP/IEP goals and objectives, (3) determine the most appropriate interventions, and (4) evaluate the child's progress (McLean et al., 1996). Each item in a CBA relates directly to a skill in the program's curriculum, thereby providing a direct link among testing, teaching, and progress evaluation (Bagnato, Neisworth, & Munson, 1997).

One thoroughly developed and empirically tested CBA tool is the Assessment, Evaluation, and Programming System: For Infants and Young Children (AEPS). The AEPS is divided into two levels: one for infants and toddlers from birth to 3 years (Bricker, 1993), one and for children from 3 to 6 years (Bricker & Pretti-Frontczak, 1996). The AEPS is divided into six domains: fine motor, gross motor, adaptive, cognitive, social-communication, and social. Each domain is divided into strands that group related behaviors and skills considered essential for infants and young children to function independently. The AEPS tests can be used in conjunction with the associated AEPS curricula (Bricker & Waddell, 1996; Cripe, Slentz, & Bricker, 1993) or with similar early childhood curricula such as the Carolina Curriculum for Preschoolers with Special Needs (Johnson-Martin, Attermeier, & Hacker, 1990).

CURRICULUM AND INSTRUCTION

CURRICULUM AND PROGRAM GOALS

Most professionals in early childhood special education agree that programs should be designed and evaluated with respect to the following outcomes or goals (Bailey & Wolery, 1992; Bricker et al., 1998; Sandall, McLean, & Smith, 2000; Wolery & Sainato, 1993, 1996):

Goals for ECSE

 Content Standards for Beginning Teachers of Early Childhood Students: Historical and philosophical foundations of services for young children both with and without exceptional learning needs (EC1K1). **PRAXIS** Special Education Core Principles: Content Knowledge: II. Legal and Societal Issues, Historical movement/trends affecting society, Accountability and meeting educational standards.

1. *Support families in achieving their own goals.* Although the child with special needs is undoubtedly the focal point, a major function of early intervention is helping families achieve the goals most important to them. Professionals realize that families function as a system and that separating the child from the system results in limited and fragmented outcomes (Turnbull & Turnbull, 2001).

2. *Promote child engagement, independence, and mastery.* Early childhood special education seeks to minimize the extent to which children are dependent on others and differ from their age mates. Intervention strategies should "promote active engagement (participation), initiative (choice making, self-directed behavior), autonomy (individuality and self-sufficiency) and age-appropriate abilities in many normalized contexts and situations" (Wolery & Sainato, 1993, p. 53). In situations in which independence is not safe, possible, or practical, support and assistance should be provided to enable the child to participate as much as she can. "For example, in getting ready for a bath, a 3-year-old child should not be expected to adjust the water to the appropriate temperature, but could be expected to help get ready for the bath (e.g., getting bath toys, assisting in taking off clothing)" (Wolery & Sainato, 1993, p. 53). (To read how preschoolers with disabilities can learn to be more independent, see *Teaching & Learning*, "Idea Bunny Helps Preschoolers Be More Independent," later in this chapter.)

3. *Promote development in all important domains.* Successful early intervention programs help children make progress in each of the key areas of development already described (e.g., cognitive, motor, communication, social). Because young children with disabilities are already behind their typically developing age mates, early childhood special educators should only use instructional strategies that lead to rapid learning (Wolery & Sainato, 1993, 1996). Strategies that produce rapid learning help the child with disabilities by saving time for other goals and moving closer to normal developmental levels.

4. *Build and support social competence.* Social skills, such as learning to get along with others and making friends, are among the most important skills anyone can learn. Most children learn such skills naturally, but many children with disabilities do not learn to interact effectively and properly simply by playing with others (Goldstein, Kaczmarek, & English, 2001; McEvoy & Yoder, 1993).

5. *Facilitate the generalization use of skills.* As effortlessly as most typically developing children seem to generalize what they learn at one time in one situation to another place and

time, many children with disabilities have extreme difficulty remembering and using previously learned skills in other situations. "Early interventionists should not be satisfied if children learn new skills; they should only be satisfied if children use those skills when and wherever they are appropriate" (Wolery & Sainato, 1993, p. 54).

6. *Prepare and assist children for normalized life experiences with their families, in school, and in their communities.* Early intervention should be characterized by the principle of normalization; that is, services should be provided in settings that are as much like the typical settings in which young children without disabilities play and learn as is possible (Cook, Tessier, & Klein, 2000). A large and growing body of published research literature demonstrates the benefits of integrated early intervention to children with disabilities and their families and suggests strategies for effective early childhood inclusion programs (Guralnick, 2001; Sainato & Strain, 1993; Sandall & Schwartz, 2002; Wolery & Wilbers, 1994).

7. *Help children and their families make smooth transitions.* A transition occurs when a child and his family move from one early intervention program or service delivery mode to another. For example, program transitions typically occur at age 3, when a child with disabilities moves from a home-based early intervention program to an early childhood special education classroom, and again at age 5, when the child moves from a preschool classroom to a regular kindergarten classroom. Preparing and assisting children and their families for smooth transitions ensure continuity of services, minimize disruptions to the family system, and are important ways to promote the success of young children with disabilities as they move into more normalized environments (Hanson et al., 2000; Fowler, Schwartz, & Atwater, 1991; La Paro, Pianta, & Cox, 2000). Cooperative planning and supports for transitions must come from professionals in both the sending and the receiving programs (Chandler, 1993; Fowler, Donegan, Lueke, Hadden, & Phillips, 2000; Hadden & Fowler, 1997).

8. *Prevent or minimize the development of future problems or disabilities.* Prevention of future problems is a major goal of early intervention. Indeed, early intervention programs that serve at-risk infants and toddlers are designed entirely with prevention as their primary goal.

 DEVELOPMENTALLY APPROPRIATE PRACTICE

Developmentally appropriate practice

Council for Exceptional Children Content Standards for Beginning Teachers of Early Childhood Students: Plan and implement developmentally and individually appropriate curriculum (EC7S2) (also CC7K2).

PRAXIS Special Education Core Principles: Content Knowledge: III. Delivery of Services to Students with Disabilities, Background knowledge, Conceptual approaches underlying service delivery.

Virtually all early childhood educators—whether they work with typically developing children or those with disabilities—share a common philosophy that learning environments, teaching practices, and other components of programs that serve young children should be based on what is typically expected of and experienced by children of different ages and developmental stages. This philosophy and the guidelines for practice based on it are called *developmentally appropriate practice* (DAP) and are described in widely disseminated materials published by the National Association for the Education of Young Children (NAEYC) (Bredekamp & Copple, 1997). The DAP guidelines were created partially in response to concerns that too many early childhood programs were focusing on academic preparedness and not providing young children with enough opportunities to engage in the less structured play and other activities that typify early childhood. "For example, some people considered it developmentally appropriate for 4- and 5-year-olds to do an hour of seatwork, toddlers to sit in high chairs with dittos, or babies in infant seats to 'do' the calendar" (Bredekamp, 1993, p. 261).

DAP recommends the following guidelines for early childhood education programs:

- Activities should be integrated across developmental domains.
- Children's interests and progress should be identified through teacher observation.
- Teachers should arrange the environment to facilitate children's active exploration and interaction.
- Learning activities and materials should be real, concrete, and relevant to the young child's life.
- A wide range of interesting activities should be provided.
- The complexity and challenges of activities should increase as the children understand the skills involved.

Most early childhood special educators view the DAP guidelines as the foundation from which to provide early intervention for children with special needs. However, the guidelines by themselves may be inadequate to ensure the individualized, specially designed instruction that such children need. A curriculum based entirely on DAP may not be sufficient for young children with disabilities for the following reasons (Wolery, Ault, & Doyle, 1992):

1. Many children with special needs have delays or disabilities that make them dependent upon others.
2. Many children with special needs have delays or disabilities that keep them from learning well on their own.
3. Many children with special needs develop more slowly than their typically developing peers do.
4. Many children with special needs have disabilities that interfere with how they interact; and as a result, they often acquire additional disabilities.

Although Bricker et al. (1998) find "a basic congruence and compatibility" (p. 213) between DAP and the focused, activity-based intervention used by many early childhood special educators, they note two significant differences between the approaches. First, special educators must target specific goals and objectives to meet the unique developmental needs of individual children, while DAP is concerned with more general developmental goals (e.g., improve language skills or self-esteem) that are applicable to a broad range of children. Second, early childhood special educators use comprehensive and repeated assessments to determine learning objectives and to monitor progress according to stated performance criteria. DAP, by contrast, does not require the use of assessment or evaluation tools.

SELECTING IFSP/IEP GOALS AND OBJECTIVES

The breadth of developmental domains and the activities that young children typically engage in provide an almost unlimited number of possibilities for instructional objectives. Consensus among many early childhood special educators is that potential IFSP/IEP goals and objectives for infants and young children should be evaluated according to five quality indicators (e.g., Notari-Syverson & Shuster, 1995; Pretti-Frontczak & Bricker, 2000):

1. *Functionality.* A functional skill (a) increases the child's ability to interact with people and objects in her daily environment and (b) may have to be performed by someone else if the child cannot do it.
2. *Generality.* In this context, a skill has generality if it (a) represents a general concept as opposed to a particular task; (b) can be adapted and modified to meet the child's disability; and (c) can be used across different settings, with various materials, and with different people.
3. *Instructional context.* The skill should be easily integrated into the child's daily routines and taught in a meaningful way that represents naturalistic use of the skill.
4. *Measurability.* A skill is measurable if its performance or a product produced by its performance can be detected (i.e., seen, heard, and/or felt). Measurable skills can be counted or timed and enable objective determination of learning progress.
5. *Relation between long-range goals and short-term objectives.* Short-term objectives should be hierarchically related; the achievement of short-term objectives should contribute directly to the attainment of long-term goals.

Figure 5.4 on page 182 shows 11 questions that can be used to assess potential IFSP/IEP objectives according to those five criteria.

INSTRUCTIONAL ADAPTATIONS AND MODIFICATIONS

Providing specialized instruction in an attempt to "remediate delays caused by the child's disabilities and prevent any secondary disabilities from developing" is the cornerstone of

IFSP/IEP goals and objectives

Council for Exceptional Children   Content Standards for Beginning Teachers of Early Childhood Students: Plan and implement developmentally and individually appropriate curriculum (EC7S2) (also CC7K1).
PRAXIS Special Education Core Principles: Content Knowledge: III. Delivery of Services to Students with Disabilities, Curriculum and instruction, IFSP/IEP development.

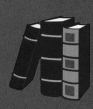

Idea Bunny Helps
Preschoolers Be More Independent

by Diane M. Sainato, Marie C. Ward, Jamie Brandt,
Jill McQuaid, and Tamara C. Timko

Picture the scene that follows:

When the flurry of the children's arrival at preschool subsided, their teacher gathered them together for morning circle time. They sang the "good morning" song, charted the weather, and handed out jobs for the day. Just before circle time ended, the teacher said, "Today during free-choice time we have many fun things to do. Please remember: only a few children at a time should be at each center. When you take an activity off the shelf, be sure to return it to the same place. Now everyone find something to do. I will be here to help you."

Most of the children immediately chose activities. The teacher had to remind some children about "waiting your turn" and "using inside voices." Most children were appropriately and actively engaged during the 15-minute center time; however, Sally, who chose a matching and sorting task, dumped a variety of colored bears onto the table and promptly forgot what to do next. Quickly frustrated by waiting for the teacher to notice her, she wandered off without finishing the task. When the teacher noticed Sally, she took her by the hand and brought her back to the table with the bears. The teacher reminded Sally about what to do, showed her how, and moved to help another child. Sally matched several bears by color. Then, growing bored with the task, she carried the bucket of bears to the water table and dumped them into the water.

The teacher sternly said, "Sally, what are you supposed to be doing?"
Sally replied, "I don't know."

Learning to perform tasks without teacher direction is necessary for successful transition and inclusion into many typical classrooms. These skills are important not only in kindergarten but throughout a child's education (Sainato & Lyon, 1989). To help preschool children develop independent performance skills, we built on the work of other researchers who had successfully used auditory prompting systems with older students with disabilities (Alberto, Sharpton, Briggs, & Stright, 1986; Trask-Tyler, Grossi, & Heward, 1994). In previous studies, students used a foot pedal or hand-operated switch to work a small tape recorder, which played instructions about performing components of tasks such as meal preparation (see "I Made It Myself and It's Good!" in Chapter 11). We adapted the auditory prompting system to make it more appropriate for preschool children and called it the Idea Bunny—a soft, stuffed toy with a small tape recorder sewn inside. A foot pedal was attached to the recorder through a small opening in the bunny's underside. The bunny was placed on a table close to a bookshelf that held a variety of activity materials.

Task Analyses and Scripts

We developed a task analysis to determine the component steps for each table-top activity. For example, these are the steps for a picture completion task:

1. Choose the basket containing picture pieces from the shelf.
2. Take the basket to the table.
3. Place the pieces on the table to show the picture.
4. Choose one piece and find another to make a picture.
5. Put the picture at the top of the table.
6. Put the pieces back into the basket.
7. Return the basket to the shelf.

We then created a script of instructions that included the steps for each learning task. The Idea Bunny "said" one step when the child pressed the foot pedal. Children were taught to use the bunny to help them complete steps in the activity. A beep sounded to signal the end of each specific

"Hello, Rondell! I'm happy you came to see Idea Bunny. Today we are going to complete pictures together."

step. At the end of the task, the Idea Bunny asked the child to stick its ears together to show the teacher that the child was finished.

The Bunny Talks!

This was the bunny's script for the picture completion task:

Hello! I'm happy you came to see Idea Bunny today. I have a great idea for you to try. Today we are going to complete pictures together. Go to the shelf and find the yellow basket of pictures that are cut in half. Bring the basket back to the table. [beep]

Take all of the pieces out of the basket and turn them around so that you can see the picture on each piece. [beep] Choose one piece and pick another piece so that it makes a picture. Match the two pieces together and put them at the top of the table. [beep]

Keep on matching the pieces together until they have all been matched to make pictures. [beep]

Great job! Now that you are finished matching the pieces, pick them up and place them in the basket. [beep]

Take the basket of picture pieces back to the shelf where you found them. [beep]

Now, put my ears together so the teacher knows you have finished your work. We had a great time today! Let's play again tomorrow. [beep]

Research Results

We have conducted three studies using the Idea Bunny as an auditory prompting device in preschool classrooms for young children with developmental disabilities (Brandt, 1992; Stemley, 1993; Ward, 1994). Results show that even though children are initially able to do the tasks, they require a great deal of teacher direction. Children have to be taught to use the Idea Bunny. At first, the children in our studies often played the whole tape just to listen to the bunny talk. Then they forgot what the bunny had first told them to do. We found that in the baseline condition (without the Idea Bunny), the children were engaged in the task but required many teacher prompts to keep on task. We then trained each child to use the Idea Bunny in a one-to-one situation with the teacher. During the intervention phase, we noted that children were much more engaged with the task and the rate of teacher prompts was low and stable.

These studies showed that preschoolers with developmental disabilities were able to learn to use the auditory prompting device. Independent engagement increased and, more important, was maintained when the prompting device was removed. Children appeared to enjoy the Idea Bunny and often patted him on the head and kissed him before they left the center. Sometimes they would talk back to the bunny. One day when the bunny said, "Hello! I'm happy you came to see Idea Bunny today," a child replied, "Hi, Bunny, I'm happy to see you, too."

Suggestions for Using Idea Bunny in the Classroom

- Begin with skills in the child's repertoire. This activity should be for practice, not for introducing new skills.
- Design a space for the center away from general play areas.
- Create a task analysis for each activity and develop scripts to match.
- Try out the scripts first to see whether the steps are too long.
- Teach children to use the prompting device.
- Monitor children to see that they understand the task.
- Place all of the materials needed to complete the task near the children.

Diane Sainato is a member of the special education faculty at The Ohio State University where she coordinates the master's degree program in early childhood special education and conducts research on ways to increase young children's independence. Marie Ward is Director of Student Services for the Delaware Union County Educational Service Center; Jamie Brandt is an itinerant teacher in the Columbus Public Schools. Jill McQuaid is the Family Coordinator for Project IMPACT, an interdisciplinary early intervention personnel preparation grant at The Ohio State University; and Tamara Timko is the Academic Director for a children's mission in Guatemala City, Guatemala.

FIGURE 5.4 Five criteria for evaluating IEP/IFSP objectives for infants, toddlers, and preschoolers with disabilities

FUNCTIONALITY	GENERALITY	INSTRUCTIONAL CONTEXT	MEASURABILITY	HIERARCHICAL RELATION BETWEEN LONG-RANGE GOAL AND SHORT-TERM OBJECTIVE
1. Will the skill increase the child's ability to interact with people and objects within the daily environment? The child needs to perform the skill in all or most of the environments in which he or she interacts. *Skill:* Places object into container. *Opportunities: Home*—Places sweater in drawer, cookie in paper bag. *School*—Places lunch box in cubbyhole, trash in trash bin. *Community*—Places milk carton in grocery cart, rocks and soil in flower pot. 2. Will the skill have to be performed by someone else if the child cannot do it? The skill is a behavior or event that is critical for completion of daily routines. *Skill:* Looks for object in usual location. *Opportunities:* Finds coat on coat rack, gets food from cupboard.	3. Does the skill represent a general concept or class of responses? The skill emphasizes a generic process, rather than a particular instance. *Skill:* Fits objects into defined spaces. *Opportunities:* Puts mail in mailbox, places crayon in box, puts cutlery into sorter. 4. Can the skill be adapted or modified for a variety of disabling conditions? The child's sensory impairment should interfere as little as possible with the performance. *Skill:* Correctly activates simple toy. *Opportunities: Motor impairments*—Activates light, easy-to-move toys (e.g., balls, rocking horse, toys on wheels, roly-poly toys). *Visual impairments:* Activates large, bright, noise-making toys (e.g., bells, drums, large rattles). 5. Can the skill be generalized across a variety of settings, materials, and/or people? The child can perform the skill with interesting materials and in meaningful situations. *Skill:* Manipulates two small objects simultaneously. *Opportunities: Home*—Builds with small interlocking blocks, threads laces on shoes. *School*—Sharpens pencil with pencil sharpener. *Community*—Takes coin out of small wallet.	6. Can the skill be taught in a way that reflects the manner in which the skill will be used in daily environments? The skill can occur in a naturalistic manner. *Skill:* Uses object to obtain another object. *Opportunities:* Uses fork to obtain food, broom to rake toy; steps on stool to reach toy on shelf. 7. Can the skill be elicited easily by the teacher/parent within classroom/home activities? The skill can be initiated easily by the child as part of daily routines. *Skill:* Stacks objects. *Opportunities:* Stacks books, cups/plates, wooden logs.	8. Can the skill be seen and/or heard? Different observers must be able to identify the same behavior. *Measurable skill:* Gains attention and refers to object, person, and/or event. *Nonmeasurable skill:* Experiences a sense of self-importance. 9. Can the skill be directly counted (e.g., by frequency, duration, distance measures)? The skill represents a well-defined behavior or activity. *Measurable skill:* Grasps pea-sized object. *Nonmeasurable skill:* Has mobility in all fingers. 10. Does the skill contain or lend itself to determination of performance criteria? The extent and/or degree of accuracy of the skill can be evaluated. *Measurable skill:* Follows one-step directions with contextual cues. *Nonmeasurable skill:* Will increase receptive language skills.	11. Is the short-term objective a developmental subskill or step thought to be critical to the achievement of the long-range goal? *Appropriate:* Short-Term Objective—Releases object with each hand. Long-Range Goal—Places and releases object balanced on top of another object. *Inappropriate:* 1. The Short-Term Objective is a restatement of the same skill as the Long-Range Goal, with the addition of an instructional prompt (e.g., Short-Term Objective—Activates mechanical toy with physical prompt. Long-Range Goal—Independently activates mechanical toy) or a quantitative limitation to the extent of the skill (e.g., Short-Term Objective—Stacks 5 1-inch blocks; Long-Range-Goal—Stacks 10 1-inch blocks). 2. The Short-Term Objective is not conceptually or functionally related to the Long-Range Goal (e.g., Short-Term Objective—Releases object voluntarily; Long-Range Goal—Pokes with index finger).

what early childhood special educators do (Sandall, Schwartz, & Joesph, 2000, p. 3). Like their colleagues who work with elementary and secondary students with disabilities, teachers who work with young children with disabilities must be skilled in using a wide range of instructional strategies and tactics.

Modifications and adaptations to the physical environment, materials, and activities themselves are often sufficient to support successful participation and learning by a child with disabilities. Such modifications range from subtle, virtually invisible supports (e.g., changing the duration or sequence of activities, using a child's preferences as a conversation topic while playing) to more obvious interventions and support (e.g., providing the child with an adaptive device, teaching peers to prompt and reward participation) (Sandall, Joseph, et al., 2000). The challenge is determining how much support a child needs for a given skill in a specific context.

> Too much support may result in children becoming over reliant on adult support. Too little support will result in children being unsuccessful, and may lead to decreasing rates of participation and increasing rates of challenging behaviors. (Sandall et al., 2000, p. 4)

Embedded Learning Opportunities One effective method for incorporating specialized instruction into typical preschool activities for children with disabilities is called embedded learning opportunities. The concept of *embedded learning opportunities* is based on the premise that although quality early childhood programs offer opportunities for learning across the day, children with disabilities often need guidance and support to learn from those opportunities (Horn, Lieber, Li, Sandall, & Schwartz, 2000). Therefore, teachers should look and plan for ways to embed brief, systematic instructional interactions that focus on a child's IEP objectives in the content of naturally occuring classroom activities. Figure 5.5 shows a teacher's plan for embedding learning opportunities into four different activity centers to support an IEP objective in the fine-motor domain for a 4-year-old boy with cerebral palsy.

Embedding learning opportunities to support young children's development of communication and language skills is an especially important teaching responsibility of an early childhood special educator. Most children learn to speak and communicate effectively with little or no formal teaching. But children with disabilities often do not acquire language in the spontaneous, seemingly effortless manner of their peers without disabilities. And as children with disabilities slip further and further behind their peers, their language deficits make social and academic development even more difficult. Preschoolers with disabilities need repeated opportunities for language use and development (Goldstein, Kaczmarek, & Hepting, 1994). In addition to providing systematic, explicit instruction of language skills to children in individual and small-group learning activities, teachers should embed meaningful opportunities for children to talk and communicate throughout the day. Even transitions between activities can provide opportunities for learning (Wolery, Anthony, & Heckathorn, 1998).

Robinson Spohn, Timko, and Sainato (1999) reported a creative and effective example of embedding language learning opportunities into mealtimes. Each child was seated at the table in front of a placemat with a picture of a food item, a cartoon character, an animal, and something silly (e.g., a cat wearing glasses and reading a book) (see Figure 5.6). There were 12 different placements, and each child sat before a different one each day. At first, the teacher played "The Talking Game" with the children while they ate breakfast in the school lunchroom. The children took turns picking an index card from a shuffled set of cards. Each card had a photo of one of the children in the group. After a child selected a card, the teacher prompted him or her to say something to the child pictured on the card. If the children could not think of anything to say, they were prompted to talk about one of the pictures on their placemat. After several weeks, the teacher no longer used the index cards and stopped prompting the children's interactions. The children continued talking with one

Modifying and adapting physical environment

 Content Standards for Beginning Teachers of Early Childhood Students: Design, implement, and evaluate environments to assure developmental and functional appropriateness (EC5S3) (also CC5K1).
PRAXIS Special Education Core Principles: Content Knowledge: III. Delivery of Services to Students with Disabilities, Structuring and managing the learning environment.

Embedded learning opportunities

 Content Standards for Beginning Teachers—Common Core: Effective management of teaching and learning (CC5K3) (also EC7S2).
PRAXIS Special Education Core Principles: Content Knowledge: III. Delivery of Services to Students with Disabilities, Structuring and managing the learning environment.

FIGURE 5.5 **Example of a plan for embedding learning opportunities into four different activity centers to support a child's IEP objective in the fine-motor domain**

Embedded Learning Opportunities at a Glance for: ___Alex___

Objective: ___Will pour liquid or other fluid material (e.g., sand, beans) from one___
___container to another with no spillage.___

Date: ___8/14___ Activity: ___Center Time___
Material: ___All centers available___

Modifications Needed:

—Water table: add a variety of containers with spouts (e.g., plastic measuring cups, teapot, play pitcher)

—Snack Center: Add to Alex's workjob pouring juice for other children

—Art Center: Place tempera paint in small pitcher, have children pour into individual bowls

—Housekeeping: Add beans to kitchen cabinet in a small pitcher for pouring into pots, cups or plates

What are you going to do?

Move through center modeling use of these new activities/materials. Provide physical guidance for Alex

What are you going to say?

Use natural cues—

Let's see you do it.

Can you do it and get all the beans in the pot?

How will you respond?

Praise, acknowledgment, feedback on accuracy

Engagement in activity created

What materials do you need?

Need to be prepared with clean-up supplies for spills—(see under modifications)

Source: "Supporting Young Children's IEP Goals in Inclusive Settings Through Embedded Learning Opportunities" by E. Horn, J. Lieber, S. Sandall, I. Schwartz, & S. Li, 2000, *Topics in Early Childhood Education, 20,* 208–223. Copyright 2000 by PRO-Ed, Inc. Reprinted with permission.

Preschool activity schedules

 Council for Exceptional Children Content Standards for Beginning Teachers–Common Core: Demands of learning environments (CC5K1) (also (EC5S3).
PRAXIS Special Education Core Principles: Content Knowledge: III. Delivery of Services to Students with Disabilities, Structuring and managing the learning environment.

another during mealtimes at rates higher than they had before, often using the pictures on their placemats as conversation starters.

PRESCHOOL ACTIVITY SCHEDULES

Teachers in preschool programs for children with disabilities face the challenge of organizing the program day into a schedule that meets each child's individual learning needs and provides children with many opportunities to explore the environment and communicate with others throughout the day. The schedule should include a balance of child-initiated and planned activities, large- and small-group activities, active and quiet times, and indoor and outdoor activities; it should allow easy transition from activity to activity (Cook et al.,

FIGURE 5.6 A placemat used to encourage preschoolers with developmental disabilities to communicate with one another during mealtime

Source: Courtesy of Diane M. Sainato, The Ohio State University.

2000). In short, the schedule should provide a framework for maximizing children's opportunities to develop new skills and practice what they have already learned while remaining manageable and flexible. In addition, how activities are scheduled and organized has considerable effect on the frequency and type of interaction that occurs between children with and without disabilities (Harris & Handleman, 2000) and on the extent to which children with disabilities benefit from instructional activities.

Bricker et al. (1998) describe an activity-planning and scheduling process that combines children's individual IFSP/IEP objectives with group activity plans. Figure 5.7 shows how children's goals and objectives in the social-communication domain were integrated into group activities in one preschool classroom.

The systematic use of play activities and the use of peer "confederates" can increase the language skills and social competence of preschoolers with disabilities.

 ### A SUPPORTIVE PHYSICAL ENVIRONMENT

The physical arrangement of the classroom itself must support the planned activities. As Kim J170 notes at the beginning of this chapter, designing an effective preschool classroom requires thoughtful planning to ensure that play areas and needed materials are accessible to and safe for all students, that boundaries between areas minimize distractions, and, most important, that the environment makes children want to explore and play. Suggestions for setting up a preschool classroom include the following (Bricker et al., 1998; Cook et al., 2000; Johnson-Martin et al., 1990; Morrison, 2001):

FIGURE 5.7 **Example of an activity schedule in the social-communication domain**

Child	Goals and objectives	Daily Program Activities: Social Communication				
		Arrival	Lunch	Outdoor play	Circle time	Discovery time
Darin Sam Mikail Aaron	Shares or exchanges objects	Shares umbrella with peer while walking from bus to classroom	Exchanges plates/bowls of food with peers	Shares or trades objects when enough are not available		• Shares watercolor palette • Trades objects in any area selected • Shares large paper to paint/write/draw • Shares big blocks • Trades puppets
Sam	Knows gender of self and others	• Walks in line with boys to classroom from bus • Places attendance card on bulletin board next to a boy's or a girl's card			Responds to song directions specifically for boys	• Plays doctor's office in dramatic area that requires practice in giving identifying information such as name, address, gender
Jamal Marisa Cody	Accurately identifies own affect/emotions	Responds to questions, "How do you feel today?" "How do you think (blank) feels today?"	Identifies likes and dislikes	Identifies affect/ emotion of children experiencing conflict or injury	Identifies affect/ emotion of people in books	
Alex	Asks what and where questions	Smells food cooking for lunch and asks, "What is for lunch?"	Notices absent peer or adult and asks, "Where is (blank)?"	Plays Hide and Seek and asks peer/adult "Where is (blank)?"	• Asks what and where questions about objects brought for sharing day • Participates in animal charades asking, "Where do you live and what do you eat?"	Asks where are objects when too few objects are present in areas
Jorge Dahlia	Uses adjectives to make comparisons	Describes texture and color of clothing on self and others	Describes textures and colors of food items served		Describes items felt in feely bag	Describes and compares completed project of peer/self

Source: Reprinted from Bricker, D., Pretti-Frontczak, K., & McComas, N. (1998). *An activity-based approach to early intervention* (2nd ed.), (pp. 103–104). Baltimore: Brookes. Used by permission.

- Organize the classroom into a number of different well-defined areas to accommodate different kinds of activities (e.g., quiet play, messy play, dramatic play, constructive play, active play).
- Locate quiet activities together, away from avenues of traffic, and loud activities together.
- Equip each area with abundant, appropriate materials that are desirable to children.
- Locate materials where children can easily retrieve them and are not dependent on adults.

- Have an open area, perhaps on a large rug, where large-group activities such as circle time and story reading can be conducted.
- Label or color-code all storage areas so that aides and volunteers can easily find needed materials.
- Arrange equipment and group areas so that students can move easily from one activity to another. Pictures or color codes can be applied to various work areas.
- Provide lockers or cubbies for students so they know where to find their belongings. Again, add picture cues to help students identify their lockers.

 ## SERVICE DELIVERY ALTERNATIVES

IDEA requires that early intervention services be provided in natural environments to the greatest extent possible. Natural environments are the same home, school, and community settings that typically developing children inhabit (Sandall & Ostrosky, 2000). Where early intervention takes place varies, depending on the age of the child and the special supports she and her family need.

Early intervention services for infants and newborns with significant disabilities are often provided in hospital settings. Most early childhood special education services, however, are provided in the child's home, in a center- or school-based facility, or in a combination of both settings.

 ### HOSPITAL-BASED PROGRAMS

Increasingly, early intervention services are being provided to hospitalized newborns and their families. Low-birth-weight and other high-risk newborns who require specialized health care are placed in neonatal intensive care units (NICUs). Many NICUs include a variety of professionals, such as neonatologists who provide medical care for infants with special needs, nurses who provide ongoing medical assistance, social workers or psychologists who help parents and families with emotional and financial concerns, and infant education specialists who promote interactions between parents and infants (Brown, Thurman, & Pearl, 1993).

 ### HOME-BASED PROGRAMS

As the name suggests, a home-based program depends heavily on the support of families. The parents typically assume the primary responsibility of being caregivers and teachers of their child with disabilities. Parents are usually supported by an early intervention specialist who visits the home regularly to model teaching procedures or other interventions for the parents, act as a consultant, evaluate the success of intervention, and regularly assess the child's progress. Home visitors (or home teachers or home advisors, as they are often called) in some programs are specially trained paraprofessionals. They may visit as frequently as several times a week but probably no less than a few times a month. They sometimes carry the results of their in-home evaluations back to other professionals, who may recommend changes in the program.

The Portage Project, one of the best-known and most widely replicated home-based programs, was begun more than 30 years ago by a consortium of 23 school districts in south-central Wisconsin (Shearer & Shearer, 1979). A project teacher typically visits the home one day each week to review the child's progress during the previous week, describe activities for the upcoming week, demonstrate to the parents how to carry out the activities with the child, observe the parent and child interacting, offer suggestions and advice as needed, summarize where the program stands, and indicate what records parents should keep during the next week. The Portage Project has produced its own assessment materials and teaching activi-

Physical arrangement of preschool classroom

Council for Exceptional Children Content Standards for Beginning Teachers of Early Childhood Students: Design, implement, and evaluate environments to assure developmental and functional appropriateness (EC5S3). **PRAXIS** Special Education Core Principles: Content Knowledge: III. Delivery of Services to Students with Disabilities, Structuring and managing the learning environment.

Differences between home-based, center-based, and combined programs

Council for Exceptional Children Content Standards for Beginning Teachers—Common Core: Family systems and the role of families in supporting development (CC2K4) (also CC5K1). **PRAXIS** Special Education Core Principles: Content Knowledge: III. Delivery of Services to Students with Disabilities, Background knowledge, Placement and program issues in early intervention.

ties, *The Portage Guide to Early Education,* based on 450 behaviors sequenced developmentally and classified into self-help, cognition, socialization, language, and motor skills.

Home-based early intervention programs have several advantages:

- The home is the child's natural environment, and it is often true that a parent can give more time and attention to the child than even the most adequately staffed center or school.
- Other family members, such as siblings and perhaps even grandparents, have more opportunity to interact with the child for both instruction and social contact. These significant others can play an important role in the child's growth and development.
- Home learning activities and materials are more likely to be natural and appropriate.
- Parents who are actively involved in helping their child learn and develop clearly have an advantage over parents who feel guilt, frustration, or defeat at their seeming inability to help their child.
- Home-based programs can be less costly to operate without the expenses of maintaining a facility and equipment and transporting children to and from the center.

Home-based programs, however, can have disadvantages:

- Because programs place so much responsibility on parents, they are not effective with all families. Not all parents are able to spend the time required to teach their children, and some who try are not effective teachers.
- Early childhood special education programs must learn to serve more effectively the large and growing number of young children who do not reside in the traditional two-parent family—especially the many thousands of children with teenage mothers who are single, uneducated, and poor. Many of these infants and preschoolers are at risk for developmental delays because of the impoverished conditions in which they live, and it is unlikely that a parent struggling with the realities of day-to-day survival will be able to meet the added demands of involvement in an early intervention program (Turnbull & Turnbull, 2001).
- Because the parent—usually the mother—is the primary service provider, children in home-based programs may not receive as wide a range of services as they would in a center-based program, where they can be seen by a variety of professionals. (Note, however, that the services of professionals such as physical therapists, occupational therapists, and speech therapists are sometimes provided in the home.)
- The child may not receive sufficient opportunity for social interaction with peers.

CENTER-BASED PROGRAMS

Center-based programs provide early intervention services in a special educational setting outside the home. The setting may be part of a hospital complex, a special day care center, or a preschool. Some children may attend a specially designed developmental center or training center that offers a wide range of services for children with varying types and degrees of disabilities. Wherever they are, these centers offer the combined services of many professionals and paraprofessionals, often from several different fields.

Most center-based programs encourage social interaction, and some try to integrate children with disabilities and typically developing children in day care or preschool classes. Some children attend a center each weekday for all or most of the day; others may come less frequently, although most centers expect to see each child at least once a week. Parents are sometimes given roles as classroom aides or encouraged to act as their child's primary teacher. A few programs allow parents to spend time with other professionals or take training while their child is somewhere else in the center. Virtually all effective programs for young children with disabilities recognize the critical need to involve parents, and they welcome parents in every aspect of the program.

A good example of a center-based program is the Precise Early Education of Children with Handicaps (PEECH) project originally developed at the University of Illinois. Designed for children ages 3 to 5 with mild to moderate disabilities, PEECH combines classroom instruction for up to 10 children with disabilities and 5 nondisabled children. A team approach to intervention and parental involvement includes a classroom teacher and a paraprofessional aide, a psychologist, a speech-language pathologist, and a social worker. Children spend 2 or 3 hours in class each day, with some time in large and small groups and individualized activities. Parents are included in all stages of the intervention, including policymaking. The project offers a lending library and a toy library for parents to use as well as a parent newsletter. The project's ultimate goal is to successfully integrate youngsters with disabilities into regular kindergarten classes whenever possible. Early childhood special educators at 200 replication sites in 36 states have received training in various components of the PEECH program (Karnes, Beauchamp, & Pfaus, 1993). (To read about another model center-based program, the Alice H. Hayden Preschool at the University of Washington, see *Teaching & Learning,* "Including Preschool Children with Autism: Five Stategies That Work," later in this chapter.)

Center-based programs generally offer three advantages that are difficult to build into home-based efforts:

- Increased opportunity for a team of specialists from different fields—education, physical and occupational therapy, speech and language pathology, medicine, and others—to observe each child and cooperate in intervention and continued assessment. Some special educators feel that the intensive instruction and related services that can be provided in a center-based program are especially important for children with severe disabilities (Rose & Calhoun, 1990).
- The opportunity for interaction with typically developing peers makes center programs especially effective for some children.
- Most parents involved in center programs feel some relief at the support they get from the professionals who work with their child and from other parents with children at the same center.

Disadvantages of a center-based program include the expense of transportation, the cost and maintenance of the center itself, and the possibility of less parent involvement than in home-based programs.

COMBINED HOME-CENTER PROGRAMS

Many early intervention programs combine center-based activities and home visitation. Few center programs take children for more than a few hours a day or more than 5 days per week. But because young children with disabilities require more intervention than a few hours a day, many programs combine the intensive help of a variety of professionals in a center with the continuous attention and sensitive care of parents at home. Intervention that carries over from center to home clearly offers many of the advantages of the two types of programs and negates some of their disadvantages.

St. Mark's Circle School in Charlotte, North Carolina, offers a combination home- and center-based early intervention program for infants and toddlers with severe/profound disabilities. The program is based on the social reciprocity model, which views the child's behavior as affecting the parent, whose behavior in turn affects the behavior of the child—hence the "circle" in the program's name. Nonresponsiveness, nonvocal behavior, irritability, lack of imitation responses, and the need for special health-care routines (e.g., tube feeding, suctioning) all present special challenges to normal infant-parent interactions; behaviors associated with these problems are often viewed negatively. The program attempts to identify and increase the frequency of alternative positive behaviors that will cause parents to want to continue their interactions with their child (Calhoun & Kuczera, 1996; Calhoun, Rose, Hanft, & Sturkey, 1991; Rose & Calhoun, 1990). The center-based

Including Preschool Children with Autism: Five Strategies That Work

by Ilene S. Schwartz, Felix F. Billingsley, and Bonnie M. McBride

Children with autism and other developmental disabilities are included in the Alice H. Hayden Preschool at the University of Washington, a comprehensive program for approximately 150 children from birth through age 6 and their families. Each classroom has 15 children: 9 qualifying for special education services, 6 typically developing. The classrooms serve children with a wide range of abilities, from severe disabilities to mild language delay to giftedness. About 30% of the children with disabilities have autism. Each class has a head teacher, an assistant teacher, and at least one aide.

We describe five strategies central to providing educational services for young children with disabilities in inclusive settings. They are tricks of the trade for helping children with autism and other developmental disabilities acquire skills, develop relationships, and participate as full class members.

Teach Communication and Social Competence

Without communication and social interactions among children, an inclusive program may provide little more than parallel instruction.

- *Use the Picture Exchange Communication System (PECS) to help children without functional verbal skills communicate effectively.* PECS teaches children to communicate with pictures and symbols (Bondy & Frost, 1994; Schwartz, Garfinkle, & Bauer, 1998). Most children with autism quickly learn to use PECS to communicate in understandable and acceptable ways about the things that are important to them while acquiring speech skills.
- *Provide systematic instruction in imitation skills.* Imitation is critical to learning from and relating to others. Embed imitation training throughout the day: in small groups, opening circle, gym, and outdoor play.
- *Plan opportunities for students with disabilities to interact directly with typically developing peers.* At opening circle, begin with a desirable toy such as bubbles and then help all children share the toy directly with other children instead of passing the toy from child to teacher to child.

Here's an example:

Mark, who has autism, sits at the art center with several classmates. He sees that his favorite painting utensil, Dot Art paints, is next to Mary, who is typically developing and new to the class. Mark uses his symbols to build the sentence "I want Dot Art paint" and extends it toward Mary. Ben, who has been in Mark's class for a year, sees that he is trying to communicate with Mary, who is painting and doesn't notice. Ben turns to Mary and says, "Mary, Mark is talking to you. Take the sentence from him and see what he wants." Mary takes Mark's sentence strip, looks at the picture, and gives him the Dot Art paint. Ben says, "If you want it back, you can just ask Mark for it. We have to share in our class."

Use Instructional Strategies That Maintain the Class's Natural Flow

Rather than isolating children with disabilities to provide individualized instruction, teach within the context of developmentally appropriate activities and routines.

- *Draw peers into the instructional situation.*
- *Use naturalistic teaching procedures.* Instruction should involve activities that are interesting to students, take advantage of child-initiated interactions, and use naturally occurring consequences.
- *Use different cues and prompts to ensure that each child receives adequate support.* Provide only what help is required so the children do not become dependent on teacher assistance.

Here's an example:

One of Jacob's IEP objectives is to learn to match similar objects. During small-group time his class made collages using various art supplies. Before the activity, his teacher placed five shapes of different colors on his collage. As the activity began, the teacher gave him five corresponding color shapes to match. The teacher provided sufficient prompts for him to complete the matching task as independently as possible. He continued to work on his collage alongside his classmates.

Teach and Provide Opportunities for Independence

While interdependence is appropriate and normal in human relationships, we also expect children to become increasingly independent as they grow.

- *Give children choices whenever possible and teach choice making when necessary.*
- *Picture schedules can help some children learn to follow the sequence and duration of daily activities.* Visual cues can ease transitions between activities, increase engagement, and provide structure for trying new activities and play materials. Over time, the schedules can be faded.
- *Because it is easy to overlook nonverbal children, give them frequent chances to respond to teacher initiations.*
- *Maintain high expectations for all children.* Celebrate small victories and immediately "up the ante," all the while believing that the child has the ability to reach the next objective.

Here's an example:

It is free-choice time in Jon's classroom, and he has been having a difficult day. Transitions are always challenging for him, but today there has been more crying and mild self-injury than we have seen in 6 weeks. When the teacher announces that everyone can make his first choice, Jon walks to the wall and looks at his schedule. It has his name and six picture/symbols on it representing activity centers that are open during free choice. The first two pictures show centers in which Jon is developing play skills; the third is his favorite—the computer center. The next two are less preferred areas, and the last picture shows "Jon's choice," which means he can pick any activity he wants. Although he is still whimpering, he looks at the schedule, touches the first picture, sets a kitchen timer next to the schedule, and walks to a center. As he engages in this routine, he calms down. He plays in the center with other children until the timer goes off. Then he walks back to the schedule, takes off the first picture and puts it in the "finished pocket" at the bottom, and repeats the routine.

Build a Classroom Community That Includes All Children

Classrooms are learning communities where everyone can make a valuable contribution and has something to learn. Both large-group activities (e.g., opening circle, songs, sto-

ries, plays) and small-group activities (e.g., cooperative games, art projects, pre-academic activities) help create a classroom community.

- *Use activities that will engage children with a large range of abilities.* Plan open-ended activities that use preferred materials, support many responses, and address the strengths of children with disabilities.
- *Allow every child to have a turn and play a role.* For example, every child, including children with autism, takes a turn being in charge of handing out materials. This puts the children with disabilities on an equal footing with others in the group and requires them to be communicative partners with peers as they request materials.

Here's an example:

It is "show and share" day, and Sophie, a 5-year-old with autism, is ready. In her lap she has a special toy from her grandmother and a cue card with words and symbols her teacher has prepared. When it's her turn, she walks to the front of the circle, holds up her toy, looks at the notecard, and follows the routine of telling her classmates two things about her toy. Then she asks, "Any questions?" After calling on classmates and answering two questions, she returns to her seat, puts her toy and cue card behind her, and picks up the notecard at her place. The teacher prepared this card with cues to support Sophie's participation as an audience member.

Promote Generalization and Maintenance of Skills

Unless skills are demonstrated across a variety of situations and maintained over time, children will have limited ability to participate meaningfully in inclusive environments.

- *Target skills that will be useful in each child's life.* Skills a child needs in many situations and those typically enjoyed by same-age children are likely to be generalized and maintained because they are frequently practiced and produce naturally reinforcing outcomes.
- *Use instructional prompts judiciously and fade them rapidly.* To keep children from depending on adult assistance and direction, use the least directive and intrusive prompt that ensures successful skill performance. Fade the prompt as quickly as possible without disrupting performance.
- *Distribute learning trials naturally.* Capitalize on teaching opportunities that occur within natural school routines and activities. This increases the likelihood of generalization and maintenance because it "duplicates the occasions in which the

continues

skill should occur after instruction ceases" (Billingsley, Liberty, & White, 1994, p. 90).

- *Use common materials for instruction.* Teach with materials frequently found in preschools, child care settings, and the homes of young children. Arrange for children to practice with these materials across many settings in the classroom.

Here's an example:

Joey has difficulty in the dramatic play area. To promote skill development, his teacher provides systematic instruction of a pretend play sequence during small-group time, using a simple play

script with pictures and words and the same materials available in the dramatic play center this week. The teacher models the sequence, following the pictures in the script book and reciting corresponding words. Then Joey takes a turn while the teacher helps. Later, during free play, he enters the dramatic play area and sees the familiar pretend play props and his picture script book. He begins following the sequence without adult assistance.

Source: Adapted from Schwartz, I. S., Billingsley, F. F., & McBride, B. M. (1998). Including children with autism in inclusive preschools: Strategies that work. *Young Exceptional Children, 1*(2), 19–26. Used by permission.

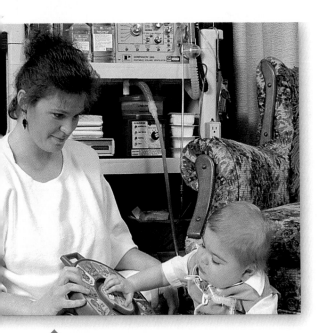

Programs like the St. Mark's Circle Project in North Carolina teach parents to identify and increase the frequency of positive behaviors by their infants such as smiling or imitating.

component of classroom instruction occurs from 9:00 A.M. to 1:00 P.M. throughout the year. The home-based/family services component entails monthly home visits; the visits include family-focused assessment and planning, demonstrations of instructional techniques, and provision of information and other support. Between regularly scheduled home visits, ongoing individualized consultation and collaboration with parents and families are available as needed.

CURRENT ISSUES AND FUTURE TRENDS

Early childhood special education has made tremendous progress over the past 20 years. The number of high-quality inclusive early childhood programs for preschoolers with disabilities increases each year, and family-centered early intervention services are available for infants and toddlers with, or at risk for, developmental disabilities than ever before. Like any young and growing field, however, early childhood special education faces numerous problems, challenges, and opportunities for improvement.

Perhaps no other area of special education presents researchers with a more important array of issues and questions in need of scientific investigation. For example, here is one fundamental question with enormous implications and from which literally hundreds of specific research questions and studies can be derived: "What type of early childhood programs and settings are most effective for which groups of children and their families?" (Holahan & Costenbader, 2000; Odom et al., 2000). Guralnick (2001) has called for a national agenda to focus research and resources on increasing the availability and quality of inclusive preschool programs for children with special needs.

To ensure that quality early childhood care is available for all children and their families and that specialized early intervention is provided to all children who have or are at risk for developmental delay, the public and elected policymakers must increase their awareness of the importance of early intervention (Kagan & Neuman, 1997; Howard, Williams, Port, & Lepper, 2001). Early intervention is expensive, especially for children with significant disabilities. More carefully controlled research on its costs and benefits is needed, and the results of these studies should be considerd in policy and funding decisions (Jacobson, Mulick, & Green, 1998; Odom et al., 2001).

FAMILIES: MOST IMPORTANT OF ALL

The success of efforts to prevent disabilities in children and to identify, assess, and intervene with children who have special needs as early as possible requires the training, experience, and cooperation of a wide range of professionals. Current best-practice guidelines for early childhood services call for a transdisciplinary approach to the delivery of related services in which parents and professionals work together in assessing needs, developing the IFSP or IEP, providing services, and evaluating outcomes (Sandall et al., 2000).

Of all the people needed to make early intervention work, parents and families are the most important. Given enough information and support, parents can help prevent many risks and causes of disabilities—before pregnancy, before birth, and certainly before a child has gone months or years without help. Given the chance, parents can take an active role in determining their children's educational needs and goals. And given some guidance, training, and support, many parents can teach their children at home and even at school.

It is no wonder, then, that all successful intervention programs for young children with disabilities take great care to involve parents (Harris & Handleman, 2000; Howard et al., 2001; Raver, 1999). Parents are the most frequent observers of their children's behavior. They usually know better than anyone else what their children need, and they can help educators set realistic goals. They can report on events in the home that outsiders might never see—for instance, how a child responds to other family members. They can monitor and report on their children's progress at home beyond the more controlled environment of the early intervention center or preschool. In short, parents can contribute to their children's programs at every stage—assessment, planning, classroom activities, and evaluation. Many parents even work in preschool classrooms as teacher aides, volunteers, or staff members.

But in our efforts to involve parents, we must recognize that while professionals come and go, parents and families are in it for the long haul. In their focus to help young children attain critical developmental gains, early childhood professionals may overlook the fact that parents are just beginning a lifetime of commitment and responsibility.

As Hutinger, Marshall, and McCarten (1983) reminded us 20 years ago, we must not forget that early childhood is supposed to be a fun, happy time for children and for the adults who are fortunate enough to work with them.

> Part of our mission as professionals in the field of early childhood special education is to possess an art of enjoyment ourselves and to help instill it in the young children and families with whom we work.
>
> Early childhood comes but once in a lifetime . . . Let's make it count!

▲ Of all the people needed to make early intervention effective, parents are the most important.

For more information on early childhood special education, go to the Web Links Module in Chapter 5 of the Companion Website at **www.prenhall.com/heward**

SUMMARY

THE IMPORTANCE OF EARLY INTERVENTION

- Early intervention consists of educational, nutritional, child care, and family supports designed to reduce the effects of disabilities or prevent the occurrence of developmental problems later in life for children at risk for such problems.

- Research has documented that early intervention can provide both intermediate and long-term benefits for young children with disabilities and those at risk for developmental delay. Benefits of early intervention include the following:

  - Gains in physical development, cognitive development, language and speech development, social competence, and self-help skills
  - Prevention of secondary disabilities
  - Reduction of family stress
  - Reduced need for special education services or placement during the school year
  - Savings to society of the costs of additional educational and social services that would be needed later without early intervention
  - Reduced likelihood of social dependence in adulthood

- The effectiveness of early intervention is increased when it begins early in life, is intensive, and lasts for a long time.

IDEA AND EARLY CHILDHOOD SPECIAL EDUCATION

- States that receive IDEA funds for early intervention services must serve all infants and toddlers birth to age 3 with developmental delays or established risk conditions. At their discretion, states may serve infants and toddlers who are at risk for acquiring disabilities because of certain biological or environmental risk conditions.
- Early intervention services for infants and toddlers are family-centered, transdisciplinary, and described by IFSPs.
- IDEA requires states to provide special education services (via IEPs) to all preschool children with disabilities ages 3 through 5.
- Preschool children do not have to be identified and reported under disability categories to receive services.

SCREENING, IDENTIFICATION, AND ASSESSMENT

- Four major types of assessment purposes/tools are used in early childhood special education:

  - Screening involves quick, easy-to-administer tests to identify children who may have a disability and who should receive further testing.
  - Diagnosis requires in-depth, comprehensive assessment of all major areas of development to determine a child's eligibility for early intervention or special education services.
  - Program planning uses curriculum-based, criterion-referenced assessments to determine a child's current skill level, identify IFSP/IEP objectives, and plan intervention activities.
  - Evaluation uses curriculum-based, criterion-referenced measures to determine progress on IFSP/IEP objectives and evaluate a program's effects.

- Many early intervention programs are moving away from assessments based entirely on developmental milestones and are incorporating curriculum-based assessment, in which each item relates directly to a skill included in the program's curriculum. This provides a direct link among testing, teaching, and program evaluation.

CURRICULUM AND INSTRUCTION

- Early intervention and education programs for children with special needs should be designed and evaluated according to these outcomes or goals:

- Support families in achieving their own goals.
- Promote child engagement, independence, and mastery.
- Promote development in all important domains.
- Build and support social competence.
- Facilitate the generalized use of skills.
- Prepare for and assist children with normalized life experiences in their families, schools, and communities.
- Help children and their families make smooth transitions.
- Prevent or minimize the development of future problems or disabilities.

- Developmentally appropriate practices provide a foundation or context from which to build individualized programs of support and instruction for children with special needs.
- IEP/IFSP objectives for infants and young children should be evaluated according to their functionality, generality, instructional context, measurability, and relation between short- and long-range goals.
- Embedded learning opportunities are brief, systematic instructional interactions that focus on a child's IEP objectives in the context of naturally occurring classroom activities.
- In addition to providing systematic, explicit instruction of language skills to children in individual and small-group learning activities, teachers should embed meaningful opportunities for children to talk and communicate throughout the day.
- Preschool activity schedules should (1) include child-initiated and planned activities, large- and small-group activities, active and quiet times, and indoor and outdoor activity; and (2) provide a framework for maximizing children's opportunities to develop new skills and practice what they have learned.
- Preschool classrooms should be designed so that play areas and needed materials are accessible to and safe for all students, boundaries between areas minimize distractions, and children want to explore and play.
- Many young children with special needs require instruction to develop social competence.

SERVICE DELIVERY ALTERNATIVES

- In home-based programs, a child's parents act as the primary teachers, with regular training and guidance from a teacher or specially trained paraprofessional who visits the home.
- In center-based programs, a child comes to the center for direct instruction, although the parents are usually involved. Center programs allow a team of specialists to work with the child and enable the child to meet and interact with other children.
- Many programs offer the advantages of both models by combining home visits with center-based programming.

CURRENT ISSUES AND FUTURE TRENDS

- The field of early childhood special education will be advanced by research investigating which combinations of program characteristics are most effective for target groups of children and their families and from studies analyzing the cost-benefit balance of early intervention.
- Parents are the most important people in an early intervention program. They can act as advocates, participate in educational planning, observe their children's behavior, help set realistic goals, work in the classroom, and teach their children at home.

To check your comprehension of chapter content, go to the Guided Review and Quiz Modules in Chapter 5 of the Companion Website at **www.prenhall.com/heward**

Chapter 6
Mental Retardation

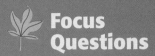

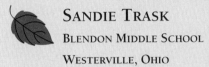

SANDIE TRASK
BLENDON MIDDLE SCHOOL
WESTERVILLE, OHIO

Education • Teaching Credentials • Experience
- B.S. in Special Education, Ohio Dominican College, 1983
- M.A. in Special Education and Applied Behavior Analysis, The Ohio State University, 1989
- Ohio Developmental Handicaps, K–12; Multiple Handicaps, K–12
- 17 years; first 6 years at The Ohio State School for the Blind teaching secondary students with visual impairments and mental retardation

Current Teaching Position and Students   The 8 sixth, seventh, and eighth graders in my self-contained classroom have a wide range of abilities and educational needs associated with mild to severe mental retardation. Most have additional disabilities, such as communication disorders or physical and motor problems, and usually remain in my classroom throughout their middle school years. Each student needs individualized instruction and supports in self-help and daily-living skills, social and communication skills, and functional academics.

Jennifer is 15 and enjoys listening to rap music, wearing stylish clothes, and socializing. She travels alone throughout the building and takes care of her personal needs. Jennifer reads and writes at a first-grade level and needs individualized instruction for all academic work. She also needs support in new situations. When problems arise, she becomes withdrawn; and she can be uncooperative about challenges.

Matthew is 12 and needs intensive supports to complete any activity. He is mobile but needs assistance with all self-help skills and prompts to complete one-step vocational activities. Matthew is nonverbal and does not read, so we use pictures to point out activities and show food choices for lunch.

The students spend most of the day in my classroom working on both individualized lessons and group activities. Two aides help me with instructional activities and accompany students when they attend general education classes such as art, physical education, and choir. Each student spends about 15 minutes a day with her reading buddy, an eighth grader without disabilities who shares reading activities. This is a wonderful social and learning opportunity for all participants.

IEP Goals and Objectives   Most of my students have 8–10 IEP goals involving reading, math, social, self-help, and vocational areas. Activities range from writing short sentences with punctuation, to adding and subtracting on the calculator, to letter and number recognition. Here are two examples of IEP goals and objectives:

Annual goal: Jennifer will learn 75 new sight words and demonstrate comprehension of the words.

Focus Questions

- What is most important in determining a person's level of adaptive functioning: intellectual capability or a supportive environment?

- What is to be gained by classifying a child with mental retardation by the intensities of supports she needs to access and benefit from education?

- What should curriculum goals for students with mental retardation emphasize?

- What are the most important features of effective instruction for students with mental retardation?

- What is necessary to make education for a student with mental retardation appropriate in an inclusive classroom?

Short-term objective 1: Jennifer will verbally read two new sight words a week and read words from her bank of previously learned words with 90% accuracy.
Short-term objective 2: Given a shopping list, recipe, or other written task, Jennifer will obtain the item and/or follow the written directions 4 out of 5 times.

Annual goal: Matthew will obtain his work supplies and work independently.
Short-term objective 1: When Matthew sees a picture of his job on his schedule, he will independently get all necessary supplies and begin his work for 4 out of 5 sessions.
Short-term objective 2: Matthew will independently place the pop cans in the box, carry them to the cafeteria, and put them into the recycling bin in the cafeteria during 4 out of 5 sessions.

To track lesson implementation and student performance, I keep a notebook for each student indexed by subject areas. I create a data collection sheet for each IEP goal and objective. I also use class attendance books to check off the dates we work on particular objectives. This helps me quickly identify what has and has not been worked on.

Functional Curriculum   My job is to prepare students for life in the community and eventual transition into the real world. Students learn to read recipes, follow bus routes, fill out applications, manage time and money, and so on. For reading, I usually choose the Edmark Functional Sight Word Series, which includes 100-word sets of fast food/ restaurant words, grocery words, and job/work words. I don't use commercially published math curricula but focus on coin recognition and values, calculator skills, time telling, price recognition, and measurement skills.

During small-group lessons, I make sure that each student has his own materials so everyone can respond and practice together. My primary strategy is repetition with feedback. We practice skills over and over and work on generalizing across settings, staff, materials, and opportunities. I make reading cards of sight words so students can bring them home to practice. I create recipes that use sight words and familiar measurements. It is exciting to see students demonstrate these skills when grocery shopping or locating and reading movie times in the newspaper.

We cook at least once a week to work on reading measurements and following directions. The students have used many kinds of kitchen equipment. We have also painted a bookshelf, découpaged a desk, and decorated pens. During community-based instruction, students check out books, buy stamps and mail packages, shop, open savings accounts, and order and pay for food. In school each student gets work-related experience with tasks such as delivering mail, filling the pop machine, watering plants, answering the telephone, collating and stapling papers, sorting and wrapping coins, and shredding paper. I emphasize the importance of starting and completing activities independently.

Motivating My Students and Me   I love the opportunity to create new experiences that make learning effective and fun. For example, I've incorporated my passion for auctions into a successful reinforcement program. Students earn money for completing their schoolwork and following the school rules. They earn bonus money when I catch them being good, such as helping one another. If they choose to break a rule, they have to pay a one-dollar fine. The students are responsible for filling out deposit slips and maintaining their account balances. I have an enlarged copy of an actual checkbook that works well. Students who have difficulty writing use deposit and withdrawal stamps as well as date and number stamps. We hold an auction every other week when they decide how much to withdraw and whether to bid on items or redeposit money for the next auction. It has been very exciting to watch them learn about handling money.

Communicating with Parents   Parents know they can call me anytime at school or home. We are fortunate to have a phone in our classroom so students can work on telephone skills. They get excited when they answer the phone and a parent is on the other end. We have a weekly class newsletter, and every student contributes at least one article per week. I use a digital camera to insert pictures of the students involved in the classroom activities, and I also include a description of the highlights for the upcoming week. All students take home a copy of the newsletter, and we e-mail it to other teachers and related services specialists and to any parents with e-mail.

To see an example of the class newsletter with stories by Ms. Trask's students, go to Teacher Feature page on the Companion Website at **www.prenhall.com/heward**

What I Like Best about Being a Special Education Teacher   One of my challenges and joys is to figure out how to meet students' changing needs and interests. The necklace business has been a wonderful activity to incorporate many student objectives into a functional skill. We live in "Buckeye Country," and a lot of people here are avid Ohio State University Buckeye fans. Two years ago, as a class activity, we made buckeye necklaces for my students to wear during the football season. When other teachers started asking us to make necklaces for them and their friends, a class business was born! It allows students at all ability levels to participate. It is exciting to watch the students build skills and self-esteem through making and selling their product. The students take turns holding job titles, such as production manager, marketing manager, and quality control manager and, as a result, learn the process of buying the materials needed, producing the product, and selling the product. The students have to manage the money for expenses and then decide how to use the profit.

A consultant colleague says he never knows what he'll see next in my classroom. He mentions the "campsite," a tent one student uses as a quiet retreat from the busy classroom; the "vending machine," where students can use classroom money to buy a treat; and the "Barnes and Noble area," a student-created nook where they can sit in soft chairs with a drink and read. His praise challenges me to think of other ways to enhance my classroom environment to better meet the needs and interests of my students.

M**ost** people have some notion of what mental retardation is and what people with mental retardation must be like. When they hear the words "special education," the first thing many people think of is mental retardation. Indeed, the first public school special education classes in 1896 were for children with mental retardation. Of course, things have changed a great deal since then. Recent years have witnessed significant improvements in the education and treatment of children and adults with mental retardation. Persons with mental retardation have enjoyed increased opportunities to experience the benefits and responsibilities of participating in the educational and community mainstream.

To better understand what will be covered in this chapter, go to the Essential Concepts and Chapter-at-a-Glance modules in Chapter 6 of the Companion Website at **www.prenhall.com/heward**

Unfortunately, although there is considerable and growing public awareness of mental retardation, much of that awareness consists of misconceptions, oversimplifications, and fear. For example, undergraduate special education majors recorded these statements from people outside the university who were making everyday references to mental retardation:

> After telling a fellow waitress about her career plans to teach children labeled as having mental retardation, . . . her co-worker's response was, "Why would you want to teach children who cannot learn?" . . .
>
> A hair dresser burned herself on a hot curling iron. "I must be retarded," she remarked. "I always burn myself on this thing." . . .
>
> Two co-workers discussed the location of a bar in another part of the city. . . . The listener . . . had some idea of where the bar was located. He asked a question to confirm his idea, "Is it across the street from the funny farm?" The co-worker confirmed that the bar was, in fact, across from the "funny farm," a residential facility for persons with mental retardation. . . .

She expressed many things to me as I explained special education including being scared of those people. . . . She told me over and over how she felt sorry for them. (Danforth & Navarro, 1998, pp. 36–40)

This chapter presents some key factors in understanding the complex concept called mental retardation. It also looks at some contemporary instructional practices that have improved educational outcomes for students with mental retardation.

DEFINITIONS

Some children are so clearly and consistently behind their peers in academic, social, language, and self-care skills that it is obvious to anyone who interacts with them that they require special education and related services. How mental retardation is defined is not much of an issue for these children; they experience pervasive and substantial limitations in all or most areas of development and functioning. But this group is only a small portion of the total population of persons with mental retardation. The largest segment consists of school-age children with mild retardation. How mental retardation is defined determines what special educational services many thousands of children are eligible (or ineligible) to receive. Thus, disagreements among professionals over what constitutes mental retardation are much more than academic exercises or philosophical debates. A subtle difference between two definitions can determine whether the label *mental retardation* is associated with a particular child and whether or not appropriate educational supports are provided (Luckasson & Reeve, 2001).

Many definitions of mental retardation have been proposed, adopted, and debated over the years. First, we will look at the most frequently used approach to defining and classifying mental retardation, one based primarily on the assessment of intellectual functioning. Then we will examine the most recent definition of mental retardation, which is based on the levels of supports needed for the individual to function effectively.

Which student has mental retardation? The term *mental retardation* identifies substantial limitations in functioning: it is not something inherent within the individual.

Definitions of MR

Council for Exceptional Children Content Standards for Beginning Teachers of Student with MR/DD: Definitions and issues related to the identification of individuals with MR/DD (MR1K1).
PRAXIS Special Education Core Principles: Content Knowledge: I. Understanding Exceptionalities, Definitions of disabilities.

AAMR'S 1983 DEFINITION IN IDEA

The American Association on Mental Retardation (AAMR), the leading professional organization concerned with the study, treatment, and prevention of mental retardation, has played a leadership role in defining mental retardation. In 1973, AAMR published a definition that was incorporated into IDEA and continues to serve today as the basis by which most states identify children for special education services under the disability category of mental retardation. That definition, with minor rewording, was published in the organization's 1983 manual on terminology and classification of mental retardation: "Mental retardation refers to significantly subaverage general intellectual functioning resulting in or associated with deficits in adaptive behavior and manifested during the developmental period" (Grossman, 1983, p. 11).

In IDEA, **mental retardation** is defined as significantly subaverage general intellectual functioning existing concurrently with deficits in adaptive behavior and manifested during the developmental period that adversely affects a child's educational performance. (34 C.R.R., Sec. 3000.7[b][5])

The definition includes three criteria. First, "significant subaverage intellectual functioning" must be demonstrated before mental retardation is diagnosed. The word *significant* refers

Level	Intelligence Test Score
Mild retardation	50–55 to approximately 70
Moderate retardation	35–40 to 50–55
Severe retardation	20–25 to 35–40
Profound retardation	Below 20–25

TABLE 6.1 Classification of mental retardation by measured IQ score

Source: Based on the AAMR's *Classification of Mental Retardation* (Grossman, 1983) and the *Diagnostic and Statistical Manual of Mental Disorders* (*DSM-IV*) (American Psychiatric Association, 1994).

to a score of two or more standard deviations below the mean on a standardized intelligence test (a score of approximately 70 or less; IQ testing will be discussed later in the chapter). Second, an individual must be well below average in both intellectual functioning *and* adaptive behavior; that is, intellectual functioning is not intended to be the sole defining criterion. Third, the definition specifies that the deficits in intellectual functioning and adaptive behavior must occur during the developmental period to help distinguish mental retardation from other disabilities (e.g., impaired performance by an adult due to head injury). The criterion "that adversely affects a child's educational performance" in the IDEA definition is automatically met when a child exhibits substantial limitations in intellectual functioning and adaptive behavior.

Persons with mental retardation have traditionally been classified by the degree or level of intellectual impairment as measured by an IQ test. The most widely used classification method cited in the professional literature consists of four levels of mental retardation according to the range of IQ scores shown in Table 6.1. The range of scores representing the high and low ends of each level indicates an awareness of the inexactness of intelligence testing and the importance of clinical judgment in determining level of severity.

Educators have often used different terms for the various degrees of mental retardation. For many years, students with mental retardation in the public schools were classified as either *educable mentally retarded* (EMR) or *trainable mentally retarded* (TMR). These terms referred to mild and moderate levels of retardation, respectively. Children with severe and profound mental retardation were not included in this two-level classification system because they were often denied a public education and were likely to reside in a state-operated institution. Although one still encounters the terms *EMR* and *TMR* today, most special educators consider them to be archaic and inappropriate because they suggest predetermined achievement limits (Beirne-Smith, Ittenbach, & Patton, 2002).

AAMR'S NEW DEFINITION BASED ON NEEDED SUPPORTS

In 1992, the AAMR published a definition and approach for diagnosing and classifying mental retardation that represented a conceptual shift from viewing mental retardation as an inherent trait or permanent condition to a description of the individual's present func-

Children with mild or moderate mental retardation are now often placed in inclusive classrooms where teachers can support their learning of academic skills in elementary years.

tioning and the environmental supports needed to improve it. That definition was revised in 2002 and reads as follows:

> Mental retardation is a disability characterized by significant limitations in both intellectual functioning and conceptual, social, and practical adaptive skills. This disability originates before age 18.

The following five assumptions are essential to the application of the definition:

1. Limitations in present functioning must be considered within the context of community environments typical of the individual's age peers and culture.
2. Valid assessment considers cultural and linguistic diversity as well as differences in communication, sensory, motor, and behavioral factors.
3. Within the individual, limitations often coexist with strengths.
4. The purpose of describing limitations is to develop a profile of needed supports.
5. With appropriate personalized supports over a sustained period, the life functioning of the person with mental retardation generally will improve. (Luckasson et al., in press)

Although Kelly needs extensive supports in some areas of life functioning, only limited supports are needed in communication and social skills.

AAMR's "2002 System" provides conceptual and procedural recommendations for functionally classifying mental retardation according to a profile of needed supports. This approach represents a change from classifying mental retardation on the basis of estimates of an individual's intellectual deficiencies to estimating the intensities of supports needed to improve functioning in her school, home, community, and work environments. Needed supports are identified and classified by an interdisciplinary team according to four levels of intensities: intermittent, limited, extensive, and pervasive (ILEP) (see Table 6.2). The ILEP system combines two prevailing theories about mental retardation:

> The system acknowledged the existence of genuine impairments in the individual but also reflected the idea that expression of the impairments is strongly affected by the life arrangements of the individual: Biology in a social context. The 1992 system changed the focus of evaluation from determining what place an individual held on the IQ continuum to what can the person do and what supports does the person need in order to function better. (Luckasson & Reeve, 2001, p. 50)

An interdisciplinary team develops a profile of the types and intensity of needed supports within each of five dimensions: intellectual abilities; adaptive behavior (conceptual, practical, social skills); participation, interactions, and social roles; health (physical health, mental health, etiological factors); and context (environments, culture, and opportunities).

It is too early to assess how AAMR's new conceptualization of mental retardation will influence special education practice. A national survey of state departments of education found that the new definition had had minimal impact on changing state guidelines for

TABLE 6.2 **Definitions of intensities of supports for individuals with mental retardation**

Intermittent	Supports on an "as needed basis." Characterized by episodic nature, person not always needing the support(s), or short-term supports needed during life-span transitions (e.g., job loss or an acute medical crisis). Intermittent supports may be high or low intensity when provided.
Limited	An intensity of supports characterized by consistency over time, time-limited but not of an intermittent nature, may require fewer staff members and less cost than more intense levels of support (e.g., time-limited employment training or transitional supports provided during the school to adult period).
Extensive	Supports characterized by regular involvement (e.g., daily) in at least some environments (such as work or home) and not time-limited (e.g., long-term support and long-term home living support).
Pervasive	Supports characterized by their constancy and high intensity; provided across environments; potential life-sustaining nature. Pervasive supports typically involve more staff members and intrusiveness than do extensive or time-limited supports.

Source: Reprinted from the American Association on Mental Retardation (AAMR). (1992). *Mental retardation: Definition, classification, and systems of supports* (9th ed., p. 26). Washington, DC: Author. Used by permission.

identifying students with mental retardation (Denning, Chamberlain, & Polloway, 2000). In an official position statement adopted by its board of directors (Smith, 1994), CEC's Division on Mental Retardation and Developmental Disabilities praises the new definition for focusing greater attention on the needs of individuals instead of on degrees of deficiency residing within the person with mental retardation and for providing the field with a positive stimulus for debate on issues critical to persons with mental retardation. The statement notes, however, that the changes required by and the implications of the new definition are so profound that they "require the most careful consideration before they are implemented in special education practices" (p. 179).

IDENTIFICATION AND ASSESSMENT

ASSESSING INTELLECTUAL FUNCTIONING

When assessing intellectual functioning as part of an evaluation for mental retardation, an intelligence (IQ) test is given by a school psychologist or other professional trained to administer and interpret such tests. An IQ test consists of a series of questions (e.g., vocabulary, similarities), problem solving (e.g., mazes, block designs), memory, and other tasks assumed to require certain degrees of intelligence to answer or solve correctly (Venn, 2000). The child's performance on those items is used to derive a score representing her intelligence.

In addition to being *standardized tests*—the same questions and tasks are always presented in a certain, specified way with the same scoring procedures used each time the test is administered—IQ tests are norm-referenced tests. When it is being developed, a *norm-referenced test* is administered to a large sample of people selected at random from the population for whom the test is intended. Test scores of persons in the norming sample are then used to represent how scores on the test are generally distributed throughout the population.

Normal Curve and Standard Deviation   IQ scores seem to be distributed throughout the population according to a phenomenon called the **normal curve**, shown in Figure 6.1. To describe how a particular score varies from the mean, or average score, of all the scores in

ILEP classification system

Council for Exceptional Children   Content Standards for Beginning Teachers of Students with MR/DD: Relate levels of support to the needs of the individual (MR3S1) (also CC2K2).
PRAXIS Special Education Core Principles: Content Knowledge: I. Understanding Exceptionalities, Classification of students with disabilities.

AAMR and CEC's Division of MR/DD

Council for Exceptional Children   Content Standards for Beginning Teachers of Students with MR/DD: Organizations and publications in the field of MR/DD (MR9K1).
PRAXIS Special Education Core Principles: Content Knowledge: III. Delivery of Services to Students with Disabilities, Professional roles, Professional organizations and associations.

Standardized tests, norm-referenced tests, the normal curve, and standard deviation

Council for Exceptional Children   Content Standards for Beginning Teachers of Students with MR/DD: Specialized terminology used in the assessment of individuals with MR/DD (MR8K1) (also CC8K1).
PRAXIS Special Education Core Principles: Content Knowledge: III. Delivery of Services to Students with Disabilities, Assessment, How to interpret standardized test results.

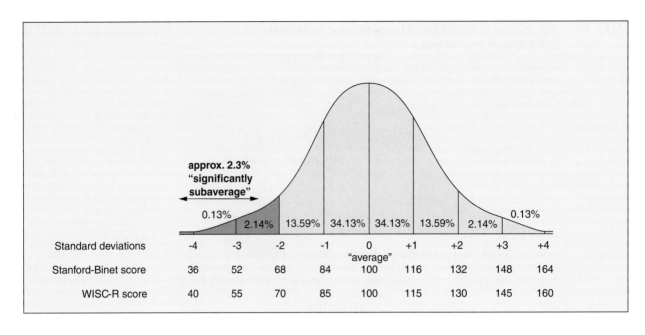

FIGURE 6.1 **Theoretical distribution of IQ scores on the normal curve**

IQ scores and diagnosis of MR

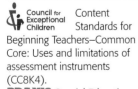 Content Standards for Beginning Teachers of Students with MR/DD: Definitions and issues related to the identification of individuals with MR/DD (MR1K1).
PRAXIS Special Education Core Principles: Content Knowledge: III. Delivery of Services to Students with Disabilities, Assessment, How to interpret standardized test results.

Issues to consider with IQ tests/scores

Council for Exceptional Children Content Standards for Beginning Teachers—Common Core: Uses and limitations of assessment instruments (CC8K4).
PRAXIS Special Education Core Principles: Content Knowledge: III. Delivery of Services to Students with Disabilities, Assessment, How to interpret standardized test results.

the norm sample, a mathematical concept called the **standard deviation** is used. An algebraic formula is applied to the scores achieved by the norm sample on a test, to determine what value equals one standard deviation for that test. A child's IQ test score can then be described in terms of how many standard deviations above or below the mean it is. Theoretically, an equal number of people score above and below the mean and about 2.3% of the population falls two or more standard deviations below the mean, which the AAMR calls "significantly subaverage."

According to the AAMR's 1983 and 2002 definitions, a diagnosis of mental retardation requires an IQ score at least two standard deviations below the mean, which is approximately 70 or less on the two most widely used intelligence tests, the Wechsler Intelligence Scale for Children—Third Edition (WISC-III) (Wechsler, 1991) and the Stanford-Binet IV (Thorndike, Hagen, & Sattler, 1986). The AAMR emphasizes that the IQ cutoff score of 70 is intended only as a guideline and should not be interpreted as a hard-and-fast requirement (Luckasson et al., 1992). A higher IQ score of 75 or more may be associated with mental retardation if, according to a clinician's judgment, the child exhibits deficits in adaptive behavior thought to be caused by impaired intellectual functioning.

Although IQ tests have been widely criticized, they can provide useful information. IQ scores are particularly useful for objectively identifying an overall performance deficit and have proven to be the best single predictor of school achievement. Because IQ tests are composed largely of verbal and academic tasks—the same things a child must master to succeed in school—they correlate highly with school achievement.

Even though the major intelligence tests are among most carefully constructed and researched psychological assessment instruments available, they are still far from perfect and have both advantages and disadvantages. Here are several more important considerations:

- *The concept of intelligence is a hypothetical construct.* No one has ever seen a thing called intelligence; it is not a precise entity but something we infer from observed performance. We assume it takes more intelligence to perform some tasks than it does to perform others.

- *An IQ test measures only how a child performs at one point in time on the items included on the test.* An IQ test samples only a small portion of an individual's skills and abilities; we infer from that performance how a child might perform in other situations (Overton, 2000).

- *Intelligence tests can be culturally biased.* The Binet and Wechsler IQ tests tend to favor children from the population on which they were normed—primarily white, middle-class children. Some of the questions may tap learning that only a middle-class child is likely to have experienced. Both the Binet and Wechsler, which are highly verbal, are especially inappropriate for children for whom English is a second language (Venn, 2000).

- *IQ scores can change significantly.* IQ scores can change, particularly in the 70–85 range that formerly constituted borderline retardation (Venn, 2000). Hence, observers are hesitant to use the label *mental retardation* on the basis of an IQ score that might increase after a period of intensive, systematic intervention.

- *Intelligence testing is not an exact science.* Among the many variables that can affect an individual's IQ score are motivation, the time and location of the test, and inconsistency or bias on the test giver's part in scoring responses that are not precisely covered by the test manual.

- *Results of an IQ test should never be used as the sole basis for making a decision on the provision or denial of special education services.* An IQ score is just one component of a multifactored, nondiscriminatory assessment.

- *Results from an IQ test should not be used to target educational objectives or design instruction.* Results of teacher-administered, criterion-referenced assessments of a student's performance of curriculum-specific skills are generally more useful for planning what to teach. Results of direct and frequent measurement of a student's performance during instruction provide needed information for evaluating and modifying teaching practices.

ASSESSING ADAPTIVE BEHAVIOR

Adaptive behavior is "the effectiveness or degree with which the individual meets the standards of personal independence and social responsibility expected of his age and social group" (Grossman, 1983, p. 157). Systematic assessment of adaptive behavior is important for reasons other than the diagnosis of mental retardation. The adaptive skills exhibited by a person with mental retardation—as well as the nature and severity of maladaptive behaviors—are critical factors in determining the supports he requires for success in school, work, community, and home environments (Rush & Francis, 2000; Schalock, 1999). A number of instruments for assessing adaptive behavior have been developed. Most consist of a series of questions that someone familiar with the individual, such as a teacher or a parent, answers.

AAMR Adaptive Behavior Scale A frequently used instrument for assessing adaptive behavior by school-age children is the AAMR Adaptive Behavior Scale—School (ABS-S) (Lambert, Nihira, & Leland, 1993). The ABS-S consists of two parts. Part 1 contains 10 domains related to independent functioning and daily living skills (e.g., eating, toilet use, money handling, numbers, time); Part 2 assesses the individual's level of maladaptive (inappropriate) behavior in seven areas (e.g., trustworthiness, self-abusive behavior, social engagement). Another form, the ABS-RC, assesses adaptive behavior in residential and community settings (Nihira, Leland, & Lambert, 1993).

Vineland Adaptive Behavior Scales The Vineland Adaptive Behavior Scales are available in three versions. The Interview Editions in Survey Form or Expanded Form are administered by an individual, such as a teacher or a direct caregiver, who is very familiar with the

Assessing adaptive behavior

Council for Exceptional Children — Content Standards for Beginning Teachers of Students with MR/DD: Adaptive behavior assessment (MR8K3).
PRAXIS Special Education Core Principles: Content Knowledge: III. Delivery of Services to Students with Disabilities, Assessment, Procedures and test materials used for referral and classification.

person being assessed (Sparrow, Balla, & Cicchetti, 1984a, 1984b). The classroom edition is designed to be completed by a teacher (Sparrow, Balla, & Cicchetti, 1985).

Assessment of Social Competence   The Assessment of Social Competence (ASC) (Meyer, Cole, McQuarter, & Reichle, 1990), which is intended to measure competence at all levels of social and intellectual functioning, consists of 252 items organized within 11 social functions (e.g., initiates interactions, follows rules, indicates preferences). Each function is further broken down into eight levels, with the highest level representing performance at an adult level of mastery.

Measurement of adaptive behavior has proven difficult, in large part because of the relative nature of social adjustment and competence: what is considered appropriate in one situation or by one group may not be in or by another (Schalock, 1999). Nowhere is there a list that everyone would agree describes exactly those adaptive behaviors all of us should exhibit. As with IQ tests, cultural bias can be a problem in adaptive behavior scales; for instance, one item on some scales requires a child to tie a laced shoe, but some children have never had a shoe with laces. Ongoing research on the measurement of adaptive behavior may help resolve these problems.

CHARACTERISTICS

Mental retardation means substantial limitations in age-appropriate intellectual and adaptive behavior. It is seldom a time-limited condition. Although many individuals with mental retardation make tremendous advancements in adaptive skills (some to the point of functioning independently and no longer being considered under any disability category), most are affected throughout their life span (Mulick & Antonak, 1994).

Many children with mild retardation are not identified until they enter school and sometimes not until the second or third grade, when more difficult academic work is required. Most students with mild mental retardation master academic skills up to about the sixth-grade level and are able to learn job skills well enough to support themselves independently or semi-independently. Some adults who have been identified with mild mental retardation develop excellent social and communication skills and once they leave school are no longer recognized as having a disability.

Children with moderate retardation show significant delays in development during their preschool years. As they grow older, discrepancies in overall intellectual development and adaptive functioning generally grow wider between these children and age mates without disabilities. People with moderate mental retardation are more likely to have health and behavior problems than are individuals with mild retardation.

Individuals with severe and profound mental retardation are almost always identified at birth or shortly afterward. Most of these infants have significant central nervous system damage, and many have additional disabilities and/or health conditions. Although IQ scores can serve as the basis for differentiating severe and profound retardation from one another, the difference is primarily one of functional impairment. Chapter 13 is devoted to the characteristics and education of students with severe disabilities.

COGNITIVE FUNCTIONING

Deficits in cognitive functioning and learning styles characteristic of individuals with mental retardation include poor memory, slow learning rates, attention problems, difficulty generalizing what they have learned, and lack of motivation.

Memory   Students with mental retardation have difficulty remembering information. As would be expected, the more severe the cognitive impairment, the greater the deficits in memory. In particular, research has found that students with mental retardation have trou-

Cognitive functioning of students with MR

Council for Exceptional Children   Content Standards for Beginning Teachers of Students with MR/DD: Psychological, social/emotional, and motor characteristics of individuals with MR/DD (MR2K3) (also CC2K2, CC3K5).

PRAXIS Special Education Core Principles: Content Knowledge: I. Understanding Exceptionalities, Characteristics of students with disabilities, Cognitive factors.

ble retaining information in short-term memory (Bray, Fletcher, & Turner, 1997). *Short-term memory,* or working memory, is the ability to recall and use information that was encountered just a few seconds to a couple of hours earlier—for example, remembering a specific sequence of job tasks an employer stated just a few minutes earlier. Merrill (1990) reported that students with mental retardation required more time than their nondisabled peers to automatically recall information and therefore have more difficulty handling larger amounts of cognitive information at one time. Early researchers suggested that once persons with mental retardation learned a specific item of information sufficiently to commit it to *long-term memory,* information recalled after a period of days or weeks, they retained that information about as well as persons without retardation (Belmont, 1966; Ellis, 1963).

More recent research on memory abilities of persons with mental retardation has focused on teaching *metacognitive* or *executive control* strategies, such as rehearsing and organizing information into related sets, which many children without disabilities learn to do naturally. Students with mental retardation do not tend to use such strategies spontaneously but can be taught to do so with improved performance on memory-related and problem-solving tasks as an outcome of such strategy instruction (Brown, Campione, & Murphy, 1974; Hughes & Rusch, 1989; Merrill, 1990).

Learning Rate   The rate at which individuals with mental retardation acquire new knowledge and skills is well below that of typically developing children. A frequently used measure of learning rate is *trials to criterion,* the number of practice or learning trials needed before a student can respond correctly to a learning task without prompts or assistance. For example, while just 2 or 3 trials with feedback may be required for a typically developing child to learn to discriminate between two geometric forms, a child with mental retardation may need 20 to 30 or more trials to learn the same discrimination.

Because students with mental retardation learn more slowly, some educators have assumed that instruction should be slowed down to match their lower rate of learning. Research has shown, however, that students with mental retardation need and benefit from opportunities to learn to "go fast." See Teaching & Learning, "How Many Can You Do in 1 Minute?" later in this chapter.

Attention   The ability to attend to critical features of a task (e.g., to the outline of geometric shapes instead of dimensions such as their color or position on the page) is a characteristic of efficient learners. Students with mental retardation often have trouble attending to relevant features of a learning task and instead may focus on distracting irrelevant stimuli. In addition, individuals with mental retardation often have difficulty sustaining attention to learning tasks (Zeaman & House, 1979). These attention problems compound and contribute to a student's difficulties in acquiring, remembering, and generalizing new knowledge and skills.

Effective instructional design for students with mental retardation must systematically control for the presence and saliency of critical stimulus dimensions as well as the presence and effects of distracting stimuli. After initially directing a student's attention to the most relevant feature of a simplified task and reinforcing correct responses, the complexity and difficulty of the task can gradually be increased. A student's selective and sustained attention to relevant stimuli will improve as he experiences success for doing so.

Generalization of Learning   Students with disabilities, especially those with mental retardation, often have trouble using their new knowledge and skills in settings or situations that differ from the context in which they first learned those skills. Such transfer or generalization of learning that occurs naturally for children without disabilities may not be evident in students with mental retardation without specific programming to facilitate it (Horner, Dunlap, & Koegel, 1988). Researchers and educators are no longer satisfied by demonstrations that individuals with mental retardation can initially acquire new knowledge or skills. One of the most important and challenging areas of contemporary research in special education is the search for strategies and tactics for promoting generalization and maintenance of learning by individuals with mental retardation. Some of the findings of that research are described later in this chapter and throughout this text.

Motivation   Some students with mental retardation exhibit an apparent lack of interest in learning or problem-solving tasks (Switzky, 1997). Some individuals with mental retardation develop *learned helplessness,* a condition in which a person who has experienced repeated failure comes to expect failure regardless of his or her efforts. In an attempt to minimize or offset failure, the person may set extremely low expectations for himself and not appear to try very hard. When faced with a difficult task or problem, some individuals with mental retardation may quickly give up and turn to or wait for others to help them. Some acquire a problem-solving approach called *outer-directedness,* in which they seem to distrust their own responses to situations and rely on others for assistance and solutions.

Rather than an inherent characteristic of mental retardation, the apparent lack of motivation may be the product of frequent failure and prompt dependency acquired as the result of other people's doing things for them. After successful experiences, individuals with mental retardation do not differ from persons without mental retardation on measures of outer-directedness (Bybee & Zigler, 1998). The current emphasis on teaching self-determination skills to students with mental retardation is critical in helping them to be self-reliant problem solvers who act upon their world rather than passively wait to be acted upon (Wehmeyer, Martin, & Sands, 1998).

 ADAPTIVE BEHAVIOR

By definition children with mental retardation have substantial deficits in adaptive behavior. These limitations can take many forms and tend to occur across domains of functioning. Limitations in self-care skills and social relationships as well as behavioral excesses are common characteristics of individuals with mental retardation.

Self-Care and Daily Living Skills   Individuals with mental retardation who require extensive supports must often be taught basic self-care skills such as dressing, eating, and hygiene. Direct instruction and environmental supports such as added prompts and simplified routines are necessary to ensure that deficits in these adaptive areas do not come to seriously limit one's quality of life. Most children with milder forms of mental retardation learn how to take care of their basic needs, but they often require training in self-management skills to achieve the levels of performance necessary for eventual independent living.

Social Development   Making and sustaining friendships and personal relationships present significant challenges for many persons with mental retardation. Limited cognitive processing skills, poor language development, and unusual or inappropriate behaviors can seriously impede interacting with others. It is difficult at best for someone who is not a professional educator or staff person to want to spend the time necessary to get to know a person who stands too close, interrupts frequently, does not maintain eye contact, and strays from the conversational topic. Teaching students with mental retardation appropriate social and interpersonal skills is one of the most important functions of special education.

Behavioral Excesses and Challenging Behavior   Students with mental retardation are more likely to exhibit behavior problems than are children without disabilities. Difficulties accepting criticism, limited self-control, and bizarre and inappropriate behaviors such as

Learned helplessness and outer-directedness

Council for Exceptional Children Content Standards for Beginning Teachers of Students with MR/DD: Psychological, social/emotional, and motor characteristics of individuals with MR/DD (MR2K3) (also CC2K2).
PRAXIS Special Education Core Principles: Content Knowledge: I. Understanding Exceptionalities, Characteristics of students with disabilities, Cognitive factors and affective and social-adaptive factors.

Adaptive behavior of individuals of individuals with MR/DD

Council for Exceptional Children Content Standards for Beginning Teachers of Students with MR/DD: Psychological, social/emotional, and motor characteristics of individuals with MR/DD (MR2K3) (also CC2K2).
PRAXIS Special Education Core Principles: Content Knowledge: I. Understanding Exceptionalities, Characteristics of students with disabilities, Cognitive factors and affective and social-adaptive factors.

aggression or self-injury are often observed in children with mental retardation. Some of the genetic syndromes associated with mental retardation tend to include abnormal behavior (e.g., children with Prader-Willi syndrome often engage in self-injurious or obsessive-compulsive behavior). In general, the more severe the retardation, the higher the incidence of behavior problems. Individuals with mental retardation and psychiatric conditions requiring mental health supports are known as "dual diagnosis" cases. Data from one report showed that approximately 10% of all persons with mental retardation served by the state of California were dually diagnosed (Borthwick-Duffy & Eyman, 1990). Although there are comprehensive treatment guidelines available for treating psychiatric and behavioral problems of persons with mental retardation (Rush & Francis, 2000), much more research is needed on how best to support this population.

POSITIVE ATTRIBUTES

Descriptions of the intellectual functioning and adaptive behavior of individuals with mental retardation focus on limitations and deficits and paint a picture of a monolithic group of people whose most important characteristics revolve around the absence of desirable traits. But individuals with mental retardation are a huge and disparate group composed of people with highly individual personalities (Smith & Mitchell, 2001b). Many children and adults with mental retardation display tenacity in learning, get along well with others, and are positive influences on those around them (Smith, 2000).

PREVALENCE

Prevalence of MR

PRAXIS Special Education Core Principles: Content Knowledge: I. Understanding Exceptionalities, Characteristics of students with disabilities, Incidence and prevalence of various types of disabilities.

Changing definitions of mental retardation, the schools' reluctance to apply the label to children with mild mental retardation, and the changing status of schoolchildren with mild mental retardation (many are no longer identified after leaving school) contribute to the difficulty of estimating the number of people with mental retardation (Larson et al., 2001). Historically, the federal government estimated the prevalence at 3% of the general population, although recent analyses find little objective support for this figure. If prevalence figures were based on IQ scores alone, theoretically 2.3% of the population would have mental retardation (see Figure 6.1).

Basing prevalence estimates on IQ scores only, however, ignores the other necessary criterion for mental retardation—deficits in adaptive functioning and the need for supports. Some professionals believe that if adaptive behavior is included with intellectual ability when estimating prevalence, the figure would drop to about 1%. In fact, two recent national studies estimated the prevalence of mental retardation at 0.78% (Larson et al., 2001) and 1.1% of the U.S. population (Fujiura & Yamaki, 1997).

The 1% estimate is consistent with data reported by the U.S. Department of Education (2002) on the number of children receiving special education. During the 2000–2001 school year, 611,878 students ages 6 through 21 received special education under the disability category of mental retardation. These students represented 10.6% of all school-age children in special education, or about 1% of the total school-age population. Mental retardation is the third largest disability category after learning disabilities and speech or language impairments.

Prevalence rates vary greatly from state to state. For example, the prevalence of mental retardation as a percentage of total school enrollment in 2000–2001 ranged from a low of 0.32% (New Jersey) to a high of 2.41% (West Virginia) (U.S.D.E., 2002). Such large differences in prevalence are no doubt a function of the widely differing criteria for identifying students with mental retardation (Denning et al., 2000). Prevalence figures also vary considerably among districts within a given state (McDermott, 1994).

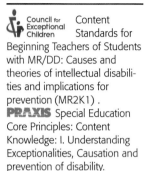
CAUSES

More than 250 causes of mental retardation have been identified. Figure 6.2 lists just some of the many hundreds of etiological factors associated with mental retardation that are categorized by the AAMR as **prenatal** (occurring before birth), **perinatal** (occurring during or shortly after birth), or **postnatal** causes. All of these etiologic factors associated with mental retardation can be classified as either biological or environmental (psychosocial). However, both biological and environmental factors are often relevant in individual cases of mental retardation (Beirne-Smith et al., 2002).

FIGURE 6.2 **Disorders in which mental retardation may occur**

I. PRENATAL CAUSES

   A. Chromosomal disorders (e.g., Trisomy 21 [Down syndrome], fragile-X syndrome, Turner's syndrome, Klinefelter syndrome)

   B. Syndrome disorders (e.g., Duchenne muscular dystrophy, Prader-Willi syndrome)

   C. Inborn errors of metabolism (e.g., phenylketonuria [PKU], Tay-Sachs disease)

   D. Developmental disorders of brain formation (e.g., anencephaly, spina bifida, hydrocephalus)

   E. Environmental influences (e.g., maternal malnutrition, fetal alcohol syndrome, juvenile diabetes mellitus, irradiation during pregnancy)

II. PERINATAL CAUSES

   A. Intrauterine disorders (e.g., maternal anemia, premature delivery, abnormal presentation, umbilical cord accidents, multiple gestation)

   B. Neonatal disorders (e.g., intracranial hemorrhage, neonatal seizures, respiratory disorders, meningitis, encephalitis, head trauma at birth)

III. POSTNATAL CAUSES

   A. Head injuries (e.g., cerebral concussion, contusion, or laceration)

   B. Infections (e.g., encephalitis, meningitis, malaria, measles, rubella)

   C. Demyelinating disorders (e.g., postinfectious disorders, postimmunization disorders)

   D. Degenerative disorders (e.g., Rett syndrome, Huntington disease, Parkinson's disease)

   E. Seizure disorders (e.g., epilepsy)

   F. Toxic-metabolic disorders (e.g., Reye's syndrome, lead or mercury poisoning)

   G. Malnutrition (e.g., protein-calorie malnutrition)

   H. Environmental deprivation (e.g., psychosocial disadvantage, child abuse and neglect, chronic social/sensory deprivation)

   I. Hypoconnection syndrome

Source: Adapted from the American Association on Mental Retardation (AAMR). (1992). *Mental retardation: Definition, classification, and systems of supports* (9th ed., pp. 81–91). Washington, DC: Author. Used by permission.

Authors of a review of 13 epidemiological studies concluded that, for approximately 50% of cases of mild mental retardation and 30% of cases of severe mental retardation, the cause is unknown (McLaren & Bryson, 1987). Nevertheless, knowledge of etiology is critical to efforts designed to prevent the incidence of mental retardation (Coulter, 1996; Moser, 2000) and may have implications for some educational interventions (Dykens, Hodapp, & Finucane, 2000; Hodapp & Dykens, 2001; Powell, Houghton, & Douglas, 1997).

Biological Causes   Specific biological causes are identified for about two-thirds of individuals with more severe forms of mental retardation (Batshaw, 1997). It is important to understand that none of the etiologic factors shown in Figure 6.2 *is* mental retardation. These conditions, diseases, and syndromes are commonly associated with mental retardation; but they may or may not result in the deficits of intellectual and adaptive functioning that define mental retardation (e.g., low birth weight due to maternal malnutrition may or may not result in mental retardation). The term *syndrome* refers to a number of symptoms or characteristics that occur together and provide the defining features of a given disease or condition.

Table 6.3 describes some of the more common prenatal conditions that often result in mental retardation. Some of the health conditions and disorders shown in Figure 6.2 require special education and related services as disabilities in their own right and/or are causes of other disabilities whether or not mental retardation is also involved. A number of these conditions are discussed in Chapter 10 (cytomegalovirus [CMV], meningitis, rubella) and Chapter 12 (diabetes, epilepsy, head injuries, hydrocephalus, muscular dystrophy, spina bifida).

Environmental Causes   Individuals with mild mental retardation, those who require less intensive supports, make up about 85% of all persons with mental retardation (APA, 1994). In the vast majority of those cases there is no demonstrable evidence of organic pathology—no brain damage or other biological problem. When no biological factor is evident in an individual with mental retardation, the cause is presumed to be *psychosocial disadvantage,* the combination of a poor social and cultural environment early in the child's life. The term *developmental retardation* is also used as a synonym for psychosocial disadvantage to refer to mental retardation thought to be caused primarily by environmental influences such as minimal opportunities to develop early language, child abuse and neglect, and/or chronic social or sensory deprivation. Although there is no direct proof that social and environmental deprivation causes mental retardation, it is generally believed that these influences are responsible for most cases of mild retardation.

Research conducted at the Juniper Gardens Children's Project has led to a hypothesis of developmental retardation as an intergenerational progression in which the cumulative experiential deficits in social and academic stimulation are transmitted to children from low socioeconomic status (SES) environments (Greenwood et al., 1992; Greenwood, Hart, Walker, & Risley, 1994). Figure 6.3 illustrates the progression of developmental retardation in terms of low academic achievement and early school failure. There are several key contributors to this cycle of environmentally caused retardation (Greenwood et al., 1994):

1. Limited parenting practices that produce low rates of vocabulary growth in early childhood
2. Instructional practices in middle childhood and adolescence that produce low rates of academic engagement during the school years
3. Lower rates of academic achievement and early school failure and early school dropout
4. Parenthood and continuance of the progression into the next generation (p. 216)

Additional support for the hypothesis of developmental retardation is provided by McDermott (1994), who has found that much of the variability in prevalence rates of mental

Psychosocial disadvantage and developmental retardation

Council for Exceptional Children   Content Standards for Beginning Teachers of Students with MR/DD: Causes and theories of intellectual disabilities and implications for prevention (MR2K1) (also CC2K3).
PRAXIS Special Education Core Principles: Content Knowledge: I. Understanding Exceptionalities, Causation and prevention of disability.

TABLE 6.3 Some prenatal conditions associated with mental retardation

Syndrome	Definition/Cause	Remarks/Characteristics
Down syndrome	Caused by chromosomal abnormality; most common of three major types is trisomy 21, in which 21st set of chromosomes is a triplet rather than a pair. Most often results in moderate level of mental retardation, although some individuals function in mild or severe range. Affects about 1 in 1,000 live births; probability of having a baby with Down syndrome increases to approximately 1 in 30 for women at age 45.	Best-known and well-researched biological condition associated with mental retardation; estimated to account for 5–6% of all cases. Characteristic physical features: short stature; flat, broad face with small ears and nose; upward slanting eyes; small mouth with short roof, protruding tongue may cause articulation problems; hypertonia (floppy muscles); heart defects common; susceptibility to ear and respiratory infections. Older persons at high risk for Alzheimer's disease.
Fetal alcohol syndrome (FAS)	Mother's excessive alcohol use during pregnancy has toxic effects on fetus, including physical defects and developmental delays. Diagnosed when the child has two or more craniofacial malformations and growth is below the 10th percentile for height and weight. Children who have some but not all of the diagnostic criteria for FAS and a history of prenatal alcohol exposure are diagnosed with fetal alcohol effect (FAE), a condition associated with hyperactivity and learning problems.	One of the leading known causes of mental retardation, FAS has an incidence higher than Down syndrome and cerebral palsy. In addition to cognitive impairments, some children experience sleep disturbances, motor dysfunctions, hyperirritability, aggression, and conduct problems. Although risk of FAS is highest during first trimester of pregnancy, pregnant women should avoid drinking alcohol in any amount.
Fragile X syndrome	A triplet, repeat mutation on the X chromosome interferes with production of FMR-1 protein, which is essential for normal brain functioning; majority of males experience mild to moderate mental retardation in childhood and moderate to severe deficits in adulthood; females may carry and transmit the mutation to their children but tend to have fewer disabilities than affected males.	Affects approximately 1 in 4,000 males; the most common inherited cause of mental retardation and the most common clinical type of mental retardation after Down syndrome. Characterized by social anxiety and avoidance (avoiding eye contact, tactile defensiveness, turning the body away during face-to-face interactions, and stylized, ritualistic forms of greeting); preservative speech often includes repetition of words and phrases.

FIGURE 6.3
Schematic illustration of the intergenerational progression of developmental retardation

Source: Reprinted from Greenwood, C. R., Hart, B., Walker, D., & Risley, T. (1994). The opportunity to respond and academic performance revisited: A behavioral theory of developmental retardation and its prevention. In R. Gardner, III, D. M. Sainato, J. O. Cooper, T. E. Heron, W. L. Heward, J. W. Eshleman, & T. A. Grossi (Eds.), *Behavior analysis in education: Focus on measurably superior instruction* (p. 216). Pacific Grove, CA: Brookes/Cole. Used by permission.

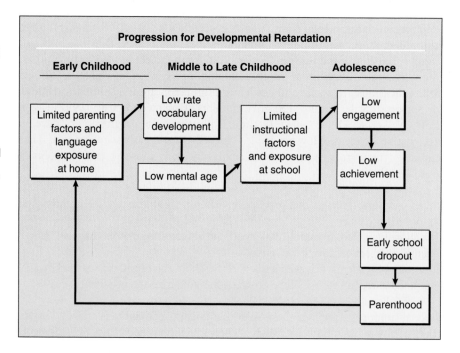

TABLE 6.3 *continued*

Syndrome	Definition/Cause	Remarks/Characteristics
Klinefelter syndrome (XXY males)	Males receive an extra X chromosome. Sterility, underdevelopment of male sex organs, acquisition of female secondary sex characteristics are common; sometimes includes mild levels of cognitive retardation.	XXY males often have problems with social skills, auditory perception, language, sometimes mild levels of cognitive retardation; more often associated with learning disabilities than with mental retardation.
Phenylketonuria (PKU)	Genetically inherited condition in which a child is born without an important enzyme needed to break down an amino acid, phenylalanine, found in many common foods; failure to break down this amino acid causes brain damage that often results in aggressiveness, hyperactivity, and severe mental retardation.	Mental retardation resulting from PKU has been virtually eliminated in the United States through widespread screening. By analyzing the concentration of phenylalanine in a newborn's blood plasma, doctors can diagnose PKU and treat it with a special diet. Most children with PKU who receive a phenylalanine-restricted diet early enough have normal intellectual development.
Prader-Willi syndrome	Caused by deletion of a portion of chromosome 15. Initially, infants have hypertonia (floppy muscles) and may have to be tube fed. Initial phase is followed by development of insatiable appetite; constant preoccupation with food can lead to life-threatening obesity if food seeking is not monitored. Affects 1 in 10,000 to 25,000 live births.	Associated with mild retardation and learning disabilities; behavior problems common: impulsivity, aggressiveness, temper tantrums, obsessive-compulsive behavior; some forms of self-injurious behavior, such as skin picking; delayed motor skills, short stature, small hands and feet, underdeveloped genitalia.
Williams syndrome	Caused by deletion of material on the seventh chromosome; range of cognitive functioning ranges from normal to mild and moderate levels of mental retardation.	Characteristic elfin-like facial features; physical features and manner of expression exudes cheerfulness and happiness; described as "overly friendly," lack of reserve toward strangers; often have uneven profiles of skills, with strengths in vocabulary and story-telling skills and weaknesses in visual-spatial skills; often hyperactive, may have difficulty staying on task and low tolerance for frustration or teasing.

Source: Beirne-Smith, Ittenbach, & Patton (2002); Belser & Sudhalter (2001); Dimitropoulos, Feurer, Butler, & Thompson (2001); Dykens (2000); Dykens & Rosner (1999); Hagerman & Cronsiter (1996); Levine & Wharton (2000); Mervis, Klein-Tasman, & Mastin (2001); Sudhalter & Belser (2001); Symons, Butler, Sanders, Feurer, & Thompson (1999); Symons, Clark, Roberts, & Bailey (2001); Thomas (2001).

retardation reported by different school districts is explained by SES status. Her findings are "consistent with the notion that a large percentage of mental retardation is based on environmental causes, most notably, deprivation in the early years of life" (p. 182). Children who live in poverty have a higher than normal chance of being identified as mentally retarded (Fujiura & Yamaki, 2000).

 PREVENTION

Probably the biggest single preventive strike against mental retardation (and many other disabling conditions, including blindness and deafness) was the development of an effective rubella vaccine in 1962. When **rubella** (German measles) is contracted by mothers during the first 3 months of pregnancy, it causes severe damage in 10% to 40% of the unborn children. Fortunately, this cause of mental retardation can be eliminated if women are vaccinated for rubella before becoming pregnant.

A simple blood test administered to virtually every baby born in the United State has drastically reduced the incidence of mental retardation caused by **phenylketonuria** (PKU).

Prevention of MR

Council for Exceptional Children Content Standards for Beginning Teachers of Students with MR/DD: Causes and theories of intellectual disabilities and implications for prevention (MR2K1).
PRAXIS Special Education Core Principles: Content Knowledge: I. Understanding Exceptionalities, Causation and prevention of disability.

How Many Can You Do in 1 Minute?

The conventional wisdom goes something like this: students with mental retardation can learn; but because they learn at a slower rate than students without disabilities, they should be given more time to complete their work. Although it is true that children with mental retardation acquire new skills more slowly, teachers may be doing students with disabilities a disservice by always providing plenty of time for them to do their work. Accuracy measures alone do not provide a complete picture of learning. For instance, whereas two students might each complete a page of math problems with 100% accuracy, the one who finishes in 2 minutes is more accomplished than the one who needs 5 minutes to answer the same problems. To be functional, many skills we use every day in the home, community, or workplace must be performed at a certain rate of speed.

Providing students with practice to build fluency is an important part of teaching. After the initial *acquisition stage of learning,* when a student learns how to perform the skill correctly, she progresses to the *practice stage of learning,* in which the focus should shift to building *fluency*—performing a skill with accuracy and speed. "The teacher does not push fluency when the student cannot yet work the problems correctly. Similarly, when teaching a student to be fluent, techniques used to promote accuracy are not used. During fluency instruction, elaborate explanations and corrections are not needed; in fact, they might even slow the student down. Instead, the teacher talks about and rewards fluency" (Howell & Lorson-Howell, 1990, p. 21).

Time trials—giving students the opportunity to perform a skill as many times as they can in a brief period—can be an excellent way to build fluency. Several studies have shown that both general and special education students not only benefit from time trials but also like to be timed. For example, Miller, Hall, and Heward (1995) evaluated the effects of two procedures for conducting 1-minute time trials on the rate and accuracy with which 11 elementary students with mild mental retardation wrote answers to single-digit math facts. During the first 2 weeks of the study, when the students were told to complete as many problems as they could during an untimed 10-minute work period, the students answered correctly an average of 8.4 problems per minute. During the next phase, in which a series of seven 1-minute time trials was

By analyzing the concentration of phenylalanine in a newborn's blood plasma, doctors can diagnose PKU and treat it with a phenylalanine-restricted diet. Most children with PKU who receive treatment have normal intellectual development (Beirne-Smith et al., 2002).

Toxic exposure through maternal substance abuse and environmental pollutants (e.g., lead poisoning) are two major causes of preventable mental retardation that can be combated with education and training (Howard, Williams, & McLaughlin, 1994; Schroeder, 1987).

Advances in medical science have enabled doctors to identify certain genetic influences strongly associated with mental retardation. One approach to prevention offered by many health service organizations is *genetic counseling,* a discussion between a specially trained medical counselor and prospective parents about the possibility that they may give birth to a child with disabilities on the basis of the parents' genetic backgrounds. For discussions of

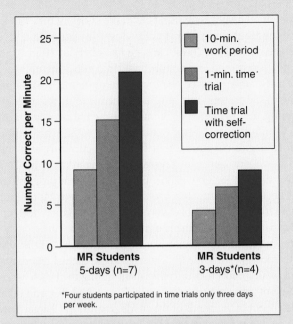

FIGURE A Mean number of math facts answered correctly per minute by elementary students with mental retardation

Source: Reprinted from Miller, A. D., Hall, S. W., & Heward, W. L. (1995). Effects of sequential 1-minute time trials with and without inter-trial feedback and self-correction on general and special education students' fluency with math facts. *Journal of Behavioral Education, 5,* p. 340. Used by permission.

Did working faster harm students' accuracy? Not at all: the students answered correctly 85% of all the problems they attempted during the 10-minute work period, but their accuracy improved to 89% when time trials were used. When asked which method they preferred, 10 of the 11 students indicated they liked time trials better than the untimed work period.

Fluency training in the form of 1-minute time trials has been used successfully to help students with disabilities improve a wide range of academic, vocational, and other skills (e.g., Beck, Conrad, & Anderson, 1995; Binder, 1996; Johnson & Layng, 1994; McCuin & Cooper, 1994; Stump et al., 1992; Weinstein & Cooke, 1992).

Guidelines for Conducting Time Trials

- Keep the time for each trial short. One minute is sufficient for most academic skills.
- Do time trials every day. For example, a series of two or three 1-minute oral reading time trials could be conducted at the end of each day's lesson.
- Make time trials fun. Time trials should not be presented as a test; they are a learning activity that can be approached like a game.
- Use time trials during the practice stage of learning, after students have learned how to do the skill correctly.
- Follow time trials with a more relaxed activity.
- Feedback to students should emphasize proficiency (total number correct), not simply accuracy (percentage correct).
- Encourage each student try to beat his own best score.
- Have students keep track of their progress by self-graphing their best score each day.

Source: Adapted from Miller, A. D., & Heward, W. L. (1992). Do your students really know their math facts? Using daily time trials to build fluency. *Intervention in School and Clinic, 28,* 98–104. Used by permission.

conducted with a 20-second rest period between each time trial (equaling a total of 10 minutes, as in the first phase), the students' correct rate increased to 13.2 per minute. Fluency improved to 17.3 problems per minute during a final phase, when immediate feedback and self-correction were conducted immediately after each of two consecutive time trials. Figure A illustrates the results.

ethical considerations of genetic testing for disabilities, see Beirne-Smith et al. (2002), Kuna (2001), and Smith and Mitchell (2001a).

Amniocentesis is a procedure in which a sample of fluid is withdrawn from the amniotic sac surrounding the fetus during the second trimester of pregnancy (usually the 14th to 17th week). Fetal cells are removed from the amniotic fluid and grown in a cell culture for about 2 weeks. At that time, a chromosome and enzyme analysis is performed to identify the presence of about 80 specific genetic disorders before birth. Many of these disorders, such as Down syndrome, are associated with mental retardation.

A new technique for prenatal diagnosis that may eventually replace amniocentesis is **chorion villus sampling** (CVS). A small amount of chorionic tissue (a fetal component of the developing placenta) is removed and tested. The most significant advantage of CVS is that it can be performed earlier than amniocentesis (during the 8th to 10th week of pregnancy). Because fetal cells exist in relatively large numbers in the chorion, they can be analyzed immediately without waiting for them to grow for 2 to 3 weeks. Although CVS is being used more often, it has been associated with a miscarriage rate of about 10 in 1,000 (compared with 2.5 in 1,000 for amniocentesis) and is still considered experimental.

These medical advances have noticeably reduced the incidence of mental retardation caused by some of the known biological factors, but huge advancements in research are needed to reach the goal of lowering the incidence of biomedical mental retardation by 50%, as stated by the President's Committee on Mental Retardation in 1976. The authors of a recent analysis of prevention strategies concluded that full use of currently available prevention measures could reduce the prevalence of severe mental retardation by 20% (Stevenson, Massey, Schroer, McDermott, & Richter, 1996). While noting that progress toward the 50% prevention goal has been significant, Stevenson et al. concluded: "At the present time, the technological capacity to prevent 50% of cases of mental retardation does not exist. The greatest shortfall is the capacity to determine causation" (p. 187).

As we have noted, most children with mental retardation are in the mild range, and their developmental delays have no clearcut etiology. These are the children whose mental retardation is thought to be primarily the result of an impoverished environment during their early years. The poor environment may be a result of parental neglect, poverty, disease, bad diet, and other factors—many of which are completely out of the hands of the child's parents. In Chapter 5 we discussed several early intervention programs aimed at reducing the incidence of developmental retardation. Although measuring the effects of programs that aim to prevent psychosocial retardation is much more difficult than measuring the decreased number of children suffering from a disease such as PKU, the preliminary results of these projects are encouraging; and some models of effective early intervention have been identified (Guralnick, 1997).

EDUCATIONAL APPROACHES

The search for effective methods for educating students with mental retardation began more than 200 years ago, when Jean Marc Gaspard Itard kept a detailed diary of his efforts to teach a young boy who was found in the woods and thought to be a feral child. Itard, whom many consider to be the father of special education, showed that intensive, systematic intervention could produce significant gains with a child thought to be incapable of learning (Itard, 1894/1962).

Since Itard's time, researchers working in mental retardation have developed numerous methods of specialized instruction, some of which have contributed to improved practice in all areas of education. Similarly, the efforts by early advocates on behalf of children and adults with mental retardation blazed trails for advocacy groups representing individuals with other disabilities. Table 6.4 highlights some key historical events and their implications for the education and treatment of children and adults with mental retardation.

CURRICULUM GOALS

What do students with mental retardation need to learn? Not too many years ago, children with mild mental retardation were presented with a slowed- and/or watered-down version of the general education curriculum that focused largely on traditional academic subjects. For example, a group of children with mild mental retardation might spend several weeks on a geography unit learning the 50 states and their capitals. Students with more severe forms of mental retardation spent many hours putting pegs into pegboards and sorting plastic sticks by color because it was believed that these isolated skills were developmental prerequisites for more meaningful activities. Unfortunately, knowing that Boise is the capital of Idaho or being able to sort by color did not help these students become more independent.

TABLE 6.4	A history of the education of children with mental retardation: Key events and implications	
Date	**Historical Event**	**Educational Implication**
1799	Jean Marc Gaspard Itard published an account of his work with Victor, the Wild Boy of Aveyron.	Itard showed that intensive treatment could produce significant learning. Many consider Itard to be the father of special education.
1848	Edouard Seguin helped establish the Pennsylvania Training School.	This was the first educational facility for persons with mental retardation in the United States.
1850	Samuel Gridley Howe began the School for Idiotic and Feeble Minded Youth.	This was the first publicly funded residential school in the United States.
1896	The first public school class for children with mental retardation began in Providence, RI.	This began the special class movement, which grew to 1.3 million children in 1974, the year before IDEA.
1905	Alfred Binet and Theodore Simon developed a test in France to screen those students not benefiting from the regular curriculum.	The test enabled empirical identification of students with mental retardation and contributed to the growth of the special class movement.
1916	Lewis Terman of Stanford University published the Stanford-Binet Intelligence Scale in the United States.	Many schools adopted IQ testing as a means of identifying children with below-average general intelligence.
1935	Edgar Doll published the Vineland Social Maturity Scale.	It provided a standardized method for assessing a person's adaptive behavior, which later became part of the definition of mental retardation.
1950	Parents formed the National Association for Retarded Children (known today as The Arc).	The Arc remains a powerful and important advocacy organization for persons of all ages with mental retardation.
1959	AAMR published its first manual on the definition and classification of mental retardation, with diagnosis based on an IQ score of one standard deviation below the mean (approximately 85) (Heber, 1959).	Many students were identified in the borderline category of mental retardation and served in special classes for "slow learners" or EMR students.
1961	John F. Kennedy established the first President's Panel on Mental Retardation.	The panel's first report (Mayo, 1962) made recommendations that helped guide national policy with respect to mental retardation (e.g., citizenship, education, prevention).
1969	Bengt Nirje published a key paper defining normalization. Wolf Wolfensberger championed normalization in the United States.	Normalization became a leading philosophy guiding the development and delivery of educational, community, vocational, and residential services for persons with mental retardation.
1973	AAMR published a revised definition that required a score on IQ tests of two standard deviations below the mean (approximately 70 or less) and concurrent deficits in adaptive behavior.	This effectively eliminated mild mental retardation.
1992	AAMR published "System '92," a radically different definition of mental retardation with a classification system based on intensities of supports.	New definition and classification system generated cautious support by some and concern by others; few states used the '92 system for identifying and planning services for students with mental retardation.
2002	AAMR published a revision of the 1992 definition; retains classification by intensities of supports; returns to IQ of approximately two standard deviations below mean; adds social participation and interactions as fifth dimension of functioning.	Impact of AAMR's newest definitional system will be determined in coming years.

![Council for Exceptional Children] Content Standards for Beginning Teachers of Students with MR/DD: Plan instruction for independent functional life skills relevant to the community, personal living, sexuality and employment (MR7S3).

PRAXIS Special Education Core Principles: Content Knowledge: III. Delivery of Services to Students with Disabilities, Curriculum and instruction, Functional academics.

Susan learns functional vocational skills in the hospital kitchen where she trains.

![Council for Exceptional Children] Content Standards for Beginning Teachers–Common Core: Integrate affective, social, and life skills with academic curricula (CC7S7).

PRAXIS Special Education Core Principles: Content Knowledge: III. Delivery of Services to Students with Disabilities, Curriculum and instruction, Self-care, daily living, and vocational skills.

Functional Curriculum   In recent years, identifying functional curriculum goals for students with mental retardation has become a major priority for special educators. Learning activities in a functional curriculum are chosen because they will maximize a student's independence, self-direction, and enjoyment in everyday school, home, community, and work environments.

Browder and Snell (2000) define functional academics as "the most useful parts of the 'three R's'—reading, writing, and arithmetic" (p. 497). Choosing functional academic targets is not as simple as it might seem. The most useful part of writing for one student (e.g., making a grocery list) may not be a functional writing skill for another student (e.g., writing the number of items packaged on the job). Careful assessment of each student's current routines must be conducted to find those skills that are required and/or could be used often. Skills that are likely to be required by future environments should also be considered.

Teachers must be on guard against the faulty assumption that a traditional academic skill cannot be functional because it is not a typical activity or learning outcome for students with mental retardation. For example, while *crystal* and *limestone* might not seem to be functional sight words, such words might be extremely functional for a student with a rock collection (Browder, 2000).

Clark (1994) suggests that teachers determine functional knowledge or skills by seeking answers to these questions:

- Does the content focus on necessary knowledge and skills to function as independently as possible in the home, school, or community?
- Does the content provide a scope and sequence for meeting future needs?
- Do the student's parents think the content is important for both current and future needs?
- Does the student think the content is important for both current and future needs?
- Is the content appropriate for the student's chronological age and current intellectual, academic, or behavioral performance level(s)?
- What are the consequences to the student of not learning the concepts and skills? (p. 37)

An even simpler approach to determining whether any given skill represents functional curriculum is to contemplate this question from the student's perspective: "Will I need it when I'm 21?" (Beck, Broers, Hogue, Shipstead, & Knowlton, 1994). The answer to this question is critical because when educators fail to relate curriculum for a student with mental retardation to outcomes with direct relevance to that student's eventual independence and quality of life, "years of valuable opportunities for meaningful learning can be wasted" (Knowlton, 1998, p. 96).

Life Skills   As students with mental retardation reach middle and secondary school, the emphasis on learning functional skills that will help them transition to adult life in the community becomes especially critical. Several models and taxonomies of adult functioning are available that can be used as the framework from which to build functional curriculum activities (e.g., Brolin, 1991; Dever, 1988). For example, *Life Skills Instruction for All Students with Special Needs* (Cronin & Patton, 1993) includes 147 major life skills structured around six domains of adult functioning. Table 6.5 shows examples of how academic and social skills instruction can be related to some of these life skills.

TABLE 6.5   Relationship of scholastic/social skills to adult life skills domains

	Employment Education	Home and Family	Leisure Pursuits	Community Involvement	Emotional–Physical Health	Personal Responsibility Relationships
Reading	Reading classified ads for jobs	Interpreting bills	Locating and understanding movie information in a newspaper	Following directions on tax forms	Comprehending directions on medication	Reading letters from friends
Writing	Writing a letter of application for a job	Writing checks	Writing for information on a city to visit	Filling in a voter registration form	Filling in your medical history on forms	Sending thank you notes
Listening	Understanding oral directions of a procedure change	Comprehending directions	Listening to a weather forecast to plan an outdoor activity	Understanding campaign ads	Attending lectures on stress	Taking turns in a conversation
Speaking	Asking your boss for a raise	Discussing morning routines with family	Inquiring about tickets for a concert	Stating your opinion at the school board meeting	Describing symptoms to a doctor	Giving feedback to a friend
Math applications	Understanding difference between net and gross pay	Computing the cost of doing laundry in a laundromat versus home	Calculating the cost of a dinner out versus eating at home	Obtaining information for a building permit	Using a thermometer	Planning the costs of a date
Problem-solving	Settling a dispute with a co-worker	Deciding how much to budget for rent	Role-playing appropriate behaviors for various places	Knowing what to do if you are the victim of fraud	Selecting a doctor	Deciding how to ask someone for a date
Survival skills	Using a prepared career-planning packet	Listing emergency phone numbers	Using a shopping-center directory	Marking a calendar for important dates (e.g., recycling, garbage collection)	Using a system to remember to take vitamins	Developing a system to remember birthdays
Personal-social	Applying appropriate interview skills	Helping a child with homework	Knowing the rules of a neighborhood pool	Locating self-improvement classes	Getting a yearly physical exam	Discussing how to negotiate a price at the flea market

Source: From *Life Skills Instruction for All Students with Special Needs: A Practical Guide for Integrating Real Life Content into the Curriculum* (p. 33) by M. E. Cronin and J. R. Patton, 1993, Austin, TX: PRO-ED. Copyright 1993 by PRO-ED. Reprinted by permission.

Self-Determination   Self-determined learners set goals, plan and implement a course of action, evaluate their performance, and make adjustments in what they are doing to reach their goals. Learning self-determination skills can serve as both a curriculum goal in its own right as well as a means to help students achieve other learning outcomes (Wehmeyer, Palmer, Agran, Mithaug, & Martin, 2000). Self-determination requires a complex set of skills and is a lofty goal for any student. However, students with mental retardation can learn self-determination skills, and those who do are more likely to achieve IEP goals and make a successful transition from school to adult life (Field, Martin, Miller, Ward, & Wehmeyer, 1998b; German, Martin, Huber Marshall, & Sale, 2000). Recently, several curriculum models and instructional materials have been developed for teaching self-determination to students with disabilities (e.g., Agran & Wehmeyer, 1999; Wehmeyer, Agran, & Hughes, 1998; Wehmeyer et al., 2000).

An important and initial component of self-determination is teaching students to take responsibility for their learning. Students should be taught to take an active role in their learning at an early age. Teaching students with disabilities to recruit assistance from the classroom teacher is one strategy for helping them succeed in general education classrooms and to take an active role in their education. For example, Craft, Alber, and Heward (1998) taught four fourth graders with mental retardation to recruit teacher attention while they worked on spelling assignments in a general education classroom. They were taught to show their work to the teacher two to three times per session and to make statements such as "How am I doing?" or "Look, I'm all finished!" Recruitment training, which was conducted in the special education classroom, increased the frequency of each student's recruiting, the frequency of teacher praise, the percentage of worksheet items completed, and the accuracy with which the students completed the assignments (see Figure 6.4). After the study the general education teacher stated, "They fit in better, they were more a part of the group, and they weren't being disruptive because they were working." (To learn more about this strategy for teaching students to take an active role in their learning, see Teaching & Learning, "'Look, I'm All Finished!' Recruiting Teacher Attention," later in this chapter.)

 INSTRUCTIONAL METHODOLOGY

Students with mental retardation learn best when instruction is explicit and systematic. **Applied behavior analysis** offers a systematic approach to the design and evaluation of instruction based on scientifically demonstrated principles that describe how the environment affects learning (Alberto & Troutman, 1999; Cooper, Heron, & Heward, 1987; Wolery, Bailey, & Sugai, 1988). Teaching methods derived from applied behavior analysis are used effectively not only with learners who experience mental retardation and other disabilities but also with students in general education (Crandall, Jacobson, & Sloane, 1997; Gardner, Sainato, et al., 1994).

Although specific teaching tactics take many forms, systematic instruction derived from principles of behavior analysis entails the following six features:

1. Precise definition and task analysis of the new skill to be learned
2. Direct and frequent measurement of the student's performance of the skill
3. Frequent opportunities for active student response during instruction
4. Immediate and systematic feedback for student performance
5. Procedures for achieving the transfer of stimulus control from instructional cues or prompts to naturally occurring stimuli
6. Strategies for promoting the generalization and maintenance of newly learned skills to different, nontraining situations and environments

Task Analysis   Task analysis means breaking down complex or multiple-step skills into smaller, easier-to-learn subtasks. The subskills or subtasks are then sequenced, either in the natural order in which they are typically performed or from the easiest to most difficult. As-

FIGURE 6.4 **Mean percentage of spelling worksheet items completed and percentage of items correct by four fourth-grade students with mental retardation before (baseline) and after they were taught to show their work to their classroom teacher (generalization/ maintenance)**

Source: From Craft, M., Alber, S. R., & Heward, W. L. (1998). Teaching elementary students with developmental disabilities to recruit teacher attention in a general education classroom: Effects on teacher praise and academic productivity. *Journal of Applied Behavior Analysis, 31,* 399–415. Used with permission.

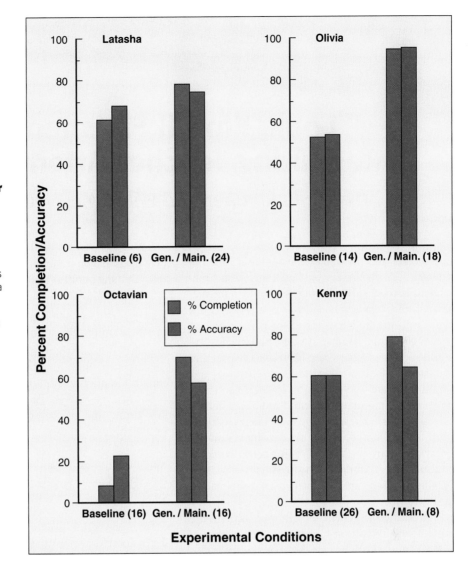

sessing a student's performance on a sequence of task-analyzed subskills helps pinpoint where instruction should begin.

During the task analysis stage of instructional planning, it is important to consider the extent to which the natural environment requires performance of the target skill for a given duration or at a minimum rate. For example, Test, Spooner, Keul, and Grossi (1990) included specific time limits for each of the 17 steps in a task analysis used to teach two secondary students with severe mental retardation to use the public telephone to call home. The specific sequence of steps and the time limit for each step were determined by having two adults without disabilities use the telephone.

Direct and Frequent Measurement   Teachers should verify the effects of their instruction by directly and frequently measuring student performance (Ysseldyke, 2001). Measurement is *direct* when it objectively records the learner's performance of the behavior of interest in the natural environment for that skill. Measurement is *frequent* when it occurs on a regular basis; ideally, measurement should take place as often as instruction occurs.

Two errors of judgment are common for [teachers] who do not collect direct and frequent measurements of their student's performance. First, many ineffective intervention programs are continued. . . . Second, many effective programs are dis-

Direct and frequent measurement

Council for Exceptional Children   Content Standards for Beginning Teachers—Common Core: Evaluate instruction and monitor progress of individuals with exceptional educational needs (CC8S8) (also CC7S13). **PRAXIS** Special Eeducation Core Principles: Content Knowledge: III. Delivery of Services to Students with Disabilities, Assessment, Procedures for ongoing program monitoring.

"Look, I'm All Finished!" Recruiting Teacher Attention

by Sheila R. Alber and William L. Heward

Preparation of students with disabilities for inclusion in general education classrooms should include instruction in classroom survival skills. Attending to instruction, following directions, and completing assigned seatwork are skills likely to enhance a student's acceptance and success in the regular classroom. Because teachers value such "good student" behaviors, students are also likely to receive teacher praise and attention for exhibiting them.

But classrooms are busy places, so teachers can easily overlook students' important academic and social behaviors. Research shows that teachers are more likely to pay attention to a disruptive student than to one who is working quietly and productively (Walker, 1997). It is hard for teachers to be aware of students who need help, especially low-achieving ones who are less likely to ask (Newman & Golding, 1990).

Although teachers in general education classrooms are expected to adapt instruction to serve students with disabilities, this is not always the case. Most secondary teachers interviewed by Schumm et al. (1995) believed that students with disabilities should take responsibility for obtaining the help they need. Thus, politely recruiting teacher attention and assistance can help students with disabilities function more independently and actively influence the quality of instruction they receive.

Recruiting Can Work

Students of various ages and abilities have learned to recruit teacher and peer attention for performing a wide range of tasks in classroom and community settings: preschoolers with developmental delays for completing pre-academic tasks and staying on task during transitions (Connell, Carta, & Baer, 1993; Stokes, Fowler, & Baer, 1978) as well as students with learning disabilities (Alber, Heward, & Hippler, 1999; Wolford, Alber, & Heward, 2001), behavioral disorders (Morgan, Young, & Goldstein, 1983), and mental retardation while performing academic tasks in regular classrooms (Craft et al., 1998) and secondary students with

mental retardation for improved work performance in vocational training settings (Mank & Horner, 1987).

Who Should be Taught to Recruit?

Withdrawn Willamena.   Willamena seldom asks a teacher anything. Because she is so quiet and well behaved, her teachers sometimes forget she's in the room. Withdrawn Willamenas are prime candidates for recruitment training.

In-a-Hurry Harry.   Harry is usually half-done with a task before his teacher finishes explaining it. Racing through his work allows him to be the first to turn it in. But his work is often incomplete and error-filled, so he doesn't hear much praise from his teacher. Harry would benefit from recruitment training that includes self-checking and self-correction.

Shouting Shelly.   Shelly has just finished her work, and she wants her teacher to look at it—right now! But Shelly doesn't raise her hand. She gets her teacher's attention—and disrupts most of her classmates—by shouting across the room. Students like Shelly should be taught appropriate ways to solicit teacher attention.

Pestering Pete.   Pete always raises his hand, waits quietly for his teacher to come to his desk, and then politely asks, "Have I done this right?" But sometimes he repeats this routine a dozen times in a 20-minute period, and his teachers find it annoying. Positive teacher attention often turns into reprimands. Recruitment training for Pete, and for all students, will teach him to limit the number of times he cues his teachers for attention.

Teaching Students to Recruit

1. *Identify target skills.*   Students should recruit teacher attention for target skills that are valued and therefore likely to be reinforced—e.g., writing neatly and legibly, working accurately, completing assigned work, cleaning up at transitions, and making contributions when working in a cooperative group.

Politely recruiting teacher attention and assistance is one way students can actively influence the quality of instruction they receive.

2. *Teach self-assessment.*   Students should self-assess their work before recruiting teacher attention (e.g., Sue asks herself, "Is my work complete?"). After the student can reliably distinguish between complete and incomplete work samples, she can learn how to check the accuracy of her work with answer keys, checklists of the steps or components of the academic skill, or spot-checking two or three items before asking the teacher to look at it.

3. *Teach appropriate recruiting.*   Teach students when, how, and how often to recruit and how to respond to the teacher after receiving attention.

- *When?*   Students should signal for teacher attention after they have completed and self-checked a substantial part of their work. Students should also be taught when not to try to get their teacher's attention (e.g., when the teacher is working with another student, talking to another adult, taking the lunch count).

- *How?*   The traditional hand raise should be part of every student's recruiting repertoire. Other methods of gaining attention should be taught depending upon teacher preferences and routines in the general education classroom (e.g., have students signal they need help by standing up a small flag on their desks; expect students to bring their work to the teacher's desk for help and feedback).

- *How often?*   While helping Withdrawn Willamena learn to seek teacher attention, don't turn her into a Pestering Pete. How often a student should recruit varies across teachers and activities (e.g., independent seatwork, cooperative learning groups, whole-class instruction). Direct observation in the classroom is the best way to establish an optimal rate of recruiting; it is also a good idea to ask the regular classroom teacher when, how, and with what frequency she prefers students to ask for help.

- *What to say?*   Students should be taught several statements that are likely to evoke positive feedback from the teacher (e.g., "Please look at my work." "Did I do a good job?" "How am I doing?"). Keep it simple, but teach the student to vary her verbal cues so she will not sound like a parrot.

- *How to respond?*   Students should respond to their teacher's feedback by establishing eye contact, smiling, and saying, "Thank you." Polite appreciation is very reinforcing to teachers and will increase the likelihood of more positive attention the next time.

4. *Model and role-play the complete sequence.*   Begin by providing students with a rationale for recruiting (e.g., the teacher will be happy you did a good job, you will get more work done, your grades might improve). Thinking aloud while modeling is good way to show the recruiting sequence. While performing each step, say, "Okay, I've finished my work. Now I'm going to check it. Did I put my name on my paper? Yes. Did I do all the problems? Yes. Did I follow all the steps? Yes. Okay, my teacher doesn't look busy right now. I'll raise my hand and wait quietly until she comes to my desk." Have another student pretend to be the regular classroom teacher and come over to you when you have your hand up. Say, "Mr. Patterson, please look at my work." The helper says, "Oh, you did a very nice job." Then smile and say, "Thank you, teacher." Role-play with praise and offer corrective feedback until the student correctly performs the entire sequence on several consecutive trials.

5. *Prepare students for alternate responses.*   Of course, not every student cue will result in teacher praise; some efforts to recruit may even be followed by criticism (e.g., "This is all wrong. Pay better attention the next time."). Use role playing to prepare students for these possibilities and have them practice polite responses (e.g., "Thank you for helping me with this.").

Politely recruiting teacher attention and assistance is one way students can actively influence the quality of instruction they receive. For more information on teaching students to recruit teacher attention, see Alber and Heward (2001).

Sheila R. Alber is a faculty member in the Department of Special Education at the University of Southern Mississippi.

Source: Adapted from Alber, S. R., & Heward, W. L. (1997). Recruit it or lose it! Training students to recruit contingent teacher attention. *Intervention in School and Clinic, 5,* 275–282. Used with permission.

continued prematurely because subjective judgment finds no improvement. For example, teachers who do not use direct and frequent measures might discern little difference between a student's reading 40 words per minute with 60% accuracy and 48 words per minute with 73% accuracy. However, direct and frequent data collected on the rate and accuracy of oral reading would show an improved performance. (Cooper et al., 1987, p. 60)

Active Student Response   Contemporary educational research is unequivocal in its support of the positive relationship between students' active engagement with academic tasks and their achievement. Providing instruction with high levels of active student participation is important for all learners, but it is particularly important for students with disabilities: "For children who are behind to catch up, they simply must be taught more in less time. If the teacher doesn't attempt to teach more in less time . . . the gap in general knowledge between a normal and handicapped student becomes even greater" (Kameenui & Simmons, 1990, p. 11).

Various terms such as *active student response, opportunity to respond,* and *academic learning time* are used to refer to this important variable.

> **Active student response** (ASR) can be defined as an observable response made to an instructional antecedent. To say it less technically, ASR occurs when a student emits a detectable response to ongoing instruction. The kinds of responses that qualify as ASR are as varied as the kinds of lessons that are taught. Depending upon the instructional objective, examples of ASR include words read, problems answered, boards cut, test tubes measured, praise and supportive comments spoken, notes or scales played, stitches sewn, sentences written, workbook questions answered, and fastballs pitched. The basic measure of how much ASR a student receives is a frequency count of the number of academic responses emitted within a given period of instruction. (Heward, 1994, p. 286)

When all variables are held constant (e.g., quality of curriculum materials, students' prerequisite skills, motivational variables), an ASR-rich lesson will generally result in more learning than does a lesson in which students make few or no responses.

Providing systematic feedback

PRAXIS Application of Core Principles Across Categories of Disability: II. Instruction, Ways to select and implement the format and components of instruction, Reinforcement, Drill and practice.

Systematic Feedback   Instructional feedback—information provided to students on some aspect of their performance—falls into two broad categories: praise and/or other forms of **positive reinforcement** for correct responses, and error correction for incorrect responses. Feedback is generally most effective when it is specific, immediate, positive, frequent, and differential (comparing the student's present performance with past performance; e.g., "You read 110 words today, Jermon. That's five more than yesterday.") (Van Houten, 1984).

Effective teachers change the focus and timing of the feedback they provide as a student progresses from initial attempts at learning a new skill through practicing a newly acquired skill. When a student is first learning a new skill or content knowledge, feedback ideally follows each response (see Figure 6.5). Feedback during this initial *acquisition stage of learning* should focus on the accuracy and topography of the student's response. By providing feedback after each response, the teacher reduces the likelihood that the student will practice errors. See Teaching & Learning, "What to Do When Students Make Mistakes," later in this chapter.

During the *practice stage of learning,* when the student can perform the new skill with accuracy, the student should be allowed to make a series of responses before feedback is provided. Feedback during the practice stage should emphasize the correct rate at which the student performs the target skill. Providing feedback after each response during the practice stage of learning may have a detrimental effect by blocking the student's chance to develop fluency by "going fast."

Transfer of Stimulus Control   Trial-and-error learning is inefficient and frustrating for students without disabilities. For students with mental retardation and other learning prob-

lems, it is likely to be a complete waste of time. Instead of waiting to see whether the student will make a correct response, the effective teacher provides a prompt (e.g., physical guidance, verbal directions, picture cues, prerecorded auditory prompts) that makes a correct response very probable. For example, Wood, Frank, and Hamre-Nietupski (1996) provided picture prompts for students to help them correctly perform each step in a task analysis for opening a combination lock found on student lockers. The correct response is reinforced, the prompt is repeated, and another correct student response is reinforced. The response prompts are then gradually and systematically withdrawn so that the student's behavior comes under the **stimulus control** of the curriculum content, or things in the natural environment that typically serve as cues for that skill (Wolery, Ault, & Doyle, 1992).

Generalization and Maintenance   *Generalization* and *maintenance* refer to the extent to which students use what they have learned across settings and over time. Although there is still much to be learned about helping students with mental retardation and other disabilities get the most out of what they learn, the promising beginnings of a reliable "technology of generalization" have been developed (Horner, Dunlap, & Koegel, 1988; Rosales & Baer, 1998). Here are three examples of many strategies for promoting generalization and maintenance:

- *Aim for naturally occurring reinforcement contingencies.*   The most basic strategy for promoting generalization and maintenance is to increase the probability that a student's new skill will be reinforced in the natural environment (e.g., the regular classroom, the playground, the community, recreational and work settings). This can be accomplished by (1) teaching only functional skills that are needed and likely to be valued by people in the student's natural environment and (2) teaching students to perform new skills with the accuracy and fluency necessary to produce reinforcement in the natural environment.
- *Program common stimuli.*   If the generalization setting differs greatly from the setting where teaching takes place, the student may not perform the new behavior. There are

Promoting generalization and maintenance

Council for Exceptional Children   Content Standards for Beginning Teachers—Common Core: Use strategies to facilitate maintenance and generalization of skills across learning environments (CC4S4).
PRAXIS Special Education Core Principles: Content Knowledge: III. Delivery of Services to Students with Disabilities, Curriculum and Instruction, Instructional development and implementation, Concept generalization.

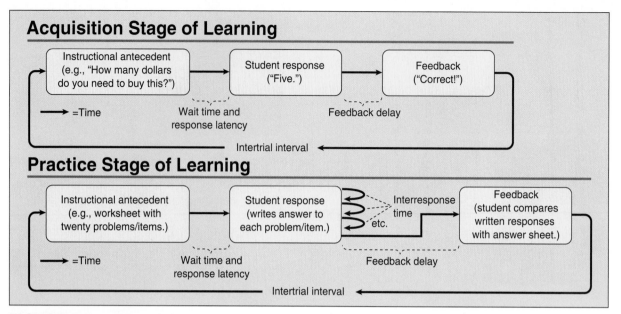

Acquisition Stage of Learning

Instructional antecedent (e.g., "How many dollars do you need to buy this?") → Student response ("Five.") → Feedback ("Correct!")

→ =Time

Wait time and response latency

Feedback delay

Intertrial interval

Practice Stage of Learning

Instructional antecedent (e.g., worksheet with twenty problems/items.) → Student response (writes answer to each problem/item.) → Interresponse time etc. → Feedback (student compares written responses with answer sheet.)

→ =Time

Wait time and response latency

Feedback delay

Intertrial interval

FIGURE 6.5 **Feedback within a series of learn trials during the acquisition and practice stages of learning**

Source: Reprinted from Heward, W. L. (1994). Three "low-tech" strategies for increasing the frequency of active student response during group instruction. In R. Gardner III, D. M. Sainato, J. O. Cooper, T. E. Heron, W. L. Heward, J. W. Eshleman, & T. A. Grossi (Eds.), *Behavior analysis in education: Focus on measurably superior instruction* (p. 284). Pacific Grove, CA: Brooks/Cole. Used with permission.

two basic ways to program common stimuli: (1) incorporate into the teaching situation as many typical features of the generalization setting as possible, and (2) create a new common stimulus that the student learns to use in the teaching setting and can transport to the generalization setting, where it prompts or assists performance of the target skill. Sandie Trask applied this technique in her master's thesis when she taught secondary students with mental retardation and visual impairments to use tape-recorded recipes to prepare snack foods. See Teaching & Learning, "I Made It Myself and It's Good!" in Chapter 11.

- *Community-based instruction.* Teaching in the actual setting where students are ultimately to use their new skills increases the probability of generalization and maintenance. Community-based instruction is a widely used practice in special education with a good research base to support it (Owens-Johnson & Hamill, 2002). However, simply conducting instruction in the community does not guarantee generalization and maintenance. A poorly designed lesson will be ineffective regardless of where it is conducted. And community-based instruction can be expensive and is typically not available on a daily basis. Morse and Schuster (2000) found that 2 days per week of community-based instruction supplemented by simulation training in the classroom was effective in teaching students with mental retardation to shop for groceries.

 EDUCATIONAL PLACEMENT ALTERNATIVES

Children with mild retardation have traditionally been educated in self-contained classrooms in the public schools. Today many children with mild and moderate mental retardation are being educated in regular classrooms, with a special educator helping the classroom teacher with individualized instruction for the child and providing extra tutoring in a resource room as needed.

Placement alternatives for students with MR

 Council for Exceptional Children Content Standards for Beginning Teachers of Students with Mr/DD: Continuum of placement services available for individuals with MR/DD (MR1K3).
PRAXIS Special Education Core Principles: Content KNowledge: III. Delivery of Services to Students with Disabilities, Background knowledge, Continuum of educational and related services.

Community-based instruction provides these secondary students with mental retardation an opportunity to acquire employment skills in a real work setting.

During the 1999–2000 school year, 14% of students with mental retardation were educated in the regular classroom, with 29.5% being served in resource room programs and 50.5% in separate classes (U.S. Department of Education, 2002). About 6% of students with mental retardation continue to attend special schools or residential facilities. Sometimes a number of small neighboring school districts pool their resources to offer a special school program for students with moderate, severe, and profound mental retardation. However, many special educators today believe that separate schools prohibit students from obtaining an education in the least restrictive environment and that all children should attend their local neighborhood schools regardless of the type or severity of their disability (e.g., Baumgart & Giangreco, 1996; Brown et al., 1989a; Snell, 1991).

As we saw in Chapter 2, simply putting a child with disabilities into a regular classroom does not necessarily mean that he will be accepted socially or receive the most appropriate and needed instructional programming. This may be especially true for students with mental retardation, whose presence in the regular classroom represents a novel challenge for many teachers. For example, although 97% of general education teachers who responded to a national survey about grading practices reported that they had taught students with learning disabilities and 73% had taught students with behavior disorders, only 23% indicated they had taught students with mental retardation (Bursuck et al., 1996).

Many special and regular educators, however, are developing programs and methods for integrating the instruction of students with mental retardation with that of their nondisabled classmates. Systematically planning for the focus student's inclusion in the classroom through team games and collaborative learning and group investigation projects and directly training all students in specific skills for interacting with one another are just some of the methods for increasing the chances of a successful regular class placement (Bauer & Brown, 2001; Dugan et al., 1995; Giangreco, 1997; Grenot-Scheyer, Fisher, & Staub, 2001; Janney & Snell, 1996, 1997, 2000; Kennedy & Fisher, 2001; Krajewski & Flaherty, 2000; Putnam, 1998). Peer tutoring and peer buddy programs have also proven effective in promoting the instructional and

Facilitating inclusion for students with MR

Council for Exceptional Children — Content Standards for Beginning Teachers of Students with MR/DD: Approaches to create positive learning environments for individuals with MR/DD (MR5K1) (also CC4S1).
PRAXIS Special Education Core Principles: Content Knowledge: III. Delivery of Services to Students with Disabilities, Curriculum and instruction and implementation across continuum of educational placements.

What to Do When Students Make Mistakes

Students make mistakes, even during carefully planned lessons using well-designed instructional materials. They answer incorrectly, give incomplete answers, or do not respond at all. The importance of providing feedback when students make errors is well documented (e.g., Brophy, 1986; Christenson, Ysseldyke, & Thurlow, 1989). Nevertheless, relatively little experimental research on error correction exists, and what does exist is inconclusive. Teachers are left knowing the importance of correcting student errors but receiving little empirically supported guidance for how to do so.

Don't Let Students Practice Errors during the Acquisition Stage of Learning

Students learn by doing, but if errors are repeated, they may be learning how to perform skills incorrectly. Students learn better by "doing with feedback." The biggest problem with delayed feedback is that it allows students to practice errors (Van Houten, 1984). Practicing errors also wastes valuable instructional time because of the reteaching and relearning that eventually must take place.

Most errors are made during the acquisition stage of learning, when the student is learning how to perform a new skill or to remember and use new knowledge correctly. It is important that feedback be provided before the student is required to use the skill/knowledge again. Feedback should be qualitative, focusing on the accuracy of the student's response. For example: "Excellent, Robin. You removed all of the leaves with dark spots. But there's still too much sand on them to serve to our customers. Let me show you again how to wash it off. Then you can show me."

For behaviors that produce a permanent product (e.g., a completed workbook page, a sanded piece of wood), it is usually not critical that feedback occur within a few seconds or minutes of a student's response. Feedback received even a day or two later may still be helpful as long as it occurs before the student must respond again.

Teachers can ensure that students receive feedback after each response by using instructional strategies such as these:

- *Collaborative learning.* Use a peer tutoring system or small-group activities in which peers provide feedback to one another after each response (Miller, Barbetta, & Heron, 1994).
- *Learning centers.* Use instructional materials and computer software that provide feedback after each response.
- *Self-correction.* Teach students to self-score their work and self-correct any errors before proceeding to the next problem or item (Goddard & Heron, 1998; Morten, Heward, & Alber, 1998).
- *Homework.* Avoid assigning homework or independent seatwork activities that do not contain self-scoring and self-correcting components until the student can perform the target skill with some accuracy.

When Errors Occur, Provide Effective and Efficient Error Correction

When handled properly, errors can provide good opportunities for teaching and learning. But too often error correction is carried out ineffectively (the student is still wrong the next time) and inefficiently (it is time-consuming and reduces the total number of learning trials that can be conducted during the lesson). Although much remains to be learned about how teachers should respond when students make mistakes during instruction, the combined results of several experimental studies provide some guidance. Research suggests that error correction will be more effective and efficient when it includes these four characteristics:

Now Instead of Later. Errors should be corrected before going to the next item or problem. Teachers may hesitate to delay instruction when a student errs during group instruction, preferring instead to work individually with her after the lesson. But this may allow the student to make the same mistake for the rest of the lesson. Two recent studies compared "right now" and "end-of-the-lesson" error correction during sight-word lessons with primary students with mental retardation and science vocabulary

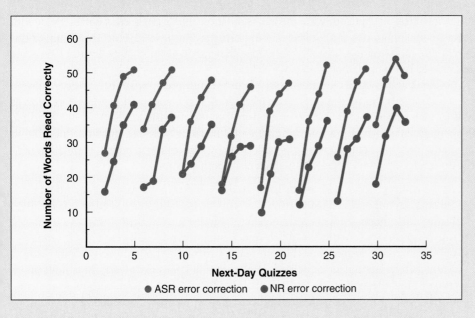

FIGURE A Total number of sight words read correctly by six primary students with mental retardation on tests given one day after instruction (breaks in data paths separate word sets)

Source: Reprinted from Barbetta, P. M. (1991). *Active error correction during sight words drills by students with developmental handicaps.* Unpublished doctoral dissertation, The Ohio State University. Used by permission.

lessons with upper elementary-age students with learning disabilities. Error correction immediately after each error was more effective, even when the postlesson error correction consisted of repeated trials (Barbetta, Heward, Bradley, & Miller, 1994; Kleinman et al., 1994).

Direct. Error correction is direct when the feedback focuses on the target skill. Several studies have shown that the effectiveness of error correction is improved when students are provided with complete information or a direct model of the missed item (Barbetta, Heward, & Bradley, 1993; Espin & Deno, 1989). That is, instead of offering incomplete or indirect feedback, tell, show, and/or guide the student through the correct response.

Brief. The teacher should rapidly tell, show, and/or demonstrate the correct response (e.g., "This word is 'circus.'"). Correcting an error in 3 or 4 seconds is better than engaging in an extended discussion of the student's mistake. In trying to help students understand their error, teachers often spend a great deal of time talking. Although detailed explanations are sometimes necessary and helpful, often students just get confused or lose interest. Time would be better used conducting several more complete learning trials.

Ends with the Student Making the Correct Response. When a student errs, teachers often hint, probe, tell, show, and eventually provide the correct response or ask another student to answer. The student who made the original error passively observes. Results from several studies show that feedback is more effective when the student who erred is given an opportunity to emit the corrected response (Barbetta & Heward, 1993; Dalrymple & Feldman, 1992; Drevno et al., 1994). For example, Barbetta, Heron, and Heward (1993) examined the effects of active student response during the correction of errors made by primary stu-

dents with mental retardation during sight-word lessons. Half of each week's set of 20 unknown words were taught with "no response" (NR) error correction (after each error, the teacher modeled the correct response while the student looked at the word); the remaining 10 words were taught with "active student response" (ASR) error correction (the student repeated the word after the teacher's model). ASR error correction was more effective for all six children on all five measures of performance: number and percentage of correct responses during instruction, same-day tests, next-day tests (see Figure A), maintenance tests given 2 weeks after instruction, and words read in sentences.

The error correction episode should end with the student making the correct response. Instead of providing or showing the correct response and then asking the student, "Now do you understand?" have the student repeat the correct response (e.g., teacher: "No. This word is 'circus'. What is this word?" Student: "Circus." Teacher: "Good.").

Evaluate the Effects of Error Correction

As with any instructional technique, teachers should evaluate their error correction procedures. First, what is the procedure's effectiveness in helping students respond correctly in the future? This can be directly and simply determined by observing how the student responds to the same item or task the next time it is presented. Second, how efficient are the error correction procedures? A complex, time-consuming procedure may be effective (the student responds correctly in the future) but inefficient because it limits the total number of learning trials during the lesson. Like most questions concerning effective instructional practices, the question of how error correction should be conducted is an empirical one. Its answer lies in student performance.

social inclusion of students with mental retardation into regular classrooms (Delquadri, Greenwood, Whorton, Carta, & Hall, 1986; Haring & Breen, 1992; Hughes, Killian, & Fischer, 1996; Mortweet et al., 1999; Staub, Spaulding, Peck, Gallucci, & Schwartz, 1996). See Teaching & Learning, "Some Things We've Learned about Inclusion," later in this chapter.

Students with mental retardation often benefit from similar programs for students who are not disabled. During the early elementary grades, students with mental retardation as well as their chronological age peers need instruction in basic academic skills. Reading, mathematical calculations, and writing are core curricular areas that should be included in programs for all students. During this period, many students with mental retardation benefit from full or partial inclusion in regular classroom settings.

> As students get older, their needs begin to differ and thus curricular differentiation becomes an important consideration. . . . Rather than being integrated into a world history class, many students with mental retardation may be better served by learning the necessary functional skills for independent living. Skills such as job readiness, how to use leisure time, how to budget and shop, how to cook and how to maintain a household are important. While all individuals must learn these skills in order to be independent, most students learn them on their own, without specific instructional activities that focus on these areas. Students with mental retardation, on the other hand, often need structured learning experiences in order to learn these skills. (Smith & Hilton, 1994, pp. 6–7)

The relative appropriateness of inclusion in the regular classroom may change for some students as they move from the elementary grades to the secondary level, when opportunities for community-based instruction in vocational and life skills are critical. The extent to which a student with mental retardation, like all students with disabilities, is educated in a general education classroom should be determined by the student's individual needs. "School inclusion can then be seen as a means (as opposed to just a goal unto itself) toward the ultimate objective of community inclusion and empowerment" (Polloway, Smith, Patton, & Smith, 1996, p. 11).

 ## CURRENT ISSUES AND FUTURE TRENDS

Two issues confronting the field of mental retardation today are the continued evolution of the definition of mental retardation and increasing the acceptance and membership of persons with mental retardation in society.

 ### THE EVOLVING DEFINITION OF MENTAL RETARDATION

The conception of mental retardation has undergone numerous changes in terminology, IQ score cutoff, and the relative role of adaptive functioning during the past 4 decades. In each case, those changes have reflected an ongoing attempt to better understand mental retardation in order to achieve more effective and reliable systems of identification, classification, research, and habilitation.

Some professionals in the field of mental retardation have criticized the AAMR's 1992/2002 definition (e.g., Borthwick-Duffy, 1994; Greenspan, 1997; Jacobsen & Mulick, 1996; MacMillan, Gresham, & Siperstein, 1993; Vig & Jedrysek, 1996). Some of the concerns are as follows:

- IQ testing will remain a primary (and in practice perhaps the only) means of diagnosis.
- Adaptive skills cannot be reliably measured with current assessment methods.
- The levels of needed supports are too subjective.
- Classification will remain essentially unchanged in practice because the four intensities of supports—intermittent, limited, extensive, and pervasive—will simply replace the four levels of retardation based on IQ scores—mild, moderate, severe, and profound.

Recognizing these criticisms and the difficulty of describing the implications of the new definition for the field of mental retardation, the AAMR's Ad Hoc Committee on Terminology and Classification concluded its presentation and discussion of its most recent definition with this observation:

> The field of mental retardation is currently in a state of flux regarding not just a fuller understanding of the condition of mental retardation, but also in the language and processes we use in naming, defining and classifying. . . . This state of flux is both frustrating and challenging. It is frustrating because it prohibits one from relying on past language, definitions, and models of mental retardation that can be a source of stability and permanence to some. However, the state is also challenging for it provides the opportunity to incorporate the current and evolving understanding of the condition of mental retardation and the factors that influence the lives of people in their societies. Whether perceived from a scientific or social perspective, the condition of mental retardation is being thought of differently today throughout the world. (Ad Hoc Committee on Terminology and Classification, 2001, p. 12)

The debate over the definition of mental retardation will surely continue. Burton Blatt, one of the field's most prolific, influential, and controversial figures, argued that when all is said and done mental retardation is best viewed as an administrative category. In his final book, *The Conquest of Mental Retardation* (1987), Blatt wrote, "Simply stated, someone is mentally retarded when he or she is 'officially' identified as such" (p. 72).

There is discussion in the field of changing the name from *mental retardation* to another term (Luckasson & Reeve, 2001). Some authors have even suggested that the entire concept of mental retardation should be eliminated because of the stigma and negative expectations attached to people who receive the label (cf. Smith & Mitchell, 2001b; Taylor & Blatt, 1999). But regardless of the term used to identify the combination of intellectual and adaptive behavior limitations currently known as mental retardation—or even if society decides not to identify and name it—substantial challenges in learning and independence constitute a real disability for the children and adults who experience them. And helping individuals with disabilities achieve to their fullest potential is what special education is all about.

ACCEPTANCE AND MEMBERSHIP

In a report to Congress nearly 30 years ago, the President's Committee on Mental Retardation (1976) outlined goals in the field of mental retardation for the remainder of the century. The report included specific objectives to be met by the year 2000 in several areas, including the following:

- Attainment of citizenship status in law and in fact for all mentally retarded individuals in the United States, exercised to the fullest degree possible under the conditions of disability
- Reduction of the incidence of mental retardation from biomedical causes by at least 50% by the year 2000
- Reduction of the incidence and prevalence of mental retardation associated with social disadvantage to the lowest level possible by the end of the century
- Adequate and humane service systems for all persons with mental retardation in need of them
- Achievement of a firm and deep public acceptance of persons with mental retardation as members in common of the social community and as citizens in their own right

Although significant accomplishments and progress were made on each of the President's Committee's goals, none was fully achieved at the turn of the century, and much work

Continuing debate and evolution of definition of MR

Council for Exceptional Children — Content Standards for Beginning Teachers of Students with Mr/DD: Trends and practices within the field of MR/DD (MR1K5) (also CC1K5).

Some Things We've Learned about Inclusion

by Martha E. Snell, University of Virginia, and Rachel E. Janney, Radford University

Inclusion involves creating a mainstream where everyone fits and learns. Inclusion affects the location of students, the supports provided, the roles school staff fill, and the ways teachers interact with each other. In inclusive schools:

- All students attend their neighborhood school.
- Students with disabilities are members of general education classrooms with their age peers; their numbers reflect the natural proportion of students with disabilities.
- Special education supports follow students into the mainstream.
- Inclusion is planned individually to enable active and meaningful participation in learning and social activities. Planning addresses classes and schedule, amount and kinds of support, accommodations and modifications, and any related services.

Benefits of Inclusion

Most educators agree that inclusion involves complex change, but knowing what inclusion is still may not convince people to make the change. Why include students with disabilities, especially those with extensive support needs? Because inclusion provides benefits to students with disabilities, typical students, and teachers.

For students with disabilities, we know that inclusion can lead to social benefits and skill improvements (Dugan et al., 1995; Fryxell & Kennedy, 1995; Hunt, Staub, Alwell, & Goetz, 1994; Kennedy, Shukla, & Fryxell, 1997; Shukla, Kennedy, & Cushing, 1998). These benefits mean not being separated from typical peers but sharing class membership; having increased social interactions; gaining positive social relationships; expanding one's peer network and making friends; and having peers who can be models for communication, social skills, dress, style, increased

alertness, and improved academic learning and motivation for learning.

For typical students, benefits cluster in the personal growth domain (Cushing & Kennedy, 1997; Kishi & Meyer, 1994; Shukla et al., 1998). Students demonstrate improvements in attitudes toward people different from themselves, increased social responsibility, and self-confidence. They have an opportunity to expand peer networks and form meaningful relationships with students in the mainstream.

General education teachers describe unanticipated rewards from their own interactions with focus students; these teachers are positively motivated by discovering that students with disabilities have personalities, can learn, and can contribute in class.

Most benefits of inclusion depend on how schools plan for, implement, and support change and then sustain outcomes. Searching the literature for supportive evidence produces a mixed bag of findings. It seems that the challenges of including students with extensive cognitive and/or physical disabilities may be fewer than those of including students prone to emotional outburst or aggression. But categorizing students as "easier to include" or "harder to include" is an error-prone strategy. Only by planning needed supports on an individual basis can educators help inclusion yield benefits.

Unwritten Agreements between Teachers

Observations and interviews with teachers and students from 10 classrooms in elementary schools practicing inclusion have taught us a great deal (Janney & Snell, 1996, 1997). For example, classroom teachers and special education teachers have unwritten contracts about the roles they play to support the students with moderate and severe disabilities included in their classrooms:

Inclusion should be planned to enable active and meaningful participation in the learning and social activities of the classroom.

- Classroom teachers continued to have primary authority for the class and the included child when he was treated like classmates—for example, during class activities, recess, P.E., circle time, reading and math, and field trips.
- Special education teachers or classroom aides assumed primary responsibility when the focus child was treated differently from classmates: for example, during individualized tutoring or related services for health or physical needs.
- When including students with more extensive support needs, the teachers would, as much as possible, (1) keep focus students near their peers, (2) treat them like their classmates, and (3) provide them with the same or similar activities and materials.

After all, as these teachers told us, inclusion is about students having membership in classrooms with nondisabled peers. So why separate them or treat them differently?

Teachers' Modifications

To implement these assumptions, teachers made three kinds of changes. First, they modified their typical roles because the focus student was shared between two teachers and the classroom teacher now had at least one new staff member in and out of the classroom. Second, they modified class routines and the classroom itself. For example, peers were allowed to walk with focus students and help them stay with the class on the way to lunch, P.E., and other activities; schedules allowed time for students with physical disabilities to make transitions; reading circles were moved so positioning equipment would fit. Third, teachers modified instructional activities to enable focus students to participate academically and socially. Sometimes changes were simplifications (fewer spelling words); sometimes they involved different materials (specialized scissors) or response modalities (listening to a taped story rather than looking at a book because of visual impairments). Sometimes instructional activities were modified to enable the focus child to participate socially, not academically: just sitting with a group doing math activities or holding a book that others were reading. Finally, special education teachers used parallel activities that differed from classmates' activities, were carried out separately but in the classroom, and in which only the focus child participated (e.g., working on money skills while classmates did addition and subtraction). Inclusion was successful when students fit in *both* socially and instructionally.

Lessons about Helping and Socialization

Observations also taught us about how teachers use peer interactions to include students with disabilities in their elementary general education classrooms. We learned that classroom teachers developed rules for peers to help the included child:

- *Who could help the focus student with class work.* Typical students could not help each other, but they could help the focus student.
- *When to help the focus student.* Typical students could help if they were "helper of the day" or asked by the teacher, but not when the teacher was teaching or if the focus student rejected assistance.
- *How to help.* Typical students could help in ways that let the focus student participate as much as he or she could. "Don't do it for her" was a guideline teachers taught peers (but did not always follow themselves).

We have repeatedly observed general and special education teachers teach three important lessons that facilitate socialization between students and their classmate with disabilities. The main teaching approach was to model lessons through their own behavior toward the focus student—to "practice what they preached."

continues

Lessons	Examples
Just another student. Treat focus students like other students as much as possible.	Use greetings, joking styles as with other students; include them in all class activities; and apply the same rules for everyone's behavior.
Age appropriate. Encourage focus students to look and act in ways that reflect their actual age, not "like babies." Use the same rule to guide peer interactions.	Use age-appropriate greetings, tone of voice, teaching and leisure materials, and clothes.
Back off. Adults should draw peers into academic or social activities with focus children and then back off to avoid hampering their interactions.	Pull peers into the activity and make it fun; then leave. Or help a focus student into the sandbox among peers; then move away and monitor from a distance.

Teachers Working Together

More recently (Snell & Janney, 2000), we observed kindergarten and first-grade teachers over a school year as they practiced inclusion in an elementary school. We found that these teachers naturally used problem-solving strategies with their teammates to address problems that arose with the children who had high support needs. Teachers' concerns clustered into several areas: disagreement about students' goals and problems, challenges with coordination and communication, and difficulties putting solutions into place and evaluating them. Their approach for addressing these concerns, while not articulated as steps, consisted of steps similar to traditional models: identify the problem, gather information, generate potential solutions, evaluate potential solutions, implement, and evaluate. Under pressure for solutions, however, they often discussed and generated ideas too quickly, which curtailed brainstorming as a team and meant that ideas were tried out before being well formed and improved through repeated application of these steps. These findings lend support for team problem solving as an essential element of the meaningful inclusion of children with disabilities; but given the logistical constraints of teaching, it is critical that school administrators lend strong support to regular team collaboration (e.g., preserving time for teaming and valuing its outcomes).

Normalization

PRAXIS Special Education Core Principles: Content Knowledge: II. Legal and Societal Issues, Historical movements/trends affecting the connections between special education and the larger society.

remains. An especially important and continuing challenge for the field, and for all of society, is moving beyond the physical integration of persons with mental retardation in society to the acceptance and membership that comes from holding valued roles.

For many years, the principle of **normalization** has provided a conceptual foundation and general approach for improving the life experiences of persons with mental retardation. Wolf Wolfensberger (1972), one of the first and best-known champions of normalization, wrote that the principle refers to the use of progressively more normal settings and procedures "to establish and/or maintain personal behaviors which are as culturally normal as possible" (p. 28). Normalization is not a single technique or set of procedures but an overriding philosophy. It says that persons with mental retardation should, to the greatest extent possible, be both physically and socially integrated into everyday society regardless of their degree or type of disability.

While the principle of normalization has helped individuals with mental retardation who are physically present in many school, community, and work settings today, it has not gained them acceptance and true membership. Wolfensberger (1983) has proposed the concept of *social role valorization* (SRV) as a necessary and natural extension of the normalization principle. He writes, "The most explicit and highest goal of normalization must be the creation, support, and defense of valued social roles for people who are at risk of social devaluation" (p. 234).

The key premise of SRV is that people's welfare depends extensively on the social roles they occupy: People who fill roles that are positively valued by others will generally be afforded by the latter the good things of life, but people who fill roles that are devalued by others will typically be badly treated by them. This implies that in the case of people whose life situations are very bad, and whose bad situations are bound up with occupancy of devalued roles, then if the social roles they are seen as occupying can somehow be upgraded in the eyes of perceivers, their life conditions will usually improve, and often dramatically so. (Wolfensberger, 2000, p. 105)

Perhaps the greatest current expression and extension of the normalization/SRV concept in special education can be found in the growing movement toward teaching self-determination skills to individuals with mental retardation. Self-determination involves acting as the primary agent in one's life and "making choices and decisions regarding one's quality of life free from undue influence or interference" (Wehmeyer, Kelchner, & Richards, 1996, p. 632). In his presidential address to the AAMR, Wagner (2000) offered this example of the relationship between self-determination and social role valorization:

> How do we really start to implement this dream of highly valued roles in society? One thing we need to do is begin to celebrate the people who, in fact, currently have highly valued roles. Let me tell you about some of my heroes. . . . there is Christina. She has big dreams. What makes Christina unique is that her dreams are really good. About 6 years ago, she was mainstreamed into a large high school. In central Louisiana. She no sooner got there than she decided that she was going to become a cheerleader. Much to our amazement, she went out for the cheerleading squad and became a cheerleader. Then, a few years later when she was a senior, Christina decided that she wanted to be Homecoming Queen. She saw no problem at all with the fact that she has Down syndrome. She was going to be the Homecoming Queen. Well, lo and behold, she ran for Homecoming Queen and won. Christina is my heroine of big dreams. She did not let her handicaps stand in the way of realizing her dreams. I think it is also a testament to that high school that they did not let her handicaps stand in the way either. (p. 442)

Among the most important things that special educators can do are helping students like Christina identify their goals and providing the instruction and supports that will enable them to pursue those goals. As support for self-determination and social role valorization grows among both educators and the public, the time draws nearer when all persons with mental retardation will experience the benefits of valued membership in integrated school, community, and employment settings.

Social role valorization and self-determination

 Content Standards for Beginning Teachers of Students with MR/DD: Trends and practices within the field of MR/DD (MR1K5) (also CC4S5).
PRAXIS Special Education Core Principles: Content Knowledge: II. Legal and Societal Issues, The school's connections with communities of students with disabilities, Developing student self-advocacy.

 For more information on mental retardation, go to the Web Links module in Chapter 6 of the Companion Website at **www.prenhall.com/heward**

SUMMARY

DEFINITIONS

- The definition incorporated into IDEA states that mental retardation involves both significantly subaverage general intellectual functioning and deficits in adaptive behavior manifested between birth and age 18. Intellectual functioning is usually measured with a standardized intelligence test and adaptive behavior with an observation checklist or scale.
- There are four degrees of mental retardation as classified by IQ score: mild, moderate, severe, and profound.
- AAMR's 1992/2002 definition of mental retardation represents a shift away from conceptualizations of mental retardation as an inherent trait or permanent state of being to a description of the individual's present functioning and the environmental supports needed to improve it.
- Classification of mental retardation according to AAMR's 1992/2002 definition is based on four levels and intensities of supports needed to improve functioning in the environments in which the individual lives: intermittent, limited, extensive, and pervasive.

IDENTIFICATION AND ASSESSMENT

- An intelligence (IQ) test consists of a series of questions (e.g., vocabulary, similarities), problem solving (e.g., mazes, blocks design), memory, and other tasks assumed to require certain amounts of intelligence to answer or solve correctly.

- IQ scores seem to be distributed throughout the population according to a phenomenon called the normal curve. Theoretically, about 2.3% of the population falls two or more standard deviations below the mean, which the AAMR calls "significantly subaverage."

- The IQ cutoff score of 70 is intended only as a guideline and should not be interpreted as a hard-and-fast requirement. A higher IQ score of 75 or more may be associated with mental retardation if, according to a clinician's judgment, the child exhibits deficits in adaptive behavior thought to be caused by impaired intellectual functioning.

- Because IQ tests are composed largely of verbal and academic tasks—the same things a child must master to succeed in school—they correlate highly with school achievement.

- Adaptive behavior is "the effectiveness or degree with which the individual meets the standards of personal independence and social responsibility expected of his age and social group" (Grossman, 1983, p. 157).

- Systematic assessment of adaptive behavior is important because the adaptive skills exhibited by a person with mental retardation—as well as the nature and severity of maladaptive behaviors—are critical factors in determining the nature and degree of supports she requires for success in school, work, community, and home environments.

- Most instruments for assessing adaptive behavior consist of a series of questions answered by someone familiar with the individual.

- Measurement of adaptive behavior has proven difficult, in large part because of the relative nature of social adjustment and competence: what is considered appropriate in one situation or by one group may not be in or by another.

CHARACTERISTICS

- Children with mild mental retardation may experience substantial performance deficits only in school. Their social and communication skills may be normal or nearly so. They are likely to become independent or semi-independent adults.

- Most children with moderate mental retardation show significant developmental delays during their preschool years.

- Research has found that students with mental retardation have trouble retaining information in short-term memory.

- Students with mental retardation do not tend to use *metacognitive* or *executive control* strategies such as rehearsing and organizing information. When taught to use such strategies, their performance on memory-related and problem-solving tasks is likely to improve.

- Students with mental retardation learn at a significantly slower rate than that of typically developing children.

- Students with mental retardation often have trouble attending to relevant features of a learning task and instead may focus on distracting irrelevant stimuli. In addition, individuals with mental retardation often have difficulty sustaining attention.

- Students with mental retardation often have trouble using their new knowledge and skills in settings or situations that differ from the context in which they first learned those skills.

- Some individuals with mental retardation develop *learned helplessness*, a condition in which a person expects failure regardless of his or her efforts.

- Some students with mental retardation exhibit *outer-directedness*; they seem to distrust their own responses to situations and rely on others for assistance and solutions.

- Children with mental retardation have substantial deficits in adaptive behavior that take many forms and tend to occur across domains of functioning. Limitations in self-care skills and social relationships as well as behavioral excesses are common characteristics of individuals with mental retardation.

PREVALENCE

- Theoretically, 2.3% of the population would score two standard deviations below the norm on IQ tests; but this does not account for adaptive behavior, the other criterion for diagnosis of mental retardation. Many experts now cite an incidence figure of approximately 1% of the total population.
- During the 2000–2001 school year, approximately 1% of the total school enrollment received special education services under the disability category of mental retardation.

CAUSES AND PREVENTION

- More than 250 causes of mental retardation have been identified.
- Etiology is unknown for most individuals with mild mental retardation. Increasing evidence, however, suggests that psychosocial disadvantage in early childhood is a major cause of mild mental retardation.
- Recent scientific advances—including genetic counseling, amniocentesis, CVS, virus vaccines, and early screening tests—are helping reduce the incidence of clinical or biologically caused retardation.
- Although early identification and intensive educational services to high-risk infants show promise, there is still no widely used technique to decrease the incidence of mental retardation caused by psychosocial disadvantage.

EDUCATIONAL APPROACHES

- Curriculum should focus on functional skills that will help the student be successful in self-care, vocational, domestic, community, and leisure domains.
- Major components of explicit systematic instruction are task analysis, direct and frequent measurement, repeated opportunities to respond, systematic feedback, transfer of stimulus control from teacher-provided cues and prompts to natural stimuli, and programming for generalization and maintenance.

EDUCATIONAL PLACEMENT ALTERNATIVES

- Approximately 50% students with mental retardation are educated in separate classrooms, 30% in resource rooms, and 15% in regular classrooms.
- During the early elementary grades, many students with mental retardation benefit from full or partial inclusion in regular classroom settings.
- Strategies for facilitating successful regular class placement include planning for the focus student's inclusion in the classroom through team games, collaborative learning and group investigation projects, and directly training all students in specific skills for interacting with one another.
- The relative appropriateness of inclusion in the regular classroom may change for some students with mental retardation as they move from the elementary grades to the secondary level when opportunities for community-based instruction in vocational and life skills are critical.
- The extent to which a student with mental retardation, like all students with disabilities, is educated in a general education classroom should be determined by the student's individual needs.

CURRENT ISSUES AND FUTURE TRENDS

- Changes and debate over the definition of mental retardation are likely to continue and reflect the ongoing need to better understand mental retardation in order to achieve more effective and reliable systems of identification, classification, research, and habilitation.
- The principles of normalization, social role valorization, and self-determination are important in helping individuals with mental retardation achieve acceptance and membership in society.

 To check your comprehension of chapter contents, go to the Guided Review and Quiz Modules in Chapter 6 of the Companion Website at **www.prenhall. com/heward**

Chapter 7
Learning Disabilities

Focus Questions

- Why has the concept of learning disabilities proven so difficult to define?

- Do most students who are identified as learning disabled have a true disability? Or are they just low achievers or victims of poor instruction?

- What are the most important skills for an elementary-age student with learning disabilities to master? A secondary student?

- How do basic academic skills and learning strategies relate to each other?

- Should all students with learning disabilities be educated in the regular classroom?

Ronni Hochman Spratt

Hastings Middle School

Upper Arlington, Ohio

Education • Teaching Credentials • Experience

- B. S., Special Education, State University College at Buffalo, New York, 1971
- M. A., Special Education, The Ohio State University, 1974
- Ohio certification in Learning Disabilities, (K–12), Emotional Disturbance (K–12), Developmental Handicaps (K–12), Reading
- 30 years of experience as special educator

My Students and Classroom   This year, 16 seventh and eighth graders spend time in my cross-categorical resource room every day. Eight students have learning disabilities, and the others have a variety of impairments and conditions: Tourette's syndrome, attention-deficit/hyperactivity disorder, Asperger's, and traumatic brain injury. Our school day consists of nine 42-minute periods. Students come and go throughout the day and are in the resource room for as few as one or as many as five periods. Most students are in the room for two or three periods each day, where they receive individual and small-group instruction in reading, writing, math, and organizational and self-control skills.

I believe it's important to create a physical and social environment where students feel safe and willing to take risks with learning. This is a place where there is mutual respect and the uniqueness of each individual is valued. The first thing my students learn is that there are high academic and behavioral standards in my classroom, for them and for me. Those standards are clearly defined, and the students know exactly what's expected of them each day. The students know it's okay to make mistakes in my classroom. They see me make mistakes every day. But they must keep trying.

I emphasize organizational skills, self-advocacy, and personal responsibility. When students first enter the room, they show me their plan books; each one has a three-ring binder, and they turn in any work that is due. Students are taught to write down their assignments in my class and their other classes. Then students get started on their work. Some do peer tutoring for vocabulary building; others begin writing on the computers. The students self-evaluate their work as much as possible. Each student sets a weekly accuracy or fluency goal for every subject or skill area. There are graphs all over the room, and the students chart their performance every day. Each student has a graph for the number of words written in his journal, another graph for vocabulary words learned in peer tutoring, a graph for scores on corrective reading worksheets, and a homework graph. Students who turn in all of their homework and in-class assignments Monday through Thursday are not assigned homework over the weekend. They like that, and so do I.

Connecting with General Education   I tell my students it's their job to find out what each of their general education teachers expects. I say, think of that teacher as an employer or boss that you want to please. If that teacher sees you trying, she'll help you. But if she sees you unprepared, slouching, and talking in class, she's much less likely to help you.

At the beginning of the year, each student writes a letter to each of his or her regular class teachers. This really helps the special education students get off to a good start in the regular classroom. Students use the letters to introduce themselves and their families, describe their interests and hobbies, and state what they hope to accomplish in each teacher's class during the year. The students must also articulate their special educational needs and describe how they think the teacher can help them learn and be successful. The general education teachers tell me the letters ease some of their concerns and give them some information with which to begin a relationship with the students. But of course, those letters don't get printed and signed until they're in respectable shape. So during that first week of school, a lot of writing, editing, and revising gets done in my classroom.

Teaching Strategies   Here are few other approaches I've found effective.

Get to know your students personally.   Each student is different as an individual, but they all respond to genuine, personal attention. Every day I try to have a brief, personal conversation with each student. I can tell you what she likes to eat, her favorite and least favorite bands, what TV shows she watches, what she's excited about, what she's worried about, and her hopes for the future. Once students trust you and know that you're not going anywhere—that you're consistent—they are very open and responsive. They know I truly care about them. So when I don't let up on them academically and demand their best efforts and signs of improvement, they're okay with it. When I have to discipline a student, they understand. They know I'm doing it because I'm *for* them. Of all the notes and letters I've received from parents and students, one of my favorites was from an eighth-grade boy who wrote, "Even though I have been bad at times, she's still there for me the whole way."

Discover and build upon each student's strengths.   I believe a key to helping students access the general education curriculum is identifying the student's strengths and then putting him back into the regular classroom only in the areas in which he can experience a great amount of success. I use the student's time in the resource room to build those skills he needs to be completely integrated into the regular classroom—whether it's learning to read faster or learning to stay on task long enough to complete independent seatwork.

Expect your students to learn and then provide the supports that enable them to do so.   Provide supports that enable students to have some success and then gradually withdraw them. Today's hot word for this approach is "scaffolding"—a strategy that effective special educators have always used.

Hold high expectations and stick to them.   Students need to know that we consistently expect them to succeed and do their best. The first time a student hands me a beautiful piece of writing, I smile and say, "Whoa, Charlotte, you just made a big mistake! You showed me how well you can do. I will never accept anything less from you." Once a student has shown me she can do quality work, I won't accept shoddy work. With all the modifications, supports, and accommodations in the world, kids will still flunk tests. I don't accept that. Laziness is not a learning disability.

Some students with learning disabilities are like unmade beds; they leave stuff all over the place. It might be cute and okay for a little while, but it's no way to achieve in school or live your whole life. Organizational and self-management skills are key.

To see some of the "Dear Teacher" letters by Ms. Spratt's students, visit the Teacher Feature module in Chapter 7 of the Companion Website at **www.prenhall.com/heward**

Whether or not those skills are on a student's IEP, I always show students how to get organized, help them set and focus on reachable short-term goals, and teach them some self-monitoring and self-evaluation skills. For example, there's Eduardo, a new student from Venezuela. He's an adorable and very friendly boy, an only child whose parents dote on him. Eduardo wasn't turning in his homework in a couple of his general education classes, and it turns out his parents were covering for him. I told him that had to change. He'd have to show me his work every day; and if it wasn't completed appropriately, he'd redo it during lunch in my room. He complained, which I ignored; but he complied, which I praised. Last grading period he earned his best grades ever, and I guarantee he'll show an achievement jump of at least two grade levels this year. He's started to take off. That's special education.

Advice for Someone Considering a Career in Special Education   Don't get into this work unless you really are excited about it. Being a special education teacher is too important and too difficult to do well if you're not committed. (And I'd say the same thing to anyone considering a career as a general education teacher.) Spend as much time in schools and classrooms as you can. Look for every opportunity to work with students with special needs. If you find out that teaching isn't what you thought or wanted it to be, that's fine. If you can't wait to get back in the classroom each time you leave—well, most days anyway—then pursue it.

After you become a licensed teacher, stay interested and active in your profession. Find a good mentor who will talk with you about curriculum and instruction and who you can come to with problems or concerns. Attend in-service workshops; better yet, help plan and present them. One of the best ways to stay current and active and to learn from others is to attend and present at conferences and teacher development programs.

You have to be able to do many things at the same time. I'm sure every special educator interviewed for this book has said that. But if you're not organized and can't time-share on multiple tasks, this job will eat you alive.

You hear a lot about teachers getting burned out. I believe that some of the teachers who state burnout as the reason they're leaving the classroom were never really that happy to be there in the first place. If you've never been lit, you can't be burned out!

Enjoy the students; they're so much fun. If you just take the time to get to know them, they'll be willing to do anything for you. And they'll teach you some things and provide lots of laughs along the way. Sure, there are some difficult days; some are downright disastrous. Have a sense of humor. And use it!

What I Like Most about Being a Special Educator   This fall, I trained my 50th student teacher, Nikia Bryant. The photo on the title page of this chapter shows Nikia working with some of my students. There's nothing more rewarding for me than helping a new teacher get started on his or her career. The fact that there is almost always a student teacher or field-experience student in my classroom means I have to be able to explain and defend everything I do. That means I'm always thinking about what I'm doing and why I'm doing it, which makes me a better teacher.

For the past 3 years, I've served as a clinical educator for The Ohio State University's special education program, spending one day every other week observing student teachers. Not only does this give me the opportunity to work with a larger number of preservice teachers, but I get to observe and pick up ideas from the cooperating teachers in all those different classrooms. The day I stop learning in this job is the day I'll give it up. I can honestly say that I am as excited about what I do now as when I began 30 years ago.

To better understand what will be covered in this chapter, go to the the Essential Concepts and Chapter-at-a-Glance modules in Chapter 7 of the Companion Website at **www.prenhall.com/heward**

ACALD

Council for Exceptional Children **Content Standards** for Beginning Teachers of Students with LD: Professional organizations and sources of information relevant to the field of LD (LD9K2).
PRAXIS Special Education Core Principles: Content Knowledge: III. Delivery of Services to Students with Disabilities, Professional roles, Use of professional organizations.

By the late 1950s most public schools had established special education programs (or at least offered some type of special service) for children with mental retardation, students with physical disabilities, children with sensory impairments, and those with emotional and behavioral disorders. But there remained a group of children who were having serious learning problems at school yet did not fit into the existing categories of exceptionality. They did not appear to be handicapped. The children seemed physically intact, yet they were unable to learn certain basic skills and subjects at school. In searching for help for their children, parents turned to physicians and psychologists. (Remember, the schools had no programs for these children.) Understandably, these professionals viewed the children from the vantage points of their respective disciplines. As a result, terms such as *brain damage, minimal brain dysfunction, neurological impairment, perceptual handicap, dyslexia,* and *aphasia* were often used to describe or account for the children's learning problems. Many of these terms are still used today because a variety of disciplines continue to influence the field of learning disabilities.

The term *learning disabilities* was coined by Samuel Kirk in a 1963 address to a group of parents whose children were experiencing serious difficulties in learning to read, were hyperactive, or could not solve math problems. The parents liked the term and that very evening voted to form the Association for Children with Learning Disabilities. Today, the organization's name is the Association for Children and Adults with Learning Disabilities (ACALD), and it is a powerful advocacy group for persons with learning disabilities. In 1975 learning disabilities was included as a special education category in IDEA.

No area of special education has experienced as much rapid growth, extreme interest, and continuing controversy as learning disabilities. The number of children identified as learning disabled has nearly tripled since the passage of IDEA, making this category the largest in special education and fueling an ongoing debate on the nature of the learning disability concept. Some believe the increase in the number of children identified as learning disabled indicates the true extent of the disability. Others contend that too many low achievers—children without a disability who are simply doing poorly in school—have been improperly identified as learning disabled, placing a severe strain on the limited resources available to serve those students challenged by a true disability.

There is considerable confusion and disagreement among professionals and parents on even the most basic question: what is a learning disability? In some ways, learning disabilities bring out both the worst and the best that special education has to offer. Learning disabilities has served as a breeding ground for fads and miracle treatments ("New Vitamin and Diet Regimen Cures Learning Disabilities!"). At the same time, some of the most innovative teachers and scholars in special education have devoted their careers to learning disabilities. And numerous methods of instruction first developed for students with learning disabilities have influenced and benefited the entire field of education.

IDEA definition of LD

Council for Exceptional Children **Content Standards** for Beginning Teachers–Common Core: Issues in definition and identification of individuals with exceptional learning needs (CC1K5).
PRAXIS Special Education Core Principles: Content Knowledge: I. Understanding Exceptionalities, Definitions of disabilities.

 DEFINITIONS

Numerous definitions for learning disabilities have been proposed, but none has been universally accepted. The two definitions that have had the most influence are the federal definition in IDEA and a definition proposed by the National Joint Committee on Learning Disabilities.

 THE IDEA DEFINITION

In IDEA, **learning disabilities** is defined as follows:

> *In General*—The term "specific learning disability" means a disorder in one or more of the basic psychological processes involved in understanding or in using language,

spoken or written, which disorder may manifest itself in an imperfect ability to listen, think, speak, read, write, spell, or to do mathematical calculations.

Disorders Included—Such term includes such conditions as perceptual disabilities, brain injury, minimal brain dysfunction, dyslexia, and developmental aphasia.

Disorders Not Included—Such term does not include a learning problem that is primarily the result of visual, hearing, or motor disabilities, of mental retardation, of emotional disturbance, or of environmental, cultural, or economic disadvantage. (Sec. 602 [26])

 ## THE NJCLD DEFINITION

The National Joint Committee on Learning Disabilities (NJCLD), a group composed of official representatives from 10 professional organizations involved with students with learning disabilities, believes that the federal definition of learning disabilities contains several inherent weaknesses (Myers & Hammill, 1990):

1. *Exclusion of adults.*   Learning disabilities can occur at all ages, and the IDEA definition refers only to school-age children.
2. *Reference to basic psychological processes.*   Use of the phrase "basic psychological processes" has generated extensive and perhaps unnecessary debate on how to teach students with learning disabilities; and how to teach is a curricular issue, not a definitional one.
3. *Inclusion of spelling as a learning disability.*   Because spelling can be subsumed under "written expression," it is redundant and should be eliminated from the definition.
4. *Inclusion of obsolete terms.*   Inclusion of terms such as dyslexia, minimal brain dysfunction, perceptual impairments, and developmental aphasia, which historically have proven difficult to define, only adds confusion to the definition.
5. *Wording of the exclusion clause.*   The final clause in the IDEA definition suggests that learning disabilities cannot occur along with other disabilities. A more accurate statement, according to the NJCLD, is that a person may have a learning disability along with another disability but not because of another disability.

In response to these problems with the federal definition, the NJCLD proposed the following definition:

Learning disabilities is a general term that refers to a heterogeneous group of disorders manifested by significant difficulties in the acquisition and use of listening, speaking, reading, writing, reasoning, or mathematical abilities. These disorders are intrinsic to the individual and presumed to be due to central nervous system dysfunction, and may appear across the life span. Problems in self-regulatory behaviors, social perception, and social interaction may exist with learning disabilities but do not themselves constitute a learning disability. Although learning disabilities may occur concomitantly with other handicapping conditions (for example, sensory impairment, mental retardation, serious emotional disturbance) or with extrinsic influences (such as cultural differences, insufficient or inappropriate instruction), they are not the result of those conditions or influences. (NJCLD, 1989, p. 1)

 ## OPERATIONALIZING THE DEFINITION

A survey of all 50 states found that the majority use the IDEA definition of learning disabilities or some variation of it (Mercer, Jordan, Allsopp, & Mercer, 1995). When operationalizing the definition for the purpose of identifying students with learning disabilities, most states and school districts require that three criteria be met:

1. A severe discrepancy between the student's intellectual ability and academic achievement
2. An exclusion criterion: the student's difficulties are not the result of another known condition that can cause learning problems
3. A need for special education services

Ability-achievement discrepancy

Council for Exceptional Children Content Standards for Beginning Teachers of Students with LD: Philosophies, theories, models and issues related to individuals with LD (LD1K2). **PRAXIS** Special Education Core Principles: Content Knowledge: I. Understanding Exceptionalities, Characteristics of student with disabilities, Cognitive factors.

Ability-Achievement Discrepancy   Children with learning disabilities exhibit an unexpected difference between general ability and achievement—a discrepancy that would not be predicted by the student's general intellectual ability (Kavale & Forness, 2000). Children who are having minor or temporary difficulties in learning should not be identified as learning disabled. According to federal guidelines that accompanied the original IDEA, only children with a true disability, as evidenced by a "severe discrepancy between achievement and intellectual ability," were to be identified as learning disabled (U.S. Office of Education, 1977, p. 65083).

The federal government proposed several mathematical formulas for determining a severe discrepancy. All of the proposed formulas were eventually rejected, and the final rules and regulations for IDEA did not contain a specific definition of and formula for determining a severe discrepancy. This left states to find their own criteria for implementing the definition of learning disabilities. Although the federal definition no longer mentions "discrepancy," the most common practice for identifying children with learning disabilities is determining if a severe discrepancy exists between their expected and actual achievement. This involves comparing a student's score on an IQ test with his score on a standardized achievement test. While such a comparison seems simple on the surface, in practice it is fraught with problems (Fletcher et al., 2001; Fuchs, Fuchs, Mathes, Lipsey, & Roberts, 2001; Gresham, 2001; Kavale, 2001).

Many students underachieve academically. How is unexpected underachievement caused by a "hidden disability" to be distinguished from underachievement that might result from factors such as poor motivation or faulty instruction? Confusion and disagreement about exactly how a severe discrepancy should be determined have led to widely differing procedures for identifying and classifying students as learning disabled (Kavale & Forness, 2000; Ysseldyke, 2001). As a result, the percentage of children identified as learning disabled ranges across states from a low of 3.0% of the total school-age population in Kentucky to 9.2% in Massachusetts (U.S. Department of Education, 2000).

Students with learning disabilities experience significant learning difficulties that cannot be explained by mental retardation, sensory impairment, emotional disturbance, or lack of educational opportunity.

Exclusion   The IDEA definition of learning disabilities is meant to identify students with significant learning problems that are not "primarily the result" of other conditions that can impede learning, such as another recognized disability or lack of opportunity to learn due to environmental, cultural, or economic conditions. The word *primarily* in the definition recognizes that learning disabilities can coexist with other disabilities; but when that is considered the case, the student typically receives services under the other disability category.

Need for Special Education   Students with learning disabilities show specific and severe learning problems despite normal educational efforts and therefore need specially designed instruction that is tailored (i.e., specially designed) to meet their unique needs (Simmons, Kame'enui, & Chard, 1998). This criterion is meant to avoid the overidentification of children who have not had the opportunity to learn (NJCLD, 1998). Such children should progress normally as soon as they receive typically effective instruction at a curricular level appropriate to their current skills.

CHARACTERISTICS

To describe the various categories of exceptionality, observers typically list the physical and psychological characteristics often exhibited by the individuals who make up that group. For example, early in the field's history a task force commissioned to identify the characteristics of children with learning disabilities (the term *minimal brain dysfunction* was used to describe these children at that time) found that 99 separate characteristics were reported in the literature (Clements, 1966). The inherent danger in such lists is the tendency to assume, or to look for, *each* of those characteristics in *all* children considered in the category. This danger is especially troublesome with learning disabilities because the category includes children who exhibit a wide range of learning, social, and emotional problems. In fact, Mercer (1997) suggests that it is theoretically possible for an individual with learning disabilities to exhibit one of more than 500,000 combinations of cognitive or socioemotional problems.

Learning disabilities are associated with problems in listening, reasoning, memory, attention, selecting and focusing on relevant stimuli, and the perception and processing of visual and/or auditory information. These perceptual and cognitive processing difficulties are assumed to be the underlying reason why students with learning disabilities experience one or more of the following characteristics: reading problems, deficits in written language, underachievement in math, poor social skills, attention deficits and hyperactivity, and behavioral problems.

READING PROBLEMS

Difficulty with reading is by far the most common characteristic of students with learning disabilities. It is estimated that 90% of all children identified as learning disabled are referred for special education services because of reading problems (Kavale & Forness, 2000). Some professionals now believe the term *learning disabilities,* which encompasses so many different types of learning problems, hinders our understanding of the causes, developmental courses, and outcomes of the reading problems experienced by many children (Fletcher et al., 2001). They recommend developing specific definitions and research bases for each type of learning disability (e.g., reading disabilities, math disabilities).

Evidence suggests that specific reading disability, also called **dyslexia,** is a persistent deficit, not simply a developmental lag in linguistic or basic reading skills (Grossen, 1998; Lyon, 1995). Dyslexia is an unexpected difficulty in learning to read characterized by difficulties in learning to recognize letters, subsequent problems in pronouncing words out of sentence context, and persistent difficulties in fluent oral reading and spelling (Berninger, 2000; Raskind, 2001). Children who fail to learn to read by the first grade tend to fall farther and farther behind their peers, not only in reading but in general academic achievement as well. For example, longitudinal studies have found that 74% of children who are diagnosed as learning disabled because of reading problems remain disabled in the ninth grade (Fletcher et al., 1994; Stanovich & Siegel, 1994).

Recent research has begun to reveal a great deal about the fundamental nature of children's reading disabilities and the type of instruction most likely to prevent and remediate reading problems (Jenkins & O'Conner, 2001; National Reading Panel, 2000; Smith, Baker, & Oudeans, 2001; Wolf, Miller, & Donnelly, 2000). In summarizing this research, Torgesen and Wagner (1998) state that (1) the "most severe reading problems of children with learning disabilities lie at the word, rather than the text, level of processing" (i.e., inability to accurately and fluently decode single words), and (2) the most common cognitive limitation of these children involves a dysfunction in the awareness of the phonological structure of words in oral language (p. 226).

Recent research suggests that children with severe reading disabilities, particularly those who are resistant to interventions effective for the majority of struggling readers, may share a second processing problem in addition to deficits in phonological awareness. Many children and adults with dyslexia show a significant deficit in *visual naming speed* (the ability to rapidly name visually presented stimuli) compared to a typical reader (Lovett, Steinbach,

Dyslexia/reading disabilities

Council for Exceptional Children — Content Standards for Beginning Teachers–Common Core: Educational implications of characteristics of various exceptionalities (CC2K2).
PRAXIS Special Education Core Principles: Content Knowledge: I. Understanding Exceptionalities, Characteristics of students with disabilities, Cognitive factors.

Phonological awareness

Council for Exceptional Children — Content Standards for Beginning Teachers of Students with LD: Effects of phonological awareness on the reading abilities of individuals with LD (LD3K2).
PRAXIS Special Education Core Principles: Content Knowledge: I. Understanding Exceptionalities, Characteristics of students with disabilities, Cognitive factors.

& Frijters, 2000; Wolf, Bowers, & Biddle, 2000). When asked to state the names of visually presented material such as letters, many individuals with reading disabilities have difficulty rapidly retrieving and stating the names of the letters, even though they know the letter names. The term *double deficit hypothesis* is used to describe children who exhibit underlying deficits in phonological awareness and rapid naming speed (Wolf & Bowers, 2000).

Of course, comprehension is the goal of reading. And comprehension lies at the phrase, sentence, paragraph, and story level, not in identifying single words. But the inability to rapidly identify words impairs comprehension in at least two ways. First, faster readers encounter more words and idea units, thereby having the opportunity to comprehend more. Second, assuming that both word recognition and comprehension consume finite cognitive processing resources, a struggling reader who devotes more processing resources to identify words has "fewer cognitive processing resources . . . available for comprehension. The less efficient word reading of students with reading disabilities overloads working memory and undermines reading comprehension" (Jenkins & O'Conner, 2001, pp. 1–2). (To learn what research tells us about how to prevent reading disabilities in young children, see Teaching & Learning, "Six Principles for Early Reading Instruction," later in this chapter.)

Reading is the most common academic problem experienced by students with learning disabilities.

Comprehension and beginning reading instruction

Council for Exceptional Children   Content Standards for Beginning Teachers of Students with LD: Relationships among reading instruction methods and LD (LD7K1) (also LD3K3). **PRAXIS** Special Education Core Principles: Content Knowledge: III. Delivery of Services to Students with Disabilities, Curriculum and instruction, Language and literacy acquisition.

Written language deficits

Council for Exceptional Children   Content Standards for Beginning Teachers Common Core: Educational implications of characteristics of various exceptionalities (CC2K2) (also LD3K3). **PRAXIS** Special Education Core Principles: Content Knowledge: I. Understanding Exceptionalities, Characteristics of students with Disabilities.

 WRITTEN LANGUAGE DEFICITS

Many students with learning disabilities have problems with writing and spelling. When compared to their peers without disabilities, students with learning disabilities perform significantly lower across most written expression tasks, especially vocabulary, grammar, punctuation, and spelling (Newcomer & Barenbaum, 1991). Some students have a specific disability with written language. For example, Table 7.1 shows the story written by a 10-year-old student when shown an illustration of prehistoric cavemen. Sean's oral reading of his story reveals a huge disparity between his written and oral language abilities.

Compounding the weak language base that many students with learning disabilities bring to the writing task is an approach to the writing process that involves minimal planning, effort, and metacognitive control (Englert et al., 1991; Graham & Harris, 1993). Many of these students use a "retrieve-and-write" approach in which they retrieve from immediate memory "whatever seems appropriate and write it down" (De La Paz & Graham, 1997, p. 295). They seldom use the self-regulation and self-assessment strategies of competent writers: setting a goal or plan to guide their writing, organizing their ideas, drafting, self-assessing, and rewriting. As a result, they produce poorly organized compositions containing a few poorly developed ideas (Sexton, Harris, & Graham, 1998).

TABLE 7.1 **Written language sample from a 10-year-old student with learning disabilities**

Sean's Written Story	Sean's Oral Reading of His Story
A loge tine ago they atene a cosnen they head to geatthere on fesee o One day tere were sane evesedbeats all gaseraned tesene in cladesn they hard a fest for 2 meanes.	A long time ago there were ancient cave men. They had to get their own food. One day there were some wildebeests. They all gathered them and killed them. They had a feast for two months.

Source: Courtesy of Timothy E. Heron, The Ohio State University.

FIGURE 7.1 Journal entries written by a seventh-grade student with learning disabilities—Before and after

November 21
Prompt: Describe your idea of the "ideal" thanksgiving dinner

MY FAVORITE FOOD IS A GRILL HOG IN A PUMPKIN IN A ROAST HAM IN A MAYBE A TURKEY my favorite DESSERT food strawberry pie THE END

February 27
Prompt: Describe your favorite clock

The clock that I have it is very old it was the first clock that my grandpa had it run off of current and it might go to the time it will go off in a little bird will comes at of the box. The box look like a house in it has a to pendulums on the bottom of the house inside of the house it has people in it. On the otside it has to door on it in it has to windows the color is color is brown on the top of the clock it is black.

Source: From Williams, S. C. (2002). How speech-feedback and word-prediction software can help students write. *Teaching Exceptional Children, 34*(3), 76. Used by permission.

Fortunately, the writing and spelling skills of most students with learning disabilities can be improved through strategy instruction, frequent opportunities to practice writing, and systematic feedback (Goddard & Heron, 1998; Graham, Harris, & Larsen, 2001; Heward, Heron, Gardner, & Prayzer, 1991; Marchisan & Alber, 2001; Williams, 2002). For example, Figure 7.1 shows the improvements in the writing of a seventh grader with learning disabilities after instruction and practice with software programs with speech feedback and word prediction components (Johnston, 1994a, 1994b).

 MATH UNDERACHIEVEMENT

Numerical reasoning and calculation pose major problems for many students with learning disabilities. Students with learning disabilities perform lower than normally achieving children with every type of arithmetic problem at every grade level (Cawley, Parmar, Foley, Salmon, & Roy, 2001). Deficits in retrieving number facts and solving story problems are particularly evident (Jordan & Hanich, 2000; Ostad, 1998). The math competence of students with learning disabilities progresses about 1 year for every 2 years in school, and the skills of many children plateau by age 10 or 12 (Cawley, Parmar, Yan, & Miller, 1998).

Given these difficulties, it is not surprising that more than 50% of students with learning disabilities have IEP goals in math (Kavale & Reese, 1992). As with reading and writing, explicit, systematic instruction that provides guided, meaningful practice with feedback usually improves the math performance of students with learning disabilities (e.g., Fuchs & Fuchs, 2001; Gagnon & Maccini, 2001; Maccini & Ruhl, 2000; Marsh & Cooke, 1996).

Caitlin's daily session at the computer in the "writing room" is spent practicing, self-evaluating, and self-editing the specific writing skills she needs to master.

 SOCIAL SKILLS DEFICITS

After reviewing 152 different studies, Kavale and Forness (1996) concluded that about 75% of students

Six Principles for Early Reading Instruction

by Bonnie Grossen

Extensive research by the National Institute of Child Health and Human Development (NICHD) over the past 30 years has produced more than 2,000 peer-reviewed journal articles about early reading acquisition and reading difficulties. (See Lyon [1995] and National Reading Panel [2000] for a review.) Six key principles of effective beginning reading instruction can be derived from this growing body of highly replicable scientific findings.

1. *Begin teaching phonemic awareness directly in kindergarten.* Phonemes are the individual sounds in words that make a difference in meaning if changed. Many children and adults who cannot read are not aware of phonemes. Children and adults who can read are aware of phonemes. A child is phonemically aware if she can do some of these things (Simmons, Kame'enui, Coyne, & Chard, 2002):

- *Phoneme deletion.* What word would be left if the /k/ sound were taken away from "cat"?
- *Word-to-word matching.* Do "pen" and "pipe" begin with the same sound?
- *Blending.* What word would we have if you put these sounds together: /s/, /a/, /t/?
- *Sound isolation.* What is the first sound in "rose"?
- *Phoneme segmentation.* What sounds do you hear in the word "hot"?
- *Phoneme counting.* How many sounds do you hear in the word "cake"?
- *Odd word out.* What word starts with a different sound: "bag," "nine," "beach," "bike"?
- *Sound-to-word matching.* Is there a /k/ sound in "bike"?

If phonemic awareness does not develop by age 5 or 6, it is unlikely to develop later without instruction. In other words, don't wait for this crucial reading readiness skill to develop. Phonemic awareness activities such as rhyming games have a positive effect on reading acquisition and spelling for nonreaders. Teachers should start teaching phonemic awareness before beginning instruction in letter-phoneme relationships and continue phonemic awareness activities while teaching the letter-phoneme relationships.

2. *Teach each letter-phoneme relationship explicitly.* Only about 40 to 50 letter-sound relationships are necessary to read. Figure A shows the 48 most regular letter-phoneme relationships. Telling children explicitly what single sound a given letter or letter combination makes prevents reading problems better than encouraging children to figure out the sounds for the letters by giving clues. Many children have difficulty figuring out the individual letter-phoneme correspondences if they hear them only in the context of words and word parts. Therefore, phonemes should be separated from words for instruction. For example, the teacher shows the children the letter "m" and says, "This letter says /mmm/."

A new phoneme and other phonemes the children have learned should be practiced for about 5 minutes each day in isolation. The rest of the lesson should use these phonemes in words and stories composed of only the letter-phoneme relationships the children have learned in isolation up to that point.

3. *Teach frequent, highly regular letter-sound relationships systematically.* To teach systematically means coordinating the introduction of the letter-phoneme relationships with the material the children are asked to read. The words and stories should be composed of only the letter-phoneme relationships the children have learned. The order of the introduction of letter-phoneme relationships should be planned to allow reading material composed of meaningful words and stories as soon as possible. For example, if the first three letter-phoneme relationships the children learn are /a/, /b/, /c/, the only real word the children can read

a as in "fat"	i as in "sit"	r	er as in "fern"
g as in "goat"	c as in "cat"	o-e as in "pole"	qu as in "quick"
v	w as in "well"	z	ai as in "maid"
m	f	ch as in "chip"	ay as in "hay"
l	b	ou as in "cloud"	sh as in "shop"
e	j	kn as in "know"	ar as in "car"
t	a-e as in "cake"	ea as in "beat"	igh as in "high"
h	n	oy as in "toy"	th as in "thank"
u-e as in "use"	i-e as in "pipe"	oa as in "boat"	au as in "haul"
s	d	ee as in "need"	ew as in "shrewd"
u	k	ph as in "phone"	ir as in "first"
p	y as in "yuck"	oi as in "boil"	aw as in "lawn"

is "cab." But if the first three letter-phoneme relationships are /m/, /a/, /s/, the children can read "am," "Sam," "mass," "ma'am."

4. *Show children exactly how to sound out words.* After children have learned two or three letter-phoneme relationships, teach them how to blend the sounds into words. Show them how to move sequentially from left to right through spellings as they sound out each word. Every day practice blending words composed of only the letter-phoneme relationships the children have learned.

5. *Give children connected, decodable text to practice the letter-phoneme relationships.* Children need extensive practice applying their knowledge of letter-sound relationships to reading. The most effective integration of phonics and reading occurs with *decodable text*—text composed of words that use the letter-phoneme relationships the children have learned to that point and a limited number of sight words that have been systematically taught. As the children learn more letter-phoneme relationships, the texts become more sophisticated.

Texts that are less decodable do not integrate phonological knowledge with actual reading. For example, the first sentence children read in one meaning-based program with an unintegrated phonics component was "The dog is up." The sound-letter relationships the children had learned up to this point were /d/, /m/, /s/, /r/, /t/. By applying their phonics knowledge, the children could only read "_____ d_____ _____ _____." But if children have learned /a/, /s/, /m/, /b/, /t/, /h/, /f/, /g/, /i/, they can read "Sam has a big fist." The sentence is 100% decodable because the phonics component has been integrated properly into the child's real reading.

Text that is less decodable requires children to use prediction or context to figure out words. Although prediction is valuable in comprehension for predicting

the next event or predicting an outcome, research indicates that it is not useful in word recognition. Consider the following sample of authentic text by Jack London. One child was able to decode approximately 80% of the text; the parts he was unable to decode accurately are omitted.

> He had never seen dogs fight as these w_____ish c_____ f_____t, and his first ex_____ t_____t him an unf_____able l_____n. It is true, it was a vi_____ ex_____, else he would not have lived to pr_____it by it. Curly was the v_____. They were camped near the log store, where she, in her friend_____ way, made ad_____ to a husky dog the size of a full-_____ wolf, th_____ not half so large as _____he. _____ere was no w_____ing, only a leap in like a flash, a met_____ clip of teeth, a leap out equal_____ swift, and Curly's face was ripped open from eye to jaw.

The use of predictable text rather than decodable text might allow children to use prediction to figure out a passage. However, the strategy would not transfer to real reading, as the London passage demonstrates. Predictable text gives children false success. While such success may motivate many children, ultimately they will not be successful readers if they rely on text predictability to read.

6. *Use interesting stories to develop language comprehension.* Research does not rule out the use of interesting, authentic stories to develop language comprehension. But it does recommend not using these stories as reading material for nonreaders. Teacher-read stories play an important role in building children's oral language comprehension, which ultimately affects their reading comprehension. Story-based activities should be structured to build comprehension skills, not decoding skills.

continues

The systematic integration of phonics and reading can occur only with decodable text.

Using real stories to develop comprehension should be balanced with the decoding instruction described in the first five principles. While children are learning to decode, instruction for comprehension and instruction for decoding should be conducted separately; but both types of instruction should occur. In other words, balance but don't mix. A common misconception is that the teacher should embed instruction of letter-phoneme relationships in the context of real stories. This mixture of decoding and comprehension instruction in the same instructional activity is clearly less effective, even when the decoding instruction is fairly structured (Foorman, Francis, Fletcher, Schatschneider, & Mehta, 1998; Torgesen, Wagner, & Rashotte, 1997).

During the early stages of reading acquisition, children's oral language comprehension level is much higher than their reading comprehension level. The stories teachers read to children to build their comprehension should be geared to their oral language comprehension level. The material used to build children's decoding should be geared to their decoding skills, with attention to meaning. Although decodable text can be meaningful and engaging, it will not build children's comprehension skills or teach them new vocabulary to the extent that might be needed. Comprehension strategies and new vocabulary should be taught using orally presented stories and texts that are more sophisticated than the early decodable text the children read. The teacher should read these stories to the children and discuss the meaning with them. After the children become fluent decoders, they can apply these comprehension strategies to their own reading.

Bonnie Grossen is a research associate at the University of Oregon. Her interests include identifying the best interventions for solving educational problems, especially in the areas of reading and science instruction, critical thinking, and problem solving for diverse learners.

Social, attention, and behavioral problems

Council for Exceptional Children Content Standards for Beginning Teachers of Students with LD: Psychological, social, and emotional characteristics of individuals with LD (LD2K3) (also CC2K2).
PRAXIS Special Education Core Principles: Content Knowledge: I. Understanding Exceptionalities, Characteristics of students with disabilities, Affective and social-adaptive factors.

with learning disabilities exhibit deficits in social skills. Poor social skills often lead to rejection, low social status, fewer positive interactions with teachers, difficulty making friends, and loneliness—all of which are experienced by many students with learning disabilities regardless of classroom placement (Haager & Vaughn, 1995; Ochoa & Palmer, 1995; Pavri & Monda-Amaya, 2000). The poor social skills of students with learning disabilities may be due to inability to perceive emotions of others, specifically nonverbal affective expressions (Most & Greenbank, 2000).

Some students with learning disabilities, however, experience no problems getting along with their peers and teachers. For example, Sabornie and Kauffman (1986) reported no significant difference in the sociometric standing of 46 learning disabled high school students and 46 peers without disabilities. Moreover, they discovered that some of the students with learning disabilities enjoyed socially rewarding experiences in inclusive classrooms.

One interpretation of these contradictory findings is that social competence and peer acceptance are not characteristics of learning disabilities but outcomes of the different social climates created by teachers, peers, parents, and others with whom students with learning disabilities interact (Vaughn, McIntosh, Schumm, Haager, & Callwood, 1993). Researchers have begun to identify the types of problems experienced by children with learning disabilities who are ranked low in social acceptance and to discover instructional arrangements that promote the social status of students with learning disabilities in the regular classroom (Bryan, 1997; Vaughn, Elbaum, & Schumm, 1996).

ATTENTION PROBLEMS AND HYPERACTIVITY

Some students with learning disabilities have difficulty attending to a task and/or display high rates of purposeless movement (hyperactivity). Children who consistently exhibit this combination of behavioral traits may be diagnosed as having *attention-deficit/hyperactivity disorder (ADHD)*. ADHD is described in some detail later in this chapter.

 BEHAVIORAL PROBLEMS

Some students with learning disabilities display behavioral problems in the classroom. Research has consistently found a higher-than-normal rate of behavioral problems among students with learning disabilities (Cullinan, 2002). In a study of 790 students enrolled in K–12 learning disabilities programs in Indiana, the percentage of students with behavioral problems (15%) remained consistent across grade levels (McLeskey, 1992). Although these data definitely show increased behavioral problems among children with learning disabilities, the relationships between the students' behavior problems and academic difficulties are not known. In other words, we do not know whether the academic deficits or the behavioral problems cause the other difficulty. And it is important to note that many children with learning disabilities exhibit no behavioral problems at all.

Regardless of the interrelationships of these characteristics, teachers and other caregivers responsible for planning educational programs for students with learning disabilities need skills in dealing with social and behavioral difficulties as well as academic deficits. Some of these important teaching skills are described in Chapter 8.

 THE DEFINING CHARACTERISTIC

Although students who receive special education under the learning disabilities category are an extremely heterogeneous group, it is important to remember that the fundamental, defining characteristic of students with learning disabilities is *specific and significant achievement deficits in the presence of adequate overall intelligence.*

Figure 7.2 compares the achievement of students with learning disabilities to the expected rate of acquiring 1 year's worth of knowledge and skills for each year in school. The difference between what students with learning disabilities "are expected to do and what they can do . . . grows larger and larger" over time (Deshler, Schumaker, Lenz , 2001, p. 97). The performance gap becomes especially noticeable and handicapping in the middle and secondary grades, when the academic growth of many students with disabilities plateaus. By the time they reach high school, students with learning disabilities are the lowest of the low achievers, performing below the 10th percentile in reading, written language, and math (Hock, Schumaker, & Deshler, 1999).

The difficulties experienced by children with learning disabilities—especially for those who cannot read at grade level—are substantial and pervasive and usually last across the life span (Mercer, 1997). The tendency to think of learning disabilities as a "mild" disability erroneously supports "the notion that a learning disability is little more than a minor inconvenience rather than the serious, life-long condition it often is detracts from the real needs of these students" (Hallahan, 1998, p. 4).

Academic achievement of students with LD

 Council for Exceptional Children | Content Standards for Beginning Teachers–Common Core: Educational implications of characteristics of various exceptionalities (CC2K2) (also LD3K3).
PRAXIS Special Education Core Principles: Content Knowledge: I. Understanding Exceptionalities, Characteristics of students with disabilities.

 ## ATTENTION-DEFICIT/HYPERACTIVITY DISORDER

All children have difficulty attending at times (attention deficit) and all children sometimes engage in high rates of purposeless or inappropriate movement (hyperactivity). Children who consistently exhibit this combination of behavioral traits may be diagnosed with **attention-**

FIGURE 7.2
Performance gap between students with learning disabilities and expected acquisition of knowledge and skills

Source: Adapted from Deshler, D. D., Schumaker, J. B., Lenz, B. K., et al. (2001). Ensuring content-area learning by secondary students with learning disabilities. *Learning Disabilities Research and Practice, 16,* 97. Reprinted by permission.

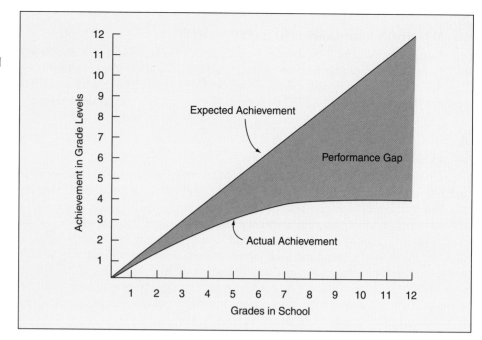

Expected Achievement

Performance Gap

Actual Achievement

Achievement in Grade Levels

Grades in School

deficit/hyperactivity disorder (ADHD). In many respects, ADHD reflects "either too much (e.g., fidgeting) or not enough (e.g., lack of impulse control or attention) of what adults expect in certain settings" (Goldstein & Goldstein, 1998, pp. 4–5). Children with ADHD present a difficult challenge to their families, teachers, and classmates. Their inability to stay on task, impulsive behavior, and fidgeting impair their ability to learn and increase the likelihood of unsatisfactory interactions with others.

Wolraich's (1999) contention that ADHD "has the distinction of being both the most extensively studied mental disorder and the most controversial" (p. 163) suggests that the condition is both well known and little understood (Bicard, 2000). Although the last decade of the 20th century witnessed an explosion of interest in ADHD, historical references to the symptoms that are diagnosed as ADHD today suggest that such children have been with us for centuries (Barkley, 1998; Conners, 2000; Goldstein & Goldstein, 1998). The first published account of the disorder in the medical or scientific literature appeared in 1902 when British physician George Still described Still's disease. Still believed that children who were restless and exhibited problems maintaining attention suffered from a "defect of moral control" that he presumed to be the result of brain injury or dysfunction. Over the years, a variety of terms has been used to refer to this combination of behavioral symptoms: *postencephalitic disorder* in the 1920s, *brain damage syndrome* in the 1940s, *minimal brain dysfunction* in the 1960s, and *hyperkinetic impulse disorder of children* in the 1970s (Mather & Goldstein, 2001). Because medical science has found no clear-cut evidence of brain damage, emphasis in defining and diagnosing the condition has focused and relied on the description and identification of a combination of behavioral symptoms.

Historical background of LD

 Council for Exceptional Children Content Standards for Beginning Teachers of Students with LD: Historical foundations, classical studies, and major contributors in the field of LD (LD1K1).

Definition of ADHD

Council for Exceptional Children Content Standards for Beginning Teachers–Common Core: Issues in definition and identification of individuals with exceptional learning needs (CC1K5).
PRAXIS Special Education Core Principles: Content Knowledge: I. Understanding Exceptionalities, Definitions of disabilities.

DEFINITION AND DIAGNOSIS

The symptoms of ADHD occur in two broad dimensions: those indicative of faulty attention and those related to hyperactivity and impulsivity. Symptoms of hyperactivity and impulsivity tend to occur together with high frequency. With regard to predicting future functioning, however, "the greater the degree of reported impulsive behavior, the more problems in the classroom and later life. Thus, it has been increasingly hypothesized that the core impairment in ADHD represents faulty inhibition or self-control, leading to a constellation of related symptoms" (Mather & Goldstein, 2001, p. 49).

FIGURE 7.3 Diagnostic criteria for attention-deficit/hyperactivity disorder (ADHD)

A. Either (1) or (2):
   1. Six (or more) of the following symptoms of *inattention* have persisted for at least 6 months to a degree that is maladaptive and inconsistent with developmental level:
   Inattention
     a. Often fails to give close attention to details or makes careless mistakes in schoolwork, work, or other activities.
     b. Often has difficulty sustaining attention in tasks or play activities.
     c. Often does not seem to listen when spoken to directly.
     d. Often does not follow through on instructions and fails to finish schoolwork, chores, or duties in the workplace (not due to oppositional behavior or failure to understand instructions).
     e. Often has difficulty organizing tasks and activities.
     f. Often avoids, dislikes, or is reluctant to engage in tasks that require sustained mental effort (such as schoolwork or homework).
     g. Often loses things necessary for tasks or activities (e.g., toys, school assignments, pencils, books, or tools).
     h. Is often easily distracted by extraneous stimuli.
     i. Is often forgetful in daily activities.
   2. Six (or more) of the following symptoms of *hyperactivity–impulsivity* have persisted for at least 6 months to a degree that is maladaptive and inconsistent with developmental level:
   Hyperactivity
     a. Often fidgets with hands or feet or squirms in seat.
     b. Often leaves seat in classroom or in other situations in which remaining seated is expected.
     c. Often runs about or climbs excessively in situations in which it is inappropriate (in adolescents or adults, may be limited to subjective feelings of restlessness).
     d. Often has difficulty playing or engaging in leisure activities quietly.
     e. Is often "on the go" or often acts as if "driven by a motor."
     f. Often talks excessively.
   Impulsivity
     g. Often blurts out answers before questions have been completed.
     h. Often has difficulty awaiting turn.
     i. Often interrupts or intrudes on others (e.g., butts into conversations or games).
B. Some hyperactive–impulsive or inattentive symptoms that caused impairment were presented before age 7 years.
C. Some impairment from the symptoms is present in two or more settings (e.g., at school [or work] and at home).
D. There must be clear evidence of clinically significant impairment in social, academic, or occupational functioning.
E. The symptoms do not occur exclusively during the course of pervasive developmental disorder, schizophrenia, or other psychotic disorder and are not better accounted for by another mental disorder (e.g., mood disorder, anxiety disorder, dissociative disorder, or a personality disorder).
Code based on type:
Attention-Deficit/Hyperactivity Disorder, Combined Type: if both Criteria A1 and A2 are met for the past 6 months.
Attention-Deficit/Hyperactivity Disorder, Predominantly Inattentive Type: if Criterion A1 is met but Criterion A2 is not met for the past 6 months.
Attention-Deficit/Hyperactivity Disorder, Predominantly Hyperactive–Impulsive Type: if Criterion A2 is met but Criterion A1 is not met for the past 6 months.
Coding note: For individuals (especially adolescents and adults) who currently have symptoms that no longer meet full criteria, "In Partial Remission" should be specified.

Source: Reprinted from American Psychiatric Association. (2000). *Diagnostic and statistical manual of mental disorders* (4th ed., Text Revision, pp. 92–93). Washington, DC: Author.

Children are diagnosed as having ADHD according to criteria found in the *Diagnostic and Statistical Manual of Mental Disorders* (DSM-IV-TR) (American Psychiatric Association, 2000). "The essential feature of attention-deficit/hyperactivity disorder is a persistent pattern of inattention and/or hyperactivity-impulsivity that is more frequent and severe than is typically observed in individuals at a comparable level of development" (p. 85). To diagnose ADHD, a physician must determine that a child consistently displays six or more symptoms of either inattention or hyperactivity-impulsivity for a period of at least six months (see Figure 7.3).

The diagnosing physician assigns one of three sub-types of ADHD, depending on a child's constellation of symptoms: ADHD, combined type; ADHD, predominantly inattentive type; and ADHD, predominantly hyperactive-impulsive type. Approximately half of the children tested for ADHD are diagnosed with the combined type, 30% the inattentive type, and 20% the hyperactive-impulsive type (Lahey et al., 1994).

The diagnostic criteria for ADHD are diverse and subjective. For example, what is the basis for deciding whether a child is "often 'on the go'"? And how can one determine that a child who avoids or dislikes schoolwork or homework does so because of an attention deficit as opposed to one of many other possible reasons? A child who is diagnosed by one physician as not having ADHD may very well be diagnosed as having it by another. Parents have been known to engage in "physician shopping," taking their child from one doctor to another until a diagnosis of ADHD is made (Reid, Maag, & Vasa, 1994). After their review of 48 articles and books on ADHD written by leading authorities revealed that 69 characteristics and 38 different causes of ADHD were proposed, Goodman and Poillion (1992) concluded that ADD was an acronym for "Any Dysfunction or Difficulty" (p. 37).

ACADEMIC ACHIEVEMENT AND COMORBIDITY WITH OTHER DISABILITIES

Most children with ADHD struggle in the classroom. They score lower than do their age-mates on IQ and achievement tests, more than half require remedial tutoring for basic skills, and about 30% repeat one or more grades (Barkley, 1998). A considerable percentage of children with ADHD—25% to 50%—are also identified as having a learning disability, depending on the school district (Shelton & Barkley, 1994). Two studies found that 15% and 26% of children with learning disabilities also were diagnosed with ADHD (Gilger, Pennington, & DeFries, 1992; Shaywitz, Fletcher, & Shaywitz, 1995).

However, it is important to stress that ADHD is not the same as a learning disability. Although some children with learning disabilities are inattentive, hyperactive, and impulsive, many are calm and work diligently at learning tasks. Many children without learning disabilities also have trouble attending and sitting still. Likewise, some children who display impulsivity, inattention, and/or hyperactivity do well in school.

Many children with ADHD experience serious emotional and behavioral problems. About 60% of adolescents with ADHD develop at least one additional behavioral problem (Barkley, Fischer, Barkley, Edelbrock, & Smallish, 1990). Forness and Kavale (in press) estimate that 43% of children receiving special education for emotional and behavioral disorders have a diagnosis of ADHD. Many students who are identified with emotional and behavioral disorders are also diagnosed with ADHD. A statewide survey in Wisconsin found that 40% of elementary school, 32% of middle school, and 25% of secondary students with emotional and behavioral disorders were taking medications for ADHD (Runnheim, Frankenberger, & Hazelkorn, 1996). In another study, approximately one fourth of a large sample of juvenile offenders reported they had been diagnosed with and received medication for ADHD (Zabel & Nigro, 1999).

ELIGIBILITY FOR SPECIAL EDUCATION

ADHD is not a disability category recognized by IDEA; however, it is estimated that more than one half of children with ADHD receive special education (Reid & Maag, 1998). A large proportion of students with ADHD are served under the learning disabilities and emotional and behavioral disorders categories. Students with ADHD can be served under the other health impairments category if the outcome of the disorder is a "heightened alertness to environmental stimuli that results in limited alertness with respect to the educational environment" that adversely affects academic performance (U.S. Department of Education, 1999, p. 12422).

Many children with ADHD who are not served under IDEA are eligible for services under Section 504 of the Rehabilitation Act. As discussed in Chapter 1, Section 504 is a civil rights law that provides certain protections for persons with disabilities. Under Section 504, schools may be required to develop and implement accommodation plans designed to help students with ADHD succeed in the general education classroom. Accommodation plans often include such adaptations and adjustments as extended time on tests, preferred seating, additional teacher monitoring, reduced or modified class or

Achievement of students with ADHD and comorbidity with LD and E/BD

 Council for Exceptional Children   Content Standards for Beginning Teachers–Common Core: Educational implications of characteristics of various exceptionalities (CC2K2) (also LD3K1).
PRAXIS Special Education Core Principles: Content Knowledge: I. Understanding Exceptionalities, Characteristics of students with disabilities.

ADHD and eligibility for special education

Council for Exceptional Children   Content Standards for Beginning Teachers–Common Core: Issues, assurances, and due process rights related to assessment, eligibility, and placement within a continuum of services (CC1K6).
PRAXIS Special Education Core Principles: Content Knowledge: II. Legal and Societal Issues, Public Law 105–97 (IDEA '97) and Section 504.

homework assignments and worksheets, and monitoring the effects of medication on the child's behavior in school.

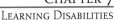

CHAPTER 7
LEARNING DISABILITIES

 PREVALENCE

The most frequently cited estimate of the prevalence of ADHD is 3% to 5% of all school-age children (American Psychiatric Association, 2000). A random national sample of family pediatricians found that 5.3% of all elementary students screened received a diagnosis of ADHD (Wolraich et al., 1990). These figures suggest that the typical classroom will have one or two children either diagnosed as ADHD or presenting the problems typically associated with ADHD.

Child count data reported by the states reveals a large increase in the numbers of students served under IDEA's other health impairments category since the federal government stipulated that students with ADHD were eligible under that disability category. Some states reported increases of 20% in the number of children served under the other health impairments category between the 1997–1998 and 1998–1999 school year (U.S. Department of Education, 2000). Nationwide, the number of children served in the other health impairments category increased more than 400% from 1989–1990 to 2000–2001, by far the biggest proportional increase of any disability category (U.S. Department of Education, 2002).

Boys are 3 to 10 times more likely to be diagnosed with ADHD than are girls, with the ratio being higher at younger ages (American Psychiatric Association, 2000; Barkley, 1998).

 CAUSES

In most cases, the specific causes of the inattention and hyperactivity-impulsivity that lead to a child's diagnosis of ADHD are not known. Although many view ADHD as primarily a biologically based disorder, clear and consistent causal evidence linking brain damage or dysfunction and behavioral symptoms of ADHD has not been found. However, there is growing evidence of genetic factors that may place individuals at a greater than normal risk of an ADHD diagnosis (Edelbrock, Rende, Plomin, & Thompson, 1995). Genetics may provide certain risk or resilience factors, and then environmental influences (i.e., life experiences) determine whether an individual receives a diagnosis of ADHD (Goldstein & Goldstein, 1998).

ADHD is associated with a wide range of genetic disorders and diseases. For example, individuals with Fragile X syndrome, Turner syndrome, and Williams syndrome (see Chapter 6) frequently have attention and impulsivity problems. Symptoms of ADHD are also associated with conditions such as fetal alcohol syndrome, prenatal exposure to cocaine, and lead poisoning.

Also, a growing body of research using neuroimaging technologies shows that some individuals with ADHD have structural or biochemical differences in their brains (e.g., Berquin et al., 1998; Filipek et al., 1997). But not all individuals diagnosed with ADHD have brains that appear different from those of individuals without ADHD. And some people without ADHD have brain structures similar to those with ADHD. It is possible that biochemical differences in the brains of children with ADHD may play a causal role in their behavioral deficits and excesses (e.g., Ernst, Cohen, Liebenauer, Jons, & Zametkin, 1997).

The causes of ADHD are not well understood. It is very possible, if not nearly certain, that behaviors leading to the diagnoses of ADHD in two different children will be caused by completely different factors or sets of factors (Maag & Reid, 1994; Goldstein & Goldstein, 1998; Gresham, 2002). It is also possible that different causal factors influence a child's inattention and/or impulsivity in different situations or environments. A full understanding of those causal factors may be necessary for interventions to be optimal and have long-lasting effects.

 TREATMENT

Drug therapy and behaviorally based interventions are the two most widely used treatment approaches used with children with ADHD.

Prevalence of ADHD

PRAXIS Special Education Core Principles: Content Knowledge: I. Understanding Exceptionalities, Incidence and prevalence of various types of disabilities.

Causes of ADHD

Council for Exceptional Children Content Standards for Beginning Teachers of Students with LD: Etiologies of LD (LD2K1).
PRAXIS Special Education Core Principles: Content Knowledge: I. Understanding Exceptionalities, Causation and prevention of disability.

Council for Exceptional Children **Content Standards for Beginning Teachers–Common Core:** Effects of various medications on individuals with exceptional learning needs (CC2K7). **PRAXIS Special Education Core Principles: Content Knowledge:** I. Understanding Exceptionalities, Characteristics of students with disabilities, Medical factors.

Drug Therapy   Prescription stimulant medication is the most common intervention for children with ADHD. Methylphenidate, sold under the trade name Ritalin, is the most frequently prescribed medication for ADHD. Other stimulants such as dextroamphetamine sulfate (Adderall), methamphetamine hydrochloride (Desoxyn), dextroamphetamine (Dexedrine), and pemoline (Cylert) are also prescribed.

The number of children on stimulant medication increased tremendously in the 1990s. An estimated 700,000 children received medication for ADHD in the late 1980s. By 1995 the number had more than doubled to 1.6 million children (Safer, Zito, & Fine, 1996). In 2000 it was estimated that more than 3 million school children in the United States were receiving drug treatment for ADHD (Jensen, 2000). Diller (1998) reports that sales of Ritalin for children in the United States account for 90% of the worldwide consumption of the drug, and the production of Ritalin has increased 700% since 1990.

Why are stimulant medications prescribed so frequently for children with ADHD? Undoubtedly, there are many reasons, but two factors seem certain. First, there are many children whose hyperactivity and impulsivity are troublesome to their parents and teachers. Second, many children with ADHD show marked improvements in behavior when taking stimulant medication.

Reviews of controlled studies show that 70% to 80% of children diagnosed with ADHD respond positively to Ritalin (Barkley, 1998, Swanson, McBurnett, Christain, & Wigal, 1995), at least in the short term. A positive response typically includes a reduction in hyperactivity, increased attention and time on task, better academic productivity, and improvements in general conduct.

Although teachers and parents generally report favorable outcomes for children taking stimulant medication, common side effects include insomnia, decreased appetite, headaches, weight loss, and irritability. These side effects are usually of short duration and can often be controlled with a reduction in dosage (Goldstein & Goldstein, 1998).

Additional problems have been reported with children not taking their medication as prescribed, trying to catch up on missed pills by taking too many pills at once, and trading or even selling their medications (Hancock, 1996; Wood & Zabel, 2001).

The popular media have created and nurtured numerous myths about Ritalin such as the following: it builds up in the child's bloodstream, it is addictive and leads to drug abuse later in life, it stunts children's growth, it can cause children to have seizures (Pancheri & Prater, 1999). None of these are supported by scientific research. When prescribed and monitored by a competent physician, Ritalin has proven to be a safe and often effective intervention.

Mather and Goldstein (2001) believe that "the immediate short-term benefits of stimulant medications far outweigh the liabilities and thus appear to justify the continued use of these medications in the treatment of ADHD" (p. 63). And based on their assessment of two meta-analyses of medication studies, Forness, Kavale, Crenshaw, and Sweeney (2000) suggest that it is unwise and could be considered malpractice not to include drug therapy as part of a comprehensive treatment program for children with ADHD.

Some professionals, however, have voiced concerns that the drugs may have little or no long-term benefits on academic achievement and that educators and parents rely too much on medical interventions (Maag & Reid, 1994). They view drug treatment as an inappropriate, easy way out that might produce short-term improvements in behavior but result in long-term harm. "When stimulants work in the short-term, pharmacological intervention may be used as a crutch and may postpone or prevent the use of non-pharmacological interventions, which may be more effective in the long run" (Swanson et al., 1993, p. 158).

It is difficult to predict the effects of stimulant medication on an individual child. Although the majority of children respond positively to stimulants, 20% to 30% show either no response or a negative response (i.e., their symptoms get worse) (Gresham, 2002). A child's response or lack of response to stimulant medication cannot be used as a basis for confirming the ADHD diagnosis (DuPaul & Stoner, 1994). Nor can a child's age, size, or weight be used to determine the optimum dosage in terms of the desired effects on hyperactivity and safety. Direct and daily measurement of a student's performance on academic tasks during alternating drug and placebo conditions is a promising technique for evaluating the effects of the drug and determining appropriate dosage levels (e.g., Northup, Fusilier, Swanson, Roane, & Borrero, 1997; Stoner, Carey, Ikeda, & Shinn, 1994).

Howell, Evans, and Gardiner (1997) provide educators with guidelines for the safe use of stimulant medications in the classroom with optimal benefits. Gadow and Nolan (1993), DuPaul and Stoner (1994), and Goldstein and Goldstein (1998) are excellent sources of information for educators on this important topic.

Behavioral Interventions   The principles and methods of applied behavior analysis, particularly positive reinforcement for on-task behavior, modifying assignments and instructional activities to promote success, and gradually teaching self-control, provide teachers and parents with practical strategies for teaching and living with children with ADHD (Flick, 2000; Goldstein & Goldstein, 1998). Teacher-administered interventions for children with ADHD include restructuring the environment (e.g., seating the child close to the teacher, breaking assignments into small, manageable chunks) and providing differential consequences for child behavior (e.g., positive reinforcement such as praise and tokens for appropriate behavior, ignoring inappropriate behavior, and time out, response cost for inappropriate behavior) (Bicard, 2000; Gordon, Thompson, Cooper, & Ivers, 1991). These and related behavioral strategies for helping children learn adaptive behavior are discussed throughout this text.

An important line of research with major implications for treating children with ADHD is exploring how to teach self-control to children whose learning is adversely affected by impulsivity. A deficit of *executive function,* or the ability to verbally control one's actions, has been hypothesized as being a primary characteristic of children diagnosed with ADHD (Barkley, 1998). According to this hypothesis, children with ADHD would be unlikely candidates for, and perhaps incapable of, learning self-control (Abikoff, 1991). Recent research has demonstrated, however, that children with ADHD can learn to self-regulate their behavior to reduce impulsiveness.

Neef, Bicard, and Endo (2002) demonstrated that children with ADHD can learn self-control when treatment regimes are directly tied to assessment. Results of a recent study demonstrate that children with ADHD can learn to follow rules and describe their own behavior provided they are given clear instructions and consistent reinforcement (Bicard & Neef, in press). Results of these studies and research on self-monitoring (e.g., Huff & DuPaul, 1998) and correspondence training, a procedure in which children are reinforced for "do-say" verbal statements about what they had done previously and "say-do" statements describing what they plan to do (e.g., Paniagua, 1992; Shapiro, DuPaul, & Bradley-King, 1998), show promise for treating children who have ADHD.

PREVALENCE

Learning disabilities is by far the largest of all special education categories. During the 2000–2001 school year, nearly 2.9 million students ages 6 to 21 received special education under the specific learning disabilities category (U.S. Department of Education, 2002). This figure represents one-half of all school-age children with disabilities and means that about 5 of every 100 students in the United States have a learning disability. Males with learning disabilities outnumber females by a 3-to-1 ratio across grade levels.

The number of students identified with learning disabilities has grown tremendously since the passage of IDEA. The current number is nearly triple the number of students with learning disabilities who received special education in 1976–1977, the first year the federal government reported such data. Swanson (2000) notes that the rising incidence of children with learning disabilities might be considered an epidemic. Each year, approximately 120,000 additional students are identified with learning disabilities, a number equal to all Americans who contracted AIDS, hepatitis, and tuberculosis in 1995 (Rousch, 1995).

Many educators are alarmed by the rising prevalence figures for learning disabilities. They believe the ever-increasing numbers of students classified as learning disabled are the result

Behavioral interventions for ADHD

 Council for Exceptional Children   Content Standards for Beginning Teachers–Common Core: Teach individuals to use self-assessment, problem solving, and other cognitive strategies to meet their needs (CC4S2) (also CC5K2). **PRAXIS** Special Education Core Principles: Content Knowledge: III. Delivery of Services to Students with Disabilities, Curriculum and Instruction, Self-management.

Prevalence of LD

PRAXIS Special Education Core Principles: Content Knowledge: I. Understanding Exceptionalities, Incidence and prevalence of various types of disabilities.

of overidentification and misdiagnosis of low-achieving students, which reduces the resources available to serve the students who are truly learning disabled. Some authorities have expressed concern that the concept of learning disabilities is poorly defined and functions as a catch-all category for any student who is experiencing learning problems and does not meet eligibility requirements for other disability categories. For example, Reid Lyon of the National Institute of Child and Human Development suggests that "learning disabilities have become a sociological sponge to wipe up the spills of general education" (cited by Gresham, 2001).

Some authorities, however, believe the current number of students being served as learning disabled may not be a gross overestimate and may be closer to the truth than most people have previously thought. Hallahan (1992) points to the newness of the field of learning disabilities and to societal/cultural changes (e.g., poverty, substance abuse by pregnant women) as two possible reasons for the increase in prevalence figures.

> Exactly what proportion of the increase represents bogus cases of learning disabilities is open for speculation and future research. In the meantime, we should be open to the idea that at least some of the increase represents students who are in very real need of learning disabilities services. (p. 528)

CAUSES

Causes of LD

 Council for Exceptional Children Content Standards for Beginning Teacher of Students with LD: Etiologies of LD (LD2K1).
PRAXIS Special Education Core Principles: Content Knowledge: I. Understanding Exceptionalities, Causation and prevention of disability.

In most cases, the cause (etiology) of a child's learning disability is unknown. Many causes have been proposed, a situation that probably reflects the highly diverse nature of students with learning disabilities. Just as there are different types of learning disabilities (e.g., dyslexia, language disabilities, math disabilities), there are likely to be different causes. Four suspected causal factors are brain damage, heredity, biochemical imbalance, and environmental causes.

BRAIN DAMAGE OR DYSFUNCTION

Some professionals believe that all children with learning disabilities suffer from some type of brain injury or dysfunction of the central nervous system. Indeed, this belief is inherent in the NJCLD definition of learning disabilities, which states that learning disorders are "presumed to be due to central nervous system dysfunction." In cases in which actual evidence of brain damage cannot be shown (and this is the situation with the majority of children with learning disabilities), the term *minimal brain dysfunction* is sometimes used, especially by physicians. This wording implies brain damage by asserting that the child's brain does not function properly.

Neurological bases of LD

 Council for Exceptional Children Content Standards for Beginning Teachers of Students with LD: Neurobiological and medical facors that may impact the learning of individuals with LD (LD2K2).
PRAXIS Special Education Core Principles: Content Knowledge: I. Understanding Exceptionalities, Characteristics of students with disabilities, Medical factors.

Recent advances in magnetic resonance imaging (MRI) technology have enabled researchers to discover that specific regions of the brains of some individuals with reading and language disabilities show activation patterns during phonological processing tasks that are different from the patterns found in the brains of nondisabled individuals (Richards, 2001; Simos, Breier, Fletcher, Bergman, & Papanicolaou, 2000). The actual structure of the brain of some children with reading disabilities is slightly different from that of children without disabilities (Leonard, 2001).

This research holds great promise for understanding the biological bases of dyslexia and other specific learning disabilities. However, as Leonard (2001) points out, we do not yet know how and to what extent the brain's neural networks are affected by the child's experiences (i.e., learning) and vice versa. Thus, we do not know whether neurobiological factors associated with learning disabilities contribute to the learning problems of children, are the product of an unstimulating environment, or a combination. There is also evidence that differences in the ways in which dyslexic and normal children's brains are activated weakens with intensive intervention and treatment (Richards, 2001).

Special educators must beware of placing too much emphasis on theories linking learning disabilities to brain damage or brain dysfunction, for three major reasons. First, not all children with learning disabilities display clinical (medical) evidence of brain damage, and not all children with brain damage have learning disabilities. The second problem is that assuming a child's learning problems are caused by a dysfunctioning brain can serve as a built-in excuse for ineffective instruction. When a student with suspected brain damage fails to learn, his teachers may be quick to presume that the brain injury prevents him from learning and be slow to analyze and change instructional variables. Third, whether "learning disabilities in an individual case are symptoms that result from brain injury or developmental delay will not essentially alter the methods of teaching the student" (Myers & Hammill, 1990, p. 22).

> Current interpretations of the role of constitutional factors show reciprocal relations with the environment, such that environmental factors (e.g., instruction) must be in place to develop the neural networks that support academic skills. Even genetic studies of reading disability show that only about 50 percent of the variability in reading skills can be explained by genetic factors—the remainder is environmental. Learning disabilities represent interplays of constitutional and environmental factors that are not yet well understood. (Fletcher et al., 2001, p. 7)

 HEREDITY

Siblings and children of persons with reading disabilities have a slightly greater than normal likelihood of having reading problems. There is growing evidence that genetics may account for at least some family links with dyslexia (Pennington, 1995; Raskind, 2001). Research has located possible chromosomal loci for the genetic transmission of phonological deficits that may predispose a child for reading problems later (Cardon et al., 1994).

 BIOCHEMICAL IMBALANCE

It was once theorized that biochemical disturbances within a child's body caused learning disabilities. For example, Feingold (1975, 1976) claimed that artificial colorings and flavorings in many of the foods children eat can cause learning disabilities and hyperactivity. He recommended a treatment for learning disabilities that consisted of a diet with no foods containing synthetic colors or flavors. In a comprehensive review of research studies that tested the special diet, Spring and Sandoval (1976) concluded that there was very little scientific evidence to support Feingold's theory. In response to the controversy over diet treatments, the American Council on Science and Health (1979) issued the following statement:

> Hyperactivity will continue to be a frustrating problem until research resolves the questions of its cause, or causes, and develops an effective treatment. The reality is that we still have a great deal to learn about this condition. We do know now, however, that diet is not the answer. It is clear that the symptoms of the vast majority of the children labeled "hyperactive" are not related to salicylates, artificial food colors, or artificial flavors. The Feingold diet creates extra work for homemakers and changes the family lifestyle . . . but it doesn't cure hyperactivity. (p. 5)

It was also suggested that learning disabilities can be caused by the inability of a child's bloodstream to synthesize a normal amount of vitamins (Cott, 1972). Some physicians began megavitamin therapy with children with learning disabilities, which consisted of massive daily doses of vitamins in an effort to overcome the suspected vitamin deficiencies. Two studies designed to test the effects of megavitamin treatment with learning disabled and hyperkinetic children found that huge doses of vitamins did not improve the children's performance (Arnold, Christopher, Huestis, & Smeltzer, 1978; Kershner, Hawks, & Grekin, 1977). Today, most professionals in learning disabilities give little credence to biochemical imbalance as a significant cause of children's learning problems.

ENVIRONMENTAL FACTORS

Although very difficult to document as primary causes of learning disabilities, environmental factors—particularly impoverished living conditions early in a child's life and poor instruction—probably contribute to the achievement deficits experienced by many children in this special education category. The tendency for learning disabilities to run in families suggests a correlation between environmental influences on children's early development and subsequent achievement in school. Evidence for this relationship can be found in longitudinal research such as that conducted by Hart and Risley (1995), who found that infants and toddlers who received infrequent communication exchanges with their parents were more likely to show deficits in vocabulary, language use, and intellectual development before entering school.

Another environmental variable that is likely to contribute to children's learning problems is the quality of instruction they receive. Many special educators today believe that Engelmann (1977) was correct when he claimed more than 25 years ago that the vast majority of "children who are labeled 'learning disabled' exhibit a disability not because of anything wrong with their perception, synapses, or memory, but because they have been seriously mistaught" (pp. 46–47).

Although the relationship between poor instruction and learning disabilities is not clear, there is a great deal of evidence showing that many students' learning problems can be remediated by direct, intensive, and systematic instruction. It would be naïve to think, however, that the achievement problems of all children with learning disabilities are caused entirely by inadequate instruction. Nevertheless, from an educational perspective, intensive, systematic instruction should be the treatment of first choice for all students with learning disabilities.

ASSESSMENT

Five forms of assessment are frequently used with students with learning disabilities: standardized achievement tests, criterion-referenced tests, informal reading inventories, curriculum-based measurement, and direct daily measurement.

STANDARDIZED TESTS

Standardized achievement tests

Council for Exceptional Children Content Standards for Beginning Teachers of Students with LD: Terminology and procedures used in the assessment of individuals with LD (LD8K1).
PRAXIS Special Education Core Principles: Content Knowledge: III. Delivery of Services to Students with Disabilities, Assessment, Use of assessment for diagnosis.

Standardized intelligence and achievement tests are widely used with children with learning disabilities because a discrepancy between intellectual ability and achievement is the primary factor in determining eligibility for special education services. Standardized tests are norm-referenced, which means they have been constructed so that one student's score can be compared with the scores of other students of the same age who have taken the test. Intelligence tests were discussed in Chapter 6. Some standardized achievement tests are designed to measure a student's overall academic achievement—e.g., the Iowa Tests of Basic Skills (Hoover, Hieronymus, Frisbie, & Dunbar, 1996), the Peabody Individual Achievement Test (Markwardt, 1998), the Woodcock-Johnson III Tests of Achievement (Woodcock & Mather, 2000), and the Wide Range Achievement Test—3 (WRAT) (Wilkinson, 1994). Scores on these tests are reported by grade level; a score of 3.5, for example, means that the student's score equaled the average score by those students in the norm group who were halfway through the third grade.

Some norm-referenced tests are designed to measure achievement in certain academic areas. Frequently administered reading achievement tests include the Durrell Analysis of Reading Difficulty (Durrell & Catterson, 1980), the Gates-MacGinitie Reading Tests (MacGinitie, MacGinitie, Maria, & Dreyer, 2000), the Gray Oral Reading Tests (Wiederholt & Bryant, 1992), the Spache Diagnostic Reading Scales (Spache, 1981), and the Woodcock Reading Mastery Test (Woodcock, 1998). Norm-referenced tests used to assess mathematics achievement include KeyMath—Revised: A Diagnostic Inventory of Essential Skills (Connolly, 1998), the Stanford Diagnostic Mathematics Test (Beatty, Madden, Gardner, & Karlsen, 1995), and the Test of Mathematical Abilities (Brown, Cronin, & McEntire, 1994).

CRITERION-REFERENCED TESTS

Criterion-referenced tests differ from norm-referenced tests in that a child's score on a criterion-referenced test is compared with a predetermined criterion, or mastery level, rather than with normed scores of other students. The value of criterion-referenced tests is that they identify the specific skills the child has already learned and the skills that require instruction. One criterion-referenced test widely used by special educators is the Brigance Diagnostic Comprehensive Inventory of Basic Skills (Brigance, 1999), which includes 140 skill sequences in four subscales: readiness, reading, language arts, and math. Some commercially distributed curricula now include criterion-referenced test items for use as both a pretest and a posttest. The pretest assesses the student's entry level to determine which aspects of the program he is ready to learn; the posttest evaluates the effectiveness of the program. Criterion-referenced tests can be, and often are, informally developed by classroom teachers.

INFORMAL READING INVENTORIES

Teachers' growing awareness of the inability of formal achievement tests to provide useful information for planning instruction has led to greater use of teacher-developed and -administered tests, particularly in the area of reading. An informal reading inventory usually consists of a series of progressively more difficult sentences and paragraphs that a student is asked to read aloud. By directly observing and recording aspects of the student's reading skills—such as mispronounced vowels or consonants, omissions, reversals, substitutions, and comprehension—the teacher can determine the level of reading material that is most suitable for the child and the specific reading skills that require remediation (Carnine, Silbert, & Kame'enui, 1997).

CURRICULUM-BASED MEASUREMENT

Curriculum-based measurement (CBM) involves frequent assessment of a student's progress in learning the objectives that make up the curriculum in which the student is participating (Deno, 1985; Fuchs & Fuchs, 1996; Howell & Nolet, 2000). CBM is a *formative evaluation* method in that it provides information on student learning as instruction takes place over time. By contrast, the result of a *summative evaluation* cannot be used to inform instruction because it is conducted after instruction has been completed (e.g., at the end of a grading period or school year). One study found that teachers who used CBM made an average of 2.5 changes in students' instructional plans over the course of 20 weeks, compared to an average of just 0.27 changes by teachers who were not using CBM (Fuchs, Fuchs, Hamlett, & Steeker, 1991). Other studies have reported that students whose teachers tailor instruction plans on CBM data perform and achieve better academically than do students whose teachers do not use CBM (Steeker & Fuchs, 2000; Wesson, 1991).

DIRECT DAILY MEASUREMENT

Direct daily measurement means observing and recording a child's performance on the specific skill being taught each day that it is taught. In a program teaching multiplication facts, for example, the student's performance of multiplication facts would be assessed each day

Criterion-referenced tests

Council for Exceptional Children Content Standards for Beginning Teachers of Students with LD: Terminology and procedures used in the assessment of individuals with LD (LD8K1) (also CC8K4).
PRAXIS Special Education Core Principles: Content Knowledge: III. Delivery of Services to Students with Disabilities, Assessment, Use of assessment for making instructional decisions.

Informal reading inventories, CBM, and direct daily measurement

Council for Exceptional Children Content Standards for Beginning Teachers of Students with LD: Terminology and procedures used in the assessment of individuals with LD (LD8K1) (also CC8K4).
PRAXIS Special Education Core Principles: Content Knowledge: III. Delivery of Services to Students with Disabilities, Assessment, Use of assessment for making instructional decisions.

that multiplication was taught. Measures such as correct rate (number of facts stated or written correctly per minute), error rate, and percent correct are often recorded.

Two advantages of direct daily measurement are clear. First, it gives information about the child's performance on the skill under instruction. Second, this information is available on a continuous basis so that the teacher can modify instruction in accordance with changing (or unchanging) performance, not because of intuition, guesswork, or the results of a test that measures something else (Bushell & Baer, 1994). Direct and frequent measurement is the cornerstone of the behavioral approach to education introduced in Chapter 6 and is becoming an increasingly popular assessment and evaluation technique in all areas of special education.

Precision Teaching   Some teachers of students with learning disabilities use a special system for direct daily measurement called **precision teaching** (Lindsley, 1996). Precision teachers make instructional decisions based on changes in the frequency of a student's performance (e.g., number of words read correctly per minute) as plotted on a standard graphic display called the *standard celeration chart* (see Figure 7.4). Precision teaching is neither a specific method of teaching nor a curriculum; it is a way of evaluating the effects of instruction and making instructional decisions. Additional information about precision teaching can be found in Beck, Conrad, and Anderson (1995); Kubina and Cooper (2001); Potts, Eshleman, and Cooper (1993); and West, Young, and Spooner (1990).

▲

Self-recording and self-graphing daily measures of academic performance are excellent ways to motivate and involve students in their own learning.

To find out how precision teaching was used to help a student with learning disabilities improve his reading skills, see "Tutoring Joe" in Chapter 7 on the Companion Website at **www.prenhall.com/heward**

History of LD

Council for Exceptional Children   Content Standards for Beginning Teachers of Students with LD: Historical foundations, classical studies, and major contributors in the field of LD (LD1K1).
PRAXIS Special Education Core Principles: Content Knowledge: II. Legal and Societal Issues, Historical movements/trends affecting the connections between special education and the larger society.

EDUCATIONAL APPROACHES

Not long ago, instruction of students with learning disabilities emphasized the remediation of basic skill deficits, often at the expense of providing opportunities for students to express themselves, learn problem-solving skills, or contact the general education curriculum in a meaningful way. "The overemphasis on the 'basics with the exclusion of any creative or cognitively complex activities provides many students with LD an unappealing intellectual diet" (Gersten, 1998, p. 163). (Table 7.2 describes some key historical events and their implications for the education of students with learning disabilities.)

In recent years, however, the field has begun to shift its instructional focus, from a remediation-only mode to an approach designed to give students with learning disabilities meaningful access to and success with the core curriculum. By incorporating the six principles of effective instructional design shown in Figure 7.5 (page 266), educators can make curriculum and instruction more effective for students with and without disabilities (Kame'enui et al., 2002; Klingner & Vaughn, 1999).

Research has also shown that students with learning disabilities (1) have difficulty organizing information on their own, (2) bring limited stores of background knowledge to many academic activities, and (3) often do not approach learning tasks in effective and efficient ways. Thus, contemporary best practice in educating students with learning disabilities is characterized by explicit instruction, content enhancements, and learning strategies (Gersten, 1998; Hock et al., 1999).

EXPLICIT INSTRUCTION

Explicit instruction involves carefully designed materials and activities that provide structures and supports that enable all students to make sense of new information and con-

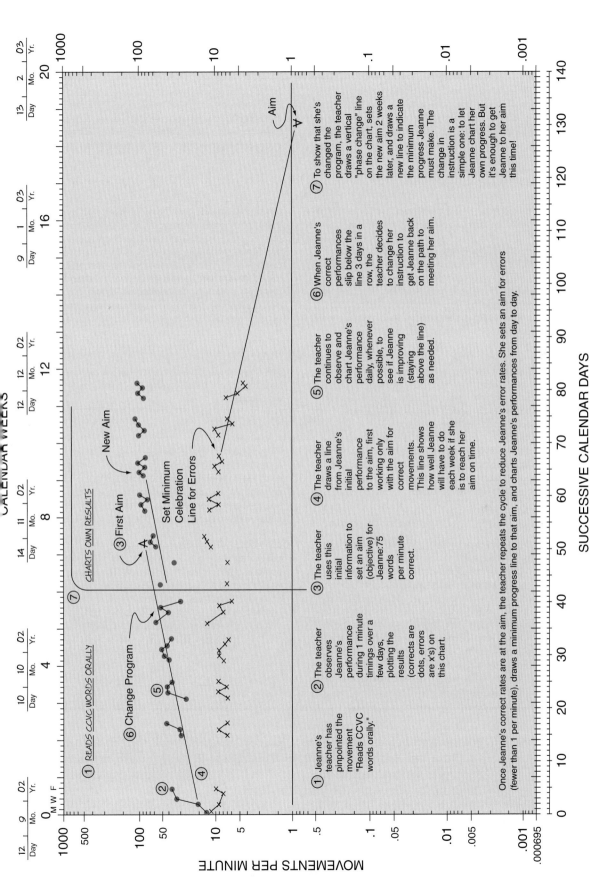

FIGURE 7.4 Standard celeration chart used in precision teaching

Source: Adapted from *Exceptional Teaching* (p. 276) by O. Whie and N. Haring, 976, New York: Merrill/Macmillan. Reprinted by permission.

TABLE 7.2 A history of the education of children with learning disabilities: Key events and implications

Date	Historical Event	Educational Implications
late 1930s– early 1940s	Research by Alfred Strauss and colleagues with children with mental retardation and brain injury at the Wayne County Training School in Michigan found relationships between brain injury and disorders that interfered with learning: perceptual disorders, perseveration, disorders of conceptual thinking, and behavioral problems such as hyperactivity and impulsivity.	In the book, *Psychopathology and Education of the Brain-Injured Child,* Strauss and Lara Lehtinen (1947) recommended strategies for relieving perceptual and conceptual disturbances of children with brain injury and thus reducing their symptomatic learning problems.
1950s– 1960s	By the early 1950s, most public schools had established special education programs for children with mental retardation, sensory impairments, physical disabilities, and behavioral disorders. But there remained a group of children who were having serious learning problems at school, yet did not fit into any of the existing categories of exceptionality. They did not "look" disabled; the children seemed physically intact, yet they were unable to learn certain basic skills and subjects at school.	In searching for help with their children's problems, parents turned to other professionals—notably doctors, psychologists, and speech and language specialists. Understandably, these professionals viewed the children from the perspectives of their respective disciplines. As a result, terms such as *brain damage, minimal brain dysfunction, neurological impairment, perceptual handicap, dyslexia,* and *aphasia* were often used to describe and to account for the children's learning and behavior problems.
1963	The term *learning disabilities* was coined by Samuel Kirk in an address to a group of parents whose children were experiencing serious difficulties in learning to read, were hyperactive, or could not solve math problems.	The parents liked the term and, that very evening, voted to form the Association for Children with Learning Disabilities (ACLD).
1966	A national task force identified 99 different characteristics of children with *minimal brain dysfunction* (the term used at the time) reported in the literature (Clements, 1966).	The inherent danger in such lists is a tendency to assume that each of those characteristics is exhibited by *all* of the children considered to be in the category. This danger is especially troublesome with learning disabilities, because the children who make up the category are an extremely heterogeneous group.
mid 1960s– 1970s	The concept of process, or ability, testing grew out of the belief that learning disabilities are caused by a basic underlying difficulty of the child to process, or use, environmental stimuli in the same way that children without disabilities do. Two of the most widely used process tests used for diagnosing and assessing learning disabilities were developed during this time: the Illinois Test of Psycholinguistic Abilities (ITPA) (Kirk, McCarthy, & Kirk, 1968) and the Marianne Frostig Developmental Test of Visual Perception (Frostig, Lefever, & Whittlesey, 1964).	The ability training approach dominated special education for children with learning disabilities, from the field's inception through the 1970s. The three most widely known ability training approaches were psycholinguistic training, based on the ITPA; the visual-perceptual approach (Frostig & Horne, 1973); and the perceptual-motor approach (Kephart, 1971).

cepts. According to Cazden (1992), teachers should be "explicit about what needs to be done, or said, or written—rather than leaving it to learners to make inferences from experiences that are unmediated by help" (p. 111). In other words, explicit instruction is anything but learning by trial and error. Teachers use explicit instruction when they do the following (Carnine, Jones, & Dixon, 1994; Gersten, 1998):

1. Provide students with a sufficient range of examples to illustrate a concept or problem-solving strategy.
2. Provide models of proficient performance, including step-by-step strategies (at times) or broad, generic questions and guidelines that focus attention and prompt deep processing.

Date	Historical Event	Educational Implications

TABLE 7.2 *continued*

Date	Historical Event	Educational Implications
1968	The National Advisory Committee on Handicapped Children drafted and presented to Congress a definition of learning disabilities.	This definition was later incorporated into IDEA and used to govern the dispersal of federal funds for support of services to children with learning disabilities.
1968	The Division for Children with Learning Disabilities (DCLD) was established within the Council for Exceptional Children (CEC).	DCLD has become the largest division of CEC.
1969	The Children with Learning Disabilities Act (part of P.L. 91–230) was passed by Congress.	This legislation authorized a five-year program of federal funds for teacher training and the establishment of model demonstration programs for students with learning disabilities.
late 1970s– early 1980s	Reviews of research showing the ineffectiveness of psycholinguistic training (Hammill & Larsen, 1978), the visual-perceptual approach (Myers & Hammill, 1976), and perceptual-motor approaches (Kavale & Mattison, 1983) are published.	Process testing and ability training gradually gave way to increased use of a skill training, or task-analysis, approach. If a student has not learned a complex skill (e.g., reading a sentence) and has had sufficient opportunity and wants to succeed, a skill trainer would conclude that the student has not learned the necessary prerequisite skills (e.g., sounding out letters, reading single words) and provides direct instruction and practice on those prerequisite skills.
1975	Congress passed the Individuals with Disabilities Education Act (P.L. 94-142)	Learning disabilities was included as one of the disability categories in IDEA.
1980s and 1990s	Research on instructional design (e.g., Kame'enui & Carnine, 1998), content enhancements (e.g., Scruggs & Mastropieri, 1992), and learning strategies (e.g., Schumaker & Deshler, 1992) provides additional knowledge on effective teaching methods for students with learning disabilities.	Skill training approach supplemented with increased emphasis on helping students with learning disabilities have meaningful contact with the general curriculum through explicit instruction, content enhancements, fluency-building, and the use of learning strategies and self-management skills.
2001	In response to concern about the large number of children identified as learning disabled, the U.S. Office of Special Education sponsored a Learning Disabilities Summit in Washington, DC. Nationally recognized experts were asked to review the most current research on key issues in learning disabilities.	Nine white papers were developed on topics dealing with diagnostic decision making, discrepancy models, classification models, early identification, and the nature and legitimacy of learning disabilities as a disability (available at http://www.air.org/LDsummit/paper.htm). The LD Summit will likely spark continued debate and possibly changes in policy and practice.

3. Have students explain how and why they make decisions.
4. Provide frequent, positive feedback for student performance so students persist in activities.
5. Provide adequate practice opportunities that entail interesting and engaging activities.

 CONTENT ENHANCEMENTS

Educating students with learning disabilities at the middle and secondary levels is particularly difficult. The majority of students with learning disabilities are "ill-prepared for high school" and have reading and language skills at the 4th- to 5th-grade level (Deshler, Schumaker, Lenz et al., 2001). Lectures and assigned readings in textbooks are widely used in middle and high school classrooms to present academic content to students. The teacher talks and assigns a portion of a high-vocabulary, content-dense text; and students are held responsible for obtaining, remembering, and using the information later (usually on a quiz

FIGURE 7.5 Six major principles of effective instructional design

Big Ideas
Highly selected concepts, principles, rules, strategies, or heuristics that facilitate the most efficient and broadest acquisition of knowledge.

Conspicuous Strategies
Sequence of teaching events and teacher actions that make explicit the steps in learning. They are made conspicuous by the use of visual maps or models, verbal directions, full and clear explanations, etc.

Mediated Scaffolding
Temporary support for students to learn new material. Scaffolding is faded over time.

Strategic Integration
Planful consideration and sequencing of instruction in ways that show the commonalities and differences between old and new knowledge.

Primed Background Knowledge
Related knowledge, placed effectively in sequence, that students must already possess in order to learn new knowledge.

Judicious Review
Sequence and schedule of opportunities learners have to apply and develop facility with new knowledge. The review must be adequate, distributed, cumulative, and varied.

Source: From Kame'enui, E. J., Carnine, D. W., & Dixon, R. C. (2002). Introduction. In E. J. Kame'enui, D. W. Carnine, R. C. Dixon, D. C. Simmons, & M. D. Coyne (Eds.), *Effective teaching strategies that accommodate diverse learners* (2nd ed.), (p. 9). Upper Saddle River, NJ: Merrill/Prentice Hall. Reprinted by permission.

Content enhancements: Guided notes, graphic organizers, and mnemonic strategies

Council for Exceptional Children Content Standards for Beginning Teachers of Students with LD: Methods for guiding individuals in identifying and organizing critical content (LD4K5).

PRAXIS Special Education Core Principles: Content Knowledge: III. Delivery of Services to Students with Disabilities, Curriculum and Instruction, Modification of materials.

or test). A combination of poor reading, listening, note taking, and study skills, compounded by a limited store of background knowledge, makes obtaining needed information from reading, lectures, and homework assignments a daunting task for students with learning disabilities. *Content enhancement* is the general name given to a wide range of techniques teachers use to enhance the delivery of critical curriculum content so that students are better able to organize, comprehend, and retain that information (Hock et al., 1999; Hudson, Lignugaris/Kraft, & Miller, 1993; Lenz & Bulgren, 1995). Let's take a brief look at several types of content enhancements helpful to students with learning disabilities.

Guided Notes   Students who take good notes and study them later consistently receive higher test scores than do students who only listen to the lecture and read the text (Baker & Lombardi, 1985; Norton & Hartley, 1986). The listening, language, and, in some cases, motor-skill deficits of many students with learning disabilities, however, make it difficult for them to identify what is important and write it down correctly and quickly enough during a lecture (Deshler, Ellis, & Lenz, 1996). While trying to choose and write one concept in a notebook, the student with learning disabilities might miss the next two points. Although various strategies and formats for effective note taking have been identified, they are seldom taught to students (Mercer & Mercer, 2001).

Guided notes is a method for organizing and enhancing curriculum content and providing students with disabilities and their regular classroom peers with a means of actively participating during a lecture (Heward, 2001; Lazarus, 1996). Guided notes are teacher-prepared handouts that guide students through a lecture with standard cues and specific spaces in which to write key facts, concepts, and/or relationships. Numerous studies have found that elementary, middle, and secondary students with and without learning disabilities earn higher test scores when using guided notes than they do when taking their own notes (e.g., Beckley, Al-Attrash, Heward, & Morrison, 1999; Courson, 1989; Hamilton, Seibert, Gardner, & Talbert-Johnson, 2000; Lazarus, 1991; see Heward [1994] for a review). Figure 7.6 lists some advantages of guided notes and suggestions for using them.

Graphic Organizers and Visual Displays   *Graphic organizers*—visual-spatial arrangements of information containing words or statements connected graphically—can help students see meaningful hierarchical and comparative relationships (Dye, 2000; Horton, Lovitt, & Bergerud, 1990). *Visual displays* can be effective for teaching abstract concepts to students with disabilities. Bulgren, Deshler, Schumaker, and Lenz (2000) have developed a graphic device and teaching routine called the concept anchoring table/routine that helps students relate a new concept to a concept and information with which they are already familiar (see Figure 7.7). Students complete the anchoring table as part of a 7-step teacher-guided instructional routine that enables students to use their background experiences and knowledge to understand the new concept. Research has shown that the concept anchoring routine helps students learn abstract or complex information such as "federalism" or "commensalism" (Bulgren et al., 2000; Deshler, Schumaker, Bulgren, et al., 2001).

Mnemonics   Research has demonstrated that mnemonics (memory-enhancing strategies) can help students with learning disabilities recall specific academic content (Brigham & Brigham, 2001; Swanson, 1999). **Mnemonic instruction**—which combines special presentation of information with explicit strategies for recall—is most often used to help students remember large amounts of unfamiliar information or make connections between two or more facts or concepts. (See Teaching & Learning, "Mnemonic Strategies," later in this chapter.)

 LEARNING STRATEGIES

Proficient learners approach tasks and problems systematically. They identify what needs to be done, make a plan, and evaluate their progress. An accomplished writer knows how to identify and organize the content of a paper to enhance its persuasiveness. When adding a series of unlike fractions, a skilled math student immediately looks to see if all of the denominators are even numbers. Unless they are explicitly taught, however, many students with learning disabilities are unaware of the learning strategies, or "tricks of the trade," that proficient learners use (Deshler & Schumaker, 1993).

A learning strategy can be defined as "an individual's approach to a learning task. A strategy includes how a person thinks and acts when planning, executing, and evaluating performance on a task and its outcomes" (Deshler & Lenz, 1989, p. 205). Donald Deshler and Jean Schumaker and their colleagues at the University of Kansas (Schumaker & Deshler, 1992) have conducted extensive research on how to help students with learning disabilities acquire and use effective learning strategies. They have developed, field-tested, and validated a learning strategies curriculum for adolescents with learning disabilities (Ellis, Deshler, Lenz, Schumaker, & Clark, 1991).

Students use task-specific strategies to guide themselves successfully through a learning task or problem. A mnemonic device might be used to help students remember the steps of the strategy. For example, Maccini and Hughes (2000) taught secondary students with learning disabilities to recite the letters in S.T.A.R. as cues for the steps in systematically solving algebra word problems (*S*earch the problem, *T*ranslate the words into an equation, *A*nswer the problem, and *R*eview the solution).

Learning strategies

 Council for Exceptional Children   Content Standards for Beginning Teachers of Students with LD: Methods for teaching individuals to independently use cognitive processing to solve problems (LD4K4).
PRAXIS Special Education Core Principles: Content Knowledge: III. Delivery of Services to Students with Disabilities, Curriculum and Instruction, Learning and strategy instruction.

FIGURE 7.6 Guided notes: Advantages and suggestions

Advantages of Guided Notes (GN)

- *Students are actively engaged with curriculum.*   To complete their GN, students must actively interact with the lesson's content by listening, looking, thinking, and writing.
- *Students produce standard and accurate lecture notes for study and review.*
- *Students can more easily identify the most imortant information.*   Because GN cue the location and number of key concepts, facts, and/or relationships, students are better able to determine if they are "getting it" and are more likely to ask the teacher to clarify.
- *Teachers must prepare the lesson or lecture carefully.*
- *Instructors are more likely to stay on task with the lecture's content and sequence.*
- *GN improve the independent note-taking skills of some students.*
- *Students retain more information and earn higher scores on quizzes and tests.*

Suggestions for Creating and Using Guided Notes

- *Include all facts, concepts, and relationships students are expected to learn.*
- *Include background information so that students' note taking focuses on the important facts, concepts, and relationships they need to learn.*
- *Produce notes on a word processor so that changes and updates can be easily made.*
- *Examine existing lecture outlines to identify the most important course content that students must learn and retain via lectures.* Remember, less can be more. Student learning is enhanced by lectures with fewer points supported by additional examples and opportunities for students to respond to questions or scenarios.
- *Delete the key facts, concepts, and relationships from the lecture outline, leaving the remaining information to provide structure and context for students' note taking.*
- *Insert formatting cues such as asterisks, bullets, and blank lines to show students where, when, and how many facts or concepts to write. For example:*

> ### Explanation of Symbols in Guided Notes
>
> ⊃, ✳, ★, ❶ Write a definition, concept, key point, or procedure next to each bullet, asterisk, star, or numbered circle.
>
> _____ Fill in blank lines with a word or phrase to complete a definition, concept, key point, or procedure during lecture/class.
>
> ☞ The pointing finger comes into play when you review and study your notes after class. It is a prompt to think of and write your own examples of a concept or ideas for applying a particular strategy.
>
> 📖 *Big Idea* 📖 Big ideas are statements or concepts with wide-ranging implications for understanding and/or applying course content.

- *Use overhead transparencies or PowerPoint slides to project key content.*   Visually projecting the key facts, definitions, concepts, and relationships helps ensure that all students access the most critical content and improves the pace of the lecture.
- *Leave ample space for students to write.*   Providing three to four times the space needed to type the content will generally leave enough room for students' handwriting.
- *Don't require students to write too much.*   Using GN should not unduly slow down the pace of the lesson.
- *Enhance GN with supporting information, resources, and additional opportunities to respond.*   Insert diagrams, illustrations, photos, highlighted statements or concepts that are particularly important, and resources such as websites into GN. Interspersing sets of questions or practice problems within the GN gives students additional opportunities to respond and receive teacher feedback during the lesson.
- *Consider gradually fading the use of guided notes to help students learn to take notes in classes in which GN are not used.*
- *Provide follow-up activities to ensure that students study and review their notes (e.g., daily quiz, collaborative review activity).*

Source: Adapted from Heward, W. L. (2001). *Guided notes: Improving the effectiveness of your lectures.* Columbus: The Ohio State University Partnership Grant for Improving the Quality of Education for Students with Disabilities.

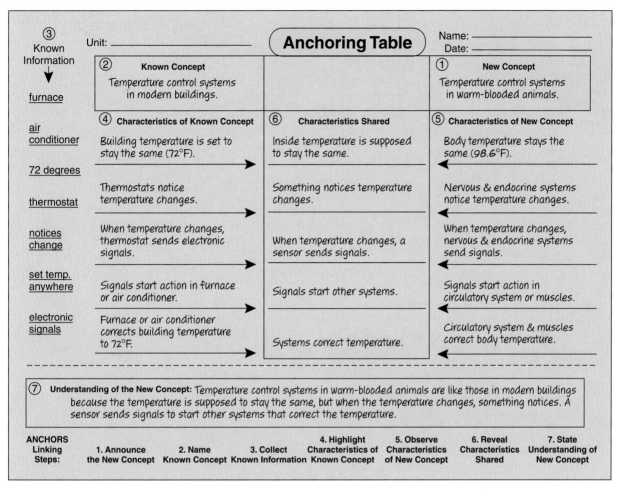

FIGURE 7.7 **Example of a concept anchoring table for the concept "temperature control systems in warm-blooded animals"**

Source: Deshler, D. D., Schumaker, J. B., Bulgren, J. A., Lenz, B. K., Jantzen, J., Adams, G., Carnine, D., Grossen, B., Davis, B., & Marquis, J. (2001). Making things easier: Connecting new knowledge to things students already know. *Teaching Exceptional Children, 33*(4), 84.

EDUCATIONAL PLACEMENT ALTERNATIVES

REGULAR CLASSROOM

IDEA requires that students with disabilities be educated with their nondisabled peers and have access to the core curriculum to the maximum extent possible and that they be removed from the regular classroom only to the extent that their disability necessitates. During the 1999–2000 school year, 45% of students with learning disabilities were educated in regular classrooms (U.S. Department of Education, 2000).

All of the methods described in the previous section for enhancing the general education curriculum help promote the success of students with learning disabilities in the regular classroom. Special educators can facilitate the success of students with learning disabilities in regular classrooms by teaching them behaviors that are valued by regular class teachers. Table 7.3 (page 273) lists the 10 things that 89 regular education high school teachers identified as most important for success in the regular education classroom. Another strategy for increasing the likelihood of successful inclusion is to interview successful students to find out their secrets for success in a particular teacher's classroom (Monda-Amaya, Dieker, & Reed, 1998).

Research on the academic achievement of students with learning disabilities in inclusive classrooms is mixed. Some studies have reported better learning outcomes for students

Placement alternatives

  Council for Exceptional Children Content Standards for Beginning Teachers–Common Core: Demands of learning environments (CC5K1).
PRAXIS Special Education Core Principles: Content Knowledge: III. Delivery of services to Students with Disabilities, Background knowledge, Placement issues/Least restrictive environment.

Mnemonic Strategies

by Margo A. Mastropieri and Thomas E. Scruggs
George Mason University

Success in school is strongly associated with the ability to learn and remember verbal information. For example, students are frequently expected to remember states and capitals, multiplication facts, U.S. presidents, science vocabulary, and mathematical formulas. Unfortunately, many students with mild cognitive disabilities have difficulty remembering verbal information. Some researchers have linked these problems to difficulties in effectively using appropriate learning strategies to improve recall by more effectively encoding, storing, and retrieving information.

We have been studying mnemonic (memory-enhancing) strategies and evaluating their effectiveness with students who have difficulty remembering academic information. We primarily have studied the use of these strategies by students with learning disabilities; however, we have also found that they can be useful for students with mild mental retardation and behavioral disorders as well as normally achieving and gifted students.

The Keyword Method

The keyword method is one of the most versatile mnemonic strategies. It is useful when linking a new, unfamiliar word with familiar information. For example, to remember that the Italian word *mela* (may-la) means "apple," first construct a keyword for *mela*. A keyword sounds like the new word but is familiar and easy to picture. In this case, "mailbox" would be a good keyword for mela because it sounds like it and is easy to picture. Next, draw (or ask students to imagine) a picture of the keyword and its referent doing something together—e.g., a mailbox with an apple in it. Finally, students study the picture and are told, when asked for the meaning of mela, to think of the keyword "mailbox," remember the picture with the mailbox in it, remember *what else* was in the picture, and retrieve the correct answer, "apple." Although there are several steps to successful retrieval, research has shown that students with learning difficulties can easily use the keyword method and remember far more information when they do so.

To help remember that George M. Cohan wrote the patriotic song "Over There" during World War I, students could use the picture shown in Figure A. In this picture, "cone" is the keyword for Cohan. When a child asks, "Where did you get the cone?" the other child points and sings, "Over there." Students who have studied the picture and its mnemonic strategy can then remember the answer to the question "Who was George M. Cohan?"

Sometimes two keywords can be used. For example, to teach that Annapolis is the capital of Maryland, construct keywords of both Annapolis ("an apple") and Maryland ("marry") and show a picture of apples getting married.

Sometimes keywords are not necessary because the words are already familiar. Sometimes pictures can be *mimetic*, or direct representations. For example, to show that sponges attach themselves to the ocean floor, draw a mimetic picture in which sponges are attached to the ocean floor. Sometimes *symbolic* pictures are needed when the information is familiar but abstract. For example, to show that birds are warm-blooded, show a picture of a bird sitting in warm sunshine. In this case, the sun is a symbol for warm-blooded. In contrast, cold-blooded fish and reptiles can be pictured in cold scenes. This method of using mimetic, symbolic, or acoustic (keyword) reconstructions has been called *reconstructive elaborations*. It can be used to adapt a wide variety of content information.

The Pegword Method

The pegword method employs rhyming words for numbers (1 is "bun," 2 is "shoe," 3 is "tree," etc.) when information to be remembered is numbered or ordered. For example, to remember that an example of a third-class lever is a rake, create a picture of a rake leaning against a tree (3). To remember that insects have six legs, create a picture of insects on sticks (6). To remember that Newton's first (or number 1) law of motion is that objects at rest tend to stay at rest, show a picture of a bun (1) resting.

Pegwords can be combined with keywords. For example, to remember that the mineral rhodochrosite is num-

George M. Cohan (Cone)   Wrote the song "Over There"

FIGURE A Mnemonic picture for remembering that George M. Cohan wrote the song "Over There"

Source: From Mastropieri, M. A., & Scruggs, T. E. (1991). *Teaching students ways to remember: Strategies for learning mnemonically* (p. 49). Cambridge, MA: Brookline. Reprinted with permission.

Central Powers (Central Park)   Turkey, Austria, Germany

FIGURE B Mnemonic picture for remembering the names of the countries in the Central Powers during World War I: Turkey, Austria-Hungary, and Germany

Source: From Mastropieri, M. A., & Scruggs, T. E. (1991). *Teaching students ways to remember: Strategies for learning mnemonically* (p. 119). Cambridge, MA: Brookline. Reprinted with permission.

ber 4 on the Mohs' hardness scale, show a picture of a road (keyword for rhodochrosite) going through a door (peg-word for 4).

Letter Strategies

Most people have used letter strategies to remember information—for example, using the acronym HOMES to remember the names of the Great Lakes: Huron, Ontario, Michigan, Erie, and Superior. However, this strategy is effective only if students are familiar with the names of the Great Lakes because they just have the first letters as a prompt. Another helpful letter strategy is the acronym

FARM-B to remember the classes of vertebrates: fish, amphibians, reptiles, mammals, birds.

Acrostics and related strategies can also be helpful. For example, the sentence "My very educated mother just served us nine pizzas" can be used to remember the planets in order: Mercury, Venus, Earth, Mars, Jupiter, Saturn, Uranus, Neptune, Pluto.

Letter strategies can also be combined with keywords. For example, the countries of the Central Powers in World War I included Turkey, Austria-Hungary, and Germany. These countries can be represented by the acronym TAG,

continues

which Figure B shows being played in Central Park, keyword for Central Powers.

Recommendations

Here are some guidelines for incorporating mnemonic strategies into classroom teaching for students with learning difficulties:

1. *Teach a small number of strategies at first.* Explain every step of the strategy very carefully and monitor for understanding. When students begin to show facility in using the method, more strategies can be included.

2. *Monitor for comprehension.* Students need to be made aware that they are learning two things: important content information and the strategies for remembering that information. This can be prompted by asking for each separately: "What is the capital of New Hampshire, Mary?" "Good. How did you remember that?" Additionally, students should not be taught to remember information they do not understand. Ensure comprehension of the information before applying memory strategies.

3. *Mnemonic pictures do not need to be great works of art.* They simply need to portray the relevant information clearly. However, if you are certain that you cannot draw at all, use stick figures or cutouts from magazines, employ a student artist, ask students to draw their own pictures, or encourage student use of imagery.

4. *Teach students to generalize mnemonic strategies to their own independent use.* However, they should first be well acquainted with a variety of teacher-developed mnemonic strategies. Promote group brainstorming of keywords and interactive pictures and carefully explain the steps to constructing mnemonic strategies. Then prompt strategy construction and provide feedback.

For further information, see Mastropieri, M. A., & Scruggs, T. E. (2000). *The inclusive classroom: Strategies for effective instruction* (Chap. 10). Upper Saddle River, NJ: Merrill/Prentice Hall.

Margo A. Mastropieri and Thomas E. Scruggs are professors in the Graduate School of Education, George Mason University. They are co-editors of the research annual *Advances in Learning and Behavioral Disabilities.*

with learning disabilities in inclusive general education classrooms than in pullout programs (e.g., Baker, Wang, & Walberg, 1995; Rea, McLaughlin, Walther-Thomas, 2002; Shulte, Osborne, & McKinney, 1990). Other studies of students with learning disabilities in the regular classroom have reported disappointing achievement results (e.g., Schumm, Moody, & Vaughn, 2000), concerns about inadequate instruction (e.g., Chard & Kame'enui, 2000), and poor acceptance by teachers and/or peers (e.g., Cook, 2001; Cook, Tankersley, Cook, & Landrum, 2000).

Some school districts employ a collaborative teaching model to support the full inclusion of students with learning disabilities. Collaborative teaching involves in-class support by a special education teacher who provides instructional assistance to students with disabilities and perhaps some co-teaching with the general education teacher (Zigmond & Magiera, 2001). Data from two studies, however, question the effectiveness of this model. Boudah, Schumaker, and Deshler (1997) found that both the general education teachers and the special education teachers devoted more than half of their time to noninstructional tasks and spent less than 10% of their time presenting curriculum content. Not surprisingly, Boudah et al. also reported disappointing outcome measures for the students with learning disabilities who were included in those classrooms. The authors of another study that examined the experiences of 25 elementary students with learning disabilities who participated in a full inclusion program concluded that "full-time placement in the general education classroom with in-class support from special education teachers is not sufficient to meet the needs of these students. They require combined services that include in-class support and daily intensive, one-on-one instruction from highly trained personnel" (Klingner, Vaughn, Hughes, Schumm, & Elbaum, 1998, p. 159).

 CONSULTANT TEACHER

A consultant teacher provides support to regular classroom teachers and other school staff who work directly with students with learning disabilities. The consultant teacher helps the regular teacher select assessment devices, curriculum materials, and instructional activities. The consultant may even demonstrate teaching methods or behavior management strate-

TABLE 7.3 The 10 most important things a student with learning disabilities should do to achieve success in a regular education classroom

Student Skill/Behavior	Mean Rating*
Follows directions in class	3.72
Comes to class prepared with materials	3.48
Uses class time wisely	3.48
Makes up assignments and tests	3.43
Treats teachers and peers with courtesy	3.40
Completes and turns in homework on time	3.37
Works cooperatively in student groups	3.19
Completes tests with a passing grade	3.19
Appears interested in subject	2.90
Takes notes in class	2.88

*Skills are ordered from most to least important as ranked by teachers; 4 is the highest possible score.

Source: Reprinted from "Instructional Practices in Mainstreamed Secondary Classrooms" by L. Ellet, 1993, *Journal of Learning Disabilities, 26,* 59. © 1993 by PRO-ED, Inc. Used by permission.

gies. A major advantage of this model is that the consultant teacher can work with several teachers and thus indirectly provide special education services to many children. A major drawback is that the consultant has little or no direct contact with the children. Heron and Harris (2001) describe procedures consultant teachers can use to increase their effectiveness in supporting children in the regular classroom.

RESOURCE ROOM

A resource room is a specially staffed and equipped classroom where students with learning disabilities come for one or several periods during the school day to receive individualized instruction. A resource room teacher serves an average of 20 students with disabilities. During the 1999–2000 school year, 39% of students with learning disabilities were served in resource rooms.

The resource teacher is a certified special educator whose primary role is to teach needed academic skills, social skills, and learning strategies to the students who are referred to the resource room. Students typically attend their general education classrooms for most of the school day and come to the resource room only for one or more periods of specialized instruction in the academic and/or social skill areas in which they need the most help. In addition to teaching students with learning disabilities, the resource teacher also works closely with each student's regular teacher(s) to suggest and help plan each student's program in the regular classroom.

Some advantages of the resource room model are that (1) students do not lose their identity with their regular class peer group; (2) students can receive the intense, individualized instruction they need every day, which might not be possible for the regular class teacher to provide; and (3) flexible scheduling allows the resource room to serve a fairly large number of students. Some disadvantages of resource rooms are that they (1) require students to spend time traveling between classrooms, (2) may result in inconsistent instructional approaches between settings, and (3) make it difficult to determine whether students should be held accountable for what they missed while out of the regular classroom.

SEPARATE CLASSROOM

During the 1999–2000 school year, 16% of students with learning disabilities were served in separate classrooms. In a separate classroom the learning disabilities teacher is responsible for

all educational programming for a group of 8 to 12 students with learning disabilities. The academic achievement deficiencies of some children with learning disabilities are so severe that they need full-time placement in a setting with a specially trained teacher. In addition, poor work habits and inappropriate social behaviors make some students with learning disabilities candidates for the separate classroom, where distractions can be minimized and individual attention stressed. As was noted in Chapter 2, it is important that IEP teams do not consider placement in a separate classroom (or any other educational setting) as permanent. A student should be placed in a separate classroom only after legitimate and supported attempts to serve her effectively in less restrictive environments have proven unsuccessful.

In a resource room, students with learning disabilities can receive intense, individualized instruction on the academic and social skills they need for success in the mainstream.

LD Summit papers

Council for Exceptional Children Content Standards for Beginning Teachers—Common Core: Models, theories, and philosophies that form the basis for special education practice (CC1K1) (also CC1K3).
PRAXIS Special Education Core Principles: Content Knowledge: II. Legal and Societal Issues, Historical movements/trends affecting the connections between special education and the larger society.

Difficulty defining and identifying LDs

Council for Exceptional Children Content Standards for Beginning Teachers of Students with LD: Philosophies, theories, models and issues related to individuals with LD (LD1K2).
PRAXIS Special Education Core Principles: Content Knowledge: I. Understanding Exceptionalities, Basic concepts, Labeling and implications of the classification process.

CURRENT ISSUES AND FUTURE TRENDS

The field of learning disabilities is so large, dynamic, and controversial that an entire volume could easily be devoted to a discussion of current issues. In response to concern about the large number of children who have been identified as learning disabled, the U.S. Office of Special Education sponsored a national Learning Disabilities Summit in Washington, DC, in 2001. Nationally recognized experts were invited to review the most current research and prepare papers discussing implications of and recommendations for policy, research, and practice on a variety of pressing issues, including discrepancy models and alternative approaches for diagnosing learning disabilities (Gresham, 2001; Kavale, 2001), classification of learning disabilities (Fletcher et al., 2001), the difficulty of differentiating students with learning disabilities from other underachieving students (Fuchs et al., 2001), and early identification and prevention of learning disabilities (Jenkins & O'Conner, 2001). All of the LD Summit papers are available on the Internet [http://www.air.org/LDsummit/paper.htm] and are important reading for anyone who wishes to seriously explore current issues and likely trends in learning disabilities.

We will briefly discuss two issues: the continuing debates about defining and identifying the true nature of learning disabilities and full inclusion. The chapter closes with an observation on the importance of maintaining a positive approach in our work with children with learning disabilities.

WILL THE STUDENT WITH REAL LEARNING DISABILITIES PLEASE STAND UP?

The field of learning disabilities continues to struggle with defining the nature of the unexpected learning problems it was created to study and treat. Although virtually everyone in education recognizes that present definitions of learning disabilities are inadequate, finding a definition that provides clearcut criteria for identification and serves as a standard by which to interpret and assess research findings has "proven easier said than done" (Conte & Andrews, 1993, p. 149).

To Tell the Truth was a popular TV game show in the 1960s. A panel of celebrities asked questions of three contestants, only one of whom was actually the person all were pretending to be. In some respects, the search to find the truly learning disabled among the many students who do poorly in school is like that TV game show. Many questions (in the form of achievement tests, intelligence tests, and still more tests) are given to the contestants (students), whose answers are judged by a panel of experts (school psychologists, teachers, and administrators) charged with picking out the students with real learning disabilities from the pretenders. The differences, of course, are also significant. On the game show, the consequences for a wrong answer were no more serious than a loud buzzer and a consolation prize; but in the game of identifying students with learning disabilities, mistakes are costly. An answer of "no, he's not learning disabled" can be devastating for the student who truly needs specially designed instruction to meet his individual learning needs. If the team of selection experts concludes "yes, there is one" when the student's underachievement is primarily a result of insufficient contact with appropriate general education curriculum and instruction, then the limited resources available to help students with learning disabilities are stretched further.

Fuchs et al. (2001) conclude the executive summary of their LD Summit paper, "Is 'Learning Disabilities' Just a Fancy Term for Low Achievement?," with these observations:

> Given that learning disabled (LD) students' reading achievement is worse than that of low-achieving students [who are not identified as LD], and assuming that many LD students' instructional needs can be addressed only by special education, why not simply use very low achievement as the primary criterion to identify LD and dispense with technically inadequate discrepancy formulas and controversial and divisive IQ tests? . . . Whether LD qualifies as a distinct diagnostic entity or occurs in varying degrees of severity, as hypertension and obesity do, findings indicate that researchers and practitioners tend to identify children with more severe reading problems as LD. Given this, it seems reasonable that special education, with its capacity to provide intensive reading instruction, be directed at this group of children. (p. 8).

The discussion of what constitutes a true learning disability will no doubt go on for some time. We close this discussion of the difficulties in defining learning disabilities by recognizing a central truth: labeling does not cause disabilities, nor will the removal of a label cure them. From an educator's standpoint, the most important issue should not revolve around whether to consider the academic deficiencies exhibited by a student as evidence of a disability (Macht, 1998). Instead, we should focus our resources and energies on determining how to go about assessing and effectively remediating the specific academic and social skill deficits in each student's repertoire. What a child's learning problem is called is not so important; what is important is that schools provide an educational program responsive to the individual needs of all children who have difficulty learning.

SHOULD ALL STUDENTS WITH LEARNING DISABILITIES BE EDUCATED IN THE REGULAR CLASSROOM?

For the majority of students with learning disabilities, the least restrictive environment for all or most of the school day is the regular education classroom attended by their same-age peers. The movement toward full inclusion of all students with disabilities in regular classrooms, however, has many professionals and advocates for students with learning disabilities worried. They think that although the full inclusion movement is based on strong beliefs and has the best intentions at heart, little research supports it ("Award-Winning Researchers Raise Questions about 'Inclusion,'" 2001; Fuchs & Fuchs, 1994; Kauffman & Hallahan, 1994; Swanson, 2000). They fear that the special education services for students with learning disabilities guaranteed by IDEA—particularly the meaningful development and implementation of IEPs and the identification of the least restrictive environment for each student along a continuum of placement options—will be lost if full inclusion becomes reality. They wonder how, for example, a high school student with learning disabilities who spends the entire school day in regular education subject matter classes will receive the individualized reading instruction at the fourth-grade level that she needs.

All of the major professional and advocacy associations concerned with the education of children with learning disabilities have published position papers against full inclusion (CLD, 1993; DLD, 1993; LDA, 1993 [see Figure 7.8]; NJCLD, 1994). Each group recognizes

Perspectives on full inclusion

 Council for Exceptional Children Content Standards for Beginning Teachers of Students with LD: Philosophies, theories, models and issues related to individuals with LD (LD1K2) (also CC5K1).
PRAXIS Special Education Core Principles: Content Knowledge: II. Legal and Societal Issues, Historical movements/trends, Inclusion.

FIGURE 7.8 Learning Disabilities Association of America position statement on full inclusion

"Full inclusion," "full integration," "unified system," and "inclusive education" are terms used to describe a popular policy/practice in which all students with disabilities, regardless of the nature or severity of their disability and need for related services, receive their total education with the regular education classroom in their home school. The Learning Disabilities Association of America does not support "full inclusion" or any policies that mandate the same placement, instruction, or treatment of all students with learning disabilities. Many students with learning disabilities benefit from being served in the regular education classroom. However, the regular education classroom is not the appropriate placement for a number of students with learning disabilities who may need alternative instructional environments, teaching strategies, and/or materials that cannot or will not be provided with the context of a regular classroom placement.

LDA believes that decisions regarding educational placement of students with learning disabilities must be based on the needs of each individual student rather than administrative convenience or budgetary considerations and must be the result of a cooperative effort involving educators, parents, and the student when appropriate.

LDA strongly supports the Individuals with Disabilities Act (IDEA) which mandates:

- a free and appropriate public education in the least restrictive environment appropriate for the student's specific learning needs
- a team-approved Individualized Education Program (IEP)
- a placement decision must be made on an individual basis and considered only after the development of the IEP
- a continuum of alternative placements to meet the needs of students with disabilities for special education and related services
- a system for the continuing education of regular and special education and related services personnel to enable these personnel to meet the needs of children with disabilities

LDA believes that the placement of all children with disabilities in the regular classroom is as great a violation of IDEA as is the placement of all children in separate classrooms on the basis of their type of disability.

Source: Reprinted from Learning Disabilities of America Association. (1993, March/April). Position paper on full inclusion of all students with learning disabilities in the regular classroom. *LDA Newsbrief, 28*(2), 1. © 1993 by the Learning Disabilities of America Association, Pittsburgh, PA. Used by permission.

CLD, DLD, LDA, & NJCLD

Council for Exceptional Children Content Standards for Beginning Teachers of Students with LD: Professional organizations and sources of information relevant to the field of LD (LD9K2).

PRAXIS Special Education Core Principles: Content Knowledge: III. Delivery of Services to Students with Disabilities, Professional roles, Use of professional organizations.

and supports the placement of students with learning disabilities in regular classrooms to the maximum extent possible, given that the instructional and related services required to meet each student's individualized educational needs are provided; but they strongly oppose policies that mandate the same placement and instruction for all students with learning disabilities. Each group believes that special education for students with learning disabilities requires a continuum of placement options that includes the possibility of some or even all instruction taking place outside the regular classroom.

The regular education classroom for some students with learning disabilities may actually be more restrictive than a resource room or special class placement when the instructional needs of the student are considered—and remember that academic deficit is the primary characteristic and remedial need of students with learning disabilities (Baker & Zigmond, 1995). It should be noted, however, that placing a student with learning disabilities in a pullout program or special class does not guarantee that student will receive the intensive, specialized instruction she needs. For example, Moody, Vaughn, Hughes, and Fischer (2000) found that only three of the six resource room teachers they observed provided differentiated reading materials and instruction to match the individualized needs of their students.

The collective message of research on outcomes for students with learning disabilities in inclusive classrooms and other settings is consistent with the findings for students with other disabilities: the location in which a student is taught is not as important as the quality of instruction that student receives.

 MAINTAINING A POSITIVE FOCUS

With its unending stream of claims, counterclaims, and controversy, the area of learning disabilities at times seems to lose sight of its fundamental goals and some commonsense truths. Tom Lovitt, who has contributed classroom-based research on virtually every aspect of the education of children with learning disabilities for more than 35 years, once wrote that, all things being equal, a teacher who imparts many skills to many children is good, and one who does not is not (Lovitt, 1977). After all, teaching is helping children learn new things. Although Lovitt believes that the development of children's academic and social skills is the primary purpose for teachers and students to come together, he also warns us to not become so concerned with fixing everything we believe is wrong with the student that we forget about recognizing and building upon all that is positive.

> Although we don't know how to really define LD youngsters (and heaven knows we've tried), we do know that often they don't do as well as their non-LD mates in oral and silent reading, reading comprehension, spelling, mathematics, history, science, geography, industrial arts, music, or family living. Because of these many deficits and deviations, we teachers, in all good faith, set out to remediate as many of the "shortfalls" as possible so that youth with learning disabilities will be as normal and wonderful as we are. We should reconsider this total remedial approach to learning disabilities. One reason for considering an alternative should be obvious if we thought of a day in the life of a student with learning disabilities. First, the teacher sets out to remediate his reading, then his math, and then his language, social skills, and soccer playing. Toward the end of the day, she attempts to remediate his metacognitive deficits. That lad is in a remediation mode throughout the day. Is it any wonder that some of these youngsters have self-concepts, self-images, self-esteems, and attributions that are out of whack?
>
> We should spend some time concentrating on these youngsters' positive qualities. If, a girl is inclined toward mechanics, or a boy to being a chef, we should nurture those skills. And if a child doesn't have a negotiable behavior, we should locate one and promote it. I can't help but think that if every youngster, LD or otherwise, had at least one trade, skill, or technique about which he or she was fairly competent, that would do more for that youngster's adjustment than would the many hours of remediation to which the child is subjected. Perhaps that accent on the positive would go a long way toward actually helping the remediation process. If children knew they could excel in something, that might help them become competent in other areas as well. (T. C. Lovitt, January 14, 2002, personal communication)

 For more information on learning disabilities, go to the Web Links module in Chapter 7 of the Companion Website at **www.prenhall.com/heward**

SUMMARY

DEFINITIONS

- There is no universally agreed-on definition of learning disabilities. Most states require that three criteria be met: (1) a severe discrepancy between potential or ability and actual achievement, (2) learning problems that cannot be attributed to other disabilities, and (3) special educational services needed to succeed in school.
- No matter which definition is used, educators should focus on each student's specific skill deficiencies for assessment and instruction.

CHARACTERISTICS

- Most students with learning disabilities show one or more of the following characteristics: reading problems, deficits in written language, underachievement in math, social skills deficits, problems with attention and hyperactivity, and behavioral problems.
- The fundamental, defining characteristic of students with learning disabilities is specific and significant achievement deficiency in the presence of adequate overall intelligence.

ATTENTION-DEFICIT/HYPERACTIVITY DISORDER

- To be diagnosed with attention-deficit/hyperactivity disorder (ADHD), a child must consistently display six or more symptoms listed in the DSM-IV of inattention or hyperactivity-impulsivity for a period of at least six months.
- ADHD is not a disability category recognized by IDEA. Many students with ADHD also have learning disabilities and/or emotional and behavioral disorders and receive special education under those categories. Students with ADHD can also be served under the other health impairments category if the disorder results a "heightened alertness to environmental stimuli" that adversely affects academic performance. Some children with ADHD are eligible for services under Section 504 of the Rehabilitation Act.
- The prevalence of ADHD is estimated to be 3% to 5% of all school-age children.
- Boys are much more likely to be diagnosed with ADHD than are girls.
- Genetic factors may place individuals at a greater than normal risk of an ADHD diagnosis. ADHD is associated with a wide range of genetic disorders and diseases such as Fragile X syndrome, Turner syndrome, Williams syndrome, fetal alcohol syndrome, prenatal exposure to cocaine, and lead poisoning.
- Some individuals with ADHD have structural or biochemical differences in their brains that may play a causal role in their behavioral deficits and excesses.
- Ritalin is the most frequently prescribed medication for children with ADHD. Approximately 70% to 80% of children diagnosed with ADHD respond positively to Ritalin. Common, but usually manageable, side effects of Ritalin include insomnia, decreased appetite, headaches, weight loss, and irritability.
- The use of stimulant medications with children is controversial. Some professionals believe the benefits outweigh the liabilities and that drug therapy should be part of a comprehensive treatment program for children with ADHD. Other professionals are concerned that stimulant medications have few long-term benefits on academic achievement and that educators and parents rely too heavily on medical interventions.
- Classroom interventions for students with ADHD included reinforcing for on-task behavior, modification of assignments and instructional activities to promote success, and teaching self-control strategies.
- About three times as many boys are identified as learning disabled as are girls

PREVALENCE

- Learning disabilities form the largest category in special education. Students with learning disabilities represent one half of all students receiving special education.
- About three times as many boys are identified as learning disabled as are girls.

CAUSES

- Although the actual cause of a specific learning disability is seldom known, four types of suspected causal factors are brain damage, heredity, biochemical imbalance, and environmental factors.
- Specific regions of the brains of some individuals with reading and language disabilities show abnormal activation patterns during phonological processing tasks.
- Genetics may account for at least some family linkage with dyslexia. Research has located possible chromosomal loci for the genetic transmission of phonological deficits that may predispose a child for reading problems later.

- Most professionals today give little credence to biochemical imbalance as a significant cause of learning disabilities.
- Environmental factors—particularly impoverished living conditions early in a child's life and poor instruction—contribute to the achievement deficits of many children with learning disabilities.

ASSESSMENT

- Norm-referenced tests compare a child's score with the scores of age mates who have taken the same test.
- Criterion-referenced tests, which compare a child's score with a predetermined mastery level, are useful in identifying specific skills the child has learned as well as skills that require instruction.
- Teachers use informal reading inventories to observe directly and record a child's reading skills.
- Curriculum-based measurement is a formative evaluation method that measures a student's progress in the actual curriculum in which she is participating.
- Direct and daily measurement involves assessing a student's performance on a specific skill each time it is taught.
- Precision teaching is a special type of direct and daily measurement in which the standard celeration chart is used to guide instructional decisions based on changes in a student's frequency of performance.

EDUCATIONAL APPROACHES

- Contemporary best practice in educating students with learning disabilities includes approaches such as explicit instruction, content enhancements, and learning strategies.
- Content enhancements, such as graphic organizers, visual displays, guided notes, and mnemonic strategies, make curriculum content more accessible to students with learning disabilities.
- Learning strategies help students guide themselves successfully through specific tasks or general problems.

EDUCATIONAL PLACEMENT ALTERNATIVES

- Most students with learning disabilities spend at least part of each school day in the regular classroom.
- In some schools, a consultant teacher helps regular classroom teachers work with children with learning disabilities.
- In the resource room, a specially trained teacher works with children on particular skill deficits for one or more periods per day.
- A few children with learning disabilities attend separate classrooms. This placement option, however, should be used only after legitimate attempts to serve the child in a less restrictive setting have failed; and it should not be considered permanent.

CURRENT ISSUES AND FUTURE TRENDS

- Discussion and debate about what constitutes a true learning disability are likely to continue. It is important for schools to respond to the individual needs of all children who have difficulty learning.
- Most professionals and advocates for students with learning disabilities do not support full inclusion, which would eliminate the continuum of service delivery options.
- In addition to their academic and social skills deficits, students with learning disabilities possess positive attributes and interests that teachers should identify and try to strengthen.

 To check your comprehension of chapter content, go to the Guided Review and Quiz modules in Chapter 7 of the Companion Website at **www.prenhall.com/heward**

Chapter 8
Emotional and Behavioral Disorders

Focus Questions

- Why should a child who behaves badly be considered disabled?

- Who is more severely disabled: the acting-out, antisocial child or the withdrawn child?

- How are behavior problems and academic performance interrelated?

- How can a teacher's efforts to defuse a classroom disturbance contribute to an escalation of misbehavior?

- What are the most important skills for teachers of students with emotional and behavioral disorders?

MICHELLE FUNDORA SAN

CENTENNIAL MIDDLE SCHOOL

DADE COUNTY PUBLIC SCHOOLS, MIAMI, FLORIDA

Education • Teaching Credentials • Experience
- A.A., Special Education, Miami Dade Community College, 1997
- B.S., Special Education/Students with Emotional Handicaps, Florida International University, 2000
- Florida certification in Emotional Handicaps (K–12)
- 2 years teaching experience

Current Teaching Position   At Centennial Middle school, a school of 1,200 sixth-through eighth-grade students in Miami, I teach students diagnosed as severely emotionally disturbed.

Students   I co-teach with another special education teacher in a self-contained classroom. I teach no more than 13 students at a time. They range from ages 11 to 13. Academically, our students range from as low as kindergarten to above grade level. There is a lot of racial and cultural diversity in our school; I have black, white, and Hispanic students in my classroom. All of our students come from low economic backgrounds and qualify for free lunches. One student is included in general education classrooms for part of the day, and I expect to have at least three other students in the regular classroom by the end of the year.

I am very surprised that we have four girls in my classroom this year. Girls are somewhat rare for this population. The students this year are very different from those of previous years, in terms of their behavior. Last year, most of my students had conduct disorders or were very withdrawn. But this year, several students are diagnosed as psychotic, and they experience visual and auditory hallucinations.

Teaching Strategies   Students with behavioral and emotional problems have extreme difficulty sitting still and listening to a lecture. I have found that I can get full participation from my students if they are actively involved in the lesson. I accomplish this by using guided notes, response cards, and plenty of hands-on projects. For example, one time we did three projects on cells, but the students did not understand the concepts until the last project, when they built a model of a cell out of candy and labeled it correctly.

During teacher-led lessons, I reinforce good behavior and participation with points toward free time. I do this at random intervals so the students can't predict when they have to be good. I set a timer on my desk to varying intervals—say, 3 minutes, then 4 minutes, then 1 minute. Because the students can't predict when they have to be good, they have to be good all the time to maximize their gains.

It also helps to have a set schedule so that students know what they are doing each day. Students with emotional and behavioral disorders need structure. Peer tutoring works well—if I've paired the right students together. My students also like to challenge themselves by writing contracts with me for meeting specific behavioral or academic goals in exchange for a favorite activity or treat.

A Collaborative Effort The Dade County Public Schools has contracted with the Bertha Abbess Children Center (BACC) to provide a variety of counseling and other support services to children with the most severe emotional and behavioral disorders. For example, BACC clinical social workers conduct daily counseling and peer support groups with the students. During these groups, the students talk about their feelings, and the therapists lead activities dealing with issues such as anger control, family problems, drug use, criminal activity, and so on. BACC therapists also see students on an individual basis. I let the BACC person know if any of my students are having a hard day or if I've noticed any odd behavior recently. The students see a music therapist once a week, and a psychiatrist visits every couple of weeks to check on the medications used by several of the students to help with their behavior. BACC also has therapists who deal with students who have been sexually abused. The center provides an effective model of positive classroom management and support for teachers to follow, and the teachers and BACC clinicians work as a team to help develop, implement, and evaluate each student's IEP.

What I Like the Most About Being a Special Educator That's easy: working with the students. Any little positive change or happy memory I can add to these students' lives makes it all worthwhile. I also enjoy the unpredictability of the day. Having to stay on my toes at all times makes this job very interesting.

A Meaningful Moment I had this student last year, I'll call him Tom, who was totally withdrawn. Tom had trouble making eye contact, could not take any kind of touch, and for the first couple months of school never once verbalized what he felt or wanted. If I took too much time to call on him, he would say, "Never mind," or "Forget it." As the year progressed, he improved a little, and near the Christmas break he was better at verbalizing what he wanted. If I sat with him for a while and fished real hard, he would let me know how he was feeling. But there was still no improvement in eye contact or touch. A few days before the break, he brought in a Christmas card for me and my team teacher. We both read it and thanked him, and I hung it up on the classroom wall.

On the last day before Christmas break, all the students were helping clean up the room, and Tom was sweeping the floor. A girl from the classroom next to ours brought a Christmas card over to me. I said, "Thank you!" and gave her a hug. Tom stopped sweeping and said, "Miss, I gave you a card, and you never gave me a hug!" At that moment I was extremely stung, as you can imagine. I said, "Tom, I never thought you would want a hug. You never even like me to touch you on the shoulder. But I will give you a hug right now if you want me to." Of course, Tom said, "Never mind," and went back to his sweeping. At the end of the day, as we walked our students out to the buses, I asked Tom if I could give him the hug I owed him. To my surprise, he turned, gave me a quick hug, and then immediately said, "Okay. That's enough. Bye!"

I laughed and said, "Bye, Tom." Tom still has trouble making eye contact, and he still doesn't like anyone to touch him. But I will never forget that hug. Tom draws me nice pictures once in a while, too.

I'm glad that Tom and I shared that great experience. My first year was a tough one because both my team-teaching partner and I were first-year teachers working alone together. In your first year in the classroom, you need a lot of reassurance because you are very insecure about how well you are doing. The feedback I got from Tom that day made my whole year.

To learn more about Michelle San's classroom, visit the Teacher Feature module in Chapter 8 of the Companion Website at **www.prenhall.com/heward**

Childhood should be a happy time: a time for playing, making friends, and learning—and for most children it is. But some children's lives are in constant turmoil. Some children strike out at others, sometimes with disastrous consequences. Others are so shy and withdrawn that they seem to be in their own worlds. In either case, playing with others, making friends, and learning all the things a child must learn are extremely difficult for them. These are children with emotional and behavioral disorders. They are referred to by a variety of terms: emotionally disturbed, socially maladjusted, psychologically disordered, emotionally handicapped, or even psychotic if their behavior is extremely abnormal or bizarre.

Many children with emotional and behavioral disorders are seldom really liked by anyone—their peers, teachers, siblings, even parents. Sadder still, they often do not even like themselves. The child with behavioral disorders is difficult to be around, and attempts to befriend him (most are boys) may lead to rejection, verbal abuse, or even physical attack. Although most children with emotional and behavioral disorders are of sound mind and body, their noxious or withdrawn behavior is as serious an impediment to their functioning and learning as are the physical and developmental disabilities that challenge other children. Children with emotional and behavioral disorders make up a significant portion of students who need special education.

To better understand what will be covered in this chapter, go to the Essential Concepts and Chapter-at-a-Glance modules in Chapter 8 of the Companion Website at **www.prenhall.com/heward**

 ## DEFINITIONS

Like their colleagues in mental retardation and learning disabilities, special educators who work with students with emotional and behavioral disorders have been struggling to reach consensus on a definition. A clear definition of behavioral disorders is lacking for numerous reasons. First, disordered behavior is a social construct; there is no clear agreement about what constitutes good mental health. All children behave inappropriately at times. How often, with how much intensity, and for how long must a student engage in a particular behavior before he is considered disabled because of the behavior? Second, different theories of emotional disturbance use concepts and terminology that do little to promote meaning from one definition to another. Third, expectations and norms for appropriate behavior are often quite different across ethnic and cultural groups. Finally, sometimes emotional and behavioral disorders occur in conjunction with other disabilities (notably mental retardation and learning disabilities), making it difficult to tell whether one condition may be the result or the cause of the other.

Although many definitions of behavioral disorders have been proposed, the two that have had the most influence are the definition in IDEA and one proposed by a coalition of professional associations concerned with children with behavior problems.

 ### IDEA DEFINITION OF EMOTIONAL DISTURBANCE

Emotional disturbance is one of the disability categories in IDEA under which children may receive special education services. IDEA defines serious emotional disturbance as follows:

(I)   The term means a condition exhibiting one or more of the following characteristics over a long period of time and to a marked degree that adversely affects educational performance:
  (a)   An inability to learn which cannot be explained by intellectual, sensory, and health factors;
  (b)   An inability to build or maintain satisfactory interpersonal relationships with peers and teachers;
  (c)   Inappropriate types of behavior or feelings under normal circumstances;

Definition of E/BD

Council for Exceptional Children   Content Standards for Beginning Teachers–E/BD: Educational terminology and definitions of individuals with E/BD (BD1K1).
PRAXIS Special Education Core Principles: Content Knowledge: I. Understanding Exceptionalities, Definitions of specific disabilities.

(d) A general pervasive mood of unhappiness or depression; or

(e) A tendency to develop physical symptoms or fears associated with personal or school problems.

(II) The term includes schizophrenia. The term does not apply to children who are socially maladjusted, unless it is determined that they have an emotional disturbance. (U.S. Department of Education, 1999, p. 12422)

At first glance, this definition may seem straightforward enough. It identifies three conditions that must be met: *chronicity* ("over a long period of time"), *severity* ("to a marked degree"), and *difficulty in school* ("adversely affects educational performance"); and it lists five types of problems that qualify. But in fact, this definition is extremely vague and leaves much to the subjective opinion of the authorities who surround the child. What do terms such as *satisfactory* and *inappropriate* really mean? Differing degrees of teacher tolerance for student behavior (Schwartz, Wolfe, & Cassar, 1997; Shinn, Tindal, & Spira, 1987), differences between teachers' and parents' expectations for student behavior (Aaroe & Nelson, 2000), and the fact that expectations for behavior vary across ethnic and cultural groups (Taylor, Gunter, & Slate, 2001) make the referral and identification of students with emotional and behavioral disorders a difficult and subjective process.

And how does one determine that some behavior problems represent "social maladjustment" whereas others indicate true "emotional disturbance"? Many children experiencing significant difficulties in school because of their behavior are ineligible for special education under IDEA because their problems are considered to be "merely" conduct disorders or discipline problems (Forness & Kavale, 2000).

The federal definition was derived from a single study conducted by Eli Bower (1960) in the Los Angeles county schools more than 40 years ago (Forness & Kavale, 2000). Bower himself never intended to make a distinction between emotional disturbance and social maladjustment. Indeed, he has stated that the five components of the definition were, in fact, meant to be indicators of social maladjustment (Bower, 1982).

It is difficult to conceive of a child who is sufficiently socially maladjusted to have received that label but who does not display one or more of the five characteristics (especially *b*) included in the federal definition. As written, the definition seemingly excludes children on the very basis for which they are included. This illogical criterion for ineligibility, the dated and arbitrary list of the five characteristics that are not supported by recent research, and the subjective wording that enables school districts to not serve many children with behavioral problems have produced strongly voiced criticism of the federal definition (e.g., Cline, 1990; Forness & Knitzer, 1992; Kauffman, 2001; Wood et al., 1997).

 CCBD DEFINITION OF EMOTIONAL OR BEHAVIORAL DISORDERS

In response to the problems many saw with the federal definition, the Council for Children with Behavioral Disorders (CCBD, 1989) drafted a new definition using the term *emotional or behavioral disorder* (see Figure 8.1). The CCBD definition was later adopted by the National Mental Health and Special Education Coalition (a group of 30 education, mental health, and child advocacy organizations) and subsequently submitted to the U.S. Congress as a proposed replacement for the IDEA definition of serious emotional disturbance. The CCBD definition reads as follows:

1. The term "emotional or behavioral disorder" means a disability that is characterized by emotional or behavioral responses in school programs so different from appropriate age, cultural, or ethnic norms that the responses adversely affect educational performance, including academic, social, vocational or personal skills; more than a temporary, expected response to stressful events in the environment; consistently exhibited in two different settings, at least one of which is school-related; and unresponsive to direct intervention in general

Council for Children with Behavior Disorders (CCBD)

Council for Exceptional Children **Content Standards for Beginning Teachers–E/BD:** Professional and Ethical Practice, Organizations and publications relevant to the field (BD9K1).
PRAXIS Special Education Core Principles: Knowledge: III. Delivery of Services to Students with Disabilities, Professional roles, Use of professional literature and organizations.

FIGURE 8.1 Emotionally disturbed or behaviorally disordered? Does it make a difference?

The Council for Children with Behavioral Disorders (CCBD) has officially adopted the position that the term *behaviorally disordered* is more appropriate than the term *emotionally disturbed*. The CCBD endorses use of *behaviorally disordered* because (1) it does not suggest any particular theory of causation or set of intervention techniques, (2) it is more representative of the students who are disabled by their behavior and are being served under IDEA, and (3) it is less stigmatizing (Huntze, 1985). The concern about stigmatization may have some merit, at least in terms of how teachers perceive children. Two studies found that the label *behaviorally disordered* implies less-negative dimensions to teachers than does *emotionally disturbed* (Feldman, Kinnison, Jay, & Harth, 1983; Lloyd, Kauffman, & Gansneder, 1987). Both pre- and in-service teachers indicated they thought children labeled as behaviorally disordered were more teachable and likely to be successful in a regular classroom than were children identified as emotionally disturbed.

education, or the condition of the child is such that general education interventions would be insufficient.

2. The term includes such a disability that co-exists with other disabilities.
3. The term includes a schizophrenic disorder, affective disorder, anxiety disorder, or other sustained disorder of conduct or adjustment, affecting a child if the disorder affects educational performance as described in paragraph (1). (*Federal Register,* February 10, 1993, p. 7938)

The proposed definition clarifies the educational dimensions of the disability; focuses directly on the child's behavior in school settings; places behavior in the context of appropriate age, ethnic, and cultural norms; and increases the possibility of early identification and intervention (McIntyre & Forness, 1996). Perhaps most important, it does not require "meaningless distinctions between social and emotional maladjustment, distinctions that often waste diagnostic resources when it is already clear that serious problems exist" (Forness & Kavale, 2000, p. 267).

 ## CHARACTERISTICS

Children with emotional or behavioral disorders are characterized primarily by behavior that falls significantly beyond the norms of their cultural and age group on two dimensions called externalizing and internalizing. Both patterns of abnormal behavior have adverse effects on children's academic achievement and social relationships.

 ### EXTERNALIZING BEHAVIORS

The most common behavior pattern of children with emotional and behavioral disorders consists of antisocial, or *externalizing behaviors.* In the classroom, children with externalizing behavior problems frequently do the following (adapted from Walker, 1997, p. 13):

- Get out of their seats
- Yell, talk out, and curse
- Disturb peers
- Hit or fight
- Ignore the teacher
- Complain
- Argue excessively
- Steal

Externalizing behavior and noncompliance

 Council for Exceptional Children Content Standards for Beginning Teachers—E/BD: Social Characteristics of Individuals with E/BD (BD2K3). **PRAXIS** Special Education Core Principles: Content Knowledge: I. Understanding Exceptionalities, Characteristics of students with disabilities, Affective and social-adaptive factors.

- Lie
- Destroy property
- Do not comply with directions
- Have temper tantrums
- Are excluded from peer-controlled activities
- Do not respond to teacher corrections
- Do not complete assignments

Rhode, Jensen, and Reavis (1998) describe noncompliance as the "king-pin behavior" around which other behavioral excesses revolve. "Noncompliance is simply defined as not following a direction within a reasonable amount of time. Most of the arguing, tantrums, fighting, or rule breaking is secondary to avoiding requests or required tasks" (p. 4). Clearly, an ongoing pattern of such behavior presents a major challenge for teachers of antisocial children. "They can make our teaching lives miserable and single-handedly disrupt a classroom" (Rhode et al., 1998, p. 3).

All children sometimes cry, hit others, and refuse to comply with requests of parents and teachers; but children with emotional and behavioral disorders do so frequently. Also, the antisocial behavior of children with emotional and behavioral disorders often occurs with little or no provocation. Aggression takes many forms—verbal abuse toward adults and other children, destructiveness and vandalism, and physical attacks on others. These children seem to be in continuous conflict with those around them. Their own aggressive outbursts often cause others to strike back. It is no wonder that children with emotional and behavioral disorders are seldom liked by others and find it difficult to establish friendships.

Many believe that most children who exhibit deviant behavioral patterns will grow out of them with time and become normally functioning adults. Although this optimistic outcome holds true for many children who exhibit problems such as withdrawal, fears, and speech impairments (Rutter, 1976), research indicates that it is not so for children who display consistent patterns of aggressive, coercive, antisocial, and/or delinquent behavior (Patterson, Cipaldi, & Bank, 1991; Trembley, 2000; Wahler & Dumas, 1986). The stability of aggressive behavior over a decade is equal to the stability of intelligence (Kazdin, 1987).

A pattern of antisocial behavior early in a child's development is the best single predictor of delinquency in adolescence.

Preschoolers who show the early signs of antisocial behavior patterns do not grow out of them. Rather, as they move throughout their school careers, they grow into these unfortunate patterns with disastrous results to themselves and others. This myth that preschoolers will outgrow antisocial behavior is pervasive among many teachers and early educators and is very dangerous because it leads professionals to do nothing early on when the problem can be effectively addressed. (Walker, Colvin, & Ramsey, 1995, p. 47)

Children who enter adolescence with a history of aggressive behavior stand a very good chance of dropping out of school, being arrested, abusing drugs and alcohol, having marginalized adult lives, and dying young (Lipsey & Derzon, 1998; Walker et al., 1995). Students with emotional and behavioral disorders are 13.3 times more likely to be arrested during their school careers than nondisabled students are (Doren, Bullis, & Benz, 1996a), and 58% are arrested within five years of leaving high school (Chesapeake Institute, 1994).

 INTERNALIZING BEHAVIORS

Some children with emotional and behavioral disorders are anything but aggressive. Their problem is the opposite—too little social interaction with others. They are said to have *internalizing* behavioral disorders. Although children who consistently act immature and withdrawn do not present the threat to others that antisocial children do, their behavior creates a serious impediment to their own development. These children seldom play with

Early pattern of antisocial behavior

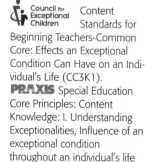

Content Standards for Beginning Teachers-Common Core: Effects an Exceptional Condition Can Have on an Individual's Life (CC3K1).
PRAXIS Special Education Core Principles: Content Knowledge: I. Understanding Exceptionalities, Influence of an exceptional condition throughout an individual's life span.

Internalizing behavior

Content Standards for Beginning Teachers–E/BD: Social characteristics of individuals with E/BD (BD2K3).
PRAXIS Special Education Core Principles: Content Knowledge: I. Understanding Exceptionalities, Characteristics of students with disabilities, Affective and social-adaptive factors.

others their own age. They usually do not have the social skills needed to make friends and have fun, and they often retreat into daydreams and fantasies. Some are fearful of things without reason, frequently complain of being sick or hurt, and go into deep bouts of depression. Obviously, such behavior limits a child's chances to take part in and learn from the school and leisure activities in which normal children participate. (Table 8.1 describes the most common types of anxiety disorders and mood disorders seen in school-age children.)

Children who exhibit the internalizing behaviors characteristic of some types of anxiety and mood disorders may be less disturbing to classroom teachers than are antisocial children. Because of this, they are in danger of not being identified. Happily, the outlook is fairly good for the child with mild or moderate degrees of withdrawn and immature behavior who is fortunate enough to have competent teachers and other school professionals responsible for his development. Carefully targeting the social and self-determination skills the child should learn and systematically arranging opportunities for and reinforcing those behaviors often prove successful.

It is a grave mistake, however, to believe that children with emotional disorders that result primarily in internalizing behaviors have only mild and transient problems. The severe anxiety and mood disorders experienced by some children not only cause pervasive impairments in their educational performance—they also threaten their very existence. Indeed, without identification and effective treatment, the extreme emotional disorders of some children can lead to self-inflicted injury or even death from substance abuse, starvation, or suicidal behavior.

Children who exhibit internalizing behavioral disorders are often limited in their chances to take part in and learn from school and leisure activities.

 ## ACADEMIC ACHIEVEMENT

Most students with emotional and behavioral disorders perform one or more years below grade level academically (Cullinan, 2002). Many of these students exhibit significant deficiencies in reading (Coleman & Vaughn, 2000; Maughan, Pickles, Hagell, Rutter, & Yule, 1996) and in math achievement (Greenbaum et al., 1996). In addition to the challenges to learning caused by their behavioral excesses and deficits, many students with emotional or behavioral disorders also have learning disabilities and/or language delays, which compound their difficulties in mastering academic skills and content (Glassberg, Hooper, & Mattison, 1999; Kaiser, Hancock, Cai, Foster, & Hester, 2000).

The following dismal academic outcomes for students with emotional and behavioral disorders are derived from several nationwide studies (Chesapeake Institute, 1994; Valdes, Williamson, & Wagner, 1990; U.S. Department of Education, 1998, 1999):

- Two-thirds cannot pass competency exams for their grade level.
- They have the lowest grade-point average of any group of students with disabilities.
- They have the highest absenteeism rate of any group of students.
- Only 20%–25% leave high school with a diploma or certificate of completion, compared to 50% of all students with disabilities and 76% of all youth in the general population.
- More than 50% drop out of high school.

The strong correlation between low academic achievement and behavioral problems is not a one-way relationship. The disruptive and defiant behavior of students with emotional and behavioral disorders "almost always leads to academic failure. This failure, in turn, predisposes them to further antisocial conduct" (Hallenbeck & Kauffman, 1995, p. 64).

Academic achievement of students with E/BD

Council for Exceptional Children — Content Standards for Beginning Teachers-Common Core: Educational implications of characteristics of exceptionalities (CC2K2).
PRAXIS Special Education Core Principles: Content Knowledge: I. Understanding Exceptionalities, Characteristics of students with disabilities.

TABLE 8.1 Types of anxiety, mood, and other emotional disorders in children

Condition	Characteristics/Symptoms	Remarks
ANXIETY DISORDERS	Maladaptive emotional state or behaviors caused by excessive and often irrational fears and worries.	
Generalized anxiety disorder	Excessive, unrealistic worries, fears, tension that lasts six months or more; in addition to chronic anxiety, symptoms include restlessness, fatigue, difficulty concentrating, muscular aches, insomnia, nausea, excessive heart rate, dizziness, and irritability.	Excessive worrying interferes with normal activities. Children tend to be very hard on themselves, striving for perfection, sometimes redoing tasks repeatedly; they may also seek constant approval or reassurance from others. Usually affects children between the ages of 6 and 11.
Phobias	Intense fear reaction to a specific object or situation (such as snakes, dogs, or heights); level of fear is inappropriate to the situation and is recognized by the person as being irrational; can lead to the avoidance of common, everyday situations.	Most phobias can be treated successfully with behavior therapy techniques such as systematic desensitization (gradual and repeated exposure to feared object or situation while relaxing) and self-monitoring.
Obsessive/compulsive disorder (OCD)	Persistent, recurring thoughts (obsessions) that reflect exaggerated anxiety or fears; typical obsessions include worry about being contaminated, behaving improperly, or acting violently. The obsessions may lead an individual to perform a ritual or routine (compulsions)—such as washing hands, repeating phrases, or hoarding—to relieve the anxiety caused by the obsession.	OCD most often begins in adolescence or early adulthood. Most individuals recognize their obsessions are irrational and that the compulsions are excessive or unreasonable. Behavioral therapy is effective in treating most cases of OCD; medications are often effective.
Anorexia nervosa	Refusal to maintain body weight at or above a minimally normal weight for age and height. Obsessive concern with body weight or shape. Intense anxiety about gaining weight or becoming fat, even though severely underweight. Two subtypes: restricting food intake by starving oneself down to an abnormal weight and binge-eating/purging.	Anorexia and bulimia (see below) are primarily disorders of females, particularly adolescent girls. Early in the course of anorexia, the person often denies the disorder. Depression, anxiety, compulsive exercise, social withdrawal, obsessive/compulsive symptoms, and substance abuse are often associated with eating disorders.
Bulimia nervosa	Recurrent episodes of (a) binge eating (eating in a discrete period of time an amount of food much larger than most people would eat under similar circumstances while feeling that one cannot stop eating) and (b) inappropriate compensatory behavior in order to prevent weight gain (e.g., self-induced vomiting, misuse of laxatives or other medications, fasting, excessive exercise).	Preoccupation with weight and shape and excessive self-evaluation are primary symptoms of both anorexia and bulimia. Many patients demonstrate a mixture of both anorexic and bulimic behaviors.
Post-traumatic stress disorder	Prolonged and recurrent emotional reactions after exposure to a traumatic event (e.g., sexual or physical assault, unexpected death of a loved one, natural disaster, witnessing or being a victim of acts of war or terrorism). Symptoms: flashbacks and nightmares of the traumatic event; avoiding places or things related to the trauma; emotional detachment from others; and difficulty sleeping, irritability, or poor concentration.	Increased recognition of PTSD in children has occurred in the U.S. since the terrorist attacks of September 11, 2001. Individual and group counseling and support activities can be helpful. Teachers can help by providing an environment in which the child with PTSD feels safe and positive social attention for the child's involvement with normal activities.
Selective mutism (also called elective mutism, speech phobia)	Child speaks normally to specific person or group (e.g., family members) but refuses to talk to others. May be a response to trauma, more often caused by anxiety or fear of speaking in certain settings or to certain individuals or groups.	Treatment uses positive approach, no attention or punishment for not speaking, reinforcement for approximations of speaking (e.g., participation in class activities, non-speech vocalizations).

MOOD DISORDERS Characterized by impaired functioning due to episodes of abnormally depressed or elevated emotional state.

Disorder	Description	Additional Information
Depression	Marked by pervasive sad mood and sense of hopelessness. Symptoms include social withdrawal; irritability; feelings of guilt or worthlessness; inability to concentrate; loss of interest in normal activities; drastic change in weight, appetite, or sleeping pattern; prolonged crying bouts; recurring thoughts of suicide. Several symptoms must be exhibited over a period of time and not be temporary, reasonable responses to life circumstances (e.g., grief over death of a family member).	It is estimated that 15% to 20% of adolescents experience depression at one time or another; adolescent girls are twice as likely as are boys to be depressed. Depression is often overlooked in children, especially when symptoms are overshadowed by externalizing behavioral disorders. Teachers should be attentive for signs of possible depression and refer students for evaluation.
Bipolar disorder (formerly called manic-depressive disorder)	Alternative episodes of depressive and manic states. During manic episodes, person is in an elevated mood of euphoria—a feeling of extraordinary elation, excitement—and exhibits three or more of the following symptoms: excessive egotism; very little sleep needed; incessant talkativeness; rapidly changing thoughts and ideas in uncontrolled order; easily distracted; agitated, "driven" activities; and participation in personally risky activities. The peak age at onset of first symptoms falls between the ages of 15–19. Five years or more may elapse between the first and second episodes, but the time periods between subsequent episodes usually narrow.	Some patients are reluctant to participate in treatment because they find the experience of mania very enjoyable. Patients often recall this experience and minimize or deny entirely the devastating features of full-blown mania or the demoralization of a depressive episode. Regular patterns of daily activities, including sleeping, eating, physical activity, and social and/or emotional stimulation may help. Medications are often effective in treating acute episodes, preventing future episodes, and in providing stabilizing moods between episodes.

OTHER DISORDERS

Disorder	Description	Additional Information
Schizophrenia	A severe psychotic disorder characterized by delusions, hallucinations (hearing voices), unfounded fears of persecution, disorganized speech, catatonic behavior (stupor and muscular rigidity), restricted range and intensity of emotional expression (affective flattening), reduced thought and speech productivity, and decreased initiation of goal-directed behavior. Affects males and females with equal frequency. Onset typically occurs during adolescence or early adulthood. Most persons with schizophrenia alternate between acute psychotic episodes and stable phases with few or no symptoms.	Although there is no cure at present, most children with schizophrenia benefit from a variety of treatments, including antipsychotic medication, behavioral therapy, and educational interventions such as social skills training. The general goals of treatment are to decrease the frequency, severity, and psychosocial consequences of psychotic episodes and to maximize functioning between episodes.
Tourette syndrome	An inherited neurological disorder characterized by motor and vocal tics (repeated and involuntary movements) such as eye blinking, facial grimacing, throat clearing or sniffing, arm thrusting, kicking, or jumping. About 15% of cases include *coprolalia* (repeated cursing, obscene language, and ethnic slurs). Symptoms typically appear before age 18; males affected 3 to 4 times more often than females. Many students with TS also have attentional problems, impulsiveness, compulsions, ritualistic behaviors, and learning disabilities.	Tics are experienced as irresistible; student may seek a secluded spot to release symptoms after delaying them. Tics are more likely during periods of tension or stress, and decrease with relaxation or when focusing on an absorbing task. Tolerance and understanding of symptoms are of paramount importance to students with TS; untimed exams (in a private room if vocal tics are a problem), and permission to leave the classroom when tics become overwhelming are often helpful.

Sources: American Psychiatric Association (1999, 2000a, 2000b, 2000c); Anxiety Disorders Association of America (2001). Brigham and Cole (1999); Cullinan (2002); Kauffman (2001); Morris and Kratochwill (1998); Stark, Bronik, Wong, Wells and Ostrander (2000); Tourette Syndrome Association (2000).

INTELLIGENCE

Many more children with emotional and behavioral disorders score in the slow learner or mildly retarded range on IQ tests than do children without disabilities. Valdes et al. (1990) reported a mean IQ of 86 for students with emotional and behavioral disorders, with about half of their sample scoring between 71 and 90. The students in a study by Cullinan, Epstein, and Sabornie (1992) had an average IQ score of 92.6. On the basis of his review of research related to the intelligence of children with emotional and behavioral disorders, Kauffman (2001) concluded that "although the majority fall only slightly below average in IQ, a disproportionate number, compared to the normal distribution, score in the dull normal and mildly retarded range, and relatively few fall in the upper ranges" (p. 251).

Whether children with emotional and behavioral disorders actually have any less real intelligence than do children without disabilities is difficult to say. An IQ test measures how well a child performs certain tasks at the time and place the test is administered. It is almost certain that the disturbed child's inappropriate behavior has interfered with past opportunities to learn many of the tasks included on the test. Rhode et al. (1998) estimate that the average student actively attends to the teacher and to assigned work approximately 85% of the time but that students with behavior disorders are on task only about 60% or less of the time. This difference in on-task behavior can have a dramatic impact on academic learning. (To learn about one strategy for keeping students actively engaged with instruction, see Teaching & Learning, "Using Response Cards to Increase Participation and Achievement," later in this chapter.)

Response cards

Council for Exceptional Children
Content Standards for Beginning Teachers-Common Core: Select, adopt, and use instructional strategies and materials according to student's exceptional learning needs (CC4S3).
PRAXIS Special Education Core Principles: Content Knowledge: III. Delivery of Services to Students with Disabilities, Teaching strategies and methods for small and large group instruction.

 SOCIAL SKILLS AND INTERPERSONAL RELATIONSHIPS

The ability to develop and maintain interpersonal relationships during childhood and adolescence is an important predictor of present and future adjustment. As might be expected, many students with emotional and behavioral disorders experience great difficulty in making and keeping friends (Cartledge & Milburn, 1995; Gresham, Lane, MacMillan, & Bocian, 1999). The results of a study by Schonert-Reichl (1993) comparing the social relationships of secondary students with behavioral disorders with those of same-age peers without disabilities is representative of much of the published literature on social skills of students with emotional and behavioral disorders. The students with behavioral disorders reported lower levels of empathy toward others, participation in fewer curricular activities, less frequent contacts with friends, and lower-quality relationships than were reported by their peers without disabilities.

 PREVALENCE

Prevalence of E/BD

PRAXIS Special Education Core Principles: Content Knowledge: I. Understanding Exceptionalities, Incidence and prevalence of various types of disabilities.

Estimates of how many children have emotional and behavioral disorders vary widely. Cullinan and Epstein (1995) suggest that a "rule of one-third" describes the prevalence of behavior disorders: that approximately 33% of children will experience behavior problems that concern their teachers at some time during any given year, that the behavior of about one-third of those children (or 10% of the school-age population) will require intervention or assistance of school personnel outside the regular classroom, and one-third of that group (about 3%) will have behavioral problems significant enough to warrant special education. After reviewing studies on prevalence, Koyanagi and Gaines (1993) concluded that between 3% and 5% of children have emotional and behavioral problems sufficient to warrant intervention. A national consortium of special educators and researchers who are developing schoolwide discipline and positive behavioral support programs estimates that between 1% and 7% of students have chronic problems with behavior that require intensive, individualized intervention and supports (Sugai, Sprague, Horner, & Walker, 2000).

Such varying estimates suggest that different criteria are being used to decide what constitutes emotional or behavioral disorders. Differences in prevalence figures, however, stem as much from how the data are collected as they do from the use of different definitions (Cullinan, 2002). Most surveys ask teachers to identify students in their classes who display behavior problems at that point in time. Many children exhibit inappropriate behavior for short periods, and such one-shot screening procedures will identify them.

Annual reports from the federal government, however, show far fewer children are being served than the most conservative prevalence estimates. The 472,932 children ages 6 to 21 who received special education under the IDEA category of emotional disturbance during the 2000–2001 school year represented only about 0.7% of the school-age population (U.S. Department of Education, 2002). Although this figure marked the greatest number of children with emotional and behavioral disorders ever served and ranked emotional disturbance as the fourth-largest disability category in special education (8.2% of all students ages 6 through 21 served under IDEA), it means that most children with emotional and behavioral disorders are not receiving special education.

The number of children being served represents less than half of the 2% estimate the federal government used previously in its estimates of funding and personnel needs for students with emotional and behavioral disorders. Kauffman (2001) believes that social policy and economic factors caused the government to first reduce its estimate of the prevalence of behavioral disorders (from 2% to 1.2%) and then to stop publishing an estimate altogether. "The government obviously prefers not to allow wide discrepancies between prevalence estimates and the actual number of children served. It is easier to cut prevalence estimates than to serve more students" (p. 50).

Regardless of what prevalence study one turns to, it is evident there are many thousands of schoolchildren whose emotional and behavior problems are adversely affecting their educational progress but who are not presently receiving the special education they need. Although IDEA clearly mandates that all children with disabilities receive individualized special education services, the uncertain meaning of many aspects of the definition allows determination of whether a child is behaviorally disordered to be more a function of a school district's available resources to provide the needed services than a function of the child's actual needs for such services.

 GENDER

The vast majority of children identified for special education because of emotional or behavioral disorders are boys (Cullinan, 2002). Boys identified as emotionally or behaviorally disordered are likely to have externalizing disorders and to exhibit antisocial, aggressive behavior. Although girls with emotional and behavioral disorders are more likely to show internalizing disorders such as anxiety and social withdrawal, research shows that girls have problems with aggression and antisocial behavior as well (Talbott & Thiede, 1999).

 JUVENILE DELINQUENCY

The word *delinquent* is a legal term; however, the offenses that an adolescent commits to be labeled delinquent constitute a behavioral disorder. In 1999, law enforcement agencies made about 2.5 million arrests of persons under the age of 18 (Snyder, 2000). Juveniles, who comprise about 20% of the total population, were involved in 16% of all violent crime arrests and 32% of all property crime arrests in 1999.

Arrest rates for juveniles increase sharply during the junior high years. This pattern probably reflects both the greater harm adolescents can cause to society as a result of their inappropriate behavior and the fact that younger children are often not arrested (and therefore do not show up on the records) for committing the same acts that lead to the arrest of an older child. Younger children, however, are being arrested, and they are committing more crimes than in the past. Children under 15, for example, accounted for 67% of all juvenile

Using Response Cards to Increase Participation and Achievement

Rashawn raised his hand for the last time. He wanted to answer several of his teacher's questions, especially when she asked whether anyone could name the clouds that look like wispy cotton. But it wasn't his day to get called on. He tried to follow along but after a while lost interest and laid his head on his desk.

Dean did get called on once, but he didn't raise his hand too often. It was easier just to sit there. If he were quiet and still like Rashawn, then he wouldn't have to think about learning all this weather stuff. But it got too hard for Dean to just sit, so he started acting out. This got his teacher's attention.

"Dean, please pay attention!"

"Stop that, Dean!"

"Dean, how do you expect to learn this material for tomorrow's test if you're not part of the group?"

The next day, Rashawn and Dean both did poorly on the test of meteorology concepts. Each boy had a long history of poor school achievement, and teachers sometimes used *slow learner, attention deficit disorder, learning disabilities, emotional disturbance,* and *behavioral disorders* as explanations for their lack of success. But perhaps their poor scores, as well as their chronic underachievement, were directly influenced by the quality of instruction they received.

Neither boy had actively participated during the previous day's lesson. Instead of being active learners who responded frequently to the lesson's content, both boys were at best passive observers. Educational research has shown that students who respond actively and often usually learn more than do students who passively attend to instruction (Fisher & Berliner, 1985; Greenwood, Delquadri, & Hall, 1984; Heward, 1994). Although most teachers recognize the importance of active student participation, it is difficult to implement during group instruction. A common strategy is for the teacher to pose a question to the entire class and then call on one student to answer. This technique often results in frequent responses by high-achieving students and few or no responses by low-achieving students such as Rashawn and Dean (Maheady, Mallete, Harper, & Saca, 1991). Response cards (RCs) are one alternative to the traditional hand-raising (HR) and one-student-participating-at-a-time method of group instruction (Heward et al., 1996).

Response Cards

Response cards are cards, signs, or items that are simultaneously held up by all students to display their responses to a question or problem presented by the teacher. There are two basic types: preprinted and write-on. When using preprinted RCs, each student selects from a personal set of cards the one with the answer he wishes to display. Examples include yes/true and no/false cards, numbers, colors, traffic signs, molecular structures, and parts of speech. Instead of a set of different cards, a single preprinted RC with multiple answers can be given to each student (e.g., a card with clearly marked sections identified as proteins, fat, carbohydrates, vitamins, and minerals for use in a lesson on healthful eating habits). In its humblest version, the preprinted RC with multiple responses is a "pinch card": the student responds by holding up the card with her fingers pinching the part displaying her answer. Brightly colored clothespins also make excellent pinching tools. Preprinted RCs may also have built-in devices for displaying answers, such as a cardboard clock with movable hour and minute hands.

When using write-on RCs, students mark their answers on blank cards that are erased between learning trials. A set of 40 durable write-on RCs can be made from a 4-by-8-foot sheet of white laminated bathroom board (available from most builders' supply stores). The cost is generally less than $20, including the charge for cutting the sheet into 9-by-12-inch RCs. Dry-erase markers are available at most office supply stores, and paper towels or tissues will easily wipe the RCs clean.

Students can also use small chalkboards as write-on RCs, but responses may be difficult for the teacher to see in a full-size classroom. Write-on RCs can be custom-made to provide background or organizing structure for responses. For example, music students might mark notes on an RC

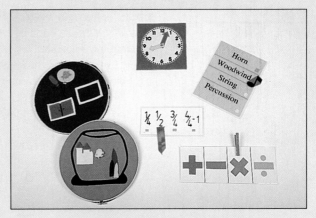

With write-on response cards, each student in the class can answer every question the teacher asks about the story just read.

that has permanent treble and bass clef scales; students in a driver's education class could draw where their car should go on RCs with permanent street intersections.

Research

RCs have been evaluated through a series of studies in regular and special education classrooms at the elementary, middle, and secondary levels (e.g., Armendariz & Umbreit, 1999; Cavanaugh, Heward, & Donelson, 1996; Lambert, 2001; Narayan, Heward, Gardner, Courson, & Omness, 1990). For example, Gardner, Heward, and Grossi (1994) compared the use of write-on RCs with HR during whole-class science lessons in an inner-city fifth-grade classroom. The study produced three major findings.

First, when RCs were used, each student responded to teacher-posed questions an average of 21.8 times per 30-minute lesson, compared to a mean of 1.5 academic responses when the teacher called on individuals. The higher participation rate takes on additional significance when its cumulative effect is calculated over the course of a 180-day school year. If RCs were used instead of HR for just 30 minutes per day, each student in the class would make an additional 3,700 academic responses during the school year.

Second, all 22 students scored higher on next-day quizzes and two-week review tests that followed lessons with RCs than they did on quizzes and tests that followed lessons with HR.

Third, all but one student preferred RCs over raising their hands to be called on.

General Suggestions for Using RCs

- Model several question-and-answer trials and give students practice on how to use RCs.
- Maintain a lively pace throughout the lesson; keep intervals between trials short.

- Give clear cues when students are to hold up and put down their cards.
- Remember that students can learn from watching others; do not let them think it is cheating to look at classmates' RCs.

Specific Suggestions for Using Preprinted RCs

- Design and construct the cards to be as easy to see as possible (e.g., consider size, print type, color codes).
- Make the cards easy for students to manipulate and display (e.g., put answers on both sides of the cards so that students can see what they are showing the teacher; attach a group of related cards to a ring).
- Begin instruction on new content with a small set of fact/concept cards (perhaps only two), gradually adding additional cards as skills improve.

Specific Suggestions for Using Write-On RCs

- Limit language-based responses to one or two words.
- Keep a few extra markers on hand.
- Be sure students do not hesitate to respond because they are concerned about making spelling mistakes: (1) provide several practice trials with new terms before the lesson begins; (2) write new terms on the chalkboard and tell students to refer to them during the lesson; and/or (3) use the "don't worry" technique, telling students to try their best but that misspellings will not count against them.
- Students enjoy doodling on their response cards. After a good lesson, let students draw on the cards for a few minutes.

arrests for arson in 1999. Although boys are generally arrested for crimes involving aggression (e.g., assault, burglary) and girls have been associated with sex-related offenses (e.g., prostitution), more and more violent offenses are being committed by girls (Siegel & Senna, 1994; Snyder, 2000). In 1999, girls accounted for 27% of all juvenile arrests.

About half of all juvenile delinquents are *recidivists* (repeat offenders). Recidivists are more likely to begin their criminal careers at an early age (usually by age 12), commit more serious crimes, and continue a pattern of repeated antisocial behavior as adults (Farrington, 1995; Tolan & Thomas, 1995). One study in Oregon found that 20% of juvenile offenders committed 87% of all crimes by juveniles (Wagner & Lane, 1998). Because only a fraction of the total number of criminal acts committed by juveniles are reported (i.e., around 12% to 15% [Henggler, 1989]), it is impossible to know the extent of the problem.

There is some good news to report. Although statistics reported by the U.S. Office of Juvenile Justice and Delinquency Prevention in the early 1990s showed alarming increases in juvenile offenses, especially violent crime, more recent data from the same agency reveal that juvenile arrests for violent crimes dropped 23% from 1995 to 1999 (Snyder, 2000). The juvenile violent crime arrest rate in 1999 was at its lowest level since 1988, 36% below the peak year of 1994. In spite of this encouraging trend, the number of children who perpetrate violent crimes or are the victims of crimes by other youth is much, much too large.

 ## CAUSES

The behavior of some children with emotional or behavioral disorders is so self-destructive and—when seen through the eyes of our own experience and understanding of how the world works—illogical that it is difficult to imagine how they got that way. We shake our heads in bewilderment and ask, "Where did that behavior come from?"

Numerous theories and conceptual models have been proposed to explain abnormal behavior. Regardless of the conceptual model from which emotional or behavioral disorders are viewed, the suspected causes can be grouped into two major categories: biological and environmental.

 ### BIOLOGICAL FACTORS

Brain Disorders   Many individuals who have brain disorders experience problems with emotion and behavior. Brain disorders are the result of either *brain dysgenesis* (abnormal brain development) or *brain injury* (caused by influences such as disease or trauma that alter the structure or function of a brain that had been developing normally up to that point). (Traumatic brain injury is discussed in Chapter 12.) For the vast majority of children with emotional and behavioral disorders, however, there is no evidence of brain disorder or injury.

Genetics   There is evidence of a genetic link to some forms of emotional and behavioral disorders (Weiner, 1999). The disorder with the strongest research support for a genetic risk factor is *schizophrenia,* a severe and debilitating form of mental illness characterized by auditory hallucinations (hearing voices), delusions, unfounded fears of persecution, and disordered speech. Relatives of schizophrenics have an increased risk of acquiring schizophrenia that cannot be explained by environmental factors alone; and the closer the relation, the higher the probability of acquiring the condition (Gottesman, 1991). However, genetics alone has not been found to cause schizophrenia. A person in either of the two highest risk groups (a child of two parents with schizophrenia or an identical twin of a sibling with the condition) still has a less than 50% chance of developing schizophrenia (Plomin, 1995).

Temperament   Some researchers believe that all children are born with a biologically determined temperament. There is no agreed-upon definition of temperament, but it is generally conceived to be a person's behavioral style or typical way of responding to situations.

Causes of E/BD

 Council for Exceptional Children   Content Standards for Beginning Teachers–E/BD: Etiology and diagnosis related to various theoretical approaches in the field of E/BD (BD2K1).
PRAXIS Special Education Core Principles: Content Knowledge: I. Understanding Exceptionalities, Causation and prevention of disability.

An infant who seldom cries but smiles and coos when passed from one person to another might be said to have an easygoing temperament. In contrast, an infant who is distractable, frequently fusses, and withdraws from new situations might show signs of a difficult temperament. There is some research evidence showing that an easy or positive temperament is correlated with resilience to stress (Smith & Prior, 1995) and that a difficult temperament at an early age increases the likelihood of behavior problems in adolescence (Caspi, Henry, McGee, Moffitt, & Silva, 1995; Morgan & Jensen, 1988).

Although a child's inborn temperament may not in itself cause a behavior problem, it may predispose the child to problems (Carey, 1998). Thus, certain events that might not produce abnormal behavior in a child with an easygoing temperament might result in disordered behavior by the child with a difficult temperament.

 ## ENVIRONMENTAL FACTORS

Dodge (1993) has identified three primary environmental factors that contribute to the development of conduct disorder and antisocial behavior: (1) an adverse early rearing environment, (2) an aggressive pattern of behavior displayed when entering school, and (3) social rejection by peers. Considerable research evidence supports Dodge's contention that these causal factors occur in sequence (Patterson, Reid, & Dishion, 1992; Sprague & Walker, 2000). The settings in which these events occur are the home, community, and school.

Home   The relationship children have with their parents, particularly during the early years, is critical to the way they learn to behave. Observation and analysis of parent-child interaction patterns show that parents who treat their children with love, are sensitive to their children's needs, and provide praise and attention for desired behaviors tend to have children with positive behavioral characteristics. More than two decades of research has shown that antisocial children are more likely to come from homes in which parents are inconsistent disciplinarians, use harsh and excessive punishment to manage behavior problems, spend little time engaged in prosocial activities with their children, do not monitor the whereabouts and activities of their children, and show little love and affection for good behavior (Biglan, 1995; McEvoy & Welker, 2000; Patterson et al., 1992; Walker et al., 1995). When such conditions are present in the home, a young child may be "literally trained to be aggressive during episodes of conflict with family members" (Forgatch & Paterson, 1998, p. 86).

Because of the research on the relationship between parental child-rearing practices and behavior problems, some mental health professionals have been quick to pin the blame for children's behavior problems on parents. But the relationship between parent and child is dynamic and reciprocal; in other words, the behavior of the child affects the behavior of the parents just as much as the parents' actions affect the child's actions (Sameroff, 2001). Therefore, at best it is not practical and at worst it is wrong to blame parents for the behavior problems of their children. Instead, professionals must work with parents to help them systematically change certain aspects of the parent-child relationship in an effort to prevent and modify those problems (Landy, 2002; Zionts, Simpson, & Zionts, 2001).

Community   When students associate with peers who exhibit antisocial behavior, they are more likely to experience additional trouble in the community and at school. Gang membership, drug and alcohol abuse, and deviant sexual behavior are community factors that contribute to the development and maintenance of an antisocial lifestyle (Biglan, 1995; Harland, 1997; Walker et al., 1995).

School   School is where children spend the largest portion of their time outside the home. Therefore, it makes sense to observe carefully what takes place in schools in an effort to identify factors that may contribute to problem behavior. Also, because most children with

Influence of home and community

 Content Standards for Beginning Teachers-Common Core: Characteristics and effects of the environmental milieu of the individual with exceptional learning needs and the family (CC2K3) (also CC2K4).

Even though the teacher is trying to help, a child's deviant behavior patterns can actually be maintained or even strengthened by what happens in the classroom.

emotional and behavioral disorders are not identified until they are in school, it seems reasonable to question whether school actually contributes to the incidence of behavioral disorders. Schooling practices that contribute to the development of emotional and behavioral problems in children include ineffective instruction that results in academic failure, unclear rules and expectations for appropriate behavior, inconsistent and punitive discipline practices, infrequent teacher praise and approval for academic and social behavior, and failure to individualize instruction to accommodate diverse learners (Colvin, Kameenui, & Sugai, 1993; Gunter, Denny, Jack, Shores, & Nelson, 1993; Lago-Delello, 1998; Mayer, 1995).

There is no question that what takes place in the classroom can maintain and actually strengthen deviant behavioral patterns even though the teacher is trying to help the child. Consider the all too common interaction between teacher and student illustrated in Figure 8.2 (Rhode et al., 1998). It begins with a teacher request that the student ignores and follows a predictable and escalating sequence of teacher pleas and threats that the student counters with excuses, arguments, and eventually a full-blown tantrum. The aggression and tantruming is so aversive to the teacher that she withdraws the task demand (thereby reinforcing and strengthening the student's disruptive behavior) so the student will stop tantruming (thereby reinforcing the teacher for withdrawing the request) (Gunter et al., 1993; Maag, 2001). This process has been called *coercive pain control* because the child learns to use painful behavior (e.g., arguing, making excuses, tantruming, property destruction, even physical aggression) to get what he wants (Patterson, 1982).

 A COMPLEX PATHWAY OF RISKS

It is impossible to identify a single factor or isolated event as the definite cause of a child's emotional or behavioral disorders. Most behavioral problems are the accumulated effect of exposure to a variety of family, neighborhood, school, and societal risk factors. And research into genetics and brain-related factors has not advanced to the point where the presence and contribution of a genetic predisposition for greater susceptability or resilience to a given risk factor can be identified. The greater the number of risk factors and the longer a child's exposure to them, the greater the probability that the child will experience negative outcomes (Sprague & Walker, 2000). Figure 8.3 illustrates this pattern of antisocial behavior development as originally conceived by Patterson and his colleagues (Patterson, 1992). Although the interplay of these risk factors is complex, and the specific contribution of any given risk factor cannot be determined, the outcome is highly predictable.

Although knowledge of these risk factors provides information necessary for planning and implementing prevention programs (Dwyer, Osher, & Hoffman, 2000; Sprague & Walker, 2000; Vance, Fernandez, & Biber, 1998), teachers should know that effective intervention and treatment of children's existing behavior problems do not require precise knowledge of etiology. Attempting to determine the extent to which various factors in a child's past are responsible for his current behavior problems is "an

Teacher's reaction to noncompliance

 Content Standards for Beginning Teachers-Common Core: Teacher attitudes and behaviors that influence behavior of individuals with exceptional learning needs (CC5K4).
PRAXIS Special Education Core Principles: Content Knowledge: III. Delivery of Services to Students with Disabilities, Structuring and managing the learning environment for consistency and positive interactions.

FIGURE 8.2
Coercive pain control

Source: Reprinted from Rhode, G., Jensen, W. R., & Reavis, H. K. (1998). *The tough kid book: Practical classroom management strategies* (p. 5). Longmont, CO: Sopris West. Used with permission.

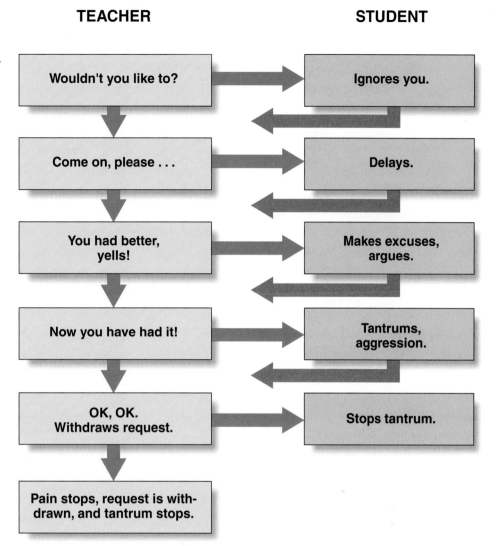

TEACHER — **STUDENT**

- Wouldn't you like to? → Ignores you.
- Come on, please . . . → Delays.
- You had better, yells! → Makes excuses, argues.
- Now you have had it! → Tantrums, aggression.
- OK, OK. Withdraws request. → Stops tantrum.
- Pain stops, request is withdrawn, and tantrum stops.

impossible *and* quite unnecessary task. Disruptive child behavior can be changed very effectively without knowing the specific, original causes for its acquisition and development" (Walker, 1997, p. 20).

 ## IDENTIFICATION AND ASSESSMENT

Assessment of emotional and behavioral disorders, as with all disabilities, should answer four basic questions concerning special education services:

1. Who might need help?
2. Who really does need help (who is eligible)?
3. What kind of help is needed?
4. Is the help benefiting the student?

The primary purpose of initial assessment is not to determine whether the child has something called an emotional and behavioral disorder but to see whether the child's behavior is different enough to warrant special services and, if so, to indicate what those services should be.

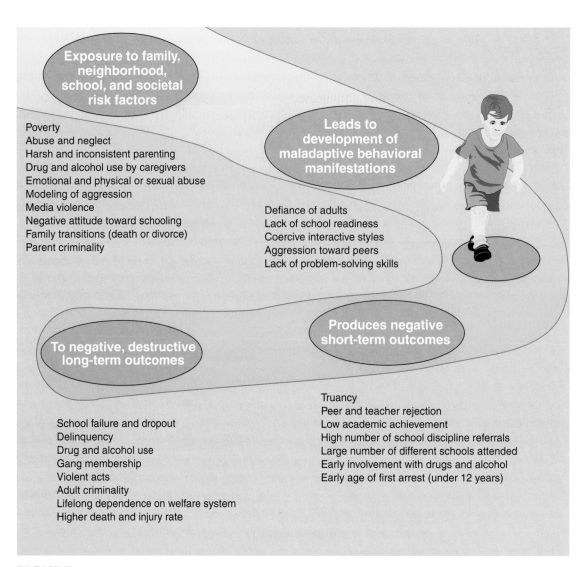

FIGURE 8.3 **The path to long-term negative outcomes for children and youth who are at risk for school failure, delinquency, and violence**

Source: Reprinted from Walker, H. M., & Sprague, J. R. (1999). The path to school failure, delinquency, and violence: Causal factors and some potential solutions. *Intervention in School and Clinic, 35,* 67.

In practice, however, many school districts do not use any systematic method for identifying children with emotional and behavioral disorders. This is because most children with emotional and behavioral disorders identify themselves. Antisocial children seldom go unnoticed: "To have one in your classroom is to recognize one" (Rhode et al., 1998, p. 3). This does not mean, however, that identification is a sure thing. Identification of emotional disturbance is always more difficult with younger children because the behavior of all young children changes quickly and often. Also, there is danger that some children with internalizing behaviors go undetected because their problems do not draw the attention of parents and teachers.

Walker (1997) recommends that school-related assessment of children with behavior problems include the following (adapted from pp. 72–73):

- Whenever possible, address the specific reason(s) underlying problematic or deficient student behavior.
- Provide a road map to guide the design and implementation of effective interventions.

- Always give high priority to the vast reservoir of information teachers have about student performance and behavioral characteristics.
- Use more than one method (e.g., rankings, checklists, direct observations) in more than one setting (e.g., classroom, playground, home), and involve more than one social agent (e.g., parents, teachers, peers).
- Consider teacher judgment as one of the most valid and valuable sources of decision-making information available for developing alternative solutions to the problem.
- Collect only the essential information necessary to understand the school-related problems.

 SCREENING TESTS

Children who display patterns of antisocial behavior upon entering school run the risk of developing more serious and long-standing behavior problems as they progress through school and life. Sprague and Walker (2000) stress the importance of systematically screening and identifying as early as possible those children who are at risk for developing serious patterns of antisocial behavior. Screening is the process of differentiating between children who are not likely to be disabled and those who either show signs of behavioral disturbance or seem to be at risk for developing behavior problems. Children identified through a screening process then undergo more thorough assessment to determine their eligibility for special education and their specific educational needs.

Most screening devices consist of behavior rating scales or checklists that are completed by teachers, parents, peers, and/or children themselves. Brief descriptions of four screening tests for emotional and behavioral disorders follow.

Behavior Rating Profile (BRP-2)   This test includes six subtests that can be used independently or in any combination (Brown & Hammill, 1990). The Teacher Rating Scale includes 30 items that teachers rate on a 4-point scale from "very much like the student" to "not at all like the student" (e.g., "Doesn't follow class rules."). Parents complete the 30-item Parent Rating Scale in a similar manner (e.g., "Is shy, clings to parents."). Students answer true/false questions on the three Student Rating Scales (Home, School, and Peer) (e.g., "Other kids don't seem to like me very much."). The Sociogram is a peer-nomination activity in which each student in the class identifies three classmates in response to questions such as "Which of the girls and boys in your class would you most (or least) like to work with on a class project?"

Child Behavior Checklist (CBCL)   This test comes in teacher report, parent report, and child report forms and can be used with children ages 5 through 18 (Achenbach & Edelbrock, 1991). The teacher's form includes 112 behaviors (e.g., "cries a lot," "not liked by other pupils") that are rated on a 3-point scale: "not true," "somewhat or sometimes true," or "very true or often true." The CBCL also includes items representing social competencies and adaptive functioning such as getting along with others and acting happy.

Systematic Screening for Behavioral Disorders (SSBD)   This test is the most systematic, fully developed instrument presently available for screening children for possible emotional and behavioral disorders. The SSBD employs a 3-step **multiple gating screening** process for progressively narrowing down the number of children suspected of having serious behavior problems (Walker & Severson, 1990). In Gate I, classroom teachers rank-order every student in their classrooms according to behavioral profiles on two dimensions: externalizing problems and internalizing problems. The top three students on each teacher's list progress to Gate II, the Critical Events Index.

Critical events are behavioral pinpoints of high salience and intensity that do not depend on frequency to define their severity. Any occurrence of these target behaviors is viewed as an indicator of major disruption of social-behavioral adjustment processes in school. Critical events have been characterized as analogous to

Screening tools for E/BD

Council for Exceptional Children   Content Standards for Beginning Teachers–E/BD: Characteristics of behavioral rating scales (BD8K1; also CC8K3).
PRAXIS Special Education Core Principles: Content Knowledge: III. Delivery of Services to Students with Diabilities, Assessment, Use of assessment for screening.

"behavioral earthquakes" in terms of their ecological disruptiveness and severity. (Todis, Severson, & Walker, 1990, pp. 75–76)

The 33 items that make up the Critical Events Index include externalizing behaviors such as "is physically aggressive with other students" and "makes lewd or obscene gestures" and internalizing behaviors such as "vomits after eating" and "has auditory or visual hallucinations." Students who exceed normative criteria on the Critical Events Index advance to Gate III of the SSBD, which consists of direct and repeated observations during independent seatwork periods in the classroom and on the playground during recess. Children who meet or exceed cutoff criteria for either or both observational measures are referred to child study teams for further evaluation to determine their eligibility for special education.

Behavioral and Emotional Rating Scale (BERS)   This test assesses a student's strengths in 52 items across 5 areas of functioning: interpersonal strengths (e.g., reacts to disappointment in a calm manner); family involvement (e.g., participates in family activities); intrapersonal strengths (e.g., demonstrates a sense of humor), school functioning (e.g., pays attention in class), and affective strengths (e.g., acknowledges painful feelings of others) (Epstein & Sharma, 1998). Data from a strength-based assessment such as the BERS may be used to present positive attributes of students in IEP meetings, as an aid in writing IEP goals and objectives, and as an outcome measure to document a student's progress on strength-related IEP goals and objectives (Epstein, Hertzog, & Reid, 2001).

 PROJECTIVE TESTS

A **projective test** consists of ambiguous stimuli (e.g., "What does this inkblot look like to you?") or open-ended tasks (e.g., "Complete this sentence for me: 'Most girls like to. . . .' "). It is assumed that responses to items that have no right or wrong answer will reveal a person's true personality characteristics. The most famous projective test is the Rorschach Test (Rorschach, 1942), which consists of a set of 10 cards, each containing an inkblot, the left and right halves being mirror images of each other. The subject is shown one card at a time and told, "Tell me what you see, what it might be for you. There are no right or wrong answers."

Another well-known projective test is the Thematic Apperception Test (TAT) (Morgan & Murray, 1935). A person taking the TAT is shown a series of pictures and asked to make up a story about each picture, telling who the people are; what they are doing, thinking, and feeling; and how the situation will turn out.

Although sometimes interesting, the results of projective tests are of minimal value in planning or evaluating special education. Projective tests assess an indirect and extremely limited sample of a child's behavioral repertoire and, just as important, they do not assess how the child typically acts over a period of time. One-time measures—whether direct or indirect—are not a sufficient basis for identifying the presence of an emotional or behavioral disorder or planning education and treatment.

 DIRECT OBSERVATION AND MEASUREMENT OF BEHAVIOR

In assessment by direct observation and measurement, the actual behaviors that cause concern about a child are clearly specified and observed in the settings in which they normally occur (e.g., in the classroom, on the playground). Behavior can be measured objectively along several dimensions: rate, duration, latency, magnitude, and topography (see Figure 8.4).

The advantage of assessing and describing emotional and behavioral disorders in terms of these dimensions is that identification, design of instructional strategies, and evaluation of the effects of treatment can all revolve around objective measurement. This approach leads to a direct focus on the child's problem—the behavior that is adversely affecting his life—and ways of dealing with it such as strengthening a desired alternative behavior as opposed to concentrating on some presumed (and unreachable) problem within the child.

FIGURE 8.4   Five measurable dimensions of behavior

RATE: how often a particular behavior occurs per standard unit of time (e.g., six talkouts per minute). All children cry, get into fights with other children, and sulk from time to time; yet we are not apt to think of them as emotionally disturbed. The primary difference between children with behavioral disorders and other children is the frequency with which these behaviors occur. Although disturbed children may not do anything their nondisabled peers do not do, they do certain undesirable things too often (e.g., crying, hitting others) and/or engage in adaptive behaviors too infrequently (e.g., playing with others).

DURATION: how long a child engages in a given activity (e.g., worked on math problems for 12 minutes). The amount of time children with behavioral disorders engage in certain activities is often markedly different—either longer or shorter—from that of other children. For example, most young children have temper tantrums, but the tantrums generally last no more than a few minutes. A child with emotional and behavioral disorders may tantrum for more than an hour at a time. The problem may also be one of too short a duration. For example, some children with emotional and behavioral disorders cannot stick to an academic task for more than a few seconds at a time.

LATENCY: the time that elapses between the opportunity to respond and the beginning of the behavior. The latency of a child's behavior may be too long (e.g., several minutes elapse before he begins to comply with the teacher's request) or too short (e.g., the child immediately begins screaming and tantruming at the slightest provocation or frustration, thus having no time to consider more appropriate alternative behaviors).

MAGNITUDE: the strength or intensity of behavior. The magnitude of a child's responses may be too little (e.g., talking in a volume so low that she cannot be heard) or too much (e.g., slamming the door).

TOPOGRAPHY: the physical shape or form of behavior. Printing your name in block letters and signing your name in cursive have different topographies. Some children with emotional and behavioral disorders emit behaviors that are seldom, if ever, seen in typical children (setting fires, self-abuse). These behaviors may be maladaptive, bizarre, or dangerous to the child or others.

 FUNCTIONAL BEHAVIORAL ASSESSMENT

Functional behavioral assessment (FBA) is a systematic process of gathering information to help IEP teams understand why a student may be engaging in challenging behavior. Interviews and direct observation are used to obtain information about the setting events and environmental factors that predict and trigger the problem behavior and the consequences for the behavior that may be maintaining it (Chandler & Dahlquist, 2002; Heckaman, Conroy, Fox, & Chait, 2000; O'Neill et al., 1997; Scott & Nelson, 1999). This information is used to generate hypotheses about what the behavior's function, or purpose, is for the student. Two major types of behavioral function are (1) to get something the student wants (positive reinforcement) (e.g., hitting other students produces one-on-one attention from the teacher), and (2) to escape or avoid something the student doesn't want (negative reinforcement) (e.g., disruptive behavior when the teacher presents academic tasks results in removal of the task). The hypotheses are then used to guide the development of an intervention plan to identify and teach more appropriate replacement behaviors and to reduce the frequency or severity of the problem behavior.

This information can be used to improve the effectiveness and efficiency of behavioral intervention (Lalli, Browder, Mace, & Brown, 1993; Umbreit, 1995). For example, knowing that a student's tantrums are maintained by teacher attention suggests a different intervention than one indicated for misbehavior that is maintained by escape from challenging academic tasks.

Functional behavioral assessment might also include a **functional analysis,** the systematic manipulation of several antecedent or consequent events surrounding the target behavior in an attempt to verify the function of the behavior for the child (e.g., systematically

Measurable dimensions of behavior

 Council for Exceptional Children Content Standards for Beginning Teachers–Common Core: Basic terminoloy used in assessment (CC8K1).
PRAXIS Special Education Core Principles: Content Knowledge: I. Understanding Exceptionalities, The nature of behaviors, including frequency, duration, and intensity.

Functional behavioral assessment

 Council for Exceptional Children Content Standards for Beginning Teachers–Common Core: Use functional assessments to develop intervention plans (CC7S4).
PRAXIS Special Education: Core Principles: Content Knowledge: III. Delivery of Services to Students with Disabilities, Structuring and managing the learning environment, Behavioral analysis/Functional analysis.

varying the difficulty of academic tasks to test if the child's oppositional behavior is triggered by difficult tasks) (Iwata, Dorsey, Slifer, Bauman, & Richman, 1994). Because functional analysis purposely results in occurrences of the problem behavior, it should be conducted only by highly trained personnel who have attained appropriate consents from parents/guardians and ensured that adequate safeguards are in place to protect the student and others from any harm. (Functional analysis is discussed further in Chapter 13.)

EDUCATIONAL APPROACHES

CURRICULUM GOALS

What should students with emotional and behavioral disorders be taught? An obvious but only partially correct answer is they should learn to control their antisocial behavior. For many years, programs serving students with behavioral disorders focused on treating maladaptive behavior at the expense of academic instruction. As a result, students who already possessed deficient academic skills fell even further behind their peers (Knitzer, Sternberg, & Fleisch, 1990). Special education for students with emotional and behavioral disorders must also include instruction in the social and academic skills required for success in school, community, and vocational settings.

Social Skills   Social skills instruction is an important curriculum component for students with emotional and behavioral disorders. Many of these students have difficulty holding a conversation, expressing their feelings, participating in group activities, and responding to failure or criticism in positive and constructive ways. They often get into fights and altercations because they lack the social skills needed to handle or defuse provocative incidents. The slightest snub, bump, or misunderstood request—which would be laughed off or ignored by most children—can precipitate an aggressive attack by some students.

Numerous social skills curricula and training programs have been published; several recommended ones are described in Figure 8.5. Television programs (Bryan & Ryan, 2001) and children's books have also been used to teach social skills to students with emotional and behavioral disorders (Brame, 2000; Sridhar & Vaughn, 2000). (To find out how teachers used a TV program to help a student become more likeable to his classmates, see Figure 8.6.)

Academic Skills   Although students with emotional and behavioral disorders require special education to work on their specific behavior problems and social skills deficits, academic instruction cannot be neglected (Edwards & Chard, 2000). Most children with emotional and behavioral disorders are already achieving below their nondisabled peers; reading, writing, and arithmetic are as important to children with emotional and behavioral disorders as they are to any child who hopes to function successfully in society.

Fortunately, most students with emotional and behavioral disorders make excellent progress when provided with explicit, systematic instruction (see Chapters 6 and 7). And effective instruction is the foundation for effective classroom management. Teachers must guard against the tendency to provide students with behavior problems limited academic instruction in the form of easier tasks, fewer opportunities to respond, and lowered expectations because they wish to avoid students' noncompliance and outbursts (Gunter et al., 1993; Wehby, Symons, Canale, & Go, 1998).

Students who are actively engaged during instruction exhibit less off-task and disruptive behavior than do students who are expected to observe passively.

FIGURE 8.5 Recommended social skills curricula

Getting Along with Others (Jackson, Jackson, & Monroe, 1983): includes 32 lessons across 17 social skills areas such as following directions, handling name calling and teasing, and offering to help. Available from Research Press, Department 95, P.O. Box 9177, Champaign, IL 61826.

Skillstreaming the Adolescent: A Structured Learning Approach to Teaching Prosocial Skills (Goldstein et al., 1997): activities designed to increase self-esteem and develop competence in dealing with peers, family, and authority figures. Skillstreaming programs for elementary and preschool children are also available. Published by Research Press (see above).

Taking Part: Introducing Social Skills to Children (Cartledge & Kleefeld, 1991): helps students in preschool classrooms through third grade learn social skills in six units: making conversation, communicating feelings, expressing oneself, cooperating with peers, playing with peers, and responding to aggression and conflict. Published by American Guidance Service, 4201 Woodland Road, Circle Pines, MN 55014.

The Prepare Curriculum: Teaching Prosocial Competencies (Goldstein, 1999): designed for students who are aggressive, withdrawn, or otherwise deficient in social competencies. Activities and materials for middle and high school students in 10 areas, such as problem solving, anger control, stress management, and cooperation. Published by Research Press (see above).

The Walker Social Skills Curriculum: includes *ACCEPTS: A Curriculum for Children's Effective Peer and Teacher Skills* (Walker et al., 1983), for children grades K–6, and *ACCESS: Adolescent Curriculum for Communication and Effective Social Skills* (Walker, Todis, Holmes, & Horton, 1988) for students at the middle and high school levels. Available from PRO-ED, 8700 Shoal Creek Boulevard, Austin, TX 78757.

Working Together (Cartledge & Kleefeld, 1994): incorporates stories and activities based on folk literature to teach social skills to students in grades 3–6 and older students with special needs. Published by American Guidance Service (see above).

FIGURE 8.6 Jacob's story

Jacob was a slight young man who had a wry sense of humor and often played the role of class clown. He sometimes made sarcastic, personal attacks on his teachers and other students. This behavior often disrupted class and frequently resulted in disciplinary referrals. For this reason, Jacob had trouble making and keeping friends in school, a problem which exacerbated the feelings of loneliness and upheaval he experienced living in foster care.

During an Amazing Discoveries lesson titled, "Does Everyone See the Same Thing?" Jacob and the other students were asked to watch a short segment of the television show, *Home Improvement.* As they watched, students kept track of the number of put-downs they heard. At the end of the segment, the students reported the number of put-downs they had counted for the characters. As is often the case, there were wide variations in what the youth perceived as insulting. The social lesson was that conflict often arises when people have different ideas about what kinds of comments are put-downs. This helped Jacob understand that sometimes he was hurting those around him without meaning to.

After this lesson, his teacher noticed that Jacob started apologizing when his funny comments seemed to hurt others' feelings. She also noticed that the other students would recall the lesson when letting Jacob know that his jokes were hurtful. After a while, Jacob began using his great sense of humor in less hurtful ways and seemed to become a more engaged member of the class.

To learn more about the Amazing Discoveries program and other projects designed to provide social, academic, and behavioral supports for secondary students with emotional and behavior disorders, go to http://www.air.org/cecp/safetynet.htm/

Social skills curricula and instruction

 Content Standards for Beginning Teachers–E/BD: Sources of specialized materials for individuals with E/BD (BD4K1).

PRAXIS Special Education: Content Knowledge: III. Delivery of Services to Students with Disabilities, Structuring and managing the learning environment, Social skills training.

Source: Bryan, T., & Ryan, A. (2001). Jacob's story: Amazing discoveries. In A. K. Ryan, *Strengthening the safety net: How school can help youth with emotional and behavioral needs complete their high school education and prepare for life after school* (p. 10). Burlington, VT: School Research Office, University of Vermont.

Schoolwide positive behavior support

Council for Exceptional Children — Content Standards for Beginning Teachers–E/BD: Prevention and intervention strategies for individuals at risk of E/BD (BD4K4).
PRAXIS Special Education: Content Knowledge: III. Delivery of Services to Students with Disabilities, Structuring and managing the learning environment for expectations, rules, consequences, consistency, and positive interactions.

▲ Proactive behavior management strategies include the use of positive reinforcement to increase the frequency of desired behavior.

★ BEHAVIOR MANAGEMENT

Discipline and Schoolwide Systems of Behavior Support Traditionally, discipline in the schools has focused on the use of punishment in an effort to control the misbehavior of specific students. Not only is punishment generally ineffective in achieving long-term suppression of problem behavior, particularly for students with chronic histories of behavior problems, it does not help students learn desired, prosocial behaviors. Among the most important advances in student discipline procedures over the past decade is the development of schoolwide behavior support systems that promote and support positive behaviors by all students. The goals of schoolwide systems are to define, teach, and support appropriate behaviors in a way that enhances the academic and social behavior success of all students (Lewis & Sugai, 1999).

Schools that implement schoolwide systems of positive behavior support use a team-based approach to teach appropriate behavior to all students in the school. All teachers and school staff participate in teaching and rewarding desired student behavior, there are clearly defined and consistently applied consequences for rule violations, and objective data are used to evaluate and continually improve the system (Algozzine, Audette, Ellis, Marr, & White, 2000; Lo & Cartledge, in press; Sugai, Sprague, Horner, & Walker, 2000).

Successful schoolwide systems of behavior support are characterized by the following (Center for Positive Behavioral Interventions & Supports, 2001):

1. *Behavioral expectations are stated.* A small number of behavioral expectations are clearly defined. These often are simple, positively framed rules such as "Be respectful, be responsible, and be safe" or "Respect yourself, respect others, and respect property."

2. *Behavioral expectations are defined and taught.* The behavioral expectations are taught to all students in the building. Specific examples are provided for behavioral expectations (e.g., "Being respectful in class means raising your hand when you want to speak or get help. During lunch or in the hall, being respectful means using a person's name when you talk to him or her."). Behavioral expectations are taught directly with a systematic format: the general rule is presented, the rationale for the rule is discussed, positive examples ("right way") are described and rehearsed, negative examples ("wrong way") are described and modeled, and students practice the "right way" until they demonstrate fluent performance.

3. *Appropriate behaviors are acknowledged.* Appropriate behaviors are acknowledged on a regular basis. Some schools do this through formal systems (tickets, rewards); others do it through social events. Schools strive to establish a ratio of four positive adult interactions with students for every one that is negative.

4. *Behavioral errors are corrected proactively.* When students violate behavioral expectations, clear procedures are needed for providing information to them that their behavior was unacceptable and preventing unacceptable behavior from resulting in inadvertent rewards.

5. *Program evaluations and adaptations are data-driven and made by a team.* Successful schools establish a simple, efficient strategy for continually assessing if they are being successful and a decision-making process that allows adaptation to behavioral challenges. At the schoolwide level, general measures of the school climate include behavior incident reports, attendance rates, tardies, detention and suspension rates, etc.

FIGURE 8.7
Continuum of effective behavior support

Source: U.S. Department of Education (2000). Twenty-second Annual Report to Congress on the Implementation of the Individual with Disabilities Education Act (p. III-16). Washington, DC: Author.

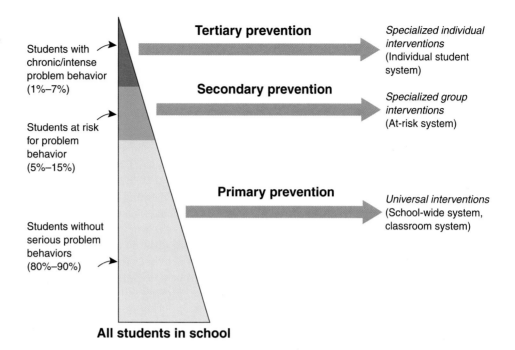

Students with chronic/intense problem behavior (1%–7%)

Students at risk for problem behavior (5%–15%)

Students without serious problem behaviors (80%–90%)

Tertiary prevention

Secondary prevention

Primary prevention

All students in school

Specialized individual interventions (Individual student system)

Specialized group interventions (At-risk system)

Universal interventions (School-wide system, classroom system)

6. *Individual student support systems are integrated with schoolwide discipline systems.* Schoolwide behavior support does not replace the need for a comprehensive set of more intensive interventions for the 1% to 7% of students in most schools who require more individualized and ongoing behavioral support (see Figure 8.7).

Classroom Management Teachers of students with emotional and behavior disorders must design and manage classroom environments that are effective in not only decreasing antisocial behavior but also increasing the frequency of positive teacher-student interactions as a basis for building positive behavior and academic success (Gunter et al., 1993; Shores, Gunter, & Jack, 1993). This is a very tall order. Fortunately, teachers can turn to a strong base of clearly defined, research-validated practices for guidance on effective classroom management (e.g., Alberto & Troutman, 1999; Algozzine & Kay, 2002; Kerr & Nelson, 2002; Sprick & Howard, 1997).

The majority of classroom behavior problems can be prevented by the use of proactive behavior management. *Proactive strategies* are preplanned interventions that anticipate behavior problems and stop them before they occur. "It is much more difficult to remediate the problems caused by a Tough Kid than to prevent them. Once a teacher has lost the management tempo in a classroom and things are out of control, it is far more difficult to reestablish control" (Rhode et al., 1998, p. 19).

Proactive strategies include structuring the physical environment of the classroom (e.g., have the most difficult students sit nearest the teacher), establishing clear rules and expectations for appropriate behavior (Bicard, 2000), scheduling and sequencing lesson activities to minimize down time, presenting instructions to students in ways that increase the probability of compliance (Walker & Sylvester, 1998), keeping students actively engaged during instruction (Gunter, Hummel, & Conroy, 1998; Heward, 1994; Sutherland & Wehby, 2001), and using praise and positive reinforcement to motivate desired behavior (Maag, 2001; Sutherland, Wehby, & Yoder, 2001; Webber & Scheuermann, 1991). (See Profiles & Perspectives, "The Power of Teacher Praise," later in this chapter.)

Managing the classroom environment for students with emotional and behavior disorders requires a great deal of knowledge and skill. In addition to the strategies already mentioned, teachers must also know when and how to use a large set of behavioral teaching

Proactive classroom management

 Council for Exceptional Children — Content Standards for Beginning Teachers–Common Core: Basic classroom management strategies for individuals with exceptional learning needs (CC5K2).
PRAXIS Special Education: Application of Core Principles: Content Knowledge: III. Delivery of Services to Students with Disabilities, Structuring and managing the learning environment for expectations, rules, consequences, consistency, and positive interactions.

Contingent teacher praise and positive reinforcement

 Council for Exceptional Children — Content Standards for Beginning Teachers–E/BD: Theory of reinforcement techniques in serving individuals with E/BD (BD1K5).
PRAXIS Special Education: Application of Core Principles: Content Knowledge: III. Delivery of Services to Students with Disabilities, Structuring and managing the learning environment, Behavioral interventions.

tools such as **shaping, contingency contracting, extinction** (ignoring disruptive behavior), **differential reinforcement of other behavior** (reinforcing any behavior except the undesirable response), **response cost, time out** (restricting students' access to reinforcement for a brief time following an inappropriate behavior), **overcorrection** (requiring restitution beyond the damaging effects of the antisocial behavior, as when a child who takes another child's cookie must return it plus one of her own). These techniques should not be implemented as isolated events but incorporated into an overall instructional and classroom management plan that includes the previously mentioned proactive strategies and perhaps a **level system** in which students access greater independence and more privileges as they demonstrate increased behavioral control (Anderson & Katsiyannis, 1997; Barbetta, 1990; Cruz & Cullinan, 2001).

When designing and implementing classroom management strategies, teachers of students with emotional and behavioral disorders must be careful not to create an environment in which coercion is the primary means by which students are motivated to participate and follow rules. In addition to promoting escape and avoidance behavior by those being coerced, coercive environments do not teach what to do as much as they focus on what not to do (Sidman, 1989). Two other methods of proactive and positive classroom management are teaching self-management skills to students and using peer mediation and support.

Self-Management   Many children with emotional and behavioral disorders believe they have little control over their lives. Things just seem to happen to them, and being disruptive is their means of reacting to an inconsistent and frustrating world. Self-management can help them learn responsibility and achieve self-determination (Wehmeyer, Agran, & Hughes, 1998). Self-management is also an important tool for promoting the generalization and maintenance of treatment gains from one setting to another.

*Self-monitoring and
self-evaluation*

Content Standards for Beginning Teachers–Common Core: Use procedures to promote individual's self-awareness, self-management, self-control, self-reliance, and self-esteem (CC4S5) (also CC4S2, CC4S4).
PRAXIS Special Education Core Principles: Content Knowledge: III. Delivery of Services to Students with Disabilities, Teaching strategies and methods, Self-management.

Of the many forms of self-management, self-monitoring and self-evaluation are the most widely used and most researched. **Self-monitoring** is a relatively simple procedure in which the student observes and records the occurrence (and sometimes the nonoccurrence) of his own behavior; **self-evaluation** involves comparing one's behavior against a standard or goal. Numerous studies have demonstrated that students with behavior problems can effectively use self-monitoring and self-evaluation to help regulate their behavior (e.g., Carr & Punzo, 1993; Dunlap et al., 1995; Peterson, Young, West, & Hill Peterson, 1999; Webber, Scheuermann, McCall, & Coleman, 1993; Wood, Murdock, Cronin, Dawson, & Kirby, 1998). (To learn about a CD-ROM program children can use to create self-management tools, see Teaching & Learning, "KidTools: Self-Management Tools for Children," later in this chapter.)

One of the most impressive studies demonstrating the effectiveness of self-management techniques for the generalization of improved behavior across classroom settings was reported 20 years ago by Rhode, Morgan, and Young (1983). Six students with emotional and behavioral disorders learned to bring their highly disruptive and off-task behaviors under control in a resource room with a combination of techniques that featured self-monitoring and self-evaluation. Initially, the teacher rated each student and awarded points at 15-minute intervals on a scale from 5 (great) to 0 (poor) for classroom behavior and academic work. Then the students began to evaluate their own behavior with the same rating system. The teacher continued to rate each student.

Teacher and students compared their ratings. If the student's rating was within one point of the teacher's, he received the number of points he had given himself. If teacher and student matched exactly, the student earned an additional bonus point. The teacher then began to fade the number of times she also rated the students. After the students were behaving at acceptable levels and accurately self-evaluating their behavior, they began to self-evaluate once every 30 minutes in the regular classroom. Eventually, the self-evaluation cards and point system were withdrawn, and students were encouraged to continue to self-evaluate themselves privately. During the study's final phase, the students' level of appropriate behavior in the regular classroom was as high as their nondisabled peers.

Peer Mediation and Support   The power of the peer group can be an effective means of producing positive changes in students with behavioral disorders (Barbetta, 1990a; Coleman & Webber, 1988). Strategies for teaching peers to help one another decrease inappropriate behavior include the following:

- *Peer monitoring.*   A student is taught to observe and record a peer's behavior and provide the peer with feedback (Fowler, Dougherty, Kirby, & Kohler, 1986; Smith & Fowler, 1984).
- *Positive peer reporting.*   Students are taught, encouraged, and reinforced for reporting each others' positive behaviors (Bowers, MicGinnis, Ervin, & Friman, 1999).
- *Peer tutoring.*   In serving as academic or social skills tutors for one another, students with emotional and behavioral disorders may also learn better social skills (Blake, Wang, Cartledge, & Gardner, 2000; Cochran, Feng, Cartledge, & Hamilton, 1993).
- *Peer confrontation.*   Peers are trained to confront one another when inappropriate behavior occurs or is about to occur, explaining why the behavior is a problem and suggesting or modeling an appropriate alternative response (Salend, Jantzen, & Giek, 1992; Sandler, Arnold, Gable, & Strain, 1987).

Implementing a peer support, or *group process,* model is much more complicated than bringing together a group of children and hoping they will benefit from positive peer influence. Most children with serious emotional and behavioral disorders have not been members of successfully functioning peer groups in which appropriate behavior is modeled and valued (Hallenbeck & Kauffman, 1995), nor have many such children learned to accept responsibility for their actions (Rockwell & Guetzloe, 1996). The teacher's first and most formidable challenge is helping promote group cohesiveness.

Although group process treatment programs take many forms, most incorporate group meetings and group-oriented contingencies. Two types of group meetings are usually held daily. A planning meeting is held each morning in which the group reviews the daily schedule, each group member states a behavioral goal for the day, peers provide support and suggestions to one another for meeting their goals, and a group goal for the day is agreed on. An evaluation meeting is held at the end of each day to discuss how well the individual and group goals were met, and each group member must give and receive positive peer comments. Problem-solving meetings are held whenever any group member, including the teacher, feels the need to discuss a problem. The group identifies the problem, generates several solutions, discusses the likely consequences of each solution, develops a plan for the best solution, and makes verbal commitments to carry out the plan. **Group-oriented contingencies** specify certain rewards and privileges that are enjoyed by the group if their behavior meets certain criteria. The criteria for earning the rewards, as well as the rewards themselves, are determined by the group.

Barbetta (2002) recommends some basic rules for fostering the development of group cohesiveness:

- Every student is an equal member of the group and, as such, is accountable and responsible to the group.
- All students have daily responsibilities to the group (e.g., classroom jobs, peer monitoring).
- Schedule daily group planning meetings (each morning) and evaluation meetings (at the end of the day) where group and individual behavioral goals can discussed, evaluated, and reinforced.
- As often as possible, the group "moves" as one.
- The group works out all major decisions and problems together using group problem-solving meetings.
- Use classroom management systems and/or classroom interventions in which reinforcers are provided based on the collective performance of the group. For example, if the class earns 90% or above of their classroom management system points as a group, they earn top-level privileges the following day.

Peer-mediated support and interventions

 Council for Exceptional Children   Content Standards for Beginning Teachers–E/BD: Functional classroom designs for individuals with E/BD (BD5K2). **PRAXIS** Special Education Core Principles: Content Knowledge: III. Delivery of Services to Students with Disabilities, Structuring and managing the learning environment for expectations, rules, consequences, consistency, and positive interactions.

The Power of Teacher Praise

Social approval, often conveyed through verbal praise, is a powerful reinforcer for most people. The positive effects of teacher praise on student performance have been known for a long time (Hall, Lund, & Jackson, 1968; Madsen, Becker, & Thomas, 1968; Zimmerman & Zimmerman, 1962)—a very long time, in fact (Gilchrist, 1916). Research has shown repeatedly the positive effects of contingent praise on the behavior of infants (e.g., Poulson & Kymissis, 1988), preschoolers (e.g., Connell, Randall, Wilson, Lutz, & Lamb, 1993; Fox, Shores, Lindeman, & Strain, 1986), school-age students (e.g., Martella, Marchand-Martella, Young, & MacFarlane, 1995; Martens, Lochner, & Kelly, 1992; McGee, Krantz, Mason, & McClannahan, 1983; Mudre & McCormick, 1989; Staub, 1990; van der Mars, 1989; Wolery, Cybriwski, Gast, & Boyle-Gast, 1991), and adults (e.g., Haseltine & Mittenburger, 1990).

Yet many educators do not appreciate that the systematic use of contingent praise and attention may be the most powerful motivational and classroom management tool they have available. Teacher praise and attention is especially important for students with learning and behavior problems.

MISGUIDED ADVICE

Some argue against the use of praise and rewards for student performance (Deci, Koestner, & Ryan, 1999; Hintz & Driscoll, 1988; Lepper, Keavney, & Drake, 1996; Ryan & Deci, 1996). Alfie Kohn (1993a; 1993b), in particular, has achieved considerable popularity by giving speeches and writing books and papers for educators and business managers, claiming that extrinsic motivators such as incentive plans, grades, and verbal praise damage the intrinsic motivation of students and employees to perform and learn. Using faulty interpretations of research of questionable validity, Kohn argues that not only is praise ineffective but it is actually harmful to students. He claims that praise increases pressure to live up to the compliment, insinuates unrealistic expectations of future success, insidiously manipulates people, establishes a power imbalance, insults

people if awarded for unchallenging behaviors, and undermines intrinsic motivation.

A careful examination of the research conducted both in classrooms and laboratories does not support Kohn's contention that students are "punished by rewards" (Cameron & Pierce, 1994, 1996; Cameron, Banko, & Pierce, 2001). Cameron et al. (2001) conducted a meta-analysis of 145 experimental studies and concluded there was no scientific evidence for detrimental effects of reward on intrinsic motivation.

> These findings are given more importance in light of the fact that the group-design experiments on rewards and intrinsic motivation were primarily designed to detect detrimental effects. The reward contingencies examined in this literature can be viewed as a subset of the many possible arrangements of the use of reward in everyday life. . . . What is clear at this time is that rewards do not inevitably have pervasive negative effects on intrinsic motivation. Nonetheless, the myth continues. (pp. 21, 27)

LOW RATES OF TEACHER PRAISE

Kohn and others concerned that teachers are praising their students too frequently need not worry. In spite of its documented effectiveness in increasing academic performance and desired student behaviors, studies over the past three decades have consistently found very low rates of teacher praise in the classroom. In a study of 104 teachers in grades 1 through 12, White (1975) found that rates of teacher praise dropped with each grade level; and in every grade after second, the rate at which teachers delivered statements of disapproval (criticisms, reproach) to students exceeded the rate of teacher approval (praise or encouragement). More recent studies have reported similar low rates of teacher praise in both regular and special education classrooms (e.g., Baker & Zigmond, 1990; Deno, Maruyama, Espin, & Cohen, 1990; Nowacek, McKinney, & Hallahan, 1990; Ysseldyke, Thurlow, Mecklenburg, & Graden, 1984). Especially discouraging are findings reported by Shores et al. (1993) that teachers' rates of praise in some classrooms for students with emotional and behavioral disorders are as low as one per hour.

FOUR POSSIBLE REASONS FOR LOW RATES OF TEACHER PRAISE

Some teachers worry that students will come to expect to be praised or rewarded. They believe students should want to learn for intrinsic reasons. Certainly it would be wonderful if all students came to school prepared to work hard and to learn for so-called intrinsic reasons. The ultimate intrinsic motivator is success itself (Skinner, 1989)—using new knowledge and skills effectively enough to enjoy control over one's environment, be it solving a never-before-seen algebra problem or reading a mystery with sufficient fluency and endurance to find out who did it. But it is both naïve and irresponsible for educators to expect students with few skills and a history of academic failure to work hard without positive consequences. Contingent teacher praise and other extrinsic motivators such as points toward a grade or slips of paper as entries in the classroom weekly lottery are proven methods for helping students attain the performance levels necessary to come into contact with the naturally existing reinforcement contingencies of success (Alberto & Troutman, 1999).

Some teachers believe that praising takes too much time away from teaching. Detecting and praising performance improvements by students, particularly low-achieving students who have experienced little academic success, is one of the most important and effective forms of teaching. It is unfortunate that some educators have been led to believe they are not teaching when they are praising student accomplishments.

Some teachers feel it is unnatural to praise. Teachers who think it is not natural to praise students' good behavior are, in some respects, quite correct. The natural contingencies of the classroom (and most other social environments) undermine the use of praise and strengthen reprimanding behavior. Teacher reprimands typically produce an immediate change in student behavior (e.g., the child stops disrupting class), which negatively reinforces reprimanding (Maag, 2001). By contrast, when a teacher praises a student for behavior, such as working quietly in class, there is usually no immediate consequence that functions as reinforcement for the teacher's praising behavior (e.g., the student just continues working as before). Although praising a student who is working quietly on an assignment may increase the future frequency of that behavior, no immediate consequences occur to reinforce the teacher's praising behavior. The pervasiveness of these nat-

urally occurring contingencies is supported by the fact that while few teachers must be taught to identify misbehaving students and issue reprimands, many teachers need help learning to catch students being good.

Classrooms are busy places, and many student behaviors worthy of praise and attention go unnoticed. Many desirable classroom behaviors may not be noticed by teachers if students do not call attention to themselves. Teachers are more likely to notice and pay attention to a disruptive student than to a student who is working quietly and productively.

TIPS FOR INCREASING THE FREQUENCY OF TEACHER PRAISE

- *Always be on the lookout for student behavior worthy of praise.* Even the most unskilled and unruly student is correct or obedient sometimes. Don't miss these critical teaching moments.
- *Arrange opportunities for students to do something well just so you can give approval.* For example, an easy and effective way to provide a low-achieving student with an opportunity to succeed in front of his classmates is to ask a question he is likely to know and then call on him to answer.
- *Don't worry about sounding wooden and unnatural at first.* Teachers are often concerned their students will think they are not being genuine. Practice four or five praise statements you can say when you observe specific behaviors or performance improvements by your students. Providing specific praise and approval is just like any other new skill; you'll get better at it with practice.
- *Use self-management to increase your praise rate.* Set a goal to give a certain number of praise statements in a given class period. Prompt yourself to praise desired student behavior by marking reminders in your lesson plan or by playing a cassette tape with randomly spaced beeps. Self-record your praising behavior by marking a card or moving pennies from one pocket to another. Reward yourself with a special treat after school for meeting your goal. Start small and gradually increase your daily goal as your praising skills improve. (To see the self-management strategies Chuck Wood used to increase his use of contingent praise in his first year of teaching, visit the *Feature Teacher* module of the Companion Website at **www.prenhall.com/heward.**)
- *Don't worry about overpraising.* Of all the mistakes a teacher might make, providing too much praise and approval for students' good academic and social behaviors is not likely to be one of them.

KidTools: Self-Management Tools for Children

by Gail Fitzgerald, University of Missouri,
and Louis Semrau, Arkansas State University

KidTools is a computer-based program that helps children create and use a variety of self-management materials at school and home. The goal of the KidTools program is to encourage children to take responsibility for changing and managing their own behaviors. The program consists of three software programs on a CD-ROM. The two children's programs, First Step KidTools (designed for children ages 7–10) and Second Step KidTools (for ages 11–14), provide computer-generated templates that let children be as independent as possible in selecting behaviors to change, picking a self-management tool, developing the steps of their personalized intervention, and printing the tool (e.g., self-monitoring cards, contracts). There is overlap between the two programs, with Second Step KidTools including some higher-level thinking and problem-solving procedures.

Three Levels of Control
KidTools includes intervention procedures for three types, or levels, of control. In all three levels, there is an empha-

sis on what children say and think to themselves as they execute their behavior plans.

External control procedures may be necessary to establish control over problematic behaviors before the child moves to shared- or self-control interventions. In these procedures, the adult provides direction and structure for appropriate behaviors. KidTools available for this level of intervention are point cards.

Shared control techniques provide a transition step for encouraging the child to develop self-control. There is an emphasis on problem solving and making plans to change or learn a behavior. The child and adult jointly participate in these procedures. KidTools available for this level of intervention are contracts, make-a-plan cards, and planning tools.

Internal control techniques assist children through cues and structure provided by self-monitoring procedures.

Helping Children Use KidTools
For these materials to be successful, teachers or parents must first provide instruction in behavior-change tech-

- All major rewards are earned and shared by the group.
- Only in rare instances is a student "removed" from the group (i.e., no longer accountable to the group for her behavior).
- When a student is "removed" from the group, there must be a plan developed and implemented immediately for the student to re-earn group membership.

The teacher functions as a member of the group but has veto power when necessary. (For one teacher's personal reflections on teaching students with emotional and behavioral disorders with a group process approach, see Profiles & Perspectives, "My Return Voyage," later in this chapter.)

 FOSTERING STRONG TEACHER-STUDENT RELATIONSHIPS

In addition to academic and behavior management skills, the teacher of children with emotional and behavioral disorders must be able to establish healthy and positive child-teacher

niques. Children need to understand the concept of a behavior as something they do or think, be able to name behaviors, understand how to monitor whether behaviors occur or not, and assume some level of responsibility for their own behaviors.

KidTools was developed around the concept of positive behavior interventions. Children are encouraged to express their behavior in positive terms. They focus on doing positive behaviors rather than stopping negative behaviors. For example, they decide "I will use my inside voice" rather than be reminded "Don't talk loudly in class."

Children will need to be taught to use self-talk cues and inner speech to give themselves directions. Each self-management procedure in KidTools has variations that will need to be taught, demonstrated, and practiced with children before they can be used independently. Once children know the prerequisite skills, the computer program can be used with a minimal amount of teacher help. Ongoing support by the teacher or parent will ensure that the process remains effective and positive for children.

Teacher Resources.

The third program, Tool Resources, contains information for adults who assist children in using KidTools. It incudes guidelines and tips for each procedure, steps for implementation, age-appropriate examples for children, troubleshooting tips, and references to related resources. A teacher can navigate through the information, return to a menu to select new strategies, or search the entire data base using the Find function.

KidTools runs on both Windows and Macintosh platforms and is available at no cost to educators who plan to use the program in the education of at-risk children or children with disabilities. The KidTools series is being expanded to include learning strategies such as time management, study skills, and organizational skills essential for school survival and success. For more information on the KidTools programs, visit the Virtual Resource Center in Behavioral Disorders website: http://www.coe.missouri.edu/~vrcbd/

relationships. William Morse (1976, 1985), one of the pioneers in the education of children with emotional and behavioral disorders, identified two important affective characteristics necessary for teachers to relate effectively and positively to students with behavior problems. Morse called these traits differential acceptance and empathetic relationship.

Differential acceptance means the teacher can receive and witness frequent and often extreme acts of anger, hate, and aggression from children without responding similarly. Of course, this is much easier said than done. But the teacher of students with emotional and behavioral disorders must view disruptive behavior for what it is—behavior that reflects the student's past frustrations and conflicts with himself and those around him—and try to help the child learn better ways of behaving. Acceptance should not be confused with approving or condoning antisocial behavior; the child must learn that he is responding inappropriately. Instead, this concept calls for understanding without condemning.

Having an *empathetic relationship* with a child refers to a teacher's ability to recognize and understand the many nonverbal cues that often are the keys to understanding the individual needs of emotionally disturbed children. Teachers should communicate directly and

Differential acceptance and empathetic relationship

Council for Exceptional Children

Content Standards for Beginning Teachers–Common Core: Teacher attitudes and behaviors that influence behavior of individuals with exceptional learning needs (CC5K4).

PRAXIS Special Education: Content Knowledge: III. Delivery of Services to Students with Disabilities, Professional roles and responsibilities of teachers, Influence of teacher attitudes, values and behaviors on the learning of exceptional students.

My Return Voyage

by Patricia M. Barbetta,
Florida International University

The power of the peer group can be an effective means of producing positive changes in children with emotional and behavioral disorders. Patty Barbetta, now chairperson of the Department of Special Education at Florida International University, spent 11 years as a teacher, teacher supervisor, and education director at the Pressley Ridge School, a special school in Pittsburgh for children and adolescents with severe emotional and behavioral disorders. Here Patty describes some of her experiences while implementing a behaviorally oriented group process model.

What was I doing returning to a frontline position in a classroom for children with emotional and behavioral disorders after 5 years as a program supervisor? My coworkers, friends, and family asked this question—and for very good reasons. They recalled my early teaching experiences with these children: the hours I spent restraining Jeremy, who never thought twice before hitting me hard; the day the fire chief threatened to fine me when Sam falsely set off the alarm once too often; the time I developed a behavioral contract for Connie to follow her mother's directions, only to have her run away from home. And my biannual trips to the emergency room for a tetanus shot necessitated by student bites.

REASONS FOR RETURNING

My reasons for returning to the classroom were many, but I will mention just two. First was the progress we had made during my first year of teaching. Don't get me wrong. We still had behavior problems right through the last day of school. But by the end of the year, the problems were less frequent and typically were resolved quickly. In our second year (we had virtually the same group), we managed to function well enough to earn money for a field trip to Washington, DC—a 3-day trip that (even though the entire group had to take a time out at Arlington Cemetery) went off without major incident. We were by far the best-behaved group at the Smithsonian (much better than some of the general education groups). Witnessing our hard-earned gains was very rewarding.

Second, I had an interest in directly implementing group process techniques as a new component of the treatment program at Pressley Ridge. I admit I didn't readily buy into the group model at first. The idea of handing over control to a group of students with behavioral disorders scared me. These students working together as a group? I simply couldn't imagine it. Most of them had never been part of a successfully functioning peer group. When they did participate as a group, they usually shoplifted, hung out on the street corner harassing passersby, or picked on timid students in the school cafeteria.

"THAT'S HIS PROBLEM, NOT MINE!"

As I had feared, things did not go well when I first tried a group approach. The students, accustomed to individualized, teacher-designed and -directed classroom management systems, resented being asked to be involved in their own treatment. And they especially resented being held accountable to each other. The students were not very good at working together, problem solving, or encouraging each other to behave appropriately. In fact, they were terrible at these skills. Most did everything they could to undermine the group effort by intentionally losing points needed to earn group activities. They often refused to get involved in each other's problems: "That's his problem, Miss, not mine!" Furthermore, many of them intentionally encouraged inappropriate behaviors by laughing at and suggesting even more creative ways for misbehaving. As for us teachers, we thought it was much simpler to just do things ourselves. There were many very unhappy students and teachers in that early transition period, but we have since learned how we could have made that transition much smoother.

THREE IMPORTANT LESSONS

I learned three very important lessons during the transition to a group programming model. First, implementing a successful group process program is much more complicated than simply bringing together a group of students. Teachers and students have to work very hard to develop well-functioning groups. Second, the peer group is an extremely powerful resource—one that we cannot afford to waste. When the groups at our school started to gel, we observed some positive and powerful group pressure at work. I remember watching Danaire, a young man with a history of acting out, calmly and effectively de-escalating Louie (a new group member) on many occasions when he was about to assault a staff person. And I recall the first time Rico, a tough inner-city kid, shook Chad's hand when he finally learned his multiplication facts. Why was this so amazing? You see, Chad was pretty much the class nerd, and it took several weeks for Rico to even recognize his existence. The two never became best friends, but they were able to help each other out on occasion. And finally, and maybe most important, I learned that involving the students in their treatment was not giving up control. As teachers, we sometimes kid ourselves into thinking we are in control. Every student in the room contributes to each other's behaviors; their influence already exists. The effective use of group process program strategies helped us guide this peer influence.

So what was my return to the classroom like? Frustrating, exciting, challenging, exhausting, and rewarding are a few descriptors that come to mind. You might think that after 8 years in the field it would have been simple. Working with students with behavioral disorders is often rewarding, but it is never simple. The Voyagers (my group that return year) reminded me of this.

THE VOYAGERS

Who were the Voyagers? Well, they were 12 very different 13- to 15-year-old boys who were referred to our program for a variety of behavior problems. Why did they decide to call themselves the Voyagers? They said it was because they would be "voyaging smoothly through their year to return quickly to their public schools." Well, not quite. Things did start out great (commonly referred to as the "honeymoon period"), but we quickly hit a few meteor storms.

Just a few examples: Eric, who referred to himself as "the King of Going Off" (the "Go-Off Master" for short) was very big for his age. He enjoyed staring down, shoving, and hitting students and staff; and he did so often. Then there was Mark, the class thief, who stole anything that wasn't tied down. Then he would hide the stolen item in a fellow Voyager's desk to try to get him in trouble. Gary lived in a rough neighborhood with his alcoholic mother. He often came to school tired and angry. On a bad day, even the simplest request would set him off. What did he do when he was "off"? Usually, he threw his desk across the room. Russell, the class clown, occasionally felt the need to run into the woods, gather sticks and leaves, attach them to his clothes, and come back into the classroom acting like Rambo. This was sometimes funny but hardly ever appropriate. And don't let me forget James, whose favorite activity was hanging and swinging from the doorway while making funny noises, combined with the most creative combinations of swear words you could imagine. Remember, I've described only 5 of the 12 Voyagers.

Were we ever able to function as a group? Yes, we were on many occasions but only after many disappointing moments, terribly difficult days, and frequent opportunities to practice pulling it together as a group. We spent numerous days with restricted privileges because of poor group performances, but no group was more pleased to earn top-level privileges. We may not have made it to the Halloween party, but we did win the Christmas door-decorating contest. And it might have taken us 55 minutes to walk back into school after we lost an intramural football game in the fall, but no group could touch us at the tug-of-war during spring field day.

Was I crazy to go back into the classroom? Probably. Was I sorry I did? No way. I learned more that year about effective strategies for teaching students with emotional and behavioral disorders than ever before. And along the way I managed to help a few troubled kids. It was a rough return voyage but a very rewarding one.

honestly with behaviorally troubled children. Many of these children have already had experience with supposedly helpful adults who have not been completely honest with them. Children with emotional and behavioral disorders can quickly detect someone who is not genuinely interested in their welfare.

The teacher of children with emotional and behavioral disorders must also realize that his actions serve as a powerful model. Therefore, it is critical that the teacher's actions and attitudes be mature and demonstrate self-control.

A FOCUS ON ALTERABLE VARIABLES

Alterable variables

Council for Exceptional Children Content Standards for Beginning Teachers–Common Core: Effective management of teaching and learning (CC5K3). **PRAXIS** Special Education Core Principles: Content Knowledge: III. Delivery of Services to Students with Disabilities, Professional roles and responsibilities of teachers, Influence of teacher attitudes, values, and behaviors on the learning of exceptional students.

The twofold task of the teacher of children with emotional and behavioral disorders is helping students (1) replace antisocial and maladaptive behaviors with more socially appropriate behaviors and (2) acquire academic knowledge and skills. The frequent displays of antisocial behavior, the absence of appropriate social skills, and the academic deficits exhibited by many students with emotional and behavioral disorders make this a staggering challenge. The challenge is made all the more difficult because the teacher seldom, if ever, can control (or even know) all of the factors affecting a student's behavior. There is typically a host of contributing factors over which the teacher can exert little or no influence (e.g., the delinquent friends with whom the student associates before and after school). But it does little good to bemoan the student's past (which no one can alter) or to use all of the things in the student's current life that cannot be changed as an excuse for failing to help the student in the classroom.

Special educators should focus their attention and efforts on those aspects of a student's life that they can effectively control. Bloom (1980) uses the term *alterable variables* to refer to things that both make a difference in student learning and can be affected by teaching practices. Alterable variables include key dimensions of curriculum and instruction such as the amount of time allocated for instruction; the sequence of activities within the overall lesson; the pacing of instruction; the frequency with which students actively respond during instruction; whether, how, and when students receive praise or other forms of reinforcement for their efforts; and the manner in which errors are corrected. The teachers who focus on the identification and systematic management of alterable variables are those most likely to make a difference in the lives of children with emotional and behavioral disorders.

EDUCATIONAL PLACEMENT ALTERNATIVES

Students with emotional and behavioral disorders are served across the continuum of educational placements. During the 1999–2000 school year, approximately 33% of school-age children with emotional and behavioral disorders were educated in separate classrooms, 23% in resource rooms, 26% in regular classrooms with consultation, 13% in special schools, and 5% in residential or homebound placements (U.S. Department of Education, 2002). Although the trend in recent years has been for increased placement of students with emotional and behavior disorders in regular classrooms, slightly more than half of all students in this disability category receive their education in separate classrooms, special schools, and residential facilities.

The relatively high proportion of students with emotional or behavior disorders who are served in more restrictive settings compared to students in most other disability categories probably reflects the fact that only students with the most severe behavioral problems are identified and served. As a result, most students receiving special education because of emotional or behavioral disorders have serious, longstanding problems that require intensive interventions in highly structured environments. Consistent implementation of the specialized supports and programming needed by these students can be very difficult in the regular classroom (Brigham & Kauffman, 1998).

A major challenge of educating students with emotional and behavioral disorders is arranging an environment in which academic as well as social skills can be learned at acceptable rates and the safety of all students is protected. Supporters of full inclusion believe that the regular classroom can be made into such an environment for all students with disabilities. Some positive outcomes have been reported for students with emotional and behavioral disorders in regular classrooms. For example, a study comparing middle school students who spent the entire school day in separate classrooms with students who participated in various classes in regular classrooms for at least one hour per day found that the students who spent part of the day in regular classrooms had better academic records and better work habits than did the students who spent the entire day in

special classes (Meadows, Neel, Scott, & Parker, 1994). Although these results seem to support the contention that students with emotional and behavioral disorders should be educated in regular classrooms, the authors point out that the students included in the regular classrooms did not exhibit the extreme aggression, lack of self-control, or degree of withdrawal that the students who stayed in the special classrooms did. They also noted that placement in general education classrooms typically represents "a major reduction, . . . if not a complete cessation, of differential programming" (p. 178). That is, the general education teachers did not make instructional or management accommodations to meet the needs of the students with behavior problems. Without specialized instruction or accommodations, it is hard to imagine how students with severe emotional and behavioral disorders would receive an appropriate education in the regular classroom.

After reviewing 25 studies comparing the progress of students with emotional and behavioral disorders in different educational placements, Schneider and Leroux (1994) concluded that special programs (which included resource rooms, self-contained classrooms, special schools, and treatment centers) appear to be more effective in promoting academic achievement than is the regular classroom, but better gains in children's self-concept are noted for less restrictive settings. Another review found that students in self-contained classrooms showed more decreases in disruptive behavior than did students placed in general education classrooms (Stage & Quiroz, 1997).

While supporting the education of students with emotional and behavioral disorders in the regular classroom when their individual needs can be met, the Council for Children with Behavioral Disorders (CCBD, 1993) does not believe that the regular classroom is the most appropriate placement for all students with emotional and behavioral disorders.

> CCBD supports a full continuum of mental health and special education services for children and youth with emotional or behavioral disorders. We believe that educational decisions depend on individual student needs. Consequently, . . . CCBD does not support the notion that all . . . students with emotional or behavioral disorders are always best served in general education classrooms. (p. 1)

When an IEP team makes the decision to place a student with emotional or behavioral disorders in a regular classroom or to transition a student from a more restrictive setting to

Placement alternatives

Council for Exceptional Children Content Standards for Beginning Teachers–E/BD: Advantages and disadvantages of placement options and the continuum of service for individuals with E/BD (BD5K1). **PRAXIS** Special Education Core Principles: Content Knowledge: III. Delivery of Services to Students with Disabilities, Placement and program issues/Continuum of educational services.

the regular classroom, it is imperative that the student and general education teacher be prepared before and supported after the placement. Preparation includes identifying the behavioral and academic expectations of the regular classroom, assessing the student's current skills against those expectations, teaching the student additional skills needed to meet those expectations, and inservice training for the teacher on special techniques of behavior management (Nelson, 2000; Rhode et al., 1998). Support following the regular class placement should include a crisis intervention support plan and ongoing consultation and in-class modeling and intervention by a special educator trained to work with students with behavioral disorders (Fuchs, Fuchs, Fernstrom, & Hohn, 1991; Shapiro, Miller, Swaka, Gardill, & Handler, 1999; Walker et al., 1995).

 ## CURRENT ISSUES AND FUTURE TRENDS

Special education for students with emotional and behavioral disorders faces a number of critical and ongoing issues. We discuss five of the most pressing of these issues here.

 ### SERVING ALL STUDENTS WITH EMOTIONAL AND BEHAVIORAL DISORDERS

A continuing concern of many advocates for children with emotional and behavioral disorders is revising the federal definition of this disability so that all children with emotional and behavioral problems that adversely affect their educational performance are eligible for special education. As we discussed earlier, the current federal definition of "seriously emotionally disturbed" distinguishes between students who exhibit a "true" emotional disturbance (considered a disability covered under IDEA) and those whose antisocial behaviors are thought to be the result of social maladjustment (and thus are not eligible for special education under the IDEA). Attempts to sort and label students as socially maladjusted or conduct disordered from those with emotional disturbances in order to deny them needed special education services is both unethical and a waste of time (Nelson, 2000). All students with behavioral problems need and deserve effective special education.

 ### PREVENTING EMOTIONAL AND BEHAVIORAL DISORDERS

In addition to serving all children who already exhibit emotional or behavioral disorders, we must greatly increase efforts to identify children who are at-risk for developing behavior problems and to prevent the development of antisocial behavior. Despite public concern over school safety and youth violence and widespread recognition that antisocial behavior is a chronic disabling condition that exacts tremendous social and financial costs for society, we do little to prevent it. Instead of intervening early when problems are small and more likely to be responsive to intervention, we wait until children are older and their antisocial behavior is well established and much more difficult to change.

Why don't we make a concerted effort to prevent behavior problems in children? Kauffman (1999) has suggested several factors that obstruct the prevention of emotional and behavioral disorders in children: a misguided optimism that children who exhibit antisocial behavior at a young age will grow out of it; worry that identifying and labeling a child as at-risk might cause stigma for the child and his family; concern that because no system of screening is perfect, some children will be misidentified; and an unwillingness to spend the money needed to pay for a comprehensive program of screening, identification, and early intervention.

The knowledge and tools for early detection and prevention are available (e.g., Sprague & Walker, 2000; Strain & Timm, 2001). What is needed is the national resolve and commitment of resources sufficient for a large-scale program of early detection and prevention.

DISCIPLINING STUDENTS WITH DISABILITIES

Disciplining students with disabilities for serious school offenses is a controversial and sometimes contentious issue. The 1997 amendments to IDEA contain a number of rules and regulations pertaining to the discipline of students with disabilities. These provisions of the law are intended to help school administrators maintain a safe school environment while protecting the rights of students with disabilities to an appropriate education. These discipline rules in IDEA are especially relevant to students with behavioral disorders, who by definition are receiving special education because of their problem behavior.

School districts are able to discipline students with disabilities in the same manner as they do students without disabilities, with a few notable exceptions (Smith, 2000; Yell, Katsiyannis, Bradley, & Rozalski, 2000). A student with disabilities can be suspended from school for disciplinary reasons for a total of 10 days per school year. A suspension in excess of 10 days is considered a change of placement, which can be done only by the IEP team.

If a student with a disability commits a serious act that would result in suspension of more than 10 days or expulsion of a student without disabilities (e.g., bringing a gun or drugs to school), the IEP team and other qualified personnel must review the relationship between the student's misconduct and his disability. This review is called a **manifestation determination**. The IEP team may conclude that the behavior which resulted in disciplinary action was *not* a manifestation of the student's disability only when all of the following criteria are met (Katsiyannis & Maag, 2001):

1. The special education services, supplementary aides and services, and behavior intervention strategies provided to the student prior to the incident were consistent with the student's IEP and placement.
2. The student's disability did not impair his ability to understand the impact and consequences of the behavior subject to the disciplinary action.
3. The disability did not impair the student's ability to control the behavior that caused the disciplinary action.

If the IEP team determines that the student's behavior is not a manifestation of his disability, the same disciplinary procedures used with other students may be imposed and the student removed to an alternative school or home instruction. However, the school must continue to provide educational services in the alternative educational setting.

Several authors have noted the extreme difficulty and apparent paradox of trying to determine whether or not the misbehavior of a student who is receiving special education because of a chronic history of such behavior is related to his disability (Katsiyannis & Maag, 2001; Smith, 1997, 2000; Yell et al., 2000). Nevertheless, schools are required by law to make exactly that decision. Currently no empirically validated methods exist for determining whether a student's misbehavior that warrants disciplinary action is related to his disability. Development of valid and reliable methods for conducting a manifestation determination and for providing continued support and treatment of students whose placement is changed as the result of suspension are immediate challenges for the field.

 IMPROVING SERVICES FOR YOUTH IN JUVENILE CORRECTIONS SYSTEM

Improving special education services for school-age youths with disabilities in correctional institutions is another important challenge. About 450,000 school-age youths are placed in detention centers or training schools each year in the United States, with another 300,000 sent to adult jails (Leone, Rutherford, & Nelson, 1991). Students with emotional and behavioral disorders are 13.3 times more likely to be arrested during their school careers than nondisabled students are (Doren, Bullis, & Benz, 1996a), and 20% of students

EMOTIONAL AND
BEHAVIORAL DISORDERS

Disciplining students with disabilities

 Content Standards for Beginning Teachers–Common Core: Laws, policies, and ethical principles regarding behavior management planning and implementation (CC1K2). **PRAXIS** Special Education Core Principles: Content Knowledge: II. Legal and Societal Issues, Federal laws and legal issues related to discipline.

with emotional and behavioral disorders are arrested at least once before they leave school, compared with 9% for all students with disabilities and 6% of all students (Chesapeake Institute, 1994). The educational outlook is bleak for juveniles with disabilities who find themselves in jails and detention centers. Although it can be argued that adjudicated delinquents are, by virtue of the behaviors that precipitated their arrest, behaviorally disordered, most juvenile offenders receive few or no special education services (McIntyre, 1993). Those incarcerated youths who do receive special education services typically receive substandard services (Leone & Meisel, 1997).

DEVELOPING WRAPAROUND SYSTEMS OF COMPREHENSIVE CARE

Many children with emotional and behavioral disorders and their families need and receive an array of mental health and social services such as foster care, child welfare, and community recreation programs. Traditionally, each of those services is provided by a separate agency, each with its own location, procedures, intake forms, and record-keeping system. Just accessing the services requires families to make a series of visits, and the services often overlap one another and leave significant areas of need unserved. An increasing trend in recent years has been the development of community-based systems of care in which mental health and social service agencies collaborate in an effort to wrap a coordinated, interwoven set of comprehensive services around the child. The most effective wraparound programs are characterized by child- and family-centered interventions and supports, interagency cooperation with shared goals, and individualized care that fits programs around a child's needs rather than fitting the child into already determined programs (Stroul & Friedman, 1996).

Increasingly, schools are participating in and, in some cases, serving as the coordinating agency for wraparound service programs (e.g., Anderson, & Matthews, 2001; Duckworth et al., 2001; Eber, Nelson, & Miles, 1997). Woodruff et al. (1999) identified several features of successful school-based wraparound programs: (1) they emphasize school-wide prevention; (2) school personnel advocate for and empower families to be partners in the services designed to help their children; (3) professionals from child and family welfare, mental health, juvenile justice, and other community agencies serve the child in the school as well as in the community; and (4) a school-based case manager coordinates the services to ensure that they support the student's learning at school, home, and in the community.

CHALLENGES, ACHIEVEMENTS, AND ADVOCACY

The issues presented here are not new. Most have been recognized, discussed, and debated for decades. And each will likely remain problems well into the future. Many other issues and problems could be added to the list. Although the challenges faced by those who work with and advocate for students with emotional and behavioral disorders appear daunting and unrelenting, the field has experienced significant advancements and successes to help guide the future (Walker, Sprague, Close, & Starlin, 1999–2000; Webber & Scheuermann, 1997). For example, the field has identified specific program components and instructional practices that, when used in combination, are likely to result in successful outcomes for students with emotional and behavioral disorders (Epstein, Kutash, & Duchnowski, 1998; Peacock Hill Working Group, 1991). Many of those achievements and best practices have been described in this chapter. We must now work diligently to close the gap between what is known about effective special education for students with emotional and behavioral disorders and what those students experience each day in the classroom.

Wraparound services

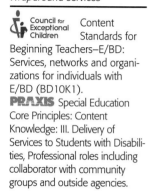

Content Standards for Beginning Teachers–E/BD: Services, networks and organizations for individuals with E/BD (BD10K1).

PRAXIS Special Education Core Principles: Content Knowledge: III. Delivery of Services to Students with Disabilities, Professional roles including collaborator with community groups and outside agencies.

For more information on emotional and behavioral disorders, go to the Web Links module in Chapter 8 of the Companion Website at **www.prenhall.com/heward**

DEFINITIONS

- There is no single, widely used definition of emotional and behavioral disorders. Most definitions require a child's behavior to differ markedly (extremely) and chronically (over time) from current social or cultural norms.
- Many leaders in the field do not like the definition of "seriously emotionally disturbed" in IDEA because students who are socially maladjusted are not eligible for special education services.
- The CCBD and the NMHSEC have proposed a definition of emotional and behavioral disorders as a disability characterized by "behavioral or emotional responses in school programs so different from appropriate age, cultural, or ethnic norms that they adversely affect educational performance."

CHARACTERISTICS

- Children with externalizing problems frequently exhibit antisocial behavior; many become delinquents as adolescents.
- Children with internalizing problems are overly withdrawn and lack social skills needed to interact effectively with others.
- As a group, students with emotional and behavioral disorders perform academically at least 1 or more years below grade level; many have difficulty in reading and math.
- A large number of students with emotional or behavioral disorders also have learning disabilities and/or language delays.
- On the average, students with emotional and behavioral disorders score somewhat below normal on IQ tests.
- Many students with emotional and behavioral disorders have difficulty developing and maintaining interpersonal relationships.

CAUSES

- Biological factors related to development of behavioral disorders include brain disorders, genetics, and temperament.
- Environmental etiological factors occur in home, community, and school.
- Although knowledge of causes is necessary for planning and implementing prevention programs, effective intervention and treatment of children's existing behavior problems does not require precise knowledge of etiology.

PREVALENCE

- Estimates of the prevalence of behavioral disorders vary widely. Several research studies suggest that 3% to 5% have emotional and behavioral problems that warrant special treatment.
- Far fewer children with emotional and behavioral disorders are receiving special education than the most conservative prevalence estimates.

IDENTIFICATION AND ASSESSMENT

- Systematic screening should be conducted as early as possible to identify children who are at risk for developing serious patterns of antisocial behavior.
- Most screening devices consist of behavior rating scales or checklists that are completed by teachers, parents, peers, and/or children themselves.
- Projective tests often yield interesting results, but they are rarely useful in planning and implementing interventions.
- Direct and continuous observation and measurement of specific problem behaviors within the classroom that indicates directly whether and for which behaviors

intervention is needed. Five measurable dimensions of behavior are rate, duration, latency, magnitude, and topography.

- Functional behavioral assessment employs interviews, direct observation, and sometimes functional analysis to identify the setting events and environmental factors that predict and trigger problem behavior and the consequences that may be maintaining it.

EDUCATIONAL APPROACHES

- Students with emotional and behavioral disorders require training in systematic social skills and academics.
- Schoolwide systems of positive behavior support and discipline focus on teaching appropriate behavior to all students in the school.
- A good classroom management system uses proactive strategies to create a positive, supportive, and noncoercive environment that promotes prosocial behavior and academic achievement.
- Self-management skills can help students develop control over their environment, responsibility for their actions, and self-direction.
- Group process approaches use the influence of the peer group to help students with emotional and behavioral disorders learn to behave appropriately.
- Teachers should concentrate their resources and energies on alterable variables–those things in a student's environment that the teacher can influence.
- Two important affective traits for teachers of students with emotional and behavioral disorders are differential acceptance and empathetic relationship.

EDUCATIONAL PLACEMENT ALTERNATIVES

- Most students with emotional and behavioral disorders are served in self-contained or resource classrooms.
- Nearly half of students with emotional and behavioral disorders spend at least part of the school day in regular classrooms.
- Comparing the behavioral and academic progress of students with emotional and behavioral disorders in different educational placements in an effort to determine which setting is the best is difficult because students with milder disabilities are included first and more often, whereas those students who exhibit more severe behavioral disturbances tend to remain in special classes.
- When a student with emotional or behavioral disorders is placed in a regular classroom, it is imperative that the student and general education teacher be prepared before and supported after the placement.

CURRENT ISSUES AND FUTURE TRENDS

- Five pressing challenges for the field of emotional and behavioral disorders are:
  - Making all students with emotional and behavioral disorders, eligible for special education services.
  - Preventing of emotional and behavioral disorders, through screening, identification, and early intervention.
  - Developing valid and reliable methods for conducting manifestation determinations required by IDEA disciplinary provisions.
  - Improving services for youths in the juvenile corrections system.
  - Developing wraparound systems of comprehensive care.

To check your comprehension of chapter content, go to the Guided Review and Quiz modules in Chapter 8 of the Companion Website at **www.prenhall.com/heward**

Chapter 9
Communication Disorders

STEVEN EVERLING
NORTHWEST ELEMENTARY SCHOOL
PINELLAS COUNTY SCHOOL DISTRICT, LARGO, FLORIDA

Education • Teaching Credentials • Experience
- B.A. in Communication Sciences and Disorders, University of South Florida, 1995
- M.S. in Speech-Language Pathology, University of South Florida, 2000
- Florida, Speech and Language Impaired, K–12; Certificate of Clinical Competence in Speech-Language Pathology from the American Speech-Language-Hearing Association
- 6 years experience as a speech-language pathologist

Current Teaching Position and Students   I've been a speech-language pathologist in the Pinellas County Schools for 6 years. My first 4 years were in a middle school. For 3 years I taught the entire academic curriculum—language arts, reading, math, science, and social studies—in a self-contained classroom for students with severe language impairments. The emphasis was on promoting language development across the curriculum. The next year, I taught language arts to students who were in the language-impaired resource program and provided pull-out speech therapy services to students with impairments of articulation, voice, and fluency. For the past 2 years, I have delivered speech and language services in a resource room at Northwest Elementary, a K–5 building of about 750 students.

The 50 students I'm serving this year are between the ages of 5 and 12 and are classified as speech and/or language impaired. Students range among grades K–5. Some of my students also receive services because of mental retardation, learning disabilities, or emotional disturbance.

IEP Goals   Here are examples of IEP goals and objectives for some of my students this year:

Annual goal.   Brian will use strategies for accessing and organizing information from print on four out of five opportunities over three consecutive sessions.
   Short-term objective 1.   Brian will use story search and mapping strategies to access and organize information from a narrative text.
   Short-term objective 2.   Brian will use story search strategies and graphic organizers to access and organize information from expository text.
Annual goal.   Sara will increase speech intelligibility by decreasing the use of a final consonant deletion pattern at the appropriate developmental level on 8 of 10 opportunities over five consecutive sessions.
   Short-term objective 1.   Sara will be able to produce the targeted speech pattern in words with or without prompts.

Focus Questions

- How are speech and language interrelated?

- How should a teacher respond to a child who says, "The dogs runned home"? To a child who says, "That foop is dood"?

- What are common elements of effective interventions for speech and language impairments?

- What are the most important functions of an alternative and augmentative communication system?

- Why are naturalistic interventions more likely to result in maintenance and generalization of a child's new speech and language skills?

Short-term objective 2.   Sara will be able to produce the targeted speech pattern in short phrases with or without prompts.

Annual goal.   Lee will improve vocal quality on 8 out of 10 opportunities over three consecutive sessions.

Short-term objective 1.   Lee will label and identify the parts of the vocal mechanism.

Short-term objective 2.   Lee will identify abusive vocal behaviors in self.

Short-term objective 3.   Lee will develop and use a system with the speech pathologist to monitor abusive vocal behaviors.

Short-term objective 4.   Lee will develop and use a system with his parent to monitor abusive vocal behaviors.

Curriculum Materials and Teaching Strategies   I try to create functional communication situations that best support my students' individual speech and language needs. For students with language-related impairments, this includes making connections to reading and spelling wherever appropriate. I help students develop meaningful strategies they can implement as active learners to construct their own meanings through both interpersonal interactions and interactions with print. Examples of thematic materials that I have found useful include the *Literature-Based Reading Activities* (Yopp & Yopp, 2001) and *The Magic of Stories: Literature-Based Language Intervention* (Strong & North, 1996), among others.

For children with language needs, strategies have to be specific to the individual child. In general, I have found that many children with language disabilities have significant problems making inferences in both the oral and print domains. For example, Brian, an 11-year-old with specific learning disabilities and language impairments, could not organize the structure of a storybook. He couldn't get the gist of a story. Brian's special education teacher and I collaborated in teaching him several ways to organize text-based information. These strategies included story search procedures to find important information and story maps and other graphic organizers to arrange key information so that reasonable inferences could be made. I try to give students with articulation, voice, or fluency problems strategies to better manage speaking in their everyday school and home environments.

Collaboration and Teaming   Every school day I work and interact with several different professionals. I collaborate with general education and special education teachers to help them become aware of the unique communication needs of students with speech and/or language impairments. I also explain and demonstrate techniques they can use to facilitate language learning and assist in the generalization of skills and strategies the students have learned in speech and language therapy. I also interact frequently with the school psychologist because the speech and language assessments I administer are often a component of the multifactored evaluations conducted whenever a student is referred for special education placements. On occasion, I interact with the occupational and physical therapists on ways we can assist each other with skill carryover for students.

What I Like Most about Being a Special Educator   There are two things I like most about being a special educator. First, I enjoy working with a variety of students, each of whom presents unique speech and/or language needs. From the student who stutters, to the student who exhibits speech sound errors, to the student who has difficulties with language-based concepts, finding the appropriate strategies for communicative success is always a welcome challenge. Second, I appreciate collaborating with other educators and school-based personnel who share a similar desire to assist students in achieving their potential.

Advice to Someone Considering a Career in Special Education   My main advice for anyone considering a career in special education is to be flexible because each day in the classroom you'll be confronted with new situations and challenges. Additionally, it is important to have an open and honest line of communication with your students' parents. Frequent communication with parents not only encourages appropriate student behavior

To see some of the strategies Mr. Everling uses to promote his students' language skills, go to the Teacher Feature module of the Companion Website at **www.prenhall.com/heward**

but also increases the likelihood that the skills you are teaching in the classroom will be practiced and reinforced in the home environment—and this is so important for students receiving special education services.

The Most Difficult Thing about Being a Special Educator   The most difficult thing about this job is finding enough time in the day to get everything accomplished: lesson planning, IEPs and related paperwork, parent conferences, schoolwide faculty duties and responsibilities, just to name a few. However, I have found that the longer I work in the school system, the more efficiently and effectively I am able to manage the multiple responsibilities of a special educator's typical school day.

Most Meaningful Accomplishments As a Special Educator   My most meaningful accomplishments occur when my students demonstrate improvement in their ability to be effective communicators. For example, a first-grade student, John, who was in both the specific learning disabilities and speech-impaired programs, presented with such a severe phonological impairment that his speech was nearly unintelligible. The characteristic of John's speech that most hindered his intelligibility was his pattern of producing most speech sounds in the front of his mouth while omitting sounds at the end of words. The impact of these patterns became clearly evident toward the end of our first therapy session, when John said, "Ti to toe." I had to ask him to repeat himself a couple of times before I realized he was trying to say, "Time to go." All of John's utterances exhibited similar speech patterns. Over the course of his first- and second-grade years, I saw John 2 hours per week for speech therapy. At the onset of his first-grade year, his reluctance to speak was a clear effect of his not being understood by parents, teachers, and friends. One can imagine John's frustration: always being asked to repeat himself and then still not being understood. By the end of his second-grade year, John's speech, while still noticeably in error, was for the most part intelligible to those with whom he most commonly interacted. By that time, John had become a much more verbal and assertive child, a result, at least partially, of his now being able to more effectively communicate with others. Students like John make my responsibilities as a speech-language pathologist real and meaningful.

To learn how Mr. Everling helped John overcome his speech problems, go to the Teacher Feature module on the Companion Website at **www.prenhall.com/heward**

Communication——the sending and receiving of information—is such a fundamental part of the human experience that we cannot stop communicating even when we want to. You may decide to say nothing, but sometimes saying nothing communicates a great deal. Still, imagine trying to go through an entire day without speaking. How would you make contact with other people? You would be frustrated when others did not understand your needs and feelings. By the end of the day, besides feeling exhausted from trying to make yourself understood, you might even start to question your ability to function adequately in the world.

Although relatively few people with communication disorders are completely unable to express themselves, an exercise such as the one just described would increase your awareness of some of the problems and frustrations faced every day by children and adults who cannot communicate effectively. Children who cannot absorb information through listening and reading and/or cannot express their desires, thoughts, and feelings in spoken words are virtually certain to encounter difficulties in their schools and communities. When communication disorders persist, it may be hard for children to learn and develop and to form satisfying relationships with other people.

To To better understand what will be covered in this chapter, go to the Essential Concepts and Chapter-at-a-Glance modules in Chapter 9 of the Companion Website at **www.prenhall.com/heward**

DEFINITIONS

Before we define communication disorders, a discussion of some basic terms is necessary.

COMMUNICATION

Communication is the interactive exchange of information, ideas, feelings, needs, and desires. It involves encoding, transmitting, and decoding messages. Each communication interaction includes three elements: (1) a message, (2) a sender who expresses the message, and (3) a receiver who responds to the message. Although intra-individual communication occurs when the same person is both sender and receiver of the same message (e.g., when we talk to ourselves or write a note to remind ourselves to do something when we read it later), communication most often involves at least two participants, each playing the dual roles of sender and receiver.

In addition to enabling some degree of control in a social environment, communication serves several important functions, particularly between teachers and children (Lindfoors, 1987; Owens, 2001).

Narrating Children need to be able to tell (and follow the telling of) a story—that is, a sequence of related events connected in an orderly, clear, and interesting manner. Five-year-old Cindy tells her teacher, "I had a birthday party. I wore a funny hat. Mommy made a cake, and Daddy took pictures." Fourteen-year-old Ian tells the class about the events leading up to Christopher Columbus's first voyage to America.

Explaining/Informing Teachers expect children to interpret the explanations of others in speech and writing and to put what they understand into words so that their listeners or readers will be able to understand it too. In a typical classroom, children must respond frequently to teachers' questions: "Which number is larger?" "How do you suppose the story will end?" "Why do you think George Washington was a great president?"

Requesting Children are expected to communicate their wishes and desires to others in socially appropriate ways. A child who has learned to state requests clearly and politely is more likely to get what she wants and less likely to engage in inappropriate behavior as a way to communicate her needs.

Expressing It is important for children to express their personal feelings and opinions and to respond to the feelings of others. Speech and language can convey joy, fear, frustration, humor, sympathy, anger. A child writes, "I have just moved. And it is hard to find a friend because I am shy." Another tells her classmates, "Guess what? I have a new baby brother!" Through such communicative interactions, children gradually develop a sense of self and an awareness of other people.

Although speech and language form the message system most often used in human communication, spoken or written words are not necessary for communication to occur. In fact, it has been estimated that between 50% and 90% of the information in some face-to-face interactions may be communicated by nonspeech means (Lue, 2001; Owens, 2001). Both paralinguistic behaviors and nonlinguistic cues play major roles in human communication. *Paralinguistic codes* include speech modifications (e.g., variations in pitch, intonation, rate of delivery, pauses) and nonlanguage sounds (e.g., "oohh," laughter) that change the form and meaning of the message. *Nonlinguistic cues* include body posture, facial expressions, gestures, eye contact, head and body movement, and physical proximity.

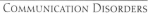

LANGUAGE

Language is a formalized code used by a group of people to communicate with one another. All languages consist of a set of abstract symbols—sounds, letters, numbers, elements of sign language—and a system of rules for combining those symbols into larger units (Hulit & Howard, 2002; Owens, 2001). There are more than 6,000 languages spoken in the world (McLaughlin, 1998). Languages are not static; they grow or contract as the cultures and regions they are part of change.

The symbols and rules governing language are essentially arbitrary no matter what language is spoken. The arbitrariness of language means there is usually no logical, natural, or required relationship between a set of sounds and the object, concept, or action it represents. The word "whale," for example, brings to mind a large mammal that lives in the sea; but the sound of the word has no apparent connection with the creature. "Whale" is merely a symbol we use for this particular mammal. A small number of *onomatopoeic* words—such as "tinkle," "buzz," and "hiss"—are considered to sound like what they represent, but most words have no such relationship. Likewise, some hand positions or movements in sign language, called *iconic signs,* look like the object or event they represent (e.g., tipping an imaginary cup to one's lips is the manual sign for "drink"). Remember, language is used to express descriptions of and relations between objects and events; it does not reproduce those objects and events.

▲ Good communicators use nonlinguistic cues such as body postures and gestures and pragmatic conversational skills such as turn taking.

Five Dimensions of Language   Language is often described along five dimensions that define its *form* (phonology, morphology, syntax), *content* (semantics), and *use* (pragmatics). **Phonology** refers to the linguistic rules governing a language's sound system. Phonological rules describe how sounds can be sequenced and combined. The English language uses approximately 45 different sound elements, called **phonemes.** Only the initial phoneme prevents the words "pear" and "bear" from being identical, for example; yet in one case we think of a fruit, in the other a large animal.

The **morphology** of a language is concerned with the basic units of meaning and how those units are combined into words. **Morphemes,** the smallest element of language that carry meaning, can be sounds, syllables, or whole words. *Free morphemes* can stand alone (e.g., "fit," "slow"). *Bound morphemes* do not carry meaning by themselves; they are grammatical markers that change the meaning of words when attached to free morphemes (e.g., "*un*fit," "slow*ly*"). The word "baseballs" consists of two free morphemes ("base" and "ball") and one bound morpheme ("s").

Syntax is the system of rules governing the meaningful arrangement of words into sentences. If morphemes could be strung together in any order, language would be an unintelligible tangle of words. Syntactical rules are language-specific (e.g., Japanese and English have different rules); and they specify the acceptable (i.e., grammatical) relationships among the subject, verb, object, and other sentence elements. The meaning of a sentence cannot be derived from the congregate meanings of the individual words; it is found in the interactive meanings of those words as the result of their grammatical and sequential relationships with one another. For example, "Help my chicken eat" conveys a meaning much different from "Help eat my chicken."

Semantics has to do with the meaning of words and combinations of words. A competent language user possesses semantic knowledge that includes vocabulary and concept development, connotative meanings by context ("hot" refers to air temperature when discussing the weather but means something else when talking about an athlete's recent performance), categories ("collies" and "beagles" are "dogs"), and relationships between words such as antonyms and synonyms.

Pragmatics is a set of rules governing how spoken language is used to communicate. There are three kinds of pragmatic skills (ASHA, 2001a): (1) using language to achieve various communicative functions and goals (e.g., greeting, informing, demanding, promising, requesting); (2) adapting or changing language to the conversational context (e.g., talking differently to a baby than to an adult, providing background information to an unfamiliar listener); and (3) following rules for conversations or narrative (e.g., beginning and ending a conversation, taking turns, staying on the topic, rephrasing when misunderstood, keeping proper distance, facial expressions, gestures). Rules may vary across languages and cultures.

 SPEECH

Speech is the oral production of language. Although it is not the only possible vehicle for expressing language (e.g., gestures, manual signing, pictures, and written symbols can also be used), speech is the fastest, most efficient method of communication by language. Speech sounds are the product of four separate but related processes (Hulit & Howard, 2002): *respiration* (breathing provides the power supply for speech); *phonation* (the production of sound when the vocal folds of the larynx are drawn together by the contraction of specific muscles, causing the air to vibrate); *resonation* (the sound quality of the vibrating air, shaped as it passes through the throat, mouth, and sometimes nasal cavities); and *articulation* (the formation of specific, recognizable speech sounds by the tongue, lips, teeth, and mouth). Figure 9.1 shows the normal speech organs.

Speech is also one of the most complex and difficult human endeavors. Hulit and Howard (2001) describe just some of what happens in speaking a single word, "statistics."

> The tip of the tongue is lifted from a resting position to an area on the roof of the mouth just behind the upper teeth called the alveolar ridge to produce the "s" sound. The tongue is pressed against the alveolar ridge hard enough to produce constriction, but not so hard as to stop the airflow altogether. As the speaker slowly contracts the muscles of exhalation under precise control, air is formed between the tip of the tongue and the alveolar ridge. Leaving the tongue in the same area, the speaker now presses a little harder to stop the air flow and then quickly releases the contact for the production of the "t" sound. The tongue drops to a neutral position and the vocal folds in the larynx vibrate to produce the vowel "a." The speaker turns off the larynx and lifts the tongue to the alveolar ridge for the next "t," then vibrates the vocal folds for the vowel "i" while the tongue stays in a forward but slightly lowered position. The speaker turns the larynx off again and moves the tongue to the alveolar ridge yet again to produce the controlled constriction for the next "s," followed by increased pressure to stop the air flow and release it for the "t." The larynx is turned on one more time and the tongue lowered to a neutral position for the "i," and then turned off as the tongue arches to the back of the mouth where it contacts

FIGURE 9.1 **Normal speech organs**

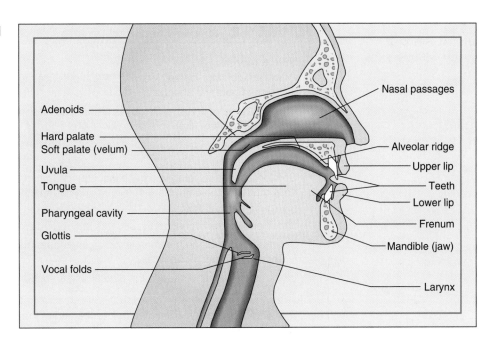

Labels (top to bottom, left): Adenoids, Hard palate, Soft palate (velum), Uvula, Tongue, Pharyngeal cavity, Glottis, Vocal folds

Labels (right): Nasal passages, Alveolar ridge, Upper lip, Teeth, Lower lip, Frenum, Mandible (jaw), Larynx

the velum, or fleshy part of the roof of the mouth, for the "k." Finally, the tongue tip darts to the alveolar ridge for the production of the final "s" sound. All of this occurs in the production of *one* word! (pp. 4–5)

Most languages begin in oral form, developed by people speaking with each other. Reading and writing are secondary language forms that use graphic symbols to represent the oral form. There is no one-to-one correspondence, however, between **graphemes** (print symbols or letters) and phonemes.

 NORMAL DEVELOPMENT OF SPEECH AND LANGUAGE

Despite the complexity of speech and language, most children, without any formal instruction, learn to talk during the first few years of life. The process of learning language is a remarkable one that is not fully understood. For centuries parents, teachers, and scholars have been fascinated by the phenomenon of language acquisition in children.

Understanding how young, normally developing children acquire language is helpful to the teacher or specialist working with children who have delayed or disordered communication. Knowledge of normal language development can help the specialist determine whether a particular child is simply developing language at a slower-than-normal rate or whether the child shows an abnormal pattern of language development. Figure 9.2 identifies some of the key features of speech and language development of a typically developing child. As we consider normal language development, remember that the ages at which children acquire certain speech and language skills are not rigid and inflexible. Children's abilities and early environments vary widely, and all of these factors affect language development. Nevertheless, most children follow a relatively predictable sequence in their acquisition of speech and language.

As the descriptions in Figure 9.2 indicate, children's words and sentences often differ from adult forms while the children are learning language. Children who use structures such as "All gone sticky" and "Where he is going?"; pronunciations such as "cwackers" and "twuck"; or word forms such as "comed," "goed," or "sheeps" gradually learn to replace them with acceptable adult forms. These early developmental forms drop out as the child

Normal language development

Council for Exceptional Children — Content Standards for Beginning Teachers–Common Core: Typical and atypical human growth and development (CC2K1).
PRAXIS Special Education Core Principles: Content Knowledge: I. Understanding Exceptionalities, Human development and behavior as related to students with disabilities, Language development.

FIGURE 9.2 Overview of normal language development

Birth to 6 months
- Infant first communicates by crying, which produces a reliable consequence in the form of parental attention.
- Different types of crying develop—a parent can often tell from the baby's cry whether she is wet, tired, or hungry.
- Comfort sounds—coos, gurgles, and sighs—contain some vowels and consonants.
- Comfort sounds develop into babbling, sounds that in the beginning are apparently made for the enjoyment of feeling and hearing them.
- Vowel sounds, such as /i/ (pronounced "ee") and /e/ (pronounced "uh"), are produced earlier than consonants, such as /m/, /b/, and /p/.
- Infant does not attach meaning to words she hears from others but may react differently to loud and soft voices.
- Infant turns eyes and head in the direction of a sound.

7 to 12 months
- Babbling becomes differentiated before the end of the first year and contains some of the same phonetic elements as the meaningful speech of 2-year-olds.
- Baby develops **inflection**—her voice rises and falls.
- She may respond appropriately to "no," "bye-bye," or her own name and may perform an action, such as clapping her hands, when told to.
- She will repeat simple sounds and words, such as "mama."

12 to 18 months
- By 18 months, most children have learned to say several words with appropriate meaning.
- Pronunciation is far from perfect; baby may say "tup" when you point to a cup or "goggie" when she sees a dog.
- She communicates by pointing and perhaps saying a word or two.
- She responds to simple commands such as "Give me the cup" and "Open your mouth."

18 to 24 months
- Most children go through a stage of **echolalia,** in which they repeat, or echo, the speech they hear. Echolalia is a normal phase of language development, and most children outgrow it by about the age of 2½.
- There is a great spurt in acquisition and use of speech; baby begins to combine words into short sentences, such as "Daddy bye-bye" and "Want cookie."
- Receptive vocabulary grows even more rapidly; at 2 years of age she may understand more than 1,000 words.
- Understands such concepts as "soon" and "later" and makes more subtle distinctions between objects such as cats and dogs and knives, forks, and spoons.

matures, usually without any special drilling or direct instruction (Hulit & Howard, 2002; Owens, 2001). It is also worth noting that children often produce speech sounds inconsistently. The clarity of a sound may vary according to factors such as where the sound occurs in a word and how familiar the word is to the child. Children whose expressive vocabularies consist of fewer than 50 words and/or produce limited word combinations at 24 months of age are considered late talkers. Kelly (1998) reviews the late talker literature and makes recommendations for serving this population of children.

A major longitudinal study has provided a great deal of information about the social and linguistic environment in which typical children learn to talk. Hart and Risley (1995, 1999)

FIGURE 9.2 *(continued)*

2 to 3 years
- The 2-year-old child talks, saying sentences such as "I won't tell you" and asking questions such as "Where my daddy go?"
- She participates in conversations.
- She identifies colors, uses plurals, and tells simple stories about her experiences.
- She can follow compound commands such as "Pick up the doll and bring it to me."
- She uses most vowel sounds and some consonant sounds correctly.

3 to 4 years
- The normal 3-year-old has lots to say, speaks rapidly, and asks many questions.
- She may have an expressive vocabulary of 900–1,000 different words, using sentences of three to four words.
- Sentences are longer and more varied: "Cindy's playing in water"; "Mommy went to work"; "The cat is hungry."
- She uses speech to request, protest, agree, and make jokes.
- She understands children's stories; grasps such concepts as funny, bigger, and secret; and can complete simple analogies such as "In the daytime it is light; at night it is. . . . "
- She substitutes certain sounds, perhaps saying "baf" for "bath" or "yike" for "like."
- Many 3-year-olds repeat sounds or words ("b-b-ball," "l-l-little"). These repetitions and hesitations are normal and do not indicate that the child will develop a habit of stuttering.

4 to 5 years
- The child has a vocabulary of more than 1,500–2,000 words and uses sentences averaging five words in length.
- She begins to modify her speech for the listener; for example, she uses longer and more complex sentences when talking to her mother than when addressing a baby or a doll.
- She can define words such as "hat," "stove," and "policeman" and can ask questions such as "How did you do that?" or "Who made this?"
- She uses conjunctions such as "if," "when," and "because."
- She recites poems and sings songs from memory.
- She may still have difficulty with consonant sounds such as /r/, /s/, /z/ and /j/ and with blends such as "tr," "gl," "sk," and "str."

After 5 years
- Language continues to develop steadily, although less dramatically, after age 5.
- A typical 6-year-old uses most of the complex forms of adult English and has an expressive vocabulary of 2,600 words and a receptive understanding of more than 20,000 words.
- Most children achieve adult speech sound production by age 7.
- Grammar and speech patterns of a child in first grade usually match those of her family, neighborhood, and region.

Sources: Adapted from American-Speech-Language-Hearing-Association (2001); Hart & Risley (1999); Hodson (1994); Hulit & Howard (2002); Owens (2002); Porter & Hodson (2001); Shames & Anderson (2002).

FIGURE 9.3 **Normal pattern of growth in talking**

Source: Hart, B., & Risley, T. R. (1999). *The social world of children learning to talk* (p. 280). Baltimore: Brookes. Used with permission.

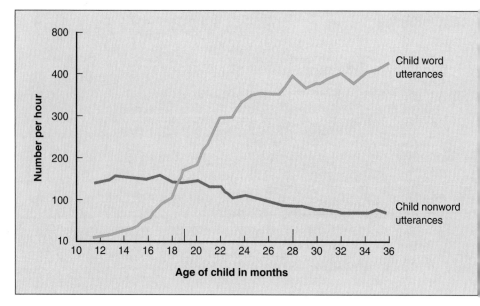

Average number per hour of child word utterances (green line) and child nonword utterances (purple line). Word utterances were those containing recognizable words. Nonword utterances were intonational sentences, babble, gibberish, emotive interjections, and strings of nonsense syllables. The vertical line at 19 months old indicates when, on average, children had become talkers: Their frequency of utterances that contained recognizable words had grown to exceed their frequency per hour of nonword utterances. The vertical line at 28 months old indicates when, on average, the children had become speakers: Their frequency of talking (word utterances per hour) had grown to match that of their parents.

conducted monthly hour-long observations over a period of 2½ years of children from 42 diverse families. The researchers recorded everything said by, to, and around each of the 42 children during unstructured activities in their daily lives at home. Of the many interesting results of this landmark study, two findings are especially notable. First, children between the ages of 11 and 36 months of age are exposed to a tremendous amount of spoken language. "Perhaps most striking of all our findings. . . was the sheer amount of children's exposure to talk and interaction among the people around them. Over the years of observation, we regularly recorded an average of 700–800 utterances per hour within the children's hearing" (Hart & Risley, 1999; p. 34).

Second, children who are learning to talk practice their new skill relentlessly, actively participating in literally thousands of learning trials every day. They say words again and again, they repeat what they hear, they describe things, they talk to themselves while playing, they say what they want, they ask questions, and they respond to questions. After the children in the Hart and Risley study said their first word at an average age of 11 months, their number of utterances per hour increased steadily. On average, at 19 months of age the children became talkers: their frequency of utterances containing recognizable words had grown to exceed the frequency of nonword utterances (see Figure 9.3). At 28 months, the children became speakers: their frequency of talking matched their parents'. At age 3, the children said an average of 1,400 words per hour, using an average of 232 different words per hour and almost 20,000 total words in a 14-hour waking day.

 COMMUNICATION DISORDERS DEFINED

The American Speech-Language-Hearing Association (ASHA, 1993) defines a **communication disorder** as "an impairment in the ability to receive, send, process, and comprehend concepts or verbal, nonverbal and graphic symbols systems. A communication disorder may be evident in the processes of hearing, language, and/or speech" (p. 40).

By how much must a child's communication abilities differ from those of others for the difference to be considered impairment? As we have already noted, the development of speech and language is a highly individual process. No child conforms exactly to precise developmental norms; some are advanced, some are delayed, and some acquire language in an unusual sequence. The range of normalcy of any dimension of speech or language is tremendous. Hulit and Howard (2002) observe:

> We have no exact standards for how much language a normal speaker has or even for how well he uses the language he has. We have vague ideas about acceptable male and female voices, but most of us have a tolerance for voices that go beyond even our own standards. We may notice that well-known television journalists such as Tom Brokaw and Barbara Walters have some problems with "r" and "l," but few of us would consider these individuals speech-defective. So how do we determine what a communication defect is? (pp. 362–363)

When does a communication difference become a communication disorder? In making such judgments, Haynes and Pindzola (1998) emphasize the impact that a communication pattern has on one's life. A communication difference would be considered a disability, they note, when any one of these criteria is met:

- The transmission and/or perception of messages is faulty.
- The person is placed at an economic disadvantage.
- The person is placed at a learning disadvantage.
- The person is placed at a social disadvantage.
- The person's self-esteem or emotional growth is negatively impacted.
- The problem causes physical damage or endangers the health of the person.

To be eligible for special education services, a child's communication disorders must have an adverse effect on learning. The definition of *speech or language impairments* in IDEA reads: "a communication disorder, such as stuttering, impaired articulation, a language impairment, or a voice impairment that adversely affects a child's educational performance" (20 U.S.C. 1401 [3], Section 300.7[c][11]).

Like all disabilities, communication disorders vary widely by degree of severity. The speech and language of some children deviate from the normal to such an extent that they have serious difficulties in learning and interpersonal relations. Children who are not able to make themselves understood or who cannot comprehend ideas that are spoken to them by others are likely to be greatly handicapped in virtually all aspects of education and personal adjustment. A severe communication disorder may lead others—teachers, classmates, people in the community—to believe the child does not care about the world around him or simply has nothing to say (Downing, 1999).

Specialists in the field of communication disorders make a distinction between speech impairments and language impairments. A child may have a speech impairment, a language impairment, or both.

Speech Impairments   A widely used definition considers speech to be impaired "when it deviates so far from the speech of other people that it (1) calls attention to itself, (2) interferes with communication, or (3) provokes distress in the speaker or the listener" (Van Riper & Erickson, 1996, p. 110). The three basic types of **speech impairments** are articulation disorders (errors in the production of speech sounds), fluency disorders (difficulties with the flow or rhythm of speech), and voice disorders (problems with the quality or use of one's voice). Each will be discussed later in the chapter.

It is always important to keep the speaker's age, education, and cultural background in mind when determining whether speech is impaired. A 4-year-old girl who says, "Pwease weave the woom" would not be considered to have a speech impairment, but a 40-year-old woman would surely draw attention to herself with that pronunciation because it differs markedly from the speech of most adults. A traveler unable to articulate the /l/ sound would

Definition of speech and language impairments

Council for Exceptional Children   Content Standards for Beginning Teachers–Common Core: Issues in definition and identification of individuals with exceptional learning needs (CC1K5).
PRAXIS Special Education Core Principles: Content Knowledge: I. Understanding Exceptionalities, Basic concepts, Definitions of disabilities.

not be clearly understood in trying to buy a bus ticket to Lake Charles, Louisiana. A male high school student with an extremely high-pitched voice might be reluctant to speak in class for fear of being mimicked and ridiculed by his classmates.

Many children have mild or moderate speech disorders. Usually their speech can be understood, but they may mispronounce certain sounds or use immature speech, like that of younger children. These problems often disappear as a child matures. If a mild or moderate articulation problem does not improve over an extended period or if it appears to have an adverse effect on the child's interaction with others, referral to a speech-language pathologist is indicated (Owens, 1999).

Language Impairments   ASHA (1993) defines a **language disorder** as "impaired comprehension and/or use of spoken, written, and/or other symbol systems. The disorder may involve (1) the form of language (phonology, morphology, and syntax), (2) the content of language (semantics), and/or (3) the function of language in communication (pragmatics) in any combination" (p. 40).

Some children have serious difficulties in understanding language or expressing themselves through language. A child with a *receptive language disorder* may be unable to learn the days of the week in proper order or may find it impossible to follow a sequence of commands such as "Pick up the paint brushes, wash them in the sink, and then put them on a paper towel to dry." A child with an *expressive language disorder* may have a limited vocabulary for her age, be confused about the order of sounds or words (e.g., "hostipal," "aminal," "wipe shield winders"), and use tenses and plurals incorrectly (e.g., "Them throwed a balls"). Children with difficulty in expressive language may or may not also have difficulty in receptive language. For instance, a child may be able to count out six pennies when asked and shown the symbol 6, but she may not be able to say the word "six" when shown the symbol. In that case, the child has an expressive difficulty, but her receptive language is adequate. She may or may not have other disorders of speech or hearing.

Most children learn patterns of speech and language appropriate to their families and neighborhoods before they enter school.

 COMMUNICATION DIFFERENCES ARE NOT DISORDERS

Before entering school, most children have learned patterns of speech and language appropriate to their families and communities. The way each of us speaks is the result of a complex mix of influences, including race and ethnicity, socioeconomic class, education, occupation, geographical region, and peer group identification (Payne & Taylor, 2002). Every language contains a variety of forms, called **dialects,** that result from historic, linguistic, geographical, and sociocultural factors. Each dialect shares a common set of rules with the standard language. Standard American English (as used by most teachers, in textbooks, and on newscasts) is an idealized form seldom used in everyday conversation. As it is spoken in North America, English includes at least 10 regional dialects (e.g., Appalachian English, Southern English, New York dialect, Central Midland) and several sociocultural dialects (e.g., African American English, Latino English) (Owens, 2001).

The dialect of any group of people is neither inferior nor superior to the dialect spoken by another group. "There are dialects of English spoken by many people and dialects spoken by fewer people, but number of speakers does not indicate superiority or correctness. Every dialect of English is linguistically correct within the rules that govern it, and every dialect of English is as valid as any other" (Hulit & Howard, 2002, p. 324). A child who uses a dialect different from the dominant culture of the school should not be treated as having a communication disorder (Battle, 1998; Seymour, Bland-Stewart, & Green, 1998; Van Keulen, Weddington, & DeBose, 1998).

If the teacher does not accept natural communication differences among children and mistakenly assumes that a speech or language impairment is present, problems may arise in the classroom and in parent-teacher communication (Reed, 1998). On the other hand, some children with communication differences have communication disorders within their dialects, and such impairments must not be overlooked (Payne & Taylor, 2002; Van Keulen et al., 1998).

Dialects and communication differences

 Council for Exceptional Children   Content Standards for Beginning Teachers–Common Core: Issues in definition and identification of individuals with exceptional learning needs (CC1K5) (also CC2K5 and CC6K1).
PRAXIS Special Education Core Principles: Content Knowledge: I. Understanding Exceptionalities, Basic concepts, Definitions of disabilities.

 ## CHARACTERISTICS

 ### SPEECH SOUND ERRORS

There are four basic kinds of speech sound errors:

- *Distortions.* A speech sound is distorted when it sounds more like the intended phoneme than another speech sound but is conspicuously wrong. The /s/ sound, for example, is relatively difficult to produce; children may produce the word "sleep" as "schleep," "zleep," or "thleep." Some speakers have a lisp; others a whistling /s/. Distortions can cause misunderstanding, although parents and teachers often become accustomed to them.
- *Substitutions.* Children sometimes substitute one sound for another, as in saying "train" for "crane" or "doze" for "those." Children with this problem are often certain they have said the correct word and may resist correction. Substitution of sounds can cause considerable confusion for the listener.
- *Omissions.* Children may omit certain sounds, as in saying "cool" for "school." They may drop consonants from the ends of words, as in "pos" for "post." Most of us leave out sounds at times, but an extensive omission problem can make speech unintelligible.
- *Additions.* The addition of extra sounds makes comprehension difficult. For example, a child might say "buhrown" for "brown" or "hamber" for "hammer."

Articulation and phonological disorders

 Council for Exceptional Children   Content Standards for Beginning Teachers–Common Core: Educational implications of characteristics of various exceptionalities (CC2K2).
PRAXIS Special Education Core Principles: Content Knowledge: I. Understanding Exceptionalities, Characteristics of students with disabilities, Linguistic factors.

Traditionally, all speech sound errors by children were identified as articulation problems and thought to be relatively simple to treat (McReynolds, 1990). Articulation refers to the movement of muscles and speech organs necessary to produce various speech sounds. Research during the past two decades, however, has revealed that many speech sound errors are not simply a function of faulty mechanical operation of the speech apparatus but are directly related to problems in recognizing or processing the sound components of language (phonology).

Articulation Disorders   An **articulation disorder** means that a child is at present not able to produce a given sound physically; the sound is not in her repertoire of sounds. A severe articulation disorder is present when a child pronounces many sounds so poorly that her speech is unintelligible most of the time; even the child's parents, teachers, and peers cannot easily understand him. The child with a severe articulation disorder may say, "Yeh me yuh a da wido," instead of "Let me look out the window," or perhaps, "Do foop is dood" for "That soup is good." The fact that articulation disorders are prevalent does not mean that teachers, parents, and specialists should regard them as simple or unimportant. On the contrary, as Haynes and Pindzola (1998) observe, an articulation disorder severe enough to interfere significantly with intelligibility is a debilitating communication problem, and articulation disorders are not necessarily easy to diagnose and treat effectively.

Phonological Disorders   A child is said to have a **phonological disorder** if she has the ability to produce a given sound and does so correctly in some instances but does not produce the sound correctly at other times. Children with expressive phonological disorders are apt to experience problems in academic areas, and they are especially at risk for difficulties in spelling (Clarke-Klein & Hodson, 1995) and reading (Larrivee & Catts, 1999).

Determining whether a speech sound error is primarily an articulation or phonological disorder is important because the treatment goals and procedures differ. Hall et al. (2001) identify three indicators that help clinicians make the distinction. Children with phonological disorders are more likely to

- make multiple sound errors, while children with articulation problems are more likely to have difficulty with only a few sounds.
- make errors consistent with a phonological process (e.g., final consonant deletion, making an error on a sound in one position but producing that sound correctly in another position, as in omitting "t" in "post" but producing "t" in "time").
- have other language delays (because phonology is a component of language).

 FLUENCY DISORDERS

Normal speech makes use of rhythm and timing. Words and phrases flow easily, with certain variations in speed, stress, and appropriate pauses. ASHA (1993) defines a *fluency disorder* as an "interruption in the flow of speaking characterized by atypical rate, rhythm, and repetitions in sounds, syllables, words, and phrases. This may be accompanied by excessive tension, struggle behavior, and secondary mannerisms" (p. 40).

Stuttering   The best-known (and probably least understood) fluency disorder is **stuttering**, a condition marked by rapid-fire repetitions of consonant or vowel sounds, especially at the beginning of words, prolongations, hesitations, interjections, and complete verbal blocks (Ramig & Shames, 2002). It is believed that approximately 3 million people in the United States stutter (Lue, 2001). Developmental stuttering is considered a disorder of childhood. It usually begins between the ages of 2 and 6, and 98% of cases begin before the age of 10 (Mahr & Leith, 1992). It is believed that 4% of children stutter for 6 months or more and that about 80% of those who have stuttered recover spontaneously. Stuttering is far more common among males than females, and it occurs more frequently among twins. The prevalence of stuttering is about the same in all western countries: regardless of what language is spoken, about 1% of the general population has a stuttering problem at any given time. The causes of stuttering remain unknown, although the condition has been studied extensively with some interesting results (Bloodstein, 1995). Stuttering tends to run in families; but it is not known whether this is the result of a genetic connection (Yairi, 1998), an environment conducive to the development of the disorder, or a combination of hereditary and environmental factors.

Stuttering is situational; that is, it appears to be related to the setting or circumstances of speech. A child may be likely to stutter when talking with people whose opinions matter most to him, such as parents and teachers, and in situations such as being called on to speak in front of the class. Most people who stutter are fluent about 95% of the time;

Although Joshua's physical disabilities make it difficult for him to articulate speech sounds well enough to be understood, his communication board has opened up social interaction for him.

a child with a fluency disorder may not stutter at all when singing, talking to a pet dog, or reciting a poem in unison with others. Reactions and expectations of parents, teachers, and peers clearly have an important effect on any child's personal and communicative development.

Cluttering   One type of fluency disorder is known as **cluttering,** a condition in which speech is very rapid, with extra sounds or mispronounced sounds. The clutterer's speech is garbled to the point of unintelligibility. Hulit and Howard (2002) point out two differences between stuttering and cluttering: (1) the stutterer is usually acutely aware of his fluency problems, while the clutterer may be oblivious to his disorder; (2) when a stutterer is asked to pay more attention to his speech, he is likely to stutter more; but the clutterer can often improve his fluency by monitoring his speech.

Fluency disorders

 Content Standards for Beginning Teachers–Common Core: Educational implications of characteristics of various exceptionalities (CC2K2). **PRAXIS** Special Education Core Principles: Content Knowledge: I. Understanding Exceptionalities, Characteristics of students with disabilities, Linguistic factors.

 ## VOICE DISORDERS

Voice is the sound produced by the larynx. A **voice disorder** is characterized by "the abnormal production and/or absences of vocal quality, pitch, loudness, resonance, and/or duration, which is inappropriate for an individual's age and/or sex" (ASHA, 1993, p. 40). A voice is considered normal when its pitch, loudness, and quality are adequate for communication and it suits a particular person. A voice—whether good, poor, or in between—is closely identified with the person who uses it.

Voice disorders are more common in adults than in children. Considering how often some children shout and yell without any apparent harm to their voices, it is evident that the vocal cords can withstand heavy use. In some cases, however, a child's voice may be difficult to understand or may be considered unpleasant (Sapienza & Hicks, 2002). *Dysphonia* describes any condition of poor or unpleasant voice quality.

The two basic types of voice disorders involve phonation and resonance. A *phonation disorder* causes the voice to sound breathy, hoarse, husky, or strained most of the time. In severe cases, there is no voice at all. Phonation disorders can have organic causes, such as growths or irritations on the vocal cords; but hoarseness most frequently comes from chronic vocal abuse, such as yelling, imitating noises, or habitually talking while under tension. Misuse of the voice causes swelling of the vocal folds, which in turn can lead to growths known as vocal nodules, nodes, or polyps. A breathy voice is unpleasant because it is low in volume and fails to make adequate use of the vocal cords.

A voice with a *resonance disorder* suffers from either too many sounds coming out through the air passages of the nose (*hypernasality*) or, conversely, not enough resonance of the nasal passages (*hyponasality*). The hypernasal speaker may be perceived as talking through her nose or having an unpleasant twang. A child with hypernasality has speech that is excessively nasal, neutral, or central-sounding rather than oral, clear, and forward-sounding (Hall et al., 2001). A child with hyponasality (sometimes called *denasality*) may sound as though he constantly has a cold or a stuffed nose, even when he does not. As with other voice disorders, the causes of nasality may be either organic (e.g., cleft palate, swollen nasal tissues, hearing impairment) or functional (perhaps resulting from learned speech patterns or behavior problems).

Voice disorders

 Content Standards for Beginning Teachers–Common Core: Educational implications of characteristics of various exceptionalities (CC2K2). **PRAXIS** Special Education Core Principles: Content Knowledge: I. Understanding Exceptionalities, Characteristics of students with disabilities, Linguistic factors.

 ## LANGUAGE IMPAIRMENTS

Language impairments can involve problems in one or more of the five dimensions of language: phonology, morphology, syntax, semantics, and pragmatics. Language impairments are usually classified as either receptive or expressive. As described previously, *receptive* language impairment interferes with the understanding of language. A child may, for example, be unable to comprehend spoken sentences or follow a sequence of directions. An *expressive* language

Receptive and expressive language impairments

Content Standards for Beginning Teachers–Common Core: Educational implications of characteristics of various exceptionalities (CC2K2). **PRAXIS** Special Education Core Principles: Content Knowledge: I. Understanding Exceptionalities, Characteristics of students with disabilities, Linguistic factors.

Language delays

 Content
Standards for
Beginning Teachers–Common
Core: Typical and atypical
human growth and develop-
ment (CC2K1).
PRAXIS Special Education
Core Principles: Content
Knowledge: I. Understanding
Exceptionalities, Human devel-
opment and behavior as
related to students with disabili-
ties, Language development.

*Prevalence of communication
disorders*

PRAXIS Special Education
Core Principles: Content
Knowledge: I. Understanding
Exceptionalities, Incidence and
prevalence of various types of
disabilities.

impairment interferes with production of language. The child may have a very limited vocabulary, may use incorrect words and phrases, or may not even speak at all, communicating only
through gestures. A child may have good receptive language when an expressive disorder is
present or may have both expressive and receptive disorders in combination. The term
language-learning disabilities (LLD) is often used to refer to children with significant receptive
and/or expressive language disorders.

To say that a child has a language delay does not necessarily mean that the child has a
language disorder. As Reed (1998) explains, a language delay implies that a child is slow to
develop linguistic skills but acquires them in the same sequence as normal children. Generally, all features of language are delayed at about the same rate. A language disorder, however, suggests a disruption in the usual rate and sequence of specific emerging language
skills. For example, a child who consistently has difficulty in responding to who, what, and
where questions but who otherwise displays language skills appropriate for her age would
likely be considered to have language impairment.

Children with serious language disorders are almost certain to have problems in school
and with social development. They frequently play a passive role in communication. Children with impaired language are less likely to initiate conversations than are their peers.
When language-disordered children are asked questions, their replies rarely provide new
information related to the topic. It is often difficult to detect children with language disorders; their performance may lead people to mistakenly classify them with disability labels
such as mental retardation, hearing impairment, or emotional disturbance, when in fact
these descriptions are neither accurate nor appropriate.

Children with oral language problems are likely to have difficulties in both reading
and writing (Westby & Clauser, 1999). Recent research suggests that a "real" reading disability (dyslexia) may be less of a contributor to the reading difficulties of many children
identified as learning disabled than is language learning disability (LLD) (Catts &
Kamhi, 1999).

PREVALENCE

Estimates of the prevalence of communication disorders in children vary widely. Reliable
figures are hard to come by because investigators often employ different definitions of
speech and language disorders and sample different populations. In the 2000–2001
school year, 1,092,105 children ages 6 to 21 received special education services under
the IDEA category of "speech or language impairments" (U.S. Department of Education,
2002). This number represents about 2.3% of the resident population and 21.6% of all
students receiving special education services, which makes speech or language impairments the second-largest category after learning disabilities.

However, the actual number of children with speech and language impairments is
much higher. It is estimated that approximately 50% of children who receive special education services because of another primary disability (e.g., mental retardation, learning
disabilities, hearing impairments) also have communication disorders (Hall, Oyer, &
Haas, 2001).

According to a national survey by ASHA (2001c), school-based speech-language
pathologists (SLPs) work with an average of 53 students each month. Approximately half
of all elementary students who are served by SLPs have speech and language production
problems (see Table 9.1). Fewer than 1 in 10 children with speech and language impairments have fluency disorders.

Speech and language impairments are more prevalent among males than females and
are about the same in each of the major geographical regions of the United States. Approximately two-thirds of school-age children served by speech-language pathologists are boys
(Hall et al., 2001). The percentage of children with speech and language disorders decreases
significantly from the earlier to the later school grades.

TABLE 9.1 Percentage of elementary children served by speech-language pathologists, by type of communication disorder

Disorder	Grades K–3 (in %)	Grades 4–6 (in %)
Speech sound production	58.2	48.7
Spoken language production	47.5	48.2
Spoken language comprehension	38.4	41.9
Intelligibility	16.9	3.6
Fluency	3.4	8.8
Pragmatics	1.7	1.6
Voice	0.6	0.5

*Percentage totals exceed 100% because many students are treated for multiple disorders.
Source: American Speech-Language-Hearing Association (2001c). *Schools survey.* [Online]. www.asha.org

 ## CAUSES

Many types of communication disorders and numerous possible causes are recognized. A speech or language impairment may be *organic*—that is, attributable to damage, dysfunction, or malformation of a specific organ or part of the body. However, most communication disorders are not considered organic but are classified as functional. A *functional communication disorder* cannot be ascribed to a specific physical condition, and its origin is not clearly known. McReynolds (1990) points out that decades of research on the causes of many speech and language impairments have produced few answers. A child's surroundings provide many opportunities to learn appropriate and inappropriate communication skills, and some specialists believe that functional communication disorders derive mainly from environmental influences.

 ### CAUSES OF SPEECH IMPAIRMENTS

Examples of physical factors that frequently result in speech impairments are **cleft palate**, paralysis of the speech muscles, absence of teeth, craniofacial abnormalities, enlarged adenoids, and traumatic brain injury. **Dysarthria** refers to a group of speech disorders caused by neuromuscular impairments in respiration, phonation, resonation, and articulation. Lack of precise motor control needed to produce and sequence sounds causes distorted and repeated sounds. An organic speech impairment may be a child's primary disability, or it may be secondary to other disabilities, such as mental retardation, impaired hearing, and cerebral palsy.

 ### CAUSES OF LANGUAGE DISORDERS

Factors that can contribute to language disorders in children include cognitive limitations or mental retardation, hearing impairments, behavioral disorders, structural abnormalities of the speech mechanism, and environmental deprivation (Hall et al., 2001). Language is so important to academic performance that it can be impossible to differentiate a learning disability from a language disorder (Silliman & Diehl, in press).

Some severe disorders in expressive and receptive language result from injury to the brain. **Aphasia** describes a loss of the ability to process and use language. Aphasia is one of the most prevalent causes of language disorders in adults, most often occurring suddenly after a cardiovascular event (stroke). Head injury is a significant cause of aphasia in children. Aphasia may be either expressive or, less commonly, receptive. Children with mild aphasia have language patterns that are close to normal but may have difficulty retrieving

Causes of communication disorders

PRAXIS Special Education Core Principles: Content Knowledge: I. Understanding Exceptionalities, Causation and prevention of disability.

certain words and tend to need more time than usual to communicate. Children with severe aphasia, however, are likely to have a markedly reduced storehouse of words and language forms.

Research indicates that genetics may contribute to communication disorders. Scientists in Britain have discovered a gene area that affects speech (Porterfield, 1998), and other researchers have reported genetic links to phonological disorders (Uffen, 1997) and stuttering (Yairi, 1998).

Environmental influences also play an important part in delayed, disordered, or absent language. The communication efforts of some children are reinforced; other children, unfortunately, are punished for talking, gesturing, or otherwise attempting to communicate. A child who has little stimulation at home and few chances to speak, listen, explore, and interact with others will probably have little motivation for communication and may well experience delays in language development.

 ## IDENTIFICATION AND ASSESSMENT

"Don't worry; she'll grow out of it."

"Speech therapists can't help a child who doesn't talk."

"He'll be all right once he starts school."

These are common examples of misguided, inaccurate, yet widely held attitudes toward communication disorders. Although some children who experience temporary, mild speech impairments or language delays do get better, many do not improve and deteriorate without intervention. To avoid the consequences of unrecognized or untreated speech and language impairments, it is especially important for children to receive professional assessment and evaluation services (Hall et al., 2001).

 ### SCREENING AND TEACHER OBSERVATIONS

In some school districts, speech-language pathologists screen the spoken language abilities of all kindergarten children. These screenings might involve norm-referenced tests, informal assessments developed by the SLP, and questionnaires or checklists for parents and teachers (McCauley, 2001). Classroom teachers also play an important role in identifying children who may have speech and language impairments. A checklist such as the one in Figure 9.4 can be used to identify children with whom the speech-language pathologist can conduct individualized screening for possible communication disorders. Children who fail a speech and language screening test are candidates for a systematic, in-depth evaluation.

 ### EVALUATION COMPONENTS

Testing procedures vary according to the suspected type of disorder. Often the specialist conducts broad screenings to detect areas of concern and then moves to more detailed testing in those areas. There is no perfect test or method of assessing children's speech and language (Silliman & Diehl, in press). Most examiners will use a variety of assessment devices and approaches in an effort to obtain as much relevant information as possible to inform diagnostic decisions and treatment plans. A comprehensive evaluation to detect the presence and extent of a communication disorder would likely include the following components:

- *Case history and physical examination.* Most professional speech and language assessments begin with the creation of a case history about the child. This typically involves completing a biographical form that includes information such as the child's birth and developmental history, health record, scores on achievement and intelligence tests, and adjustment to school. The parents may be asked when the child first

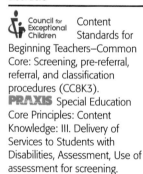

Screening for communication disorders

Council for Exceptional Children Content Standards for Beginning Teachers—Common Core: Screening, pre-referral, referral, and classification procedures (CC8K3).
PRAXIS Special Education Core Principles: Content Knowledge: III. Delivery of Services to Students with Disabilities, Assessment, Use of assessment for screening.

Assessment and diagnosis of communication disorders

Council for Exceptional Children Content Standards for Beginning Teachers—Common Core: Screening, pre-referral, referral, and classification procedures (CC8K3) (also CC8K1).
PRAXIS Special Education Core Principles: Content Knowledge: III. Delivery of Services to Students with Disabilities, Assessment, Use of assessment for diagnosis.

FIGURE 9.4 A checklist for identifying speech and language problems in the classroom

Directions: The following behaviors may indicate that a child in your classroom has a language impairment that is in need of language intervention. Please check the appropriate items.

_____ Child mispronounces sounds and words.

_____ Child omits words, endings, such as plural -s and past tense -ed.

_____ Child omits small, unemphasized words, such as auxiliary verbs or prepositions.

_____ Child uses an immature vocabulary, overuses empty words, such as "one" and "thing," or seems to have difficulty recalling or finding the right word.

_____ Child had difficulty comprehending new words and concerns.

_____ Child's sentence structure seems immature or over-reliant on forms, such as subject-verb-object. It's unoriginal, dull.

_____ Child has difficulty with one of the following:

_____ Verb tensing	_____ Articles	_____ Auxiliary verbs
_____ Pronouns	_____ Irreg. verbs	_____ Prepositions
_____ Word order	_____ Irreg. plurals	

_____ Child has difficulty relating sequential events.

_____ Child has difficulty following directions.

_____ Child's questions often poorly formed.

_____ Child has difficulty answering questions.

_____ Child's comments often off topic or inappropriate for the conversation.

_____ There are long pauses between a remark and the child's reply or between successive remarks by the child. It's as if the child is searching for a response or is confused.

_____ Child appears to be attending to communication but remembers little of what is said.

Source: From Owens, R. E. (1999). *Language disorders: A functional approach to assessment and intervention* (4th ed.), (p. 373). Boston: Allyn & Bacon. Used by permission.

crawled, walked, and uttered words. Social skills, such as playing readily with other children, may also be considered. The specialist carefully examines the child's mouth, noting any irregularities in the tongue, lips, teeth, palate, or other structures that may affect speech production. If the child has an organic speech problem, the child is referred for possible medical intervention.

- *Articulation test.*   Speech errors by the child are assessed. A record is kept of the sounds that are defective, how they are being mispronounced, and the number of errors. Examples of articulation tests include the Photo Articulation Test (Pendergast, Dickey, Selmar, & Soder, 1984) and the Goldman-Fristoe Test of Articulation (Goldman & Fristoe, 1986).

- *Hearing test.*   Hearing is usually tested to determine whether a hearing problem is causing the suspected communication disorder. Audiometry, a formal procedure for testing hearing, is discussed in Chapter 10.

- *Auditory discrimination test.*   This test is given to determine whether the child is hearing sounds correctly. If unable to recognize the specific characteristics of a given sound, the child will not have a good model to imitate. The Test of Auditory Discrimination (Goldman, Fristoe, & Woodcock, 1990) is frequently used.

- *Phonological awareness and processing.* Included in the many phonological skills of children who are competent speakers and users of language is the ability to distinguish the presence and absence of speech sounds, differences between and among sounds, and when individual sounds begin and end. They can remember language sounds and reproduce them at a later time. Children without phonological awareness and processing skills not only have problems with receptive and expressive oral language but have great difficulties in learning to read. Phonological processing measures include the Test of Phonological Awareness (Torgeson & Bryant, 1994) and the Comprehensive Test of Phonological Processing (Wagner, Torgeson, & Rahsotte, 1999).

- *Vocabulary and overall language development test.* The amount of vocabulary a child has acquired is generally a good indicator of language competence. Frequently used tests of vocabulary include the Peabody Picture Vocabulary Test—III (Dunn & Dunn, 1997) and the Comprehensive Receptive and Expressive Vocabulary Test (Wallace & Hammill, 1994). An overall language test, such as the Test of Language Development (Hammill & Newcomer, 1997) and the Clinical Evaluation of Language Fundamentals (Semel, Wiig, & Seord, 1995), assesses the child's understanding and production of language structures (e.g., important syntactical elements such as the concept that conjunctions show relations between the sentence elements they connect).

- *Language samples.* An important part of any evaluation procedure is obtaining accurate samples of the child's expressive speech and language. The examiner considers factors such as intelligibility and fluency of speech, voice quality, and use of vocabulary and grammar. Some speech-language pathologists use structured tasks to evoke language samples. They may, for example, ask a child to describe a picture, tell a story, or answer a list of questions. Most specialists, however, use informal conversation to obtain language samples, believing that the child's language sample will be more representative if the examiner uses natural conversation rather than highly structured tasks (Hadley, 1998). Open-ended questions such as "Tell me about your family" are suggested rather than yes-no questions or questions that can be answered with one word, such as "What color is your car?" To ensure a complete and accurate record of the talk and reduce distractions for the child caused by note taking, examiners usually tape-record the child's language samples.

▲ A comprehensive assessment of communication disorders includes articulation, auditory discrimination, vocabulary tests, and a language sample.

- *Observation in natural settings.* Objective observation and measurement of children's language use in social contexts is an important element of assessment for communication disorders. It is imperative that the observer samples the child's communication behavior across various settings rather than limit it to a clinic or examining room. A parent-child observation is frequently arranged for young children. The specialist provides appropriate toys and activities and requests the parent to interact normally with the child.

After all the data from the multifactored evaluation have been gathered, the speech-language pathologist reviews the results of the case. Because there is often so much assessment information, some SLPs use computer programs to help organize and analyze the results (Hall et al., 2001). A treatment plan is then developed in cooperation with the child's parents and teachers to set up realistic communication objectives and determine the methods that will be used.

EDUCATIONAL APPROACHES

Various approaches are employed in the treatment of children with communication disorders. *Speech-language pathologist (SLP)* is the preferred term for the school-based professional with primary responsibility for identifying, evaluating, and providing therapeutic services to children with communication disorders (ASHA, 2001c). But terms such as *speech therapist, speech clinician,* and *speech teacher* are still used in some schools. As a key member of a child's IEP team, the SLP's goal is to correct the child's speech and/or language problems or to help the child achieve the maximum communicative potential, which may involve compensatory techniques and/or augmentative and alternative means of communication (Hall et al., 2001). Speech-language pathology addresses both organic and functional causes and encompasses practitioners with numerous points of view and a wide range of accepted intervention techniques.

Some SLPs employ structured exercises and drills to correct speech sounds; others emphasize speech production in natural language contexts. Some prefer to work with children in individual therapy sessions; others believe that group sessions are advantageous for language modeling and peer support. Some encourage children to imitate the therapist's speech; others prefer to have the child listen to tapes of his own speech. Some specialists follow a structured, teacher-directed approach in which targeted speech and language behaviors are precisely prompted, recorded, and reinforced; others favor less structured methods. Some SLPs focus on a child's expressive and receptive communication; others devote attention to other aspects of the child's behavior and environment, such as self-confidence and interactions with parents and classmates. Clearly, many possible options can be explored in devising effective, individualized treatment plans for students with communication disorders.

TREATING SPEECH SOUND ERRORS

A general goal of specialists in communication disorders is to help the child speak as clearly and pleasantly as possible so that a listener's attention will focus on the child's message rather than how he says it.

Articulation Errors   The goals of therapy for articulation problems are acquisition of the correct speech sound(s), generalization of the sound(s) to all speaking settings and contexts (especially the classroom), and maintenance of the correct sound(s) after therapy has ended. Traditional articulation therapy involves discrimination and production activities.

Discrimination activities are designed to improve the child's ability to listen carefully and detect the differences between similar sounds (e.g., the /t/ in "take," the /c/ in "cake") and to differentiate between correct and distorted speech sounds. The child learns to match his speech to that of a standard model by using auditory, visual, and tactual feedback. A generally consistent relationship exists between children's ability to recognize sounds and their ability to articulate them correctly.

Production is the ability to produce a given speech sound alone and in various contexts. Therapy emphasizes the repetitive production of sounds in various contexts, with special attention to the motor skills involved in articulation. Exercises are employed to produce sounds with differing stress patterns. The SLP may have the child carefully watch how sounds are produced and then use a mirror to monitor his own speech production. Children are expected to accurately produce problematic sounds in syllables, words, sentences, and stories. They may tape-record their own speech and listen carefully for errors. Therapy progresses from having the child articulate simple sounds in isolation; then in syllables, words, phrases, sentences, and structured conversation; and finally in unstructured conversation. As in all communication training, it is important for the teacher, parent, or specialist to provide a good language model, reinforce the child's improving performance, and encourage the child to talk.

Phonological Errors   When a child's spoken language problem includes one or more phonological errors, the goal of therapy is to help the child identify the error pattern(s) and gradually produce more linguistically appropriate sound patterns (Barlow, 2001). For example, a child who frequently omits final consonants might be taught to recognize the difference between minimally contrastive words—perhaps using a set of cards with the words "sea," "seed," "seal," "seam," and "seat" (Hall et al., 2001). Therapeutic tasks are constructed so that the child is rewarded for following directions (e.g., "Pick up the 'seal' card") and speaking clearly enough for the therapist to follow his or her directions (e.g., the child directs the SLP to give him the "seat" card). To respond correctly, the child must attend to and use the information in the final consonant sound.

Sounds are not taught in isolation. Children with phonological problems can often articulate specific sounds but are not using those sounds in proper linguistic context.

Although the distinction between articulation errors and phonological errors is important, many children with communication disorders have problems with both. The therapeutic approaches for articulation and phonological disorders are not incompatible and can be used in conjunction for some children.

 TREATING FLUENCY DISORDERS

Throughout history, people who stutter have been subjected to countless treatments—some of them unusual, to say the least. Past treatments included holding pebbles in the mouth, sticking fingers into a light socket, talking out of one side of the mouth, eating raw oysters, speaking with the teeth clenched, taking alternating hot and cold baths, and speaking on inhaled rather than exhaled air (Ham, 1986; Hulit & Howard, 2002). For many years, it was widely thought that a tongue that was unable to function properly in the mouth caused stuttering. As a result, it was common for early physicians to prescribe ointments to blister or numb the tongue or even to remove portions of the tongue through surgery!

Application of behavioral principles has strongly influenced recent practices in the treatment of fluency disorders. A therapist using this methodology regards stuttering as learned behavior and seeks to eliminate it by establishing and encouraging fluent speech. For example, one stuttering treatment program called the Lidcombe Program trains parents to positively reinforce their child's fluent utterances in the home. Packman and Onslow (1998) cite six different studies in which the effectiveness of the Lidcombe Program has been demonstrated.

Children may learn to manage their stuttering by deliberately prolonging certain sounds or by speaking slowly to get through a "block." They may increase their confidence and fluency by speaking in groups, where pressure is minimized and successful speech is positively reinforced. They may learn to monitor their own speech and to reward themselves for periods of fluency. They may learn to speak to a rhythmic beat or with the aid of devices that mask or delay their ability to hear their own speech. Tape recorders are often used for drills, simulating conversations, and documenting progress.

Children often learn to control their stuttering and produce increasingly fluent speech as they mature. No single method of treatment has been recognized as most effective. Stuttering frequently decreases when children enter adolescence, regardless of which treatment method was used. Often, the problem disappears with no treatment at all. Results from studies of the phenomenon of spontaneous recovery from stuttering have reported that 65% to 80% of children diagnosed as stutterers apparently outgrow or get over their dysfluencies without formal intervention (Curlee & Yairi, 1998). Nevertheless, a speech-language pathologist should be contacted when a child exhibits signs of stuttering or when the parents are concerned about speech fluency. Although some children who stutter get better without help, many do not. Early intervention may prevent the child from developing a severe stutter. In its initial stages, stuttering can almost always be treated successfully by teachers, parents, and a speech-language pathologist working together. When interacting with a child who stutters, a teacher should pay primary attention to what the child is saying rather than to his difficulties in saying it. When the child experiences a verbal block, the teacher should be patient and calm, say nothing, and maintain eye contact with the child until he finishes speaking. (For additional suggestions for how classroom teachers can help children with speech dysfluencies, see Teaching & Learningl, "Helping the Child Who Stutters in the Classroom," later in this chapter.)

TREATING VOICE DISORDERS

A thorough medical examination should always be sought for a child with a voice disorder. Surgery or other medical interventions can often treat organic causes. In addition, SLPs sometimes recommend environmental modifications; a person who is consistently required to speak in a noisy setting, for example, may benefit from the use of a small microphone to reduce vocal straining and shouting (Sapienza & Hicks, 2002). Most remedial techniques, however, offer direct vocal rehabilitation, which helps the child with a voice disorder gradually learn to produce more acceptable and efficient speech. Voice therapy often begins with teaching the child to listen to his own voice and learn to identify those aspects that need to be changed. Depending on the type of voice disorder and the child's overall circumstances, vocal rehabilitation may include activities such as exercises to increase breathing capacity, relaxation techniques to reduce tension, or procedures to increase or decrease the loudness of speech (Harris & Harris, 1997; Johnston & Umberger, 1996).

Because many voice problems are directly attributable to vocal abuse, behavioral principles can be used to help children and adults break habitual patterns of vocal misuse. For example, a child might self-monitor the number of abuses he commits in the classroom or at home, receiving reinforcement for gradually lowering the number of abuses over time. Computer technology has also been successfully applied in the treatment of voice disorders. Some instruments enable speakers to see visual representations of their voice patterns on a screen or printout; speakers are thus able to monitor their own vocalizations visually as well as auditorily and to develop new patterns of using their voices more naturally and efficiently (Bull & Rushakoff, 1987).

TREATING LANGUAGE DISORDERS

Treatments for language disorders are also extremely varied. Some programs focus on pre-communication activities that encourage the child to explore and that make the environment conducive to the development of receptive and expressive language. Clearly, children must have something they want to communicate. And because children learn through imitation, it is important for the teacher or specialist to talk clearly, use correct inflections, and provide a rich variety of words and sentences.

The changing and expanding role of school-based SLPs today includes connecting children's oral language to literacy components of the curriculum as much as possible (ASHA, 2001b; Merritt & Culatta, 1998). This is done in a variety of ways. For example, children with very limited oral language might be taught how to orally "read" pictures as a language enhancement activity (Alberto & Fredrick, 2000). Children with language impairments might develop written language skills by exchanging e-mail letters to penpals (Harmston, Strong, & Evans, 2001).

Speech-language pathologists are increasingly employing naturalistic interventions to help children develop and use language skills. Naturalistic approaches were developed as

>

Interacting with a child who stutters

 Council for Exceptional Children   Content Standards for Beginning Teachers–Common Core: Teacher attitudes and behaviors that influence behavior of individuals with exceptional learning needs (CC5K4).
PRAXIS Special Education Core Principles: Content Knowledge: III. Delivery of Services to Students with Disabilities, Structuring and managing the learning environment for consistency, attitudes, and positive interactions.

Helping the Child Who Stutters in the Classroom

There is no single treatment for stuttering because the causation, type, and severity of nonfluencies vary from child to child. Despite this variability, teachers can significantly help a child who stutters by providing a good speech model, improving the child's self-esteem, and creating a good speech environment.

Provide a Good Speech Model

- *Reduce your rate of speech.* Young children often imitate the speech rate of their parents and other significant adults. This rate may be inappropriately fast for the child's motoric and linguistic competencies. Slower speech provides the child with time needed to organize thoughts, choose vocabulary and grammatical form, and plan the speech act motorically.

- *Create silences in your interactions.* Pauses placed at appropriate places in conversation help create a relaxed communication environment, slower rate of speech, and a more natural speech cadence. Pause for 2 to 3 seconds before responding to a child's questions and statements.
- *Model simple vocabulary and grammatical forms.* Stuttering is more likely to occur in longer words, words that are used less frequently, and more grammatically complex sentences.
- *Model normal nonfluencies.* You may need to make a conscious effort to use normal nonfluencies, such as interjections ("um" or "ah") or an occasional whole-word repetition, phrase repetition, or pause. Knowing that even fluent speech contains nonfluen-

---

Naturalistic interventions/milieu teaching strategies

Council for Exceptional Children Content Standards for Beginning Teachers—Common Core: Design learning environments that encourage active participation in individual and group activities (CC5S4). **PRAXIS** Special Education Core Principles: Content Knowledge: III. Delivery of Services to Students with Disabilities,Curriculum and Instruction, Language and literacy acquisition.

an alternative to didactic language interventions, because children often experienced difficulties in generalizing new skills from the structured teaching settings to everyday contexts. In contrast to didactic teaching approaches, which use contrived materials and activities (e.g., pictures, puppets) and massed trials to teach specific skills, *naturalistic interventions* are characterized by dispersed learning trials carried out in the natural environment as opportunities occur for teaching functional communication. Naturalistic approaches occur in the context of normal conversational interchanges that follow the child's "attentional lead" (Goldstein, Kaczmarek, & Hepting, 1994).

Kaiser (2000) makes the following recommendations about naturalistic interventions, which are also known as **milieu teaching strategies:**

- Teach when the child is interested.
- Teach what is functional for the student at the moment.
- Stop while both the student and the teacher are still enjoying the interaction.

Naturalistic interventions involve structuring the environment to create numerous opportunities for desired child responses (e.g., holding up a toy and asking, "What do you want?") and structuring adult responses to a child's communication (e.g., the child points outside and says, "Go with me," and the teacher says, "Okay, I'll go with you."). "Successful

cies will help children accept nonfluencies and reduce the fear of speaking.

Improve the Child's Self-Esteem

- *Disregard moments of nonfluency.* Reinforce occurrences of fluency and ignore nonfluencies. Do not give instructions such as "Slow down," "Take a deep breath," or "Stop and start over," which imply that the child is not doing enough. This might increase guilt and diminish self-confidence.
- *Show acceptance of what the child expresses rather than how it is said.* Ask the child to repeat only the parts of the utterance that were not understood rather than those that were nonfluent. This request indicates that you did listen and that the message is important.
- *Treat the child who stutters like any other child in the class.* Do not reduce your expectations because of the nonfluencies.
- *Acknowledge nonfluencies without labeling them.* Do not refer to the problem of stuttering. Instead, use words that the child uses to describe her speech, such as "bumpy" or "hard." Assure the child that it is okay to have dysfluencies; everyone does.
- *Help the child feel in control of speech.* Follow the child's lead in conversation. Speech will more likely be fluent if the child can talk about areas of interest.
- *Accept nonfluencies.* Try not to be overly concerned about normal nonfluencies because you see the child as a stutterer. Maintain eye contact and remain patient.

Create a Good Speech Environment

- *Establish good conversational rules.* Interruptions may distract the child and increase nonfluencies. Ensure that no one interrupts and that everyone gets a chance to talk.
- *Listen attentively.* Active listening lets the child know that content is important. Use naturalistic comments (e.g., "Yes, Johnny, that is a large blue truck.") in place of absent-minded "uh-huhs" and generic statements (e.g., "Good talking!").
- *Suggest that the child cease other activities while speaking.* It is sometimes difficult to perform two different motoric acts, such as coloring and talking, simultaneously. Asking the child to stop other activities while speaking may improve fluency.
- *Prepare the child for upcoming events.* The emotionality of birthdays, holidays, field trips, and changes in the daily schedule may cause apprehension and increase stuttering. Discussing upcoming events can reduce fear associated with the unknown and should enhance the child's fluency.

Source: From LaBlance, G. R., Steckol, K. F., & Smith, V. L. (1994). Stuttering: The role of the classroom teacher. *Teaching Exceptional Children, 26*(2), 10–12. Adapted by permission.

milieu teaching more closely resembles a conversation than a rote instructional episode" (Kaiser, 2000, p. 459). However, good naturalistic teaching does not mean the teacher should wait patiently to see whether and when opportunities for meaningful and interesting language use by children occur. Environments in which language teaching takes place should be designed to catch students' interest and increase the likelihood of communicative interactions that can be used for teaching purposes. Six strategies for arranging environments that create naturally occurring language teaching opportunities are described in Figure 9.5.

No matter what the approach to treatment, children with language disorders need to be around children and adults with something interesting to talk about. As Reed (1998) points out, it was assumed for many years that a one-to-one setting was the most effective format for language intervention. Emphasis was on eliminating distracting stimuli and focusing a child's attention on the desired communication task. Today, however, it is generally recognized that language is an interactive, interpersonal process and that naturally occurring intervention formats should be used to expose children with language disorders to a wide range of stimuli, experiences, contexts, and people that cannot be replicated in one-to-one therapy.

Whatever intervention methods they use, effective speech-language pathologists establish specific goals and objectives, keep precise records of their students' performance, and arrange the learning environment so that each child's efforts at communication will be rewarded and enjoyable.

FIGURE 9.5 Six strategies for increasing naturalistic opportunities for language teaching

1. **Interesting materials.** Students are likely to communicate when things or activities in the environment interest them. *Example:* James lay quietly on the rug, with his head resting on his arms. Ms. Davis sat at one end of the rug and rolled a big yellow ball right past James. James lifted his head and looked around for the ball.

2. **Out of reach.** Students are likely to communicate when they want something that they cannot reach. *Example:* Mr. Norris lifted a drum off the shelf and placed it on the floor between Judy and Annette, who were both in wheelchairs. Mr. Norris hit the drum three times and then waited, looking at his two students. Judy watched and clapped her hands together. Then, she reached for the drum with both arms outstretched.

3. **Inadequate portions.** Students are likely to communicate when they do not have the necessary materials to carry out an instruction. *Example:* Mr. Robinson gave every student except Mary a ticket to get into the auditorium for the high school play. He told his students to give their tickets to the attendant. Mr. Robinson walked beside Mary toward the entrance. When Mary reached the attendant, Mr. Robinson paused and looked at Mary. She pointed to the tickets in his hand and signed "give me." Mr. Robinson gave her a ticket and she handed it to the attendant who said "Thank you. Enjoy the play."

4. **Choice-making.** Students are likely to communicate when they are given a choice. *Example:* Peggy's favorite pastime is listening to tapes on her tape recorder. On Saturday morning, Peggy's father said to her, "We could listen to your tapes" (pointing to the picture of the tape recorder on Peggy's communication board) "or we could go for a ride in the car" (pointing to the picture of the car). "What would you like to do?" Peggy pointed to the picture of the tape recorder. "OK, let's listen to this new tape you like," her father said as he put the tape in and turned on the machine.

5. **Assistance.** Students are likely to communicate when they need assistance in operating or manipulating materials. *Example:* Tammy's mother always places three clear plastic containers with snacks (cookies, crackers, popcorn) on the kitchen table before Tammy returns from school. When Tammy arrives home and is ready for a snack, she goes to the table and chooses what she wants. The containers are hard to open, so Tammy usually brings the container with her chosen snack to her mother. Her mother responds to this nonverbal request by modeling a request form that specifies Tammy's choice (e.g., "Open popcorn.")

6. **Unexpected situations.** Students are likely to communicate when something happens that they do not expect. *Example:* Ms. Esser was helping Kathy put on her socks and shoes after rest time. After assisting with the socks, Ms. Esser put one of the shoes on her own foot. Kathy stared at the shoe for a moment and then looked up at her teacher, who was smiling. "No," laughed Kathy, "my shoe."

Source: From Kaiser, A. P. (2000). Teaching functional communication skills. In M. E. Snell & F. Brown (Eds.), *Instruction of students with severe disabilities* (5th ed.), (p. 467). Upper Saddle River, NJ: Merrill/Prentice Hall. Reprinted by permission.

 ## AUGMENTATIVE AND ALTERNATIVE COMMUNICATION

Augmentative and alternative communication (AAC) refers to a diverse set of strategies and methods to assist individuals who are unable to meet their communication needs through speech or writing. AAC has three components (Kangas & Lloyd, 2002):

1. A representational symbol set or vocabulary
2. A means for selecting the symbols
3. A means for transmitting the symbols

Each of the three components of AAC may be unaided or aided. *Unaided techniques* do not require a physical aid or device. They include oral speech, gestures, facial expressions, general body posture, and manual signs. Of course, individuals without disabilities use a wide range of unaided augmentative communication techniques. *Aided techniques* of communication involve an external device or piece of equipment. ACC devices can be simple, low-tech affairs or sophisticated electronic equipment (Lahm & Everington, 2002).

Individuals who do not speak so that others can understand must have access to vocabulary that matches as nearly as possible the language they would use in various situations if they could speak. Beukelman and Miranda (1998) suggest that decisions about what items to include in a student's augmentative vocabulary should take into account the following:

This communication device enables the user to select and transmit synthesized speech via a wand attached to the head.

- Vocabulary that peers in similar situations and settings use
- What communication partners (e.g., teachers, parents) think will be needed
- Vocabulary the student is already using in all modalities
- Contextual demands of specific situations

Symbol Sets and Symbol Systems After selecting the vocabulary for an AAC system, a collection of symbols must be chosen or developed to represent the vocabulary. There are numerous commercially available *symbol sets,* a collection of pictures or drawings in which each symbol has one or more specified meanings, from which a person's AAC vocabulary might be constructed. Symbol sets—such as the Oakland Picture Dictionary (Kirsten, 1981), Picture Communication Symbols (Mayer-Johnson, 1986), and the Pictogram Ideogram Communication symbols (Johnson, 1985)—are graphic, which means that the symbols look like the object or concept they represent as much as possible. Mayer-Johnson has an electronic version of its symbols that can be incorporated into picture overlays. Symbol sets may also be homemade, consisting of photos, pictures, and perhaps words and the alphabet.

In contrast to symbol sets, *symbol systems* are structured around an internal set of rules that govern how new symbols are added to the system. One of the best-known symbol systems is Blissymbolics, which represents concepts through a combination of geometric shapes. The user of Blissymbolics combines multiple symbols to create new meanings (e.g., "school" is communicated by selecting the symbols "house-gives-knowledge"). Because many of the Blissymbolics are abstract, however, and do not look like the concept they represent, some individuals have difficulty learning the system. Figure 9.6 shows how common concrete and abstract vocabulary can be represented by Bliss symbols and six other symbol sets.

Selecting the Symbols Symbols are selected in augmentative communication by direct selection, scanning, or encoding responses (Kangas & Lloyd, 2002). *Direct selection* involves pointing to the symbol one wishes to express with a finger or fist or sometimes with a wand attached to the head or chin. With a limited number of selections widely spaced from one another, the user can select symbols by "eye pointing." *Scanning* techniques present choices to the user one at a time, and the user makes a response at the proper time to indicate which item or group of selections she wants to communicate. Scanning can be

Augmentative and alternative communication

Council for Exceptional Children Content Standards for Beginning Teachers–Common Core: Augmentative and assistive communication strategies (CC6K4).
PRAXIS Special Education Core Principles: Content Knowledge: III. Delivery of Services to Students with Disabilities, Technology for teaching and learning, Augmentative and alternative communication.

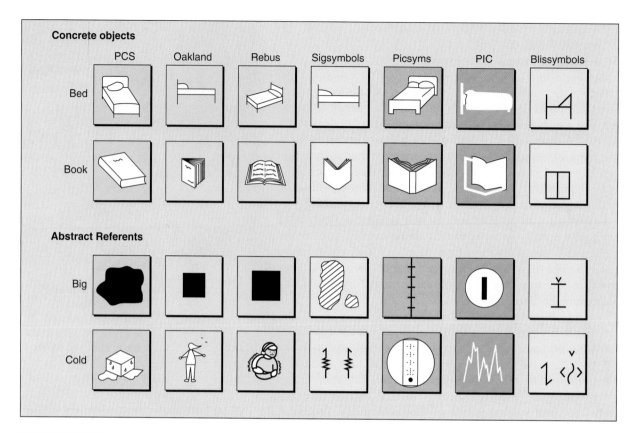

FIGURE 9.6 Examples from widely used graphic symbol sets (PCS = Picture Communication Symbols; PIC = Pictogram Ideogram Communication)

Source: From Vanderheiden, G. C., & Lloyd, L. L. (1986). Non-speech modes and systems. In S. W. Blackstone (Ed.), *Augmentative communication* (ff. 49–161). Rockville, MD: American Speech-Language-Hearing Association. Reprinted by permission.

machine- or listener-assisted (e.g., the listener may point to symbols one at a time while watching for the user's eye blink, which signals selection). *Encoding* involves giving multiple signals to indicate the location of the symbol or item to be selected. Usually, the user makes a pair of responses that directs the listener to a specific printed message on a reference list. In a display in which symbols are organized by color and number, for example, a student can first touch one card (to select the red group of messages) and then make a second pointing response to indicate which number message in the red group is intended. (Figure 9.7 gives suggestions on how to communicate with a person who uses AAC.)

Transmitting the Symbols Once vocabulary and a symbol set have been selected, a method of transmitting the symbols must be determined. The most common tool for augmentative communication display and transmission is the *communication board,* a flat area (often a tray or table attached to a wheelchair) on which the symbols are arranged for the user to select. A student may have a basic communication board of common words, phrases, numbers, and so forth for use across many situations. He may also have various situational boards, or miniboards, with specific vocabulary for certain situations (e.g., at a restaurant, in science class). Symbols can also be transported and displayed in a wallet or photo album.

A variety of electronic devices offer a wide range of alternatives for transmitting communication symbols. Dedicated communication aids—such as the Prentke Romich Intro Talker, the Prentke Romich Liberator, DECtalk by Digital Equipment Company, and Sentinent System's Dynavok—offer computerized speech selection and transmission. To learn

FIGURE 9.7 How to talk with a person who uses AAC

Communicating with someone who does not speak can be a challenging, even unnerving, experience for many natural speakers. Here are 10 suggestions for those who use speech to communicate that will help improve the quality of their conversations with people who use AAC:

- Introduce yourself.
- Ask the person to show you how the communication system works.
- Pause to let the person construct a message. Be patient; it might take a while.
- Relax and give yourself a chance to get used to a slower rhythm of communication. Don't feel like you have to fill all the silent spaces by talking all the time.
- Be sure to give your new friend a chance to ask you questions or to make comments.
- Even though you might guess what's coming next from context, don't finish the person's sentences unless given permission or prompted to do so.
- Interact at eye-to-eye level if you can. If the person's in a wheelchair, you might grab a chair and sit across from her.
- Pay attention to facial expressions and gestures, just as you would with someone who communicates by speech.
- Don't be afraid to say you don't understand something and to ask to have it repeated.
- Talk directly to the person; don't communicate with her through someone else.

Source: Adapted from Blackstone, S. W. (1991). Beyond public awareness: The road to involvement! *Augmentative Communication News, 4*(2), 6. Used by permission of Augmentative Communication, Inc., Monterey, CA.

how the Dynavok and other assistive technology were used to help an 11-year-old boy who was unable to speak participate in the regular classroom, see Erickson and Koppenhaver (1998). (Physicist Stephen Hawking describes his AAC device in Profiles & Perspectives, "My Communication System," later in this chapter.)

A student might need more than one ACC device.

Anna, a second grader with severe disabilities, uses her BIGmack, with its voice output to respond "I'm here" when her teacher takes the attendance every morning. She also uses another voice-output communication aid with 8 messages (Message Mate) to request specific things she wants or needs throughout the day (e.g., water, a break, time on the computer). Although she makes good use of facial expressions and vocalizations, Anna also relies on an adapted photo album that contains pictures from magazines, postcards, and photographs with different comments written underneath them to serve as a conversation book during social times with her classmates. (Downing, 2000, p. 35)

EDUCATIONAL PLACEMENT ALTERNATIVES

During the 1999–2000 school year, approximately 87.5% of children with speech or language impairments were served in the regular classroom—6.7% in resource rooms and 5.3% in separate classes (U.S. Department of Education, 2002). A wide variety of service delivery models for students with communication disorders are used within these three educational placement options. ASHA recognizes the following seven service delivery models (ASHA Ad Hoc Committee on the Roles and Responsibilities of the School-Based Speech-Language Pathologist, 1999).

Placement alternatives

Council for Exceptional Children Content Standards for Beginning Teachers–Common Core: Issues, assurances, and due process right related to assessment, eligibility, and placement with a continuum of services (CC1K6).
PRAXIS Special Education Core Principles: Content Knowledge: III. Delivery of Services to Students with Disabilities, Background knowledge, Placement issues/Continuum of educational services.

My Communication System

by Stephen W. Hawking

Stephen W. Hawking is Lucasian Professor of Mathematics and Theoretical Physics at the University of Cambridge. He has amyotrophic lateral sclerosis (ALS). Sometimes called Lou Gehrig's disease, ALS is a motor neuron disease of middle or late life that involves progressive degeneration of nerve cells that control voluntary motor functions. Initial symptoms usually entail difficulty in walking, clumsiness of the hands, slurred speech, and an inability to swallow normally. The muscles of the arms and legs waste away; eventually, walking is impossible and control of the hands is lost, although sensation remains normal. There is no known cause or cure for ALS. Professor Hawking responded to our request to describe the augmentative communication system he uses by writing the following story.

In my third year at Oxford, I noticed that I seemed to be getting clumsier, and I fell over once or twice for no apparent reason. Shortly after my 21st birthday, I went into the hospital for tests. I was in for two weeks, during which time I had a wide variety of tests. After all that, they didn't tell me what I had, except that it was not multiple sclerosis and that I was an atypical case. I didn't feel like asking for more details because they were obviously bad.

The realization that I had an incurable disease that was likely to kill me in a few years was a bit of a shock. But I didn't die. In fact, although there was a cloud hanging over my future, I found, to my surprise, that I was enjoying life in the present more than before. I began to make progress with my research.

Up to 1974, I was able to feed myself and get in and out of bed. However, things were getting more difficult, so in 1980 we changed to a system of community and private nurses, who came in for an hour or two in the morning and evening. This lasted until I caught pneumonia in 1985 and had to have a tracheotomy operation. After this, I had to have 24-hour nursing care.

Before the operation, my speech had been getting more slurred, so only a few people who knew me well could understand me. But at least I could communicate. I wrote scientific papers by dictating to a secretary, and I gave seminars through an interpreter, who repeated my words more clearly. However, the tracheotomy removed my ability to speak altogether. For a time, the only way I could communicate was to spell out words letter by letter, by raising my eyebrows when someone pointed to the right letter

MONITORING

The SLP monitors or checks on the student's speech and language performance in the regular classroom. This option is often used just before a student is dismissed from therapy.

PULLOUT

The traditional and still most prevalent model of service delivery is the pullout approach, sometimes called *intermittent direct service*. The child may be seen individually or in small groups of up to three children. Depending upon the needs of the individual child, pullout may involve sessions of up to 1 hour 5 days per week.

According to ASHA (2001c), most of the students receiving services from school-based speech-language pathologists during the 1999–2000 school year met with the SLP at least two times a week, most often for 21–30 minute sessions. The classroom teacher and the SLP collaborate so that curriculum materials used in the classroom can be incorporated into the child's speech and language therapy sessions.

Physicist Stephen W. Hawking

right angle. I run a program called Living Center, written by a company called Words Plus of Sunnyvale, California. A cursor moves across the upper part of the screen. I can stop it by pressing a switch in my hand. In this way, I can select words that are printed on the lower part of the screen. This system allows me to communicate much better than I could before; I can manage up to 15 words a minute. I can either speak what I have written or save it on a disk. I can then print it out or call it back and speak it sentence by sentence, like I'm doing now. Using this system, I have written a book and a dozen scientific papers. I have also given a number of scientific and popular talks. They have been well received. I think that is in large part due to the quality of my speech synthesizer, made by Speech Plus, also of Sunnyvale, California.

One's voice is very important. If you have a slurred voice, people are likely to treat you as mentally deficient: "Does he take sugar?" This synthesizer is by far the best I have heard because it varies the intonation and doesn't speak like a Dalek. The only trouble is that it gives me an American accent; however, the company is working on a British version.

I have had motor neuron disease for practically all my adult life, and I am often asked, "How do you feel about having ALS?" The answer is, "Not a lot." I try to lead as normal a life as possible and not think about my condition or regret the things it prevents me from doing, which are not that many. It has not prevented me from having a very attractive family and being successful in my work. This is thanks to the help I have received from my wife, my children, and a large number of other people and organizations. I have been lucky, in that my condition has progressed more slowly than is often the case. But it shows that one need not lose hope.

on a spelling card. It is pretty difficult to carry on a conversation like that, let alone write a scientific paper.

Today, I communicate with a computer system. A computer expert in California, Walter Woltosz, sent me a program he had written called Equalizer. This program allowed me to select words from a series of menus on the screen by pressing a switch in my hand. A switch operated by head or eye movement could also control the program. When I have built up what I want to say, I can send it to a speech synthesizer. At first, I just ran the Equalizer program through a desktop computer. However, David Mason, of Cambridge Adaptive Communications, who is also the husband of one of my nurses, put together the system I now use. I have a Datavue 25 computer mounted to the back of my wheelchair that runs from a battery under the chair's seat. The screen is mounted where I can see it, though you have to view it from the

Many speech-language professionals believe it is impossible to adequately serve a child with speech or language impairments with an isolated, pullout approach (two or three 30-minute sessions each week with a specialist) (Harn, Bradshaw, & Ogletree, 1999). Because communication is seen as occurring most appropriately in the natural environment, remedial procedures are increasingly carried out in the regular classroom during ongoing routines rather than in a special speech room.

 COLLABORATIVE CONSULTATION

There is an increasing tendency for communication disorders specialists to serve as consultants for regular and special education teachers (and parents) rather than spend most of their time providing direct services to individual children (Dohan & Schulz, 1998). Speech-language pathologists who work in school settings more often function as team members concerned with children's overall education and development. The speech-language pathologist often provides training and consultation for the regular classroom teacher, who may do much of the direct work with a child with communication disorders.

Collaboration with SLPs

 Council for Exceptional Children — Content Standards for Beginning Teachers–Common Core: Models and strategies of consultation and collaboration (CC10K1).

PRAXIS Special Education Core Principles: Content Knowledge: III. Delivery of Services to Students with Disabilities, Professional roles, Teacher as a multidisciplinary team member.

The specialist concentrates on assessing communication disorders, evaluating progress, and providing materials and techniques. Teachers and parents are encouraged to follow the specialist's guidelines.

CLASSROOM-BASED

Increasingly, SLPs are working as educational partners in the classroom, mediating between students' communication needs and the communication demands of the curriculum. Other terms used for speech and language services provided directly in the regular classroom include curriculum-based, transdisciplinary, interdisciplinary, and inclusive programming. Language and speech goals can be integrated into daily curriculum activities when SLPs become classroom collaborators. The advantage is that services are brought to the child and teacher, and communication connections with the curriculum are made more directly. Hall et al. (2001) and Lue (2001) offer numerous suggestions for how teachers can help children with communication disorders in the classroom. (Later in the chapter, Teaching & Learning, "Active Learning Dialogues for Students with Language Learning Disabilities," describes how SLPs can use instructional discourse in the classroom to increase children's language competence.)

SELF-CONTAINED CLASSROOM

Students with the most severe communication disorders are served in self-contained special classrooms for children with speech or language impairments. During the 1999–2000 school year, approximately 1 in 20 children with speech or language impairments were served in separate classes (U.S. Department of Education, 2001).

COMMUNITY-BASED

In community-based models, speech and language therapy is provided outside of the school, usually in the home. This model is most often used with preschoolers and sometimes for students with severe disabilities, with an emphasis on teaching functional communication skills in the community.

COMBINATION

There are variations of all these models, and many schools and SLPs serve children using combinations of two or more models (Borsch & Oaks, 1993; Blosser & Kratcoski, 1997).

CURRENT ISSUES AND FUTURE TRENDS

In the future, specialists in communication disorders will probably function even more indirectly than they do today. They will continue to work as professional team members, assisting teachers, parents, physicians, and other specialists in recognizing potential communication disorders and in facilitating communication skills. In-service training will become an ever-more-important aspect of the specialist's responsibilities.

SPEECH-LANGUAGE THERAPIST OR
LANGUAGE-RELATED EDUCATION CONSULTANT?

A growing controversy among some members of the SLP profession is the extent to which services for students with speech and language impairments provided in inclusive classrooms should take "a therapeutic focus" versus an "educational focus" (Prelock, 2000a, 2000b). Although speech-language pathologists in the schools are being encouraged to provide services within inclusive models, they often express concern that they are becoming more like classroom teachers and that the therapy they should be providing to students on their caseloads is getting watered down as a result. Ehren (2000) discusses these concerns and offers solutions to the role confusion and dissatisfaction of many SLPs who provide in-classroom speech-language services. Ehren suggests that SLPs can preserve their role identity and the integrity of services provided by maintaining a therapeutic focus and sharing the responsibility for student success with classroom teachers.

 ## CHANGING POPULATIONS

Speech-language pathologists who work in schools are likely to find themselves working with increasing numbers of children with severe and multiple disabilities who previously did not receive specialized services from speech-language pathologists. Caseloads have grown in many school districts, and financial restrictions make it virtually impossible for all students with speech or language impairments to receive adequate services from the relatively few specialists who are employed. Even though all students with disabilities are entitled to receive all of the special education and related services they need, the schools' limited resources necessitate difficult decisions at the local level. Some programs may choose to provide special services only to those students with the most severe speech and language impairments. Others may concentrate their professional resources on higher-functioning students who are considered to have the best potential for developing communication skills. Parents, advocates, and professional organizations will play an instrumental role in determining which children will receive specialized speech and language services.

Paraprofessional personnel may, in the future, be more widely trained to work directly with children who have speech and language disorders, while professionals will concentrate on diagnosis, prescriptive programming, evaluation, and the use of technology. Peer tutoring or therapy approaches using students without disabilities as language models are likely to become more prevalent. These approaches may allow more students to receive specialized help.

Currently, speech and language intervention programs are heavily oriented toward the preschool and school-age population. Although early detection and intervention will clearly remain a high priority among communication disorders specialists, there is a need for long-term studies to document the effectiveness of early intervention on later speech and language development. Professionals are also becoming increasingly aware of the special speech and language needs of adolescents and adults, many of whom have untreated communication problems. The future will likely see greater attention to the assessment and treatment of speech and language disorders caused by the aging process.

 ## ACROSS-THE-DAY INTERVENTIONS

The traditional role of the speech-language pathologist will probably continue to change, from that of offering direct therapy to students to "facilitating the implementation of communication interventions in the classroom environment" (Goldstein et al., 1994, p. 106). As we have discussed, naturalistic interventions that take place in the actual environments in which children use language are gradually becoming the norm.

But naturalness is no guarantee of effectiveness. As Goldstein et al. (1994) point out, the real challenge lies in designing and implementing across-the-day interventions that can be used effectively by teachers and other significant persons in the child's life. The most effective communication disorders specialist of the future will be expert not only in designing interventions that can be implemented in the classroom and home but also in training and supporting teachers and parents in carrying out those interventions.

 For more information on communication disorders, go to the Web Links module in Chapter 9 of the Companion Website at **www.prenhall.com/heward**

Active Learning Dialogues for Students with Language Learning Disabilities

by Elaine R. Silliman and Jill L. Beasman, University of South Florida

Dramatic changes continue in how speech-language pathologists (SLPs) work in schools. Traditionally, the SLP was seen as an outside expert who intervened with children who had language and communication disabilities. Children's needs were typically addressed by pulling them out of the classroom; they were brought to the services. Although pullout services still continue as the primary model of service delivery, studies show that this model is not an effective or efficient way to facilitate real language learning in relation to the curriculum (ASHA, 1996). Because SLPs have knowledge about the oral language basis of reading, writing, and spelling, they are assuming new roles and responsibilities in the classroom (ASHA, 2001b; Silliman, Ford, Beasman, & Evans, 1999). Thus, more SLPs are working as educational partners in the classroom because language and speech goals can be more fully integrated into daily curriculum activities when SLPs become classroom collaborators (Ehren, 2000; Hadley, Simmerman, Long, & Luna, 2000). The advantage is that services are brought to children and teachers, and communication connections with the curriculum are made more directly.

The major purpose of verbal communication is to create understanding between people. This understanding is made possible through dialogue, the active exchange of messages between speakers and listeners or writers and readers. All classroom teaching and learning consists of dialogue between teachers (or SLPs) and students (Stone, 2002). But not all dialogue is good teaching and learning.

Passive Learning Dialogues
The dialogue in Figure A is an excerpt from a lesson on community workers taught by an SLP. The SLP was the classroom teacher for this kindergarten–grade 1 special education group of eight children with language learning disabilities (LLD). This lesson characterizes traditional language learning activities: the dialogue creates the illusion that real learning is taking place (Silliman, Bahr, Beasman, & Wilkinson, 2000; Stone, 2002).

Learning through language is presented in fragmented, discrete skills. Students are involved in "language experience time," which treats language and communication as a subject area rather than a learning tool that can be applied across the curriculum.

Learning is a one-way activity in which the SLP is a knowledge transmitter. Students are expected to pay attention and respond to the adult's frame of reference. The purpose of adult communication is to assess continually what students know by asking known-answer questions such as "Who can tell me what the chef's job is?" and "What else does a chef do?" Students' contributions are limited to short responses such as "To cook food" and "Make food."

The SLP assumes a power role. The SLP controls who can talk, when talking can take place, and what will be talked about. Language learning tends to be reduced to students' recalling what they know; it does not relate to any real communication purposes.

Passive learning dialogues teach students that learning means giving the right answer, creating the illusion that meaningful learning occurs. For example, the major reason for students to participate in the dialogue is to provide accurate answers to the knowledge-testing questions. In contrast, active learning dialogues teach students that learning through language and communication is a process of discovering possible answers to questions.

Active Learning Dialogues.
Active learning dialogues are guided by theme-based learning in which the communication goals for a student with an LLD are integrated across the curriculum and into all classroom activities. Active learning dialogues are linked to

FIGURE A Sample of instructional dialogue from "The Chef Lesson"

students' real-world experience through problem solving. Outcomes are functional. Children learn that listening, speaking, reading, and writing always have real purposes, such as understanding what others have to say and communicating to others what they want to say. "Lesson talk should sound like conversation, . . . not recitation" (Englert, Tarrant, Mariage, & Oxer, 1994, p. 167).

In the active learning dialogue in Figure B, students have just read a science book on spiders. They are developing a semantic web to organize their reading comprehension. Tom, who has a severe LLD, is attempting to write about what he has learned and becomes orally engaged in persuading Jerry, another student with an LLD, about the importance of having specific knowledge about spiders. The SLP facilitates. This dialogue demonstrates some of the shared interactional features that build active learning contexts (Brookes & Brookes, 1993; Silliman, Mills, & Murphy, 1997).

Integrating primary sources of information and good literature into curriculum/intervention activities. Students draw on a variety of information sources from the Internet to scientific literature.

Viewing students as critical thinkers. The SLP mediates the many ways that students can think, analyze, and communicate about what they are learning (e.g., through discussion, cooperative writing, drawing). Responsibility for learning is shared between the SLP and the students. This division of power communicates to students that, first,

FIGURE B Sample of instructional conversations from "The Spider Dialogue"

they must take responsibility for what is learned and how, and, second, they are viewed as competent to do so.

Using dialogue that promotes instructional conversations. Students' reasons for decisions are sought, relative to their individual comprehension levels, to advance cognitive,

continues

linguistic, and communicative abilities. Jimmy challenges Tom to explain how spiders can "live in dinky little tubes" and "how they [the spiders] can get in there."

Supporting student collaboration. Students often work in cooperative groups to (1) develop ownership of their own learning, (2) explore ideas through talking together, (3) discover similarities that relate concepts, and (4) make new applications (Palincsar, Collins, Marano, & Magnusson, 2000). Tom demonstrates these four outcomes of cooperative learning. He clearly views himself as knowledgeable about the attributes of spiders and their habitats. He attempts to explain his reasoning to Jerry, a process that Amanda and Beatrice reaffirm throughout the interactions with their questions and comments. He draws on real-world knowledge to offer an analogy for Jerry (although the analogy lacks some linguistic clearness—"those play set thingies"). Finally, he can apply what he has learned from reading (and, to a lesser extent, writing) to inform others.

 SUMMARY

DEFINITIONS

- Communication is any interaction that transmits information. Narrating, explaining, informing, requesting, and expressing are major communicative functions.
- A language is an arbitrary symbol system that enables a group of people to communicate. Each language has rules of phonology, morphology, syntax, semantics, and pragmatics that describe how users put sounds and ideas together to convey meaning.
- Speech is the oral production of language; it is the fastest and most efficient method of communication by language.
- Normal language development follows a relatively predictable sequence. Most children learn to talk and use language without any formal instruction; by the time they enter first grade, their grammar and speech patterns match those of the adults around them.
- A communication disorder is "an impairment in the ability to receive, send, process, and comprehend concepts or verbal, nonverbal and graphic symbol systems" (ASHA, 1993, p. 40).
- A child has a speech impairment if his speech draws unfavorable attention to itself, interferes with the ability to communicate, or causes social or interpersonal problems.
- The three basic types of speech impairments are articulation disorders (errors in the production of speech sounds), fluency disorders (difficulties with the flow or rhythm of speech), and voice disorders (problems with the quality or use of one's voice).
- Some children have trouble understanding language (receptive language disorders); others have trouble using language to communicate (expressive language disorders); still others have language delays.
- Speech or language differences based on regional or cultural dialects are not communication disorders. However, children with dialects may also have speech or language disorders.

CHARACTERISTICS

- There are four basic kinds of sound speech errors: distortions, omissions, substitutions, and additions.
- A child with an articulation disorder is not able to produce a given sound physically.
- A child with a phonological disorder has the ability to produce a given sound and does so correctly in some instances but not at other times.
- Stuttering, the most common fluency disorder, is marked by rapid-fire repetitions of consonant or vowel sounds, especially at the beginning of words, prolongations, hesitations, interjections, and complete verbal blocks.
- A voice disorder is characterized by abnormal vocal quality, pitch, loudness, resonance, and/or duration for the speaker's age and sex.
- Language impairments involve problems in phonology, morphology, syntax, semantics, and/or pragmatics; they are usually classified as either receptive or expressive.

PREVALENCE

- A little more than 2% of school-age children receive special education for speech and language impairments, the second-largest disability category under IDEA.
- Nearly twice as many boys as girls have speech impairments.
- Children with articulation and spoken language problems represent the largest category of speech-language impairments.

CAUSES

- Although some speech and language impairments have physical (organic) causes, most are functional disorders that cannot be directly attributed to physical conditions.

IDENTIFICATION AND ASSESSMENT

- Assessment of a suspected communication disorder may include some or all of the following components: (1) case history and physical examination, (2) articulation test, (3) hearing test, (4) auditory test, (5) phonological awareness and processing, (6) vocabulary and overall language development test, (7) language samples, and (8) observation in natural settings.

EDUCATIONAL APPROACHES

- A speech language pathologist (SLP) employs a wide range of techniques for identifying, evaluating, and providing therapeutic services to children. These include structured exercises and drills as well as individual and group therapy sessions.
- A general goal of treating speech and sound errors is to help the child speak as clearly as possible. Addressing articulation and phonological errors involves discrimination and production activities. Fluency disorders can be treated with the application of behavioral principles and self-monitoring, although many children recover spontaneously.
- Voice disorders can be treated surgically or medically if the cause is organic. Most remedial techniques offer direct vocal rehabilitation. Behavioral principles help break habitual patterns of misuse.
- Language disorder treatments vary widely. Precommunication activities encourage exploration of expressive language. SLPs connect oral language to literacy components of the curriculum. Naturalistic interventions disperse learning trials throughout the natural environment and normal conversation.
- Augmentative and alternative communication may be aided or unaided and consists of three components: a representational symbol set or vocabulary, a means for selecting the symbols, and a means for transmitting the symbols.

EDUCATIONAL PLACEMENT ALTERNATIVES

- Most children with speech and language problems attend regular classes.
- ASHA recognizes seven service delivery models: monitoring, pullout, collaborative consultation, classroom-based, self-contained classroom, community-based, and combination.

CURRENT ISSUES AND FUTURE TRENDS

- Specialists will probably function even more indirectly in the future. In-service training will become even more important.
- SLP professionals will deal with the controversy as to whether services should take a therapeutic versus educational focus.
- Changing populations mean growing caseloads and more children with severe and multiple disabilities receiving therapy for communication disorders.
- Across-the-day interventions mean that interventions must be applicable not only in the classroom but also by teachers and parents.

To check your comprehension of chapter content, go to the Guided Review and Quiz modules in Chapter 9 of the Companion Website at **www.prenhall.com/heward**

Chapter 10
Hearing Loss

Focus Questions

- In what ways do the child who is deaf and the child who is hard of hearing differ?

- How do students whose cultural identity is with the Deaf community view hearing loss?

- Why can't reading simply replace speech as a means of learning and understanding English?

- How do oral/aural, total communication, and bilingual-bicultural approaches differ in their philosophies and teaching methods?

- Why has American Sign Language (ASL) not been fully accepted as the language of instruction in educational programs for deaf children?

DOUGLAS JACKSON

EL PASO REGIONAL DAY SCHOOL PROGRAM FOR THE DEAF

HILLSIDE ELEMENTARY SCHOOL, EL PASO, TEXAS

Education • Teaching Credentials • Experience
- B.A., Social Studies Education, University of Northern Colorado, 1978
- M.S., Education of the Deaf University of Rochester/NTID, New York, 1982
- Texas and Florida certifications in hearing impaired (K–12), social studies (secondary), and gifted (K–12)
- 17 years teaching students with special needs

Current Teaching Position   For the past 7 years, I have taught science, social studies, and art to elementary-age deaf students at Hillside Elementary. Texas is divided into regional day school programs as far as deaf ed is concerned. The El Paso regional program is housed in the El Paso Independent School District. At Hillside Elementary, a regular neighborhood school of about 700 students, eleven deaf ed. teachers, two speech therapists, and an interpreter serve 70 deaf students. Our program serves students from all of the surrounding school districts. One of my students rides an hour each way from Ft. Hancock. This is not unusual. Hearing impairment is a low-incidence disability and a very cost-intensive one. It would not be possible for the other districts to provide all of these expensive services.

My Students   I have nine students in my fifth-grade homeroom, all of whom receive special education and related services under the IDEA categories of hearing and speech or language impairments. Almost all of our students are Hispanic, and some come from homes in which Spanish is the primary or only language. A couple of our students have deaf parents who were born in Mexico. Socioeconomically, we run the gamut. Some of our students come from middle-class families, and some come from poor families—sometimes desperately so. We get to know our students very well, and our students get to know each other better than their own siblings do sometimes.

Curriculum Materials and Teaching Strategies   We try to parallel the materials and the units that are covered in the regular classes, adapting a lot of the language in the texts. I often turn textbook content into plays that incorporate the students' personalities and interests and take advantage of the great resource of local culture. Sometimes students draw backgrounds and create props, and we videotape these plays. I use participatory theater as a teaching tool for several reasons: (1) plays help the students understand the material better; (2) active learning is always better than passive attending; (3) plays personalize the material, helping the students understand that the events and concepts they're learning about are central to the history and current life of their world; (4) plays bring out the students' natural creativity; and (5) plays help the students feel less

daunted by the textbook. We also use technology—video letters with deaf students in other places, distance learning sessions with the Texas School for the Deaf, and structured Internet research assignments.

I incorporate activities that help our students teach each other. This year we're incorporating the Pillars of Character across the curriculum. Our upper elementary students are working in small groups to create puppet plays involving situations that require responsibility. To get started, we wrote and performed a prototypical video puppet play. It involved an old lady who was too sick to walk her dogs every day. One of the students played a student who promised to walk her dogs every day. Later that week some of his friends tried to talk him into a mall trip that would have caused him to shirk his responsibility. We performed these plays for our preschool, kindergarten, first-, and second-grade students.

You may be wondering how kids sign and manipulate puppets at the same time. Obviously they can't sign and hold the puppets simultaneously, so we cheat. We tape the puppets to the set we have created, orient the audience to the characters and the set before the play begins, and then the students read the parts. It seems to work. I do the same thing every year for a series of Puppet Economics plays I use before my fifth graders play the Stock Market Game Worldwide.

Personal Qualities Important for Special Educators   I guess the first impulse is to list "patience," "dedication," and so on, and those are wonderful qualities, but for me, being a great teacher is like being a great lawyer, doctor, chef, or artist. You can't tell where the self ends and the profession begins. I mean, look at a van Gogh or a Picasso or a Renoir. They were always painters and always themselves—every brushstroke was a fingerprint. Great teachers do that, and I aspire to be like them. Great teachers aren't content to simply look at the state standards and try to decide how they will cover them. They're always seeing the world through the eyes of a teacher; and when something new and interesting happens to them, they automatically think how they can share that experience with their students. I would be lying if I said that I had this skill from day one. Many of my early efforts as a teacher were 10 steps forward and 9 steps back, sometimes 9 steps forward and 10 steps back. It is something that I am still working on now—I am very much a work in progress.

A Memorable Moment   There have been many. I'll share the first one that comes to mind. Our students love school. One big reason they do is that school is an oasis of communication for them. Once, while gathering for a field trip, we passed the marquee in front of school. One of my students looked at the sign and read, "Saturday School," which referred, of course, to a mandatory program for students who had misbehaved during the week. Several other students gasped, "Saturday school! Can we come?" It's always great to hear that the customers want more, not less, of your service. 🍃

To learn more about how Mr. Jackson uses plays, collaborative learning, and the Internet as teaching tools, go to the Teacher Feature module on the Companion Website at **www.prenhall. com/heward**

To better understand what will be covered in this chapter, go to the Essential Concepts and Chapter-at-a-Glance modules in Chapter 10 of the Companion Website at **www.prenhall. com/heward**

AS Lou Ann Walker, the child of deaf parents, observes in her autobiography, people who have normal hearing usually find it difficult to fully appreciate the enormous importance of the auditory sense in human development and learning: "Nature attaches an overwhelming importance to hearing. As unborns we hear before we can see. Even in deep comas, people often hear what is going on around them. For most of us, when we die, the sense of hearing is the last to leave the body" (Walker, 1986, p. 165).

A sighted person can simulate blindness by closing her eyes or donning a blindfold, but it is virtually impossible for a hearing person to turn off his ears. The basic structure of the inner ear is present in the fetus at 6 months, and hearing begins before birth (Brownell, 1999). Throughout life, all hearing animals obtain information about the world around them, from all directions, 24 hours a day. When a twig snaps behind us, we don't have to be looking to know that we are not alone.

In addition to its tremendous survival advantage, hearing plays the lead role in the natural, almost effortless manner by which most children acquire speech and language. Newborns respond to sounds by startling or blinking. At a few weeks of age, infants with normal hearing can listen to quiet sounds, recognize their parents' voices, and pay attention to their own gurgling and cooing sounds. At 1 month, hearing infants prefer natural speech sounds over nonlanguage sounds (Mehler et al., 1988). By 6 months, hearing infants can discriminate the speech sounds of the language to which they have been exposed from the sounds of other languages (Werker & Lalonde, 1988). By the time they are 1 year old, hearing children can produce many of the sounds of their language and are speaking their first words. Children develop language by constantly hearing people talk and by associating these sounds with innumerable activities and events. Sound acquires meaning, and children quickly learn that people convey information and communicate their thoughts and feelings by speaking and hearing.

In contrast, for children who cannot hear speech sounds, learning a spoken language is anything but natural or effortless. Children who are deaf simply do not have access to an auditorally based language. As we will see, however, when children who are deaf are exposed to a visual, sign-based language as their first language, they acquire language and communication skills in a manner quite similar to the acquisition of speech by hearing children. Some children with hearing loss can hear speech with hearing aids or other technologies, and techniques such as speech training and speechreading enable many children with hearing loss to communicate effectively. Whether a child's hearing loss is mild or profound, early identification and assessment are keys to providing needed special education services.

It may be impossible for a person with normal hearing to fully comprehend the immense difficulties a prelingually deaf child faces trying to learn language.

DEFINITIONS

Like other disabilities, hearing loss can be defined and classified from different perspectives and for different purposes. A medical definition describes the degree of hearing loss on a continuum from mild to profound. Educational definitions focus on the child's ability to use his hearing to understand speech and learn language and the effects on educational performance. For example, IDEA uses the category label *hearing impairment* to indicate a hearing loss that adversely affects educational performance and thereby makes the child eligible for special education. Most special educators distinguish between children who are deaf and those who are hard of hearing.

Normal hearing generally means that a person has sufficient hearing to understand speech. Under adequate listening conditions, a person with normal hearing can interpret speech in everyday situations without using any special device or technique. A child who is **deaf** is not able to use hearing to understand speech. Even with a hearing aid, the hearing loss is too great to allow a deaf child to understand speech through the ears alone. Although a deaf person may perceive some sounds through **residual hearing**, she uses vision as the primary modality for learning and communication.

A child who is **hard of hearing** has a significant hearing loss that makes some special adaptations necessary. Children who are hard of hearing are able to use their hearing to

Definitions: hearing impairment, deaf, residual hearing, hard of hearing

Council for Exceptional Children — Content Standards for Beginning Teachers–D/HH: Educational definitions and identification criteria for individuals who are D/HH (DH1K1). **PRAXIS** Special Education Core Principles: Content Knowledge: I. Understanding Exceptionalities, Definitions of disabilities.

Deaf culture and community

Council for Exceptional Children — Content Standards for Beginning Teachers–D/HH: Cultural dimensions of hearing loss that may affect the individual (DH3K2) (also DH1K2). **PRAXIS** Special Education Core Principles: Content Knowledge: II. Legal and Societal Issues, Schools connections with families and communities of students with disabilities, Cultural and community influences.

understand speech, generally with the help of a hearing aid. Though they may be delayed or deficient, the speech and language skills of a hard-of-hearing child are developed mainly through the auditory channel.

Many persons who are deaf do not view their hearing loss as a disability and consider the term *hearing impairment* inappropriate and demeaning because it suggests a deficiency or pathology. Like other cultural groups, members of the Deaf community share a common language and social practices. When the cultural definition of hearing loss is used, Deaf is spelled with a capital *D,* just as an uppercase letter is used to refer to a person who is French, Japanese, or Jewish. While person-first language is considered the appropriate way to refer to individuals with disabilities, persons who identify with the Deaf culture prefer terms such as teacher of the Deaf, school for the Deaf, and Deaf person. (See Profiles & Perspectives, "Defiantly Deaf," later in this chapter.)

HOW WE HEAR

Audition, the sense of hearing, is a complex and not completely understood process. The function of the ear is to gather sounds (acoustical energy) from the environment and to analyze and transform that energy into a form (neural energy) that can be interpreted by the brain. Figure 10.1 shows the major parts of the human ear. The outer ear consists of the external ear and the auditory canal. The part of the ear we see, the **auricle,** funnels sound waves into the **auditory canal (external acoustic meatus)** and helps a person determine the direction from which the sound is coming.

When sound waves enter the external ear, they are slightly amplified as they move toward the **tympanic membrane** (eardrum). Variations in sound pressure cause the eardrum to move in and out. These movements of the eardrum change the acoustical energy into mechanical energy, which is transferred to the three tiny bones of the *middle ear* (the *hammer, anvil,* and *stirrup*). The base (called the *footplate*) of the third bone in the sequence, the stirrup, rests in an opening called the *oval window,* the path through which sound energy enters the inner ear. The vibrations of the three bones (together called the **ossicles**) transmit energy from the middle ear to the inner ear with little loss.

The most critical and complex part of the entire hearing apparatus is the *inner ear,* which is covered by the temporal bone, the hardest bone in the entire body. The inner ear contains the **cochlea,** the main receptor organ for hearing, and the *semicircular canals,* which control the sense of balance. The cochlea, named for its resemblance to a coiled snail shell, consists of two fluid-filled cavities that contain 30,000 tiny hair cells arranged in four rows. Energy transmitted by the ossicles moves the fluid in the cochlea, which in turn stimulates the hair cells. When the hair cells are stimulated they send minute electrical signals which are transmitted along the auditory nerve to the brain. High tones are picked up by the hair cells at the basal, or lowest turn, of the cochlea; and low tones stimulate hair cells at the apex, or top, of the cochlea.

THE NATURE OF SOUND

Sound is measured in units that describe its intensity and frequency. Both dimensions of sound are important in considering the needs of a child with a hearing loss. The intensity or loudness of sound is measured in **decibels (dB).** Zero dB represents the smallest sound a person with normal hearing can perceive, which is called the *zero hearing-threshold level* (HTL), or **audiometric zero.**

Larger dB numbers represent increasingly louder sounds. A low whisper 5 feet away registers about 10 dB, a running automobile about 65 dB, and Niagara Falls about 90 dB. Conversational speech 10 to 20 feet away ranges from approximately 20 to 55 dB. A sound of about 125 dB or louder will cause pain to the average person.

FIGURE 10.1 Basic anatomy of the human ear

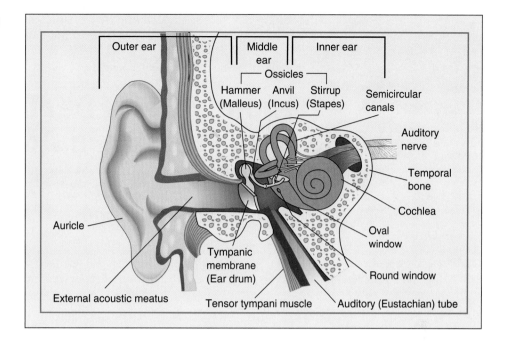

The frequency, or pitch, of sound is measured in cycles per second, or **hertz (Hz)**; 1 hertz equals 1 cycle per second. The lowest note on a piano has a frequency of about 30 Hz, middle C about 250 Hz, and the highest note about 4,000 Hz. Human hearing is limited to a range of about 20 to 20,000 Hz, but many audible sounds are outside the speech range, the frequency range of ordinary conversation. Although a person who cannot hear very low sounds (e.g., a foghorn) or very high sounds (e.g., a piccolo) may suffer some inconvenience, she will encounter no significant problems in the classroom or everyday life. A person with a severe hearing loss in the speech range, however, is at a great disadvantage in acquiring and communicating in a spoken language.

The frequency range generally considered most important for hearing spoken language is 500 to 2,000 Hz, but some speech sounds have frequencies below or above that range. For example, the /s/ phoneme (as in the word "sat") is a high-frequency sound, typically occurring between 4,000 and 8,000 Hz (Northern & Downs, 1991). A student whose hearing loss is more severe at the higher frequencies will thus have particular difficulty in discriminating the /s/ sound. Conversely, phonemes such as /dj/ (the sound of the "j" in "jump") and /m/ occur at low frequencies and will be more problematic for a student with a low-frequency hearing loss. As you might expect, a student with a high-frequency hearing loss tends to hear men's voices more easily than women's voices.

Degree and frequency range of hearing loss

 Council for Exceptional Children — Content Standards for Beginning Teachers–D/HH: Effects of sensory input on the development of language and cognition (DH6K3) (also, CC2K2).

PRAXIS Special Education Core Principles: Content Knowledge: I. Understanding Exceptionalities, Characteristics of students with disabilities, Sensory factors.

CHARACTERISTICS

Any discussion of characteristics of students who are deaf or hard of hearing should include three qualifications. First, students who receive special education because of hearing loss comprise an extremely heterogeneous group (Easterbrooks, 1999). It is a mistake to assume that a commonly observed behavioral characteristic or average level of academic achievement is representative of all children with hearing loss.

Second, the effects of hearing loss on a child's communication and language skills, academic achievement, and social and emotional functioning are influenced by many factors, including the type and degree of hearing loss, the age at onset, the attitudes of the child's parents and siblings, opportunities to acquire a first language (whether through speech or sign), and the presence or absence of other disabilities (Moores, 2001; Schirmer, 2002).

Defiantly Deaf: Deaf People Live, Proudly, in Another Culture, but Not a Lesser One

by Andrew Soloman

The protest at the Lexington Center, which includes New York's oldest Deaf school, is an important stage in the Deaf struggle for civil rights, and on April 25, the first day of student demonstrations, I ask an African-American from the 11th grade whether she has also demonstrated for race rights. "I'm too busy being Deaf right now," she signs. "My two older brothers aren't Deaf, so they're taking care of being black. Maybe if I have time I'll get to that later."

Another student intercedes. "I am black and Deaf and proud and I don't want to be white or hearing or different in any way from who I am." Her signs are pretty big and clear. The first student repeats the sign "proud"—her thumb, pointing in, rises up her chest—and then suddenly they are overcome with giggles and go back to join the picket line.

This principle is still new to me, but it has been brewing in the Deaf community for some time: while some deaf people feel cut off from the hearing world, or disabled, for others, being Deaf is a culture and a source of pride. ("Deaf" denotes culture, as distinct from "deaf," which is used to describe pathology.) A steadily increasing number of deaf people have said that they would not choose to be hearing. To them, the word "cure"—indeed the whole notion of deafness as pathology—is anathema.

The Deaf debates are all language debates. "When I communicate in A.S.L., my native language," M. J. Bienvenu, a political activist, said to me, "I am living my culture. I don't define myself in terms of 'not hearing' or of 'not' anything else." A founder of the Bicultural Center (a sort of Deaf think tank), M. J. is gracious, but also famously terrifying: brilliant, striking-looking and self-possessed, with signing so swift, crisp and perfectly controlled that she seems to be rearranging the air in front of her into a more acceptable shape. Deaf of Deaf (that is, children who are deaf with deaf parents), with Deaf sisters, she manifests, like many other activists, a pleasure in American Sign Language that only poets feel for English. "When our language was acknowledged," she says, "we gained our freedom." In her hands "freedom"—clenched hands are crossed before the body, then swing apart and face out—is like an explosion.

A "FAMILY" GATHERING

I attended the National Association of the Deaf convention in Knoxville, Tennessee, with almost 2,000 Deaf participants. At Lexington, I saw Deaf people stand up to the hearing world. I learned how a TTY works, met pet dogs who understood sign, talked about mainstreaming and oralism and the integrity of visual language. I became accustomed to doorbells that flashed lights instead of ringing. But none of this could have prepared me for the immersion that is the NAD convention, where the brightest, most politicized, most committed Deaf gather for political focus and social exchange. There, it is not a question of whether the hearing will accept the existence of Deaf culture, but of whether Deaf culture will accept the hearing.

I arrive the night of the president's reception. There are 1,000 people in the grand ballroom of the Hyatt Regency, the lights turned up because these people are unable to communicate in darkness. The crowd is nearly soundless; you hear the claps that are part of the articulation of A.S.L., the clicks and puffing noises the deaf make when they sign, and occasionally their big uncontrolled laughter. People greet each other as if they have been waiting forever for these encounters—the Deaf community is close, closed and affectionate.

Deaf people touch each other far more than the hearing, and everyone here hugs friends. I, too, find myself hugging people as if I have known them forever. Yet I

In 1988, students at Gallaudet University, the world's only university dedicated exclusively to the education of deaf students, successfully demonstrated for a deaf person to be appointed president after a hearing person who was unable to use sign language had been selected for the position.

must be careful of the difference between a friendly and a forward embrace; how you touch communicates a world of meaning in Deaf circles. I must be careful of looking abstractedly at people signing; they will think I am eavesdropping. I do not know any of the etiquette of these new circumstances. "Good luck with the culture shock," more than one person says to me, and I get many helpful hints.

As I look across the room it seems as if some strange human sea is breaking into waves and glinting in the light, as thousands of hands move at stunning speed, describing a spatial grammar with sharply individual voices and accents. The association is host to the Miss Deaf America pageant, and the young beauties, dressed to the nines and sporting their state sashes, are objects of considerable attention. "Look how beautifully she expresses herself," says someone, pointing to one contestant, and then, of another: "Can you believe that blurry Southern signing? I didn't think anyone really signed like that!" (Regional variations of sign can be dangerous: the sign that in New York slang means "cake" in some Southern states means "sanitary napkin.")

The luminaries of the Deaf world—activists, actors, professors—mix comfortably with the beauty queens. I am one of perhaps a dozen hearing people at this party. I have heard Deaf people talk about how their "family" is the Deaf community. Rejected in so many instances by parents with whom they cannot communicate, united by their struggle with a world that is seldom understanding

of them, they have formed inviolable bonds of love of a kind that are rare in hearing culture. At the National Association of the Deaf, they are unmistakable. Disconcerting though it may sound, it is impossible, here, not to wish you were Deaf. I had known that Deaf culture existed, but I had not guessed how heady it is.

The Association members are a tiny minority, less than 10 percent of the nation's Deaf; most deaf people are what the Deaf call "grass roots." The week after the convention, the national Deaf bowling championships in Baltimore will attract a much larger crowd, people who go to Deaf clubs, play cards and work in blue-collar jobs. Below them in the Deaf status structure are the peddlers (the Deaf word for the mendicants who "sell" cards with the manual alphabet on subways—the established Deaf community tried as early as the 40's to get them off the streets).

At the V.I.P. party after the radiant Miss Deaf Maryland has won, I am talking to Alec Naiman, a world traveler who was one of the pilots at this year's Deaf fly-in at the Knoxville airport. We are discussing a trip he made to China. "I met some Deaf Chinese people my first day, and went to stay with them. Deaf people never need hotels; you can always stay with other Deaf people. We spoke different signed languages, but we could make ourselves understood. Though we came from different countries, Deaf culture held us together. By the end of the evening we'd talked about Deaf life in China, and about Chinese politics, and we'd understood each other linguistically and culturally. No hearing American could do that in China," he says. "So who's disabled then?"

MAKING THE IRREGULAR REGULAR

How to reconcile this Deaf experience with the rest of the world? Should it be reconciled at all? M. J. Bienvenu has been one of the most vocal and articulate opponents of the language of disability. "I am Deaf," she says to me in Knoxville, drawing out the sign for "Deaf," the index finger moving from chin to ear, as though she is tracing a broad smile. Considerably gentler now than in her extremist heyday in the early 80's, she acknowledges that "for some deaf people, being deaf is a disability. Those who learn forced English while being denied sign emerge semi-lingual rather than bilingual, and they are disabled people. But for the rest of us, it is no more a disability than being Japanese would be."

I have heard of a couple who opted for an abortion when they heard that their child was hearing, so strong a view did they hold on the superiority of Deaf ways. But I also met many Deaf individuals who objected to the way

continues

that the Deaf leadership (focused around the National Association of the Deaf) have presumed to speak for all the deaf people of America. There were plenty who said that being deaf is of course a disability, and that anything you could do about it would be welcome. They were righteously indignant at the thought of a politically correct group suggesting that their problems weren't problems.

It is tempting in the end, to say that there is no such thing as a disability. Equally, one might admit that almost everything is a disability. There are as many arguments for correcting everything as there are for correcting nothing. Perhaps it would be most accurate to say that "disability" and "culture" are really matters of degree. Being

Deaf is a disability and a culture in modern America; so is being gay, so is being black; so is being female; so even, increasingly, is being a straight white male. So is being paraplegic, or having Down syndrome. What is at issue is which things are so "cultural" that you wouldn't think of "curing" them, and which things so "disabling" that you must "cure" them—and the reality is that for some people each of these experiences is primarily a disability experience while for others it is primarily a cultural one.

Source: Excerpt from Soloman, A. (1994, August 28). Defiantly deaf. *The New York Times.* © 1994 by the New York Times Company. Reprinted by permission.

Third, generalizations of how deaf people are supposed to act and feel must be viewed with extreme caution. Lane (1988), for example, makes a strong case against the existence of the so-called psychology of the deaf. He shows the similarity of the traits attributed to deaf people in the professional literature to traits attributed to African people in the literature of colonialism and suggests that those traits do not "reflect the characteristics of deaf people but the paternalistic posture of the hearing experts making these attributions" (p. 8). In addition, he argues that the scientific literature on the psychology of the deaf is flawed in terms of test administration, test language, test scoring, test content and norms, and its description of subject populations, arguments that have been noted by other researchers as well (Moores, 2001; Paul & Quigley, 1990).

 ## ENGLISH LITERACY

English literacy skills

 Council for Exceptional Children Content Standards for Beginning Teachers–D/HH: Effects of sensory input on the development of language and cognition (DH6K3) (also, CC2K1, CC2K2, DH3K4). **PRAXIS** Special Education Core Principles: Content Knowledge: I. Understanding Exceptionalities, Characteristics of students with disabilities, Sensory factors.

A child with a hearing loss—especially a prelingual loss of 90 dB or greater—is at a great disadvantage in acquiring English language skills. Hearing children typically acquire a large vocabulary and a knowledge of grammar, word order, idiomatic expressions, fine shades of meaning, and many other aspects of verbal expression by listening to others and to themselves from early infancy. A child who, from birth or soon after, is unable to hear the speech of other people will not learn speech and language spontaneously, as do children with normal hearing. Since reading and writing involve graphic representations of a phonologically based language, the deaf child must strive to decode and produce text based on a language for which she may have little or no understanding.

Students with hearing loss have smaller vocabularies than do with peers with normal hearing, and the gap widens with age (ASHA, 2001). Children with hearing loss learn concrete words such as "tree," "run," "book," and "red" more easily than abstract words such as "tired," "funny," "equal to," and "freedom." They also have difficulty with function words and verb phrases such as "the," "an," "are," and "have been." They may omit endings of words, such as the plural "-s," "-ed," or "-ing." Because the grammar and structure of English often do not follow logical rules, a person with prelingual hearing loss must exert a great deal of effort to read and write with acceptable form and meaning. For example, if the past tense of "talk" is "talked," then why doesn't "go" become "goed"? If the plural of "man" is "men," then shouldn't the plural of "pan" be "pen"? Learning words with multiple meanings is difficult. It is not easy to explain the difference between the expressions "He's beat" (tired) and "He was beaten" to a person who has never had normal hearing.

Deaf students often have difficulty differentiating questions from statements. Most have difficulty understanding and writing sentences with passive voice (*The assignment was given yesterday*) and relative clauses (*The gloves I left at home are made of leather*). Many students who are deaf write sentences that are short, incomplete, or improperly arranged. The following sentences taken from stories written by elementary deaf students illustrate some of the English literacy problems attributable to not hearing spoken language:

Bobby is walked.

The boy sees a brown football on the hold hand.

The trees is falling a leaves.

The happy children is friending.

To learn how the Internet can be used to help deaf students become better writers, see Teaching & Learning, "Internet Chat Environment," later in this chapter.

 SPEAKING

Atypical speech is common in many children who are deaf or hard of hearing. In addition to all of the challenges that hearing loss poses to learning the vocabulary, grammar, and syntax of English, not being able to hear one's own speech makes it difficult to assess and monitor it. As a result, children with hearing loss may speak too loudly or not loudly enough. They may speak in an abnormally high pitch or sound like they are mumbling because of poor stress, poor inflection, or poor rate of speaking. The speech of children with hearing loss may be difficult to understand because they omit quiet speech sounds such as "s," "sh," "f," "t," and "k," which they cannot hear.

 ACADEMIC ACHIEVEMENT

Most children with hearing loss have difficulty with all areas of academic achievement, especially reading and math. Studies assessing the academic achievement of students with hearing loss have routinely found them to lag far behind their hearing peers, and the gap in achievement between children with normal hearing and those with hearing loss usually widens as they get older (ASHA, 2001). The average deaf student who leaves high school at age 18 or 19 is reading at about the fourth-grade level (Allen, 1994; Holt, 1993; Kuntze, 1998), and their mathematics performance is in the range of fifth to seventh grade (Allen, 1986, 1994). Approximately 30% of deaf students are functionally illiterate when they leave school, compared to fewer than 1% of hearing students (Paul & Jackson, 1993).

Paul and Quigley (1990) summarize this dismal state of affairs:

No general improvement in achievement in most students who are severely to profoundly hearing-impaired has been observed since the . . . early years of the 20th century. The average student completing a secondary education program is still reading and writing at a level commensurate with the average 9- to 10-year-old hearing student. Achievement in mathematics is about one or two grades higher. (p. 227)

It is important not to equate academic performance with intelligence. Deafness itself imposes no limitations on the cognitive capabilities of individuals (Moores, 2001), and some deaf students read very well and excel academically (Lichtenstein, 1998). The problems that students who are deaf often experience in education and adjustment are largely attributable to the mismatch between their perceptual abilities and the demands of spoken and written English.

 SOCIAL FUNCTIONING

Hearing loss can influence a child's behavior and socioemotional development. Children with hearing losses often report feeling isolated, friendless, and unhappy in school, particularly when their socialization with other children with hearing loss is limited. These social

Speech skills

Council for Exceptional Children Content Standards for Beginning Teachers–D/HH: Effects of sensory input on the development of language and cognition (DH6K3) (also, CC2K2, DH3K4).
PRAXIS Special Education Core Principles: Content Knowledge: I. Understanding Exceptionalities, Characteristics of students with disabilities, Sensory factors.

Academic achievement

Council for Exceptional Children Content Standards for Beginning Teachers–D/HH: Impact of hearing loss on learning and experience. (DH3K4) (also, CC2K2, DH2K2).
PRAXIS Special Education Core Principles: Content Knowledge: I. Understanding Exceptionalities, Characteristics of students with disabilities, Sensory factors.

Internet Chat Environment: Online Conversations between Deaf and Hearing Students

by Barbara R. Schirmer and Albert L. Ingram

Conversation is the milieu of language acquisition for all children. For children to learn language, they need a considerable amount of experience in conversation with adults. Through many conversations about mutually interesting topics, children discern the underlying rules of the language. For deaf children, face-to-face spoken conversations are typically fraught with inconsistent and incomplete language models because they miss the elements they cannot hear or speechread. If they are conversing in American Sign Language, the structure is unlike English, so they learn the structure of ASL but not that of English.

Written English can offer consistent and complete models of English but not the give-and-take of conversation. The qualities of conversation that promote language development in young hearing and deaf children are well-formed and short sentences, redundancy, and a focus on shared perceptions (Garton & Pratt, 1998; Masataka, 1996; Reilly & Bellugi, 1996; Schirmer, 2000). Although books and stories can offer the first two, sharing perceptions is unique to conversations. Written conversations in the form of dialogue journals and e-mail have been used by teachers, but there is little evidence in the literature that these strategies result in improved written language of deaf students (Johnson, 1997; Lieberth, 1991; Weiserbs, 2000).

Online chats can provide a closer match to face-to-face conversation because the dialogue can take place in real time. A teacher can monitor instructional conversations and incorporate linguistic features that are targeted language goals for the child. Online chat environments have the added advantage of being highly motivating to students. Educators are increasingly using them to provide an interactive learning experience and to extend the educational experience beyond the classroom (Ingram, Hathorn, & Evans, 2000; Kearsley, 2000).

We set up online chats between deaf and hearing students separated by distance and even by time zone. We used The Palace software, which was free to upload from the Internet. When the students logged on to our Palace server, they could see a visual depiction of White Hall at Kent State University. Each student's name appeared below an avatar, which the student could dress up with props. Typed comments appeared for a few seconds in dialogue balloons above the avatar's head and also in a log window on the right of the screen, which maintained a record of the entire conversation. Each day, teams of one deaf student and one hearing student met with the online teacher for 10–20 minutes apiece. The teacher assigned each team a science project. They discussed the project online and looked up information on the Internet when their team was not interacting on The Palace. The online teacher used an intervention strategy that encouraged the deaf students to use language features such as descriptors and conjunctions, which were identified as linguistic goals for these students. We found that the targeted language features appeared with greater frequency and the students highly enjoyed conversing with peers in real time. Figure A is an interview with one of the deaf students that was conducted at the conclusion of the study.

The following guidelines can facilitate successful online chats between students:

- *Age or grade level.* Students should be beyond the emergent or beginning stages of reading and writing development.

Teacher: What do you think of the astronomy activity?

Student: I think it was pretty cool, fun to learn, different. Class is always the same. Think math, science, etc. Pah! Learning about the stars was fun.

Teacher: How do you feel about doing this activity online?

Student: I enjoyed it but it was hard to search the Internet.

Teacher: What were the positive and negative things about the activity?

Student: Negative, it was hard to find Internet information. Positive, learning information, then writing from Internet research.

Teacher: What do you think about using The Palace?

Student: I like it. It was neat, different, plus I never had fun like that before.

Teacher: What did you contribute and what did your team member contribute?

Student: We went back and forth. Answer, then ask, then answer, then ask questions.

Teacher: How did Dr. Schirmer help with your discussion online?

Student: If my partner typed an impossible word I didn't understand, then I asked Barbara what that meant, then I understood and it helped me.

Teacher: How did you change your writing during the activity?

Student: I learned from hearing culture.

Teacher: What influenced your writing?

Student: I read different kinds of writing.

Teacher: Would you do this kind of activity again if you had the opportunity?

Student: Possibly. If I have time in the future, I would prefer, yes.

FIGURE A. Interview with one of the deaf students at the conclusion of the study

- *Technology skills.* Students must have relatively fluent keyboarding skills to keep up with an online conversation. They also should have some knowledge of how to search the Internet.
- *Cooperative learning.* It is helpful if the students have participated in cooperative learning activities in their classrooms so that they understand how to work with a partner in carrying out a project.
- *Online teacher.* An adult should monitor the online conversation. The online teacher can provide instruction and direction, as well as focus on the deaf child's linguistic skills. The online teacher can be a parent volunteer, aide, or older student.
- *Learning unit.* The learning unit should be a topic that is relevant and motivating to all of the students. We found that middle and high school students liked the topic of astronomy, began with many conceptions (and misconceptions) about the stars and planets, and could find much information on the Internet.
- *Scheduling.* The schedule needs to be planned carefully, and everyone needs to be flexible about unforeseen problems. Student absences, schoolwide activities, and unreliable Internet connections occurred frequently during our research study.
- *Software.* We chose The Palace software because it is easy to use, visually appealing, relatively secure from others joining our conversations, and cost-free. Other Internet chat software is available, enabling text-only rooms or adding two-dimensional or three-dimensional visual environments. It is crucial to make sure that the school does not have a firewall in place that prevents access or that a request to remove the firewall is made before beginning the project. We found that having a laptop available that could gain access through a modem and telephone line was helpful.
- *Writing goals and growth.* The online chat environment can provide substantial opportunity for the deaf student to actively participate during instruction. The more the student responds in writing and receives feedback from a skilled peer or the online teacher during the instructional conversation, the more likely it is that the student's language and writing skills will improve.

Barbara R. Schirmer is Dean of the School of Education and Allied Professions and Professor of Special Education at Miami University in Oxford, Ohio. She is the author of *Language and Literacy Development in Children Who Are Deaf* (Allyn and Bacon, 2000). Albert L. Ingram is Assistant Professor of Educational Technology at Kent State University.

problems appear to be more frequent in children with mild or moderate hearing losses than in those with severe to profound losses (ASHA, 2001). Concerns about lack of friendship and acceptance were reported by 50% of the 40 deaf and hard-of-hearing children in one study (Davis, Elfenbein, Schum, & Bentler, 1986). Data obtained from parents in the same study suggested that children with hearing loss were more likely to have behavioral difficulties in school and social situations than were children with normal hearing. Even a slight hearing loss can cause a child to miss important auditory information, such as the tone of a teacher's voice while telling students to get out their spelling workbooks, which can lead to the child's being considered inattentive, distractible, or immature (Easterbrooks, 1999).

Children with hearing loss frequently express feelings of depression, withdrawal, and isolation, particularly those whose hearing loss is acquired (Meadow-Orlans, 1985). A study of more than 1,000 deaf adolescents who were considered disruptive in the classroom (Kluwin, 1985) found that the most frequently related factor was reading ability; that is, students who were poorer readers were more likely to exhibit problem behaviors in school.

Research has not provided clear insights into the effects of hearing loss on behavior; however, it appears that the extent to which a child with hearing loss successfully interacts with family members, friends, and people in the community depends largely on others' attitudes and the child's ability to communicate in some mutually acceptable way (Ita & Friedman, 1999; Marschark & Clark, 1998). Children who are deaf with deaf parents are thought to have higher levels of social maturity and behavioral self-control than do deaf children of hearing parents, largely because of the early use of manual communication between parent and child that is typical in homes with deaf parents.

Many individuals who are deaf choose to work, live, and socialize primarily with other deaf people; members of hearing society may mistakenly view this as clannishness. Certainly, communication plays a major role in anyone's adjustment. Most individuals with hearing loss are fully capable of developing positive relationships with their hearing peers when a satisfactory method of communication can be used.

Social functioning

Council for
Exceptional
Children   Content
Standards for
Beginning Teachers–D/HH:
Impact of educational
placement options with regard
to cultural identity and
linguistic, academic, and social-
emotional development
(DH3K1) (also DH3K2, CC2K5,
CC2K6).

PRAXIS Special Education
Core Principles: Content
Knowledge: I. Understanding
Exceptionalities, Characteristics
of students with disabilities,
Affective and social-adaptive
factors.

 ## PREVALENCE

According to ASHA (2001), 95 of every 1,000 people have a chronic hearing loss, and about 28 million Americans experience some difficulty in receiving and processing aural communication. The large majority of persons with hearing loss are adults; it is estimated that 54% of persons over age 65 experience some limitations in hearing (Benson & Marano, 1998). The U.S. Public Health Service (1990) estimates that 83 out of every 1,000 children in the United States have an educationally significant hearing loss and that severe to profound hearing loss occurs in about 9 of every 1,000 school-age children.

During the 2000–2001 school year, 70,662 students ages 6 to 21 received special education services under the disability category of hearing impairments (U.S. Department of Education, 2002). This represents 1.2% of all school-age students who received special education services and about 0.11% of the resident student population. The actual number of school-age children with hearing loss in special education programs is somewhat higher because some children with hearing impairments are counted under another primary disability category (e.g., mental retardation, cerebral palsy, deaf-blind). It is not known precisely the percentage of these students who are deaf or hard of hearing. A national survey of early intervention programs serving children with hearing loss reported that 46% of the children were deaf and 54% hard of hearing (Meadow-Orlans, Mertens, Sass-Lehrer, & Scott-Olson, 1997).

About 25% of students who are deaf or hard of hearing have another disabling condition, most notably learning disabilities (9%), mental retardation (8%), vision problems (4%), and emotional or behavioral disorders (4%) (Holden-Pitt & Diaz, 1998). It is estimated that 9% of students with hearing loss have two or more additional disabilities (Shildroth & Hotto, 1994).

Prevalence of hearing loss

PRAXIS Special Education
Core Principles: Content
Knowledge: I. Understanding
Exceptionalities, Incidence and
prevalence of various types of
disabilities.

TYPES AND AGE OF ONSET

The two main types of hearing loss are conductive and sensorineural. **Conductive hearing loss** results from abnormalities or complications of the outer or middle ear. A buildup of excessive wax in the auditory canal can cause a conductive hearing loss, as can a disease that leaves fluid or debris. Some children are born with incomplete or malformed auditory canals. A hearing loss can also be caused if the eardrum or ossicles do not move properly. As its name implies, a conductive hearing loss involves a problem with conducting, or transmitting, sound vibrations to the inner ear. If the rest of the auditory system is intact, conductive hearing losses can often be corrected through surgical or medical treatment. Hearing aids are usually beneficial to persons with conductive impairments.

Sensorineural hearing loss refers to damage to the auditory nerve fibers or other sensitive mechanisms in the inner ear. The cochlea converts the physical characteristics of sound into corresponding neural information that the brain can process and interpret; impairment of the cochlea may mean that sound is delivered to the brain in a distorted fashion or not delivered at all. Amplification (making the source of sound louder) may not help the person with a sensorineural hearing loss. Surgery or medication cannot correct most sensorineural hearing loss. The combination of both conductive and sensorineural impairments is called a *mixed hearing loss.*

Hearing loss is also described in terms of being *unilateral* (present in one ear only) or *bilateral* (present in both ears). Most students who receive special education for hearing loss have bilateral losses, although the degree of impairment may not be the same in both ears. Children with unilateral hearing loss generally learn speech and language without major difficulties, although they tend to have problems localizing sounds and listening in noisy or distracting settings.

It is important to consider the age of onset—whether a hearing loss is **congenital** (present at birth) or **acquired** (appears after birth). The terms *prelingual hearing loss* and *postlingual hearing loss* identify whether a hearing loss occurred before or after the development of spoken language. A child who, from birth or soon after, is unable to hear the speech of other people will not learn speech and language spontaneously, as do children with normal hearing. A good way to approximate the experience of a child who is deaf from birth or early childhood is to watch a television program in which a foreign language is being spoken—with the sound on the TV set turned off (Furth, 1973). You would face the double problem of being unable to read lips and understand an unfamiliar language. Of the deaf and hard-of-hearing children served in special education programs, 95% have a prelingual hearing loss (Commission on Education of the Deaf, 1988).

A child who acquires a hearing loss after speech and language are well established, usually after age 2, has educational needs very different from the prelingually deaf child. The educational program for a child who is prelingually deaf usually focuses on acquisition of language and communication, whereas the program for a child who is postlingually deaf usually emphasizes the maintenance of intelligible speech and appropriate language patterns.

 CAUSES OF CONGENITAL HEARING LOSS

Although more than 400 causes of hearing loss have been identified, the exact cause is listed as "unknown" for up to 50% of children with hearing loss in some studies (Gallaudet University, 1998; Moores, 2001).

Genetic Factors   About one half of all congenital deafness is caused by genetic abnormalities (Tran & Grunfast, 1999). Genetic hearing loss may be autosomal dominant, auto-

Types of hearing loss

Council for Exceptional Children   Content Standards for Beginning Teachers–D/HH: Educational definitions and identification criteria for individuals who are D/HH (DH1K1). **PRAXIS** Special Education Core Principles: Content Knowledge: I. Understanding Exceptionalities, Characteristics of students with disabilities, Sensory factors.

Age of onset

Council for Exceptional Children   Content Standards for Beginning Teachers–D/HH: Impact of the onset of hearing loss, age of identification, and provisions of services on the development of the individual who is D/HH (DH2K2). **PRAXIS** Special Education Core Principles: Content Knowledge: I. Understanding Exceptionalities, Human development related to students with disabilities, Language development.

Causes of hearing loss

Council for Exceptional Children   Content Standards for Beginning Teachers–D/HH: Etiologies of hearing loss that can result in additional sensory, motor, and/or learning differences (DH1K3). **PRAXIS** Special Education Core Principles: Content Knowledge: I. Understanding Exceptionalities, Causation and prevention of disability.

somal recessive, or X-linked (related to the sex chromosome). *Autosomal dominant hearing loss* exists when one parent, who carries the dominant gene for hearing loss and typically has a hearing loss, passes the gene on to the child. In this case there is at least a 50% probability that the child will also have a hearing loss. The probability is higher if both parents have the dominant gene or if both grandparents on one side of the family have hearing loss due to genetic causes.

Approximately 80%–90% of inherited hearing loss is caused by *autosomal recessive hearing loss* in which both parents typically have normal hearing and carry a recessive gene (Tran & Grunfast, 1999). In this case the probability is 25% that the child will have a hearing loss. Because both parents usually have normal hearing, and because no other family members have hearing loss, there is no prior expectation that the child may have a hearing loss.

In *X-linked hearing loss,* the mother carries the recessive trait for hearing loss on the sex chromosome and passes it on to male offspring but not to females. This kind of hearing loss is rare, accounting for only about 1%–2% of hereditary hearing loss.

Even though 90% of children who are deaf are born to hearing parents, about 30% of the school-age population of students who are deaf have relatives with hearing loss (Moores, 2001). Because most hereditary deafness is the result of recessive genetic traits, the marriage of two deaf persons results in only a "slightly increased risk of deafness in their children because there is a small chance that both parents would be affected by the same exact genetic deafness" (Northern & Downs, 1991, p. 90). Hearing loss is one of the known characteristics of more than 200 genetic syndromes, such as Down syndrome, Usher syndrome, Treacher Collins syndrome, and fetal alcohol syndrome.

Maternal Rubella Although rubella (also known as German measles) has relatively mild symptoms, it can cause deafness, visual impairment, heart disorders, and a variety of other serious disabilities in the developing child when it affects a pregnant woman, particularly during the first trimester. A major epidemic of rubella in the United States and Canada between 1963 and 1965 accounted for more than 50% of the students with hearing loss in special education programs in the 1970s and 1980s. Since an effective vaccine was introduced in 1969, the incidence of hearing loss caused by rubella has decreased significantly.

Congenital Cytomegalovirus (CMV) Both rubella and cytomegalovirus (CMV) are members of a group of infectious agents known as TORCHES (toxoplasmosis, rubella, cytomegalovirus, herpes simplex, and syphilis). CMV is a common viral infection, and most people who are infected with it experience minor symptoms such as respiratory infections that soon disappear. Approximately 1% of infants have CMV in their saliva; and 10% of those may later develop various conditions, including mental retardation, visual impairment, and, most often, hearing impairment. It is estimated that 4,000 children are born in the United States each year with significant hearing impairments caused by CMV infection (Strauss, 1999). At present, there is no known prevention or treatment for CMV. However, a blood test can determine if a woman of childbearing age is at risk for developing an initial CMV infection during pregnancy.

Prematurity It is difficult to precisely evaluate the effects of prematurity on hearing loss, but early delivery and low birth weight are more common among children who are deaf than among the general population.

 CAUSES OF ACQUIRED HEARING LOSS

Otitis Media A temporary, recurrent infection of the middle ear, **otitis media** is the most common medical diagnosis for children. In 1990, it accounted for 6 million office visits to the doctor for children under the age of 5 (Stool et al., 1994). Nearly 90% of all children will experience otitis media at least once, and about one-third of children have three episodes (Roberts, Wallace, & Henderson, 1997). Antibiotics usually are an effective treatment; but if untreated, otitis media can result in a buildup of fluid and a ruptured eardrum, which causes permanent conductive hearing loss.

Meningitis   The leading cause of postlingual hearing loss is meningitis, a bacterial or viral infection of the central nervous system that can, among its other effects, destroy the sensitive acoustic apparatus of the inner ear. Children whose deafness is caused by meningitis generally have profound hearing losses. Difficulties in balance and other disabilities may also be present.

Ménière's Disease   A fairly rare disorder of the inner ear, Ménière's disease is characterized by sudden and unpredictable attacks of vertigo (dizziness), fluctuations in hearing, and *tinnitus* (a ringing in the ears without external stimulation). In its severest form, Ménière's disease can be incapacitating. Little is understood about the mechanisms underlying the condition, and at present there is no reliable treatment or known cure (Schessel, 1999). Ménière's disease most often appears in people between the ages of 40 and 60, but it can affect children under the age of 10.

Noise Exposure   Noise pollution—repeated exposure to loud sounds, such as industrial noise, jet aircraft, guns, and amplified music—is increasingly recognized as a cause of hearing loss. Exposure to excessive noise is probably the cause in a significant portion of the 28 million Americans with permanent hearing loss (ASHA, 2001).

 ## IDENTIFICATION AND ASSESSMENT

 ### ASSESSMENT OF INFANTS

The earlier a hearing loss is identified, the better a child's chances are for receiving early intervention and treatment and for developing good language and communication skills (Calderon & Naidu, 2000). Unfortunately, hearing loss goes undetected in many children, and detection does not always lead quickly to intervention. A national survey of parents of preschool children with hearing loss found that parents suspected their baby had a hearing loss at an average age of 17 months and had the diagnosis confirmed at a mean age of 22 months (Meadow-Orlans et al., 1997). Half of the hard-of-hearing children in this study did not have their hearing loss diagnosed until they were 2.5 years old. More discouraging are the data on the lag time between diagnosis and intervention: children waited an average of 8 months for a hearing aid, 10 months for speech and auditory services, and 11 months to begin sign language.

All infants, hearing and deaf alike, babble, coo, and smile. Later on, children who are deaf tend to stop babbling and vocalizing because they cannot hear themselves or their parents, but the baby's increasing silence may go unnoticed for a while and then be mistakenly attributed to other causes. Figure 10.2 lists some common auditory behaviors emitted by infants with normal hearing. Failure to demonstrate these responses may mean that an infant has a hearing loss, and an audiological exam is recommended.

The two most widely used methods of screening for hearing loss in infants measure physiological reactions to sound. With *auditory brain stem response,* sensors placed on the scalp measure electrical activity as the infant responds to auditory stimuli. In *otoacoustic emission* screening, a tiny microphone placed in the baby's ear detects the echoes of hair cells in the cochlea as they vibrate to sound. As of 1999, the legislatures of 29 states had mandated the screening of all newborn infants (Diefendorf, 1999).

Early identification of hearing loss

 Council for Exceptional Children   Content Standards for Beginning Teachers–D/HH: Specialized terminology used in assessing individuals who are D/HH (DH8K1) (also DH2K2). **PRAXIS** Special Education Core Principles: Content Knowledge: III. Delivery of Services to Students with Disabilities, Assessment, Use of assessment for screening and diagnosis.

*Typical development of
behaviors related to sound*

 Content
Standards for
Beginning Teachers–D/HH:
Effects of sensory input on the
development of language and
cognition (DH6K3) (also,
DH6K2, CC2K5).
PRAXIS Special Education
Core Principles: Content
Knowledge: I. Understanding
Exceptionalities, Human devel-
opment related to students
with disabilities, Language
development.

FIGURE 10.2 Expected auditory behaviors

1 Month
- Jumps or startles in response to loud noises
- Begins making gurgling sounds
- Responds to voice

3 Months
- Coos, babbles
- Turns to voices
- May quiet down to familiar voices close to ear
- Stirs or awakens from sleep when there is a loud sound relatively close by

6 Months
- Makes vocal sounds when alone; engages in vocal play
- Turns head toward sounds or when name is called and speaker is not visible
- Vocalizes when spoken to directly
- Imitates sounds

9 Months
- Responds differently to a cheerful versus angry voice
- Tries to copy the speech sounds of others
- Babbling acquires inflection

12 Months
- Locates a sound source by turning head (whether the sound is at the side, above, or below level)
- Ceases activity when parent's voice is heard
- Responds to own name
- Uses single words such as *mama* or *dada* correctly
- Vocalizes emotions
- Laughs spontaneously
- Disturbed by nearby noise when sleeping
- Imitates sounds and words
- Understands some familiar phrases or words
- Responds to music or singing
- Increases type and amount of babbling

18 Months
- Comes when called
- Responds to *no*
- Follows simple commands
- Uses 4–10 words in addition to *mama* or *dada*

24 Months
- Has vocabulary of more than 50 words
- Uses two words together
- Follows simple directions
- Responds to rhythm of music
- Uses voice for a specific purpose
- Shows understanding of many phrases used daily in life
- Plays with sound-making objects
- Uses well-inflected vocalization
- Refers to himself/herself by name
- Names a picture or object

Source: Adapted from Cleeland (1984); Gleason (1999); Northern and Downs (1991).

PURE-TONE AUDIOMETRY

A procedure called *pure-tone audiometry* is used to assess the hearing of older children and adults. The examiner uses an **audiometer,** an electronic device that generates sounds at different levels of intensity and frequency. The child, who receives the sound either through earphones (air conduction) or through a bone vibrator (bone conduction), is instructed to hold up a finger when he hears a sound and to lower it when he hears no sound. The test seeks to determine how loud sounds at various frequencies must be before the child is able to hear them. Most audiometers deliver tones in 5-dB increments, from 0 to 120 dB, with each dB level presented in various frequencies, usually starting at 125 Hz and increasing in octave intervals (doubling in frequency) to 8,000 Hz. The results of the test are plotted on a chart called an **audiogram** (see Figure 10.3).

An audiometer generates tones of precise intensity and frequency.

To obtain a hearing level on an audiogram, the child must be able to detect a sound at that level at least 50% of the time. For example, a child who has a 60-dB hearing loss cannot detect a sound until it is at least 60 dB loud, in contrast to a child with normal hearing, who would detect that same sound at a level between 0 and 10 dB.

SPEECH AUDIOMETRY

Speech audiometry tests a person's detection and understanding of speech. A list of one- and two-syllable words is presented at different dB levels. The **speech reception threshold (SRT),** the dB level at which the individual can understand half of the words, is measured and recorded for each ear. It is important to recognize that while a child might identify single words 50% of the time when spoken at a given volume and frequency, that does not always translate into ability to follow conversational speech (Woolsey, 1999).

ALTERNATIVE AUDIOMETRIC TECHNIQUES

Several alternative techniques have been developed for testing the hearing of children and individuals with severe disabilities who are not able to understand and follow conventional audiometry procedures (Roeser & Yellin, 1987). In **play audiometry**, the child is taught to perform simple but distinct activities, such as picking up a toy or putting a ball into a cup, whenever she hears the signal, either pure tones or speech. A similar procedure is **operant conditioning audiometry,** in which the child is reinforced with a token or small candy when he pushes a lever in the presence of a light paired with a sound. No reinforcer is given for pushing the lever when the light and sound are off. Next, the sound is presented without the light. If the child pushes the lever in response to the sound alone, the examiner knows the child can hear that sound. **Behavior observation audiometry** is a passive assessment procedure in which the child's reactions to sounds are observed. A sound is presented at an increasing level of intensity until a response, such as head turning, eye blinking, or cessation of play, is reliably observed.

Audiometry and audiograms

Council for Exceptional Children — Content Standards for Beginning Teachers–D/HH: Specialized terminology used in assessing individuals who are D/HH (DH8K1) (also DH8K2).
PRAXIS Special Education Core Principles: Content Knowledge: III. Delivery of Services to Students with Disabilities, Assessment, Use of assessment for diagnosis and making instructional decisions.

Mild Loss (41 to 55 dB)

Vicki:

- Is able to understand face-to-face conversation with little difficulty
- Misses much of the discussion that goes on in her classroom—particularly if several children are speaking at once or if she cannot see the speaker clearly
- Has some classmates who are unaware she has a hearing loss
- Benefits from wearing a hearing aid
- Receives occasional speech and language assistance from a speech-language pathologist

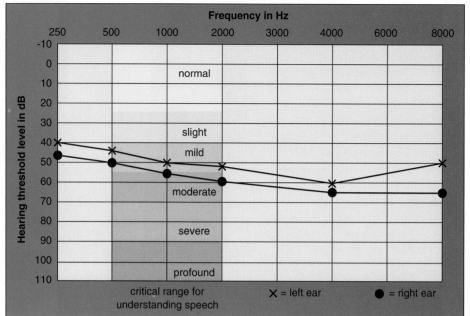

Audiogram for Vicki, who has a mild hearing loss

Moderate Loss (56 to 70 dB)

Antoine:

- Without a hearing aid can only hear conversation if it is loud and clear
- Can hear male voices more easily than female voices (loss is less pronounced in the lower frequencies)
- Finds it impossible to follow most class discussions, even though his teacher arranges favorable seating for him
- Has impaired but intelligible speech
- Attends a part-time special class for children with hearing loss and is in a regular classroom for part of the day

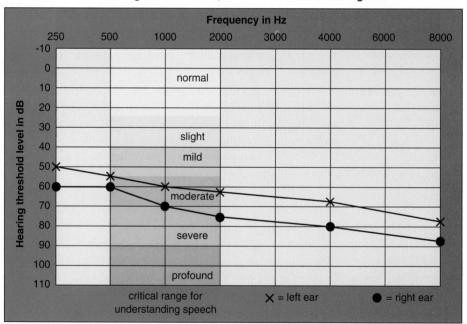

Audiogram for Antoine, who has a moderate hearing loss

FIGURE 10.3 **Effects of different degrees of hearing loss on speech and language and probable educational needs**

DEGREES OF HEARING LOSS

Hearing loss is usually described by the terms *slight, mild, moderate, severe,* and *profound,* depending on the average hearing level, in decibels, throughout the frequencies most important for understanding speech (500 to 2,000 Hz). It is important to recognize, however, that no two children have exactly the same pattern of hearing, even if their responses on a hear-

Severe Loss (71 to 90 dB)

Brante:

- Can hear voices only if they are very loud and 1 foot or less from her ear
- Wears a hearing aid, but it is unclear how much she gains from it
- Can distinguish most vowel sounds but hears only a few consonants
- Can hear a door slamming, a vacuum cleaner, and an airplane flying overhead
- Communicates by speech and signs
- Must always pay close visual attention to a person speaking with her
- Splits her school day between a special class and a regular classroom with an educational interpreter

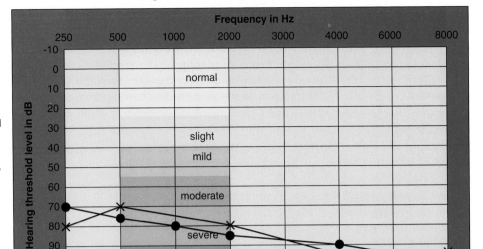

Audiogram for Brante, who has a severe hearing loss

Profound Loss (91 dB or more)

Steve:

- Cannot hear conversational speech at all
- Has a hearing aid that helps him be aware of certain loud sounds, such as a fire alarm or a bass drum
- Uses vision as his primary modality for learning
- Uses American Sign Language as his first language and principal means of communication
- Has not developed intelligible speech
- Attends a residential school for the deaf

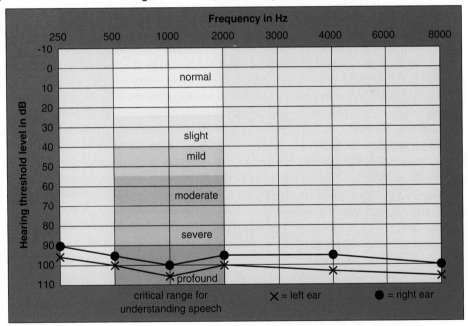

Audiogram for Steve, who has a profound hearing loss

FIGURE 10.3 *(continued)*

ing test are similar. Just as a single intelligence test cannot provide sufficient information to plan a child's educational program, the special education needs of a child with hearing loss cannot be determined from an audiometric test alone. Children hear sounds with differing degrees of clarity, and the same child's hearing ability may vary from day to day. Some children with very low levels of measurable hearing are able to benefit from hearing aids and can learn to speak. On the other hand, some children with less apparent hearing loss are not able to function well through the auditory channel and must rely on vision as their primary means of communication. Figure 10.3 shows the audiograms of four children with mild, moderate, severe, and profound hearing loss and describes some of the effects.

Degree and frequency range of hearing loss

 Council for Exceptional Children   Content Standards for Beginning Teachers–D/HH: Effects of sensory input on the development of language and cognition (DH6K3) (also CC2K2).

TECHNOLOGIES AND SUPPORTS THAT AMPLIFY, PROVIDE, SUPPLEMENT, OR REPLACE SOUND

In years past, it was assumed that individuals who were deaf simply did not hear at all. But hearing loss occurs in many degrees and patterns, and nearly all deaf children have some amount of residual hearing. Modern methods of testing hearing and improved technology for the amplification of sound enable many children, even those with severe and profound hearing loss, to use their residual hearing productively.

TECHNOLOGIES THAT AMPLIFY OR PROVIDE SOUND

Hearing aids

Content Standards for Beginning Teachers–D/HH: Strategies for stimulating and using residual hearing (DH6K8).

PRAXIS Special Education Core Principles: Content Knowledge: III. Delivery of Services to Students with Disabilities, Curriculum and Instruction, Technology for sensory disabilities.

Hearing Aids   A hearing aid is an amplification device; it makes sounds louder. Early versions indiscriminately amplified all sounds, which made them ineffective for most children with sensorineural hearing loss. Modern hearing aids can differentially amplify selected frequencies and therefore can be tailored to each child's individual pattern of hearing loss (House, 1999).

There are dozens of kinds of hearing aids; they can be worn behind the ear, in the ear, or on the body, or they can be incorporated into eyeglass frames. Children can wear hearing aids in one or both ears (monaural or binaural aids). Whatever its shape, power, or size, a hearing aid picks up sound, magnifies its energy, and delivers this louder sound to the user's middle ear. In many ways, the hearing aid is like a miniature public address system, with a microphone, an amplifier, and controls to adjust volume and tone.

Although hearing aids help many children increase their awareness of sound, it is important to understand that hearing aids make sounds louder but not necessarily clearer. Thus, children who hear sounds with distortion will still experience distortion with hearing aids. The effect is similar to turning up the volume on an old transistor radio: you can make the music louder, but you cannot make it clearer. Even the most powerful hearing aids generally cannot enable children with severe and profound hearing losses to hear speech sounds beyond a distance of a few feet. A hearing aid cannot correct a hearing loss in the same way that eyeglasses or contact lenses correct vision or by itself enable a deaf child to function without additional special education services or supports. In all cases, the wearer of the hearing aid, not the aid itself, does most of the work in interpreting conversation.

The earlier in life a child can be fitted with an appropriate hearing aid, the more effectively he will learn to use hearing for communication and awareness. Today, it is not at all unusual to see infants and preschool children wearing hearing aids; the improved listening conditions become an important part of the young child's speech and language development. To derive the maximum benefit from a hearing aid, a child should wear it throughout the day. Residual hearing cannot be effectively developed if the aid is removed or turned off outside the classroom.

It is difficult for any child to learn in a noisy classroom, but children who are deaf or hard of hearing are especially reliant on good classroom acoustics in order to hear and comprehend spoken language. Hearing aids offer minimal benefit in noisy and reverberant classrooms (Nelson, 2001). A *signal-to-noise ratio* (SNR) of at least +15 dB is considered necessary for students to achieve maximum benefit from a personal amplification device and their residual hearing (ASHA, 1995). An ambient noise level of 35 dB or less

▲ To derive maximum benefit from a hearing aid, a child should wear it throughout the day.

will generally allow all speakers' voices to reach all students at the desired +15 dB SNR. However, classrooms today are more active and noisier than ever. When Knecht, Whitelaw, and Nelson (2000) recorded noise levels in 32 unoccupied elementary classrooms, they found only four with background noise levels within the recommended limit. The average ambient noise in most of the other classrooms was 10 dB to 15 dB above the ASHA guideline.

Assistive Listening Devices   Group assistive listening devices can solve the problems caused by distance, noise, and reverberation in the classroom. In most systems, a radio link is established between the teacher and the children with hearing loss, with the teacher wearing a small microphone transmitter (often on the lapel, near the lips) and each child wearing a receiver that doubles as a personal hearing aid (Crandell & Smaldino, 2001). An FM radio frequency is usually employed, and wires are not required, so teacher and students can move freely around the classroom. The FM device creates a listening situation comparable to the teacher's "being only 6 inches away from the child's ear at all times" (Ireland, Wray, & Flexer, 1988, p. 17).

Cochlear Implants   Unlike hearing aids, which deliver amplified sound to the ear, a **cochlear implant** bypasses damaged hair cells and stimulates the auditory nerve directly. The implant is surgically placed under the skin behind the ear. An implant has four basic parts: an external *microphone*, which picks up sound from the environment; an external *speech processor,* which selects and arranges sounds picked up by the microphone; a *transmitter;* and a *receiver/stimulator*, which receives signals from the speech processor and converts them into electric impulses. *Electrodes* collect the impulses from the stimulator and send them directly to the brain via the auditory nerve (see Figure 10.4).

Cochlear implant surgery usually takes 2–3 hours, and the child stays overnight in the hospital. About 4 weeks later, the child returns to the implant center for the initial stimulation of the device and tune-up sessions over 2–3 days. An implant does not restore or create normal hearing. It can, however, give a deaf person a useful auditory understanding of the environment and help him or her to understand speech. Approximately 25,000 people worldwide have received cochlear implants since their approval by the Food and Drug Administration in 1989 (NIDCD, 2001). In the United States, some 14,000 people have implants; about half of these are children, most between the ages of 2 and 6.

When coupled with intensive post-implantation therapy, cochlear implants can help young children acquire speech, language, developmental, and social skills. While there are still many questions to be answered about cochlear implants, initial research reports have described significant improvements in speech perceptions, speech production, and language skills compared to peers without cochlear implants (Spencer, 2001; McKinley & Warren, 2000). It is not yet known if there is an optimal age for implantation, but earlier implantation seems to yield better outcomes.

Tremendous controversy surrounds cochlear implants. Many members of the Deaf community are vehemently against cochlear implants and consider the procedure to be a form of genocide of the Deaf culture (e.g., Lane & Bahan, 1998). Luterman (1999) offers the following explanation of a position that is difficult for most hearing people to understand:

> People who have never heard do not experience hearing impairment as a loss. This is why they can believe, much to the consternation of the normally hearing population, that deafness is a cultural difference rather than a deficit. It would be analogous, for example, to those who had ESP thinking that the rest of us were terribly handicapped in our communication abilities, while we who do not possess ESP and have never had it do not feel the least handicapped. The only way we would is if those with ESP constantly reminded us of our deficiency and tried to "fix" us. (p. 75)

Group listening devices

Council for Exceptional Children   Content Standards for Beginning Teachers–D/HH: Strategies for stimulating and using residual hearing (DH6K8).
PRAXIS Special Education Core Principles: Content Knowledge: III. Delivery of Services to Students with Disabilities, Curriculum and Instruction, Technology for sensory disabilities.

Cochlear implants

Council for Exceptional Children   Content Standards for Beginning Teachers–D/HH: Issues and trends in the field of education of individuals who are D/HH (DH1K4) (also DH3K2).
PRAXIS Special Education Core Principles: Content Knowledge: II. Legal and Societal Issues, Historical movements/trends affecting the connections between special education and the larger society.

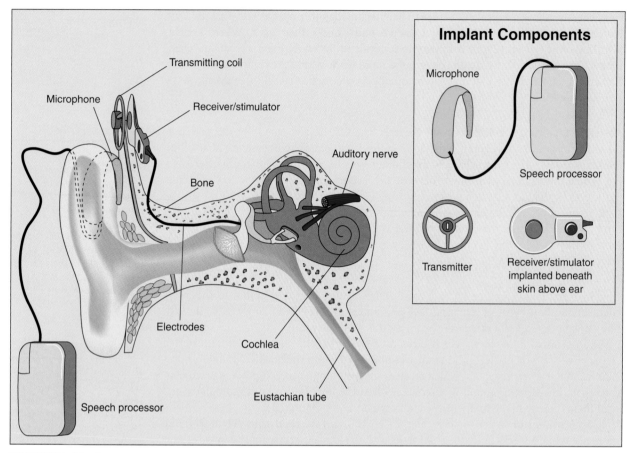

FIGURE 10.4 **Internal and external components of the cochlear implant**

To read more about the contrasting views of deafness as a cultural difference or as a sensory impairment to be remedied, see Profiles & Perspectives, "Defiantly Deaf," previously in this chapter, and "Deafness: The Dilemma," which follows later in this chapter.

 SUPPORTS AND TECHNOLOGIES THAT SUPPLEMENT OR REPLACE SOUND

Interpreters

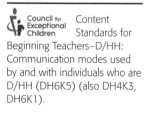 Content Standards for Beginning Teachers–D/HH: Communication modes used by and with individuals who are D/HH (DH6K5) (also DH4K3, DH6K1).

Interpreters *Interpreting*—signing the speech of a teacher or other speaker for a person who is deaf—began as a profession in 1964 with the establishment of a professional organization called the Registry of Interpreters for the Deaf (RID). Many states have programs for training interpreters, who must meet certain standards of competence to be certified by the RID. For the most part, the organization was initially composed of *freelance interpreters*, who interpret primarily for deaf adults in situations such as legal or medical interactions.

The role of the *educational interpreter* (sometimes referred to as an *educational transliterator*) has made it possible for many students with hearing loss to enroll in and successfully complete postsecondary programs. There has also been greater use of educational interpreters in elementary and secondary classrooms (Schick, Williams, & Bolster, 1999). Duties of interpreters vary across schools; they are likely to perform tasks such as tutoring, assisting regular and special education teachers, keeping records, and supervising students with hearing loss (Cawthon, 2001).

Speech-to-Text Translation   A fast-developing technology that promises to increase deaf students' access during live presentations, such as public or classroom lectures, is computer-aided speech-to-text translation. A leading example of this technology is the C-Print speech-to-text service developed at the National Technical Institute for the Deaf at the University of Rochester (Stinson, Elliot, McKee, & Francis, 2001). A trained captionist types the teacher's lecture and students' comments into a laptop computer using a shorthand code. Special software translates the code (e.g., typing "kfe" produces "coffee"), and the text is instantly displayed on a screen or a student's personal laptop computer monitor. The captionist does not produce a verbatim translation of the lecture but keeps as close as possible to the original. C-Print and similar technologies enable the student to print a hard copy of the lecture transcript for study as notes.

Speech-to-text translation and TV captioning

Council for Exceptional Children   Content Standards for Beginning Teachers–D/HH: Communication modes used by and with individuals who are D/HH (DH6K5) (also DH4K3, DH6K1).

Television Captioning   Today most regular programming on commercial and public network television, as well as many live newscasts and sporting events, is captioned (printed text appears at the bottom of the screen, similar to watching a film with subtitles), giving deaf people access to televised news and entertainment. Since 1993, a federal law has required that all new television sets sold in the United States be equipped with an internal device that allows the user to position captions anywhere on the screen.

Lewis and Jackson (2001) found that deaf students comprehended more of scripts that were accompanied by video than they did by reading the scripts alone. This finding suggests that visual stimuli provide essential information deaf viewers can use to improve their comprehension. Lewis and Jackson suggest that acquiring "television literacy" (through the use of captioned videos in the classroom) might advance the reading skills of deaf students by exposing them to English vocabulary and syntax.

Text Telephones   The telephone served as a barrier to deaf people in employment and social interaction for many years, but acoustic couplers now make it possible to send immediate messages over conventional telephone lines in typed or digital form. Text telephones (TT) (see photo at right) enable the user to send a typed message over telephone lines to anyone else who has a TT (originally called TTY or TDD systems). As a result of the Americans with Disabilities Act, TTs are now available in most public places such as airports and libraries, and every state has a relay service that enables TT users to communicate with a person on a conventional telephone via an operator who relays the messages. Relay numbers are published in every phone directory.

"Hearing dogs" are trained to alert a deaf person to important sounds in the environment such as a ringing telephone.

Alerting Devices   Some individuals who are deaf or hard of hearing use special devices to alert them to certain sounds or events. For example, to signal the doorbell, a fire alarm, or alarm clock, a sound-sensitive switch can be connected to a flashing light or a vibrator. Hearing-ear dogs alert a deaf person to important sounds in the environment.

Deafness:
The Dilemma

by Bonnie Tucker

During the last twenty years, technological advances to assist people with hearing loss surpassed the expectation of many. Hearing aids improved tremendously, both with respect to quality and aesthetics. The newer aids block out background noise and emphasize sound in the speech range, which has enabled some severely hearing-impaired people to benefit from aids for the first time. . . . Cochlear implants have enabled some profoundly deaf people, both children and adults, to understand speech without having to rely on speechreading or interpreters; some cochlear implantees are able to converse on the voice telephone with strangers.

Twenty years ago I, for one, did not foresee these almost Orwellian transformations. Today, however, my vision for the future is unlimited. Given the rapidly advancing state of technology in this area, it is not unrealistic to assume that twenty years hence the technological advances of the past two decades will seem outmoded, even ancient. It is

not unrealistic to assume that in twenty years cochlear implants will enable profoundly deaf people to understand speech in most circumstances, including on the telephone. We are not there yet, but we are on our way.

Many members of the Deaf community, including leaders of the National Association of the Deaf (NAD) . . . do not want cochlear implants. They do not want to hear. They want their children to be Deaf, and to be a part of the Deaf world. "We like being Deaf," they state. "We are proud of our Deafness. . . . " They claim the right to their own "ethnicity, with our own language and culture, the same way that Native Americans or Italians bond together"; they claim the right to "personal diversity," which is "something to be cherished rather than fixed and erased." And they strongly protest the practice of placing cochlear implants in children. . . . These same individuals, however, are among the strongest advocates for laws and special programs to protect and assist people with

---

History of education of students who are D/HH

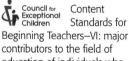 Council for Exceptional Children Content Standards for Beginning Teachers–VI: major contributors to the field of education of individuals who are D/HH (DH1K5) (also DH7K1).
PRAXIS Special Education Core Principles: Content Knowledge: II. Legal and Societal Issues, Historical movements/trends affecting connections between special education and the larger society.

 ## EDUCATIONAL APPROACHES

Over the years, many philosophies, theories, and specialized methods and materials have been developed for teaching children who are deaf and hard of hearing. Most of these approaches have been enthusiastically promoted by their advocates and critically denounced by others. Indeed, for more than 100 years, people have waged an impassioned debate over how best to teach children who do not hear. Table 10.1 highlights some key historical events and implications for the education of students with hearing loss.

The three major approaches to teaching deaf and hard-of-hearing students today are the oral/aural approach, total communication, and the bilingual-bicultural approach. Regardless of instructional approach or the academic subject area at hand, the primary objective of all teachers of students with hearing loss is the development and use of language and communication skills.

For the teacher of deaf and hard-of-hearing students, language is the curricular foundation on which the school day is built. The child's acquisition of language in face-to-face communication, reading, and writing is the focal point of instruction. The opportunity that content area instruction provides deaf and hard-of-hearing students to use language expressively and receptively is at least as important, and often considerably more important, than the specific concepts taught within individual subject areas. (Schirmer, 1997, p. 53)

hearing loss. They argue fiercely for the need for inter- preters, TTYs, telephone relay services, specially funded educational programs, and closed-captioning, at no cost to themselves. On the one hand, therefore, they claim that deafness is not a disability, but a state of being, a "right" that should not be altered. On the other hand, they claim that deafness is a disability that society should compensate for by providing and paying for services to allow deaf people to function in society. . . .

Do Deaf people have the right to refuse to accept new technology, to refuse to "fix" their Deafness if such repair becomes possible? Yes, absolutely. They do have the right, if they wish to exercise that right, to cherish their Deaf culture, their Deaf ethnicity, their "visually oriented" personal diversity. They have every right to choose not to fix their Deafness. . . . Do Deaf people have the right to demand that society pay for the resulting cost of that choice, however? No, I do not believe they do.

By way of analogy, suppose that blindness and quad- riplegia were "curable" due to advanced technology. Blind people could be made to "see" via artificial means such as surgical implantation or three-dimensional eye- glasses; quadriplegic individuals could be made to "walk" and use their arms via artificial means such as surgical nerve implantation or specially built devices. Oh, the blind people might not see as perfectly as sighted peo- ple—they might still miss some of the fine print. And the quadriplegic individuals might walk with a limp or move their arms in a jerky fashion. But, for the most part, they would require little special assistance.

Suppose that 10 blind people chose not to make use of available technology for the reason that blindness is not a "disability," not something to be fixed, but that blind people are simply "auditory oriented," and 20 quadriplegic people chose not to make use of available technology for the reason that quadriplegics are simply "out-of-body oriented." How long will society agree to pay for readers, attendants, and other services and de- vices to assist those blind and quadriplegic individuals who have exercised their right to be diverse? More im- portant, how long should society be asked to pay for such services and devices?

When technology advances to the extent that pro- foundly deaf people could choose to "hear"—which, eventually, it surely will—Deaf people will have to re- solve the dilemma, both for reasons of practicality and morality. . . . Deaf people will have to decide whether to accept hearing or to remain Deaf. They have every right to choose the latter course. If they do so, however, they must assume responsibility for that choice and bear the resultant cost, rather than thrust that responsibility upon society. . . . As our grandparents used to say, "You can't have your cake and eat it too."

Bonnie Tucker is a professor of law at Arizona State University. Deaf since infancy, and unable to wear hearing aids, Dr. Tucker had cochlear implant surgery at the age of 52. She is the Editor and part author of *Cochlear Implants: A Handbook* (Tucker, 1998).

Source: From Tucker, B. (1993). Deafness: 1993–2013—The dilemna. *Volta Review, 95,* 105–108. Reprinted by permission.

ORAL/AURAL APPROACHES

Educational programs with an oral/aural emphasis view speech as essential if students who are deaf are to function in the hearing world. Training in producing and understanding speech and language is incorporated into virtually all aspects of the child's education. A purely oral approach without any manual communication was used widely in the United States before the 1970s. Today, only about one-fourth of educational programs for students with hearing loss identify themselves as solely oral/aural programs (Meadow-Orlans et al., 1997).

A child who attends a program with an oral emphasis typically uses several means to develop residual hearing and the ability to speak as intelligibly as possible (Stone, 1997). Auditory, visual, and tactile methods of input are frequently used. Much attention is given to amplification, auditory training, speechreading, the use of technological aids, and, above all, talking. A few schools and classes maintain a purely oral environment and may even prohibit children from pointing, using gestures, or spelling out words to communicate. Children in these programs must express themselves and learn to understand others through speech alone. Other oral/aural programs also emphasize speech and listening skills but are more flexible and may use and encourage a variety of approaches to help students produce and understand spoken language.

Educators who use an oral approach acknowledge that teaching speech to children who are deaf is difficult, demanding, and time-consuming for the teacher, the parents, and—

Oral/aural approach

Council for Exceptional Children

Content Standards for Beginning Teachers–D/HH: Models, theories, and philoso- phies that provide the basis for education practice for individ- uals who are D/HH (DH1K2) (also DH4K2, DH4K3, DH6K5). **PRAXIS** Special Education Core Principles: Content Knowledge: II. Legal and Societal Issues, Historical movements/trends affecting connections between special education and the larger society.

TABLE 10.1 A history of the education of children who are deaf or hard of hearing: Key events and implications

Date	Historical Event	Educational Implications
Late 16th century	Pedro Ponce de Leon (1520–1584), an Augustinian monk and scholar, established in Spain a school for the deaf children of noble families.	This was the first educational program for exceptional children of any kind.
18th century	Schools for children who were deaf were set up in England, France, Germany, Holland, and Scotland.	Both oral and manual methods of instruction were used.
1817	The American Asylum for the Education of the Deaf and Dumb (renamed the American School for the Deaf) opened in Hartford, CT, under the leadership of Thomas Gallaudet and Laurent Clerc, a deaf French educator.	Children with hearing loss were among the first in the United States to receive special education. Gallaudet and Clerc used sign language as their method of instruction at the school. Some consider Clerc to be the father of deaf education in the United States.
Early 19th century	Students who were deaf were considered to be most appropriately served in asylums or special sanctuaries and removed from normal society.	The prevailing philosophy of the early 19th century was that persons who were deaf were incapable of benefiting from oral instruction.
Mid- to late 19th century	Instruction in speech and speechreading became widely available to students who were deaf throughout the United States. Several day schools were established for deaf children. Alexander Graham Bell criticized residential schools and the use of sign language, which he believed contributed to the segregation of deaf people.	Oral approaches dominated to such a great degree that the use of sign language in schools was officially prohibited at an international conference in 1880. It was not until many years later that schools relaxed their restrictions against the use of sign language. This era marked the beginning of what some have called "the Hundred Years War" over what methods of communication are best for deaf children.
Mid- to late 20th century	The majority of students whose deafness was caused by the rubella epidemics of the mid-1960s departed from the school-age population.	Enrollments in public residential schools for children with hearing impairments in the United States declined sharply as public school programs became more widely available.
1960s	Reserach by linguist William Stokoe at Gallaudet showed that sign language used by the deaf community was a legitimate language in its own right.	What had been called "the Sign Language" was given a new name, American Sign Language (ASL).

most of all—the student. Speech comes hard to the deaf child. The rewards of successful oral communication, however, are thought to be worth the effort. And indeed, most students with hearing losses no worse than severe can learn speech well enough to communicate effectively with hearing people. The best results are obtained with students with hearing loss who are enrolled in indisputably comprehensive oral programs or who are integrated most of the school day into regular education programs (Paul & Quigley, 1990).

Auditory Learning   Listening comprises 45% of daily communication for adults, and children spend up to 60% of the school day in situations where they are expected to be listening effectively (Crandell & Smaldino, in press). Many children with hearing loss have much more auditory potential than they actually use, and their residual hearing can be improved in the context of actual communication and daily experiences. All children with hearing loss, regardless of whether their preferred method of communication is oral (speech) or manual (signs), should receive training and practice to improve their listening skills.

Auditory training for young children with hearing loss begins by teaching awareness of sound. Parents might direct their child's attention to sounds such as a doorbell ringing or water running. They might then focus on localization of sound—for example, by hiding a radio somewhere in the room and encouraging the child to look for it. Discrimination of

Auditory training/learning

Council for Exceptional Children   Content Standards for Beginning Teachers–D/HH: Strategies to facilitate cognitive and communicative development in individuals who are D/HH (DH6K7) (also DH4K3).

TABLE 10.1 *continued*		
Date	**Historical Event**	**Educational Implications**
1968	Congress funded the National Technical Institute for the Deaf (NTID) at the Rochester Institute for Technology.	NTID offers technical and vocational degree programs for deaf students.
1970s	Total communication (TC) was adopted as the method of communication and instruction by the majority of deaf education programs.	TC attempts to present instructional content via simultaneous use of speech and sign language. While TC is still used frequently today, it has not raised the academic achievement of deaf students.
1986	In response to concerns about the academic and employment outcomes of deaf students, Congress established the Commission on Education of the Deaf (CED) with the Education of the Deaf Act of 1986.	CED began its 1988 report to Congress: "The present state of education for persons who are deaf in the United States is unsatisfactory. Unacceptably so" (p. viii). The report included 52 recommendations for improving the education of students with hearing loss.
1988	Students at Gallaudet University protested the hiring of a hearing president at their college in the Deaf President Now movement.	The movement led to the hiring of I. King Jordan as the first deaf president of Gallaudet, galvanized the deaf community, and increased the awareness of many in hearing society of the concerns and issues facing the Deaf culture.
1989	FDA approves use of cochlear implant surgery as means of bypassing the inner ear and providing a sense of sound directly through the auditory nerve for those with sensorineural hearing loss.	Educators have to find the most effective methods for helping deaf children receive maximum benefit from cochlear implants. There has been much controversy; many in the Deaf community view cochlear implants as a threat to the existence of their language and culture.
1990s	The Deaf community increased its activism and self-advocacy, especially with regard to ASL as a Deaf child's first language.	There is increased interest in and use of a bilingual/bicultural (bi-bi) approach, in which ASL is the language of instruction and English is taught as a second language.

sounds is another important part of auditory training; a child might learn to notice the differences between a man's voice and a woman's voice, between a fast song and a slow song, or between the words "rack" and "rug." Identification of sounds comes when a child is able to recognize a sound, word, or sentence through listening.

The focus today is on *auditory learning*—that is, teaching the child to learn to listen and to learn by listening instead of simply learning to hear (Ling, 1986). Advocates of auditory learning contend that the first three levels of auditory training—detecting, discriminating, and identifying sounds—are important but insufficient for developing the student's residual hearing. Auditory learning emphasizes a fourth and highest level of listening skills—the comprehension of meaningful sounds.

Some teachers find it helpful to conduct formal auditory training/learning sessions in which a child is required to use only hearing: he would have to recognize sounds and words without looking at the speaker. In actual practice, however, the student gains useful information from vision and the other senses to supplement the information received from hearing. Consequently, all senses should be effectively developed and constantly used.

Speechreading **Speechreading** is the process of understanding a spoken message by observing the speaker's face. Children with hearing loss, whether they have much or little residual hearing and whether they communicate primarily through oral or manual means, use their vision to help them understand speech. Some sounds are readily distinguished by watching the speaker's lips. For example, the word "pail" begins with the lips in a shut position, whereas the lips are somewhat drawn together and puckered at the corners for the

Speechreading

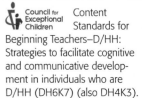

Council for Exceptional Children Content Standards for Beginning Teachers–D/HH: Strategies to facilitate cognitive and communicative development in individuals who are D/HH (DH6K7) (also DH4K3).

word "rail." Paying careful attention to a speaker's lips may help an individual with hearing loss derive important clues—particularly if she is also able to gain additional information through residual hearing, signs or gestures, facial expressions, and the context or situation.

Speechreading, however, is extremely difficult and has many limitations. About half of all English words have some other word(s) that appear the same in pronunciation; that is, although they sound quite different, they look alike on the lips. Words such as "bat," "mat," and "pat," for example, look exactly alike and simply cannot be discriminated by watching the speaker's lips. To complicate matters, visual clues may be blocked by a hand or a pencil, chewing gum, or a mustache. Many speakers are virtually unintelligible through speechreading; they may seem not to move their lips at all. In addition, it is extremely tiring to watch lips for a long time, and it may be impossible to do so at a distance, such as during a lecture.

Walker (1986) estimates that even the best speechreaders detect only about 25% of what is said through visual clues alone; "the rest is contextual piecing together of ideas and expected constructions" (p. 19). Shanny Mow (1973), a teacher who is deaf, graphically describes the frustrations of speechreading:

> Like the whorls on his fingertips, each person's lips are different and move in a peculiar way of their own. When young, you build confidence as you guess correctly "ball," "fish," and "shoe" on your teacher's lips. This confidence doesn't last. As soon as you discover there are more than four words in the dictionary, it evaporates. Seventy percent of the words when appearing on the lips are no more than blurs. Lipreading is a precarious and cruel art which rewards a few who have mastered it and tortures the many that have tried and failed. (pp. 21–22)

The combination of amplification and auditory training can help a child make the most of his residual hearing.

Despite the problems inherent in speechreading, it can be a valuable tool in a deaf or hard-of-hearing person's communication repertoire. Research shows that speechreading skills can be improved when deaf persons practice speechreading their own speech and that of others via computer-assisted video instruction (DeFilippo, Sims, & Gottermeier, 1995; Sims & Gottermeier, 1995). Initial evaluations of a computer-based, interactive videodisc program developed at Bloomsburg (Pennsylvania) University show promise in helping people with hearing loss make better use of their vision to decode speech (Slike, Thornton, Hobbis, Kokoska, & Job, 1995; Slike & Hobbis, 1998). (For tips on making your speech more accessible to someone who is speechreading, see Teaching & Learning, "Communicating with Someone Who Is Deaf," later in this chapter.)

Cued Speech   **Cued speech** is a method of supplementing oral communication. It supplies a visual representation of spoken language by adding cues, in the form of hand signals near the chin, to assist in identifying syllabic and phonetic features of speech that cannot be distinguished through speechreading (Caldwell, 1997). The hand signals must be used in conjunction with speech; they are neither signs nor manual alphabet letters and cannot be read alone. Eight hand shapes are used to identify consonant sounds, and four locations identify vowel sounds. A hand shape coupled with a location gives a visual indication of a syllable. According to Cornett (1974), who developed the system, cued speech can give intensive language input to young children because it clarifies the patterns of spoken English and does not disrupt the natural rhythm of speech.

TOTAL COMMUNICATION

Educational programs with an emphasis on **total communication** (also called *simultaneous communication*, or *simcom*) advocate the use of a variety of forms of communication to teach English to students with hearing loss. Practitioners of total communication maintain that the simulta-

---

Cued speech

Council for Exceptional Children   Content Standards for Beginning Teachers–D/HH: Strategies to facilitate cognitive and communicative development in individuals who are D/HH (DH6K7) (also DH4K2).

Total communication

Council for Exceptional Children   Content Standards for Beginning Teachers–D/HH: Models, theories, and philosophies that provide the basis for education practice for individuals who are D/HH (DH1K2) (also DH4K2, DH4K3, DH6K5). **PRAXIS** Special Education Core Principles: Content Knowledge: II. Legal and Societal Issues, Historical movements/trends affecting connections between special education and the larger society.

neous presentation of English by speech and manual communication (signing and finger-spelling) makes it possible for children to use either one or both types of communication (Hawkins & Brawner, 1997). Since its introduction as a teaching philosophy in the 1960s, total communication has become the most widely used method of instruction in schools for the deaf. A survey of 137 early intervention programs for deaf and hard-of-hearing students in 39 states found that 66% of the programs used total communication (Meadow-Orlans et al., 1997).

Manually Coded English   Teachers who practice total communication generally speak as they sign and make a special effort to follow the form and structure of spoken English as closely as possible. Several English-based sign systems have been designed for educational purposes, with the intention of facilitating the development of reading, writing, and other language skills in students with hearing loss. *Manually coded English* refers to several educationally oriented sign systems, such as Signing Essential English (commonly known as SEE I) (Anthony, 1971), Signing Exact English (SEE II) (Gustason, Pfetzing, & Zawolkow, 1980), and Signed English (Bornstein, 1974). While manually coded English borrows many signs and incorporates some of the features of American Sign Language (to be discussed), it also seeks to follow correct English usage and word order. Unfortunately, deaf students must often learn and use two or more sign language systems, depending on the person with whom they are communicating.

Manually coded English and fingerspelling

Council for Exceptional Children   Content Standards for Beginning Teachers–D/HH: Strategies to facilitate cognitive and communicative development in individuals who are D/HH (DH6K7) (also DH4K2).

Fingerspelling   *Fingerspelling,* or the manual alphabet, is used to spell out proper names for which no signs exist and to clarify meanings. It consists of 26 distinct hand positions, one for each English letter. A one-hand manual alphabet is used in the United States and Canada (see Figure 10.5). Some manual letters—such as "C," "L," and "W"—resemble the

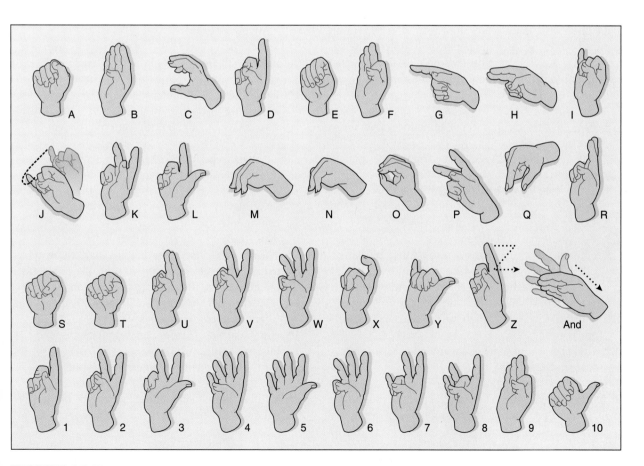

FIGURE 10.5   The manual alphabet used to fingerspell English in North America

Communicating with Someone Who Is Deaf

It is not unusual for a businessperson, bank teller, student, police officer, or anyone else to have the opportunity to communicate with a person who is deaf. Yet many people with normal hearing are unsure of themselves. As a result, they may avoid deaf people altogether or use ineffective and frustrating strategies when they do attempt to communicate.

The following tips for facilitating communication were suggested by the Community Services for the Deaf program in Akron, Ohio. These tips provide basic information about three commmon ways that deaf persons communicate: through speechreading, with sign language or the assistance of an interpreter, and by written communication. Usually, the person will indicate the approach with which he is most comfortable. If the person relies mainly on speechreading, here are things you can do to help.

- Face the person and stand or sit no more than four feet away.
- The room should have adequate illumination, but don't seat yourself in front of a strong or glaring light.
- Try to keep your whole face visible.
- Speak clearly and naturally, and not too fast.
- Don't exaggerate your mouth movements.
- Don't raise the level of your voice.
- Some words are more easily read on the lips than others are. If you are having a problem being understood, try substituting different words.
- It may take a while to become used to the deaf person's speech. If at first you can't understand what she is saying, don't give up.
- Don't hesitate to write down any important words that are missed.

If the deaf person communicates best through sign language (and you do not), it will probably be necessary to use an interpreter. Here are some considerations to keep in mind:

- The role of the interpreter is to facilitate communication between you and the person who is deaf. The interpreter should not be asked to give opinions, advice, or personal feelings.
- Maintain eye contact with the deaf person and speak directly to him. The deaf person should not be made to take a back seat in the conversation. For example, say, "How are you today?" instead of "Ask him how he is today."
- Remain face to face with the deaf person. The best place for the interpreter is behind you and a little to your side. Again, avoid strong or glaring light.
- Remember, it is the interpreter's job to communicate everything that you and the deaf person say. Don't say anything that you don't want interpreted.

Written messages can be helpful in exchanging information. Consider the following:

- Avoid the temptation to abbreviate your communication.
- Write in simple, direct language.
- The deaf person's written English may not be grammatically correct, but you will probably be able to understand it. One deaf person, for example, wrote "Pay off yesterday, finish me" to convey the message "I paid that loan off yesterday."
- Use visual aids, such as pictures, diagrams, and business cards.
- Don't be afraid to supplement your written messages with gestures and facial expressions.
- Written communication has limitations, but it is often more effective than no communication at all.

shape of printed English letters, whereas others—such as "A," "E," and "S"—have no apparent similarity. As in typewriting, each word is spelled out letter by letter.

Some educators have expressed concern about the quality of signing in many total communication classrooms, noting the linguistic inconsistency in the signing behavior of teachers. Although English is promoted as the primary language base in total communication programs, *Pidgin signed English* (PSE)—a mixture of English, ASL, and invented signs that represents no standard language—best describes the way most teachers tend to sign (Stewart, 1992).

Schirmer (2002) gives two reasons why she believes total communication is going out of favor in deaf education:

> One reason is that the idea of using every communication technique and mode available seems unrealistic. Teachers typically emphasize speech and audition at the expense of sign language, or vice versa. And students attend more to one mode than the other. A second reason total communication as a method has become controversial is that it was predicated on having the teacher use speech and sign language simultaneously, and, . . . it is not possible to speak and use ASL at the same time. (p. 539)

AMERICAN SIGN LANGUAGE AND THE BILINGUAL-BICULTURAL APPROACH

American Sign Language (ASL) is the language of the Deaf culture in the United States and Canada. Although the sign languages used by native deaf speakers were once thought to be nonlanguages (alinguistic), work by the linguist William Stokoe (Stokoe, 1960; Stokoe, Armstrong, & Wilcox, 1995) showed that ASL is a legitimate language in its own right rather than an imperfect variation of spoken English. ASL is a visual-spatial language in which the shape, location, and movement pattern of the hands; the intensity of motions; and the signer's facial expressions all communicate meaning and content. Because ASL has its own rules of phonology, morphology, syntax, semantics, and pragmatics, it does not correspond to spoken or written English (Drasgow, 1998). Articles, prepositions, tenses, plurals, and word order are expressed differently from English. It is as difficult to make precise word-for-word translations between ASL and English as it is to translate many foreign languages into English word for word.

Some ASL signs are *iconic;* that is, they convey meaning through hand shapes or motions that look like or appear to imitate or act out their message. In making the sign for "cat," for example, the signer seems to be stroking feline whiskers on her face; in the sign for "eat," the hand moves back and forth into an open mouth. Most signs, however, have little or no iconicity; they do not resemble the objects or actions they represent. If sign language were simply a form of pantomime, then most nonsigners would be able to understand it with relative ease. But the vast majority of signs cannot be guessed by people who are unfamiliar with sign language.

Several researchers have found that children as young as 5 months of age are able to produce and understand signs effectively (e.g., Maestas y Moores & Moores, 1980; Orlansky & Bonvillian, 1985). "When deaf children have full visual access to a natural signed language, they acquire it in the same effortless manner as hearing children acquire a spoken language" (Drasgow, 1998, p. 334).

During the 1990s, the Deaf community as well as a growing number of both hearing and deaf special educators began calling for the use of ASL as the language of instruction (Baker & Baker, 1997; Drasgow, 1998; Mahshie, 1995; Pittman & Huefner, 2001; Strong, 1995). They believe that ASL provides a natural pathway to linguistic competence and that English is better learned in the context of a *bilingual-bicultural (bi-bi) education* after the child has mastered his native or first language (ASL). Proponents of this model view deafness as a cultural and linguistic difference, not a disability, and recognize ASL as the deaf

ASL

Council for Exceptional Children Content Standards for Beginning Teachers–D/HH: Communication modes used by and with individuals who are D/HH (DH6K5) (also DH4K3, DH6K1).

Bilingual-bicultural approach

Council for Exceptional Children Content Standards for Beginning Teachers–D/HH: Models, theories, and philosophies that provide the basis for education practice for individuals who are D/HH (DH1K2) (also DH4K2, DH4K3, DH6K5). **PRAXIS** Special Education Core Principles: Content Knowledge: II. Legal and Societal Issues, Historical movements/trends affecting connections between special education and the larger society.

child's natural language. The goal of the bilingual-bicultural education approach is to help deaf students become bilingual adults who are competent in their first language, ASL, and can read and write with competence in their second language, English.

The basic theoretical argument for bilingual education is that students who have a solid foundation in their native language (L1) will be able to use their literacy-related L1 skills as a springboard for learning the majority second language (L2) (Cummins, 1989). Ewoldt (1996) suggests that a top-down bilingual-bicultural approach that encourages deaf students to pursue "the construction of meaning through relevant, enjoyable, natural communication" (p. 294) will overcome their lack of knowledge of sentence form and print characteristics.

Some related support for the bi-bi approach can be found in research correlating early exposure to and development of fluency in ASL and increased competence and English literacy (Prinz et al., 1996; Strong & Prinz, 1997). However, Mayer and Akamatsu (1999) question the extent of L1-L2 interdependence when the two languages under consideration are a native sign language and the written form of an oral language. They also point out the logical inconsistency and danger of not providing deaf students with direct instruction and practice in the bottom-up literacy skills such as English language principles and phonics just because those are the skills with which they have the most difficulty. To date, although the rhetoric advocating for bi-bi is high and many programs have been implemented, there are few objective data reporting outcomes and evaluating what features of such programs are and are not effective (Schirmer, 2001). IEP teams most consider and document the in-

Increasing numbers of deaf children are being taught with bilingual educational approaches in which ASL is the language of instruction.

Some signs, such as "cat" (left) and "eat" (right) are iconic; they look like the objects or actions they represent.

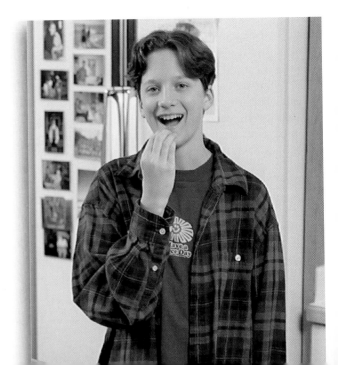

dividual communication needs of each student who is deaf or hard of hearing, One systematic way of doing so is described in Teaching & Learning, "Considering the Communication Needs of Students Who Are Deaf or Hard of Hearing," later in this chapter.

EDUCATIONAL PLACEMENT ALTERNATIVES

In most areas of the United States, parents and students now have the option of choosing between local public school programs and residential school placement. Today, approximately 84% of children who are deaf or hard of hearing attend local public schools: 40% receive most of their education in regular classrooms, 19% attend resource rooms for part of the school day, 25% are served in separate classrooms, and 16% attend special schools (U.S. Department of Education, 2002). Most students with hearing loss who are included in regular classrooms are hard of hearing and have hearing losses of less than 90 dB.

Of the 8.6% of students with hearing loss who attend residential schools, about one-third live at home with their families and commute to the school. Over 90% of the students currently enrolled in residential schools have severe and profound prelingual hearing loss. Nearly one-third of the students with hearing loss served in residential schools have additional disabilities.

American Sign Language (ASL) is a legitimate language with its own vocabulary, syntax, and grammatical rules. It does not correspond to spoken or written English.

Examining the question of where students who are deaf should be educated yields some research evidence—and much strong opinion—to support both inclusive and segregated settings. With the increased emphasis on inclusion, some question the effectiveness and appropriateness of residential placements for any student. Research, however, has not found that residential schools for the deaf contribute to academic or social deficits in students. On the contrary, some studies suggest that residential schooling may be the most effective placement for certain students. For example, Braden, Maller, and Paquin (1993) report that the performance IQs of children with hearing loss who were educated in residential schools increased over a 3- to 4-year period but that the scores of similar students in regular school day programs did not.

> The results of this study clearly disprove the belief that placement in residential, segregated programs invariably inhibits cognitive abilities. The assumption that children with hearing loss are best served in mainstream settings should be suspended until additional information is available regarding placement effects on such children's cognitive, social and academic development. (p. 432)

As Bat-Chava (2000) notes, where a child who is deaf is educated also influences the likelihood of his or her cultural identity. In schools in which oral English is the language of instruction, supplemented by fingerspelling and English-based sign systems, students are more likely to view hearing loss as a disability. Schools in which ASL is the language of instruction foster the perspective of deafness as a culture.

In a study of the effects of inclusion on the academic achievement of high school students who are deaf, Kluwin (1993) reported that, although those students who were

Placement options

Council for Exceptional Children   Content Standards for Beginning Teachers–Common Core: Demands of learning environments (CC5K1) (also DH1K4, DH5K2).
PRAXIS Special Education Core Principles: Content Knowledge: III. Delivery of Services to Students with Disabilities, Background knowledge, Placement and program issues, Least restrictive environment/Continuum of educational services.

Considering the Communication Needs of Students Who Are Deaf or Hard of Hearing

by Susan R. Easterbrooks and Sharon K. Baker

According to IDEA '97, students' IEPs must contain a written statement of how the IEP team considered the communication needs of each student who is deaf or hard of hearing. This is a wonderful addition to the requirements for appropriately serving students with hearing losses because it brings important questions to the attention of those unfamiliar with the field. Unless done well, however, such a statement will miss the mark of its intention. This seemingly simple question is actually complex and challenges schools and districts to broaden their perspectives.

Students who are deaf or hard of hearing form a heterogeneous group whose needs vary greatly. Some have cochlear implants and communicate orally. Some use an English-based sign system or American Sign Language (ASL). Others have additional disabilities or come from homes where the spoken language is not English. Educators need to use many approaches and philosophies to meet all variations within the population (e.g., Baker & Baker, 1997; Goldberg, 1997; Gustason, 1997; Stone, 1997). IEP teams need to address several questions when considering the communication needs of students who have hearing losses. Team members should ask these questions at each IEP meeting, and answers should lead to decisions regarding placement, language mode, use of technology, and access to appropriate language models.

We developed the matrix shown in Figure A to help IEP teams consider pertinent information relevant to the communication needs of students who are deaf or hard of hearing. In schools for the deaf, such a matrix may not be needed given the expertise available on site. Local school systems, however, especially those with few students with hearing losses and, consequently, few teachers of the deaf, may benefit from such guidance.

Using the Matrix

Begin by answering each question and placing an *X* in the column corresponding to the evidence gathered by observing the student's behavior or noting his or her family history. For example, if a child has deaf parents, then his or her early experiences are likely to be with ASL. If a child received a cochlear implant and sufficient auditory instruction as a preschooler, then his or her early experiences were more auditory than visual. If the child shows evidence of further neurological impairment, he may be at risk for poor auditory processing or for poor development of an auditory-based communication system. Each of these situations will have had a significant effect on the child's present communication needs.

Next, tally the *X*'s at the bottom of each column to get a sense of where the school, family, and child's relative strengths lie. Third, use this information to engage in a discussion of the student's communication needs. Be sure to have at least two people with training and experience in deaf education participate in this discussion. Finally, after discussion of the information gathered to complete the form, include decisions on the IEP. Retain the matrix in the student's file as a means of documenting that you have met the IDEA '97 requirement to consider the communication needs of a student who is deaf or hard of hearing.

Place an X in the most appropriate column corresponding to the question. Provide descriptive evidence to document your consideration. Tally the number of Xs in each column to suggest a response to communication needs.

Name: CH   Date: 11-11-98

Question	Listens: Oral A-V Cues	Looks: English Orientation (word order) E.g. English Signs/Cued Speech	Looks: American Sign Language Orientation (spatial)	Tactile:	Other:
What is the Child's Current Style/Mode of Understanding the World?	Understands less than 1/2 of auditory message.	Watches others. Lipreads. Comprehends signs well. Understand >75%. X			
What is the Child's Current Style/Mode of Responding to the World?	Speech is understandable approx. 75% of the time. X	Supports speech with signs. Speaks to parents Signs to friends. X			
In Which Mode/Style Does the Child Show Best Autonomy?		Most comfortable when he can support his speech with signs X			
What is the Parents' Present Communication Mode/Style?	Most of their interactions are spoken X	Are learning to sign X			
What Mode/Style Do the Parents State They Prefer or Support?	X	Parents are learning to sign. Very committed to English word order & reading. X	Do not support ASL.		
What Were the Child's Earliest Communication Experiences?	Heard until age 2 yrs. 4 mos. (CA = 9-4) X				
What Resources are Available for Family/School/Community Development?	No oral program nearby	Community college has sign classes X			
What Information Is Available from a Psychological Evaluation?		WISC-III Pic Arr = 13 Coding = 10 X	WISC-III Pic Compl = 7 Obj Assemb = 8		
What Skills in Languages/Modes Do the Teachers in This System Have?		X	X		
In Which Mode/Style Is There the Highest Degree of Likelihood of Consistency from School to Home to Community?		Mom reports neighbors and church members are learning to sign X	No deaf family members. Rural Community. No ASL users in community.		
TALLYS	4	9	1	0	0

Needs Relative to Mode/Style:

Uses total communication receptively and expressively. In group situations, needs sign. One-on-one can communicate in oral mode. Continue interaction with other deaf students.

Needs Relative to Family Development:

Family is working hard to help him learn to read. Reads at beginning 2nd grade level. Oriented to English syntax. Family needs access to sign instruction

Classroom Modifications:

Needs classroom buddy system to help him keep up with printed work. Teacher needs to check comprehension of instruction and directions frequently. One-on-one reading support. Interpreter situationally.

Technology Related to Communication:

Assistive listening device.

FIGURE A   Matrix for considering the communication needs of students who are deaf or hard of hearing

Source: Adapted from S. R. Easterbrooks & S. K. Baker. (2001). Considering the communication needs of students who are deaf or hard of hearing. *Teaching Exceptional Children, 33*(3), 70–76. Reprinted with permission.

Inclusion

 Content
Standards for
Beginning Teachers–D/HH:
impact of educational
placement options with regard
to cultural identity and
linguistic, academic, and social-
emotional development
(DH3K1) (also DH1K4,
DH5K1).
PRAXIS Special Education
Core Principles: Content
Knowledge: III. Delivery of
Services to Students with
Disabilities, Background
knowledge, Placement and
program issues, Least restrictive
environment/Continuum of
educational services.

included in regular classrooms for academic content fared better on achievement measures than did students who spent all or most of the day in a separate class, the difference may have been the result of curriculum programming and class selection, not the actual placement where instruction took place. After assessing the self-concepts of 90 deaf secondary students across different educational placements, van Gurp (2001) concluded there were academic advantages to more integrated, resource room-like placements and social advantages in attending segregated schools.

Cawthon (2001) found that elementary teachers in inclusive classrooms directed about half as many utterances to deaf students as they did to hearing students and that educational interpreters were critical factors in how well the deaf students understood and participated in classroom discourse and learning activities. The skill level of an educational interpreter plays a major role in the success and appropriateness of a regular classroom placement for students who are deaf (Schick et al., 1999). An educational interpreter must provide the deaf or hard-of-hearing student with all speech and other auditory information in the classroom, a formidable task for the most highly skilled interpreter. In one study, only 15% of 221 educational interpreters had an associate's degree in interpreting (Jones, Clark, & Soltz, 1997); another study found that only 4 of 30 interpreters had attended an interpreter training program (Schick & Williams, 1994). After examining videotaped performances of 59 educational interpreters, Schick et al. (1999) reported that fewer than half performed at a level considered minimally acceptable. They concluded that "many deaf children receive an interpretation of classroom discourse that may distort and inadequately represent the information being communicated" (p. 144).

In an effort to identify strategies to overcome barriers to meaningful participation of students with hearing loss in general education classrooms, Stinson and Liu (1999) conducted observations and focus groups with elementary general education teachers, teachers of the deaf, interpreters, notetakers, deaf and hard-of-hearing students, and their hearing classmates. The authors organized their findings into a list of 16 specific strategies to make placement in the regular classroom educationally beneficial. They suggested several strategies for each type of individual in the classroom (e.g., teacher, interpreter, hearing peers). Stinson and Liu recommend that students with hearing loss should

- be responsible for taking initiative in the classroom and believe the outcome will be at least somewhat successful.
- have and use communication skills for participating in the regular classroom (e.g., repairing miscommunications, taking turns).
- when participating in small-group learning activities, carry out a specific task and share the information with the group.

While full inclusion in regular classrooms has benefited some deaf students, all of the professional and parent organizations involved with educating students who are deaf have issued position statements strongly in favor of maintaining a continuum of placement options (e.g., Commission on Education of the Deaf, 1988; Consumer Action Network, 1994). Moores (1993), a respected leader in the field of deaf education, voiced the perspective of many deaf educators and parents:

> For many deaf children the concept of total inclusion, as currently promulgated, could in reality be exclusionary in practice. Placing a deaf child in a classroom in physical contiguity to hearing children does not automatically provide equal access to information. In fact, it can be isolating, both academically and socially. (p. 251)

As with all learners, we should never overlook the most fundamental factor in determining how successful a student will be in the regular classroom (or any other placement): quality of instruction. After studying the math achievement of 215 secondary students with hearing loss who were either in self-contained classrooms or mainstreamed into regular classes with or without an interpreter, Kluwin and Moores (1989) concluded, "Quality of instruction is the prime determinant of achievement, regardless of placement" (p. 327).

 POSTSECONDARY EDUCATION

A growing number of educational opportunities are available to students with hearing loss after completion of high school. The oldest and best known is Gallaudet University in Washington, DC, which offers a wide range of undergraduate and graduate programs in the liberal arts, the sciences, education, business, and other fields. The National Technical Institute for the Deaf (NTID), located at the Rochester Institute of Technology, provides wide-ranging programs in technical, vocational, and business-related fields such as computer science, hotel management, photography, and medical technology. Both Gallaudet and NTID are supported by the federal government, and each enrolls approximately 1,500 students who are deaf or hard of hearing.

More than 150 other institutions of higher education have developed accredited programs specifically for students with hearing loss (Rawlings, Karchmer, Allen, & DeCaro, 1999). Among these are four regional postsecondary programs that enroll substantial numbers of students with hearing loss: St. Paul (Minnesota) Technical-Vocational Institute, Seattle (Washington) Central Community College, the Postsecondary Education Consortium at the University of Tennessee, and California State University at Northridge.

The percentage of students with hearing loss who attend postsecondary educational programs has risen dramatically in the past 20 years. It is hoped that the increase in postsecondary programs will expand vocational and professional opportunities for deaf adults.

 CURRENT ISSUES AND FUTURE TRENDS

Given the large percentage of children with hearing loss who are educated in regular classrooms for most of the day, it is likely that oral/aural and total communication methods of instruction will continue to be used. Speech, after all, is the most widely used form of communication among teachers and students in regular classes. At the same time, an increasing percentage of the deaf children served in special schools and self-contained classrooms will be taught with the bilingual-bicultural approach, where ASL is the language of instruction.

Educators, scientists, philosophers, and parents—both hearing and deaf—have for many years debated the most appropriate instructional methods for children who are deaf. The controversy continues today. In the past, however, fundamental disagreement focused on the extent to which deaf children should express language through speech and perceive the communication of others through speechreading and residual hearing. Today, the focal point has switched to which language modality—auditory or visual—best suits a child's acquisition of an initial language. Research has yet to provide (and perhaps never will provide) a definitive answer to the question of which communication method is best. There is general agreement, however, that educational programs for students who are deaf leave much room for improvement.

Different children communicate in different ways. Some children with hearing loss, unfortunately, have experienced deep frustration and failure because of rigid adherence to an oral-only program. They have left oral programs without having developed a usable avenue of communication. Equally unfortunate is the fact that other children with hearing loss have not been given an adequate opportunity to develop their auditory and oral skills because they were placed in educational programs that did not provide good oral instruction. In both cases, children have been unfairly penalized. Every child who is deaf should have access to an educational program that uses a communication method best suited to her unique abilities and needs. Mahshie (1995) recommends letting the child choose her first language:

Gallaudet University and NTID

 Content Standards for Beginning Teachers–D/HH: Model programs, including career/vocational and transition, for individuals who are D/HH (DH7K1) (also DH10K2).
PRAXIS Special Education Core Principles: Content Knowledge: III. Delivery of Services to Students with Disabilities, Professional roles, Use of professional organizations.

Choosing auditory or visual language modality

 Content Standards for Beginning Teachers–D/HH: Issues and trends in the field of education of individuals who are D/HH (DH1K4) (also DH6K1, DH6K5).
PRAXIS Special Education Core Principles: Content Knowledge: II. Legal and Societal Issues, Historical movements/trends affecting connections between special education and the larger society.

For more information on hearing loss, go to the Web Links module in Chapter 10 of the Companion Website at **www.prenhall.com/heward**

In environments where the Deaf child encounters both spoken and signed language separately—as whole languages—during the course of natural interactions, it has become apparent to both parents and professionals that the child will be the guide regarding his or her predisposition toward a more oral or more visual language. In this win-win situation, the choice of a first language is clearly the child's. (p. 73)

Early and continued access to language and the communication modality best suited to their individual needs and preferences, effective instruction with meaningful curriculum, and self-advocacy are the keys to increasing the percentage of deaf or hard-of-hearing people who are able to access and enjoy the full spectrum of educational, social, vocational, and recreational opportunities society has to offer.

SUMMARY

DEFINITIONS

- Hearing loss exists on a continuum from mild to profound, and most special educators distinguish between children who are deaf and those who are hard of hearing. A deaf child is not able to understand speech through the ears alone. A hard-of-hearing child is able to use hearing to understand speech, generally with the help of a hearing aid.
- Many Deaf persons do not view hearing loss as a disability. Like other cultural groups, members of the Deaf community share a common language (ASL) and social practices.
- Sound is measured by its intensity (decibels [dB]) and frequency (hertz [Hz]); both dimensions are important in considering the special education needs of a child with a hearing loss. The frequencies most important for understanding speech are 500–2,000 Hz.

CHARACTERISTICS

- Deaf children—especially those with a prelinguistic loss of 90 dB or greater—are at a great disadvantage in acquiring English literacy skills, especially reading and writing.
- The speech of children with hearing loss may be difficult to understand because they omit speech sounds they cannot hear, speak too loudly or softly, speak at an abnormally high pitch, speak with poor inflection, and/or speak at an improper rate.
- As a group, deaf and hard-of-hearing students lag far behind their hearing peers in academic achievement, and the achievement gap usually widens as they get older.
- Children with severe to profound hearing losses often report feeling isolated and unhappy in school, particularly when their socialization with other children with hearing loss is limited.
- Many deaf individuals choose membership in the Deaf community and culture.

PREVALENCE

- Students with hearing loss represent about 1.2% of all school-age students receiving special education.

TYPES AND CAUSES

- Hearing loss is described as conductive (outer or middle ear) or sensorineural (inner ear) and as unilateral (in one ear) or bilateral (in both ears).
- A prelingual hearing loss occurs before the child has developed speech and language; a postlingual hearing loss occurs after that time.
- Causes of congenital hearing loss include genetic factors, maternal rubella, heredity, congenital cytomegalovirus (CMV), and prematurity.

- Causes of acquired hearing loss include otitis media, meningitis, Ménière's disease, and noise exposure.

IDENTIFICATION AND ASSESSMENT

- Auditory brain stem response and otoacoustic emission are two methods of screening for hearing loss in infants.
- A formal hearing test generates an audiogram, which graphically shows the intensity of the faintest sound an individual can hear 50% of the time at various frequencies.
- Hearing loss is classified as slight, mild, moderate, severe, or profound, depending on the degree of hearing loss.

TECHNOLOGIES AND SUPPORTS THAT AMPLIFY, PROVIDE, SUPPLEMENT, OR REPLACE SOUND

- Technologies that amplify or provide sound include hearing aids, assistive listening devices, and cochlear implants.
- Technologies and supports that enhance or replace sound include educational interpreters, speech-to-text translation, television captioning, text telephones, and alerting devices.
- Although technology holds much promise for addressing the communication problems faced by deaf and hard-of-hearing people, many leaders of Deaf culture do not view deafness as a disability and oppose efforts to "cure" it or make them more like members of the mainstream hearing culture.

EDUCATIONAL APPROACHES

- The oral/aural approach views speech as essential if students are to function in the hearing world; much emphasis is given to amplification, auditory training, speechreading, the use of technological aids, and, above all, talking.
- Total communication uses speech and simultaneous manual communication via signs and fingerspelling in English word order.
- In the bilingual-bicultural approach, deafness is viewed as a cultural and linguistic difference, not a disability, and ASL is used as the language of instruction.

EDUCATIONAL PLACEMENT ALTERNATIVES

- Forty percent of children with hearing loss attend regular classrooms, 19% attend resource rooms for part of the school day, 25% are served in separate classrooms, and 16% attend special schools.
- All of the professional and parent organizations involved in deaf education have issued position statements strongly in favor of maintaining a continuum of placement options.

CURRENT ISSUES AND FUTURE TRENDS

- Given the large percentage of children with hearing loss who are educated in regular classrooms for most of the day, it is likely that oral/aural and total communication methods of instruction will continue to be used.
- The bilingual-bicultural approach will probably be used with a growing percentage of the deaf children served in special schools and self-contained classrooms.
- Access to the language and communication modality best suited to their individual needs and preferences, effective instruction with meaningful curriculum, and self-advocacy are the keys to improving the future for people who are deaf or hard of hearing.

To check your comprehension of chapter content, go to the Guided Review and Quiz modules in Chapter 10 of the Companion Website at **www.prenhall.com/heward**

Chapter 11
Blindness and Low Vision

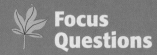

Focus Questions

- In what ways does loss of vision affect learning?

- How does the age at which vision is lost affect the student?

- Normally sighted children enter school with a great deal of knowledge about trees. How can a teacher help a student who is congenitally blind learn about trees?

- What compensatory skills do students with visual impairments need most?

- How do the educational goals and instructional methods for children with low vision differ from those for children who are blind?

JEANNA MORA DOWSE

PINON AND GANADO UNIFIED SCHOOL DISTRICTS

APACHE COUNTY, ARIZONA

Education • Teaching Credentials • Experience

- A.A. in Nursing, New Mexico State University, 1986
- B.S. in Elementary Education, Texas Tech University, 1991
- M.A. in Visual Impairment, University of Arizona, 1997
- Arizona Standard Elementary Education, K–8; Arizona English as a Second Language, K–12; Arizona Standard Visually Impaired, K–12
- 4 years as a teacher of students with visual impairments

Current Teaching Position and Students   I am an itinerant teacher of children with visual impairments (VI) in two rural school districts in Apache County. I have a caseload of nine students in the Pinon Unified School District and eight students in Ganado. My students range in age from 4 to 17 years old and are in preschool through ninth grade. All of my students are members of the Navajo tribe. Many are from families that receive welfare. Some of my students speak both Navajo and English, some have been identified as Limited English Proficient, and some are not fluent in either language.

IEP Goals   The Arizona State Department of Education requires that 75% of a student's IEP goals be based on the Arizona State Curriculum Standards. Most of my students are able to access the general curriculum with adaptations or modifications. It is very important for me to consult with the classroom teachers in order to identify IEP goals and objectives that will accomplish this. Most of my students need help with literacy skills, understanding their visual impairment, and learning how to self-advocate for needed accommodations. Here are some examples of IEP goals and objectives for several of my students this year:

Annual goal.   The student will complete the braille program "Patterns: Reading-Readiness Level" (red) with 90% accuracy as documented by program guidelines and recorded by a certified VI teacher.

Short-term objective 1.   The student will tactually identify and then verbalize the letters *a–m* in braille as documented by mastery tests.

Short-term objective 2.   The student will tactually identify and then verbalize the letters *n–z* in braille as documented by mastery tests.

Annual goal.   The student will identify characters in a story and retell the story in sequence with 90% accuracy when five different stories are read aloud on five different occasions.

Short-term objective 1.   The student will listen to a variety of story boxes and verbally and tactually identify the main characters in the story with 90% accuracy.

Short-term objective 2.   The student will listen to a variety of story boxes and will verbally retell a story in sequence with 90% accuracy.

Annual goal.   The student will use interpersonal skills to express to teachers and coaches the need for adaptations or modifications for his visual impairment.

Short-term objective 1.   The student will research his visual impairment on the Internet and document in writing four details regarding his visual impairment.

Short-term objective 2.   The student will interview at least two individuals with the same type of visual impairment and write a short essay documenting information obtained from the interviews.

Curriculum Materials and Teaching Strategies   My students need hands-on activities. I have found that students enjoy story boxes with objects from the stories inside a box. They are able to feel the objects and act out the story. My students need many opportunities to listen to language and books. I encourage parents and teachers to expose my students to as many real-life experiences as possible. They learn the importance of writing when they are able to write or dictate their own books and letters to family and friends. My students who are emergent readers/writers make books from objects they have collected from a walk or from things they bring from home.

Collaboration and Teaming   We are required by the state of Arizona to write multidisciplinary team reports. That is, we no longer write individual reports but must collaborate to write one assessment report. We also consult with each other when we are providing services to the same student. I am lucky to work with some very good school psychologists, physical therapists (PTs), occupational therapists (OTs), and speech-language pathologists (SLPs). We often work with the same student at one time and explain what each person can do to enhance the student's sessions. For example, the PT and OT have given me ideas about positioning, and the SLP has suggested how I can elicit spontaneous speech. When a student is having difficulty in a particular area, we brainstorm about how we can help. For example, the PT was working to help a student use her walker to travel independently from one classroom to another. The student had the ability to move faster, but she seemed to purposely take more time than necessary. We created a special "telephone book" for her with pictures of her teachers and their 4-digit phone numbers. Each time she reached a classroom, she was to use her book to call her teacher to let them know she had made it. There were no more problems with her arriving late to class. She loved using the phone, and her teachers would praise her for walking so independently and promptly.

Advice for Someone Considering a Career in Special Education   Special education is a very challenging and worthwhile endeavor. Treat every student as an individual and search for a key to unlock his unique way of learning and interpreting the world. Parents and administrators are not the enemy, and every effort should be made to include them in meeting the special needs of your students. Remember that you are part of a team; you should not feel as though you are alone. A positive attitude takes less energy then a negative one.

To learn about teaching methods used by Mrs. Dowse and what it's like to teach students in schools hundreds of miles apart, go to the Teacher Feature module of Chapter 11 on the Companion Website at **www.prenhall.com/heward**

The Most Difficult Thing about Being a Special Educator   The most difficult thing for me is ensuring that classroom teachers and special education teachers follow through with my recommendations. I frequently have to remind the teachers to adhere to the modifications and adaptations needed for my students. I also have to ensure that teaching assistants understand why they are doing certain things that I have recommended. It takes a lot of patience and instruction to make sure that school personnel follow through.

Meaningful Accomplishments   During my first year, I worked with a 3-year-old boy who was congenitally blind. His parents were extremely protective of him, and it took a lot of instruction to educate the parents about their child's capabilities and that it was okay to let him explore and discover the world. This student is now in the first grade and flourishing.

I am a certified Irlen screener for scotopic sensitivity syndrome, which is a visual perceptual problem that causes words on a page to become distorted and causes physical symptoms while an individual is reading. Recently, I screened a student who was receiving special education services because of an identified learning disability. I discovered that she had severe scotopic sensitivity syndrome, and I referred her for a lens evaluation. She was fitted for Irlen lenses and immediately began reading everything she could get her hands on. After just 3 months, her scores on a standardized reading test went from the third-grade to the seventh-grade level.

S ixteen-year-old Maria is a bright, college-bound student who has been totally blind since birth. She recently took a series of intellectual and psychological tests and performed well, scoring at about her expected age and grade level. Something unusual happened, however, on one of the test items. The examiner handed Maria an unpeeled banana and asked, "What is this?" Maria held the banana and took several guesses but could not answer correctly. The examiner was astonished, as were Maria's teachers and parents. After all, this section of the test was intended for young children. Even though Maria had eaten bananas many times, she had missed out on one important aspect of the banana experience: she had never held and peeled a banana by herself.

This true story (adapted from Swallow, 1978) illustrates the tremendous importance of vision in obtaining information about the world in which we live. Many concepts that children with normal vision seem to acquire effortlessly may not be learned at all by children with visual impairments—or may be learned incorrectly—unless someone deliberately teaches them. Teachers who work with children with visual impairments find it necessary to plan and present a great many firsthand experiences, enabling children with visual impairments to learn by doing things for themselves. Good teachers understand, however, that even when a concept is deliberately presented to children with visual impairments, they may not learn it in exactly the same way that children with normal vision would.

This is true because, although students with visual impairments may learn to make good use of their other senses (hearing, touch, smell, and taste) as channels for contacting the environment, they do not totally compensate for loss of vision. Touch and taste cannot tell a child much about things that are far away or even just beyond her arms' reach. And while hearing can tell her a good deal about the near and distant environment, it seldom provides information that is as complete, continuous, or exact as the information people obtain from seeing their surroundings.

Vision plays a critical role in learning in the classroom. For example, normally sighted students are routinely expected to exercise several important visual skills. They must be able to focus on different objects and shift their vision from near to far as needed. They must have good hand-to-eye coordination, maintain visual concentration, discriminate among colors and letters, see and interpret many things simultaneously, and remember what they have seen. Children with visual impairments, however, have deficits in one or more of these abilities. As a result, they need special equipment and/or adaptations in instructional materials or procedures to function effectively in school.

Importance of visual experience

 Council for Exceptional Children Content Standards for Beginning Teachers–VI: Impact of visual impairment on learning and experience (VI2K4). **PRAXIS** Special Education Core Principles: Content Knowledge: I. Understanding Exceptionalities, Characteristics of students with disabilities, Sensory factors.

 To better understand what will be covered in this chapter, go to the Essential Concepts and Chapter-at-a-Glance modules in Chapter 11 on the Companion Website at **www.prenhall.com/heward**

Visual acuity, field of vision, tunnel vision

 Council for Exceptional Children | Content Standards for Beginning Teachers–VI: Specialized terminology used in assessing individuals with VI (VI8K1) (also VI1K5).
PRAXIS Special Education Core Principles: Content Knowledge: I. Understanding Exceptionalities, Characteristics of students with disabilities, Sensory factors.

DEFINITIONS

Unlike other disabilities covered by IDEA, visual impairment has both legal and educational definitions.

LEGAL DEFINITION OF BLINDNESS

The legal definition of blindness is based on visual acuity and field of vision. **Visual acuity**—the ability to clearly distinguish forms or discriminate details—is most often measured by reading letters, numbers, or other symbols from the Snellen chart. A peson with normal vision can read a 3/8" letter at 20 feet. The familiar phrase "20/20 vision" does not, as some people think, mean perfect vision; it simply indicates that at a distance of 20 feet, the eye can see what a normally seeing eye sees at that distance. As the bottom number increases, visual acuity decreases.

A person whose visual acuity is 20/200 or less in the better eye after the best possible correction with glasses or contact lenses is considered **legally blind** by the federal government (Social Security Administration, 2000). If Jane has 20/200 vision while wearing her glasses, she needs to stand at a distance of 20 feet to see what a normally sighted person can see from 200 feet. In other words, Jane must get much closer than normal to see things clearly. Her legal blindness means that she will likely find it difficult to use her vision in many everyday situations. But many children with 20/200, or even 20/400, visual acuity succeed in the regular classroom with special help. Some students' visual acuity is so poor they are unable to perceive fine details at any distance, even while wearing glasses or contact lenses. An individual with visual acuity of no better than 20/70 in the better eye after correction is considered **partially sighted** for legal and governmental purposes.

A person may also be considered legally blind if his **field of vision** is extremely restricted. When gazing straight ahead, a normal eye is able to see objects within a range of approximately 160 to 170 degrees. A person whose vision is restricted to an area of 20 degrees or less is considered legally blind. Some people with **tunnel vision** de-

FIGURE 11.1 A street scene as it might be viewed by persons with 20/20 or 20/200 visual acuity or a restricted field of vision

scribe their perception as viewing the world through a narrow tube; they may have good central vision but poor peripheral vision at the outer ranges of the visual field. Conversely, some eye conditions make it impossible for people to see things clearly in the center of the visual field but allow relatively good peripheral vision. Because a person's visual field often deteriorates gradually over a period of years without notice, a thorough visual examination should always include measurement of the visual field as well as visual acuity. Figure 11.1 shows what a person might see with normal or poor visual acuity or a limited field of vision.

Children who are legally blind are eligible to receive a wide variety of educational services, materials, and benefits from governmental agencies. They may, for example, obtain Talking Books and playback devices from the Library of Congress. Their schools may be able to buy books and educational materials from the American Printing House for the

Blind because the federal government allots states and local school districts a certain financial allowance for each legally blind student. A person who is legally blind is also entitled to vocational training, free U.S. mail service, and an income tax exemption. (To learn about services available to persons with visual impairments, go to the WebLinks for Chapter 11 in the Companion Website and click on the American Printing House for the Blind and American Federation of the Blind.)

Even though these services and benefits are important to know about, the legal definition of blindness is not especially useful to teachers. Some children who do not meet the criteria for legal blindness have visual impairments severe enough to require special education. Other students whose visual impairments qualify them as legally blind have little or no need for special education services.

Federal entitlements for children who are legally blind

 Council for Exceptional Children Content Standards for Beginning Teachers–VI: Federal entitlements that provide specialized equipment and materials for individuals with VI (VI1K1).

EDUCATIONAL DEFINITIONS OF VISUAL IMPAIRMENTS

The definition of *visual disability including blindness* in IDEA emphasizes the relationship between vision and learning: "an impairment in vision that, even with correction, adversely affects a child's educational performance." Students with visual impairments display a wide range of visual abilities—from total blindness to relatively good vision. The precise clinical measurements of visual acuity and visual field used to determine legal blindness have limited relevance for educators. Instead, educators classify students with visual impairments based on the extent to which they use vision and/or auditory/tactile means for learning (Bishop, 1996).

- A student who is *totally blind* receives no useful information through the sense of vision and must use tactile and auditory senses for all learning.
- A child who is *functionally blind* has so little vision that she learns primarily through the auditory and tactile senses; however, she may be able to use her limited vision to supplement the information received from the other senses and to assist with certain tasks (e.g., moving about the classroom).
- A child with **low vision** uses vision as a primary means of learning but may supplement visual information with tactile and auditory input.

Definitions of visual impairment

 Council for Exceptional Children Content Standards for Beginning Teachers–VI: Educational definitions, identification criteria, labeling issues, and incidence and prevalence figures for individuals with VI (VI1K3).
PRAXIS Special Education Core Principles: Content Knowledge: I. Understanding Exceptionalities, Definitions of disabilities.

AGE AT ONSET

Like other disabilities, visual impairment can be congenital (present at birth) or adventitious (acquired). Most visual impairments of school-age children are congenital. It is useful for a teacher to know the age at which a student acquired a visual impairment. A child who has been blind since birth naturally has quite a different perception of the world than does a child who lost his vision at age 12. The first child has a background of learning through hearing, touch, and the other nonvisual senses, whereas the second child has a large background of visual experiences on which to draw.

Children who have been blind since birth have a background of learning through hearing, touch, and the other nonvisual senses.

Most people who are adventitiously blind retain a visual memory of things they formerly saw. This memory can be helpful in a child's education; an adventitiously blind child may, for instance, remember the appearance of colors, maps, and printed letters. At the same time, however, the need for emotional support and acceptance may be greater than it might be for a congenitally blind child, who does not have to make a sudden adjustment to the loss of vision.

 ## PREVALENCE

Children with visual impairments constitute a very small percentage of the school-age population—fewer than 2 children in 1,000. During the 2000–2001 school year, 25,927 children ages 6 to 21 received special education services under IDEA within the category of visual impairments (U.S. Department of Education, 2002). According to Sacks (1998), almost one-half of the school-age population of students with visual impairments have at least one additional disability. Thus, the total number of students with visual impairments is somewhat higher than the data reported for IDEA because some students with visual impairments are served and counted under other disability categories such as deaf-blindness and multiple disabilities. Still, visual impairment is a low-incidence disability.

Even when viewed as a percentage of the population of students who receive special education services, the prevalence of visual impairments is very small: only about 0.4%, or 1 in 200, of all school-age children with IEPs are served under the disability category of visual impairments. Educators and parents of children with visual impairments frequently express concern about this low prevalence because they fear that when financial resources are limited, students with visual impairments may not receive adequate services from specially trained teachers. It can be particularly difficult for a local public school to provide comprehensive services for a child with visual impairment who resides in a rural area. Small school districts often cooperate with each other in employing special teachers for students with visual impairments.

 ## TYPES AND CAUSES OF VISUAL IMPAIRMENTS

 ### HOW WE SEE

Effective vision requires proper functioning of three anatomical systems of the eye: the optical system, the muscular system, and the nervous system. A simplified diagram of the eye appears in Figure 11.2. The eye's optical system collects and focuses light energy reflected from objects in the visual field. As light passes through the eye, several structures bend, or refract, the light to produce a clear image. The light first hits the **cornea,** the curved transparent membrane that protects the eye (much as an outer crystal protects a watch face). It then passes through the **aqueous humor,** a watery liquid that fills the front chamber of the eye. Next the light passes through the **pupil,** a circular hole in the center of the colored **iris;** the pupil contracts or expands to regulate the amount of light entering the eye. The light then passes through the **lens,** a transparent, elastic structure. After the light passes through the **vitreous humor,** a jellylike substance that fills most of the eye's interior, it reaches the innermost layer of the eye, the **retina.** This multilayered sheet of nerve tissue at the back of the eye has been likened to the film in a camera: for a clear image to be seen, the light rays must come to a precise focus on the retina.

The eye's muscular system enables **ocular motility,** the eye's ability to move. Six muscles attached to the outside of each eye enable it to search, track, converge, and fixate on images. These muscles also play a significant part in depth perception (**binocular vision**), the ability to fuse the separate images from each eye into a single, three-dimensional image. Inside the eye, tiny muscles adjust the shape of the lens, making it thicker or thinner, so the eye can bring objects at different distances into sharp focus (**accommodation**).

Age of onset

 Council for Exceptional Children Content Standards for Beginning Teachers–VI: Development of secondary senses when vision is impaired (VI2K2) (also, VI2K5).
PRAXIS Special Education Core Principles: Content Knowledge: I. Understanding Exceptionalities, Characteristics of students with disabilities, Sensory factors.

Prevalence of visual impairment

 Council for Exceptional Children Content Standards for Beginning Teachers–VI: Educational definitions, identification criteria, labeling issues, and incidence and prevalence figures for individuals with VI (VI1K3).
PRAXIS Special Education Core Principles: Content Knowledge: I. Understanding Exceptionalities, Incidence and prevalence of various types of disabilities.

Anatomy and function of the eye

 Council for Exceptional Children Content Standards for Beginning Teachers–VI: Basic terminology related to the structure and function of the human visual system (VI1K4).
PRAXIS Special Education Core Principles: Content Knowledge: I. Understanding Exceptionalities, Human development, Sensory development.

FIGURE 11.2   Basic parts of the human eye

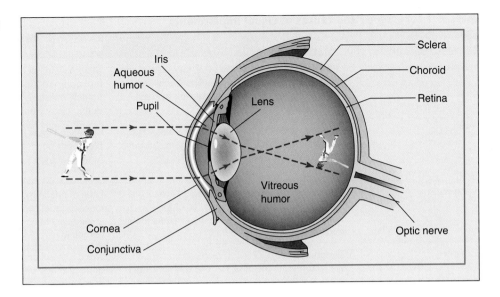

The eye's nervous system converts light energy into electrical impules and transmits that information to the brain, where it is processed into visual images. The retina consists of millions of light receptors called cones and rods. The **cones** enable detection of color and detail necessary for tasks such as reading and are located in the center of the retina and function best in good light. The **rods,** which are responsible for peripheral vision, detection of movement, and vision in dim light, are distributed around the periphery of the retina. The **optic nerve** carries the electrical messages from the cones and rods directly to the **visual cortex** at the base of the brain.

 CAUSES OF VISUAL IMPAIRMENTS

Damage or disturbances to any part of the eye's optical, muscular, or nervous systems can result in impaired vision. Causes of visual impairments are grouped into three broad categories: refractive errors, structural impairments, and cortical visual impairments (Sacks, 1998; Stiles & Knox, 1996).

Refractive Errors   **Refraction** is the process of bending light rays when they pass from one transparent structure into another. As just described, the normal eye refracts, or bends, light rays so that a clear image falls directly on the retina. However, for many people—perhaps half the general population—the size and shape of the eye prevent the light rays from focusing clearly on the retina. In **myopia,** or *nearsightedness,* the eye is longer than normal from front to back, causing the image to fall in front of the retina instead of exactly on it. A child with myopia can see near objects clearly; but more distant objects, such as a chalkboard or a movie, are blurred or not seen at all. The opposite of myopia is **hyperopia,** commonly called *farsightedness.* The hyperopic eye is shorter than normal, preventing the light rays from converging on the retina. A child with hyperopia has difficulty seeing near objects clearly but is able to focus well on more distant objects. Glasses or contact lenses can compensate for many refractive errors by changing the course of light rays to produce as clear a focus as possible.

Structural Impairments   Visual impairments can be caused by poor development of, damage to, or malfunction of one or more parts of the eye's optical or muscular systems. Cataracts and glaucoma are two of the numerous causes of visual impairment due to damage or disintegration of the eye itself. A **cataract** is a cloudiness in the lens of the eye that

Types and causes of visual impairment

Council for Exceptional Children   Content Standards for Beginning Teachers–VI: Basic terminolgy related to diseases and disorders of the human visual system (VI1K5).
PRAXIS Special Education Core Principles: Content Knowledge: I. Understanding Exceptionalities, Causation and prevention of disability.

TABLE 11.1 Types and causes of visual impairments

Condition	Definition/Cause	Remarks/Educational Implications
Albinism	Lack of pigmentation in the eyes, skin, and hair; results in moderate to severe visual impairment by reducing visual acuity and causing nystagmus; heredity	Children with albinism almost always have photophobia, a condition in which the eyes are extremely sensitive to light; eye fatigue may occur during close work
Amblyopia	Reduction in or loss of vision in the weaker eye from lack of use; caused by strabismus, unequal refractive errors, or opacities of the lens or cornea	Close work may result in eye fatigue, loss of place, poor concentration; seating should favor functional eye
Astigmatism	Distorted or blurred vision caused by irregularities in the cornea or other surfaces of the eye that produce images on retina not in equal focus (refractive error)	Loss of accommodation when object brought close to face; avoid long periods of reading or close tasks that cause discomfort; child may complain of headaches and fluctuating vision
Cataract	Blurred, distorted, or incomplete vision caused by cloudiness in the lens; caused by injury, malnutrition or rubella during pregnancy, glaucoma, retinitis pigmentosa, heredity, aging	Avoid glare of any kind; light source behind child; good contrast between print and paper; variation in near and distant tasks can prevent tiring
Color deficiency or color blindness	Difficulty distinguishing certain colors; red-green confusion is most common; caused by cone malformation or absence, macular deficiency, heredity	Usually not an educationally significant visual impairment; teach alternative ways to discriminate objects usually identified by color (e.g., tags for clothing colors, position of red and green on traffic lights)
Cortical visual impairment (CVI)	Impaired vision due to damage to or malfunction of the visual cortex and/or optic nerve; causes include anoxia, head injury, and infections of the central nervous system; many children with CVI have additional disabilities, such as cerebral palsy, seizure disorders, mental retardation	Visual functioning may fluctuate depending upon lighting conditions and attention; vision usually does not deteriorate, improvement sometimes occurs over a period of time; some children with CVI use their peripheral vision; some are photophobic; some are attracted to bright light and will gaze at the sun; visual images should be simple and presented singly
Diabetic retinopathy	Impaired vision as a result of hemorrhages and the growth of new blood vessels in the area of the retina due to diabetes; leading cause of blindness for people ages 20 to 64	Provide good lighting and contrast; magnification; pressure to perform can affect blood glucose
Glaucoma	Abnormally high pressure within the eye due to disturbances or blockages of the fluids that normally circulate within the eye; vision is impaired or lost entirely when the increased pressure damages the retina and optic nerve	Fluctuations in visual performance may frustrate child; be alert to symptoms of pain; eye drops administered on schedule; child may be subjected to teasing because of bulging eyes
Hyperopia (farsightedness)	Difficulty seeing near objects clearly but able to focus well on distant objects; caused by elongated eye that focuses images in front of the retina (refractive error)	Loss of accommodation when object brought close to face; avoid long periods of reading or close tasks that cause discomfort

blocks the light necessary for seeing clearly. **Glaucoma** is abnormally high pressure within the eye caused by disturbances or blockages of the fluids that normally circulate within the eye. Central and peripheral vision are impaired or lost entirely when the increased pressure damages the optic nerve.

Dysfunction of the muscles that control and move the eyes can make it difficult or impossible for a child to see effectively. **Nystagmus**, a rapid, involuntary, back-and-forth movement of the eyes in a lateral, vertical, or rotary direction, can cause problems in focusing and reading. **Strabismus** is an inability to focus on the same object with both eyes because imbalance of the eye muscles creates an inward or outward deviation of one or both

TABLE 11.1 *continued*

Condition	Definition/Cause	Remarks/Educational Implications
Macular degeneration	Central area of the retina gradually deteriorates, causing loss of clear vision in the center of the visual field; common in older adults but fairly rare in children	Tasks such as reading and writing difficult; prescribed low-vision aid or closed-circuit TV; good illumination; avoid glare
Myopia (nearsightedness)	Distant objects are blurred or not seen at all but can see near objects clearly; caused by elongated eye that focuses images in front of the retina (refractive error)	Encourage child to wear prescribed glasses or contact lens; for near tasks child may be more comfortable working without glasses and bringing work close to face
Nystagmus	Rapid, involuntary, back-and-forth movement of the eyes, which makes it difficult to focus on objects; when the two eyes cannot focus simultaneously, the brain avoids a double image by suppressing the visual input from one eye; the weaker eye (usually the one that turns inward or outward) can actually lose its ability to see; can occur on its own but is usually associated with other visual impairments	Close tasks for extended period can lead to fatigue; some children turn or tilt head to obtain the best focus; do not criticize this
Retinitis pigmentosa (RP)	The most common genetic disease of the eye; causes gradual degeneration of the retina; first symptom is usually difficulty seeing at night, followed by loss of peripheral vision; heredity	High illumination with no glare; contracting visual field causes difficulties with scanning and tracking skills necessary for tasks such as reading; teach student to locate visual objects with systematic search grid; as RP is progressive, curriculum should include mobility training, especially at night, and braille training if prognosis is loss of sight
Retinopathy of prematurity (ROP)	Caused by administering high levels of oxygen to at-risk infants; when the infants are later removed from the oxygen-rich incubators, the change in oxygen levels can produce an abnormally dense growth of blood vessels and scar tissue in the eyes, leading to visual impairment and often total blindness	High illumination, magnifiers for close work; telescopes for distance viewing; students may have brain damage resulting in mental retardation and/or behavior problems
Strabismus	Inability to focus on the same object with both eyes due to an inward or outward deviation of one or both eyes; caused by muscle imbalance; secondary to other visual impairments	Classroom seating should favor student's stronger eye; some students may use one eye for distance tasks, the other eye for near tasks; frequent rest periods may be needed during close work; may need more time to adjust to unfamiliar visual tasks

Sources: From Levack, Stone, & Bishop (1994); Mason (1997); Sacks (1998).

eyes. If left untreated, strabismus and other disorders of ocular motility can lead to permanent loss of vision.

Cortical Visual Impairments   Some children with visual impairments have nothing wrong with their eyes. The term **cortical visual impairments** (CVI) refers to decreased vision or blindness due to known or suspected damage to or malfunction of the parts of the brain that interpret visual information. Causes of CVI include insuficient oxygen at birth (anoxia), head injury, hydrocephalus, and infections of the central nervous system. Visual functioning may fluctuate depending upon environment, lighting conditions, and activities. Some children with CVI use their peripheral vision; some are photophobic; some are attracted to bright light; and some will gaze at the sun.

Table 11.1 summarizes some of the most common types and causes of visual impairments. Although a teacher seldom needs detailed knowledge concerning the etiology of a child's visual impairment, understanding how a student's visual impairment affects class-room performance is important. It is useful to know, for example, that Linda's cataracts make it difficult for her to read under strong lights, that Derek has only a small amount of central vision in his right eye, or that Yoko will need to administer eye drops to relieve the pressure caused by her glaucoma before leaving on a class field trip.

 # CHARACTERISTICS

 ## COGNITION AND LANGUAGE

*Cognition and language
development*

 Content Standards for Beginning Teachers–VI: Effects of visual impairment on development (VI2K3) (also, CC2K2). **PRAXIS** Special Education Core Principles: Content Knowledge: I. Understanding Exceptionalities, Characteristics of students with disabilities, Cognitive and linguistic factors.

This chapter began with a story about a bright teenage girl without sight who could not identify the object she was holding as a banana. Maria had eaten bananas many times, she could spell and read the word *banana,* and she could explain the best climate for growing bananas. But because she'd never held an unpeeled banana, Maria was not able to identify it.

Consider what two children, one with normal vision and one with limited or absent vision, might learn from everyday experiences with a family pet.

> Children with normal vision see a cat's mouth open when it meows or spits, so they can connect the sound to the cat. When they pet the kitty, they feel the soft fur and see the cat's entire body simultaneously. When Dad tells the cat to stop scratching the couch, they look at Dad, see that he is looking at the cat, and follow his gaze over to where the cat is pawing at the couch.
>
> The experience is different for children with visual impairments. They have no way of knowing what the meow, growl, or purr is. They can pinpoint where the sound is coming from, but they cannot see what it is coming from. When the cat remains still long enough, they can feel its soft fur, but they can feel only part of the cat at a time. They can't see that the cat has a head with ears, a body, four legs, four paws with claws, and a tail. . . . And if they get scratched, the paw comes out of and returns to nowhere. Children with visual impairments can still learn the concept of cat, but if they rely on incidental learning, it will take quite a while to put this jumble of isolated experiences together. (Ferrell, 1996, pp. 79–80)

Sighted children without other disabilities are constantly learning from their experiences and interactions with their environment. As they move about, the sense of sight provides a steady stream of detailed information about their environment and about relationships between things in that environment. Without any effort on their part or on the part of others, children with normal sight produce great stores of useful knowledge from everyday experiences. Visual impairments, however, preclude most such incidental learning.

The sense of vision gives children the ability to organize and make connections between different experiences, connections that help the child make the most of those experiences. Children who are blind perform more poorly than sighted children do on cognitive tasks requiring comprehension or relating different items of information. Impaired or absent vision makes it difficult to see (literally, of course, but also cognitively) the connections between experiences. "It is as though all the educational experiences of the blind child are kept in separate compartments" (Kingsley, 1997, p. 27).

This makes learning even simple language concepts such as "cats have tails" and "bananas are smooth" difficult. Abstract concepts, analogies, and idiomatic expressions can be particularly difficult for children who cannot see. Jeanna Mora Dowse shared this experience:

> One morning, the OT was working with a 4-year-old student who was blind. This student was taking his time walking to the therapy room, so the OT told him to "Shake a leg!" The student stopped, shook his right leg, and then continued walk-

ing as slowly as before. The OT had to explain to him that "Shake a leg!" was just an expression for "Hurry up."

There is no evidence that these challenges to learning restrict the potential of children with visual impairments. They do, however, magnify the importance of repeated, direct contact with concepts through nonvisual senses.

 ## MOTOR DEVELOPMENT AND MOBILITY

Blindness or severe visual impairment often leads to delays or deficits in motor development. Stone (1997) explains two reasons for this. First, a significant portion of the purposeful movements of fully sighted babies involves reaching for things they see. The child's efforts to grasp objects, especially those that are just out of reach, strengthen muscles and improve coordination, which in turn enable more effective movement. The absence of sight or clear vision, however, reduces the baby's motivation to move. For the child who is blind, the world is no more interesting when sitting up and turning her head from side to side than it is when she is lying on the floor. Second, a child without clear vision may move less often because movements in the past have resulted in painful contact with the environment.

In addition to limiting a child's opportunities to learn though contact and experience with the physical environment, decreased motor development and movement can lead to physical and social detachment. Children who are blind "may put their natural energy, which would otherwise have found purposeful outlets, into rocking, poking or flapping, all of which can affect their learning and social acceptability" (Stone, 1997, p. 89).

Even limited vision can have negative effects on motor development. Children with low vision have poorer motor skills than do children who are sighted. Their gross motor skills, especially balance, are weak. They frequently are unable to perform motor activities through imitation, and they are usually more careful of space (Bouchard & Tétreault, 2000).

 ## SOCIAL ADJUSTMENT AND INTERACTION

Compared with normally sighted children, children with visual impairments interact less during free time and are often delayed in the development of social skills (Erin, Dignan, & Brown, 1991; Skellenger, Hill, & Hill, 1992). Some young children with sensory impairments experience difficulty in receiving and expressing affection, behaviors that have been shown to facilitate future development in other areas of social competence (Compton & Niemeyer, 1994). Although many adolescents with visual impairments have best friends, many also struggle with social isolation and must work harder than their sighted peers to make and maintain friendships (Leigh & Barclay, 2000; Rosenblum, 1998, 2000; Sacks, Wolffe, & Tierney, 1998).

Students with visual impairments are often not invited to participate in group activities such as going to a ball game or a movie because sighted peers just assume they are not interested. Over time students with visual impairments

Motor development

 Content Standards for Beginning Teachers–VI: Effects of visual impairment on development (VI2K3) (also, CC2K2). **PRAXIS** Special Education Core Principles: Content Knowledge: I. Understanding Exceptionalities, Human development, Motor development.

Social and emotional development

Content Standards for Beginning Teachers–VI: Effects of visual impairment on development (VI2K3) (also, CC2K2). **PRAXIS** Special Education Core Principles: Content Knowledge: I. Understanding Exceptionalities, Characteristics of students with disabilities, Affective and social-adaptive factors.

There are virtually no limits to the kinds of activities in which students with visual impairments can participate. This spelunker is totally blind.

and their sighted age mates have fewer and fewer shared experiences and common interests as bases for conversation, social interactions, and friendships.

Rosenblum (2000) identifies several issues influencing the limited social involvement of many adolescents with visual impairments. Because of the low incidence of the disability, many children with visual impairments are unable to benefit from peers or adult role models who are experiencing the same challenges because of visual impairments. Social isolation becomes particularly pronounced for many teenagers with visual impairments when sighted peers obtain driver's licenses.

Another factor contributing to social difficulties is that the inability to see and respond to the social signals of others reduces opportunities for reciprocal interactions (Frame, 2000; Kirkwood, 1997). During a conversation, for example, a student who is blind cannot see the gestures, facial expressions, and changes in body posture used by his conversation partner. This inability to see important components of communication hampers the blind student's understanding of the conversation partner's message. And his failure to respond with socially appropriate eye contact, facial expressions, and gestures suggests lack of interest in his partner's communicative efforts and makes it unlikely that the individual will seek out his company in the future.

Some individuals with visual impairments engage in repetitive body movements or other behaviors such as body rocking, eye rubbing, hand flapping, and head weaving. These behaviors were traditionally referred to in the visual impairment literature as "blindisms" or "blind mannerisms" (Kingsley, 1997). *Stereotypic behavior* (stereotypy) is a more clearly defined term that subsumes blindisms and mannerisms. It is also a more appropriate term: such behaviors are also exhibited by other children and do not occur among all children who are blind (Gense & Gense, 1994).

Although not usually harmful, stereotypic behavior can place a person with visual impairments at a great social disadvantage because these actions are conspicuous and may call negative attention to the person. It is not known why many children with visual impairments engage in stereotypic behaviors (Bak, 1999). However, various behavioral interventions such as reinforcement of incompatible behaviors and self-monitoring have been used to help individuals with visual impairments reduce stereotypic behaviors such as repetitive body rocking (McAdam, O'Cleirigh, & Cuvo, 1993) or head drooping during conversation (Raver, 1984).

Many persons who have lost their sight report that the biggest difficulty socially is dealing with the attitudes and behavior of those around them. The beliefs, superstitions, and mythology that form "the folklore of blindness" no doubt influence some of those attitudes and behaviors.

> The influence of the folklore of blindness generally is expressed in attitudes towards (and by) blind people that sound absurd but are genuinely felt. . . . One finds that folk beliefs are divided into two groups. On the negative side of this dichotomy are the beliefs that blind people are either helpless and pathetic or evil and contagious and probably deserve their fate. On the more positive side are the beliefs that blind people have special or even magical abilities, special powers of perception, and deserve special attention. (Wagner-Lampl & Oliver, 1994, pp. 267–268)

 ## EDUCATIONAL APPROACHES

Numerous specialized teaching methods and curriculum materials have been developed in an effort to overcome the obstacles to learning presented by blindness and low vision. Advances in instructional methodology and, in particular, technology have greatly increased access to the general education curriculum and academic success among students with visual impairments. As one high school student who is blind remarked, "By taking advantage of technology around me, I am able to have an education equal to my sighted peers" (Leigh & Barclay, 2000, p. 129). However, the education of students with visual impairments is a field with a history of more than 150 years, and today's developments were made possible by the contributions of many teachers and researchers who came before. Table 11.2 highlights some key historical events and their implications for the education of students with visual impairments.

Stereotypic behavior

Council for Exceptional Children   Content Standards for Beginning Teachers–VI: Effects of visual impairment on development (VI2K3) (also, CC2K2). **PRAXIS** Special Education Core Principles: Content Knowledge: I. Understanding Exceptionalities, Characteristics of students with disabilities, Affective and social-adaptive factors.

History of education of students with VI

Council for Exceptional Children   Content Standards for Beginning Teachers–VI: Historical foundations of education of individuals with VI (VI1K2). **PRAXIS** Special Education Core Principles: Content Knowledge: II. Legal and Societal Issues, Historical movements/trends affecting the connections between special education and the larger society.

TABLE 11.2	A history of the education of children with visual impairments: Key events and implications	
Date	**Historical Event**	**Educational Implications**
1784	Shocked at seeing people who were blind performing as jesters or begging on the streets of Paris, Victor Hauy resolved to teach them more dignified ways of earning a living. He started the first school for children who were blind. Hauy's curriculum included reading and writing (using embossed print), music, and vocational skills.	The competence of Hauy's students influenced the establishment of other residential schools in Europe and Russia in the early 19th century.
1821	Samuel Gridley Howe founded the Perkins School for the Blind, the oldest and best-known residential school for students who are blind.	Many methods and materials for teaching students with visual impairments were first developed at Perkins. Anne Sullivan and her famous pupil, Helen Keller, spent several years at Perkins.
1829	The first draft of a tactile method of reading created by Louis Braille was published. He was a student at a Paris school for children who were blind.	Braille's system of embossed six-dot cells proved the most efficient of several methods of reading by touch and is the primary means of literacy for the blind today.
1862	The Snellen chart was developed by a Dutch ophthalmologist.	The chart provided a fast, standardized test of visual acuity; it is still used today as a visual screening tool for schoolchildren.
1900; 1909/1913	The first public school class for children who were blind opened in Chicago; the first classes for children with low vision began in Cleveland and Boston.	Students with visual impairments were educated in public schools; children with low vision were educated in special "sight-saving classes" in which all instruction was conducted orally.
1932	The Library of Congress made Talking Books available to any person who is legally blind.	Availability of recorded books and other print materials enhanced the range of curriculum content accessible to students with visual impairments.
1938	The first itinerant teaching program for children with visual impairments attending regular classrooms began in Oakland, California.	This marked the beginning of the long and relatively successful history of including children with visual impairments in regular classrooms.
1940s–1950s	Thousands of children became blind or severely visually impaired by retinopathy of prematurity (ROP) caused by the increased use of oxygen with premature infants.	Residential schools were not able to accommodate the large influx of visually impaired children; thus, special education programs and services for students with visual impairments became much more widely available in the public schools in the 1950s and 1960s.
1944	Richard Hoover developed a system for teaching orientation and mobility (O&M) skills to persons with visual impairments. It featured a long white cane.	This system of O&M and the "Hoover cane" become standard parts of the curriculum for students with visual impairments.
1951	The Perkins brailler was invented.	The first fast and easy method for writing braille improved access to and participation in education.
Mid-1960s	Natalie Barraga published research showing that children with low vision do not lose their remaining sight by using it and that visual functioning can be improved by use.	Barraga's (1964, 1970) work was instrumental in ending the sight-saving classes attended by children with low vision for more than 50 years.

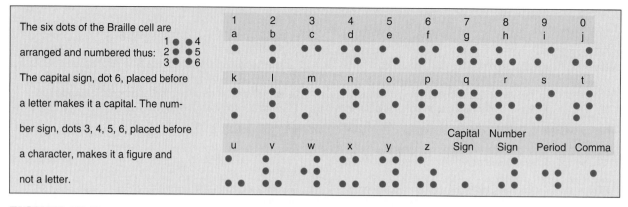

FIGURE 11.3 **The braille system for representing numbers and letters**
Source: From the Division for the Blind and Physically Handicapped, Library of Congress, Washington, DC.

 SPECIAL ADAPTATIONS FOR STUDENTS WHO ARE BLIND

Because they must frequently teach skills and concepts that most children acquire through vision, teachers of students who are blind must plan and carry out activities that will help their students gain as much information as possible through the nonvisual senses and by participation in active, practical experiences. For example, a blind child may hear a bird singing but get no concrete idea of the bird itself from the sound alone. A teacher interested in teaching such a student about birds might plan a series of activities that has the student touch birds of various species and manipulate related objects such as eggs, nests, and feathers. The student might assume the responsibility for feeding a pet bird at home or in the classroom. Through such experiences, the child with visual impairments can gradually obtain a more thorough and accurate knowledge of birds than she could if her education were limited to reading books about birds, memorizing vocabulary, or feeling plastic models.

Braille, brailler, slate and stylus

Council for Exceptional Children — Content Standards for Beginning Teachers–VI: Strategies for teaching Braille reading and writing (VI4K1).
PRAXIS Special Education Core Principles: Content Knowledge: III. Delivery of Services to Students with Disabilities, Curriculum and Instruction, Technology for sensory disabilities.

Braille Braille is the primary means of literacy for people who are blind. **Braille** is a tactile system of reading and writing in which letters, words, numbers, and other systems are made from arrangements of raised dots (see Figure 11.3). In some ways, braille is like the shorthand that secretaries use. A set of 189 abbreviations, called *contractions*, helps save space and permits faster reading and writing. For example, when the letter *r* stands by itself, it means "rather." The word "myself" in braille is written "myf." Frequently used words, such as "the," "and," "with," and "for," have their own special contractions. For example, the "and" symbol ⠯ appears four times in the following sentence:

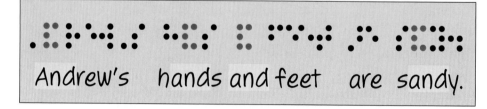

Andrew's hands and feet are sandy.

Students who are blind can read braille much more rapidly than they can read the raised letters of the standard alphabet. The speed of braille reading varies a great deal from student to student; however, it is almost always much slower (about 100 words per minute for good braille readers) than the speed of print reading. Most children who are blind are introduced to braille in the first grade. Rex, Koenig, Wromsley, and Baker (1994) recommend that children receive 1½ to 2 hours of instruction in reading and writing braille each day since this is the same amount of time typically devoted to literacy skills for sighted children in the primary grades. Rather than have the child learn to write out every word, letter by letter, and later un-learn this approach, teachers introduce contractions early in the program. Of course, it is important for the child to eventually know the full and correct spelling of words, even if every letter does not appear separately in braille.

Although it usually takes several years for children to become thoroughly familiar with braille, it is no more difficult than learning to read print for sighted children.

> True, some people claim that the braille code is more *complex* than the print code because more symbols are used. But if a child receives good reading instruction and has a rich variety of background experiences, learning to read braille should not be "difficult." If a child says that braille is difficult to read, it is probably because she has heard an adult say so. (Koenig, 1996, pp. 233–234)

Young children generally learn to write braille by using a *brailler*, a six-keyed, mechanical device that somewhat resembles a typewriter. Older students are usually introduced to the *slate and stylus*, in which the braille dots are punched out one at a time by hand, from right to left. The slate-and-stylus method has certain advantages in note taking; for example, it is much smaller and quieter than the brailler.

Braille Technological Aids   Most braille books are large, expensive, and cumbersome. It can be difficult for students to retrieve information quickly when they must tactually review many pages of braille books or notes. Technological developments have made braille more efficient, thus enabling many students who are blind to function more independently in regular classrooms, universities, and employment settings.

Braille 'n Speak is a battery-powered, pocket-sized device for note taking with a keyboard for braille entry and voice output. It can translate braille into synthesized speech or print.

The Mountbatten Brailler is an electronic brailler that is easier to use than the manual, mechanical brailler. Braille embossers print braille from digital text, and some printers produce pages with both braille and print formats, enabling blind and sighted readers to use the same copy.

Declining Braille Literacy   The vast majority of employed adults who are blind use braille at work; and congenitally blind adults who learn to read braille have higher employment rates, attain greater educational levels, earn more income, and spend more time reading than do those who learn to read print (Ryles, 1996). Nevertheless, there has been a decline in braille literacy over the years (Wittenstein, 1994). In comparison to the early 1960s, when it was estimated that nearly half of blind students could read and write braille, a national census in 1992 found that only 10% of legally blind students in grades K through 12 were braille readers (American Printing House for the Blind, 1992). Visual readers—students who primarily use regular or large-print materials—made up the largest group (27%), with 10% being auditory readers, who use recorded materials or are read to aloud. Nonreaders (31%)—students with visual impairments with additional severe disabilities—and prereaders (22%) made up the rest of the student population.

In response to the concern about declining braille literacy, the 1997 amendments to IDEA specified for the first time that IEP teams for students with visual impairments make a determination of the student's preferred reading medium and that instruction in braille must be considered. In addition, at least 27 states have passed legislation, called "braille bills," making braille equipment and instruction available for students if the parents or any other member of the IEP team indicates it is needed and requiring teachers of students with visual impairments to be proficient in braille. IEP teams can use the Learning Media Assessment to help determine the most appropriate reading medium for students with visual impairments (Koenig & Holbrook, 1993).

Tactile Aids and Manipulatives   Manipulatives are generally recognized as effective tools in teaching beginning mathematics skills to elementary students. When using most

Braille technological aids

 Content Standards for Beginning Teachers–VI: Strategies for teaching Braille reading and writing (VI4K1).
PRAXIS Special Education Core Principles: Content Knowledge: III. Delivery of Services to Students with Disabilities, Curriculum and Instruction, Technology for sensory disabilities.

Tactile aids and manipulatives

Content Standards for Beginning Teachers–VI: Strategies for teaching use of the abacus, talking calculator, tactile graphics, and adapted science equipment (VI4K7).
PRAXIS Special Education Core Principles: Content Knowledge: III. Delivery of Services to Students with Disabilities, Curriculum and Instruction, Technology for sensory disabilities.

The brailler is a six-keyed device that punches the raised braille dots in special paper.

manipulatives, such as Cuisenaire rods, however, sighted students use length and color to distinguish the various numerical values of the rods. Belcastro (1989) has developed a set of rods that enables students who are blind to quickly identify different values by feeling the lengths and tactile markings associated with each number.

Another mathematical aid for students who are blind is the Cranmer abacus. Long used in Japan, the abacus has been adapted to assist students who are blind in learning number concepts and making calculations. Manipulation of the abacus beads is particularly useful in counting, adding, and subtracting.

For more advanced mathematical functions, the student is likely to use the Speech-Plus talking calculator, a small electronic instrument that performs most of the operations of any standard calculator. It "talks" by voicing entries and results aloud and also presents them visually in digital form. This is only one of many instances in which the development of synthetic speech technology has helpful implications for people who are blind. Talking clocks and spelling aids are also available.

In the sciences and social studies, several adaptations encourage students who are blind to use their tactile and auditory senses for firsthand manipulation and discovery. Examples are embossed relief maps and diagrams, three-dimensional models, and electronic probes that give an audible signal in response to light. Curriculum modification projects, such as MAVIS (Materials Adaptation for Students with Visual Impairments in the Social Studies) and SAVI (Science Activities for the Visually Impaired), emphasize how students with visual impairments can, with some modifications, participate in learning activities along with normally sighted students.

Technological Aids for Reading Print The Optacon (optical-to-tactile converter) is a small, hand-held electronic device that converts regular print into a readable vibrating form. The Optacon does not convert print into braille but into a configuration of raised pins representing the letter the camera is viewing. When the tiny camera of the Optacon is held over a printed *E*, for example, the user feels on the tip of one finger a vertical line and three horizontal lines. Although extensive training and practice are required, many children and adults who are blind are able to read regular print effectively with the aid of the Optacon. The Optacon II enables the user to scan print on computer screens.

The L&H Kurzweil 1000 is a sophisticated computer-based reading system that uses an optical character recognition (OCR) system to scan and read printed text with synthetic speech. The user can regulate the speed, have the machine spell out words letter by letter if desired, and even choose from 14 different voices. The "intelligence" of the Kurzweil reading machines is constantly being improved; and the machines are currently in use at most residential schools and also in many public school programs, public libraries, rehabilitation centers, and colleges and universities. The first Kurzweil Reading Machine weighed more than 300 pounds and cost $50,000. But the costs of Reading Machines have decreased greatly, and machines manufactured by L&H Kurzweil, IBM, and Arenstone with computer accessories can be purchased for about $1,000.

Computer Access   Assistive technology that provides access to personal computers offers tremendous opportunities for the education, employment, communication, and leisure enjoyment of individuals with visual impairments. These technologies include (1) hardware and sofware that magnify screen images, (2) speech recognition software that enables the user to tell the computer what to do, and (3) software that converts text files to synthesized speech.

Keyboarding is an important means of communication between children who are blind and their sighted classmates and teachers and is also a useful skill for further education and employment. Instruction in keyboarding should begin as early as feasible in the child's school program. Today, handwriting is seldom taught to students who are totally blind, with the noteworthy exception of learning to sign one's name in order to assume responsibilities such as maintaining a bank account, registering to vote, and applying for a job.

 SPECIAL ADAPTATIONS FOR STUDENTS WITH LOW VISION

Between 75% and 80% of school-age children enrolled in educational programs for visually impaired students have some potentially useful vision. Learning by students with low vision need not be restricted to the nonvisual senses, and they generally learn to read print (Corn & Koenig, 1996).

Functional Vision   *Visual efficiency* and *functional vision* are related terms denoting how well a person uses whatever vision he has (Barraga & Erin, 1992; Corn, 1989). A child's functional vision cannot be determined or predicted by measurements of visual acuity or visual field. Some children with severe visual impairments use the limited vision they have very capably. Other children with relatively minor visual impairments are unable to function as visual learners; they may even behave as though they were blind.

Utley, Roman, and Nelson (1998) suggest that vision is functional when one or more visual-motor skills (e.g., fixation, scanning, tracking, gaze shift; see Table 11.3) (1) are essential steps in the accurate and efficient performance of a task; (2) promote more independent performance in home, school, vocational, or community environments; or (3) enhance the degree of choice and autonomy of an individual, thereby enhancing her quality of life. The fundamental premises underlying the development of functional vision is that children learn to see, that functional vision is teachable behavior, and that children must be actively involved in using their own vision (Utley et al., 1998).

Merely furnishing a classroom with attractive things for children to see is not sufficient. A child with low vision may, without training, be unable to derive much meaningful information through vision. Forms may be perceived as vague masses and shapeless, indistinct blobs. Systematic training in visual recognition and discrimination is needed to help children learn to use their visual impressions intelligently and effectively, to make sense out of what they see. Instruction in use of vision skills should not be limited to isolated "visual stimulation sessions" but incorporated into all parts of the visually impaired student's program (Ferrell & Muir, 1996), and visual skills should be taught within the context of meaningful activities for the student (Downing & Bailey, 1990). For example, instead of having the child with low vision practice her visual skills by sorting miscellaneous junk objects, she could use those skills while learning to make a fruit and ice cream drink.

Optical Devices   Many ophthalmologists and optometrists specialize in the assessment and treatment of low vision. A professional examination can help determine which types of optical aids, if any, can benefit a particular child with low vision. These special devices might include glasses and contact lenses, small hand-held telescopes, and magnifiers placed on top of printed pages. Such aids cannot give normal vision to children with visual impairments but may help them perform better at certain tasks, such as reading small print or seeing distant objects.

Computer access and keyboarding

 Council for Exceptional Children   Content Standards for Beginning Teachers–VI: Strategies for teaching technology skills to individuals with VI (VI4K6) (also, VI4K5). **PRAXIS** Special Education Core Principles: Content Knowledge: III. Delivery of Services to Students with Disabilities, Curriculum and Instruction, Technology for sensory disabilities.

Visual efficiency/visual functioning

 Council for Exceptional Children   Content Standards for Beginning Teachers–VI: Strategies for teaching visual efficiency skills and use of print adaptations, optical devices, and non-optical devices (VI4K9).

Optical devices

 Council for Exceptional Children   Content Standards for Beginning Teachers–VI: Strategies for teaching visual efficiency skills and use of print adaptations, optical devices, and non-optical devices (VI4K9).

TABLE 11.3 Definitions and examples of four visual and visual-motor skills

Visual and Visual-Motor Skills	Definitions and Examples
Fixation	*Definition:* Active alignment of the line of sight (i.e., visual axis) in one or both eyes on a stationary object or person. *Example:* Looking at a tube of toothpaste while reaching to pick it up and apply it to the toothbrush.
Scanning	*Definition:* Visually searching for an object or person among a display of visual stimuli. *Example:* Visually locating the appropriate bus or van at dismissal time.
Tracking	*Definition:* Visually following a moving stimulus. *Example:* Watching the trajectory of coins as they are sorted into the appropriate locations in the cash drawer.
Gaze shift	*Definition:* Shifting fixation in space from one location to another. *Example:* Fixating on one type of cutlery and then others (i.e., first soup spoons; then forks, knives, and teaspoons) as the appropriate silverware for a particular meal is selected.

Source: From Utley, B. L., Roman, C., & Nelson, G. L. (1998). Functional vision. In S. Z. Sacks & R. K. Silberman (Eds.). *Educating students who have visual impairments with other disabilities* (p. 399). Baltimore: Paul H. Brookes Publishing Co., adapted with permission.

Optical aids are usually specialized rather than all-purpose, and children whose vision is extremely limited are more likely to use monocular (one-eye) than binocular (two-eye) aids, especially for seeing things at a distance. Juanita might, for example, use her glasses for reading large print, a magnifier stand for reading smaller print, and a monocular (one-eye) telescope for viewing the chalkboard. A usual disadvantage of corrective lenses and magnifiers is that the more powerful they are, the more they tend to distort or restrict the peripheral field of vision. Some field-widening lenses and devices are now available for students with limited visual fields. These include prisms and fish-eye lenses designed to make objects appear smaller so that a greater area can be perceived on the unimpaired portions of a student's visual field. It is usually a good idea to furnish optical aids on a trial or loan basis so that the student can gradually learn to use and evaluate them in natural settings. A follow-up session should then be scheduled.

Closed-circuit television systems are used in some classrooms to enable students with low vision to read regular-sized printed materials. These systems usually include a sliding table on which a book is placed, a television camera with a zoom lens mounted above the book, and a television monitor nearby. The student is able to adjust the size, brightness, and contrast of the material and can select either an ordinary black-on-white image or a negative white-on-black image, which many students prefer. The teacher may also have a television monitor that lets him see the student's work without making repeated trips to the student's desk. A disadvantage of closed-circuit television systems is that they are usually not portable, so the student who uses television as a primary reading medium is largely restricted to the specially equipped classroom or library.

Reading Print   Students with low vision use three basic approaches for reading print: (1) *approach magnification* (reducing the distance between the eye and the page of print from 40 cm to 5 cm results in 8× magnification) (Jose, 1983), (2) *lenses* (optical devices), and (3) *large print* (Corn & Ryser, 1989). Many books and other materials are available in large print for children with low vision. The American Printing House for the Blind produces books in 18-point type. Some states and other organizations produce large-type materials, but the size and style of the print fonts, spacing, paper, and quality of production vary widely. The sentence you are reading now is set in 10-point type. Here are four examples of different large-print type sizes:

CHAPTER 11

BLINDNESS AND LOW VISION

Reading print

 Council for Exceptional Children   Content Standards for Beginning Teachers–VI: Strategies for teaching visual efficiency skills and use of print adaptations, optical devices, and non-optical devices (VI4K9). **PRAXIS** Special Education Core Principles: Content Knowledge: III. Delivery of Services to Students with Disabilities, Curriculum and Instruction, Modification of materials and equipment.

This is 14 point type.
This is 18 point type.
This is 20 point type.
This is 24 point type.

Although print size is an important variable, other equally important factors to consider are the quality of the printed material, the contrast between print and page, the spacing between lines, and the illumination of the setting in which the child reads. It is generally agreed that a child with visual impairments should use the smallest print size that she can read comfortably. A child may be able to transfer from large print to smaller print as reading efficiency increases, just as most normally sighted children do. Table 11.4 compares the advantages and disadvantages of large-print materials and optical devices.

A significant number of children with low vision are able to learn to read using regular-sized print with or without the use of optical aids. This permits a much wider variety of materials and eliminates the added cost of obtaining large-print books or enlarging texts with special duplicating machines. Corn and Ryser (1989) obtained information from the teachers of 399 students with low vision on variables such as reading speed and achievement, fatigue, and access to various materials. They concluded that, in most instances, reading regular print with an optical device is preferable to large-print materials.

Classroom Adaptations   A number of minor classroom adaptations can be very important for students with low vision. As Bennett (1997) points out, the most effective low vision device is proper light. Most regular classrooms have adequate lighting, but special lamps may still be helpful for some children. Many students benefit from desks with adjustable or tilting tops so that they can read and write at close range without constantly bending over and casting a shadow. Writing paper should have a dull finish to reduce glare; an off-white color such as buff or ivory is generally better than white. Worksheets photocopied on colored paper can be difficult for students with low vision to use; if needed, an aide or classmate can first go over the worksheet with a dark pen or marker. Some teachers have found it helpful to give students with low vision chairs with wheels so that they can easily move around the chalkboard area or other places in the classroom where instruction is taking place without constantly getting up and down. A teacher can make many other modifications using common sense and considering the needs of the individual student with low vision. (For suggestions on helping students with low vision in the classroom, see (Teaching & Learning, "Helping the Student with Low Vision," later in this chapter.)

EXPANDED CURRICULUM PRIORITIES

In addition to learning to use braille, functional vision skills, and low vision aids, the "expanded core curriculum" (Hatlen, 1996) for students with visual impairments includes orientation and mobility, listening skills, and functional life skills.

TABLE 11.4 **Large-print materials and optical devices: Advantages and disadvantages**

Large-Print Materials	Optical Devices
Advantages	**Advantages**
• Little or no instruction is needed to use a large-print book or other materials.	• Users have access to materials of various sizes, such as regular texts, newspapers, menus, and maps.
• A low vision clinical evaluation is not needed.	• Optical devices have a lower cost per child than large-print materials do.
• Students carry large-print books like other students carry books in their classes.	• Devices are lighter weight and more portable than large-print materials are.
• Funds for large-print books come from school districts that may require parental or other funding for optical devices.	• There is no ordering or waiting time for production or availability.
	• Users have access to distant print and objects, such as chalkboards, signs, and people.
Disadvantages	**Disadvantages**
• Fewer words can be seen at once; large-print materials are more difficult to read smoothly with a natural sweep of eye movements.	• A low vision clinical evaluation must be obtained for the prescription of optical devices.
• Enlarging print by photocopy emphasizes imperfect letters.	• Funding for clinical evaluation and optical devices must be obtained.
• Pictures are in black, white, and shades of gray.	• Instruction in the use of the optical devices is needed.
• Fractions, labels on diagrams, maps, and so forth are enlarged to a print size smaller than 18-point type.	• The cosmetics of optical devices may cause self-consciousness.
• The size and weight of large-print texts make them difficult to handle.	• Optical problems associated with the optics of devices need to be tolerated.
• Large-print materials are not readily available after the school years, and students may be nonfunctional readers with regular-size type.	

Source: A. Corn & G. Ryser, "Access to Print for Students with Low Vision." *Journal of Visual Impairment & Blindness, 83,* 340–349. Reprinted with permission from American Foundation for the Blind, 15 West 16th St., New York, NY 10011.

Orientation and Mobility **Orientation** is knowing where you are, where you are going, and how to get there by interpreting information from the environment. **Mobility** involves moving safely and efficiently from one point to another. Although the two sets of skills are complementary, orientation and mobility are not the same thing (Hill & Snook-Hill, 1996). A person can know where he is but not be able to move safely in that environment, and a person may be mobile but get disoriented or lost.

Orientation and mobility (O&M) instruction is considered a related service by IDEA and is included in the IEP of virtually all children with significant visual impairments. *O&M specialists* have developed many specific techniques (e.g., trailing, squaring off, using arms as bumpers) and mobility devices (e.g., a shopping cart, suitcase on wheels) to teach students with visual impairments to understand their environment and maneuver through it safely and effectively (Perla & Ducret, 1999; Tellefson, 2000; Tolla, 2000).

For most students, more time and effort are spent in orientation training than in learning specific mobility techniques. It is extremely important that, from an early age, children with visual impairments be taught basic concepts that will familiarize them with their own bodies and their surroundings. For example, they must be taught that the place where the leg bends is called a "knee" and that rooms have walls, doors, windows, corners, and ceilings.

Cane Skills   The long cane is the most widely used device for adults with severe visual impairments who travel independently (Jacobson, 1993). The traveler does not tap the cane but sweeps it lightly in an arc while walking to gain information about the path ahead. Properly used, the cane serves as both a bumper and a probe. It acts as a bumper by protecting the body from obstacles such as parking meters and doors; it is also a probe to detect in advance things such as drop-offs or changes in travel surface (e.g., from grass to concrete or from a rug to a wooden floor).

Even though mastery of cane skills can do much to increase a person's independence and self-esteem, cane use exacts physical effort and poses certain disadvantages (Gitlin, Mount, Lucas, Weirich, & Gramberg, 1997). The cane cannot detect overhanging obstacles such as tree branches and provides only fragmentary information about the environment, particularly if the person who is blind is in new or unfamiliar surroundings. Unfortunately, many adventitiously blinded persons do not begin learning cane travel skills until 1 to 2 years after losing their sight; they mention concern about acceptance by others and the negative stigmas they believe are associated with the cane (Wainapel, 1989).

Until recently, formal O&M instruction, especially for cane use, was seldom given to children younger than about 12 years of age. However, the importance of early development of travel skills and related concepts is now generally recognized. Today, it is not at all unusual for preschool children to benefit from the services of an O&M specialist, but there is disagreement over which, if any, mobility device is most suitable for initial use by very young children (Dykes, 1992). Professionals recognize the long cane's benefits of increased protection and confidence while traveling but question whether preschoolers can handle the motor and conceptual demands of long cane use. These concerns have led to the development of a variety of alternative mobility devices, including modified and smaller canes such as the Connecticut precane (Foy, Von Scheden, & Waiculonis, 1992) and the kiddy cane (Pogrund, Fazzi, & Schreier, 1993).

Under the watchful eyes of an orientation and mobility specialist, Matthew is learning how to gain information about the path ahead by sweeping his cane in an arc.

Guide Dogs   Fewer than 2% of people with visual impairments travel with the aid of guide dogs (Hill & Snook-Hill, 1996). Like the cane traveler, the guide dog user must have good O&M skills to select a route and to be aware of the environment. The dog wears a special harness and has been trained to follow several basic verbal commands, to provide protection against obstacles, and to ensure the traveler's safety. Guide dogs are especially helpful when a person must travel over complicated or unpredictable routes, as in large cities. Several weeks of intensive training at special guide dog agencies are required before the person and the dog can work together effectively. Guide dogs are not usually available to children under 16 years of age or to people with multiple disabilities. Young children, however, should have exposure to and positive experiences with dogs so they are comfortable with them and can make informed choices later about the possibilities of working with a guide dog (Young, 1997).

Helping the Student with Low Vision

What does a child with low vision actually see? It is difficult for us to know. We can obtain some idea of total blindness by wearing a blindfold, but the majority of children with visual impairments are not totally blind. Even when two children share the same cause of visual impairment, it is unlikely that they see things in exactly the same way. And each child may see things differently at different times.

Corn (1989; Corn & Koenig, 1996) believes that curriculum development and instructional planning for children with low vision should be guided by some basic premises about low vision and its effects on a person:

- *Children with congenital low vision view themselves as whole.* Although it may be proper to speak of residual vision in reference to those who experience adventitious low vision, those with congenital low vision do not have a normal vision reference. They view the world with all of the vision they have ever had.
- *Children with low vision generally view the environment as stationary and clear.* Although there are exceptions, it is a misconception that people with low vision live in an impressionistic world in which they are continuously wanting to clear the image.
- *Low vision offers a different aesthetic experience.* Low vision may alter an aesthetic experience, but it does not necessarily produce a lesser one.

- *The use of low vision is not always the most efficient or preferred method of functioning.* For some tasks, the use of vision alone or in combination with other senses may reduce one's ability to perform. For example, using vision may not be the most efficient method for determining how much salt has been poured on one's food.
- *Those who have low vision may develop a sense of visual beauty, enjoy their visual abilities, and use vision to learn.*

Suggestions for Teachers

The following suggestions for teachers of students with low vision are from the Vision Team, a group of specialists in visual impairment who work with regular classroom teachers in 13 school districts in Hennepin County, Minnesota.

- Using the eyes does not harm them. The more children use their eyes, the greater their efficiency will be.
- Holding printed material close to the eyes may be the child with low vision's way of seeing best. It will not harm the eyes.
- Although eyes cannot be strained from use, a child with low vision's eyes may tire more quickly. A change of focus or activity helps.
- Copying is often a problem for children with low vision. The child may need a shortened assignment or more time to do classwork.

Although owning a guide dog is a major responsibility and sometimes inconvenient, many owners report increased confidence and independence in traveling and say that their dogs often serve as ice breakers for interactions with sighted people (Hill & Snook-Hill, 1996; Minor, 2001). However, guide dogs are not pets but working companions for their owners, and sighted people should abide by the following guidelines (Ulrey, 1994):

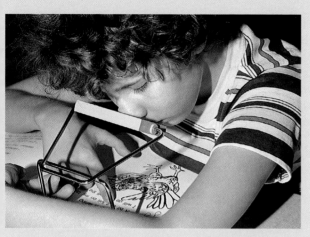
Low-vision aids should be portable and easy to use.

- It is helpful if the teacher verbalizes as much as possible while writing on the chalkboard or using the overhead projector.
- The term *legally blind* does not mean educationally blind. Most children who are legally blind function educationally as sighted children.
- Contrast, print style, and spacing can be more important than the size of the print.
- One of the most important things a child with low vision learns in school is to accept the responsibility of seeking help when necessary rather than waiting for someone to offer help.
- In evaluating quality of work and applying discipline, the teacher best helps the child with low vision by using the same standards that are used with other children.

Using Low-Vision Aids
Children who have low-vision aids, such as special eyeglasses, magnifiers, and telescopes, may need instruction and assistance in learning how to use them most effectively. Here are some tips for children to help them become accustomed to low-vision aids:

- *Low-vision aids take time to get used to.* At first, it seems like just a lot more things to take care of and carry around, but each aid you have will help you with a special job of seeing. You will get better with practice. In time, reaching for your telescope to read the chalkboard will seem as natural as picking up a pencil or pen to write. It's all a matter of practice.
- *Lighting is very important.* Always work with the most effective light for you. It makes a big difference in how clear things will look. Some magnifiers come with a built-in light, but most times you will have to use another light. A desk lamp is best. (The overhead light casts a shadow on your book or paper as you get close enough to see it.) Be sure the light is along your side, coming over your shoulder.
- *Be sure to keep your aids clean.* Dust, dirt, and fingerprints are hard to see through. Clean the lenses with a clean, soft cloth (never paper). Always be sure your hands are clean to begin with.
- *Keep your aids in their cases when you are not using them.* They will be more protected and always ready for you to take with you wherever you go.
- *Carry your low-vision aids with you.* Most of them are small and lightweight. In that way, you will have them when you need them. If you have aids you use only at school, you may want to ask your teacher to keep them in a safe place for you.
- *Experiment in new situations.* Can you see the menu at McDonald's? Watch the football game? See prices on toys? Find your friend's house number? The more often you use your low-vision aid, the better you will get at using it.
- *Try out different combinations of aids with and without your glasses or contact lenses.* In this way, you will find the combination that works best for you.

Source: Tips for using low-vision aids, from Dean, M. *A Closer Look at Low Vision Aids.* Connecticut State Board of Education and Services for the Blind, Division of Children's Services, 170 Ridge Road, Wethersfield, CT 06109. Reprinted by permission.

- Do not pet a guide dog without first seeking the owner's permission.
- Do not take hold of the dog's harness, as this might confuse the dog and the owner.
- If a person with a guide dog appears to need assistance, approach on his or her right side (guide dogs are usually on the left side) and ask if he or she needs help.

Sighted Guides   Most people who are blind find it necessary to rely occasionally on the assistance of others. The *sighted guide technique* is a simple method of helping a person with visual impairments to travel:

- When offering assistance to a person who is blind, speak in a normal tone of voice and ask directly, "May I help you?" This helps the person locate you.
- Do not grab the arm or body of the person who is blind. Permit him to take your arm.
- The person with visual impairment should lightly grasp the sighted person's arm just above the elbow and walk half a step behind in a natural manner. Young children might hold on to the index finger or pinky of an adult sighted guide.
- The sighted person should walk at a normal pace, describing curbs or other obstacles and hesitating slightly before going up or down. Never pull or push a person who is blind when you are serving as a sighted guide.
- Do not try to push a person who is blind into a chair. Simply place his hand on the back of the chair, and the person will seat himself.

When students with visual impairments attend regular classes, it may be a good idea for one of the students and the O&M specialist to demonstrate the sighted guide technique to classmates. To promote independent travel, however, overreliance on the sighted guide technique should be discouraged once the student has learned to get around the classroom and school.

Electronic Travel Aids   Several electronic travel aids have been developed to facilitate the orientation and mobility of individuals with visual impairments. The laser beam cane converts infrared light into sound as the light beam strikes objects in the traveler's path. Different levels of vibration in the cane signal relative proximity to an obstacle. Other electronic travel aids are designed for use in conjunction with a standard cane or guide dog. The Mowat Sensor is a flashlight-sized device that bounces ultrasound off objects and gives the traveler information about the distance and location of obstacles through changes in vibration. The SonicGuide, which is worn on the head, converts reflections of ultrasound into sounds of varied pitch, amplitude, and tone that enable the traveler to determine distance, direction, and characteristics of objects in the environment.

Whatever the preferred method of travel, most students with visual impairments can generally learn to negotiate familiar places, such as school and home, on their own. Many students with visual impairments can benefit from learning to use a systematic method for obtaining travel information and assistance with street crossing. Good orientation and mobility skills have many positive effects. A child with visual impairments who can travel independently is likely to develop more physical and social skills and more self-confidence than will a child who must continually depend on other people to get around. Good travel skills also expand a student's opportunities for employment and independent living.

Listening skills

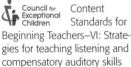
Council for Exceptional Children   Content Standards for Beginning Teachers–VI: Strategies for teaching listening and compensatory auditory skills (VI4K4).

Listening Skills   Children with visual impairments, especially those who are blind, must obtain an enormous amount of information by listening. Vision is thought to be the coordinating sense, and it has been estimated that 80% of information received by a normally sighted person comes through the visual channel (Arter, 1997; Best, 1992). Children who are blind must use other senses, predominately touch and hearing, to contact and comprehend their environment. A widely held misconception is that persons who are blind automatically develop a better sense of hearing to compensate for their loss of sight. Children with visual impairments do not have a super sense of hearing, nor do they necessarily listen better than their normally sighted peers do. It is more accurate to say that, through proper instruction and experiences, children with visual impairments learn to use their hearing more efficiently (Koenig, 1996).

The systematic development of listening skills is an important component of the educational program of every child with visual impairments. Listening is not the same thing as hearing; it is possible to hear a sound without understanding it. Listening involves being aware of sounds, discriminating differences in sounds, identifying the source of sounds, and attaching meaning to sounds (Heinze, 1986).

Learning-to-listen activities can take an almost unlimited variety of forms. Young children, for example, might learn to discriminate between sounds that are near and far, loud and soft, high-pitched and low-pitched. A teacher might introduce a new word into a sentence and ask the child to identify it or ask children to clap each time a key word is repeated. In the "shopping game," a child begins by saying, "I went to the store and I bought _____." Each player repeats the whole list of items purchased by previous students and then adds his or her own item to the list (Arter, 1997). It is important to arrange the rules of such games so that children who fail to remember the list are not eliminated, which would result in fewer oportunties to practice for the children with the weakest listening and auditory memory skills (Mangold, 1982). Older students might practice higher-order listening skills such as identifying important details with distracting background noises, differentiating between fact and opinion, or responding to verbal analogies.

Students with visual impairments, particularly in high school, make frequent use of recorded materials. In addition to using recordings of texts, lectures, and class discussions, students with visual impairments and their teachers can obtain on a free-loan basis thousands of recorded books and magazines and playback equipment through the Library of Congress, the American Printing House for the Blind, the Canadian National Institute for the Blind, Recordings for the Blind, and various other organizations. But a listener can process auditory information at more than twice the speed of the average oral reading rate of about 120 words per minute (Aldrich & Parkin, 1989). Variable-speed cassette tape recorders available from the American Printing House for the Blind (APH) accelerate the playback rate of recorded text without significantly distorting the quality of the speech. In addition to tactile markings on the controls and a window that allows users to feel with their fingertip if the tape is playing, the APH Handicassette has built-in pitch control and a speech compression feature that electronically shortens the length of selected words. With practice, students can listen to accelerated and compressed speech at speeds of up to 275 words per minute without affecting comprehension (Arter, 1997).

Functional Life Skills   Some special educators have expressed concern that efforts to help students with visual impairments match the academic achievement of sighted age mates have too often come at the expense of sufficient opportunities to learn daily living and career skills (Miller, 1993; Sacks et al., 1998). Specific instruction and ongoing supports should be provided to ensure that students with visual impairments learn skills such as cooking, personal hygiene and grooming, shopping, financial management, transportation, and recreational activities that are requisites for an independent and enjoyable adulthood (Corn, 2000; Kaufman, 2000; Rosenblum, 2000). (To find out how three secondary students who are blind were taught to prepare some of their favorite snack foods, see Teaching & Learning, "I Made It Myself, and It's Good!" later in this chapter.)

Some students with visual impairments will also benefit from direct instruction on how to deal with strangers, how to interpret and explain their visual impairments to other people, and how to make socially acceptable gestures in conversation.

EDUCATIONAL PLACEMENT ALTERNATIVES

In the past, most children with severe visual impairments were educated in residential schools. Today, however, 86% of children with visual impairments are educated in public schools, and two out of three receive at least some of their education in regular school classrooms: 49% of all school-age students with visual impairments are members of regular classes, and 19% attend resource rooms for part of each day (U.S. Department of Education, 2002). Separate classrooms in public schools serve another 18% of the school-age population of children with visual impairments.

Functional life skills

Council for Exceptional Children   Content Standards for Beginning Teachers–VI: Strategies for teaching social, daily living, and functional life skills to individuals with VI (VI4K15). **PRAXIS** Special Education Core Principles: Content Knowledge: III. Delivery of Services to Students with Disabilities, Curriculum and Instruction, Self-care and daily living skills.

Placement alternatives and service models

PRAXIS Special Education Core Principles: Content Knowledge: III. Delivery of Services to Students with Disabilities, Background knowledge, Placement and program issues, Least restrictive environment/Continuum of educational services.

I Made It Myself, and It's Good!

For special education to contribute to meaningful lifestyle changes for students, it must help them gain functional skills for postschool environments. Being able to prepare one's own food is a critical skill for independent living. Steve, Lisa, and Carl were 17 to 21 years old and enrolled in a class for students with multiple disabilities at a residential school for the blind. They were living in an on-campus apartment used to teach daily living skills. Several unsuccessful attempts had been made to teach basic cooking skills to the three. None possessed any functional vision or braille skills, and their IQ scores ranged from 64 to 72 on the Perkins Binet Test of Intelligence for the Blind.

To learn new skills, especially those involving long chains of responses such as following the steps of a recipe, students like Steve, Lisa, and Carl require intensive instruction over many trials. Once a skill is learned, its generalization to other settings and situations and maintenance over time are often lacking. The challenge was to discover a method for teaching cooking skills that would be effective initially but also would enable the students to prepare recipes for which they had not received instruction and that resulted in long-term maintenance of their new skills.

A "Walkman Cookbook"

Because Steve, Lisa, and Carl were blind, it was not possible to use picture cookbooks or color-coded recipes, which have been used successfully with learners with mental retardation and other disabilities (Book, Paul, Gwalla-Ogisi, & Test, 1990; Johnson & Cuvo, 1981). Instead, tape-recorded recipes were used. Each student wore a cooking apron on which two pockets had been sewn. One pocket at the waist held a small tape recorder; the second pocket, located at the chest, held a switch that the students pushed to turn the tape player on and off. Each step from the task-analyzed recipes was prerecorded in sequence on a cassette tape. ("Open the bag of cake mix by tearing it at the tab.") A beep signaled the end of each direction.

Performance Measures

The number of recipe steps each student independently completed was measured during preinstruction (baseline), instruction, and maintenance phases. To assess generalization, probes were conducted on two classes of recipes on which the students received no training. Simple generality recipes could be prepared with the same set of cooking skills learned in a related trained item. Complex generality recipes required a combination of skills learned in two different trained recipes. The relationship between the trained recipes and the two types of recipes used to assess generality is shown in Figure A. As a measure of social validity, each trial was also scored as to whether the food prepared was edible.

Baseline

To objectively assess whether learning has occurred, student performance must be measured before instruction begins. The first baseline trial was conducted without the tape-recorded recipes to determine which food preparation steps, if any, each student could already perform without any assistance or adaptive equipment. It was then necessary to find out whether the students could successfully prepare the food items if they were simply given the tape-recorded recipes. After being shown how to operate the tape recorder to play back the instructions, each student was asked to prepare each recipe but was given no other prompts, assistance, or feedback.

Instruction

Students were told that the taped recipes explained exactly what to do and where to find the food items and utensils. They practiced using the remote switch to control the rate of instructions by stopping the tape each time they heard a beep. Training for each step of the task analysis consisted of a three-component least-to-most prompt hierarchy (verbal, physical, and hand-over-hand guidance) following errors and verbal praise for correct responses. Training on a recipe continued until a student correctly performed all steps on two consecutive trials over two sessions.

Results

Lisa, Carl, and Steve needed a total of 12, 19, and 35 instructional trials, respectively, to learn the three different recipes. (Steve required a high number of trials to master the coffee and cheesecake recipes due to repeated spills when pouring liquids. This problem was solved by teaching Steve to use his fingers to feel where and how much liquid he was pouring.) Additionally, after mastering the trained recipes, each student was able to prepare both the simple and the complex generality recipes with the tape recorder, even though they had not received any instruction on those recipes.

The ultimate evaluation of cooking skills instruction is whether or not the food prepared can be eaten. A mistake on any one of several crucial steps in the 27-step task analysis for making microwave cake (e.g., not stirring the egg into the batter) would result in a cake no one would want to eat. Before training, none of Steve's 13 attempts to make any of the trained recipes could be eaten, whereas all 6 of his posttraining attempts were edible. Before he learned how to prepare the related trained recipes, Steve was unsuccessful in all 20 of his attempts to make the simple generality recipes and on each of 4 attempts to prepare the complex generality recipes. After learning how to make the related recipes, he was able to follow tape-recorded recipes to successfully prepare the recipes for which he had received no direct training: on 82% of the trials (9 out of 11) with the simple generality recipes and on all 3 trials with the complex generality recipes. In follow-up probes

Steve has learned to accurately pour and measure the milk for his cake by placing his fingers in the bowl.

conducted 6 weeks and 4 months after the study ended, Steve was still able to prepare each of the recipes successfully. Lisa and Carl showed similar gains in their ability to prepare food for themselves.

Individualized, Normalized, and Self-Determined

A self-operated audio prompting system (also see Barfels, Al-Attrash, & Heward, 1998; Briggs et al., 1990; Davis, Brady, Williams, & Burta, 1992; Grossi, 1998; Mechling & Gast, 1997; "The Idea Bunny" in Chapter 5) offers several advantages. First, the prerecorded prompts can be individualized. For example:

- Tape-recorded instructions can be as precise or general as necessary, depending on known or probable tasks and environments.
- Vocabulary can be modified, pacing of instructions speeded up or slowed down, and instructions for particularly difficult steps repeated or given in more detail.
- Students might use their own voice to record special prompts or reminders relevant to certain steps of the task (e.g., "Have I checked for spills?").

Relationship Between Trained Recipes and Two Classes of Untrained Recipes Used to Assess Generalized Outcomes of Instruction

Simple Generality	Trained Recipes	Complex Generality
French fries (11)[a] Pizza (13)	Pizza (13) [Lisa & Carl] French fries (11) [Steve]	
Popcorn (10) [Lisa & Steve]		Brownies
Tea (10)	Coffee (10)	Cake (27)
Pudding (13)	Cheesecake(21)	

Trained Recipes - These recipes were taught directly.

Simple Generality - Preparation of these recipes required the same preparation skills as trained recipes.

Complex Generality - Preparation of these recipes required a combination of the food preparation skills learned in two of the three trained recipes.

[a] = Numbers in parentheses indicate number of steps in task analysis.

FIGURE A

continues

- Verbal praise and encouragement from teachers, parents, friends, or the student himself could also be included in the instructions.

Second, individuals with disabilities are currently using a variety of assistive devices to increase their independence in domestic, community, and employment settings. Some assistive devices, however, may not be used by the learner in natural settings. A student in a crowded restaurant, for example, may hesitate to remove a laminated ordering card from her pocket or purse because it marks her as different. By contrast, the popularity of Walkman-like personal stereos enables the wearer of audio headphones to listen to a series of self-delivered prompts in a private,

unobtrusive, and normalized manner that does not impose on or bother others.

The self-operated feature of the system puts the student in control of the environment, thereby increasing the probability of independent functioning and level of self-determination. As Carl remarked when sharing with his girlfriend the microwave cake he had just made, "I made it myself, and it's good!"

Source: Adapted from Trask-Tyler, S. A., Grossi, T. A., & Heward, W. L. (1994). Teaching young adults with developmental disabilities and visual impairments to use tape-recorded recipes: Acquisition, generalization, and maintenance of cooking skills. *Journal of Behavioral Education, 4,* 283–311. Used by permission.

 ## ITINERANT TEACHER MODEL

Most students with visual impairments who are included in general education classrooms receive support from itinerant teacher-consultants, sometimes called *vision specialists.* These specially trained teachers may be employed by the school district; a nearby residential school; or a regional, state, or provincial education agency. Although their roles and caseloads vary widely from program to program, most itinerant teacher-consultants are expected to assume some or all of the following responsibilities (Flener, 1993; Willoughby & Duffy, 1989):

- Collaboratively develop with the regular classroom teacher curricular and instructional modifications according to the child's individual needs
- Provide direct instruction on compensatory skills to the student with visual impairments (e.g., listening, typing skills)
- Obtain or prepare specialized learning materials
- Adapt reading assignments and other materials into braille, large-print, or tape-recorded form or arrange for readers

Patrick is getting along fine in the regular classroom—thanks to the instructional adaptations jointly planned by his itinerant vision specialist and his classroom teacher.

- Make referrals for low-vision aids services; train students in the use and care of low-vision aids
- Interpret information about the child's visual impairment and visual functioning for other educators and parents
- Help plan the child's educational goals, initiate and maintain contact with various agencies, and keep records of services provided
- Consult with the child's parents and other teachers

The itinerant teacher-consultant may or may not provide instruction in orientation and mobility. Some schools, particularly in rural areas, employ dually certified teachers who are also O&M specialists. Other schools employ one teacher for educational support and another for O&M training. Students on an itinerant teacher's caseload may range from infants to young adults and may include children who are blind, those with low vision, and students with multiple disabilities.

Some public school programs have special resource rooms for students with visual impairments. In contrast with the itinerant teacher-consultant who travels from school to school, the resource room teacher remains in one specially equipped location and serves students with visual impairments for part of the school day. Usually, only large school districts have resource rooms for students with visual impairments.

The amount of time the itinerant teacher-consultant or resource room teacher spends with a visually impaired student who attends regular classes varies considerably. Some students may be seen every day because they require a great deal of specialized assistance. Others may be seen weekly, monthly, or even less frequently because they are able to function well in the regular class with less support.

Inclusive education for students with visual impairments has had advocates for many years. Cruickshank (1986), for example, suggested that "the blind child is perhaps the easiest exceptional child to integrate into a regular grade in the public schools" (p. 104). To make inclusion successful, however, a full program of appropriate educational and related services must be provided (Pugh & Erin, 1999).

The key person in the program for a child with visual impairments is the regular classroom teacher. An extensive study of the elements of successful inclusion of children with visual impairments in public school classes found that the single most important factor was the regular classroom teacher's flexibility (Bishop, 1986). Other aspects of the school situation found to be highly important were peer acceptance and interaction, availability of support personnel, and adequate access to special supplies and equipment. (To find out how teachers and sighted classmates supported the inclusion of a young child with visual impairment in a community-based preschool, see Teaching & Learning, "Including Ryan," later in this chapter.)

For inclusion to be successful, a child with visual impairments needs a skilled and supportive regular classroom teacher. This was underscored by a study that asked adolescents to assess the impact of visual impairments on their lives (Rosenblum, 2000). All 10 students in the study attended public school general education classrooms for at least 50% of the school day. Several students reported that a general education teacher made it difficult for them to use disability-specific skills such as braille or computerized speech output in the classroom. ("It took him about a quarter to get the stuff [tests and worksheets] to the braillist in the first place" [p. 439].) Other participants reported that insensitive teachers caused them to feel humiliation and frustration about having a visual impairment. ("The science teacher wanted me to identify rocks by a visual method and I told her I can't. She goes, 'Well, you're going to have to if you want to get a good grade'" [p. 439].) Several other participants reported that general education teachers treated them like younger children. ("The teachers talk to me differently like I'm more of a 6 year old rather than a 13 year old" [p. 43].)

RESIDENTIAL SCHOOLS

About 7.5% of school-age children with visual impairments attend residential schools (U.S. Department of Education, 2002). Residential schools continue to meet the needs of a sizable number of children with visual impairments. The current population of residential schools consists largely of children with visual impairments with additional disabilities, such as mental retardation, hearing impairment, behavioral disorders, and cerebral palsy. (See Chapter 13 for information on children with multiple disabilities, including those who are deaf-blind.) Some parents are not able to care for their children adequately at home; others prefer the greater concentration of specialized personnel, facilities, and services that a residential school usually offers.

Importance of regular classroom teacher

 Content Standards for Beginning Teachers–VI: Attitudes and actions of teachers that affect the behaviors of individuals with VI (VI3K3).
PRAXIS Special Education Core Principles: Content Knowledge: III. Delivery of Services to Students with Disabilities, Professional roles, Influence of teacher attitudes, values and behaviors on the learning of exceptional students.

Including Ryan: Using Natural Supports to Make Inclusion Natural

*I*ncluding young children with disabilities in preschool class-rooms with their nondisabled peers is widely recognized as a critical component of early childhood special education ser-vices. Although efforts have been made to establish more natural preschool settings to accommodate children with disabilities throughout the country, parents of children with visual impair-ments often have few choices of general early childhood programs that will provide the necessary supports and services for their chil-dren. In practice, however, the kinds of inclusive supports of most value are those that are common sense, casual, and unobtrusive. Elizabeth Erwin describes how classroom staff and sighted peers made effective use of natural supports with Ryan, a 3-year-old boy with visual impairments, to facilitate his membership and mean-ingful participation in a community-based preschool.

The preschool teacher, teacher aides, and Ryan's sighted classmates supported his membership and active participation in the most natural ways possible. We defined natural supports as assistance intended to create connec-tions, competence, or teamwork in unobtrusive and indi-vidualized ways that lead to the achievement of a task or the provision of important contextual input about the en-vironment. Equally important was acceptance by adults and classmates of the unique adaptive strategies that Ryan used to accomplish tasks and negotiate the classroom en-vironment.

Adult Interventions

All three adults in the classroom (the classroom teacher; Kima, the full-time assistant; and Dan, a part-time assis-tant) provided supports for Ryan in several ways.

Contextual cues. They provided him with frequent and consistent information about the environment and ongoing activities. For example, during snack time, Dan told Ryan, "I put your cup in front of you but not on the place mat. The other kids have it that way, so if the mat moves, the cup won't fall over." When Ryan and four classmates were at the sand table, Kima sat behind Ryan providing verbal information: "You have to put more in your cup; it is still empty." or "Keep your hand inside the table; otherwise, the sand will fall on the floor. Feel the difference?"

Although Kima's responsibilities were to provide assis-tance to all of the children in the class, she frequently fur-nished Ryan with information about her physical location. For example, she would alert Ryan that she was returning to or leaving the room or the immediate area and give him contextual information about others in the vicinity (e.g., "Ryan, Sue and Melissa are sitting here").

Spontaneous events. The staff took advantage of naturally occurring spontaneous events to promote learning and help Ryan make connections between pieces of information that other children acquired visually. For example, during show-and-tell, Ryan stood in front of the circle with the teacher and answered her questions about the Barney doll he had brought in that day. Toward the end of Ryan's turn, the teacher asked Laurie to come up and stand close to Ryan. She then asked Ryan to look at Laurie's shirt and tell the group what was on it. Ryan bent down and touched Laurie's shirt with his nose because he was so close to her. Then he exclaimed, "It's Barney!" The teacher made a big deal about the fact that the same Barney that Ryan had brought in was also on Laurie's shirt. Ryan and the other children got a big kick out of the coincidence.

Detailed verbal directions and explanations. The adults supported Ryan's independence by providing detailed ex-planations on how he could accomplish tasks. For example, when Ryan finished painting, the teacher told him, "Walk over to the rug, and when you feel the rug you'll see a bright yellow toy in front of you." Ryan followed the instruction and walked cautiously to the rug. He was a little bent over as if he was looking at the ground for cues. When he found the rug, he sat down to play with the yellow toy.

Simple verbal cues and prompts.   Ryan usually needed explicit instructions or a demonstration only when learning a new behavior. After that, the adults used simple verbal cues to help him anticipate what might be happening next. For example, when another song began, Kima provided prompts like "Don't forget: elbows next" or "Now comes the tricky part." Ryan independently carried out the approximate body movements that corresponded to the song.

Physical cues.   Physical cues were a natural means to give Ryan specific input about how to carry out a task or activity. He really seemed to like music time. He had a big smile on his face as he moved his body to the music. Kima used physical prompts like positioning his hands straight out in front of him as the song indicated. Once she showed him, he was able to perform the movement correctly and independently the next time the song was played.

Peer Supports

Ryan's peers were another viable and natural source of information about and assistance in the environment. At the beginning of the school year, the children did not offer support frequently or spontaneously. Kima said: "At the beginning, they wouldn't come close to Ryan. His movements were a little different at times, and they would just watch him. Eventually, they understood that Ryan was putting his face right into theirs, and I would say this is this person or that person. Now, most of them will say, 'It's me, Ken,' or 'I'm Ronnie.'"

The children did not usually identify themselves to other classmates, but they seemed to recognize that this way of sharing information was useful to Ryan. They also realized that Ryan gained access to certain types of information or needed assistance in ways that might be different from theirs. For example, during show-and-tell it was Sue's turn to show a toy to the group. She first gave the toy to Ryan. Hillary, who was seated next to Ryan, leaned closer to him and guided his hands over the toy, purposely showing him the knobs and buttons.

At other times, the adults orchestrated encounters between Ryan and his classmates to promote positive social and communicative interactions and to reduce the amount of adult intervention. For example, during transitions Kima often enlisted the help of classmates: "I will often say,

'Cathy, can you take Ryan's hand and bring him to the rug?' The children know right away that they need to bring him through a clear path. I have noticed that they don't run him into a chair. They seem to love to do this. He loves it, too. Ryan will take someone's hand and say, 'Well, hi there,' and start a conversation."

Ryan's Adaptive Strategies

To compensate for his visual impairment, Ryan used a variety of adaptive strategies that enabled him to move freely within the classroom and gain access to information. His father described one such strategy: "Ryan becomes physically close to people because that is his means of really figuring out what they are doing. He doesn't know how to regard other people's physical space, and he will have to learn that. Right now, he comes very close to other children, and I think that scares them a little bit." Ryan also maintained close physical proximity when he explored objects in his immediate environment. The classroom staff was cognizant of his need to use this distinctive strategy that his sighted peers did not use, and they never discouraged him from bringing objects close to his face or reprimanded him for standing close to others.

Traveling independently and making choices were age-appropriate and meaningful preschool tasks that Ryan, like his preschool classmates, needed to learn. The difference was in the way the children accomplished those goals. Ryan used familiar landmarks and signals in the classroom to orient himself, which fostered his independent mobility within the environment. Kima said: "He leads himself by touching everything. Lonie [Ryan's vision specialist] told us that he can find the light in the window, so we fostered that right from the beginning. Ryan uses the light from the window to know where the rug is. Also, he can feel the difference when he is on the floor and when he is on the rug. So he can go over and find his toys on the shelf by using the window and rug as guides."

Ryan also used verbal skills to gain information available to his classmates by vision. Kima said: "He will walk over to a group of children, and he always uses his words. If he asks a question, he will not always get an answer. But he will go over and, rather than just join in, say, 'What are you doing?' 'Who are you?' or 'What have you guys got?'"

Source: Adapted from Erwin, E. J. (1996). Meaningful participation in early childhood general education using natural supports. *Journal of Visual Impairment and Blindness, 90,* 400–411. Used by permission.

Residential schools

Council for Exceptional Children Content Standards for Beginning Teachers–VI: Historical foundations of education of individuals with VI (VI1K2) (also, VI1K6).
PRAXIS Special Education Core Principles: Content Knowledge: III. Delivery of Services to Students with Disabilities, Background knowledge, Placement and program issues, Continuum of educational services.

Parents and educators who support residential schools for children with visual impairments frequently point to the leadership that such schools have provided over a long period, with their "wealth and broad range of expertise" (Miller, 1985, p. 160). These supporters argue that a residential school can be the least restrictive environment for some students with visual impairments and multiple disabilities. A follow-up study of students with visual impairments at a state school for the blind found that parents, local education agencies, and the students themselves generally considered the residential school placement to have been appropriate and beneficial (Livingston-White, Utter, & Woodard, 1985). Among the advantages cited were specialized curriculum and equipment, participation in extracurricular activities, individualized instruction, small classes, and improved self-esteem.

Like placement at any other point in the continuum of educational settings, placement in a residential school should not be regarded as permanent. Many children with visual impairments move from residential schools into public schools (or vice versa) as their needs change. Some students in residential schools attend nearby public schools for part of the school day. Most residential schools encourage parent involvement and have recreational programs that bring students with visual impairments into contact with sighted peers. Independent living skills and vocational training are important parts of the program at virtually all residential schools.

In several states, there is close cooperation between public school and residential school programs that serve children with visual impairments. A residential school for students who are blind has an opportunity to work closely with consumers, parents, professionals, and funding agencies in developing a wide array of community-based services. Cooperative working relationships and creative short- and long-term planning efforts have the potential to generate positive and reality-based services that respond to present-day needs within the context of community integration. Residential schools—primarily because of the expertise of their staff but also because of their location, centralization of resources, and availability of facilities—have the potential to become responsive resource centers on regional and state levels.

Residential schools have long played an important role in training teachers of children with visual impairments on both a preservice and in-service basis. The residential school is usually well equipped to serve as a resource center for instructional materials and as a place where students with visual impairments can receive specialized evaluation services. An increasing number of residential schools now offer short-term training to students with visual impairments who attend regular public schools. One example is a summer workshop emphasizing braille, mobility, and vocational training.

 These students with visual impairments at a residential school are reading print materials in various large-size type.

CURRENT ISSUES AND FUTURE TRENDS

Children with visual impairments constitute a very small portion of the school-age population, but they have many unique needs. Although the current trend toward inclusion of children with visual impairments into regular public school classrooms is generally welcomed, some educators caution against wholesale placement of children with visual impairments in regular schools without adequate support. Many vision professionals resist noncategorical special education programs for students with visual impairments. It is unrealistic, they argue, to expect regular teachers or teachers trained in other areas of special education to be competent in specialized techniques such as braille, orientation and mobility, and visual efficiency. (See Profiles & Perspectives, "A Paper on the Inclusion of Students with Visual Impairments," later in this chapter.)

SPECIALIZATION OF SERVICES

Although financial restrictions may require some public school and residential school programs for children with visual impairments to close down or consolidate with programs for children with other disabilities, strong support exists for the continuation of highly specialized services. It is likely that both public school and state-run residential programs for children with visual impairments will continue to operate well into the future, occasionally challenging each other for the privilege of serving the relatively small number of available students. The results of this competition may well prove favorable if both types of programs are encouraged to improve the quality of their educational services.

EMERGING TECHNOLOGY AND RESEARCH

New and emerging electronic and biomedical technologies will continue to aid children and adults with visual impairments, particularly in the areas of mobility, communication, and use of low vision. The U.S. Department of Education and the National Institute on Disability, Rehabilitation, and Research have jointly funded a research and development project to develop accessible and affordable talking global positioning system (GPS) technologies for people with visual impairments. The goal of the 5-year collaborative project involving engineers, designers, O&M specialists, special educators, and rehabilitation professionals is to develop GPS and other way-finding products that can announce present location, provide audible cues for the location of pay phones and restrooms, interpret traffic signals, read street signs, give distance and direction information, and so on.

Although research in artificial sight is in the early experimental stages, it holds much promise. In the future, it may even be possible to provide a form of artificial sight to people who are totally blind by implanting electrodes into the brain and connecting them to a miniature television camera built into an artificial eye.

A number of research teams are exploring a process called *tactile vision sensory substitution*, in which tactile images are projected onto an area of the body that enable the person who is blind to perceive a visionlike sensation. An example of this line of research is work by Kathi Kamm, a professor of occupational therapy at the University of Wisconsin—Milwaukee (Griffin, 2001). Kamm's device sends images from a digital camera to a 144-pixel array of electrodes that are activated according to how bright the image is in that location of the array. In early tactile vision sensory substitution research, the electrode array was placed on a person's back, abdomen, fingers, or toes. But those locations were uncomfortable and impractical and required too much voltage to be felt. Kamm places the electrode array on the tongue because it is more sensitive and requires less voltage. And because the tongue has no sweat glands, there is no pain.

Kamm has begun using the system to teach congenitally blind children to recognize lines, letters, and faces. After 10 to 25 hours of training, the children usually begin to perceive objects in space, not on their tongues, and will begin to reach out for them.

FIGHTING AGAINST DISCRIMINATION AND FOR SELF-DETERMINATION

Like other groups of individuals with disabilities, people with visual impairments are becoming increasingly aware of their rights as citizens and consumers and are fighting discrimination based on their disabilities. Many people—even some who work with students

Inclusion

  Content Standards for Beginning Teachers–VI: Issues and trends in special education and the field of VI (VI1K6).
PRAXIS Special Education Core Principles: Content Knowledge: III. Delivery of Services to Students with Disabilities, Background knowledge, Placement and program issues, Least restrictive environment/Continuum of educational services.

Emerging technologies for individuals with VI

PRAXIS Special Education Core Principles: Content Knowledge: III. Delivery of Services to Students with Disabilities, Curriculum and Instruction, Technology for sensory disabilities.

A Paper on the Inclusion of Students with Visual Impairments

American Foundation for the Blind

"Inclusion," "full inclusion" and "inclusive education" are terms which recently have been narrowly defined by some (primarily educators of students with severe disabilities) to espouse the philosophy that ALL students with disabilities, regardless of the nature or the severity of their disability, receive their TOTAL education within the regular education environment. This philosophy is based on the relatively recent placement of a limited number of students with severe disabilities in regular classrooms. Research conducted by proponents of this philosophy lacks empirical evidence that this practice results in programs which are better able to prepare ALL students with visual impairments to be more fully included in society than the current practice, required by federal law, of providing a full range of program options.

Educators and parents of students with visual impairments have pioneered special education and inclusive program options for over 164 years. It is significant that the field of education of visually impaired students was the first to develop a range of special education program options, beginning with specialized schools in 1829 and extending to inclusive (including "full inclusion") public school program options since 1900.

Experience and research clearly support the following three position statements outlining the essential elements which must be in place in order to provide an appropriate education in the least restrictive environment for students with visual impairments.

I. *Students with visual impairments have unique educational needs which are most effectively met using a team approach of professionals, parents and students.* In order to meet their unique needs, students must have specialized services, books and materials in appropriate media (including braille), as well as specialized equipment and technology to assure equal access to the core and specialized curricula, and to enable them to most effectively compete with their peers in school and ultimately in society.

The unique educational needs of all students with visual impairments cannot be met in a single environment, even with unlimited funding. It is critical that a team approach be used in identifying and meeting these needs and that the team must include staff who have specific expertise in educating students with visual impairments. The proposal that ALL of the needs of ALL students can

with visual impairments—tend to underestimate their students' capacities and deny them a full range of occupational and personal choices. The future should bring a shift away from some of the vocations and settings in which people with visual impairments have traditionally worked (e.g., piano tuning, rehabilitation counseling) in favor of a more varied and rewarding range of employment opportunities.

Some years ago, a reporter asked a prominent blind woman, "What is it that blind people would want from society?" The woman replied, "The opportunity to be equal and the right to be different."

What did this woman mean by two remarks that seem diametrically opposite? Perhaps she meant that print and braille are equal, but very different; that the need for independent travel is similar for sighted and blind persons, but the skills are learned very differently by blind people; and that concepts and learning that occur for sighted people in a natural, spontaneous manner require different learning experiences for blind persons. Perhaps she was emphasizing that blind persons should have the opportunity to learn the same knowledge and skills as sighted people, but that their manner of learning will be different. (Hatlen, 1996)

 For more information on blindness and low vision, go to the Web Links module in Chapter 11 on the Companion Website at **www.prenhall.com/heward**

be met in one environment, the regular classroom, violates the spirit as well as the letter of the law—IDEA.

II. *There must be a full range of program options and support services so that the Individualized Education Program (IEP) team can select the most appropriate placement in the least restrictive environment for each individual student with a visual impairment.* The right of every student with a visual impairment to an appropriate placement in the least restrictive environment, selected by the IEP team from a full range of program options and based upon each student's needs, is nothing more or less than is mandated by federal law.

III. *There must be adequate personnel preparation programs to train staff to provide specialized services that address the unique academic and non-academic curriculum needs of students with visual impairments.* There must also be ongoing specialized personnel development opportunities for all staff working with these students as well as specialized parent education.

Students with visual impairments have the right to an appropriate education that is guided by knowledgeable specialists who work collaboratively with parents, the student and other education team members. Access to training on an ongoing basis is essential for all team members, especially parents who provide the necessary continuity and support in their child's education.

PLACEMENT DOES NOT NECESSARILY PROVIDE ACCESS

Providing equal access to all individuals with disabilities is the key element of the Rehabilitation Act of 1973 and the Americans with Disabilities Act of 1992. Access involves much more than providing ramps. Access is also the key element of inclusion, which involves much more than placement in a particular setting. The relationship of access and inclusion may not be obvious to individuals who are not familiar with the educational and social impact of a vision loss. Placing a student with a visual impairment in a regular classroom does not, necessarily, provide access and the student is not, necessarily, included. A student with a visual impairment, who does not have access to social and physical information because of the visual impairment, is not included, regardless of the physical setting. Students with visual impairments will not be included unless their unique educational needs for access are addressed by specially trained personnel in appropriate environments and unless these students are provided with equal access to core and specialized curricula through appropriate specialized books, materials and equipment.

Conclusion: Students with visual impairments need an educational system that meets the individual needs of ALL students, fosters independence, and is measured by the success of each individual in the school and community. Vision is fundamental to the learning process and is the primary basis upon which most traditional education strategies are based. Students who are visually impaired are most likely to succeed in educational systems where appropriate instruction and services are provided in a full array of program options by qualified staff to address each student's unique educational needs, as required by Public Law 101-476, The Individuals with Disabilities Education Act (IDEA).

Source: From "A Paper on the Inclusion of Students with Visual Impairments," September 26, 2001. From the American Federation of the Blind's Joseph L. Taylor Leadership Institute, Education Work Group. [http://www.afb.org/info_document_view.asp?documentid51344]

SUMMARY

DEFINITIONS

- Legal blindness is defined as visual acuity of 20/200 or less in the better eye after correction with glasses or contact lenses or a restricted field of vision of 20% or less.
- An educational definition classifies students with visual impairments based on the extent to which they use vision and/or auditory/tactile means for learning.
- A student who is totally blind receives no useful information through the sense of vision and must use tactile and auditory senses for all learning.
- A child who is functionally blind has so little vision that she learns primarily through the auditory and tactile senses; however, she may be able to use her limited vision to supplement the information received from the other senses.
- A child with low vision uses vision as a primary means of learning.
- The age at onset of a visual impairment affects a child's educational and emotional needs.

PREVALENCE

- Visual impairment is a low-incidence disability affecting approximately 2 of every 1,000 children in the school-age population. About one-half of all students with visual impairments have additional disabilities.

TYPES AND CAUSES OF VISUAL IMPAIRMENT

- The eye collects light reflected from objects and focuses the objects' image on the retina. The optic nerve transmits the image to the visual cortex of the brain. Difficulty with any part of this process can cause vision problems.
- Refractive errors mean that the size and shape of the eye prevent the light rays from focusing clearly on the retina.
- Structural impairments are visual impairments caused by poor development of, damage to, or malfunction of one or more parts of the eye's optical or muscular systems.
- Cortical visual impairment (CVI) refers to decreased vision or blindness due to damage to or malfunction of the parts of the brain that interpret visual information.

CHARACTERISTICS

- Children with severe visual impairments do not benefit from incidental learning that normally sighted children obtain in everyday experiences and interactions with the environment.
- Visual impairment often leads to delays or deficits in motor development.
- Some students with visual impairments experience social isolation and difficulties in social interactions due to limited common experiences with sighted peers; inability to see and use eye contact, facial expressions, and gestures during conversations; and/or stereotypic behaviors.
- The behavior and attitudes of sighted persons can be unnecessary barriers to the social participation of individuals with visual impairments.

EDUCATIONAL APPROACHES

- Braille—a tactile system of reading and writing in which letters, words, numbers, and other systems are made from arrangements of embossed six-dot cells—is the primary means of literacy for students who are blind.
- Students who are blind may also use special equipment to access standard print through touch, reading machines, and prerecorded materials.
- Children with low vision should be taught to use visual efficiency or functioning.
- Students with low vision use three basic methods for reading print: approach magnification, optical devices, and large print.
- Students who are blind or have severe visual impairments need instruction in orientation (knowing where they are, where they are going, and how to get there) and mobility (moving safely and efficiently from one point to another).
- Systematic development of listening skills is an important component of the educational program of every child with visual impairments.
- The curriculum for students with visual impairments should also include systematic instruction in functional living skills such as cooking, personal hygiene and grooming, shopping, financial management, transportation, and recreational activities.

EDUCATIONAL PLACEMENT ALTERNATIVES

- Two out of three children with visual impairments spend at least part of each school day in regular classes with sighted peers.
- In many districts, a specially trained itinerant vision specialist provides support for students with visual impairments and their regular classroom teachers.
- Some programs also have separate orientation and mobility instructors or separate resource rooms for students with visual impairments.

- About 7.5% of children with visual impairments, especially those with other disabilities, attend residential schools.
- Most parents can choose between public day and residential schools for their children with visual impairments.

CURRENT ISSUES AND FUTURE TRENDS

- Children with visual impairments are likely to receive specialized services in the future in both regular and residential schools. Greater emphasis will be placed on intervention with visually impaired infants and young children and on training older students for independence.
- It is hoped that all people with visual impairments will benefit from new technological and biomedical developments. Artificial sight may be possible in the future.
- Career opportunities will likely expand as individuals with visual impairments become more aware of their legal and human rights.

To check your comprehension of chapter content, go to the Guided Review and Quiz modules in Chapter 11 on the Companion Website at **www.prenhall.com/heward**

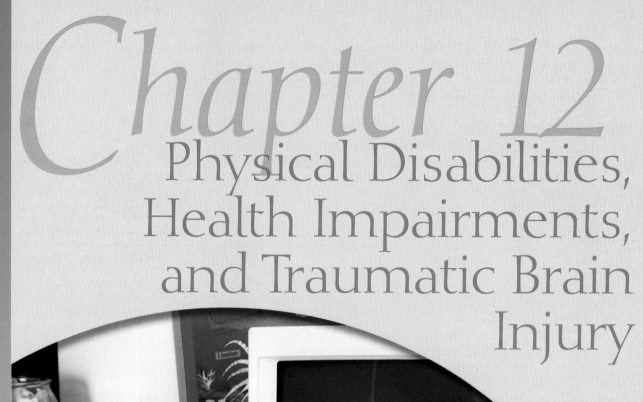

Chapter 12

Physical Disabilities, Health Impairments, and Traumatic Brain Injury

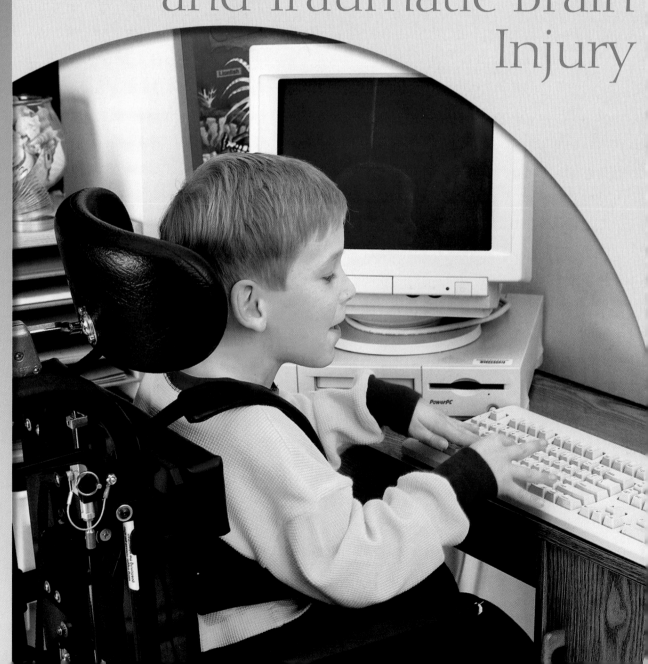

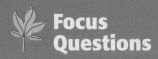
- In what ways might the visibility of a physical or health impairment affect a child's self-perception, social development, and level of independence?

- How do the nature and severity of a child's physical disability affect IEP goals and objectives?

- What must members of transdisciplinary teams for students with severe physical disabilities and multiple health needs guard against?

- How might an assistive technology device be a hindrance as well as a help?

- How can the classroom environment be modified to support the inclusion of students with disabilities described in this chapter?

MARY KATE RYAN-GRIFFITH

JUDITH A. RESNIK ELEMENTARY SCHOOL

MONTGOMERY COUNTY PUBLIC SCHOOLS

GAITHERSBURG, MARYLAND

Education • Teaching Credentials • Experience

- B.S. in Special Education/Elementary Education, Peabody College for Teachers, Vanderbilt University, 1980
- M.A. in Education of the Hearing Impaired, Gallaudet University, 1984
- Maryland Professional Certificates: Special Education K–12, Hearing Impaired K–12, and Elementary Education K–6
- 4 years as fourth-grade teacher; 10 years as a special educator

Current Teaching Position and Students   For the first six years of my special education career, I was the resource teacher for the entire elementary school, with a caseload of up to 50 students. Our model for service delivery of special education has changed dramatically in the past several years. We have moved from the traditional model of separate programs with pullout resource services to a departmentalized approach, assigning each special educator in the building to a grade level. The special educator serves all children with special needs on her grade level in an inclusion model, with minimal pullout for specialized groups or differentiation. I am currently assigned to the fourth grade. I co-teach in three classrooms and have two pullout reading groups. I currently work with 16 students with a range of disabilities: physical challenges caused by cerebral palsy and bone defects, learning disabilities, traumatic brain injury, emotional disabilities, and one child who is hard of hearing. The children come from low- to middle-income families. They are white, African American, Hispanic, Native American, and Native African. Several speak Spanish or Ghanaian as their first language.

Adaptations and Teaching Strategies   These children can function within the regular classroom, but they require support, which can range from academic to physical. Some children in wheelchairs require desks with a cutout that they can get in and under. Tables and desks may need to be raised, and special seats in bathrooms are sometimes necessary. Walkers, standers, and leg braces are everyday pieces of equipment. If children's hands are not fully functional, special pencil grips and eating utensils are a great help.

The computer has been a great advance for improving academic abilities. Bridget's cerebral palsy causes spasticity in her hands, which makes writing or standard keyboarding very difficult. For her I work with the occupational therapist to create *overlays*—pages fitted to a special type of keyboard that run on a special software program. Each overlay is created with specific types of information about a subject, such as different kinds of maps, or generic sentence parts relating to a book we are reading. By touching the keyboard, Bridget can cre-

ate sentences related to the subject. She can do this independently and really enjoys her schoolwork since she is relieved of the drudgery of writing or typing and creates it herself. My students use a variety of typing/voice programs. Tim has learning disabilities and severe motoric impact in his hands. His writing is basically illegible, so he types on a program that gives him choices for words and then voices his paragraph back to him. In this way he can work independently and monitor his own spelling and grammar. We also use programs that create graphic organizers for children. This helps to improve comprehension, especially when children are writing reports. I also use low-tech devices and strategies to aid reading and writing such as raised-line paper; multicolored paper; rulers, index cards, or papers to help children maintain their place; or, for the extremely distracted, a cut-out window in a long page so they only see one line at a time.

We also accommodate children in the classroom by reading books and tests to them and having them dictate their responses. Some children use this approach as a crutch, so I transition them: first, I write everything, then they each write a line and then a paragraph, and finally they write it all themselves with support for spelling and mechanics. Sometimes the desire for me to write reflects a lack of confidence, so building a positive attitude is paramount to success.

Advice to Someone Considering a Career in Special Education   Attitude is everything. I broke my neck in a car accident one week after completing student teaching for my master's degree from Gallaudet University. Clinically, I am an *incomplete quadriplegic* since I traumatized my spinal cord rather than severed it. I am paralyzed from the chest down and have some slight impairment of the arms and hands. However, I am very independent. I drive myself to work using hand controls, and my van has a special seat and a lift. My husband and I adapted our house with a ramp, a larger bathroom, and a tub seat for showers. I frequently use a reacher—a long metal rod with a clamp at the end—to get things that are out of my reach; but otherwise, I don't require much special equipment. I tend to use things in the environment to help me. Anything that can extend my reach is subject to use, whether it be a spatula in the kitchen or a ruler in school. I am relatively healthy, although I do take daily medication for spasticity. I can take out any bully when my legs go into spasm.

I have been in a wheelchair for 17 years. For years after my accident I went through all the stages of grief, from denial to acceptance. Much like I would grieve over the death of a loved one, I grieved for the loss of my ability to dance, run, and walk. Those losses still pain me occasionally. However, I have always believed that when a door closes, somewhere a window opens, and that human beings are the most adaptable creatures on earth. I have learned to perform cherished activities from my chair. I get a kick out of people's surprised looks when I take to the dance floor.

In my job I work with parents as well as children who are dealing with challenges. Some parents have children who were born with challenges and medically diagnosed at birth. Others have children who qualified for special education after encountering academic difficulties. At some point, all of these parents must go through the grief process. They need to grieve for the loss of a "perfect child" and get through the guilt that makes them believe they have done something to damage their child. In some cases, they need to get past denying that there is a problem at all. I can relate to parents going through this process and help them understand their child on another level. For example, even though I'm in a wheelchair and a child may be learning disabled, we both need to do things differently and understand that coping is a lifelong process. Special education teachers need to be sensitive to parents' feelings. Not only do parents have to deal with the disability, but they must also handle meetings, paperwork, the everyday needs of the child, and the question "Where do we go from here?"

Children experience the same grief process but more on a level of "I can't do what others are doing," whether it be running or reading. I try to relate my experience of hav-

To see examples of some of the adaptive materials and activities used by Ms. Ryan-Griffith, go to the Teacher Feature page on the Companion Website at **www.prenhall. com/heward**

440

ing to do things differently to whatever they are concerned with at the time. I explain that even though they have to do things differently, they are not stupid. Everyone has their own special way of learning, and my job is to find out how they learn so I can teach them better. To older kids I explain their test scores and what an IEP means. I bring them into their challenges so that they own them. Getting vested in and positive about their progress is extremely important. Another important way I get through to kids is by talking about myself. When I encounter a new group of students, I always begin by telling about myself, bringing them into my challenges. I explain why I'm in a wheelchair and let them ask questions. This way they also start to talk about themselves, and we can relate our experiences about doing things differently and feelings about our challenges. I also give my talk to the general education classes so they can become more aware of and sensitive to challenges of others. In this way they can start to see people, not chairs. Then we all go out and take a ride on my lift.

Children with physical disabilities, health impairments, and traumatic brain injury are an extremely varied population. Describing them with a single set of characteristics would be impossible, even if we used very general terms. Their physical disabilities may be mild, moderate, or severe. Some children with special health care needs are extremely restricted in their activities and intellectual functioning; others have no major limitations on what they can do and learn. Some appear entirely normal; others have highly visible disabilities. Children may have a single impairment or a combination of disabilities. They may have lived with the physical disability or health impairment since birth or have acquired it recently. Some children must use special assistive devices that call attention to their disability; others display behaviors they cannot control. Some disabilities are always present; others occur only from time to time. Over an extended period, the degree of disability may increase, decrease, or remain about the same.

As you can see, the students whose special education needs we consider in this chapter have a great many individual differences. Linda, for example, has undergone long periods of hospitalization and finds it difficult to keep up with her academic work. Gary takes medication that controls his seizures most of the time, but it also tends to make him drowsy in the classroom. Brian, who uses a wheelchair for mobility, is disappointed that he is unable to compete with his classmates in football, baseball, and track. Yet he participates fully in all other aspects of his high school program with no special modifications other than the addition of a few ramps in the building and a newly accessible washroom. Most of Brian's teachers and friends, in fact, do not think of him as needing special education at all. Janice becomes tired easily and attends school for only 3 hours per day. Kencel does his schoolwork in a specially designed chair that helps him sit more comfortably in the classroom.

An appropriate education for children with physical and health impairments may require modifications in the classroom environment, use of specialized teaching techniques, assistive devices for communication or mobility, and/or provision of related health services in the classroom. It is important for teachers (and often for other students as well) to understand how a particular condition may affect a child's learning, development, and behavior. Because some physical and health impairments may cause possible complications or emergencies to arise in the classroom, it is equally important for the teacher to know how to manage such situations effectively and when and how to seek help. Although we can make general statements about some physical disabilities, health impairments, and traumatic brain injury, numerous variations occur in the degree and severity of the conditions and how they may affect a child and his educational needs. Thus, basic information and

To better understand what will be covered in this chapter, go to the Essential Concepts and Chapter-at-a-Glance modules in Chapter 12 of the Companion Website at **www.prenhall.com/heward**

suggested guidelines shape our basic approach to the topic of students with physical disabilities and traumatic brain injury.

PHYSICAL DISABILITIES AND HEALTH IMPAIRMENTS

DEFINITIONS

Definitions of orthopedic impairment and other health impairments

 Council for Exceptional Children Content Standards for Beginning Teachers–P&HD: Issues and educational definitions of individuals with P&HD (PH1K1).
PRAXIS Special Education Core Principles: Content Knowledge: I. Understanding Exceptionalities, Definitions of disabilities.

Children with physical disabilities and health conditions who require special education are served under two IDEA disability categories: orthopedic impairments and other health impairments. According to IDEA, an **orthopedic impairment**

> adversely affects a child's educational performance. The term includes impairments caused by congenital anomaly (e.g., clubfoot, absence of some member, etc.), impairments caused by disease (e.g., poliomyelitis, bone tuberculosis, etc.), and impairments from other causes (e.g., cerebral palsy, amputations, and fractures or burns that cause contractures). (C.F.R. Sec. 300.7 [b] [7])

Although IDEA uses the term orthopedic impairments, children with physical disabilities may have orthopedic impairments or neuromotor impairments. An **orthopedic impairment** involves the skeletal system—bones, joints, limbs, and associated muscles. A **neuromotor impairment** involves the central nervous system, affecting the ability to move, use, feel, or control certain parts of the body. Although orthopedic and neurological impairments are two distinct and separate types of disabilities, they may cause similar limitations in movement. Many of the same educational, therapeutic, and recreational activities are likely to be appropriate for students with orthopedic and neurological impairments (Bigge, Best, & Heller, 2001). And there is a close relationship between the two types: for example, a child who is unable to move his legs because of damage to the central nervous system (neuromotor impairment) may also develop disorders in the bones and muscles of the legs (orthopedic impairment), especially if he does not receive proper therapy and equipment.

Children served under the IDEA category of *other health impairments* have

> limited strength, vitality, or alertness due to chronic or acute health problems such as a heart condition, tuberculosis, rheumatic fever, nephritis, asthma, sickle cell anemia, hemophilia, epilepsy, lead poisoning, leukemia, or diabetes that adversely affects a child's educational performance. (20 U.S.C., 1400 et seq.)

Health impairments include diseases and special health conditions that affect a child's educational activities and performance, such as cancer, diabetes, and cystic fibrosis. Some children with attention deficit/hyperactivity disorder (ADHD) are served under the other health impairments category of IDEA, with the reasoning that their condition results in a heightened alertness that adversely affects their educational performance. However, most children with ADHD who meet eligibility requirements for special education are served under other disability categories, most often specific learning disabilities or emotional disturbance. ADHD is discussed in Chapter 7.

Chronic and acute conditions

 Council for Exceptional Children Content Standards for Beginning Teachers–P&HD: Medical terminology related to P&HD (PH2K1).
PRAXIS Special Education Core Principles: Content Knowledge: I. Understanding Exceptionalities, Characteristics of students with disabilities, Medical factors.

Note the common clause in each definition: *that adversely affects a child's educational performance.* According to IDEA, a child is entitled to special education services if her educational performance is adversely affected by a physical disability or health-related condition. Physical disabilities and health conditions may be congenital (a child is born with a missing limb) or acquired (a child without disabilities sustains a spinal cord injury at age 15). Not all students with physical disabilities and health conditions need special education. Most physical disabilities and health conditions that result in special education are *chronic conditions;* that is, they are long-lasting, most often permanent conditions (e.g., cerebral palsy is a permanent disability that will affect a child throughout his life). By contrast, an *acute condition,* while it may produce severe and debilitating symptoms, is of limited duration (e.g., a child who acquires pneumonia will experience symptoms, but the disease itself is not permanent). Some chronic physical disabilities and health conditions have flare-ups or episodes of acute symptoms (e.g., a child with cystic fibrosis may experience periods of acute respiratory difficulties).

PREVALENCE

It is estimated that chronic medical conditions affect up to 20%—approximately 12 million—school-age children in the United States (Sexson & Dingle, 2001). However, during the 2000–2001 school year, just 73,011 children between the ages of 6 and 21 received special education services under the disability category of orthopedic impairments, compared with 291,474 children with other health impairments (U.S. Department of Education, 2002). Together, these two disability categories represent 6.4% of all school-age children receiving special education services.

Two factors make the actual number of children with physical disabilities much higher than the number of children receiving special education services under these two IDEA categories. First, because physical and health impairments often occur in combination with other disabilities, children may be counted under other categories, such as learning disabilities, speech or language impairments, or mental retardation. For example, for the purpose of special education eligibility, a diagnosis of mental retardation usually takes precedence over a diagnosis of physical impairment. Second, there are numerous children whose physical impairments and chronic health conditions do not adversely affect their educational performance sufficiently to warrant special education (Hill, 1999).

Prevalence of physical disabilities and health impairments

PRAXIS Special Education Core Principles: Content Knowledge: I. Understanding Exceptionalities, Incidence and prevalence of various types of disabilities.

TYPES AND CAUSES

Literally hundreds of physical impairments and health conditions can adversely affect children's educational performance. Here we address only those that are encountered most frequently in school-age children. For a more extensive discussion of the many physical impairments and chronic health conditions that may result in special education, see Batshaw (1997), Bigge et al. (2001), or Hill (1999).

Cerebral Palsy Cerebral palsy—a disorder of voluntary movement and posture—is the most prevalent physical disability in school-age children. In some programs, half or more of the students considered to have physical or health impairments have cerebral palsy. Cerebral palsy is a permanent condition resulting from a lesion to the brain or an abnormality of brain growth. Many diseases can affect the developing brain and lead to cerebral palsy (Batshaw, 1997). Children with cerebral palsy experience disturbances of voluntary motor functions that may include paralysis, extreme weakness, lack of coordination, involuntary convulsions, and other motor disorders. They may have little or no control over their arms, legs, or speech, depending on the type and degree of impairment. The more severe forms of cerebral palsy are often diagnosed in the first few months of life. In many other cases, however, cerebral palsy is not detected until the child is 2 to 3 years old, when parents notice that their child is having difficulty crawling, balancing, or standing. The motor dysfunction usually does not get progressively worse as a child ages. Cerebral palsy can be treated but not cured; it is not a disease, not fatal, not contagious, and, in the great majority of cases, not inherited.

About one-third of children with cerebral palsy have intelligence within or above the normal range, one-third have mild cognitive impairment, and one-third have moderate to severe mental retardation (e.g., Whaley & Wong, 1995). Sensory impairments are also common in children with cerebral palsy; 5% to 15% have hearing loss (Nechring & Steele,

Types and causes of physical disabilities and health impairments

 Content Standards for Beginning Teachers–P&HD: Etiology and characteristics of P&HD across the life span (PH2K2) (also, PH2K1).
PRAXIS Special Education Core Principles: Content Knowledge: I. Understanding Exceptionalities, Causation and prevention of disability.

1996), and up to 50% have impaired vision (Dzienkowski, Smith, Dillow, & Yucha, 1996). It is important to note that no clear relationship exists between the degree of motor impairment and the degree of intellectual impairment (if any) in children with cerebral palsy (or other physical disabilities). A student with only mild motor impairment may experience severe developmental delays, whereas a student with severe motor impairments may be intellectually gifted (Willard-Holt, 1998).

The causes of cerebral palsy are varied and not clearly known (Pellegrino, 1997). It has most often been attributed to the occurrence of injuries, accidents, or illnesses that are *prenatal* (before birth), *perinatal* (at or near the time of birth), or *postnatal* (soon after birth) that result in decreased oxygen to low-birth-weight newborns. Recent improvements in obstetrical delivery and neonatal care, however, have not decreased the incidence of cerebral palsy, which has remained steady during the past 20 years or so at about 1.5 in every 1,000 live births (Evans & Smith, 1993). An additional 1,200 to 1,500 children acquire cerebral palsy through postbirth trauma or accidents (Heller, Alberto, Forney, & Schwartzman, 1996). Factors most often associated with cerebral palsy are mental retardation of the mother, premature birth (gestational age of 32 weeks or less), low birth weight, and a delay of 5 minutes or more before the baby's first cry.

Because the location and extent of brain damage is so variable in individuals with cerebral palsy, a diagnosis of the condition is not descriptive of its effects. Cerebral palsy is classified in terms of the affected parts of the body and by its effects on movement (Best & Bigge, 2001). The term *plegia* (from the Greek "to strike") is often used in combination with a prefix indicating the location of limb involvement:

With a little help from a classmate, another musician joins the marching band.

Limbs affected by cerebral palsy

Council for Exceptional Children Content Standards for Beginning Teachers–P&HD: Medical terminology related to P&HD (PH2K1).
PRAXIS Teaching Students with Orthopedic Impairments: I. Overview, General and technical medical aspects related to orthopedically disabling conditions.

- *Monoplegia.* Only one limb (upper or lower) is affected.
- *Hemiplegia.* Two limbs on same side of the body are involved.
- *Triplegia.* Three limbs are affected.
- *Quadriplegia.* All four limbs (both arms and legs) are involved; movement of the trunk and face may also be impaired.
- *Paraplegia.* Only legs are impaired.
- *Diplegia.* Impairment primarily involves the legs, with less severe involvement of the arms.
- *Double hemiplegia.* Impairment primarily involves the arms, with less severe involvement of the legs.

Cerebral palsy is classified by its effects on movement according to its effects on muscle tone (hypertonia or hypotonia) and quality of movement (athetosis or ataxia) (Pellegrino, 1997). Approximately 50% to 60% of all individuals with cerebral palsy have *spastic cerebral palsy,* which is characterized by tense, contracted muscles (**hypertonia**). Their movements may be jerky, exaggerated, and poorly coordinated. They may be unable to grasp objects with their fingers. When they try to control their movements, they may become even jerkier. If they are able to walk, they may use a scissors gait, standing on the toes with knees bent and pointed inward. Deformities of the spine; hip dislocation; and contractures of the hand, elbow, foot, and knee are common.

Athetosis occurs in about 20% of all cases of cerebral palsy. Children with *athetoid cerebral palsy* make large, irregular, twisting movements they cannot control. When they are at rest or asleep, there is little or no abnormal motion. An effort to pick up a pencil, however, may result in wildly waving arms, facial grimaces, and extension of the tongue. These children may not be able to control the muscles of their lips, tongue, and throat and may drool. They may also seem to stumble and lurch awkwardly as they walk. At times their muscles may be tense and rigid; at other times, they may be loose and flaccid. Extreme difficulty in expressive oral language, mobility, and activities of daily living often accompanies this form of cerebral palsy.

Ataxia is noted as the primary type of involvement in only 1% to 10% of cases of cerebral palsy (Hill, 1999). Children with *ataxic cerebral palsy* have a poor sense of balance and hand use. They may appear to be dizzy while walking and may fall easily if not supported. Their movements tend to be jumpy and unsteady, with exaggerated motion patterns that often overshoot the intended objects. They seem to be constantly attempting to overcome the effect of gravity and stabilize their bodies.

Rigidity and *tremor* are additional but much less common types of cerebral palsy. Children with the rare rigidity type of cerebral palsy display extreme stiffness in the affected limbs; they may be fixed and immobile for long periods. Rhythmic, uncontrollable movements mark tremor cerebral palsy; the tremors may actually increase when the children attempt to control their actions.

Most infants born with cerebral palsy have **hypotonia,** or weak, floppy muscles, particularly in the neck and trunk. When hypotonia persists throughout the child's first year without being replaced with spasticity or athetoid involvement, the condition is called generalized hypotonia. Hypotonic children typically have low levels of motor activity, are slow to make balancing responses, and may not walk until 30 months of age (Bleck, 1987). Severely hypotonic children must use external support to achieve and maintain an upright position.

Because most children with cerebral palsy have diffuse brain damage, pure types of cerebral palsy are rare. Children may also be described as having *mixed cerebral palsy,* consisting of more than one of these types, particularly if their impairments are severe. The motor impairment of children with cerebral palsy often makes it frustrating, if not impossible, for them to play with toys. (See Teaching & Learning, "Adapting Toys for Children with Cerebral Palsy," later in this chapter.)

Because cerebral palsy is such a complex condition, it is most effectively managed through the cooperative involvement of physicians, teachers, physical therapists, occupational therapists, communication specialists, counselors, and others who work directly with children and families. Dormans and Pellegrino (1998) have compiled a detailed handbook to guide the education of children with cerebral palsy by interdisciplinary teams. Regular exercise and careful positioning in school settings help the child with cerebral palsy move as fully and comfortably as possible and prevent or minimize progressive damage to muscles and limbs. Most children with cerebral palsy are capable of learning to walk, although many need to use wheelchairs, braces, and other assistive devices, particularly for moving around outside the home. Orthopedic surgery may increase a child's range of motion or obviate complications such as hip dislocations and permanent muscle contractions.

Spina Bifida   Congenital malformations of the brain, spinal cord, or vertebrae are known as *neural tube defects.* The most common neural tube defect is **spina bifida,** a condition in which the vertebrae do not enclose the spinal cord. As a result, a portion of the spinal cord and the nerves that normally control muscles and feeling in the lower part of the body fail to develop normally. Of the three types of spina bifida, the mildest form is **spina bifida occulta,** in which only a few vertebrae are malformed, usually in the lower spine. The defect is usually not visible externally. It is estimated that up to 10% of the general population may have spina bifida occulta (Liptak, 1997). If the flexible casing (meninges) that surrounds the spinal cord bulges through an opening in the infant's back at birth, the condition is called **meningocele.** These two forms do not usually cause any loss of function for the child.

In **myelomeningocele**—the most common and most serious form of spina bifida—the spinal lining, spinal cord, and nerve roots all protrude. The protruding spinal cord and nerves are usually tucked back into the spinal column shortly after birth. This condition carries a high risk of paralysis and infection. In general, the higher the location of the lesion

Hypertonia, athetosis, ataxia, and hypotonia

Council for Exceptional Children   Content Standards for Beginning Teachers–P&HD: Medical termionology related to P&HD (PH2K1) (also, PH2K2, PH3K1, CC2K1).
PRAXIS Teaching Students with Orthopedic Impairments: I. Overview, General and technical medical aspects related to orthopedically disabling conditions.

Spina bifida and related terms

Council for Exceptional Children   Content Standards for Beginning Teachers–P&HD: Medical terminology related to P&HD (PH2K1) (also, PH2K2, PH3K1).
PRAXIS Teaching Students with Orthopedic Impairments: I. Overview, General and technical medical aspects related to orthopedically disabling conditions.

Adapting Toys for Children with Cerebral Palsy

Spontaneous and independent use of commercially available toys is not possible for many children with cerebral palsy. The toys often require more coordination or strength than these youngsters have. Continuous inability to engage in physical activity and gain mastery over the environment may cause the child to lose motivation and become passive. Because playing is an integral part of intellectual, social, perceptual, and physical development, growth in these areas may be limited when the child cannot actively play.

Fortunately, toys can be adapted to make them more accessible to children with physical disabilities. Six types of modifications are most effective in promoting active, independent use of play materials.

Stabilization. Stabilizing a toy enhances its function in two ways. First, it prevents the child's uncontrolled movements and difficulty directing the hand to desired locations from moving objects out of reach or knocking them over. Second, many children with cerebral palsy have difficulty performing tasks that require holding an object with one hand while manipulating it in some way with the other hand. Toys with a base can be clamped to a table. Masking tape is an inexpensive and effective way to secure many toys. Velcro is another. The hook side of Velcro can be placed on the toy, while the loop side is mounted on a clean surface. Suction cups can also stabilize a toy for a short time on a clean, nonwood surface.

Boundaries. Restricting the movement of toys such as cars or trains makes it easier for some children to use and retrieve them if pushed out of reach. Boundaries can be created in various ways depending upon how the object is to be moved. For example, push toys can be placed in the top of a cardboard box or on a tray with edges to create a restricted area. Pull toys can be placed on a track, and items that require a banging motion, such as a tambourine, can be held in a wood frame with springs.

Grasping aids. The ability to hold objects independently can be facilitated in a variety of ways. A Velcro strap can be placed around the child's hand, with Velcro also placed on the materials to be held, thus creating a bond between the hand and the object. A universal cuff can be used for holding sticklike objects such as crayons or pointers. Simply enlarging an item by wrapping foam or tape around it may make it easier to hold.

Manipulation aids. Some toys require isolated finger movements, use of a pincer grasp, and controlled movements of the wrist, which are too difficult for a child with

on the spine, the greater the effect on the body and its functioning. About 6 in 10,000 live births in the United States result in myelomeningocele; and it affects girls at a much higher rate than boys (Liptak, 1997).

About 80% to 90% of children born with myelomeningocele develop **hydrocephalus,** the accumulation of cerebrospinal fluid in tissues surrounding the brain (Hill, 1999). Left untreated, this condition can lead to head enlargement and severe brain damage. Hydrocephalus is treated by the surgical insertion of a **shunt,** a one-way valve that diverts the cerebrospinal fluid away from the brain and into the bloodstream. Replacements of the shunt are usually necessary as a child grows older. Teachers who work with children who have shunts should be aware that blockage, disconnection, or infection of the shunt may result in increased intracranial pressure. Warning signs such as drowsiness, vomiting, headache,

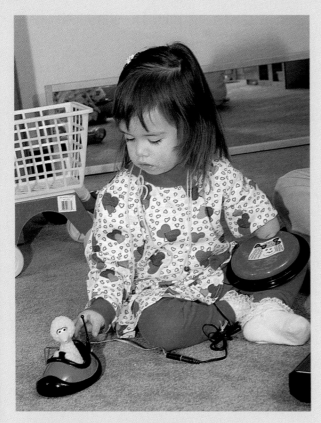

An adapted switch makes battery-operated toys accessible and fun for Madelyn.

ified to operate by adapted switches. Teachers can make and adapt their own switches and toys (Burkhardt, 1981; Wright & Momari, 1985) or purchase them from a number of firms that serve persons with disabilities. After determining some physical action (such as moving a knee laterally, lifting a shoulder, or making a sound) that the child can perform consistently and with minimum effort, one selects the type of switch best suited to that movement. The switch is always positioned in the same place, which facilitates automatic switch activation and allows the child to give full attention to the play activity rather than concentrating on using the switch.

Positioning.   An occupational or physical therapist should determine the special positioning needs of each child. Good positioning will maximize freedom of movement; improve the ability to look at a toy; and facilitate controlled, relaxed movement. Placement of the toy is crucial. It should be within easy reach and require a minimum of effort to manipulate. The child should not become easily fatigued or have to struggle. The child must be able to look at the toy while playing.

General considerations.   Activities should be interesting and facilitate cognitive growth yet not be beyond the child's conceptual capabilities. Toys should be sturdy and durable. Avoid toys with sharp edges or small pieces that can be swallowed.

These principles for adapting toys can be applied to other devices, such as communication aids, computers, environmental controls, and household items, to make them easier to use. Making an educational environment more accessible gives children with physical disabilities greater control of their surroundings and the opportunity to expand the scope of their learning experiences.

physical disabilities. Various adaptations can help compensate for deficits in these movements. Extending and widening pieces of the toy will make swiping and pushing easier. Flat extensions, knobs, or dowels can be used to increase the surface area. A crossbar or dowel, placed appropriately, can compensate for an inability to rotate the wrist.

Switches.   Some children have such limited hand function that they can only operate toys that are activated by a switch. Commercially available, battery-operated toys can be mod-

Source: Adapted from Schaeffler, C. (1988, Spring). Making toys accessible for children with cerebral palsy. *Teaching Exceptional Children, 20,* 26–28. Used by permission.

irritability, and squinting should be heeded because a blocked shunt can be life threatening (Charney, 1992). Shunts can be removed in many school-age children when the production and absorption of cerebrospinal fluid are brought into balance.

Usually children with spina bifida have some degree of paralysis of the lower limbs and lack full control of bladder and bowel functions. In most cases, these children have good use of their arms and upper body (although some children experience fine motor problems). Children with spina bifida usually walk with braces, crutches, or walkers; they may use wheelchairs for longer distances. Some children need special help in dressing and toileting; others are able to manage these tasks on their own.

Because the spinal defect usually occurs above where nerves that control the bladder emerge from the spinal cord, most children with spina bifida have urinary incontinence and

Clean intermittent catherization

 Council for Exceptional Children Content Standards for Beginning Teachers–P&HD: Specialized healoth care intervetions for individuals with P&HD (PH5K2).
PRAXIS Teaching Students with Orthopedic Impairments: I. Overview, General and technical medical aspects related to orthopedically disabling conditions.

need to use a *catheter* (tube) or bag to collect their urine. **Clean intermittent catheterization (CIC)** is taught to children with urinary complications so that they can empty their bladders at convenient times (Ault, Rues, Graff, & Holvoet, 2000). This technique is effective with both boys and girls, works best if used every 2 to 4 hours, and does not require an absolutely sterile environment (McLone & Ito, 1998).

Muscular Dystrophy   **Muscular dystrophy** refers to a group of inherited diseases marked by progressive *atrophy* (wasting away) of the body's muscles. **Duchenne muscular dystrophy (DMD)** is the most common and most severe of the more than 40 types. DMD affects only boys (1 in 3,500 male births), but about one-third of cases are the result of genetic mutation in families with no history of the disease (Best, 2001). The child appears normal at birth, but muscle weakness is usually evident between the ages of 2 and 6, when the child begins to experience difficulty in running or climbing stairs. The child may walk with an unusual gait, showing a protruding stomach and hollow back. The calf muscles of a child with muscular dystrophy may appear unusually large because the degenerated muscle has been replaced by fatty tissue.

Children with muscular dystrophy often have difficulty getting to their feet after lying down or playing on the floor. They may fall easily. By age 10 to 14, the child loses the ability to walk; the small muscles of the hands and fingers are usually the last to be affected. Some doctors and therapists recommend the early use of electrically powered wheelchairs; others suggest employing special braces and other devices to prolong walking as long as possible.

At this time, there is no known cure for muscular dystrophy, and in most cases this progressive disease is fatal in adolescence or young adulthood. Death is often caused by heart failure or respiratory failure due to atrophied chest muscles. Treatment focuses on maintaining function of unaffected muscles for as long as possible, facilitating ambulation, helping the child and family cope with limitations imposed by the disease, and providing emotional support and counseling to the child and family (Hill, 1999). Regular physical therapy, exercise, and the use of appropriate aids and appliances can help the child maintain a good deal of independence. The child should be encouraged to be as active as possible. However, a teacher should be careful not to lift a child with muscular dystrophy by the arms: even a gentle pull may dislocate the child's limbs.

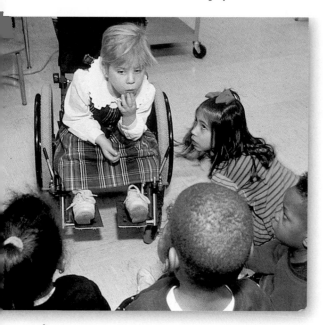

"Well, I think the best part of the story was when. . . ." Learning self-catheterization has given Kristine more control over her classroom schedule and increased her participation.

Location and effects of spinal cord injuries

Council for Exceptional Children   Content Standards for Beginning Teachers–P&HD: Medical terminology related to P&HD (PH2K1).
PRAXIS Teaching Students with Orthopedic Impairments: I. Overview, General and technical medical aspects related to orthopedically disabling conditions.

Spinal Cord Injuries   Spinal cord injuries are usually the result of a lesion to the spinal cord caused by a penetrating injury (e.g., gunshot wound), stretching of the vertebral column (e.g., whiplash during an auto accident), fracture of the vertebrae, or compression of the spinal cord (e.g., a diving accident). Vehicular accidents, sports injuries, and violence are the most common causes of spinal cord injuries in school-age children (Apple, Anson, Hunter, & Bell, 1995). Injury to the spinal column is generally described by letters and numbers indicating the site of the damage; for example, a C5–6 injury means the damage has occurred at the level of the fifth and sixth cervical vertebrae, a flexible area of the neck susceptible to injury from whiplash and diving or trampoline accidents. A T12 injury refers to the 12th thoracic (chest) vertebra and an L3 to the third lumbar (lower back) area. In general, paralysis and loss of sensation occur below the level of the injury. The higher the injury on the spine and the more the injury (lesion) cuts through the entire cord, the greater the paralysis (Hill, 1999).

Males represent 80% of the approximately 7,000 to 10,000 persons in the United States who are victims of traumatic spinal cord injuries each year, and most are 15 to 30 years old (National Spinal Cord Injury Association, 2001). Students who have sustained spinal cord injuries usually use wheelchairs for mobility. Motorized wheelchairs, though expensive, are recommended for those with quadriplegia, whereas children with paraplegia can use self-propelled wheelchairs. Children with quadriplegia may have severe breathing problems because the muscles of the chest, which normally govern respiration, are affected. In most cases, children with spinal cord injuries lack bladder and bowel control and need to follow a careful management program to maintain personal hygiene and avoid infection and skin irritation.

Rehabilitation programs for children and adolescents who have sustained spinal cord injuries usually involve physical therapy, the use of adaptive devices for mobility and independent living, and psychological support to help them adjust to a sudden disability. *Personal care attendants* (PCAs) assist many individuals with spinal cord injury, particularly those with quadriplegia, with activities of daily living. Adolescents and adults are often particularly concerned about sexual function. Even though most spinal cord injuries do affect sexuality, understanding partners and positive attitudes toward themselves mean that many people with spinal cord injuries are able to enjoy satisfying sexual relationships.

Epilepsy   Whether we are awake or asleep, there is always electrical activity occurring in the brain. A *seizure* is a disturbance of movement, sensation, behavior, and/or consciousness caused by abnormal electrical discharges in the brain. "Some have likened the event, known as a seizure, to an engine misfiring or to a power surge in a computer" (Hill, 1999, p. 231). Anyone can have a seizure. It is common for a seizure to occur when someone has a high fever, drinks excessive alcohol, or experiences a blow to the head.

When seizures occur chronically and repeatedly, however, the condition is known as a *seizure disorder* or, more commonly, **epilepsy.** Epilepsy is not a disease, and it constitutes a disorder only while a seizure is actually in progress. It is estimated that 1% of the general population has epilepsy (Brumback, Mathews, & Shenoy, 2001).

The cause of epilepsy for approximately 30% of cases is identified from among at least 50 different conditions known to result in seizure activity, such as cerebral palsy, infections of the brain or central nervous system, metabolic disorders such as hypoglycemia, alcohol or lead poisoning, an underlying lesion caused by scar tissue from a head injury, high fever, an interruption in blood supply to the brain, or rough handling of a baby (shaken-baby syndrome) (Evans & Smith, 1993; Lowenthal, 2001). Epilepsy can occur at any stage of life but most frequently begins in childhood. A wide variety of psychological, physical, and sensory factors are thought to trigger seizures in susceptible persons—for example, fatigue, excitement, anger, surprise, hyperventilation, hormonal changes (as in menstruation or pregnancy), withdrawal from drugs or alcohol, and exposure to certain patterns of light, sound, or touch.

Many unfortunate misconceptions about epilepsy have circulated in the past and are still prevalent today. Negative public attitudes, in fact, have probably been more harmful to people with epilepsy than has the condition itself. During a seizure, a dysfunction in the electrochemical activity of the brain causes a person to lose control of the muscles temporarily. Between seizures (that is, most of the time), the brain functions normally. Teachers, school health care personnel, and perhaps classmates need to be aware that a child is affected by a seizure disorder so that they can be prepared to deal with a seizure if one should occur in school. There are several types of seizures.

The **generalized tonic-clonic seizure** (formerly called *grand mal*) is the most conspicuous and serious type of seizure. A generalized tonic-clonic seizure can be disturbing and frightening to someone who has never seen one. The affected child has little or no warning that a seizure is about to occur; the muscles become stiff, and the child loses consciousness and falls to the floor. Then the entire body shakes violently as the muscles alternately contract and relax. Saliva may be forced from the mouth, legs and arms may jerk, and the bladder and bowels may be emptied. In most cases, the contractions diminish in 2 to 3 minutes, and the child either goes to sleep or regains consciousness in a confused or drowsy state. Generalized tonic-clonic seizures may occur as often as several times a day or as seldom as once a year. They are more likely to occur during the day than at night. A tonic-clonic

Epilepsy and types of seizures

   Council for Exceptional Children   Content Standards for Beginning Teachers–P&HD: Medical terminology related to P&HD (PH2K1) (also, PH2K2, PH3K1).
PRAXIS Teaching Students with Orthopedic Impairments: I. Overview, General and technical medical aspects related to orthopedically disabling conditions.

FIGURE 12.1 Procedures for handling tonic-clonic seizures

The typical seizure is not a medical emergency, but knowledgeable handling of the situation is important. When a child experiences a generalized tonic-clonic seizure in the classroom, the teacher should follow these procedures:

- Keep calm. Reassure the other students that the child will be fine in a minute.

- Ease the child to the floor and clear the area around him of anything that could hurt him.

- Put something flat and soft (like a folded coat) under his head so it will not bang on the floor as his body jerks.

- You cannot stop the seizure. Let it run its course. Do not try to revive the child and do not interfere with his movements.

- Turn him gently onto his side. This keeps his airway clear and allows saliva to drain away.

  DON'T try to force his mouth open.

  DON'T try to hold on to his tongue.

  DON'T put anything in his mouth.

- When the jerking movements stop, let the child rest until he regains consciousness.

- Breathing may be shallow during the seizure, and may even stop briefly. In the unlikely event that breathing does not begin again, check the child's airway for obstruction and give artificial respiration.

Some students recover quickly after this type of seizure; others need more time. A short period of rest is usually advised. If the student is able to remain in the classroom afterwards, however, he should be encouraged to do so. Staying in the classroom (or returning to it as soon as possible) allows for continued participation in classroom activity and is psychologically less difficult for the student. If a student has frequent seizures, handling them can become routine once teacher and classmates learn what to expect. If a seizure of this type continues for longer than five minutes, call for emergency assistance.

Source: Adapted from the Epilepsy Foundation of America. (1987). *Epilepsy school alert.* Washington, DC: Author.

Procedures for handling seizures

Council for Exceptional Children Content Standards for Beginning Teachers–P&HD: Specialized health care interventions for individuals with P&HD (PH5K2).
PRAXIS Teaching Students with Orthopedic Impairments: I. Overview, General and technical medical aspects related to orthopedically disabling conditions.

seizure, although very frightening to someone who has not witnessed such an episode, is not a medical emergency (Hill, 1999). Figure 12.1 describes procedures for handling seizures in the classroom.

The **absence seizure** (previously called *petit mal*) is far less severe than the generalized tonic-clonic seizure but may occur much more frequently—as often as 100 times per day in some children. Usually there is a brief loss of consciousness, lasting anywhere from a few seconds to half a minute or so. The child may stare blankly, flutter or blink her eyes, grow pale, or drop whatever she is holding. She may be mistakenly viewed as daydreaming or not listening. The child may or may not be aware that she has had a seizure, and no special first aid is necessary. The teacher should keep the child's parents advised of seizure activity and may also find it helpful to explain it to the child's classmates.

A **complex partial seizure** (also called *psychomotor*) may appear as a brief period of inappropriate or purposeless activity. The child may smack her lips, walk around aimlessly, or shout. She may appear to be conscious but is not actually aware of her unusual behavior. Complex partial seizures usually last from 2 to 5 minutes, after which the child has amnesia about the entire episode. Some children may respond to spoken directions during a complex partial seizure.

A **simple partial seizure** is characterized by sudden jerking motions with no loss of consciousness. Partial seizures may occur weekly, monthly, or only once or twice a year. The teacher should keep dangerous objects out of the child's way and, except in emergencies, should not try to physically restrain him.

Many children experience a warning sensation, known as an *aura*, a short time before a seizure. The aura takes different forms in different people; distinctive feelings, sights, sounds, tastes, and even smells have been described. The aura can be a useful safety valve, enabling the child to leave the class or group before the seizure actually occurs. Some children report that the warning provided by the aura helps them feel more secure and comfortable about themselves.

In some children, absence and partial seizures can go undetected for long periods. An observant teacher can be instrumental in detecting the presence of a seizure disorder and in referring the child for appropriate medical help. The teacher can also assist parents and physicians by noting both the effectiveness and the side effects of any medication the child takes. With proper medical treatment and the support of parents, teachers, and peers, most students with seizure disorders lead full and normal lives. Antiepileptic drugs may largely or wholly control epileptic seizures in 60% to 70% of children (Pedley, Scheuer, & Walczak, 1995). Some children require such heavy doses of medication, however, that their learning and behavior are adversely affected; and some medications have undesirable side effects, such as drowsiness, nausea, weight gain, and thickening of the gums. All children with seizure disorders benefit from a realistic understanding of their condition and accepting attitudes on the part of teachers and classmates. Although the student with seizure disorders may be uncomfortable about letting friends know about the condition, classmates should be aware so that they will know how to, and how not to, respond in the event of a seizure (Hill, 1999).

Diabetes   Diabetes—a chronic disorder of metabolism—is a common childhood disease, affecting about 1 in 600 school-age children; so it is likely that most teachers will encounter students with diabetes at one time or another (Sexson & Dingle, 2001). Without proper medical management, the diabetic child's system is not able to obtain and retain adequate energy from food. Not only does the child lack energy, but many important parts of the body—particularly the eyes and the kidneys—can be affected by untreated diabetes. Early symptoms of diabetes include thirst, headaches, weight loss (despite a good appetite), frequent urination, and cuts that are slow to heal.

Children with **Type I diabetes** (formerly called *juvenile diabetes* or *early-onset diabetes*) have insufficient insulin, a hormone normally produced by the pancreas and necessary for the metabolism of glucose, a form of sugar produced when food is digested. To regulate the condition, insulin must be injected daily under the skin. Most children with diabetes learn to inject their own insulin—in some cases as frequently as four times per day—and to determine the amount of insulin they need by testing the level of sugar and other substances in their urine. Children with diabetes must follow a specific and regular diet prescribed by a physician or nutrition specialist. A regular exercise program is also usually suggested.

Teachers who have a child with diabetes in their classrooms should learn how to recognize the symptoms of both too little sugar or too much sugar in the child's bloodstream and the kind of treatment indicated by each condition (Yousef, 1995). *Hypoglycemia* (low blood sugar), also called *insulin reaction* or *diabetic shock,* can result from taking too much insulin, unusually strenuous exercise, or a missed or delayed meal. (The blood sugar level is lowered by insulin and exercise and raised by food.) Symptoms of hypoglycemia include faintness, dizziness, blurred vision, drowsiness, and nausea. The child may appear irritable or have a marked personality change. In most cases, giving the child some form of concentrated sugar (e.g., a sugar cube, a glass of fruit juice, a candy bar) ends the insulin reaction within a few minutes. The child's doctor or parents should inform the teacher and school health personnel of the appropriate foods to give in case of insulin reaction.

Diabetes and related terms

Council for Exceptional Children   Content Standards for Beginning Teachers–P&HD: Medical terminology related to P&HD (PH2K1) (also, PH2K2, PH3K1).
PRAXIS Teaching Students with Orthopedic Impairments: I. Overview, General and technical medical aspects related to orthopedically disabling conditions.

Hyperglycemia (high blood sugar) is more serious; it indicates that too little insulin is present and the diabetes is not under control. Its onset is gradual rather than sudden. The symptoms of hyperglycemia, sometimes called *diabetic coma,* include fatigue; thirst; dry, hot skin; deep, labored breathing; excessive urination; and fruity-smelling breath. A doctor or nurse should be contacted immediately if a child displays such symptoms.

Asthma   **Asthma** is a chronic lung disease characterized by episodic bouts of wheezing, coughing, and difficulty breathing. An asthmatic attack is usually triggered by allergens

(e.g., pollen, certain foods, pets), irritants (e.g., cigarette smoke, smog), exercise, or emotional stress, which results in a narrowing of the airways in the lungs. This reaction increases the resistance to the airflow into and out of the lungs, making it harder for the individual to breathe. The severity of asthma varies greatly: the child may experience only a period of mild coughing or extreme difficulty in breathing that requires emergency treatment. Many asthmatic children experience normal lung functioning between episodes.

Asthma is the most common lung disease of children; estimates of its prevalence range from 6% to as high as 12% of school-age children (Sexson & Dingle, 2001). The causes of asthma are not completely known, although most consider it the result of an interaction of heredity and environment. Symptoms generally begin in early childhood but sometimes do not develop until late childhood or adolescence. Asthma tends to run in families, which suggests that an allergic intolerance to some stimulus may be inherited. Symptoms of asthma might also first appear following a viral infection of the respiratory system.

Primary treatment for asthma begins with a systematic effort to identify the stimuli and environmental situations that provoke attacks. The number of potential allergens and irritants is virtually limitless, and in some cases it can be extremely difficult to determine the combination of factors that results in an asthmatic episode. Changes in temperature, humidity, and season (attacks are especially common in autumn) are also related to the frequency of asthmatic symptoms. Rigorous physical exercise produces asthmatic episodes in some children. Asthma can be controlled effectively in most children with a combination of medications and limiting exposure to known allergens. Most children whose breathing attacks are induced by physical exercise can still enjoy physical exercise and sports through careful selection of activities (e.g., swimming generally provokes less exercise-induced asthma than running) and/or taking certain medications before rigorous exercise. Although asthma is biochemical in origin, an interrelationship exists between emotional stress and asthma. Periods of psychological stress or higher emotional responses increase the likelihood of asthmatic attacks, and asthmatic episodes produce more stress. Treatment often involves counseling or an asthma teaching program (Hill, 1999) in which children and their families are taught how to reduce and cope with emotional stress.

Asthma is the leading cause of absenteeism in school. It is estimated that 10 million school days are lost each year because of asthma (Asthma and Allergy Foundation of America, 2001). Chronic absenteeism makes it difficult for the child with asthma to maintain performance at grade level, and homebound instructional services may be necessary. The majority of children with asthma who receive medical and psychological support, however, successfully complete school and lead normal lives. By working cooperatively with parents and medical personnel to minimize the child's contact with provoking factors and constructing a plan to assist the child during attacks, the classroom teacher can play an important role in reducing the impact of asthma (Getch & Neuharth-Pritchett, 1999).

This special educator does not allow Jamika's chronic illness to prevent her from participating in developmentally appropriate play activities.

Causes, characteristics, and effects of asthma

Council for Exceptional Children   Content Standards for Beginning Teachers–P&HD: Impact of P&HD on individuals, families, society (PH3K1) (also, PH2K2, CC2K2).

PRAXIS Teaching Students with Orthopedic Impairments: I. Overview, General and technical medical aspects related to orthopedically disabling conditions.

Cystic Fibrosis   **Cystic fibrosis** is a genetic disorder of children and adolescents in which the body's exocrine glands excrete thick mucus that can block the lungs and parts of the digestive system. It is a hereditary disease found predominantly in Caucasians—affecting approximately 1 in 3,500 live Caucasian births, 1 in 11,500 Hispanic births, and 1 in 14,500 African American births (FitzSimmons, 1993). Children with cystic fibrosis often have difficulty breathing and are susceptible to pulmonary disease (lung infections). Malnutrition and poor growth are common characteristics of children with cystic fibrosis because of pancreatic insufficiency that causes inadequate digestion and malabsorption of nutrients, especially fats. They often have large and frequent bowel movements because food passes through the system only partially digested. Getting children with cystic fibrosis to consume enough calories is critical to their health and development. The symptoms may result from a missing chemical or substance in the body. Medical research has not determined exactly how cystic fibrosis functions, and no reliable cure has yet been found. Medications prescribed for children with cystic fibrosis include enzymes to facilitate digestion and solutions to thin and loosen the mucus in the lungs. Children with cystic fibrosis undergo daily physiotherapy in which the chest is vigorously thumped and vibrated to dislodge mucus, followed by positioning the body to drain loosened secretions.

Many children and young adults with cystic fibrosis are able to lead active lives. During vigorous physical exercises, some children may need help from teachers, aides, or classmates to clear their lungs and air passages. The life expectancy of people with cystic fibrosis used to be very short; 30 years ago the median life expectancy was about 8 years. The long-range outlook for children affected by cystic fibrosis is improving; and with current treatment, the average life expectancy of individuals with cystic fibrosis is 32.5 years (Cystic Fibrosis Foundation, 2001).

Human Immunodeficiency Virus and Acquired Immunodeficiency Syndrome   Persons with **acquired immunodeficiency syndrome (AIDS)** are not able to resist and fight off infections because of a breakdown in the immune system. Opportunistic infections such as tuberculosis, pneumonia, and cancerous skin lesions attack the person's body, grow in severity, and ultimately result in death. At present, there is no known cure or vaccine for AIDS, although there have been recent advances in drugs such as AZT.

AIDS is caused by the **human immunodeficiency virus (HIV),** which is found in the bodily fluids of an infected person (blood, semen, vaginal secretions, and breast milk). HIV is transmitted from one person to another through sexual contact and blood-to-blood contact (e.g., intravenous drug use with shared needles, transfusions of unscreened contaminated blood). Pregnant women can also transmit HIV to newborn children. Most people who become infected with HIV show no symptoms of AIDS for 8 to 12 years, and not all persons who have HIV get AIDS (Centers for Disease Control and Prevention, 2001a).

The number of people worldwide who have contracted HIV/AIDS is staggering. It is estimated that 30 million people worldwide carry the HIV virus, with as many as 3 million new cases per year. Although the incidence rate for new cases of AIDS in the United States has decreased in recent years, the disease is still of epidemic proportions. Of the nearly 800,000 cumulative cases of HIV-positive cases reported in the United States through December 2000, approximately 9,000 involved children under the ages of 13 (Centers for Disease Control and Prevention, 2001a).

In addition to health problems and significant weight loss, serious neurological complications and developmental delays have been noted in children with HIV/AIDS, particularly in expressive language, attention, memory, and motor functioning (National Institute of Allergy and Infectious Diseases, 2001; Wolters, Brouwers, & Moss, 1995). These complications may be caused by the direct effect of the HIV virus on the brain, opportunistic infections that arise because of the weakened immune system, the powerful regimen of medications taken to combat the spread of HIV, or a combination of these factors (Sexson & Dingle, 2001).

Cystic fibrosis

 Council for Exceptional Children   Content Standards for Beginning Teachers–P&HD: Impact of P&HD on individuals, families, society (PH3K1) (also, PH2K2, CC2K2).
PRAXIS Teaching Students with Orthopedic Impairments: I. Overview, General and technical medical aspects related to orthopedically disabling conditions.

HIV/AIDS

Council for Exceptional Children   Content Standards for Beginning Teachers–P&HD: types and transmission routes of infectious and communicable diseases (PH2K4) (also, PH2K1, PH3K1).
PRAXIS Teaching students with Orthopedic Impairments: I. Overview, General and technical medical aspects related to orthopedically disabling conditions.

Because of fear generated by misconceptions about the spread of the disease, some school districts have barred children with HIV/AIDS from attending school in defiance of the IDEA principle of zero reject (Turnbull & Turnbull, 2000). However, HIV is not transmitted by saliva, nasal secretions, sweat, tears, urine, or vomit unless blood is visible; and the presence of a child with HIV/AIDS in the classroom presents no undue health risks to other children (Centers for Disease Control and Prevention, 1998). Children with HIV/AIDS cannot legally be excluded from attending school unless they are deemed a direct health risk to other children (e.g., exhibit biting behavior or open lesions).

Because children with HIV/AIDS and their families often face discrimination, prejudice, and isolation, teachers and school personnel should actively facilitate school/peer acceptance and the social adjustment of a child with HIV/AIDS (Hill, 1999). Additionally, all teachers and school personnel must be trained in *universal precautions* for dealing with blood and bodily fluids from any child (e.g., how to safely administer first aid for a cut or tend to a child's nose bleed) (Porter, Haynie, Bierle, Caldwell, & Palfrey, 1997). Parents are not required to inform the school that their child has HIV (or any other medical or health condition), and a particular student or staff member may have HIV without knowing it.

To prevent the disease from spreading further in the preadolescent and adolescent populations, HIV/AIDS prevention must be included in the curriculum. Students receiving special education services may be more prone to contracting HIV because of a lack of knowledge about the disease. For recommendations on developing and implementing an HIV/AIDS prevention and education curriculum for students with disabilities, see Kelker, Hecimovic, and LeRoy (1994) and Lerro (1994).

 ## CHARACTERISTICS

The characteristics of children with physical disabilities and health impairments are so varied that attempting to describe them is nearly impossible. Knowing the underlying cause of a student's physical impairment or health condition provides limited guidance in planning needed special education and related services. One student with cerebral palsy may require few special modifications in curriculum, instruction, or environment, while the severe limitations in movement and intellectual functioning experienced by another student with cerebral palsy require a wide array of curricular and instructional modifications, adaptive equipment, and related services. Some children with health conditions have chronic but relatively mild health conditions; others have extremely limited endurance and vitality and require sophisticated medical technology and around-the-clock support to maintain their very existence. A given physical or health condition may take markedly different *trajectories* in the same child (Best, 2001). For example, treatment of cancer may have little or no positive effect on a child's life, prolong and enhance the life of a child, or lead to complete remission of the disease. The treatment itself (e.g., the extent to which hospitalization is required, the immediate effects of chemotherapy on the child's physical and emotional condition) and its outcome will both have significant effects on when and what type of special education and related services are needed.

The combined effects of all of these variables render lists of learning and behavioral characteristics of children with physical disabilities and health impairments highly suspect at best. Nevertheless, two cautiously qualified statements can be made concerning the academic and socioemotional characteristics of children with physical disabilities and health impairments. Although many individual students with physical disabilities or health impairments achieve well above grade level—indeed, some are intellectually gifted—as a group these children function below grade level academically. In addition to the neurological, motor, and other impairments that hamper their academic performance, the medications and daily health care routines that some children must endure have negative side effects on academic achievement. Educational progress is also hampered by frequent and sometimes prolonged absences from school for medical treatment when flare-ups or relapses require hospitalization (Kline, Silver, & Russell, 2001).

Effects of P&HD on academic achievement and social/emotional development

Council for Exceptional Children Content Standards for Beginning Teachers–Common Core: Educational implications of various exceptionalities (CC2K2) (also, PH3K1). **PRAXIS** Teaching students with Orthopedic Impairments: II. Effects of Disabling Conditions on Various Aspects of Development; physical, social, emotional, interpersonal, cognitive, perceptual, and language.

Coping emotionally with a physical disability or a chronic health impairment presents a major problem for some children. Maintaining peer relationships and a sense of belonging to the group can be difficult for a child who must frequently leave the instructional activity or classroom to participate in therapeutic or health care routines. Anxiety about fitting in at school may be created by prolonged absences from school (Olsen & Sutton, 1998). Students with physical disabilities and health impairments frequently identify concerns about physical appearance as reasons for emotional difficulties and feelings of depression (Sexson & Dingle, 2001).

VARIABLES AFFECTING THE IMPACT OF PHYSICAL DISABILITIES AND HEALTH IMPAIRMENTS ON CHILDREN'S EDUCATIONAL PERFORMANCE

It is both possible and useful to identify the effects of general variables that influence the characteristics of children across various types of physical disabilities and health impairments. Many factors must be taken into consideration in assessing the effects of a physical disability or health impairment on a child's development and behavior. Perrin et al. (1993) have developed a noncategorical system for classifying and understanding children's chronic physical and medical conditions in which the characteristics or effects of 13 dimensions of a child's condition are judged (see Figure 12.2). A physical impairment or medical condition can limit a child's ability to engage in age-appropriate activities, mobility, cognitive functioning, social and emotional development, sensory functioning, and communication across a continuum ranging from normal functioning (no impact) to extremely impaired. A minor or transient physical or health impairment, such as those most children experience while growing up, is not likely to have lasting effects; but a severe,

Factors that affect impact of P&HD

Council for Exceptional Children — Content Standards for Beginning Teachers–P&HD: Impact of P&HD on individuals, families, society (PH3K1) (also, PH2K2).
PRAXIS Special Education Core Principles: Content Knowledge: I. Understanding Exceptionalities, Characteristics of students with disabilities.

FIGURE 12.2 **Dimensions of a noncategorical system for classifying and describing the effects of a physical disability or a chronic health condition**

Dimension	Effects Continuum		
Duration	Brief	←——→	Lengthy
Age of onset	Congenital	←——→	Acquired
Limitation of age-appropriate activities	None	←——→	Unable to conduct
Visibility	Not visible	←——→	Highly visible
Expected survival	Usual longevity	←——→	Immediate threat to life
Mobility	Not impaired	←——→	Extremely impaired
Physiologic functioning	Not impaired	←——→	Extremely impaired
Cognition	Normal	←——→	Extremely impaired
Emotional/social	Normal	←——→	Extremely impaired
Sensory functioning	Not impaired	←——→	Extremely impaired
Communication	Not impaired	←——→	Extremely impaired
Course	Stable	←——→	Progressive
Uncertainty	Episodic	←——→	Predictable

Source: Reprinted from Perrin, E. C., Newacheck, P., Pless, B., Drotar, D., Gortmaker, S. L., Leventhal, J., Perrin, J. M., Stein, R. E. K., Walker, D. K., & Weitzman, M. (1993). Issues involved in the definition and classification of chronic health conditions. Reproduced by permission of *Pediatrics,* Vol. 91, pp. 787–793. © 1993.

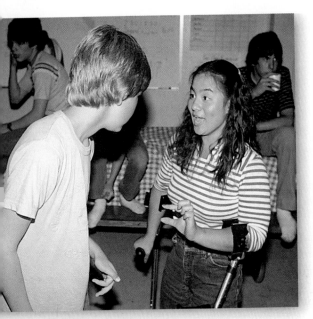

chronic impairment can greatly limit a child's range of experiences. In addition to the severity with which the condition affects different areas of functioning, two particularly important factors are age of onset and visibility.

Age of Onset Some conditions are congenital (present at birth); other conditions are acquired during the child's development as a result of illness, accident, or unknown cause. As with all disabilities, it is important for the teacher to be aware of the child's age at the time he acquired the physical or health impairment. A child who has not had the use of his legs since birth may have missed out on some important developmental experiences, particularly if early intervention services were not provided. In contrast, a teenager who suddenly loses the use of her legs in an accident has likely had a normal range of experiences throughout childhood but may need considerable support from parents, teachers, specialists, and peers in adapting to life with this newly acquired disability.

The severity, visibility, and age of acquisition of a physical or health impairment all affect an individual's adaptation and development.

Visibility Physical impairments and health conditions range from highly visible and conspicuous to not visible. How children think about themselves and the degree to which they are accepted by others often are affected by the visibility of a condition. Some children use a variety of special orthopedic appliances, such as wheelchairs, braces, crutches, and adaptive tables. They may ride to school on a specially equipped bus or van. In school they may need assistance using the toilet or may wear helmets. Although such special devices and adaptations help children meet important needs, they often have the unfortunate side effect of making the physical impairment more visible, thus making the child look even more different from nondisabled peers.

The visibility of some physical disabilities may cause other children and adults to underestimate the child's abilities and limit opportunities for participation. By contrast, many health conditions such as asthma or epilepsy are not visible, and others may not perceive the child as needing or deserving of accommodations. This misperception is supported by the fact that the child functions normally most of the time (Best, 2001).

TRAUMATIC BRAIN INJURY

Definition of TBI

Council for Exceptional Children Content Standards for Beginning Teachers–P&HD: Issues and educational definitions of individuals with P&HD (PH1K1).
PRAXIS Special Education Core Principles: Content Knowledge: I. Understanding Exceptionalities, Definitions of disabilities.

 DEFINITION

When it was originally passed, IDEA did not specifically mention the needs of children who have experienced head trauma and/or coma. However, when the law was amended in 1990 (P.L. 101-476), traumatic brain injury was added as a new disability category under which children could be eligible for special education services. IDEA defines **traumatic brain injury** as

an acquired injury to the brain caused by an external physical force, resulting in total or partial functional disability or psychosocial impairments, or both, that adversely affects a child's educational performance. The term applies to open or closed head injuries resulting in impairments in one or more areas, such as cognition; language; memory; attention; reasoning; abstract thinking; judgment; problem-solving; sensory, perceptual, and motor abilities; psychosocial behavior; physical functions; information processing; and speech. The term does not apply to brain injuries that are congenital or generative, or brain injuries induced by birth trauma. (34 C. F. R. Sec. 300.7 [6] [12])

As with the IDEA definitions of orthopedic impairments and other health impairments, the key phrase in the definition of traumatic brain injury is *that adversely affects a child's educational performance.* It is also important to note that traumatic brain injury is an *acquired* condition. Although the effects of some types of traumatic brain injury on learning and behavior are similar to the effects of other disabilities, children whose learning or behavioral problems are caused by disease or congenital malformation of the brain (e.g., cerebral palsy, some causes of mental retardation) are not considered to have traumatic brain injury.

PREVALENCE

Injuries to the head are common in children and adolescents. Head injuries occur in the pediatric population (1 month to 15 years) at a rate of about 1 million per year (Heller et al., 1996). It is estimated that each year 1 in 500 school-age children will be hospitalized with traumatic head injuries, 1 in 30 children will sustain a significant head injury by the age of 15, and 1 in 10,000 children will die as the result of head trauma (Hill, 1999; Whaley & Wong, 1995). Traumatic brain injury is the leading cause of death in children, accounting for approximately one-third of all accidental deaths in children (Centers for Disease Control, 2001b); and it is the most common acquired disability in childhood (Brain Injury Association, 2001).

In spite of the sobering statistics on head injuries, the number of children receiving special education under the category of traumatic brain injury is very small. In 1991–1992, the first school year after traumatic brain injury was added to IDEA as a separate disability category, only 330 school-age students were served nationally. By the 2000–2001 school year, the number of children with traumatic brain injury between the ages of 6 and 21 served in special education programs had increased dramatically to 14,829 (U.S. Department of Education, 2002).

While it is likely that greater numbers of children with traumatic brain injury will be identified and served in the future as educators increase their understanding and recognition of head injuries, the gap between incidence and children served is huge. What accounts for the significant difference between the incidence of head injuries to children and the number of children receiving special education for head injuries? First, recovery is good following most brain injuries. The skull is very good at protecting the brain, and the human brain has a remarkable capacity to naturally compensate for injury. Second, the vast majority of head injuries sustained by children are mild and do not result in obvious adverse effects on educational performance. Third, many students with mild brain injuries are identified and served under another disability category, most likely learning disabiities or emotional or behavioral disorders. Fourth, students with severe head injuries are often served under other disability categories.

TYPES AND CAUSES

Head injuries are classified by the type of injury (open or closed), by the kind of the damage sustained by the brain, and by the location of the injury. An **open head injury** is the result of penetration of the skull as through a bullet wound or a forceful blow to the head with a hard or sharp object. Open head injuries that are not fatal often result in specific deficits or problems with specific behavioral or sensory functions controlled by the particular parts of the brain where the injury occurred (see Figure 12.3 on page 460).

The most common type of head injury does not involve penetration of the skull. A **closed head injury** occurs when the head hits a stationary object with such force that the brain slams against the inside of the cranium. The stress of this rapid movement and impact pulls apart and tears nerve fibers or axons, breaking connections between different

Prevalence of TBI

PRAXIS Special Education Core Principles: Content Knowledge: I. Understanding Exceptionalities, Incidence and prevalence of various types of disabilities.

Types and causes of TBI

Content Standards for Beginning Teachers–P&HD: Etiology and characteristics of P&HD across the life span (PH2K2) (also, PH2K1).
PRAXIS Special Education Core Principles: Content Knowledge: I. Understanding Exceptionalities, Causation and prevention of disability.

Abuse and Neglect of Children with Disabilities

onsider the following cases:

Travis hit all the kids on the school bus, on the playground and everyone he could reach as he bounded into my kindergarten class. Every day. Travis had witnessed his mother deliberately scalding his 3-year-old sister with a kettle of boiling water. She was injured terribly.

Brevard's drug-addicted mother had burned his genitalia with her cigarette. She has blond hair. He was frightened of every blond-haired woman, among his many emotional problems.

Kim said Christmas wasn't as much fun as usual, with the cops coming and taking Daddy to jail for stabbing Mommy's tummy.

Ernestine never smiled or laughed the whole year, not even when going down the slide or catching a ball. Her arms twitched nervously most of the time. Her mom had left her with a neighbor "while she went to the store." She never returned. Ernestine has lived in the green house, the white one, the apartment and had been in three schools before she entered my kindergarten from the brown house. (Craig Wall, kindergarten teacher, Columbus, OH; quoted in the *Columbus Dispatch*, August 28, 1998, p. 7A)

Child maltreatment covers a spectrum of behaviors committed by parents or significant others. It includes verbally intimidating or shaming a child, neglecting a child's physical and health care needs, causing physical harm by striking or burning a child, and sexually abus-

ing a child. Maltreatment takes a tremendous toll on a child's development. "Other than malnutrition or disease, there is probably no risk factor for children that has greater consequences for their development than maltreatment by their parents" (Groves, 1997, p. 86).

Child abuse and neglect occur with alarming frequency in the United States. Here are some statistics for a single year (U.S. Department of Health and Human Services, 1998):

- State child protection service agencies investigated an estimated 2 million reports that involved the alleged maltreatment of approximately 3 million children.
- Almost 1 million children were victims of substantiated or indicated child abuse and neglect, an approximate 18% increase since 1990.
- The national rate of victimization was 15 victims per 1,000 children.
- An estimated 1,077 child maltreatment fatalities occurred in the 50 states and the District of Columbia.

Because the majority of child abuse and neglect cases are never reported, it is impossible to know the true extent of the problem. Some professionals think the number of actual cases is at least twice the number of those reported (Lowenthal, 2001). In 77% of cases, the perpetrators are parents and relatives of the child (National Center on Child Abuse and Neglect, 1995).

Children with disabilities are 1.7 times more likely to be victims of abuse and neglect than are children without

parts of the brain. Car and bicycle accidents are the primary causes of closed head injuries. *Shaken-baby syndrome* is another unfortunate but common cause of traumatic brain injury in children. The rough handling and violent shaking of the baby causes rapid acceleration and deceleration of the head, which in turn causes the brain to be whipped back and forth, bouncing off the inside of the skull. (See Profiles & Perspectives, "Abuse and Neglect of Children with Disabilities," later in this chapter.)

The effects of traumatic brain injury on learning and behavior are determined by the severity of the injury and the part of the brain that sustained damaged. A mild brain injury results

disabilities (National Center on Child Abuse and Neglect, 1996). Not only are children with disabilities overrepresented in child abuse samples (Sullivan & Knutson, 1994), but they are more likely to be abused for a longer period. "Whereas the infant with colic may increase family stress for a limited period, the child with cerebral palsy, or any other long-term or permanent handicap, presents a potential long-term family crisis. . . . It is no wonder, then, that children with handicaps are disproportionately represented in child abuse samples" (Zirpoli, 1987, p. 44).

Is a child abused and neglected because of a disability, or do abuse and neglect produce a disability in an otherwise normally developing child? In most instances, it would be a mistake to say simply that a child's disability caused the abuse and neglect. Researchers have concluded that child abuse and neglect have no single cause but are the product of complex interactions among numerous variables, only one of which concerns the child's characteristics (Kairys, 1996; Lowenthal, 2001; Sobsey, 1994). Factors also include a parent's own abuse as a child, alcohol or drug dependency, unemployment, poverty, and marital discord; seldom is any one factor the lone cause of child abuse. For example, although poverty increases the probability of abuse and neglect, most children from poor families receive loving and nurturing care from their parents. Likewise, the great majority of parents of children with disabilities provide a loving and nurturing environment.

EDUCATORS' RESPONSIBILITY TO REPORT SUSPECTED ABUSE

There must be greater awareness of the problem of child abuse and neglect, especially among professionals who work with children and families. Because teachers see children daily for most of the year, they are in the best position to identify and report suspected cases of abuse. All 50 states require that teachers and other professionals who frequently deal with children report suspected cases of abuse and neglect. Indeed, many state laws require any citizen who sus-

pects abuse and neglect to report it, and most states impose criminal penalties for failure to do so. People who, in good faith, report suspected cases are immune from civil or criminal liability. All educators should become familiar with child abuse laws in their state and learn how to recognize and report indicators of abuse and neglect. Lowenthal (2001) provides specific information on detecting and reporting signs of physical abuse, sexual abuse, and neglect and describes classroom policies and practices to protect teachers from unwarranted allegations of abuse.

SUPPORT FOR FAMILIES WITH HISTORIES OF ABUSE AND NEGLECT

One successful program for preventing and treating child abuse and neglect is Project 12-Ways, developed by Lutzker and colleagues at the University of Southern Illinois (Lutzker & Campbell, 1994). The project's guiding philosophy is that family problems can be eased by eliminating stress-producing factors (e.g., unemployment) and teaching both children and parents the skills necessary for getting along without abuse and neglect. Recognizing the multidimensional factors involved and understanding the entire family as a dynamic system, the project employs an ecobehavioral approach to treatment. That is, rather than prescribing a standard treatment regimen consisting of one or two components, a counselor conducts a thorough assessment of the family's needs and resources. After assessment, family and counselor jointly determine goals and then implement an individualized program of family support services.

Repucci, Britner, and Wollard (1997) have studied 25 programs for helping abusive and neglectful parents and offer numerous suggestions for planning, conducting, and evaluating such programs.

- Information on detecting signs of child abuse and neglect can be obtained from Child Help USA. Anyone can and should report a suspected case of child abuse; reports can be filed anonymously. If you do not know the appropriate local agency to contact, call the toll-free Child Help USA hotline: (800) 422-4453.

in a *concussion,* a brief or momentary loss of consciousness without any subsequent complications or damage. Even a mild concussion, however, is often followed by post-concussion syndrome, which can include temporary headaches, dizziness spells, and fatigue.

Contusions (bruising, swelling, and bleeding) usually accompany a moderate brain injury. Blood vessels in the brain may also rupture, causing a *hematoma* (aggregation or clotting of blood) that may grow and put pressure on vital brain structures. A moderate brain injury usually results in a loss of consciousness lasting from a few minutes to a few hours followed by a few days or weeks of confusion. Individuals who sustain a moderate brain in-

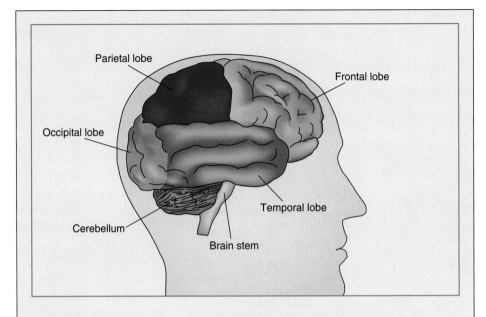

FIGURE 12.3 Parts of the brain and some of their functions

Frontal lobe

- Emotions
- Expressive language
- Word associations
- Memory for habits and motor activities
- Problem solving
- Reasoning

Parietal lobe

- Integration of different senses
- Location for visual attention
- Location for touch perception
- Manipulation of objects

Occipital lobe

- Vision

Cerebellum

- Balance and equilibrium
- Some memory for reflex motor acts

Brain stem

- Regulates body functions (e.g., breathing, heart rate, swallowing)
- Reflexes to seeing and hearing (e.g., startle response)
- Controls autonomic nervous system (e.g., sweating, blood pressure, digestion, internal temperature)
- Affects level of alertness

Temporal lobe

- Hearing
- Speech
- Memory acquisition
- Categorization of objects

jury will experience significant cognitive and behavioral impairments for many months. Most, however, will make a complete or nearly complete recovery.

Severe head trauma almost always results in a *coma*, a state of prolonged unconsciousness lasting days, weeks, or even longer. Persons in a coma cannot be awakened, and there is no meaningful response to external stimulation. In addition to brain contusions and hematomas or damage to the nerve fibers or axons, a person with severe brain injury may have suffered from *anoxia* (loss of oxygen to the brain for a period of time). Although many individuals with severe brain injuries make significant improvements during the first year after their injury and continue to improve at a more gradual pace for many years, most will have permanent physical, behavioral, and/or cognitive impairments.

 CHARACTERISTICS

Although not always visible and sometimes seemingly minor or inconsequential, traumatic brain injury is complex. Depending on the extent and location of the injury, symptoms caused by a brain injury vary widely. Impairments caused by brain injuries may be temporary or lasting and fall into three main categories: (1) physical and sensory changes (e.g., lack of coordination, spasticity of muscles); (2) cognitive impairments (e.g., short- and

FIGURE 12.4 Possible signs and effects of traumatic brain injury

Physical and sensory changes

- Chronic headaches, dizziness, light-headedness, nausea
- Vision impairments (e.g., double vision, visual field defects, blurring, sensitivity to light)
- Hearing impairment (e.g., increased sensitivity to sound)
- Alterations in sense of taste, touch, and smell
- Sleep problems (e.g., insomnia, day/night confusion)
- Stress-related disorders (e.g., depression)
- Poor body temperature regulation
- Recurrent seizure activity
- Poor coordination and balance
- Reduced speed of motor performance and precision of movement

Cognitive changes and academic problems

- Difficulty keeping up with discussions, instructional presentations, note taking
- Difficulty concentrating or attending to task at hand (e.g., distractible, confused)
- Difficulty making transitions (e.g., home to school, class to class, switching from fractions to decimal problems on same math worksheet)
- Inability to organize work and environment (e.g., difficulty keeping track of books, assignments, lunch box)
- Problems in planning, organizing, pacing tasks and activities
- Extremely sensitive to distraction (e.g., unable to take a test in a room with other students)
- Tendency to perseverate; inflexible in thinking
- Impairments in receptive oral language (e.g., difficulty following directions; misunderstanding what is said by others)
- Inability to perceive voice inflections or nonverbal cues
- Impairments in reading comprehension
- Impairments in expressive oral or written language (e.g., aphasia, difficulty retrieving words, poor articulation, slow speech, difficulty in spelling or punctuation)

Social, emotional, and behavioral problems

- Chronically agitated, irritable, restless, or anxious
- Increased aggressiveness
- Impaired ability to self-manage; lowered impulse control; poor anger control
- Difficulty dealing with change (i.e., rigid); poor coping strategies
- May overestimate own ability (often evidenced as "bragging")
- Decreased insight into self and others; reduced judgment
- Decreased frustration tolerance; frequent temper outbursts and overreactions to events
- May talk compulsively and excessively
- Inability to take cues from the environment (often leading to socially inappropriate behavior)

Source: Adapted from Hill, J. L. (1999). *Meeting the needs of children with special physical and health care needs* (pp. 259–260). Upper Saddle River, NJ: Merrill/Prentice Hall. © 1999 by Merrill/Prentice Hall. Used by permission.

Signs and effects of TBI

Council for Exceptional Children. Content Standards for Beginning Teachers–Common Core: Educational implications of various exceptionalities (CC2K2) (also, PH3K1). **PRAXIS** Special Education Core Principles: Content Knowledge: I. Understanding Exceptionalities, Characteristics of students with disabilities, Cognitive, affective and social-adaptive, linguistic, motor, and sensory factors.

long-term memory deficits, difficulty maintaining attention and concentration); and (3) social, behavioral, and emotional problems (e.g., mood swings [emotional lability], self-centeredness, lack of motivation). Figure 12.4 provides additional examples of characteristics that may be signs of traumatic brain injury.

The educational and lifelong needs of students with head injuries are likely to require comprehensive programs of academic, psychological, and family support (Savage & Wolcott,

1994). Recovery from a brain injury is often inconsistent. A student might make excellent progress, then regress to an earlier stage, then make a rapid series of gains. Individuals with brain injuries sometimes reach plateaus in their recovery during which no improvements occur for some time. A plateau does not signal the end of functional improvement.

Students who have been hospitalized with head injuries reenter school with deficits from their injuries compounded by an extended absence from school. Ylvisaker (1986) recommends that the child with a head injury return to school when she is physically capable, can respond to instructions, and can sustain attention for 10 to 15 minutes. Tyler and Mira (1993) suggest a number of ways in which school programs can assist the student with traumatic brain injury during the reentry period:

- A shortened school day, concentrating academic instruction during peak performance periods; frequent breaks; and a reduced class load may be necessitated by the chronic fatigue that some students with head injury experience for a year or more.
- A special resource period at the beginning and end of each school day when a teacher, counselor, or aide helps the student plan or review the day's schedule, keep track of assignments, and monitor progress may be required because of problems with loss of memory and organization.
- Modifications such as an extra set of textbooks at home, a peer to help the student move efficiently from class to class, and early dismissal from class to allow time to get to the next room can help the student who has difficulties with mobility, balance, or coordination. (Adaptive physical education is often indicated.)
- Behavior management and/or counseling interventions may be needed to help with problems such as poor judgment, impulsiveness, overactivity, aggression, destructiveness, and socially uninhibited behavior often experienced by students with head injury.
- Modifications of instruction and testing procedures such as tape-recording lectures, assigning a note taker, and allowing extra time to take tests may be needed.
- IEP goals and objectives may need to be reviewed and modified as often as every 30 days because of the dramatic changes in behavior and performance by some children during the early stages of recovery.

Accommodations for students with TBI

Council for Exceptional Children Content Standards for Beginning Teachers–P&HD: Adaptations of educational environments necessary to accommodate individuals with P&HD (PH5K1) (also, CC5K1). **PRAXIS** Special Education Core Principles: Content Knowledge: III. Delivery of Services to Students with Disabilities, Curriculum and Instruction, Modification of materials and equipment.

History of education of students with P&HD

Council for Exceptional Children Content Standards for Beginning Teachers–P&HD: Historical foundations related to knowledge and practices in P&HD (PH1K2) . **PRAXIS** Special Education Core Principles: Content Knowledge: II. Legal and Societal Issues, Historical movements/trends affecting the connections between special education and the larger society.

 EDUCATIONAL APPROACHES

Special education of children with physical disabilities and health impairments in the United States has a history of more than 100 years (see Table 12.1). While some students with physical and health impairments can fully access and benefit from education with minimal accommodations or environmental modifications, the intensive health and learning needs of other students require a complex and coordinated array of specialized instruction, therapy, and related services. In addition to progressing in the general education curriculum to the maximum extent possible, many students with physical disabilities, health impairments, or traumatic brain injuries also need intensive instruction in a parallel curriculum on ways of "coping with their disabilities" (Bowe, 2000, p. 75). Similar in function to the expanded core curriculum for students with visual impairments, the parallel curriculum for students with physical and health impairments includes items such as using adaptive methods and assistive technologies for mobility, communication, and daily-living tasks; increasing independence by self-administering special health care routines; and learning self-determination and self-advocacy skills.

TABLE 12.1 A history of the education of children with physical disabilities, health impairments, and traumatic brain injury: Key events and implications

Date	Historical Event	Educational Implications
1893	Industrial School for Crippled and Deformed Children was established in Boston.	This was the first special institution for children with physical disabilities in the United States (Eberle, 1922).
Circa 1900	The first special classes for children with physical impairments began in Chicago.	This was the first time children with physical disabilities were educated in public schools (La Vor, 1976).
Early 1900s	There were serious outbreaks of tuberculosis and polio in the United States.	This led to increasing numbers of children with physical impairments being educated by local schools in special classes for the "crippled" or "delicate" (Walker & Jacobs, 1985).
Early 20th century	Winthrop Phelps demonstrated that children could be helped through physical therapy and the effective use of braces. Earl Carlson (who himself had cerebral palsy) was a strong advocate of developing the intellectual potential of children with physical disabilities through appropriate education.	The efforts of these two American physicians contributed to increased understanding and acceptance of children with physical disabilities and to recognition that physical impairment did not preclude potential for educational achievement and self-sufficiency.
Early 20th century to 1970s	Decisions to "ignore, isolate, and institutionalize these children were often based on mental incompetence presumed because of physical disabilities, especially those involving communication and use of upper extremities" (Conner, Scandary, & Tullock, 1988, p. 6).	Increasing numbers of children with mild physical disabilities and health conditions were educated in public schools. Most children with severe physical disabilities were educated in special schools or community agencies (e.g., the United Cerebral Palsy Association).
1975	P.L. 94-142 mandated a free, appropriate public education for all children with disabilities and required schools to provide related services (e.g., transportation services, physical therapy, school health services) necessary for students to be educated in the least restrictive environment.	No longer could a child be denied the right to attend the local public school because there was a flight of stairs at the entrance, bathrooms were not accessible, or school buses were not equipped to transport wheelchairs. The related services provision of IDEA transformed schools from "solely scholastic institutions into therapeutic agencies" (Palfrey, 1995, p. 265).
1984	The Supreme Court ruled in *Independent School District v. Tatro* that schools must provide intermittent catheterization as a supportive or related service if necessary to enable a student with disabilities to receive a public education.	The *Tatro* ruling expanded the range of related services that schools are required to provide and clarified the differences between school health services, which can be performed by a nonphysician, and medical services, which are provided by physicians for diagnostic or eligibility purposes.
1984	The World Institute on Disability was co-founded by Ed Roberts, an inspirational leader for self-advocacy by persons with disabilities.	This was a major milestone in the civil rights and self-advocacy movement by people with disabilities (Stone, 1995).
1990	Americans with Disabilities Act (P.L. 101-336) was passed.	ADA provided civil rights protections to all persons with disabilities in private sector employment and mandated access to all public services, accommodations, transportation, and telecommunications.
1990	Traumatic brain injury was added as a new disability category in the reauthorization of IDEA (P.L. 101-476).	There were increased awareness, services, research, and resources for teachers concerning the educational needs of children with TBI.
1999	The U.S. Supreme Court ruled in *Cedar Rapids v. Garret F.* that a local school district must pay for the one-on-one nursing care for a medically fragile student who required continuous monitoring of his ventilator and other health-maintenance routines.	The decision reaffirmed and extended the Court's ruling in the 1984 *Tatro* case that schools must provide any and all health services needed for students with disabilities to attend school, as long as performance of those services does not require a licensed physician.

TEAMING AND RELATED SERVICES

The transdisciplinary team approach has special relevance for students with physical disabilities, health impairments, and traumatic brain injury. No other groups of exceptional children come into contact, both in and out of school, with as many different teachers, physicians, therapists, and other specialists. Because the medical, educational, therapeutic, vocational, and social needs of these students are often complex and frequently affect each other, it is especially important that educational and health care personnel openly communicate and cooperate with one another. Two particularly important members of the interdisciplinary team for many children with physical disabilities, health impairments, and traumatic brain injury are the physical therapist and the occupational therapist. Each is a licensed health professional who must complete a specialized training program and meet rigorous standards.

Physical therapists (PTs) are involved in the development and maintenance of motor skills, movement, and posture. They may prescribe specific exercises to help a child increase her control of muscles and use specialized equipment, such as braces, effectively. Massage and prescriptive exercises are perhaps the most frequently applied procedures; but physical therapy can also include swimming, heat treatment, special positioning for feeding and toileting, and other techniques. PTs encourage children to be as motorically independent as possible; help develop muscular function; and reduce pain, discomfort, or long-term physical damage. They may also suggest dos and don'ts for sitting positions and activities in the classroom and may devise exercise or play programs that children with and without disabilities can enjoy together.

Occupational therapists (OTs) are concerned about a child's participation in activities, especially those that will be useful in self-help, employment, recreation, communication, and aspects of daily living (e.g., dressing, eating, personal hygiene). They may help a child learn (or relearn) diverse motor behaviors such as drinking from a modified cup, buttoning clothes, tying shoes, pouring liquids, cooking, and typing on a computer keyboard. These activities can enhance a child's physical development, independence, vocational potential, and self-concept. OTs conduct specialized assessments and make recommendations to parents and teachers regarding the effective use of appliances, materials, and activities at home and school. Many OTs also work with vocational rehabilitation specialists in helping students find opportunities for work and independent living after completion of an educational program.

Figure 12.5 shows how a PT and an OT worked with a third-grade student with spastic cerebral palsy and other members of the student's IEP team in support of five learning outcomes.

Other specialists who frequently provide related services to children with physical disabilities, health impairments, and traumatic brain injury include the following:

PTs, OTs, and other related-services specialists

Council for Exceptional Children Content Standards for Beginning Teachers–P&HD: Roles and responsibilities of school and community-based medical and related services personnel (PH10K3). **PRAXIS** Special Education Core Principles: Content Knowledge: III. Delivery of Services to Students with Disabilities, Professional roles, Teacher as multidisciplinary team member.

- *Speech-language pathologists (SLPs)* provide speech therapy, language interventions, oral motor coordination (e.g., chewing and swallowing), and augmentative and alternative communication (AAC) services.
- *Adaptive physical educators* provide physical education activities designed to meet the individual needs of students with disabilities.
- *School nurses* provide certain health care services to students, monitor students' health, and inform IEP teams of the effects of medical conditions on students' educational programs.
- *Prosthetists* make and fit artificial limbs.
- *Orthotists* design and fit braces and other assistive devices.
- *Biomedical engineers* develop or adapt technology to meet a student's specialized needs.
- *Health aides* carry out medical procedures and health care services in the classroom.
- *Counselors and medical social workers* assist students and families in adjusting to disabilities.

One	Two	Three	Four	Five
Learning Outcomes				
Maddie will independently complete her morning routine from exiting school bus to storing her belongings, and preparing for class.	Maddie will use computer at desk to complete 25% of her work independently.	Maddie will attend to educator and focus on task at hand 70% of the time during classroom activities, requiring only minimal assistance 25% of the time to refocus attention despite competing sounds, sights, or actions.	Maddie will participate with classmates in 50% of the physical education activities.	Maddie will participate at least 25% with basic self-care tasks during school.
Physical Therapy Direct Service				
Instruction in maneuvering wheel chair off bus, over school grounds, and into classroom.	Work on postural control and stabilization of upper body to improve use of hands and head control for desktop work.	Work on postural control to improve head, torso, and shoulder stability to allow eyes and hands to move yet still attend to class activity; work on coordination of breathing during activity to maintain focus on task.	Instruct in maneuvering and positioning self during activities; assist in teaching various gross-motor activities.	Work on increasing independence with transfers on/off toilet.
Physical Therapy Indirect Service				
Work with bus driver to assure safe exit from bus.	Instruct aide in techniques to facilitate proper posture at desk.	Consult with educator regarding strengths and limitations during class.	Work with educator to supplement activities with components appropriate for inclusion; train educator and aide to facilitate participation in group activities; work with administrators to ensure accessibility to both indoor and outdoor activity areas.	Teach aide toilet transfers; recommendations made for adaptive toilet and sink to be installed in bathroom.
Occupational Therapy Direct Service				
Work on organizational skills and efficiency during routine.	Introduce computer at desk with adaptations; work on fine motor coordination and equipment use.	Work during class on attention to task—refocusing techniques.	Work on upper extremity coordination to increase participation during group play.	Introduce and instruct in use of adaptive and modified equipment to facilitate independence in hygiene activities of daily living.
Occupational Therapy Indirect Service				
Work with teacher to set up achievable AM schedule; suggest reorganization of materials in classroom to make them more accessible; instruct classroom aide in routine and necessary cues to initially assist with completion of routine.	Instruct educators and aide in computer use, adaptations needed and current limitations; instruct aide and family in technidques to assist with use of device.	Instruct educators and aide in cues to assist with attention to task and identify appropriate reinforcers; make recommendations for environmental changes that will reduce distractions.	Instruct aide to assist with participation in activities. Work with educator to supplement activities with components appropriate for inclusion.	Teach aide use of adaptive equipment and how to assist with the activities of daily living.

Source: From Szabo, J. L. (2000). Maddie's story: Inclusion through physical and occupational therapy. *Teaching Exceptional Children, 33*(2), p. 15. Reprinted by permission.

 ## ENVIRONMENTAL MODIFICATIONS

Environmental modifications are frequently necessary to enable a student with physical and health impairments to participate more fully and independently in school. Environmental modifications include adaptations to provide increased access to a task or activity, modifying the way in which instruction is delivered, and changing the manner in which the task is done (Bigge et al., 2001; Heller, Dangel, & Sweatman, 1995). Although barrier-free architecture is the most publicly visible type of environmental modification for making community buildings and services more accessible, some of the most functional adaptations require little or no cost. For example:

- Installing paper cup dispensers near water fountains so they can be used by students in wheelchairs
- Moving a class or an activity to an accessible part of a school building so that a student with a physical impairment can be included
- Providing soft-tip pens that require less pressure for writing
- Providing a head-mounted pointer stick and keyboard guard that enables a student with limited fine-motor control to strike one computer key at a time
- Changing desk- and tabletops to appropriate heights for students who are very short or who use wheelchairs
- Providing a wooden pointer to enable a student to reach the upper buttons on an elevator control panel
- Modifying the response requirements by allowing written responses instead of spoken responses or vice versa

 ## ASSISTIVE TECHNOLOGY

Although the term *technology* often conjures up images of sophisticated computers and other hardware, technology includes any systematic method for accomplishing a practical task or purpose based on scientific principles. **Assistive technology** is defined in IDEA as

> any item, piece of equipment, or product system, whether acquired commercially off the shelf, modified, or customized, that is used to increase, maintain, or improve functional capabilities of a child with a disability. (20 U.S.C., 1401, Section 602[1])

The types of assistive technology used by persons with disabilities are often the same as those used by individuals without disabilities: "For example, a flexible drinking straw used by persons without disabilities may be viewed as a convenience for drinking purposes. For a student with physical disabilities who cannot grasp and tilt a cup to drink from it, the straw facilitates a functional daily living skill (i.e., drinking from a cup) with little or no assistance from others" (Williams, 1991, p. 206).

Individuals with physical disabilities use both low-tech assistive devices (e.g., adapted eating utensils, picture communication books) and high-tech assistive devices (e.g., computerized synthetic speech devices, electronic switches that can be activated by eye movements) for a wide variety of purposes, including mobility, performing daily life skills, improved environmental manipulation and control, better communication, access to computers, recreation and leisure, and enhanced learning (Parette, 1998).

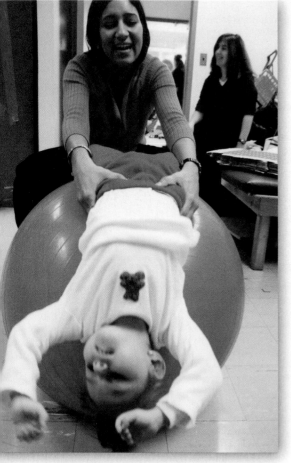

A physical therapist has prescribed specific exercises to increase Laura's muscular control and range of movement.

Education team members should not view a student's acquisition and use of assistive technology as an educational outcome in itself but as a means of increasing the student's independence and access to various activities and opportunities (Reed & Best, 2001).

Some students are unable to move freely from place to place without the assistance of a mobility device. Advances in wheelchair design have made manual chairs lighter and stronger, powered chairs have been adapted for use in rural areas, and new environmental controls have put the wheelchair user in contact with both immediate and distant parts of their world. Many children as young as 3 to 5 years old can learn to explore their environment with freedom and independence in "energy efficient, creative, wheeled scooter boards and wheeled go-carts that provide mobility without restricting upper or lower extremity functions" (Evans & Smith, 1993, p. 1418).

Incidentally, a student should not be described as being "confined to a wheelchair." This expression suggests that the person is restrained or even imprisoned. Most students who use wheelchairs leave them from time to time to exercise, travel in an automobile, or lie down. It is preferable to say that a student "has a wheelchair" or "uses a wheelchair to get around."

New technological aids for communication are used increasingly by children whose physical impairments prevent them from speaking clearly. For students who are able to speak but have limited motor function, voice input/output products enable them to access computers (Lahm & Everington, 2002). Such developments allow students with physical impairments to communicate expressively and receptively with others and to take part in a wide range of instructional programs. Telecommunications technology is used by many individuals with physical disabilities to expand their world, gain access to information and services, and meet new people. Many children and adults with disabilities use e-mail and instant messaging to communicate with others, make new friends, and build and maintain relationships.

Technology can seldom be pulled off the shelf and serve a student with disabilities with maximum effectiveness. Before purchasing and training a child to use any assistive technology device, the education team should carefully consider certain characteristics of the child and of the potential technologies that might be selected as well as the impact of using those technologies on the child's family (Hourcade, Parette, & Huer, 1997; Parette, 1998; Reed & Best, 2001). An assessment of the child's academic skills, social skills, and physical capabilities should help identify the goals and objectives for the technology as well as narrow down the kinds of devices that may be effective. The child's preferences for certain types of technology should also be determined. At that point, the characteristics of potentially appropriate technologies should be considered, including availability, simplicity of operation, initial and ongoing cost, adaptability to meet the changing needs of the child, and the reliability and repair record of the device. Several excellent handbooks on designing, selecting, and using assistive technology are also available (e.g., Chuch & Glennen, 1992; Cook & Hussey, 1995; Gray, Quartrano, & Liberman, 1998).

Assistive technology includes low-tech devices such as this simple chalk holder.

Assistive technology

 ## SPECIAL HEALTH CARE ROUTINES

Many students with physical disabilities have special health care needs that require specialized procedures such as taking prescribed medication or self-administering insulin shots (Harchik, 1994), clean intermittent catheterization (CIC), tracheostomy care, ventilator/respirator care (Lehr & Macurdy, 1994), and managing special nutrition and dietary needs

FIGURE 12.6 Example of IHCP objectives included in an IEP for a student with special health care needs

Tube feeding:
- Student will explain (orally, in writing, or through other means) reasons for alternative eating method.
- Student will describe steps necessary in implementing the procedure.
- Student will indicate desire to eat.
- Student will measure feeding liquid to be placed in feeding bag or syringe.
- Student will pour food in feeding bag or syringe.
- Student will direct cleaning of feeding equipment.
- Student will clean equipment.
- Student will feed self.

Tracheostomy suctioning:
- Student will indicate need to be suctioned.
- Student will turn on suction machine.
- Student will hold suction tube while procedure is being implemented.
- Student will describe steps necessary to suction.
- Student will explain to others the indicators of need for suctioning.

Catheterization:
- Student will indicate time to be catheterized.
- Student will self-catheterize.
- Student will describe steps in implementing the process.
- Student will wash materials necessary.
- Student will assemble materials necessary.
- Student will hold catheter steady during procedure.
- Student will describe indicators of problems related to catheterization.

Source: From Lehr, D. H., & Macurdy, S. (1994). Meeting special health care needs of students. In M. Agran, N. E. Marchand-Martella, & R. C. Martella (Eds.), *Promoting health and safety: Skills for independent living* (p. 82). Baltimore, MD: Paul H. Brookes. Reprinted by permission.

ICHPs

 Council for Exceptional Children Content Standards for Beginning Teachers–P&HD: Integrate an individual's health care plan into daily programming (PH7S5).

(Heller, Bigge, & Allgood, 2001). These special health-related needs are prescribed in an *Individualized Health Care Plan (IHCP)*, which is included as part of the student's IEP. According to Poulton (1996), an IHCP is "the written, preplanned and ongoing plan of care for students requiring special health services developed by licensed health personnel and the education team. It includes the nursing process of assessment, nursing diagnosis, planning, intervention, and evaluation. It also includes a plan for emergencies" (p. 1). Figure 12.6 provides examples of possible IHCP objectives that might be included in a student's IEP. Teachers and school personnel must be provided with training on how to safely administer health care procedures they are expected to perform (Heller, Fredrick, Best, Dykes, & Cohen, 2000).

Often, well-meaning teachers, classmates, and parents tend to do too much for a child with physical or health impairments. It may be difficult, frustrating, and/or time-consuming for the child to learn to care for his own needs; but the confidence and skills gained from independent functioning are well worth the effort in the long run (Ault et al., 2000). Students who learn to perform all or part of their daily health care needs increase their ability to function independently in normal environments and lessen their dependence on caregivers (Bosner & Belfiore, 2001; Neef, Parrish, Egel, & Sloan, 1986).

Importance of Positioning, Seating, and Movement Proper positioning, seating, and regular movement are critically important for children with physical disabilities. Proper positioning and movement encourage the development of muscles and bones and help maintain healthy skin (Heller, Forney, Alberto, Schwartzman, & Goeckel, 1999). In addition to the health-related issues, positioning can influence how a child with physical disabilities is perceived and accepted by others. Simple adjustments can contribute to improved appearance and greater comfort and increased health for the child with physical disabilities (Best, Bigge, & Reed, 2001):

- Good positioning results in alignment and proximal support of the body.
- Stability positively affects use of the upper body.
- Stability promotes feelings of physical security and safety.
- Good positioning can reduce deformity.
- Positions must be changed frequently.

Proper seating helps combat poor circulation, muscle tightness, and pressure sores; and it contributes to proper digestion, respiration, and physical development. Be attentive to the following (Heller et al., 1996):

- Face should be forward, in midline position.
- Shoulders should be in midline position and not hunched over.
- Trunk should be in midline position; maintain normal curvature of spine.
- Seatbelt, pommel or leg separator, and/or shoulder and chest straps may be necessary for shoulder/upper trunk support and upright positions.
- Pelvic position: hips should be placed as far back in the chair as possible and weight distributed evenly on both sides of the buttocks.
- Foot support: both feet should be level and supported on the floor or wheelchair pedals.

Skin care is a major concern for many children with physical disabilities. The skin underneath braces or splints should be checked daily to identify persistent red spots that indicate an improper fit. Skin checks should be performed by someone on the student's team at least twice daily. Students who are capable of conducting self-checks of their skin should be taught to do so. Use of a long-handled mirror can reduce the student's dependence on others for this self-care task (Ricci-Balich & Behm, 1996). A health care professional should be contacted if any spot does not fade within 20 minutes after the pressure is relieved (Campbell, 2000). Students who are able to use their arms should be taught to perform "chair pushups" in which they lift their buttocks off the seat for 5 to 10 seconds. Doing chair pushups every 30 to 60 minutes may prevent pressure sores. Children who cannot perform pushups can shift their weight by bending forward and sideways.

Lifting and Transferring Students To prevent the development of pressure sores and help students maintain proper seating and positioning, teachers must know how to move and transfer students with physical disabilities. Routines for lifting, transferring, and repositioning children with physical disabilities should be developed for each child and entail standard procedures for (1) making contact with the child, (2) communicating what is going to happen in a manner the child can understand, (3) preparing the child physically for the transfer, and (4) requiring the child to participate in the routine as much as possible (Stremel et al., 1990). Figure 12.7 shows an example of an individualized routine for lifting and carrying a preschool child with cerebral palsy and spastic quadriplegia. Posting charts and photos of recommended positions for individual students can help remind teachers, paraprofessionals, and other staff to use proper transferring and positioning techniques. Guidelines for shifting the position of students in their wheelchairs and for moving students to and from a wheelchair to toilets and to the classroom floor are provided by Parette and Hourcade (1986).

Positioning, seating, and movement

 Content Standards for Beginning Teachers–P&HD: Use positioning techniques that decrease inappropriate tone and facilitate appropriate postural reactions to enhance participation (PH5S3) (also, PH2K3).
PRAXIS Special Education Core Principles: Content Knowledge: III. Delivery of Services to Students with Disabilities, Curriculum and Instruction, Positioning for students with physical disabilities.

Lifting and transferring students

Content Standards for Beginning Teachers–P&HD: Demonstrate appropriate body mechanics to ensure student and teacher safety in transfer, lifting, positioning, and seating (PH5S2).

FIGURE 12.7 Example of a routine for lifting and carrying a child with physical disabilities

Name: ___Tommy___ **Date:** ___5/11/02___

Lifting and Carrying Routine

Follow these steps each time you up pick Tommy up from the floor or move him from one piece of equipment to another, or move him in the classroom from one location to another.

Step	Activity	Desired Response
Contacting	Touch Tommy on his arm or shoulder & tell him you are going to move him from _____ to _____ .	Wait for Tommy to relax.
Communicating	Tell Tommy where you are going and show him a picture or object that represents where he is going. For example, show him his coat and say, "we are going outside now to play."	Wait for Tommy to respond with facial expressions and vocalizations. (Try not to get him so hyped that he becomes more spastic.)
Preparing	Make sure Tommy's muscle tone is not stiff before you move him. Use deep pressure touch with a flat hand on his chest area to help relax him.	Wait to make sure that Tommy's body is relaxed and in alignment (as much as possible).
Lifting	Place Tommy in a sitting position and lift him from sitting unless he is in the stander, where he will need to be lifted from standing. Tell him that you are going to lift him. Put your arms around Tommy's back and under his knees and bend his knees to his chest so that you maintain him in a flexed position.	Wait for Tommy to reach his arms forward toward you and facilitate at his shoulders if he does not initiate reach within 10 sec.
Carrying	Turn Tommy away from you so that he is facing away and can see where you are moving. Lean his back against your body to provide support, and hold him with one arm under his hips with his legs in front. If his legs become stiff, use your other arm to hold his legs apart by coming under one leg and between the two legs to hold them gently apart.	Tommy will be able to see where he is going and can use him arms to indicate location (grossly).
Repositioning	Put Tommy in the next position he is to use for the activity. Tell him what is happening: "Music is next and you are going to sit on the floor so you can play the instruments with Jilly and Susan."	Tommy is ready to partici-pate in the next activity.

Source: From Campbell, P. H. (2000). Promoting participation in natural environments by accommodating motor disabilities. In M. E. Snell & F. Brown, *Instruction of students with severe disabilities* (5th ed.), (p. 305). Upper Saddle River, NJ: Merrill/Prentice Hall. © 2000 by Merrill/Prentice Hall. Reprinted by permission.

INDEPENDENCE AND SELF-ESTEEM

All children, whether or not they face the challenges presented by a physical disability, chronic health condition, or traumatic brain injury, need to develop respect for themselves and feel that they have a rightful place in their families, schools, and communities. Effective teachers accept and treat children with physical impairments and special health care needs as worthwhile and whole individuals rather than as disability cases. They encourage the children to develop a positive, realistic view of themselves and their physical conditions. They enable the children to experience success, accomplishment, and, at times, failure. They expect the children to meet reasonable standards of performance and behavior. They help the children cope with disabilities wherever possible and realize that, beyond their physical impairments, these children have many qualities that make them unique individuals.

Students with physical limitations should be encouraged to develop as much independence as possible (Enright, 2000; McGill & Vogle, 2001). Nevertheless, most persons with physical disabilities find it necessary to rely on others for assistance at certain times, in certain situations. Effective teachers can help students cope with their disabilities, set realistic expectations, and accept assistance gracefully when it is needed.

Many people without disabilities tend to feel uncomfortable in the presence of a person with a visible disability and react with tension and withdrawal. This response is probably attributable to lack of previous contact with individuals with disabilities: people may fear that they will say or do the wrong thing. Belgrave and Mills (1981) found that when people with physical disabilities specifically mentioned their disabilities in connection with a request for help ("Would you mind sharpening my pencil for me? There are just some things a person can't do from a wheelchair"), they were perceived more favorably than they were when no mention was made of the disability.

Many people with disabilities report that their hardware (wheelchairs, artificial limbs, communication devices, and other apparatus) creates a great deal of curiosity and leads to frequent, repetitive questions from strangers. Learning how to explain their physical disabilities or health condition and respond to questions can be an appropriate component of the educational programs for some children. They may also benefit from discussing concerns such as when to ask for help from others and when to decline offers of assistance.

Developing independence and self-esteem

 Content Standards for Beginning Teachers–P&HD: Barriers to accessibility and acceptance of individuals with P&HD (PH5K3) (also, CC5K4). **PRAXIS** Special Education Core Principles: Content Knowledge: III. Delivery of Services to Students with Disabilities, Professional roles, Influence of teacher attitudes, values, and behavior on the learning of exceptional children.

EDUCATIONAL PLACEMENT ALTERNATIVES

For no group of exceptional children is the continuum of educational services and placement options more relevant than for students with physical impairments and special health needs. Most children with physical and health impairments today spend at least part of the school day in regular classrooms. During the 2000–2001 school year, about 44% of all school-age students who receive special education services under the disability category orthopedic impairments, 45% of those with other health impairments, and 31% of those with traumatic brain injury were educated in the regular classroom (U.S. Department of Education, 2002). The percentage of students in each disability category served in resource rooms was 22%, 33%, and 27%.

Many children with physical disabilities are also served in special classes in the public schools. During the 1999–2000 school year, about 28% of all school-age students who receive special education services under the disability category orthopedic impairments, 17% of those with other health impairments, and 32% of those with traumatic brain injury were educated in separate classrooms (U.S. Department of Education, 2002). Some districts have entire schools designed or adapted especially for students with physical disabilities, whereas in others special classrooms are housed within regular elementary or secondary school buildings. Special classes usually provide smaller class size, more adapted equipment, and easier access to the services of professionals such as physicians, physical and occupational therapists, and specialists in communication disorders and therapeutic recreation. To find out the percentage of school-age students with orthopedic impairments, other health impairments, and traumatic brain injury served in six different educational environments during the 2000–2001 school year, see Table 1.2 in Chapter 1.

Some children with the most severe physical and health impairments are served in homebound or hospital education programs. If a child's medical condition necessitates hospitalization or treatment at home for a lengthy period (generally 30 days or more), the local school district is obligated to develop an IEP and provide appropriate educational services to the child through a qualified teacher. Some children need home- or hospital-based instruction because

Placement alternatives

 Content Standards for Beginning Teachers–Common Core: Demands of learning environments (CC5K1). **PRAXIS** Special Education Core Principles: Content Knowledge: III. Delivery of Services to Students with Disabilities, Background knowledge, Placement issues/Least restrictive environment.

their life-support equipment cannot be made portable. Such *technology-dependent students* are in need of "both a medical device to compensate for the loss of a vital body function and substantial and ongoing nursing care to avoid death or further disability" (Office of Technology Assessment, 1987, p. 3). The term *medically fragile* is also used to refer to students who are dependent on life-support medical technology. As Lehr and McDaid (1993) point out, however, many of these children are "incredibly strong—survivors of many adverse conditions, who in fact are not fragile at all, but remarkably strong to be able to rebound from periods of acute illness" (p. 7).

Home or hospital settings are usually regarded as the most restrictive levels of special education service because little or no interaction with nondisabled students is possible. Most large hospitals and medical centers employ educational specialists who cooperate with the hospitalized student's home school district in planning and delivering instruction. Homebound children are visited regularly by itinerant teachers or tutors hired by the school district. Some school programs use a closed-circuit TV system to enable children to see, hear, and participate in class discussions and demonstrations from their beds.

One should not assume that a technology-dependent child cannot be educated in the public schools. After examining the experiences of 77 families of children who are ventilator-assisted, the authors of a study on the educational placements of such children concluded that "barriers to the integration of these children into school-based programs are attitudinal more than technological" (Jones, Clatterbuck, Marquis, Turnbull, & Moberly, 1996, p. 47).

 ## INCLUSIVE ATTITUDES

Attitudes and practices that hinder or support inclusion of students with P&HD

Council for Exceptional Children Content Standards for Beginning Teachers–P&HD: Barriers to accessibility and acceptance of individuals with P&HD (PH5K3) (also, CC5K4). **PRAXIS** Special Education Core Principles: Content Knowledge: III. Delivery of Services to Students with Disabilities, Professional roles, Influence of teacher attitudes, values, and behavior on the learning of exceptional children.

After health care objectives are met, acceptance is the most basic need of children with physical disabilities, health impairments, and traumatic brain injury. How parents, teachers, classmates, and others react to a child with physical disabilities is at least as important as the disability itself. Many children with physical disabilities suffer from excessive pity, sympathy, and overprotection; others are cruelly rejected, stared at, teased, and excluded from participation in activities with nondisabled children. Turner-Henson, Holaday, Corser, Ogletree, and Swan (1994) conducted interviews with the parents of 365 children with chronic illnesses and reported that one-third (34.5%) of the parents had experienced specific incidences of discrimination concerning their children. Although the study did not focus on the schools, more than half (55%) of the problems cited by the parents occurred at school (e.g., child not allowed to participate in play activities because of a brace or excluded from parties because of food limitations; teacher thinks child is faking low blood sugar). Peers were the second most common source of discrimination (36%).

The classroom can be a useful place to discuss disabilities and to encourage understanding and acceptance of a child with a physical disability, health impairment, or traumatic brain injury. Some teachers find that simulation or role-playing activities are helpful. Classmates might, for example, have the opportunity to use wheelchairs, braces, or crutches to expand their awareness of some barriers a classmate with physical disabilities faces. As Pieper (1983) notes, most children with physical and health impairments are "neither saintly creatures nor pitiable objects" (p. 8). She suggests that teachers emphasize cooperation rather than competition by choosing tasks that require students to work together. It is important to give praise when earned but not to make the child with a physical impairment a teacher's pet who will be resented by other students. Factual information can also help build a general understanding of impairment. Classmates should learn to use accurate terminology and offer the correct kind of assistance when needed.

Including Children with Chronic Illness   Some students with chronic illnesses are absent from school for extended periods because of flare-ups or scheduled medical treatment. Successful reentry of a child who has missed extended periods of school because of illness

FIGURE 12.8 Suggestions for helping peers maintain relationships with and prepare for return of a child who has been absent due to a serious illness or disease

Explain and allow discussion of the child's illness before treatment and before the child's return.

Common questions asked by children include

- What is the child's condition?
- Is it contagious?
- Will the child die?
- Will the child look different?
- Will the child act differently? (e.g., act "funny," bleed, faint, cough, vomit)?
- Can the child still do regular activities? (e.g., attend school, play, spend the night with friends, go out?)
- Should we talk about the illness, or should we ignore it?
- What will other children think if we stay friends with the child?

Update the class at least weekly on the child's progress.

Encourage and provide opportunities for classmates to maintain contact with the child (e.g., cards, visits, audiotapes, calls).

Encourage and provide opportunities for the child to visit the classroom.

Provide educational materials so that the child feels involved and can keep up with the class.

Have another period of discussion for the class shortly before the child returns to school:

- Consult with child, family, and health care team about what information should be conveyed.
- Consider involving the child and/or a health care team member in the discussion.

Have a welcome-back activity for the child on the day of his or her return.

Monitor peer responses and interactions with the child after the child's return.

Source: From Sexson, S. B., & Dingle, A. D. (2001). Medical disorders. In F. M. Kline, L. B. Silver, & S. C. Russell (Eds.), *The educator's guide to medical issues in the classroom* (p. 47). Baltimore: Paul H. Brookes. Reprinted by permission.

or the contraction of a disease requires preparation of the child, her parents, classmates, and school personnel (Sexson & Madan-Swain, 1993). The student's classmates should be given information about the child and the disease, encouraged to ask questions, and kept informed of the child's progress. Figure 12.8 shows questions that peers often ask about a classmate with a health problem and suggests several strategies for preparing the child and her peers for the child's return to the class.

There is a need for improved programs of education and counseling for students with terminal illnesses. These programs should give realistic support to the child and family in dealing with death and in making the best possible use of the time available (Ault et al., 2000). When a child dies, teachers and classmates are seriously affected; and their needs should be considered and talked about. For a discussion of ways in which classroom teachers can help themselves, classmates, and parents deal with the death of a student, see Cassini and Rodgers (1989), McHutchion (1991), Peckham (1993), Thornton and Krajewski (1993), and Wrenn (1994).

CURRENT ISSUES AND FUTURE TRENDS

Children with physical disabilities, health impairments, and traumatic brain injury are being included in regular educational programs as much as possible today. No longer do professionals believe that the regular classroom is an inappropriate environment for a child with physical limitations. Although architectural and attitudinal barriers still exist in some areas, inclusive public school programs are gradually becoming the norm instead of the exception.

RELATED SERVICES IN THE CLASSROOM

We will likely see a continuation of the present trend to serve children with physical and health impairments in regular classrooms as much as possible. Therapists and other support personnel will come into the classroom to assist the teacher, child, and classmates (Szabo, 2000). For example, some school districts in North Carolina employ health aides who carry out medical care plans in the classroom, assist OTs or PTs, help students get lunch trays, or act as teachers' assistants if not needed elsewhere (*CEC Today*, 1998). This appears to be a more effective and economical use of professional time and skill than removing a child with disabilities from the classroom to provide services in an isolated setting. Wherever and by whomever needed health and other related services are carried out, we must heed Orelove and Sobsey's (1991) caution:

> The challenge for the team is to determine how to work with and around the student's medical and physical needs to provide an appropriate education, rather than turning the school day into an extended therapy session. Therapy and specialized health care procedures should facilitate, not replace, instruction. (pp. 3–4)

Including students with physical impairments and special health care needs, however, has raised several controversial issues. Many questions center on the extent of responsibility properly assumed by teachers and schools for providing for a child's physical and health care needs. Some educators and school administrators believe that services such as catheterization, tracheotomy care, and tube feeding are more medical than educational and should not be the school's responsibility. The expense of such services, the training and supervision of personnel, and the availability of insurance pose potential problems for school districts. Similar questions have been raised with regard to the assistive devices and special therapeutic services that children with physical or health impairments may need to access and benefit from a public education. For example, who should bear the cost of an expensive computerized communication system for a child with cerebral palsy—the parents, the school, both, or some other agency?

Tatro and Garret cases

 Council for Exceptional Children Content Standards for Beginning Teachers–P&HD: Laws and policies related to specialized health care in the educational setting(PH1K3). **PRAXIS** Special Education Core Principles: Content Knowledge: II. Legal and Societal Issues, Tatro re: related services.

Two landmark U.S. Supreme Court cases have made clear the government's position. In *Irving Independent School District v. Tatro* (1984), the U.S. Supreme Court decided that a school district was obligated to provide clean intermittent catheterization to a young child with spina bifida. The Court considered catheterization to be a related service necessary for the child to remain in the least restrictive educational setting and able to be performed by a trained layperson.

Cedar Rapids Community School District v. Garret F. (1999) involved nursing care for a middle school student who was paralyzed from a motorcycle accident since the age of 4 and could breathe only with an electric ventilator or by someone pumping an air bag attached to his tracheotomy tube. In addition to having someone monitor and check the settings on his ventilator, Garret required continuous assistance with his tracheotomy, positioning in his wheelchair, observations to determine if he was in respiratory distress, catheterization, assessments of his blood pressure, and assistance with food and drink.

Garret's mother had used money from insurance and a settlement with the motorcycle company to hire a nurse to care for his medical needs. When Garret reached middle school, his mother asked the school district to assume the cost of his physical care during the school day. The school district refused, believing they were not responsible under IDEA for providing continuous nursing care. The Supreme Court agreed with lower courts that the nursing services were related services because Garret could not attend school without them and ruled that the school district had to pay for continuous one-on-one nursing care. These two rulings used what is known as a "bright-line test" for making decisions about related services (Katsiyannis & Yell, 2000). A bright-line test is a test that is clearly stated and easy to follow (Thomas & Hawke, 1999). The bright-line test established in the *Tatro* case and upheld by the *Garret* case is that if a licensed physician is required to perform a service, the school district is not responsible for paying for it. If a nurse or health aide can perform the service, even if it is medical in nature, it is considered a related service that the school district must provide under IDEA to give the child access to a free, appropriate public education.

The Supreme Court's interpretation of related services places a huge financial burden on schools and may contribute to increased pressure on Congress to help relieve the burden by raising the level of federal funding for IDEA (Katsiyannis & Yell, 2000). Reviews and discussions of special education law and legal precedents concerning the schools' responsibility for providing assistive technology and special health care services can be found in Heller et al. (2000), Katsiyannis and Yell (2000), Rapport (1996), and Weiss and Dykes (1995).

Emerging technologies for P&HD

 Council for Exceptional Children Content Standards for Beginning Teachers–P&HD: Barriers to accessibility and acceptance of individuals with P&HD (PH5K3).
PRAXIS Special Education Core Principles: Content Knowledge: III. Delivery of Services to Students with Disabilities, curriculum and Instruction, Power mobility for students with physical disabilities.

NEW AND EMERGING TECHNOLOGIES FOR PERSONS WITH SEVERE PHYSICAL DISABILITIES

Over the past several decades, the use of technology to "minimize disadvantages associated with disabilities has blossomed from a promise that benefited a few individuals to a reality that has improved many people's lives" (Sobsey, 1996, p. 207). New and emerging developments in technology and biomedical engineering hold even more exciting implications for many individuals with physical disabilities. People with paralysis resulting from spinal cord injury and other causes are already benefiting from sophisticated microcomputers that can stimulate paralyzed muscles by bypassing damaged nerves. In 1982 Nan Davis became the first human being to walk with permanently paralyzed muscles; she was able to control a computer with her brain and transmit impulses to sensors placed on her paralyzed muscles. Such systems have become more efficient and widespread, helping many people with various kinds of physical impairments. *Myoelectric (bionic) limbs* are battery-powered artificial limbs that pick up electrical signals from the brain and enable the user to perform certain movements and functions. *Robotics* also holds promise for increasing the independent functioning of students with physical disabilities. A robot is "any mechanical device operated automatically, especially by remote control, to perform in a seemingly human way" (*Webster's New World Dictionary*, 1986, p. 1231). Robots have great potential as assistive tools for students with disabilities by enabling independent manipulation of the environment and providing increased educational access and opportunities (Howell, 2000).

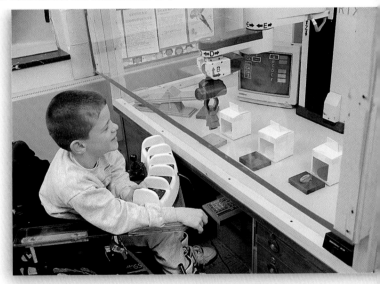

Which object weighs the most? As his skills at controlling the robot increase, Troy comes into contact with ever more complex and exciting learning experiences.

 **ANIMAL ASSISTANCE**

Using animals to assist people with physical disabilities has also generated much recent interest. Animals can help children and adults with physical disabilities in many ways. Nearly everyone is familiar with guide dogs, which can help people who are blind travel independently. Some agencies now train hearing dogs to assist people who are deaf by alerting them to sounds. Another recent and promising approach to the use of animals by people with disabilities is that of a helper or service dog. Depending on a person's needs, dogs can be trained to carry books and other objects (in saddlebags), pick up telephone receivers, turn light switches on or off, and open doors. Dogs can also be used for balance and support—for example, to help a person propel a wheelchair up a steep ramp or to help a person stand up from a seated position. And dogs can be trained to contact family members or neighbors in an emergency.

Monkeys have been trained to perform complex tasks such as preparing food, operating record and tape players, and turning the pages of books. Sometimes technological and animal assistance are combined, as when a person uses a laser beam (emitted from a mouth-held device) to show a monkey which light switch to turn on.

In addition to providing practical assistance and enhancing the independence of people with disabilities, animals also appear to have social value as companions. People frequently report that their helper animals serve as icebreakers in opening up conversations and contacts with nondisabled people in the school and community. In addition, the responsibility of caring for an animal is a worthwhile and rewarding experience for many people, with or without disabilities.

 "Helper" or "service" dogs can be trained to assist with many daily living and work-related tasks.

 **EMPLOYMENT, LIFE SKILLS, AND SELF-ADVOCACY**

A major area of concern is employment, one of the most meaningful aspects of adult life. Many studies show that successful and remunerative work is one of the most important variables in enabling people with disabilities to lead satisfying, productive, and independent lives. Yet negative attitudes persist on the part of many employers. Vocational and professional opportunities must be expanded to include individuals with disabilities more equitably. While children are in school, their education should help them investigate practical avenues of future employment; and there should be ongoing contact between educators and vocational rehabilitation specialists.

Traditionally, children and adults with disabilities were viewed as society's responsibility, and it was assumed they should be grateful for the services (i.e., charity) bestowed upon them by a benevolent society (Wolfensberger, 2000). Persons with disabilities neither want nor need charity; rather, they need and deserve equal access to the same educational, employment, housing, and recreational opportunities as persons without disabilities (Giangreco, 1996). Legislation and litigation over the past 20 years have mandated equal access and provided funding for improved opportunities, but many of those advancements have been the direct product of self-advocacy.

Telethons and other fund-raising activities on behalf of persons with disabilities have become controversial in recent years. Some self-advocacy groups and professionals believe they perpetuate negative stereotypes and portray people with disabilities as objects of pity (see the November 1993 issue of the *TASH Newsletter*).

There are many self-help groups for people with disabilities. These groups can help provide information and support to children affected by similar disabilities. It is usually encouraging for a child and parent to meet and observe capable, independent adults who have disabilities, and worthwhile helping relationships can be established. Teachers can promote self-knowledge and self-confidence in their students with physical disabilities by introducing them to such adults and groups. Some self-advocacy groups operate centers for independent living, which emphasize adaptive devices, financial benefits, access to jobs, and provision of personal care attendants. Other groups are active as advocates for social change, countering instances in which people with disabilities are excluded from meaningful participation in society.

We all must work to improve the quality of education, increase physical access to public buildings, improve public attitudes, and provide greater support for parents and families. As these needs are met, the opportunity to participate fully in all facets of everyday community life will be open to all people with physical disabilities and health impairments.

Promoting self-advocacy

 PRAXIS Special Education Core Principles: Content Knowledge: III. Delivery of Services to Students with Disabilities, Professional roles, Teacher as collaborator with community groups, Directing parents to other groups and resources.

To check your comprehension of chapter content, go to the Guided Review and Quiz modules in Chapter 12 of the Companion Website at **www.prenhall.com/heward**

 SUMMARY

DEFINITIONS OF PHYSICAL DISABILITIES AND HEALTH IMPAIRMENTS

- Children with physical disabilities and health impairments are eligible for special education under two disability categories of IDEA: orthopedic impairments and other health impairments.
- Orthopedic impairments involve the skeletal system; a neurological impairment involves the nervous system. Both are frequently described in terms of the affected parts of the body.
- Physical disabilities and health impairments may be congenital or acquired, chronic or acute.

PREVALENCE OF PHYSICAL DISABILITIES AND HEALTH IMPAIRMENTS

- In 2000–2001, 6.4% of all school-age students who received special education services were reported under the disability categories of orthopedic impairments and other health impairments. This figure does not include all children with physical or health impairments because some are reported under other disability categories, and some do not require special education services.

TYPES AND CAUSES OF PHYSICAL DISABILITIES AND HEALTH IMPAIRMENTS

- Cerebral palsy is a long-term condition arising from impairment to the brain and causing disturbances in voluntary motor functions.
- Spina bifida is a congenital condition that may cause loss of sensation and severe muscle weakness in the lower part of the body. Children with spina bifida can usually participate in most classroom activities but need assistance in toileting.
- Muscular dystrophy is a long-term condition; most children gradually lose the ability to walk independently.

- Spinal cord injuries are caused by a penetrating injury, stretching of the vertebral column, fracture of the vertebrae, or compression of the spinal cord and usually result in some form of paralysis below the site of the injury.
- Epilepsy produces disturbances of movement, sensation, behavior, and/or consciousness.
- Diabetes is a disorder of metabolism that can often be controlled with injections of insulin.
- Children with cystic fibrosis, asthma, HIV/AIDS, and other chronic health conditions may require special education and other related services, such as health care services and counseling.

CHARACTERISTICS OF CHILDREN WITH PHYSICAL DISABILITIES AND HEALTH IMPAIRMENTS

- Perrin et al. (1993) have proposed a noncategorical system for classifying and understanding children's chronic physical and medical conditions; it includes 13 dimensions that are judged on a continuum from mild to profound.
- Many factors must be taken into consideration when assessing the effects of a physical impairment or health condition on a child's development and behavior. Two particularly important variables are the age of onset and the visibility of the impairment.

DEFINITION OF TRAUMATIC BRAIN INJURY

- Traumatic brain injury is an acquired injury to the brain caused by an external physical force, resulting in total or partial functional disability or psychosocial impairments, or both, that adversely affects a child's educational performance.

PREVALENCE OF TRAUMATIC BRAIN INJURY

- Each year, 1 in 500 school-age children will be hospitalized with traumatic head injuries.
- Traumatic brain injury is the leading cause of death in children and the most common acquired disability in childhood.

TYPES AND CAUSES OF TRAUMATIC BRAIN INJURY

- Open head injuries are the result of penetration of the skull. Closed head injuries are more common and result from the head hitting a stationary object with such force that the brain slams against the inside of the cranium.
- Major causes of traumatic brain injury in children are car and bicycle accidents, gunshot wounds, shaken-baby syndrome, falls, and accidents during contact sports.
- A mild brain injury results in a concussion, a brief or momentary loss of consciousness, usually without any subsequent complications.
- A moderate brain injury usually results in contusions (bruising, swelling, and bleeding), hematomas (aggregation or clotting of blood), loss of consciousness, and significant cognitive and behavioral impairments for many months.
- In addition to brain contusions, hematomas, and damage to the nerve fibers or axons, a severe brain injury results in a coma and often permanent impairments in functioning.

CHARACTERISTICS OF CHILDREN WITH TRAUMATIC BRAIN INJURY

- Impairments caused by brain injuries fall into three main categories: (1) physical and sensory changes (e.g., lack of coordination, spasticity of muscles); (2) cognitive impairments (e.g., short- and long-term memory deficits, difficulty maintaining attention and concentration); and (3) social, behavioral, and emotional problems (e.g., mood swings [emotional lability], self-centeredness, lack of motivation).

EDUCATIONAL APPROACHES

- Children with physical disabilities, health impairments, and traumatic brain injury typically require services from an interdisciplinary team of professionals.
- Physical therapists (PTs) use specialized knowledge to plan and oversee a child's program in making correct and useful movements. Occupational therapists (OTs) are concerned with a child's participation in activities, especially those that will be useful in self-help, employment, recreation, communication, and other aspects of daily living.
- Modifications to the physical environment and classroom activities can enable students with physical and health impairments to participate more fully in the school program.
- Assistive technology is any piece of equipment or device used to increase, maintain, or improve the functional capabilities of individuals with disabilities.
- Students can increase their independence by learning to take care of their personal health care routines such as clean intermittent catheterization and self-administration of medication.
- Proper positioning and seating are important for children with physical disabilities. All teachers and other staff should follow a standard routine for lifting and moving a child with physical disabilities.
- How parents, teachers, classmates, and others react to a child with physical disabilities is at least as important as the disability itself.
- Students with physical limitations should be encouraged to develop as much independence as possible. Effective teachers help students cope with their disabilities, set realistic expectations, and accept help gracefully when it is needed.

EDUCATIONAL PLACEMENT ALTERNATIVES

- About 45% of students with physical impairments and chronic health conditions are served in regular classrooms.
- The amount of supportive help that may be required to enable a student with physical disabilities to function effectively in a regular class varies greatly according to each child's condition, needs, and level of functioning.
- Special classes usually provide smaller class size, more adapted equipment, and easier access to the services of professionals such as physicians, physical and occupational therapists, and specialists in communication disorders and therapeutic recreation.
- Some technology-dependent children require home- or hospital-based instruction because their life-support equipment cannot be made portable.
- Successful reentry of children who have missed extended periods of school because of illness or the contraction of a disease requires preparation of the child, his parents, classmates, and school personnel.

CURRENT ISSUES AND FUTURE TRENDS

- The education of students with physical and health impairments in regular classrooms has raised several controversial issues, especially with regard to the provision of medically related procedures in the classroom.
- New and emerging technologies such as bionic body parts and robotics offer exciting possibilities for the future.
- Animals, particularly dogs and monkeys, can assist people with physical disabilities in various ways.
- Children with physical disabilities can gain self-knowledge and self-confidence by meeting capable adults with disabilities and joining self-advocacy groups.

For more information on physical disabilities, health impairments, and traumatic brain injury, go to the Web Links module in Chapter 12 of the Companion Website at **www.prenhall.com/heward**

Chapter 13
Autism and Severe Disabilities

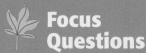

Focus Questions

- Why is a curriculum based on typical developmental stages inappropriate for students with severe disabilities?

- Why is it so critical to select functional and age-appropriate curriculum objectives for students with autism or severe disabilities?

- Can a teacher increase the learning potential of students with autism and severe disabilities? How?

- What are the most important skills for a teacher of students with severe disabilities? Why?

- How much time should a student with autism or severe disabilities spend in the general education classroom with his or her nondisabled peers?

Diane K. Ellis
Bellevue Public School District
Bellevue, Nebraska

Education • Certification • Experience
- B.S., Special Education and Elementary Education, University of South Dakota, 1982
- M.A., Early Childhood Special Education, University of South Dakota, 1988
- Nebraska Teacher Certification, Severe/Multiple Disabilities, K–12; Preschool Handicapped; Visually Impaired, K–12; Mild/Moderate Handicapped, K–12, Elementary
- 20 years of teaching children and adults with a variety of disabilities

Teaching Position and Students   I am the assistive technology and augmentative communication (AAC) consultant for the Bellevue Public School District. I began teaching in the Bellevue Schools 14 years ago as lead teacher for CHAP School, which served students with multiple or severe/profound disabilities. I serve a caseload of 70 students. The children who receive the majority of my direct service time are those with severe physical disabilities, moderate to profound mental handicaps, and autism. The students range in age from 2 to 14, and they are educated in a wide range of placements in six school buildings throughout the district. Several children are served in home-based placements.

I'll introduce you to several of my students with the caution that each is unique and these descriptions and disability labels do not begin to identify his or her strengths or challenges, needs or potential. Jeremy, a 10-year-old with autism, has a beautiful smile and some significantly challenging behaviors. When interacting with others, Jeremy gets frustrated because of his limited communication skills, which often lead to full-blown tantrums with head banging, biting, and screaming. Gary is a second grader with traumatic brain injury who exhibits significant communicative, cognitive, and behavioral challenges but has excellent gross motor skills. This results in some serious safety issues as he can climb fences and pull away from an adult's hand to escape while not recognizing common dangers. Cory is a fifth grader with significant physical disabilities due to cerebral palsy. He uses a motorized wheelchair, and his difficulty with oral communication often results in frustration when trying to interact with unfamiliar listeners or peers. Dawn is a first grader with profound mental retardation, visual impairment, severe physical disability, and numerous medical and health concerns. She requires adult assistance to participate in any activity and functions in the 1–6 month age range.

IEP Goals and Objectives   Many of the IEP goals for these students focus on their use of assistive technology or AAC supports to function more independently within their educational environments. This may mean the use of

alternate keyboards with customized overlays so that they can use software or type their names. Some students need a switch to activate the computer with adaptive software. Students learn to use switches to activate tape recorders, blenders, or radios. Here are examples of IEP goals and objectives designed to influence the functional communication and classroom independence of students with significant disabilities.

Annual goal. Using sign language, verbalizations, voice output device, and/or Picture Exchange Communication System (PECS) book, Jeremy will initiate interactions with others at least 10 times in a 20-minute observation for 4–5 sessions by January 2003.

Short-term objective 1. Jeremy will activate voice output device (sequential communicator) to initiate a play interaction with a peer at least five times in a 20-minute observation for 4–5 sessions by September 2002.

Short-term objective 2. Given PECS book and open-hand cue, Jeremy will exchange a picture symbol to request desired items from a listener at least 10 times during a 20-minute observation for 4–5 sessions by May 2002.

Annual goal. Given switch access and alternate keyboard (i.e., Intellikeys), Cory will use the devices to access the classroom computer for academic lessons on 4 of 5 sessions by January 2003.

Short-term objective 1. When given switch access and verbal prompt, Cory will activate cause-and-effect software five times on 4 of 5 sessions by May 2002.

Short-term objective 2. When given alternate keyboard access (Intellikeys) and name overlay, Cory will type the first two letters of his name correctly on 4 of 5 sessions by September 2002.

[*Note:* Subsequent objectives for Jeremy and Cory increase the performance criteria, fade the open-hand cue or verbal prompt, and/or increase the number of letters typed.]

Services/Instructional Strategies Assistive technology or AAC supports should be considered whenever a child is experiencing difficulty participating in his educational program or demonstrates frustration with communication. Communication is necessary in every environment and for classroom independence. My intervention efforts focus on developing functional communication skills and integrating these skills throughout the school day.

I give students direct, one-to-one instruction on using AAC and other assistive technologies with specific plans for integrating the use of those supports into their daily activities at school and home. The AAC systems include voice output devices, communication boards/overlays, sign language, and the Picture Exchange Communication System (PECS) (Bondy & Frost, 1994). Teachers always pair spoken language with the AAC system. In addition to working directly with students, I provide consultation and training support to school staff and parents on the use of assistive technology for children.

I also help teach weekly literacy and language lessons to small groups of students in eight special education classrooms. We read a book and complete related language activities using graphic symbol supports. For example, one of the students' favorite books is *The Little Old Lady Who Wasn't Afraid of Anything.* I've created communication boards with graphic symbol software to support expressive and receptive language skills. I may point to the graphic symbols as I read the story to support receptive understanding. The communication overlay may be placed on a voice output device, function as a communication board, or be used as individual symbols on a PECS book. Students then use the graphic symbols to initiate or respond to questions about the story. Related activities include using clothing props to dress up as scarecrows and making a classroom book with graphic symbols using the story's repetitive lines. Students then "read" the created classroom book by using the graphic symbols as cues to the written word.

Another part of my role on IEP teams is helping conduct functional behavioral assessments to determine if a child's challenging behavior has a communicative function. It is common for students who have significant difficulties in communicating to engage in

To see examples of assistive technologies and instructional materials used by Ms. Ellis, go the Teacher Feature module of the Companion Website at **www.prenhall.com/heward**

challenging behaviors such as tantrums, aggression, and noncompliance. When students learn alternate ways to communicate with others, the frequency and/or duration of their behavioral outbursts usually decrease.

What I Like Most about Being a Special Educator   I have never wanted to be anything other than a special education teacher. The challenges of teaching students with severe disabilities can be daunting, but the rewards are tremendous with each step a student takes: The smile and laughter of Davy when he discovered that he controlled the action of the characters on the computer screen. The joy of Christopher's parents when their son finally said, "I love you!" with his voice output device. And then there is Janey, who changed from an aggressive loner into a child who sought out others to play and even learned to compromise by developing functional communication skills!

The progress students make, no matter how small, sustains a teacher during the more challenging periods. Seeing a student become more independent and knowing that her newfound success is due in part to my involvement is an awesome feeling that can't be described. Knowing that I have positively influenced a student and her family provides the incentive I need to hang in there during the more challenging periods.

Advice for Someone Considering a Career in Special Education   A teacher of children with severe disabilities must learn to accept that progress is measured in tiny steps. However, the impact of those tiny steps can be enormous. The children who challenge us the most are the ones who will give us the most personal reward. No matter what population you teach, I believe you can never know enough. The knowledge base of special education—our collective understanding of empirically derived best practices—has changed during the 20 years I've been in the field, and it will surely continue to change in the future. I continue to look for new information and ways to expand my knowledge and increase my skills as a teacher. So prepare yourself to be a teacher but also prepare yourself to be a student—learning new ways to improve the life of each child you serve.

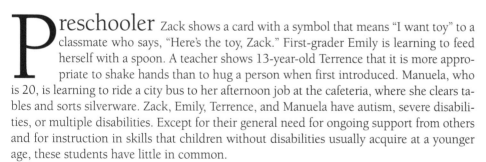

Preschooler Zack shows a card with a symbol that means "I want toy" to a classmate who says, "Here's the toy, Zack." First-grader Emily is learning to feed herself with a spoon. A teacher shows 13-year-old Terrence that it is more appropriate to shake hands than to hug a person when first introduced. Manuela, who is 20, is learning to ride a city bus to her afternoon job at the cafeteria, where she clears tables and sorts silverware. Zack, Emily, Terrence, and Manuela have autism, severe disabilities, or multiple disabilities. Except for their general need for ongoing support from others and for instruction in skills that children without disabilities usually acquire at a younger age, these students have little in common.

Students with autism and severe disabilities are a highly diverse population. Each student often has a combination of obvious and not-so-obvious disabilities. Because of differences in their intellectual, physical, and behavioral limitations, each student requires different additions to or adaptations in their education. Without direct and systematic instruction, however, many individuals with autism or severe disabilities are not able to perform the most basic, everyday tasks we take for granted, such as eating, toileting, and communicating our needs and feelings to others.

Having autism or a severe disability does not preclude meaningful achievements. Despite the severity and multiplicity of their disabilities, these students can and do learn. An ever-growing body of evidence demonstrates that individuals with autism or severe disabilities can learn and function effectively in integrated school, work, and community settings.

To better understand what will be covered in this chapter, go to the Essential Concepts and Chapter-at-a-Glance modules in Chapter 13 of the Companion Website at **www.prenhall.com/heward**

AUTISM

 DEFINITION

Autism is one of the most intriguing, fascinating, and "baffling" of childhood disorders (Simpson, 2001, p. 68). Leo Kanner, a psychiatrist at Johns Hopkins Hospital in Baltimore, was the first to describe and name the condition when he when he published case reports on a group of 11 children in 1943. He wrote that the children displayed behaviors that differed "so markedly and uniquely from anything reported so far, that each case merits . . . a detailed consideration of its fascinating peculiarities" (Kanner, 1985, p. 11). The children Kanner described shared the following characteristics:

- Difficulty relating to others in a typical manner
- Extreme aloneness that seemed to isolate the child from the outside world
- Resistance to being picked up or held by parents
- Significant speech deficits including mutism and echolalia
- In some cases, very good rote memory
- Early specific food preferences
- Obsessive desire for repetition and sameness
- Bizarre, repetitive behavior such as rocking back and forth
- Lack of imagination, few spontaneous behaviors such as typical play
- Normal physical appearance

Kanner called this condition *early infantile autism.* He based the term on the Greek word *autos* (self), because the children seemed to be locked inside themselves and detached from the world.

Autism is a severe developmental disability marked by impairments of communication, social, and emotional functioning. According to the definition endorsed by the Autism Society of America (2000), the essential features of the condition typically appear before 30 months of age and consist of disturbances in (1) developmental rates and/or sequences; (2) responses to sensory stimuli; (3) speech, language, and cognitive capacities; and (4) capacities to relate to people, events, and objects (Sturmey & Sevin, 1994).

Autism is defined in IDEA as

> a developmental disability affecting verbal and nonverbal communication and social interaction, generally evident before age 3, that affects a child's performance. Other characteristics often associated with autism are engagement in repetitive activities and stereotyped movements, resistance to environmental change or change in daily routines, and unusual responses to sensory experiences. The term does not apply if a child's educational performance is adversely affected primarily because the child has a serious emotional disturbance. (34 C.F. R., Part 300, 300.7[b][1])

Parents of children with autism commonly report that their baby developed in typical fashion for the first year or more, acquiring some meaningful communication skills and enjoying cuddling and hugging. But between 12 and 15 months, the child began showing an oversensitivity to certain sounds or touch; no longer seemed to understand even simple words or gestures; and became increasingly withdrawn, aimless, and perseverative (Greenspan, 1992).

 DIAGNOSIS

There is no medical test for autism; a diagnosis is made according to criteria described in the *Diagnostic and Statistical Manual of Mental Disorders* (American Psychiatric Association,

Definition of autism

Council for Exceptional Children Content Standards for Beginning Teachers–INDEP CURR: Definitions and issues related to the identification of individuals with disabilities (IC1K1) (also, CC1K5). **PRAXIS** Special Education Core Principles: Content Knowledge: I. Understanding Exceptionalities, Definitions of specific disabilities.

FIGURE 13.1 Diagnostic criteria for autism

A. A total of six (or more) items from (1), (2), and (3), with at least two from (1), and one each from (2) and (3):

1. Qualitative impairment in social interaction, as manifested by at least two of the following:
   a. Marked impairment in the use of multiple nonverbal behaviors such as eye-to-eye gaze, facial expression, body postures, and gestures to regulate social interaction.
   b. Failure to develop peer relationships appropriate to developmental level.
   c. A lack of spontaneous seeking to share enjoyment, interests, or achievements with other people (e.g., by a lack of showing, bringing, or pointing out objects of interest).
   d. Lack of social or emotional reciprocity.

2. Qualitative impairments in communication as manifested by at least one of the following:
   a. Delay in, or total lack of, the development of spoken language (not accompanied by an attempt to compensate through alternative modes of communication such as gestures or mime).
   b. In individuals with adequate speech, marked impairments in the ability to initiate or sustain a conversation with others.
   c. Stereotyped and repetitive use of language or idiosyncratic language.
   d. Lack of varied, spontaneous make-believe play or social imitative play appropriate to developmental level.

3. Restricted repetitive and stereotyped patterns of behavior, interests, and activities, as manifested by at least one of the following:
   a. Encompassing preoccupation with one or more stereotypic and restricted patterns of interest that is abnormal either in intensity or focus.
   b. Apparently inflexible adherence to specific, nonfunctional routines or rituals.
   c. Stereotypic and repetitive motor mannerisms (e.g., hand or finger flapping or twisting, or complex whole-body movements).
   d. Persistent preoccupation with parts of objects.

B. Delays or abnormal functioning in at least one of the following areas, with onset prior to age 3 years: (1) social interaction, (2) language as used in social communication, or (3) symbolic or imaginative play.

C. The disturbance is not better accounted for by Rett's Disorder or Childhood Disintegrative Disorder.

Source: Reprinted from American Psychiatric Association. (2000). *Diagnostic and statistical manual of mental disorders* (4th ed., text rev., p. 92). Washington, DC: Author.

2000) (see Figure 13.1). Autism is one of five developmental disabilities of childhood included under the umbrella term *pervasive developmental disorder (PDD)* (American Psychiatric Association, 2000). Many professionals now use the term *autism spectrum disorders* instead of PDD. The five subtypes of PDD are autistic disorder, Asperger disorder, Rett's disorder, childhood disintegrative disorder, and pervasive developmental disorder not otherwise specified. These related disorders are differentiated from autistic disorder primarily by the age of onset and severity of various symptoms.

At the mild end of the autism spectrum is **Asperger syndrome**, sometimes referred to as "high-functioning autism." Children with Asperger syndrome do not have general language delay, and many have average or even above average intelligence. Characteristics of Asperger syndrome include poor communication and social skills, repetitive and stereotyped behaviors, intense interest or preoccupation in atypical things or parts of things (e.g., tractors or

PDD, autism spectrum disorders, Asperger's syndrome

Council for Exceptional Children Content Standards for Beginning Teachers–INDEP CURR: Definitions and issues related to the identification of individuals with disabilities (IC1K1) (also, IC2K4, CC1K5, CC2K6).
PRAXIS Special Education Core Principles: Content Knowledge: I. Understanding Exceptionalities, Definitions of specific disabilities.

washing machines) (Barnhill et al., 2000; Safran, 2001; Simpson & Myles, in press). Their peculiarities and lack of social skills make it very hard for these children to develop and maintain friendships.

CHARACTERISTICS

The combination of behavioral deficits (e.g., inability to relate to others, lack of functional language) and behavioral excesses (e.g., self-stimulation, bizarre and challenging behaviors) makes children with autism stand out as strikingly different from most children. Written nearly 30 years ago, Lovaas and Newsom's (1976) description of six frequently observed characteristics of children with autism provides a graphic picture of the pervasive nature of this disorder:

- *Apparent sensory deficit.* We may move directly in front of the child, smile, and talk to him, yet he will act as if no one is there. We may not feel that the child is avoiding or ignoring us, but rather that he simply does not seem to see or hear. . . . As we get to know the child better, we become aware of the great variability in this obliviousness to stimulation. For example, although the child may give no visible reaction to a loud noise, such as a clapping of hands directly behind his ears, he may orient to the crinkle of a candy wrapper or respond fearfully to a distant and barely audible siren.
- *Severe affect isolation.* Another characteristic that we frequently notice is that attempts to love and cuddle and show affection to the child encounter a profound lack of interest on the child's part. Again, the parents relate that the child seems not to know or care whether he is alone or in the company of others.
- *Self-stimulation.* A most striking kind of behavior in these children centers on very repetitive stereotyped acts, such as rocking their bodies when in a sitting position, twirling around, flapping their hands at the wrists, or humming a set of three or four notes over and over again. The parents often report that their child has spent entire days gazing at his cupped hands, staring at lights, spinning objects, etc.
- *Tantrums and self-mutilatory behavior.* Often the parents report that the child sometimes bites himself so severely that he bleeds, or that he beats his head against walls or sharp pieces of furniture so forcefully that large lumps rise and his skin turns black and blue. He may beat his face with his fists . . . Sometimes the child's aggression will be directed outward against his parents or teachers in the most primitive form of biting, scratching, and kicking. Some of these children absolutely tyrannize their parents by staying awake and making noises all night, tearing curtains off the window, spilling flour in the kitchen, etc.
- *Echolalic and psychotic speech.* Most of these children are mute; they do not speak, but they may hum or occasionally utter simple sounds. The speech of those who do talk may be echoes of other people's attempts to talk to them. For example, if we address a child with the question, "What is your name?" the child is likely to answer, "What is your name?" (preserving, perhaps, the exact intonation of the one who spoke to him). At other times the echolalia is not immediate but delayed; the child may repeat statements he has heard that morning or on the preceding day, or he may repeat TV commercials or other such announcements.
- *Behavior deficiencies.* Although the presence of the behaviors sketched above is rather striking, it is equally striking to take note of many behaviors that the autistic child does not have. At the age of 5 or 10, he may, in many ways, show the behavioral repertoire of a 1-year-old child. He has few if any self-help skills but needs to be fed and dressed by others. (pp. 308–309)

Children who display these symptoms are sometimes described as having "low functioning" autism. Not all children with autism exhibit each of the characteristics described

Characteristics of autism

Council for
Exceptional
Children   Content
Standards for
Beginning Teachers–INDEP
CURR: Psychological and social-
emotional characteristics of
individuals with disabilities
(IC2K4) (also, CC2K2).
PRAXIS Special Education
Core Principles: Content
Knowledge: I. Understanding
Exceptionalities, Characteristics
of students with disabilities,
Cognitive and affective and
social-adaptive factors.

by Lovaas and Newsom (1976). Many children with autism are "quite loving and caring, thoughtful and creative" (Greenspan & Weider, 1997, p. 88).

Although autism occurs across the full range of intellectual abilities, between 70% and 80% of individuals with autism also have mental retardation (Romanczyk, Weinter, Lockshin, & Ekdahl, 1999). Uneven skill development is a common characteristic of autism, and some children exhibit "splinter skills," areas of relatively superior performance that are unexpected compared to other domains of functioning. For example, a child may draw very well or remember things that were said a week before but have no functional language and make no eye contact with others.

A very few persons with autism exhibit **savant syndrome,** an extraordinary ability in an area such as memorization, mathematical calculations, or musical ability while functioning at the mental retardation level in all other areas (Kelly, Macaruso, & Sokol, 1997; Treffert, 1989). The betting calculations by Raymond in the movie *Rain Man* is an example of savant syndrome.

PREVALENCE

Students with autism constitute the fastest growing category in special education. Although historically considered a rare disorder, in 1996 autism was estimated to occur in 15 of every 10,000 children (Dawson & Osterling, 1997), a prevalence rate three times higher than figures cited in the 1970s. More recently the Autism Society of America (2000) has estimated that autism occurs in as many as 1 in 500 people, a figure consistent with data reported by one state (California Department of Developmental Services, 1999). This would make autism more common than childhood cancer or Down syndrome. Boys are affected about four times more often than are girls (Fombonne, 1999).

In the 2000–2001 school year, 78,717 students ages 6 to 21 received special education services under the IDEA category of autism (U.S. Department of Education, 2002). This represents an increase of 131% in the number of students served just 4 years before. It is not clear what factors are responsible for the huge increase in the number of students served under this category. It may be due to increased awareness, better assessment procedures, availability of services via diagnostic category, and may or may not reflect an actual increase in the true incidence of autism spectrum disorders.

CAUSES

Numerous causes of autism have been proposed over the years. For many years, it was widely thought that parents who were indifferent to the emotional needs of their children caused autism. This notion may have had its beginnings in Kanner's (1943/1985) observations that many of the parents of his original "autistic" group were preoccupied and that "there were very few really warmhearted fathers and mothers" (p. 50).

During the 1950s and 1960s Bruno Bettelheim perpetuated the notion that autism could be attributed to the psychopathology of parents. Bettelheim's (1967) theory of *psychogenesis* claimed that autism was an outcome of uninterested, "cold" parents who were unable to develop an emotional bond with their children. Sadly, mothers of children with autism were called "refrigerator mothers" and led to believe they were the cause of their children's disability.

The idea that they are to blame creates a great deal of guilt on top of the grief already experienced by parents who find their toddler exhibiting the disturbing behaviors characteristic of autism. No causal link between parental personality and autism was ever discovered, and in 1977 the National Society for Autistic Children (today the Autism Society of America) stated, "No known factors in the psychological environment of a child have been shown to cause autism."

Prevalence of autism

PRAXIS Special Education Core Principles: Content Knowledge: I. Understanding Exceptionalities, Incidence and prevalence of various types of disabilities.

Causes of autism

Council for Exceptional Children Content Standards for Beginning Teachers–INDEP CURR: Etiologies and medical aspects of conditions affecting individuals with disabilities (IC2K3).
PRAXIS Special Education Core Principles: Content Knowledge: I. Understanding Exceptionalities, Causation and prevention of disability.

Recent research shows a clear biological origin for autism in the form of abnormal brain development, structure, and/or neurochemistry (Akshoomoff, 2000; Mauk, Reber, & Batshaw, 1997). Numerous genetic links to autism have been established, but a complete understanding of the causal relationships has yet to be found (Autism Research Institute, 1998; Mueller & Courchesne, 2000). Autism might best be viewed as a behavioral syndrome which may be produced by multiple biological causes (Berney, 2000; Mueller & Courchesne, 2000).

EDUCATION AND TREATMENT

Until recently, the prognosis for children with autism was extremely poor, with problems of daily living persisting into adulthood for more than 90% of cases (Bristol et al., 1996; Matson, 1994). This reality combined with the "uniqueness of autism and the myriad ways in which persons with autism spectrum disorders manifest their disability" has made the area "fertile ground" for the advancement of countless strategies (Simpson, 2001, p. 68). Many controversial treatments and cures for autism have been promoted (e.g., holding therapy, facilitated communication, colored lenses, dolphin-assisted therapy), most without scientific evidence of their effects and benefits (Heflin & Simpson, 2002; Jacobson, Mulick, & Schwartz, 1995; Romanczyk et al., 1999). For one parent's perspectives on the anguish of trying to separate unsubstantiated claims from scientifically validated treatments for her two children, see Profiles & Perspectives, "The Autism Wars" later in this chapter.

On the brighter side, however, a great deal of exciting and promising research predicts better futures for children with autism (e.g., Dawson & Osterling, 1997; Green, 2001; Panerai, Ferrante, Caputo, & Impellizzeri, 1998; Simpson, 2001; Schwartz, Sandall, Garfinkle, & Bauer, 1998). Intensive, behaviorally based early intervention has helped some children with autism learn communication, language, and social skills that have enabled them to succeed in general education classrooms (Jacobson, Mulick, & Green, 1998).

One powerful example of the potential of systematic early intervention on the lives of children with autism is the work of Ivar Lovaas and his colleagues at the University of California at Los Angeles. Lovaas (1987) provided a group of 19 children with autism with an intensive early intervention program of one-on-one behavioral treatment for more than 40 hours per week for 2 years or more before they reached age 4. Intervention also included parent training and mainstreaming into a regular preschool environment. When compared with a control group of 19 similar children at age 7, children in the early intervention group had gained 20 IQ points and had made major advances in educational achievement. Nine of the children were able to move from first to

Intensive, behaviorally based early intervention has helped some children with autism learn communication and social skills.

second grade in a regular classroom and were considered by their teachers to be well adjusted.

Follow-up evaluations of the same group of 19 children several years later at the average age of 11.5 years showed that the children had maintained their gains (McEachin, Smith, & Lovaas, 1993). In particular, 8 of the 9 "best outcome" children were considered to be "indistinguishable from average children on tests of intelligence and adaptive behavior" (p. 359). In discussing the outcomes of this research, Lovaas (1994) states:

> After 1 year of intensive intervention, fifty percent of the children can be integrated into regular kindergarten classrooms. Then, we have them repeat kindergarten to get a head start on first grade. Successful passing of first grade is the key. Those that pass first grade are likely to obtain normal IQ scores and normal functioning. The children who don't make it into first grade are likely to need intensive supports for their entire life. (n.p.)

Although some have questioned the validity and generality of this research (e.g., Gresham & MacMillan, 1997), the work of Lovaas and his colleagues represents a landmark accomplishment in the education of children with autism. First, they have discovered and validated at least some of the factors that can be controlled to help children with autism achieve normal functioning in a regular classroom. Second, the successful results offer real hope and encouragement for the many teachers and parents who are desperate to learn how to help children with autism.

The teaching methods used in the Lovaas early intervention project were derived from applied behavior analysis (ABA). As we learned in Chapter 6, ABA is a systematic approach for designing, conducting, and evaluating instruction based upon scientifically verified principles describing how the environment affects learning. From the perspective of ABA, "autism is a syndrome of behavioral deficits and excesses that have a biological basis but are nonetheless amenable to change through carefully orchestrated, constructive interactions with the physical and social environment" (Green, 2001, p. 73).

Because of the documented accomplishments of some children with autism after receiving intensive ABA therapy, many parents and practitioners have been advocating for ABA programs and services for children with autism. However, misunderstandings about ABA are widespread, and many teachers and parents have a very narrow view of what ABA is and is not. They have been led to believe that ABA consists only of *discrete trial training* (DTT), one-on-one sessions during which a routinized sequence of contrived learning trials is presented. For example, an item or instruction is presented (e.g., "Clap your hands."), the child responds, and reinforcement is provided for a correct response. Each sequence of antecedent stimulus, child response, and consequence is a trial.

DTT is an important part of ABA programming for children with autism and a teaching tool that special educators should know how to use correctly and skillfully. However, DTT is just one type of teaching arrangement, and ABA programming uses a variety of procedures to help individuals with autism acquire and generalize new skills (Anderson & Romanczyk, 1999; Green, 2001; Sundberg & Partington, 1999). Just a partial list of systematic strategies for teaching students with autism based on ABA include the following:

- Picture Exchange Communication System (Bondy & Frost, 1994; Schwartz, Garfinkle, & Bauer, 1998)
- Stimulus control strategies; building stimulus equivalence classes (Green, 2001; Sidman, 1994)
- Peer-mediated interventions for social relationships (Strain & Schwartz, 2001)
- Functional assessment of challenging behavior (Cipani, 1998)
- Pivotal response intervention (Koegel, Koegel, Harrower, & Carter, 1999)
- Naturalistic language strategies (McGee, Morrier, & Daly, 1999) (see Teaching & Learning, "Teaching Communication Skills to Students with Autism," later in this chapter)

ABA and DTT

Council for Exceptional Children   Content Standards for Beginning Teachers–INDEP CURR: Prevention and intervention strategies for individuals with disabilities (IC4K2) (also, IC1K7).
PRAXIS Special Education Core Principles: Content Knowledge: III. Delivery of Services to Students with Disabilities, Curriculum and Instruction, Modeling, skill drill, guided practice, concept generalization.

The Autism Wars

by Catherine Maurice

Many parents I know, as well as many researchers and clinicians, routinely use the phrase "the autism wars." We know what we're talking about, but people unfamiliar with the politics of autism diagnosis and treatment might not. Briefly, "the autism wars" refers to the fierce infighting and conflicting claims of individuals or groups, each of whom claims to know how best to treat children with autism and derides the theories and methods of the other camps. In an environment where funding is scarce, fear and passion run high, and children's futures are at stake, the autism wars can generate much rancor, to say nothing of confusion.

On Monday, for example, a parent may consult one doctor and be told to place her child in a "therapeutic nursery." The doctor will tell the parent to avoid at all costs any program based on behavior analysis because such programs are "manipulative, damaging, and tantamount to dog training." On Tuesday, the parent might be told that therapeutic nurseries have little impact on autistic behaviors and often reinforce such behaviors, in spite of their warm and fuzzy talk about "nurturing the whole child" and "finding the hidden child within the autistic shell." On Wednesday, the parent is informed (say, by another parent writing on the Internet) that massive doses of vitamin B6 can produce meaningful language in the child or that an injection of gamma globulin can repair the child's damaged immune system. In the course of hearing or reading these recommendations, the parent learns that professionals are "not to be trusted" and that parents should always "trust their own instincts" and "follow their hearts" when it comes to selecting autism treatments. On Thursday, the same parent is advised to try "an eclectic approach: a little of this and a little of that." (Soon, because of fear and longing, "a little of this and a little of that" becomes an astonishing array of "treatments" levied onto 3- and 4-year-old children.) Finally, on Friday, the parent is told that there is not a whole lot that anyone can do for autism anyway, so why not come to a weekly support group to discuss "coping" and "feelings" with a "coping facilitator"?

For a parent of a newly diagnosed child or for a young person just starting out in a career in which he wishes to be of service to a child or an adult with autism, the barrage of conflicting messages can produce frustration, fear, and even despair. It is nothing short of outrageous that the organizations and individuals to whom parents and caregivers turn for help have not yet produced a set of clear, strong, discriminatory guidelines based on sound scientific principles as well as humanitarian concerns to lead people through the morass of so-called "options" for autism treatments.

Instead, many experts have tolerated, even encouraged, this frantic, time-consuming, expensive experimentation on our children—perhaps to remain popular with parents, who love anyone who gives them hope. But if my child is diagnosed with cancer, I need hope laced with truth. Otherwise, I will chase every apricot pit and bottle of shark cartilage I can afford as long as there is someone, anyone, who tells me that these things might help. If my child had cancer, I could presumably go to a reputable cancer center and find out which treatments have solid empirical research behind them; which treatments are still experimental; which are "alternative" (an unfortunate euphemism for "no data"); which are known to cause harm. A reputable cancer treatment center, in other words, would give me the objective information I needed to make a truly informed choice for my child's well-being.

But with autism, anything goes. I have had two children diagnosed with autism—meaning that, according to the prevailing opinion, my sweet little girl and my beloved little boy would never hold a meaningful conversation with me; never attend regular schools; never play with other children; never know how to use language to comfort a friend, heal a hurt, or tell a joke. When my daughter received this terrifying diagnosis, many people, both professionals and parents, told me how "expert" they were in autism. I was told about their degrees, their far-flung reputations, and their personal experience. But very few people had ever bothered to read, much less refer me to, published data in reputable, peer-reviewed, science-based journals. All was opinion; all was anecdote; all was theory.

Through the grace of God, I managed to stumble my way through many deviations, mistakes, and wrong turns until I found the program and the people who could truly help my children. Although I was told that applied behavior analysis was cold and harmful, that autism was lifelong, severe, and incurable, I managed somehow to hold onto a little flame of reason in the face of opinion and ideology. The research was there. The data were there. None of the other saviors and experts had anywhere close to the 30-year history of empirical evidence that the field of behavior analysis has accrued. In the end, after trembling through all the tears and the nightmarish uncertainty that other parents have endured, I closed my eyes, said a prayer, and chose to use not only my heart but also that other gift: my head. I chose to believe that sometimes we should follow the gift of reason, the faculty of logic. Men and women in the behavioral sciences have researched for decades how human beings learn, and their exercise of reason and logic have led to monumental strides in understanding how children with autism can learn, sometimes to the point where they can make very significant progress or even recover.

Today, 10 years after they were diagnosed, both my daughter and my son have been reevaluated (by the same people who first diagnosed them) and have been found to have "no significant residua of autism." They attend regular schools where they do not receive any special services. They get good grades, have friends, and have now officially entered the years where they are deeply embarrassed by their mother, especially if I do something mortifying like sing in front of their friends.

No, recovery does not happen to all families who choose intensive behavioral intervention. So far, studies indicate that at best only 30% to 40% of children will reach this level of functioning. However, it does appear that virtually all children can make some appreciable progress if they are treated in a program informed by qualified professionals in the field of applied behavior analysis. Most children will develop some level of meaningful language, even if some behavioral problems remain. Today, I know many families who delight in their children's ever-growing capacity to communicate verbally with them, to learn, and to love. No, their children have not fully recovered, and perhaps they may never do so, but these families have survived the autism wars and

have emerged stronger by learning how to sort authority from authoritarianism, fact from opinion.

What do I draw from my own war with autism? Many things, but among them figures the sorrow of a survivor—one who knows that others still endure a dangerous political climate where misinformation and disinformation abound and children do not receive the services they so desperately need. I want other parents to have the same chance that I did: a real chance, with real choices, not bogus "options" that bleed money and time and steal opportunity from their children. There is hope for meaningful improvement in autism, for communication, for true learning—but that hope does not spring from dolphin therapies, facilitated communication, Ouija boards, or pumping our kids full of vitamins or Prozac. That hope springs, at the present time, from the science of applied behavior analysis, and no amount of furious invective about "the training of robots" will succeed for long in blurring the fierce power of that truth.

Do I believe that applied behavior analysis is the only worthwhile treatment for autism? It is not a question of what I or anyone else believes. It is a question of what objective data exist to back up any treatment claim. The education and treatment of children with autism should be based on scientific research, not on belief. Maybe one day science will produce a biomedical intervention that will lead to cure or recovery for most children. I hope so—for the sake of the children I know whose progress under applied behavior analysis is relatively slow, and for the sake of their parents. I hope that careful, responsible research, not media-hyped crazes about substances manufactured from pigs' intestines (cf. the recent "secretin" fad), will one day lead us to that cure. But for today, it is incumbent upon all of us to seek the treatments that can help the children who are alive today. It is incumbent upon us to seek the science—the hard science, not the pseudo-science that abounds in popular books, newsletters, or Internet chat rooms. And for the sake of all our children, we should never just accept at face value what anyone tells us about research. We need to ask for that research, check it out, read it, find out where it was published. Find out the reputation of the journal in which it was published. Find out if there was any peer review of the research. Find out whether or not there were control groups, intake evaluations, outcome data, and independent confirmation of findings.

Reason and tenderness can walk hand in hand. Judgment, intelligence, compassion, and mercy all have their place in autism treatment. We parents love our children. That's a given. We owe it to them to figure out sense from nonsense, hope from hype.

continues

FIGURING OUT SENSE FROM NONSENSE

Recommended readings about science, pseudo-science, and discriminatory thinking:

The Demon-Haunted World: Science As a Candle in the Dark by Carl Sagan. Random House: New York, 1995.

Crazy Therapies: What Are They? Do They Work? by Margaret Thaler Singer and Janja Lalich. San Francisco: Jossey-Bass, 1996.

Behavioral Intervention for Young Children with Autism: A Manual for Parents and Professionals edited by C. Maurice, G. Green, and S. C. Luce. Austin, TX: PRO-ED, 1996.

Science in Autism Treatment: The Newsletter of the Association for Science in Autism Treatment. 175 Great Neck Road, Suite 406, Great Neck, New York, 11021, (516) 466-4400 or http://www.asatonline.org.

Catherine Maurice, Ph.D., is the author of the best-selling book *Let Me Hear Your Voice: A Family's Triumph over Autism* (Knopf, 1993; Ballantine, 1994). She lectures widely about the importance of bringing more accountability and scientific rigor into the education and treatment of children with autism.

Excellent descriptions of a variety of teaching methods based on ABA for children with autism can be found in Harris and Handleman (2000); Koegel and Koegel (1995); Maurice, Green, and Foxx (2001); and Scheuermann and Webber (2002).

 # SEVERE DISABILITIES

 ## DEFINITIONS

Definitions of severe disabilities

Council for Exceptional Children Content Standards for Beginning Teachers–INDEP CURR: Definitions and issues related to the identification of individuals with disabilities (IC1K1) (also, CC1K5). **PRAXIS** Special Education Core Principles: Content Knowledge: I. Understanding Exceptionalities, Definitions of specific disabilities.

Severe Disabilities As used by most special educators, the term *severe disabilities* generally encompasses students with significant disabilities in intellectual, physical, and/or social functioning. Autism, multiple disabilities, and deaf-blindness—three IDEA disability categories described in this chapter—as well as severe mental retardation, severe emotional disturbance, and severe orthopedic and health impairments are included under the term.

There is no single, widely accepted definition of severe disabilities. Most definitions are based on tests of intellectual functioning, developmental progress, or the extent of educational need. According to the system of classifying levels of mental retardation previously used by the American Association on Mental Retardation, persons receiving IQ scores of 35 to 40 and below were considered to have severe mental retardation; scores of 20 to 25 and below resulted in a classification of profound mental retardation. In practice, however, the term *severe disabilities* often includes many individuals who score in the moderate level of mental retardation (IQ scores of 40 to 55) (Wolery & Haring, 1994).

Traditional methods of intelligence testing are virtually useless with children whose disabilities are profound. Imagine the difficulty, as well as the inappropriateness, of giving an IQ test to a student who cannot hold up his head or point, let alone talk. If tested, such students tend to be assigned IQ scores at the extreme low end of the continuum. Knowing that a particular student has an IQ of 25, however, is of no value in designing an appropriate educational program. Thus, educators of students with severe and profound disabilities tend to focus on the specific skills a child needs to learn rather than on intellectual level.

It was once common to take a developmental approach to the definition of severe disabilities. For example, Justen (1976) proposed that individuals with severe disabilities are "those individuals age 21 and younger who are functioning at a general developmental level of half or less than the level which would be expected on the basis of chronological age" (p. 5). Most educators now maintain that developmental levels have little relevance to this population and instead emphasize that a student with severe disabilities—regardless of age—is one who needs instruction in basic skills, such as getting from place to place independently, communicating with others, controlling bowel and bladder functions, and self-feeding. Most children without disabilities are able to acquire these basic skills in the first five years of life, but the student with severe disabilities needs special instruction to do so. The basic-skills definition makes it clear that special education for students with severe disabilities must not focus on traditional academic instruction.

Although severe disabilities is not recognized as a separate disability category in IDEA, the law's regulations governing programs and services for students who need "highly specialized" services and who experience "intense" problems state the following:

> The term "children with severe disabilities" refers to children with disabilities who, because of the intensity of their physical, mental, or emotional problems, need highly specialized education, social, psychological, and medical services in order to maximize their full potential for useful and meaningful participation in society and for self-fulfillment. The term includes those children with disabilities with severe emotional disturbance (including schizophrenia), autism, severe and profound mental retardation, and those who have two or more serious disabilities such as deaf-blindness, mental retardation and blindness, and cerebral palsy and deafness. Children with severe disabilities may experience severe speech, language, and/or perceptual-cognitive deprivations, and evidence abnormal behavior such as failure to respond to pronounced social stimuli, self-mutilation, self-stimulation; manifestation of intense and prolonged temper tantrums, and the absence of rudimentary forms of verbal control; and may also have extremely fragile physiological conditions. (34 C.F.R. Sec. 315.4[d])

The inclusion of extremely challenging behavioral problems, such as self-stimulation and self-injurious behavior, in the federal definition is not intended to imply that all children with severe disabilities exhibit such characteristics; most do not. Rather, the inclusion of such examples makes it clear that *all* children are entitled to a free public education in the least restrictive environment no matter how complicated or challenging their learning, behavioral, or medical problems—"even those students who, in the judgment of some people, seem to be 'ineducable'" (Turnbull & Cilley, 1999, p. 9).

The Association for Persons with Severe Handicaps (TASH) defines people with severe disabilities as

> individuals of all ages who require extensive ongoing support in more than one major life activity in order to participate in integrated community settings and to enjoy a quality of life that is available to citizens with fewer or no disabilities. Support may be required for life activities such as mobility, communication, self-care, and learning, as necessary for independent living, employment and self-sufficiency. (Lindley, 1990, p. 1)

Compared with other areas of special education—mental retardation, learning disabilities, and behavioral disorders, in particular—there has been less concern and debate about the definition of severe disabilities. This does not indicate that professionals are uninterested in defining the population of students they serve but reflects two inherent features of severe disabilities. First, there is little need for a definition that precisely describes who is and is not to be identified by the term *severe disabilities*. Although the specific criteria a school district uses to define learning disabilities have a major impact on who will be eligible for special education services, whether or not special education is needed by any student who might be considered severely disabled is never an issue. Second, because of the tremendous diversity of learning and physical challenges experienced by such students, any single set of descriptors is inadequate. Statements that specify the particular educational goals and support needs of individual students are more meaningful.

Profound Disabilities   Some professionals make a distinction between children with profound disabilities and those with severe disabilities. Sternberg (1994) believes that a distinction between severe and profound disabilities is necessary because the "expectations and implications for each are different. These differences are related not only to one's capability for independent functioning but also to the utility of specific educational or training models and methods" (p. 7). According to Sternberg, an individual with *profound disabilities* is one who

> exhibits profound developmental disabilities in all five of the following behavioral-content areas: cognition, communication, social skills development, motor-mobility, and activities of daily living (self-help skills); and requires a service structure with continuous monitoring and observation. . . . This definition also posits a ceiling of 2 years of age for each area of functioning (6 years of age for those classified as severely disabled). If the individual functions above that level, the individual cannot be classified as profoundly disabled. (p. 6)

Thus, an individual with profound disabilities, according to Sternberg, functions at a level no higher than that of a typically developing 2-year-old in all five areas (whereas the functioning of a student with severe disabilities in one or more of these areas may be less delayed, up to the level of a typical 6-year-old). Some educators question whether children with profound disabilities can benefit from education. See Profiles & Perspectives, "Are All Children Educable?" later in this chapter.

Definitions of profound disabilities, multiple disabilities, and deaf-blindness

 Council for Exceptional Children   Content Standards for Beginning Teachers–INDEP CURR: Definitions and issues related to the identification of individuals with disabilities (IC1K1) (also, CC1K5).
PRAXIS Special Education Core Principles: Content Knowledge: I. Understanding Exceptionalities, Definitions of specific disabilities.

Joey's enthusiasm and determination are evident each time his teacher uses music in a lesson.

▼

MULTIPLE DISABILITIES AND DEAF-BLINDNESS

IDEA defines **multiple disabilities** as follows:

> Multiple disabilities means concomitant impairments (such as mental retardation–blindness, mental retardation–orthopedic impairment, etc.), the combination of which causes such severe educational problems that they cannot be accommodated in special education programs solely for one of the impairments. The term does not include deaf-blindness. (34 C. F. R., Sec. 300: [b][6])

A particularly challenging group of students with severe disabilities includes those with dual sensory impairments. "There is perhaps no condition as disabling as deaf-blindness, the loss of part or all of one's vision and hearing" (Bullis & Otos, 1988, p. 110). IDEA defines **deaf-blindness** as a combination of both auditory and visual disabilities that causes

> such severe communication and other developmental and learning needs that the persons cannot be appropriately educated in special education programs solely for children and youth with hearing impairments, visual impairments, or severe disabilities, without supplementary assistance to address their educational needs due to these dual, concurrent disabilities. (IDEA, 1990, sec. 1422)

The majority of children who have both visual and hearing impairments at birth experience major difficulties in acquiring communication and motor skills, mobility, and appropriate social behavior.

Because these individuals do not receive clear and consistent information from either sensory modality, a tendency exists to turn inward to obtain the desired level of stimulation. The individual therefore may appear passive, nonresponsive, and/or noncompliant. Students with dual sensory impairments may not respond to or initiate appropriate interactions with others and often exhibit behavior that is considered socially inappropriate (e.g., hand flapping, finger flicking, head rocking). (Downing & Eichinger, 1990, pp. 98–99)

Although 94% of individuals who are deaf-blind have some functional hearing and/or vision (Baldwin, 1995), the combined effects of the dual impairments severely impede the development of communication and social skills. An educational program for children who are deaf is often inappropriate for a child who also has limited vision because many methods of instruction and communication rely heavily on the use of sight. On the other hand, programs for visually impaired students usually require good hearing because much instruction is auditory.

Therefore, educational programs for students with dual sensory impairments who require instruction in basic skills are generally similar to those for other students with severe disabilities. Although most students with dual sensory impairments can make use of information presented in visual and auditory modalities, when used in instruction these stimuli must be enhanced and the students' attention directed toward them. Tactile teaching techniques involving the sense of touch are used to supplement the information obtained through visual and auditory modes (Engelman, Griffin, Griffin, & Maddox, 1999).

A man who is deaf-blind vividly describes the importance of supplementing information about the world with other sensory modes:

The senses of sight and hearing are unquestionably the two primary avenues by which information and knowledge are absorbed by an individual, providing a direct access to the world in which he lives . . . . When these senses are lost or severely limited, the individual is drastically limited to a very small area of concepts, most of which must come to him through his secondary senses or through indirect information supplied by others. The world literally shrinks; it is only as large as he can reach with his fingertips or by using his severely limited sight and hearing, and it is only when he learns to use his remaining secondary senses of touch, taste, smell, and kinesthetic awareness that he can broaden his field of information and gain additional knowledge. (Smithdas, 1981, p. 38)

Teaching techniques involving the sense of touch are used to provide and supplement instructional stimuli for students with dual sensory impairments.

Impact of deaf-blindness

Council for Exceptional Children — Content Standards for Beginning Teachers—INDEP CURR: Impact of sensory impairments, physical and health disaiblities on individuals, families and society (IC2K2) (also, CC2K2, CC2K6). PRAXIS Special Education Core Principles: Content Knowledge: I. Understanding Exceptionalities, Characteristics of students with disabilities, Cognitive, linguistic, and sensory factors.

CHARACTERISTICS

Throughout this book, we have seen how definitions and lists of characteristics used to describe a disability category have limited meaning at the level of the individual student. And, of course, it is at the level of the individual student where special education takes place, where decisions about what and how to teach should be made. As various physical, behavioral, and

Are All Children Educable?

Some educators, other professionals, and citizens question the wisdom of spending large amounts of money, time, and human resources attempting to educate children who have such serious and profound disabilities that they may never be able to function independently. Some would prefer to see resources spent on children with higher apparent potential—especially when economic conditions limit the quality of educational services for all children in the public schools. "Why bother with children who fail to make meaningful progress?" they ask.

Accelerating a response rate may indeed be a worthy first goal in an educational program if there is reasonable hope of shaping the response into a meaningful skill. Nevertheless, after concerted and appropriate effort by highly trained behavior therapists, for a reasonable period of time, a child's failure to make significant progress toward acquisition of a meaningful skill could reasonably be taken as an in-

dication that the child is ineducable. . . . Granted, all children probably are educable if education is defined as acceleration of any operant response. But such a definition trivializes the meaning of the term education and, even without consideration of benefit, moots the question of educability. . . . We suggest that public response to the questions "What is education?" "What skills are meaningful?" "What rate of progress is significant?" and "What cost/benefit ratios are acceptable?" sampled with sufficient care, could be invaluable in deciding who is educable and who is not. (Kauffman & Krouse, 1981, pp. 55–56)

A parent of a daughter with severe disabilities disagrees:

If anyone were to be the judge of whether a particular behavior change is "meaningful," it should certainly not be only the general taxpayer, who has no

learning characteristics associated with severe disabilities are described, keep in mind that students with severe disabilities constitute the most heterogeneous group of all exceptional children. As Westling and Fox (2000) point out, the differences among students with severe disabilities are greater than their similarities.

Most students with severe disabilities exhibit extreme deficits in intellectual functioning. Many need special services and supports because of motor impediments; communication, visual, and auditory impairments; and medical conditions such as seizure disorders. Many have medical and physical problems that require frequent attention (Ault, Rues, Graff, & Holvoet, 2000). Many students with severe disabilities have more than one disability. Even with the best available methods of diagnosis and assessment, it is often difficult to identify the nature and intensity of a child's multiple disabilities or to determine how combinations of disabilities affect a child's behavior. Some children, for example, do not respond in any observable way to visual stimuli, such as bright lights or moving objects. Is this because the child is blind as a result of eye damage, or is the child unresponsive because of profound mental retardation due to brain damage? Such questions arise frequently in planning educational programs for students with severe disabilities.

The one defining characteristic of students with severe disabilities is that they exhibit significant and obvious deficits in multiple life-skill or developmental areas. No specific

idea how rewarding it is to see your 19-year-old acquire the skill of toilet flushing on command or pointing to food when she wants a second helping. I suspect that the average taxpayer would not consider it "meaningful" to him or her for Karrie to acquire such skills. But in truth, it is "meaningful" to that taxpayer whether he recognizes it or not, in the sense that it is saving him or her the cost of Karrie's being institutionalized, which she certainly would have been by now if she never showed any progress.

The complexity, cost, and hopelessness of evaluating fairly the "meaningfulness" of various types and degrees of learning leads me to conclude that no one should be denied an education. . . . I would be very resistant to the idea that we should now, at this infant stage of the science and technology of education for severely retarded students, give up intensive skill training for anyone. (Hawkins, 1984, p. 285).

In many ways, our knowledge of the learning and developmental processes of individuals with severe and profound disabilities is still primitive and incomplete. We do know, however, that children with severe disabilities are capable of benefiting significantly from appropriate and carefully implemented educational programs. Even in cases in which little or no progress has been observed, it would be wrong to conclude that the student is incapable of learning. It may instead be that our teaching methods are imperfect and that the future will bring improved methods and materials to enable that student to learn useful skills. Children, no matter how severe their disabilities, have the right to the best possible public education and training society can offer them.

There are still many unanswered questions in the education of children whose disabilities are complex and pervasive. Even though their opportunities for education and training are expanding rapidly, nobody really knows their true learning potential. What we do know is that students with the most severe disabilities will go no farther than we let them; it is up to us to open doors and to raise our sights, not to create additional barriers.

Don Baer, professor of human development at the University of Kansas and a pioneer in the development of effective teaching methods for persons with severe disabilities, offers this perspective on educability:

Some of us have ignored both the thesis that all persons are educable and the thesis that some persons are ineducable, and instead have experimented with ways to teach some previously unteachable people. Over a few centuries, those experiments have steadily reduced the size of the apparently ineducable group relative to the obviously educable group. Clearly, we have not finished that adventure. Why predict its outcome, when we could simply pursue it, and just as well without a prediction? Why not pursue it to see if there comes a day when there is such a small class of apparently ineducable persons left that it consists of one elderly person who is put forward as ineducable. If that day comes, it will be a very nice day. And the next day will be even better. (D. M. Baer, February 15, 2002, personal communication)

set of behaviors is common to all individuals with severe disabilities. Although each student presents a unique combination of physical, intellectual, and social characteristics, the following behaviors and skill deficits are frequently observed in students with severe disabilities (Brown et al., 1991; Kim & Arnold, 2002; Westling & Fox, 2000; Wolery & Haring, 1994):

- *Slow acquisition rates for learning new skills.* Compared to other students with disabilities, students with severe disabilities learn at a slower rate, require more instructional trials to learn a given skill, learn fewer skills in total, and have difficulty learning abstract skills or relationships.
- *Poor generalization and maintenance of newly learned skills.* Generalization refers to the performance of skills under conditions different from those in which they initially were learned. Maintenance refers to the continued use of a new skill after instruction is terminated. For students with severe disabilities, generalization and maintenance seldom occur without instruction that is meticulously planned to facilitate it.
- *Limited communication skills.* Almost all students with severe and multiple disabilities are limited in their abilities to express themselves and to understand others. Some cannot talk or gesture meaningfully and might not respond when communication is attempted; some are not able to follow even the simplest requests.

Characteristics of severe disabilities

Council for Exceptional Children Content Standards for Beginning Teachers–INDEP CURR: Psychological and social-emotional characteristics of individuals with disabilities (IC2K4) (also, CC2K2). PRAXIS Special Education Core Principles: Content Knowledge: I. Understanding Exceptionalities, Characteristics of students with disabilities, Cognitive and affective and social-adaptive factors.

- *Impaired physical and motor development.* Many children with severe disabilities have limited physical mobility. Many cannot walk; some cannot stand or sit up without support. They are slow to perform basic tasks such as rolling over, grasping objects, and holding up their heads. Physical impairments are common and may worsen without consistent physical therapy.

- *Deficits in self-help skills.* Some children with severe disabilities are unable to independently care for their most basic needs, such as dressing, eating, exercising bowel and bladder control, and maintaining personal hygiene. They usually require special training involving prosthetic devices and/or adapted skill sequences to learn these basic skills.

- *Infrequent constructive behavior and interaction.* Nondisabled children and those whose disabilities are less severe typically play with other children, interact with adults, and seek out information about their surroundings. Some children with severe disabilities do not. They may appear to be completely out of touch with reality and may not show normal human emotions. It may be difficult to capture the attention of or evoke any observable response from a child with profound disabilities.

- *Stereotypic and challenging behavior.* Some children with severe disabilities engage in behaviors that are ritualistic (e.g., rocking back and forth, waving fingers in front of the face, twirling the body), self-stimulatory (e.g., grinding the teeth, patting the body), self-injurious (e.g., head banging, hair pulling, eye poking, hitting or scratching or biting oneself), and/or aggressive (e.g., hitting or biting others). The high frequency with which some children emit these challenging behaviors is a serious concern because they interfere with learning more adaptive behaviors and with acceptance and functioning in integrated settings.

Descriptions of behavioral characteristics, such as those just mentioned, can easily give an overly negative impression. Despite the intense challenges their disabilities impose on them, many students with severe disabilities also exhibit warmth, persistence, determination, a sense of humor, sociability, and various other desirable traits (Forest & Lusthaus, 1990; Stainback & Stainback, 1991). Many teachers find great satisfaction in working with students who have severe disabilities and observing their progress in school, home, and community settings.

 PREVALENCE

Prevalence of severe disabilities

PRAXIS Special Education Core Principles: Content Knowledge: I. Understanding Exceptionalities, Incidence and prevalence of various types of disabilities.

Because there is no universally accepted definition of severe disabilities, there are no accurate and uniform figures on prevalence. Estimates of the prevalence of severe disabilities range from 0.1% to 1% of the population (Kim & Arnold, 2002). Brown (1990) considers students with severe disabilities to be those who function intellectually in the lowest functioning 1% of the school-age population.

Because severe disabilities is not one of the disability categories under which the states make their annual report to the federal government, the number of students with severe disabilities who receive special education services under IDEA cannot be determined from data supplied by the U.S. Department of Education. Students who have severe disabilities are served and reported under other disability categories, including mental retardation, multiple disabilities, other health impairments, autism, and deaf-blindness. The available information, however, shows that this is neither a small nor an isolated population.

In the 2000–2001 school year, 121,954 school-age students received special education and related services under the IDEA disability category of multiple disabilities, and 1,318 students with deaf-blindness were served (U.S. Department of Education, 2002). Before the passage of IDEA in 1975, fewer than 100 children with dual sensory impairments were receiving specialized education services, virtually all of which were located at residential schools for children who are blind.

CAUSES

Severe intellectual disabilities can be caused by a wide variety of conditions, largely biological, that may occur before (prenatal), during (perinatal), or after birth (postnatal). In almost every case, a brain disorder is involved. Brain disorders are the result of either *brain dysgenesis* (abnormal brain development) or *brain damage* (caused by influences that alter the structure or function of a brain that had been developing normally up to that point). From a review of 10 epidemiological studies, Coulter (1994) estimated that prenatal brain dysgenesis accounts for most cases of severe cognitive limitations and that perinatal and postnatal brain damage account for a minority of cases. Coulter (1994) states that a brain disorder is "the only condition that will account for the existence of profound disabilities" (p. 41).

A significant percentage of children with severe disabilities are born with chromosomal abnormalities, such as Down syndrome, or with genetic or metabolic disorders that can cause serious problems in physical or intellectual development. Complications of pregnancy—including prematurity, Rh incompatibility, and infectious diseases contracted by the mother—can cause or contribute to severe disabilities. A pregnant woman who uses drugs, drinks alcohol excessively, or is poorly nourished has a greater risk of giving birth to a child with severe disabilities. Because their disabilities tend to be more extreme and more readily observable, children with severe disabilities are more frequently identified at or shortly after birth than are children with mild disabilities.

Severe disabilities also may develop later in life from head trauma caused by automobile and bicycle accidents, falls, assaults, or abuse. Malnutrition, neglect, ingestion of poisonous substances, and certain diseases that affect the brain (e.g., meningitis, encephalitis) also can cause severe disabilities. Although hundreds of medically related causes of severe disabilities have been identified, in about one-sixth of all cases, the cause cannot be clearly determined (Coulter, 1994).

Causes of severe disabilities

Council for Exceptional Children Content Standards for Beginning Teachers–INDEP CURR: Etiologies and medical aspects of conditions affecting individuals with disabilities (IC2K3).
PRAXIS Special Education Core Principles: Content Knowledge: I. Understanding Exceptionalities, Causation and prevention of disability.

 EDUCATIONAL APPROACHES

How does one go about teaching students with autism or severe disabilities? To answer this question, three fundamental and interrelated questions must be considered:

1. What skills should be taught?
2. What methods of instruction should be employed?
3. Where should instruction take place?

Of course, each of these questions must be asked for all students; but when a student is challenged by autism or severe disabilities, the answers take on enormous importance. During the past 30 years, major changes and advancements in the education of students with severe disabilities have led to new responses to the questions of curriculum, teaching methods, and placement.

 CURRICULUM: WHAT SHOULD BE TAUGHT?

Not long ago, a student's "mental age" as determined by norm-referenced tests of development played a significant role in the selection of curriculum content and teaching activities. This practice led to an emphasis on activities thought to be essential prerequisites for higher-level skills because typical children of a given age did such skills. As a result, students with severe disabilities spent many hundreds of hours working on artificially contrived activities that had no immediate value and, because they were not age-appropriate (e.g., teenage students sorting blocks by color or clapping their hands to the rhythm of a

Learning to shop is one of the functional vocational skills identified by Sheila's IEP team.

Functional and age-appropriate skills

Council for Exceptional Children Content Standards for Beginning Teachers–Common Core: Theories and research that form the basis of curriculum development and instructional practice (CC7K1) (also, CC4S4, CC7K2, IC5S2, IC5S12).

PRAXIS Special Education Core Principles: Content Knowledge: III. Delivery of Services to Students with Disabilities, Curriculum and Instruction, Criteria of ultimate functioning.

song for preschoolers), may have contributed to the perception of students with severe disabilities as eternal children (Bellamy & Wilcox, 1982).

Today, most educators recognize that students with severe disabilities do not acquire skills in the same sequence that nondisabled students do and that developmental "ages" should not serve as the basis for determining curriculum activities. For example, a 16-year-old student who is learning to feed and toilet herself should not be taught in the same way or with the same materials as a nondisabled 2-year-old who is learning to feed and toilet herself. Even though both individuals need to learn the same skill, their past experiences, present environments, and future prospects are significantly different and demand different instructional activities and materials.

Contemporary curriculum content for students with severe disabilities is characterized by its focus on functional skills that can be used in immediate and future domestic, vocational, community, and recreational/leisure environments. Educational programs are future-oriented in their efforts to teach skills that will enable students with severe disabilities to participate in integrated settings as meaningfully and independently as possible after they leave school.

Functionality Functional skills are immediately useful to a student, are frequently required in school and nonschool environments, result in less dependence on others, and allow the student to participate in less restrictive environments (Slaton, Schuster, Collins, & Carnine, 1994). Placing pegs into a pegboard or sorting wooden blocks by color do not meet any of these criteria. Examples of functional skills for many students with severe disabilities include activities such as learning to dress oneself, prepare a snack, ride a public bus, purchase items from coin-operated vending machines, and recognize common sight words in community settings. Whenever possible, functional instructional activities should employ authentic materials (Westling & Fox, 2000). For example, students learning to use money to make purchases should practice with real bills and coins instead of simulated money. See Profiles & Perspectives, "My Brother Darryl," later in this chapter.

Age-Appropriateness Students with severe disabilities should participate in activities that are appropriate for same-age peers without disabilities. Adolescents with severe disabilities should not use the same materials as young, nondisabled children; in fact, having teenagers sit on the floor and play clap-your-hands games or cutting and pasting cardboard snowmen highlights their differences and discourages integration. It is more appropriate to teach recreation and leisure skills, such as bowling and CD player operation, or to engage the students in holiday projects, such as printing greeting cards. Teachers of secondary students with severe disabilities should avoid decorating classroom walls with child-oriented cartoon characters and should not refer to their students as "boys," "girls," or "kids" when "young men," "young women," or "students" are more age-appropriate.

It is critically important to build an IEP for a student with severe disabilities around functional and age-appropriate skills. Because nonschool settings demand such skills and nondisabled peers exhibit them, functional and age-appropriate behaviors are more likely to be reinforced in the natural environment and, as a result, maintained in the student's repertoire.

Making Choices Imagine going through an entire day without being able to make a choice, any choice at all. Someone else—a teacher, a staff person, a parent—will decide what you will wear, what you will do next, what you will eat for lunch, whom you will sit next to, and so on throughout the day, every day. In the past, students with severe disabil-

My Brother Darryl:
A Case for Teaching Functional Skills

by Preston Lewis

Eighteen years old, moderately/severely handicapped. Been in school for 12 years. Never been served in any setting other than an elementary school. He has had a number of years of "individualized instruction." He has learned to do a lot of things! Darryl can now do lots of things he couldn't do before.

He can put 100 pegs in a board in less than 10 minutes while in his seat with 95% accuracy, but he can't put quarters in a vending machine.

Upon command he can "touch" his nose, shoulder, leg, hair, ear. He is still working on wrist, ankle, hips, but he can't blow his nose when needed.

He can do a 12-piece Big Bird puzzle with 100% accuracy and color an Easter bunny and stay in the lines. He prefers music, but has never been taught to use a radio or record player.

He can now fold primary paper in half and even quarters, but he can't sort clothes, white from colors, for washing.

He can roll Play-Doh and make wonderful clay snakes, but he can't roll bread dough and cut out biscuits.

He can string beads in alternating colors and match it to a pattern on a DLM card, but he can't lace his shoes.

He can sing his ABCs and tell me the names of all the letters in the alphabet when presented on a card in upper case with 80% accuracy, but he can't tell Men's room from Ladies' when we go to McDonald's.

He can be told it's cloudy/rainy and take a black felt cloud and put it on the day of the week on an enlarged calendar (with assistance), but he still goes out in the rain without a raincoat or hat.

He can identify with 100% accuracy 100 different Peabody Picture Cards by pointing, but he can't order a hamburger by pointing to a picture or gesturing.

He can walk a balance beam forward, sideways, and backward, but he can't walk up the steps of the bleachers unassisted in the gym or go to basketball games.

He can count to 100 by rote memory, but he doesn't know how many dollars to pay the waitress for a $2.59 McDonald coupon special.

He can put a cube in the box, under the box, beside the box, and behind the box, but he can't find the trash bin in McDonald's and empty his trash into it.

He can sit in a circle with appropriate behavior and sing songs and play Duck Duck Goose, but nobody else in his neighborhood his age seems to want to do that.

I guess he's just not ready yet.

Source: Preston Lewis is a curriculum specialist in the Kentucky Department of Education.

---

ities had few opportunities to express preferences and make choices; the emphasis was on establishing instructional control over students. Traditionally, persons with severe disabilities were simply cared for and taught to be compliant.

> Some caregivers might feel that to complete tasks for persons with disabilities is easier and faster than allowing them to do it for themselves; while others may have the attitude that the person already has enough problems coping with his or her disability. Regardless of the underlying intention, the result can be to overprotect, to encourage learned helplessness, and to deprive the individual of potentially valuable life experiences. (Guess, Benson, & Siegel-Causey, 1985, p. 83)

Special educators are recognizing the importance of choice making as a way of making activities meaningful and as an indicator of quality of life for students with severe disabilities (Brown & Lehr, 1993; Newton, Horner, & Lund, 1991). Increasing efforts are being

Teaching choice-making

Council for Exceptional Children Content Standards for Beginning Teachers–INDEP CURR: Teach individuals to give and receive meaningful feedback from peers and adults (IC5S5) (also, IC4K3, CC4S5).

made to help students with severe disabilities express their preferences and make decisions about matters that will affect them. For example, a child might be presented with pictures of two activities and asked to point to the one she would rather engage in. Another child might be asked, "Who would you like to be your partner?" Or the teacher might say, "Should we do this again?" Of course, in presenting such choices, the teacher must be prepared to accept whichever alternative the student selects and to follow through accordingly. Bambara and Koger (1996) describe procedures for providing increased opportunities for choice making throughout the day.

Several studies have found that nonverbal students with severe disabilities can learn to use picture activity schedules to indicate their preferences for learning and leisure-time activities (e.g., Bryan & Gast, 2000; Morrison, 1999). Other researchers have discovered ways to help individuals with severe disabilities express preferences for where they will live (Faw, Davis, & Peck, 1996), what foods they will purchase and eat (Cooper & Browder, 1998; Parsons, McCarn, & Reid, 1993), leisure activities (Browder, Cooper, & Lim, 1998), and whether or not they want to participate in daily routines and activities (Bambara & Ager, 1992; Bannerman, Sheldon, Sherman, & Harchik, 1990).

Communication Skills   Effective communication is essential to our quality of life, enabling us to express our desires and choices, to obtain and give information, and, most important, to form and maintain relationships with others. Early research and training in communication for persons with autism and severe disabilities focused on remediation of specific forms of communication, such as the production of speech sounds, words, and descriptive phrases (Kaiser & Goetz, 1993). However, the focus of and methods used to teach communication skills to students with severe disabilities have undergone significant changes during the past 20 years. Two changes in perspective regarding the nature of communication are shaping contemporary research and instructional practices in communication for persons with severe disabilities (Ferguson, 1994; Kaiser, 2000; Kaiser & Goetz, 1993):

1. Communication is independent of the specific mode that is used as a channel for communication.
2. Communication occurs when communication partners establish shared meanings.

To be functional, communication must "work"; that is, it must influence the behavior of others to "bring about effects that are appropriate and natural in a given social context" (Calculator & Jorgensen, 1991, p. 204). The responsibility for successful communication rests with both communication partners. However, shared meaning is more likely when the communication partner who is relatively more skilled uses the principles of responsive interaction, such as following the lead of the less skilled speaker, balancing turns between conversation partners, and responding with interest and affect.

Many students with severe disabilities are able to learn to understand and produce spoken language. Speech is always a desirable goal, of course, for those who can attain it. A student who can communicate verbally is likely to have a wider range of educational, employment, residential, and recreational opportunities than is a student who is unable to speak. Because of sensory, motor, cognitive, or behavioral limitations, some students with severe disabilities may not learn to speak intelligibly even after extensive instruction. Many systems of augmentative and alternative communication (AAC) have proven useful—including gestures, various sign language systems, pictorial communication boards, symbol systems, and electronic communication aids. AAC is described in detail in Chapter 9.

The Picture Exchange Communication System (PECS) (Frost & Bondy, 1994) is a widely used form of AAC among children with autism. With PECS, children learn to communicate with others by selecting and showing cards with pictures and symbols representing their

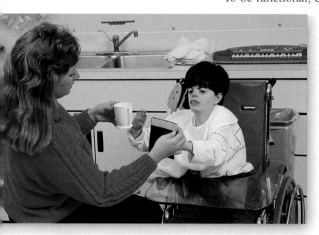

▲ Since she has learned to make choices and express her preferences, Kimberly's quality of life has improved greatly.

wishes. For example, a children who wants more orange juice during snack time puts the picture for juice next to the "I want" symbol on his Velcro talking strip and shows it to his teacher. Teachers, peers, and family members always use spoken language during the exchange. Schwartz, Garfinkle, and Bauer (1998) reported on the use of PECS with 31 children with autism and said that all of the children learned to use PECS and 56% of the children began to spontaneously use speech during their communicative interactions with peers and teachers.

Communication is achieved only with great difficulty by persons who are deaf-blind and requires greater effort on the part of communication partners (Tedder, Warden, & Sikka, 1993). The use of dual communication boards can help students who are deaf-blind discriminate the receptive or expressive functions of responses from a communication partner (Heller & Bigge, 2001). When a communication partner points to pictures or symbols on her board, a receptive message is provided to the student, requiring a response from the student on his board. The communication partner can point to the student's board and provide imitative prompts or corrective feedback to help the student make expressive messages.

Although the specialized forms of communication used by some individuals with severe disabilities limit the number of people with whom they can communicate (Heller & Bigge, 2001), these systems do enable many students with severe disabilities to receive and express basic information, feelings, needs, and wants. Sign language and other communication systems also can be learned by a student's teachers, peers, parents, and employers, thus encouraging use outside the classroom. Some students—after learning to communicate through PECS, sign language, communication boards, or other strategies—later are able to acquire speech skills. Researchers are working to develop partner-friendly forms of communication.

Recreational and Leisure Skills   Most children develop the ability to play and later to occupy themselves constructively and pleasurably during their free time. But children with severe disabilities may not learn appropriate and satisfying recreational skills unless they are specifically taught. Teaching appropriate leisure and recreational skills helps individuals with severe disabilities interact socially, maintain their physical skills, and become more involved in community activities. Many persons with severe disabilities do not use their unstructured time appropriately; rather than participate in enjoyable pursuits, they may spend excessive time sitting, wandering, or looking at television. A variety of programs to teach recreational and leisure skills have recently been developed; this area is now generally acknowledged as an important part of the curriculum for students with severe disabilities.

In one study, task analysis, picture prompts, and modified game materials were used to help young elementary children with moderate and severe disabilities learn to independently play the board game Candyland (Raschke, Dedrick, Heston, & Farris, 1996). Sometimes modifying the rules by which some team games are played can provide enough supports to enable an individual with severe disabilities to participate (Krebs & Coultier, 1992). For example, Figure 13.2 shows how the rules of a girls' softball league were modified to accommodate the skill limitations of a player with severe disabilities. For information and guidelines for selecting and teaching community-based recreational and leisure activities, see Macias, Best, Bigge, and Musante (2001); Moon (1994); Schlein, Meyer, Heyne, and Brandt (1995); and Schlein and Ray (1998).

Prioritizing and Selecting Instructional Targets   Teachers must learn good choice-making skills too. Students with autism and severe disabilities present numerous skill deficits often compounded by the presence of challenging behaviors, and each of those could (but not necessarily should) be targeted as an IEP goal or instructional objective. However, it is seldom, if ever, possible to design and implement a teaching program to deal simultaneously with all of the learning needs and challenging behaviors presented by a student with severe disabilities. (In the rare instance in which the resources to do so might be available, such an all-at-once approach would not be recommended anyway.) One of the greatest responsibilities a special educator undertakes in his role as a member of an IEP team is the selection of instructional objectives.

AAC and PECS

Council for Exceptional Children   Content Standards for Beginning Teachers–Common Core: Augmentative and assistive communication strategies (CC6K4) (also, IC6K2). **PRAXIS** Special Education Core Principles: Content Knowledge: III. Delivery of Services to Students with Disabilities, Curriculum and Instruction, Augmentative and alternative communication.

Prioritization of instructional targets

Council for Exceptional Children   Content Standards for Beginning Teachers–Common Core: Identify and prioritize areas of the general curriculum and accommodations for individuals with exceptional learning needs (CC7S1) (also, CC7S2, CC7S3). **PRAXIS** Special Education Core Principles: Content Knowledge: III. Delivery of Services to Students with Disabilities, Assessment, How to effectively use evaluation results in IFSP/IEP development.

FIGURE 13.2 Modifications that enabled Katie, a player with severe disabilities, to participate in a girls' softball league

1. Defensively, it was decided to play *Katie in center field*. This was more of a safety decision than a modification because Katie could not field a hit ball. Children at this age have a tendency to make contact with the ball either too early or too late, resulting in more balls being hit toward the left and right fields and fewer to center field. Also, there would be three other outfielders (natural supports) who could back-up and overshadow Katie's position in front, to her left and right (in softball there are four outfield positions: left field, center field, right field, and short center). Thus, the chances of Katie's being hit by the ball would be minimized if she were put into a position where balls are less likely to be hit.

2. Katie is slow and deliberate when she fields the ball, and she rarely stops balls even when they are hit directly to her. Therefore, out of fairness to Katie and her team, *the offense could only advance two bases if the ball were hit directly to her*. It should be noted that this particular modification was suggested by the coaches and approved by 87% of the players without disabilities.

3. Offensively, it was decided to *allow Katie to hit a ball off a tee because she could not hit* a pitched ball. Katie was allowed three attempts to hit the ball from the tee. The possibility, therefore, for a base on balls and being hit by a pitch did not exist for her. If she did not hit the ball in three attempts she was called "out." When Katie hit the ball, she ran unassisted to first base.

4. For baserunning, *the distance to first base was shortened* to account for Katie's running ability. Prior to the beginning of the season, some of Katie's teammates were timed on how fast they could run to first base, and an average time was computed. Using this average time as a standard, Katie was asked to run toward first base. While her teammates could make it all the way to first base in the given time, Katie only made it about halfway. Thus, the distance to first base for Katie was approximately half the distance to regular first base.

5. In consideration of Katie's safety and out of fairness to Katie's hitting and running ability, *the defense had to play at normal depths*. If Katie made contact with the ball and the ball was in fair territory, the fielder had to throw the ball to the first baseman positioned at regulation first base. If the fielder threw the ball to regulation first base before Katie stepped on her modified first base, Katie was called out. Otherwise, she was called "safe." As a result of a safe call, a pinch runner took Katie's place at regulation first base. At this point, Katie was taken back to the dugout.

Source: Reprinted from Bernabe, E. A., & Block, M. E. (1994). Modifying rules of a regular girls softball league to facilitate the inclusion of a child with severe disabilities. *Journal of The Association for Persons with Severe Handicaps, 19,* 26. Used by permission.

Judgments about how much a particular skill ultimately will contribute to a student's overall quality of life are difficult to make. In many cases, we simply do not know how useful or functional a behavioral change will prove to be. Whichever skills are chosen for instruction, they ultimately must be meaningful for the learner and her family. Several methods have been devised to help IEP team members prioritize the relative significance of suggested skills or learning activities. For example, Figure 13.3 shows a form on which parents rate and prioritize potential learning outcomes as one step in the IEP planning process developed by Giangreco et al. (1998).

 INSTRUCTIONAL METHODS: HOW SHOULD STUDENTS WITH AUTISM AND SEVERE DISABILITIES BE TAUGHT?

Care and concern for the well-being of students with autism or severe disabilities and assurance that they have access to educational programs are important. By themselves, however,

FIGURE 13.3 **A method for rating and prioritizing potential learning outcomes in the area of communication skills**

Step 1.2

Mark only one box to indicate if the family wants to discuss this set of learning outcomes in:
Step 1 (Family Interview; priority this year?) ☒; Step 2 (Additional Learning Outcomes) ☐; Skip for Now ☐

Currently, in what ways does the student communicate?

Expressively: _facial expressions, eye movements, vocalizations_

Receptively: _speech_

#	Learning Outcomes	Step 1.3 Circle Score	Needs Work?	Step 1.4 Rank up to 5 Priorities
1	Expresses Continuation or "More" (e.g., makes sounds or movement when desired interaction stops to indicate he or she would like eating, playing, etc., to continue)	E P Ⓢ	Ⓝ Y	
2	Makes Choices When Given Options	E Ⓟ S	N Ⓨ	1
3	Makes Requests (e.g., for objects, food, interactions, activities, assistance)	Ⓔ P S	N Ⓨ	3
4	Summons Others (e.g., has a way to call others to him or her)	Ⓔ P S	N Ⓨ	
5	Expresses Rejection/Refusal (e.g., indicates when he or she wants something to stop or does not want something to begin)	E P Ⓢ	Ⓝ Y	
6	Expresses Greetings and Farewells	E Ⓟ S	N Ⓨ	4
7	Follows Instructions (e.g., one step, multistep)	Ⓔ P S	N Ⓨ	
8	Sustains Communication with Others (e.g., takes turns, attends, stays on topic, perseveres)	E Ⓟ S	N Ⓨ	5
9	Initiates Communication with Others	Ⓔ P S	Ⓝ Y	
10	Responds to Questions (e.g., if asked a question, he or she attempts to answer)	Ⓔ P S	N Ⓨ	2
11	Comments/Describes (e.g., expands vocabulary for events, objects, interactions, feelings)	Ⓔ P S	Ⓝ Y	
12	Asks Questions of Others	Ⓔ P S	Ⓝ Y	
		E P S	N Y	

Comments: ③ _Needs communication system to make requests_
⑦ _Instructions must be those he can physically do_
⑧ _Yes/no using eye & head movement_

Scoring Key (use scores for Step 1.3 alone or in combination):
E = Early/Emerging Skill (1% – 25%)   **P** = Partial Skill (25% – 80%)   **S** = Skillful (80% – 100%)

Source: Reprinted from Giangreco, M. J., Cloninger, C. J., & Iverson, V. S. (1998). _Choosing outcomes and accommodations for children: A guide to educational planning for students with disabilities_ (2nd ed., p. 87). Baltimore: Brookes. Used by permission.

care and access are not enough. To learn effectively, students with severe disabilities need more than love, care, and a supportive classroom environment. They seldom acquire complex skills through imitation and observation alone; they are not likely to blossom on their own.

The learning and behavioral problems of students with autism and severe disabilities are so extreme and significant that instruction must be carefully planned, systematically executed, and continuously monitored for effectiveness. The teacher must know what skill to teach, why it is important to teach it, how to teach it, and how to recognize that the student has achieved or performed the skill. Collectively, the authors of leading texts on teaching students with autism and severe disabilities recommend that attention should be given to the following components of an instructional program (Cipani & Spooner, 1994; Maurice, Green, & Foxx, 2001; Orelove & Sobsey, 1996; Snell & Brown, 2000; Scheuermann & Webber, 2002; Westling & Fox, 2000):

Elements of systematic instruction

Council for Exceptional Children — Content Standards for Beginning Teachers–Common Core: Theories and research that form the basis of curriculum development and instructional practice (CC7K1) (also, CC4S4, CC7S5, CC7S13, IC1K7, IC4S6).
PRAXIS Special Education Core Principles: Content Knowledge: III. Delivery of Services to Students with Disabilities, Curriculum and Instruction, Teaching Strategies and methods.

- *The student's current level of performance must be precisely assessed.* Precise assessment of current performance is necessary to determine which skills to teach and at what level instruction should begin. Is Keeshia able to hold her head up without support? For how many seconds? Under what conditions? In response to what verbal or physical signals? Unlike traditional assessment procedures, which may rely heavily on standardized scores and developmental levels, assessment of students with severe disabilities emphasizes each learner's ability to perform specific, observable behaviors. Assessment should not be a one-shot procedure but should take place at different times, in different settings, and with different persons. The fact that a student with autism or severe disabilities does not demonstrate a skill at one particular time or place does not mean that she is incapable of demonstrating that skill.

- *The skill to be taught must be defined clearly.* "Carlos will feed himself" is too broad a goal for many students with severe disabilities. A more appropriate statement might be "When applesauce is applied to Carlos's right index finger, he will put the finger in his mouth within 5 seconds." A clear statement like this enables the teacher and other observers to determine whether Carlos attains this objective. If, after repeated trials, he has not, a different method of instruction should be tried.

- *The skill may need to be broken down into smaller component steps.* An effective teacher of students with severe disabilities knows how to use task analysis (described in Chapter 6) to break down a skill into a series of specific, observable steps. Assessment of student performance on each step of the task analysis helps the teacher determine where to begin instruction. She can gradually teach each required step until the student can accomplish the entire task independently. Without this sort of structure and precision in teaching, a great deal of time is likely to be wasted.

- *The teacher must provide a clear prompt or cue to the child.* It is important for the child to know what action or response is expected. A cue can be verbal; the teacher might say, "Bev, say apple," to indicate what Bev must do before she will receive an apple. Or a cue can be physical; the teacher might point to a light switch to indicate that Bev should turn on the light. It also may be necessary for the teacher to demonstrate an activity many times and to physically guide the child through some or all of the tasks required in the activity. To learn more about delivering and fading instructional prompts to students with autism and severe disabilities, see Doyle, Wolery, Ault, and Gast (1988); Green (2001); and Wolery, Ault, and Doyle (1992).

- *The student must receive feedback and reinforcement.* Students with severe disabilities must receive immediate and clear information about their performance; and like all students, they are more likely to repeat an action if it is followed immediately by a reinforcing consequence. It is critical that effective reinforcers be identified for students with severe disabilities. Unfortunately, it is not always easy to determine what items or events a noncommunicative child finds motivating. Many teachers devote extensive efforts to reinforcer sampling; that is, they attempt to find out which items and activities are reinforcing to a particular child, and they keep careful records of what is and is not effective. Methods for assessing stimuli that may serve as reinforcers for individuals with severe disabilities are described in Lohrmann-O'Rouke and Browder (1998).

- *Strategies that promote generalization and maintenance must be used.* Most students with autism and severe disabilities have difficulty generalizing the skills they learn. Thus, an effective teacher has students perform targeted skills in different settings and with different instructors, cues, and materials before concluding with confidence that the student has acquired and generalized a skill. Several strategies for facilitating generalization are discussed in Chapter 6. More detailed information can be found in Cooper, Heron, and Heward, (1987); Snell and Brown (2000); and Westling and Fox (2000). Using naturalistic teaching strategies is one of the best ways to facilitate a student's generalization and maintenance of importance skills. See Teaching & Learning, "Teaching Communication Skills to Students with Autism," later in this chapter.

- *The student's performance must be directly and frequently assessed.* Because the progress of students with severe disabilities most often occurs in very small steps, it is important to measure performance frequently and precisely. Collecting data on a student's performance of each step of a task-analyzed skill or routine gives the teacher precise information about skill learning, which is shown most clearly by student performance data collected every day. Some programs keep videotaped records of students' performance on specific tasks. This record can add an important dimension to documenting behavioral changes over extended periods. Denham and Lahm (2001) describe how students with severe disabilities can use computer and assistive technologies to create alternative portfolios as a means to document their achievement.

Naturalistic teaching strategies

Council for Exceptional Children — Content Standards for Beginning Teachers–INDEP CURR: Strategies for integrating student initiated learning experiences into ongoing instruction (IC4K3) (also, CC4S4).
PRAXIS Special Education Core Principles: Content Knowledge: III. Delivery of Services to Students with Disabilities, Curriculum and Instruction, Instructional activities.

Partial participation

Council for Exceptional Children — Content Standards for Beginning Teachers–Common Core: Use procedures to increase the individual's self-awareness, self-management, self-control, self-reliance, and self-esteem (CC4S5) (also, IC5S6).
PRAXIS Special Education Core Principles: Content Knowledge: III. Delivery of Services to Students with Disabilities, Curriculum and Instruction, Criteria of ultimate functioning.

Partial Participation The principle of partial participation, first described by Baumgart et al. (1982), acknowledges that even though some individuals with severe disabilities are not able to independently perform all steps of a given task or activity, they often can be taught to perform selected components or an adapted version of the task. Partial participation can be used to help a learner be more active in a task, make more choices in how the task will be carried out, and provide more control over the activity. Table 13.1 is an example of how partial participation could be used within each step of a task analysis for making a blender drink.

TABLE 13.1 Using partial participation within each step of a task analysis for making a blender drink

Task: Making a blender drink **Teacher's Assistance**	*Learner:* Saundra **Learner's Participation**	**Goal**
1. Announces activity	Lifts her head to listen	Active
2. Wheels Saundra to the cabinet	—	—
3. Gets out the utensils	Grasps a spoon	Active
4. Wheels Saundra to the table	Releases the spoon on the table	Active
5. Shows fruits	Selects one fruit by grasping it and pushing it to the teacher	Choice
6. Shows beverages	Selects one beverage by grasping it and pushing it to the teacher	Choice
7. Puts the ingredients in the blender	Operates the blender with a switch when the chosen ingredients are in	Control
8. Spoons the blender drink into a glass	Indicates if ready to drink	Control
9. Holds out a straw	Places the straw in the glass and drinks	Active Control

Key: Partial participation may have the goal of encouraging the learner to be more active in the routine (Active), to make more choices (Choice), or to have more control of the routine (Control). These goals are shown for each step of the task analysis.

Source: Reprinted from Browder, D. M., & Snell, M. E. (1993). Daily living and community skills. In M. E. Snell (Ed.), *Instruction for students with severe disabilities* (4th ed.) (p. 494). Upper Saddle River, NJ: Merrill/Prentice Hall. Used by permission.

Teaching Communication Skills to Students with Autism

by Jo Webber and Brenda Scheuermann

Mark is an 11-year-old student with autism. Although he is able to talk, he generally shuns social interaction. When someone tries to talk to him, he closes one eye, turns to the side, and flaps his hands repeatedly. When Mark wants something, he usually points or whines. His communication primarily consists of one-word replies to others' questions. Mark attends a special class for most of the school day. However, he goes to lunch and art with general education students from Ms. Jacobs's class. Mark's teachers and parents have identified spontaneous communication as his highest-priority IEP goal: they want him to initiate verbal requests and begin conversations with his peers. Following the recommendations of the speech-language pathologist, Ms. Jacobs is using naturalistic teaching techniques to teach Mark to use spontaneous language.

Students like Mark have extensive communication and social deficits requiring systematic and intensive instructional intervention. Unfortunately, these students are usually not motivated to learn these skills. Even if they do master some skills during class instruction, they often fail to use them in their daily lives, rendering the skills nonfunctional.

Naturalistic teaching directly addresses the problems of low motivation and generalization. As you read in Chapter 9, naturalistic teaching is based on the notion of a "teachable moment," which means that when students demonstrate interest in something, that's a great time to teach them related skills. For example, if Mark gets up from his desk and heads for the water fountain, Ms. Jacobs should use this opportunity to prompt him to ask for a drink of water. This notion of the teachable moment applies to all students, but it is particularly pertinent for students with autism and other severe disabilities who learn slowly, do not participate readily in learning activities, and frequently fail to generalize what they have learned. For these students, every teachable moment is a precious learning opportunity.

Naturalistic teaching includes several components. First, it requires environmental conditions that capture student attention and interest. These can be naturally occurring conditions or situations contrived by the teacher (e.g., putting a desired object out of reach). Second, the teacher must be able to control those conditions: blocking access, for example, to the water fountain. Finally, it is important to provide natural reinforcement after desired student responses. Mark was motivated by the presence of the water fountain and his own thirst. In a naturalistic teaching situation, Ms. Jacobs will block his access to the water, prompt him to communicate what he wants, and, when he complies, allow him to get a drink of water (natural reinforcement). Spontaneously asking for water should occur more often in the future, which is the goal.

Naturalistic Teaching Strategies

Several teaching strategies are associated with naturalistic teaching and can be used alone or in combination. Each teaching session should be short and positive (Kaiser, 2000). Teachers should (1) observe students and note attempts to obtain desired outcomes (e.g., get a toy or food), (2) obtain student attention, and (3) use a responsive interactive style. Specific strategies include the following:

- *Mand.* A *mand* is a verbal instruction that cues students to perform a behavior that they may know how to perform but do not. For example, after blocking Mark's access to the water, Ms. Jacobs obtains his attention and says (mand), "Tell me what you want." After telling Mark what to do, she waits for him to say, "Water." If he complies, she praises him and expands his response (e.g., "Good, Mark. You want a drink of water") and allows him to get a drink.

Mark enters Ms. Jacobs's general education classroom just as her students are lining up for lunch. Ms. Jacobs quickly steps in front of Mark, who is heading for a favorite spot in the corner. "Hi, Mark. Tell me what you need to do" (mand).
Mark responds, "Lunch."
"Good, Mark. Yes, it's time for lunch" (praise and expanded language). "Line up so we can go." (mand). Mark lines up. "Good lining up," says Ms. Jacobs and allows the students to walk to the cafeteria (natural reinforcement).

- *Mand-prompt.* Often, even with a mand, students do not perform a desired behavior. In this case teachers need to add prompts. For example, if Mark does not comply with the mand, Ms. Jacobs provides a prompt by saying, "Water" or "I want water." Then she waits for Mark to talk. Once again, teachers need to first gain the student's attention and then repeat the mand-prompt-wait sequence no more than three times. At this point, access to the water (reinforcement) should follow, regardless of Mark's response, so as not to discourage him from trying to obtain a drink of water in the future (another teachable moment).

As he goes through the cafeteria line, Mark's peer buddy tells him, "Tell the lady what you want, Mark" (mand) at each food selection site and prompts by saying, "I want. . . ." As Mark requests food (e.g., "I want Jell-O," the peer buddy says, "Good, you want the Jell-O" (praise and expanded language). Mark receives the designated food item (natural reinforcement) and moves down the line.

- *Model.* When students are able to perform the behavior but hesitate, teachers may dispense with mands and just model the correct behavior for students to imitate.

The peer buddy notices that Mark cannot reach the chocolate milk carton in the lunch line. He gains Mark's attention and says, "Please help me," or "I want the milk, please" (model) and then waits for a response. When Mark imitates the model, his buddy praises him, repeats the correct response, and helps him retrieve the milk. If two models result in incorrect responses, teachers should add a mand and/or a prompt or end the teaching interaction and use a mand and/or prompt procedure at the next opportunity. At the end of the line, the peer buddy again provides a model for Mark by handing the cashier his money and saying, "You're welcome," when the cashier says, "Thank you." When Mark imitates these responses, the peer praises him and leads him to his seat (natural reinforcement).

Making Naturalistic Teaching Successful

Teachers must regularly take advantage of natural teaching opportunities for naturalistic teaching to be effective. Following are some pointers for successful implementation:

- *Attend to the students.* Teachers should be good observers of student preferences, anticipating student needs and searching for communicative intent in all student behavior.
- *Teach functional skills at opportune moments.* Teach during lunchtime, free time, transition time, before and after class time, and on the bus if possible.
- *Establish a stimulating environment.* Provide many situations in which students will be motivated to produce communicative and social behaviors.
- *Refrain from providing too much assistance.* Require that students use functional behaviors to make requests or protest. Provide only as much assistance as is necessary for successful responding.
- *Reinforce appropriate communicative and social behaviors.* Begin with frequent reinforcement and fade to less frequent reinforcement and natural consequences.
- *Assess results.* As with all teaching, collect data to determine if the student has learned spontaneous communication and social skills.

Brenda Scheuermann and Jo Webber are professors of special education at Southwest Texas State University in San Marcos, Texas. They are the authors of *Autism: Teaching DOES Make a Difference* (Wadsworth, 2002).

Ferguson and Baumgart (1991) describe and offer suggestions for avoiding four types of errors or common misapplications of partial participation: (1) passive participation—the learner is present but not actively participating; (2) myopic participation—the student's participation is limited to only some parts of the activity, which are chosen more for the convenience of others; (3) piecemeal participation—partial participation and the accompanying concepts of functional, activity-based, age-appropriate curriculum activities are used only part of the time; and (4) missed participation—in trying to help students become independent, the teacher misses the point of partial participation altogether.

Positive Behavioral Support   Notable changes have occurred in how teachers respond to disruptive, aggressive, or socially unacceptable behaviors by students with disabilities. In the not-too-distant past, a student who engaged in stereotypic head weaving may have had his head restrained or perhaps had a teacher manipulate his head up and down for several minutes, and a student who tantrumed or screamed may have been "treated" with the application of aversive consequences (e.g., being sprayed with water mist) or extended time out from instruction. These were "modes of intervention which most people would reject as absolutely unacceptable if they were used with a person who does not have disabilities" (Center on Human Policy, 1986, p. 4).

Today, a growing number of special education programs are responding to challenging, excessive, or unacceptable behaviors of students with a nonaversive treatment approach called positive behavioral support. Elements of positive behavior support include (1) understanding the meaning that a behavior has for a student, (2) teaching the student a positive alternative behavior, (3) using environmental restructuring to make the undesired behaviors less likely to occur, and (4) using strategies that are socially acceptable and intended for integrated school and community settings (Carr et al., in press).

Positive behavioral support begins with a functional assessment of the problem behavior. Although **functional assessment** refers to a variety of behavior assessment methodologies for determining the environmental variables that are setting the occasion for and maintaining challenging behaviors, it usually consists of these three steps (Chandler & Dahlquist, 2002; Conroy & Davis, 2000; Horner & Carr, 1997):

1. *Structured interviews* are conducted with teachers, family members, and others who know the child well to find out the circumstances that typically surround the occurrence and nonoccurrence of the problem behavior and the reactions the behavior usually evokes from others.
2. *Systematic observations* of the child are conducted to learn (a) the environmental context and events that covary with the problem behavior (e.g., transitions from one classroom or activity to another, task difficulty); (b) the intensity, duration, and form of the problem behavior; and (c) the events that follow the problem behavior and may function to maintain it (e.g., teacher attention, withdrawal of task demands).
3. *Functional analysis* (i.e., experimental manipulation) of the variables identified in steps 1 and 2 is carried out to verify their function in either triggering or maintaining the problem behavior. For an extensive collection of research and conceptual papers on functional analysis, see Neef (1994).

Results of functional assessments are used to guide the development of positive behavior support plans. For example, functional assessments conducted by Lalli, Browder, Mace, and Brown (1993) revealed that the self-injury and aggressive outbursts by three nonvocal

---

Immediate positive reinforcement is especially critical for students with severe disabilities.

Positive behavioral support

Council for Exceptional Children   Content Standards for Beginning Teachers–Common Core: Laws, policies, and ethical principles regarding behavior management planning and implementation (CC1K2) (also, CC5S5).
PRAXIS Special Education Core Principles: Content Knowledge: III. Delivery of Services to Students with Disabilities, Structuring and managing the learning environment, Behavioral intervention.

Functional assessment, functional analysis

Council for Exceptional Children   Content Standards for Beginning Teachers–Common Core: Use functional assessments to develop intervention plans (CC7S4) (also, CC8K1, IC7S1, IC8S1).
PRAXIS Special Education Core Principles: Content Knowledge: III. Delivery of Services to Students with Disabilities, Structuring and managing the learning environment, Behavioral analysis/ Functional analysis.

students with severe disabilities during instructional activities were maintained by teacher attention (in the form of reprimands) and/or escape (misbehavior often resulted in termination of the academic task). This information led to the design of successful interventions that included frequent positive comments for appropriate behaviors, withholding attention for problem behavior, and teaching the students a socially acceptable behavior for communicating their wishes (e.g., choosing the next activity by pointing to a picture schedule, tapping the teacher on the shoulder). Several books provide guidelines for developing positive behavioral support plans (e.g., Carr et al., 1994; Janney & Snell, 2000; Koegel, Koegel, & Dunlap, 1996; O'Neill et al., 1997). (To read firsthand applications of functional assessment and positive behavioral support, see Teaching & Learning, "Functional Assessment–Based Intervention in a School Setting," later in this chapter, and "A Parent-Professional Partnership in Positive Behavioral Support" in Chapter 4.)

Problem behaviors such as noncompliance, aggression, acting out, and self-injury can sometimes be reduced through relatively simple modifications of curriculum or the way in which learning activities are presented (Ferro, Foster-Johnson, & Dunlap, 1996; Munk & Repp, 1994). For example:

- Providing students with a choice of tasks or task sequence (Kern, Mantegna, Vorndran, Bailin, & Hilt, 2001; Peck Peterson, Caniglia, & Royster, 2001)
- Interspersing easy or high-probability tasks or requests with more difficult items or low-probability requests (Harchik & Putzier, 1990; Horner, Day, Sprague, O'Brien, & Tuesday-Heathfield, 1991)
- Maintaining a rapid pace of instruction (Dunlap, Dyer, & Koegel, 1983; Ernsbarger et al., 2001)
- Using a response-prompting procedure that results in fewer errors (Heckaman, Alber, Hooper, & Heward, 1998)
- Reducing task difficulty (Carr & Durand, 1985)

Positive behavioral support should not be confused with relationship-based approaches that do not provide systematic environmental arrangements and differential consequences for behavior. For example, gentle teaching is a philosophy and approach for treating problem behaviors by individuals with disabilities that relies on "valuing" the person and "giving warm assistance and protection when necessary" (McGee & Gonzalez, 1990, p. 244). McGee (1992), the major proponent of gentle teaching, claims, "Behavior problems will evaporate like the morning dew if we express unconditional valuing" (McGee & Menolascino, 1992, p. 109). Although gentle teaching and other relationship-based approaches such as holding therapy (Tinbergen & Tinbergen, 1983) may sound wonderful, there is little scientific evidence of their effectiveness (Bailey, 1992; Mudford, 1995; Heflin & Simpson, 2002; Romanczyk, Weinter, Lockshin, & Ekdahl, 1999).

Small-Group Instruction   For many years, most professionals believed that one-to-one instruction was the only effective teaching arrangement for students with severe disabilities. The rationale was that one-to-one teaching minimized distractions and increased the likelihood of the student's responding only to the teacher.

Although a one-to-one teaching format allows for the intensive, systematic instruction known to be effective with students who have severe disabilities, small-group instruction also has potential advantages (Kamps, Dugan, Leonard, & Daoust, 1994; Keel & Gast, 1992; Munk, Van Laarhoven, Goodman, & Repp, 1998; Snell & Brown, 2000):

- Skills learned in small-group instruction may be more likely to generalize to group situations and settings.
- Small-group instruction provides opportunities for social interaction and peer reinforcement that are missed when a student is taught alone and isolated from other students.

Small-group instruction

 Council for Exceptional Children   Content Standards for Beginning Teachers–INDEP CURR: Methods for ensuring individual academic success in one-to-one, small-group, and large-group settings (IC5K4) (also, CC5K3).
PRAXIS Special Education Core Principles: Content Knowledge: III. Delivery of Services to Students with Disabilities, Curriculum and Instruction, Small-group Instruction.

Functional Assessment–Based Intervention in a School Setting

by John Umbreit

Why would a child suddenly hit another child without being provoked? Or spit at other children? Or bite them? Or scream? Why would a child pick objects off tables and throw them on the floor? Why would he run away sometimes but lie down on the floor and refuse to get up at other times? If this were a typically developing child, we might think he was a brat or a bully, or even disturbed and in need of counseling. But if this were a child with mental retardation or autism, we would be much more likely to think these behaviors were just a part of his disability. After all, a lot of people with developmental disabilities do those kinds of things. At least that is what we thought for many years.

Today, we take a very different approach, one that assumes that challenging behaviors actually are learned behaviors that occur because they produce desirable consequences, such as attention from other people or escape from unpleasant situations. This approach has important implications for treatment. For instance, take the case of the child who hits others to gain attention. With our old way of thinking, we might have "treated" the hitting by ignoring it altogether or by using a negative consequence, such as loss of privileges or time out, that was intended to eliminate the hitting or reduce its frequency. But if we saw that the hitting actually was an effective way for a child with few social skills to gain attention from others, our "treatment" would focus on teaching this child more socially appropriate ways of getting attention.

One of the most interesting children with whom we have used this approach (called functional assessment) was Reggie, an 11-year-old boy with moderate to severe retardation, seizures, and behavior disorders. Reggie regularly engaged in a variety of challenging behaviors: he hit, spit, bit, threw objects, screamed, ran away, threw himself on the floor and refused to get up. He did these things frequently throughout the day, including at school,

which is where Dr. Kwang-Sun Blair and I worked with him and his teachers.

Reggie began school at age 6 and spent the first 3 years in a separate class for students with severe emotional disabilities. During that time, he often hit his classmates and teachers. He was then placed in a cross-categorical classroom for a year and then into an inclusion program. In the year before our study began, Reggie's challenging behaviors had escalated so much that school district officials were considering removing him from the program. His teachers had attempted a variety of interventions to reduce these problems, including reinforcing alternative behavior, giving choices, time out, physical restraints, and redirection. None of these procedures had been effective.

We began the process of functional assessment by defining Reggie's challenging behaviors and the appropriate behaviors his teachers wanted him to use instead. Then we conducted structured interviews with 10 people who knew Reggie well (often only two or three people are needed). These people included several of his current and former teachers, the school principal, and both of Reggie's parents. Next, we conducted structured observations to identify the situations in which each challenging behavior occurred and the consequences it produced. These 15-minute observation sessions were conducted in multiple environments: in the classroom, on the playground, in the lunchroom, in the library. The interviews and observations revealed clear and important patterns in Reggie's behavior. Specifically, we learned that Reggie displayed one or more challenging behaviors when an activity was something he didn't like to do, when he was required to engage in an activity (i.e., had no choice in the matter), and when he received little attention from staff. In addition, observational data showed that Reggie's challenging behaviors produced considerably more attention than his appropriate behaviors did.

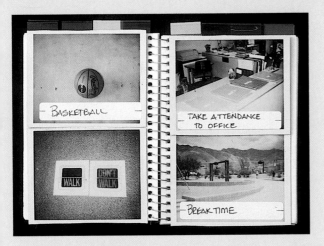

Reggie's communication book helped him interact positively with others.

We hypothesized that Reggie's behavior would improve if he (1) took part in preferred activities, (2) was allowed to choose activities whenever possible, and (3) received frequent social attention from staff for appropriate behavior. Next, we tested each hypothesis within the context of naturally occurring routines and activities at school. To do this, we conducted a series of assessment sessions, ranging from 8 to 15 minutes long. Some were baseline sessions in which the typical conditions that existed before the study were in place. Baseline sessions were alternated with the hypothesis-testing conditions we expected would improve Reggie's behavior. For example, in one session, he might be required to engage in a nonpreferred activity. In the next session, he would be allowed to engage in a preferred activity. Throughout each session, we recorded how often Reggie emitted both challenging and appropriate behaviors. We tested and repeated various combinations of our hypotheses until a clear picture emerged of the situations and consequences that reliably controlled his behavior.

The experimental data supported all three hypotheses: Reggie behaved much better in preferred activities, when he had choices, and when he received frequent attention for appropriate behavior. We used this information to design an intervention package for him consisting of four components. Whenever possible, desired skills were taught through preferred activities that Reggie was allowed to choose, and frequent attention was provided for appropriate behavior. When nonpreferred activities could not be avoided, his teachers tried to give him some choice among these activities and interacted with him frequently when he behaved appropriately.

Instruction in appropriate social and communication skills was included as the fourth component of the intervention because Reggie's teachers and parents told us in the interviews that his limited skills in these areas restricted his ability to interact appropriately with others. This intervention element took two forms. First, the teachers designed a small communication book that included photographs with a written word or phrase related to objects and activities that Reggie encountered during his school day. He carried the book with him wherever he went at school, and his teachers always provided instruction in context (i.e., when the object or activity was encountered naturally). At first, there were only about 10 items in the book, but this number quickly increased to more than 40. Second, the teaching staff was instructed to respond to every occurrence of challenging behavior by immediately teaching Reggie appropriate behavior that he should use instead. For example, he tried to use a computer game in the school's library; but when the game did not boot correctly, he hit the computer screen. Instead of scolding him or using time out, the teacher immediately taught him to ask the school librarian for help, which he got. Thereafter, whenever he needed help, he asked for it independently.

To test the effectiveness of the intervention package, we began with one week of baseline conditions. During the second week, the teachers implemented the intervention only during the afternoon of each day, continuing baseline conditions during the morning. At the end of this week, the afternoon results were very encouraging, so teachers began implementing the intervention throughout the day. They continued to implement the intervention for the remaining 5 months of the school year. Figure A shows the power of an intervention that is based on a clear understanding of why a person is engaging in challenging behaviors.

Although no formal data have been collected since the study ended, we do know that Reggie's improved behavior continued as he transitioned to middle school and, recently, to high school. During this time, the program we developed has been continued, aided greatly by the school district's willingness to let last year's teachers train Reggie's new teachers at the beginning of each new school year. According to the teachers, the training has focused on both how to work with Reggie and why it is important to work with him that way.

Reggie is now nearly 18 years old. He spends part of each day at school and part in a community-based program that targets self-sufficiency and work-skill development. The only time he has significant problems is when he interacts with new staff who have not yet learned how

continues

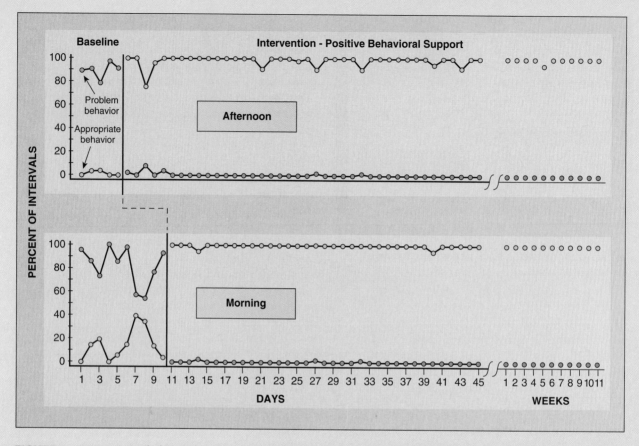

FIGURE A Percentage of observation intervals in which Reggie exhibited problem and appropriate behaviors in school during baseline and intervention conditions

to work with him. These problems are always quickly resolved. Without functional assessment and its resulting intervention, Reggie's problem behaviors would have led to a more restrictive placement with limited opportunities for school and community involvement.

Data from this study (Umbreit & Blair, 1996) and several others like it are teaching us that challenging behaviors of people with developmental disabilities are functional behaviors that, though inappropriate, give them an effective way to influence their world. Func-

tional assessment–based intervention offers us a way to understand these behaviors and to improve the quality of life for students and their families, teachers, and friends.

John Umbreit is a professor in the Special Education Program at the University of Arizona, where he directs the university's participation in the Arizona Behavioral Initiative, a statewide effort to improve schoolwide discipline. His research and teaching focus on applied behavior analysis, functional assessment, and positive behavioral support in natural, community-based environments.

- Small-group instruction provides opportunities for incidental or observation learning from other students.
- In some instances, small-group instruction may be a more cost-effective use of the teacher's time.

The effectiveness of small-group instruction is enhanced when teachers do the following (Kamps et al., 1994; Munk et al., 1998; Snell & Brown, 2000):

- Ensure that students possess basic prerequisite skills such as (1) sitting quietly for a period of time, (2) maintaining eye contact, and (3) following simple instructions or imitating simple responses.

- Encourage students to listen and watch other group members and then praise them for doing so.
- Keep instruction interesting by keeping individual turns short, giving all members turns, giving turns contingent on attending, and using demonstrations and a variety of materials that can be handled.
- Use methods such as choral responding and response cards (see Chapter 8), which enable every student in the group to respond to each instructional trial.
- Involve all members by using multilevel instruction individualized to each student's targeted skills and mode of response.
- Use partial participation and material adaptation to enable all students to respond.
- Keep waiting time to a minimum by controlling the group size and limiting the amount of teacher talk and the amount/length of student response in a single turn.
- Promote cooperation among group members.

WHERE SHOULD STUDENTS WITH SEVERE DISABILITIES BE TAUGHT?

Benefits of the Neighborhood School   What is the least restrictive and most appropriate educational setting for a student with severe disabilities? This important question continues to be the subject of much debate and discussion. Lou Brown (who has long championed the inclusion of persons with severe disabilities in integrated school, vocational, and community settings) and his colleagues at the University of Wisconsin make a strong case for why students with severe disabilities should attend the same school they would attend if they were not disabled:

> The environments in which students with severe intellectual disabilities receive instructional services have critical effects on where and how they spend their postschool lives. Segregation begets segregation. We believe that when children with intellectual disabilities attend separate schools, they are denied opportunities to demonstrate to the rest of the community that they can function in integrated environments and activities; their nondisabled peers do not know or understand them and too often think negatively of them; their parents become afraid to risk allowing them opportunities to learn to function in integrated environments later in life; and taxpayers assume they need to be sequestered in segregated group homes, enclaves, work crews, activity centers, sheltered workshops, institutions, and nursing homes. (Brown et al., 1989, p. 1)

Brown and his colleagues offer four reasons why they believe neighborhood schools should replace segregated and clustered schools. They define a clustered school as "a regular school attended by an unnaturally large proportion of students with intellectual disabilities, but it is not the one any or most would attend if they were not labeled disabled" (1989, p. 1). First, when students without disabilities go to an integrated school with peers who are disabled, they are more likely to function responsibly as adults in a pluralistic society. Second, various sources of information support integrated schools as more meaningful instructional environments. Hunt, Goetz, and Anderson (1986), for example, compared the IEP objectives for students with severe disabilities who were taught at integrated versus segregated schools. They found the quality of IEP objectives—in terms of age-appropriateness, functionality, and the potential for generalization of what was being taught to other environments—was higher for the students educated in integrated schools. Third, parents and families have greater access to school activities when children are attending their home schools. Fourth, attending one's home school provides greater opportunities to develop a wide range of social relationships with nondisabled peers. Table 13.2 presents examples of 11 kinds of social relationships that might develop between students with severe disabilities and their nondisabled peers when they attend the same school.

Benefits of neighborhood schools

 Council for Exceptional Children   Content Standards for Beginning Teachers—INDEP CURR: Advantages and disadvantages of placement options and programs on the continuum of services for individuals with disabilities (IC5K5) (also, IC1K6, CC5K1).
PRAXIS Special Education Core Principles: Content Knowledge: III. Delivery of Services to Students with Disabilities, placement and program issues, Least restrictive environment.

TABLE 13.2 Social relationships that can develop between students with severe disabilities and their nondisabled peers when they attend the same school

Social Relationship	Example
Peer tutor	Leigh role-plays social introductions with Margo, providing feedback and praise for Margo's performance.
Eating companion	Jennifer and Rick eat lunch with Linda in the cafeteria and talk about their favorite music groups.
Art, home economics, industrial arts, music, physical education companion	In art class, students were instructed to paint a sunset. Tom sat next to Dan and offered suggestions and guidance about the best colors to use and how to complete the task.
Regular class companion	A fifth-grade class is doing a "Know Your Town" lesson in social studies. Ben helps Karen plan a trip through their neighborhood.
During-school companion	"Hangs out" and interacts on social level: after lunch and before the bell for class rang, Molly and Phyllis went to the student lounge for a soda.
Friend	David, a member of the varsity basketball team, invites Ralph, a student with severe disabilities, to his house to watch a game on TV.
Extracurricular companion	Sarah and Winona prepare their articles for the school newspaper together and then work on the layout in the journalism lab.
After-school-project companion	The sophomore class decided to build a float for the homecoming parade. Joan worked on it with Maria, a nondisabled companion, after school and on weekends in Joan's garage.
After-school companion	On Saturday afternoon, Mike, who is not disabled, and Bill go to the shopping mall.
Travel companion	David walks with Ralph when he wheels from last-period class to the gym, where Ralph helps the basketball team as a student manager.
Neighbor	Interacts with student in everyday environments and activities. Parents of nondisabled students in the neighborhood regularly exchange greetings with Mary when they are at school, around the neighborhood, at local stores, at the mall, at the grocery.

Source: Adapted from Brown, L., Long, E., Udvari-Solner, A., Davis, L., VanDeventer, P., Ahlgren, C., Johnson, F., Gruenewald, L., & Jorgensen, J. (1989). The home school: Why students with severe disabilities must attend the schools of their brothers, sisters, friends, and neighbors. *Journal of the Association for Persons with Severe Handicaps, 14,* 4. Used by permission.

Inclusion and social relationships

 Council for Exceptional Children Content Standards for Beginning Teachers–INDEP CURR: Advantages and disadvantages of placement options and programs on the continuum of services for individuals with disabilities (IC5K5) (also, IC5K2, CC5K1). **PRAXIS** Special Education Core Principles: Content Knowledge: III. Delivery of Services to Students with Disabilities, placement and program issues, Least restrictive environment/Inclusion.

Social Relationships   Establishing and maintaining a network of social relationships is one of the desired outcomes of inclusive educational practices for students with severe disabilities (Schwartz, 2000). Although research has shown that simply placing students with disabilities into regular schools and classrooms does not necessarily lead to increased positive social interactions, regular class participation can provide additional opportunities for positive social contacts and the development of friendships (e.g., Hanline, 1993; Staub, Spaulding, Peck, Gallucci, & Schwartz, 1996).

For example, Kennedy and Itkonen (1994) studied the effects of regular class participation on social contacts with peers without disabilities for three high school students with severe and multiple disabilities. Don was 18 years old and classified as having severe intellectual retardation, along with paraplegia, cerebral palsy, and visual impairments. He used a wheelchair to move himself for short distances and lived in a 50-person facility for people with multiple disabilities and intensive health care needs. Manny was also 18 years old and classified as having severe retardation. He communicated with two- or three-word sentences and had a 10-year history of hitting and pinching others. Ann was 19 years old with moderate mental retardation. Her communications ranged from a few words to elaborate sentences. She was receiving instruction regarding appropriate topics of conversation and maintaining physical distance when interacting with others. Ann received medication for generalized tonic-clonic seizures and often yelled, ran away, and hit others during transitions from one class or activity to another. Contingency contracts were in effect for both Manny and Ann as a preventive behavior management procedure; they could earn privileges for not engaging in problem behaviors.

A social contact was defined as a student with disabilities interacting with a peer(s) within the context of a meaningful activity (e.g., eating lunch, conducting a science project) for a minimum of 15 minutes. Each of the three students participated in a different regular classroom (average size: 25 students) for one period each school day, five days per week. Several aspects of this study deserve special comment. First, regular class participation increased the number of social contacts for each student, even though ongoing opportunities to contact nondisabled peers were provided through "friendship" and peer tutoring programs during those weeks when the students were not in the regular classroom. Second, the increases in social contacts were the result of participation for only one class period per day. It might be presumed that additional participation (e.g., two or three periods per day) would result in even more frequent contacts. Third, the increased social contacts were obtained without an elaborate training program or intensive intervention. Each student simply began participating in the regular classroom after a "circle of friends" introduction by the special education teacher to the regular class peers that stressed the similarities among all students, the need for students to support one another, and the importance of social relationships.

Friendships and after-school relationships between students with disabilities and their nondisabled peers are more likely to develop when all students attend their home school.

A wide variety of strategies for promoting desired social relationships has been developed (Strain & Schwartz, 2001). One strategy is to give the student with disabilities a skill for initiating and maintaining interaction. For example, two nonverbal boys with severe and profound mental retardation and multiple physical disabilities learned to initiate play activities with nondisabled peers by showing badges with photographs of activities (Jolly, Test, & Spooner, 1993). Other strategies focus on teaching classmates without disabilities to initiate social contacts during free time, cooperative learning, or peer tutoring and peer buddy activities (Eichinger, 1990; Hughes et al., 2001; Hughes, Killian, & Fischer, 1996; Putnam, 1998; Romer, White, & Haring, 1996). Still other approaches involve changes in the roles and responsibilities of instructional faculty, such as teaching teams (Ferguson, Meyer, Jeanchild, Juniper, & Zingo, 1992; Giangreco, Cloninger, Dennis, & Edelman, 2000; Janney & Snell, 2000; Kochar, West, & Taymans, 2000). Many of these strategies for facilitating the regular classroom inclusion of students with severe disabilities are compatible with one another; and it is typical for a program to incorporate multiple, concurrent methods for identifying and providing supports for students, their teachers, and their peers. To learn about a collaborative method for building social supports for students with disabilities in regular classrooms, see Teaching & Learning, "Planning for Inclusion with MAPS," later in this chapter.

Planning inclusion with MAPS

 Council for Exceptional Children Content Standards for Beginning Teachers–Common Core: Use strategies to facilitate integration into various settings (CC4S1) (also, CC5S1, CC5S3).
PRAXIS Special Education Core Principles: Content Knowledge: III. Delivery of Services to Students with Disabilities, Background knowledge, Placement issues/Least restrictive environment.

Experiences and Transformations of General Education Teachers To find out how regular education teachers reacted to having a student with severe disabilities placed in their classrooms, Giangreco, Dennis, Cloninger, Edelman, and Shattman (1993) interviewed 19 K–9 general education teachers. They found that regardless of how the child with severe

Planning for Inclusion with MAPS

by Marsha Forest and Jack Pearpoint

The movement to integrate children with disabilities into ordinary classrooms is founded on a simple yet profound philosophy: everyone belongs. The McGill Action Planning System (MAPS) is a systems approach to problem solving that has helped many schools welcome and support children with disabilities in regular classrooms.

Who Goes to a MAP? Friends!

The size of the group that gathers for a MAP session can vary from two to two dozen. The key ingredients for participants are intimate and personal contact with the individual who is being mapped. A grandmother or neighbor, a friend—all are on equal footing with professionals, who are welcomed and needed, but as individuals, not as therapists. Parents and family members usually have the most to offer. Their perspectives are welcome in a MAP.

Peer participation is critical. Classmates have enormous untapped energy and creative capacity. Their straight talk often offers teachers new ideas. Adults must be careful not to constrain or downgrade the participation of children: they are critical and equal partners in the MAPS process.

Should the individual who is being mapped be present? This is a judgment call; it works both ways. We lean toward full participation. People understand an enormous amount, more than we think. Also, a MAP is a real boost for an individual who previously has been excluded. Full participation also saves time in trying to explain the process later.

What Happens at a MAP?

Mapping is a collaborative problem-solving process aided by a facilitator and a recorder. The facilitator, positioned at the open end of a half-circle formed by the participants, presents eight key questions to the group. The facilitator must be skilled in group process and have a problem-solving orientation. Most important, the facilitator must be committed to building an integrated school community. The information and ideas generated during the session are marked by the recorder on a large piece of chart paper. Public charting is vital to the MAPS process: it generates images that help participants visualize the relationships among people and actions, thus promoting the creation of additional problem-solving strategies. It also serves as a permanent record of the plans and commitments made by the group. The recorder need not be an artist; but it is vital that the MAP be printed or written clearly, using the participants' words. The chart should include contributions from everyone in the group.

MAPS planning typically occurs in one or two sessions, and approximately three hours are required to fully address these questions:

1. *What's a MAP?* The facilitator begins the MAPS process by asking participants, "What is a map?" A recent group gave these answers:
   - Something that gives direction
   - A thing that helps you get somewhere
   - Routes to different places
   - A way to find a new way
2. *What is the individual's history?* The participants most intimate with the child being mapped (e.g., parents and family members) are asked to give a 10- to 15-minute history focusing on key milestones and events in the individual's life.
3. *What is your dream for the individual?* This question is intended to get people, especially parents, to imagine their vision for the child's future. Many parents of children with disabilities have lost their ability to dream about what they really want for their child. This question helps the group focus on the direction in which the individual is now heading and encourages concrete action plans for realizing the vision.
4. *What is your nightmare?* This question is the hardest to ask but is very important to get on the table. We must understand the nightmare to prevent it. No parent has ever said, "I'm worried that my child won't attend a

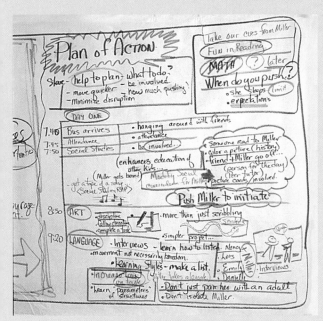

A portion of Miller's MAP

university, won't get an A on the next test, or won't learn to spell." Instead, the question brings out what is in the heart of virtually every parent of a child with a severe disability: "We're afraid our child will end up in an institution, work in a sheltered workshop, and have no one to care for her when we die."

5. *Who is the individual?* With this question, the MAPS process shifts into a no-holds-barred brainstorming mode. Participants are asked to give words or phrases that describe the person being mapped. The rule is no jargon, no labels; just describe how you see the person. The image of a unique and distinct personality should emerge. Here are examples from a recent MAP for Miller, a 14-year-old who, to some, is "severely handicapped and mentally retarded."

- She has a brother.
- She gets around in a wheelchair.
- She's lots of fun.
- She's active like crazy.
- She's radical/bad (really means good).
- She's temperamental.
- She likes to touch.
- She wants to be involved.
- She looks at you.
- She can talk some.

6. *What are the individual's strengths, abilities, gifts, and talents?* It is vital to build upon strengths and abilities. Yet all too often we focus on the things a child with a

disability cannot do. This can be a difficult question for parents, who have been struggling with negatives for so long. This question also is intended to produce a brainstormed list from the entire group. Here is part of the list generated for Miller:

- She can make us laugh.
- She moves her arms, can throw a ball.
- She likes to listen to music.
- She's persistent, tries real hard.
- She can count and remember numbers.
- She enjoys stories and movies.

7. *What are the individual's needs?* This, too, is a brainstorm. Don't let people stop each other, but don't get bogged down either. Keep it short and record people's words and perceptions. Parents, teachers, and peers often have different perceptions about needs. For Miller, it was decided that what she needed most of all was

- A communication system that lets her express her wants and feelings
- More independence with dressing and other self-care skills
- To be with her own age group
- Places to go and things to do after school
- Teenage clothes

8. *What is the plan of action?* This is the final and most important question of all. The MAPS planning group imagines what the individual's ideal day at school would look like and what must be done to make it a reality. Step by step, the MAPS group goes through an entire day, envisioning the various environments and activities the individual will experience and what kinds of resources, supports, and adaptations can be created to make the day successful. For example, a peer volunteers to meet the taxi that brings Miller to school each morning and to walk with her to the classroom. During language arts period, a classmate will help Miller practice with her communication board. The principle of partial participation will be used on the playground when Miller bats in the softball game and a teammate runs the bases for her.

A MAP Is Not . . .

- A trick, a gimmick, or a quick-fix solution to complex human problems. It is not a one-shot session that blasts a vulnerable person into the everyday life and fabric of school and community. MAPS is a problem-solving process; the plans for action are not set in stone but must be reviewed and changed as often as needed.
- A replacement for an IEP. A MAP session may provide useful information for an IEP, but it is not a substitute for the IEP process and must not be treated as such.

continues

- A tool to make any segregated setting better. MAPS was designed to liberate people from segregated settings; it is for people and organizations who are committed to figuring out together how to get a person fully included in life.
- An academic exercise. It is a genuine, personal approach to problem solving with and on behalf of real individuals who are vulnerable. A MAP produces outcomes that have real implications for how the person will live his life.
- Just talk. MAPS is talk and action. A MAP gives clear directions and action steps for inclusion.

The metaphor for MAPS is a kaleidoscope, a beautiful instrument whose design changes constantly. We see the kaleidoscope as the outcome of each MAP. It is a medley of people working together to make something unique and better happen. It is more than anyone can do alone.

For additional information and training materials on MAPS, write to the Centre for Integrated Education and Community, 24 Thome Crescent, Toronto, Ontario, Canada, M6H 2S5. Forest and Lusthaus (1990) and Vandercook, York, and Forest (1989) also describe the MAPS approach.

Changing attitudes of general education teachers

Council for Exceptional Children Content Standards for Beginning Teachers–Common Core: Teacher attitudes and behaviors that influence behavior of individuals with exceptional learning needs (CC5K4) (also, IC5K2). PRAXIS Special Education Core Principles: Content Knowledge: III. Delivery of Services to Students with Disabilities, Professional roles, Influence of teacher attitudes, values and behavior on the learning of exceptional children.

disabilities was placed in the general education classroom, most teachers initially described the placement in cautious or negative terms (e.g., "reluctant," "nervous," "unqualified," "angry"). Despite their initial negative reactions, 17 of the teachers experienced "increased ownership and involvement" with the child with severe disabilities as the school year progressed. Giangreco et al. refer to this process of changing attitude and perspective as transformation.

Transformations were gradual and progressive, rather than discrete and abrupt. . . . A number of teachers who had these experiences reportedly came to the realization they could be successful and that including the student was not as difficult as they had originally imagined. . . . The following quotes typify the comments of teachers who underwent significant transformation.

"I started seeing him as a little boy. I started feeling that he's a person too. He's a student. Why should I not teach him? He's in my class. That's my responsibility. I'm a teacher!"

"I made the full swing of fighting against having Bobbi Sue placed in my room to fighting for her to be in a mainstream classroom working with kids in the way that she had worked with them all year long. I'm a perfect example of how you have to have an open mind."

"I started watching my own regular classroom students. They didn't treat him any differently. They went about their business like everything was normal. So I said, 'If they can do it, I can do it.' He's not getting in their way. They're treating him like everybody else."

"They were always letting me know when I forgot something. 'You didn't remember to include Sarah.' So they were very good at letting me know."

"The kids help you figure it out." (Giangreco et al., 1993, pp. 359–372)

For detailed information about administrative, curricular, and instructional strategies designed to support the education of students with severe disabilities in regular schools, see Bauer and Brown (2001); Fisher and Ryndak (2001); Giangreco and Doyle (2000); Kennedy and Fisher (2001); Sailor, Gee, and Karasoff (2000); and Snell and Janney (2000b).

How Much Time in the Regular Classroom?   Although the social benefits of regular class participation for students with disabilities—as well as for their peers without disabilities—have been clearly shown, the effects of full inclusion on the attainment of IEP goals and objectives is not yet known. The functional IEP goals and objectives for students with severe disabilities are seldom reflected in the academic curriculum of the regular classroom (especially at the secondary level). Available instruction time is especially valuable to students who by definition require direct, intensive, and ongoing instruction to acquire basic skills that students without disabilities learn without instruction. A major challenge for both special and general educators is to develop models and strategies for including students with severe disabilities in regular classroom activities without sacrificing their opportunities to acquire, practice, and generalize the functional skills they need most.

In the end, the best inclusion facilitators are the students themselves.

The question of how much time students with severe disabilities should spend in the regular classroom is an important one. Although a few full inclusion advocates might argue that every student with disabilities should have a full-time regular class placement regardless of the nature of her educational needs, most special educators probably would agree with Brown et al. (1991), whose position is that students with severe disabilities should be based in the same schools and classrooms they would attend if they were not disabled but that they should also spend some time elsewhere.

There are substantial differences between being based in and confined to regular education classrooms. "Based in" refers to being a member of a real class, where and with whom you start the school day, you may not spend all your time with your class, but it is still your group and everyone knows it. . . . It is our position that it is unacceptable for students with severe disabilities to spend either 0% or 100% of their time in regular education classrooms. . . . How much time should be spent in regular classes? Enough to ensure that the student is a member, not a visitor. A lot, if the student is engaged in meaningful activities. Quite a bit if she is young, but less as she approaches 21. There is still a lot we do not know. (pp. 40, 46)

THE CHALLENGE AND REWARDS OF TEACHING STUDENTS WITH AUTISM AND SEVERE DISABILITIES

Virtually every parent of a child with autism or severe disabilities has heard a host of negative predictions from educators, doctors, and concerned friends and family. Parents often are offered such discouraging forecasts as "Your child will never talk" or "Your child will never be toilet-trained." Yet in many instances those children make gains that far exceed the professionals' original predictions. Despite predictions to the contrary, many children have learned to walk, talk, toilet themselves, and perform other "impossible" tasks.

Teachers—both special and general educators—who are providing instruction to students with autism and severe disabilities can rightfully be called pioneers on an exciting new frontier of education. Twenty years ago, Orelove (1984) stated that professionals who were involved in educating students with severe disabilities could "look back with pride, and even awe, at the advances they have made. In a relatively brief period, educators, psychologists, and other professionals have advocated vigorously for additional legislation and funds, extended the service delivery model into the public schools and community, and developed a training technology" (p. 271).

Although significant progress has been made in the two decades since Orelove's positive assessment, a great deal more must be accomplished. Future research must increase our understanding of how students with severe disabilities acquire, maintain, and generalize functional skills (Simpson, 2001). As more effective techniques for changing behavior are developed, they must be balanced with concern for the personal rights and dignity of individuals with severe disabilities. Current and future teachers of students with severe disabilities have the opportunity to be at the forefront of those developments.

Teaching students with severe disabilities is difficult and demanding. The teacher must be well organized, firm, and consistent. He must be able to manage a complex educational operation, which usually involves supervising paraprofessional aides, student teachers, peer tutors, and volunteers. The teacher must be knowledgeable about one-to-one and small-group instruction formats and be able to work cooperatively with other teachers and related service professionals. He must maintain accurate records and constant planning for the future needs of his students. Effective communication with parents and families, school administrators, vocational rehabilitation personnel, and community agencies is also vital.

Students with the most severe disabilities sometimes give little or no apparent response, so their teachers must be sensitive to small changes in behavior. The effective teacher is consistent and persistent in designing and implementing strategies to improve learning and behavior (even if some of the students' previous teachers were not). The effective teacher should not be too quick to remove difficult tasks or requests that result in noncompliance or misbehavior. It is better to teach students to request assistance and to intersperse tasks that are easy for the student to perform.

There is a difference between either expecting miracles or being passively patient and simply working each day at the job of designing, implementing, and evaluating systematic instruction and supports. It can be a mistake to expect a miracle:

> In the beginning, we were expecting a sudden step forward, that we might somehow turn a cognitive, emotional, or social key inside the child's mind that would produce a giant leap ahead. . . . Such a leap would have been so gratifying, and it would have made our work so much easier. But it never happened. Instead, progress followed a slow, step-by-step progression, with only a few and minor spurts ahead from time to time. We learned to settle in for hard work. (Lovaas, 1994, n.p.)

Some might consider it undesirable to work with students with autism and severe disabilities because of the extent of their behavioral challenges and learning problems. Yet working with students who require instruction at its very best can offer many highly rewarding teaching experiences. Much satisfaction can be felt in teaching a child to feed and dress herself independently; helping a student make friends with nondisabled peers; and supporting a young adult's efforts to live, travel, and work as independently as possible in the community. Both the challenge and the potential rewards of teaching students with severe disabilities are great.

 For more information on autism and severe disabilities, go to the Web Links module in Chapter 13 of the Companion Website at **www.prenhall.com/heward**

 **SUMMARY**

DEFINITION OF AUTISM

- The essential features of autism typically appear prior to 30 months of age and consist of disturbances of (1) developmental rates and/or sequences; (2) responses to sensory stimuli; (3) speech, language, and cognitive capacities; and (4) capacities to relate to people, events, and objects.

- Autism is one of five developmental disabilities of childhood included under the umbrella term *pervasive developmental disorder* (PDD). Many professionals now use the term *autism spectrum disorders* instead of PDD.
- A diagnosis of autism is made according to criteria described in the DSM-IV.
- Asperger syndrome is sometimes referred to as "high-functioning autism." Children with Asperger syndrome do not have a general language delay, and many have average or even above-average intelligence. They have poor communication and social skills, engage in repetitive and stereotyped behaviors, and display an intense interest in or preoccupation with atypical things or parts of things.

CHARACTERISTICS OF STUDENTS WITH AUTISM

- Frequently observed characteristics of children with autism are apparent sensory deficit, severe affect isolation, self-stimulation, challenging behavior such as tantrums and self-injurious behavior, echolalic and psychotic speech, and skill deficiencies.
- Although autism occurs across the full range of intellectual abilities, between 70% and 80% of individuals with autism also have mental retardation.
- Uneven skill development is a common characteristic of autism; and some children exhibit "splinter skills," areas of relatively superior performance that are unexpected compared to other domains of functioning.
- A very few persons with autism exhibit savant syndrome, an extraordinary ability in a specific area or skill while functioning at the mental retardation level in all other areas.

PREVALENCE OF AUTISM

- Historically considered a rare disorder, recent estimates are that autism occurs in as many as 1 in 500 people.
- Boys are affected about four times more often than are girls.

CAUSES OF AUTISM

- For many years, it was widely thought that parents who were indifferent to the emotional needs of their children caused autism. However, no causal link between parental personality and autism was ever discovered.
- Recent research shows a clear biological origin for autism in the form of abnormal brain development, structure, and/or neurochemistry.

EDUCATION AND TREATMENT OF STUDENTS WITH AUTISM

- Numerous controversial treatments and cures for autism have been promoted, most without scientific evidence of their effects and benefits.
- Although the prognosis for children with autism has traditionally been poor, some children have achieved normal functioning by the primary grades as a result of an intensive, behaviorally oriented program of early intervention.
- From the perspective of applied behavior analysis, "autism is a syndrome of behavioral deficits and excesses that have a biological basis but are nonetheless amenable to change through carefully orchestrated, constructive interactions with the physical and social environment" (Green, 2001, p. 73).
- Discrete trial training (DTT) is an important part of ABA programming for children with autism. However, DTT is just one type of teaching arrangement, and ABA programming uses a variety of procedures to help individuals with autism acquire and generalize new skills, such as PECS, stimulus control strategies, peer-mediated interventions, functional assessment, pivotal response intervention, and naturalistic teaching strategies.

DEFINITIONS AND PREVALENCE OF SEVERE AND MULTIPLE DISABILITIES

- Students with severe disabilities need instruction in many basic skills that most children without disabilities acquire without instruction in the first 5 years of life.
- Students with profound disabilities have pervasive delays in all domains of functioning and reach a developmental level no higher than 2 years of age in any domain.
- TASH defines persons with severe disabilities as "individuals of all ages who require extensive ongoing support in more than one major life activity in order to participate in integrated community settings and to enjoy a quality of life that is available to citizens with fewer or no disabilities."
- Students with severe disabilities frequently have multiple disabilities, including physical problems, and usually look and act markedly different from children without disabilities.
- Students with severe and multiple disabilities are served and counted under several disability categories, making prevalence figures hard to determine.
- Estimates of the prevalence of severe disabilities range from 0.1% to 1% of the population.

CHARACTERISTICS OF STUDENTS WITH SEVERE AND MULTIPLE DISABILITIES

- Students with severe disabilities need intensive instruction in many basic skills that most children without disabilities learn without instruction. Children with severe disabilities may show some or all of the following behaviors or skill deficits: slow acquisition rates for learning new skills, difficulty in generalizing and maintaining newly learned skills, severe deficits in communication skills, impaired physical and motor development, deficits in self-help skills, infrequent constructive behavior and interaction, and frequent inappropriate behavior.
- Despite their intense challenges, students with severe disabilities often exhibit many positive characteristics, such as warmth, humor, sociability, and persistence.
- Students with dual sensory impairments cannot be accommodated in special education programs designed solely for students with hearing or visual impairments. Although the vast majority of children labeled deaf-blind have some functional hearing and/or vision, the dual impairments severely impede learning of communication and social skills.
- Despite their limitations, children with severe disabilities can and do learn.

CAUSES OF SEVERE DISABILITIES

- Brain disorders, which are involved in most cases of severe intellectual disabilities, are the result of either brain dysgenesis (abnormal brain development) or brain damage (caused by influences that alter the structure or function of a brain that had been developing normally up to that point).
- Severe and profound disabilities most often have biological causes, including chromosomal abnormalities, genetic and metabolic disorders, complications of pregnancy and prenatal care, birth trauma, and later brain damage.
- In about one-sixth of all cases of severe disabilities, the cause cannot be clearly determined.

EDUCATIONAL APPROACHES

- A curriculum based on typical developmental milestones is inappropriate for most students with autism or severe disabilities.
- Students with autism and severe disabilities must be taught skills that are functional, age-appropriate, and directed toward the community. Interaction with typically developing students should occur regularly.

- Students with severe disabilities should be taught choice-making skills.
- The emphasis of research and training in communication for persons with severe disabilities has shifted from the remediation of specific forms of communication to a focus on functional communication in any mode that enables communication partners to establish shared meanings.
- Some students with severe disabilities use augmentative and alternative systems of communication (AAC), such as gestures, various sign language systems, pictorial communication boards, PECS, and electronic communication aids.
- Students with autism or severe disabilities should also be taught age-appropriate recreation and leisure skills.
- Because each student with autism or severe disabilities has many learning needs, teachers must carefully prioritize and choose IEP objectives and learning activities that will most benefit the student and his family.
- Effective instruction of students with autism or severe disabilities is characterized by these elements:
  - The student's current level of performance is precisely assessed.
  - The skill to be taught is defined clearly.
  - The skills are ordered in an appropriate sequence.
  - The teacher provides clear prompts or cues to the student.
  - The student receives immediate feedback and reinforcement from the teacher.
  - Strategies that promote generalization of learning are used.
  - The student's performance is carefully measured and evaluated.
- Partial participation is both a philosophy for selecting activities and a method for adapting activities and supports to enable students with severe disabilities to actively participate in meaningful tasks they are not able to perform independently.
- The teacher of students with severe disabilities must be skilled in positive, instructionally relevant strategies for assessing and dealing with challenging and problem behaviors.
- Research and practice are providing increasing support for the use of integrated small-group instruction arrangements for students with severe disabilities.
- Students with severe disabilities are more likely to develop social relationships with students without disabilities if they attend their home school and are included at least part of the time in the regular classroom.
- Although the initial reactions of many general education teachers who have a student with severe disabilities placed in their classrooms are negative, those apprehensions and concerns often transform into positive experiences as the student becomes a regular member of their classroom.

THE CHALLENGE AND REWARDS OF TEACHING STUDENTS WITH AUTISM AND SEVERE DISABILITIES

- Teachers must be sensitive to small changes in behavior. The effective teacher is consistent and persistent in evaluating and changing instruction to improve learning and behavior.
- Working with students who require instruction at its very best can be highly rewarding to teachers.

To check your comprehension of chapter content, go to the Guided Review and Quiz modules in Chapter 13 of the Companion Website at **www.prenhall.com/heward**

Chapter 14
Giftedness and Talent
by Jane Piirto and William L. Heward

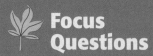

- Why do students who are very bright need special education?

- How has the evolving definition of giftedness changed the ways in which students are identified and served?

- What provisions should be made to accurately identify students with outstanding talents who are from diverse cultural groups or have disabilities?

- In what ways should the pace and depth of curriculum be differentiated for gifted and talented students?

- How can grouping help the regular classroom teacher plan for the educational needs of students of various abilities?

Patricia Concepcion Lambert

Hunter College Elementary School
New York, New York

Education • Teaching Credentials • Experience
- B.A., Psychology, Hunter College, 1974
- M.S., Elementary Education, Hunter College, 1981
- Postgraduate degree in Administration and Supervision, Hunter College, 1996
- New York State Teaching Certificate, Nursery–6
- 22 years of experience as educator of gifted and talented children

I was walking in Central Park one day when a very tall man came up to me and said, "Ms. Lambert?" I looked up at him, a little perplexed, and he said, "I'm sure you don't recognize me because the last time you saw me I was up to your knee. You were my first-grade teacher, and my family moved to Virginia the next year."

As he smiled, I instantly remembered his little face in my classroom more than 15 years ago. "How are you, Ali?" I asked. "And how are your parents? I remember your mom worked at a university, and your dad was an artist."

"I can't believe you remember my name, let alone the occupations of my parents! We are all fine. I've graduated from college with a degree in computer science and now work for Bill Gates. I never forgot you and how much you made me feel that I could do whatever it was that I set my mind to do. I remember how you got me interested in so many things, especially Ancient Egypt."

Ali and I stood there for about 30 minutes reminiscing about his time at Hunter Elementary and catching up on life. Finally we said our good-byes, promising to keep in touch. He took a couple of steps away and then turned around and said, "Oh yeah, I still have the canopic jar that I made in your class, and I keep it right next to my diploma! Thanks for everything." It was a day that I will never forget.

I have been a teacher of the gifted for 22 years. All of that time has been spent in various positions at the Hunter College Elementary School in New York City. This school is unique. The average IQ of our students is about 150, and they come from all racial and ethnic groups in the borough of Manhattan.

Here in New York City, and, I'm sure, elsewhere, there seems to be a public assumption that teaching gifted children is an elitist position and that they are members of an elitist population. I beg to differ. *All* children deserve an education that is developmentally appropriate and differentiated in a manner that meets their needs. Gifted children are entitled to the same services that one would provide to any other category of child in need. Each year we welcome bright little children to an elementary school experience that focuses on fast-paced, in-depth learning not available in most elementary schools. The school is tuition-free, and we help train many student teachers not only from Hunter College but also from Teachers College at Columbia University and other city colleges.

After teaching in kindergarten, first grade, second grade, and several mixed-age early childhood classes, and after a stint as the after-school program coordinator, I am now the principal of Hunter. The students are taught in self-contained classrooms of 24 students each with a head teacher (and an assistant teacher in the primary grades). We have specialists in science, mathematics, the arts, music, chess, learning disabilities (yes, some gifted children have learning disabilities), foreign languages, and physical education.

We have several objectives for our students. These encompass not only academic intelligence but emotional intelligence. Students are guided to become independent thinkers who can work both critically and creatively. We plan interdisciplinary instruction so that the depth and breadth of educational experiences will afford students opportunities to see and make connections across and within curricula areas. For example, among the mathematics goals in kindergarten are that the child should understand the meaning of numbers in the real world. The concept of symmetry should be introduced. Whole numbers through 20, sorting by attributes, tallying and organizing information, graphing, picture graphs, bar graphs, estimation, comparison of sets, number patterns, introduction of addition and subtraction algorithms, addition facts to 10, and counting by numbers other than 1 should be part of the kindergarten mathematics curriculum for academically talented children. As the reader can see, these are advanced academic objectives because gifted children are precocious—that is, they have academic abilities similar to children who are several years older than they are.

Based on the work of Daniel Goleman (1985), we have created a parallel curriculum in emotional intelligence that determines how well one uses the raw intellect that he or she possesses. The following goals are important in educating the young gifted child for emotional intelligence:

1. *Children will be able to see things from another's point of view (empathy).* When reading books, children are asked to find alternative endings based on another character's point of view. Reading the book *The True Story of the Three Little Pigs* by Jon Scieszka is a wonderful way to introduce children to this concept.
2. *Children will be able to control impulsive behavior (self-awareness).* Using a traffic light as a metaphor, children are asked to take a signal from themselves whenever they are feeling upset. The upset feeling is like the red light: they should stop and take a moment to take note of what they are feeling. Next comes the yellow light, a time to use a few moments to think about several ways in which they might respond to that feeling. Finally, they are encouraged to choose the best response from the ones that they've thought of; and like the green light, they go with the best decision.
3. *Children will be able to communicate clearly and effectively (communication and cooperation).* Students are given many opportunities each day to respond to one another's questions during reading, social studies, and math lessons.

We also collaborate with families. I have always had an open-door policy and encourage parents to be contributors to the educational process. Each year I send out a parent survey. I try to ensure that all families participate in a classroom activity every year. Parents may accompany the class on a field trip, bind student books, make costumes for a class play, give a lecture on a specific area of study (e.g., one parent doctor came in to discuss the human heart), etc.

What I like most about being a special educator is that it allows me to specialize in an area and become an expert in a field. I can focus on securing information and resources. My most meaningful accomplishment is moving from simply attending conferences to learn about gifted education to being a speaker at gifted conferences. Thus, I am able to give back to the community. On a personal teacher/child level, the love that one receives from the children in the class is incomparable. What I like least is common to most teachers. The remuneration for the countless hours that one puts into activities such as developing lessons, individualizing instruction, attending work-related functions, and continuing education is not commensurate with the position.

However, having been an educator for such a long time, I have difficulty imagining doing anything else with my life. Being not only a teacher but a counselor, a nurturer, a role model, a nurse, an arbitrator, a politician, and all the other roles that one must assume when teaching a special population of children is physically demanding, but I have developed stamina over time. Teachers of the gifted and talented also need humility, for there is always a child who's smarter than you in some area. Teaching the gifted and talented is an intense experience that takes much more time than a day holds.

After spending seven years with us, most of our students attend Hunter College High School, which shares our building. They then go to academically challenging colleges, many in the Ivy League. They start with their special education as four-year-olds and continue throughout their academic lives.

For more information about Patricia Lambert and Hunter College Elementary School, go to the Teacher Feature module on the Companion Website at **www.prenhall.com/heward**

Our study of exceptional children thus far has focused on students with intellectual, behavioral, sensory, or physical disabilities—children who require specially designed instruction to benefit from education. Gifted and talented students lie on the other end of the continuum of cognitive, academic, artistic, and social abilities. Gifted and talented children may find that a traditional curriculum is inappropriate; it may not provide the advanced and unique challenges they require to learn most effectively. They, too, need special education to reach their potential.

Janie has just completed her report on the solar system and is word-processing it for class tomorrow. She looks out her bedroom window and wonders what might be happening on the countless planets that circle all of those stars. And she thinks about the circumstances that made life possible on the third planet from the star called Sol. What Janie is doing may not seem special; after all, most students type school reports and wonder about extraterrestrial life—until we learn that she is just 6 years old. Janie is functioning years ahead of her peers. She writes in complete sentences, expresses herself exceptionally well, and has a powerful urge to know the answers to many and varied problems.

To better understand what will be covered in this chapter, go to the Essential Concepts and Chapter-at-a-Glance modules in Chapter 14 of the Companion Website at **www.prenhall.com/heward**

Toney Jojola saunters down a dusty back road near his home in the southwestern United States. Toney is excited because today his mentor and great-aunt has promised to teach him the process of applying the rich charcoal slip to the pottery he is making. His people have been making pottery for hundreds of years, but somehow it seems to take on multiple meanings in his hands. He notices and uses small variations in color and texture to embed his favorite symbol of the winged serpent into his pieces. Toney does not say much in school or express himself very well in writing, but he understands everything that is being said and talked about. During class he dreams of the pottery designs he will someday create.

Malcolm, a ninth grader, runs from school to the bus stop for the bus that will take him to the local university, where he is taking his second course in creative writing. He is excited about showing his latest short story to the professor. He believes he has a message that must be heard; he is powerfully moved to reach out to the disaffected, the disenfranchised, as well as the ambivalent of all races. He has many ideas for changing what he believes is wrong with his government. Bursting with energy and desire, Malcolm struggles to sit still while the bus moves him ever closer to his training ground for the future.

Janie, Toney, and Malcolm need special education—in the form of curriculum modifications and specialized instructional activities—to enhance and develop their individual talents. These precocious youngsters, and others like them, will become the outstanding scientists, artists, writers, inventors, and leaders of the future. Understanding and working to develop the talents of these exceptional children is an important undertaking of special educators who work in the area of gifted and talented education.

DEFINITIONS

Intelligence, creativity, and talent have been central to the various definitions of giftedness that have been proposed over the years. Lewis Terman (1925), one of the pioneers of the field, defined the gifted as those who score in the top 2% on standardized tests of intelligence. Guilford (1967) called for the identification of people with creative potential. Witty (1951), recognizing the value of including special skills and talents, described gifted and talented children as those "whose performance is consistently remarkable in any potentially valuable area" (p. 62). These three concepts continue to be reflected in the current and still-evolving definitions of gifted and talented children.

FEDERAL DEFINITIONS

The first federal definition of the gifted and talented came with the 1972 Marland Report. This definition said that gifted and talented children were found in six areas:

> Children capable of high performance include those with demonstrated and/or potential ability in any of the following areas, singly or in combination:
>
> - General intellectual ability
> - Specific academic aptitude
> - Creative or productive thinking
> - Leadership ability
> - Ability in the visual or performing arts
> - Psychomotor ability (Marland, 1972, p. 5)

The Marland definition had a strong influence on early state definitions. Since its beginnings, the field of the gifted and talented education has sought to include multiple kinds of giftedness in its definitions, not just the high IQ or superior cognitive type of giftedness. In 1978, the federal definition was revised to eliminate psychomotor ability and to include preschool children and adolescents.

In 1991, a revised definition of gifted and talented children was motivated by new cognitive research and concerns about the inequity in participation in programs for the intellectually gifted. In this report, called *National Excellence: A Case for Developing America's Talent,* the word *gifted* was eliminated, and the terms *outstanding talent* and *exceptional talent* were embraced. The definition proposed that giftedness—or talent—occurs in all groups across all cultures and is not necessarily revealed in test scores but in a person's "high performance capability" in the intellectual, creative, and artistic realms. Giftedness is said to connote "a mature power rather than a developing ability." Talent is to be found by "observing students at work in rich and varied educational settings." The best way to find talented children is by "providing opportunities and observing performance" (pp. 54, 55). Here is how the new federal definition goes:

> Children and youth with outstanding talent perform or show the potential for performing at remarkably high levels of accomplishment when compared with others of their age, experience, or environment.
>
> These children and youth exhibit high performance capability in intellectual, creative, and/or artistic areas, possess an unusual leadership capacity, or excel in specific academic fields. They require services or activities not ordinarily provided by the schools.
>
> Outstanding talents are present in children and youth from all cultural groups, across all economic strata, and in all areas of human endeavor. (*National Excellence,* 1993, pp. 54–57)

A recent survey (Stephens & Karnes, 2000) found that many state departments of education have incorporated components of the *National Excellence* definition into their defini-

---

Early definitions of G&T and Marland report

 Content Standards for Beginning Teachers–G&T: Historical foundations of gifted and talented education (GT1K1) (also, CC1K5).

Current federal definition of G&T

 Content Standards for Beginning Teachers–G&T: Issues in definition and identification of individuals with gifts and talents, including those from culturally and linguistically diverse backgrounds (GT1K5).

tions of giftedness and talent. Although the general intelligence test element of the definition prevails (39 states consider superior cognitive ability as giftedness), 33 states include specific academic ability, 30 include creative thinking, 20 include the visual and performing arts, and 18 include leadership in their definitions of giftedness and talent.

OTHER KEY CONTEMPORARY AND COMPLEMENTARY DEFINITIONS

This new conception of giftedness shows our growing recognition of the importance of balancing theoretical with practical definitions of giftedness that emphasize situated problem solving (Sternberg, 1988; Sternberg & Grigorenko, 2000); talents that are context- and domain-related (Gagné, 1995; Gardner, 1983; Piirto, 1999, 2001); and the influence of sustained, deliberate practice on the realization of a child's talent (Ericsson, 2001; Ericsson & Charness, 1994). The following four definitions of gifted and talented students are widely cited examples of this contemporary view.

Renzulli's Three-Trait Definition Renzulli's (1978) definition of giftedness is based on an interaction among three basic clusters of human traits: (1) above-average general intellectual abilities, (2) a high level of task commitment, and (3) creativity. Gifted and talented children are those

> possessing or capable of developing this composite set of traits and applying them to any potentially valuable area of human performance. Children who manifest or are capable of developing an interaction among the three clusters require a wide variety of educational opportunities and services that are not ordinarily provided through regular instructional programs. (p. 184)

Figure 14.1 illustrates how the three components of ability (actual or potential), task commitment, and creative expression are jointly applied to a valuable area of human endeavor. Like the federal definition, Renzulli's definition provides a great deal of freedom in determining who is considered gifted and talented, depending on the interpretation of

Renzulli's, Piirto's, Maker's, and Sternberg's conceptions of G&T

Council for Exceptional Children   Content Standards for Beginning Teachers–G&T: Issues in definition and identification of individuals with gifts and talents, including those from culturally and linguistically diverse backgrounds (GT1K5).

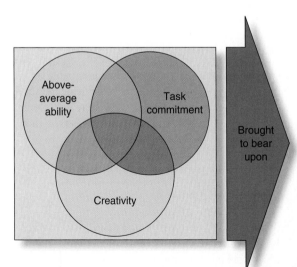

General Performance Areas

Mathematics • Visual Arts • Physical Sciences • Philosophy • Social Sciences • Law • Religion • Language Arts • Music • Life Sciences • Movement Arts

Specific Performance Areas

Cartooning • Astronomy • Public Opinion Polling • Jewelry Design • Map Making • Choreography • Biography • Film Making • Statistics • Local History • Electronics • Musical Composition • Landscape Architecture • Chemistry • Demography • Microphotography • City Planning • Pollution Control • Poetry • Fashion Design • Weaving • Play Writing • Advertising • Costume Design • Meteorology • Puppetry • Marketing • Game Design • Journalism • Electronic Music • Child Care • Consumer Protection • Cooking • Ornithology • Furniture Design • Navigation • Genealogy • Sculpture • Wildlife Management • Set Design • Agricultural Research • Animal Learning • Film Criticism • etc.

FIGURE 14.1 Renzulli's three-component definition of giftedness

Source: Reprinted from Renzulli, J. S. (1978). What makes giftedness? Reexamining a definition. *Phi Delta Kappan, 60,* 184. Used by permission.

"valuable human performance." In a general sense, Renzulli's model merges some acknowledged components of superior performance, including fundamentally high levels of intellectual capability, the ability to innovate and synthesize information, and the motivation necessary to spend a great deal of time working with media and materials.

Maker characterizes the gifted person as a creative problem solver who enjoys the challenge of complexity.

Piirto's Concept of Talent Development   Piirto (1999b) defines the gifted as

> those individuals who, by way of having certain learning characteristics such as superior memory, observational powers, curiosity, creativity, and the ability to learn school-related subject matters rapidly and accurately with a minimum of drill and repetition, have a right to an education that is differentiated according to those characteristics. (p. 28)

Such children become apparent early and should be served throughout their educational lives, from preschool through college. While they may or may not become producers of knowledge or makers of novelty, their education should give them the background to become adults who do produce knowledge or make new artistic and social products. Piirto's pyramid model emphasizes (1) a foundation of genetic endowment; (2) personality attributes such as drive, resilience, intuition, perception, intensity, and the like; (3) the minimum intelligence level necessary to function in the domain in which the talent is demonstrated; (4) talent in a specific domain such as mathematics, writing, visual arts, music, science, or athletics; and (5) the environmental influences of five "suns": (a) the sun of home, (b) the sun of community and culture, (c) the sun of school, (d) the sun of chance, and (e) the sun of gender (see Figure 14.2). Which talent is developed depends on the "thorn" of passion, calling, or sense of vocation

Maker's Problem-Solving Perspective   Maker's dynamic perspective incorporates the three elements that appear most often within contemporary definitions of the gifted and talented: high intelligence, high creativity, and excellent problem-solving skills (Maker, 1996). She characterizes a gifted person as

> a problem solver—one who enjoys the challenge of complexity and persists until the problem is solved in a satisfying way. Such an individual is capable of: a) creating a new or more clear definition of an existing problem, b) devising new and more efficient or effective methods, and c) reaching solutions that may be different from the usual, but are recognized as being effective, perhaps more effective, than previous solutions. (Maker, 1993, p. 71)

Sternberg's Triarchic Model   According to Sternberg's (1985) triarchic theory, intelligent behavior consists of three components or subprocesses:

1. *Practical intelligence:* how to get along in the world and adapt, select, and shape environments; includes the ability most often called common sense.
2. *Creative ability:* the ability to produce novel products, which are often made after a person learns something to the point at which it is automatic.
3. *Executive ability:* the metacognitive ability to monitor one's internal thinking processes.

Combining these three subprocesses to a high degree leads to what Sternberg calls "successful intelligence" (Sternberg & Grigorenko, 2000).

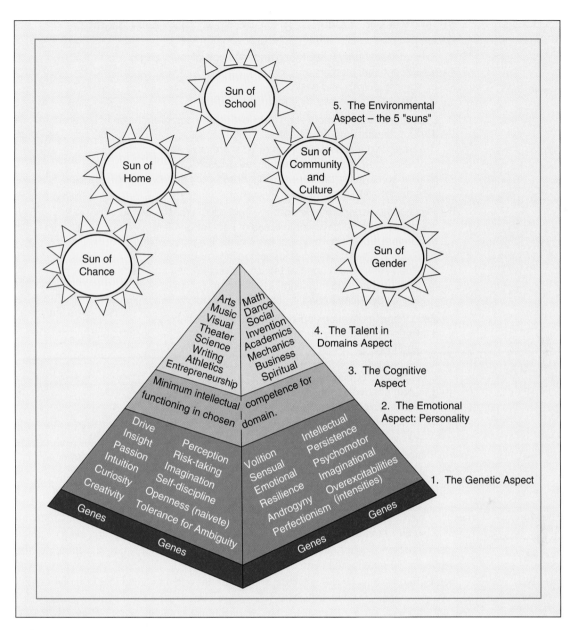

FIGURE 14.2 **Piirto pyramid of talent development**

Source: From Piirto, J. (2001). *"My teeming brain": Understanding creative writers.* Cresskill NJ: Hampton Press. Originally from Piirto, J. (1994). *Talented children and adults: Their development and education.* Upper Saddle River, NJ: Merrill/Prentice Hall. Used with permission.

To summarize, each of these definitions offers a perspective on the new conception of intelligence and giftedness that radically departs from previous definitions by broadening the understanding of talents, reducing the focus on IQ, and focusing on certain environmental and personality areas as well as specific talents.

 ## CHARACTERISTICS

Giftedness is a complex human condition covering a wide range of abilities and traits. While the definitions of giftedness are social constructions—that is, they are not absolute but vary according to situation—there is no doubt that advanced students have special educational needs. Some students have special talents, but rarely do these match the stereotypes that many people have of giftedness. These students may not be outstanding in academics, but

FIGURE 14.3 Identifiers of young gifted and talented children

1. *Exceptional learner* (acquisition and retention of knowledge)
   a. Exceptional memory
   b. Learns quickly and easily
   c. Advanced understanding/meaning of area

2. *Exceptional user of knowledge* (application and comprehension of knowledge)
   a. Exceptional use of knowledge
   b. Advanced use of symbol systems: expressive and complex.
   c. Demands a reason for unexplained events
   d. Reasons well in problem-solving: draws from previous knowledge and transfers it to other areas

3. *Exceptional generator of knowledge* (individual creative attributes)
   a. Highly creative behavior in areas of interest of talent
   b. Does not conform to typical ways of thinking, perceiving
   c. Enjoys self-expression of ideas, feelings or beliefs
   d. Keen sense of humor that reflects advanced, unusual comprehension of relationships and meaning
   e. Highly developed curiosity about causes, future, the unknown

4. *Exceptional motivation* (individual motivational attributes)
   a. Perfectionism: striving to achieve high standards, especially in areas of talent and interest
   b. Shows initiative; self-directed
   c. High level of inquiry and reflection
   d. Long attention span, when motivated
   e. Leadership: desire and ability to lead
   f. Intense desire to know

Source: From Shaklee et al. (1989). *Early assessment for educational potential and/or economically disadvantaged students.* Washington, DC: U.S. Department of Education.

Cognitive and learning characteristics of G&T

 Council for Exceptional Children   Content Standards for Beginning Teachers–G&T: Cognitive characteristics of individuals with gifts and talents in intellectual, academic, creative, leadership, and artistic domains (GT2K7).

they may have special abilities in areas such as music, dance, art, or leadership. Gifted and highly talented individuals are found across gender, cultural, linguistic, and even disability groups. Figure 14.3 identifies learning and intellectual characteristics of young children considered to be gifted and talented.

Some children may have intellectual abilities found only in 1 child in 1,000 or 1 child in 10,000. Silverman (1995) identifies the following characteristics for the highly gifted—children with IQ scores 3 standard deviations or greater above the mean (IQ greater than 145):

- Intense intellectual curiosity
- Fascination with words and ideas
- Perfectionism
- Need for precision
- Learning in great intuitive leaps
- Intense need for mental stimulation
- Difficulty conforming to the thinking of others
- Early moral and existential concern
- Tendency toward introversion (pp. 220–221)

We must also realize that many lists of gifted characteristics portray gifted children as having only virtues and no flaws. The very attributes by which we identify gifted children, however, can cause problems. High verbal ability, for example, may prompt gifted students to talk themselves out of troublesome situations or allow them to dominate class discussions. High curiosity may give them the appearance of being aggressive or snoopy as they

INDIVIDUAL DIFFERENCES AMONG GIFTED AND TALENTED STUDENTS

Awareness of individual differences is also important in understanding gifted students. Like other children, gifted children show both inter- and intraindividual differences. For example, if two students are given the same reading achievement test and each obtains a different score, we can speak of *interindividual* differences in reading achievement. If a student who obtains a high reading achievement score obtains a much lower score on an arithmetic achievement test, we say the student has an *intraindividual* difference across the two areas of performance. A graph of any student's abilities would reveal some high points and some lower points; scores would not be the same across all dimensions. The gifted student's overall pattern of performance, however, may be well above the average for that grade and/or age, as we see in Figure 14.4. Leslie performs higher in vocabulary and social studies than Jackie does, and Jackie shows higher performance in science and mathematics than Leslie does. These are interindividual differences. Each student also has intraindividual differences in scores. For example, Leslie has the vocabulary of an 11th grader but scores only at a 7th-grade equivalent in mathematics; Jackie earned grade equivalents of 10th grade in science and mathematics and 7th grade in writing.

Inter- and intraindividual differences

Council for Exceptional Children
Content Standards for Beginning Teachers–G&T: Similarities and differences of individuals with and without gifts and talents and the general population of learners (GT2K2). Similarities and differences among individuals with and without gifts and talents (GT2K3).

CREATIVITY

Many writers and teachers believe that creative ability is central to the definition of giftedness. Clark (1997) calls creativity "the highest form of giftedness" (p. 64) and Sternberg (1988) suggests that "gifted individuals who make the greatest long-range contributions to society are probably those whose gifts involve coping with novelty—specifically, in the area of insight. Creative and insightful individuals make discoveries and devise the inventions that ultimately change society" (p. 74).

Although we all profess to know creativity when we see it, there is no universally accepted definition of it. Guilford (1959, 1967, 1987), who studied the emergence of creativity as one aspect of his overall theory concerning human intelligence, describes these dimensions of cognitive creative behavior, which he called *divergent production,* in his structure of intellect model:

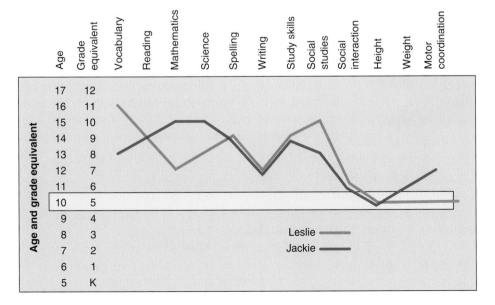

FIGURE 14.4
Profiles of two gifted and talented students, both age 10 and in fifth grade

Guildford's elements of creativity

 Council for Exceptional Children Content Standards for Beginning Teachers–G&T: Cognitive characteristics of individuals with gifts and talents in intellectual, academic, creative, leadership, and artistic domains (GT2K7) (also, GT2K2, GT7K3).

- *Fluency.* The creative person is capable of producing many ideas per unit of time.
- *Flexibility.* A wide variety of ideas, unusual ideas, and alternative solutions are offered.
- *Novelty/originality.* Unique, low-probability words and responses are used; the creative person has novel ideas.
- *Elaboration.* The ability to provide details is evidenced.
- *Synthesizing ability.* The person has the ability to juxtapose unlikely ideas.
- *Analyzing ability.* The person has the ability to organize ideas into larger, inclusive patterns. Symbolic structures must often be broken down before they can be reformed into new ones.
- *Ability to reorganize or redefine existing ideas.* The ability to transform an existing object into one of different design, function, or use is evident.
- *Complexity.* The ability to manipulate many interrelated ideas at the same time is shown.

Piirto (1998, 2001) studied creative individuals in a variety of areas and summarized the characteristics of highly creative individuals within their fields of creativity, thus linking their high abilities to particular areas of expertise. She reports that (1) each of these fields has specific predictive behaviors in childhood, (2) there is a developmental process in the emergence of talents in various domains, and (3) IQ scores should be minimized in importance and subsumed into a more contextual view of children who are performing tasks within specific domains. Piirto maintains that all people are creative, that creativity is more an aspect of personality than a type of giftedness, and that testing for creative potential is often invalid and unreliable.

Although many gifted and talented students do become scientists, physicians, inventors, and great artists and performers, they have no obligation to do so. Providing them with the differentiated education they need should not be predicated on an expectation that they "owe society" any more than all children do.

> These children have no greater obligation than any other children to be future leaders or world-class geniuses. They should just be given a chance to be themselves, children who might like to classify their collection of baseball cards by the middle initial of the players, or who might like to spend endless afternoon hours in dreamy reading of novels, and to have an education that appreciates and serves these behaviors. (Piirto, 1999a, pp. 28–29)

It is often difficult to differentiate between the concepts of talent and creativity, perhaps because they may exist on a continuum rather than as separate entities. If we examine the life of a highly talented individual, such as the famous dancer Martha Graham, we can see the relationship between creativity and talent. Her creativity is evident in her pioneering modern dance techniques and her innovative methods of expression in the choreography of the dance. However, her great talent as a dancer, seen in her elegant movements, is equally impressive and serves notice that not only was she a talented dancer but she also created new dances with great meaning and impact on the viewer. Gifted and talented children are most often identified by creativity, talent, and/or extreme intellectual ability that is atypical for their age. See Profiles & Perspectives, "Precocity As a Hallmark of Giftedness," later in this chapter.

Gifted and talented children can often be identified by their precociousness. Although just 16 years old, Alexandra Nechita is one of the world's most recognized artists. Her unique abstract style was evident at the age of four.

PREVALENCE

Using the normal curve, one would predict that 3 to 5 percent of students would be gifted and talented in the category of superior cognitive ability, scoring 2 standard deviations or

Precocity As a Hallmark of Giftedness

by Jane Piirto

Four-year-old Maria has been waiting and waiting to go to school. She plays school all the time. She is the teacher, and her dolls are the students. At her day care center, she is the one who always leads the other kids in games because she is the only one who can read. The other kids look up to her, except when she tries to make them do things they really don't want to do, such as count by twos. The day care center teacher told Maria's mother that Maria was very bright. When Maria went for her preschool screening, the district recommended that the school psychologist test her. The school psychologist told Maria's mother that Maria had an IQ of 145 on the Stanford-Binet Intelligence Scale, a score that put her in the 99th percentile. This score would qualify her for the district's program for the academically talented, which starts at the third grade, although they do have enrichment lessons in first and second grade.

Finally, Maria turns 5, and it is the first day of school. She wears her new dress and new shoes. Her mother braids her hair and fastens it with new barrettes. When she gets to school, she is anxious for her mother to leave yet feels shy among all of the children. As they come into the room, the children are given large nametags. Half of them are crying as their parents leave them. Maria looks around the room and sees a shelf of books. She always reads when she doesn't know what else to do, so she goes over to the shelf and waits for things to calm down.

After all of the parents have gone, the teacher tells the children to sit on a line painted on the floor. She sits on a small chair with the children in a semicircle around her and says, "My name is Mrs. Miller, boys and girls. Welcome to kindergarten. In kindergarten, we will learn our letters and our numbers so that we can learn to read in first grade."

"I can read already," Maria says, jumping up.

"That's nice," says Mrs. Miller. "Maria, when we want to talk, first we must stand, and then we must wait until Mrs. Miller calls on us."

"But I can read already!" Maria's voice gets petulant, and tears form in the corners of her eyes.

"Maria, that's nice," said Mrs. Miller. "But in kindergarten, we will learn how to read right. Please sit down now."

Maria is chagrined. Feeling shame and embarrassment, she sits down. She has taken the first step to underachievement.

Underachievement is the prevailing situation in the education of academically talented young children in most schools today. By the time she has been socialized into the kindergarten milieu, Maria will have learned to keep quiet about her abilities and even to suppress that she can read. In first grade, she will comply with the reading tasks in order to fit in. By second grade, even though she will be getting all of her work right, she will have learned that she doesn't have to put forth any effort in school in order to be the best student. By third grade, she will have learned that boredom (as long as she's quietly bored) and waiting (as long as she's not disruptive while she's waiting) are what the school seems to expect of her. By fourth grade, when she gets into a pullout program for academically talented students, she will resent it when the teacher of the academically talented tries to challenge her and, in challenging her, stretches her capabilities. Maria's story, unfortunately, is typical of many young academically talented children who enter the public school system.

Maria's scenario indicates the types of precocious behavior talented students might display when their abilities are great. Like other young gifted and talented children, Maria can easily do things typically seen only in older children. Even without special testing, their talents can be spotted by teachers who are sensitive to the concept of *precocity*. In fact, I believe the main way to recognize talented students is by their precocity: achievements resembling those of older children. I call these behaviors *predictive behaviors*. These children are often difficult to locate because they might wish to fit in and not to create disturbances; but their talents can be found by teachers, parents, and educators who look closely.

Prevalence of G&T

 Content
Standards for
Beginning Teachers–G&T:
Incidence and prevalence of
individuals with gifts and talents
(GT1K6).

more above the mean on a standardized intelligence test. If we include those students regarded as highly talented, estimates for the prevalence of giftedness can range as high as 10 to 15 percent of the total school-age population (Renzulli & Reis, 1997).

During the 1998–1999 school year, 43 states reported serving more than 2 million students in K–12 gifted programs (Council of State Directors of Programs for the Gifted, 2000). This number ranks gifted and talented students as the second-largest group of exceptional children receiving special education services. The number and percentage of students identified as gifted and talented vary widely from state to state; for instance, six states identified more than 10% of the student population as gifted and talented, and six states identified 3% or less.

On the basis of an estimate that gifted and talented children comprise 5% of the school-age population, approximately 2.5 million additional gifted and talented children may need special education (Clark, 2002). This discrepancy between need and the level of service may make gifted and talented children the most underserved group of exceptional children.

IDENTIFICATION AND ASSESSMENT

A multifactored assessment approach that uses information from a variety of sources is considered to be more accurate and equitable in identification of the gifted and talented. This approach includes data from a variety of sources, including the following:

- Group and individual intelligence tests
- Achievement tests
- Portfolios of student work
- Teacher nomination based on reports of student behavior in the classroom
- Parent nomination
- Self-nomination
- Peer nomination
- Extracurricular or leisure activities

*Multidimensional screening for
G&T students*

 Content
Standards for
Beginning Teachers–G&T:
Screening, pre-referral, referral,
and identification procedures
for individuals with gifts and
talents (GT8K4).

Each state has its own identification procedures. Figure 14.5 illustrates one comprehensive approach for identifying students who require specialized services for their talents. Based on an identification process first developed by the California Association for Gifted Children, this model features a progressive filtering process that refines a large pool of potentially gifted students to a smaller, formally identified group. The process is time-consuming and thorough, beginning with the development of a large pool of potentially gifted students in the initial stage (screening); testing, consulting, and analyzing data (development of profile and case study); identification decisions and placement (committee meeting for consideration, placement in gifted program); and finally the development of an appropriate educational program for the child.

We can demonstrate how this process would work with a student thought to have great potential—say, the little girl Janie described at the beginning of this chapter. First, Janie's highly refined intellectual behaviors would have to be noticed by a teacher, parent, her peers, or another person, who would then forward a nomination for additional screening. Figure 14.6 shows questions that Janie's teacher might ask. The teacher's report would contribute to the multidimensional, or multifactored, screening approach that is gaining in popularity among educators of the gifted and talented.

Multidimensional screening also involves a rigorous examination of teacher reports, family history, student inventories, and work samples and perhaps the administration of group achievement or group or individual intelligence tests. The coordinator of gifted services at the school or district level reviews this information and determines whether the results indicate a potential for giftedness and justify the referral of the case to a placement committee. If the coordinator believes there is sufficient evidence to continue, the parents are asked if they would like to refer Janie for more extensive testing to determine whether she qualifies for gifted services. The coordinator then manages the development of a case

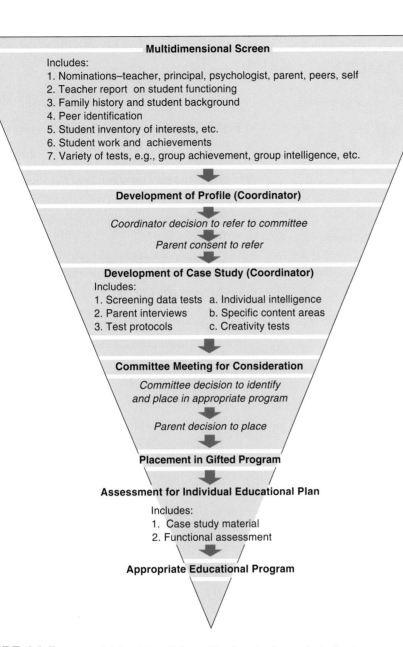

Multidimensional Screen

Includes:
1. Nominations–teacher, principal, psychologist, parent, peers, self
2. Teacher report on student functioning
3. Family history and student background
4. Peer identification
5. Student inventory of interests, etc.
6. Student work and achievements
7. Variety of tests, e.g., group achievement, group intelligence, etc.

Development of Profile (Coordinator)

Coordinator decision to refer to committee

Parent consent to refer

Development of Case Study (Coordinator)

Includes:
1. Screening data tests   a. Individual intelligence
2. Parent interviews   b. Specific content areas
3. Test protocols   c. Creativity tests

Committee Meeting for Consideration

*Committee decision to identify
and place in appropriate program*

Parent decision to place

Placement in Gifted Program

Assessment for Individual Educational Plan

Includes:
1. Case study material
2. Functional assessment

Appropriate Educational Program

FIGURE 14.5   A model for identifying gifted and talented students

Source: From Clark, B. A. (2002). *Growing up gifted* (6th ed.), (p. 333). Upper Saddle River, NJ: Merrill/Prentice Hall. Reprinted by permission.

study that includes screening data, parent interviews, test protocols, an individual intelligence test, tests in specific content areas, and creativity tests. These data are compiled, organized, and presented to the placement committee for consideration. The committee determines whether Janie qualifies for services and what type of program would be best suited for her particular pattern of giftedness. The parents are an integral part of this meeting and have to agree with the results and placement decisions that are developed in committee. Janie is then placed in a gifted program, and the special education teacher or person in charge of the program initiates special services. This level of assessment is more focused and uses all of the previous case study materials and other assessment data to determine where Janie should start in the program and the overall focus of the special education services she will receive.

FIGURE 14.6 Questions about classroom behavior that can guide a teacher's efforts to identify students who may be gifted and talented

In the classroom does the child

- Ask a lot of questions?
- Show a lot of interest in progress?
- Have lots of information on many things?
- Want to know why or how something is so?
- Become unusually upset at injustices?
- Seem interested and concerned about social or political problems?
- Often have a better reason than you do for not doing what you want done?
- Refuse to drill on spelling, math facts, flash cards, or handwriting?
- Criticize others for dumb ideas?
- Become impatient if work is not "perfect"?
- Seem to be a loner?
- Seem bored and often have nothing to do?
- Complete only part of an assignment or project and then take off in a new direction?
- Stick to a subject long after the class has gone on to other things?
- Seem restless, out of seat often?
- Daydream?
- Seem to understand easily?
- Like solving puzzles and problems?
- Have his or her own idea about how something should be done? And stay with it?
- Talk a lot?
- Love metaphors and abstract ideas?
- Love debating issues?

This child may be showing giftedness cognitively.

Does the child

- Show unusual ability in some area? Maybe reading or math?
- Show fascination with one field of interest? And manage to include this interest in all discussion topics?
- Enjoy meeting or talking with experts in this field?

- Get math answers correct, but find it difficult to tell you how?
- Enjoy graphing everything? Seem obsessed with probabilities?
- Invent new obscure systems and codes?

This child may be showing giftedness academically.

Does the child

- Try to do things in different, unusual, imaginative ways?
- Have a really zany sense of humor?
- Enjoy new routines or spontaneous activities?
- Love variety and novelty?
- Create problems with no apparent solutions? And enjoy asking you to solve them?
- Love controversial and unusual questions?
- Have a vivid imagination?
- Seem never to proceed sequentially?

This child may be showing giftedness creatively.

Does the child

- Organize and lead group activities? Sometimes take over?
- Enjoy taking risks?
- Seem cocky, self-assured?
- Enjoy decision making? Stay with that decision?
- Synthesize ideas and information from a lot of different sources?

This child may be showing giftedness through leadership ability.

Does the child

- Seem to pick up skills in the arts—music, dance, drama, painting, etc.—without instruction?
- Invent new techniques? Experiment?
- See minute detail in products or performances?
- Have high sensory sensitivity?

This child may be showing giftedness through visual or performing arts ability.

Source: From Clark, B. A. (2002). *Growing up gifted* (6th ed.), (p. 332). Upper Saddle River, NJ: Merrill/Prentice Hall. Reprinted by permission.

MULTICULTURAL ASSESSMENT AND IDENTIFICATION

Biases inherent in the identification process are primarily to blame for the underrepresentation of students from groups such as African Americans, Latinos, and Native Americans in gifted programs nationally (Ford, 1998; Montgomery, 2001; Plummer, 1995; Van Tassel-Baska, Patton, & Prillaman, 1991). In addition, minorities are not entering many important fields requiring mathematics and science skills. For example, although African Americans make up 12% of the population, they earn just 5% of the bachelor's degrees awarded each year in mathematics and science, receive only 1% of the doctoral degrees, and make up just 2% of all employed scientists and engineers in this country. Hispanics comprise 9% of the population but represent just 3% of the bachelor's degrees in science and mathematics, 2% of the doctoral degrees, and 2% of all employed scientists in this country (U.S. Department of Education, 1991).

Many youth from special populations have not had extensive opportunities to develop a broad pattern of giftedness, but they have often developed special talents within a particular domain. The identification process should be designed to find those special talents. Subsequent educational services should focus on facilitating growth in the talent areas. Current best practices for identifying gifted and talented students from diverse cultural groups involve a multifactored, or multidimensional, assessment process that meets these criteria (Clark, 2002; Ford, 1998; Frasier, Garcia, & Passow, 1995; Frasier et al., 1995; Maker, 1996; Montgomery, 2001; Ortiz & Gonzales, 1991; Plummer, 1995; Tonemah, 1987; Woliver & Woliver, 1991):

▲ Assessment of young children's abilities to solve mathematical-spatial problems might include the time used to complete puzzles, the number of puzzles completed, and the particular problem-solving strategies used by the child.

- Identification should have a goal of inclusion rather than exclusion.
- Information should be gathered from multiple sources providing both objective and subjective data (e.g., parent interviews, individual intelligence testing, performance on group problem-solving tasks, motivational and behavioral factors, individual conferences with candidates).
- A combination of formal and informal testing techniques, including teacher referrals, the results of intelligence tests, and individual achievement tests, should be used.
- A generally greater sensitivity to aspects of acculturation and assimilation that allows for multiple perspectives to be identified and honored should be demonstrated.
- Identification procedures should begin as early as possible—before children are exposed to prejudice and stereotyping—and be continuous.
- Unconventional measures involving arts and aesthetic expression such as dance, music, creative writing, and crafts should be used.
- Information gathered during the identification process should help determine the curriculum.

Issues and procedures for identifying G&T children from diverse cultural groups

 Council for Exceptional Children — Content Standards for Beginning Teachers–G&T: Issues in definition and identification of individuals with gifts and talents, including those from culturally and linguistically diverse backgrounds (GT1K5) (also, GT3K7, GT8K5).

Maker (1997) developed a procedure called DISCOVER, which has been used to assess children from diverse cultural groups and females in an equitable fashion. Based on Gardner's theoretical framework of multiple intelligences, the DISCOVER assessment process involves a series of five progressively more complex problems that provide children with various ways to demonstrate their problem-solving competence by interacting with the content and one another.

Problem Types I and II require convergent thinking and are most similar to the types of question found on standardized intelligence and achievement tests. Type I problems are highly structured. The solver knows the solution method and must recall or derive the correct answer and involve convergent thinking. Type II problems also are highly structured, but the solver must decide on the correct method to use. Type III problems are clearly structured, but a range of methods can be used to solve them and they have a range of acceptable answers. Type IV and V problems are more open ended, less structured, and require much more divergent thinking. . . . Type IV problems are commonly found in tests of creativity. Type V problems are extremely ill structured. The solver must explore the possibilities, identify the questions to be answered, and determine the criteria by which an effective solution will be recognized. (Maker, Nielson, & Rogers, 1994, p. 7)

Figure 14.7 shows an example of DISCOVER problem-solving activities for four types of intelligences for children in grades K–2. Children use a Pablo kit, a 21-piece set of tangrams (geometric shapes), to demonstrate their problem-solving abilities with mathematical-spatial problems. Observers record the time used to complete the puzzles, the number of puzzles

DSCOVER problem-solving activities

Council for Exceptional Children — Content Standards for Beginning Teachers–G&T: Differing learning styles of individuals with gifts and talents including those from culturally diverse backgrounds and strategies for addressing these styles (GT3K7) (also, GT8K4, GT8K5).

FIGURE 14.7 Examples of activities for assessing K–2 children's problem-solving competence across four different types of intelligence

Activities and Intelligences	Problem Type				
	Type I	Type II	Type III	Type IV	Type V
Spatial	Find a piece shaped like a ____. (Teacher shows a shape.)	Find pieces that look like a rainbow. (Observer shows pictures.)	Find pieces and make mountains. (Observer shows pictures.)	Make any animal with as many pieces as you need. Tell about your animal if you want. (Observer provides connectors.)	Make anything you want to make. Tell about it if you wish.
Mathematical-Spatial	Complete simple tangram puzzles with a one-to-one correspondence between the tangram pieces and the puzzles.	Complete simple tangram puzzles with more than one solution that works.	Complete complex tangram puzzles with multiple solutions.	Make a square with as many tangram pieces as you can.	Make a design or a pattern with the pieces.
Mathematical	Complete one- and two-digit addition and subtraction problems.	Complete magic squares using addition and subtraction.	Write correct number sentences using numbers given (in any order).	Write as many correct number problems as you can with an answer of 10.	None
Linguistic	Provide a label for toys given.	Make groups of toys and tell how items in the group are alike. (Some are obvious.)	Make different groups of toys and tell how items in each group are alike. (Encourage going beyond the obvious.)	Tell a story that includes all your toys.	Write a story about a personal experience, something you made up, or anything you wish.

Source: From "Giftedness, Diversity, and Problem-Solving" by C. J. Maker, A. B. Nielson, & J. A. Rogers. *Teaching Exceptional Children, 27*(1), 1994, p. 9. © 1994 by the Council for Exceptional Children. Reprinted with permission.

completed, and particular problem-solving strategies used by the child. A bag of toys provides the materials for assessing the child's linguistic (storytelling) skills.

Maker et al. (1994; Sarouphim, 2001) report positive results from using the DISCOVER model to assess the problem-solving abilities of students from African American, Navajo, Tohono O'Odham, and Mexican American cultural groups: (1) the children identified by the process closely resemble the cultural characteristics of the communities from which they come; (2) equitable percentages of children from various ethnic, cultural, linguistic, and economic groups are identified; (3) the process is equally effective with boys and girls; and (4) students identified through the process make gains equal to or greater than those of students who were identified by traditional standardized tests when placed in special enrichment programs.

 ## GIFTED AND TALENTED GIRLS

Cultural barriers; test and social biases; organizational reward systems; sex-role stereotyping; and conflicts among career, marriage, and family all act as external impediments to the advancement of gifted and talented women (Kerr, 1985). In reviewing the topic of gifted women, Silverman (1986) points out that the history of genius and women's roles has been contradictory (eminent contributions cannot be made from a subservient status) and that identification procedures reflect masculine (product-oriented) versus feminine (development-oriented) concepts of giftedness.

Thus, some of the key issues that appear in the literature concerning the identification and education of females who are gifted and talented involve conflicts concerning role definitions (McCormick & Wolf, 1993; Piirto, 1991; Rimm, 2000, 2002), extreme stress related to a lack of self-esteem (Genshaft, Greenbaum, & Borovosky, 1995), poor course selection based on academic choices made in middle school and high school (Clark, 2002), and a lack of parental and general community support for female achievements (Hollinger, 1995).

Identification of G&T girls and boys

 Council for Exceptional Children — Content Standards for Beginning Teachers–G&T: Issues in definition and identification of individuals with gifts and talents, including those from culturally and linguistically diverse backgrounds (GT1K5).

 ## GIFTED AND TALENTED BOYS

Recently, the problems and situations of gifted and talented boys have been highlighted as well (Kerr & Cohn, 2001). Among these are negative stereotyping for boys who have talent in and want to enter the arts, a boy code (Pollack, 1998) that operates against the expression of feelings and emotions, and a reluctance on the part of parents and teachers to permit boys' creative behaviors. "Gifted boys are confronted with the same pressures that all men in our society face, to become independent, strong, and competitive. However, being gifted puts a special burden on boys, not only to prove their masculinity, but also to develop their gifts" (Kerr & Cohn, p. 11).

 ## GIFTED AND TALENTED STUDENTS WITH DISABILITIES

It may be surprising to learn that the incidence of giftedness and talent among a large proportion of students with disabilities mirrors that of the larger general education population. So we would expect to have almost as many gifted students within the subpopulation of all students with disabilities. However, the combination of a disability and giftedness brings with it an even more complicated set of behaviors and attitudes to challenge educators and parents (Reis, Neu, & McGuire, 1995).

Whitmore and Maker (1985) conducted in-depth case studies of the needs and accomplishments of five gifted and talented students with visual, hearing, physical, and learning disabilities. They concluded that teachers and parents can foster the intellectual and talent development of children with disabilities by conveying positive, realistic expectations; encouraging independence; guiding constructive coping strategies; providing daily opportunities to build abilities and enjoy success; and pursuing positive social experiences for the child. Willard-Holt (1998), who reported case study analyses of the academic and personality characteristics of gifted students with cerebral palsy and no speech, drew similar implications for practice. (World-famous theoretical physicist Stephen W. Hawking talks about his views of the Big Bang singularity and quantum mechanics in Profiles & Perspectives, "I Was Thinking about Black Holes," later in this chapter.)

Identification of G&T students with disabilities

Council for Exceptional Children — Content Standards for Beginning Teachers–G&T: Issues in definition and identification of individuals with gifts and talents, including those from culturally and linguistically diverse backgrounds (GT1K5) (also, GT3K4, GT3K5).

I Was Thinking about Black Holes

by Stephen W. Hawking

Stephen W. Hawking is Lucasian Professor of Mathematics and Theoretical Physics at the University of Cambridge in England. He is considered by many to be the foremost theoretical physicist in the world today. His goal is to develop a grand unifying theory of the entire universe. Such a theory would encompass all known laws of science and describe how the universe began. While a student in college, he was diagnosed with amyotrophic lateral sclerosis (ALS), a degenerative disease of the nervous system sometimes called Lou Gehrig's disease. He uses a wheelchair for mobility and a computer-assisted synthetic speech generator to communicate (see "My Communication System" in Chapter 9).

I was born on January the 8th, 1942, exactly 300 years after the death of Galileo. However, I estimate that about 200,000 other babies were also born that day; I don't know whether any of them were later interested in astronomy. I was a fairly normal small boy, slow to learn to read, and very interested in how things worked. I was never more than about halfway up the class at school (it was a very bright class). When I was 12, one of my friends bet another friend a bag of sweets that I would never come to anything. I don't know if this bet was ever settled, and, if so, which way it was decided.

My father would have liked me to do medicine. However, I thought that biology was too descriptive and not sufficiently fundamental. Maybe I would have thought differently if I had been aware of molecular biology, but that was not generally known about at the time. Instead, I wanted to do mathematics, more mathematics, and physics. My father thought, however, that there would not be any jobs in mathematics, apart from teaching. He therefore made me do chemistry, physics, and only a small amount of mathematics. Another reason against mathematics was that he wanted me to go to his old College, University College, Oxford, and they did not do mathematics at that time. I duly went to University College in 1959 to do physics, which was the subject that in-terested me most, because it governs how the universe behaves. To me, mathematics is just a tool with which to do physics.

At that time, the physics course at Oxford was arranged in a way that made it particularly easy to avoid work. I did one exam before I went up and then had 3 years at Oxford, with just the final exam at the end. I once calculated that I did about 1,000 hours of work in the 3 years I was at Oxford, an average of an hour a day. I'm not proud of this lack of work, I'm just describing my attitude of complete boredom and feeling that nothing was worth making an effort for. One result of my illness has been to change all that; when you are faced with the possibility of an early death, it makes one realize that life is worth living and that there are lots of things you want to do.

Because of my lack of work, I had planned to get through the final exam by doing problems in theoretical physics and avoiding any questions that required factural knowledge, However, I didn't sleep the night before the exam because of nervous tension. So I didn't do very well. I was on the borderline between a first- and second-class degree, and I had to be interviewed by the examiners to determine which I should get. In the interview they asked me about my future plans. I replied I wanted to do research. If they gave me a first, I would go to Cambridge. If I only got a second, I would stay in Oxford. They gave me a first.

I thought there were two possible areas of theoretical physics that were fundamental and in which I might do research. One was cosmology, the study of the very large. The other was elementary particles, the study of the very small. However, I thought that elementary particles were less attractive because, although scientists were finding lots of new particles, there was no proper theory of elementary particles. All they could do was arrange the particles in families, like in botany. In cosmology, on the other hand, there was a well-defined theory, Einstein's General Theory of Relativity.

I had not done much mathematics at school or at Oxford, so I found General Relativity very difficult at first.

Also, during my last year at Oxford, I had noticed that I was getting rather clumsy in my movements. Soon after I went to Cambridge, I was diagnosed as having ALS, amyotrophic lateral sclerosis, or motor neuronic disease, as it is known in England. The doctors could offer no cure or assurance that it would not get worse. The only consolation they could give me was that I was not a typical case.

At first the disease seemed to progress fairly rapidly. There did not seem much point in working at my research because I didn't expect to live long enough to finish my Ph.D. However, as time went by, the disease seemed to slow down. I also began to understand General Relativity and to make progress with my work. However, what really made the difference was that I got engaged to a girl whom I had met about the time I was diagnosed with ALS. This gave me something to live for. If I were to get married, I had to get a job. And to get a job, I had to finish my Ph.D. I therefore started working hard for the first time in my life. To my surprise, I found I liked it. Maybe it is not really fair to call it work.

My research up to 1970 was in cosmology, the study of the universe on a large scale. My most important work in this period was on singularities. Observations of distant galaxies indicate that they are moving away from us: The universe is expanding. This implies that the galaxies must have been closer together in the past. The question then arises: Was there a time in the past when all of the galaxies were on top of each other and the density of the universe was infinite? Or was there a previous contracting phase, in which the galaxies managed to avoid hitting each other? Maybe they flew past each other and started to move away from each other. To answer this question required new mathematical techniques. These were developed between 1965 and 1970, mainly by Roger Penrose and myself. We used these techniques to show that there must have been a state of infinite density in the past, if the General Theory of Relativity was correct.

This state of infinite density is called the Big Bang singularity. It would be the beginning of the universe. All of the known laws of science would break down at a singularity. This would mean that science would not be able to predict how the universe would begin, if General Relativity is correct. However, my more recent work indicates that it is possible to predict how the universe would begin if one takes into account the theory of quantum mechanics, the theory of the very small.

General Relativity also predicts that massive stars will collapse in on themselves when they have exhausted their nuclear fuel. The work that Penrose and I had done showed that they would continue to collapse until they reached a singularity of infinite density. This singularity would be an end of time, at least for the star and anything on it. The gravitational field of the singularity would be so strong that light could not escape from a region around it, but would be dragged back by the gravitational field. The region from which it is not possible to escape is called a black hole, and its boundary is called the event horizon. Anything or anyone who falls into the black hole through the event horizon will come to an end of time at the singularity.

Stephen W. Hawking

I was thinking about black holes as I got into bed one night in 1970, shortly after the birth of my daughter, Lucy. Suddenly, I realized that many of the techniques that Penrose and I had developed to prove singularities could be applied to black holes.

In particular, the area of the event horizon, the boundary of the black hole, could not decrease with time. And when two black holes collided and joined together to form a single hole, the area of the horizon of the final hole would be greater than the sum of the areas of the horizons of the original black holes. This placed an important limit on the amount of energy that could be emitted in the collision. I was so excited that I did not get much sleep that night.

From 1970 to 1974, I worked mainly on black holes. But in 1974, I made perhaps my most surprising discovery: Black holes are not completely black! When one takes the small-scale behavior of matter into account, particles and radiation can leak out of a black hole. The black hole emits radiation as if it were a hot body.

Since 1974, I have been working on combining General Relativity and quantum mechanics into a consistent theory. One outcome of that work was a proposal I made with Jim Hartle that both space and time are finite in extent but they don't have any boundary or edge. They would be like the surface of the Earth, but with two more dimensions. The Earth's surface is finite in area, but it doesn't have any boundary.

If this proposal is correct, there would be no singularities, and the laws of science would hold everywhere, including at the beginning of the universe. The way the universe began would be determined by the laws of science. I would have succeeded in my ambition to discover how the universe began. But I still don't know why it began.

CURRICULUM AND INSTRUCTION

CURRICULAR GOALS

The overall goal of educational programs for gifted and talented students should be the fullest possible development of every child's actual and potential abilities. In the broadest terms, the educational goals for these youngsters are no different from those for all children. Feelings of self-worth, self-sufficiency, civic responsibility, and vocational and avocational competence are important for everyone. However, some additional specific educational outcomes are especially desirable for gifted and talented students.

Gifted students need both content knowledge and the abilities to develop and use that knowledge effectively. Most educators of gifted and talented students agree that the most important concern in developing appropriate curriculum is to match the students' specific needs with a qualitatively different curricular intervention. According to Kaplan (1988), a *differentiated curriculum* should do the following:

1. be responsive to the needs of the gifted student as both a member of the gifted population and as a member of the general population.
2. include or subsume aspects of the regular curriculum.
3. provide gifted students with opportunities to exhibit those characteristics that were instrumental in their identification as gifted individuals.
4. not academically or socially isolate these students from their peers.
5. not be used as either a reward or a punishment for gifted students. (p. 170)

Curriculum and instruction for gifted and talented students should also have the following characteristics:

- *Be based on learning characteristics of academically talented students in their area of strength.* These characteristics include "their ability to learn at a faster rate; their ability to think abstractly about content that is challenging; their ability to think productively, critically, creatively, and analytically; and their ability to constantly and rapidly increase their store of knowledge, both knowledge of facts and knowledge of processes and procedures" (Piirto, 1999b, p. 365).
- *Possess academic rigor.* The widespread abuse of grading practices, the dumbing down of the curriculum, and the lowered expectations of teachers have all sapped curriculum of its strength and rigor. Research skills, keyboarding and computer use, speed reading, at least one foreign language, and interpersonal and affective development should be systematically taught as part of the curriculum. There is a distinct need to increase the relevance, discipline, and depth of current curriculum, primarily within the regular education setting, where most gifted students are for most of the day. (See Profiles & Perspectives "Dumbing Down," later in this chapter.)
- *Be thematic and interdisciplinary.* Academically talented students should be exposed to the structures, terminologies, and methodologies of various disciplines. The

Functions and characteristics of differentiated curriculum

Council for Exceptional Children — Content Standards for Beginning Teachers–G&T: Differential curriculum needs of individuals with gifts and talents (GT7K6) (also, GT7K2, GT7K5).

The intellectual abilities and talents of children with disabilities can be fostered by providing daily opportunities for practicing superior abilities and for enjoying the feelings of success.

skills of systematic investigation are fundamental abilities that gifted students use throughout a lifetime of learning. These skills include the use of references, the use of the library, the gathering of information (data), and the reporting of findings in a variety of ways. These skills may ultimately be used in diverse settings, such as law and medical libraries, museums, chemical and electrical laboratories, theatrical archives, and national parks.

- *Be balanced and articulated.* Often a curriculum scope and sequence is not written for the education of the gifted and talented, and teachers do not know why, when, or what they should teach.

Gifted and talented students need exposure to a challenging and conceptually rich curriculum. Far too many gifted children are "languishing in the regular classroom, unable to focus their attention on material that was mastered long ago, is unbearably simplistic, and has been reiterated beyond their tolerance level" (Silverman, 1995, p. 220).

Feldhusen and Moon (1995) advocate the development of an individualized growth plan designed to develop a broad program of services for gifted and talented students. In some states (for example, Florida and Ohio), an individualized curriculum plan designed to develop a broad program of services for gifted and talented students is required or suggested. These plans differ from an IEP along several important dimensions: (1) they are not a requirement for services to be provided; (2) they are more flexible, having no time restrictions, reporting requirements, or physical boundaries; and (3) they are primarily collaboratively planned but essentially student-directed. The growth plan should include assessment information, student-generated goals (in consultation with others), and the recommended activities for accomplishing these goals. A key feature of this approach is that the student is guided toward the establishment of her own goals and is an active participant in all instructional and evaluative activities.

DIFFERENTIATING CURRICULUM: ACCELERATION AND ENRICHMENT

Differentiation is a broad term referring to a variety of strategies for providing gifted and talented students with a challenging and conceptually rich curriculum. Because gifted students learn at a faster rate and can absorb and reconfigure more concepts than most students, they benefit from a differentiated curriculum that is modified in both its pace and depth (Piirto, 1999b). **Acceleration** is the general term for modifying the pace at which the student moves through the curriculum; **enrichment** means probing or studying a subject at a greater depth than would occur in the regular curriculum.

Acceleration Acceleration is permitting a student to move as swiftly as possible through required curriculum content. Academically talented students often need less explanation; they just need to know the next step. What the classroom teacher decides to do to differentiate for the academically talented student depends on the subject matter. Subjects that are sequential are the most appropriate candidates for acceleration. In mathematics, a child must learn to add before subtracting, must learn to multiply before dividing. By the time an academically talented child is in the fourth grade, he or she will probably have mastered the skills of reading; enrichment with more difficult reading matter is a way of differentiation. However, in mathematics, the child must be taught; and the sequence of mathematics proceeds from arithmetic to algebra to calculus, and so on.

A young academically talented student attending a university summer program told how he had sat, bored, during a plane geometry class that was required at his school for intellectually and academically talented students but where testing out of a course was not permitted. To this student, plane geometry consisted of nothing but "two points on a line, two points on a line." Even though the plane geometry class was being offered to eighth graders (although in most schools it is offered to high school sophomores), this student had already mastered the material and was interested in fractal geometry. The high point in his

Acceleration

Council for
Exceptional
Children Content
Standards for
Beginning Teachers—G&T:
Acceleration, enrichment, and
counseling within a continuum
of service options for individuals with gifts and talents
(GT5K4) (also, GT7K2).

Dumbing Down: Pretending That All Students Are Equal Doesn't Make It So

by Robin Marantz Henig

Last summer, I ran into my neighbor when I dropped by the pool for an evening swim. She was sitting in the slanting sunshine, a closed paperback on her lap, and she and the other swim-team mothers waited for practice to end. I asked how her sons were enjoying the summer and she told me how well they were doing on the team. She even told me their best lap times, in seconds, down to the hundredths. This was not bragging—simply the way things are around here. Yet when she asked about my daughters, I didn't tell her that both had been accepted for the highly selective academic programs in their respective schools. This was also the way things are around here.

My neighbor and I are both products of our national ambivalence about ability: it's O.K. to extol athletic excellence, but there's something elitist, or at least unseemly, about even acknowledging intellectual excellence. The notion of intellectual accomplishment, as opposed to performance in other spheres, must be uniquely threatening to the American egalitarian spirit. How else to explain the offensive attitude of many public schools—the very places where academic achievement should be cultivated and celebrated—toward our brightest children?

School officials seem to make decisions based on the belief that no child is smarter than any other child. But of course some are smarter, just as some are better athletes or musicians. The school system's lie hurts everyone, but especially the kids with the greatest intellectual promise.

When the boy across the street asked for harder work in sixth-grade math, he was told he couldn't get too far ahead of the rest of the class—it would run counter to the school's group-oriented philosophy. Yet he was capable of working at an eighth-grade level or higher, while some kids in his class were still mastering third-grade skills.

What perverse logic would force him to tread water for an entire year so as not to outdistance the others? If he were a 12-year-old Michael Jordan, would his coach caution him not to make too many baskets so the others would have a chance to score?

Very bright kids are victims of the trend toward "heterogeneous classrooms," which lump together children who perform at, above, and below grade level. And though experts say high achievers are a good influence on slower kids and though teachers may intend to offer "differentiated instruction," in practice this rarely happens. Sometimes simple logistics make it impossible. Sometimes accelerating an individual goes against some inexplicable educational philosophy.

My own daughters, who are now 10 and 14, wasted a lot of time in heterogeneous classrooms while the lesson was repeated again and again until everyone got it.

When my younger one was in third grade, the teacher said she wouldn't call on her when she raised her hand because the teacher knew she knew the answer. So my daughter sat quietly, trying hard to focus on the lesson even though she couldn't participate. Expecting her to blossom intellectually in such a setting is like expecting the young Jordan to get better at basketball just by showing up at a gym. My older daughter suffered similarly until in fifth grade she moved to a homogeneous class, one of the few our school system still grudgingly offers. Finally, she could learn something each day that she didn't already know. "It's perfect—I love it—everyone's like me," she said after her first day. They weren't, really; they were white and black and Indian and Chinese and Hispanic and Sri Lankan.

By spending all day with intellectual peers, my daughter and her classmates have learned that their brainpower is not only admirable but something to revel in. This is a rare and wonderful lesson in a community that hands out trophies for sports but not for schoolwork. So is the corollary: that intelligence, like the muscles of a powerful swimmer, can be exercised and stretched, so that all kids can achieve their personal best.

Source: Excerpted from Henig, R. M. (1994, October 23). Dumbing down. *New York Times,* pp. 34, 36. © 1994 by the New York Times Company. Reprinted by permission.

day was being able to ask the teacher one or two questions about fractal geometry at the end of the period when the students began their homework. Although the teacher kept him pointed in the right direction and he experimented with fractal geometry on his home computer, an accelerated curriculum would have prevented him from having to sit through plane geometry day after day.

Silverman (1995) believes that acceleration is a "necessary response to a highly gifted student's faster pace of learning" (p. 229). Southern and Jones (1991) listed 15 types of acceleration options:

1. Early entrance
2. Grade skipping
3. Continuous progress
4. Self-paced instruction
5. Subject-matter acceleration
6. Combined classes
7. Curriculum compacting
8. Telescoping curriculum
9. Mentorships
10. Extracurricular programs
11. Concurrent enrollment
12. Advanced placement
13. Credit by examination
14. Correspondence courses
15. Early entrance into junior high, high school, or college

One commonly heard concern is that early admission and grade skipping will lead to social or emotional problems because the child will be in a classroom with older students who are more advanced physically and emotionally. Although this concern is understandable, some research shows that if acceleration is done properly, few, if any, socioemotional problems result (Southern & Jones, 1991). After reviewing a decade of longitudinal research on the academic acceleration of mathematically precocious youths, Swiatek and Benbow (1991) found no evidence that acceleration harms willing students either academically or socially. In a meta-analysis of 23 studies of acceleration, Kulik (1992a, 1992b) found that students whose classes were accelerated generally outperformed those who were not accelerated but were of the same ability levels.

Enrichment   Enrichment, or adding more to the traditional subject matter content (e.g., foreign language, anthropology, law, art, music), is another way to differentiate curriculum for students of high ability. Enrichment experiences let students investigate topics of interest in greater detail than is ordinarily possible with the standard school curriculum. Topics of investigation may be based on the ongoing activities of the classroom but permit students to go beyond the limits of the day-to-day instructional offerings. By allowing students to help define the area of interest and independently access a variety of information and materials, the teacher can facilitate the development of gifted and talented students' competencies and skills. High-ability students who have enriched curricula will achieve more than high-ability students who do not have enriched curricula (Kulik, 1992a, 1992b).

An excellent example of an enrichment activity was carried out at the Applied Sciences and Engineering Laboratories of the A.T. duPont Institute (Barner, Howell, & Mahoney, 1996). A special project matched 20 students with disabilities with 20 mentors who all worked together in a virtual project environment aimed at cooperatively creating a website for high school–age students with disabilities. The website was meant to provide college application and funding information for students with disabilities throughout the

Enrichment

Council for
Exceptional
Children   Content Standards for Beginning Teachers–G&T: Acceleration, enrichment, and counseling within a continuum of service options for individuals with gifts and talents (GT5K4) (also, GT7K2).

United States. The website was also envisioned as a means of communicating among groups of students with disabilities. The project involved smaller teams of students and mentors working on different components of the page. A great deal of on-line searching, writing, and reporting produced a website that facilitates information exchange among a specific group of students.

Enrichment is not a "do-your-own-thing" approach with no structure or guidance. Children involved in enrichment experiences should not be released to do a random, haphazard project. A basic framework that defines limits and sets outcomes is necessary. Projects should have purpose, direction, and specified outcomes. A teacher should provide guidance as needed to keep students working efficiently.

Although acceleration and enrichment are often viewed as separate options for talented students, as Southern and Jones (1991) point out, the two strategies are intertwined: "advanced study in any discipline may entail the kind of activities normally associated with enrichment" (p. 22). Enrichment is supposed to broaden the curriculum and include material that is not in the regular course of study. However, acceleration may also involve advanced material not contained in the regular course of study.

OTHER METHODS FOR DIFFERENTIATING CURRICULUM AND INSTRUCTION

Curriculum compacting

Council for Exceptional Children Content Standards for Beginning Teachers–G&T: Acceleration, enrichment, and counseling within a continuum of service options for individuals with gifts and talents (GT5K4) (also, GT7K2).

Curriculum Compacting   Many gifted and talented students have already mastered much of the content of the regular curriculum when the school year begins. In fact, one study found that 60% of all fourth graders in a certain school district were able to attain a score of 80% correct or higher on a test of mathematics content before they had even opened their books in September (EPIE, 1980). **Curriculum compacting** involves compressing the instructional content and materials so that academically able students have more time to work on more challenging materials. Curriculum compacting is a useful technique for adapting and developing curriculum for talented students in subjects such as mathematics and science, although it is not so effective in social studies or in literature, where depth of understanding is required. One study showed that when teachers compacted the curriculum, gifted and talented students scored significantly higher on tests of mathematics and science concepts after the content was altered (Reis, 1995).

There are three steps are involved in curriculum compacting: (1) assess the target content areas, (2) determine the content to be eliminated, and (3) substitute more appropriate content. When pretesting academically talented students to find out what they already know, the most difficult problems or content should be presented first. Students who can solve the most difficult problems do not need to do the other, easier problems (Winebrenner, 2001).

For curriculum compacting to be effective, teachers must have a substantial understanding of the curricular content and not only condense the material but also modify its presentation, create more meaningful instruction, and evaluate that instruction for individual students. For example, Juan's teacher, Mr. Dominguez, suspects that the fourth grader is as many as two grade levels ahead in mathematics. To discover if Juan is a good candidate for curricular compacting, Mr. Dominguez first determines the scope and sequence of concepts and skills in mathematics curriculum that fourth-, fifth-, and sixth-grade students are expected to master. Then he constructs a test to evaluate which of those curriculum components Juan is able to perform. If Juan is found to have mastered the content and strategies of the higher-level math, then Mr. Dominguez must design and provide replacement activities that are a more challenging and productive use of Juan's time.

Tiered Lessons   A tiered lesson provides different extensions of the same basic lesson for groups of students of differing abilities. For example, after the whole class is exposed to a basic lesson on a poem, three groups of students might work on follow-up activities or assignments of basic, middle, and high difficulty. Figure 14.8 shows an example of a tiered lesson on riddles.

Bloom's Taxonomy   Asking questions that require students to demonstrate different types of knowledge about a given topic or problem is another way to differentiate curriculum. The taxonomy of educational objectives developed by Bloom and his colleagues (Bloom, 1956) provides a useful framework for differentiating instruction. The taxonomy includes six different levels or types of cognitive understanding. At the *knowledge* and *comprehension* levels, a student can identify, define, explain, and summarize and restate a concept or fact but is not required to relate the information to other concepts or material. Teachers most often ask knowledge and comprehension questions.

Bloom's taxonomy

Council for Exceptional Children   Content Standards for Beginning Teachers–G&T: Theories and research that form the basis of curriculum development and instructional pratice (GT7K3).

At the *application level,* the student uses general principles or abstract concepts in new concrete situations without being told which principle or rule is the proper one. At the *analysis level,* the student can break a concept or communication into its elements or parts, making hierarchical and other types of relationships between the parts explicit and clear. Analysis requires students to recognize unstated assumptions, check the consistency of hypotheses, and recognize the use of propaganda techniques, thus demonstrating an understanding of the underlying structure, effect, or theoretical basis of the content.

Synthesis involves putting together parts to form a whole so that the student can produce a unique communication either through writing or speaking, produce a plan or set of operations—a proposal, a unit of instruction, a blueprint—and show an understanding of abstract relations, classification schemes, hypotheses, and an inductive discovery of principles or generalizations. At the *evaluation level,* the student is able to make judgments about the value of something (e.g., a theory, idea, method) for a given purpose using evidence from a variety of sources.

Figure 14.9 shows examples of how a teacher could differentiate instruction on the Cinderella story through various questions and learning activities based on Bloom's taxonomy. Although both average and high-ability students should have learning opportunities at all levels of Bloom's taxonomy, opportunities and expectations to work at the advanced levels of the taxonomy are especially important for academically talented students. However, as Clark (2002) points out, it is a mistake to think that gifted learners do not need instructional activities at the lower levels of the taxonomy. In order to analyze, synthesize, and evaluate information, students must possess basic knowledge and comprehension of that information.

⭐ CURRICULUM DIFFERENTIATION OUTSIDE THE CLASSROOM

For some students with outstanding talents, learning opportunities outside the classroom may be more important and rewarding than much of the instruction that takes place within it. Teachers should always attempt to connect with both human and physical resources available in the community. Options for learning outside the school include the following.

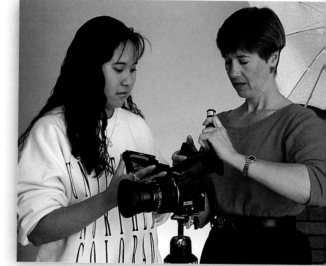

A good mentor provides students with exceptional talents opportunities to develop both their conceptual and performance skills in a real-world setting.

Internships and Mentor Programs   The value and power of a viable mentor to the realization of talent or creativity have been recognized since the Middle Ages. The importance of mentors cannot be underestimated in certain artistic and scientific fields, where the development of both performance and conceptual skills is critical to success. Internships and mentorships allow students with exceptional talents to be exposed to powerful and proven

FIGURE 14.8   A tiered lesson using riddles to promote thinking and problem solving skills

Author: Ms. Erin Morris Miller (National Research Center/Gifted and Talented)	**Author's e-mail:** HOTLINX@virginia.edu
Curriculum area(s): math, science, social studies	Grade Level: 3
Time required : 30 minutes	Instructional grouping: heterogeneous

Overview

This is a thinking skills lesson to help students practice thinking openly and flexibly. This lesson can be used as a mental warm-up session before beginning a challenging lesson that requires the students to think flexibly or counterintuitively. Use this lesson to prepare the students for times when making assumptions would be bad. Examples include solving word problems in math, finding patterns in math, drawing conclusions from reading selections, and making decisions during a unit on economy. (This idea was inspired by a high school advanced placement calculus teacher, Fred Pence, who began each class with a puzzle to get the students in the mood to problem-solve. The concept was adapted for younger students.) In this lesson students first solve a riddle as a whole class and then are divided into small groups to solve additional riddles. The groups are formed according to the students' readiness to read and understand difficult vocabulary. Each group works independently, with the teacher moving from group to group facilitating their discussions.

Standards

This lesson helps students develop the skills necessary to achieve any standard that involves problem solving. Examples include math and science problems as well as dilemmas in social studies and analysis of literature.

Materials

There are three level of riddles. Level 1 consists of three simple riddles, level 2 consists of one medium-hard riddle, and level 3 consists of one difficult riddle.

Differentiating curriculum outside the classroom

Council for Exceptional Children — Content Standards for Beginning Teachers–G&T: Community-based and service learning opportunities for individuals with gifts and talents (GT7K7).

educational strategies—modeling, practice, and direct feedback and reinforcement of important behaviors—within a real-world setting.

Special Courses   Specialized courses and workshops are offered at local colleges and universities, arts and cultural events, museums, and recreation centers. These courses, which may or may not have high school or college continuing education credits attached to them, form a rich variety of additional opportunities for students to encounter mentors, make new friends, and be exposed to concepts that may not be included in the school curriculum.

Competitions   Competitions such as Odyssey of the Mind, Invention Convention, History Day, Power of the Pen, and the like are regularly offered, usually by regional offices of education. These programs provide a differentiated opportunity for all students, and gifted and talented students often find a way to express their passions and talents in these competitions.

Junior Great Books   This is a highly structured educational program in which students read selections from a number of areas, including classics, philosophy, fiction, and poetry, and then discuss their meaning with teachers. Teachers who participate in Junior Great Books receive special training on how to use specific questioning techniques to evoke high-quality responses from the students.

FIGURE 14.8 *Continued*

As a result of this lesson, students should
know . . .
Riddles are written puzzles.
understand . . .
Riddles require people to think creatively.
Riddles require people to not make assumptions.
be able to do . . .
Students should be able to solve riddles.

Preassessment
One main difference between the riddles is the difference in the vocabulary involved. Groups should be formed based on the students' verbal proficiency.

Basic riddles
What can go up a chimney down but can't go down a chimney up? (an umbrella)

If a rooster laid a brown egg and a white egg, what kind of chicks would hatch? (None. Roosters don't lay eggs!)

What needs an answer, but doesn't ask a question? (the phone)

Medium-hard riddle
I can sizzle like bacon,
I am made with an egg,
I have plenty of backbone but lack a good leg,
I peel layers like onions but still remain whole,
I can be long like a flagpole yet fit in a hole.
What am I?
(a snake)

Challenging riddle
This thing devours all,
Birds, beasts, trees, flowers,
Gnaws iron, bites steel,
Grinds hard stones to meal,
Slays kings, ruins towns,
And beats high mountains down.
(time)
(by J. R. R. Tolkien)

Summer Programs Many summer programs are available to gifted and talented students that offer educational experiences as diverse as environmental studies and space and aeronautical studies. Summer programs are usually relatively brief but intense learning experiences that concentrate on specific areas of intellectual, artistic, or cultural affairs.

International Experiences New Zealanders have a cultural rite of passage they refer to as "the trek," wherein they pack their bags and travel in modest fashion to the far reaches of the planet. It is an eye-opening experience for people from a tiny Pacific island and one that gives them an exceptional opportunity to see and touch the world in an intimate fashion. An international curricular experience can merge this act of exploration with the demands of a structured learning experience such as the International Baccalaureate Program. Numerous international programs offer academic credit for study at participating educational agencies around the world. They are excellent opportunities to develop global interactional skills with academically rigorous studies.

FIGURE 14.9 Using Bloom's taxonomy as a guide for differentiating instruction based on the Cinderella Story

Level	Common verbs to use in questions	Examples from Cinderella story	Possible student products
Knowledge	know, collect, cite, repeat, recall, define, enumerate, list, name, label, tell, recount, relate, specify, identify	• How many stepsisters did Cinderella have? • What was the slipper made of?	List, definition, fact, reproduction
Comprehension	restate, recognize, locate, summarize, explain, report, convert, discuss, express, retell, describe, identify, translate, estimate	• Discuss the events on the night of the ball. • Describe what happened to the pumpkin.	Same as for knowledge level
Application	exhibit, apply, dramatize, solve, employ, practice, compute	• Make an exhibit of the ball gowns that Cinderella's two sisters and stepmother wore. • Dramatize what happened when the prince came to Cinderella's house with the glass slipper.	illustration, diagram, map, diary, model, collection, diorama, puzzle
Analysis	interpret, categorize, dissect, analyze, classify, diagram, outline, compare, group, arrange, contrast, examine, inventory, subdivide	• Compare and contrast Cinderella's treatment by her stepmother and by the prince. • Why was the stepmother so cruel to Cinderella?	questionnaire, survey, report, graph, chart, outline
Synthesis	compose, propose, produce, invent, imagine, formulate, create, design, predict, construct, create, improve, develop, rearrange	• Compose a song that Cinderella would sing while she did her work in the cinders. • Design Cinderella's ball gown, chariot, or slipper.	formula, invention, film, new game, story, poem, art product, machine, advertisement
Evaluation	judge, criticize, prove, decide, assess, revise, appraise, estimate, rate, evaluate, determine, conclude	• Prove that Cinderella deserved to go to the ball. • Determine what would have happened if Cinderella had run away but had not lost her slipper.	panel discussion, evaluation scale, report, survey, editorial, verdict, recommendation

 THREE CURRICULUM MODELS FOR GIFTED EDUCATION

Numerous models and programs for meeting the special curricular needs of gifted and talented students have been developed. The three models described in this section are excellent examples of how special education for gifted and talented students can truly be differentiated from the regular education curriculum. Each model encourages and supports independent exploration and inquiry, provides substantial modifications to the learning environment, and leads to tangible products as outcomes of students' learning activities.

Schoolwide Enrichment Model   The Schoolwide Enrichment Model (SEM) not only attempts to meet the needs of gifted and talented students within the regular classroom setting but is meant to be used with the other students in the classroom (Renzulli & Reis, 1986; Tomlinson et al., 2001).

The Schoolwide Enrichment Model (SEM) focuses on applying the know-how of gifted education to a systematic plan for total school improvement. This plan is not intended to replace existing services to students who are identified as gifted according to various state or local criteria. Rather, the model should be viewed as an umbrella under which many different types of enrichment and acceleration services are made available to targeted groups of students, as well as all students within a given school or grade level. (Renzulli, 1998, p. 1)

The first step of the SEM is identifying a talent pool of high-ability students (usually about 15% to 25% of the school's enrollment) by using a multifactored assessment approach, including achievement tests, teacher and peer nominations, and creativity assessments. Once the students are identified, they are able to take part in specialized services, many of which are also available and appropriate for other learners in the same classroom. Reis (1995) discusses some of the relevant features of this instructional approach:

Schoolwide Enrichment Model

 Council for Exceptional Children Content Standards for Beginning Teachers–G&T: Models, theories, and philosophies that form the basis of gifted education (GT1K2) (also, GT7K3).

- Interest and learning styles assessments are used with talent pool students. Informal and formal methods are used to create and/or identify an individual student's interests and to encourage students to further develop and pursue their interests in various ways.
- Curriculum compacting is offered to all eligible students. The regular curriculum of the classroom is modified by eliminating redundant or repetitious information and materials.
- Three types of enrichment activities are offered to students: Type I, general exploratory experiences; Type II, purposefully designed instructional methods and materials; and Type III, advanced-level studies with greater depth and complexity.

Reis and Cellerino (1983) recommend using a "revolving door" identification model that allows all children in the talent pool to participate in Type I and Type II enrichment activities. Only students who show serious interest in a specific topic evolve into Type III investigators. Students are never compelled to begin Type III projects; the level remains an open option for them.

Maker's Active Problem Solver Model
Maker (1993) builds her curricular interventions around a conception of the gifted student as "a problem solver—one who enjoys the challenge of complexity and persists until the problem is solved in a satisfying way" (p. 7). The role of the teacher in this model is to facilitate high achievement and creativity by making four types of modifications:

Letting students choose the kinds of problems they wish to study and how they will go about their investigations is one method for differentiating curriculum for students with outstanding academic abilities.

- *Content modifications.* The content of a curriculum is the type of subject matter being taught. In general, the goal is to develop content that is more advanced, complex, innovative, and original than what is usually encountered in the classroom.
- *Process modifications.* The strategies and methods used in delivering the content to learners are key features of instruction. The goal is to provide students with many opportunities to actively respond to the content, including independent research, cooperative learning, peer coaching, simulations, and apprenticeships.

*Maker's Problem-Solving
Model*

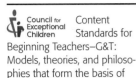

Content Standards for Beginning Teachers–G&T: Models, theories, and philosophies that form the basis of gifted education (GT1K2) (also, GT7K3).

- *Product modifications.*   The products of learning are the outcomes associated with instruction. The goal is to encourage a variety of ways through which students can present their thoughts, ideas, and results.
- *Environment modifications.*   The learning environment is both the physical characteristics of the setting(s) and the ambiance created by the teachers or facilitators. The goal is first to establish a positive working environment and then to rearrange the layout. Ideas such as peer tutoring, learning centers, self-management sheets, and learning packets can help students take more active control over and interest in their learning.

One teacher who uses Maker's model of curriculum design and delivery is Shirly Begay, a high school English teacher at the Rock Point Community School in Rock Point, Arizona. She discusses how she integrates a problem-solving emphasis into various aspects of the curriculum:

> We follow a problem-solving model. When I presented the first lesson, I wanted the students to become familiar with what I was talking about, so I used illustrations. I said, "You can't be hasty about solving a problem, or you'll be considered a sloppy problem solver. You'll come up with sloppy solutions, sloppy alternatives, and sloppy options." I wanted them to spend plenty of time gathering ideas and thinking about the answers to the questionnaires they sent out.
>
> Most of the time when we introduce problem solving to children, we want them to imagine and make up problems, but this time I wanted them to think of the problems faced by teenagers in this remote area. They brainstormed and then selected problems they didn't want their children to have. We are hoping to remedy some of these problems. I know we can't do away with most of them, but we can lessen the pressure of some, especially if we look at them in different ways. I don't want the students' ideas to stop in the classroom. I want them to write the results for publication in the school's newspaper or to read them to the chapter presidents, chapter officers, or the school board.
>
> For this problem-solving experience, I wanted the students to create a "before" picture and another after they found solutions and remedied the problem. Most Navajo students like to incorporate artwork into whatever they do. I allow them to do artwork and visual/imaginative things with whatever they have read. Most of the students who are gifted hate to write, but a few of them love to write poems and essays, so I encourage them to use both language and visual art. (cited by Maker et al., 1994, p. 16)

Problem-Based Learning Units

Content Standards for Beginning Teachers–G&T: Models, theories, and philosophies that form the basis of gifted education (GT1K2) (also, GT4K1).

Problem-Based Learning   Problem-based learning (PBL) challenges students to "learn to learn" while working cooperatively in groups to seek solutions to real-world problems. These problems are used to engage students' curiosity and initiate learning the subject matter. PBL prepares students to think critically and analytically and to find and use appropriate learning resources. In the mid-1990s, Joyce Van Tassel-Baska at the College of William and Mary served as overall project director for a series of federally funded grants to develop thematic, interdisciplinary, problem-based curriculum for gifted students. Gifted educators throughout the country created and field-tested units in science, language arts, and the social sciences (Figure 14.10 describes several examples).

An ill-formed, real-world problem serves as the basis for each of the science units, and understanding and applying the concept of *systems* is the overarching theme. These units give students experience in collecting, organizing, analyzing, and evaluating scientific data and learning to communicate their understanding to others. The PBL language arts units feature *change* as the overarching theme; the social studies units focus on the concept of *interdependence*.

The PBL units have won many major curriculum awards from discipline-based subject matter groups as well as the National Association for Gifted Children's "red apple" award for excellence. In addition to wide use in the United States, PBL units are used by teachers

FIGURE 14.10 Examples of College of William and Mary problem-based learning units in science, language arts, and social studies

SCIENCE

Acid, Acid Everywhere
This unit poses an ill-structured problem that leads the students into an interdisciplinary inquiry about the structures of and interaction between several systems, centering around the study of an acid spill on a local highway.

The Chesapeake Bay
This unit focuses on the various systems involved in the pollution of the Chesapeake Bay. The systems included in this unit are ecosystems, chemical reaction systems, government systems, and economic systems.

What a Find!
An exploration of the field of archaeology. Students are put in the role of junior archaeologists at a research museum and discover that construction work as been halted on a new school because of the discovery of historic artifacts.

For more information on problem-based units in scence, go to www.wm.edu/education/gifted-ed/Curriculum/Science_materials.htm

LANGUAGE ARTS

Literary Reflections on Personal and Social Change
Grades 4–6
This unit involves students' interacting with literature while enhancing reading comprehension and textual analysis skills. The literature selections, including *The Secret Garden* and world-class short stories by such authors as Tolstoy and Singer, serve as a basis for discussion.

Literature of the 1940's: A Decade of Change
Grades 7–9
This unit looks at the historical events and social issues of the 1940s through the literature of the decade. The unit is rich in materials that highlight the concept of change, including works such as Hersey's *Hiroshima, The Diary of Anne Frank,* and McCuller's *The Member of the Wedding.*

Change Through Choices: A Literature Unit for High School Students
(Grades 10–12)
This unit focuses on catalytic choices that determine change in a variety of situations. This unit attempts to give the student a chance to question real-world choices and problems and decide what valuable lessons can be learned through careful individual examination of options.

For more information on problem-based units in language arts, go to www.wm.edu/education/gifted-ed/Curriculum/Language_Arts_materials.htm

SOCIAL STUDIES

Ancient China: The Middle Kingdom
(Grades 2–3)
Human civilizations develop and sustain themselves as a collection of interdependent systems. The unit provides opportunities for students to broaden their understanding by comparing ancient Chinese civilization with aspects of their own lives and communities.

A House Divided? The Civil War, Its Causes and Effects
(Grades 5–6)
The concept of cause and effect serves as a central organizing theme of this unit, which explores the events and perspectives leading to the American Civil War and the chronology and context of the war itself, using primary-source documents.

The 1930s in America: Facing Depression
(Grades 6–7)
The unit explores Depression-era America from the perspective of many different groups of people, using a variety of primary sources to illustrate events and the social-political context.

For more information on problem-based units in social studies, go to www.wm.edu/education/gifted-ed/Curriculum/Social_Studies_materials.htm

in 18 countries and have been adopted by the American Embassy Schools and the Department of Defense schools. Although the PBL units were developed initially for gifted and talented students, they can be used with students of all ability levels by modifying the activities up or down depending on student ability.

EDUCATIONAL PLACEMENT ALTERNATIVES AND ABILITY GROUPING

Placement alternatives

 Content Standards for Beginning Teachers–G&T: Issues, assurances, and due process rights related to assessment, eligibility, and placement within a continuum of services (GT1K7).

SPECIAL SCHOOLS

Special schools for gifted and talented students have a long history. Special high schools for students of both genders began in the early 20th century with the establishment of Stuyvesant High School in New York City. The establishment of the Hunter College High School for Gifted Girls came even earlier. The Hunter College Elementary School for gifted students opened in l941. Children are selected for admission to these schools on the basis of competitive examinations and scores on individual IQ tests. These arrangements for academically talented children became popular in the 1980s as mandates for desegregation caused urban school systems to change the concept of the neighborhood school to the concept of the magnet school. Even on the elementary school level in many urban areas, special magnet schools emphasize various themes: for example, Columbus, Ohio, has a French language school; most larger cities have a special high school for the visual and performing arts and special schools for mathematics and science.

SELF-CONTAINED CLASSROOMS

There is always the option of creating a self-contained room for gifted and talented students. The primary advantage of the self-contained classroom is that all curriculum and instruction can be focused on needs of high-ability students. Other advantages of self-contained classrooms are that students are more likely to work at a pace commensurate with their abilities, and membership in a class of intellectual equals may challenge some gifted students to excel even further. The self-contained classroom model may also be more efficient because gifted education teachers do not have to move from classroom to classroom or school to school to serve students.

In addition to sharing many of the disadvantages of self-contained classrooms for students with disabilities (e.g., limited opportunity to develop friendships with peers in general education), self-contained classroom programs for gifted and talented students must often deal with the stigma of being viewed as elitist. Some districts may be too small to support the self-contained classroom option, even multi-age or across-grade-level classes.

RESOURCE ROOM OR PULLOUT PROGRAMS

Some educators of the gifted and talented believe that the resource room or pullout model is the best option for serving these students. While resource room programs offer many of the advantages of a self-contained classroom without the disadvantages of complete segregation from the regular classroom, they pose a number of challenges and disadvantages as well (see Figure 14.11). Administrators and teachers in schools that provide resource room/pullout services for gifted and talented students should recognize that these children do not stop being gifted when they leave the resource room and return to the regular classroom. Although the learning opportunities and instruction provided to talented students in the resource room may be of the highest quality, it does not eliminate the need to differentiate curriculum for these students when they are in the regular classroom during the remaining parts of the school day.

REGULAR CLASSROOM

For gifted and talented students, inclusion in the regular classroom has not been an issue as it has been with other exceptional children. Most academically or otherwise talented stu-

FIGURE 14.11 Advantages and disadvantages of the resource room and pullout models for gifted and talented students

Advantages	Disadvantages
1. Pullout programs are quite easy to set in motion.	1. Costs more as extra teachers have to be hired and special facilities provided.
2. The teacher in the regular classroom has more time to work with the other students.	2. The regular classroom teachers get frustrated and often feel that students leaving disrupts their instructional plan.
3. Students who are left in the classroom have a chance to shine.	3. Students in the regular classroom might feel resentful.
4. The teacher in the pullout program can focus on critical and creative thinking since the teacher in the regular classroom focuses on the standard curriculum.	4. The academically talented students might have to make up work in the regular classroom while having more work in the pullout classroom.
5. The differentiation of curriculum is separated from the classroom flow.	5. Curriculum may have no relationship to curriculum in the regular classroom.
6. Students receive special help in areas of strength.	6. Students are treated differently according to ability.
7. Teachers can feel as if they have "their" kids.	7. Teachers are isolated from the other teachers.
8. Students can have time with other students to discuss intellectual interests that may not be shared by students in the regular classroom.	8. Students may feel different from the rest of the students in their regular classroom.
9. Collaboration with other teachers is encouraged.	9. Students are academically talented all the time, and not just during pullout time.
10. Small groups of students can do special projects that would not be possible in the regular classroom.	10. Small groups of students may receive special privileges other students don't receive (e.g., access to computers, field trips).
11. Teachers of the talented can provide intensive instruction in areas of expertise (e.g., the arts, foreign language).	11. Turf issues with regular classroom teacher may arise (e.g., homework, lessons and assemblies missed).

Source: From Piirto, J. (1999). *Talented children and adults: Their development and education* (2nd ed.), (p. 73). Upper Saddle River, NJ: Merrill/Prentice Hall. Used by permission.

dents are served in regular classrooms. If the school district has a program for gifted and talented students, a teacher with special training in gifted education provides direct and indirect support for the regular classroom teacher. Working in consultation with the regular classroom teacher, this special educator—sometimes called a facilitator, consulting teacher, or intervention specialist for the gifted—might provide specialized instruction in science, math, the humanities, or other subjects to flexible groups of students. She may work with a high-ability reading or math group while the rest of class is working in these domains. She may mentor projects and displays, design special learning centers, and help plan special field trips.

An advantage of this model is that the gifted education teacher is no longer isolated and alone, working in her resource room or pullout classroom without knowledge of what the students are doing in their home classrooms. She is in partnership with regular classroom teachers, collaborating on curriculum planning teams and helping plan lessons that are multileveled. Another important advantage of the consultant teacher model is that students of all ability levels in the regular classroom can benefit from smaller student-teacher ratios, participating in multitiered lessons and learning activities on creativity, critical thinking, or study strategies that the gifted specialist may teach to the whole classroom.

Consulting teacher model

 Council for Exceptional Children

Content Standards for Beginning Teachers–G&T: Models and strategies for consultation and collaboration (GT10K4).

However, many schools do not have a specialist in the education of the gifted and talented, and the regular classroom teacher is responsible for differentiating curriculum for students with advanced educational needs.

 ABILITY GROUPING

An issue of considerable debate and strong opinions over the years is the extent to which academically talented students should be taught in groups composed of their intellectual equals or in heterogeneous groups of students of all abilities. Social injustices and upheavals have resulted in increased calls for equity in all of society's institutions. For some, equity in education includes the idea that all students should be taught in heterogeneous groups so that no group of students can progress faster than any other group of students. Others, including most educators and researchers in the field of gifted education, believe that heterogeneous group instruction means that the talented students will not be able to reach their potential. (See Figure 14.12.)

Ability grouping has been used in schools, both formally and informally, for more than a hundred years. As soon as the number of students in any classroom or school got to be so large that the differences in their abilities to learn stood out, teachers automatically put students into groups for subject matter instruction. These groups were often informal, consisting of two or more students who could keep pace with each other. When students started to be grouped according to chronological age and when developmental experts cautioned that students should remain in classes only with their age mates, ability grouping began to be the norm rather than the exception.

XYZ Grouping or Tracking *XYZ grouping* places students into different levels of curriculum requirements or offerings according to high, middle, and low ability based on test scores or other indicators or predictors of performance. Detroit had such a plan as early as 1919. Students had the same curricula and the same textbooks; the only differences were in pace of instruction and depth of enrichment. Students in the top 20% in achievement were placed in the "X" classes, students in the next 60% were placed in the "Y" classes, and the lowest 20% were placed in "Z" classes. Another name for "XYZ" grouping is *tracking.* Well-founded concern over the potential dangers (e.g., reduced expectations and limited learning opportunities for children in lower tracks, placement in lower tracks at an early age being permanent) and abuses of tracking (e.g., as a procedure for de facto segregation of students by race, culture, and/or socioeconomic status) have caused some critics to call for an elimination of all forms of ability grouping for instruction (e.g., Oakes, 1985).

Within-Class Grouping In contrast to tracking, a second type of ability grouping is *within-class grouping,* in which students within the same heterogeneous class are grouped for instruction according to their achievement. The most common form of within-class grouping is regrouping by subject; students are generally grouped into three or more levels, and they study material from different textbooks at different levels. Meta-analytic studies from the University of Michigan (Kulik & Kulik, 1984a, 1984b, 1987, 1990, 1992; Kulik, 1992a, 1992b) and from Johns Hopkins University (Slavin, 1987, 1991) found that this type of ability grouping had positive results, with gains for low-, middle-, and high-ability students averaging 1.2 years in a school year. Students should be grouped by ability for reading and mathematics.

Another form of within-class grouping is *cluster grouping,* in which several talented students receive specialized instruction from a teacher who treats them as talented. Four to six talented students should make up a cluster. Cluster grouping can be used effectively at all grade levels and in all subject areas. It can be especially effective when there are not enough students to form an advanced placement offering section for a particular subject. Cluster grouping is also a welcome option in rural settings or wherever small numbers of gifted stu-

Ability grouping issues and concerns

Council for Exceptional Children — Content Standards for Beginning Teachers–G&T: Relationship of gifted education to the organization and function of educational agencies (GT1K4).

Within-class ability groupings

Council for Exceptional Children — Content Standards for Beginning Teachers–G&T: Grouping practices that support differentiated learning environments (GT5K5).

FIGURE 14.12 **Position statement on ability grouping by the National Association for Gifted Children**

Ability Grouping

The National Association for Gifted Children (NAGC) is fully committed to national goals that advocate both excellence and equity for all students, and we believe that the best way to achieve these goals is through *differentiated* educational opportunities, resources, and encouragement for all students.

The practice of grouping, enabling students with advanced abilities and/or performance to be grouped together to receive appropriately challenging instruction, has recently come under attack. NAGC wishes to reaffirm the importance of grouping for instruction of gifted students. Grouping allows for more appropriate, rapid, and advanced instruction, which matches the rapidly developing skills and capabilities of gifted students.

Special attention should be given to the identification of gifted and talented students who may not be identified through traditional assessment methods (including economically disadvantaged individuals, individuals of limited English proficiency, and individuals with handicaps), to help them participate effectively in special grouping programs.

Strong research evidence supports the effectiveness of ability grouping for gifted students in accelerated classes, enrichment programs, advanced placement programs, etc. Ability and performance grouping has been used extensively in programs for musically and artistically gifted students, and for athletically talented students with little argument. Grouping is a necessary component of every graduate and professional preparation program, such as law, medicine, and the sciences. It is an accepted practice that is used extensively in the education programs in almost every country in the western world.

NAGC does not endorse a tracking system that sorts all children into fixed layers in the school system with little attention to particular content, student motivation, past accomplishment, or present potential.

To abandon the proven instructional strategy of grouping students for instruction at a time of educational crisis in the U.S. will further damage our already poor competitive position with the rest of the world, and will renege on our promise to provide an appropriate education for all children. (Approved 11/91)

Source: National Association for Gifted Children, Washington, DC. Reprinted by permission.

dents make appropriate accommodations difficult. The advantage of this type of grouping is that it fits philosophically with the special educational practice of inclusion yet still provides talented students with a peer group. Teachers have found that cluster grouping helps the achievement of the other students as well.

Cross-grade grouping is another type of ability grouping. This was first tried in the Joplin Plan in Missouri in the 1950s. In this model, students in the fourth, fifth, and sixth grades were broken into nine groups reading from the second-grade to the ninth-grade level. Students went to reading class at the same hour but to the level of instruction at which they were achieving. Other types of cross-grade grouping are (1) ability-grouped class assignments, (2) ability grouping for selected subjects, (3) nongraded plans, and (4) special classes. Cross-grade grouping is an effective means of delivering differentiated instruction, and achievement gains similar to those of within-grade grouping have been found (Lloyd, 1999).

Cross-grade ability grouping

 Council for Exceptional Children

Content Standards for Beginning Teachers–G&T: Grouping practices that support differentiated learning environments (GT5K5).

Grouping is not going to go away, but it should always be flexible. That is, students should be able to move into and out of groups depending on task and subject and even on whim. The days of a child's being put into the "redbird" reading group in first grade and remaining with the same students until high school graduation are over. Ability grouping, when used properly, produces academic gains for academically talented students when challenging materials are also used. If students are grouped across grades for high-level instruction, there seem to be no lasting social or emotional effects (Rogers, 1991).

Shore, Cornell, Robinson, and Ward (1991) suggest that when identifying who should be grouped, educators should "err, if one must, on the side of providing differentiated service for too many rather than too few students" (pp. 86–87). Languages and mathematics seem most amenable for ability grouping. And if there is to be grouping, the curriculum should be adapted as well. While this may seem obvious, some teachers seem to think that just putting children into different ability groups is enough, and they do not provide differentiated curriculum.

The National Research Center on the Gifted and Talented recommends the following guidelines for ability grouping:

Guideline 1: Although some school programs that group children by ability have only small effects, other grouping programs help children a great deal. Schools should therefore resist calls for the wholesale elimination of ability grouping.

Guideline 2: Highly talented youngsters profit greatly from work in accelerated classes. Schools should therefore try to maintain programs of accelerated work.

Guideline 3: Highly talented youngsters also profit greatly from an enriched curriculum designed to broaden and deepen their learning. Schools should therefore try to maintain programs of enrichment.

Guideline 4: Bright, average, and slow youngsters profit from grouping programs that adjust the curriculum to the aptitude levels of the groups. Schools should try to use ability grouping in this way.

Guideline 5: Benefits are slight from programs that group children by ability but prescribe common curricular experiences for all ability groups. Schools should not expect student achievement to change dramatically with either establishment or elimination of such programs.

CURRENT ISSUES AND FUTURE TRENDS

The current ethos surrounding the development and provision of special education services to gifted and talented students involves movement on several fronts:

- The conceptual and definitional nature of giftedness and talent is being more intensively questioned.
- There is a possibility that almost all services for gifted and talented students may originate from the regular teacher within the regular classroom.
- There is increased need to identify and serve gifted and talented students from underserved populations, including different cultural groups, females, students with disabilities, and children from disadvantaged environments.

Advocates and writers in the field are growing increasingly wary of the term *gifted,* realizing that in some ways it perpetuates the myth that talent is predetermined and not the result of extensive effort on the part of students, teachers, parents, and communities. It simply makes it too easy for society as a whole to ignore these students' needs and to ascribe their growth and development (or lack thereof) to uncontrollable factors beyond the reach of instructional interventions. An unintended result is that both individuals and societal institutions can assert that because these students can easily make it on their own, they need no extra help from society. If only the misconception that all of these students make it was true! The available data indicate that large numbers of students who would qualify for gifted and talented services drop out of school and that many more students who are culturally different, disabled, or economically disadvantaged are never even identified. Estimates of this group of underachieving gifted students range from 10% to 20% of all high school dropouts (Davis & Rimm, 1994).

There is a growing awareness that gifted advocates need to reconceptualize special services to gifted and talented students in a manner that differs from the traditional model of a gifted teacher in a segregated gifted classroom (Hertzog, 1998). Most of the newer instructional models (e.g., Renzulli's schoolwide enrichment model, Maker's active problem solver model, problem-based learning) occur within the regular classroom and depend heavily on interactions within the community, with few requiring a special teacher or classroom. There are obvious and important impacts on teacher training, classroom management, and curriculum if the regular classroom becomes the dominant educational service setting for academically talented students. It is likely there will be an increased emphasis on collaboration between teachers of the gifted and regular classroom educators to provide special education to gifted and talented students. The increasingly sophisticated use of technological tools and related methods will provide gifted students with greater connectivity and independence in the future. This ability to communicate with persons from distant and differing cultures and languages will provide new avenues of expression for gifted and talented students. In addition, the ability to explore topics in greater depth through the use of global data bases and to create interactive presentations about their discoveries will allow gifted and talented students to become more independent and exert greater self-determination over their own learning.

Increasing numbers of persons are advocating for more accurate and inclusive identification procedures that provide access to special education for gifted students who are members of underserved populations. Persons who have high ability or talent comprise a very different group of exceptional learners; but it is important to remember that all talent, including exceptional talent, can suffer from a lack of quality educational experiences, informative feedback, and emotional support. Students who exhibit high ability and talent are susceptible to the same fears and frustrations that come with a lack of interest or understanding of their needs and abilities, regardless of race, gender, socioeconomic status, and disability status.

In addition, there is a need to provide counseling services to gifted and talented students. Our track record of understanding and then facilitating the emotional growth of gifted and talented students is weak to nonexistent. As with all children and adults, a number of predictable and unpredictable crises will occur throughout their lives. With their heightened sense of social justice and greater awareness of the needs of others, students who are gifted and talented often experience confusion and estrangement with more depth than their peers do. Teachers are not counselors, but they often become aware of issues specific to their individual students' needs.

Gifted and talented students need special education; they need differentiated curriculum, instructional strategies, materials, and experiences that allow them to realize their potential. As we face increasingly complex problems in the global society of the future, we will need as much help as we can get from our citizenry. There are new approaches and perspectives concerning the manner in which students are identified and services are delivered that reflect insights into the way in which humans learn and create. These innovations promise to provide students with high ability and talents a brighter learning future that returns benefits to their country and their world.

Evolving models of G&T education

 Content Standards for Beginning Teachers–G&T: Relationship of gifted education to the organization and function of educational agencies (GT1K4) (also, GT1K12).

Need for increased identification and services for G&T children from underserved populations

 Content Standards for Beginning Teachers–G&T: Issues in definition and identification of individuals with gifts and talents, including those from culturally and linguistically diverse backgrounds (GT1K5) (also, GT1K12).

 For more information on gifted and talented students, go to the Web Links module in Chapter 14 of the Companion Website at **www.prenhall.com/heward**

SUMMARY

DEFINITIONS

- The federal government defines gifted and talented children as those exhibiting high performance capability in intellectual, creative, and/or artistic areas; possessing an unusual leadership capacity; or excelling in specific academic fields.

- Renzulli's definition of giftedness is based on the traits of above-average general abilities, high level of task commitment, and creativity.
- Piirto defines the gifted as having superior memory, observational powers, curiosity, creativity, and ability to learn.
- Maker defines the gifted and talented student as a problem solver who is capable of (1) creating a new or clearer definition of an existing problem, (2) devising new and more efficient or effective methods, and (3) reaching solutions that may be different from the usual.
- Sternberg's triarchic theory of intelligent behavior consists of three components or subprocesses: practical intelligence, creative ability, and executive ability.

CHARACTERISTICS

- Learning and intellectual characteristics of gifted and talented students include the ability to do the following:
  - Rapidly acquire, retain, and use large amounts of information
  - Relate one idea to another
  - Make sound judgments
  - Perceive the operation of larger systems of knowledge that may not be recognized by the ordinary citizen
  - Acquire and manipulate abstract symbol systems
  - Solve problems by reframing the question and creating novel solutions
- Gifted children are by no means perfect, and their unusual talents and abilities may make them either withdrawn or difficult to manage in the classroom.
- Gifted students need both basic and advanced content knowledge and the abilities to use and develop that knowledge effectively.
- Many gifted children are creative. Although there is no universally accepted definition of creativity, we know that creative children have knowledge, examine it in a variety of ways, critically analyze the outcomes, and communicate their ideas.
- Guilford includes dimensions of fluency, flexibility, originality, and elaboration in his definition of creativity.

PREVALENCE

- The most commonly cited prevalence estimate is that high-IQ gifted students make up 3% to 5% of the school-age population.
- There are many forms of talents that do not require a high IQ. Perhaps 10% to 15% of students possess such talents.

IDENTIFICATION AND ASSESSMENT

- IQ tests are one, but not necessarily the best, means for identifying students with high intellectual ability. The usual means of identification include a combination of IQ scores; achievement measures; checklists; teacher, parent, community, and peer nominations; self-nomination; and leisure interests.
- Maker's DISCOVER procedure can be used to equitably identify gifted and talented females as well as students from diverse cultural groups.
- Teachers and parents can foster the intellectual and talent development of children with disabilities by conveying positive, realistic expectations; encouraging independence; guiding constructive coping strategies; providing daily opportunities to build abilities and enjoy success; and pursuing positive social experiences for the child.

EDUCATIONAL APPROACHES

- Curriculum should consider the learning characteristics of gifted and talented students, preserve academic rigor, be thematic and interdisciplinary, consider various curriculum orientations, and be balanced and articulated.

- *Differentiation* is a broad term referring to a variety of strategies for providing gifted and talented students with a challenging and conceptually rich curriculum.
- *Acceleration* is the general term for modifying the pace at which the student moves through the curriculum.
- *Enrichment* means probing or studying a subject at a greater depth than would occur in the regular curriculum.
- Curriculum compacting involves compressing instructional content so students have more time to work on more challenging materials.
- Tiered lessons provide extensions of the same basic lesson for groups of students of differing abilities.
- Bloom's taxonomy of educational objectives provides a framework for differentiating curriculum by asking questions and assigning activities that require students to demonstrate different types of knowledge.
- Options for learning outside of school include internships and mentorships, special courses and workshops in the community, competitions such as Odyssey of the Mind, Junior Great Books, summer programs, and international experiences.
- Three models for differentiating curriculum for gifted students are Renzulli's school-wide enrichment model, Maker's active problem solver model, and the problem-based learning units.

EDUCATIONAL PLACEMENT ALTERNATIVES AND ABILITY GROUPING

- Special schools for gifted and talented students have a long history, starting with the 20th century. Students are selected for admission based on competitive examinations and IQ test scores. Magnet schools emphasize themes such as foreign language, performing arts, or math and science.
- Curriculum and instruction in self-contained classrooms can focus on the needs of high-ability students. In addition to sharing many of the disadvantages of self-contained classrooms for students with disabilities, self-contained classroom programs for gifted and talented students may be viewed by some as elitist.
- Some schools use a resource room or pullout model for serving gifted and talented students. Although resource room programs offer many advantages, they pose a number of challenges and disadvantages as well.
- Most gifted and talented students are served in regular classrooms. A consultant teacher trained in gifted education often helps the regular classroom teacher plan and deliver specialized instruction.
- Most educators and researchers in the field of gifted education believe that ability grouping is necessary if gifted and talented students are to reach their potential. Within-class grouping and cross-age grouping are two forms of ability grouping that offer effective means of delivering differentiated instruction to students according to their achievement and interests.

CURRENT ISSUES AND FUTURE TRENDS

- The conceptual and definitional nature of giftedness is being more intensively questioned.
- Most services for gifted and talented students will probably originate from the regular teacher within the regular classroom.
- The importance of realizing the needs of gifted and talented girls and boys, individuals with disabilities, and diverse cultural groups is now recognized. We need better procedures for identifying, assessing, teaching, and encouraging these children.
- As we have seen with other exceptional children, we must improve society's attitudes toward gifted and talented children if we are to improve their futures.

To check your comprehension of chapter content, go to the Guided Review and Quiz modules in Chapter 14 of the Companion Website at
www.prenhall.com/heward

Chapter 15
Transition to Adulthood

Barbara Horvath

Transition Coordinator

Monroe County Community School Corporation

Bloomington, Indiana

Education • Teaching Credentials • Experience
- B.S., Special Education, Western Michigan University, 1971
- M.S., Special Education, Learning Disabilities and Emotional Disabilities, Indiana University, 1981
- Indiana certification in mental disabilities, learning disabilities, emotional disabilities (K–12); Texas, mental disabilities (K–12)
- 10 years as classroom teacher, 15 years as coordinator of special education services

As the school year draws to an end, a group of school and adult agency staff members gather to discuss students' transitions from school to adult life. As transition coordinator for the school district, I begin by suggesting we review the accomplishments of some of our exiting students. Kris, a vocational rehabilitation (VR) counselor, asks about Tom. A great kid, he has worked hard during the past two years. Tom realizes that his learning disability will continue to be an issue for him in college, but Kris has worked with him to obtain needed services through the college's disability office. Tom's special education teacher, Gary, has helped Tom learn to advocate for the accommodations he will need in his courses. During school time, Gary and Tom worked on college applications; and Tom's family helped him meet deadlines for applications and federal financial assistance. Gary and I have worked with Tom and his parents to make a list of the skills he needs to hone over the summer: doing laundry, budgeting, maintaining a checkbook, and scheduling and using his time well. I have also given Tom information about organizations and activities on campus since he is shy and may find it difficult to make friends. Tom and his parents think they are ready for this huge step to independent living at college. But Tom has Gary's e-mail address and knows he can count on Gary, Kris, and me for help.

Susan, another VR counselor, suggests we talk about Char. During her sophomore year, Char's case conference committee (which included Char and her father) determined that she would leave school with a certificate of achievement rather than a diploma. Char struggles with reading and clearly would not be able to meet graduation requirements. Karen, our work-study coordinator, has arranged a variety of unpaid work experiences for Char over the last three years. Real-work experience in a variety of job settings has helped her determine the type of work she most enjoys and is skilled in, the social and physical environments that are most comfortable for her, and the speed at which she is most successful. Even though Char thought she wanted to work in a burger joint, she quickly learned that its rushed pace wasn't for her. Clerking at a small grocery store was better, but

Focus Questions

- What can teachers of elementary children with disabilities do to help prepare them for successful lives as adults?

- Why should postschool outcomes drive educational programming for secondary students with disabilities?

- What are the most important factors in determining the success of an individualized transition plan?

- How can programs that are intended to help adults with disabilities limit their participation and enjoyment of adulthood?

- Should quality of life for adults with disabilities be the ultimate outcome measure for special education?

dealing with so many people was stressful. Toward the end of a 2-hour shift, Char found it difficult to keep being polite to the customers. Now she is enjoying her job stocking shelves and taking inventory in a small shop. She hopes to work more than 4 hours a day and is glad that she is leaving school with a job.

Char's father was concerned about his daughter's safety traveling to and from work, but with Karen's help Char has learned the bus routes without difficulty. If she does miss a connection, she calls her father on her new cell phone so she won't have to wait for the next bus.

Char will benefit from follow-along services provided by an adult service agency. Brenda, the school district's primary contact with the agency, is at our meeting today. As we review Char's transition timeline, Brenda talks about Char's relationship with Tammy, the agency's job coach. Tammy has been getting to know Char during the past 4 weeks, dropping in to see her at work and school. As we fade support from the school district job coach, the adult service job coach provides more and more services. At first Tammy will spend an hour a day on the job with Char. As Char gains independence in job tasks, Tammy will fade her visits to once a week.

Char wants to move to a place of her own within 2 years, and Susan and I are gathering information on low-cost housing since she is not eligible for residential services through the Medicaid waiver program. She wants an apartment on a bus line because she knows that it will be several years before she can afford a car. She would like to have a roommate—preferably her best friend, Beth. The transition team has worked with them on how to proceed after high school.

Now our group turns to Steve, a young man with a traumatic brain injury. At age 15, Steve was in a car accident. He was hospitalized for several months and then underwent several more months of intensive physical therapy. Although he can walk, his gait is uneven, he falls easily, and his stamina is limited. Steve did not receive special education services before the accident. He continues to struggle with the changes in his life, loss of friends, and anger control. His dreams for his future are radically different from what they were 3 years ago. Due to his intense mental health and emotional needs, our team has made connections with a variety of residential, mental health, and employment agencies.

Like many other 18-year-olds, Steve is interested in women, cars, shooting pool, and getting married someday. Although he can carry on a conversation, his short-term memory is poor. He forgets to take his medicine, gets confused about his schedule, often misses his bus, and forgets to set his alarm. He has angry outbursts at his parents, teachers, and peers. Steve has lost several work-study jobs because of trouble taking criticism. He is now working at a job that gives him some freedom to choose which tasks to do first. However, he needs to take a midday break because he tires easily.

Steve has had difficulty, especially during the summer, in making good choices about his free time. Although we hope he will someday take advantage of adult education classes, he is not presently interested in more school. He wants to take guitar lessons and perhaps an art class, so his special education teacher is helping him explore those options.

The group turns to a discussion of Mike. Because his family had not participated in his case conferences for the last 3 years, they had missed a great deal of information about planning for life after high school. Although Mike had attended all of his conferences and will be graduating with a diploma and a decent grade-point average, he had no real plan for his future. According to his special education teacher, Mike had not shown any interest in postsecondary opportunities. He has never had a job and seems content to let his parents take care of him.

Then Mike's father showed up at a case conference. He called me the next day to ask if I could meet with him, his wife, and Mike to talk about the future. It is not unusual for families to put off planning until the last minute. The comfort and routine of school can lull families into a false sense of security. When I met with the family at their home one evening, it was clear that planning for the future was a frightening new topic. I thought we needed to focus on Mike's strengths, his hopes and potential barriers to them, and the beginning of a plan. I asked who might be able to help with the planning: friends, other family members, teachers? The family compiled a list and agreed on a time for our next planning meeting.

Participants at that meeting included Mike's parents, his grandfather, his older sister, two friends of his, one family friend, his landscaping teacher, and his special education teacher. Everyone contributed to the list of his strengths, a very empowering time for him. He talked about his dreams: traveling, working with his hands, being outdoors, staying with his girlfriend, playing golf, and so on. Then we talked about careers. Mike was uncertain until the talk turned to his love of driving and his desire to travel. When one of his friends joked, "Drive semis!" Mike immediately agreed. Someone else mentioned his tendency to fix things. Being an electrician became an option.

When we discovered that Mike was not eligible for vocational rehabilitation services, Kris, the VR counselor, offered information about technical schools for electricians and schools that offered truck-driver training. His high school counselor began helping him apply to those schools. Mike is now excited about the future and is becoming proactive in making contacts and following them up.

Next the group moved to a review of our work on the community transition council (CTC), which meets 4 times per year. Participants include high school work-study coordinators, parents, VR counselors, and representatives from adult service providers and the mental health center. The CTC reviews its task forces and plans for future activities. The task forces meet as needed to prepare the quarterly family newsletter, offer information or professional development opportunities to teachers and counselors, and develop materials and activities about planning transitions to adult life.

After 12 years of CTC activities, we still have unfinished work. Mike is a good example. Students should not be at the end of their school careers before planning begins. Each year a few of our 60 exiting students see their plans crumble after graduation. So while we recognize that we cannot control everything, our long-term plan is to ensure that all of our students step into the adult life they desire. This doesn't mean locking a student into a life plan. It means that each student will leave high school recognizing her personal strengths, knowing where to turn for support, and looking toward adult life with confidence.

 To see examples of transition planning tools developed by Ms. Horvath and her colleagues, go to the Teacher Feature module of Chapter 15 on the Companion Website at **www.prenhall.com/heward**

W**hat** does it mean to become an adult? Ferguson and Ferguson (2000) suggest that adulthood is expressed through autonomy, membership, and change. Adults express autonomy by self-sufficiency (e.g., having the financial and emotional resources to take care of themselves), self-determination, and completeness (a sense of having "arrived"). Adults experience and enjoy membership in the form of connectedness with the community, citizenship activities, and affiliations. Adulthood is characterized by change rather than stasis (e.g., moving to a new community, going back to school, taking a new job, watching old friends move away, and making new friends). Becoming an adult can be tough work for anyone.

However it is conceptualized, transition from high school to adulthood—with its increased privileges and responsibilities—is especially challenging for youth with disabilities. Skill deficits, limited opportunities created by low expectations or discrimination, and the absence of needed supports are just some of the obstacles to successful transition for many youth with disabilities.

We begin our discussion of transition by looking at the results of several studies that focus on what is perhaps the most important question of all regarding the ultimate effectiveness of special education: what do students with disabilities do after they leave school?

 To better understand what will be covered in this chapter, go to the Essential Concepts and Chapter-at-a-Glance modules in Chapter 15 of the Companion Website at **www.prenhall.com/heward**

HOW DO FORMER SPECIAL EDUCATION STUDENTS FARE AS ADULTS?

What happens to students with disabilities when they leave high school and enter the adult world? Do graduates of special education programs find work? Where do they live? How do the lives of adults with disabilities compare with the expectations and experiences of most citizens? How do adults with disabilities rate their quality of life? Are they happy?

Obtaining answers to such questions has become one of the highest priorities in special education today. More than 50 studies of graduates and leavers of secondary special education programs provide enlightening information on their experiences as young adults. Before we look at some of the results of these studies on employment, postsecondary education, and overall success of young adults with disabilities, let's examine the percentage of special education students who complete high school.

COMPLETING HIGH SCHOOL

Students who do not complete high school are likely to face more difficulties in adult adjustment than are those who do. Special education students who do not complete school are more likely to have lower levels of employment and wages and higher rates of problems with the criminal justice system (Malian & Love, 1998; Wagner, Blackorby, Cameto, & Newman, 1994; Yelin & Katz, 1994). The percentage of students with disabilities who graduate with a standard high school diploma has remained at about 25% for more than a decade (U.S. Department of Education, 2000). The percentage of students with disabilities varies greatly by state, ranging from a low of 6.8% (Mississippi) to a high of 45.4% (New Jersey). A "staggering number" of special education students drop out of school (Patton, Cronin, & Jairrels, 1997, p. 295). Although many high school dropouts resume their secondary education or obtain a general education development (GED) diploma, only 3% of youth with disabilities had completed a program to earn a high school diploma within 3 to 5 years after they had dropped out (Wagner et al., 1994).

EMPLOYMENT STATUS

The largest and most comprehensive study of the adult adjustment of youth with disabilities after they leave secondary special education programs is the National Longitudinal Transition Study (NLTS). The NLTS is an ongoing effort to assess and monitor changes in the lives of 8,000 youths with disabilities who left U.S. secondary special education programs between 1985 and 1987 (Blackorby & Wagner, 1996).

Data from the NLTS show an unemployment rate of 46% for all youth with disabilities who have been out of school for less than 2 years. The unemployment rate for young adults with disabilities drops to 36.5% when they have been out of school for 3 to 5 years, but nearly one in five persons (19.6%) states she has given up looking for work (NLTS).

The employment outlook is much worse for students with physical, sensory, severe, and multiple disabilities. The NLTS found extremely low employment rates 3 to 5 years after secondary school for young adults with orthopedic impairments (22%), visual impairments (29%), and multiple disabilities (17%) (NLTS).

Between one-half and two-thirds of young adults with disabilities who are employed work in part-time jobs (Frank & Sitlington, 2000; Sitlington, Frank, & Carson, 1993). The incomes of many individuals with disabilities hover near the poverty level (Scuccimarra & Speece, 1990); and relatively few receive health insurance, sick leave, or vacation benefits (Frank & Sitlington, 2000). On average, youth with disabilities in the NLTS earned a median hourly wage of $5.72, less than $12,000 per year for full-time, year-round employment. Only 40% of the young adults with disabilities who had jobs 3 to 5 years after school earned more than $6.00 per hour.

Although the employment earnings of high school graduates with learning disabilities are slightly higher than those of peers without disabilities for the first 4 years after leaving school (because most of their peers are attending college), by the 5th year the earnings of graduates without disabilities "increasingly outpaced those of their peers with LD" (Goldstein, Murray, & Edgar, 1998, p. 60).

A nationwide survey of Americans with disabilities ages 16 to 64 by Louis Harris and Associates (2000) reported even more discouraging findings than did follow-up studies of youth who have recently left high school: approximately two-thirds are unemployed, only 20% have full-time jobs, and 11% are working part time. These results reaffirm a conclusion of a similar Harris poll in 1986 that "not working is perhaps the truest definition of what it means to be disabled" (p. 81). Like other minority groups, persons with disabilities are often in the position of being the last hired and first fired (Trupin, Sebesta, Yelin, & LaPlante, 1997).

POSTSECONDARY EDUCATION

Attending college and postsecondary vocational programs greatly increases the likelihood of obtaining employment and generally experiencing success as an adult. Compared with their peers without disabilities, fewer former special education students pursue postsecondary education. A follow-up of 1,242 youths with disabilities who had been out of school for one year found that 15% had taken at least one postsecondary course compared with 56% of youth without disabilities (Fairweather & Shaver, 1991). NLTS found that 27% of young adults who had left high school had enrolled in postsecondary education programs within 3 to 5 years compared with 68% of the general same-age population (Blackorby & Wagner, 1996).

Brian's job gives him a sense of autonomy and connectedness with the community.

OVERALL ADJUSTMENT AND SUCCESS

Being a successful adult involves much more than holding a job; it means achieving status as an independent and active member of society. Independence for an adult includes the ability to participate in society, work, have a home, raise a family, and share the joys and responsibilities of community life (Ferguson & Ferguson, 2000). Adults with disabilities face numerous obstacles in day-to-day living that affect where and how they live, how well they can use community resources, and what opportunities they have for social interaction. After being out of high school for 3 to 5 years, only 37% of youth with disabilities were living independently (alone, with a spouse or roommate, in a college dormitory or military housing; that is, not as a dependent) compared with 60% of the general population (NLTS).

The NLTS includes a measure of adult adjustment that assesses independent functioning in three domains: (1) employment (competitively employed in a full-time job or engaged in job training or postsecondary education), (2) residential arrangements (living alone or with a spouse or roommate), and (3) social activities (having friends, belonging to social groups). When assessed at a period less than 2 years out of school, only 6.4% of all youth with disabilities met these three criteria. When the same measures are assessed after individuals have been out of school for 3 to 5 years, 20% were judged to be independent in all three domains (Wagner et al., 1994). Even with this significant improvement after several years, four out of every five former special education students had still not achieved the status of independent adulthood after being out of high school for up to 5 years.

It is important to note that the very small percentage of young adults who met the criteria for successful transition to adult life in this study had graduated from secondary special education programs. Young adults who leave secondary programs by routes other than graduation do not fare as well as those who do complete school with a diploma or certificate (Blackorby & Wagner, 1996; Malian & Love, 1998).

A follow-up study of graduates of secondary special education programs in Iowa evaluated whether or not transition to adulthood was successful as defined by four criteria: (1) employed (full or part time) in a competitive job, a homemaker, a full-time student, or in a job-training program; (2) buying a home, living independently, or living with a friend or spouse; (3) paying at least a portion of one's living expenses; and (4) being involved in more than three different leisure activities (Sitlington et al., 1993). This study found that only 5.8% of 737 students with learning disabilities, 5 of 142 students with mental retardation (3.5%), and just 1 of 59 students with behavioral disorders could be judged as having made a successful adult adjustment 1 year after they had completed high school.

There is some evidence that outcomes are improving slightly for graduates of secondary special education programs. A study of postschool outcomes for high school graduates with mental retardation in Iowa found that the class of 1993 was slightly better off than the class of 1985 (Frank & Sitlington, 2000). For example, 74% of the 1993 graduates were employed compared to 66% of the 1985 graduates; 28% of the 1993 graduates lived independently compared to 21% of the 1985 graduates; and 39% of the 1993 graduates were enrolled in some type of postsecondary education or training program compared to 21% of the 1985 graduates.

Such findings have focused attention on what has become a dominant issue in special education today—the transition from school to adult life in the community. Many youth who leave secondary special education programs discover to their dismay and discouragement that "the fiscal and logistical demands of daily life [are] far more complex than what they learned in functional math, home-economics, or life skills classes . . . [and that the] protective nature of their experiences in special education had left them ill-prepared for the real world" (Knoll & Wheeler, 2001, pp. 502–503). And it is not just students with major cognitive limitations or severe physical, sensory, or behavioral disabilities who have trouble adjusting to life after high school. Former special education students with disabilities considered mild face significant challenges in every aspect of adult life (Tymchuk, Lakin, & Luckasson, 2001).

No longer can special educators be satisfied with students' improved performance on classroom-related tasks. We must work equally hard to ensure that the education students receive during their school years plays a direct and positive role in helping them deal successfully with the multifaceted demands of adulthood.

Will's Bridges model

Council for Exceptional Children — Knowledge and Skill Base for Beginning Special Education Transition Specialists: Theoretical and applied models of transition (TS1K1) (also, TS1K3). **PRAXIS** Special Education Core Principles: Content Knowledge: II. Legal and Societal Issues, Historical movements/trends affecting connections between special education and the larger society, transition.

TRANSITION SERVICES AND MODELS

WILL'S BRIDGES MODEL OF SCHOOL-TO-WORK TRANSITION

In response to growing concern over the failure of so many young adults with disabilities in the job market and community living, Congress authorized funding for secondary education and transitional services for youth with disabilities when it amended IDEA in 1983 (P.L. 98-199). In 1984, Madeline Will, director of the U.S. Office of Special Education and Rehabilitation Services, proposed a model of transition services that encompassed three levels of service, each conceptualized as a bridge between the secondary special education curriculum and adult employment (Will, 1986). Each level differs in terms of the nature and extent of the services an individual with disabilities needs to make a successful transition from school to work. At the first level are students who require no special transition services. On graduation from an appropriate secondary special education curriculum, these young adults, presumably those with mild disabilities, would make use of the generic employment services already available to people without disabilities in the community (e.g., job placement agencies). At the second level are persons with disabilities who require the time-limited transitional services offered by vocational rehabilitation or adult service agencies that are specially designed to help individuals with disabilities gain competitive, independent employment. The third level of transitional services consists of ongoing employment services that are necessary to enable persons with severe disabilities to enjoy the benefits of meaningful paid work.

HALPERN'S THREE-DIMENSIONAL MODEL

Because it showed the federal government's recognition of the need to improve the employment outcomes for special education students, Will's bridges model for school-to-work transition was viewed as a move in the right direction. Many special educators, however, thought that it offered a too-limited perspective on transition. Halpern (1985) wrote that it is a mistake to focus on adult employment as the sole purpose and outcome of transition services: "Living successfully in one's community should be the primary target of transitional services" (p. 480). Halpern proposed a transition model that directed Will's generic, time-limited, and ongoing support services toward helping students with disabilities adjust to adult life in the community in three domains: (1) the quality of residential environment, (2) adequacy of social and interpersonal network, and (3) meaningful employment (see Figure 15.1).

Halpern's model influenced subsequent definitions of transition services in the 1990 and 1997 amendments to IDEA. The view that transition must focus on all domains of adult functioning characterizes the field today.

Halpren's transition model

Council for Exceptional Children Knowledge and Skill Base for Beginning Special Education Transition Specialists: Theoretical and applied models of transition (TS1K1) (also, TS1K3).
PRAXIS Special Education Core Principles: Content Knowledge: II. Legal and Societal Issues, Historical movements/trends affecting connections between special education and the larger society, transition.

DEFINITION OF TRANSITION SERVICES IN IDEA

Transition services are defined in IDEA as

> a coordinated set of activities for a student with a disability that:
>
> (a) is designed within an outcome-oriented process, which promotes movement from school to post-school activities, including postsecondary education, vocational training, integrated employment (including supported employment), continuing and adult education, adult services, independent living, or community participation;
>
> (b) is based upon the individual student's needs, taking into account the student's preferences and interests; and
>
> (c) includes instruction, related services, community experiences, the development of employment and other post-school adult living objectives, and, when appropriate, acquisition of daily living skills and functional vocational evaluation. (P.L. 105-17, Sec. 602[30])

IDEA definition of transition services

Council for Exceptional Children Knowledge and Skill Base for Beginning Special Education Transition Specialists: Transition-related laws and policies (TS1K2).
PRAXIS Special Education Core Principles: Content Knowledge: II. Legal and Societal Issues, Federal laws and legal issues related to special education, Public Law 105-17 (IDEA 1997).

INDIVIDUALIZED TRANSITION PLAN

In contrast to IEP goals and objectives, which address one year at a time, transition planning requires the IEP team to think and plan several years ahead (deFur, 2000). When a student reaches the age of 14, IDEA requires the IEP team to thoughtfully consider the student's post-school goals.

> Beginning at age 14, and updat[ing] annually, [the team should create] a statement of the transition service needs of the child under the applicable components of the child's

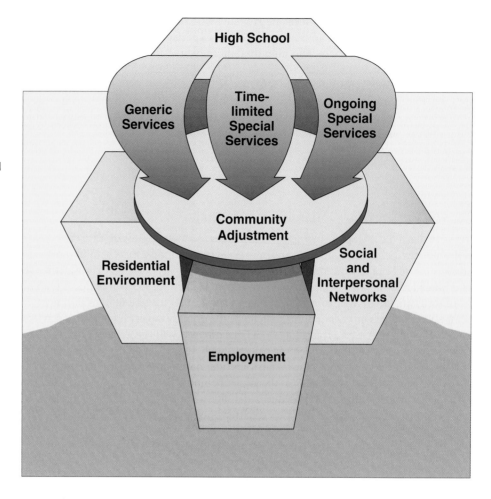

FIGURE 15.1
Halpern's three-dimensional conceptualization of transition

Source: From "Transition: A Look at the Foundation" by A. S. Halpern. *Exceptional Children, 51,* 1985, p. 481. © 1985 by the Council for Exceptional Children. Reprinted with permission.

IEP that focuses on the child's courses of study (such as participation in advanced-placement courses or a vocational education program). [P.L. 105-17, Sec. 602[30])

The intent of this provision is to focus the IEP team's attention on secondary curriculum and course planning related to postschool success.

When a student reaches the age of 16, an *individualized transition plan* (ITP) must be developed. The ITP may be written at an earlier age if the IEP team determines it is appropriate for an individual student. Developed and included as part of the IEP process, a student's ITP outlines actions, events, and resources that will affect and support her move from school to adulthood. A well-written ITP details the types of curricular programming and supports that will prepare the student for a smooth and successful transition to adult life.

Transition plans are designed within an outcome-oriented process based on the student's and family's vision of the future. The student's IEP/ITP team specifies postschool outcomes and goals in four major areas—employment, postsecondary education/training, residential, and recreation/leisure—and then develops an individualized program of instruction and activities designed to reach those outcomes. Decisions about needed transition services should be guided by answers to questions such as the following (deFur, 2000; Flexer, Simmons, Luft, & Baer, 2001; Martin & Marshall, 1995; Sitlington, Clark, & Kolstoe, 2000; Wehman, 2002; West et al., 1999) :

- What are the student's dreams and vision of his life as a young adult?
- What are his strengths? How will he build upon them to facilitate a successful transition?

Individualized transition plan (ITP)

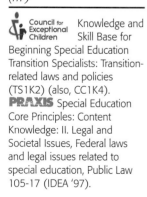

Council for Exceptional Children **Knowledge and Skill Base for Beginning Special Education Transition Specialists:** Transition-related laws and policies (TS1K2) (also, CC1K4).
PRAXIS Special Education Core Principles: Content Knowledge: II. Legal and Societal Issues, Federal laws and legal issues related to special education, Public Law 105-17 (IDEA '97).

- What skills does the student need to develop or improve to make progress toward her postschool goals?
- Will the student seek a regular high school diploma? If so, what course of study and proficiency tests will be required?
- Will she work toward a vocational certificate of completion instead of a regular diploma?
- Does he have an expressed career interest now? If not, what can the team do to help him explore career possibilities and discover his preferences?
- Is the student likely to remain in high school through the maximum age of eligibility for special education services? If so, what curriculum and work experiences will be needed after age 18?
- In what school and community activities will the student participate?

A well-written transition plan ensures that parents are aware of available adult services and employment options in the community, improves the chances that adult services will be available with few disruptions to the graduating student, and provides school and adult-service personnel with a set of procedures and timelines to follow. After graduation, the ITP can be incorporated into an individual rehabilitation plan if the young adult is served by vocational rehabilitation or made part of an individualized habilitation plan if the young adult is served by a community adult services agency (e.g., a county program for people with developmental disabilities).

Like IEPs, transition plans can take many formats as long as they contain the necessary information. Figure 15.2 shows the ITP developed for Jeff, a 10th grader with learning disabilities. Jeff and his parents share a vision for the future in which Jeff has a good job and lives as independently as possible. He is very interested in obtaining his driver's license; and based on some of his community-work experiences, he thinks he might like to work in the heating and air conditioning field. Jeff also sees himself getting married someday, but first he wants to live on his own for a while, probably in an apartment with a roommate or two. He has also expressed the desire to continue his education after high school; therefore, one of the activities on his ITP is to obtain information about community and technical colleges.

The goals and objectives numbers on the ITP refer to the goals and objectives on Jeff's IEP that support the transition plan (IEP objectives are at the bottom of the figure). Academic goals for Jeff, such as reading comprehension, use the content area from the transition plan—e.g., a heating and air conditioning textbook and the driver's education manual. Jeff frequently relies on adults to assist him in decision making and to request information about days off at work, and he needs to better understand his disability. His self-advocacy goal relates to more self-reliance. Although specific skills will be taught, Jeff will practice his self-advocacy skills at his part-time job.

TRANSITION TEAMING

Transition planning requires a team—special education teachers, general education teachers, vocational education teachers, school counselors, related services personnel, personnel from community and adult services agencies such as vocational rehabilitation, higher education, and/or developmental disabilities adult services agencies—that can help the student identify and reach her postschool goals. All people involved must build and maintain communication links and supports among the team members.

Transition involves the coordination, delivery, and transfer of services from the secondary school program to receiving agencies (e.g., employers, postsecondary education and vocational training programs, residential service providers). Although work-study and vocational training programs for special education students and vocational rehabilitation services for adults with disabilities have long existed in every state, systematic coordination of and communication between schools and community-based adult services have

Relating transition services to IEP goals and objectives

Council for Exceptional Children — Knowledge and Skill Base for Beginning Special Education Transition Specialists: Methods for linking academic content to transition goals (TS4K2) (also, CC4S6).
PRAXIS Special Education Core Principles: Content Knowledge: III. Delivery of Services to Students with Disabilities, Curriculum and Instruction, Career development and transition issues as related to curriculum design and implementation.

FIGURE 15.2 Example of an individualized transition plan (ITP)

STATEMENT OF NEEDED TRANSITION SERVICES

Name of Student ___Jeff Grace___ Date ___1-14-02___

Person Responsible for Coordinating Transition Services ___Nancy Long___

Title ___Work Study Coordinator___

INSTRUCTION: Goals and objectives for transition should be indicated below in the following areas and be incorporated into the body of the IEP (pages 2 and 3).

See IEP goals and objectives for curriculum modifications and adaptations

EMPLOYMENT & POSTSECONDARY OUTCOME(S): _Full-time job in heating/air conditioning_

ACTIVITIES AND SERVICES	Goal Number for Transition Goals and Objectives	Responsible Person/Provider	Initiation/Duration
Heating/air cond. voc. class	1.a, 1.b, 1.c	Voc Educ. Teacher	1/02 to 2/03
Explore Technical colleges	NA	Jeff, guidance coun.	1/02 to 6/02
Part-time job	2.a, 2.b, 2.c	Jeff, work study coord.	1/02 to 2/03

POSTSCHOOL/ADULT LIVING OUTCOME(S): _Live independently in apartment with roommate_

ACTIVITIES AND SERVICES	Goal Number for Transition Goals and Objectives	Responsible Person/Provider	Initiation/Duration
Family Planning Class	1.a, 1.b, 1.c	SPED Teacher/Reg. Teacher	1/02 to 6/02
Money management	3.a 3.b	SPED Teacher	1/02 to 1/03
Self-advocacy skills trn.	2.a, 2.b, 2.c	Jeff, SPED Teacher	1/02 to 2/03

COMMUNITY PARTICIPATION OUTCOME(S): To participate in the community through social relationships and transportation.

ACTIVITIES AND SERVICES	Goal Number for Transition Goals and Objectives	Responsible Person/Provider	Initiation/Duration
Drivers Ed.	1.a 1.b 1.c	Driver Ed Teacher / SPED Teacher	1/02 to 6/03
Register to vote	NA	Jeff and parents	1/02 to 6/03
Interact Club	NA	Jeff	1/02 to 6/03

Jeff's Transition-Related IEP Objectives

1. **Reading comprehension.** Goal: Jeff will increase his reading skills.
   a. When given a reading passage from the driver's education manual or heating and air conditioning textbook, Jeff will increase his reading comprehension skills by using the SQ3R study skills method.
   b. Given 10 functional vocabulary words from the course text, Jeff will identify and define each word.
   c. Given an unfamiliar/unknown word in the heating and air conditioning text (or other course texts), Jeff will decode the word using word attack skills.
2. **Self-advocacy.** Goal: Jeff will increase his self-advocacy skills.
   a. Jeff will increase his understanding of his disability by identifying and stating his strengths and areas of difficulty.
   b. When given various community and work situations, Jeff will identify and demonstrate appropriate decision-making skills.
   c. When given various community and work problem situations, Jeff will identify people who can assist him with difficult or unfamiliar situations.
3. **Money management.** Goal: Jeff will manage his personal finances.
   a. Jeff will construct and use a monthly personal budget for his present income.
   b. Jeff will record personal major income and expenses for three months.

Source: ITP form from Ohio Department of Education. (1998). *Model policies and procedures for the education of children with disabilities* (p. 608b). Columbus: Author.

not typically occurred. Although interagency cooperation is critical to the success of transition, the amendments to IDEA "made it clear that the initial and ultimately most significant transition responsibilities lie with schools" (Moon & Inge, 1993, p. 583).

Nowhere in special education are teaming and collaboration more important than when planning and delivering transition services for secondary students. The validity and likely effectiveness of the transition services described on a student's ITP depend on the student's involvement, family involvement, and the collaboration of professionals who are helping the student and family plan and implement transition services. Cooperation and communication between and among professionals and families are keys to effective transition planning. See Profiles & Perspectives, "Removing Transition Hurdles with Effective Communication," later in this chapter.

BEGINNING TRANSITION ACTIVITIES AND CAREER EDUCATION EARLY

Numerous models for conceptualizing and guiding the delivery of transition services have been developed (e.g., Kohler, 1998; Sitlington et al., 2000). All stress the importance of providing career education at an early age, the student's choosing goals, a functional secondary school curriculum that offers work experience in integrated community job sites, systematic coordination between the school and adult service providers, and parental involvement and support.

The Council for Exceptional Children's Division on Career Development and Transition (DCDT) believes that career development and transition services should begin in the elementary grades for all children with disabilities. According to DCDT's position statement, three basic principles underlie the provision of career education and transition services:

1. *Education for career development and transition is for individuals with disabilities of all ages.*
2. *Career development is a process begun at birth and continues throughout life.*
3. *Early career development is essential for making satisfactory choices later.* A frequent criticism of secondary employment training programs is that there are too few choices and that professionals too often end up making those choices for students . . . . The best way to prepare individuals for self-knowledge (interests, abilities, limiting barriers) and decision-making is to begin the process of self-awareness and choice-making as early as possible. (Clark, Carlson, Fisher, Cook, & D'Alonzo, 1991, pp. 115–116)

Developing career awareness and vocational skills during the elementary years does not mean, of course, that 6-year-old children should be placed on job sites for training. Appropriate transition-related objectives should be selected at each age level (Brolin, 1997; Cronin & Patton, 1993; Johnson & Wehman, 2001). For example, elementary students might sample different types of jobs through classroom responsibilities such as watering plants, cleaning chalkboards, or taking messages to the office. Young children with disabilities might also visit community work sites where adults with disabilities are employed. Middle school students should begin to spend time at actual community job sites, with an increasing amount of in-school instruction devoted to the development of associated work skills, such as being on time, staying on task, and using interpersonal skills (Beakley & Yoder, 1998).

Developing and operating a school-based business enterprise can help high school students learn functional academic, work, problem-solving, and social skills. For example, Lindstrom, Benz, and Johnson (1997) describe four school-based businesses—an espresso and baked goods bar, a take-out meals operation, a mail-order seed business, and a winter produce garden—that students with disabilities in several high schools in Oregon have helped develop and operate. Secondary students with moderate and severe disabilities should also spend an increasing amount of time receiving instruction at actual community job sites (Moon & Inge, 2000). The remaining hours of in-school instruction should focus on acquisition of functional skills needed in the adult work, domestic, community, and recreational/leisure environments toward which the student is headed (Benz & Lindstrom, 1997; Patton et al., 1997). Table 15.1 on page 581 shows examples of transition-related curriculum activities in the domestic, community, leisure, and vocational domains that might be incorporated into a student's IEP.

Removing Transition Hurdles with Effective Communication

by Sue Brewster and Lyn Dol

Let us introduce ourselves: Sue is a job-training coordinator and transition specialist for an urban school system; Lyn is the mother of Karen, a young adult with a disability. We would like to share what we have learned about helping young adults with disabilities transition from school to adult life from our experience with a transition-planning meeting for Karen.

Karen Karen, challenged by mental retardation, epilepsy, and osteoporosis, which requires her to use a wheelchair, was in her last year of high school. Throughout high school, Karen had participated in a variety of work experiences in the community, such as at a restaurant, a child care facility, two different nursing homes, and a large general department store. Karen's strengths include her desire to work in the community, social skills, and quality of work. Staying on task, poor productivity, and short-term memory were areas of difficulty.

Karen and her family were feeling the many stresses that occur with leaving high school and moving into the adult world. The county board of mental retardation and developmental disabilities (MR/DD), which provides vocational, residential, recreation, and other services to individuals with disabilities, had presented Karen and her family with two options: community-based employment or a sheltered workshop environment. At the time, community-based employment was an option only for persons who could work at least 20 hours per week with minimal support, such as having a job coach stop in every week or so. Individuals whose disabilities prevented them from working the required hours or who needed more support were automatically placed on the waiting list for the sheltered workshop. Karen's seizure disorder and physical disability made it difficult for her to meet the required number of hours for community placement, yet she had frequently expressed her desire to work in the community.

To help prepare Karen for community placement, Sue had found her a nonpaying work experience at a restaurant on a nearby university campus. Karen's duties were to bus tables and clean off trays. Grant funds to increase transition services for youths with disabilities were used to provide transportation to and from the job site and for a maximum of 100 job-coaching hours. Karen and her job coach, Chris, began working at the restaurant for 8 hours per week. It was hoped that this nonpaid work experience would lead to paid employment and possibly additional working hours after graduation.

As the 100 hours of grant-funded job coaching neared completion, Chris thought that Karen would continue to need support services on the job. Lyn preferred that Karen work in the community, but she had many questions concerning the feasibility of community work. Sue, who had visited Karen at the job site, thought that things were going pretty well; and the restaurant manager had indicated the possibility of offering Karen competitive employment. Sue was also concerned that the grant funding might be lost for other students if this placement failed. At this point, Sue arranged a transition-planning meeting for all interested parties in an effort to determine what support services Karen would need after graduation and to try to solidify the employment placement.

Karen's Transition Meeting The meeting was held at the restaurant with all interested parties present: Karen; Lyn and Bill, Karen's parents; Mark, Karen's older brother; Sue, the job training coordinator; Chris, the job coach; Jim, the restaurant manager; two people from the county MR/DD program; and a representative from the Bureau of Vocational Rehabilitation (BVR).

After all had introduced themselves, Sue began the meeting by asking Chris, "How is Karen doing since you've been with her for 6 weeks on the job?" Knowing what the stakes were and who was present around the table (parents and restaurant manager), Chris hesitated and then said something positive while admitting that Karen had some "slow days." When Bill, Karen's father, asked Jim, the restaurant manager, whether he would have to hire somebody else to do the job if Karen didn't get it, he sounded as if he didn't really expect that Karen would ever work in the community.

Throughout the meeting, it seemed that people were saying one thing and meaning another. Everyone seemed to be communicating at cross purposes, to have his own agenda and objective. The meeting ended with everyone feeling very negative, exhausted, and perplexed.

Most important, the meeting ended without a community job for Karen.

Bubble Heads   Two months after the meeting, Sue, feeling as though she had failed, met with Lyn to figure out what had gone wrong at the meeting. They decided to ask each participant to remember what she was thinking during the meeting and to compare that with the statements they had actually said. After talking with the participants and comparing what was said with what they "were really saying," Sue and Lyn learned some important lessons about effective communication during transition planning. Figure A shows actual statements made by members of the planning team; the bubbles show what each person was really thinking.

FIGURE A   Karen's ITP meeting: What people said and what they were really thinking

(continued)

COMMUNICATION BREAKDOWN

- The seating arrangement is important. The meeting had been conducted at a long, narrow table. A round table would have helped ensure that each team member had equal opportunity to talk and be heard by everyone and to see and hear the person speaking.
- Too many people hamper effective communication. Both the family and the employer expressed the feeling of being overwhelmed by the number of people (10) who were present at the meeting.
- Listen to what people are saying they want and need, even if their request differs from what you think should occur. For example, Lyn was saying to Sue that she would like to see Karen working in the community rather than in a sheltered workshop. At the same time, her husband and her son were voicing skepticism and were being protective of Karen. Sue did not consider the interactions among the family members and considered only what she thought would be best for Karen. Sue should have met with the family before the transition meeting to help the family sort out and determine what they wanted.
- Because Lyn was surrounded with negative beliefs about Karen's ability to work in the community, she left the meeting thinking that perhaps her husband and son had been right all along. The family gave up hope of community work for Karen. This made it easy for the business to not offer Karen the job.
- Sue may not have been really listening to the family because of her job-placement requirement. She may have been more concerned with meeting her placement quota than with the concerns of the family.
- Not once during the meeting did anyone ask Karen where she wanted to work and what she thought her strengths, weaknesses, and support needs were. Service providers have to step outside their realm and place the individual with a disability in the center of the planning to ensure that her requests and desires are addressed.

PROFESSIONALS SOMETIMES BUILD THEIR OWN HURDLES

- Even though they want to do the right thing, service providers often get trapped by their own rules and regulations and their usual way of doing business. BVR and MR/DD gave up by stating that they could not provide services to Karen if she was not going to get paid at least minimum wage or work at least 20 hours per week.
- Potential employers will avoid getting involved when they deal with too many professionals, bureaucratic tangles, or turf fighting between agencies.

Karen's New Job   Everyone except Karen seemed to have given up after that fateful meeting. But Karen persisted in expressing her preference for a job in the community. Sue brought the transition team together again to address the requests and needs of Karen and her family. By being flexible and creative, Sue has worked during the last 2 years to create jobs for Karen and others with significant challenges. Karen is now doing meaningful work in an integrated job in the community. She is currently working at Anderson's General Store in a group placement (enclave) with three other individuals with significant challenges. Her job entails moving and facing items to the front of the shelves. Karen works 3 days per week for 3 hours per day with the support of a job coach. To help alleviate the family's concerns about Karen struggling in the community, Sue arranged for them to observe Karen at work.

Karen's production rate currently keeps her from earning minimum wage, but she has the opportunity to do meaningful work for pay and to interact with nondisabled peers. In the last year, Karen has made another transition. She has moved from her parents' home to a group home with four other adults with disabilities. With her supports and effective communication among service providers and the family, Karen is continuing her transition to independence.

Sue Brewster is a job-training coordinator for the Toledo (Ohio) Public School System. Lyn Dol, a coordinator for the local Interagency Transition Team and a parent mentor for adult issues, ensures that services for individuals with disabilities are family-driven.

TABLE 15.1 Examples of transition-related curriculum activities in four domains that might be included in a student's IEP

	Domestic	Community	Leisure	Vocational
Elementary	Picking up toys Washing dishes Making bed Dressing Grooming Eating skills Toileting skills Sorting clothes Vacuuming Setting the table at mealtime	Eating meals in a restaurant Using restroom in a local restaurant Putting trash into container Choosing correct change to ride city bus Giving the clerk money to purchase an item Responding appropriately to pedestrian safety signs Going to neighbor's house for lunch	Climbing on swing set Playing board games Playing tag with neighbors Coloring Playing kickball Croquet Riding bicycles Playing with age-appropriate toys Community soccer league	Returning toys to appropriate storage spaces Cleaning the room at the end of the day Working on a task for a designated period Wiping tables after meals Following 2- to 4-step instructions Answering the telephone Emptying trash Taking messages to people
Middle School	Washing clothes Preparing simple meals (soup, salad, and sandwich) Keeping bedroom clean Making snacks Mowing lawn Raking leaves Making grocery lists Purchasing items from a list Vacuuming and dusting Setting an alarm clock at night and turning it off when waking	Crossing streets safely Purchasing an item from a department store Purchasing a meal at a restaurant Using local transportation system to get to and from recreational facilities Participating in local scout troop Going to a neighbor's house for lunch on Saturday	Playing volleyball Taking aerobics classes Playing checkers with a friend Playing miniature golf Cycling Attending high school or local college basketball games Hanging out at local mall Swimming Attending crafts class at city recreation center	Mopping/waxing floors Cleaning windows Hanging and bagging clothes Busing tables Working for 1–2 hours Operating machinery (e.g., dishwasher, buffer) Cleaning sinks, bathtubs, and fixtures Internship with school janitor or office staff Following a job sequence
High School	Cleaning all rooms in place of residence Developing a weekly budget Cooking meals Operating thermostat to regulate heat or air Doing yard maintenance Maintaining personal needs Caring for and maintaining clothing	Using bus system to move about the community Depositing checks into bank account Using community department stores Using community grocery stores Using community health facilities (e.g., physician, pharmacist)	Jogging Boating Watching college basketball game Video games Card games YMCA swim class Gardening Going on a vacation Collecting tapes or CDs Reading magazines or comics Hanging out/sleeping over with friends	Janitorial duties (at J. C. Penney) Housekeeping duties (at Days Inn) Grounds keeping duties at local college campus Food service at mall cafeteria Laundry duties at local laundromat Performing job duties to company standards

Source: Adapted from Johnson, S., & Wehman, P. (2001). Teaching for transition. In P. Wehman, *Life beyond the classroom: Transition strategies for young people with disabilities* (3rd ed.), (pp. 156–157). Baltimore: Brookes. Used by permission.

 EMPLOYMENT

Work can be defined as using one's physical and/or mental energies to accomplish something productive. Our society is based on a work ethic; we place a high value on work and on people who contribute. Besides providing economic support, work offers opportunities for social interaction and a chance to use and enhance skills in a chosen area. Work generates the respect of others and provides a sense of pride and self-satisfaction.

All young adults face important questions about what to do with their lives—whether to attend college or technical school, whether to work as a bricklayer or an accountant—but for the person without disabilities, answering those questions involves choosing from a number of options. By contrast, the young adult with disabilities often has fewer options from which to choose. Occupational choices decrease if the person with disabilities has limited skills; they may decrease even more due to the nature of the disability and still further because of employers' (needless) prejudices and misconceptions about people with disabilities. For most adults with disabilities, obtaining and holding a job is a major life challenge and goal.

Secondary school programs can facilitate the transition to the world of work by providing functional curricula and real work experiences in integrated community job sites.

Characteristics of secondary school programs and competitive employment outcomes

 Council for Exceptional Children

Knowledge and Skill Base for Beginning Special Education Transition Specialists: Research on relationships between individual outcomes and transition practices (TS1K4).

PRAXIS Special Education Core Principles: Content Knowledge: III. Delivery of Services to Students with Disabilities, Curriculum and Instruction, Career development and transition issues as related to curriculum design and implementation.

COMPETITIVE EMPLOYMENT

A person who is competitively employed performs work valued by an employer, functions in an integrated setting with nondisabled co-workers, earns at or above the federal minimum wage, and is working without support from an outside human service agency. Virtually all special educators who have studied the transition of students with disabilities from school to adult life believe that only through significant revision of the public school curriculum and improved coordination of school and adult vocational habilitation services can the prospects of competitive employment be enhanced for young adults with disabilities (e.g., Flexer et al., 2001; Johnson & Wehman, 2001; Patton et al., 1997; Sitlington et al., 2000).

Three characteristics are critical to good secondary school programs. First, the curriculum must stress functional skills; that is, students must learn vocational skills that they will actually need and use in local employment situations. Second, school-based instruction must be carried out in integrated settings as much as possible. Students with disabilities must be given ample opportunities to learn the interpersonal skills necessary to work effectively with co-workers in integrated work sites. Third, community-based instruction should ideally begin as early as age 10–13 for students with severe disabilities and must be used for progressively extended periods as students near graduation. While on work sites in the community, students should receive direct instruction in areas such as specific job skills, ways to increase production rates, and transportation to and from employment sites. Students should train and work in the community whenever possible so they learn "the communication, behavior, dress and other codes critical for success in integrated environments . . . [and] to get to and from important places on time or to produce consistently" (Brown, Farrington, Suomi, & Zeigler, 1999, p. 6).

Several follow-up studies have found a positive correlation between paid work experiences during high school and postschool employment (e.g., Benz, Lindstrom, & Yavanoff, 2000; Benz, Yovanoff, & Doren, 1997; D'Amico, 1991; Kohler, 1994; Scuccimarra & Speece, 1990). Unpaid and volunteer work experience is also valuable for students with disabilities (Brown et al., 1999). Unfortunately, the NLTS found that only 39% of young adults with disabilities had been enrolled in work experience programs during high school.

SUPPORTED EMPLOYMENT

A new type of vocational opportunity has emerged that helps adults with severe disabilities, who have historically been unemployed or restricted to sheltered settings, earn real wages for real work. The supported employment movement recognizes that many adults with severe disabilities require ongoing, often intensive support to obtain, learn, and hold a job.

Supported employment is defined in the Rehabilitation Act Amendments of 1986 (P.L. 99-506) as

- competitive work in integrated work settings;
- for persons with the most severe disabilities;
- for whom competitive employment has not traditionally occurred;
- or for whom competitive employment has been interrupted or intermittent as a result of a severe disability; and
- who, because of the severity of their disability, need intensive support services; or
- extended services in order to perform such work. (P.L. 102-569, Sec. 635[b][6] [c][iii])

Definition of supported employment

Council for Exceptional Children — Knowledge and Skill Base for Beginning Special Education Transition Specialists: Transition-related laws and policies (TS1K2).
PRAXIS Special Education Core Principles: Content Knowledge: II. Legal and Societal Issues, Federal laws and legal issues related to special education.

Supported employment has grown rapidly since its inception. In 1986, fewer than 10,000 individuals were working in federally assisted supported employment demonstration projects in 20 states. Just 2 years later, the supported employment movement had grown to a total of 32,342 participants nationally; and the cumulative wages these workers earned grew from $1.4 million to $12.4 million in the 15 states that reported earnings data (Wehman, Kregel, Shafer, & West, 1989). By 1995, it was estimated that more than 139,000 persons with disabilities were working through supported employment with an average hourly wage of $4.70 (Wehman, Revell, & Kregel, 1998). These employees earned more than $750 million in annual wages in 1995, many becoming taxpayers for the first time in their lives.

The success of supported employment depends in large part on job development, the identification and creation of community-based employment opportunities for individuals with disabilities. Four distinct models of supported employment have evolved: small business enterprise, mobile work crew, work enclave, and individual placement model. A national survey of supported employment programs found that 80% of supported employees were working in the individual placement model (Revell, Wehman, Kregel, West, & Rayfield, 1994).

The supported employment movement is enabling tens of thousands of individuals like Barry to experience, for the first time in their lives, the benefits of real work for real wages.

Small Business Enterprise This model provides supported employment for persons with disabilities by establishing a business that takes advantage of existing commercial opportunities within a community. The business hires a small number of individuals with disabilities as well as several employees without disabilities.

Mobile Work Crew A mobile work crew involves a small group of supported employees organized around a small single-purpose business, such as building or grounds maintenance, working in an integrated community employment setting. A general manager may be responsible for finding and coordinating the work of several small crews of three to eight individuals, with each crew supervised by a supported employment specialist. Mobile work crews are organized as not-for-profit corporations; the extra costs the organizations incur because their employees do not work at full productivity levels are covered by public funds. Such costs are usually less than would be needed to support the work crew employees in activity centers, which provide little or no real work or reimbursement.

Supported employment models

Council for Exceptional Children — Knowledge and Skill Base for Beginning Special Education Transition Specialists: Theoretical and applied models of transition (TS1K1).

Enclave (or Workstation) In this model of supported employment, a small group of no more than eight persons with disabilities performs work with special training or job supports within a normal business or industry. Work enclave employees typically receive wages commensurate with their productivity rates. The work enclave provides a useful alternative to traditional segregated sheltered employment, offering many of the benefits of community-based integrated employment as well as the ongoing supports necessary for long-term job success.

With respect to interaction with nondisabled co-workers, program developers and industrial managers contemplating the enclave model must ensure that

> employees not become segregated from the rest of the working community (much like the "handicapped wing" of a public school). A balance must be attained in providing the structure to support training interventions, to address low productivity, and insure adaptability to changing work demands, without sacrificing the advantages of a normal industrial environment. (Rhodes & Valenta, 1985, p. 18)

Individual Placement   The individual placement model of supported employment consists of developing jobs with employers in the community, systematically assessing clients' job preferences, carefully placing employees on jobs they want, intensive job-site training and advocacy, building systems of natural supports on the job site, ongoing monitoring of client performance, and a systematic approach to long-term job retention and follow-up (Wehman, Brooke, & Inge, 2001; Wehman & Kregel, 1998).

The supported employment specialist is the key to making a supported work program effective. The supported employment specialist, sometimes called a job coach, is a community-based professional who works in a nonprofit job placement program, a public vocational or adult services program, or a secondary special education program. The employment specialist is "the most integral aspect in making supported employment work" (Wehman & Revell, 1997, p. 630). Figure 15.3 identifies the major activities and responsibilities of a supported employment specialist in each component of the supported work model. To perform all of these functions, the employment specialist "must move comfortably in and out of a variety of roles associated with a consumer-driven approach to supported employment: planner, consultant, head hunter, technician, and community resource" (Wehman et al., 2001).

In a typical supported employment program, the employment specialist provides direct, on-site job training to the employee with disabilities and serves as the primary source of support and assistance to the supported employee. Although the job coach gradually reduces the time spent in direct, on-site training and support, this model of outside assistance has several inherent drawbacks (Chadsey, Linneman, Rusch, & Cimera, 1997; Mank, Cioffi, & Yovanoff, 2000; Simmons & Whaley, 2001):

Roles of employment specialist/job coach

Council for Exceptional Children   Knowledge and Skill Base for Beginning Special Education Transition Specialists: Scope and role of agency personnel related to transition services (TS9K2) (also, TS9K1).

- The arrival and presence of the job coach can be disruptive to the natural work setting.
- The supported employee may perform differently in the presence of her job coach.
- The job coach's presence can reduce the frequency of interaction between the supported employee and co-workers without disabilities.
- It is difficult for the employment specialist to be sensitive to the changing demands of the job over time and to provide continued support and training consistent with those changes.
- The cost of providing training and support by an employment specialist who must travel to the job site is higher and the efficiency of the approach is lower than one that takes advantage of the natural interactions of co-workers.
- The always-on-call job coach may also prevent the employer and co-workers from figuring out and implementing natural solutions to problems.
- This approach may foster too much dependence on the job coach, working against the supported employee's learning how to solve problems on the job and assuming responsibility for her own management.

FIGURE 15.3 Sample description of a job coach's responsibilities

Job Description: Employment Specialist

General Description

The employment specialist is involved in all aspects of community-based vocational training, placement, and follow-along for persons with an array of severe disabilities as part of the Excel Rehabilitation Program. The successful candidate will meet the employers to secure placements, provide one-on-one training for job and other related skills, and maintain systematic and regular contact with employers after job training has been completed. The employment specialist will work as part of a team and will interact frequently with other professionals related to specific cases.

Specific Duties/Responsibilities

1. *Job Development.* The employment specialist will complete job market screening activities and regularly present the employment program to prospective employers until adequate numbers of appropriate open positions have been identified. The specialist will analyze job duties and requirements of potential jobs.
2. *Consumer Assessment.* The employment specialist will complete and/or secure assessment and evaluation information as necessary to assist the consumer with informed decision making. This may include referral to other professionals/ agencies and subsequent interpretation of reports, observations, and interviewing persons knowledgeable about the consumer.
3. *Job Placement.* The employment specialist will complete activities to secure placement of individuals with disabilities that include vocational guidance, assistance with application procedures, support during interview processes, advice regarding job offers and negotiation, and initial planning for work.
4. *Job Site Training.* The employment specialist will work with the consumer on and off the job site until the consumer can maintain employment without regular or frequent assistance from the specialist. These duties may include development and implementation of instructional and/or behavioral programming strategies, conferences with the employer, co-workers, and/or consumer, and collection of performance information such as measures of quality and rate of work.
5. *Follow-Along.* The employment specialist will establish and maintain periodic contact with consumers, employers, and others as necessary to facilitate continued successful placement of the employee with disabilities. The employment specialist will be on call to assist in the resolution of obstacles to continued employment.
6. *Other.* The employment specialist will perform other related duties including but not limited to participating in agency meetings, attending training and professional development meetings, developing materials, coordinating consumer services as necessary for continued placement, and maintaining accurate consumer case files.

Source: Reprinted from Wehman, P., & Revell, W. G., Jr. (1997). Transition from school to adulthood: Looking ahead. In P. Wehman (Ed.), *Exceptional individuals in school, community, and work* (p. 631). Austin, TX: PRO-ED. Used by permission.

Natural Supports   The role of the employment specialist/job coach is evolving from one of primary supporter for the employee with disabilities to one of working with the employer and co-workers to help identify, develop, and facilitate the typical or indigenous supports of the workplace (Mank, Cioffi, & Yovanoff, 1999). Rogan, Hagner, and Murphy (1993) define natural supports as "any assistance, relationships or interactions that allow a person to secure or maintain a community job . . . in a way that corresponds to the typical work routines and social interactions of other employees" (p. 275).

Co-worker support and influence

Council for Exceptional Children   Knowledge and Skill Base for Beginning Special Education Transition Specialists: Identify and facilitate modifications within work and community environments (TS5S1) (also, CC5K1).

Importance of Co-Workers   Social interaction is a natural feature of a typical workplace. Social interaction provides an important source of support for any employee, with or without disabilities, and it is associated with job performance and job satisfaction. Because of their consistent presence in the work environment, co-workers can be a potentially powerful source of natural support for workers with disabilities (Rusch & Minch, 1988). Rusch, Hughes, McNair, and Wilson (1990) define a co-worker as an employee who works in the proximity of the supported employee, performs the same or similar duties, and/or takes breaks or eats meals in the same area as the supported employee. Six types of co-worker involvement beneficial to supported employees are described in Figure 15.4.

A skilled and friendly co-worker can provide information, answer questions, demonstrate job tasks, provide assistance and repeat instructions as needed, give social praise and feedback for performance, and serve as an important contact point for the supported employee's entry into the social fabric of the workplace (Curl, Hall, Chisholm, & Rule, 1992; Lee, Storey, Anderson, Goetz, & Zivolich, 1997). Although some co-workers provide support naturally, observations in the workplace indicate that some formal training is usually necessary to make co-workers' "help" effective in maintaining successful employment. For example, Curl, Lignugaris/Kraft, Pawley, and Salzberg (1988) found that co-workers typically presented more than 100 instructions in the first 2 hours of employment training—a frequency likely to overwhelm a newly hired employee with disabilities. Several approaches for co-worker training have been developed. Co-workers can be taught how to provide support during brief, 15- to 20-minute sessions during breaks or before or after work. Curl (1990) has developed a program in which co-workers learn to use a simple 4-step procedure in which they (1) provide instructions, (2) demonstrate the job task, (3) observe the supported employee performing the same task, and (4) deliver praise and evaluative feedback on the trainee's performance.

Natural Cues and Self-Management   The belief that employees with disabilities should be taught independence in the workplace has gained widespread acceptance among supported employment professionals and has spawned exciting and promising research in the

---

FIGURE 15.4   Six types of co-worker involvement

1. **Advocating.**   A co-worker advocates for a supported employee by optimizing, backing, and supporting a supported employee's employment status. *Optimizing* refers to encouraging a supervisor to assign high-status and relevant tasks to a supported employee; *backing* refers to supporting a supported employee's rights, for example, by attempting to prevent practical jokes aimed at her. It also includes speaking up for a supported employee or offering explanations during differences of opinion. *Supporting* relates to providing emotional support to a supported employee in the form of friendship, association, etc.

2. **Associating.**   A co-worker interacts socially with a supported employee at the workplace.

3. **Befriending.**   A co-worker interacts socially with a supported employee outside the workplace.

4. **Collecting data.**   A co-worker collects data by observing and recording social and/or work performance.

5. **Evaluating.**   A co-worker appraises a supported employee's work performance and provides (written/oral) feedback to him.

6. **Training.**   A co-worker supports a supported employee by providing on-the-job skill training.

Source: Adapted from Rusch, F. R., Hughes, C., McNair, J., & Wilson, P. G. (1990). *Co-worker involvement scoring manual and index.* Champaign: University of Illinois Press. Used by permission.

use of natural cues and self-management. Natural cues are features that already exist in the work environment that the employee can see, hear, touch, or smell and use to signal what to do next (Moon & Inge, 2000). For example, clocks or whistles may signal going to a job station, co-workers' stopping work and leaving the job station might be the prompt for break time, and a growing pile of dirty dishes should be the cue to increase the rate of dishwashing. The employment specialist's role expands from training the employee how to perform various vocational and social skills to teaching the supported employee how to respond independently to the cues that occur naturally in the workplace. When naturally occurring cues are insufficient to prompt the desired behavior, the supported employee can be taught to respond to contrived cues, such as picture prompts depicting individual steps in a multiple-step task (Wilson, Schepis, & Mason-Main, 1987) or prerecorded verbal prompts interspersed within favorite music that the employee might listen to on a Walkman-type cassette player (Barfels, Al-Attrash, & Heward, 1999; Grossi, 1998; West, Rayfield, Clements, Unger, & Thornton, 1994).

Self-monitoring can also be effectively used in employment training. Research has shown that employees with disabilities can use self-monitoring (observing and recording one's performance) and self-evaluation (comparing self-monitored performance with a goal or production criterion) to increase their job productivity and independence (Grossi & Heward, 1998; Sowers, Verdi, Bourbeau, & Sheehan, 1985; Wheeler, Bates, Marshall, & Miller, 1988). For example, Allen, White, and Test (1992) developed a picture/symbol form that employees with disabilities can use to self-monitor their performance on the job (see Figure 15.5).

Employees with disabilities can also learn to self-manage their work performance by providing their own verbal prompts and self-instructions (Hughes, 1997). For example, Salend, Ellis, and Reynolds (1989) used a self-instructional strategy to teach four adults with severe mental retardation to "talk while you work." Productivity increased dramatically and error rates decreased when the women verbalized to themselves, "Comb up, comb down, comb in bag, bag in box" while packaging combs in plastic bags. Hughes and Rusch (1989) taught two supported employees working at a janitorial supply company how to solve problems by using a self-instructional procedure consisting of four statements:

1. Statement of the problem (e.g., "Tape empty")
2. Statement of the response needed to solve the problem (e.g., "Need more tape")
3. Self-report (e.g., "Fixed it")
4. Self-reinforcement (e.g., "Good")

SHELTERED EMPLOYMENT

A **sheltered workshop** is a common type of vocational setting for adults with severe disabilities. Sheltered workshops serve individuals with a wide variety of disabilities, although about half are persons with mental retardation. Sheltered workshops provide one or more of three types of programs: (1) evaluation and training for community-based employment (commonly referred to as transitional workshops), (2) extended or long-term employment, and (3) work activities.

A **work activity center** offers programs of activities for individuals whose disabilities are viewed by local decision makers as too severe for productive work. Rehabilitation and training revolve around concentration and persistence at a task. Intervals of work may be short, perhaps only an hour long, interspersed with other activities—such as training in social skills, self-help skills, household skills, community skills, and recreation. There are approximately 5,000 sheltered work and day activity centers in the United States (Butterworth, Gilmore, Kiernan, & Shalock, 1999).

Many sheltered work programs offer both transitional and extended employment within the same building. Transitional workshops try to place their employees in community-based

Natural and contrived cues, self-monitoring, and self-instruction in the workplace

Council for Exceptional Children — Content Standards for Beginning Teachers–Common Core: Use procedures to increase the individual's self-awareness, self-management, self-control, self-reliance, and self-esteem (CC4S5) (also, CC4S6, TS5S1, TS8S5).
PRAXIS Special Education Core Principles: Content Knowledge: III. Delivery of Services to Students with Disabilities, Curriculum and Instruction, Self-management.

Sheltered employment

Council for Exceptional Children — Knowledge and Skill Base for Beginning Special Education Transition Specialists: Range of post-school options within specific outcome areas (TS7K3).
PRAXIS Special Education Core Principles: Content Knowledge: II. Legal and Societal Issues, Historical movements/trends affecting connections between special education and the larger society, transition.

Task Sheet

Student: _____   Week of: _____   Observer: _____

		M	T	W	Th	Comments
	1. Job needs (e.g., name tag, lunch).					
	2. Get work assignment.					
	3. Get cart.					
	4. Find and enter room.					
	5. Check drapes.					
	6. Check TV.					
	7. Make bed.					
	8. Dust.					
	9. Stock amenities.					
	10. Empty wastebaskets.					
	11. Clean bathroom.					
	12. Vacuum.					
	13. Fill out hotel checklist					

jobs. Extended employment workshops are operated to provide whatever training and support services are necessary to enable individuals with severe disabilities to work productively within the sheltered environment. The Wage and Hour Division of the U.S. Department of Labor requires that persons working in an extended sheltered workshop receive at least 50% of the minimum wage; they may be paid an hourly wage or a piecework rate.

All sheltered workshops have at least two elements in common. First, they offer rehabilitation, training, and—in some instances—full employment. Second, to provide meaningful work for clients, a sheltered workshop must operate as a business. Sheltered workshops generally engage in one of three types of business ventures: contracting, prime manufacturing, or reclamation.

Contracting is the major source of work in most workshops. A contract is an agreement that a sheltered workshop will complete a specified job (e.g., assembling and packaging a company's product) within a specified time for a given price. Most sheltered workshops have one or more professional staff members, called contractors or contract procurement persons, whose sole job is to obtain and negotiate contracts with businesses and industries in the community.

Prime manufacturing involves the designing, producing, marketing, and shipping of a complete product. The advantage of prime manufacturing over contracting, assuming a successful product is being manufactured, is that the workshops do not have problems with downtime when they are between contracts. They can plan their training and labor requirements more directly. Most sheltered workshops, however, are neither staffed nor equipped to handle the more sophisticated business venture of prime manufacturing.

In a *reclamation,* or salvage, operation, a workshop purchases or collects salvageable material, performs the salvage or reclamation operation, and then sells the reclaimed product. Salvage and reclamation operations have proven successful for many sheltered workshops because they require a lot of labor, are low in overhead, and can usually continue indefinitely.

Problems with Sheltered Employment   Sheltered workshops and work activity centers are no longer considered appropriate transition outcomes for young people with disabilities (Block, 1997). The theoretical purpose of sheltered workshops is to train individuals in specific job-related skills that will enable them to obtain competitive employment; however, few employees of sheltered workshops are ever placed in jobs in the community. Only about 10% of sheltered workshop employees were placed in community jobs from 1977 to 1987 (U.S. Congress, 1987; U.S. Department of Labor, 1979), and many who are placed do not keep their jobs for long (Brickey, Campbell, & Browning, 1985). By contrast, approximately 50% of all supported employees are still earning wages and paying taxes 1 year after placement alongside nondisabled co-workers (Rusch, 1990).

Many professionals believe that the poor competitive employment record of sheltered workshop graduates may be more indicative of limitations inherent in sheltered workshops than of the employment potential of persons with disabilities (Mank, Cioffi, & Yovanoff, 1998; Wehman et al., 2001). Because sheltered workshop employment is conducted in segregated settings, affords limited opportunities for job placement in the community, and provides extremely low pay, it has been called a dead-end street for individuals with mental retardation (Frank & Sitlington, 1993). West, Revell, and Wehman (1998) discuss the challenges faced by agencies that operate sheltered work programs when converting their programs to supported employment.

Poor prospects for sheltered employees

 Council for Exceptional Children   Knowledge and Skill Base for Beginning Special Education Transition Specialists: Research on relationships between individual outcomes and transition practices (TS1K4).

 ## POSTSECONDARY EDUCATION

Many high school students look ahead to college. However, access to postsecondary education may be even more important for persons with disabilities than it is for individuals without them. Postsecondary education significantly improves chances of meaningful employment. Among adults with disabilities, only 15.6% of those without a high school diploma are employed; participation in the labor force doubles to 30.2% for those who have completed high school and triples to 45.1% for those with some postsecondary education (Yelin & Katz, 1994). Individuals with disabilities who had completed a 4-year college degree were four times more likely to be employed than were persons with disabilities who had never attended college (Harris & Associates, 1986).

Individuals with disabilities who are graduates of postsecondary education programs—technical training, a community college 2-year associate's degree, or a 4-year bachelor's degree—enjoy increased vocational options and greater lifetime earnings (Gajar, Goodman, & McAfee, 1995). Increasingly, jobs require technical training, problem solving, and interpersonal skills

Relationship between postsecondary education and employment

 Council for Exceptional Children   Knowledge and Skill Base for Beginning Special Education Transition Specialists: Research on relationships between individual outcomes and transition practices (TS1K4).

that can be attained through postsecondary education (Webster, Clary, & Griffith, 2001). In 1950, 60% of jobs were classified as unskilled, but it is estimated that only 12% to 15% of jobs did not require specific skills or training in the year 2000 (Hoye, 1998).

The percentage of first-time, full-time freshmen enrolled in college who indicate they have a disability has increased significantly, from 3% in 1978 to more than 9% in 1998 (Henderson, 1999). Students with learning disabilities comprise the largest number of postsecondary students with disabilities. Even youth with moderate and severe disabilities can participate in some aspects of traditional college life, including auditing academic classes and enjoying recreation and physical education activities in an integrated setting with same-age peers (Hall, Kleinert, & Kerns, 2000).

Although the range and availability of services offered by colleges and universities for students with disabilities have increased greatly in recent years, the success of students with disabilities as measured by graduation is well below that of students without disabilities. One study found that 80% of students with learning disabilities who had attended postsecondary education programs had not graduated 5 years after high school compared to 56% of students without disabilities (Murray, Goldstein, Nourse, & Edgar, 2000). Ten years after they had left high school, 56% of the students with learning disabilities had not graduated from postsecondary education compared to 32% of those without disabilities.

Several studies have reported that preparation for postsecondary education was frequently lacking in students' transition plans (Grigal, Test, Beattie, & Wood, 1997; Hitchings, Luzzo, Retish, Horvath, & Ristow, 1998). In one study, only 8 out of 97 college students with learning disabilities could remember meeting annually with their high school counselors to discuss courses for the following year and the steps for selecting a college (Hitchings et al., 2001). These results reveal the need for increased emphasis on postsecondary education goals and outcomes during transition planning.

Mull, Sitlington, and Alper (2001) concluded their review of 26 published articles describing or reporting on services for postsecondary students with learning disabilities with the following suggestions:

Needs of post-secondary students with LD

 Council for Exceptional Children Knowledge and Skill Base for Beginning Special Education Transition Specialists: Implications of individual characteristics with respect to post-school outcomes and support needs (TS2K1).

- High school students need to be prepared to determine which of the accommodations and supports used at the secondary level they will need at the postsecondary level and how to access these supports as needed.
- Students need to be trained how to use assistive technology devices that will increase their access to and ability to manipulate curriculum content.
- Secondary teachers need to be aware of the demands of postsecondary education environments so they can help students acquire the skills, supports, and accommodations to be successful in those environments.
- As a field, special education needs to deal with the issue of documentation of disabilities, which is required for postsecondary students to access the accommodations and support services they need. This is a concern because many secondary special education programs are no longer using specific disability labels and formal psychological testing to diagnose disabilities (p. 106).

For additional information on promoting the success of postsecondary education for students with learning disabilities, see Brinckerhoff, Shaw, and McGuire (1993); Garten, Rumrill, and Serebreni (1996); and Skinner (1998).

RESIDENTIAL ALTERNATIVES

Where one lives determines a great deal about *how* one lives. Where a person lives influences where she can work, what community services and resources will be available, who her friends will be, what the opportunities for recreation and leisure will be, and, to a great extent, what feelings of self and place in the community will develop. Not long ago, the only place someone with severe disabilities could live, if she did not live with family, was a large, state-operated institution. Although she had done no wrong to society, an institution was considered the best place for the person. There were no other options—no such thing as residential alternatives.

Historically, segregation and institutionalization were the only options for persons with severe disabilities (Howe, Horner, & Newton, 1998). Today, most communities provide a variety of residential options for adults with disabilities. Increased community-based residential services have meant a greater opportunity for adults with severe disabilities to live in a more normalized setting.

 ## GROUP HOMES

Group homes provide family-style living for a small group of individuals, usually three to six persons. Most group homes serve adults with mental retardation, although some have residents with other disabilities. Some group homes are principally residential and represent a permanent home for their residents. Staff persons in this type of home help the people who live there develop self-care and daily living skills, form interpersonal relationships, and participate in recreation and leisure skills. During the day, most residents work in the community or in a sheltered workshop.

Other group homes operate more as halfway houses. Their primary function is to prepare individuals with disabilities for a more independent living situation, such as a supervised apartment. These transitional group homes typically serve residents who have recently left institutions, bridging the gap between institutional and community living.

Two aspects of group homes make them a much more normalized place to live: their size and their location. Most people grow up in a typical family-sized group where there is opportunity for personal attention, care, and privacy. The congregate-living arrangement of an institution cannot offer a typical, normalized lifestyle, no matter how much effort a hardworking, caring staff makes. By keeping the number of people in a group home small, there is a greater chance for a family-like atmosphere. Size is also directly related to the neighborhood's ability to assimilate the members of the group home into typical activities within the community. Large groups tend to become self-sufficient, orienting inward and thereby resisting movement outward into the community. In groups larger than six or eight, care providers can no longer relate properly to individuals. Large group homes tend to acquire the characteristics of a place of work for direct care staff rather than a home where people live (Ferguson & Ferguson, 2000). Indeed, some evidence suggests that quality of life is better for persons residing in smaller rather than larger group homes (Burchard, Hasazi, Gordon, & Yoe, 1991; Conroy, 1996).

The location and physical characteristics of the group home itself are also vital determinants of its ability to provide a normalized lifestyle. A group home must be located within the community in a residential area, not a commercially zoned district. It must be in an area where the people who live there can conveniently access shopping, schools, churches, public transportation, and recreational facilities. In other words, a group home must be located in a normal residential area where any one of us might live. And it must look like a home not conspicuously different from the other family dwellings on the same street.

Research has shown not only that the architectural features of the home influence the degree to which residents and others give it a high rating of homelikeness but also that some interior design features of a home correlate with the frequency of certain adaptive and maladaptive behaviors by residents (Thompson, Robinson, Dietrich, Farris, & Sinclair, 1996a, 1996b). For example, a laundry room located in the basement may present challenges for residents that create behavioral problems, and a cafeteria-style dining room table is not conducive to conversations during meals.

Residential options

Council for Exceptional Children   Knowledge and Skill Base for Beginning Special Education Transition Specialists: Range of post-school options within specific outcome areas (TS7K3).
PRAXIS Special Education Core Principles: Content Knowledge: II. Legal and Societal Issues, Historical movements/trends affecting connections between special education and the larger society, transition.

FOSTER HOMES

When a family opens its home to an unrelated person for an extended period, the term *foster home* applies. Although foster homes have provided temporary residential services and family care for children (usually wards of the court) for many years, more and more families have begun to share their homes with adults with disabilities. In return for providing room and board for their new family member, foster families receive a modest financial reimbursement.

Life in a foster family home can have numerous advantages for an adult with disabilities. Instead of interacting with paid group home staff who may or may not actually live at the same address, the person with disabilities lives in a residence that is owned or rented by individuals or families as their primary domicile. The person can participate and share in day-to-day family activities, receive individual attention from people vitally interested in his continued growth and development, and develop close interpersonal relationships. As part of a family unit, the adult with disabilities also has more opportunities to interact with and be accepted by the community at large. In their survey of small group homes and foster homes, Hill et al. (1989) found that 80% of foster home caregivers perceived residents with disabilities primarily as family members. In contrast, group home staff were more likely to view persons with disabilities as trainees or friends.

 APARTMENT LIVING

A rented apartment is one of the most common living arrangements for people without disabilities in our society. Today, an increasing number of adults with disabilities are enjoying the freedom and independence that apartment living offers. Apartment living offers them an even greater opportunity for integration into the community than do group homes. Whereas the resident of a group home interacts primarily with other persons with disabilities, in an apartment-living arrangement (assuming the apartment is in a regular apartment complex), the likelihood of interacting with persons without disabilities is greater. Burchard et al. (1991) found that people who lived in supervised apartments had about twice as many social and leisure activities in the community as did individuals who lived in small group homes or with their natural parents. They also found that persons living in supervised apartments were more likely to be accompanied in the community by peers who are not disabled than those living in group homes were. Another study followed seven young adults with mental retardation who had moved from a campus-type residential setting to community-based apartments (Rose, White, Conroy, & Smith, 1993). Assessments of the young adults' social/communication skills, community-living skills, and general independence conducted at 6 and 12 months after the move found significant and continued gains over pre-move measures.

"What's for dinner?" Judy and Kathy, who spent most of their lives in a state institution for people with mental retardation, have shared an apartment for the past ten years.

Three types of apartment living for adults with disabilities are common: the apartment cluster, the co-residence apartment, and the maximum-independence apartment. An *apartment cluster* consists of a small number of apartments housing persons with disabilities and another nearby apartment for a support person or staff member. An apartment cluster allows for a great deal of flexibility in the amount and degree of support needed by residents in the various apartments. Whereas some people might require direct help with such things as shopping, cooking, or even getting dressed, others need only limited assistance or suggestions and prompts. To facilitate social integration, persons without disabilities may also occupy some apartments in an apartment cluster.

A *co-residence apartment* is shared by an individual with disabilities and a roommate without disabilities. Although this arrangement is sometimes permanent, most co-residence apartments are used as a step toward independent living. The live-in roommates are often unpaid volunteers.

Two to four adults with disabilities usually cohabit *maximum-independence apartments.* These adults have all of the self-care and daily living skills required to take care of themselves and their apartment on a day-to-day basis. A supervisory visit is made once or twice a week to help them deal with any special problems they may be having.

SUPPORTED LIVING

Several innovative models for residential services for adults with disabilities have been developed based on the belief that residential placements must be adapted to the needs of the person with disabilities, not vice versa (Klein, 1994; Knoll & Wheeler, 2001). **Supported living** is the term used to describe a growing movement of helping people with disabilities live in the community as independently and normally as they possibly can. Similar to the way in which supported employment provides ongoing, individualized supports to help a person with disabilities perform meaningful work in a community-based employment setting, supported living involves a personalized network of various kinds and levels of natural supports. Supported living is neither a place nor a single set of procedures to be provided for a person with disabilities.

Klein (1994) explains what supported living is by describing what it is not. Supported living does not revolve around a professional program. People should not live in a place referred to by an agency name or provider name (e.g., UCP Group Home, New Life Center). There are no criteria for participation (e.g., persons in this program must be able to cook for themselves, have a physical disability, need more or less than 3 hours per day of attendant care, have visual impairments). Supported living is not based on readiness and movement through a continuum. Participation in traditional residential services is based on a professional's assessment of the person's readiness or ability to live in a particular program, and a person must perform well (learn new skills on her individual habilitation plan) in order to move ("earn" the right) to the next, less restrictive rung on the continuum.

Supported living

Council for Exceptional Children — Knowledge and Skill Base for Beginning Special Education Transition Specialists: Range of post-school options within specific outcome areas (TS7K3).

PRAXIS Special Education Core Principles: Content Knowledge: II. Legal and Societal Issues, Historical movements/trends affecting connections between special education and the larger society, transition.

Supported living provides flexible supports when and as they are needed. Twice per month, Judy and Kathy pay their bills and review their budget with the help of a support person.

Rather than a single approach or model, supported living is a philosophy about the kind of living experiences appropriate for citizens with disabilities and about commitment to figuring out how to best approximate the ideal for each individual. Supported living, according to Klein (1994), is guided by these nine principles:

1. *Individualization.* Supported living must be something that is for one person without exception. This does not mean that everyone has to live alone. It does

mean that if people want to live with someone else, they choose with whom they live. The magic number becomes one.

2. *Everybody is ready.* There are no criteria to receive support because what occurs is individually designed. We must give up trying to make people ready by simulating how it is to live in a home and begin supporting people to have that home.

3. *Future planning.* People who are assisting others must get to know the individuals they are supporting. What are their desires and preferences? What would an ideal living situation look like for each person? After answers to these questions are determined, the people who care about the person get together regularly to develop a plan for getting as close as possible to that ideal living situation.

4. *Use of connections.* Traditional residential services rely on system solutions to problems, referring to the procedures and policy manual to find out what rules and regulations suggest. Supported living relies on the assistance of all who want to and can help. This means that professional care providers and staff are replaced by friends, family members, and neighbors whenever possible. "Who do we know who can help?" becomes a key question for planning and arranging needed supports.

5. *Flexible supports.* Supports are based and provided on the individual's schedule and needs, not on a program's schedule. Persons receive support where, when, how, and with whom it is needed. Supports must be flexible enough to be adjusted on the basis of the individual's changing needs, preferences, and desires.

6. *Combining natural supports, learning, and technology.* As much as possible, supports used are natural to the time, place, and person. Individuals are given opportunities to learn to provide their own support and to use technology to gain control over their environment as much as possible.

7. *Focusing on what people can do.* Traditional residential programs often focus on what people cannot do and design treatment programs to try to remediate those skill deficiencies. Supportive living focuses on what people can do, provides support for things they cannot do, and provides opportunities for them to learn how to do the things they want to do.

8. *Using language that is natural to the setting.* The language of supported living is natural and promotes inclusion in the community. The places where people live are described as Joe's home or Mary's home. People clean their homes and do their laundry rather than learn programs; people live with roommates, not with staff or care providers; friends, not volunteers, come over to visit; and people with disabilities are referred to as neighbors, friends, and citizens rather than as clients, consumers, and residents.

9. *Ownership and control.* Last and most important, the home is the person's, and that person controls the support that is received. Home ownership does not mean that most individuals with disabilities who do not have many financial resources will hold the mortage to a home. It does mean, however, that they sign the lease, that things in the home belong to them, and that the place is their home. Roommates sublet from the person, support people are hired by the person, and support people respond to the need for assistance when, where, and how it is needed as determined by the person. (adapted from Klein, 1994, pp. 17–18)

 **INSTITUTIONS**

Most of the large, state-operated institutions in this country were founded in the 19th or early 20th century, when it was generally believed that people with mental retardation could not be educated or trained. Large custodial institutions (many institutions once housed hundreds or even a thousand or more people with mental retardation and other disabilities) kept people with disabilities segregated from the rest of society; the institutions were never designed to help people learn to live in the community. In the 1960s and 1970s, these institutions came under intense criticism for their inability to provide individualized residential services in a comfortable, humane, and normalized environment (Blatt, 1976; Blatt & Kaplan, 1966; Kugel & Wolfensberger, 1969; Wolfensberger, 1969). The complaints were not leveled against the concept of residential programs; there will probably always be persons whose disabilities are so severe that they require the kind of 24-hour support that residential facilities can offer. The problem lies with the inherent inability of an institutional environment to allow a person to experience a normal lifestyle.

Tremendous improvements have been made in the abysmal living conditions in institutions that Blatt and Kaplan exposed more than 35 years ago in their book *Christmas in Purgatory* (1966). During the 1970s, the U.S. Department of Health, Education, and Welfare and the Joint Commission on the Accreditation of Hospitals developed extensive standards for residential facilities for individuals with mental retardation. A residential facility must meet these standards—which cover topics as diverse as building construction, staffing, and habilitative and educational programming—to qualify for federal and state Medicaid funding. Residential units that meet the standards are referred to as ICF-MR Medicaid facilities. Today, an ICF-MR facility serving 16 or more residents is considered an institution. Although the ICF-MR Medicaid system of rules and regulations has eliminated the inhumane and filthy conditions and the overcrowding that had been defining features of institutional life, the system has become the target of increasing criticism in terms of residents' quality of life and the high cost (e.g., Stancliffe & Hayden, 1998; Stancliffe & Lakin, 1998).

Deinstitutionalization—the movement of people with mental retardation out of large institutions and into smaller, community-based living environments such as group homes or apartments—has been an active reality during the past 35 years. The number of persons with mental retardation living in large state institutions has decreased steadily from a high of 194,650 in 1967 to 47,580 persons in 2000 (Lakin, Smith, Prouty, & Polister, 2001).

Several studies indicate generally positive outcomes for residents transferred from institutions to group homes to smaller, community-based living arrangements (Conroy & Bradley, 1985; Larson & Lakin, 1989). For example, Conroy (1996) compared 35 quality-of-life measures over a 5-year period for individuals living in small institutions serving an average of eight people with outcomes for persons living in community-based living apartments or group homes of three people. Higher quality was found in the community living arrangements on 10 of the indicators (e.g., choice making, normalization, individualized treatment, family satisfaction). Higher quality was not found in the ICF-MR facilities on any of the indicators.

 ## RECREATION AND LEISURE

Recreation and the enjoyable use of leisure time are important components of a self-satisfying lifestyle. Most of us take for granted our ability to pursue leisure and recreational activities. We benefit from a lifetime of learning how to play and how to enjoy personal hobbies or crafts.

But recreation and leisure activities do not come easily for many adults with disabilities. To use community recreational resources, one must have transportation, the physical ability or skills to play the game, and, usually, other willing and able friends to play with. These three variables, alone or in combination, often work to limit the recreation and leisure activities available to the adult with disabilities. Transportation is not available; the person's disability does not allow him to swim, bowl, or play tennis; and he has no friends with similar skills and interests. Because of these problems, the majority of

Deinstitutionalization

 Council for Exceptional Children

Knowledge and Skill Base for Beginning Special Education Transition Specialists: Range of post-school options within specific outcome areas (TS7K3).

PRAXIS Special Education Core Principles: Content Knowledge: II. Legal and Societal Issues, Historical movements/trends affecting connections between special education and the larger society, transition.

recreation and leisure experiences for many adults with disabilities have consisted of segregated, disabled-only outings.

Too often, the so-called leisure activities for adults with disabilities consist of watching great amounts of television, listening to music in the solitude of their rooms, and spending discretionary time socially isolated (Strand & Kreiner, 2001). Choice is a crucial element for meaningful leisure activities (Browder, Cooper, & Lim, 1998).

> Without choice, activities become simply tasks rather than providing elements of control that lead to leisure satisfaction. If television is the only offering, choice is neglected . . . . Leisure education programs should focus on development of all of the knowledge, skills, and attitudes necessary to facilitate choice—not only traditional group activity skills, but also those individual skills that will have lifetime applications. (Macias, Best, Bigge, & Musante, 2001, pp. 478–479)

Tom loves to fish. Choice is crucial to the enjoyment of leisure activities.

Teaching recreation and leisure activities

Council for Exceptional Children Knowledge and Skill Base for Beginning Special Education Transition Specialists: Arrange and evaluate instructional activities in relation to post-school goals (TS7S2) (also, TS4S1). **PRAXIS** Special Education Core Principles: Content Knowledge: III. Delivery of Services to Students with Disabilities, Curriculum and Instruction, Transition issues as related to curriculum design and implementation.

Special educators must realize the importance of including training for recreation and leisure in curricula for school-age children with disabilities. Macias et al. (2001) describe how numerous games, hobbies, crafts, and projects can be adapted to become enjoyable, worthwhile leisure-time pursuits for persons with disabilities. Areas they suggest include raising guinea pigs, music appreciation and study, photography, card games, and nature study. Suggestions are also available for adapting leisure activities for young adults who are deaf-blind, such as using permanent tactile prompts (e.g., attaching fabric to the flipper buttons of a pinball machine), adequately stabilizing materials, enhancing the visual or auditory input provided by the materials (e.g., using large-print, low-vision playing cards), and simplifying the requirements of the task (e.g., raising the front legs on a pinball machine, thereby reducing the speed with which the ball approaches the flippers).

Learning appropriate leisure skills is particularly important for adults with severe disabilities (Browder & Bambara, 2000). Most persons with severe disabilities have ample free time, but many do not use it constructively and may instead engage in inappropriate behaviors such as body rocking, hand flapping, or bizarre vocalizations. A number of studies have been reported in which age-appropriate leisure skills have been taught to secondary students and adults with moderate and severe mental retardation (Collins, Hall, & Branson, 1997; Nietupski & Svoboda, 1982; Schleien, Kiernan, & Wehman, 1981). Schleien, Wehman, and Kiernan (1981) successfully taught three adults with severe and multiple disabilities to throw darts. Vandercook (1991) taught five high school students with severe mental retardation and physical disabilities to play pinball and bowl with nondisabled peer partners. In another study, four adults with moderate mental retardation learned to order drinks in an Irish pub (O'Reilly, Lancioni, & Kiernans, 2000).

Participating in community recreation and leisure activities with an adult with disabilities can be an excellent way to appreciate the importance of a functional curriculum for school-age students. See Teaching & Learning, "A Friendship Program for Future Special Education Teachers," later in this chapter.

QUALITY OF LIFE

Without question, significant strides have been made in the lives of many people with disabilities. Tens of thousands of people who previously were relegated to life in an institution now live in real homes in regular neighborhoods. Many thousands who never had an opportunity to learn meaningful job skills go to work each day and bring home a paycheck each week. But living in a community-based residence and having a job in an integrated setting do not translate automatically into a better life.

Most advocates and professionals now realize that the physical presence of individuals with disabilities in integrated residential, work, and community settings is an important first step but that the only truly meaningful outcome of human service programs must be an improved quality of life. How highly would we rate the quality of life for a woman who always sits alone during lunch and breaks at work because she has not developed a social relationship with her co-workers? Recent research on social interaction patterns in integrated work settings suggests that this is an all-too-common scenario. Several studies have found that most contact between employees with disabilities and their nondisabled co-workers involves task performance; disabled workers are less involved in good-natured teasing and joking, and few workers with disabilities are befriended by their co-workers (e.g., Lignugaris/Kraft, Rule, Salzberg, & Stowitscheck, 1988; Rusch, Johnson, & Hughes, 1990).

And what is the quality of life for a young man who lives in a group home in a residential neighborhood but who seldom or never gets to choose what will be served for dinner or when he will go to bed and whose only "friends" are the paid staff responsible for supervising him on his weekly trip to the shopping mall? One measure of the quality of a person's life is the extent to which he can make choices. The choices we make play a significant role in defining our individual identities—from everyday matters, such as what to eat or wear, to the choices we make on larger matters, such as where to live or what kind of work to do (Ferguson & Ferguson, 2000).

There are numerous conceptions and definitions of quality of life, debates over how or whether it can be measured, and recommendations of what should or must be done to improve it (e.g., Dennis, Williams, Giangreco, & Cloninger, 1993; Halpern, 1993; Hatton, 1998; Sands & Kozleski, 1994; Schalock, Bonham, & Marchand, 2000; Syzmanski, 2000; Wehmeyer, 1994).

Schalock, Keith, Hoffman, and Karan (1989) have proposed an objective measure of quality of life. They present 28 criterion-referenced questions that comprise the Quality of Life Index. The questions are organized under three aspects: control of one's environment, involvement in the community, and social relationships. They note that the Quality of Life Index is more appropriate for living rather than work environments and that generalizations across all types of living environments are not possible. A sample of the 28 questions follows:

- How many people sleep in your bedroom?
- How much control do you have when you go to bed and when you get up?
- Who plans your meals?
- Can you do what you want to do?
- Who decides how you spend your money?

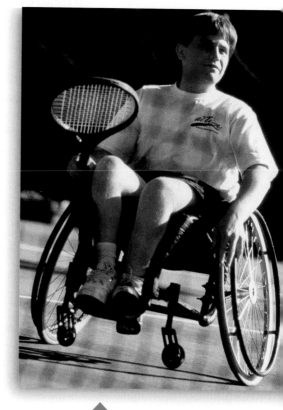

Karen does not let paraplegia get in the way of her quality of life. She enjoys an active lifestyle that includes tennis and other fitness activities.

- When can friends visit your home?
- Does your job make you feel good?
- How often do you use public transportation?
- How frequently do you spend time in recreational activities in town? (from Schalock et al., 1989, p. 27)

MISGUIDED AND LIMITING PRESUMPTIONS

A continuing problem for many adults with disabilities is lack of acceptance as full members of our society, with all the rights, privileges, and services granted to any citizen (Taylor, Bogdan, & Lutfiyya, 1995). Progress has been made in this regard (witness the litigation and legislation on behalf of persons with disabilities that have been discussed throughout this book), but we still have a long way to go. Courts can decree and laws can require, but neither can alter the way in which individuals treat people with disabilities. People with disabilities often seem "in the community but not of it" (Ferguson & Ferguson, 2000, p. 645).

Most adults with disabilities believe the biggest barriers to full integration into society are not inaccessible buildings or the actual restrictions imposed by their disabilities but the differential treatment afforded them by nondisabled people. Just as the terms *racism* and *sexism* indicate prejudiced, discriminatory treatment of racial groups and women, the term *handicapism* has been coined to describe biased reactions toward a person with a disability. Those reactions are not based on an individual's qualities or performance but on a presumption of what the person with a disability must feel or be like because of the disability (Bogdan & Taylor, 1994).

Only when a man or woman with a disability is allowed to be simply an ordinary person—given the opportunity to strive and perhaps succeed but also allowed the freedom and dignity to strive and sometimes fail—can full membership and participation in society become a reality. Only then can people with disabilities enjoy a quality of life that citizens without disabilities take for granted.

> The truth is that every human being has some ordinary ways of being and some unusual ways. Everyone suffers sometimes and has burdens and sometimes burdens others. Everyone also has times of joy, sometimes gives something to someone else, and has the possibility of creating opportunity for others in the world. Paradoxically the most common thing about people is that everyone has unique ways of being himself or herself. (Snow, 2001, p. 8)

Handicapism

 Council for Exceptional Children — Content Standards for Beginning Teachers–Common Core: Teacher attitudes and behaviors that influence behavior of individuals with exceptional learning needs (CC5K4).
PRAXIS Special Education Core Principles: Content Knowledge: III. Delivery of Services to Students with Disabilities, Professional Roles, Influence of teacher attitudes, values and behaviors on the learning of exceptional children.

Self-advocacy: responsibility for the utilization and protection of one's rights.

▼

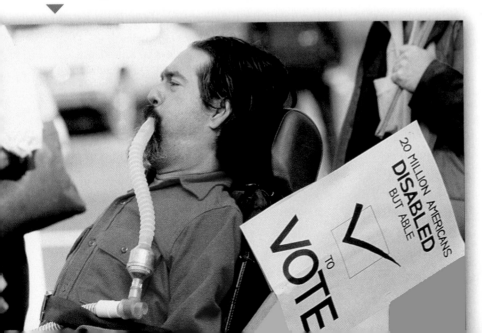

SELF-ADVOCACY

Advocacy on behalf of children and adults with disabilities has had a tremendous impact, especially during the past 30 years. Indeed, most of the pervasive changes in education, employment opportunities, and residential services have occurred because of the efforts of advocates. Family members, friends, professionals, and attorneys have traditionally undertaken advocacy for persons with disabilities. Like a growing number of professionals and most individuals with disabilities, Bigge (1991) believes that the age of "doing for" a person with a disability is rapidly diminishing. Increasingly, our society is viewing individuals with disabilities as integral and contributing members of the community in which they are a part. Federal and state legislation have provided and supported equal access of individuals with disabilities into all walks of life . . . . Along with the acquisition of these equal rights has come the responsibility for the utilization and protection of these rights. It is now necessary for those with disabilities, as individuals and as groups, to assert themselves as self-advocates. (p. 493)

Persons with disabilities have begun to assert their legal rights, challenging the view that persons with disabilities are incapable of speaking for themselves. Perhaps most conspicuous has been the self-advocacy of individuals with physical disabilities, who have been highly effective in their lobbying as part of the independent living movement. Individuals with sensory impairments have also engaged in self-advocacy. A striking and successful example is students' refusal at Gallaudet University to accept the appointment of a hearing president who did not know American Sign Language. Persons with mental retardation, however, have engaged in little self-advocacy, perhaps because many have not learned to recognize when their rights are being violated and because they lack the verbal skills to advocate on their behalf.

Self-advocacy requires self-determination:

Self-determined people know how to choose. They know what they want and how to get it. From an awareness of personal needs, self-determined individuals choose goals, then doggedly pursue them. This involves asserting an individual's presence, making his or her needs known, evaluating progress toward meeting goals, adjusting performance, and creating unique approaches to solve problems. (Martin & Marshall, 1995, p. 147)

This is a tall order for anyone with or without disabilities. But along with these skills comes freedom.

Freedom to choose, what kind of job to have, where to live, to have relationships, to make all of the everyday decisions (big and small), and the freedom to make mistakes. Dignity of failure.

Tony Coehlo, chair of the President's Committee on Employment of People with Disabilities, opened the 1994 National Self-Advocacy Conference, "Voices for Choices'" with these remarks:

We want everything we are entitled to as citizens, nothing more, but nothing less. We want the privileges of full citizenship, but we also welcome its responsibilities. We want the respect we deserve, and we demand the rights we have been denied. We now recognize that empowerment is not a gift to be given, but a right to be demanded. (Cone, 1994, p. 445)

 ## STILL A LONG WAY TO GO

In general, the quality of life for most adults with disabilities is better today than it has ever been. Not only do more adults with disabilities live, work, and play in community-based, integrated environments, but more adults with disabilities have acquired or are acquiring the personal, social, work, and leisure skills that enable them to enjoy the benefits of those settings. But *more* persons with disabilities does not mean *all* persons with disabilities. And individuals don't live life "in general"; they experience specific instances of joy and sadness, success and failure. There is still a long way to go.

True, the quality of life for someone who now has his own bedroom in a group home and works for wages in a sheltered workshop may be appreciably better than it was before he left the institution where he ate and slept communally and his "work" consisted of an endless series of arts-and-crafts projects. But do the unacceptable standards of the past mean that a relatively better quality of life today is therefore good? Would it be good enough for you?

 Self-advocacy

Council for Exceptional Children — Knowledge and Skill Base for Beginning Special Education Transition Specialists: Use support systems to facilitate self-advocacy in transition planning (TS5S2).
PRAXIS Special Education Core Principles: Content Knowledge: II. Legal and Societal Issues, School's connections with students with disabilities, Developing student self-advocacy.

 To check your comprehension of chapter content, go to the Guided Review and Quiz modules in Chapter 15 of the Companion Website at **www.prenhall.com/heward**

A Friendship Program for Future Special Education Teachers

by Jill C. Dardig

Scott and Ted, both big sports fans, attended several local basketball and baseball games together. They cheered for the Pickerington High School Lady Tigers in the state tournament and scarfed frank after frank on Dime-a-Dog Night at a Columbus Clippers game. Kelly and Kami went out to dinner at several of their favorite restaurants. They also spent some quiet nights at home baking brownies, looking at family pictures, and just talking. Paula and Todd attended a concert, went to the mall, and spent an evening with popcorn and a video at Todd's apartment.

Scott, Kelly, and Paula, all college students learning to become special education teachers, were doing their fieldwork for a required course called "Focus on Adults with Disabilities." Each student in this class is paired with an adult with developmental disabilities living in a group home, family home, or supported living apartment in the community. Each student gets to know her new friend on an informal and personal basis by planning some at-home and community-based activities they can enjoy together during the semester. Students function as friends or companions. In this way, they are able to look at their special friends in a different light—not as a school-age child but as a similar-aged peer who is learning to be an independent adult.

After meeting with his friend (and sometimes group home or supported living staff) to determine what the friend might enjoy doing, each college student designs a calendar or schedule of planned activities. The schedule may be written; but if the friend cannot read, the scheduled activities are illustrated by photos, pictures, symbols, or objects (e.g., a menu, a K-Mart ad, a puzzle piece, or a page from *TV Guide*). This schedule allows the friend to anticipate and prepare for each activity and provides cues for friends, family, and caregivers to ask questions and discuss the person's weekly activities.

We Both Had a Good Time

Students also keep a journal. They record and reflect on their activities and pay special attention to identifying which skills their friend is lacking that she could have learned in school

to enable her to become more independent as an adult. Here are some journal entries from a recent class:

We visited the Northland Mall, where we wandered in and out of stores. Mary and I tried on a pair of high heels, and we both had a good time laughing as we attempted to walk. (Norma Bernstein)

Upon returning to his apartment, Ted was very happy, almost ecstatic. He acted out dribbling and shooting a basketball, to let everyone know that he and his "Special Friend" had gone to a game. This made me feel fantastic, and I could sense that we were starting to bond. (Scott Martin)

I did not know what to expect on my first "date" with Jack. Nothing had been planned, and I expected to stay around the home so that we could get acquainted. Jack must have seen me pull in because he was waiting outside with his hat and jacket on. He wanted to see my truck. I don't just mean looking at my truck, I mean getting in, listening to the radio, and examining everything. It was a good icebreaker, and we sat outside for some time. (Dean Scheiderer)

After dinner, Kami and I went shopping at the Target department store. Kami picked out a card for her brother's birthday and helped me choose a present for my newborn nephew. After Target, we went to a pet store, since she loves animals. (Kelly Byers)

If Edna Could Redo Her Education

Aside from having a good time, students gain many valuable insights from this experience. Their most frequent observation and strongest recommendation had to do with many of their friends' lack of social skills. Several students noticed that basic social skills, such as saying "please" when requesting items, greeting the student when she arrived, and shaking hands and saying "thank you" at the end of the evening, were lacking. Students thought that many of these important skills could have been acquired easily and naturally if their friends had experienced early inclusion with their nondisabled peers while participating in informal school and community activities.

Edna and I spent a lot of our time at the City Center Mall—an activity she had expressed an interest in. Edna had a difficult time navigating her way around people; she would just "bulldoze" ahead without going around people. We browsed in many stores and had pizza there too, and had a great time. As soon as we got back to her home, however, Edna vanished without a word. . . . Later, during a trip to the movies and out to dinner, Edna spoke very loudly and annoyed other customers. Edna can be such a pleasant and nice young woman, but she seems oblivious to others around her. . . . If Edna could redo her education, I think she would have benefited from spending time, both in and outside school, with her nondisabled peers. (Barbara Miller)

Another critical skill that many of the friends lacked was the ability to make choices.

Today, Kami and I went to dinner at Pizza Hut. We continued to talk about our families and our work. I noticed Kami waits for me to do everything. Open the door, serve the food, anything that requires a decision. (Kelly Byers)

A really big difference was that [in spending time with Ted] I always took the lead with decision making. I had to be sure to wait and prompt responses from him, or else I would not have known which store he wanted to visit or what flavor of ice cream he preferred. (Scott Martin)

Future teachers can keep this in mind and give students repeated opportunities to choose snacks, books, and leisure-time activities.

Appropriate affect and expression of feelings were other areas in which many adults had some difficulty.

Todd lacks a sense of humor. I usually associate with people who like to have fun and laugh. It was very hard for me to relate to Todd, who hardly ever laughed or seemed to want to have a good time. (Paula Kruer)

Many students observed that their adult friends, even if they were quite verbal, did not have adequate conversation skills. Some adults could answer questions but did not ask questions of the students or initiate conversation.

Edna apparently has little or no concept of friendship. Her life experiences have provided her with the model that adults are "providers." Our conversation was usually one-sided, with me asking her a lot of questions,

Feb. 19	4:00 - 7:00	Drawing & Painting
Feb. 26	4:00 - 7:00	Winter Hike/Sharon Woods
Mar. 5	4:00 - 7:00	Videos & Popcorn
Mar. 19	4:00 - 7:00	Wal-Mart Shopping/Dining
Mar. 26	4:00 - 7:00	PUZZLES Games & Puzzles
Apr. 2	4:00 - 7:00	Movie/Dining
Apr. 9	4:00 - 7:00	Walk in the Park/Dining
Apr. 16	4:00 - 7:00	Popcorn & Video
Apr. 23	4:00 - 7:00	The Mall/Dining
Apr. 30	4:00 - 7:00	Surprise? ?????

Using computer-generated icons, Susan Snyder prepared this schedule of activities for her friend Terry.

but rarely was the reverse true. She never asked me when she would see me again. (Barbara Miller)

Money-handling skills were also identified as critically important in making a person more adept in the community, and many of the adults experienced difficulty paying for items independently.

Ben could have been taught basic skills that would have been helpful in integrating him into society. Handling money transactions and telling time could have prevented the need for someone to keep track of Ben's every move in stores and restaurants. (Beth Wahl)

Self-care skills were another area in which some of the adults were weak.

I believe that Mary could have been taught basic hygiene, housekeeping, and social skills during her school years so that she could enjoy more independence and less frustration as she deals with these issues now. (Norma Bernstein)

This placement helped me realize the need for an emphasis in schools to be placed on daily living skills, skills that students will need when they become adults

(continues)

living in the community. It will be helpful to remember this when I become a teacher. (Beth Wahl)

Thinking beyond Today's Activities and Experiences
Although the students who take this course will be certified to teach K–12 students, spending time with an adult will help them as teachers to become more future-oriented in their instruction—to think beyond the day's lessons or the week's goals for a particular child with a disability. This experience will help teachers select and teach functional skills to their school-age students so that eventually they will be as fully integrated into the community as possible.

This experience will enable me to visualize students as adults and thus to think ahead to behaviors that may or may not be appropriate when my student is 22 years old and beyond. No matter what grade level I teach, I will have a much clearer view of which skills are functional, which are not, and which will allow my students to take full advantage of the world around them. (Janet Fleming)

If your teacher-training program does not offer a course such as this one, you can arrange to get to know a special friend as a volunteer through a local group home or an advocacy agency. Developing a friendship with an adult with disabilities will help you become a more responsive and effective teacher of children and youth with special needs.

Jill C. Dardig is a professor of education at Ohio Dominican College in Columbus, where she trains special education teachers.

SUMMARY

HOW DO FORMER SPECIAL EDUCATION STUDENTS FARE AS ADULTS?

- The percentage of students with disabilities who graduate with a standard school diploma has remained at about 25% for more than a decade.
- Data from the National Longitudinal Transition Study (NLTS) show an unemployment rate of 46% for all youth with disabilities who have been out of school for less than 2 years; most of the young adults who had found competitive employment were working in part-time, low-paying jobs.
- The unemployment rate for young adults with disabilities drops to 36.5% when they have been out of school for 3 to 5 years, but nearly one in five (19.6%) states she has given up looking for work (NLTS).
- NTLS found that 27% of young adults who had left high school had enrolled in post-secondary education programs within 3 to 5 years compared with 68% of the general same-age population.
- Although the percentage of college students who indicate they have a disability has increased in recent years, compared to their peers without disabilities, fewer former special education students pursue postsecondary education.
- NLTS reported that four out of every five former special education students had still not achieved the status of independent adulthood after being out of high school for up to 5 years.

TRANSITION MODELS AND SERVICES

- Transition from school to life in the community has become perhaps the most challenging issue in special education today. Models for school-to-adult-life transition stress the importance of a functional secondary school curriculum that provides work experience in integrated community job sites, systematic coordination between school and adult service agencies, parental involvement and support, and a written individualized transition plan (ITP) to guide the entire process.
- Development of career awareness and vocational skills should begin in the elementary grades for children with severe disabilities.

- Middle school students should begin to spend time on actual community job sites.
- Secondary students should spend more time on actual community job sites, with in-school instruction focusing on the functional skills needed in the adult work, domestic, community, and recreational/leisure environments.

EMPLOYMENT

- Secondary school programs can enhance the competitive employment prospects for young adults with disabilities by (1) stressing functional, vocational skills; (2) conducting school-based instruction in integrated settings as much as possible; and (3) beginning community-based instruction as early as age 12 for students with severe disabilities and for progressively extended periods as the student nears graduation.
- Supported employment is a relatively new concept that recognizes that many adults with severe disabilities require ongoing support to obtain and hold a job. Supported employment is characterized by performance of real paid work in regular, integrated work sites; it requires ongoing support from a supported work specialist.
- The role of the employment specialist/job coach is evolving from one of primary supporter for the employee with disabilities to one who works with the employer and co-workers to create innovative and natural support networks.
- Self-monitoring, self-evaluation, learning how to respond independently to naturally occurring cues in the workplace, and self-instructions are four ways that employees with disabilities can increase their independence and job productivity in the workplace.
- Many adults with severe disabilities work in sheltered workshops that provide one or a combination of three kinds of programs: training for competitive employment in the community, extended or long-term employment, and work activities.

POSTSECONDARY EDUCATION

- Participation in postsecondary education significantly improves chances of meaningful employment for persons with disabilities.
- Although the percentage of postsecondary students who indicate they have a disability has tripled in the past 25 years, graduation rates of college students with disabilities is far below that of students without disabilities.
- The difficulties reported by many college students with disabilities reveal the need for greater emphasis on postsecondary education goals and outcomes during high school transition planning.

RESIDENTIAL ALTERNATIVES

- Group homes provide family-style living for three to six persons. Most group homes serve adults with mental retardation, although some have residents with other disabilities. Staff persons in this type of home help the people who live there develop self-care and daily living skills, form interpersonal relationships, and participate in recreation and leisure skills.
- Foster home placement allows the adult with disabilities to participate in day-to-day activities of family life, receive attention from people interested in his development, and experience close personal relationships.
- Apartment living offers the greatest opportunities for integration into the community and interaction with people without disabilities. Three common forms of apartment living for adults with disabilities are the apartment cluster, the co-residence apartment, and the maximum-independence apartment.
- Supported living is an approach toward helping people with disabilities live in the community as independently and normally as they can by providing a network of various kinds and levels of natural supports.

- Despite deinstitutionalization—the movement of persons with mental retardation out of large public institutions and into smaller, community-based residences such as group homes—in 2000, approximately 47,580 persons, mostly adults with severe or profound mental retardation, still lived in large institutions.

RECREATION AND LEISURE

- Learning to participate in age-appropriate recreation and leisure activities is necessary for a self-satisfying lifestyle.

THE ULTIMATE GOAL: A BETTER LIFE

- Adults with disabilities continue to face lack of acceptance as full members of society.
- Handicapism—discriminatory treatment and biased reactions toward someone with a disability—occurs on personal, professional, and societal levels. It must be eliminated before normalization can become a reality for every man and woman with a disability.
- Persons with disabilities have begun to assert their legal rights, challenging the view that they are incapable of speaking for themselves.

For more information on transition to adulthood, go to the Web Links module in Chapter 15 of the Companion Website at **www.prenhall.com/heward**

Postscript

Developing Your Own Personal View of Special Education

All introductory textbooks contain a great deal of information. In that respect, this book is no different from others. I hope, however, that you have gained more than just some basic facts and information about learners with exceptional educational needs and special education, the discipline dedicated to meeting those needs. I hope you have examined your own attitudes toward and relationships with children and adults with disabilities. At the beginning of the book, I shared eight beliefs that provide the foundation for my personal, but by no means unique, view of special education. I would like to repeat those beliefs, after which I will offer some encouragement and recommendations.

- People with disabilities have a fundamental right to live and participate in the same settings and programs—in school, at home, in the workplace, and in the community—as do people without disabilities. People with and without disabilities have a great deal to contribute to and learn from one another. We cannot do that in the absence of regular, meaningful interaction.
- Individuals with disabilities have the right to as much self-determinaton as we can help them achieve. Special educators have no more important teaching mission than helping children and adults with disabilities learn how to increase their level of decision making and control over their own lives.
- Special education must expand and improve its efforts to serve effectively all learners with exceptional educational needs. These include the gifted and talented child, the preschooler with disabilities and the infant who is at risk for a future learning problem, the exceptional child from a different cultural or ethnic background, and the adult with disabilities.
- School and family partnerships enhance both the meaningfulness and the effectiveness of special education.
- The efforts of special educators are most effective when they incorporate the input and services of all of the disciplines in the helping professions.
- All students have the right to an effective education. As educators, our primary responsibility is to design and implement effective instruction for personal, social, vocational, and academic skills. Instruction is ultimately effective when it helps the students we serve acquire and maintain positive lifestyle changes. To put it another way, the proof of the process is in the product. Therefore . . .
- Teachers must demand effectiveness from the curriculum materials and instructional tools they use. The belief that special educators require unending patience is a disservice to students with special needs and to the educators— both special and general education teachers—whose job it is to teach them. Teachers should not wait patiently for exceptional children to learn, attributing lack of progress to some inherent attribute or faulty process within the child, but should modify the instructional program to improve its effectiveness.
- Finally, the future for individuals with disabilities holds great promise. We have only begun to discover the myriad ways to improve teaching,

Personal view of special education

 Council for Exceptional Children Content Standards for Beginning Teachers–Common Core: Articulate personal philosophy of special education (CC1S1).
PRAXIS Special Education Core Principles: Content Knowledge: III. Delivery of Services to Students with Disabilities, Professional roles, Reflecting on one's own teaching.

increase learning, prevent and minimize the conditions that cause disabilities, encourage acceptance, and use technology to compensate for disabilities. We have not come as far as we can and will in learning how to help exceptional individuals build and enjoy fuller, more independent lives in the school, community, and workplace.

AS A MEMBER OF THE PROFESSION

If you consider yourself a prospective special educator, view special education as a profession and yourself as a professional. View yourself as someone with special skills and knowledge. Upon completion of your teacher preparation program, you will be different from people without your special training. This has nothing to do with arrogance; it is about recognizing that each of us must develop and responsibly use all of the professional competence we can muster.

Professional competence begins with an objective sense of the job to be done. Be wary of the conception of disabilities as merely socially constructed phenomena: that all children who are identified as disabled would achieve success and behave well if others simply viewed them more positively. This romantic ideology is seldom, if ever, promoted by individuals with disabilities themselves or by their parents and families. Children with disabilities have skill deficits and difficulties in acquiring and generalizing new knowledge and skills—real disabilities that won't be "deconstructed" away. Don't let the needs of exceptional children and their families get lost in such postmodern ideologies. Exceptional children need and deserve systematic, effective special education.

If you have a commitment and a desire to teach children with exceptional educational needs, that is commendable. You will probably hear often that you are "wonderful" or "patient" because of this. Good intentions are fine, but desire, commitment, and patience are only a beginning. What learners with disabilities need more than anything are teachers who are impatient—impatient with methods, materials, and policies that do not help their students acquire and subsequently use the knowledge and skills required for successful functioning in the home, school, workplace, and community. So don't be patient; be effective.

You will increase your effectiveness as a teacher by using only instructional materials and methods backed by sound, empirical research evidence. Teaching not only can but must be informed by science if students with disabilities are to learn as much as they can. When considering a new curriculum, program, or instructional method, ask questions such as the following:

Has this program been tested in the classroom?

What is the evidence showing this program works?

What measures of student performance were used to evaluate this program?

Has any research on this program been published in peer-reviewed journals?

Is there any evidence to suggest the program will be successful if modified to meet the skill levels and ages of my students?

Asking for evidence of effectiveness and professional development

 Council for Exceptional Children Content Standards for Beginning Teachers–Common Core: Methods to remain current regarding research-validated practice (CC9K4) and Continuum of lifelong professional development (CC9K3). **PRAXIS** Special Education Core Principles: Content Knowledge: III. Delivery of Services to Students with Disabilities, Professional roles, Critical evaluation and use of professional literature and organizations.

Teaching students with disabilities requires systematic instruction. It is demanding work. Prepare yourself for that work the best way you can. Demand relevant, up-to-date information and hands-on practical experiences from your teacher-education program. Continue your education and professional development throughout your career. Stay informed of developments in special education by reading professional journals, participating in inservice training opportunities, and attending conferences. Even better, experiment with instructional methods and share the results of your research with colleagues through presentations and publications.

Special education is not a grim, thankless business. Quite the opposite: special education is an exciting, dynamic field that offers personal satisfaction and feelings of accomplishment unequaled in most areas of endeavor. Welcome aboard!

AS A MEMBER OF THE COMMUNITY

The degree of success and happiness that a person with disabilities enjoys in the normal routines of everyday life does not depend solely on his or her skills and abilities. In large measure, the integration of people with disabilities into society depends on the attitudes and actions of citizens with little knowledge of or experience with exceptional learners. How can people come to accept and support a group they do not know?

Society controls who enters and who is kept out, much as a gatekeeper lets some visitors pass but refuses passage to others. For a particular individual, society's gatekeeper may have been a doctor who urged parents to institutionalize their child or a teacher who resisted having any difficult-to-teach kids in class. It may have been an employer who refused to hire workers with disabilities. It may have been a social worker, a school board member, a voter. Saddest of all, it may have been a parent whose low expectations kept the gate closed.

How society views people with disabilities influences how individual members of the community respond. Society's views are changing gradually for the better—they are being changed by people who believe that our past practices of exclusion and denial of opportunities were primitive and unfair. But to have maximum impact, the movement toward integration and opportunities described in this book must ultimately translate into personal terms for those of you who will not choose careers in special education. People with disabilities and people without disabilities do experience certain aspects of life differently, but they are more like one another than they are different. And the conclusion I hope you have reached is this: every child and adult with disabilities must be treated as an individual, not as a member of a category or a labeled group.

 ## IN SUM

Viewing every individual with disabilities first as a person and second as a person with disabilities may be the most important step in including the individual into the mainstream of school and community life. But a change in attitude will not diminish the disability. What it will do is give us a new outlook—more objective and more positive—and allow us to see a disability as a set of special needs. Viewing exceptional people as individuals with special needs tells us much about how to respond to them—and how we respond is the essence of special education.

Glossary

Absence seizure A type of epileptic seizure in which the individual loses consciousness, usually for less than half a minute; can occur very frequently in some children.

Acceleration An educational approach that provides a child with learning experiences usually given to older children; most often used with gifted and talented children.

Accommodation The adjustment of the eye for seeing at different distances; accomplished by muscles that change the shape of the lens to bring an image into clear focus on the retina.

Acquired immune deficiency syndrome (AIDS) A fatal illness in which the body's immune system breaks down. At present there is no known cure for AIDS or a vaccine for the virus that causes it (see *human immunodeficiency virus*).

Acquisition stage of learning The initial phase of learning when the student is learning how to perform a new skill or use new knowledge; feedback should focus on the accuracy and topography of the student's response.

Active student response (ASR) A frequency-based measure of a student's active participation during instruction; measured by counting the number of observable responses made to an ongoing lesson or to curriculum materials.

Adaptive device Any piece of equipment designed to improve the function of a body part. Examples include standing tables and special spoons that can be used by people with weak hands or poor muscle control.

Adventitious A disability that develops at any time after birth, from disease, trauma, or any other cause; most frequently used with sensory or physical impairments (contrasts with *congenital*).

Advocate Someone who pleads the cause of a person with disabilities or group of people with disabilities, especially in legal or administrative proceedings or public forums.

Albinism A congenital condition marked by deficiency in, or total lack of, pigmentation. People with albinism have pale skin; white hair, eyebrows, and eyelashes; and eyes with pink or pale blue irises.

Amblyopia Dimness of sight without apparent change in the eye's structures; can lead to blindness in the affected eye if not corrected.

American Sign Language (ASL) A visual-gestural language with its own rules of syntax, semantics, and pragmatics; does not correspond to written or spoken English. ASL is the language of the Deaf culture in the United States and Canada.

Amniocentesis The insertion of a hollow needle through the abdomen into the uterus of a pregnant woman. Used to obtain amniotic fluid in order to determine the presence of genetic and chromosomal abnormalities. The sex of the fetus can also be determined.

Anencephaly Congenital malformation of the skull with absence of all or part of the brain.

Anoxia A lack of oxygen severe enough to cause tissue damage; can cause permanent brain damage and mental retardation.

Aphasia Loss of speech functions; often, but not always, refers to inability to speak because of brain lesions.

Applied behavior analysis "The science in which procedures derived from the principles of behavior are systematically applied to improve socially significant behavior to a meaningful degree and to demonstrate experimentally that the procedures employed were responsible for the improvement in behavior" (Cooper, Heron, & Heward, 1987, p. 14).

Aqueous humor Fluid that occupies the space between the lens and the cornea of the eye.

Arena assessment A group assessment procedure sometimes used with infants and preschoolers; professionals from different disciplines (e.g., early childhood specialist, speech-language pathologist, psychologist, physical therapist) seat themselves in a circle around the child and conduct simultaneous evaluations while the child interacts with parent or play materials.

Articulation The production of distinct language sounds by the vocal organs.

Asperger's syndrome Children have normal cognitive and language development but share some of the characteristics of autism, social and emotional impairment, and restricted patterns of activities and interest; may display poor motor clumsiness; sometimes referred to as high-functioning autism.

Assistive technology Any item, piece of equipment, or product system, whether acquired commercially off the shelf, modified, or customized, that is used to increase, maintain, or improve the functional capabilities of children with disabilities. (IDEA regulations, 34 C.F.R. § 300.5)

Asthma A chronic respiratory condition characterized by repeated episodes of wheezing, coughing, and difficulty breathing.

Astigmatism A defect of vision usually caused by irregularities in the cornea; results in blurred vision and difficulties in focusing. Can usually be corrected by lenses.

Ataxia Poor sense of balance and body position and lack of coordination of the voluntary muscles; characteristic of one type of cerebral palsy.

At risk A term used to refer to children who are not currently identified as disabled but are considered to have a greater-than-usual chance of developing a disability. Physicians use the terms *at risk* or *high risk* to refer to pregnancies with a greater-than-normal probability of producing a baby with disabilities.

Athetosis A type of cerebral palsy characterized by large, irregular, uncontrollable twisting motions. The muscles may be tense and rigid or loose and flaccid. Often accompanied by difficulty with oral language.

Attention deficit disorder (ADD) See *attention deficit/hyperactivity disorder (ADHD)*.

Attention deficit/hyperactivity disorder (ADHD) Diagnostic category of the American Psychiatric Association for a condition in which a child exhibits developmentally inappropriate inattention, impulsivity, and hyperactivity.

Audiogram A graph of the faintest level of sound a person can hear in each ear at least 50% of the time at each of several frequencies, including the entire frequency range of normal speech.

Audiologist A professional who specializes in the evaluation of hearing ability and the treatment of impaired hearing.

Audiology The science of hearing.

Audiometer A device that generates sounds at specific frequencies and intensities; used to examine hearing.

Audiometric zero The smallest sound a person with normal hearing can perceive; also called the zero hearing-threshold level (HTL).

Audition The act or sense of hearing.

Auditory canal (external acoustic meatus) Slightly amplifies and transports sound waves from the external ear to the middle ear.

Auditory training A program that works on listening skills by teaching individuals with hearing impairments to make as much use as possible of their residual hearing.

Augmentative and alternative communication (AAC) A diverse set of nonspeech communication strategies and methods to assist individuals who are unable to meet their communication needs through speech; includes sign language, symbol systems, communication boards, and synthetic speech devices.

Auricle External part of the ear; collects sound waves into the auditory canal.

Autism A pervasive developmental disorder marked by severe impairment of intellectual, social, and emotional functioning. The essential features of the condition typically appear prior to 30 months of age and consist of disturbances of (1) developmental rates and/or sequences; (2) responses to sensory stimuli; (3) speech, language, and cognitive capacities; and (4) capacities to relate to people, events, and objects (Autism Society of America; Ritvo & Freeman, 1978).

Baseline A measure of the level or amount of a specific target behavior prior to implementation of an intervention designed to change the behavior. Baseline data are used as an objective measure against which to compare and evaluate the results obtained during intervention.

Behavior observation audiometry A method of hearing assessment in which an infant's reactions to sounds are observed; a sound is presented at an increasing level of intensity until a response, such as head turning, eye blinking, or cessation of play, is reliably observed.

Behavioral contract A written agreement between two parties in which one agrees to complete a specified task (e.g., a child agrees to complete a homework assignment by the next morning) and in return the other party agrees to provide a specific reward (e.g., the teacher allows the child to have 10 minutes of free time) upon completion of the task.

Behavioral disorder A disability characterized by behavior that differs markedly and chronically from current social or cultural norms and adversely affects educational performance.

Bilingual special education Using the child's home language and home culture along with English in an individually designed program of special education.

Binocular vision Vision using both eyes working together to perceive a single image.

Blind Having either no vision or only light perception; learning occurs through other senses.

Blindness, legal See *legally blind*.

Braille A system of writing letters, numbers, and other language symbols with a combination of six raised dots. A person who is blind reads the dots with his fingertips.

Cataract A reduction or loss of vision that occurs when the crystalline lens of the eye becomes cloudy or opaque.

Catheter A tube inserted into the body to permit injections or withdrawal of fluids or to keep a passageway open; often refers to a tube inserted into the bladder to remove urine from a person who does not have effective bladder control.

Cerebral palsy Motor impairment caused by brain damage, which is usually acquired during the prenatal period or during the birth process. Can involve a wide variety of symptoms (see *ataxia, athetosis, rigidity, spasticity,* and *tremor*) and range from mild to severe. Neither curable nor progressive.

Choral responding Each student in the class or group responding orally in unison to a question, problem, or item presented by the teacher.

Chorion villus sampling (CVS) A procedure for prenatal diagnosis of chromosomal abnormalities that can be conducted during the first 8 to 10 weeks of pregnancy; fetal cells are removed from the chorionic tissue, which surrounds the fetus, and directly analyzed.

Clean intermittent catheterization (CIC) A clean (not sterile) catheter (tube) is inserted into the urethra and advanced into the bladder; catheter remains in place until urine is released into a bag.

Cleft palate A congenital split in the palate that results in an excessive nasal quality of the voice. Can often be repaired by surgery or a dental appliance.

Closed head injury Caused by the head hitting a stationary object with such force that the brain slams against the inside of the cranium; stress of this rapid movement and impact pulls apart and tears nerve fibers or axons of the brain.

Cluttering A type of fluency disorder in which speech is very rapid, with extra sounds or mispronounced sounds; speech may be garbled to the point of unintelligibility.

Cochlea Main receptor organ for hearing located in the inner ear; tiny hairs within the cochlea transform mechanical energy into neural impulses that then travel through the auditory nerve to the brain.

Communication An interactive process requiring at least two parties in which messages are encoded, transmitted, and decoded by any means, including sounds, symbols, and gestures.

Communication disorder "An impairment in the ability to receive, send, process, and comprehend concepts or verbal, non-verbal and graphic symbols systems . . . disorder may be evident in the processes of hearing, language, and/or speech" (ASHA, 1993, p. 40).

Complex partial seizure A type of seizure in which an individual goes through a brief period of inappropriate or purposeless activity (also called psychomotor seizure). Usually lasts from two to five minutes, after which the person has amnesia about the entire episode.

Conduct disorder A group of behavior disorders including disobedience, disruptiveness, fighting, and tantrums, as identified by Quay (1975).

Conductive hearing loss Hearing loss caused by obstructions in the outer or middle ear or malformations that interfere with the conduction of sound waves to the inner ear. Can often be corrected surgically or medically.

Cones Light receptors that enable detection of color and detail; located in the center of the retina and function best in good light.

Congenital Any condition that is present at birth (contrasts with *adventitious*).

Constant time delay A procedure for transferring stimulus control from teacher-provided response prompts to the instructional item itself. The teacher begins by simultaneously presenting the stimulus being taught and a controlling response prompt (e.g., as the teacher holds up a flashcard with the word "ball" printed on it, she says, "Ball"). After a number of zero-second-delay trials the teacher waits for a fixed amount of time (e.g., four seconds) between presentation of the instructional stimulus and the response prompt. Practice trials are repeated with the constant delay until the student begins to respond correctly prior to the teacher's prompt.

Contingency contract A document that specifies an if-then relationship between performance of a specified behavior(s) and access to or delivery of a specified reward.

Continuum of services The range of different placement and instructional options that a school district can use to serve children with disabilities. Typically depicted as a pyramid, ranging from the least restrictive placement (regular classroom) at the bottom to the most restrictive placement (residential school or hospital) at the top.

Convulsive disorder See *epilepsy*.

Cornea The transparent part of the eyeball that admits light to the interior.

Cortical visual impairments (CVI) Decreased vision or blindness due to known or suspected damage or malfunction of the parts of the brain that interpret visual information.

Cri-du-chat syndrome A chromosomal abnormality resulting from deletion of material from the fifth pair of chromosomes. It usually results in severe retardation. Its name is French for "cat cry," named for the high-pitched crying of the child due to a related larynx dysfunction.

Cued speech A method of supplementing oral communication by adding cues in the form of eight different hand signals in four different locations near the chin.

Cultural-familial mental retardation See *psychosocial disadvantage*.

Cultural pluralism The value and practice of respecting, fostering, and encouraging the cultural and ethnic differences that make up society.

Culture The established knowledge, ideas, values, and skills shared by a society; its program of survival and adaptation to its environment.

Curriculum-based assessment Evaluation of a student's progress in terms of her performance on the skills that comprise the curriculum of the local school.

Cystic fibrosis An inherited disorder that causes a dysfunction of the pancreas, mucus, salivary, and sweat glands. Cystic fibrosis causes severe, long-term respiratory difficulties. No cure is currently available.

Deaf The result of a hearing loss severe enough so that speech cannot be understood through the ears alone, even with a hearing aid; some sounds may still be perceived.

Decibel (dB) The unit of measure for the relative intensity of sound on a scale beginning at zero. Zero dB refers to the faintest sound a person with normal hearing can detect.

Deinstitutionalization The social movement to transfer individuals with disabilities, especially persons with mental retardation, from large institutions to smaller, community-based residences and work settings.

Diabetes See *juvenile diabetes mellitus*.

Diabetic retinopathy Visual impairment caused by hemorrhages on the retina and other disorders of blood circulation in people with diabetes.

Dialect A variety within a specific language; can involve variation in pronunciation, word choice, word order, and inflected forms.

Differential reinforcement of other behavior (DRO) A procedure in which any behavior except the targeted inappropriate response is reinforced; results in a reduction of the inappropriate behavior.

Diplegia Paralysis that affects the legs more often than the arms.

Disability Condition characterized by functional limitations that impede typical development as the result of a physical or sensory impairment or difficulty in learning or social adjustment.

Double hemiplegia Paralysis of the arms, with less severe involvement of the legs.

Down syndrome A chromosomal anomaly that often causes moderate to severe mental retardation, along with certain physical characteristics such as a large tongue, heart problems, poor muscle tone, and a broad, flat bridge of the nose.

Duchenne muscular dystrophy   The most common form of muscular dystrophy, a group of long-term diseases that progressively weaken and waste away the body's muscles.

Due process   Set of legal steps and proceedings carried out according to established rules and principles; designed to protect an individual's constitutional and legal rights.

Duration (of behavior)   Measure of how long a person engages in a given activity.

Dysarthia   A group of speech disorders caused by neuromuscular impairments in respiration, phonation, resonation, and articulation.

Dyslexia   A specific language-based disorder of constitutional origin characterized by difficulties in single word decoding, usually reflecting insufficient phonological processing. These difficulties, which are not the result of generalized developmental disability or sensory impairment, are often unexpected in relation to age and other cognitive and academic abilities and severely impair the individual's ability to read (Orton Dyslexia Society Research Committee, 1994).

Echolalia   The repetition of what other people say as if echoing them; characteristic of some children with delayed development, autism, and communication disorders.

Electroencephalograph (EEG)   Device that detects and records brain wave patterns.

Encephalitis   Inflammation of the brain; can cause permanent damage to the central nervous system and mental retardation.

Endogenous   Refers to an inherited cause of a disability or impairment.

Enrichment   Educational approach that provides a child with extra learning experiences that the standard curriculum would not normally include. Most often used with gifted and talented children.

Epilepsy   A condition marked by chronic and repeated seizures, disturbances of movement, sensation, behavior, and/or consciousness caused by abnormal electrical activity in the brain (see *generalized tonic-clonic seizure, complex partial seizure, simple partial seizure,* and *absence seizure*). Can usually be controlled with medication, although the drugs may have undesirable side effects. May be temporary or lifelong.

Equal protection   Legal concept included in the 14th Amendment to the Constitution of the United States, stipulating that no state may deny any person equality or liberty because of that person's classification according to race, nationality, or religion. Several major court cases leading to the passage of P.L. 94–142 (IDEA) found that children with disabilities were not provided with equal protection if they were denied access to an appropriate education solely because of their disabilities.

Ethnocentrism   The view that the practices of one's own culture are natural and correct, while perceiving the practices of other cultures as odd, amusing, inferior, and/or immoral.

Etiology   The cause(s) of a disability, impairment, or disease. Includes genetic, physiological, and environmental or psychological factors.

Evoked-response audiometry   A method of testing hearing by measuring the electrical activity generated by the auditory nerve in response to auditory stimulation. Often used to measure the hearing of infants and children considered difficult to test.

Exceptional children   Children whose performance deviates from the norm, either below or above, to the extent that special educational programming is needed.

Exogenous   Refers to a cause of a disability or impairment that stems from factors outside the body such as disease, toxicity, or injury.

Extinction   A procedure in which reinforcement for a previously reinforced behavior is withheld. If the actual reinforcers that are maintaining the behavior are identified and withheld, the behavior will gradually decrease in frequency until it no longer, or seldom, occurs.

Facilitated communication (FC)   A type of augmentative communication in which a "facilitator" provides assistance to someone in typing or pointing to vocabulary symbols; typically involves an alphanumeric keyboard on which the user types out his message one letter at a time. To date, research designed to validate FC has repeatedly demonstrated either facilitator influence (correct or meaningful language is produced only when the facilitator "knows" what should be communicated) or no unexpected language competence compared to the participants' measured IQ or a standard language assessment.

Fetal alcohol effects (FAE)   Term used to identify the suspected etiology of developmental problems experienced by infants and toddlers who have some but not all of the diagnostic criteria for fetal alcohol syndrome (FAS) and have a history of prenatal alcohol exposure.

Fetal alcohol syndrome (FAS)   A condition sometimes found in the infants of alcoholic mothers; can involve low birth weight, developmental delay, and cardiac, limb, and other physical defects. Caused by excessive alcohol use during pregnancy; often produces serious physical defects and developmental delays; diagnosed when the child has two or more craniofacial malformations and growth is below the 10th percentile for height and weight. FAS is one of the leading known causes of mental retardation. In addition to physical problems, many children with FAS have neurological damage that contributes to cognitive and language delays.

Field of vision   The expanse of space visible with both eyes looking straight ahead, measured in degrees; 180 degrees is considered normal.

Fluency   A performance measure that includes both the accuracy and the rate with which a skill is performed; a fluent performer is both accurate and fast. In communication, the term refers to the rate and smoothness of speech; stuttering is the most common fluency disorder in speech.

Foster home   A living arrangement in which a family shares its home with a person who is not a relative. Long used with children who for some reason cannot live with their parents temporarily, foster homes are now being used with adults with disabilities as well.

Fragile-X syndrome   A chromosomal abnormality associated with mild to severe mental retardation. Thought to be the most common known cause of inherited mental retardation. Affects males more often and more severely than females; behavioral characteristics are sometimes similar to individuals with autism. Diagnosis can be confirmed by studies of the X chromosome.

Functional analysis   Refers to a variety of behavior assessment methodologies for determining the environmental variables that are setting the occasion for and maintaining challenging behaviors such as self-injury (see Iwata et al., 1994).

Generalization   Using previously learned knowledge or skill under conditions other than those under which it was originally learned. Stimulus generality occurs when a student performs a behavior in the presence of relevant stimuli (people, settings, instructional materials) other than those that were present originally. For instance, stimulus generality occurs when a child who has learned to label baseballs and beach balls as "ball" identifies a basketball as "ball." Response generality occurs when a person performs relevant behaviors that were never directly trained but are similar to the original trained behavior. For example, a child may be taught to say, "Hello, how are you?" and "Hi, nice to see you," as greetings. If the child combines the two to say, "Hi, how are you?" response generality has taken place.

Generalized tonic-clonic seizure   The most severe type of seizure, in which the individual has violent convulsions, loses consciousness, and becomes rigid. Formerly called grand mal seizure.

Genetic counseling   A discussion between a specially trained medical counselor and persons who are considering having a baby about the chances of having a baby with a disability, based on the prospective parents' genetic backgrounds.

Glaucoma   An eye disease characterized by abnormally high pressure inside the eyeball. If left untreated, it can cause total blindness, but if detected early most cases can be arrested.

Grand mal seizure   See *generalized tonic-clonic seizure.*

Group home   A community-based residential alternative for adults with disabilities, most often persons with mental retardation, in which a small group of people live together in a house with one or more support staff.

Group-oriented contingency   A type of behavior management and motivation procedure in which consequences (rewards and/or penalties) are applied to the entire group or class of students and are contingent upon the behavior of selected students or the entire group.

Guided notes   A handout that guides students through a lecture, presentation, or demonstration by providing a format that includes basic information and cues students to note key points.

Handicap   Refers to the problems a person with a disability or impairment encounters in interacting with the environment. A disability may pose a handicap in one environment but not in another.

Handicapism   Prejudice or discrimination based solely on a person's disability, without regard for individual characteristics.

Hard of hearing   Level of hearing loss that makes it difficult, although not impossible, to comprehend speech through the sense of hearing alone.

Hearing impaired   Describes anyone who has a hearing loss significant enough to require special education, training, and/or adaptations; includes both deaf and hard-of-hearing conditions.

Hemiplegia   Paralysis of both the arm and the leg on the same side of the body.

Hemophilia   An inherited deficiency in blood-clotting ability, which can cause serious internal bleeding.

Hertz (Hz)   A unit of sound frequency equal to one cycle per second; used to measure pitch.

Human immunodeficiency virus (HIV)   The virus that causes acquired immune deficiency syndrome (AIDS).

Hydrocephalus   An enlarged head caused by cerebral spinal fluid accumulating in the cranial cavity; often causes brain damage and severe retardation. A condition present at birth or developing soon afterward. Can sometimes be treated successfully with a shunt.

Hyperactive   Excessive motor activity or restlessness.

Hyperopia   Farsightedness; condition in which the image comes to a focus behind the retina instead of on it, causing difficulty in seeing near objects.

Hypertonia   Muscle tone that is too high; tense, contracted muscles.

Hypotonia   Muscle tone that is too low; weak, floppy muscles.

Immaturity   Group of behavior disorders, including short attention span, extreme passivity, daydreaming, preference for younger playmates, and clumsiness, as identified by Quay (1975).

Impedance audiometry   Procedure for testing middle ear function by inserting a small probe and pump to detect sound reflected by the eardrum.

Incidence   The percentage of people who, at some time in their lives, will be identified as having a specific condition. Often reported as the number of cases of a given condition per 1,000 people.

Individualized education program (IEP)   Written document required by the Individuals with Disabilities Education Act (P.L. 94-142) for every child with a disability; includes statements of present performance, annual goals, short-term instructional objectives, specific educational services needed, relevant dates, regular education program participation, and evaluation procedures; must be signed by parents as well as educational personnel.

Individualized family services plan (IFSP)   A requirement of P.L. 99-457, Education of the Handicapped Act Amendments of 1986, for the coordination of early intervention services for infants and toddlers with disabilities from birth to age 3. Similar to the IEP, which is required for all school-age children with disabilities.

Inflection   Change in pitch or loudness of the voice to indicate mood or emphasis.

In-service training   Any educational program designed to provide practicing professionals (e.g., teachers, administrators, physical therapists) with additional knowledge and skills.

Interdisciplinary team Group of professionals from different disciplines (e.g., education, psychology, speech and language, medicine) who work together to plan and implement an individualized education program (IEP) for a child with disabilities.

Interindividual differences Differences between two or more people in one skill or set of skills.

Interobserver agreement The degree to which two or more independent observers record the same results when observing and measuring the same target behavior(s); typically reported as a percentage of agreement.

Interrater agreement See *interobserver agreement.*

Intervention Any effort made on behalf of children and adults with disabilities; may be preventive (keeping possible problems from becoming a serious disability), remedial (overcoming disability through training or education), or compensatory (giving the individual new ways to deal with the disability).

Intraindividual differences Differences within one individual on two or more measures of performance.

Iris The opaque, colored portion of the eye that contracts and expands to change the size of the pupil.

Kinesics The study of bodily movement, particularly as it relates to and affects communication.

Klinefelter syndrome A chromosomal anomaly in which males receive an extra X chromosome; associated with frequent social retardation, sterility, underdevelopment of male sex organs, development of secondary female sex characteristics, and borderline or mild levels of mental retardation.

Language A system used by a group of people for giving meaning to sounds, words, gestures, and other symbols to enable communication with one another. Languages can use vocal (speech sounds) or nonvocal symbols, such as American Sign Language, or use movements and physical symbols instead of sounds.

Language disorder Impaired comprehension and/or use of spoken, written, and/or other symbol systems.

Learning channel A description of the modes with which a learner receives and sends information in performing a given learning task. Orally reading sight words, for example, uses the "see/say" learning channel; the "hear/write" learning channel is involved in taking a spelling test.

Learning trial Consists of three major elements: (1) antecedent (i.e., curricular) stimuli, (2) the student's response to those stimuli, and (3) consequent stimuli (i.e., instructional feedback) following the response; serves as a basic unit of analysis for examining teaching and learning from both the teacher's perspective, as an opportunity to teach, and the student's perspective, as an opportunity to learn (Heward, 1994). Sometimes called a *practice trial or learn unit.*

Least restrictive environment (LRE) The educational setting that most closely resembles a regular school program and also meets the child's special educational needs. For many students with disabilities, the regular classroom is the LRE; however, the LRE is a relative concept and must be determined for each individual student with disabilities.

Legally blind Visual acuity of 20/200 or less in the better eye after the best possible correction with glasses or contact lenses, or vision restricted to a field of 20 degrees or less. Acuity of 20/200 means the eye can see clearly at 20 feet what the normal eye can see at 200 feet.

Lens The clear part of the eye that focuses rays of light on the retina.

Longitudinal study A research study that follows one subject or group of subjects over an extended period of time, usually several years.

Low-incidence disability A disability that occurs relatively infrequently in the general population; often used in reference to sensory impairments, severe and profound mental retardation, autism, and multiple disabilities.

Low vision Visual impairment severe enough so that special educational services are required. A child with low vision is able to learn through the visual channel and generally learns to read print.

Macular degeneration A deterioration of the central part of the retina, which causes difficulty in seeing details clearly.

Magnitude (of behavior) The force with which a response is emitted.

Mainstreaming The process of integrating children with disabilities into regular schools and classes.

Manifestation determination A review of the relationship between a student's misconduct and his disability conducted by the IEP team and other qualified personnel. Required by the IDEA amendments of 1997 when school officials seek to discipline a student with disabilities in a manner that would result in a change of placement, suspension, or expulsion in excess of 10 days.

Meningitis An inflammation of the membranes covering the brain and spinal cord; can cause problems with sight and hearing and/or mental retardation.

Meningocele Type of spina bifida in which the covering of the spinal cord protrudes through an opening in the vertebrae but the cord itself and the nerve roots are enclosed.

Mental retardation A disability characterized by significant limitations in both intellectual functioning and conceptual, social, and practical adaptive skills. This disability originates before age 18 (AAMR, 2002).

Microcephalus A condition characterized by an abnormally small skull with resulting brain damage and mental retardation.

Milieu teaching strategies A variety of strategies used to teach speech and language that naturally occur during real or simulated activities in the home, school, or community environments in which a child normally functions; characterized by dispersed learning trials, following the child's attentional lead within the context of normal conversational interchanges, and teaching the form and content of language in the context of normal use.

Minimal brain dysfunction A once-popular term used to describe the learning disabilities of children with no clinical (organic) evidence of brain damage.

Mobility The ability to move safely and efficiently from one point to another.

Model program   A program that implements and evaluates new procedures or techniques in order to serve as a basis for development of other similar programs.

Monoplegia   Paralysis affecting one limb.

Morpheme   The smallest element of a language that carries meaning.

Morphology   Concerned with the basic units of meaning in a language and how those units are combined into words.

Multicultural education   An educational approach in which a school's curriculum and instructional methods are designed and implemented so that all children acquire an awareness, acceptance, and appreciation of cultural diversity and recognize the contributions of many cultures.

Multifactored assessment   Assessment and evaluation of a child with a variety of test instruments and observation procedures. Required by IDEA when assessment is for educational placement of a child who is to receive special education services. Prevents the misdiagnosis and misplacement of a student as the result of considering only one test score.

Multiple-gating screening   A multistep process for screening children who may have disabilities. The initial step casts the broadest net (e.g., a multiple-gated screening for children who may have emotional and behavior problems might begin with teacher nominations); children identified in the first step are assessed more closely in a second step (e.g., a behavior checklist); children who have passed through the first two "gates" are screened further (e.g., direct observations in the classroom).

Muscular dystrophy   A group of diseases that gradually weakens muscle tissue; usually becomes evident by the age of 4 or 5.

Myelomeningocele   A protrusion on the back of a child with spina bifida, consisting of a sac of nerve tissue bulging through a cleft in the spine.

Myopia   Nearsightedness; results when light is focused on a point in front of the retina, resulting in a blurred image for distant objects.

Neurologic impairment   Any physical disability caused by damage to the central nervous system (brain, spinal cord, ganglia, and nerves).

Neuromotor impairment   Involves the central nervous system, affecting the ability to move, use, feel, or control certain parts of the body.

Normal curve   A mathematically derived curve depicting the theoretical probability or distribution of a given variable (such as a physical trait or test score) in the general population. Indicates that approximately 68% of the population will fall within one standard deviation above and below the mean; approximately 27% will fall between one and two standard deviations either above or below the mean; and less than 3% will achieve more extreme scores of more than two standard deviations in either direction.

Normalization   As a philosophy and principle, the belief that individuals with disabilities should, to the maximum extent possible, be physically and socially integrated into the mainstream of society regardless of the degree or type of disability. As an approach to intervention, the use of progressively more normal settings and procedures "to establish and/or maintain personal behaviors which are as culturally normal as possible" (Wolfensberger, 1972, p. 28).

Nystagmus   A rapid, involuntary, rhythmic movement of the eyes that may cause difficulty in reading or fixating on an object.

Occupational therapist   A professional who programs and/or delivers instructional activities and materials to help children and adults with disabilities learn to participate in useful activities.

Ocular motility   The eye's ability to move.

Open head injury   Result of penetration of the skull, such as caused by a bullet or a forceful blow to the head with a hard or sharp object.

Operant conditioning audiometry   Method of measuring hearing by teaching the individual to make an observable response to sound. For example, a child may be taught to drop a block into a box each time a light and a loud tone are presented. Once this response is learned, the light is no longer presented and the volume and pitch of the tone are gradually decreased. When the child no longer drops the block into the box, the audiologist knows the child cannot hear the tone. Sometimes used to test the hearing of nonverbal children and adults.

Ophthalmologist   A physician who specializes in the diagnosis and treatment of diseases of the eye.

Optic nerve   The nerve that carries impulses from the eye to the brain.

Optometrist   A vision professional who specializes in the evaluation and optical correction of refractive errors.

Oral approach   A philosophy and approach to educating deaf children that stresses learning to speak as the essential element for integration into the hearing world.

Orientation   The ability to establish one's position in relation to the environment.

Orthopedic impairment   Impairment of the skeletal system—bones, joints, limbs, and associated muscles.

Ossicles   Three small bones (hammer, anvil, and stirrup) that transmit sound energy from the middle ear to the inner ear.

Osteogenesis imperfecta   A hereditary condition in which the bones do not grow normally and break easily; sometimes called brittle bones.

Otitis media   An infection or inflammation of the middle ear that can cause a conductive hearing loss.

Otologist   A physician who specializes in the diagnosis and treatment of diseases of the ear.

Overcorrection   A procedure in which the learner must make restitution for, or repair, the effects of his undesirable behavior and then put the environment in even better shape than it was prior to the misbehavior. Used to decrease the rate of undesirable behaviors.

Paraplegia   Paralysis of the lower part of the body, including both legs; usually results from injury to or disease of the spinal cord.

Paraprofessionals (in education)   Trained classroom aides who assist teachers; may include parents.

Partial participation Teaching approach that acknowledges that even though an individual with severe disabilities may not be able to independently perform all the steps of a given task or activity, she can often be taught to do selected components or an adapted version of the task.

Perceptual handicap A term formerly used to describe some conditions now included under the term *learning disabilities;* usually referred to problems with no known physical cause.

Perinatal Occurring at or immediately after birth.

Peripheral vision Vision at the outer limits of the field of vision.

Personality disorder A group of behavior disorders, including social withdrawal, anxiety, depression, feelings of inferiority, guilt, shyness, and unhappiness, as identified by Quay (1975).

Petit mal seizure See *absence seizure.*

Phenylketonuria (PKU) An inherited metabolic disease that can cause severe retardation; can now be detected at birth and the detrimental effects prevented with a special diet.

Phoneme The smallest unit of sound that can be identified in a spoken language. There are 45 phonemes, or sound families, in the English language.

Phonological disorder A language disorder in which the child produces a given sound correctly in some instances but does not produce the sound correctly at other times.

Phonology Refers to the linguistic rules governing a language's sound system.

Photophobia Extreme sensitivity of the eyes to light; occurs most notably in albino children.

Physical therapist (PT) A professional trained to help people with disabilities develop and maintain muscular and orthopedic capability and make correct and useful movement.

Play audiometry A method for assessing a child's hearing ability by teaching the child to perform simple but distinct activities, such as picking up a toy or putting a ball into a cup whenever he hears the signal, either pure tones or speech.

Positive reinforcement Presentation of a stimulus or event immediately after a behavior has been emitted, which has the effect of increasing the occurrence of that behavior in the future.

Postlingual Occurring after the development of language; usually used to classify hearing losses that begin after a person has learned to speak.

Postnatal Occurring after birth.

Practice stage of learning After the student has learned how to perform a new skill, she should work to develop fluency with the target skill. Feedback during the practice stage of learning should emphasize the rate or speed with which the student correctly performs the skill.

Prader-Willi syndrome A condition linked to chromosomal abnormality that is characterized by delays in motor development, mild to moderate mental retardation, hypogenital development, an insatiable appetite that often results in obesity, and small features and stature.

Pragmatics Study of the rules that govern how language is used in a communication context.

Precision teaching An instructional approach that involves (1) pinpointing the skills to be learned; (2) measuring the initial fluency with which the student can perform those behaviors; (3) setting an aim, or goal, for the child's improvement; (4) using direct, daily measurement to monitor progress made under an instructional program; (5) charting the results of those measurements; and (6) changing the program if progress is not adequate.

Prelingual Describes a hearing impairment acquired before the development of speech and language.

Prenatal Occurring before birth.

Prenatal asphyxia A lack of oxygen during the birth process usually caused by interruption of respiration; can cause unconsciousness and/or brain damage.

Prevalence The number of people who have a certain condition at any given time.

Primary prevention Intervention designed to eliminate or counteract risk factors so that a disability is never acquired; aimed at all relevant persons.

Projective tests Psychological tests that require a person to respond to a standardized task or set of stimuli (e.g., draw a picture or interpret an ink blot). Responses are thought to be a projection of the test taker's personality and are scored according to the given test's scoring manual to produce a personality profile.

Prosthesis Any device used to replace a missing or impaired body part.

Psychomotor seizure See *complex partial seizure.*

Psychosocial disadvantage Category of causation for mental retardation that requires evidence of subaverage intellectual functioning in at least one parent and one or more siblings (when there are siblings). Typically associated with impoverished environments involving poor housing, inadequate diets, and inadequate medical care. Often used synonymously with cultural-familial retardation; suggests that mental retardation can be caused by a poor social and cultural environment.

Pupil The circular hole in the center of the iris of the eye, which contracts and expands to let light pass through.

Quadriplegia Paralysis of all four limbs.

Rate (or *frequency of behavior*) A measure of how often a particular action is performed; usually reported as the number of responses per standard unit of time (e.g., 5 per minute).

Refraction The bending or deflection of light rays from a straight path as they pass from one medium (e.g., air) into another (e.g., the eye). Used by eye specialists in assessing and correcting vision.

Regular education initiative (REI) A position advocated by some special educators that students with disabilities can and should be educated in regular classrooms under the primary responsibility of the general education program.

Rehabilitation A social service program designed to teach a newly disabled person basic skills needed for independence.

Reinforcement See *positive reinforcement.*

Related services Developmental, corrective, and other supportive services required for a child with disabilities to benefit from special education. Includes special transportation services, speech and language pathology, audiology, psychological services, physical and occupational therapy, school health services, counseling and medical services for diagnostic and evaluation purposes, rehabilitation counseling, social work services, and parent counseling and training.

Remediation   An educational program designed to teach a person to overcome a disability through training and education.

Residual hearing   The remaining hearing, however slight, of a person who is deaf.

Resource room   Classroom in which special education students spend part of the school day and receive individualized special education services.

Response cards   Cards, signs, or items that are simultaneously held up by all students to display their response to a question or problem presented by the teacher; response cards enable every student in the class to respond to each question or item.

Response cost   A procedure for reducing the frequency of inappropriate behavior by withdrawing a specific amount of reinforcement contingent upon occurrence of the behavior.

Retina   A sheet of nerve tissue at the back of the eye on which an image is focused.

Retinitis pigmentosa (RP)   An eye disease in which the retina gradually degenerates and atrophies, causing the field of vision to become progressively more narrow.

Retinopathy of prematurity (ROP)   A condition characterized by an abnormally dense growth of blood vessels and scar tissue in the eye, often causing visual field loss and retinal detachment. Usually caused by high levels of oxygen administered to premature infants in incubators. Also called retrolental fibroplasia (RLF).

Retrolental fibroplasia (RLF)   See *retinopathy of prematurity*.

Reye's syndrome   A relatively rare disease that appears to be related to a variety of viral infections; most common in children over the age of 6. About 30% of children who contract it die; survivors sometimes show signs of neurological damage and mental retardation. The cause is unknown, although some studies have found an increased risk after the use of aspirin during a viral illness.

Rigidity   A type of cerebral palsy characterized by increased muscle tone, minimal muscle elasticity, and little or no stretch reflex.

Rods   Light receptors for peripheral vision, detection of movement, and vision in dim light; located around the periphery of the retina.

Rubella   German measles; when contracted by a woman during the first trimester of pregnancy, may cause visual impairments, hearing impairments, mental retardation, and/or other congenital impairments in the child.

Schizophrenic   Describes a severe behavior disorder characterized by loss of contact with one's surroundings and inappropriate affect and actions.

Screening   A procedure in which groups of children are examined and/or tested in an effort to identify children who are most likely to have a disability; identified children are then referred for more intensive examination and assessment.

Secondary prevention   Intervention directed at reducing or eliminating the effects of existing risk factors; aimed at individuals exposed to or displaying specific risk factors.

Selective mutism   Speaking normally in some settings or situations and not speaking in others.

Self-contained class   A special classroom, usually located within a regular public school building, that includes only exceptional children.

Self-monitoring   A behavior change procedure in which an individual observes and records the frequency and/or quality of his own behavior.

Semantics   The study of meaning in language.

Sensorineural hearing loss   A hearing loss caused by damage to the auditory nerve or the inner ear.

Severe disabilities   Term used to refer to challenges faced by individuals with severe and profound mental retardation, autism, and/or physical/sensory impairments combined with marked developmental delay. Persons with severe disabilities exhibit extreme deficits in intellectual functioning and need systematic instruction for basic skills such as self-care and communicating with others.

Shaping   A process for teaching new behavior through reinforcement of successive approximations of targeted performance.

Sheltered workshop   A structured work environment where persons with disabilities receive employment training and perform work for pay. May provide transitional services for some individuals (e.g., short-term training for competitive employment in the community) and permanent work settings for others.

Shunt   Tube that diverts fluid from one part of the body to another; often implanted in people with hydrocephalus to remove extra cerebrospinal fluid from the head and send it directly into the heart or intestines.

Simple partial seizure   A type of seizure characterized by sudden jerking motions with no loss of consciousness. Partial seizures may occur weekly, monthly, or only once or twice a year.

Snellen chart   A chart used to test visual acuity; developed by a Dutch ophthalmologist in 1862 and still used today. Consists of rows of letters, or Es facing up, down, left, or right; each row corresponds to the distance that a normally sighted person can discriminate the letters.

Social validity   A desirable characteristic of the objectives, procedures, and results of intervention, indicating their appropriateness for the learner. For example, the goal of riding a bus independently would have social validity for students residing in most cities but not for those in small towns or rural areas.

Socialized aggression   A group of behavior disorders, including truancy, gang membership, theft, and delinquency, as identified by Quay (1975).

Spasticity   A type of cerebral palsy characterized by tense, contracted muscles.

Special education   Individually planned, specialized, intensive, outcome-directed instruction. When practiced most effectively and ethically, special education is also characterized by the systematic use of research-based instructional methods, the application of which is guided by frequent measures of student performance.

Speech   A system of using breath and muscles to create specific sounds for communicating.

Speech audiometry   Tests a person's detection and understanding of speech by presenting a list of two-syllable words at different decibel (sound volume) levels.

Speech impairment   Speech that "deviates so far from the speech of other people that it (1) calls attention to itself, (2) interferes with communication, or (3) provokes distress in the speaker or the listener" (Van Riper & Erickson, 1996, p. 110). The three basic types of speech disorders are articulation, fluency, and voice.

Speechreading   Process of understanding a spoken message by observing the speaker's lips in combination with information gained from facial expressions, gestures, and the context or situation.

Speech reception threshold (SRT)   The decibel (sound volume) level at which an individual can understand half of the words during a speech audiometry test; the SRT is measured and recorded for each ear.

Spina bifida   A congenital malformation of the spine in which the vertebrae that normally protect the spine do not develop fully; may involve loss of sensation and severe muscle weakness in the lower part of the body.

Spina bifida occulta   A type of spina bifida that usually does not cause serious disability. Although the vertebrae do not close, there is no protrusion of the spinal cord and membranes.

Standard celeration chart   Chart for graphically displaying a student's learning progress from day to day in terms of changes in the frequency of correct and incorrect responses per minute.

Standard deviation   A descriptive statistic that shows the average amount of variability among a set of scores. A small standard deviation indicates that the scores in the sample are distributed close to the mean; a larger standard deviation indicates that more scores in the sample fall farther from the mean.

Stereotype   An overgeneralized or inaccurate attitude held toward all members of a particular group, on the basis of a common characteristic such as age, sex, race, or disability.

Stereotypic behavior (stereotypy)   Repetitive, nonfunctional movements (e.g., hand flapping, rocking).

Stimulus control   Occurs when a behavior is emitted more often in the presence of a particular stimulus than it is in the absence of that stimulus.

Strabismus   A condition in which one eye cannot attain binocular vision with the other eye because of imbalanced muscles.

Stuttering   A complex fluency disorder of speech, affecting the smooth flow of words; may involve repetition of sounds or words, prolonged sounds, facial grimaces, muscle tension, and other physical behaviors.

Supported employment   Providing ongoing, individualized supports to persons with disabilities to help them find, learn, and maintain paid employment at regular work sites in the community.

Syntax   The system of rules governing the meaningful arrangement of words in a language.

Systematic replication   A strategy for extending and determining the generality of research findings by changing one or more variables from a previous study to see if similar results can be obtained. For example, testing a particular instructional method with elementary students that a previous study found effective with secondary students.

Task analysis   Breaking a complex skill or chain of behaviors into smaller, teachable units.

Tay-Sachs disease   A progressive nervous system disorder causing profound mental retardation, deafness, blindness, paralysis, and seizures. Usually fatal by age 5. Caused by a recessive gene; blood test can identify carrier; analysis of enzymes in fetal cells provides prenatal diagnosis.

Tertiary prevention   Intervention designed to minimize the impact of a specific condition or disability; aimed at individuals with a disability.

Time out   A behavior management technique that involves removing the opportunity for reinforcement for a specific period of time following an inappropriate behavior; results in a reduction of the inappropriate behavior.

Time trials   A fluency-building procedure in which a student performs a new skill as many times as she can during a short period of time; one-minute time trials are effective for most academic skills.

Token economy (token reinforcement system)   An instructional and behavior management system in which students earn tokens (e.g., stars, points, poker chips) for performing specified behaviors. Students accumulate their tokens and exchange them at prearranged times for their choice of activities or items from a menu of backup rewards (e.g., stickers, hall monitor for a day).

Topography (of behavior)   The physical shape or form of a response.

Total communication   An approach to educating deaf students that combines oral speech, sign language, and fingerspelling.

Traumatic brain injury   An acquired injury to the brain caused by an external physical force, resulting in total or partial functional disability, psychosocial impairments, or both that adversely affects a child's educational performance.

Tremor   A type of cerebral palsy characterized by regular, strong, uncontrolled movements. May cause less overall difficulty in movement than other types of cerebral palsy.

Triplegia   Paralysis of any three limbs; relatively rare.

Tunnel vision   Visual impairment in which a person has good central vision but poor peripheral vision.

Turner's syndrome   A sex chromosomal disorder in females, resulting from an absence of one of the X chromosomes; lack of secondary sex characteristics, sterility, and short stature are common. Although not usually a cause of mental retardation, it is often associated with learning problems.

Tymphonic membrane (eardrum)   Located in the middle ear, the eardrum moves in and out to variations in sound pressure, changing acoustical energy to sound energy.

Type I diabetes (formerly called *juvenile diabetes* or *early-onset diabetes*)   A disease characterized by inadequate secretion or use of insulin and the resulting excessive sugar in the blood and urine. Managed with diet and/or medication but can be difficult to control. Can cause coma and eventually death if left untreated or treated improperly. Can also lead to visual impairments and limb amputation. Not curable at the present time.

Usher's syndrome   An inherited combination of visual and hearing impairments. Usually, the person is born with a profound hearing loss and loses vision gradually in adulthood because of retinitis pigmentosa, which affects the visual field.

Visual acuity   The ability to clearly distinguish forms or discriminate details at a specified distance.

Visual cortex   Interprets electrical signals from the optic nerve into visual images; located in the occipital lobe at the back of the brain.

Visual efficiency   A term used to describe how effectively a person uses his vision. Includes such factors as control of eye movements, near and distant visual acuity, and speed and quality of visual processing.

Vitreous humor   The jellylike fluid that fills most of the interior of the eyeball.

Vocational rehabilitation   A program designed to help adults with disabilities obtain and hold employment.

Voice disorder   "Abnormal production and/or absences of vocal quality, pitch, loudness, resonance, and/or duration, which is inappropriate for an individual's age and/or sex" (ASHA, 1993, p. 40).

Work activity center   A sheltered work and activity program for adults with severe disabilities; teaches concentration and persistence, along with basic life skills, for little or no pay.

References

Aaroe, L., & Nelson, J. R. (2000). A comparative analysis of teachers', Caucasian parents', and Hispanic parents' view of problematic school survival behaviors. *Education and Treatment of Children, 23,* 314–324.

Abikoff, H. (1991). Cognitive training in ADHD children: Less to it than meets the eye. *Journal of Learning Disabilities, 24,* 205–209.

Achenbach, T. M., & Edelbrock, C. S. (1991). *Manual for the child behavior checklist.* Burlington: University of Vermont, Department of Psychiatry.

Ad Hoc Committee on Terminology and Classification. (2001). Request for comment on proposed new edition of *Mental Retardation: Definition, classification, and systems of supports. AAMR News and Notes, 14*(5), 1, 9–12.

Ad Hoc Committee on the Roles and Responsibilities of the School-Based Speech-Language Pathologist. (1999). *Guidelines for the roles and responsibilities of the school-based speech-language pathologist.* Rockville, MD: American Speech-Language-Hearing Association.

Adelman, H. S. (1994). Intervening to enhance home involvement in schooling. *Intervention in School and Clinic, 29*(5), 276–284.

Adelman, H. S. (1996). Appreciating the classification dilemma. In W. Stainback & S. Stainback (Eds.), *Controversial issues confronting special education: Divergent perspectives* (2nd ed.) (pp. 96–111). Boston: Allyn & Bacon.

Agran, M., & Wehmeyer, M. L. (1999). *Teaching problem solving to students with mental retardation.* Washington, DC: American Association on Mental Retardation.

Aiello, B. (1976, April 25). Up from the basement: A teacher's story. *New York Times,* p. 14.

Akshoomoff, N. (2000). *Neurological underpinnings of autism* (Vol. 9). Baltimore: Brookes.

Alabama Institute for the Deaf and Blind. (1989). *Helping kids soar.* Talladega: Author.

Alber, M. B. (1974). *Listening: A curriculum guide for teachers of visually impaired students.* Springfield: Illinois Office of Education.

Alber, S. R., & Heward, W. L. (1997). Recruit it or lose it! Training students to recruit contingent teacher attention. *Intervention in School and Clinic, 5,* 275–282.

Alber, S. R., & Heward, W. L. (2001). Teaching students to recruit positive attention: A literature review with recommendations for practice and future research. *Journal of Behavioral Education.*

Alber, S. R., Heward, W. L., & Hippler, B. J. (1999). Training middle school students with learning disabilities to recruit positive teacher attention. *Exceptional Children, 65,* 253–270.

Alberto, P. A., & Fredrick, L. D. (2000). Teaching picture reading as an enabling skill. *Teaching Exceptional Children, 33*(6), 60–64.

Alberto, P. A., & Troutman, A. C. (1999). *Applied behavior analysis for teachers* (5th ed.). Upper Saddle River, NJ: Merrill/Prentice Hall.

Alberto, P., Sharpton, W., Briggs, A., & Stright, M. (1986). Facilitating task acquisition through the use of a self-operated auditory prompting system. *Journal of The Association for Persons with Severe Handicaps, 11,* 85–91.

Alder, N. (2000). Teaching diverse students. *Multicultural Perspectives, 2*(2), 28–31.

Aldrich, F. K., & Parkin, A. J. (1989). Listening at speed. *British Journal of Visual Impairment, 7*(1), 16–18.

Algozzine, B., & Kay, P. (Eds.). (2002). *Preventing problem behaviors: A handbook of successful prevention strategies.* Thousand Oaks, CA: Corwin Press.

Algozzine, B., Audette, B., Ellis, E., Marr, M. B., & White, R. (2000). Supporting teacher, principals, and students, through unified discipline. *Teaching Exceptional Children, 33*(2), 42–47.

Allen, C. P., White, J., & Test, D. W. (1992). Using a picture/symbol form for self-monitoring within a community-based training program. *Teaching Exceptional Children, 24*(2), 54–56.

Allen, D. A., & Affleck, G. (1985). Are we stereotyping parents? A postscript to Blacher. *Mental Retardation, 23,* 200–202.

Allen, T. (1986). Patterns of academic achievement among hearing impaired students: 1974 and 1983. In A. Schildroth & M. Karchmer (Eds.), *Deaf children in America* (pp. 161–206). San Diego: Little, Brown.

Allen, T. E. (1994). *Who are the deaf and hard-of-hearing students leaving high school and entering postsecondary education?* Unpublished manuscript, Gallaudet University, Center for Assessment and Demographic Studies, Washington, DC.

Al-Hassan, S., & Gardner III, R. (in press). Involving immigrant parents of students with disabilities in the educational process. *Teaching Exceptional Children.*

American Council on Science and Health. (1979, May). *Diet and hyperactivity: Is there a relationship?* New York: Author.

American Foundation for the Blind. (2000). *Position paper on the inclusion of students with visual impairments.* www.afb.org

American Printing House for the Blind. (1992). *Annual report.* Louisville, KY: Author.

American Psychiatric Association. (1999). *Obsessive-compulsive disorder.* Washington, DC: Author. [On-line]. Available: http://www.psych.org

American Psychiatric Association. (2000a). *Diagnostic and statistical manual of mental disorders, text revision: DSM-IV-TR* (4th ed.). Washington, DC: Author.

American Psychiatric Association. (2000b). *Practice guideline for the treatment of patients with schizophrenia.* Washington, DC: Author. [On-line]. Available: http://www.psych.org/clin_res/pg_schizo.cfm

American Psychiatric Association. (2000c). *Practice guideline for the treatment of patients with bipolar disorder.* Washington, DC: Author. [On-line]. Available: http://www.psych.org/clin_res/pg_bipolar.cfm

American Speech-Language-Hearing Association. (1983). Position paper on social dialects. *ASHA, 25*(9), 23–27.

American Speech-Language-Hearing Association. (1993). Definitions of communication disorders and variations. *ASHA, 35* (Suppl. 10), 40–41.

American Speech-Language-Hearing Association. (1995). Position paper and guidelines for acoustics in educational settings. *ASHA, 37*(Suppl. 14), 15–19.

American Speech-Language-Hearing Association (1996, Spring). Inclusive practices for children and youths with communication disorders: Position statement and technical report). *ASHA, 38* (Suppl. 16), 33–44.

American Speech-Language-Hearing Association (ASHA). (2001a). *Pragmatics, socially speaking.* www.asha.org

American Speech-Language-Hearing Association (ASHA). (2001b). Roles and responsibilities of speech-language pathologists with respect to reading and writing in children and adolescents. (Position statement, executive summary of guidelines, technical report). *ASHA Supplement 21,* 17–27. Rockville, MD: Author.

American Speech-Language-Hearing Association (ASHA). (2001c). *Schools survey.* www.asha.org

American Speech-Language-Hearing Association. (2001). *Effects of hearing loss.* http://www.asha.org/

American Speech-Language-Hearing Association. (2001d). *Language and literacy development.* Washington, DC: U. S. Department of Education and

American Speech-Language-Hearing Association. http://www.asha.org/speech/development/languagedevelopment.cfm

Anderegg, M. L., Vergason, G. A., & Smith, M. C. (1992). A visual representation of the grief cycle for use by teachers with families of children with disabilities. *Remedial and Special Education, 13*(2), 17–23.

Anderson, C., & Katsiyannis, A. (1997). By what token economy: A classroom learning tool for inclusive settings. *Teaching Exceptional Children, 29*(4), 65–67.

Anderson, J. A., & Matthews, B. (2001). We CARE for students with emotional and behavioral disabilities and their families. *Teaching Exceptional Children, 33*(5), 34–39.

Anderson, S. R., & Romancyzk, R. G. (1999). Early intervention for young children with autism: Continuum–based models. *Journal of The Association for Persons with Severe Handicaps, 24,* 162–173.

Anthony, D. (1971). *Signing essential English.* Anaheim, CA: Anaheim School District.

Antunez, B. (2000). *When everyone is involved: Parents and communities in school reform.* National Council for Bilingual Education. http://www.ncbe.gwu.edu/ncbepubs/tasynthesis/framing/6parents.htm

Anxiety Disorders Association of America (2001). *Brief overview of anxiety disorders.* Rockville, MD: Author. [On-line]. Available: http://www.adaa.org/AnxietyDisorderInfor/OverviewAnxDis.cfm

Apple, D. F., Anson, C. A., Hunter, J. D., & Bell, R. B. (1995). Spinal cord injury in youth. *Clinical Pediatrics, 34,* 90–95.

Armendariz, F., & Umbreit, J. (1999). Using active responding to reduce disruptive behavior in a general education classroom. *Journal of Positive Behavior Interventions, 1,* 152–158.

Arnold, L. E., Christopher, J., Huestis, R. D., & Smeltzer, D. J. (1978). Megavitamins for minimal brain dysfunction: A placebo controlled study. *Journal of the American Medical Association, 240,* 2642–2643.

Arter, C. (1997). Listening skills. In H. Mason & S. McCall (Eds.), *Visual impairment: Access to education for children and young people* (pp. 143–148). London: Fulton.

Artiles, A. J., & Trent, S. C. (1994). Overrepresentation of minority students in special education: A continuing debate. *Journal of Special Education, 27,* 410–437.

Artiles, A. J., Aguirre-Munoz, Z., & Abedi, J. (1998). Predicting placement in learning disabilities programs: Do predictors vary by ethnic group? *Exceptional Children, 64,* 543–559.

Artiles, A., & Zamora-Durán, G. (1997). *Reducing disproportionate representation of culturally diverse students in special and gifted education.* Reston, VA: Council for Exceptional Children.

Asthma and Allergy Foundation of America. (2001). *Facts and figures.* Washington, DC: Author. www.aafa.org

Ault, M. M., Rues, J. P., Graff, J. C., & Holvoet, J. F. (2000). Special health care

procedures. In M. E. Snell & F. Brown (Eds.), *Instruction of students with severe disabilities* (5th ed.), (pp. 245–290). Upper Saddle River, NJ: Merrill/Prentice Hall.

Autism Research Institute. (1998). Another genetic defect linked to autistic behavior, retardation. *Autism Research Review International, 12*(1), 4.

Autism Society of America. (2000). *Advocate, 33*(1), 3.

Award-winning researchers raise questions about "inclusion." (2001). *DLD Times, 18*(2), 4.

Baca, L. M., & Cervantes, H. T. (1998). *The bilingual special education interface* (3rd ed.). Upper Saddle River, NJ: Merrill/Prentice Hall.

Bagnato, S. J., Neisworth, J. T., & Munson, S. M. (1997). *LINKing assessment and early intervention: An authentic curriculum-based approach.* Baltimore: Brookes.

Bailey, D. B., & Simeonsson, R. J. (1988). *Family assessment in early intervention.* Upper Saddle River, NJ: Merrill/Prentice Hall.

Bailey, D. B., & Wolery, M. (1992). *Teaching infants and preschoolers with disabilities* (2nd ed.). Upper Saddle River, NJ: Merrill/Prentice Hall.

Bailey, D., Skinner, D., Correa, V., Arcia, E., Reyes-Blanes, M., Rodriguez, P., Vazquez, E., & Skinner, M. (1999). Needs and supports reported by Latino families of young children with developmental disabilities. *American Journal on Mental Retardation, 104,* 437–451.

Bailey, D., Skinner, D., Correa, V., Blanes, M., Vasquez, E., & Rodriguez, P. (1999). Awareness, use, and satisfaction with services for Latino parents of young children with disabilities. *Exceptional Children, 65,* 367–381.

Bailey, J. S. (1992). Gentle teaching: Trying to win friends and influence people with euphemism, metaphor, smoke, and mirrors. *Journal of Applied Behavior Analysis, 25,* 879–883.

Bak, S. (1999). Relationships between inappropriate behaviors and other factors in young children with visual impairments. *RE:view, 31,* 84–91.

Baker, B. L. (1989). *Parent training and developmental disabilities.* Washington, DC: American Association on Mental Retardation.

Baker, E., Wang, M., & Walberg, H. (1995). The effects of inclusion in learning. *Educational Leadership, 52*(4), 33–34.

Baker, J. M., & Zigmond, N. (1990). Are regular education classes equipped to accommodate students with learning disabilities. *Exceptional Children, 56,* 516–526.

Baker, J. M., & Zigmond, N. (1995). The meaning and practice of inclusions for students with learning disabilities: Themes and implications for the five cases. *Journal of Special Education, 29,* 163–180.

Baker, L., & Lombardi, B. R. (1985). Students' lecture notes and their relation

to test performance. *Teaching of Psychology, 12,* 28–32.

Baker, S., & Baker, K. (1997). Educating children who are deaf or hard of hearing: Bilingual-bicultural education. *ERIC Digest #553.* (ERIC Document Reproduction Service No. ED 416 671).

Baldwin, V. (1995). *Annual deaf-blind census.* Monmouth: Western Oregon State College, Teacher Research.

Bambara, L. M., & Ager, C. (1992). Using self-scheduling to promote self-directed leisure activity in home and community settings. *Journal of The Association for Persons with Severe Handicaps, 17,* 67–76.

Bambara, L., & Koger, F. (1996). *Innovations: Providing opportunities for choice throughout the day.* Washington, DC: American Association on Mental Retardation.

Banks, J. A. (1994a). *An introduction to multicultural education.* Boston: Allyn & Bacon.

Banks, J. A. (1994b). *Multiethnic education: Theory and practice* (3rd ed.). Boston: Allyn & Bacon.

Banks, J. A., & Banks, C. A. M. (Eds.). (1995). *Handbook of research on multicultural education.* New York: Macmillan.

Banks, J. A., & Banks, C. A. M. (Eds.). (2001). *Multicultural education: Issues and perspectives* (4th ed.). Boston: Allyn & Bacon.

Bannerman, D. J., Sheldon, J. B., Sherman, J. A., & Harchik, A. E. (1990). Balancing the right to habilitation with the right to personal liberties: The rights of people with developmental disabilities to eat too many doughnuts and take a nap. *Journal of Applied Behavior Analysis, 23,* 79–89.

Barbetta, P. M. (1990a). GOALS: A group-oriented adapted levels system for children with behavior disorders. *Academic Therapy, 25,* 645–656.

Barbetta, P. M. (1990b). Red light—green light: A classwide management system for students with behavior disorders in the primary grades. *Preventing School Failure, 34*(4), 14–19.

Barbetta, P. M. (2002, January). Personal communication.

Barbetta, P. M., & Heron, T. E. (1991). Project SHINE: Summer home instruction and evaluation. *Intervention in School and Clinic, 26,* 276–281.

Barbetta, P. M., & Heward, W. L. (1993). Effects of active student response during error correction on the acquisition and maintenance of geography facts by elementary students with learning disabilities. *Journal of Behavioral Education, 3,* 217–233.

Barbetta, P. M., Heron, T. E., & Heward, W. L. (1993). Effects of active student response during error correction on the acquisition, maintenance, and generalization of sight words by students with developmental disabilities. *Journal of Applied Behavior Analysis, 26,* 111–119.

Barbetta, P. M., Heward, W. L., & Bradley, D. M. C. (1993). Relative effects of whole-word and phonetic error correction on the acquisition and maintenance of sight words by students with developmental disabilities. *Journal of Applied Behavior Analysis, 26,* 99–110.

Barbetta, P. M., Heward, W. L., Bradley, D. M. C., & Miller, A. D. (1994). Effects of immediate and delayed error correction on the acquisition and maintenance of sight words by students with developmental disabilities. *Journal of Applied Behavior Analysis, 27,* 177–178.

Barfels, M., Heward, W. L., & Al-Attrash, M. (1999). Using audio prompts to improve work performance by adults with developmental disabilities in an enclave supported employment setting. Manuscript submitted for publication.

Barkley, R. A. (1998). *Attention-deficit/hyperactivity disorder: A handbook for diagnosis and treatment* (2nd ed.). New York: Guilford.

Barkley, R. A., Fischer, M., Edelbrock, C. S., & Smallish, L. (1990). The adolescent outcome of hyperactive children diagnosed by research criteria: I. An eight-year prospective follow-up study. *Journal of the American Academy of Children and Adolescent Psychiatry, 29,* 546-557.

Barlow, J. A. (2001). Prologue: Recent advances in phonological theory and treatment. *Language, Speech, and Hearing Services in Schools, 32,* 225–228.

Barner, K., Howell, R. D., & Mahoney, R. (1996). Telementoring and collaborative learning for students with disabilities. *Proceedings of the 20th Annual Meeting of the Society for Advancement of Rehabilitation Technologies* (pp. 176–179). Salt Lake City, UT.

Barnett, S. W., & Boyce, G. C. (1994). Effects of children with Down syndrome on parents' activities. *American Journal of Mental Retardation, 100,* 115–127.

Barnhill, G. P., Hagiwara, T., Myles, B. S., Simpson, R. L., Brick, M. L., & Griswold, D. E. (2000). Parent, teacher, and self–report of problems and adaptive behaviors in children and adolescents with Asperger syndrome. *Diagnostique, 25*(2), 147–167.

Barraga, N. C., & Erin, J. N. (1992). *Visual handicaps and learning* (3rd ed.). Austin, TX: PRO-ED.

Barrera, I. (1995). To refer or not to refer: Untangling the web of diversity, "deficit," and disability. *New York State Association for Bilingual Education Journal, 10,* 54–66.

Bateman, B. D., & Linden, M. L. (1998). *Better IEPs: How to develop legally correct and educationally useful programs* (3rd ed.). Longmont, CO: Sopris West.

Batshaw, M. L. (Ed.). (1997). *Children with disabilities* (4th ed.). Baltimore: Brookes.

Battle, D. E. (Ed.). (1998). *Communication disorders in multicultural populations* (2nd ed.). Boston: Butterworth-Heinemann.

Bat–Chava, Y. (2000). Diversity of deaf identities. *American Annals of the Deaf, 145,* 420–428.

Bauer, A. M., & Brown, G. M. (2001). *Adolescents and inclusions: Transforming secondary schools.* Baltimore: Brookes.

Baumgart, D., & Giangreco, M. F. (1996). Key lessons learned about inclusion. In D. H. Lehr & F. Brown (Eds.), *People with disabilities who challenge the system* (pp. 79–97). Baltimore: Brookes.

Baumgart, D., Brown, L., Pumpian, I., Nisbet, J., Ford, A., Sweet, M., Messina, R., & Schroeder, J. (1982). Principle of partial participation and individualized adaptations in educational programs for severely handicapped students. *Journal of The Association for Persons with Severe Handicaps, 7,* 17–27.

Bayley, N. (1993). *Bayley Scales of Infant Development manual—Second edition manual.* San Antonio, TX: Psychological Corporation.

Beakley, B. A., & Yoder, S. L. (1998). Middle schoolers learn community skills. *Teaching Exceptional Children, 30*(3), 16–21.

Beatty, L. S., Madden, R., Gardner, E. F., Karlsen, B. (1995). *Stanford Diagnostic Mathematics Test—Fourth Edition.* San Antonio, TX: Harcourt Brace Educational Measurement.

Beck, J., Broers, J., Hogue, E., Shipstead, J., & Knowlton, E. (1994). Strategies for functional community-based instruction and inclusion for children with mental retardation. *Teaching Exceptional Children, 26*(2), 44–48.

Beck, R., Conrad, D., & Anderson, P. (1995). *Skill builders handbook.* Longmont, CO: Sopris West.

Becker, W. C., Engelmann, S., & Thomas, D. R. (1971). *Teaching: A course in applied psychology.* Chicago: Science Research Associates.

Beckley, C. G., Al-Attrash, M., Heward, W. L., & Morrison, H. (1999). Using guided notes in an eighth-grade social studies class: Effects on next-day quiz scores and notetaking accuracy. Manuscript submitted for publication.

Behr, S. K., Murphy, D. L., & Summers, J. A. (1992). *User's manual: Kansas Inventory of Parental Perceptions (KIPP).* Lawrence: University of Kansas, Beach Center on Families and Disability.

Beirne-Smith, M., Ittenbach, R. F., & Patton, J. R. (2002). *Mental retardation* (6th ed.). Upper Saddle River, NJ: Merrill/Prentice Hall.

Belcastro, F. P .(1989). Use of Belcastro Rods to teach mathematical concepts to blind students. *RE:view, 21,* 71–79.

Belgrave, F. Z., & Mills, J. (1981). Effect upon desire for social interaction with a physically disabled person of mentioning the disability in different contexts. *Journal of Applied Social Psychology, 11,* 44–57.

Bellamy, G. T., & Wilcox, B. (1982). Secondary education for severely handicapped students: Guidelines for quality services. In K. P. Lynch, W. E. Kiernan, & J. A. Stark (Eds.), *Prevocational and vocational education for special needs youth: A blueprint for the 1980s.* Baltimore, Brookes.

Belmont, J. M. (1966). Long term memory in mental retardation. *International Review of Research in Mental Retardation, 1,* 219–255.

Belser, R. C., & Sudhalter, V. (2001). Conversational characteristics of children with Fragile X syndrome: Repetitive speech. *American Journal of Mental Retardation, 106,* 28–38.

Beninghof, A. M. (1998). *Ideas for inclusion: The classroom teacher's guide to integrating students with severe disabilities.* Longmont, CO: Sopris West.

Bennett, C. (1999). *Comprehensive multicultural education: Theory and practice* (4th ed.). Boston: Allyn & Bacon.

Bennett, D. (1997). Low vision devices for children and young people with a visual impairment. In H. Mason & S. McCall (Eds.), *Visual impairment: Access to education for children and young people* (pp. 64–75). London: Fulton.

Bennett, W. J. (1986). *First lessons: A report on elementary education in America.* Washington, DC: U. S. Department of Education.

Benson, V., & Marano, M. A. (1998, October). Current estimates from the National Health Interview Survey, 1995. National Center for Health Statistics. *Vital Health Stat 10, 199.*

Benz, M. R., & Lindstrom, L. E. (1997). *Building school-to-work programs: Strategies for youth with special needs.* Austin, TX: PRO-ED.

Benz, M. R., Lindstrom, L., & Yavanoff, P. (2000). Improving graduation and employment outcomes of students with disabilities: Predictive factors and student perspectives. *Exceptional Children, 66,* 509–529.

Benz, M. R., Yovanoff, P., & Doren, B. (1997). School-to-work components that predict postschool success for students with and without disabilities. *Exceptional Children, 63,* 151–165.

Berney, T. P. (2000). Autism: An evolving concept. *British Journal of Psychiatry, 176,* 20–25.

Berninger, V. (2000). Dyslexia, the invisible, treatable disorder: The story of Einstein's Ninja Turtles. *Learning Disability Quarterly, 23,* 175–195.

Berquin, P. C., Giedd, J. N., Jacobson, L. K., Hamburger, S. D., Krain, A. L., Rappaport, J. L., & Castellanos, E. X. (1998). Cerebellum in attention-deficit/hyperactivity disorder: A Morphometric MRI study. *Neurology, 50,* 1087–1093.

Best, A. B. (1992). *Teaching children with visual impairments.* Milton Keynes, England: Open University Press.

Best, S. J. (2001). Physical disabilities. In J. L. Bigge, S. J. Best, & K. W. Heller, *Teaching individuals with physical, health, or multiple disabilities* (4th ed.), (pp. 34–64). Upper Saddle River, NJ: Merrill/Prentice Hall.

Best, S., Bigge, J., & Reed, P. (2001). Supporting physical and sensory capabilities through assistive technology. In J. L. Bigge, S. J. Best, & K. W. Heller, *Teaching individuals with physical, health, or multiple disabilities* (4th ed.), (pp. 195–228). Upper Saddle River, NJ: Merrill/Prentice Hall.

Bettelheim, B. (1967). *The empty fortress: Infantile autism and the birth of the self.* London: Collier-Macmillan.

Beukelman, D. R., & Miranda, P. (1998) *Augmentative and alternative communication: Management of severe communication disorder in children and adults* (2nd ed.). Baltimore: Brookes.

Bicard, D. F. (2000). *Behavior analysis and ADHD: A review of the literature.* Unpublished manuscript, The Ohio State University, Columbus.

Bicard, D. F. (2000). Using classroom rules to construct behavior. *Middle School Journal, 31*(5), 37–45.

Bicard, D. F., & Neef, N. A. (in press). History effects of strategic versus tactical rules on adaptation to changing contingencies in children with ADHD. *Journal of Applied Behavior Analysis.*

Bigge, J. L. (1991). *Teaching individuals with physical and multiple disabilities* (3rd ed.). Upper Saddle River, NJ: Merrill/Prentice Hall.

Bigge, J. L., Best, S. J., & Heller, K. W. (2001). *Teaching individuals with physical, health, or multiple disabilities* (4th ed.). Upper Saddle River, NJ: Merrill/Prentice Hall.

Bigge, J. L., Stump, C. S., Spagna, M. E., & Silberman, R. K. (1999). *Curriculum, assessment, and instruction for students with disabilities.* Belmont, CA: Wadsworth.

Biglan, A. (1995). Translating what we know about the context of antisocial behavior into a lower prevalence of such behavior. *Journal of Applied Behavior Analysis, 28,* 479–492.

Billingsley, F. F., Liberty, K. A., & White, O. R. (1994). The technology of instruction. In E. C. Cipani & F. Spooner (Eds.), *Curricular and instructional approaches for persons with severe disabilities* (pp. 81–116). Boston: Allyn & Bacon.

Binder, C. (1996). Behavioral fluency: Evolution of a new paradigm. *Behavior Analyst, 19,* 163–197.

Bishop, V. E. (1986). Identifying the components of successful mainstreaming. *Journal of Visual Impairment and Blindness, 80,* 939–946.

Bishop, V. E. (1996). *Teaching visually impaired children* (2nd ed.). Springfield, IL: Thomas.

Blacher, J. (1984). A dynamic perspective on the impact of a severely handicapped child on the family. In J. Blacher (Ed.), *Severely handicapped children and their families* (pp. 3–50). Orlando, FL: Academic Press.

Blacher, J. (2001). Transition to adulthood: Mental retardation, families, and culture. *American Journal of Mental Retardation, 106,* 173–188.

Blackorby, J., & Wagner, M. (1996). Longitudinal postschool outcomes of youth with disabilities: Findings from the National Longitudinal Transition Study. *Exceptional Children, 62,* 399–413.

Blake, C., Wang, W., Cartledge, G., & Gardner, R. (2000). Middle school students with serious emotional disturbances serve as social skills trainers and reinforcers for peers with SED. *Behavioral Disorders, 25,* 280–298.

Blatt, B. (1976). *Revolt of the idiots: A story.* Glen Ridge, NJ: Exceptional Press.

Blatt, B. (1987). *The conquest of mental retardation.* Austin, TX: PRO-ED.

Blatt, B., & Kaplan, F. (1966). *Christmas in purgatory: A photographic essay on mental retardation.* Boston: Allyn & Bacon.

Bleck, E. E. (1987). Orthopedic management of cerebral palsy—Clinics in developmental medicine No. 99/100. Philadelphia: Lippincott.

Block, S. R. (1997). Closing the sheltered workshop: Toward competitive employment opportunities for persons with developmental disabilities. *Journal of Vocational Rehabilitation, 9,* 267–275.

Bloodstein, O. (1995). *A handbook on stuttering* (5th ed.). San Diego: Singular.

Bloom, B. S. (1980). The new direction in educational research: Alterable variables. *Phi Delta Kappan, 61,* 382–385.

Bloom, B. S. (Ed.). (1956). *Taxonomy of educational objectives. Handbook I: Cognitive domain.* New York: McKay.

Blosser, J. L., & Kratcoski, A. (1997). PACs: A framework for determining appropriate service delivery options. *ASHA, 28,* 99–107.

Board of Education of the Hendrick Hudson Central School District v. Rowley, 102 S. Ct. 3034 (1982).

Bogdan, R., & Taylor, S. J. (1994). *The social meaning of mental retardation.* New York: Teachers College Press.

Bondurant-Utz, J. (2002). *Practical guide to assessing infants and preschoolers with special needs.* Upper Saddle River, NJ: Merrill/Prentice Hall.

Bondy, A., & Frost, L. (1994). PECS: The picture exchange communication system. *Focus on Autistic Behavior, 9,* 1–9.

Book, D., Paul, T. L., Gwalla-Ogisi, N., & Test, D. W. (1990). No more bologna sandwiches. *Teaching Exceptional Children, 22*(2), 62–64.

Bornstein, H. (1974). Signed English: A manual approach to English language development. *Journal of Speech and Hearing Disorders, 3,* 330–343.

Borsch, J., & Oaks, R. (1993). *The collaboration companion: Strategies and activities in and out of the classroom.* East Moline, IL: LinguiSystems.

Borthwick-Duffy, S. (1994). Review of mental retardation: Definition, causes, and systems of supports. *American Journal on Mental Retardation, 98,* 541–544.

Borthwick-Duffy, S. A., & Eyman, R. K. (1990). Who are the dually diagnosed? *American Journal on Mental Retardation, 94,* 586–595.

Bosner, S. M., & Belfiore, P. J. (2001). Strategies and considerations for teaching an adolescent with Down syndrome and type I diabetes to self-administer insulin. *Education and Treatment in Mental Retardation and Developmental Disabilities, 36,* 94–102.

Bouchard, D., & Tétreault, S. (2000). The motor development of sighted children and children with moderate low vision aged 8–13. *Journal of Visual Impairments and Blindness, 94,* 564–573.

Boudah, D. J., Schumaker, J. B., & Deshler, D. D. (1997). Collaborative instruction: Is it an effective option for inclusion in secondary classrooms? *Learning Disability Quarterly, 4,* 293–316.

Boulware, G. L., Schwartz, I. S., & McBride, B. M. (1999). Addressing challenging behavior at home: Working with families to find solutions. In S. R. Sandall & M. Ostrosky (Eds.), *Practical ideas for addressing challenging behaviors.* Monograph of *Young Exceptional Children* (pp. 29–40). Denver: Sopris West.

Bowe, F. (2000). *Teaching individuals with physical and multiple disabilities* (4th ed.). Upper Saddle River, NJ: Merrill/Prentice Hall.

Bowen, J., Olympia, D., & Jensen, W. (1996). *Study buddies: Parent tutoring tactics.* Longmont, CO: Sopris West.

Bower, E. M. (1960). *Early identification of emotionally handicapped children in the schools.* Springfield, IL: Thomas.

Bower, E. M. (1982). Defining emotional disturbance: Public policy and research. *Psychology in the Schools, 19,* 55–60.

Bowers, F. E., McGinnis, J. C., Ervin, R. A., & Friman, P. C. (1999). Merging research and practice: the example of positive peer reporting applied to social rejection. *Education and Treatment of Children, 22,* 218–226.

Braden, J. P., Maller, S. J., & Paquin, M. M. (1993). The effects of residential versus day placement on the performance IQs of children with hearing impairment. *Journal of Special Education, 26,* 423–433.

Bradley, V. J., Knoll, J., & Agosta, J. M. (Eds.). (1992). *Emerging issues in family support.* Washington, DC: American Association on Mental Retardation.

Brain Injury Association. (2001). *Brain injury and you.* Alexandria, VA: Author. http://www.bia.org

Brame, P. (2000). Using picture storybooks to enhance the social skills training of special needs students. *Middle School Journal, 32*(1), 41.

Brandt, J. (1992). Idea Bunny: Teaching special needs preschool children independent work skills with an audio prompt recording device. Unpublished master's thesis, The Ohio State University, Columbus.

Bray, N. W., Fletcher, K. L., & Turner, L. A. (1997). Cognitive competencies and strategy use in individuals with mental retardation. In W. W. MacLean, Jr. (Ed.), *Ellis' handbook of mental deficiency, psychological theory, and research* (3rd ed.), (pp. 197–217). Mahwah, NJ: Erlbaum.

Bredekamp, S. (1993). The relationship between early childhood education and early childhood special education: Healthy marriage or family feud? *Topics in Early Childhood Special Education, 13,* 258–273.

Bredekamp, S., & Copple, C. (Eds.). (1997). *Developmentally appropriate practice in* early childhood programs. Washington, DC: National Association for the Education of Young Children.

Brewer, J., & Kieff, J. (1996). Fostering mutual respect for play at home and school. *Childhood Education, 7,* 92–96.

Bricker, D. (1986). An analysis of early intervention programs: Attendant issues and future directions. In R. J. Morris & B. Blatt (Eds.), *Special education: Research and trends* (pp. 28–65). New York: Pergamon.

Bricker, D. (1993). *AEPS measurement for birth to three years.* Baltimore: Brookes.

Bricker, D., & Pretti-Frontczak, K. (1996). *AEPS measurement for three to six years.* Baltimore: Brookes.

Bricker, D., & Squires, J. (1999). *Ages & stages questionnaires: A parent-completed, child-monitoring system* (2nd ed.). Baltimore: Brookes.

Bricker, D., & Waddell, M. (1996). *AEPS curriculum for three to six years.* Baltimore: Brookes.

Bricker, D., Pretti-Frontczak, K., & McComas, N. (1998). *An activity-based approach to early intervention* (2nd ed.). Baltimore: Brookes.

Brickey, M. P., Campbell, K. M., & Browning, L. J. (1985). A five-year follow-up of sheltered workshop employees placed in competitive jobs. *Mental Retardation, 23,* 67–73.

Brigance, A. H. (1999). *Brigance Diagnostic Comprehensive Inventory of Basic Skills— Revised.* N. Billerica, MA: Curriculum Associates.

Briggs, A., Alberto, P., Sharpton, W., Berlin, K., McKinley, C., & Ritts, C. (1990). Generalized use of a self-operated audio prompt system. *Education and Training in Mental Retardation, 25,* 381–389.

Brigham, F. J., & Cole, J. E. (1999). Selective mutism: Developments in definition, etiology, assessment and treatment. In T. Scruggs, & M. Mastropieri (Eds.), *Advances in learning and behavioral disabilities* (Vol.13, p. 183–216). Greenwich, CT: JAI.

Brigham, F. J., & Kauffman, J. M. (1998). Creating supportive environments for students with emotional or behavioral disorders. *Effective School Practices, 17*(2), 25–35.

Brigham, R., & Brigham, M. (2001). *Current practice alerts: Mnemonic instruction.* Reston, VA: Division for Learning Disabilities and Division for Research of the Council for Exceptional Children.

Bright, J., Hidalgo, N., Siu, S., Swap, S., & Epstein, J. (1995). Research on families, schools, and communities: A multicultural perspective. In J. A. Banks (Ed.), *Handbook of research on multicultural education* (pp. 498–524). New York: Macmillan.

Brinkerhoff, L. C., McGuire, J. M., & Shaw, S. F. (1998). *Postsecondary education and transition for students with learning disabilities* (2nd ed.). Austin, TX: PRO-ED.

Brinkerhoff, L. C., Shaw, S. F., & McGuire, J. M. (1993). *Promoting postsecondary

education for students with learning disabilities.* Austin, TX: PRO-ED.

Bristol, M., Cohen, D., Costello, J., Denckla, M., Eckberg, T., Kallen, R., Kraemer, H., Lord, C. Maurer, R., McIlvane, W., Minshew, N. Sigman, M., & Spence, M. (1996). State of the science in autism: Report to the National Institute of Health. *Journal of Autism and Developmental Disorders, 26,* 121–154.

Brolin, D. E. (1991). *Life-centered career education: A competency-based approach* (3rd ed.). Reston, VA: Council for Exceptional Children.

Brolin, D. E. (1997). *Life-centered career education: A competency based approach* (5th ed.). Reston, VA: Council for Exceptional Children.

Bronicki, G. J., & Turnbull, A. P. (1987). Family-professional interactions. In M. E. Snell (Ed.), *Systematic instruction of persons with severe handicaps* (3rd ed.) (pp. 9–35). Upper Saddle River, NJ: Merrill/ Prentice Hall.

Brookes, J., & Brookes, M. (1993). In search of understanding: The case for constructivist classrooms. Alexander, VA: Association for Supervision and Curriculum Development.

Brophy, J. (1986). Teacher influences on student achievement. *American Psychologist, 41,* 1069–1077.

Browder, D. M. (2000). *Comments made as guest faculty for OSU teleconference seminar: Contemporary issues in special education.* Columbus, OH: The Ohio State University.

Browder, D. M., & Bambara, L. M. (2000). Home and community. In M. E. Snell & F. Brown (Eds.), *Instruction of students with severe disabilities* (5th ed.), (pp. 543–589). Upper Saddle River, NJ: Merrill/Prentice Hall.

Browder, D. M., & Snell, M. E. (2000). Functional academics. In M. E. Snell & F. Brown, *Instruction of students with severe disabilities* (5th ed.), (pp. 493–542). Upper Saddle River, NJ: Merrill/Prentice Hall.

Browder, D. M., Cooper, K. J., & Lim, L. (1998). Teaching adults with severe disabilities to express their choice of settings for leisure activities. *Education and Training in Mental Retardation and Developmental Disabilities, 33,* 228–238.

Brower, I. C. (1983). Counseling Vietnamese. In D. R. Atkinson, G. Morten, & D. W. Sue (Eds.), *Counseling American minorities* (2nd ed.) (pp. 107–121). Dubuque, IA: Brown.

Brown v. Board of Education of Topeka, 347 U. S. 483 (1954).

Brown, F., & Lehr, D. H. (1993). Making activities meaningful for students with severe multiple disabilities. *Teaching Exceptional Children, 25*(4), 12–16.

Brown, J. R. (1982). Assessment of the culturally different and disadvantaged child. In G. Ulrey & S. J. Rogers (Eds.), *Psychological assessment of handicapped infants and young children* (pp. 163–171). New York: Thieme-Stratton.

Brown, L. (1990). Who are they and what do they want? An essay on TASH. *TASH Newsletter, 16*(9), 1.

Brown, L. F., Campione, J. C., & Murphy, M. D. (1974). Keeping track of changing variables: Long-term retention of a trained rehearsal strategy by retarded adolescents. *American Journal of Mental Deficiency, 78,* 453–466.

Brown, L. L., & Hammill, D. D. (1990). *Behavior rating profile: An ecological approach to behavioral assessment* (2nd ed.). Austin, TX: PRO-ED.

Brown, L., Farrington, K., Suomi, J., & Zeigler, M. (1999). Work-wage relationships and individuals with disabilities. *Journal of Vocational Rehabilitation, 13,* (1), 5–13.

Brown, L., Ford, A., Nisbet, J., Sweet, M., Donnellan, A., & Gruenewald, L. (1983). Opportunities available when severely handicapped students attend chronological age appropriate regular schools. *Journal of the Association for Persons with Severe Handicaps, 8,* 16–24.

Brown, L., Long, E., Udvari-Solner, A., Davis, L., VanDeventer, P., Ahlgren, C., Johnson, F., Gruenewald, L., & Jorgensen, J. (1989a). The home school: Why students with severe disabilities must attend the schools of their brothers, sisters, friends, and neighbors. *Journal of The Association for Persons with Severe Handicaps, 14,* 1–7.

Brown, L., Long, E., Udvari-Solner, A., Davis, L., VanDeventer, P., Ahlgren, C., Johnson, F., Gruenewald, L., & Jorgensen, J. (1989b). Should students with severe intellectual disabilities be based in regular or in special education classrooms in home schools? *Journal of The Association for Persons with Severe Handicaps, 14,* 8-12.

Brown, L., Schwartz, P., Udvari-Solner, A., Kampschroer, E. F., Johnson, F., Jorgensen, J., & Gruenewald, L. (1991). How much time should students with severe intellectual disabilities spend in regular education classrooms and elsewhere? *Journal of The Association for Persons with Severe Handicaps, 16,* 39–47.

Brown, V. L., Cronin, M. E., & McEntire, E. (1994). *Test of Mathematical Abilities—2.* Austin, TX: PRO-ED.

Brown, W., Thurman, S. K., & Pearl, L. W. (1993). *Family-centered intervention with infants and toddlers: Innovative cross-disciplinary approaches.* Baltimore: Brookes.

Brownell, W. E. (1999). How the ear works: Nature's solutions for listening. *The Volta Review, 99*(5), 9–28.

Bruder, M. B. (2000, December). *The Individual Family Service Plan (IFSP).* Reston, VA: ERIC Clearinghouse on Disabilities and Gifted Education. (EDO-EC-00-14)

Brumback, R. A., Mathews, S., & Shenoy, S. R. (2001). Neurological disorders. In F. M. Kline, L. B. Silver, & S. C. Russell, (Eds.), *The educator's guide to medical issues in the classroom* (pp. 49–64). Baltimore: Brookes.

Bruns, D. A. (2000). Leaving home at an early age: Parents' decisions about out-of-home placement for young children with complex medical needs. *Mental Retardation, 38,* 50–60.

Bryan, L. C., & Gast, D. L. (2000). Teaching on-task and on-schedule behaviors to high-functioning children with autism via picture activity schedules. *Journal of Autism and Developmental Disorders, 30,* 553–567.

Bryan, T., & Ryan, A. (2001). Jacob's story: Amazing discoveries. In A. K. Ryan, Strengthening the safety net: How school can help youth with emotional and behavioral needs complete their high school education and prepare for life after school (p. 10). Burlington, VT: School Research Office, University of Vermont.

Bryan, T. (1997). Assessing the personal and social status of students with learning disabilities. *Learning Disabilities Research and Practice, 12,* 63–76.

Bulgren, J. A., Deshler, D. D., Schumaker, J. B., & Lenz, B. K. (2000). The use and effectiveness of analogical instruction in diverse secondary content classrooms. *Journal of Educational Psychology, 16,* 426–441.

Bull, G. L., & Rushakoff, G. E. (1987). Computers and speech and language disordered individuals. In J. D. Lindsey (Ed.), *Computers and exceptional individuals* (pp. 83–104). Upper Saddle River, NJ: Merrill/Prentice Hall.

Bullis, M., & Otos, M. (1988). Characteristics of programs for children with deaf-blindness: Results of a national survey. *Journal of The Association for Persons with Severe Handicaps, 13,* 110–115.

Burchard, S. N., Hasazi, J. S., Gordon, L. R., & Yoe, J. (1991). An examination of lifestyle and adjustment in three community residential alternatives. *Research in Developmental Disabilities, 12,* 127–142.

Burkhardt, L. J. (1981). *Homemade battery powered toys and educational devices for severely disabled children.* Millville, PA: Burkhardt.

Bursuck, W., Polloway, E. A., Plante, L., Epstein, D. H., Jayanthi, M., & McConeghy, J. I. (1996). Report card grading and adaptations: A national survey of classroom practices. *Exceptional Children, 62,* 301–318.

Bushell, D., Jr., & Baer, D. M. (1994). Measurably superior instruction means close, continual contact with the relevant outcome data. Revolutionary! In R. Gardner III, D. M. Sainato, J. O. Cooper, T. E. Heron, W. L. Heward, J. Eshleman, & T. A. Grossi (Eds.), *Behavior analysis in education: Focus on measurably superior instruction* (pp. 3–10). Pacific Grove, CA: Brooks/Cole.

Butterworth, J., Gilmore, D., Kiernan, W. E., & Shalock, R. (1999). *Day and employment service in developmental disabilities: State and national trends.* Washington, DC: American Association on Mental Retardation.

Bybee, J., & Zigler, E. (1998). Outerdirectedness in individuals with and without mental retardation: A review. In J. A. Burack, R. M. Hodapp, & E. Zigler (Eds.), *Handbook of mental retardation* (pp. 434–460). Cambridge: Cambridge University Press.

Calculator, S. N., & Jorgensen, C. M. (1991). Integrating augmentative and alternative communication instruction into regular education settings: Expounding on best practices. *Augmentative and Alternative Communication, 7,* 204–214.

Calderon, R., & Naidu, S. (2000). Further support for the benefits of early identification and intervention for children with hearing loss. *The Volta Review, 100*(5), 53–84.

Caldwell, B. (1997). Educating children who are deaf or hard of hearing: Cued speech. *ERIC Digest #555.* (ERIC Document Reproduction Service No. ED 414 673).

Calhoun, M. L., & Kuczera, M. (1996). Increasing social smiles of young children with disabilities. *Perceptual and Motor Skills, 82,* 1265–1266.

Calhoun, M. L., Rose, T. L., Hanft, B. & Sturkey, C. (1991). Social reciprocity interventions: Implications for developmental therapists. *Physical and Occupational Therapy in Pediatrics, 11,* 45–46.

California Department of Developmental Services (1999). *A report to the legislature: Changes in the populations of persons with autism and pervasive developmental disorders in California's Department of Developmental Services system: 1987 through 1998.* Sacramento, CA: California Health and Human Service Agency.

Callahan, K., Rademacher, J. A., & Hildreth, B. L. (1998). The effect of parent participation in strategies to improve the homework performance of students who are at risk. *Remedial and Special Education, 19*(3), 131–141.

Callister, J. P., Mitchell, L., & Talley, G. (1986). Profiling family preservation efforts in Utah. *Children Today, 15,* 23–25, 36–37.

Cameron, J., & Pierce, W. D. (1994). Reinforcement, reward, and intrinsic motivation: A meta-analysis. *Review of Educational Research, 64,* 363–423.

Cameron, J., & Pierce, W. D. (1996). The debate about rewards and intrinsic motivation: Protests and accusations do not alter the results. *Review of Educational Research, 66,* 39–51.

Cameron, J., Banko, K. M., & Pierce, W. D. (2001). Pervasive negative effects of rewards on intrinsic motivation: The myth continues. *The Behavior Analyst, 24,* 1–44.

Campbell, C., Campbell, S., Collicott, J., Perner, D., & Stone, J. (1988). Individualized instruction. *Education New Brunswick, 3,* 17–20.

Campbell, P. H. (2000). Promoting participation in natural environments by accommodating motor disabilities. In M. E. Snell & F. Brown (Eds.), *Instruction of students with severe disabilities* (5th ed.),

(pp. 291–329). Upper Saddle River, NJ: Merrill/Prentice Hall.

Cardon, L. R., Smith, S. D., Fulker, D. W., Kimberling, B. F., Pennington, B. F., & DeFries, J. C. (1994) Quantitative trait locus for reading disability on chromosome 6. *Science, 226,* 276–279.

Carey, W. B. (1998). Temperament and behavior problems in the classroom. *School Psychology Review, 27,* 522–533.

Carnine, D. (1997). Bridging the research to practice gap. *Exceptional Children, 63,* 513–521.

Carnine, D. W., Silbert, J., & Kame'enui, E. J. (1997). *Direct instruction reading* (3rd ed.). Upper Saddle River, NJ: Merrill/Prentice Hall.

Carnine, D., Jones, E., & Dixon, R. (1994). Mathematics: Educational tools for diverse learners. *School Psychology Review, 23,* 406–427.

Caro, P., & Derevensky, J. L. (1997). An exploratory study using the sibling interaction scale: Observing interactions between siblings with and without disabilities. *Education and Treatment of Children, 20*(4), 383–403.

Carr, E. G., & Durand, V. M. (1985). Reducing behavior problems through functional communication training. *Journal of Applied Behavior Analysis, 18,* 111–126.

Carr, E. G., Dunlap, G., Horner, R. H., Koegel, R. L., Turnbull, A. P., Sailor, W., Anderson, J., Albin, R. W., Koegel, L. K., & Fox, L. (in press). Positive behavioral support: Evolution of an applied science. *Journal of Positive Behavior Interventions.*

Carr, E. G., Levin, L., McConnachie, G., Carlson, J. I., Kemp, D. C., & Smith, C. E. (1994). *Communication-based intervention for problem behavior: A user's guide for producing positive change.* Baltimore: Brookes.

Carr, J. (1988). Six-weeks to twenty-one years old: A longitudinal study of children with Down syndrome and their families. *Journal of Child Psychology and Psychiatry, 29*(4), 407–431.

Carr, S. C., & Punzo, R. P. (1993). The effects of self-monitoring of academic accuracy and productivity on the performance of students with behavioral disorders. *Behavioral Disorders, 18,* 241–250.

Carta, J. J., Atwater, J. B., Greenwood, C. R., McConnell, S. R., McEvoy, M. A., & Williams, R. (2001). Effects of cumulative prenatal substance exposure and environmental risks on children's developmental trajectories. *Journal of Clinical Child Psychology, 30*(3), 327–337.

Cartledge, G., & Cochran, L. L. (1993). Developing cooperative learning behavior in students with behavior disorders. *Preventing School Failure, 37,* 5–10.

Cartledge, G., & Kiarie, M. W. (2001). Learning social skills through literature for children and adolescents. *Teaching Exceptional Children, 34*(2), 40–47.

Cartledge, G., & Kleefeld, J. (1991). *Taking part: Introducing social skills to children.*

Circle Pines, MN: American Guidance Service.

Cartledge, G., & Kleefeld, J. (1994). *Working together: Building social skills through folk literature.* Circle Pines, MN: American Guidance Service.

Cartledge, G., & Milburn, J. F. (1995). *Teaching social skills to children and youth: Innovative approaches* (3rd ed.). Boston: Allyn & Bacon.

Cartledge, G., Kea, C. D., & Ida, D. J. (2000). Anticipating differences—celebrating strengths: Providing culturally competent services for students with serious emotional disturbance. *Teaching Exceptional Children, 32*(3), 6–12.

Caspi, A., Henry, B., McGee, R. O., Moffitt, T. W., & Silva, P. A. (1995). Temperamental origins of child and adolescent behavior problems: From age three to age fifteen. *Child Development, 66,* 55–68.

Cassini, K. K., & Rodgers, J. L. (1989). *Death in the classroom: A teacher's guide to assist grieving students.* Cincinnati, OH: Griefwork of Cincinnati.

Catts, H. W., & Kamhi, A. G. (1999). *Language and reading disabilities.* Boston: Allyn & Bacon.

Cavanaugh, R. A., Heward, W. L., & Donelson, F. (1996). Effects of response cards during lesson closure on the academic performance of secondary students in an earth science course. *Journal of Applied Behavior Analysis, 29,* 403–406.

Cawley, J. F., Parmar, R. S., Foley, T. E., Salmon, & Roy, S. (2001). Arithmetic performance of students: Implications for standards and programming. *Exceptional Children, 67,* 311–328.

Cawley, J. F., Parmar, R. S., Yan, W., & Miller, J. H. (1998). Arithmetic computation performance of students with learning disabilities: Implications for curriculum. *Learning Disabilities Research and Practice, 13,* 68–74.

Cawthon, S. W. (2001). Teaching strategies in inclusive classrooms with deaf students. *Journal of Deaf Studies and Deaf Education, 6,* 212–225.

Cazden, C. B. (1992). *Whole language plus: Essays on literacy in the United States and New Zealand.* New York: Teachers College Press.

CEC Today. (1998). Growing challenge for teachers—Providing medical procedures for students. 5(3), 1, 5, 15.

Cedar Rapids Community School District v. Garret F., 119 S.Ct.992 U. S. (1999). http://supct.law.cornell.edu/supct/html/96-1793.ZO.html

Cedar Rapids Community School District v. Garret, F., 67 U. S. L. W. 4165 (1999).

Center for Positive Behavioral Interventions & Supports. (2001). *School-wide behavioral support.* [Online]. http://www.pbis.org/

Center on Human Policy. (1986, December). Positive interventions for challenging behavior. *The Association for Persons with Severe Handicaps Newsletter, 12*(12), 4.

Centers for Disease Control and Prevention. (1998). HIV/AIDS prevention: Frequently asked questions. *CDC Update.* http://www.cdc.gov.hiv/pubs/facts/hivre/pfs/htm

Centers for Disease Control and Prevention. (2001a). Divisions of HIV/AIDS prevention. *Surveillance Report, 12*(2) http://www.cdc.gov.hiv/stats/hasr1202

Centers for Disease Control and Prevention. (2001b). *National health statistics.* Atlanta: Author.

Chadsey, J. G., Linneman, D., Rusch, F. R., & Cimera, R. E. (1997). The impact of social integration interventions and job coaches in work settings. *Education and training in Mental Retardation and Developmental Disabilities, 32,* 281–292.

Chaikind, S., Danielson, L. C., & Brauen, M. L. (1993). What do we know about the costs of special education? A selected review. *Journal of Special Education, 26,* 344–370.

Chandler, L. K. (1993). Steps in preparing for transition: Preschool to kindergarten. *Teaching Exceptional Children, 25*(4), 52–55.

Chandler, L. K., & Dahlquist, C. M. (2002). *Functional assessment: Strategies to prevent and remediate challenging behavior in school settings.* Upper Saddle River, NJ: Merrill/Prentice Hall.

Chard, D. J., & Kame'enui, E. J. (2000). Struggling first-grade readers: The frequency and progress of their reading. *Journal of Special Education, 34,* 28–38.

Charney, E. B. (1992). Neural tube defects: Spina bifida and myelomeningocele. In M. L. Batshaw & Y. M. Perret, *Children with disabilities: A medical primer* (3rd ed.) (pp. 471–488). Baltimore: Brookes.

Chesapeake Institute. (1994, September). *National agenda for achieving better results for children and youth with serious emotional disturbance.* Washington, DC: U. S. Department of Education.

Chesley, G. M., & Calaluce, P. D. (1997). The deception of inclusion. *Mental Retardation, 35,* 488–490.

Children's Defense Fund. (2000). *Overall child poverty rate dropped in 2000 but poverty rose for children in full-time working families.* Washington, DC: Author.

Christensen, C. M. (1992). Multicultural competencies in early intervention: Training professionals for a pluralistic society. *Infants and Young Children, 4,* 49–83.

Christensen, S. L., Ysseldyke, J. E., & Thurlow, M. L. (1989). Critical instructional factors for students with mild handicaps: An integrative interview. *Remedial and Special Education, 10,* (5), 21–23.

Chuch, G., & Glennen, S. (1992). *The handbook of assistive technology.* San Diego: Singular.

Cipani, E. (1998). Three behavioral functions of classroom noncompliance: Diagnostic and treatment implications. *Focus on Autism and Other Developmental Disabilities, 13*(2), 66–72.

Cipani, E. C., & Spooner, F. (Eds.). (1994). *Curricular and instructional approaches for persons with severe disabilities.* Boston: Allyn & Bacon.

Clark, B. (1997). *Growing up gifted: Developing the potential of children at home and at school* (5th ed.). Upper Saddle River, NJ: Merrill/Prentice Hall.

Clark, B. A. (2002). *Growing up gifted* (6th ed.). Upper Saddle River, NJ: Merrill/Prentice Hall.

Clark, G. M. (1994). Is a functional curriculum approach compatible with an inclusive education model? *Teaching Exceptional Children, 26*(2), 36–39.

Clark, G. M., Carlson, B. C., Fisher, S., Cook, I. D., & D'Alonzo, B. J. (1991). Career development for students with disabilities in elementary schools: A position statement of the division on career development. *Career Development for Exceptional Individuals, 14,* 109–120.

Clark, S. G. (2000). The IEP process as a tool for collaboration. *Teaching Exceptional Children, 33*(2), 56–66.

Clarke-Klein, S., & Hodson, B. W. (1995). A phonologically based analysis of misspellings by third graders with disordered-phonology histories. *Journal of Speech and Hearing Research, 38,* 839–849.

Cleeland, L. K. (1984). The function of the auditory system in speech and language development. In R. K. Hull & K. I. Dilka (Eds.), *The hearing-impaired child in school* (pp. 15–16). Orlando, FL: Grune & Stratton.

Clements, S. D. (1966). *Minimal brain dysfunction in children* (NINDS Monograph No. 3, Public Health Service Bulletin No. 1415). Washington, DC: U. S. Department of Health, Education, and Welfare.

Cline, D. H. (1990). Interpretations of emotional disturbance and social maladjustment as policy problems: A legal analysis of initiatives to exclude handicapped/disruptive students from special education. *Behavioral Disorders, 15,* 159–173.

Coburn, J., Locke, P., Pfeiffer, A., Ridley, J., Simon, S., & Mann, H. (1995). American Indians (pp. 225–254). In Carl A. Grant (Ed.), *Educating for diversity: An anthology of multicultural voices.* Boston: Allyn & Bacon.

Cochran, L., Feng, H., Cartledge, G., & Hamilton, S. (1993). The effects of cross-age tutoring on the academic achievement, social behaviors, and self-perceptions of low-achieving African-American males with behavioral disorders. *Behavioral Disorders, 18,* 292–302.

Cohen, S., Agosta, J., Cohen, J., & Warren, R. (1989). Supporting families of children with severe disabilities. *Journal of The Association for Persons with Severe Handicaps, 14,* 155–162.

Coleman, M., & Vaughn, S. R. (2000). Reading interventions with students with emotional/behavioral disorders. *Behavioral Disorders, 25,* 93–104.

Coleman, M., & Webber, J. (1988). Behavior problems? Try groups! *Academic Therapy, 23,* 265–274.

Collicott, J. (1991). Implementing multi-level instruction: Strategies for classroom teachers. In G. Porter & D. Richler (Eds.), *Changing Canadian Schools: Perspectives on disability and inclusion* (pp. 191–218). Ottawa, Ontario, Canada: Roeher Institute.

Collins, B. C., Hall, M., & Branson, T. A. (1997). Teaching leisure skills to adolescents with moderate disabilities. *Exceptional Children, 63,* 499–512.

Colvin, G., Kame'enui, E., & Sugai, G. (1993). Reconceptualizing behavior management and school-wide discipline in general education. *Education and Treatment of Children, 16,* 361–381.

Commission on Education of the Deaf. (1988). *Toward equality: Education of the deaf.* Washington, DC: U. S. Government Printing Office.

Compton, M. V., & Niemeyer, J. A. (1994). Expressions of affection in young children with sensory impairments: A research agenda. *Education and Treatment of Children, 17,* 68–85.

Cone, A. A. (1994). Reflections on "Self-advocacy: Voices for choices." *Mental Retardation, 32,* 444–445.

Connell, M. C., Carta, J. J., & Baer, D. M. (1993). Programming generalization of in-class transition skills: Teaching preschoolers with developmental delays to self-assess and recruit contingent teacher praise. *Journal of Applied Behavior Analysis, 26,* 3.

Connell, M. C., Randall, C., Wilson, J., Lutz, S., & Lamb, D. R. (1993). Building independence during in-class transitions: Teaching in-class transition skills to preschoolers with developmental delays through choral-response-based self-assessment and contingent praise. *Education and Treatment of Children, 16,* 160–174.

Conner, E. P., Scandary, J., & Tullock, D. (1988). Education of physically handicapped and health impaired individuals: A commitment to the future. *DPH Journal, 10*(1), 5–24.

Conners, C. K. (2000). Attention-deficit/hyperactivity disorder: Historical development and overview. *Journal of Attention Disorders, 3,* 173–191.

Connolly, A. J. (1998). *KeyMath—Revised: A Diagnostic Inventory of Essential Skills.* Circle Pines, MN: American Guidance Services.

Connor, L. E. (1986). Oralism in perspective. In D. M. Luterman (Ed.), *Deafness in perspective* (pp. 116–129). San Diego: College-Hill.

Conroy, J. W. (1996). The small ICF/MR program: Dimensions of quality and cost. *Mental Retardation, 34,* 13–26.

Conroy, J. W., & Bradley, V. J. (1985). *The Pennhurst longitudinal study: A report on five years of research and analysis.* Philadelphia: Temple University Developmental Disabilities Center.

Conroy, M. A., & Davis, C. A. (2000). Early elementary-aged children with challenging behaviors: Legal and educational issues related to IDEA and assessment. *Preventing School Failure, 44,* 163–168.

Conte, R., & Andrews, J. (1993). Social skills in the context of learning disability definitions: A reply to Gresham and Elliott and directions for the future. *Journal of Learning Disabilities, 26,* 146–153.

Cook, A. M., & Cavalier, A. R. (1999). Young children using assistive robotics for discovery and control. *Teaching Exceptional Children, 31*(5), 72–78.

Cook, A. M., & Hussey, S. M. (1995). *Assistive technologies: Principles and practice.* St. Louis: Mosby.

Cook, B. G. (2001). A comparison of teachers' attitudes toward their included students with mild and severe disabilities. *Journal of Special Education, 34,* 203–213.

Cook, B. G., & Semmel, M. I. (1999). Peer acceptance of included students with disabilities as a function of severity of disability and classroom composition. *Journal of Special Education, 33,* 50–61.

Cook, B. G., Tankersley, M., Cook, L., & Landrum, T. J. (2000). Teachers' attitudes toward their included students with disabilities. *Exceptional Children, 67,* 115–135.

Cook, R. E., Tessier, A., & Klein, M. D. (2000). *Adapting early childhood curricula for children in inclusive settings* (5th ed.). Upper Saddle River, NJ: Merrill/Prentice Hall.

Cooke, N. L., Heron, T. E., & Heward, W. L. (1983). *Peer tutoring: Implementing classwide programs in the primary grades.* Columbus, OH: Special Press.

Cooke, N. L., Heron, T. E., Heward, W. L., & Test, D. W. (1982). Integrating a Down syndrome student into a classwide peer tutoring system. *Mental Retardation, 20,* 22–25.

Cooke, N. L., Heward, W. L., Test, D. W., Spooner, F., & Courson, F. H. (1991). Student performance data in the special education classroom: Measurement and evaluation of student progress. *Teacher Education and Special Education, 13,* 155–161.

Cooper, J. O., Heron, T. E., & Heward, W. L. (1987). *Applied behavior analysis.* Upper Saddle River, NJ: Merrill/Prentice Hall.

Cooper, K. J., & Browder, D. M. (1998). Enhancing choice and participation for adults with severe disabilities in community-based instruction. *Journal of The Association for Persons with Severe Handicaps, 23,* 252–260.

Corn, A. L. (1989). Instruction in the use of vision for children and adults with low vision: A proposed program model. *RE:view, 21,* 26–38.

Corn, A. L. (2000). *Finding wheels: A curriculum for non-drivers with visual impairments for gaining control of transportation needs.* Austin: PRO–ED.

Corn, A. L., & Koenig, A. J. (1996). *Foundations of low vision: Clinical and functional perspectives.* New York: AFB Press.

Corn, A., & Ryser, G. (1989). Access to print for students with low vision. *Journal of Visual Impairment and Blindness, 83,* 340–349.

Cornett, R. O. (1974). What is cued speech? *Gallaudet Today, 5*(2), 3–5.

Correa, V. I., Blanes-Reyes, M., & Rapport, M. J. (1995). Minority issues. In H. R. Turnbull & A. P. Turnbull (Eds.), *A compendium report to Congress.* Lawrence, KS: Beach Center.

Correa, V. I., Gollery, T., & Fradd, S. (1988). The handicapped undocumented alien student dilemma: Do we advocate or abdicate? *Journal of Educational Issues of Language Minority Students, 3,* 41–47.

Correa, V., & Jones, H. (2000). Multicultural issues related to families of children with disabilities. In M. J. Fine (Ed.), *Collaboration with parents of exceptional children* (2nd ed.), (pp. 133–154). Austin, TX: PRO-ED.

Cost-benefit estimates for early intensive behavioral intervention for young children with autism: General model and single state case. *Behavioral Interventions, 13,* 201–226.

Cott, A. (1972). Megavitamins: The orthomolecular approach to behavioral disorders and learning disabilities. *Academic Therapy, 7,* 245–258.

Coulter, D. L. (1994). Biomedical conditions: Types, causes, and results. In L. Sternberg (Ed.), *Individuals with profound disabilities: Instructional and assistive strategies* (3rd ed.) (pp. 41–58). Austin, TX: PRO-ED.

Coulter, D. L. (1996). Prevention as a form of support: Implications for the new definition. *Mental Retardation, 34,* 108–116.

Council for Children with Behavioral Disorders. (1989). Best assessment practices for students with behavioral disorders: Accommodation to cultural diversity and individual differences. *Behavioral Disorders, 14,* 263–278.

Council for Children with Behavioral Disorders (1993, June). Staff position statement: Inclusion. *CCBD Newsletter,* p. 1.

Council for Exceptional Children (CEC). (2002). *What every special educator must know: The standards for the preparation and licensure of special educators* (5th ed.). Arlington, VA: Author.

Council for Learning Disabilities (1993). Concerns about the full inclusion of students with learning disabilities in regular education classrooms. *Journal of Learning Disabilities, 26,* 595.

Council of State Directors of Programs for the Gifted. (2000). *1998–99 state of the states gifted and talented education report.* Longmont, CO: Author.

Courson, F. H. (1989). Comparative effects of short- and long-form guided notes on social studies performance by seventh grade learning disabled and at-risk students. Unpublished doctoral dissertation, The Ohio State University, Columbus.

Courson, F. H., & Hay, G. H. (1996). Parents as partners. *Beyond Behavior, 7*(3), 19–23.

Craft, M. A., Alber, S. R., & Heward, W. L. (1998). Teaching elementary students with developmental disabilities to recruit teacher attention in a general education classroom: Effects on teacher praise and academic productivity. *Journal of Applied Behavior Analysis, 31,* 399–415.

Craig, S., Hall, K., Haggart, A. G., & Perez-Selles, M. (2000). Promoting cultural competence through teacher assistance teams. *Teaching Exceptional Children, 32*(3), 6–12.

Crandall, J., Jacobson, J., & Sloane, H. (Eds.). (1997). *What works in education.* Cambridge, MA: Cambridge Center for Behavioral Studies.

Crandell, C. C., & Smaldino, J. J. (2001). Improving classroom acoustics: Utilizing hearing-assistive technology and communication strategies in the educational setting. *The Volta Review, 101*(5), 47–64.

Crandell, C. C., & Smaldino, J. J. (in press). Rehabilitative technologies for individuals with hearing loss and normal hearing. In J. Katz (Ed.), *Handbook of audiology.* New York: Williams & Wilkins.

Crawford, J. (1992). Language loyalties: A source book on the official English controversy. Chicago: University of Chicago Press.

Cripe, J., Slentz, K., & Bricker, D. (1993). *AEPS curriculum for birth to three years.* Baltimore: Brookes.

Cronin, M. E., Slade, D. L., Bechtel, C., & Anderson, P. (1992). Home-school partnerships: A cooperative approach to intervention. *Intervention in School and Clinic, 27,* 286–292.

Cronin, M. S., & Patton, J. R. (1993). *Life skills instruction for all students with special needs: A practical guide for integrating real-life content into the curriculum.* Austin, TX: PRO-ED.

Cruickshank, W. M. (1986). *Disputable decisions in special education.* Ann Arbor: University of Michigan Press.

Cruz, L. & Cullinan, D. (2001). Awarding points, using levels to help children improve behavior. *Teaching Exceptional Children, 33*(3), 16–23.

Cullihan, D. (2002). *Students with emotional and behavioral disorders: an introduction for teachers and other helping professionals.* Upper Saddle River, NJ: Merrill/Prentice Hall.

Cullinan, D., & Epstein, M. H. (1995). Behavior disorders. In N. G. Haring & L. McCormick (Eds.), *Exceptional children and youth* (6th ed.). Upper Saddle River, NJ: Merrill/Prentice Hall.

Cullinan, D., Epstein, M. H., & Sabornie, E. J. (1992). Selected characteristics of a national sample of seriously emotionally disturbed adolescents. *Behavioral Disorders, 17,* 273–280.

Cummins, J. (1989). A theoretical framework for bilingual special education. *Exceptional Children, 56,* 111–119.

Curl, R. M. (1990). A demonstration project for teaching entry-level job skills: The Co-Worker Transition Model for Youths with Disabilities. *Exceptional News, 13*(3), 3–7.

Curl, R. M., Hall, S. M., Chisholm, L. A., & Rule, S. (1992). Co-workers as trainers for entry-level workers: A competitive employment model for individuals with developmental disabilities. *Rural Special Education Quarterly, 11,* 31–35.

Curl, R. M., Lignugaris/Kraft, B., Pawley, J. M., & Salzberg, C. L. (1988). "What's next?" A quantitative and qualitative analysis of the transition for trainee to valued worker. Unpublished manuscript.

Curlee, R., & Yairi, E. (1998). Treatment of early childhood stuttering: Advances and research needs. *American Journal of Speech-Language Pathology, 7,* 20–26.

Cusher, K., McClelland, A., & Stafford, P. (1992). *Human diversity in education.* New York: McGraw–Hill.

Cushing, L. S., & Kennedy, C. H. (1997). Academic effects of providing peer support in general education classrooms on students without disabilities. *Journal of Applied Behavior Analysis, 30,* 139–152.

Cystic Fibrosis Foundation. (2001). *Facts about cystic fibrosis.* Bethesda, MD: Author. www.cff.org

D'Amico, R. (1991). The working world awaits. In M. Wagner, L. Newman, R. D'Amico, E. D. Jay, P. Butler-Nalin, C. Marder, & R. Cox (Eds.), *Youth with disabilities: How are they doing? A comprehensive report from Wave 1 of the National Longitudinal Transition Study of special education students.* Menlo Park, CA: SRI International.

Dalaker, J., & Naifeh, M. (1998). Poverty in the United States: 1997. *Current Population Reports, Series P60-201.* Bureau of the Census, Washington, DC: U. S. Government Printing Office.

Dale, D. M. C. (1984). *Individualized integration: Studies of deaf and partially-hearing children and students in ordinary schools and colleges.* London: Hodder & Stoughton.

Dalrymple, A. J., & Feldman, M. A. (1992). Effects of reinforced directed rehearsal on expressive sign language learning by persons with mental retardation. *Journal of Behavioral Education, 2,* 1–16.

Danforth, S., & Navarro, V. (1998). Speech acts: Sampling the social construction of mental retardation in everyday life. *Mental Retardation, 36,* 31–43.

Danforth, S., & Rhodes, W. C. (1997). On what basis hope? Modern progress and postmodern possibilities. *Remedial and Special Education, 18,* 357–366.

Daniels, V. (2001). Responding to the learning needs of multicultural learners with gifts and talents. In C. Utley & F. Obiakor (Eds.), *Special education, multicultural education, and school reform: Components of quality education for learners with mild disabilities* (pp. 140–154). Springfield, IL: Thomas.

Darling-Hammond, L. (1995). Inequality and access to knowledge. In J. A. Banks (Ed.), *Handbook of research on multicultural education* (pp. 465–483). New York: Macmillan.

Daugherty, D. (2001). IDEA '97 and disproportionate placement. http://www.naspcenter.org/teachers/IDEA_disp.html

Davis, C. A., Brady, M. P., Williams, R. E., & Burta, M. (1992). The effects of self-operated auditory prompting tapes on the performance fluency of persons with severe mental retardation. *Education and Training in Mental Retardation, 27,* 39–50.

Davis, G. A., & Rimm, S. B. (1994). *Education of gifted and talented* (3rd ed.). Boston: Allyn & Bacon.

Davis, J. M., Elfenbein, J., Schum, R., & Bentler, R. A. (1986). Effects of mild and moderate hearing impairments on language, educational, and psychological behavior of children. *Journal of Speech and Hearing Disorders, 51,* 53–62.

Dawson, G., & Osterling, J. (1997). Early intervention in autism. In M. J. Guralnick (Ed.), *The effectiveness of early intervention* (pp. 307–326). Baltimore: Brookes.

De La Paz, S., & Graham, S. (1997). Strategy instruction in planning: Effects on the writing performance and behavior of students with learning difficulties. *Exceptional Children, 63,* 167–181.

DeAvila, E. (1976). Mainstreaming ethnically and linguistically different children: An exercise in paradox or a new approach? In R. I. Jones (Ed.), *Mainstreaming and the minority child* (pp. 93–108). Reston, VA: Council for Exceptional Children.

Deci, E. L., Koestner, R., & Ryan, R. M. (1999). A meta-analytic review of experiments examining the effects of extrinsic rewards on intrinsic motivation. *Psychological Bulletin, 125,* 627–668.

DeFilippo, C. L., Sims, D. G., & Gottermeier, L. (1995). Linking visual and kinesthetic imagery in lipreading instruction. *Journal of Speech and Hearing Research, 38,* 244–256.

deFur, S. (2000). Designing Individualized Education (IEP) Transition Plans. *ERIC Digest* (EDO-EC-00-7). Reston, VA: Council for Exceptional Children/ERIC Clearinghouse on Disabilities and Gifted Education.

Delaney, E. M., & Kaiser, A. P. (2001). The effects of teaching parents blended communication and behavior support strategies. *Behavior Disorders, 26,* 93–116.

Delpit, L. (1995). *Other people's children: Cultural conflict in the classroom.* New York: New Press.

Delquadri, J., Greenwood, C. R., Whorton, D., Carta, J. J., & Hall, R. V. (1986). Classwide peer tutoring. *Exceptional Children, 52,* 535–542.

Denham, A., & Lahm, E. A. (2001). Using technology to construct alternate portfolios of students with moderate and severe disabilities. *Teaching Exceptional Children, 33*(5), 10–17.

Denning, C. B., Chamberlain, J. A., & Polloway, E. A. (2000). An evaluation of state guidelines for mental retardation: Focus on definition and classification practices. *Education and Training in Mental Retardation and Developmental Disabilities, 35,* 226–232.

Dennis, R. E., & Giangreco, M. F. (1996). Creating conversation: Reflections on cultural sensitivity in family interviewing. *Exceptional Children, 53,* 103–116.

Dennis, R. E., Williams, W., Giangreco, M. F., & Cloninger, C. J. (1993). Quality of life as context for planning and evaluation of services for people with disabilities. *Exceptional Children, 53,* 499–512.

Deno, S. L. (1985). Curriculum-based measurement: The emerging alternative. *Exceptional Children, 52,* 219–232.

Deno, S. L. (1997). Whether thou goest ... perspectives on progress monitoring. In J. W. Lloyd, E. J. Kame'enui, & D. Chard (Eds.), *Issues in educating students with disabilities* (pp. 77–99). Mahwah, NJ: Erlbaum.

Deno, S., Maruyama, G., Espin, C., & Cohen, C. (1990). Educating students with mild disabilities in general education classrooms: Minnesota alternatives. *Exceptional Children, 57,* 150–161.

Deshler, D. D., & Lenz, B. K. (1989). The strategies instructional approach. *International Journal of Disability, Development, and Education, 6*(3), 203–244.

Deshler, D. D., & Schumaker, J. B. (1993). Strategy mastery by at-risk students: Not a simple matter. *Elementary School Journal, 94,* 153–157.

Deshler, D. D., Ellis, E. S., & Lenz, B. K. (1996) *Teaching adolescents with learning disabilities: Strategies and methods.* Denver: Love Publishing Co.

Deshler, D. D., Schumaker, J. B., Bulgren, J. A., Lenz, B. K., Jantzen, J., Adams, G., Carnine, D., Grossen, B., Davis, B., & Marquis, J. (2001). Making things easier: Connecting new knowledge to things students already know. *Teaching Exceptional Children, 33*(4), 82–85.

Deshler, D. D., Schumaker, J. B., Lenz, B. K., Bulgren, J. A., Hock, M. F., Knight, J., & Ehren, B. J. (2001). Ensuring content-area learning by secondary students with learning disabilities. *Learning Disabilities Research and Practice, 16,* 96–108.

Dever, R. B. (1988). *Community living skills: A taxonomy.* Washington, DC: American Association on Mental Retardation.

Díaz–Rico, L. T., & Weed, K. Z. (2002). *The cross-cultural, language, and academic development handbook: A complete K–12 reference guide* (2nd ed.). Boston: Allyn & Bacon.

Diefendorf, A. O. (1999). Screening for hearing loss in infants. *The Volta Review, 99*(5), 43–61.

Diller, L. H. (1998). *Running on Ritalin.* New York: Bantam Books.

Dilworth, M. E. (1998). *Being responsive to cultural differences: How teachers learn.* Thousand Oaks, CA: Corwin/Sage.

Dimitropoulos, A., Feurer, I. D., Butler, M. G., & Thompson, T. (2001). Emergence of compulsive behavior and tantrums in children with Prader-Willi syndrome. *American Journal of Mental Retardation, 106,* 39–51.

Dinsmore, J. A. (2000). Preparing teachers for diversity in rural America. *Action in Teacher Education, 22*(1), 19–23.

Division for Learning Disabilities. (2001). Award-winning researchers raise questions about "inclusion." *DLD Times, 18*(2), 4.

Division for Learning Disabilities of the Council for Exceptional Children. (1993). *Inclusion: What does it mean for students with learning disabilities?* Reston, VA: Author.

Dodd, A. W. (1996). Involving parents, avoiding gridlock. *Educational Leadership, 53*(7), 50–54.

Dodge, K. (1993). The future of research on conduct disorder. *Development and Psychopathology, 5*(1/2), 311–320.

Dohan, M., & Schulz, H. (1998). The speech-language pathologist's changing role: Collaboration with the classroom. *Journal of Children's Communication Development, 20,* 9–18.

Donley, C. R., & Williams, G. (1997). Parents exhibit children's progress at a poster session. *Teaching Exceptional Children, 29*(4), 46–51.

Doren, B., Bullis, M., & Benz, M. R. (1996a). Predicting the arrest status of adolescents with disabilities in transition. *Journal of Special Education, 29,* 363–380.

Doren, B., Bullis, M., & Benz, M. R. (1996b). Predictors of victimization experiences of adolescents with disabilities in transition. *Exceptional Children, 63,* 7–18.

Dormans, J. P., & Pellegrino, L. (Ed.) (1998). *Caring for children with cerebral palsy: A team approach.* Baltimore: Brookes.

Downing, J. (1999). *Teaching communication skills to students with severe disabilities.* Baltimore: Brookes.

Downing, J. (2000). Augmentative communication services: A critical aspect of assistive technology. *Journal of Special Education Technology, 15*(3) 35–38.

Downing, J., & Bailey, B. (1990). Developing vision use within functional daily activities for students with visual and multiple disabilities. *RE:view, 21,* 209–221.

Downing, J., & Eichinger, J. (1990). Instructional strategies for learners with dual sensory impairments in integrated settings. *Journal of The Association for Persons with Severe Handicaps, 15,* 98–105.

Doyle, P. M., Wolery, M., Ault, M. J., & Gast, D. L. (1988). System of least prompts: A literature review of procedural parameters. *Journal of The Association for Persons with Severe Handicaps, 13,* 28–40.

Drasgow, E. (1998). American Sign Language as a pathway to linguistic competence. *Exceptional Children, 64,* 329–342.

Drasgow, E., Yell, M. L., & Robinson, T. R. (in press). Developing legally correct and educationally appropriate IEPs: Federal law and lessons learned from the Lovaas hearings and cases. *Remedial and Special Education.*

Drevno, G. E., Kimball, J. W., Possi, M. K., Heward, W. L., Gardner, R., III, & Barbetta, P. M. (1994). Effects of active student response during error correction on the acquisition, maintenance, and generalization of science vocabulary by elementary students: A systematic replication. *Journal of Applied Behavior Analysis, 27,* 179–180.

Duckworth, S., Smith-Rex, S., Okey, S., Brookshire, M. A., Rawlinson, D., Rawlinson, R., Castillo, S., & Little, J. (2001). Wraparound services for young school children with emotional and behavior disorders. *Teaching Exceptional Children, 33*(4), 54–60.

Dugan, E., Kamps, D., Leonard, B., Watkins, N., Rheinberger, A., & Stackhaus, J. (1995). Effects of cooperative learning groups during social studies for students with autism and fourth-grade peers. *Journal of Applied Behavior Analysis, 28,* 175–188.

Dunlap, G., & Fox, L. (1996). Early intervention and serious problem behavior: A comprehensive approach. In L. K. Koegel, R. L. Koegel, & G. Dunlap (Eds.), *Positive behavioral support: Including people with difficult behavior in the community* (pp. 31–50). Baltimore: Brookes.

Dunlap, G., Clarke, S., Jackson, M., Wright, S., Ramos, E., & Brinson, S. (1995). Self-monitoring of classroom behaviors with students exhibiting emotional and behavioral challenges. *School Psychology Quarterly, 10,* 165–177.

Dunlap, G., Dyer, K., & Koegel, R. L. (1983). Autistic self-stimulation and intertrial interval duration. *American Journal of Mental Deficiency, 88,*194–204.

Dunlap, G., Robbins, F. R., & Darrow, M. A. (1994). Parents' reports of their children's challenging behaviors: Results of a statewide survey. *Mental Retardation, 32,* 206–212.

Dunn, L. M., & Dunn, L. M. (1997). *Peabody Picture Vocabulary Test—III.* Circle Pines, MN: American Guidance Services.

Dunst, C. (2001). Participation of young children with disabilities in community learning activities. In M. Guralnick (Ed.), *Early childhood inclusion: Focus on change* (pp. 307–333). Baltimore: Brookes.

Dunst, C. J., Trivette, C. M., & Deal, A. G. (1988). *Enabling and empowering families: Principles and guidelines for practice.* Cambridge, MA: Brookline Books.

DuPaul, G. J., & Stoner, G. (1994). *ADHD in the schools: Assessment and intervention strategies.* New York: The Guilford Press.

Duran, E. (1988). Teaching the moderately and severely handicapped student and autistic adolescent: With particular attention to bilingual special education. Springfield, IL: Thomas.

Durrell, D. D., & Catterson, J. H. (1980). *Durrell Analysis of Reading Difficulty* (3rd ed.). San Antonio, TX: Harcourt Brace Educational Measurement.

Dwyer, K. P., Osher, D., & Hoffman, C. C. (2000). Creating responsive schools:

Contextualizing early warning, timely response. *Exceptional Children, 66,* 347–365.

Dye, G. A. (2000). Graphic organizers to the rescue! Helping student link—and remember—information. *Teaching Exceptional Children, 32*(3), 72–76.

Dykens, E. M. (2000). Contaminated and unusual food combinations: What do people with Prader-Willi syndrome choose? *Mental Retardation, 38,* 163–171.

Dykens, E. M., & Rosner, B. A. (1999). Refining behavioral phenotypes: Personality-motivation in Williams and Prader-Willi syndromes. *American Journal of Mental Retardation, 104,* 158–169.

Dykens, E. M., Hodapp, R. M., & Finucane, B. M. (2000). *Genetics and mental retardation syndromes: A new look at behavior and interventions.* Baltimore: Brookes.

Dykes, J. (1992). Opinions of orientation and mobility instructors about using the long cane with preschool-age children. *RE:view, 24,* 85–92.

Dyson, L. L. (1996). The experiences of families of children with learning disabilities: parental stress, family functioning, and sibling self-concept. *Journal of Learning Disabilities, 29*(3), 280–286.

Dyson, L., Edgar, E., & Crnic, K. (1989). Psychological predictors of adjustment by siblings of developmentally disabled children. *American Journal of Mental Retardation, 94,* 292–302.

Dzienkowski, R. C., Smith, K. K., Dillow, K. A., & Yucha, C. B. (1996). Cerebral palsy: A comprehensive review. *Nurse Practitioner, 21*(2), 45–59.

Easterbrooks, S. (1999). Improving practices for students with hearing impairments. *Exceptional Children, 65,* 537–554.

Eber, L., Nelson, C. M., & Miles, P. (1997). School-based wraparound for students with emotional and behavioral challenges. *Exceptional Children, 63,* 539–555.

Eberle, L. (1922). The maimed, the halt and the race. Reprinted in R. H. Bremner (Ed.), *Children and youth in America: A documentary history. Vol. 2: 1866–1832* (pp. 1026–1028). Cambridge: Harvard University Press.

Edelbrock, C., Rende, R., Plomin, R., & Thompson, L. A. (1995). A twin study of competence and problem behavior in childhood and early adolescence. *Journal of Child Psychology and Psychiatry, 36,* 775–785.

Eden-Piercy, G. V. S., Blacher, J. B., & Eyman, R. K. (1986). Exploring parents' reactions to their young child with severe handicaps. *Mental Retardation, 24,* 285–291.

Edens, J. F. (1997). Home visitation programs with ethnic minority families: Cultural issues in parent consultation. *Journal of Educational and Psychological Consultation, 8*(4), 373–383.

Education Trust. (1996). *Education watch: The 1996 Education Trust state and national data book.* Washington, DC: Author.

Edwards, L., & Chard, D. J. (2000). Curriculum reform in a residential treatment program: Establishing high academic expectations for students with emotional and behavior disorders. *Behavioral Disorders, 25,* 259–263.

Ehren, B. J. (2000). Maintaining a therapeutic focus and sharing responsibility for student success: Keys to in-classroom speech-language services. *Language, Speech, and Hearing Services in Schools, 31,* 219–229.

Eichinger, J. (1990). Effects of goal structure on social interaction between elementary level nondisabled students and students with severe disabilities. *Exceptional Children, 56,* 408–417.

Eikeseth, S., & Lovaas, O. I. (1992). The autistic label and its potentially detrimental effect on the child's treatment. *Journal of Behavioral Therapy and Experimental Psychiatry, 23*(3), 151–157.

Ellis, E. S., Deshler, D. D., Lenz, B. K., Schumaker, J. B. & Clark, F. L. (1991). An instructional model for teaching learning strategies. *Focus on Exceptional Children, 24*(1), 1–14.

Ellis, N. R. (1963). The stimulus trace and behavior inadequacy. In N. R. Ellis (Ed.), *Handbook of mental deficiency* (pp. 134–158). New York: McGraw-Hill.

Ellwein, M. C., & Graue, M. E. (2001). Knowing children. In C. Grant & M. L. Gomez (Ed.), *Campus and classroom: Making education multicultural* (2nd ed.), (pp. 65–92). New York: Macmillan.

Emlen, A. C. (1998). *AFS consumer survey: From parents receiving child care assistance.* Portland, OR: Regional Research Institute for Human Services, Portland State University.

Engelman, M. D., Griffin, H. C., Griffin, L. W., & Maddox, J. I. (1999). A teacher's guide to communicating with students with deaf-blindness. *Teaching Exceptional Children, 31*(5), 64–70.

Engelmann, S. (1977). Sequencing cognitive and academic tasks. In R. D. Kneedler & S. G. Tarver (Eds.), *Changing perspectives in special education* (pp. 46–61). Upper Saddle River, NJ: Merrill/Prentice Hall.

Englert, C. S., Tarrant, K. L., Mariage, T. V., & Oxer, T. (1994). Lesson talk as the work of reading groups: The effectiveness of two interventions. *Journal of Learning Disabilities, 27,* 165–186.

Englert, C., Raphael, T., Anderson, L., Anthony, H., Stevens, D., & Fear. (1991). Making writing strategies and self-talk visible: Cognitive strategy instruction in writing in regular and special education classrooms. *American Educational Research Journal, 28,* 337–373.

Enright, R. (2000). If life is a journey, make it a joyride: Some tips for young people. *Exceptional Parent, 31*(7), 50–51.

Epstein, M. H., & Sharma, J. (1998). *Behavioral and Emotional Rating Scale.* Austin, TX: PRO-ED.

Epstein, M. H., Hertzog, M. A., & Reid, R. (2001). The Behavioral and Emotional Rating Scale: Long term test-retest reliability. *Behavioral Disorders, 26,* 314–320.

Epstein, M. H., Kutash, K., & Duchnowski, A. (1998). *Outcomes for children and youth with emotional and behavioral disorders and their families: Programs and evaluation of best practices.* Austin, TX: PRO-ED.

ERIC/OSEP Special Project. (2001). *Family involvement in special education.* Research Connections in Special Education (no. 9). Arlington, VA: ERIC Clearinghouse on Disabilities and Gifted Education. Available on line at www.ericcec.org.

Erickson, K. A., & Koppenhaver, D. A. (1998). Using the "write talk-nology" with Patrick. *Teaching Exceptional Children, 31*(1), 58–64.

Ericsson, A. (2001). The acquired nature of expert performance: Implications for conceptions of giftedness and innate talent? In N. Colangelo & S. Assouline (Eds.), *Talent development IV: Proceedings from the 1998 Henry B. and Jocelyn Wallace National Research Symposium on Talent Development,* (pp. 11–26). Scottsdale, AZ: Great Potential Press.

Ericsson, K. A., & Charness, N. (1994). Expert performance. Its structure and acquisition. *American Psychologist, 49*(8), 725–747.

Erin, J. N., Dignan, K., & Brown, P. A. (1991). Are social skills teachable? A review of the literature. *Journal of Visual Impairment and Blindness, 85,* 58–61.

Ernsbarger, S. C., Frazier-Trotman, S., Harrison, T. J., Simmons-Reed, E., Tincani, M. J., & Heward, W. L. (2001). *Teacher pacing and the performance of elementary students during group instruction.* Twenty-seventh annual Association for Behavior Analysis International Convention, New Orleans, LA.

Ernst, M., Cohen, R. M., Liebenauer, L. L., Jons, P. H., & Zametkin, A. J. (1997). Cerebral glucose metabolism in adolescent girls with attention-deficit/hyperactivity disorder. *Journal of Child Psychology and Psychiatry, 36,* 1399–1406.

Espin, C. A., & Deno, S. L. (1989). The effects of modeling and prompting feedback strategies on sight word reading of students labeled learning disabled. *Education and Treatment of Children, 12,* 219–231.

Evans, J. C., & Smith, J. (1993). Nursing planning, intervention, and evaluation for altered neurologic function. In D. B. Jackson & R. B. Saunders (Eds.), *Child health nursing: A comprehensive approach to the care of children and their health* (pp. 1353–1430). Philadelphia: Lippincott.

Ewolt, C. (1996). Deaf Bilingualism: A holistic perspective. *Australian Journal of the Education of the Deaf, 2,* 5–9.

Fairweather, J. S., & Shaver, D. M. (1991). Making the transition to postsecondary education and training. *Exceptional Children, 57,* 264–270.

Farlow, L. J., & Snell, M. E. (1994). *Making the most of student performance data.*

Washington, DC: American Association on Mental Retardation.

Farrington, D. P. (1995). The development of offending and antisocial behavior from childhood: Key findings from the Cambridge Study in Delinquent Development. *Journal of Child Psychology and Psychiatry, 36,* 929–964.

Faw, G. D., Davis, P. K., & Peck, C. (1996). Increasing self-determination: Teaching people with mental retardation to evaluate residential options. *Journal of Applied Behavior Analysis, 29,* 173–188.

Feingold, B. F. (1975). *Why your child is hyperactive.* New York: Random House.

Feingold, B. F. (1976). Hyperkinesis and learning disabilities linked to ingestion of artificial food colors and flavorings. *Journal of Learning Disabilities, 9,* 551–559.

Feldhusen, J. F., & Moon, S. (1995). The educational continuum and delivery of services. In J. L. Genshaft, M. Bireley, & C. L. Hollinger (Eds.), *Serving gifted and talented students: A resource for school personnel* (pp. 103–121). Austin, TX: PRO-ED.

Feldman, D., Kinnison, L., Jay, R., & Harth, R. (1983). The effects of differential labeling on professional concepts and attitudes toward the emotionally disturbed/behaviorally disordered. *Behavioral Disorders, 8,* 191–198.

Ferguson, D. L. (1994). Is communication really the point? Some thoughts on interventions and membership. *Mental Retardation, 1,* 7–18.

Ferguson, D. L., & Baumgart, D. (1991). Partial participation revisited. *Journal of The Association for Persons with Severe Handicaps, 16,* 218–227.

Ferguson, D. L., Meyer, G., Jeanchild, L., Juniper, L., & Zingo, J. (1992). Figuring out what to do with the grownups: How teachers make inclusion "work" for students with disabilities. *Journal of The Association for Persons with Severe Handicaps, 17,* 218–226.

Ferguson, P. M., & Ferguson, D. L. (2000). The promise of adulthood. In M. E. Snell & F. Brown (Eds.), *Instruction of students with severe disabilities* (5th ed.), (pp. 629–656). Upper Saddle River, NJ: Merrill/Prentice Hall.

Ferrell, K. A. (1996). Your child's development. In M. C. Holbrook (Ed.), *Children with visual impairments: A parents' guide* (pp. 73–96). Bethesda, MD: Woodbine House.

Ferrell, K. A., & Muir, D. W. (1996). A call to end vision stimulation training. *Journal of Visual Impairments and Blindness, 90,* 364–366.

Ferro, J., Foster-Johnson, L., & Dunlap, G. (1996). Relations between curricular activities and problem behaviors of students with mental retardation. *American Journal on Mental Retardation, 101,* 184–194.

Field, S., Hoffman, A., & Spezia, S. (1998). *Self-determination strategies for adolescents in transition.* Austin, TX: PRO-ED.

Field, S., Martin, J., Miller, R., Ward, M., & Wehmeyer, M. L. (1998a). *A practical guide for teaching self-determination.* Reston, VA: Council for Exceptional Children.

Field, S., Martin, J., Miller, R., Ward, M., & Wehmeyer, M. (1998b). Self-determination for persons with disabilities: A position statement of the Division on Career Development and Transition. *Career Development for Exceptional Individuals, 21,* 113–128.

Figueroa, R. A. (1989). Psychological testing of linguistic-minority students: Knowledge gaps and regulations. *Exceptional Children, 56,* 145–152.

Filipek, P. A., Semrud-Clikmann, M., Steingard, R. J., Renshaw, P. F., Kennedy, D. N., & Biederman, J. (1997). Volumetric MRI analysis comparing subject having attention-deficit/hyperactivity disorder with normal controls. *Neurology, 48,* 589–601.

Finn, C. E., Rotherham, A. J., & Hokanson, C. R., Jr. (Eds.). (2001). *Rethinking special education for a new century.* Washington, DC: Thomas B. Fordham Foundation and the Progressive Policy Institute.

Fischer, M., Barley, R. A., Edelbrock, C. S., & Smallish, L., (1990). The adolescent outcome of hyperactive children diagnosed by research criteria: II. Academic, attentional and neuropsychological status. *Journal of Consulting and Clinical Psychology, 58,* 550–588.

Fisher, C. W., & Berliner, D. C. (Eds.). (1985). *Perspectives on instructional time.* New York: Longman.

Fisher, D., & Ryndak, D. L. (Eds.). (2001). *The foundations of inclusive education: A compendium of articles on effective strategies to achieve inclusive education.* Baltimore: The Association for Persons with Severe Handicaps.

FitzSimmons, S. C. (1993). The changing epidemiology of cystic fibrosis. *Journal of Pediatrics, 122,* 1–9.

Flener, B. S. (1993). The consultative-collaborative teacher for students with visual handicaps. *RE:view, 25,* 173–182.

Fletcher, J. M., Lyon, G. R., Barnes, M., Stuebing, K. K., Francis, D. J., Olson, R. K., Shaywitz, S. E., & Shaywitz, B. A. (2001). *Classification of learning disabilities: An evidence–based evaluation* (Executive Summary). Paper presented at the LD Summit, Washington, DC. http://www.air.org/LDsummit/paper.htm

Fletcher, J. M., Shaywitz, S. E., Shankweiler, D. P., Katz, L., Liberman, I. Y., Fowler, A., Francis, D. J., Stuebing, K. K., & Shaywitz, B. A. (1994). Cognitive profiles of reading disability: Comparisons of discrepancy and low achievement definitions. *Journal of Educational Psychology, 86,* 1–18.

Flexer, R. W., Simmons, T. J., Luft, P., & Baer, R. M. (2001). *Transition planning for secondary students with disabilities.* Upper Saddle River, NJ: Merrill/Prentice Hall.

Flick, G. L. (2000). *How to reach & teach teenagers with ADHD.* West Nyack, NY: The Center for Applied Research in Education.

Fombonne, E. (1999). The epidemiology of autism: A review. *Psychological Medicine, 29,* 769–786.

Foorman, B., Francis, D., Fletcher, J., Schatschneider, C., & Mehta, P. (1998). Early interventions for children with reading problems: Study designs and preliminary findings. *Journal of Educational Psychology, 90*(1), 1–12.

Ford, B. A. (2000). *Multiple voices for ethnically diverse exceptional learners, 2000.* Reston, VA: Council for Exceptional Children.

Ford, D. Y. (1998). The underrepresentation of minority students in gifted education. *Journal of Special Education, 32*(1), 4–14.

Forest, M., & Lusthaus, E. (1990). Everyone belongs with the MAPS Action Planning System. *Teaching Exceptional Children, 22*(2), 32–35.

Forgatch, M. S., & Paterson, G. R. (1998). Behavioral family therapy. In F. M. Dattilo (Ed.), *Case studies in couple and family therapy: Systematic and cognitive perspectives* (pp. 85–107). New York: Guilford Press.

Forness, S. R., & Kavale, K. A. (1997). Defining emotional or behavioral disorders in school and related services. In J. W. Lloyd, E. J. Kame'enui, & D. Chard (Eds.), *Issues in educating students with disabilities* (pp. 45–61). Mahwah, NJ: Erlbaum.

Forness, S. R., & Kavale, K. A. (2000). Emotional or behavior disorders: Background and current status of the E/BD terminology and definition. *Behavioral Disorders, 25,* 264–269.

Forness, S. R., & Kavale, K. A. (in press). Impact of ADHD on school systems. In P. S. Jensen & J. R. Cooper (Eds.), *Findings from the NIH Consensus Conference on ADHD.* Bethesda, MD: National Institutes of Health.

Forness, S. R., Kavale, K. A., Crenshaw, T. M., & Sweeney, D. P. (2000). Best practice in treating children with ADHD: Does not using medication in a comprehensive intervention program verge on malpractice? *Beyond Behavior, 10*(2), 4–7.

Forness, S., & Knitzer, J. (1992). A new proposed definition and terminology to replace "serious emotional disturbance" in the Individuals with Disabilities Education Act. *School Psychology Review, 21,* 12–20.

Fowler, S. A., Donegan, M., Lueke, B., Hadden, D. S., & Phillips, B. (2000). Evaluating community collaboration in writing interagency agreements on the age 3 transition. *Exceptional Children, 67,* 35–50.

Fowler, S. A., Dougherty, S. B., Kirby, K. C., & Kohler, F. W. (1986). Role reversals: An analysis of therapeutic effects achieved with disruptive boys during their appointments as peer monitors. *Journal of Applied Behavior Analysis, 19,* 437–444.

Fowler, S. A., Schwartz, I., & Atwater, J. (1991). Perspectives on the transition from preschool to kindergarten for children with disabilities and their families. *Exceptional Children, 58,* 136–145.

Fox, J., Shores, R., Lindeman, D., & Strain, P. (1986). Maintaining social initiations of withdrawn handicapped and nonhandicapped preschoolers through a response-dependent fading tactic. *Journal of Abnormal Child Psychology, 14,* 387–396.

Fox, W., & Gay, G. (1995). Integrating multicultural and curriculum principles in teacher education. *Principles in Teacher Education, 70*(3), 64–82.

Foy, C. J., Von Scheden, M., & Waiculonis, J. (1992). The Connecticut pre-cane: Case study and curriculum. *Journal of Visual Impairment and Blindness, 86,* 178–181.

Fradd, S. H., & McGee, P. L. (1994). *Instructional assessment: An integrative approach to evaluating student performance.* Reading, MA: Addison-Wesley.

Frame, M. J. (2000). The relationship between visual impairment and gestures. *Journal of Visual Impairments and Blindness, 94,* 155–171.

Frank, A. R., & Sitlington, P. L. (1993). Graduates with mental disabilities: The story three years later. *Education and Training in Mental Retardation, 28,* 30–37.

Frank, A. R., & Sitlington, P. L. (2000). Young adults with mental disabilities—Does transition planning make a difference? *Education and Training in Mental Retardation and Developmental Disabilities, 35,* 119–134.

Frankenburg, W. K., & Dodds, J. B. (1990). *The Denver II training manual.* Denver: Denver Developmental Materials.

Frasier, M., Garcia, J., & Passow, A. (1995). *A review of assessment issues in gifted education and their implications for identifying gifted minority students.* Storrs: University of Connecticut, National Research Center on the Gifted and Talented. (Research Monopoly RM95204).

Frasier, M., Hunsaker, S., Lee, J., Mitchell, S., Cramond, B., Krisel, S., Garcia, J., Martin, D., Frank, E., & Finley, S. (1995). *Core attributes of giftedness: A foundation for recognizing the gifted potential of minority and economically disadvantaged students.* Storrs: University of Connecticut, National Research Center on the Gifted and Talented.

Freeman, D. E., & Freeman, Y. S. (1993). Strategies for promoting the primary language of all students. *Reading Teacher, 46,* 552–558.

Freeman, F., & Alkin, M. (2000). Academic and social attainments of children with mental retardation in general education and special education settings. *Remedial and Special Education, 21,* 3–18.

French, N. K. (2001). Supervising paraprofessionals: A survey of teacher practices. *Journal of Special Education, 35,* 41–53.

Frey, K. S., Fewell, R. R. & Vadasy, P. F. (1989). Parental adjustment and changes in child outcomes among families of young handicapped children. *Topics in Early Childhood Special Education, 8*(4), 38–57.

Friend, M. (2000). Myths and misunderstandings about professional collaboration. *Remedial and Special Education, 21,* 130–132.

Friend, M., & Bursuck, W. D. (1999). *Including students with special needs: A practical guide for classroom teachers* (2nd ed.). Needham Heights, MA: Allyn & Bacon.

Frostig, M., & Horne, D. (1973). The Frostig program for the development of visual perception (rev. ed.). Chicago: Follett.

Frostig, M., Lefever, D. W., & Whittlesey, J. R. B. (1964). The Marianne Frostig Development Test of Visual Perception. Palo Alto, CA: Consulting Psychologists Press.

Fryxell, D., & Kennedy, C. H. (1995). Placement along the continuum of services and its impact on students' social relationships. *Journal of The Association for Persons with Severe Handicaps, 20,* 259–269.

Fuchs, D., & Fuchs, L. S. (1994). Inclusive schools movement and the radicalization of special education reform. *Exceptional Children, 60,* 294–309.

Fuchs, D., Fuchs, L. S., Bahr, M. W., Fernstrom, P., & Stecker, P. (1990). Prereferral intervention: A prescriptive approach. *Exceptional Children, 56,* 493–513.

Fuchs, D., Fuchs, L. S., Fernstrom, P., & Hohn, M. (1991). Toward a responsible reintegration of behaviorally disordered students. *Behavioral Disorders, 16,* 133–147.

Fuchs, D., Fuchs, L. S., Mathes, P. G., Lipsey, M. W., & Roberts, P. H. (2001). *Is "learning disabilities" just a fancy term for low achievement? A meta–analysis of reading differences between low achievers with and without the label* (Executive Summary). Paper presented at the LD Summit, Washington, DC. http://www.air.org/LDsummit/paper.htm

Fuchs, D., Fuchs, L. S., Thompson, A., Svenson, E., Yen, L. Al Otaiba, S., Yang, N., McMaster, K. N., Prentice, K., Kazdan, S., & Saenz, L. (2001). Peer-assisted learning strategies in reading: Extension for kindergarten, first grade, and high school. *Remedial and Special Education, 22,* 15–21.

Fuchs, L. S., & Fuchs, D. (1996). Combining performance assessment and curriculum-based measurement to strengthen instructional planning. *Learning Disabilities Research and Practice, 11*(3), 183–192.

Fuchs, L. S., & Fuchs, D. (2001). Principles for the prevention and intervention of mathematics disabilities. *Learning Disabilities Research and Practice, 16,* 85–95.

Fuchs, L. S., Fuchs, D., & Bishop, N. (1992). Teacher planning for students with learning disabilities: Differences between general and special education. *Learning Disabilities Research and Practice, 7,* 120–128.

Fuchs, L. S., Fuchs, D., Hamlett, C. L., & Steecker, P. M. (1991). Effects of curriculum-based measurement and consultation on teacher planning and student achievement in mathematics operations. *American Educational Research Journal, 28,* 617–641.

Fujiura, G. T., & Yamaki, K. (2000). Trends in demography of childhood poverty and disability. *Exceptional Children, 66,* 187–199.

Fujiura, J. E., & Yamaki, K. (1997). Analysis of ethnic variations in developmental disability prevalence and household economic status. *Mental Retardation, 35,* 286–294.

Fulk, B. M., & King, K. (2001). Classwide peer tutoring at work. *Teaching Exceptional Children, 34*(2), 49–53.

Furth, H. G. (1973). *Deafness and learning: A psychosocial approach.* Belmont, CA: Wadsworth.

Gable, R. A., Hendrickson, J. M., Young, C. C., Shores, R. E., & Stowitschek, J. J. (1983). A comparison of teacher approval and disapproval statements across categories of exceptionality. *Journal of Special Education Technology, 6,* 15–21.

Gadow, K. D., & Nolan, E. E. (1993). Practical considerations in conducting school-based medication evaluations for children with hyperactivity. *Journal of Emotional and Behavioral Disorders, 1,* 118–126.

Gagné, F. (1995). Hidden meaning of the "talent development" concept. *Educational Forum, 59*(4), 350–362.

Gagnon, J. C., & Maccini, p. (2001). Preparing students with disabilities for algebra. *Teaching Exceptional Children, 34*(1), 8–15.

Gajar, A., Goodman, L., & McAfee, J. (1993). *Secondary schools and beyond: Transition of individuals with mild disabilities.* Upper Saddle River, NJ: Merrill/Prentice Hall.

Gallagher, J. J. (1984). The evolution of special education concepts. In B. Blatt & R. J. Morris (Eds.), *Perspectives in special education: Personal orientations* (pp. 210–232). Glenview, IL: Scott, Foresman.

Gallaudet University. (1998). *1996–1997 annual survey of deaf and hard-of-hearing children and youth.* Washington, DC: Gallaudet University, Center for Assessment and Demographic Studies.

Gallegos, A., & McCarty, L. L. (2000). Bilingual multicultural special education: An integrated personnel preparation program. *Teacher Education and Special Education, 23*(4), 264–270.

Gallimore, R., Boggs, J., & Jordan, C. (1974). *Culture, behavior, and education.* Beverly Hills, CA: Sage.

Gallivan-Fenlon, A. (1994). Integrated transdisciplinary teams. *Teaching Exceptional Children, 26*(3), 16–20.

Garber, H., & Heber, R. (1973). *The Milwaukee Project: Early intervention as a* technique to prevent mental retardation [Technical paper]. Storrs: University of Connecticut.

Gardner, H. (1983). *Frames of mind.* New York: Basic Books.

Gardner, R. III, Cartledge, G., Seidl, B., Woolsey, M. L., Schley, G. S., & Utley, C. A. (2001). Mt. Olivet after-school program. *Remedial and Special Education, 22,* 22–33.

Gardner, R., III, Heward, W. L., & Grossi, T. A. (1994). Effects of response cards on student participation and academic achievement: A systematic replication with inner-city students during whole-class science instruction. *Journal of Applied Behavior Analysis, 27,* 63–71.

Gardner, R., III., Sainato, D. M., Cooper, J. O., Heron, T. E., Heward, W. L., Eshleman, J., & Grossi, T. A. (Eds.). (1994). *Behavior analysis in education: Focus on measurably superior instruction.* Pacific Grove, CA: Brooks/Cole.

Garten, B. C., Rumrill, P., & Serebreni, R. (1996). The higher education transition model: Guidelines for facilitating college transition among college-bound students with disabilities. *Teaching Exceptional Children, 29*(3), 30–33.

Gartland, D. (1993). Elementary teacher-parent partnerships: Effective communication strategies. *LD Forum, 18*(3), 40–42.

Garton, A., & Pratt, C. (1998). *Learning to be literate: The development of spoken and written language.* Oxford: Blackwell.

Geenen, S., Powers, L., & Lopez-Vasquez, A. (2001). Multicultural aspects of parent involvement in transition planning. *Exceptional Children, 67,* 265–282.

Gelb, S. A. (1997). The problem of typological thinking in mental retardation. *Mental Retardation, 35,* 448–457.

Gense, M. H., & Gense, D. J. (1994). Identifying autism in children with blindness and visual impairments. *RE:view, 26,* 55–62.

Genshaft, J. L., Greenbaum, S., & Borovosky, S. (1995). Stress and the gifted. In J. L. Genshaft, M. Bireley, & C. L. Hollinger (Eds.), *Serving gifted and talented students: A resource for school personnel* (pp. 257–268). Austin, TX: PRO-ED.

German, S. L., Martin, J. E., Huber Marshall, L., & Sale, R. P. (2000). Promoting self-determination: Using Take Action to teach goal attainment. *Career Development for Exceptional Individuals, 23,* 27–38.

Gersten, R. (1998). Recent advances in instructional research for students with learning disabilities: An overview. *Learning Disabilities Research and Practice, 13,* 162–170.

Gersten, R. (2001). Sorting out the roles of research in the improvement of practice. *Learning Disabilities Research and Practice, 16,* 45–50.

Gersten, R., & Baker, S. (2000). What we know about effective instructional practices for English-language learners. *Exceptional Children, 66,* 454–470.

Getch, Y. Q., & Heuharth-Pritchett, S. (1999). Children with asthma: Strategies for educators. *Teaching Exceptional Children, 31*(3), 30–36.

Giangreco, M. F. (1992). Curriculum in inclusion–oriented schools: Trends, issues, challenges, and potential solutions. In S. Stainback & W. Stainback (Eds.), *Curriculum considerations in inclusive classrooms: Facilitating learning for all students* (pp. 239–263). Baltimore: Brookes.

Giangreco, M. F. (1996). "The stairs don't go anywhere!" A self-advocate's reflections on specialized services and their impact on people with disabilities [An invited interview]. *Physical Disabilities and Related Services, 14*(2), 1–12.

Giangreco, M. F. (1997). *Quick-guides to inclusion: Ideas for educating students with disabilities.* Baltimore, MD: Brookes.

Giangreco, M. F. (2001). Interactions among program, placement, and services in educational planning for students with disabilities. *Mental Retardation, 39,* 341–350.

Giangreco, M. F., & Doyle, M. B. (2000). Curricular and instructional considerations for teaching students with disabilities in general education classrooms. In S. Wade (Ed.), *Inclusive education: A casebook of readings for prospective and practicing teachers* (Vol 1), (pp.51–69). Hillsdale, NJ: Erlbaum.

Giangreco, M. F., & Meyer, L. H. (1988). Expanding service delivery options in regular schools and classrooms for students with severe disabilities. In J. L. Graden, J. E. Zins, & M. J. Curtis (Eds.), *Alternative educational delivery systems: Enhancing instructional options for all students* (pp. 241–267). Washington DC: National Association of School Psychologists.

Giangreco, M. F., & Putnam, J. W. (1991). Supporting the education of students with severe disabilities in regular education environments. In L. H. Meyer, C. A. Peck, & L. Brown (Eds.), *Critical issues in the lives of people with severe disabilities* (pp.245–270). Baltimore: Brookes.

Giangreco, M. F., Cloninger, C. J., & Iverson, V. S. (1998). *Choosing options and accommodations for children: A guide to educational planning for students with disabilities* (2nd ed.). Baltimore: Brookes.

Giangreco, M. F., Cloninger, C. J., Dennis, R. E., & Edelman, S. W. (2000). Problem-solving methods to facilitate inclusive education. In R. A. Villa & J. S. Thousand (Eds.), *Restructuring for caring and effective education: Piecing the puzzle together* (2nd ed.), (pp. 293–327). Baltimore: Brookes.

Giangreco, M. F., Dennis, R., Cloninger, C., Edelman, S., & Schattman, R. (1993). "I've counted Jon": Transformational experiences of teachers educating students with disabilities. *Exceptional Children, 59,* 359–372.

Giangreco, M. F., Edelman, S., & Dennis, R. (1991). Common professional practices that interfere with the integrated delivery of related services. *Remedial and Special Education, 12*(2), 16–24.

Gibb, G. S., & Dyches, T. T. (2000). *Guide to writing quality individualized education programs.* Boston: Allyn & Bacon.

Giek, K. A. (1992). Monitoring student progress through efficient record keeping. *Teaching Exceptional Children, 24*(3), 22–26.

Gilchrist, E. (1916). The extent to which praise and reproof affect a pupil's work. *School and Society, 4,* 872–874.

Gilger, J. W., Pennington, B. F., & DeFries, J. C. (1992). A twin study of the etiology of comorbidity: Attention deficit-hyperactivity disorder and dyslexia. *Journal of the American Academy of Children and Adolescent Psychiatry, 31,* 343–348.

Gitlin, L. N., Mount, J., Lucas, W., Weirich, L. C., & Gramberg, L. (1997). The physical costs and psychosocial benefits of travel aids for persons who are visually impaired or blind. *Journal of Visual Impairment and Blindness, 91,* 347–359.

Glassberg, L. A., Hooper, S. R., & Mattison, R. E. (1999). Prevalence of learning disabilities at enrollment in special education students with behavioral disorders. *Behavioral Disorders, 26,* 164–172.

Gleason, J. B. (1999). *The development of language* (4th ed.). Boston: Allyn & Bacon.

Goddard, Y. I., & Heron, T. E. (1998). Please teacher: Help me learn to spell better, teach me self-correction. *Teaching Exceptional Children, 30*(6), 38–43.

Goldberg, D. (1997). *Educating children who are deaf/hard of hearing: Auditory/verbal option.* ERIC Digest #E552. ERIC Clearinghouse on Disabilities and Gifted Education, Reston, VA. (ERIC Document Reproduction Service No. ED 414 670)

Goldman, R., & Fristoe, M. (1986). *Goldman-Fristoe Test of Articulation.* Austin, TX: PRO-ED.

Goldman, R., Fristoe, M., & Woodcock, R. W. (1990). *Goldman-Fristoe-Woodcock Test of Auditory Discrimination.* Austin, TX: PRO-ED.

Goldstein, A. P. (1999). *The prepare curriculum: Teaching prosocial competencies* (2nd ed.). Champaign, IL: Research Press.

Goldstein, A. P., & McGinnis, E. (1997). *Skillstreaming the adolescent: New strategies and perspectives for teaching prosocial skills* (2nd ed.). Champaign, IL: Research Press.

Goldstein, D. E., Murray, C., & Edgar, E. (1998). Employment earnings and hours of high school graduates with learning disabilities through the first decade after graduation. *Learning Disabilities Research and Practice, 13,* 53–64.

Goldstein, H., Kaczmarek, L. A., & English, K. M. (2001). *Promoting social communication: Children with developmental disabilities from birth to adolescence.* Baltimore: Brookes.

Goldstein, H., Kaczmarek, L., & Hepting, N. (1994). Communication interventions: The challenges of across-the-day implementation. In R. Gardner III, D. M. Sainato, J. O. Cooper, T. E. Heron, W. L. Heward, J. Eshleman, & T. A. Grossi

(Eds.), *Behavior analysis in education: Focus on measurably superior instruction* (pp. 101–113). Pacific Grove, CA: Brooks/Cole.

Goldstein, S., & Goldstein, M. (1998). *Managing attention-deficit hyperactivity disorder in children: A guide for practitioners* (2nd ed.). New York: Wiley.

Gollnick, D. M., & Chinn, P. G. (2002). *Multicultural education in a pluralistic society* (6th ed.). Upper Saddle River, NJ: Merrill/Prentice Hall.

Gonzalez, V., Brusca-Vega, R., & Yawkey, T. (1997). Assessment and instruction of culturally and linguistically diverse students with or at-risk of learning problems: From research to practice. Boston: Allyn & Bacon.

Gonzalez-Mena, J. (2002). *The child in the family and the community.* Upper Saddle River, NJ: Merrill/Prentice Hall.

Goodman, L. V. (1976). A bill of rights for the handicapped. *American Education, 12*(6), 6–8.

Gordon, M., Thompson, D., Cooper, S., & Ivers, C. L. (1991). Nonmedical treatment of ADHDE/hyperactivity: The attention training system. *Journal of School Psychology, 29,* 151–159.

Gottesman, I. I. (1991). *Schizophrenia genesis: The origins of madness.* New York: Freeman.

Graham, S., & Harris, K. R. (1993). Self-regulated strategy development: Helping students with learning problems develop as writers. *Elementary School Journal, 94,* 169–181.

Graham, S., Harris, K. R., & Larsen, L. (2001). Prevention and intervention of writing difficulties for students with learning disabilities. *Learning Disabilities Research and Practice, 16,* 74–84.

Grant, C. A., & Gomez, M. L. (2001). *Campus and classroom: Making schooling multicultural* (2nd ed.) Upper Saddle River, NJ: Merrill/Prentice Hall.

Grant, C. A., & Sleeter, C. E. (1989). Race, class, gender, exceptionality, and educational reform. In J. A. Banks & C. A. M. Banks (Eds.), *Multicultural education: Issues and perspectives* (pp. 46–65). Boston: Allyn & Bacon.

Grant, G., & McGrath, M. (1990). Need for respite-care services for caregivers of persons with mental retardation. *American Journal on Mental Retardation, 94,* 638–648.

Gray, D. B., Quartrano, L. A., & Liberman, M. L. (1998). *Designing and using assistive technology.* Baltimore: Brookes.

Green, G. (2001). Behavior analytic instruction for learners with autism: Advances in stimulus control technology. *Focus on Autism and Other Developmental Disabilities, 16,* 72–85.

Green, S. K., & Shinn, M. R. (1995). Parent attitudes about special education and reintegration: What is the role of student outcomes? *Exceptional Children, 61,* 269–281.

Greenbaum, P. E., Dedrick, R. F., Friedman, R. M., Kutash, K., Brown, E. C., Lardieri,

S. P., & Pugh, A. M. (1996). National adolescent and children treatment study (NACTS): Outcomes for children with serious emotional and behavior disturbance. *Journal of Emotional and Behavioral Disorders, 4,* 130–146.

Greenen, S., Powers, L. E., & Lopez-Vasquez, A. (2001). Multicultural aspects of parent involvement in transition planning. *Exceptional Children, 67,* 265–282.

Greenspan, S. (1997). Dead manual walking? Why the 1992 AAMR definition needs redoing. *Education and Training in Mental Retardation and Developmental Disabilities, 32,* 179–190.

Greenspan, S. I. (1992). Reconsidering the diagnosis and treatment of very young children with autistic spectrum or pervasive developmental disorder. *Zero to Three, 13*(2), 1–9.

Greenspan, S. I., & Weider, S. W. (1997). Developmental patterns and outcomes in infants and children with disorders in relating and communicating: A chart review of 200 cases of children with autistic spectrum diagnoses. *Journal of Developmental and Learning Disorders, 1,* 87–141.

Greenwood, C. R., & Maheady, L. (1997). Measurable change in student performance: Forgotten standard in teacher preparation? *Teacher Education and Special Education, 20,* 265–275.

Greenwood, C. R., Carta, J. J., Hart, B., Kamps, D., Terry, D., Delquadri, J. C., Walker, D., & Risley, T. (1992). Out of the laboratory and into the community: Twenty-six years of applied behavior analysis at the Juniper Gardens Children's Center. *American Psychologist, 47,* 1464–1474.

Greenwood, C. R., Delquadri, J., & Carta, J. J. (1997). *Together we can: Classwide peer tutoring to improve basic academic skills.* Longmont, CO: Sopris West.

Greenwood, C. R., Delquadri, J., & Hall, R. V. (1984). Opportunity to respond and student academic achievement. In W. L. Heward, T. E. Heron, D. S. Hill, & J. Trap-Porter (Eds.), *Focus on behavior analysis in education* (pp. 58–88). Upper Saddle River, NJ: Merrill/Prentice Hall.

Greenwood, C. R., Hart, B., Walker, D., & Risley, T. (1994). The opportunity to respond and academic performance revisited: A behavioral theory of developmental retardation and its prevention. In R. Gardner III, D. M. Sainato, J. O. Cooper, T. E. Heron, W. L. Heward, J. Eshleman, & T. A. Grossi (Eds.), *Behavior analysis in education: Focus on measurably superior instruction* (pp. 213–223). Pacific Grove, CA: Brooks/Cole.

Grenot-Scheyer, M., Fisher, M., & Staub, D. (2001). *Lessons learned in inclusive education at the end of the day.* Baltimore: Brookes.

Gresham, F. (2001). *Responsiveness to intervention: An alternative approach to the identification of learning disabilities* (Executive Summary). Paper presented at

the LD Summit, Washington, DC. http://www.air.org/LDsummit/paper.htm

Gresham, F. M. (2002). Caveat emptor: Considerations before buying in to the "new" medical model. *Behavioral Disorders, 27,* 158–167.

Gresham, F. M., & MacMillan, D. L. (1997). Autistic recovery? An analysis and critique of the empirical evidence on the Early Intervention Project. *Behavioral Disorders, 22,* 185–201.

Gresham, F. M., Lane, K. L., MacMillan, D.L., & Bocian, K. M. (1999). Social and academic profiles of externalizing and internalizing groups; Risk factors for emotional and behavioral disorders. *Behavioral Disorders, 24,* 231–245.

Griffin, K. L. (2001, October 7). Blind "see" via camera that tickles tongue. *Columbus Dispatch,* p. C6.

Grigal, M., Test, D. W., Beattie, J., & Wood, W. (1997). An evaluation of transition components of individualized education programs. *Exceptional Children, 63,* 357–372.

Grossen, B. (1998). *Child-directed teaching methods: A discriminatory practice of western education.* http://darkwing. uoregon.edu/~bgrossen/cdp.htm

Grossi, T. A. (1998). Using a self-operated auditory prompting system to improve the work performance of two employees with severe disabilities. *Journal of The Association for Persons with Severe Handicaps, 23,* 149–154.

Grossi, T. A., & Heward, W. L. (1998). Using self-evaluation to improve the work productivity of trainees in a community-based restaurant training program. *Education and Training in Mental Retardation and Developmental Disabilities, 33,* 248–263.

Grossman, H. (1995). *Teaching in a diverse society.* Boston: Allyn & Bacon.

Grossman, H. (Ed.). (1983). *Classification in mental retardation.* Washington, DC: American Association on Mental Deficiency.

Groves, B. M. (1997). Growing up in a violent world: The impact of family and community violence on young children and their families. *Topics in Early Childhood Special Education, 17*(1), 74–102.

Guess, D., Benson, H. A., & Siegel-Causey, E. (1985). Concepts and issues related to choice-making and autonomy among persons with severe disabilities. *Journal of The Association for Persons with Severe Handicaps, 10,* 79–86.

Guilford, J. P. (1959). Traits of creativity. In H. H. Anderson (Ed.), *Creativity and its cultivation* (pp. 142–161). New York: Harper.

Guilford, J. P. (1967). *The nature of human intelligence.* New York: McGraw-Hill.

Guilford, J. P. (1987). Creativity research: Past, present and future. In S. Isaksen (Ed.), *Frontiers of creativity research* (pp. 33–66). Buffalo, NY: Bearly.

Gunter, P. L., Denny, R. K., Jack, S. L., Shores, R. E., & Nelson, C. M. (1993). Aversive stimuli in academic interactions between students with serious emotional disturbance and their teachers. *Behavioral Disorders, 18,* 265–274.

Gunter, P. L., Hummel, J. H., & Conroy, M. A. (1998). Increasing correct academic responding: An effective intervention strategy to decrease behavior problems. *Effective School Practices, 17*(2), 55–62.

Guralnick, M. J. (1997). *The effectiveness of early intervention.* Baltimore: Brookes.

Guralnick, M. J. (1998). Effectiveness of early intervention for vulnerable children: A developmental perspective. *American Journal of Mental Retardation, 102*(4), 319–345.

Guralnick, M. J. (2001). *Early childhood inclusion: Focus on change.* Baltimore: Brookes.

Gustason, G. (1997). Educating children who are deaf or hard of hearing: English-based sign systems. *ERIC Digest #556.* (ERIC Document Reproduction Service No. ED 414 674).

Gustason, G., Pfetzing, D., & Zawolkow, E. (1980). *Signing exact English.* Los Alamitos, CA: Modern Signs.

Haager, D., & Vaughn, S. (1995). Parent, teacher, peer, and self-reports of the social competence of students with learning disabilities. *Journal of Learning Disabilities, 28,* 205–231.

Hadden, S., & Fowler, S. A. (1997). Preschool: A new beginning for children and parents. *Teaching Exceptional Children, 30*(1), 36–39.

Hadley, P. A. (1998). Language sampling protocols for eliciting text-level discourse. *Language, Speech, and Hearing Services in the Schools, 29,* 132–147.

Hadley, P. A., Simmerman, A., Long, M., & Luna, M. (2000). Facilitating language development for inner-city children: Experimental evaluation of a collaborative classroom-based intervention. *Language, Speech, and Hearing Services in Schools, 31,* 280–295.

Hagerman, R. J., & Cronister, A. (Eds.). (1996). *Fragile X syndrome: Diagnosis, treatment, and research* (2nd ed.). Baltimore: Johns Hopkins University Press.

Hall, B. J., Oyer, H. J., & Haas, W. H. (2001). *Speech, language, and hearing disorders: A guide for the teacher* (3rd ed.). Boston: Allyn & Bacon.

Hall, M., Kleinert, H. L., & Kerns, J. F. (2000). Going to college! Postsecondary programs for students with moderate and severe disabilities. *Teaching Exceptional Children, 32*(2), 58–65.

Hall, R. V., Lund, D., & Jackson, D. (1968). Effects of teacher attention on study behavior. *Journal of Applied Behavior Analysis, 1,* 1–12.

Hallahan, D. P. (1992). Some thoughts on why the prevalence of learning disabilities has increased. *Journal of Learning Disabilities, 25,* 523–528.

Hallahan, D. P. (1998). Teach. Don't flinch. *DLD Times, 16*(1), 1, 4.

Hallenbeck, B. A., & Kauffman, J. M. (1995). How does observational learning affect the behavior of students with emotional or behavioral disorders? A review of research. *Journal of Special Education, 29,* 43–71.

Halpern, A. S. (1985). Transition: A look at the foundations. *Exceptional Children, 51,* 479–486.

Halpern, A. S. (1993). Quality of life as a conceptual framework for evaluating transition outcomes. *Exceptional Children, 59,* 486–498.

Ham, R. (1986). *Techniques of stuttering therapy.* Upper Saddle River, NJ: Prentice Hall.

Hamilton, S. L., Seibert, M. A., Gardner, R., III, & Talbert-Johnson, C. (2000). Using guided notes to improve the academic achievement of incarcerated adolescents with learning and behavior problems. *Remedial and Special Education, 21,* 133–140.

Hammill, D. D., & Larsen, S. (1978). The effectiveness of psycholinguistic training: A reaffirmation of position. *Exceptional Children, 44,* 402–417.

Hammill, D., & Newcomer, P. L. (1997). *Test of Language Development—3.* Austin, TX: PRO–ED.

Hanline, M. F. (1993). Inclusion of preschoolers with profound disabilities: An analysis of children's interactions. *Journal of The Association for Persons with Severe Handicaps, 18,* 28–35.

Hanson, M. J., Beckman, P. J., Horn, E., Marquart, J., Sandall, S., Greig, D., & Breenan, E. (2000). Entering preschool: Family and professional experiences in this transition process. *Journal of Early Intervention, 23,* 279–293.

Hanson, M. J., Horn, E., Sandall, S., Beckman, P., Morgan, M., Marquart, J., Barnwell, D. K., & Chou, H. (2001). After preschool inclusion: Children's educational pathways over the early school years. *Exceptional Children, 68,* 65–83.

Harchik, A. E. (1994). Self-medication skills. In M. Agran, N. E. Marchand-Martella, & R. C. Martella (Eds.), *Promoting health and safety: Skills for independent living* (pp. 55–69). Pacific Grove, CA: Brooks/Cole.

Harchik, A. E., & Putzier, V. S. (1990). The use of high–probability requests to increase compliance with instructions to take medication. *Journal of The Association for Persons with Severe Handicaps, 15,* 40–43.

Hardin, D. M., & Littlejohn, W. (1995). Family-school collaboration: Elements of effectiveness and program models. *Preventing School Failure, 39*(1), 4–8.

Hardman, M. L., McDonnell, J., & Welch, M. (1997). Perspectives on the future of IDEA. *Journal of The Association for Persons with Severe Handicaps, 22,* 61–77.

Haring, T. G., & Breen, C. G. (1992). A peer-mediated social network intervention to enhance the social integration of persons with moderate and severe disabilities. *Journal of Applied Behavior Analysis, 25,* 319–334.

Harland, V. T. (1997). *Youth street gangs: Breaking the gangs cycles in urban America.* San Francisco: Austin & Winfield.

Harmston, K. A., Strong, C. J., & Evans, D. D. (2001). International pen-pal correspondence for students with language-learning disabilities. *Teaching Exceptional Children, 33*(3), 46–51.

Harn, W., Bradshaw, M., & Ogletree, B. (1999). The speech-language pathologist in the schools: Changing roles. *Intervention in School and Clinic, 34,* 7.

Harris, H., & Harris, S. (1997). *The voice clinic handbook.* London: Whurr.

Harris, L., & Associates. (1986). *The ICD survey of disabled Americans: Bringing disabled Americans into the mainstream.* New York: Author.

Harris, S. L., & Handleman, J. S. (Eds.). (1994). *Preschool programs for children with autism.* Austin, TX: PRO-ED.

Harris, S. L., & Handleman, J. S. (Eds.). (2000). *Preschool programs for children with autism* (2nd ed.). Austin, TX: PRO-ED.

Harry, B. (1992a). *Cultural diversity, families, and the special education system: Communication and empowerment.* New York: Teachers College Press.

Harry, B. (1992b). Making sense of disability: Low-income, Puerto Rican parents' theories of the problem. *Exceptional Children, 59,* 27–40.

Harry, B. (1994). *The disproportionate representation of minority students in special education: Theories and recommendations.* Alexandria, VA: National Association of State Directors of Special Education.

Harry, B., Kalyanpur, M., & Day, M. (1999). *Building cultural reciprocity with families: Case studies in special education.* Baltimore: Brookes.

Harry, B., Rueda, R., & Kalyanapur, M. (1999). Cultural reciprocity in sociocultural perspective: Adapting the normalization principle for family collaboration. *Exceptional Children, 66,* 123–136.

Hart, B., & Risley, T. R. (1995). *Meaningful differences in the everyday experience of young American children.* Baltimore: Brookes.

Hart, B., & Risley, T. R. (1999). *The social world of children learning to talk.* Baltimore: Brookes.

Haseltine, B., & Mittenburger, R. G. (1990). Teaching self-protection skills to persons with disabilities. *American Journal of Mental Retardation, 95,* 188–197.

Hatlen, P. (1996). *The core curriculum for blind and visually impaired students, including those with additional disabilities.* New York: American Foundation for the Blind.

Hatton, C. (1998). What is quality of life anyway? Some problems with the emerging quality of life consensus. *Mental Retardation, 36,* 104–115.

Hawkins, L., & Brawner, J. (1997). *Educating children who are deaf/hard of hearing: Total communication.* ERIC Digest #E559. ERIC Clearinghouse on Disabilities and Gifted Education, Reston, VA. (ERIC Document Reproduction Service No. ED 414 677).

Haynes, W., & Pindzola, R. (1998). *Diagnosis and evaluation in speech pathology* (5th ed.). Needham Heights, MA: Allyn & Bacon.

Heber, R. F., & Garber, H. (1971). An experiment in prevention of cultural-familial mental retardation. In D. A. Primrose (Ed.), *Proceedings of the Second Congress of the International Association for the Scientific Study of Mental Deficiency*. Warsaw: Polish Medical Publishers.

Heckaman, K. A., Alber, S. R., Hooper, S., & Heward, W. L. (1998). A comparison of least-to-most prompts and progressive time delay on the disruptive behavior of students with autism. *Journal of Behavior Education, 8*, 171–201.

Heckaman, K., Conroy, M., Fox, J., & Chait, A. (2000). Functional assessment-based interventions research on students with or at risk for emotional and behavioral disorders in school settings. *Behavioral Disorders, 25*, 196–210.

Heflin, L. J., & Simpson, R. L. (2002). Understanding intervention controversies. In B. Scheuermann & J. Webber, *Autism: Teaching Does Make a Difference* (pp. 248–277). Belmont, CA: Wadsworth.

Heinze, T. (1986). Communication skills. In G. T. Scholl (Ed.), *Foundations of education for blind and visually handicapped children and youth: Theory and practice* (pp. 301–314). New York: American Foundation for the Blind.

Heller, K. W., & Bigge, J. (2001). Augmentative and alternative communication. In J. L. Bigge, S. J. Best, & K. W. Heller, *Teaching individuals with physical, health, or multiple disabilities* (4th ed.), (pp. 229–277). Upper Saddle River, NJ: Merrill/Prentice Hall.

Heller, K. W., Alberto, P. A., Forney, P. E., & Schwartzman, M. N. (1996). *Understanding physical, sensory and health impairments*. Pacific Grove, CA: Brooks/Cole.

Heller, K. W., Bigge, J., & Allgood, P. (2001). Adaptations for personal independence. In J. L. Bigge, S. J. Best, & K. W. Heller, *Teaching individuals with physical, health, or multiple disabilities* (4th ed.), (pp. 536–565). Upper Saddle River, NJ: Merrill/Prentice Hall.

Heller, K. W., Dangel, H., & Sweatman, L. (1995). Systematic selection of adaptations for students with muscular dystrophy. *Journal of Developmental and Physical Disabilities, 7*, 253–265.

Heller, K. W., Forney, P. E., Alberto, P. A., Schwartzman, M. N., & Goeckel, T. M. (1999). *Meeting physical and health needs of children with disabilities*. Belmont, CA: Wadsworth.

Heller, K. W., Fredrick, L. D., Best, S., Dykes, M. K., & Cohen, E. T. (2000). Specialized health care procedures in the schools: Training and service delivery. *Exceptional Children, 66*, 173–186.

Henderson, C. (1992). *College freshmen with disabilities: A statistical profile*. Washington, DC: American Council on Education, HEATH Resource Center. (ERIC No. ED354792).

Henderson, C. (1999). *1999 college freshmen with disabilities: A biennial statistical profile*. Washington, DC. American Council on Education, HEATH Resource Center.

Henderson, L. W., & Meisels, S. J. (1994). Parental involvement in the developmental screening of their young children: A multiple-source perspective. *Journal of Early Intervention, 18*, 141–154.

Henggler, S. (1989). *Delinquency in adolescence*. Beverly Hills, CA: Sage.

Hernandez, H. (2001). *Multicultural education: A teacher's guide to linking context, process, and content* (2nd ed.). Upper Saddle River, NJ: Merrill/Prentice Hall.

Heron, T. E., & Harris, K. C. (2001). *The educational consultant: Helping professionals, parents, and students in inclusive classrooms* (4th ed.). Austin, TX: PRO-ED.

Heron, T. E., & Harris, K. C. (in press). *The educational consultant: Helping professionals, parents, and students in inclusive classrooms* (4th ed.). Austin, TX: PRO-ED.

Heron, T. E., & Heward, W. L. (2000). *Total tutoring for special and general educators [Instructor's manual]*. Columbus: The Ohio State University Special Education Program.

Hertzog, N. B. (1998). The changing role of the gifted education specialist. *Teaching Exceptional Children, 30*(3), 39–43.

Heward, W. L. (1994). Three "low-tech" strategies for increasing the frequency of active student response during group instruction. In R. Gardner III, D. M. Sainato, J. O. Cooper, T. E. Heron, W. L. Heward, J. Eshleman, & T. A. Grossi (Eds.), *Behavior analysis in education: Focus on measurably superior instruction* (pp. 283–320). Pacific Grove, CA: Brooks/Cole.

Heward, W. L. (2001). *Guided notes: Improving the effectiveness of your lectures*. Columbus, OH: The Ohio State University Partnership Grant for Improving the Quality of Education for Students with Disabilities.

Heward, W. L., & Cavanaugh, R. A. (2001). Educational equality for students with disabilities. In J. A. Banks & C. A. M. Banks (Eds.), *Multicultural education: Issues and perspectives* (4th ed.), (pp. 295–326). Needham Heights, MA: Allyn & Bacon.

Heward, W. L., & Chapman, J. E. (1981). Improving parent-teacher communication through recorded telephone messages: Systematic replication in a special education classroom. *Journal of Special Education Technology, 4*, 11–19.

Heward, W. L., & Dardig, J. C. (2001, Spring). What matters most in special education. *Education Connection*, 41–44.

Heward, W. L., Gardner, R., III, Cavanaugh, R. A., Courson, F. H., Grossi, T. A., & Barbetta, P. M. (1996). Everyone participates in this class: Using response cards to increase active student response. *Teaching Exceptional Children, 28*(2), 4–10.

Heward, W. L., Heron, T. E., & Cooke, N. L. (1982). Tutor huddle: Key element in a classwide peer tutoring system. *Elementary School Journal, 83*, 115–123.

Heward, W. L., Heron, T. E., Gardner, R., III, & Prayzer, R. (1991). Two strategies for improving students' writing skills. In G. Stoner, M. R. Shinn, & H. M. Walker (Eds.), *A school psychologist's interventions for regular education* (pp. 379–398). Washington DC: National Association of School Psychologists.

Hidalgo, N. M. (1997). A layering of family and friends. *Education and Urban Society, 30*, 20–41.

Hill, B. K., Lakin, K. C., Bruininks, R. H., Amado, A. N., Anderson, D. J., & Copher, J. I. (1989). *Living in the community: A comparative study of foster homes and small group homes for people with mental retardation* (Report No. 28). Minneapolis: University of Minnesota, Center for Residential and Community Services.

Hill, E. W., & Snook-Hill, M. (1996). Orientation and mobility. In M. C. Holbrook (Ed.), *Children with visual impairments: A parents' guide* (pp. 259–286). Bethesda, MD: Woodbine House.

Hill, J. L. (1999). *Meeting the needs of students with special physical and health care needs*. Upper Saddle River, NJ: Merrill/Prentice Hall.

Hilliard, A. G. (1980). Cultural diversity and special education. *Exceptional Children, 46*, 584–588.

Hintz, R., & Driscoll, A. (1988). Praise or encouragement? New insights into praise: Implications for early childhood teachers. *Young Children, 16*, 6–13.

Hitchings, W. E., Luzzo, D. A., Retish, P., Horvath, M., & Ristow, R. (1998). Identifying the needs of college students with disabilities. *Journal of College Student Development, 39*(1), 23–32.

Hitchings, W. E., Luzzo, D. A., Ristow, R., Horvath, M., Retish, P., & Tanners, A. (2001). The career development needs of college students with learning disabilities: In their own words. *Learning Disabilities Research and Practice, 16*, 8–17.

Hock, M. F., Schumaker, J. B., & Deshler, D. D. (1999). Closing the gap to success in secondary schools: A model for cognitive apprenticeship. In S. Graham, K. R. Harris, & M. Pressley (Series Eds.) & D. D. Deshler, K. R. Harris, & S. Graham (Vol. Eds.), *Advances in teaching and learning, teaching every child every day: Learning in diverse schools and classrooms* (pp.1–52). Cambridge, MA: Brookline Books.

Hodapp, R. M., & Dykens, E. M. (2001). Strengthening behavioral research on genetic mental retardation syndromes. *American Journal of Mental Retardation, 106*, 4–15.

Hodgkinson, H. (2000). Educational demographics: What teachers should know. *Educational Leadership, 58*(4), 1–5.

Hodson, B. W. (1994). Helping individuals become intelligible, literate, and articulate: The role of phonology. *Topics in Language Disorders, 14*(2), 1–16

Holahan, A., & Costenbader, V. (2000). A comparison of developmental gain for preschool children with disabilities in inclusive and self-contained classrooms. *Topics in Early Childhood Special Education, 20*, 224–235.

Holden-Pitt, L., & Diaz, J. (1998). Thirty years of the annual survey of deaf and hard-of-hearing children and youth: A glance over the decades. *American Annals of the Deaf, 142*(2), 72–76.

Hollinger, C. L. (1995). Counseling gifted young women about educational and career choices. In J. L. Genshaft, M. Bireley, & C. L. Hollinger (Eds.), *Serving gifted and talented students: A resource for school personnel* (pp. 269–283). Austin, TX: PRO-ED.

Holt, J. (1993). Stanford Achievement Test—8th edition: Reading comprehension subgroup results. *American Annals of the Deaf, 138,* 172–175.

Honig v. Doe, 485 U. S. 305, 108 S.Ct. 592, 98 L.Ed. 2d 686 (1988).

Hoover, H. D., Hieronymus, A. N., Frisbie, D. A., & Dunbar, S. B. (1996). *Iowa Tests of Basic Skills.* Chicago: Riverside.

Horn, E., Lieber, J., Li, S., Sandall, S., & Schwartz, I. (2000). Supporting young children's IEP goals in inclusive settings through embedded learning opportunities. *Topics in Early Childhood Special Education, 20,* 208–223.

Horn, L., & Berktold, J. (1999). *Students with disabilities in postsecondary education: A profile of preparation, participation, and outcomes. NCES 1999–187.* Washington, DC: National Center for Education Statistics.

Horner, R. H., & Carr, E. G. (1997). Behavioral support for students with severe disabilities: Functional assessment and comprehensive intervention. *Journal of Special Education, 31,* 84–104.

Horner, R. H., Day, H. M., Sprague, J. R., O'Brien, M., & Tuesday-Heathfield, L. (1991). Interspersed requests: A non-aversive procedure for reducing aggression and self-injury during instruction. *Journal of Applied Behavior Analysis, 24,* 265–278.

Horner, R. H., Dunlap, G., & Koegel, R. L. (1988). *Generalization and maintenance: Life-style changes in applied settings.* Baltimore: Brookes.

Horton, S. V., Lovitt, T. C., & Bergerud, D. (1990). The effectiveness of graphic organizers for three classifications of secondary students in content area classes. *Journal of Learning Disabilities, 23,* 12–22.

Hourcade, J. J., Parette, H. P., & Huer, M. B. (1997). Family and cultural alert! Considerations in assistive technology assessment. *Teaching Exceptional Children, 30*(1), 40–44.

House, J. W. (1999). Hearing loss in adults. *The Volta Review, 99*(5), 161–166.

Howard, V. F., Williams, B. F., & McLaughlin, T. F. (1994). Children prenatally exposed to alcohol and cocaine: Behavioral solutions. In R. Gardner III, D. M. Sainato, J. O. Cooper, T. E. Heron, W. L. Heward, J. Eshleman, & T. A. Grossi (Eds.), *Behavior analysis in education: Focus on measurably superior instruction* (pp. 131–146). Pacific Grove, CA: Brooks/Cole.

Howard, V. F., Williams, B. F., Port, P. D., & Lepper, C. (2001). *Very young children with special needs: A formative approach for the 21st century* (2nd ed.). Upper Saddle River, NJ: Merrill/Prentice Hall.

Howe, J., Horner, R. H., & Newton, J. S. (1998). Comparison of supported living and traditional residential services in the state of Oregon. *Mental Retardation, 36,* 1–11.

Howell, K. W. (1998). *Curriculum-based evaluation: Teaching and decision making* (3rd ed.). Monterey, CA: Brooks/Cole.

Howell, K. W., & Lorson-Howell, K. A. (1990). What's the hurry? Fluency in the classroom. *Teaching Exceptional Children, 22*(3), 20–23.

Howell, K. W., & Nolet, V. (2000). *Curriculum-based evaluation: Teaching and decision making* (3rd ed.). Belmont, CA: Wadsworth/Thompson Learning.

Howell, R. D. (2000). Grasping the future with robotic aids. In W. L. Heward, *Exceptional children: An introduction to special education* (6th ed.), (pp. 478–480). Upper Saddle River, NJ: Merrill/Prentice Hall.

Hoye, J. D. (1998, July). *Integrating school-to-work into preservice teacher education.* Paper presented at Conference for Professors of Education in Ohio, Kent, OH.

Huber Marshall, L., Martin, J. E., Maxson, L. L., Hughes, W., Miller, T. L., McGill, T., & Jerman, P. (1999). *Take action: Making goals happen.* Longmont, CO: Sopris West.

Hudson, P., & Miller, S. P. (1993). Home and school partnerships: Parent as teacher. *LD Forum, 18*(2), 31–33.

Hudson, P., Lignugaris/Kraft, B., & Miller, T. (1993). Using content enhancements to improve the performance of adolescents with learning disabilities in content classes. *Learning Disabilities Research and Practice, 8,* 106–126.

Huefner, D. S. (2000). The risks and opportunities of the IEP requirements under IDEA '97. *Exceptional Children, 63,* 195–204.

Huff, K. E., & DuPaul, G. J. (1998). Reducing disruptive behavior in general education classrooms: The use of self-management strategies. *School Psychology Review, 27,* 290–303.

Hughes, C. (1997). Self-instruction. In M. Agran (Ed.), *Student directed learning: Teaching self-determination skills* (pp. 144–170). Pacific Grove, CA: Brooks/Cole.

Hughes, C., & Rusch, F. R. (1989). Teaching supported employees with severe mental retardation to solve problems. *Journal of Applied Behavior Analysis, 22,* 365–372.

Hughes, C., Copeland, S. R., Guth, C., Rung, L. L., Hwang, B., Kleeb, G., & Strong, M. (2001). General education students' perspective on their involvement in a high school peer buddy program. *Education and Training in Mental Retardation and Developmental Disabilities, 36,* 343–356.

Hughes, C., Killian, D. J., & Fischer, G. M. (1996). Validation and assessment of a conversational interaction intervention. *American Journal on Mental Retardation, 100,* 493–509.

Hughes, F., Elicker, J., & Veen, L. (1995, January). A program of play for infants and their caregivers. *Young Children,* 52–58.

Hulit, L. M., & Howard, M. R. (2002). *Born to talk: An introduction to speech and language development* (3rd ed.), Boston: Allyn & Bacon.

Hunt, P., Goetz, L., & Anderson, J. (1986). The quality of IEP objectives associated with placement on integrated versus segregated school sites. *Journal of The Association for Persons with Severe Handicaps, 11,* 125–130.

Hunt, P., Staub, D., Alwell, M., & Goetz, L. (1994). Achievement by all students within the context of cooperative learning groups. *Journal of The Association for Persons with Severe Handicaps, 19,* 290–301.

Huntze, S. L. (1985). A position paper of the Council for Children with Behavioral Disorders. *Behavioral Disorders, 10,* 167–174.

Hutinger, P. L., Marshall, S., & McCarten, K. (1983). *Core curriculum: Macomb 0–3 regional project* (3rd ed.). Macomb: Western Illinois University.

Ingram, A. L., Hathorn, L. G., and Evans, A. D. (2000). Beyond chat on the Internet. *Computers and Education, 35*(1), 21–35.

Ireland, J. C., Wray, D., & Flexer, C. (1988). Hearing for success in the classroom. *Teaching Exceptional Children, 20*(2), 15–17.

Irving Independent School District v. Tatro, 104 S. Ct. 3371, 82 L.Ed. 2d 664 (1984).

Iscoe, I., & Payne, S. (1972). Development of a revised scale for the functional classification of exceptional children. In E. P. Trapp & P. Himelstein (Eds.), *Readings on the exceptional child* (pp. 7–29). New York: Appleton-Century-Crofts.

Ishil-Jordan, S. (1997). When behavior differences are not disorders. In A. Artiles & G. Zamora-Durán (Eds.), *Reducing disproportionate representation of culturally diverse students in special and gifted education* (pp. 27–46). Reston, VA: Council for Exceptional Children.

Ita, C. M., & Friedman, H. A. (1999). The psychological development of children who are deaf or hard of hearing: A critical review. *The Volta Review, 101,* 165–181.

Itard, J. M. G. (1894/1962). *The wild boy of Aveyron.* (G. Humphrey & M. Humphrey, Eds. and Trans.). New York: Appleton Century Crofts.

Iwata, B. A., Dorsey, M., Slifer, K., Bauman, K., & Richman, G. (1994). Toward a functional analysis of self-injury. *Journal of Applied Behavior Analysis, 27,* 197–209.

Jackson, N. F., Jackson, D. A., & Monroe, C. (1983). *Getting along with others: Teaching social effectiveness to children.* Champaign, IL: Research Press.

Jacobsen, J. J., & Mulick, J. (1996). *Manual on diagnosis and professional practice in mental retardation.* Washington, DC: American Psychological Association.

Jacobson, J. W., Mulick, J. A., & Green, G. (1998). Cost-benefit estimates for early intensive behavioral intervention for young children with autism: General model and single state case. *Behavioral Interventions, 13,* 201–226.

Jacobson, J. W., Mulick, J. A., & Schwartz, A. A. (1995). A history of facilitated communication: Science, pseudoscience, and antiscience. *American Psychologist, 50,* 750–765.

Jacobson, W. H. (1993). *The art and science of teaching orientation and mobility to persons with visual impairments.* New York: American Federation for the Blind.

Janney, R. E., & Snell, M. E. (1996). Using peer interactions to include students with extensive disabilities in elementary general education classes. *Journal of The Association for Persons with Severe Handicaps, 21,* 72–80.

Janney, R. E., & Snell, M. E. (1997). How teachers include students with moderate and severe disabilities in elementary classes: The means and meaning of inclusion. *Journal of The Association for Persons with Severe Handicaps, 42*(3), 159–169.

Janney, R., & Snell, M. E. (2000). *Modifying schoolwork.* Baltimore: Brookes.

Janney, R., & Snell, M. E. (2000). *Teacher's guides to inclusive practices: Behavioral support.* Baltimore: Brookes.

Jayanthi, M., Bursuck, W., Epstein, M. H., & Polloway, E. A. (1997). Strategies for successful homework. *Teaching Exceptional Children, 30*(1), 4–7.

Jenkins, J., & O'Conner, R. (2001). *Early identification and intervention for young children with reading/learning disabilities* (Executive Summary). Paper presented at the LD Summit, Washington, DC. http://www.air.org/LDsummit/paper.htm

Jensen, P. S. (2000). Pediatric psychopharmacology in the United States: Issues and challenges in the diagnosis and treatment of attention-deficit/hyperactivity disorder. In L. L. Greenhill & B. B. Osman (Eds.), *Ritalin: Theory and practice* (2nd ed.) Larchmont, NY: Mary Ann Liebert, Inc.

Jensen, W. R., Sheridan, S. M., Olympia, D., & Andrews, D. (1994). Homework and students with learning disabilities and behavior disorders: A practical, parent-based approach. *Journal of Learning Disabilities, 27*(9), 538–548.

Johnson, B., & Cuvo, A. (1981). Teaching mentally retarded adults to cook. *Behavior Modification, 12,* 69–73.

Johnson, H. A. (1997, June). Internet use within deaf education: Current status, trends and applications. Paper presented at the CAID/CEASD Conference, Hartford, CT.

Johnson, H. L. (1993). Stressful family experiences and young children: How the classroom teacher can help. *Intervention in School and Clinic, 28*(3), 165–171.

Johnson, R. (1985). *The picture communication symbols—Book II.* Solana Beach, CA: Mayer-Johnson.

Johnson, S., & Wehman, P. (2001). Teaching for transition. In P. Wehman (Ed.), *Life beyond the classroom: Transition strategies for young people with disabilities* (3rd ed.). Baltimore: Brookes.

Johnson, T. P. (1986). *The principal's guide to the educational rights of handicapped students.* Reston, VA: National Association of Secondary School Principals.

Johnson-Martin, N. M., Attermeier, S. M., & Hacker, B. (1990). *The Carolina Curriculum for preschoolers with special needs.* Baltimore: Brookes.

Johnston, D. (1994a). Co:Writer (Version 2.0) [Computer software]. Wauconda, IL: Don Johnston, Inc.

Johnston, D. (1994b). Write:OutLoud (Version 2.0) [Computer software]. Wauconda, IL: Don Johnston, Inc.

Johnston, K. R., & Layng, T. V. J. (1994). The Morningside model of generative instruction. In R. Gardner III, D. M. Sainato, J. O. Cooper, T. E. Heron, W. L. Heward, J. Eshleman, & T. A. Grossi (Eds.), *Behavior analysis in education: Focus on measurably superior instruction* (pp. 173–197). Pacific Grove, CA: Brooks/Cole.

Johnston, R., & Umberger, R. (1996). *The voice companion.* East Moline, IL: LinguiSystems.

Jolly, A. C., Test, D. W., & Spooner, F. (1993). Using badges to increase initiations of children with severe disabilities in a play setting. *Journal of The Association for Persons with Severe Handicaps, 18,* 46–51.

Jones, B. E., Clark, G. M., & Soltz, D. F. (1997). Characteristics and practices of sign language interpreters in inclusive education programs. *Exceptional Children, 63,* 257–268.

Jones, C. J. (2001). Teacher-friendly curriculum-based assessment in spelling. *Teaching Exceptional Children, 34*(3), 32–38.

Jones, D. E., Clatterbuck, C. C., Marquis, J., Turnbull, H. R., & Moberly, R. L. (1996). Educational placements for children who are ventilator assisted. *Exceptional Children, 63,* 47–57.

Jones, T. M., Garlow, J. A., Turnbull, H. R., & Barber, P. A. (1996). Family empowerment in a family support program. In G. H. S. Singer, L. E. Powers, & A. L. Olson (Eds.), *Redefining family support: Innovations in public-private partnerships* (p. 91). Baltimore: Brookes.

Jordan, L., Reyes-Blane, M. E., Peel, B. B., Peel, H. A., & Lane, H. B. (1998). Developing teacher–parent partnerships: Effective parent conferences. *Intervention in School and Clinic, 33,* 141–147.

Jordan, N. C., & Hanich, L. B. (2000). Mathematical thinking in second-grade children with different forms of LD. *Journal of Learning Disabilities, 33,* 567–578.

Jose, R. (1983). *Understanding low vision.* New York: American Foundation for the Blind.

Justen, J. E. (1976). Who are the severely handicapped? A problem in definition. *AAESPH Review, 1*(2), 1–12.

Kagan, S. L., & Neuman, M. J. (1997, September). Highlights of the Quality 2000 Initiative: Not by chance. *Young Children,* pp. 54–62.

Kairys, S. (1996). Family support in cases of child abuse and neglect. In G. H. S. Singer, L. E. Powers, & A. L. Olson (Eds.), *Redefining family support: Innovations in public-private partnerships* (pp. 171–188). Baltimore: Brookes.

Kaiser, A. P. (2000). Teaching functional communication skills. In M. E. Snell & F. Brown, *Instruction of students with severe disabilities* (5th ed.), (pp. 453–492). Upper Saddle River, NJ: Merrill/Prentice Hall.

Kaiser, A. P., Hancock, T. B., Cai, X., Foster, E. M., & Hester, P. P. (2000). Parent-reported behavioral problems and language delays in boys and girls enrolled in head start classrooms. *Behavioral Disorders, 26,* 26–41.

Kaiser, A. P., & Goetz, L. (1993). Enhancing communication with persons labeled severely disabled. *Journal of The Association for Persons with Severe Handicaps, 18,* 137–142.

Kame'enui, E. J., Carnine, D. W., Dixon, R. C., Simmons, D. C., & Coyne, M. D. (Eds.), (2002). *Effective teaching strategies that accommodate diverse learners* (2nd ed.). Upper Saddle River, NJ: Merrill/Prentice Hall.

Kame'enui, E. J., & Carnine, D. W. (1998). *Effective teaching strategies that accommodate diverse learners.* Upper Saddle River, NJ: Merrill/Prentice Hall.

Kame'enui, E. J., & Simmons, D. C. (1990). *Designing instructional strategies: The prevention of academic learning problems.* Upper Saddle River, NJ: Merrill/Prentice Hall.

Kamps, D. M., Dugan, E. P., Leonard, B. R., & Daoust, P. M. (1994). Enhanced small group instruction using choral responding and student interactions for children with autism and developmental disabilities. *American Journal on Mental Retardation, 99,* 60–73

Kangas, K. A., & Lloyd, L. L. (2002). Augmentative and alternative communication. In G. H. Shames & N. B. Anderson (Eds.), *Human communication disorders: An introduction* (6th ed.), (pp. 545–593). Boston: Allyn & Bacon.

Kanner, L. (1943). Autistic disturbance of affective contract. *Nervous child, 2,* 217–250.

Kanner, L. (1985). Autistic disturbance of affective contract. In A. M. Donnellan (Ed.), *Classic readings in autism* (pp. 11–53). New York: Teachers College Press.

Kaplan, S. (1988). Maintaining a gifted program. *Roeper Review, 11*(1), 35–37.

Karnes, K. B., Beauchamp, K. D. F., & Pfaus, D. B. (1993). PEECH: A nationally validated early childhood special education model. *Topics in Early Childhood Special Education, 13,* 120–135.

Katsiyannis, A., & Maag, J. W. (2001). Manifestation determination as a golden fleece. *Exceptional Children, 68,* 85–96.

Katsiyannis, A., & Yell, M. L. (2000). The Supreme Court and school health services: Cedar Rapids v. Garret F. *Exceptional Children, 66*, 317–326.

Kauffman, J. M. (1999). How we prevent the prevention of emotional and behavioral disorders. *Exceptional Children, 65*, 448–468.

Kauffman, J. M. (2001). *Characteristics of emotional and behavioral disorders of children and youth* (7th ed.). Upper Saddle River, NJ: Merrill/Prentice Hall.

Kauffman, J. M., & Hallahan, D. K. (1994). *The illusion of full inclusion: A comprehensive critique of a current special education bandwagon.* Austin, TX: PRO-ED.

Kauffman, J. M., & Krouse, J. (1981). The cult of educability: Searching for the substance of things hoped for; the evidence of things not seen. *Analysis and Intervention in Developmental Disabilities, 1*(1), 53–61.

Kaufman, A. (2000). Clothing–selection habits of teenage girls who are sighted and blind. *Journal of Visual Impairments and Blindness, 94*, 527–531.

Kavale, K. A. (2001). *Discrepancy models in the identification of learning disability* (Executive Summary). Paper presented at the LD Summit, Washington, DC. http://www.air.org/LDsummit/paper.htm

Kavale, K. A., & Forness, S. R. (1996). Social skills deficits and learning disabilities: A meta-analysis. *Journal of Learning Disabilities, 29*, 226–237.

Kavale, K. A., & Forness, S. R. (2000). History, rhetoric and reality: Analysis of the inclusion debate. *Remedial and Special Education, 21*, 279–296.

Kavale, K. A., & Mattison, P. D. (1983). One jumped off the balance beam: Meta-analysis of perceptual-motor training. *Journal of Learning Disabilities, 16*, 165–173.

Kavale, K. A., & Reese, J. H. (1992). The character of learning disabilities: An Iowa profile. *Learning Disability Quarterly, 15*, 74–94.

Kay, P. J., & Fitzgerald, M. (1997). Parents + teachers + action research = Real parent involvement. *Teaching Exceptional Children, 30*(1), 8–11.

Kazdin, A. (1987). *Conduct disorders in childhood.* Newbury Park, CA: Sage.

Kearsley, G. (2000). *Online education: Learning and teaching in cyberspace.* Belmont, CA: Wadsworth.

Keel, M. C., & Gast, D. L. (1992). Small-group instruction for students with learning disabilities: Observational and incidental learning. *Exceptional Children, 58*, 357–368.

Keith, T., Keith, P., Quirk, K., Sperduto, J., Santillo, S., & Killings, S. (1998). Longitudinal effects of parent involvement on high school grades: Similarities and differences across gender and ethnic groups. *Journal of School Psychology, 36*, 335–363.

Kelker, K., Hecimovic, A., & LeRoy, C. H. (1994). Designing a classroom and school environment for students with AIDS: A

checklist for teachers. *Teaching Exceptional Children, 26*(4), 52–55.

Keller, H. (1903). *The story of my life.* New York: Dell.

Kelly, D. J. (1998). A clinical synthesis of the "late talker" literature: Implications for service delivery. *Language, Speech and Hearing Services in the School, 29*, 76–84.

Kelly, M. L. (1990). *School-home notes.* New York: Guilford.

Kelly, S. J., Macaruso, P., & Sokol, S. M. (1997). Mental calculations in an autistic savant: A case study. *Journal of Clinical and Experimental Neuropsychology, 19*(2), 172–184.

Kennedy, C. H., & Fisher, D. (2001). *Inclusive middle schools.* Baltimore: Brookes.

Kennedy, C. H., & Itkonen, T. (1994). Some effects of regular class participation on the social contacts and social network of high school students with disabilities. *Journal of The Association for Persons with Severe Handicaps, 19*, 1–10.

Kennedy, C. H., Shukla, S., & Fryxell, D. (1997). Comparing the effects of educational placement on the social relationships of intermediate school students with severe disabilities. *Exceptional Children, 64*, 31–47.

Kephart, N. C. (1971). *The slow learner in the classroom* (2nd ed.). Columbus, OH: Merrill.

Kern, L., Mantegna, M. E., Vorndran, C. M., Bailin, D., & Hilt, A. (2001). Choice of task sequence to reduce problem behaviors. *Journal of Positive Behavior Interventions, 3*, 3–10.

Kerr, B. (1985). Smart girls, gifted women: Special guidance concerns. *Roeper Review, 8*(1), 30–33.

Kerr, B., & Cohen, S. (2001). *Smart boys.* Tempe, AZ: Great Potential Press.

Kerr, M. M., & Nelson, C. M. (2002). *Strategies for addressing behavior problems in the classroom* (4th ed.). Upper Saddle River, NJ: Merrill/Prentice Hall.

Kershner, J., Hawks, W., & Grekin, R. (1977). Megavitamins and learning disorders: A controlled double-blind experiment. Unpublished manuscript, Ontario Institute for Studies in Education.

Kim, S. H., & Arnold, M. B. (2002). Characteristics of Persons with Severe Mental Retardation. In M. Beirne-Smith, R. F. Ittenbach, & J. R. Patton, *Mental retardation* (6th ed.), (pp. 276–309). Upper Saddle River, NJ: Merrill/Prentice Hall.

Kingsley, M. (1997). The effects of a visual loss. In H. Mason & S. McCall (Eds.), *Visual impairment: Access to education for children and young people* (pp. 23–29). London: Fulton.

Kirk, S. A., McCarthy, J. J., & Kirk, W. D. (1968). Illinois Test of Psycholinguistic Abilities (rev. ed.). Urbana, IL: University of Illinois Press.

Kirkwood, R. (1997). The adolescent. In H. Mason & S. McCall (Eds.), *Visual impairment: Access to education for children and young people* (pp. 110–123). London, Fulton.

Kirsten, I. (1981). *The Oakland picture dictionary.* Wauconda, IL: Johnston.

Kishi, G. S., & Meyer, L. H. (1994). What children report and remember: A six-year follow-up of the effects of social contact between peers with and without severe disabilities, *Journal of The Association for Persons with Severe Handicaps, 19,* 277–289.

Klein, J. (1994). Supported living: Not just another "rung" on the continuum. *TASH Newsletter, 20*(7), 16–18.

Kleinman, D., Heckaman, K. A., Kimball, J. W., Possi, M. K., Grossi, T. A., & Heward, W. L. (1994, May). A comparative analysis of two forms of delayed feedback on the acquisition, generalization, and maintenance of science vocabulary by elementary students with learning disabilities. Poster presented at the 20th annual convention of the Association for Behavior Analysis, Atlanta.

Kline, F. M., Silver, L. B., & Russell, S. C. (Eds.). (2001). *The educator's guide to medical issues in the classroom.* Baltimore: Brookes.

Klingner, J. K., & Vaughn, S. (1999). Students' perceptions of instruction in inclusion classrooms: Implications for students with learning disabilities. *Exceptional Children, 66*, 23–37.

Klingner, J. K., Vaughn, S., Hughes, M. T., Schumm, J. S., & Elbaum, B. (1998). Outcomes for students with and without learning disabilities in inclusive classrooms. *Learning Disabilities Research and Practice, 13*, 153–161

Kluwin, T. N. (1985). Profiling the deaf student who is a problem in the classroom. *Adolescence, 20*, 863–875.

Kluwin, T. N. (1993). Cumulative effects of mainstreaming on the achievement of deaf adolescents. *Exceptional Children, 60*, 73–81.

Kluwin, T. N., & Moores, D. F. (1989). Mathematics achievement of hearing impaired adolescents in different placements. *Exceptional Children, 55*, 327–335.

Knecht, H. A., Whitelaw, G. M., & Nelson, P. B. (2000). *Structural variables and their relationship to background noise levels and reverberation times in unoccupied classrooms.* Manuscript in preparation (cited by Nelson, 2001).

Knitzer, J., Sternberg, Z., & Fleisch, B. (1990). *At the school house door: An examination of programs and policies for children with behavioral and emotional problems.* New York: Bank Street College of Education Press.

Knoll, J. A., & Wheeler, C. B. (2001). My home: Developing skills and supports for adult living. In R. W. Flexer, T. J. Simmons, P. Luft, & R. M. Baer, *Transition planning for secondary students with disabilities* (pp. 499–539). Upper Saddle River, NJ: Merrill/Prentice Hall.

Knowlton, E. (1998). Considerations in the design of personalized curricula supports for students with developmental disabilities. *Education and Training in Mental Retardation and Developmental Disabilities, 33*, 95–107.

Kochar, C. A., West, L. L., & Taymans, J. M. (2000). *Successful inclusion: Practical strategies for a shared responsibility*. Upper Saddle River, NJ: Merrill/Prentice Hall.

Koegel, L. K., Koegel, R. L., & Dunlap, G. (1996). *Positive behavioral support: Including people with difficult behavior in the community*. Baltimore: Brookes.

Koegel, L. K., Koegel, R. L., Harrower, J. K., & Carter, C. M. (1999). Pivotal response intervention I: Overview of approach. *Journal of The Association for Persons with Severe Handicaps, 24,* 174–185.

Koegel, R. L., & Koegel, L. (1995). *Teaching children with autism*. Baltimore: Brookes.

Koenig, A. J. (1996). Growing into literacy. In M. C. Holbrook (Ed.), *Children with visual impairments: A parents' guide* (pp. 227–257). Bethesda, MD: Woodbine House.

Koenig, A. J., & Holbrook, M. C. (2000). Ensuring high–quality instruction for students in Braille literacy programs. *Journal of Visual Impairments and Blindness, 94,* 677–694.

Kohler, P. D. (1994). On-the-job training: A curricular approach to employment. *Career Development for Exceptional Individuals, 17,* 29–40.

Kohler, P. D. (1998). Implementing a transition perspective of education: A comprehensive approach to planning and delivering secondary education and transition service. In F. R. Rusch & J. G. Chadsey (Eds.), *Beyond high school: Transition from school to work* (pp. 179–205). New York: Wadsworth.

Kohn, A. (1993a). *Punished by rewards.* Boston: Houghton Mifflin.

Kohn, A. (1993b). Why incentive plans cannot work. *Harvard Business Review, 71*(5), 54–63.

Koyanagi, C., & Gaines, S. (1993). *All systems failure: An examination of the results of neglecting the needs of children with serious emotional disturbance*. Alexandria, VA: National Mental Health Association.

Kozloff, M. A., & Rice, J. (1999). Parent and family issues: Stress and Knowledge. In P. Accardo (Ed.), *Autism: Clinical and research issues* (pp. 303–325). Timonium, MD: York.

Krajewski, J. J., & Flaherty, T. (2000). Attitudes of high school students toward individuals with mental retardation. *Mental Retardation, 38,* 154–162.

Krajewski, J. J., & Hyde, M. S. (2000). Comparison of teen attitudes toward individuals with mental retardation between 1987 and 1998: Has inclusion made a difference? *Education and Training in Mental Retardation and Developmental Disabilities, 35.*

Krebs, P., & Coultier, G. (1992). Unified sports: I've seen the light. *Palaestra, 8*(2), 42–45.

Kroth, R. L., & Edge, D. (1997). *Strategies for communicating with parents of exceptional children* (3rd ed.). Denver: Love.

Kubina, R., & Cooper, J. O. (2001). Changing learning channels: An efficient strategy to facilitate instruction and learning. *Intervention in School and Clinic, 35,* 161–166.

Kugel, R. B., & Wolfensberger, W. (Eds.). (1969). *Changing patterns in residential services for the mentally retarded*. Washington, DC: Superintendent of Documents.

Kulik, J. A. (1992a). Ability grouping and gifted students. In N. Colangelo, S. G. Assouline, & D. L. Ambroson (Eds.), *Talent development: Proceedings from the 1991 Henry B. and Jocelyn Wallace National Research Symposium on Talent Development* (pp. 261–266). Unionville, NY: Trillium.

Kulik, J. A. (1992b). An analysis of the research on ability grouping: Historical and contemporary perspectives. *Research-Based Decision Making Series*. Storrs: University of Connecticut, National Research Center on the Gifted and Talented.

Kulik, J. A., & Kulik, C. L. C. (1982). Effects of ability grouping on secondary school students: A meta-analysis of evaluation findings. *American Educational Research Journal, 19,* 415–428.

Kulik, J. A., & Kulik, C. L. C. (1984a). Effects of accelerated instruction on students. *Review of Educational Research, 54,* 409–425.

Kulik, J. A., & Kulik, C. L. C. (1984b). Synthesis of research of effects of accelerated instruction. *Educational Leadership, 42,* 84–89.

Kulik, J. A., & Kulik, C. L. C. (1987). Effects of ability grouping on student achievement. *Equity and Excellence, 23,* 22–30.

Kulik, J. A., & Kulik, C. L. C. (1990). Ability grouping and gifted students. In N. Colangelo & G. A. Davis (Eds.), *Handbook of gifted education* (pp. 178–196). Boston, MA: Allyn & Bacon.

Kuna, J. (2001). The Human Genome Project and eugenics: Identifying the impact on individuals with mental retardation. *Mental Retardation, 39,* 158–160.

Kuntze, M. (1998). Literacy and deaf children: The language question. *Topics in Language Disorders, 18*(4), 1–15.

La Paro, K. M., Pianta, R. C., & Cox, M. J. (2000). Teachers' reported transition practices for children transitioning into kindergarten and first grade. *Exceptional Children, 67,* 7–20.

Lago-Delello, E. (1998). Classroom dynamics and the development of serious emotional disturbance. *Exceptional Children, 64,* 479–492.

Lahey, B. B., Applegate, B., McBurnett, K., Biederman, J., Greenhill, L., Hynd, G. W., Barkley, R. A., Newcorn, J., Jensen, P., Richters, J., Garfinkel, B., Kerdyk, L., Frick, P. J., Ollendick, T., Perez, D., Hart, E. L., Waldman, I., & Shaffer, D. (1994). DSM-IV field trials for attention deficit hyperactivity disorder in children and adolescents. *American Journal of Psychiatry, 151,* 1673–1685.

Lahm, E. A., & Everington, C. (2002). Communication and technology supports. In L. Hamill & C. Everington, *Teaching students with moderate to severe disabilities: An applied approach for inclusive environments* (pp. 51–79). Upper Saddle River, NJ: Merrill/Prentice Hall.

Lake, J. F., & Billingsley, B. S. (2000). An analysis of factors that contribute to parent-school conflict in special education. *Remedial and Special Education, 21,* 240–251.

Lakin, K. C., Smith, J., Prouty, R., & Polister, B. (2001). State institutions during the 1990s: Changes in the number of facilities, average, daily populations, and expenditures between fiscal years 1991 and 2000. *Mental Retardation, 39,* 72–75.

Lalli, J. S., Browder, D. M., Mace, F. C., & Brown, D. K. (1993). Teacher use of descriptive analysis data to implement interventions to decrease students' problem behaviors. *Journal of Applied Behavior Analysis, 26,* 227–238.

Lambert, M. C. (2001). Effects of increasing active student responding with response cards on disruptive behavior in the classroom during math instruction for urban learners. Unpublished dissertation. Columbus, OH: The Ohio State University.

Lambert, N., Nihira, K., & Leland, H. (1993). *Adaptive Behavior Scale—School* (2nd ed.). Austin, TX: PRO-ED.

Lambie, R. (2000). *Family systems within educational contexts: Understanding at-risk special needs students*. Denver: Love.

Lancaster, J. (1806). Improvement in education. London: Collins & Perkins.

Landesman, S., & Ramey, C. T. (1989). Developmental psychology and mental retardation: Integrating scientific principles with treatment practices. *American Psychologist, 44,* 409–415.

Landy, S. (2002). *Pathways to competence: Encouraging healthy social and emotional development in young children*. Baltimore: Brookes.

Lane, H. L. (1988). Is there a "psychology of the deaf"? *Exceptional Children, 55,* 7–19.

Lane, H. L., & Bahan, B. (1998). Ethics of cochlear implantation in young children: A review and reply from a Deaf-World perspective. *Otolaryngology Head and Neck Surgery, 119,* 297–308.

Langdon H. W., Novak, J. M., Quintanar, R. S. (2000). Setting the teaching-learning wheel in motion in assessing language minority students. *Multicultural Perspectives, 2*(2), 3–9.

Lanigan, K. J., Audette, R. M. L., Dreier, A. E., & Kobersy, M. R. (2001). In C. E. Finn, A. J. Rotherham, & C. R. Hokanson, Jr. (Eds.), *Rethinking special education for a new century* (pp. 213–232). Washington, DC: Thomas B. Fordham Foundation and the Progressive Policy Institute.

Larrivee, L. S., & Catts, H. W. (1999). Early reading achievement in children with expressive phonological disorders. *American Journal of Speech-Language Pathology, 8*(2), 118–128.

Larson, S. A., & Lakin, K. C. (1989). Deinstitutionalization of persons with mental retardation. *Journal of The Association for Persons with Severe Handicaps, 14,* 324–332.

Larson, S. A., Lakin, K. C., Anderson, L., Kwak, N., Hak Lee, J., & Anderson, D. (2001). Prevalence of mental retardation and developmental disabilities: Estimates from the 1994/1995 National Health Interview Survey Disability Supplements. *American Journal of Mental Retardation, 105,* 231–252.

Lazarus, B. D. (1991). Guided notes, review, and achievement of secondary students with learning disabilities in mainstream content courses. *Education and Treatment of Children, 14,* 112–127.

Lazarus, B. D. (1996). Flexible skeletons: Guided notes for adolescents with mild disabilities. *Teaching Exceptional Children, 28*(3), 37–40.

Leach, D. J., & Siddall, S. W. (1992). Parental involvement in the teaching of reading: A comparison of Hearing Reading, Paired Reading, Pause, Prompt, Praise and Direct Instruction methods. *ADI News, 11*(2), 14–19.

Learning Disabilities of America Association. (1993, March/April). Position paper on full inclusion of all students with learning disabilities in the regular classroom. *LDA Newsbrief, 28*(2), 1.

Lee, M., Storey, K., Anderson, J. L., Goetz, L., & Zivolich, S. (1997). The effect of mentoring versus job coach instruction on integration in supported employment settings. *Journal of The Association for Persons with Severe Handicaps, 22,* 151–158.

Lehr, D. H., & Macurdy, S. (1994). Meeting special health care needs of students. In M. Agran, N. E. Marchand-Martella, & R. C. Martella (Eds.), *Promoting health and safety: Skills for independent living* (pp. 71–84). Pacific Grove, CA: Brooks/Cole.

Lehr, D. H., & McDaid, P. (1993). Opening the door further: Integrating students with complex health needs. *Focus on Exceptional Children, 25*(6), 1–7.

Leigh, S. A., & Barclay, L. A. (2000). High school Braille readers: Achieving academic success. *RE:view, 32,* 123–131.

Lenz, B. K., & Bulgren, J. A. (1995). Promoting learning in content classes. In P. A. Cegelka & W. H. Berdine (Eds.), *Effective instruction for students with learning problems* (pp. 385–417). Needham Heights, MA: Allyn & Bacon.

Leonard, C. M. (2001). Imaging brain structure in children: Differentiating language disability and reading disability. *Learning Disability Quarterly, 24,* 158–176.

Leone, P. E., & Meisel, S. (1997). Improving education services for students in detention and confinement facilities. *Children's Legal Rights Journal, 17,* (1), 2–12.

Leone, P. E., Rutherford, R. B., & Nelson, C. M. (1991). *Special education and juvenile corrections.* Reston, VA: Council for Exceptional Children.

Lepper, M. R., Keavney, M., & Drake, M. (1996). Intrinsic motivation and extrinsic rewards: A commentary on Cameron and Pierce's Meta-Analysis. *Review of Educational Research, 66,* 5–32.

Lerro, M. (1994). Teaching adolescents about AIDS. *Teaching Exceptional Children, 26*(4), 49–51.

Leung, E. K. (1988). Cultural and acultural commonalities and diversities among Asian Americans: Identification and programming considerations. In A. A. Ortiz & B. A. Ramirez (Eds.), *Schools and the culturally diverse exceptional student: Promising practices and future directions* (pp. 86–95). Reston, VA: Council for Exceptional Children.

Levack, N., Stone, G., & Bishop, V. (1994). *Low vision: A resource guide with adaptations for students with visual impairments* (2nd ed.) Austin, TX: Texas School for the Blind and Visually Impaired.

Levine, K., & Wharton, R. (2000). Williams syndrome and happiness. *American Journal of Mental Retardation, 105,* 363–371.

Lewis, M. S., & Jackson, D. W. (2001). Television literacy: Comprehension of program content using closed captions for the deaf. *Journal of Deaf Studies and Deaf Education, 5,* 43–53.

Lewis, R. B., & Doorlag, D. H. (1999). *Teaching special students in general education classrooms* (5th ed.). Upper Saddle River, NJ: Merrill/Prentice Hall.

Lewis, T., & Sugai, G. (1999). *Safe schools: School-wide discipline practices.* Reston, VA: Council for Exceptional Children.

Lian, M. G. J., & Fontánez-Phelan, S. M. (2001). Perceptions of Latino parents regarding cultural and linguistic issues and advocacy for children with disabilities. *Journal of The Association for Persons with Severe Handicaps, 26,* 189–194.

Lichtenstein, E. H. (1998). The relationships between reading processes and English skills of deaf college students. *Journal of Deaf Studies and Deaf Education, 3,* 80–134.

Lieberth, A. K. (1991). Use of scaffolded dialogue journals to teach writing to deaf students. *Teaching English to Deaf and Second-Language Students, 9*(1), 10–13.

Lignugaris/Kraft, B., Marchand-Martella, N. & Martella, R. C. (2001). Writing better goals and short-term objectives or benchmarks. *Teaching Exceptional Children, 34*(1), 52–58.

Lignugaris/Kraft, B., Rule, S., Salzberg, C. L., & Stowitschek, J. J. (1988). Social-vocational skills of handicapped and nonhandicapped adults at work. *Journal of Employment Counseling, 23,* 20–31.

Lin, S. (2000). Coping and adaptations in families of children with cerebral palsy. *Exceptional Children, 66,* 201–218.

Lindfors, J. W. (1987). *Children's language and learning* (2nd ed.). Upper Saddle River, NJ: Prentice Hall.

Lindley, L. (1990, August). Defining TASH: A mission statement. *TASH Newsletter, 16*(8), 1.

Lindsley, O. R. (1996). The four free-operant freedoms. *Behavior Analyst, 19,* 199–210.

Lindstrom, L. E., Benz, M. R., & Johnson, M. D. (1997). From school grounds to coffee grounds: An introduction to school-based enterprises. *Teaching Exceptional Children, 29*(4), 20–24.

Ling, D. (1986). Devices and procedures for auditory learning. *Volta Review, 88*(5), 19–28.

Lipsey, M. W., & Derzon, J. H. (1998). Predictors of violent or serious delinquency in adolescence and early adulthood: A synthesis of longitudinal research. In R. Loeber & D. P. Farrington (Eds.), *Serious and violent juvenile offenders: Risk factors and successful interventions* (pp. 6–105). Thousand Oaks, CA: Sage.

Lipsky, D. K., & Garter, A. (1991). Restructuring for quality. In J. W. Lloyd, A. C. Repp, & N. N. Singh (Eds.), *The regular education initiative: Alternative perspectives on concepts, issues, and models* (pp. 43–56), Sycamore, IL: Sycamore.

Liptak, G. S. (1997). Neural tube defects. In M. L. Batshaw (Ed.), *Children with disabilities* (4th ed.) (pp. 529–552). Baltimore: Brookes.

Little Soldier, L. (1990). The education of Native American students: Where makes a difference. *Equity and Excellence, 24*(4), 66–69.

Livingston-White, D., Utter, C., & Woodard, Q. E. (1985). Follow-up study of visually impaired students of the Michigan School for the Blind. *Journal of Visual Impairment and Blindness, 79,* 150–153.

Lloyd, J. W., Kauffman, J. M., & Gansneder, B. (1987). Differential teacher response to descriptions of aberrant behavior. In R. B. Rutherford, C. M. Nelson, & S. R. Forness (Eds.), *Severe behavior disorders of children and youth* (pp. 41–52). Boston: College Hill Press.

Lloyd, L. (1999). Multi-age classes and high ability students. *Review of Educational Research, 69*(2), 187–212.

Lo, Y., & Cartledge, G. (in press). More than just reports: Using office referral data to improve school discipline programs. *Principal Magazine.*

Loeber, R. & Farrington, D. (1998). *Serious and violent juvenile offenders: Risk factors and successful interventions.* Beverly Hills, CA: Sage.

Logan, K. R., Hansen, C. D., Nieminen, P. K., & Wright, E. H. (2001). Student support teams: Helping students succeed in general education classrooms or working to place students in special education? *Education and Training in Mental Retardation and Developmental Disabilities, 36,* 280–292.

Lohrmann-O'Rouke, S., & Browder, D. M. (1998). Empirically based methods to assess the preferences of individuals with severe disabilities. *American Journal on Mental Retardation, 103,* 146–161.

Louis Harris and Associates. (2000). *The National Organization of Disability/Harris survey program on participation and attitudes: Survey of Americans with disabilities.* New York: Author.

Lovaas, O. I. (1987). Behavioral treatment and normal educational and intellectual functioning in young autistic children. *Journal of Consulting and Clinical Psychology, 55,* 3–9.

Lovaas, O. I. (1994, October). Comments made during Ohio State University teleconference on applied behavior analysis, The Ohio State University, Columbus.

Lovett, M. W., Steinbach, K. A., & Frijters, J. C. (2000). Remediating the core deficits of developmental reading disability: A double–deficit perspective. *Journal of Learning Disabilities, 33,* 334–358.

Lovitt, T. C. (1977). *In spite of my resistance ... I've learned from children.* Upper Saddle River, NJ: Merrill/Prentice Hall.

Lovitt, T. C. (1982). *Because of my persistence ... I've learned from children.* Upper Saddle River, NJ: Merrill/Prentice Hall.

Lovitt, T. C. (2000). *Preventing school failure: Tactics for teaching adolescents* (2nd ed.). Austin, TX: PRO-ED.

Lowenthal, B. (2001). *Abuse and neglect: The educator's guide to the identification and prevention of child maltreatment.* Baltimore: Brookes.

Luckasson, R., & Reeve, A. (2001). Naming, defining, and classifying in mental retardation. *Mental Retardation, 39,* 47–52.

Luckasson, R., Borthwick-Duffy, S., Buntinx, W. H. E., Coulter, D. L., Craig, E. M., Reeve, A., Schalock, R. L., Snell, M. E., Spitalnik, D. M., Spreat, S., & Tasse, M. J. (in press) *Mental retardation: Definition, classification, and systems of supports* (10th ed.) Washington, DC: American Association on Mental Retardation.

Luckner, J. (1994). Developing independent and responsible behaviors in students who are deaf or hard of hearing. *Teaching Exceptional Children, 26*(2), 13–17.

Lue, M. S. (2001). *A survey of communication disorders for the classroom teacher.* Boston: Allyn & Bacon.

Luiselli, J. K., & Downing, J. N. (1980). Improving a student's arithmetic performance using feedback and reinforcement procedures. *Education and Treatment of Children, 3,* 45–49.

Luterman, D. (1999). Emotional aspects of hearing loss. *The Volta Review, 99*(5), 75–83.

Lutzker, J. R., & Campbell, R. (1994). *Ecobehavioral family interventions in developmental disabilities.* Pacific Grove, CA: Brooks/Cole.

Lynas, W. (1986). *Integrating the handicapped into ordinary schools: A study of hearing-impaired pupils.* London: Croom Helm.

Lynch, E., & Hanson, M. (1998). *Developing cross-cultural competence* (2nd ed.). Baltimore: Brookes.

Lyon, G. R. (1995). Toward a definition of dyslexia. *Annals of Dyslexia, 45,* 3–27.

Lytle, R. K., & Bordin, J. (2001). Enhancing the IEP team: Strategies for parents and professionals. *Teaching Exceptional Children, 33*(5), 28–33.

Maag, J. W. (2000). Managing resistance. *Intervention in School and Clinic, 35,* 131–140.

Maag, J. W. (2001). Rewarded by punishment: Reflections on the disuse of positive reinforcement in schools. *Exceptional Children, 67,* 173–186.

Maag, J. W., & Reid, R. (1994). Attention-Deficit Hyperactivity Disorder: A functional approach to assessment and treatment. *Behavioral Disorders, 20,* 5–23.

Maccini, P., & Hughes, C. A. (2000). Effects of problem-solving strategy on the algebraic subtraction of integers by secondary students with learning disabilities. *Learning Disabilities Research and Practice, 15,* 10–15.

Maccini, P., & Ruhl, K. L. (2000). Effects of a graduated instructional sequence on the introductory algebra performance of secondary students with learning disabilities. *Education and Treatment of Children, 23,* 465–489.

MacGinitie, W. H., MacGinitie, R. K., Maria, K., & Dreyer, L. G. (2000). *Gates-MacGinitie Reading Tests-Fourth Edition.* Itasca, IL: Riverside.

Macht, J. (1998). *Special education's failed system: A question of eligibility.* Westport, CT: Bergin & Garvey.

Macias, C. M., Best, S., Bigge, J., & Musante, P. (2001). Adaptations in physical education, leisure education, and recreation. In J. L. Bigge, S. J. Best, & K. W. Heller, *Teaching individuals with physical, health, or multiple disabilities* (4th ed.), (pp. 467–503) Upper Saddle River, NJ: Merrill/Prentice Hall.

MacMillan, D. L., & Reschly, D. J. (1998). Overrepresentation of minority students: The case for greater specificity or reconsideration of the variables examined. *Journal of Special Education, 32,* 15–24.

MacMillan, D. L., Gresham, F. M., & Siperstein, G. N. (1993). Conceptual and psychometric concerns about the 1992 AAMR definition of mental retardation. *American Journal on Mental Retardation, 98,* 325–335.

MacMillan, D. L., Gresham, F. M., Bocian, K. M., & Lambros, K. M. (1998). Current plight of borderline students: Where do they belong? *Education and Training in Mental Retardation and Developmental Disabilities, 33,* 83–94.

MacMillan, D. L., Gresham, F. M., Siperstein, G. N., & Bocian, K. M. (1996). The labyrinth of IDEA: School decisions on referred students with subaverage general intelligence. *American Journal on Mental Retardation, 101,* 161–174.

Madsen, C. H., Jr., Becker, W. C., & Thomas, D. R. (1968). Rules, praise, and ignoring: Elements of elementary classroom control. *Journal of Applied Behavior Analysis, 1,* 343–353.

Maestas y Moores, J., & Moores, D. F. (1980). Language training with the young deaf child. In D. Bricker (Ed.), *Early language intervention with handicapped children.* San Francisco: Jossey-Bass.

Maheady, L., Harper, G. F., & Mallete, B. (2001). Peer-mediated instruction and interventions and students with mild

disabilities. *Remedial and Special Education, 22,* 4–14.

Maheady, L., Mallete, B., Harper, G. F., & Saca, K. (1991). Heads together: A peer-mediated option for improving the academic achievement of heterogeneous learning groups. *Remedial and Special Education, 12*(2), 25–33.

Mahr, G., & Leith, W. (1992). Psychogenic stuttering of adult onset. *Journal of Speech and Hearing Research, 35,* 283–286.

Mahshie, S. N. (1995). *Educating deaf children bilingually.* Washington, DC: Gallaudet University Press.

Maker, C. J. (1993). Creativity, intelligence, and problem solving: A definition and design for cross-cultural research and measurement related to giftedness. *Gifted Education International, 9*(2), 68–77.

Maker, C. J. (1996). Identification of gifted minority students: A national problem, needed changes, and a promising solution. *Gifted Child Quarterly, 40,* 41–50

Maker, C. J. (1997). DISCOVER problem solving assessment. *Quest, 8*(1), 3, 4, 7.

Maker, C. J., Nielson, A. B., & Rogers, J. A. (1994). Giftedness, diversity, and problem-solving. *Teaching Exceptional Children, 27*(1), 4–19.

Malian, I. M., & Love, L. L. (1998). Leaving high school: An ongoing transition study. *Teaching Exceptional Children, 30*(3), 4–10.

Mangold, S. (1982). Art experience is fundamental to create thinking. In S. Mangold (Ed.), *A teacher's guide to the special educational needs of blind and visually handicapped children.* New York: American Foundation for the Blind.

Mank, D. M., & Horner, R. H. (1987). Self-recruited feedback: A cost-effective procedure for maintaining behavior. *Research in Developmental Disabilities, 8,* 91–112.

Mank, D., Cioffi, A., & Yovanoff, P. (1998). Employment outcomes for people with severe disabilities: Opportunities for improvement. *Mental Retardation, 36,* 205–216.

Mank, D., Cioffi, A., & Yovanoff, P. (1999). The impact of coworker involvement with supported employees on wage and integrated outcomes. *Mental Retardation, 37,* 383–394.

Mank, D., Cioffi, A., & Yovanoff, P. (2000). Direct support in supported employment and its relation to job typicalness, coworker involvement, and employment outcomes. *Mental Retardation, 38,* 506–516.

Mann, D. (1996). Serious play. *Teachers College Record, 97*(3), 447–469.

Marchisan, M. L., & Alber, S. R. (2001). The write way: Tips for teaching the writing process to resistant writers. *Intervention in School and Clinic, 36*(3), 154–162.

Margolis, H., & Brannigan, G. (1990). Calming the storm. *Learning, 18,* 40–42.

Markwardt, F. C., Jr. (1998). *Peabody Individual Achievement Test-Revised.* Circle Pines, MN: American Guidance Services.

Marland, S. (1972). Education of the gifted and talented (Vol. 1). [Report to the U. S. Congress by the U. S. Commissioner of Education.] Washington, DC: Office of Education (DHEW). (ERIC Document Reproduction Service No. ED 056 243)

Marschark, M., & Clark, M. D. (Eds.) (1998). *Psychological perspectives on deafness* (Vol. 2). Mahwah, NJ: Erlbaum.

Marsh, L. G., & Cooke, N. L. (1996). The effects of using manipulatives in teaching math problem solving to students with learning disabilities. *Learning Disabilities Research and Practice, 11*(1), 58–65.

Martella, R. C., Marchand-Martella, N. E., Young, K. R., & MacFarlane, C. A. (1995). Determining the collateral effects of peer tutoring on a student with severe disabilities. *Education and Treatment of Children, 19,* 170–191.

Martens, B. K., Lochner, D. G., & Kelly, S. Q. (1992). The effects of variable interval reinforcement on academic engagement: A demonstration of matching theory. *Journal of Applied Behavior Analysis, 25,* 143–151.

Martin, J. E., & Marshall, L. H. (1995). ChoiceMaker: A comprehensive self-determined transition program. *Intervention in School and Clinic, 30,* 147–156.

Martin, J. E., Hughes, W., Huber Marshall, L., Jerman, P., & Maxson, L. L. (1999). *Choosing personal goals.* Longmont, CO: Sopris West.

Martin, J. R. (1985). *Reclaiming a conversation: The ideal of the educated woman.* New Haven: Yale University Press.

Martin, S. L., Ramey, C. T., & Ramey, S. L. (1990). The prevention of intellectual impairment in children of impoverished families: Findings of a randomized trial of educational daycare. *American Journal of Public Health, 80,* 844–847.

Masataka, N. (1996). Perception of mothers in a signed language by 6-month-old deaf infants. *Developmental Psychology, 32,* 874–879.

Mason, H. (1997). Common eye defects and their educational implications. In H. Mason & S. McCall (Eds.), *Visual impairment: Access to education for children and young people* (pp. 38–50). London: Fulton.

Mastropieri, M. A., & Scruggs, T. E. (2000). *The inclusive classroom: Strategies for effective instruction.* Upper Saddle River, NJ: Merrill/Prentice Hall.

Mather, N., & Goldstein, S. (2001). *Learning disabilities and challenging behaviors.* Baltimore: Brookes.

Matson, J. L. (Ed.). (1994). *Autism in children and adults: Etiology, assessment, and intervention.* Pacific Grove, CA: Brooks/Cole.

Maughan, B., Pickles, A., Hagell, A., Rutter, M., & Yule, W. (1996). Reading problems and antisocial behavior: Developmental trends in comorbidity. *Journal of Child Psychology and Psychiatry, 37,* 405–418.

Mauk, J. E., Reber, M., & Batshaw, M. L. (1997). Autism. In M. L. Batshaw (Ed.), *Children with disabilities* (pp. 425–448). Baltimore: Brookes.

Maurice, C., Green, G., & Foxx, R. M. (2001). *Making a difference: Behavioral intervention for autism.* Austin, TX: PRO-ED.

Mayer, C., & Akamatsu, C. T. (1999). Bilingual-bicultural models of literacy education for deaf students: Considering the claims. *Journal of Deaf Studies and Deaf Education, 4,* 1–8.

Mayer, G. R. (1995). Preventing antisocial behavior in schools. *Journal of Applied Behavior Analysis, 28,* 467–478.

Mayer-Johnson, R. (1986). *The picture communications symbols—Book 1.* Solana Beach, CA: Mayer-Johnson.

McAdam, D. B., O'Cleirigh, C. M., & Cuvo, A. J. (1993). Self-monitoring and verbal feedback to reduce stereotypic body rocking in a congenitally blind adult. *RE:view, 24,* 163–172.

McCauley, R. J. (2001). *Assessment of language disorders in children.* Mahwah, NJ: Erlbaum.

McConnell, S. R. (1994). Social context, social validity, and program outcome in early intervention. In R. Gardner III, D. M. Sainato, J. O. Cooper, T. E. Heron, W. L. Heward, J. Eshleman, & T. A. Grossi (Eds.), B*ehavior analysis in education: Focus on measurably superior instruction* (pp. 75–85). Pacific Grove, CA: Brooks/Cole.

McCormick, M. E., & Wolf, J. S. (1993). Intervention programs for gifted girls. *Roeper Review, 16,* 85–88.

McCuin, D., & Cooper, J. O. (1994). Teaching keyboarding and computer skills to persons with developmental disabilities. *Behaviorology, 2*(1), 63–78.

McDermott, S. (1994). Explanatory model to describe school district prevalence rates for mental retardation and learning disabilities. *American Journal on Mental Retardation, 99,* 175–185.

McEachin, J. J., Smith, T., & Lovaas, I. O. (1993). Long-term outcome for children with autism who received early intensive behavioral treatment. *American Journal on Mental Retardation, 97,* 359–372.

McEvoy, A., & Welker, R. (2000). Antisocial behavior, academic failure, and school climate: A critical review. *Journal of Emotional and Behavioral Disorders, 8,* 130–140.

McEvoy, M. A., & Yoder, P. (1993). Interventions to promote social skills and emotional development. In *DEC Recommended Practices* (pp. 77–81). Reston, VA: Council for Exceptional Children, Division for Early Childhood.

McGee, G. G., Krantz, P. J., Mason, D. & McClannahan, L. E. (1983). A modified incidental teaching procedure for autistic youth: Acquisition and generalization of receptive object labels. *Journal of Applied Behavior Analysis, 16,* 329–338.

McGee, G. G., Morrier, M. J., & Daly, T. (1999). An incidental teaching approach to early intervention for toddlers with autism. *Journal of the Association for the Severely Handicapped, 24,* 133–146.

McGee, J. J. (1992). Gentle teaching's assumptions and paradigm. *Journal of Applied Behavior Analysis, 25,* 869–872.

McGee, J. J., & Gonzalez, L. (1990). Gentle teaching and the practice of human interdependence: A preliminary group study of 15 persons with severe behavioral disorders and their caregivers. In A. C. Repp & N. N. Singh (Eds.), *Current perspectives on the use of nonaversive and aversive interventions for persons with developmental disabilities* (pp. 237–254). Sycamore, IL: Sycamore.

McGee, J. J., & Menolascino, F. J. (1991). *Beyond gentle teaching: A nonaversive approach to helping those in need.* New York: Plenum.

McGill, T., & Vogle, L. K. (2001). Driver's education for students with physical disabilities. *Exceptional Children, 67,* 455–466.

McGonigel, M. J., Woodruff, G., & Roszmann-Millican, M. (1994). The transdisciplinary team: A model for family-centered early intervention. In L. J. Johnson, R. J. Gallagher, M. J. LaMontagne, J. B. Jordan, J. J. Gallagher, P. L. Hutinger, & M. B. Karnes (Eds.) *Meeting early intervention challenges: Issues from birth to three* (pp. 95–131). Baltimore: Brookes.

McHale, S. M., & Gamble, W. W. (1989). Sibling relationships of children with disabled and nondisabled brothers and sisters. *Developmental Psychology, 25*(3), 421–429.

McHutchion, M. E. (1991). Student bereavement: A guide for school personnel. *Journal of School Health, 61,* 363–366.

McIntosh, R., Vaughn, S., Schumm, J. S., Haager, D., & Lee, O. (1993). Observations of students with learning disabilities in general education classrooms. *Exceptional Children, 60,* 249–261.

McIntyre, T. (1993a).Behaviorally disordered youth in correctional settings: Prevalence, programming, and teacher training. *Behavioral Disorders, 18,* 167–176.

McIntyre, T. (1993b). Reflections on the new definition for emotional or behavioral disorders: Who still falls through the cracks and why. *Behavioral Disorders, 18,* 148–160.

McIntyre, T., & Forness, S. R. (1996). Is there a new definition yet or are kids still seriously emotionally disturbed? *Beyond Behavior, 7*(3), 4–9.

McKinley, A. M., & Warren, S. F. (2000). The effectiveness of cochlear implants for children with prelingual deafness. *Journal of Early Intervention, 23,* 252–263.

McLaren, J., & Bryson, S. E. (1987). Review of recent epidemiological studies of mental retardation: Prevalence, related disorders and etiology. *American Journal on Mental Retardation, 92,* 243–254.

McLaughlin, S. (1998). *Introduction to language development*. San Diego: Singular.

McLean, M., Bailey, D. B., & Wolery, M. (1996). *Assessing infants and preschoolers with special needs* (2nd ed.) Upper Saddle River, NJ: Merrill/Prentice Hall.

McLeskey, J. (1992). Students with learning disabilities at primary, intermediate, and secondary grade levels: Identification and characteristics. *Learning Disability Quarterly, 15*, 13–19.

McLone, D. G., & Ito, J. (1998). *An introduction to spina bifida*. Chicago: Children's Memorial Hospital Spina Bifida Team.

McReynolds, L. V. (1990). Articulation and phonological disorders. In G. H. Shames & E. H. Wiig (Eds.), *Human communication disorders* (3rd ed.) (pp. 30–73). Upper Saddle River, NJ: Merrill/Prentice Hall.

Meadow-Orlans, K. P. (1985). Social and psychological effects of hearing loss in adulthood: A literature review. In H. Orlans (Ed.), *Adjustment to adult hearing loss* (pp. 35–57). San Diego: College-Hill.

Meadow-Orlans, K. P., Mertens, D. M., Sass-Lehrer, M. A., & Scott-Olson, K. (1997). Support services for parents and their children who are deaf or hard of hearing. *American Annals of the Deaf, 142,* 278–288.

Meadows, N. B., Neel, R. S., Scott, C. M., & Parker, G. (1994). Academic performance, social competence, and mainstream accommodations: A look at mainstreamed and nonmainstreamed students with serious behavioral disorders. *Behavioral Disorders, 19*, 170–180.

Mechling, L. C., & Gast, D. L. (1997). Combination audio/visual self-prompting system for teaching chained tasks to students with intellectual disabilities. *Education and Training in Mental Retardation and Developmental Disabilities, 32,* 138–153.

Mehler, J., Jusczyk, P. W., Lambertz, G., Halsted, N., Bettoncini, J., & Ameil-Tison, C. (1988). A precursor of language acquisition in young infants. *Cognition, 29,* 143–178.

Menlove, R. R., Hudson, P. J., & Suter, D. (2001). A field of IEP dreams: Increasing general education teacher participation in the IEP development process. *Teaching Exceptional Children, 33*(5), 28–33.

Mercer, C. D. (1997). *Students with learning disabilities* (5th ed.). Upper Saddle River, NJ: Merrill/Prentice Hall.

Mercer, C. D., & Mercer, A. (2001). *Teaching students with learning disabilities* (6th ed.). Upper Saddle River, NJ: Merrill/Prentice Hall.

Mercer, C. D., Jordan, L., Allsopp, D. H., & Mercer, A. R. (1995). Learning disabilities definitions and criteria used by state education departments. Unpublished manuscript.

Merrill, E. C. (1990). Attentional resource allocation and mental retardation. In N.

W. Bray (Ed.), *International review of research in mental retardation: Vol. 16* (pp. 51–88). San Diego: Academic Press.

Merritt, D. D., & Culatta, B. (1998). *Language intervention in the classroom*. San Diego: Singular.

Mervis, C. B., Klein-Tasman, B. P., & Mastin, M. E. (2001). Adaptive behavior of 4-through 8-year-old children with Williams syndrome. *American Journal of Mental Retardation, 106,* 82–93.

Meyer, D. (1995). *Uncommon fathers: Reflections on raising a child with a disability*. Bethesda, MD: Woodbine House.

Meyer, L. H., Cole, D. A., McQuarter, R., & Reichle, J. (1990). Validation of the Assessment of Social Competence (ASC) for children and young adults with developmental disabilities. *Journal of The Association for Persons with Severe Handicaps, 15,* 57–68.

Meyers, A. R. (2000). From function to felicitude: Physical disability and the search for happiness in health services research. *American Journal on Mental Retardation, 105,* 342–351.

Miller, A. D., Barbetta, P. M., & Heron, T. E. (1994). START tutoring: Designing, training, implementing, adapting, and evaluating tutoring programs for school and home settings. In R. Gardner III, D. M. Sainato, J. O. Cooper, T. E. Heron, W. L. Heward, J. Eshleman, & T. A. Grossi (Eds.), *Behavior analysis in education: Focus on measurably superior instruction* (pp. 75–85). Pacific Grove, CA: Brooks/Cole.

Miller, A. D., Hall, S. W., & Heward, W. L. (1995). Effects of sequential 1-minute time trials with and without intertrial feedback and self-correction on general and special education students' fluency with math facts. *Journal of Behavioral Education, 5,* 319–345.

Miller, G. (1993). Expanding vocational options. *RE:view, 25*(1), 27–31.

Miller, W. H. (1985). The role of residential schools for the blind in educating visually impaired students. *Journal of Visual Impairment and Blindness, 79,* 160.

Minner, S., Beane, A., & Prater, J. (1986). Try telephone answering machines. *Teaching Exceptional Children, 19*(1), 62–63.

Minor, R. J. (2001). The experience of living with and using a dog guide. *RE:view, 32,* 183–190.

Moaven, L. D., Gilbert, G. L., Cunningham, A. L., & Rawlinson, W. D. (1995). Amniocentesis to diagnose congenital cytomegalovirus infection. *Medical Journal of Australia, 162,* 334–335.

Montgomery, D. (2001). Increasing Native American Indian enrollment in gifted programs in rural schools. *Psychology in the Schools, 38*(5), 467–475.

Montgomery, W. (2001). Creating culturally responsive, inclusive classroooms. *Teaching Exceptional Children, 33*(4), 4–9.

Moody, S. W., Vaughn, S., Hughes, M. T., & Fischer, M. (2000). Reading instruction in

the resource room: Set up for failure. *Exceptional Children, 66,* 305–316.

Moon, M. S. (1994). *Making school and community recreation fun for everyone: Places and ways to integrate*. Baltimore: Brookes.

Moon, M. S., & Inge, K. (1993). Vocational preparation and transition. In M. E. Snell (Ed.), *Instruction of students with severe disabilities* (4th ed.) (pp. 556–587). Upper Saddle River, NJ: Merrill/Prentice Hall.

Moon, M. S., & Inge, K. (2000). Vocational preparation and transition. In M. E. Snell & F. Brown (Eds.), *Instruction of students with severe disabilities* (5th ed.), (pp. 591–628). Upper Saddle River, NJ: Merrill/Prentice Hall.

Moores, D. F. (1993). Total inclusion/zero rejection models in general education: Implication for deaf children. *American Annals of the Deaf, 138,* 251.

Moores, D. F. (2001). *Educating the deaf: Psychology, principles, and practices* (5th ed.). Boston: Houghton Mifflin.

Morgan, C. D., & Murray, H. A. (1935). A method for investigating fantasies: The Thematic Apperception Test. *Archives of Neurology and Psychiatry, 34,* 289–306.

Morgan, D. P., & Jensen, W. R. (1988). *Teaching behaviorally disordered students*. Upper Saddle River, NJ: Merrill/Prentice Hall.

Morgan, D., Young, K. R., Goldstein, S. (1983). Teaching behaviorally disordered students to increase teacher attention and praise in mainstreamed classrooms. *Behavioral Disorders, 8,* 265–273.

Morris, R. J., & Kratochwill, T. R. (1998). Childhood fears and phobias. In R. J. Morris & T. R. Kratochwill (Eds.), *The practice of child therapy* (3rd ed.). Boston: Allyn & Bacon.

Morrison, G. S. (2001). *Early childhood education today* (8th ed.). Upper Saddle River, NJ: Merrill/Prentice Hall.

Morrison, R. S. (1999). *Effects of correspondence training with photographic activity schedules on toy play by young children with pervasive developmental disorders*. Unpublished doctoral dissertation, The Ohio State University, Columbus.

Morse, T. E., & Schuster, J. W. (2000). Teaching elementary students with moderate intellectual disabilities how to shop for groceries. *Exceptional Children, 66,* 273–288.

Morse, W. C. (1976). Worksheet on life-space interviewing for teachers. In N. Long, W. Morse, & R. Newman (Eds.), *Conflict in the classroom* (pp. 337–341). Belmont, CA: Wadsworth.

Morse, W. C. (1985). *The education and treatment of socioemotionally impaired children and youth*. Syracuse, NY: Syracuse University Press.

Morten, W. L., Heward, W. L., & Alber, S. R. (1998). When to self-correct?: A comparison of two procedures on spelling performance. *Journal of Behavioral Education, 8,* 321–335.

Mortweet, S. L., Utley, C. A., Walker, D., Dawson, H. L., Delquadri, J. C., Reddy, S. S., Greenwood, C. R., Hamilton, S., & Ledford, D. (1999). Classwide peer tutoring: Teaching students with mild mental retardation in inclusive classrooms. *Exceptional Children, 65,* 524–536.

Moser, H. W. (2000). Genetics and gene therapies. In M. L. Wehmeyer & J. R. Patton (Eds.), *Mental Retardation in the 21st century* (pp. 235–250). Austin, TX: PRO-ED.

Most, T., & Greenbank, A. (2000). Auditory, visual, and auditory-visual perception of emotions by adolescents with and without learning disabilities, and their relationship to social skills. *Learning Disabilities Research and Practice, 15,* 171–178.

Mow, S. (1973). How do you dance without music? In D. Watson (Ed.), *Readings on deafness* (pp. 20–30). New York: New York University School of Education, Deafness Research and Training Center.

Mudford, O. C. (1995). Review of the gentle teaching data. *American Journal on Mental Retardation, 99,* 345–355.

Mudre, L. H., & McCormick, S. (1989). Effects of meaning-focused cues on underachieving readers' context use, self-corrections, and literal comprehension. *Reading Research Quarterly, 14,* 89–113.

Mueller, R. A., & Courchesne, E. (2000). Autism's home in the brain: Reply. *Neurology, 54*(1), 270.

Mulick, J. A., & Antonak, R. (Eds.). (1994). *Life styles: Transitions in mental retardation* (vol. 5). Norwood, NJ: Ablex.

Mull, C., Sitlington, P. L., & Alper, S. (2001). Postsecondary education for students with learning disabilities: A synthesis of the literature. *Exceptional Children, 68,* 97–118.

Munk, D. D., & Repp, A. C. (1994). The relationship between instructional variables and problem behavior: A review. *Exceptional Children, 60,* 390–401.

Munk, D. D., Van Laarhoven, T., Goodman, S., & Repp, A. C. (1998). Small-group Direct Instruction for students with moderate to severe disabilities. In A. Hilton & R. Ringlaben (Eds.), *Best and promising practices in developmental disabilities* (pp. 127–138). Austin, TX: PRO-ED.

Murdick, N., Gartin, B., & Crabtree, T. (2002). *Special education law.* Upper Saddle River, NJ: Merrill/Prentice Hall.

Murray, C., Goldstein, D. E., Nourse, S., & Edgar, E. (2000). The postsecondary school attendance and completion rates of high school graduates with learning disabilities. *Learning Disabilities Research and Practice, 15,* 119–127.

Myers, P. I., & Hammill, D. D. (1982). *Methods for learning disorders* (2nd ed.). New York: John Wiley.

Myers, P. I., & Hammill, D. D. (1990). *Learning disabilities: Basic concepts, assessment practices, and instructional strategies* (3rd ed.). Austin, TX: PRO-ED.

Narayan, J. S., Heward, W. L., Gardner, R., III, Courson, F. H., & Omness, C. (1990). Using response cards to increase student participation in an elementary classroom. *Journal of Applied Behavior Analysis, 23,* 483–490.

Naseef, R. A. (2001). *Special Children, challenged parents: The struggles and rewards of raising a child with a disability* (rev. ed.). Baltimore: Brookes.

National Center for Education Statistics. (1994). *The condition of education, 1994.* Washington, DC: U. S. Department of Education.

National Center for Education Statistics. (2000). *2000 dropout rates in the United States: 1999 statistical analysis report.* Washington, DC: U. S. Department of Education.

National Center on Children's Abuse and Neglect. (1995). *Child abuse and neglect fact sheet, 1993.* Washington, DC: U. S. Government Printing Office.

National Center on Children's Abuse and Neglect. (1996). *Child abuse and neglect fact sheet, 1994.* Washington, DC: U. S. Government Printing Office.

National Education Association. (2001). *Teacher shortages.* http://www.nea.org/teaching/shortage.html

National excellence: A case for developing America's talent. (1993). Washington, DC: U. S. Department of Education, Office of Educational Research and Improvement.

National Institute of Allergy and Infectious Diseases. (2001). Fact sheet: HIV infection and adolescents http://www.niaid.nih.gov/factsheets/hivadolescent.htm

National Institute on Deafness and Other Communication Disorders. (2001). Cochlear implants. In *Health information: Hearing and balance.* http://www.nih.gov/nidcd/health/pubs_hb/coch.htm

National Joint Committee on Learning Disabilities (1989, September 18). Letter from NJCLD to member organizations. Topic: Modifications to the NJCLD definition of learning disabilities.

National Reading Panel. (2000). *Teaching children to read: An evidence-based assessment of the scientific research literature on reading and its implications for reading instruction.* Washington, DC: National Institute of Child Health and Human Development.

National Research Council. (2000). *Testing English-language learners in U. S. schools: Report and workshop summary.* http://www.nap.edu

National School Boards Association (1992, July 15). Group urges new definition of emotional disorders: NSBA opposes any change that would dilute scare resources. *NSBA Newsletter,* p. 2.

National Society for Autistic Children, Board of Directors and Professional Advisory Board. (1977). *A short definition of autism.* Albany, NY: Author.

National Spinal Cord Injury Association. (2001). *Facts and figures.* Birmingham: University of Alabama.

Nechring, W. M., & Steele, S. (1996). Cerebral palsy. In P. L. Jackson & J. A. Vessey (Eds.), *Primary care of the child with a chronic condition* (2nd ed.), (pp. 232–254). St. Louis: Mosby.

Neef, N. A. (Guest Ed.). (1994). *Journal of Applied Behavior Analysis, 27*(2) [Special issue], 196–418.

Neef, N. A., Bicard, D. F., & Endo, S. (2001). Assessment of impulsivity and the development of self-control in students with attention-deficit hyperactivity disorder. *Journal of Applied Behavior Analysis, 34, 397–407.*

Neef, N. A., Parrish, J. M. Egel, A. L., & Sloan, M. E. (1986). Training respite care providers for families with handicapped children: Experimental analysis and validation of an instructional package. *Journal of Applied Behavior Analysis, 19,* 105–124.

Neisworth, J. T., & Bagnato, S. J. (2000). Recommended practices in assessment. In S. Sandall, M. E. McLean, & B. J. Smith (Eds.), *DEC recommended practices in early intervention/ early childhood special education* (pp. 29–33). Reston, VA: Council for Exceptional Children, Division for Early Childhood.

Nelson, C. M. (2000). Educating students with emotional and behavioral disabilities in the 21st century: Looking through windows, opening doors. *Education and Treatment of Children, 23,* 204–222.

Nelson, J. R., Crabtree, M., Marchand-Martella, N., & Martella, R. (1998). Teaching behavior in the whole school. *Teaching Exceptional Children, 30*(4), 4–9.

Nelson, P. (2001). The changing demand for improved acoustics in our schools. *The Volta Review, 101*(5), 23–32.

Newborg, J., Stock, J., Wnek, J., Guidubaldi, & Suinicki, J. (1988). *Battelle Developmental Inventory.* Chicago: Riverside.

Newcomer, P. L., & Barenbaum, E. M. (1991). The written composing ability of children with learning disabilities: A review of the literature from 1980 to 1990. *Journal of Learning Disabilities, 24,* 578–593.

Newman, R. S., & Golding, L. (1990). Children's reluctance to seek help with school work. *Journal of Educational Psychology, 82,* 92–100.

Newton, J. S., Horner, R. H., & Lund, L. (1991). Honoring activity preferences in individualized plan development. *Journal of The Association for Persons with Severe Handicaps, 16,* 207–212.

Nieto, S. (2000a). *Affirming diversity: The sociopolitical context of multicultural education* (3rd ed.). New York: Addison Wesley Longman.

Nieto, S. (2000b). *Puerto Rican students in U. S. schools.* Mahwah, NJ: Erlbaum.

Nietupski, J., & Svoboda, R. (1982). Teaching a cooperative leisure skill to severely handicapped adults. *Education and Training of the Mentally Retarded, 17,* 38–43.

Nihira, K., Leland, H., & Lambert, N. K. (1993). *Adaptive Behavior Scale—*

Residential and Community (2nd ed.). Austin, TX: PRO-ED.

Nisbet, J., & Vincent, L. (1986). The differences in inappropriate behavior and instructional interactions in sheltered and nonsheltered work environments. *Journal of The Association for Persons with Severe Handicaps, 11,* 19–27.

Northern, J. L., & Downs, M. P. (1991). *Hearing in children* (4th ed.). Baltimore: Williams & Wilkins.

Norton, L. S., & Hartley, J. (1986). What factors contribute to good examination marks? The role of notetaking in subsequent examination performance. *Higher Education, 15,* 355–371.

Notari-Syverson, A. R., & Shuster, S. L. (1995). Putting real-life skills into IEP/IFSPs for infants and young children. *Teaching Exceptional Children, 27*(2), 29–32.

Nover, S. M. (1995). Full inclusion for deaf students: An ethnographic perspective. In B. Snider (Ed.), *Inclusion? Defining quality education for deaf and hard of hearing students* (pp. 33–50). Washington, DC: Gallaudet University, College for Continuing Education.

Nowacek, E. J., McKinney, J. D., & Hallahan, D. P. (1990). Instructional behaviors of more and less effective beginning regular and special educators. *Exceptional Children, 57,* 140–149.

O'Neill, R. E., Horner, R. H., Albin, R. W., Sprague, J. R., Storey, K., & Newton, J. S. (1997). *Functional assessment and program development for problem behavior: A practical handbook.* Pacific Grove, CA: Brooks/Cole.

O'Reilly, M. F., Lancioni, G. E., & Kierans, I. (2000). Teaching leisure social skills to adults with moderate mental retardation: An analysis of acquisition, generalization, and maintenance. *Education and Training in Mental Retardation and Developmental Disabilities, 35,* 250–258.

Oakes, J. (1985). *Keeping track.* New Haven, CT: Yale University Press.

Obiakor, F. E., Algozzine, B., & Ford, B. A. (1993). Urban education, the General Education Initiative, and service delivery to African-American students. *Urban Education, 28,* 313–327.

Ochoa, S. H., & Palmer, D. J. (1995). A meta-analysis of peer rating sociometric studies with learning disabled pupils. *Journal of Special Education, 29,* 1–9.

Odom, S. L., Hanson, M. J., Lieber, J., Marquart, J., Sandall, S., Wolery, R., Horn, E., Wolfberg, P., Schwartz, I., Beckman, P., Hikido, C., & Chambers, J. (2001). The costs of preschool inclusion. *Topics in Early Childhood Special Education, 21,* 146–155.

Odom, S. L., Horn, E., Marquart, J. M., Hanson, M. J., Wolfberg, P., Beckman, P., Lieber, J., Li, S., Schwartz, I., Janko, S., & Sandall, S. (2000). On the forms of inclusion: Organization context and individualized service models. *Journal of Early Intervention, 22,* 185–199.

Office of Technology Assessment. (1987). *Technology-dependent children: Hospital v.*

home care—A technical memorandum. OTA-TM-H-38. Washington, DC: Author.

Olsen, R., & Sutton, J. (1998). More hassle, more alone: Adolescents with diabetes and the role of formal and informal support. *Child: Care, Health, and Development, 24*(1), 31–39.

Olympia, D., Andrews, D., Valum, L., & Jensen, W. (1993). *Homework teams: Homework management strategies for the classroom.* Longmont, CO: Sopris West.

Orelove, F. P. (1984). The educability debate: A review and a look ahead. In W. L. Heward, T. E. Heron, D. S. Hill, & J. Trap-Porter (Eds.), *Focus on behavior analysis in education* (pp. 271–281). Upper Saddle River, NJ: Merrill/Prentice Hall.

Orelove, F. P., & Sobsey, D. (1996). *Educating children with multiple disabilities: A transdisciplinary approach* (3rd ed.). Baltimore: Brookes.

Orlansky, M. D., & Bonvillian, J. D. (1985). Sign language acquisition: Language development in children of deaf parents and implications for other populations. *Merrill-Palmer Quarterly, 31,* 127–143.

Orsillo, S. M., McCaffrey, R. J., & Fisher, J. M. (1993). Siblings of head-injured individuals: A population at risk. *Journal of Head Trauma Rehabilitation, 8*(1), 102–115.

Orsmond, G. I., & Seltzer, M. M. (2000). Brothers and sisters of adults with mental retardation: Gendered nature of the sibling relationship. *American Journal of Mental Retardation, 105,* 486–508.

Ortiz, A. (1997). Learning disabilities occurring concomitantly with linguistic differences. *Journal of Learning Disabilities, 30,* 321–333.

Ortiz, A. A. (1991a). *AIM for the BESt: Assessment and intervention model for the bilingual exceptional student. A technical report for the Innovative Approaches Research Project.* Austin: University of Texas (ERIC Document No. 341 194).

Ortiz, A. A. (1991b). *AIM for the BESt: Assessment and intervention model for the bilingual exceptional student. A handbook for teachers and planners from the Innovative Approaches Research Project.* Austin: University of Texas (ERIC Document No. 341 195).

Ortiz, V., & Gonzales, A. (1991). Gifted Hispanic adolescents. In M. Bireley & J. Genshaft (Eds.), *Understanding the gifted adolescent* (pp. 240–247). New York: Teachers College Press.

Ostad, S. A. (1998). Developmental differences in solving simple arithmetic word problems and simple number-fact problems: A comparison of mathematically normal and mathematically disabled children. *Mathematical Cognition, 4,* 1–20.

Oswald, D. P., & Coutinho, M. J. (2001). Trends in disproportionate representation: Implications for multicultural education. In C. Utley & F. Obiakor (Eds.), *Special education, multicultural education, and school reform: Components of quality education for learners with mild disabilities* (pp. 53–73). Springfield: Thomas.

Oswald, D. P., Coutinho, M. J., Best, A. M., & Singh, N. N. (1999). Ethnic representation in special education: The influence of school-related economic and demographic variables. *Journal of Special Education, 32,* 194–206.

Overton, T. (2000). *Assessment in special education: An applied approach* (3rd ed.). Upper Saddle River, NJ: Merrill/Prentice Hall.

Owens, R. E. (1999). *Language disorders: A functional approach to assessment and intervention.* (4th ed.). Boston: Allyn & Bacon.

Owens, R. E. (2001). *Language development: An introduction* (5th ed.). Boston: Allyn & Bacon.

Owens, R. E. (2002). Development of communication, language, and speech. In G. H. Shames & N. B. Anderson (Eds.), *Human communication disorders: An introduction* (6th ed.), (pp. 28–69). Boston: Allyn & Bacon.

Owens-Johnson, L., & Hamill, L. B. (2002). Community-based instruction. In L. Hamill & C. Everington, *Teaching students with moderate to severe disabilities: An applied approach for inclusive environments* (pp. 347–378). Upper Saddle River, NJ: Merrill/Prentice Hall.

Packman, A., & Onslow, M. (1998). What is the take-home message from Curlee and Yairi? *American Journal of Speech-Language Pathology, 7,* 5–9.

Padden, C., & Ramsey, C. (1998). Reading ability in signing deaf children. *Topics in Language Disorders, 18*(4), 30–46.

Page, E. B. (1972). Miracle in Milwaukee: Raising the IQ. *Educational Researcher, 15,* 8–16.

Palincsar, A. L. (1998). Keeping the metaphor of scaffolding fresh. *Journal of Learning Disabilities, 31,* 370–373.

Palincsar, A. S., Collins, K. M., Marano, N. L., & Magnusson, S. J. (2000). Investigating the engagement and learning of students with learning disabilities in guided inquiry science teaching. *Language, Speech, and Hearing Services in Schools, 31.*

Palmer, D. S., Fuller, K., Arora, T., & Nelson, M. (2001). Taking sides: Parents' views on inclusion for their children with severe disabilities. *Exceptional Children, 67,* 467–484.

Pancheri, C., & Prater, M. A. (1999). What teachers and parents should know about Ritalin. *Teaching Exceptional Children, 31*(4), 20–26.

Panerai, S., Ferrante, L., Caputo, V., & Impellizzeri, C. (1998). Use of structured teaching for the treatment of children with autism and severe and profound mental retardation. *Education and Training in Mental Retardation and Developmental Disabilities, 33,* 367–374.

Paniagua, F. A. (1992). Verbal–nonverbal correspondence training with ADHD children. *Behavior Modification, 16,* 226–252.

Parette, H. P. (1998). Assistive technology effective practices for students with mental retardation and developmental disabilities. In A. Hilton and R. Ringlaben (Eds.), *Best and promising practices in developmental disabilities* (pp. 205–224). Austin, TX: PRO-ED.

Parette, H. P., & Brotherson, M. J. (1996). Family participation in assistive technology assessment for young children with mental retardation and developmental disabilities. *Education and Training in Mental Retardation and Developmental Disabilities, 31*, 29–43.

Parette, H. P., & Petch–Hogan, B. (2000). Approaching families: Facilitating culturally/linguistically diverse family involvement. *Teaching Exceptional Children, 33*(2), 4–10.

Parette, H. P., Jr., & Hourcade, J. J. (1986). Management strategies for orthopedically handicapped students. *Teaching Exceptional Children, 18*(4), 282–286.

Park, J., Turnbull, A. P., & Park, H. S. (2001). Quality of partnerships in service provision for Korean American parents of children with disabilities: A qualitative inquiry. *Journal of The Association for Persons with Severe Handicaps, 26*, 158–170.

Parrish, T. B. (in press). Who's paying the rising cost of special education? *Journal of Special Education Leadership.*

Parsons, M. B., McCarn, J. E., & Reid, D. H. (1993). Evaluating and increasing meal-related choices throughout a service setting for people with severe disabilities. *Journal of The Association for Persons with Severe Handicaps, 18*, 253–260.

Patterson, G. R. (1982). *Coercive family process.* Eugene, OR: Castilia.

Patterson, G. R., Cipaldi, D., & Bank, L. (1991). An early starter model for predicting delinquency. In D. J. Pepler & K. H. Rubin (Eds.), *The development and treatment of childhood aggression* (pp. 139–168). Hillsdale, NJ: Erlbaum.

Patterson, G. R., Reid, J. B., & Dishion, T. J. (1992). *Antisocial boys.* Vol. 4: A social interactional approach. Eugene, OR: Castalia.

Patterson, J. M., & Leonard, B. J. (1994). Caregiving and children. In E. Kahan, D. Biegel, & M. Wykle (Eds.), *Family caregiving across the lifespan* (pp. 133–158). Beverly Hills, CA: Sage.

Patterson, J. M., Barber, P. A., & Ault, M. M. (1994). Young children with special health-care needs. In P. L. Safford, B. Spodek, & O. N. Saracho (Eds.), *Yearbook in early childhood education.* Vol. 5: *Early childhood special education* (pp. 165–191). New York: Teachers College Press.

Patton, J. M. (1998). The disproportionate representation of African Americans in special education: Looking behind the curtain for understanding and solutions. *Journal of Special Education, 32*, 25–31.

Patton, J. R., Cronin, M. E., & Jairrels, V. (1997). Curricular implications of transition: Life-skills instruction as an integral part of transition education. *Remedial and Special Education, 18*, 294–306.

Paul, P. V. (1998). *Literacy and deafness: The development of reading, writing, and literate thought.* Needham Heights, MA: Allyn & Bacon.

Paul, P. V., & Jackson, D. (1993). *Towards a psychology of deafness* (2nd ed.). San Diego: Singular.

Paul, P. V., & Quigley, S. P. (1990). *Education and deafness.* New York: Longman.

Pavri, S. (2001). Developmental delay or cultural differences? Developing effective child find practices for young children from culturally and linguistically diverse families. *Young Exceptional Children, 4,* 2–9.

Pavri, S., & Monda-Amaya, L. (2000). Loneliness and students with learning disabilities in inclusive classrooms: Self-perceptions, coping strategies, and preferred interventions. *Learning Disabilities Research and Practice, 15*(2), 22–33.

Payne, K. T., & Taylor, O. L. (2002). Multicultural influences on human communication. In G. H. Shames & N. B. Anderson (Eds.), *Human communication disorders: An introduction* (6th ed.) (pp. 106–140). Boston: Allyn & Bacon.

Peacock Hill Working Group. (1991). Problems and promises in special education and related services for children and youth with emotional or behavioral disorders. *Behavioral Disorders, 16,* 299–313.

Peck Peterson, S. M., Caniglia, C., & Royster, A. J. (2001). Application of a choice-making intervention for a student with multiply maintained problem behavior. *Focus on Autism and Other Developmental Disabilities, 16,* 240–246.

Peck Peterson, S. M., Derby, K. M., Harding, J. W., Weddle, T., & Barretto, A. (in press). Behavioral support for children with developmental disabilities and problem behavior. In J. Luchshyn, G. Dunlap, & R. Albin, (Eds.), *Families and positive behavioral support: Addressing the challenge of problem behavior in family contexts.* Baltimore: Brookes.

Peckham, V. C. (1993). Children with cancer in the classroom. *Teaching Exceptional Children, 26*(1), 27–32.

Pedley, T. A., Scheuer, M. L., & Walczak, T. S. (1995). Epilepsy. In L. P. Rowland (Ed.), *Merritt's textbook of neurology* (9th ed.) (pp. 845–868). Baltimore: Williams & Wilkins.

Pellegrino, L. (1997). Cerebral palsy. In M. L. Batshaw (Ed.), *Children with disabilities* (4th ed.) (pp. 499–528). Baltimore: Brookes.

Pendergast, K., Dickey, S., Selmar, J., & Soder, A. (1984). *Photo Articulation Test.* Austin, TX: PRO-ED.

Pennington, B. F. (1995). Genetics of learning disabilities. *Journal of Child Neurology, 10,* 69–77.

Pennsylvania Association for Retarded Children v. Commonwealth of Pennsylvania, 343 F. Supp. 279 (1972).

Perl, J. (1995). Improving relationship skills for parent conferences. *Teaching Exceptional Children 28*(1), 29–31.

Perla, F., & Ducret, W. D. (1999). Guidelines for teaching orientation and mobility to children with multiple disabilities. *RE:view, 31,* 113–119.

Perlmutter, J., & Burrell, L. (1995, January). Learning through play as well as work. *Young Children,* pp. 14–21.

Perrin, E. C., Newacheck, P., Pless, B., Drotar, D., Gortmaker, S. L., Leventhal, J., Perrin, J. M., Stein, R. E. K., Walker, D. K., & Weitzman, M. (1993). Issues involved in the definition and classification of chronic health conditions. *Pediatrics, 91,* 787–793.

Peterson, L. D., Young, K. R., West, R. P., & Hill Peterson, M. (1999). Effects of student self-management on generalization of student performance to regular classrooms. *Education and Treatment of Children, 19,* 170.

Pieper, E. (1983). *The teacher and the child with spina bifida* (2nd ed.). Rockville, MD: Spina Bifida Association of America.

Piirto, J. (1991). Why are there so few? (Creative women: mathematicians, visual artists, musicians). *Roeper Review, 13*(3), 142–147.

Piirto, J. (1998). *Understanding those who create* (2nd ed.). Scottsdale, AZ: Gifted Psychology Press.

Piirto, J. (1999a). Implications of postmodern curriculum theory for the education of the talented. *Journal for the Education of the Gifted, 22*(4), 386–406.

Piirto, J. (1999b). *Talented children and adults: Their development and education* (2nd ed.) Upper Saddle River, NJ: Merrill/Prentice Hall.

Piirto, J. (2001). "My teeming brain": *Understanding creative writers.* Cresskill, NJ: Hampton.

Pittman, P., & Huefner, D. S. (2001). Will the courts go bi-bi? IDEA '97, the courts, and deaf education. *Exceptional Children, 67,* 187–198.

Plomin, R. (1995). Genetics and children's experiences in the family. *Journal of Child Psychology and Psychiatry, 36,* 33–68.

Plummer, D. (1995). Serving the needs of gifted children from a multicultural perspective. In J. L. Genshaft, M. Bireley, & C. L. Hollinger (Eds.), *Serving gifted and talented students: A resource for school personnel* (pp. 285–300). Austin, TX: PRO-ED.

Pogrund, R. L., Fazzi, D. L., & Schreier, E. M. (1993). Development of a preschool "kiddy cane." *Journal of Visual Impairment and Blindness, 87,* 52–54.

Pollack, W. (1998). *Real boys: Rescuing our sons from the myths of boyhood.* New York: Holt.

Polloway, E. A., Smith, J. D., Patton, J. R., & Smith, T. E. C. (1996). Historic changes in mental retardation and developmental disabilities. *Education and Training in Mental Retardation and Developmental Disabilities, 31,* 3–12.

Porter, J. H., & Hodson, B. W. (2001). Collaborating to obtain phonological acquisition data for local schools. *Language, Speech, and Hearing Services in Schools, 32,* 165–171.

Porter, S., Haynie, M., Bierle, T., Caldwell, T. H., & Palfrey, J. S. (1997). *Children and youth: Assisted by medical technology in educational settings: Guidelines for care* (2nd ed.). Baltimore: Brookes.

Porterfield, K. (1998). British researchers identify genetic area affecting speech. *ASHA Leader, 3*(4), 1, 4.

Potts, L., Eshleman, J. W., & Cooper, J. O. (1993). Ogden R. Lindsley and the historical development of precision teaching. *Behavior Analyst, 16,* 177–189.

Poulson, C. L., & Kymissis, E. (1988). Generalized imitation in infants. *Journal of Experimental Child Psychology, 46,* 324–336.

Poulton, S. (1996). Guidelines to writing individualized healthcare plans. http://www.nursing.uiowa.edu/www/ nursing/courses/96–22/students/sp1996/ 96–222WEguideline/htm

Powell, D. S., Batsche, C. J., Ferro, J., Fox, L., & Dunlap, G. (1997). A strength-based approach in support of multi-risk families: Principles and issues. *Topics in Early Childhood Special Education, 17*(1), 1–26.

Powell, L., Houghton, S., & Douglas, J. (1997). Comparison of etiology-specific cognitive functioning profiles for individuals with fragile X and individuals with Down syndrome. *Journal of Special Education, 34,* 362–376.

Poyadue, F. S. (1993). Cognitive coping at Parents Helping Parents. In A. P. Turnbull, J. M. Paterson, S. K. Behr, D. L. Murphy, J. G. Marquis, & M. J. Blue-Banning (Eds.), *Cognitive coping, families, and disability* (pp. 95–110). Baltimore: Brookes.

Prelock, P. A. (2000a). Prologue: Multiple perspectives for determining the roles of speech-language pathologists in inclusionary classrooms. *Language, Speech, and Hearing Services in Schools, 31,* 213–218.

Prelock, P. A. (2000b). Epilogue: An intervention focus for inclusionary practice. *Language, Speech, and Hearing Services in Schools, 31,* 296–298.

President's Committee on Mental Retardation. (1976). *Mental retardation: Century of decision.* Washington, DC: U. S. Government Printing Office.

Pretti–Frontczak, K. L., & Bricker, D. (2000). Enhancing the quality of Individualized Education Plan (IEP) goals and objectives. *Journal of Early Intervention, 23,* 92–105.

Prinz, P. M., Strong, M., Kuntze, M., Vincent, J., Friedman, J., Moyers, P. P., & Helman, E. (1996). A path to literacy through ASL and English for deaf children. In C. E. Johnson & J. H. V. Gilbert (Eds.), *Children's language* (Vol. 9) (pp. 235–251). Mahwah, NJ: Erlbaum.

Public Law 95–561. Gifted and Talented Children's Education Act. *Congressional Record* (1978, October 10). H–12179.

Pugh, G. S., & Erin, J. (1999). (Eds.). *Blind and visually impaired students: Education service guidelines.* Watertown, MA: Perkins School for the Blind.

Putnam, J. W. (1998). *Cooperative learning and strategies for inclusion: Celebrating diversity in the classroom* (2nd ed.). Baltimore: Brookes.

Ramey, C. T., & Ramey, S. L. (1992). Effective early intervention. *Mental Retardation, 30,* 337–345.

Ramey, C. T., Bryant, D. M., Wasik, B. H., Sparling, J. J., Fendt, K. H., & LaVange, L. M. (1992). The Infant Health and Development Program for low birthweight, premature infants: Program elements, family participation, and child intelligence. *Pediatrics, 89,* 454–465.

Ramig, P. R., & Shames, G. H. (2002). Stuttering and other disorders of fluency. In G. H. Shames & N. B. Anderson (Eds.), *Human communication disorders: An introduction* (6th ed.) (pp. 258–302). Boston: Allyn & Bacon.

Rao, S. S. (2000). Perspectives of an African American mother on parent-professional relationships in special education. *Mental Retardation, 38,* 475–488.

Rapport, M. J. K. (1996). Legal guidelines for the delivery of health care services in schools. *Exceptional Children, 62,* 537–549.

Raschke, D. B., Dedrick, C. V. L., Heston, M. L., & Farris, M. (1996). Everyone can play! Adapting the Candy Land board game. *Teaching Exceptional Children, 28*(4), 28–33.

Raskind, W. H. (2001). Current understanding of the genetic basis of reading and spelling disability. *Learning Disability Quarterly, 24,* 141–157.

Raver, S. (1984). Modification of head droop during conversation in a 3-year-old visually impaired child: A case study. *Journal of Visual Impairment and Blindness, 78,* 307–310.

Raver, S. A. (1999). *Intervention strategies for infants and toddlers with special needs: A team approach* (2nd ed.) Upper Saddle River, NJ: Merrill/Prentice Hall.

Rawlings, B. W., & King, S. J. (1986). Postsecondary educational opportunities for deaf students. In A. N. Schildroth & M. A. Karchmer (Eds.), *Deaf children in America* (pp. 231–257). San Diego: College-Hill.

Rawlings, B. W., Karchmer, M. A., Allen, T. E., & DeCaro, J. J. (1999). *College and career programs for deaf students* (10th ed.). Washington, DC, and Rochester, NY: Gallaudet University and National Technical Institute for the Deaf.

Rea, P. J., McLaughlin, V. L., & Walther-Thomas, C. (2002). Outcomes for students with learning disabilities in inclusive and pullout programs. *Exceptional Children, 68,* 203–222.

Reed, P., & Best, S. (2001). Assessment for assistive technology. In J. L. Bigge, S. J. Best, & K. W. Heller, *Teaching individuals with physical, health, or multiple disabilities* (4th ed.), (pp. 149–194). Upper Saddle River, NJ: Merrill/Prentice Hall.

Reed, V. A. (1998). *An introduction to children with language disorders* (3rd ed.). Needham Heights, MA: Allyn & Bacon.

Reid, R., & Maag, J. W. (1994). How many fidgets in a pretty much: A critique of behavior rating scales for identifying students with AD/HD. *Journal of School Psychology, 32,* 339–354.

Reid, R., & Maag, J. W. (1998). Functional assessment: A method for developing classroom–based accommodations and interventions. *Reading & Writing Quarterly, 14,* 7–15.

Reilly, J. S., & Bellugi, U. (1996). Competition on the face: Affect and language in ASL mothers. *Journal of Child Language, 23,* 219–239.

Reis, S. (1995). What gifted education can offer the reform movement: Talent development. In J. L. Genshaft, M. Bireley, & C. L. Hollinger (Eds.), *Serving gifted and talented students: A resource for school personnel* (pp. 371–387). Austin, TX: PRO-ED.

Reis, S. M., & Cellerino, M. (1983). Guiding gifted students through independent study. *Teaching Exceptional Children, 15,* 136–139.

Reis, S. M., Neu, T. W., & McGuire, J. M. (1995). *Talents in two places: Case studies of high ability students with learning disabilities who have achieved* (Research Monograph 95114). Storrs: University of Connecticut, National Research Center on the Gifted and Talented.

Renzulli, J. (1998). *Relationship between gifted programs and total school improvement using the schoolwide enrichment model.* Storrs: University of Connecticut, National Resource Center on the Gifted and Talented.

Renzulli, J. S. (1978). What makes giftedness?: Reexamining a definition. *Phi Delta Kappan, 61,* 180–184.

Renzulli, J. S., & Reis, S. M. (1997). The schoolwide enrichment model: New directions for developing high-end learning. In N. Colangelo & G. A. Davis (Eds.), *Handbook of gifted education* (2nd ed.) (pp. 136–154) Needham Heights, MA: Allyn & Bacon.

Renzulli, J., & Reis, S. (1986). The enrichment triad/revolving door model: A schoolwide plan for the development of creative productivity. In J. Renzulli (Ed.), *Systems and models for developing programs for the gifted and talented.* Mansfield Center, CT: Creative Learning Press.

Repucci, N. D., Britner, P. A., & Wollard, J. L. (1997). *Preventing children abuse and neglect through parent education.* Baltimore: Brookes.

Reschly, D. J. (1996). Identification and assessment of students with disabilities. *Future of Children, 6*(1), 40–53.

Revell, W. G., Wehman, P., Kregel, J., West, M., & Rayfield, R. (1994). Supported employment for persons with severe disabilities: Positive trends in wages, models, and funding. *Education and Training in Mental Retardation, 29,* 256–264.

Rex, E. J., Koenig, A. J., Wromsley, D. P., & Baker, R. L. (1994). *Foundations of Braille literacy.* New York: American Foundation for the Blind.

Reyes-Blanes, M., Rodriguez, P., Vázquez, E., & Skinner, M. (1999). Needs and supports reported by Latino families of young children with developmental disabilities. *American Journal on Mental Retardation, 104,* 437–451.

Reynolds, M. C., & Heistad, D. (1997). 20/20 analysis: Estimating school effectiveness in serving students at the margins. *Exceptional Children, 63,* 439–449.

Reynolds, M. C., Zetlin, A. G., & Heistad, D. (1996). *A manual for 20/20 analysis.* Philadelphia: Temple University, Center for Research in Human Development and Education. [ERIC Document Reproduction Service No. ED 358 183]

Rhode, G., Jensen, W. R., & Reavis, H. K. (1998). *The tough kid book: Practical classroom management strategies.* Longmont, CO: Sopris West.

Rhode, G., Morgan, D. P., & Young, K. R. (1983). Generalization and maintenance of treatment gains of behaviorally handicapped students from resource rooms to regular classrooms using self-evaluation procedures. *Journal of Applied Behavior Analysis, 16,* 171–188.

Rhodes, L. E., & Valenta, L. (1985). Industry-based supported employment: An enclave approach. *Journal of The Association for Persons with Severe Handicaps, 10,* 12–20.

Ricci-Balich, J., & Behm, J. A. (1996). Pediatric rehabilitation nursing. In S. P. Hoeman (Ed.), *Rehabilitation nursing: Process and application* (pp. 660–682). St. Louis: Mosby.

Richards, T. L. (2001). Functional magnetic resonance imaging and spectroscopic imaging of the brain: Application of fMRI and fMRS to reading disabilities and education. *Learning Disability Quarterly, 24,* 189–203.

Rimland, B. (1993a). Beware the advozealots: Mindless good intentions injure the handicapped. *Autism Research Review International, 7*(4), 1.

Rimland, B. (1993b). Inclusive education: Right for some. *Autism Research Review International, 7*(1), 3.

Rimm, S. (2000). *See Jane win.* New York: Crown.

Rimm, S. (2002). *How Jane won.* New York: Crown.

Roberts, J. E., Wallace, I. F., & Henderson, F. W. (1997). *Otitis media in young children: Medical, developmental, and education considerations.* Baltimore: Brookes.

Robins, K. N., Lindsey, R. B., Lindsey, D. B., & Terrell, R. D. (2002). *Culturally proficient instruction: A guide for people who teach.* Thousand Oaks, CA: Corwin.

Robinson Spohn, J. R., Timko, T. C., & Sainato, D. M. (1999). Increasing the social interactions of preschool children with disabilities during mealtimes: The effects of an interactive placemat game. *Education and Treatment of Children, 22,* 1–18.

Rock, M. L. (2000). Parents as equal partners: Balancing the scales in IEP development. *Teaching Exceptional Children, 32*(6), 30–37.

Rockwell, S., & Guetzloe, E. (1996). Group development for students with emotional/behavioral disorders. *Teaching Exceptional Children, 29*(1), 38–43.

Roeser, R., & Yellin, W. (1987). Pure-tone tests with preschool children. In F. Martin (Ed.), *Hearing disorders in children: Pediatric audiology* (pp. 217–264). Austin, TX: PRO-ED.

Rogan, P., Hagner, D., & Murphy, S. (1993). Natural supports: Reconceptualizing job coach roles. *Journal of The Association for Persons with Severe Handicaps, 18,* 275–281.

Rogers, K. B. (1991). *The relationship of grouping practices to the education of the gifted and talented learner.* Storrs: University of Connecticut, National Research Center on the Gifted and Talented.

Romanczyk, R. G., Weinter, T., Lockshin, S., & Ekdahl, M. (1999). Research in autism: Myths, controversies, and perspectives. In D. B. Zager (Ed.), *Autism: Identification, education, and treatment* (2nd ed.), (pp. 23–61). Mahwah, NJ: Erlbaum.

Romer, L. T., White, J., & Haring, N. G. (1996). The effect of peer mediated social competency training on the type and frequency of social contacts with students with deaf-blindness. *Education and Training in Mental Retardation and Developmental Disabilities, 31,* 324–338.

Rorschach, H. (1942). *Rorschach psychodiagnostic plates.* New York: Psychological Corporation.

Rosales, J., & Baer, D. M. (1998). *How to plan for generalization* (2nd ed.). Austin, TX: PRO-ED.

Rose, K. C., White, J. A., Conroy, J., & Smith, D. M. (1993). Following the course of change: A study of adaptive and maladaptive behaviors in young adults living in the community. *Education and Training in Mental Retardation, 28,* 149–154.

Rose, T. L., & Calhoun, M. L. (1990). The Charlotte Circle Project: A program for infants and toddlers with severe/profound disabilities. *Journal of Early Intervention, 14,* 175–185.

Rosenblum, L. P. (1998). Best friendships of adolescents with visual impairments: A descriptive study. *Journal of Visual Impairments and Blindness, 92,* 593–608.

Rosenblum, L. P. (2000). Perceptions of the impact of visual impairments on the lives of adolescents. *Journal of Visual Impairments and Blindness, 94,* 434–445.

Rousch, W. (1995). Arguing over why Johnny can't read. *Science, 267,* 1896–1898.

Rueda, R. (1997). Changing the context of assessment: The move to portfolios and authentic assessment. In A. Artiles & G. Zamora-Durán (Eds.), *Reducing disproportionate representation of culturally diverse students in special and gifted education* (pp. 7–26).

Rumberger, R. W., Ghatak, R., Polous, G., Ritter, P. L., & Dornbush, S. M. (1990). Family influences on dropout behavior in one California high school. *Sociology of Education, 63,* 283–299.

Runnheim, V., Frankenberger, W. R., & Hazelkorn, M. N. (1996). Medicating students with emotional and behavioral disorders and ADHD: A state survey. *Behavioral Disorders, 21,* 306–314.

Rusch, F. (1990). *Supported employment: Models, methods, and issues.* Sycamore, IL: Sycamore.

Rusch, F. R., & Minch, K. E. (1988). Identification of co-worker involvement in supported employment: A review and analysis. *Research in Developmental Disabilities, 9,* 247–254.

Rusch, F. R., Hughes, C., McNair, J., & Wilson, P. G. (1990). *Co-worker involvement scoring manual and instrument.* Champaign: University of Illinois, Board of Trustees.

Rusch, F. R., Johnson, J. R., & Hughes, C. (1990). Analysis of co-worker involvement in relations to level of disability versus placement approach among supported employees. *Journal of The Association for Persons with Severe Handicaps, 15,* 32–39.

Rush, A. J., & Francis, A. (Eds.). (2000). Expert consensus guideline series: Treatment of psychiatric and behavioral problems in mental retardation. *American Journal of Mental Retardation, 105,* 159–228.

Rutter, M. (1976). *Helping troubled children.* New York: Plenum.

Ryan, R. M., & Deci, E. L. (1996). When paradigms clash: Comments on Cameron and Pierce's claim that rewards do not undermine intrinsic motivation. *Review of Educational Research, 66,* 33–38.

Ryles, R. (1996). The impact of braille reading skills on employment, income, education, and reading habits. *Journal of Visual Impairment and Blindness, 90,* 219–226.

Ryndak, D. L., & Alper, S. (1996). *Curriculum content for students with moderate and severe disabilities in inclusive settings.* Boston: Allyn & Bacon.

Sabornie, E. J., & Kauffman, J. M. (1986). Social acceptance of learning disabled adolescents. *Learning Disabilities Quarterly, 9,* 55–60.

Sack, J. (1997, April 16). Disruptive special education students get own school. *Education Week on the Web,* 1–7.

Sacks, S. Z., & Silberman, R. K. (Eds.).(1998). *Educating students who have visual impairments with other disabilities:* Baltimore: Brookes.

Sacks, S. Z., Wolffe, K. E., & Tierney, D. (1998). Lifestyles of students with visual impairments adolescents. Preliminary studies of social networks. *Exceptional Children, 64,* 463–478.

Safer, D. J., Zito, J. M., & Fine, E. M. (1996) Increased methylphenidate usage for attention-deficit disorder in the 1990s. *Pediatrics, 98,* 1084–1088.

Safford, P. L., & Safford, E. J. (1996). *A history of childhood disability.* New York: Teachers College Press.

Safran, S. P. (2001). Asperger syndrome: The emerging challenge to special education. *Exceptional Children, 67,* 151–160.

Sailor, W., Gee, K., & Karasoff, P. (2000). Inclusion and school restructuring. In M.

E. Snell & F. Brown (Eds.), *Instruction of students with severe disabilities* (5th ed.), (pp. 1–29). Upper Saddle River, NJ: Merrill/Prentice Hall.

Sainato, D. M., & Lyon, S. L. (1989). Promoting successful mainstreaming transitions for handicapped preschool children. *Journal of Early Intervention, 13*(4), 305–314.

Sainato, D. M., & Strain, P. S. (1993). Increasing integration success for preschoolers with disabilities. *Teaching Exceptional Children, 25*(2), 36.

Salend, S. J. (2001). *Creating inclusive classrooms: Effective and reflective practices* (4th ed.). Upper Saddle River, NJ: Merrill/Prentice Hall.

Salend, S. J., Ellis, L. L., & Reynolds, C. J. (1989). Using self-instruction to teach vocational skills to individuals who are severely retarded. *Education and Training of the Mentally Retarded, 24,* 248–254.

Salend, S. J., Jantzen, N. R., & Giek, K. (1992). Using a peer confrontation system in a group setting. *Behavioral Disorders, 17,* 211–218.

Salvia, J., & Ysseldyke, J. E. (2001). *Assessment in special and remedial education* (8th ed.). Boston: Houghton Mifflin.

Sameroff, A. (2001). *Rick and resilience from infancy to adolescence: Is it better to change the child or the context?* Keynote address at Research Project Directors' Conference, U.S. Office of Special Education Programs, Washington, DC. (July 11).

Sandall, S., & Ostrosky, M. (2000). *Natural environments and inclusion: Young exceptional children.* Monograph series No. 2. Reston, VA: Council for Exceptional Children, Division for Early Childhood.

Sandall, S., & Schwartz, I. (2002). *Building blocks for teaching preschoolers with special needs.* Baltimore: Brookes.

Sandall, S., Joseph, G., Chou, H. Y., Schwartz, I. S., Horn, E., Lieber, J., Odom, S. L., & Wolery, R. (2000). *Talking to practitioners: Focus group report on curriculum modifications in inclusive preschool classrooms.* Unpublished manuscript.

Sandall, S., McLean, M. E., & Smith, B. J. (Eds.). (2000). *DEC recommended practices in early intervention/early childhood special education.* Reston, VA: Council for Exceptional Children, Division for Early Childhood.

Sandall, S., Schwartz, I., & Joseph, G. (2000). A building blocks model for effective instruction in inclusive early childhood settings. *Young Exceptional Children, 4*(3), 3–9.

Sandler, A. G., & Mistretta, L. A. (1998). Positive adaptation in parents of adults with disabilities. *Education and Training in Mental Retardation and Developmental Disabilities, 33,* 123–130.

Sandler, A. G., Arnold, L. B., Gable, R. A., & Strain, P. S. (1987). Effects of peer pressure on disruptive behavior of behaviorally disordered students. *Behavioral Disorders, 16,* 9–22.

Sands, D. J., & Kozleski, E. B. (1994). Quality of life differences between adults with and without disabilities. *Education and Training in Mental Retardation, 29,* 90–101.

Sansone, J., & Zigmond, N. (1986). Evaluating mainstreaming through an analysis of students' schedules. *Exceptional Children, 52,* 452–458.

Santelli, B., & Poyadue, F. S. (2001). *The parent to parent handbook: Connecting families of children with special needs.* Baltimore: Brookes.

Santelli, B., Turnbull, A., Marquis, J., & Lerner, E. (1997). Parent-to-parent programs: A resource for parents and professionals. *Journal of Early Intervention, 21,* 73–83.

Sapienza, C., & Hicks, D. M. (2002). Voice disorders. In G. H. Shames & N. B. Anderson (Eds.), *Human communication disorders: An introduction* (6th ed.), (pp. 349–393). Boston: Allyn & Bacon.

Sarouphim, K. M. (2001). DISCOVER: Concurrent validity, gender differences, and identification of minority students. *Gifted Child Quarterly, 45*(2), 130–139.

Sasso, G. (2001). The retreat from inquiry and knowledge in special education. *Journal of Special Education, 34,* 178–193.

Savage, R. C., & Wolcott, G. F. (Eds.). (1994). *Educational dimensions of acquired brain injury.* Austin, TX: PRO-ED.

Scarcella, R. (1990). *Teaching language minority students in the multicultural classroom.* Upper Saddle River, NJ: Merrill/Prentice Hall.

Schalock, R. L. (Ed.). (1999). *Adaptive behavior and its measurement: Implications for the field of mental retardation.* Washington, DC: American Association on Mental Retardation.

Schalock, R. L., Bonham, G. S., & Marchand, C. B. (2000). Consumer based quality of life assessment: A path model of perceived satisfaction. *Evaluator and Program Planning, 23,* 75–85.

Schalock, R. L., Keith, K. D., Hoffman, K., & Karan, O. C. (1989). Quality of life: Its measurement and use. *Mental Retardation, 27,* 25–31.

Schessel, D. A. (1999). Ménière's disease. *The Volta Review, 99*(5), 177–183.

Scheuermann, B., & Webber, J. (2002). *Autism: Teaching Does Make a Difference.* Belmont, CA: Wadsworth.

Schick, B., & Williams, K. (1994). The evaluation of educational interpreters. In B. Schick & M. P. Moeller (Eds.), *Sign language in the schools: Current issues and controversies.* Omaha, NE: Boys Town Press.

Schick, B., Williams, K., & Bolster, L. (1999). Skill levels of educational interpreters working in public schools. *Journal of Deaf Studies and Deaf Education, 4,* 144–155.

Schirmer, B. R. (1997). Boosting reading success: Language, literacy, and content area instruction for deaf and hard-of-hearing students. *Teaching Exceptional Children, 30*(1), 52–55.

Schirmer, B. R. (2000). Language and literacy development in children who are deaf (2nd ed.). Boston: Allyn & Bacon.

Schirmer, B. R. (2001). *Psychological, social, and educational dimensions of deafness.* Boston: Allyn & Bacon.

Schirmer, B. R. (2002). Hearing loss. In A. Turnbull, R. Turnbull, M. Shank, S. Smith, & D. Leal (Eds.), *Exceptional Lives: Special education in today's schools* (3rd ed.), (pp. 516–554). Upper Saddle River, NJ: Merrill/Prentice Hall.

Schleien, S. J., Kiernan, J., & Wehman, P. (1981). Evaluation of an age-appropriate leisure skills program for moderately retarded adults. *Education and Training of the Mentally Retarded, 16,* 13–19.

Schleien, S. J., Meyer, L. H., Heyne, L. A., & Brandt, B. B. (1995). *Lifelong leisure skills and lifestyles for persons with developmental disabilities.* Baltimore: Brookes.

Schleien, S. J., Wehman, P., & Kiernan, J. (1981). Teaching leisure skills to severely handicapped adults: An age-appropriate darts game. *Journal of Applied Behavior Analysis, 14,* 513–519.

Schleien, S. J., & Ray, M. T. (1998). *Community recreation and persons with disabilities: Strategies for integration* (2nd ed.). Baltimore: Brookes.

Schneider, B. H., & Leroux, J. (1994). Educational environments for the pupil with behavioral disorders: A "best evidence" synthesis. *Behavioral Disorders, 19,* 192–204.

Schnorr, R. (1990). "Peter? He comes and he goes . . .": First-graders' perspectives of a part-time mainstream student. *Journal of the Association for Persons with Severe Handicaps, 15,* 231–240.

Schön, D. A. (1983). *The reflective practitioner: How professionals think in action.* New York: Basic Books.

Schonert-Reichl, K. A. (1993). Empathy and social relationships in adolescents with behavioral disorders. *Behavioral Disorders, 18,* 189–204.

Schroeder, S. (Ed.). (1987). *Toxic substances and mental retardation: Neurobiological toxicology and teratology.* Washington, DC: American Association on Mental Retardation.

Schulz, J. B. (1985). The parent-professional conflict. In H. R. Turnbull & A. P. Turnbull (Eds.), *Parents speak out: Then and now* (pp. 3–11). Upper Saddle River, NJ: Merrill/Prentice Hall.

Schumaker, J. B., & Deshler, D. D. (1992). Validation of learning strategy interventions for students with learning disabilities: Results of a programmatic research effort. In B. Y. L. Wong (Ed.), *Contemporary intervention research in learning disabilities* (pp. 22–46). New York: Springer-Verlag.

Schumm, J. S., Moody, S. W., & Vaughn, S. (2000). Grouping for reading instruction: Does one size fit all? *Journal of Learning Disabilities, 33,* 477–488.

Schumm, J. S., Vaughn, D., Haager, D., McDowell, J., Rothlein, L., & Saumell, L. (1995). General education teacher planning: What can students with learning disabilities expect? *Exceptional Children, 61,* 335–352.

Schwartz, I. (2000). Standing on the shoulders of giants: Looking ahead to facilitating membership and relationships for children with disabilities. *Topics in Early Childhood Special Education, 20,* 123–128.

Schwartz, I. S., & Baer, D. M. (1991). Social validity assessments: Is current practice state of the art? *Journal of Applied Behavior Analysis, 24,* 189–204.

Schwartz, I. S., Garfinkle, A. N., & Bauer, J. (1998). The picture exchange communication system: Communication outcomes for young children with disabilities. Manuscript submitted for publication.

Schwartz, I., Garfinkle, A. N., & Bauer, J. (1998). The Picture Exchange Communication System: Communicative outcomes for young children with disabilities. *Topics in Early Childhood Special Education, 18,* 144–159.

Schwartz, I., Sandall, S. R., Garfinkle, A. N., & Bauer, J. (1998). Outcomes for children with autism: Three case studies. *Topics in Early Childhood Special Education, 18,* 132–143.

Schwartz, Wolfe, & Cassar, 1997; Feb BD p. 151.

Scorgie, K., & Sobsey, D. (2000). Transformational outcomes associated with parenting children who have disabilities. *Mental Retardation, 38,* 195–206.

Scott, T. M., & Nelson, C. M. (1999). Using functional behavioral assessment to develop effective intervention plans: Practical classroom applications. *Journal of Positive Behavioral Interventions, 1,* 242–251.

Scruggs, T. E., & Mastropieri, M. A. (1992). Classroom applications of mnemonic instruction: Acquisition, maintenance, and generalization. *Exceptional Children, 58,* 219–229.

Scuccimarra, D. J., & Speece, D. L. (1990). Employment outcomes and social integration of students with mild handicaps: The quality of life two years after high school. *Journal of Learning Disabilities, 23,* 213–219.

Semel, E., Wiig, E. H., & Secord, W. (1995). *Clinical evaluation of language fundamentals* (3rd ed.). San Antonio, TX: Psychological Corporation.

Sexson, S. B., & Dingle, A. D. (2001). Medical disorders. In F. M. Kline, L. B. Silver, & S. C. Russell, (Eds.), *The educator's guide to medical issues in the classroom* (pp. 29–48). Baltimore: Brookes.

Sexson, S. B., & Madan-Swain, A. (1993). School reentry for the child with chronic illness. *Journal of Learning Disabilities, 26,* 115–125.

Sexton, M., Harris, K. R., & Graham, S. (1998). Self-regulated strategy development and the writing process: Effects on essay writing and attributions. *Exceptional Children, 64,* 295–311.

Seymour, H. N., Bland-Stewart, L., & Green, L. J. (1998). Difference versus deficit in child African American English. *Language, Speech, and Hearing Services in the Schools, 29,* 96–108.

Shade, B. J., & New, C. A. (1993). Cultural influences on learning: Teaching implications. In J. A. Banks & C. A. M. Banks (Eds.), *Multicultural education: Issues and perspectives* (2nd ed.) (pp. 317–331). Needham Heights, MA: Allyn & Bacon.

Shaklee, B., Whitmore, J., Barton, L. Barbour, N., Ambross, R., & Viechnicki, K. (1989). Early assessment for exceptional potential for young and/or economically disadvantaged students. Washington, DC: Office of Educational Research and Improvement, U. S. Department of Education Grant No. R206A00160.

Shames, G. H. & Anderson, N. B. (2002). *Human communication disorders: An introduction* (6th ed.). Boston: Allyn & Bacon.

Shapiro, E. S., DuPaul, G. J., & Bradley-King, K. L. (1998). Self-management as a strategy to improve the classroom behavior of adolescents with ADHD. *Journal of Learning Disabilities, 31,* 545–555.

Shapiro, E. S., Miller, D. N., Swaka, K., Gardill, M. C., & Handler, M. W. (1999). Facilitating the inclusion of students with EBD into general education classrooms. *Journal of Emotional and Behavioral Disorders, 7,* 83–93.

Shaywitz, B. A., Fletcher, J. M., & Shaywitz, S. E. (1995). Defining and classifying learning disabilities and attention-deficit/hyperactivity disorder. *Journal of Child Neurology, 10,* 50–57.

Shearer, M. S., & Shearer, D. E. (1979). *The Portage Project: A model for early childhood education.* Portage, WI: Portage Project.

Sherman, T. M., & Cormier, W. H. (1974). An investigation of the influence of student behavior on teacher behavior. *Journal of Applied Behavior Analysis, 7,* 11–21.

Shildroth, A. N., & Hotto, S. A. (1994). Inclusion or exclusion? Deaf students and the inclusion movement. *American Annals of the Deaf, 139,* 239–242.

Shinn, M. R., Tindal, G. A., & Spira, D. A. (1987). Special education referrals as an index of teacher tolerance: Are teacher imperfect tests? *Exceptional Children, 54,* 32–40.

Shonkoff, J. P., & Meisels, S. J. (Eds.). (2000). *Handbook of early childhood intervention* (2nd ed.). New York: Cambridge University Press.

Shore, B. M., Cornell, D. G., Robinson, A., & Ward, V. (1991). *Recommended practices in gifted education: A critical analysis.* New York: Teachers College Press.

Shores, R. E., Gunter, P. L., & Jack, S. L. (1993). Classroom management strategies: Are they setting events for coercion? *Behavioral Disorders, 18,* 92–102.

Shores, R. E., Jack, S. L., Gunter, P. L., Ellis, D. N., DeBriere, T. J., & Wehby, J. H. (1993). Classroom interactions of children with disorders. *Journal of Emotional and Behavioral Disorders, 1,* 27–39.

Shukla, S., Kennedy, C. H., & Cushing, L. S. (1998). Adult influence on the participation of peers without disabilities in peer support programs. *Journal of Behavioral Education, 8,* 397–413.

Shulte, A., Osborne, S., & McKinney, J. (1990). Academic outcomes for students with learning disabilities in consultation and resource programs. *Exceptional Children, 77,* 162–172.

Sicley, D. (1993). Effective methods of communication: Practical interventions for classroom teachers. *Intervention in School and Clinic, 29,* 105–108.

Sidman, M. (1989). *Coercion and its fallout.* Boston: Authors Group.

Sidman, M. (1994). *Equivalence relations and behavior: A research story.* Boston: Authors Cooperative.

Siegel, I. J., & Senna, J. J. (1994). *Juvenile delinquency: Theory, practice, and law* (5th ed.). St. Paul, MN: West.

Sievert, A. L., Cuvo, A. J., & Davis, P. K. (1988). Training self-advocacy skills to adults with mild handicaps. *Journal of Applied Behavior Analysis, 21,* 299–309.

Silliman, E. R., & Diehl, S. F. (in press). Assessing children with language learning disabilities. In D. K. Berstein & E. Tiegerman-Farber (Eds.), *Language and communication disorders in children* (5th ed.). Needham Heights, MA: Allyn & Bacon.

Silliman, E. R., Bahr, R., Beasman, J., & Wilkinson, L. C. (2000). Scaffolds for learning to read in an inclusion classroom. *Language, Speech, and Hearing Services in Schools, 31,* 265–269.

Silliman, E. R., Ford, C. S., Beasman, J., & Evans, D. (1999). An inclusion model for children with language learning disabilities: Building classroom partnerships. *Topics in Language Disorders, 19*(3), 1–18.

Silliman, E. R., Mills, L. R., & Murphy, M. M. (1997). How to start? One story of change in a middle school. In N. W. Nelson & B. Hoskins (Eds.), *Strategies for supporting classroom success* (pp. 1–22). San Diego: Singular.

Silverman, L. K. (1986). Parenting young gifted children. *Journal of Children in Contemporary Society, 18,* 73–87.

Silverman, L. K. (1995). Highly gifted children. In J. L. Genshaft, M. Bireley, & C. L. Hollinger (Eds.), *Serving gifted and talented students: A resource for school personnel* (pp. 124–160). Austin, TX: PRO-ED.

Simmons, D. C., Kame'enui, E. J., & Chard, D. J. (1998). General education teachers' assumptions about learning and students with learning disabilities: Design-of-instruction analysis. *Learning Disability Quarterly, 21,* 6–21.

Simmons, D. C., Kame'enui, E. J., Coyne, M. D., & Chard, D. J. (2002). In E. J. Kame'enui, D. W. Carnine, R. C. Dixon, D. C. Simmons, & M. D. Coyne, (Eds.), *Effective teaching strategies that accommodate diverse learners* (2nd ed.), (pp. 53–92). Upper Saddle River, NJ: Merrill/Prentice Hall.

Simmons, T. J., & Whaley, B. (2001). Transition to employment. In R. W. Flexer, T. J. Simmons, P. Luft, & R. M. Baer. *Transition planning for secondary students with disabilities* (pp. 416–438). Upper Saddle River, NJ: Merrill/Prentice Hall.

Simon, R. (1987). *After the tears: Parents talk about raising a child with a disability.* San Diego: Harcourt Brace Jovanovich.

Simos, P. G., Breier, J. I., Fletcher, J. M., Bergman, E., & Papanicolaou, A. C. (2000). Cerebral mechanisms involved in word reading in dyslexic children: A magnetic source imaging approach. *Cerebral Cortex, 10,* 809–816.

Simpson, R. L. (1996). *Working with families and parents of exceptional children and youth: Techniques for successful conferencing and collaboration* (3rd ed.). Austin, TX: PRO-ED.

Simpson, R. L. (2001). ABA and students with autism spectrum disorders: Issues and considerations for effective practice. *Focus on Autism and Other Developmental Disabilities, 16,* 68–71.

Simpson, R. L., & Myles, B. S. (in press). Effective practices for students with Asperger syndrome. *Focus on Exceptional Children.*

Sims, D. G., & Gottermeier, L. (1995). Computer-assisted, interactive video methods for speechreading instruction: A review. In K. Erik-Spens & G. Plant (Eds.), *Speech, communication and profound deafness* (pp. 220–241). London: Whurr.

Singer, G. H. S., Powers, L. E., & Olson, A. (1996). *Redefining family support: Innovations in public/private partnerships.* Baltimore: Brookes.

Sitlington, P. L., Clark, G. M., & Kolstoe, O. P. (2000). *Comprehensive transition education and services for adolescents with disabilities* (3rd ed.). Needham Heights, MA: Allyn & Bacon.

Sitlington, P. L., Frank, A. R., & Carson, R. (1993). Adult adjustment among high school graduates with mild disabilities. *Exceptional Children, 59,* 221–233.

Skeels, H. M., & Dye, H. B. (1939). A study of the effects of differential stimulation on mentally retarded children. *Convention Proceedings, American Association on Mental Deficiency, 44,* 114–136.

Skellenger, A., Hill, E., & Hill, M. (1992). The social functioning of children with visual impairments. In S. L. Odom, S. R. McConnell, & M. A. McEvoy (Eds.), *Social competence of young children with disabilities: Issues and strategies for intervention* (pp. 165–188). Baltimore: Brookes.

Skinner, B. F. (1989). *Recent issues in the analysis of behavior.* Columbus, OH: Merrill.

Skinner, D. G., Correa, V., Skinner, M., & Bailey, D. (2001). Role of religion in the lives of Latino families of young children with developmental delays. *American Journal on Mental Retardation, 106,* 297–313.

Skinner, D., Bailey, D. D., Jr., Correa, V. I., & Rodriguez, P. (1999). Narrating self and disabilities: Latino mothers' construction of identities vis-à-vis their children with special needs. *Exceptional Children, 65,* 481–495.

Skinner, M. (1998). Promoting self-advocacy among college students with learning disabilities. *Intervention in School and Clinic, 33*(5), 278–283.

Slade, J. C., & Conoley, C. W. (1989). Multicultural experiences for special educators. *Teaching Exceptional Children, 22*(1), 60–64.

Slaton, D. E., Schuster, J., Collins, B., & Carnine, D. (1994). A functional approach to academic instruction. In E. Cipani & F. Spooner (Eds.), *Curricular and instructional approaches for persons with severe disabilities* (pp. 149–183). Boston: Allyn & Bacon.

Slavin, R. (1987). Ability grouping and student achievement in elementary schools: A best-evidence synthesis. *Review of Educational Research, 57,* 293–336.

Slavin, R. (1991). Synthesis of research on cooperative learning. *Educational Leadership, 47*(4), 3.

Slike, S. B., & Hobbs, D. H. (1998, March). *The development of a CD-ROM to teach speechreading skills.* Paper presented at the Association of College Educators of the Deaf and Hard of Hearing, Lexington, KY.

Slike, S. B., Thornton, N. E., Hobbis, D. H., Kokoska, S. M., & Job, K. A. (1995). The development and analysis of interactive videodisc technology to teach speechreading. *American Annals of the Deaf, 140*(4), 346–351.

Smith, A. (2001). A faceless bureaucrat ponders special education, disabilities, and white privilege. *Journal of The Association for Persons with Severe Handicaps, 26,* 180–188.

Smith, C. R. (1997). Advocacy for students with emotional and behavior disorders: One call for redefined efforts. *Behavioral Disorders, 22,* 96–105.

Smith, C. R. (2000). Behavioral and discipline provisions of IDEA '97: Implicit competencies yet to be confirmed. *Exceptional Children, 66,* 403–412.

Smith, J. D. (1994). The revised AAMR definition of mental retardation: The MRDD position. *Education and Training in Mental Retardation, 29,* 179–183.

Smith, J. D. (2000). The power of mental retardation: Reflections on the value of people with disabilities. *Mental Retardation, 38,* 70–72.

Smith, J. D., & Hilton, A. (1994). Program design for students with mental retardation. *Education and Training in Mental Retardation and Developmental Disabilities, 29,* 3–8.

Smith, J. D., & Hilton, A. (1997). The preparation and training of the educational community for the inclusion of students with developmental disabilities: The MRDD position. *Education and Training of Mental Retardation and Developmental Disabilities, 32,* 3–10.

Smith, J. D., & Mitchell, A. L. (2001a). Disney's Tarzan, Edgar Rice Burroughs' eugenics, and visions of utopian perfection. *Mental Retardation, 39,* 221–225.

Smith, J. D., & Mitchell, A. L. (2001b). "Me? I'm not a drooler. I'm the assistant": Is it time to abandon mental retardation as a classification? *Mental Retardation, 39,* 144–146.

Smith, J., & Prior, M. (1995). Temperament and stress resilience in school-age children: A within-families study. *Journal of the American Academy of Children and Adolescent Psychiatry, 34,* 168–179.

Smith, L., & Fowler, S. A. (1984). Positive peer pressure: The effects of peer monitoring on children's disruptive behavior. *Journal of Applied Behavior Analysis, 17,* 213–227.

Smith, S. B., Baker, S., & Oudeans, M. K., Sr. (2001). Making a difference in the classroom with early literacy instruction. *Teaching Exceptional Children, 33*(6), 8–14.

Smith, S. W. (1990a). Comparison of Individualized Education Programs (IEPs) of students with behavioral disorders and learning disabilities. *Journal of Special Education, 24*(1), 85–100.

Smith, S. W. (1990b). Individualized Education Programs (IEPs) in special education—From intent to acquiescence. *Exceptional Children, 57,* 6–14.

Smith, S. W., & Brownell, M. T. (1995). Individualized education programs: From intent to acquiescence. *Focus on Exceptional Children, 28*(1), 1–12.

Smith, S. W., & Simpson, R. L. (1989). An analysis of individualized education programs (IEPs) for students with behavioral disorders. *Behavioral Disorders, 14,* 107–116.

Smith, T. E. C., & Hilton, A. (1994). Program design for students with mental retardation. *Education and Training in Mental Retardation, 29,* 3–8.

Smithdas, R. (1981). Psychological aspects of deaf-blindness. In S. R. Walsh & R. Holzberg (Eds.), *Understanding and educating the deaf-blind/severely and profoundly handicapped: An international perspective.* Springfield, IL: Thomas.

Snell, M. E. (1991). Schools are for all kids: The importance of integration for students with severe disabilities and their peers. In J. W. Lloyd, A. C. Repp, & N. N. Singh (Eds.), *The regular education initiative: Alternative perspectives on concepts, issues, and models* (pp. 133–148). Sycamore, IL: Sycamore.

Snell, M. E., & Beckman-Brindley, S. (1984). Family involvement in intervention with children having severe handicaps. *Journal of The Association for Persons with Severe Handicaps, 9,* 213–230.

Snell, M. E., & Brown, F. (Eds.). (2000). *Instruction of students with severe disabilities* (5th ed.). Upper Saddle River, NJ: Merrill/Prentice Hall.

Snell, M. E., & Janney, R. E. (2000a). *Practices for inclusive schools: Collaborative teaming.* Baltimore: Brookes.

Snell, M. E., & Janney, R. E. (2000b). Teachers' problem-solving about children with moderate and severe disabilities in elementary classrooms. *Exceptional Children, 66,* 472–490.

Snow, J. (2001, May). Thoughts on self–determination. *Common Sense,* Issue 8, pp. 7–9. Durham, NH: University of New Hampshire, Institute on Disability.

Snyder, H. N. (2000). *Juvenile Arrests 1999.* Washington, DC: Office of Juvenile Justice and Delinquency Prevention.

Sobsey, D. (1994). *Violence and abuse in the lives of people with disabilities: The end of silent acceptance?* Baltimore: Brookes.

Sobsey, D. (1996). Review of assistive technologies: Principles and practice by A. M. Cook & S. M. Hussey. *Journal of The Association for Persons with Severe Handicaps, 21,* 207–209.

Social Security Administration. (2000). *Titles II and XVI: Basic disability.* www.ssa.gov/disability

Sonnenschein, S. (1981). Parents and professionals: An uneasy relationship. *Teaching Exceptional Children, 14,* 62–65.

Sontag, E., Sailor, W., & Smith, J. (1977). The severely/profoundly handicapped: Who are they? Where are we? *Journal of Special Education, 11*(1), 5–11.

Soodak, L., & Erwin, E. (2000). Valued member or tolerated participant: Parents' experience in inclusive early childhood settings. *Journal of the Association for Persons with Severe Handicaps, 25,* 29–41.

Southern, W. T., & Jones, E. (1991). *The academic acceleration of gifted children.* New York: Teachers College Press.

Sowers, J., Verdi, M., Bourbeau, P., & Sheehan, M. (1985). Teaching job independence to mentally retarded students through the use of a self-control package. *Journal of Applied Behavior Analysis, 18,* 81–85.

Spache, G. D. (1981). *Diagnostic Reading Scales.* Monterey, CA: CTB McGraw-Hill.

Sparks, S. (2000). Classroom and curriculum accommodations for Native American students. *Intervention in School and Clinic, 35*(5), 259–263.

Sparrow, S. S., Balla, D. A., & Cicchetti, D. V. (1984a). *Vineland Adaptive Behavior Scales: Interview edition, expanded form.* Circle Pines, MN: American Guidance Service.

Sparrow, S. S., Balla, D. A., & Cicchetti, D. V. (1984b). *Vineland Adaptive Behavior Scales: Interview edition, survey form.* Circle Pines, MN: American Guidance Service.

Sparrow, S. S., Balla, D. A., & Cicchetti, D. V. (1985). *Vineland Adaptive Behavior Scales: Classroom edition form.* Circle Pines, MN: American Guidance Service.

Spear-Swerling, L., & Sternberg, R. J. (2001). What science offers teachers of reading. *Learning Disabilities Research and Practice, 16,* 51–57.

Spencer, P. E. (2001, July). *Cochlear implants for children: Language, culture, and education.* Paper presented at Office of Special Education Program Project Director's Conference, Washington, DC.

Sprague, J., & Walker, H. (2000). Early identification and intervention for youth with antisocial and violent behavior. *Exceptional Children, 66,* 367–379.

Sprick, R. S., & Howard, L. M. (1997). *The teacher's encyclopedia of behavior management: 100 problems/500 plans.* Longmont, CO: Sopris West.

Spring, C., & Sandoval, J. (1976). Food additives and hyperkinesis: A critical evaluation of the evidence. *Journal of Learning Disabilities, 9,* 560–569.

Squires, J., Bricker, D., & Twombly, E. (2002). *Ages and Stages Questionnaires: Social–Emotional (ASQ:SE).* Baltimore: Brookes.

Sridhar, D., & Vaughn, S. (2000). Bibliotherapy for all: enhancing reading comprehension, self-concept, and behavior. *Teaching Exceptional Children, 33*(2), 74–82.

Stainback, S., & Stainback, W. (Eds.). (1991). *Teaching in the inclusive classroom: Curriculum design, adaptation and delivery.* Baltimore: Brookes.

Stainback, S., & Stainback, W. (Eds.). (1992). *Inclusion: A guide for educators.* Baltimore: Brookes.

Stainback, S., & Stainback, W. (Eds.) (1996). *Inclusion: A guide for educators* (2nd ed.). Baltimore: Brookes.

Stainton, T., & Besser, H. (1998). The positive impact of children with an intellectual disability on the family. *Journal of Intellectual and Developmental Disability, 23,* 57–70.

Stancliffe, R. J., & Hayden, C. (1998). Longitudinal study of institutional downsizing: Effects on individuals who remain in the institution. *American Journal on Mental Retardation, 102,* 500–510.

Stancliffe, R. J., & Lakin, K. C. (1998). Analysis of expenditures and outcomes of residential alternatives for persons with developmental disabilities. *American Journal on Mental Retardation, 102,* 552–568.

Stanovich, K. E., & Siegel, L. S. (1994). The phenotypic performance profile of reading-disabled children: A regression-based test of the phonological-core variable-difference model. *Journal of Educational Psychology, 86,* 24–53.

Stark, K. D., Bronik, M. D., Wong, S., Wells, G., & Ostrander, R. (2000). Depressive disorders. In M. Hersen & R. T. Ammerman (Eds.), *Advanced abnormal child psychology* (2nd ed.) (pp. 291–326). Hillsdale, NJ: Erlbaum.

Staub, D., Spaulding, M., Peck, C. A., Gallucci, C., & Schwartz, I. S. (1996). Using nondisabled peers to support the inclusion of students with disabilities at the junior high school level. *Journal of The Association for Persons with Severe Handicaps, 21,* 194–205.

Staub, R. W. (1990). The effects of publicly posted feedback on middle school students' disruptive hallway behavior. *Education and Treatment Children, 13,* 249–257.

Steeker, P. M., & Fuchs, L. S. (2000). Effecting superior achievement using curriculum-based measurement: The importance of individual progress monitoring. *Learning Disabilities Research and Practice, 15,* 128–134.

Stemley, J. (1993). Idea Puppy: Teaching preschool age children with disabilities to build independent work skills with the use of a self-operated audio prompt recording device. Unpublished master's thesis, The Ohio State University, Columbus.

Stephens, K. R., & Karnes, F. A. (2000). State definitions for the gifted and talented revisited. *Exceptional Children, 66*(2), 219–238.

Stephens, T. M., & Wolf, J. S. (1989). *Effective skills in parent/teacher conferencing* (2nd ed.). Columbus: The Ohio State University, College of Education, School Study Council of Ohio.

Sternberg, L. (Ed.). (1994). *Individuals with profound disabilities: Instructional and assistive strategies.* Austin, TX: PRO-ED.

Sternberg, R. (1988). *The triarchic mind: A new theory of human intelligence.* New York: Viking.

Sternberg, R. J. (1985). *Beyond IQ: A triarchic theory of human intelligence.* New York: Cambridge University Press.

Sternberg, R., & Grigorenko, E. (2000). *Teaching for successful intelligence.* Upper Saddle River, NJ: Merrill/Prentice Hall.

Stevenson, R. E., Massey, P. S., Schroer, R. J., McDermott, S., & Richter, B. (1996). Preventable fraction of mental retardation: Analysis based on individuals with severe mental retardation. *Mental Retardation, 34,* 182–188.

Stewart, D. A. (1992). Initiating reform in total communication programs. *Journal of Special Education, 26,* 68–84.

Stewart, J. L. (1977). Unique problems of handicapped Native Americans. In *The White House Conference on Handicapped Individuals* (vol. 1) (pp. 438–444). Washington, DC: U. S. Government Printing Office.

Stiles, S., & Knox, R. (1996). Medical issues, treatments, and professionals. In M. C. Holbrook (Ed.), *Children with visual impairments: A parents' guide* (pp. 21–48). Bethesda, MD: Woodbine House.

Stinson, M. S., & Liu, Y. (1999). Participation of deaf and hard-of-hearing students in classes with hearing students. *Journal of Deaf Studies and Deaf Education, 4,* 191–202.

Stinson, M. S., Elliot, L. B., McKee, B. G., & Francis, P. G. (2001). Accessibility in the classroom: The pros and cons of C-Print. *Volta Voices, 8*(3), 16–19.

Stokes, T. F., Fowler, S. A., & Baer, D. M. (1978). Training preschool children to recruit natural communities of reinforcement. *Journal of Applied Behavior Analysis, 11,* 285–303.

Stokoe, W. (1960). *The calculus of structure.* Washington, DC: Gallaudet University Press.

Stokoe, W. C., Armstrong, D. F., & Wilcox, S. (1995). *Gesture and the nature of language.* New York: Cambridge University Press.

Stone, C. A. (2002). Promises and pitfalls of scaffolded instruction for students with language learning disabilities. In K. G. Butler & E. R. Silliman (Eds.), *Speaking, reading, and writing in children with language learning disabilities: New paradigms for research and practice* (pp. 175–198). Mahwah, NJ: Erlbaum.

Stone, J. (1997). The preschool child. In H. Mason & S. McCall (Eds.), *Visual impairment: Access to education for children and young people* (pp. 87–96). London: Fulton.

Stone, P. (1997). Educating children who are deaf or hard of hearing: Auditory-oral option. *ERIC Digest #551.* (ERIC Document Reproduction Service No. ED 414 669).

Stoneman, Z. (1998). Research on siblings of children with mental retardation: Contributions of developmental theory and etiology. In J. A. Burach, R. M. Hodapp, & E. Zigler (Eds.), *Handbook of mental retardation and development* (pp. 669–692) Cambridge: Cambridge University Press.

Stoneman, Z., Brody, G. H., Davis, C. H., & Crapps, J. M. (1989). Mentally retarded children and their older same-sex siblings: Naturalistic in-home observations. *American Journal of Mental Retardation, 92,* 290–298.

Stool, S. E., Berg, A. O., Berman, S., et al. (1994). *Otitis media with effusion in young children. Clinical Practice Guideline, Number 12.* (AHCPR Publication No. 94-0622). Rockville, MD: Agency for Health Care Policy and Research, Public Health Service, U.S. Department of Health and Human Services.

Strain, P. S., & Schwartz, I. (2001). ABA and the development of meaningful social relations for young children with autism. *Focus on Autism and Other Developmental Disabilities, 16,* 120–128.

Strain, P. S., & Smith, B. J. (1986). A counter-interpretation of early intervention effects: A response to Casto and Mastropieri. *Exceptional Children, 53,* 260–265.

Strain, P. S., & Timm, M. A. (2001). Remediation and prevention of aggression: An evaluation of the Regional Intervention Program over a quarter century. *Behavioral Disorders, 26,* 297–313.

Strand, J., & Kreiner, J. (2001). Recreation and leisure in the community. In R. W. Flexer, T. J. Simmons, P. Luft, & R. M. Baer, *Transition planning for secondary students with disabilities* (pp. 474–498). Upper Saddle River, NJ: Merrill/Prentice Hall.

Strauss, A. A., & Lehtinen, L. E. (1947). *Psychopathology and education of the brain-injured child.* New York: Grune & Stratton.

Strauss, M. (1999). Hearing loss and cytomegalovirus. *The Volta Review, 99*(5), 71–74.

Stremel, K., Molden, V., Leister, C., Matthews, J., Wilson, R., Goodall, D. V., & Hoston, J. (1990). *Communication systems and routines: A decision making process.* Washington, DC: U. S. Office of Special Education.

Strickland, B. B., & Turnbull, A. P. (1993). *Developing and implementing Individualized Education Programs* (3rd ed.). Upper Saddle River, NJ: Merrill/Prentice Hall.

Strickland, S. P. (1971). Can slum children learn? *American Education, 7*(6), 3–7.

Strong, C. J. & North, K. H. (1996). *The magic of stories: Literature–based language intervention.* Eau Claire, WI: Thinking Publications.

Strong, M. (1995). A review of bilingual/bicultural programs for deaf children in North America. *American Annals of the Deaf, 140*(2), 84–94.

Strong, M., & Prinz, P. M. (1997). A study of the relationship between American Sign Language and English literacy. *Journal of Deaf Studies and Deaf Education, 2,* 36–46.

Stroul, B. A., & Friedman, R. M. (1996). *A system of care for children and adolescents with severe emotional disturbance* (rev. ed.). Washington, DC: National Technical Assistance Center for Child Mental Health, Georgetown University Child Development Center.

Stuart v. Nappi, 443 F. Supp. 1235 (D. Conn. 1978).

Stump, C. S., Lovitt, T. C., Fister, S., Kemp, K., Moore, R., & Schroeder, B. (1992). Vocabulary intervention for secondary-level youth. *Learning Disability Quarterly, 15,* 207–222.

Sturmey, P., & Sevin, J. A. (1994). Defining and assessing autism. In J. L. Matson (Ed.), *Autism in children and adults: Etiology, assessment, and intervention* (pp. 13–36). Pacific Grove, CA: Brooks/Cole.

Sudhalter, V., & Belser, R. C. (2001). Conversational characteristics of children with fragile X syndrome: Tangential language. *American Journal of Mental Retardation, 106,* 389–400.

Sugai, G., Sprague, J. R., Horner, R. H., and Walker, H. M. (2000). Preventing school violence: The use of office discipline referrals to assess and monitor school-wide discipline interventions. *Journal of Emotional and Behavioral Disorders, 8,* 94–101.

Sullivan, P. M., & Knutson, J. F. (1994). *The relationship between child abuse and neglect and disabilities: Implications for research and practice.* Omaha, NE: Boys Town National Research Hospital.

Sundberg, M. L. & Partington, J. W. (1999). The need for both discrete trial and natural environment training for children with autism. In P. M. Ghezzi, W. L. Williams, & J. Carr (Eds.), *Autism: Behavior Analytic Perspectives* (pp. 139–156). Reno, NV: Context.

Sutherland, K. S. (2000). Promoting positive interactions between teachers and students with emotional and behavior disorders. *Preventing School Failure, 44,* 110–115.

Sutherland, K. S., & Wehby, J. H. (2001). Exploring the relationship between increased opportunities to respond to academic requests and the academic and behavioral outcomes of students with EBD: A review. *Remedial and Special Education, 22,* 113–121.

Sutherland, K. S., Wehby, J. H., & Copeland, S. R. (2000). Effects of varying rates of behavior specific praise on the on-task behavior of students with emotional and behavioral disorders. *Journal of Emotional and Behavioral Disorders, 8,* 2–8.

Sutherland, K. S., Wehby, J. H., & Yoder, P. J. (in press). An examination of the relation between teacher praise and students with emotional/behavioral disorders opportunities to respond to academic requests. *Journal of Emotional and Behavioral Disorders.*

Swallow, R. M. (1978, May). Cognitive development. Paper presented at the North American Conference on Visually Handicapped Infants and Preschool Children, Minneapolis.

Swanson, H. L. (1999). *Interventions for students with learning disabilities: A meta-analysis of treatment outcomes.* New York: Guilford.

Swanson, H. L. (2000). Issues facing the field of learning disabilities. *Learning Disability Quarterly, 23,* 37–50.

Swanson, J., McBurnett, K., Christain, D., & Wigal, T. (1995). Stimulant medication and treatment of children with ADHD. In T. H. Ollendick & R. J. Prinz (Eds.), *Advances in Clinical Child Psychology* (Vol. 17, pp. 265–322). New York: Plenum.

Swiatek, M. A., & Benbow, C. P. (1991, November). Acceleration: Does it cause academic or psychological harm? Paper presented at the meeting of the National Association for Gifted Children, Little Rock, AR.

Swisher, K. (1992). Learning styles: Implications for teachers. In C. Diaz (Ed.), *Multicultural education for the 21st century* (pp. 72–84). Washington, DC: National Education Association.

Swisher, K. (1994). American Indian learning styles survey: An assessment of teacher knowledge. *Journal of Educational Issues of Language Minority Students, 13,* 59–78.

Switzky, H. N. (1997). Mental retardation and the neglected construct of motivation. *Education and Training in Mental Retardation and Developmental Disabilities, 32,* 194–196.

Symons, F. J., Butler, M. G., Sanders, Feurer, I. D., & Thompson, T. (1999). Self-injurious behavior in Prader-Willi syndrome: Behavioral forms and body location. *American Journal of Mental Retardation, 104,* 260–269.

Symons, F. J., Clark, R. D., Roberts, J. P., & Bailey, Jr., D. B. (2001). Classroom behavior of elementary school-age boys with fragile X syndrome. *Journal of Special Education, 34,* 194–202.

Syzmanski, L. S. (2000). Happiness as a treatment goal. *American Journal of Mental Retardation, 105,* 352–362.

Szabo, J. L. (2000). Maddie's story: Inclusion through physical and occupational therapy. *Teaching Exceptional Children, 33*(2), 26–32.

Talbott, E., & Thiede, K. (1999). Pathways to antisocial behavior among adolescent girls. *Journal of Emotional and Behavioral Disorders, 7,* 31–39.

Taylor, P. B., Gunter, P. L., & Slate, J. R. (2001). Teachers' perceptions of inappropriate student behaviors as a function of teachers' and students' gender and ethnic background. *Behavioral Disorders, 26,* 146–151.

Taylor, S. J. (1988). Caught in the continuum: A critical analysis of the principle of the least restrictive environment. *Journal of The Association for Persons with Severe Handicaps, 13,* 41–53.

Taylor, S. J., & Blatt, S. D. (Eds.). (1999). *In search of the promised land: The collected papers of Burton Blatt.* Washington, DC: American Association on Mental Retardation.

Taylor, S. J., Bogdan, R., & Lutfiyya, Z. M. (1995). *The variety of community experience: Qualitative studies of family and community life.* Baltimore: Brookes.

Tedder, N. E., Warden, K., & Sikka, A. (1993). Prelanguage communication of students who are deaf-blind and have other severe impairments. *Journal of Visual Impairment and Blindness, 87,* 302–307.

Tellefson, M. (2000). Suitcase mobility: A case study packed with opportunities for learning. *RE:view, 32,* 25–33.

Terman, L. (Ed.). (1925). *Genetic studies of genius* (vol. 1). Stanford, CA: Stanford University Press.

Test, D. W., Cooke, N. L., Weiss, A. B., Heward, W. L., & Heron, T. E. (1986). A home-school communication system for special education. *Pointer, 30,* 4–7.

Test, D. W., Spooner, F. H., Keul, P. K., & Grossi, T. A. (1990). Teaching adolescents with severe disabilities to use the public telephone. *Behavior Modification, 14,* 157–171.

Thomas, C., Correa, V., & Morsink, C. (2001). *Interactive teaming: Enhancing programs for students with special needs* (3rd ed.). Upper Saddle River, NJ: Merrill/Prentice Hall.

Thomas, L. A. (2001). Living with Prader-Willi: The "starving syndrome." *Exceptional Parent, 31*(11), 66–72.

Thomas, S. B., & Hawke, C. (1999). Health care standards for children with disabilities: Emerging standards and implications. *Journal of Special Education, 32,* 226–237.

Thompson, T., Robinson, J., Dietrich, M., Farris, M., & Sinclair, V. (1996a). Architectural features and perceptions of community residences for people with mental retardation. *American Journal on Mental Retardation, 101,* 292–314.

Thompson, T., Robinson, J., Dietrich, M., Farris, M., & Sinclair, V. (1996b). Interdependence of architectural features and program variables in community residences for people with mental retardation. *American Journal on Mental Retardation, 101,* 315–327.

Thorndike, R. L., Hagen, E. P., & Sattler, J. M. (1986). *Technical manual, the Stanford-Binet Intelligence Scale: Fourth edition.* Chicago: Riverside.

Thornton, C., & Krajewski, J. (1993). Death education for teachers: A refocused

concern relative to medically fragile children. *Intervention in School and Clinic, 29,* 31–35.

Thurlow, M., & Liu, K. (2001). *State and district assessments as an avenue to equity and excellence for English language learners with disabilities (LEP Projects Report 2).* Minneapolis: University of Minnesota, National Center on Educational Outcomes. http://education.umn.edu/NCEO/OnlinePubs/LEP2.html

Thurlow, M., Graden, J., Greener, J., & Ysseldyke, J. (1983). LD and Non-LD Students Opportunities to Learn. *Learning Disability Quarterly, 6,* 172–183.

Thurston, L. P., & Dasta, K. (1990). An analysis of in-home parent tutoring in children's academic behavior at home and in school and on parents' tutoring behaviors. *Remedial and Special Education, 11*(4), 41–52.

Timothy W. v. Rochester, N. H., School District, 875 F.2d 954 (1st Cir. 1989), cert. Denied 493 U. S. 983, 110 S.Ct. 519 (1989).

Tinbergen, N., & Tinbergen, E. A. (1983). "Autistic" children: New hope for a cure. London: Allen & Unwin.

Todis, B., Severson, H. H., & Walker, H. M. (1990). The critical events scale: Behavioral profiles of students with externalizing and internalizing behavior disorders. *Behavioral Disorders, 15,* 75–86.

Tolan, P. H., & Thomas, P. (1995). The implications of age of onset for delinquency risk II: Longitudinal data. *Journal of Abnormal Child Psychology, 23,* 157–181.

Tolla, J. (2000). Follow that bear! Encouraging mobility in a young child with visual impairment and multiple disabilities. *Teaching Exceptional Children, 32*(5), 72–77.

Tomlinson, C. A., Kaplan, S. N., Renzulli, J. S., Purcell, J., Leppien, J., & Burns, D. (2002). *The parallel curriculum: A design to develop high potential and challenge high-ability learners.* Thousand Oaks, CA: Sage/Corwin.

Tonemah, S. A. (1987). Assessing American Indian gifted and talented student's abilities. *Journal for the Education of the Gifted, 10,* 181–194.

Torgesen, J. K. (1998). Catch them before they fall: Identification and assessment to prevent reading failure in young children. *American Educator, 22*(1&2), 32–41.

Torgesen, J. K., & Bryant, B. (1994). *Test of Phonological Awareness.* Austin, TX: PRO-ED.

Torgesen, J. K., & Wagner, R. K. (1998). Alternative diagnostic approaches for specific developmental reading disabilities. *Learning Disabilities Research and Practice, 13,* 220–232.

Torgesen, J. K., Wagner, R. K., & Rashotte, C. A. (1997). Prevention and remediation of severe reading disabilities: Keeping the end in mind. *Scientific Studies of Reading, 1,* 217–234.

Tourette Syndrome Association. (2000). *What is Tourette syndrome.* Bayside, NY: Author.

[On-line]. Available: http://www.tsa-usa.org.

Townsend, B. L. (2000). The disproportionate discipline of African American learners: Reducing school suspensions and expulsions. *Exceptional Children, 66,* 381–391.

Tran, L. P., & Grunfast, K. M. (1999). Hereditary hearing loss. *The Volta Review, 99*(5), 63–69.

Trask-Tyler, S. A., Grossi, T. A., & Heward, W. L. (1994). Teaching young adults with developmental disabilities and visual impairments to use tape-recorded recipes: Acquisition, generalization, and maintenance of cooking skills. *Journal of Behavioral Education, 4,* 283–311.

Treanor, R. B. (1993). *We overcame: The story of civil rights for disabled people.* Falls Church, VA: Regal Direct.

Treffert, D. A. (1989). *Extraordinary people: Understanding "idiots savants."* New York: Harper & Row.

Trembley, R. E. (2000). The development of aggressive behavior during childhood: What have we learned in the past century? *International Journal of Behavioral Development, 24,* 129–141.

Trupin, L., Sebesta, D., Yelin, E., & LaPlante, M. (1997). *Trends in labor force participation among persons with disabilities, 1983–1994.* San Francisco: University of California, Disabilities Statistics Rehabilitation Research and Training Center, Institute for Health and Aging.

Tucker, B. P. (Ed.). (1998). *Cochlear implants: A handbook.* McFarland.

Turnbull, A. P., & Turnbull, H. R. (2001). *Families, professionals, and exceptionality: Collaborating for empowerment* (4th ed.). Upper Saddle River, NJ: Merrill/Prentice Hall.

Turnbull, A. P., & Ruef, M. (1996). Family perspectives on problem behavior. *Mental Retardation, 34,* 280–293.

Turnbull, H. R., & Cilley, M. (1999). *Explanations and implications of the 1997 amendments to IDEA.* Upper Saddle River, NJ: Merrill/Prentice Hall.

Turnbull, H. R., & Turnbull, A. P. (2000). *Free appropriate public education: The law and children with disabilities* (6th ed.). Denver: Love.

Turner-Henson, A., Holaday, B., Corser, N., Ogletree, G., & Swan, J. H. (1994). The experiences of discrimination: Challenges for chronically ill children. *Pediatric Nursing, 20,* 571–577.

Tyler, J. S., & Mira, M. P. (1993). Educational modifications for students with head injuries. *Teaching Exceptional Children, 25*(3), 24–27.

Tymchuk, A. J., Lakin, K. C., & Luckasson, R. (2001). *The forgotten generation: The status and challenges of adults with mild cognitive limitations.* Baltimore: Brookes.

U. S. Congress. (1987). *Promotion opportunities for blind and handicapped workers in sheltered workshops under the Javitz-Wagner-O'Day act.* Washington, DC: U. S. Government Printing Office.

U. S. Department of Education. (1991). *America 2000, an education strategy sourcebook.* Washington, DC: Author.

U. S. Department of Education. (1993). *To assure the free appropriate public education of all children with disabilities: Fifteenth annual report to Congress on the implementation of the Individuals with Disabilities Education Act.* Washington, DC: Government Document Services.

U. S. Department of Education. (1996). *Eighteenth annual report to Congress on the implementation of the Individuals with Disabilities Education Act.* Washington, DC: Author.

U.S. Department of Education. (1998). *Twenty-first annual report to Congress on the implementation of the Individuals with Disabilities Education Act.* Washington, DC: Author.

U.S. Department of Education. (1999). Assistance to states for the education of children with disabilities and the early intervention program for infants and toddlers with disabilities: Final regulations. *Federal Register, 64*(48), CFR Parts 300 and 303.

U. S. Department of Education. (2000). *Guide to the individualized education program.* Washington, DC: Author.

U. S. Department of Education. (2000). *Twenty-second annual report to Congress on the implementation of the Individuals with Disabilities Education Act.* Washington, DC: Author.

U. S. Department of Education. (2001). *Twenty-third annual report to Congress on the implementation of the Individuals with Disabilities Education Act.* Washington, DC: Author.

U. S. Department of Education. (2002). *Twenty-fourth annual report to Congress on the implementation of the Individuals with Disabilities Education Act.* Washington, DC: Author.

U. S. Department of Health and Human Services. (1998). *Child maltreatment 1996: Reports from the states to the National Child Abuse and Neglect Data System.* Washington, DC: U. S. Government Printing Office.

U. S. Department of Labor. (1979). *Study of handicapped clients in sheltered workshops (vol. 2).* Washington, DC: Author.

U. S. Office of Education. (1977a). Implementation of Part B of the Education of the Handicapped Act. *Federal Register, 42,* 42474–42518.

U. S. Office of Education. (1977b). Procedures for evaluating specific learning disabilities. *Federal Register, 42,* 65082–65085.

U. S. Public Health Service. (1990). *Healthy people 2000.* Washington, DC: Government Printing Office.

Uffen, E. (1997). Speech and language disorders: Nature or nurture? *ASHA Leader, 2*(14), 8.

Ulrey, P. (1994). When you meet a guide dog. *RE:view, 26,* 143–144.

Umbreit, J. (1995). Functional assessment and intervention in a regular classroom setting for the disruptive behavior of a student with attention-deficit hyperactivity disorder. *Behavioral Disorders, 20,* 267–278.

Umbreit, J., & Blair, K. C. (1996). The effects of preference, choice, and attention on problem behavior at school. *Education and Training in Mental Retardation and Developmental Disabilities, 31,* 151–161.

Utley, B. L., Roman, C., & Nelson, G. L. (1998). Functional vision. In S. Z. Sacks & R. K. Silberman (Eds.), *Educating students who have visual impairments with other disabilities* (pp. 371–412). Baltimore: Brookes.

Utley, C. (1995). Culturally and linguistically diverse students with mild disabilities. In C. A. Grant (Ed.), *Educating for diversity: An anthology of multicultural voices* (pp. 301–324). Boston: Allyn & Bacon.

Utley, C. A., & Obiakor, F. E. (2001). Learning problems or learning disabilities of multicultural learners: Contemporary perspectives. In C. Utley & F. Obiakor (Eds.), *Special education, multicultural education, and school reform: Components of quality education for learners with mild disabilities* (pp. 90–117). Springfield, IL: Thomas.

Valdés, G. (1996). *Con respecto: Bridging the distances between culturally diverse families and schools.* New York: Teachers College Press.

Valdes, K. A., Williamson, C. L., & Wagner, M. (1990). *The national longitudinal transition study of special education students. Vol. 3: Youth categorized as emotionally disturbed.* Palo Alto, CA: SRI International.

van der Mars, H. (1989). Effects of specific verbal praise on off-task behavior of second grade students in physical education. *Journal of Teaching in Physical Education, 8,* 162–169.

Van Gurp, S. (2001). Self-concept of deaf secondary school students in different educational settings. *Journal of Deaf Studies and Deaf Education, 6,* 54–69.

Van Houten, R. (1984). Setting up performance feedback systems in the classroom. In W. L. Heward, T. E. Heron, D. S. Hill, & J. Trap-Porter (Eds.), *Focus on behavior analysis in education* (pp. 114–125). Upper Saddle River, NJ: Merrill/Prentice Hall.

Van Keulen, J. E., Weddington, G. T., & DeBose, C. E. (1998). *Speech, language, learning, and the African American child.* Boston: Allyn & Bacon.

Van Reusen, A. K., & Bos, C. S. (1990). IPLAN: Helping students communicate in planning conferences. *Teaching Exceptional Children, 22*(4), 30–32.

Van Riper, C., & Erickson, R. L. (1996). *Speech correction: An introduction to speech pathology and audiology* (9th ed.). Boston: Allyn & Bacon.

Van Tassel-Baska, J., Patton, J. M., & Prillaman, D. (1991). *Gifted youth at risk: A report of a national study.* Reston, VA: Council for Exceptional Children.

Vance, J., Fernandez, G., & Biber, M. (1998). Educational progress in a population of youth with aggression and emotional disturbance: the role of risk and protective factors. *Journal of Emotional and Behavioral Disorders, 6,* 214–221.

Vandercook, T. (1991). Leisure instruction outcomes: Criterion performance, positive interactions, and acceptance by typical high school peers. *Journal of Special Education, 25,* 320–339.

Vandercook, T., York, J., & Forest, M. (1989). The McGill Action Planning System (MAPS): A strategy for building the vision. *Journal of The Association for Persons with Severe Handicaps, 14,* 205–215.

Vargas, J. S. (1977). *Behavioral psychology for teachers.* New York, NY: Harper & Row.

Vaughn, B. J., Clarke, S., & Dunlap, G. (1997). Assessment-based intervention for severe behavior problems in a natural family context. *Journal of Applied Behavior Analysis, 30,* 713–716.

Vaughn, B. J., Dunlap, G., Fox, L., Clarke, S., & Bucy, M. (1997). Parent-professional partnership in behavioral support: A case study in community-based intervention. *Journal of The Association for Persons with Severe Handicaps, 22,* 186–197.

Vaughn, S., Elbaum, B. E., & Schumm, J. S. (1996). The effects of inclusion on the social functioning of students with learning disabilities. *Journal of Learning Disabilities, 29,* 598–608.

Vaughn, S., Gersten, R. L., & Chard, D. J. (2000). The underlying message in LD intervention research: Findings from research syntheses. *Exceptional Children, 67,* 99–114.

Vaughn, S., Klingner, J., Hughes, M. (2000). Sustainability of research-based practices. *Exceptional Children, 66,* 163–171.

Vaughn, S., McIntosh, R., Schumm, J. S., Haager, D., & Callwood, D. (1993). Social status, peer acceptance, and reciprocal friendships revisited. *Learning Disabilities Research and Practice, 8,* 82–88.

Vaughn, S., Schumm, J. S., & Brick, J. B. (1998). Using a rating scale to design and evaluate inclusion programs. *Teaching Exceptional Children, 30*(4), 41–45.

Venn, J. J. (2000). *Assessing students with special needs* (2nd ed.). Upper Saddle River, NJ: Merrill/Prentice Hall.

Vig, S., & Jedrysek, E. (1996). Application of the 1992 AAMR definition: Issues for preschool children. *Mental Retardation, 34,* 244–246.

Villegas, A. M. (1988). School failure and cultural mismatch: Another view. *Urban Review, 20*(4), 253–265.

Voltz, D. L. (1994). Developing collaborative parent-teacher relationships with culturally diverse parents. *Intervention in School and Clinic, 29*(5), 288–291.

Voltz, D. L. (1998). Cultural diversity and special education teacher preparation: Critical issues confronting the field. *Teacher Education and Special Education, 21*(1), 63–70.

Voltz, D. L., & Damiano-Lantz, M. (1993). Developing ownership in learning. *Teaching Exceptional Children, 25,* 18–28.

Wagner, B. W. (2000). Presidential address 2000—Changing visions into reality. *Mental Retardation, 38,* 436–443.

Wagner, L., & Lane, L., (1998). Lane County Department of Youth Services: 1997 report: Juvenile justice services. Eugene, OR Department of Youth Services.

Wagner, M., Blackorby, J., Cameto, R., & Newman, L. (1994). *What makes a difference? Influences on postschool outcomes of youth with disabilities.* Menlo Park, CA: SRI International.

Wagner, R. K., Torgeson, J. K., & Rahsotte, C. A. (1999). *Comprehensive Test of Phonological Processing.* Austin, TX: PRO-ED.

Wagner-Lampl, A., & Oliver, G. W. (1994). Folklore of blindness. *Journal of Visual Impairment and Blindness, 88,* 267–276.

Wahler, R. G., & Dumas, J. E. (1986). "A chip off the old block": Some interpersonal characteristics of coercive children across generations. In P. S. Strain, M. J. Guralnick, & H. M. Walker (Eds.), *Children's social behavior: Development, assessment, and modification* (pp. 49–91). Orlando, FL: Academic Press.

Wainapel, S. F. (1989). Attitudes of visually impaired persons toward cane use. *Journal of Visual Impairment and Blindness, 83,* 446–448.

Walker, D. K., & Jacobs, F. H. (1985). Where there is a way, there is not always a will: Technology, public policy, and the school integration of children who are technology-assisted. *Children's Health Care, 20,* 68–74.

Walker, H. M. (1997). *The acting out child: Coping with classroom disruption* (2nd ed.). Longmont, CO: Sopris West.

Walker, H. M., & Severson, H. H. (1990). *Systematic screening for behavior disorders.* Longmont, CO: Sopris West.

Walker, H. M., & Sprague, J. R. (1999). The path to school failure, delinquency, and violence: Causal factors and some potential solutions. *Intervention in School and Clinic, 35*(2), 67–73.

Walker, H. M., & Sylvester, R. (1998). Reducing student refusal and resistance. *Teaching Exceptional Children, 30*(6), 52–57.

Walker, H. M., Colvin, G., & Ramsey, E. (1995). *Antisocial behavior in schools: Strategies and best practices.* Pacific Grove, CA: Brooks/Cole.

Walker, H. M., McConnell, S., Holmes, D., Todis, B., Walker, J., & Golden, N. (1983). *ACCESS: Adolescent curriculum for communication and effective social skills.* Austin, TX: PRO-ED.

Walker, H. M., Sprague, J. R., Close, D. W., & Starlin, C. M. (1999–2000). What is right with behavior disorders: Seminal achievements and contributions of the behavior disorders field. *Exceptionality, 8,* 13–28.

Walker, H. M., Todis, B., Holmes, D., & Horton. (1988). *The Walker social skills curriculum: The ACCEPTS program.* Austin, TX: PRO-ED.

Walker, L. A. (1986). *A loss for words: The story of deafness in a family.* New York: Harper & Row.

Wallace, G. & Hammill, D. D. (1994). Comprehensive Receptive and Expressive Vocabulary Test. Austin, TX: PRO-ED.

Walsh, J. M. (2001). Getting the "big picture" of IEP goals and state standards. *Teaching Exceptional Children, 33*(5), 18–26.

Walther-Thomas, C., Korinek, L., McLaughlin, V., & Williams, B. (2000). *Collaboration for inclusive education.* Boston: Allyn & Bacon.

Ward, M. C. (1994). Effects of a self-operated auditory prompt system on the acquisition, maintenance and generalization of independent work skills of preschoolers with developmental disabilities. Unpublished doctoral dissertation, The Ohio State University, Columbus.

Wardle, F. (2000). Multiracial and multiethnic students: How they must belong. *Multicultural Perspectives, 2*(4), 11–16.

Warfield, M. E., & Hauser-Cram, P. (1996). Child care needs, arrangements, and satisfaction of mothers of children with developmental disabilities. *Mental Retardation, 34,* 294–302.

Wasik, B. H., Ramey, C. T., Bryant, D. M., & Sparling, J. J. (1990). A longitudinal study of two early intervention strategies: Project CARE. *Child Development, 61,* 1682–1692.

Webber, J., & Scheuermann, B. (1991). Managing behavior problems: Accentuate the positive . . . Eliminate the negative! *Teaching Exceptional Children, 24,* 13–19.

Webber, J., & Scheuermann, B. (1997). A challenging future: current barriers and recommended actions for our field. *Behavioral Disorders, 22,* 167–178.

Webber, J., Scheuermann, B., McCall, C., & Coleman, M. (1993). Research on self-monitoring as a behavior management technique in special education classrooms: A descriptive review. *Remedial and Special Education, 14*(2), 38–56.

Weber, C., Behl, D., & Summers, M. (1994). Watch them play—watch them learn. *Teaching Exceptional Children, 27*(1), 30–35.

Webster's New World Dictionary of the American Language (2nd ed.). (1986). New York: Simon & Schuster.

Webster, D. D., Clary, G., & Griffith, P. L. (2001). Postsecondary education and career paths. In R. W. Flexer, T. J. Simmons, P. Luft, & R. M. Baer, *Transition planning for secondary students with disabilities* (pp. 439–473). Upper Saddle River, NJ: Merrill/Prentice Hall.

Wedel, J. W., & Fowler, S. A. (1984). "Read me a story, Mom": A home-tutoring program to teach prereading skills to language-delayed children. *Behavior Modification, 8,* 245–266.

Wehby, J. H., Symons, F. J., Canale, J. A., & Go, F. J. (1998). Teaching practices in classrooms for students with emotional and behavioral disorders: Discrepancies between recommendations and observations. *Behavioral Disorders, 24,* 51–56.

Wehman, P. (Ed.). (2002). *Individual transition plans: The teacher's curriculum guide for helping youth with special needs* (2nd ed.). Austin, TX: PRO-ED.

Wehman, P., & Kregel, J. (1998). *More than a job: Securing satisfying careers for people with disabilities.* Baltimore: Brookes.

Wehman, P., & Revell, G. (1997). Transition from school to adulthood: Looking ahead. In P. Wehman (Ed.), *Exceptional individuals in school, community, and work* (pp. 597–648). Austin, TX: PRO-ED.

Wehman, P., Brooke, V., & Inge, K. J. (2001). Vocational placements and careers. In P. Wehman (Ed.), *Life beyond the classroom: Transition strategies for young people with disabilities* (3rd ed.), (pp. 211–246). Baltimore: Brookes.

Wehman, P., Kregel, J., Shafer, M., & West, M. (1989). *Emerging trends in supported employment: A preliminary analysis of 27 states.* Richmond: Virginia Commonwealth University, Rehabilitation Research and Training Center.

Wehman, P., Revell, G., & Kregel, J. (1998). Supported employment: A decade of rapid growth and impact. *American Rehabilitation, 24*(1), 31–43.

Wehmeyer, M. L. (1994). Perceptions of self-determination and psychological empowerment of adolescents with mental retardation. *Education and Training in Mental Retardation, 29,* 9–21.

Wehmeyer, M. L., Agran, M., & Hughes, C. (1998). *Teaching self-determination to students with disabilities.* Baltimore: Brookes.

Wehmeyer, M. L., Kelchner, K., & Richards, S. (1996). Essential characteristics of self-determined behavior of individuals with mental retardation. *American Journal on Mental Retardation, 100,* 632–642.

Wehmeyer, M. L., Martin, J. E., & Sands, D. J. (1998). Self-determination for children and youth with developmental disabilities. In A. Hilton & R. Ringlaben (Eds.), *Best and promising practices in developmental disabilities* (pp. 191–203). Austin, TX: PRO-ED.

Wehmeyer, M. L., Palmer, S. B., Agran, M., Mithaug, D. E., & Martin, J. E. (2000). Promoting causal agency: The self-determined learning model of instruction. *Exceptional Children, 66,* 273.

Weiner, J. (1999). *Time, love, and memory: a great biologist and his quest for the origins of behavior.* New York: Knopf.

Weinstein, G., & Cooke, N. L. (1992). The effects of two repeated reading interventions on generalization of fluency. *Learning Disability Quarterly, 15,* 21–28.

Weintraub, F. J., & Abeson, A. (1974). New education policies for the handicapped: The quiet revolution. *Phi Delta Kappan, 55,* 526–529, 569.

Weiserbs, B. (2000). Social and academic integration using e-mail between children with and without hearing impairments. *Computers in the Schools, 16*(2), 29–44.

Weiss, K. W., & Dykes, M. K. (1995). Legal issues in special education: Assistive technology and supportive services. *Physical Disabilities: Education and Related Services, 14*(1), 29–36.

Weisz, J. R., Bromfield, R., Vines, D. L., & Weiss, B. (1985). Cognitive development, helpless behavior, and labeling effects in the lives of the mentally retarded. *Applied Developmental Psychology, 2,* 129–167.

Werker, J. E., & Lalonde, C. E. (1988). Cross language speech perception: Initial capabilities and developmental change. *Developmental Psychology, 24,* 672–683.

Weschler, D. (1991). *Weschler Intelligence Scale for Children–Revised.* San Antonio, TX: Psychological Corporation.

Wesson, C. L. (1991). Curriculum-based measurement and two models of follow-up consultation. *Exceptional Children, 77,* 246–256.

Wesson, C. L., & King, R. P. (1996). Portfolio assessment and special education students. *Teaching Exceptional Children, 28*(2), 44–48.

Wesson, C., Wilson, R., & Higbee Mandlebaum, L. (1988). Learning games for active student responding. *Teaching Exceptional Children, 20*(2), 12–14.

West, L. L., Corbey, S., Boyer-Stephens, A., Jones, B., Miller, R. J., & Sarkees-Wircenski, M. (1999). *Integrating transition planning into the IEP process* (2nd ed.). Reston, VA: Council for Exceptional Children.

West, M. D., Rayfield, R. G., Clements, C., Unger, D., & Thornton, T. (1994). An illustration of positive behavioral support in the workplace for individuals with severe mental retardation. *Journal of Vocational Rehabilitation, 4*(4), 265–271.

West, M., Revell, G., & Wehman, P. (1998). Conversion from segregated services to supported employment: A continuing challenge to the VR service system. *Education and Training in Mental Retardation and Developmental Disabilities, 33,* 239–247.

West, R. P., Young, K. R., & Spooner, F. (1990). Precision teaching: An introduction. *Teaching Exceptional Children, 22,* 4–9.

Westby, C. E., & Clauser, P. S. (1999). The right stuff for writing: Assessing and facilitating written language. In H. W. Catts & A. G. Kamhi (Eds.), *Language and reading disabilities* (pp. 259–324). Boston: Allyn & Bacon.

Westling, D. L., & Fox, L. (2000). *Teaching students with severe disabilities* (2nd ed.). Upper Saddle River, NJ: Merrill/Prentice Hall.

Whaley, L. F., & Wong, D. L. (1995). *Nursing care of infants and children* (5th ed.). St. Louis: Mosby.

Wheeler, J. J., Bates, P., Marshall, K. J., & Miller, S. R. (1988). Teaching appropriate social behaviors to a young man with moderate mental retardation in a supported competitive employment setting. *Education and Training in Mental Retardation, 23,* 105–116.

White, B. L. (1975). *The first three years of life.* Upper Saddle River, NJ: Prentice Hall.

White, M. A. (1975). Natural rates of teacher approval and disapproval in the classroom. *Journal of Applied Behavior Analysis, 8,* 367–372.

Whitmore, J. R., & Maker, C. J. (1985). *Intellectual giftedness in disabled persons.* Rockville, MD: Aspen.

Wiederholt, J. L., & Bryant, B. R. (1992) *Gray Oral Reading Tests—3rd edition.* Austin, TX: PRO-ED.

Wilkinson, G. S. (1994). *Wide Range Achievement Test—3.* Austin, TX: PRO-ED.

Will, M. C. (1986). Educating children with learning problems: A shared responsibility. *Exceptional Children, 52,* 411–415.

Willard-Holt, C. (1998). Academic and personality characteristics of gifted students with cerebral palsy: A multiple case study. *Exceptional Children, 65,* 37–50.

Williams, J. (1977). The impact and implication of litigation. In G. Markel (Ed.), *Proceedings of the University of Michigan Institute on the Impact and Implications of State and Federal Legislation Affecting Handicapped Individuals.* Ann Arbor: University of Michigan, School of Education.

Williams, R. R. (1991). Assistive technology and people with disabilities: Separating fact from fiction. *A. T. Quarterly, 2*(3), 6–7.

Williams, S. C. (2002). How speech-feedback and word-prediction software can help students write. *Teaching Exceptional Children, 34*(3), 72–78.

Williams, V. L., & Cartledge, G. (1997). Passing notes to parents. *Teaching Exceptional Children, 30*(1), 30–34.

Williamson, G. G. (1978). The individualized education program: An interdisciplinary endeavor. In B. Sirvis, J. W. Baken, & G. G. Williamson (Eds.), *Unique aspects of the IEP for the physically handicapped, homebound, and hospitalized.* Reston, VA: Council for Exceptional Children.

Willoughby, D. M., & Duffy, S. (1989). *Handbook for itinerant and resource teachers of blind and visually impaired students.* Baltimore: National Federation of the Blind.

Wilson, C. L. (1995). Parents and teachers: "Can we talk?" *LD Forum, 20*(2), 31–33.

Wilson, C. L., & Hughes, M. (1994). Involving linguistically diverse parents. *LD Forum, 19*(3), 25–27.

Wilson, J., Blacher, J., & Baker, B. L. (1989). Siblings of children with severe handicaps. *Mental Retardation, 27,* 167–173.

Wilson, P. G., Schepis, M. M., & Mason-Main, M. (1987). In vivo use of picture prompt training to increase independent work at a restaurant. *Journal of The Association for Persons with Severe Handicaps, 12,* 145–150.

Winebrenner, S. (2001). *Teaching gifted kids in the regular classroom* (2nd ed). Minneapolis: Free Spirit.

Winzer, M. A., & Mazurek, K. (1998). *Special education in multicultural contexts.* Upper Saddle River, NJ: Merrill/Prentice Hall.

Wittenstein, S. H. (1994). Braille literacy: Preservice training and teachers' attitudes. *Journal of Visual Impairment and Blindness, 88,* 516–524.

Witty, P. A. (Ed.). (1951). *The gifted child.* Boston: Heath.

Wolery, M., & Haring, T. G. (1994). Moderate, severe, and profound disabilities. In N. G. Haring, L. McCormick, & T. G. Haring (Eds.), *Exceptional children and youth* (6th ed.) (pp. 258–299). Upper Saddle River, NJ: Merrill/Prentice Hall.

Wolery, M., & Sainato, D. M. (1993). General curriculum and intervention strategies. In *DEC Recommended Practices* (pp. 50–57). Reston, VA: Council for Exceptional Children, Division for Early Childhood.

Wolery, M., & Sainato, D. M. (1996). General curriculum and intervention strategies. In S. L. Odom & M. McClean (Eds.), *Recommended practices in early intervention* (pp. 125–158). Austin, TX: PRO-ED.

Wolery, M., & Wilbers, J. S. (1994). *Including young children with special needs in early childhood programs.* Washington, DC: National Association for the Education of Young Children.

Wolery, M., Anthony, L., & Heckathorn, J. (1998). Transition-based teaching: Effects on transitions, teachers' behavior, and children's learning. *Journal of Early Intervention, 21,* 117–131.

Wolery, M., Ault, M. J., & Doyle, P. M. (1992). *Teaching students with moderate to severe disabilities.* New York: Longman.

Wolery, M., Bailey, D., & Sugai, G. (1988). *Effective teaching: Principles and procedures of applied behavior analysis with exceptional students.* Boston: Allyn & Bacon.

Wolery, M., Cybriwski, C. A., Gast, D. L., & Boyle-Gast, K. (1991). Use of constant time delay and attentional responses with adolescents. *Exceptional Children, 57,* 462–474.

Wolf, M., & Bowers, P. G. (2000). Naming-speed processes and developmental reading disabilities: An introduction to the special issue on the double-deficit hypothesis. *Journal of Learning Disabilities, 33,* 322–324.

Wolf, M., Bowers, P. G., & Biddle, K. (2000). Retrieval, automaticity, vocabulary elaboration, orthography (RAVE-O): A comprehensive, fluency-based reading intervention program. *Journal of Learning Disabilities, 33,* 375–386.

Wolf, M., Miller, L., & Donnelly, K. (2000). Naming-speed processes and developmental reading disabilities: An introduction to the special issue on the double-deficit hypothesis. *Journal of Learning Disabilities, 33,* 322.

Wolfensberger, W. (1969). The origin and nature of our institutional models. In R. B. Kugel & W. Wolfensberger (Eds.), Changing patterns in residential services for the mentally retarded (pp. 59–71). Washington, DC: President's Committee on Mental Retardation.

Wolfensberger, W. (1972). *Normalization: The principle of normalization in human services.* Toronto: National Institute on Mental Retardation.

Wolfensberger, W. (1983). Social role valorization: A proposed new term for the principle of normalization. *Mental Retardation, 21*, 234–239.

Wolfensberger, W. (2000). A brief overview of social role valorization. *Mental Retardation, 38*, 105–123.

Wolford, T., Alber, S. R., & Heward, W. L. (2001). Teaching middle school students with learning disabilities to recruit peer assistance during cooperative learning group activities. *Learning Disabilities and Research & Practice, 16*, 161–173.

Woliver, R., & Woliver, G. M. (1991). Gifted adolescents in the emerging minorities: Asians and Pacific Islanders. In M. Bireley & J. Genshaft (Eds.), *Understanding the gifted adolescent* (pp. 248–258). New York: Teachers College Press.

Wolraich, M. L., (1999). Attention-deficit hyperactivity disorder: The most studied yet most controversial diagnosis. *Mental Retardation and Development Disabilities Research Reviews, 5*, 163–168.

Wolters, P., Brouwers, P., & Moss, H. (1995). Pediatric HIV disease: Effect on cognition, learning, and behavior. *School Psychology Quarterly, 10*, 305–328.

Wood, B. A., Frank, A. R., & Hamre-Nietupski, S. M. (1996). How do you work this lock? Adaptations for teaching combination lock use. *Teaching Exceptional Children, 28*(2), 35–39.

Wood, F. H., Cheney, C. O., Cline D. H., Sampson, K., Smith, C. R., & Guetzloe, E. C. (1997). *Conduct disorders and social maladjustments: Policies, politics, and programming.* Reston, VA: Council for Children with Behavioral Disorders.

Wood, J. G. & Zabel, R. H. (2001). Adderall: special education's new (?) fix-it drug. *Beyond Behavior, 11*(1), 39–41.

Wood, J. W. (2002). *Adapting instruction to accommodate students in inclusive settings* (4th ed.). Upper Saddle River, NJ: Merrill/Prentice Hall.

Wood, S. J., Murdock, J. Y., Cronin, M. E., Dawson, N. M., & Kirby, P. C. (1998). Effects of self-monitoring on on-task behaviors of at-risk middle school students. *Journal of Behavioral Education, 8*, 263–279.

Woodcock, R. W. (1998). *Woodcock Reading Mastery Tests-Revised.* Circle Pines, MN: American Guidance Services.

Woodcock, R. W., & Mather, N. (2000). *Woodcock-Johnson III Tests of Achievement.* Itasca, IL: Riverside.

Woolsey, M. L. (1999, January). Personal communication.

Wrenn, R. L. (1994). A death at school: Issues and interventions. *Counseling and Human Development, 26*(7), 1–7.

Wright, C., & Momari, M. (1985). *From toys to computers: Access for the physically disabled child.* San Jose, CA: Wright.

Wright, J. E., Cavanaugh, R. A., Sainato, D. M., & Heward, W. L. (1995). Somos todos ayudantes y estudiantes: Evaluation of a classwide peer tutoring program in a modified Spanish class for secondary students identified as learning disabled or academically at-risk. *Education and Treatment of Children, 18*, 33–52.

Yairi, E. (1998). Is the basis for stuttering genetic? *American Speech-Language-Hearing Association, 70*(1), 29–32.

Yelin, E., & Katz, P. (1994). Labor force trends of persons with and without disabilities. *Monthly Quarterly, 72*, 593–620.

Yell, M. L. (1995). Least restrictive environment, inclusion, and students with disabilities: A legal analysis. *Journal of Special Education, 28*, 389–404.

Yell, M. L. (1998). *The law and special education.* Upper Saddle River, NJ: Merrill/Prentice Hall.

Yell, M. L., & Drasgow, E. (2000). Litigating a free appropriate public education: The Lovaas hearing and cases. *Journal of Special Education, 33*, 205–214.

Yell, M. L., Katsiyannis, A., Bradley, R., & Rozalski, M. (2000). Ensuring compliance with the discipline provisions of IDEA '97: Challenges and opportunities. *The Journal of Special Education Leadership, 13*(1), 3–18.

Ylvisaker, M. (1986). Language and communication disorders following pediatric head injury. *Journal of Head Trauma Rehabilitation, 1*, 48–56.

Yopp, R. H. & Yopp, H. K. (2001). *Literature-based reading activities.* Boston: Allyn & Bacon.

Young, J. L. (1997). Positive experiences with dogs: An important addition to the curriculum for blind and visually impaired children. *RE:view, 29*(2), 55–61.

Yousef, J. M. S. (1995). Insulin-dependent diabetes mellitus: Education implications. *Physical Disabilities: Education and Related Services, 13*(2), 43–53.

Ysseldyke, J. (2001). Reflections on a research career: Generalizations from 25 years of research on assessment and instructional decision making. *Exceptional Children, 67*, 295–309.

Ysseldyke, J. E., Thurlow, M. L., Mecklenburg, C., & Graden, J. (1984). Opportunity to learn for regular and special education students during reading instruction. *Remedial and Special Education, 5*, 29–37.

Zabel, R. H., & Nigro, F. A. (1999). Juvenile offenders with behavioral disorders, learning disabilities, and no disabilities: Self-reports of personal, family, and school characteristics. *Behavioral Disorders, 25*, 22–40.

Zawaiza, T. W. (1995). Stand and deliver: Multiculturalism and special education report in the early 21st century. In S. Walker, K. A. Turner, M. Haile-Michael, A. Vincent, & M. D. Miles (Eds.), *Disability and diversity: New leadership for a new era.* Washington, DC: President's Committee on Employment of People with Disabilities.

Zeaman, D., & House, B. J. (1979). A review of attention theory. In N. R. Ellis (Ed.), *Handbook of mental deficiency: Psychological theory and research* (2nd ed.), (pp. 63–120). Hillside, NJ: Erlbaum.

Zigmond, N., & Magiera, K. (2001). *Current practice alerts: Co-teaching.* Reston, VA: Division for Learning Disabilities and Division for Research of the Council for Exceptional Children.

Zimmerman, E. H., & Zimmerman, T. (1962). The alteration of behavior in a special classroom situation. *Journal of the Experimental Analysis of Behavior, 5*, 59–60.

Zionts, P., Simpson, R., & Zionts, L. (2001). *Emotional and behavioral problems: A handbook for understanding and handling students.* Thousand Oaks, CA: Corwin Press.

Zirpoli, T. J. (1987). Child abuse and children with handicaps. *Remedial and Special Education, 7*(2), 39–48.

Zirpoli, T. J., & Melloy, K. J. (2001). *Behavior management: Applications for teachers* (3rd ed.). Upper Saddle River, NJ: Merrill/Prentice Hall.

Name Index

Subject Index

PRAXIS PRAXIS™ Series of Professional Assessments for Beginning Teachers

Many states require a passing score on one or more PRAXIS II tests for licensure or certification as a special education teacher. PRAXIS II tests—the Subject Assessment/Specialty Area Tests of the PRAXIS Series of Professional Assessments for Beginning Teachers—assess students' knowledge of fundamental concepts and issues related to curriculum and instruction for students with disabilities. Margin notes throughout the text link critical text content to material covered on PRAXIS II tests and to CEC's Performance-Based Standards for Beginning Teachers (see inside front cover). Topics covered by the PRAXIS II test, Special Education Core Principles: Content Knowledge (0353), are shown here.

Special Education Core Principles: Content Knowledge

Descriptions of each of the content areas covered by the test are provided below. For each content area, the approximate percentage of examination questions pertaining to that area is shown. Not every sub-topic in a given content area appears on any one form of the test, but every form of the test contains questions on a broad range of subtopics

Familiarity with the definitions set forth in IDEA '97 (the 1997 amendments to the Individuals with Disabilities Education Act) is assumed.

I. **Understanding Exceptionalities (25%-30% of test questions)**
    - Human development and behavior as related to students with disabilities, including
        - Social and emotional development and behavior
        - Language development and behavior
        - Cognition
        - Physical development, including motor and sensory
    - Characteristics of students with disabilities, including the influence of
        - Cognitive factors
        - Affective and social-adaptive factors, including cultural, linguistic, gender, and socioeconomic factors
        - Genetic, medical, motor, sensory, and chronological-age factors
    - Basic concepts in special education, including
        - Definitions of all major categories and specific disabilities, including attention deficit/hyperactivity disorder (ADHD), as well as the incidence and prevalence of various types of disabilities
        - The causation and prevention of disability
        - The nature of behaviors, including frequency, duration, intensity, and degrees of severity
        - The classification of students with disabilities (classifications as represented in the 1997 amendments to the Individuals with Disabilities Education Act [IDEA '97]; labeling of students; ADHD; the implications of the classification process for the persons classified, etc.)
        - The influence of level of severity and presence of multiple exceptionalities on students with disabilities
    - The influence of (an) exceptional condition(s) throughout an individual's life span.

II. **Legal and Societal Issues (15%-20% of test questions)**
    - Federal laws and legal issues related to special education, including
        - Public Law 94-142
        - Public Law 105-17 (IDEA '97)
        - Section 504
        - Americans with Disabilities Act (ADA)
        - Important legal issues, such as those raised by the following cases: Rowley re: program appropriateness, Tatro re: related services, Honig re: discipline, Oberti re: inclusion
    - The school's connections with the families, prospective and actual employers, and communities of students with disabilities, for example
        - Teacher advocacy for students and families, developing student self-advocacy
        - Parent partnerships and roles
        - Public attitudes toward individuals with disabilities
        - Cultural and community influences on public attitudes toward individuals with disabilities
        - Interagency agreements
        - Cooperative nature of the transition planning process
    - Historical movements/trends affecting the connections between special education and the larger society, for example
        - Deinstitutionalization and community-based placements
        - Inclusion
        - Application of technology
        - Transition
        - Advocacy
        - Accountability and meeting educational standards